# INTERNATIONAL MARKETING

## AN ASIA–PACIFIC PERSPECTIVE

# 4

# INTERNATIONAL MARKETING

## AN ASIA–PACIFIC PERSPECTIVE

4

**RICHARD FLETCHER AND LINDEN BROWN**

PEARSON

Education
Australia

Pearson Education Australia
Unit 4, Level 3
14 Aquatic Drive
Frenchs Forest NSW 2086

www.pearsoned.com.au

Acquisitions Editor: Paul Burgess
Project Editor: Katie Millar
Editorial Coordinators: Jo Davis and Louise Cavander
Copy Editor: Joy Window
Proofreader: Ron Buck
Copyright and Pictures Editor: Liz de Rome
Cover and internal design by Natalie Bowra
Cover photograph from Getty Images
Typeset by Midland Typesetters, Australia

Printed in China

1 2 3 4 5 12 11 10 09 08

National Library of Australia
Cataloguing-in-Publication Data

Fletcher, Richard.
International marketing: an asia-pacific perspective.

4th ed.
Includes index.
ISBN 9780733992377 (pbk).

1. Export marketing — Asia.  2. Export marketing — Pacific
Area.  I. Brown, Linden.  II. Title.

658.84

An imprint of Pearson Education Australia
(a division of Pearson Australia Group Pty Ltd)

# BRIEF CONTENTS

# DETAILED CONTENTS

# PREFACE

For the last decade both students and teachers of international marketing in Australia and New Zealand have been complaining at the lack of a comprehensive textbook on this subject that reflects the needs of marketers and managers in the region. Texts currently available, written by North American and, to a lesser extent, European academics, are largely irrelevant as they focus for the most part on the needs of the transnational company. Their treatment of the problems faced by small and medium-sized firms in undertaking international marketing is cursory.

Yet it is small and medium-sized exporters which make up the vast bulk of firms involved in international business in the Australasian region. There are very few transnational firms, but many branches or subsidiaries of such firms. Hence, coverage of transnational firms in a text designed to address the abovementioned shortcomings should focus on the role of the transnational firm as an international competitor and the role in international activities of managers of their local subsidiary or branch operations.

The problem cannot be addressed simply by adapting an American text. An adaptation cannot fully reflect this and other problems, as well as the unique characteristics of undertaking business in the region. For this reason it was decided to write a totally new textbook. The perspective in this fourth edition of the book is that of firms in Australia and New Zealand looking outwards—principally, but not exclusively—towards the Asia–Pacific region, as this is the major focus of their international business activities. As many of the case studies and examples used in this text involve countries in Asia, the text is also relevant for courses in international marketing delivered in Asian countries in the region.

A problem encountered with many current texts in international marketing is that almost all the examples, case studies and anecdotes relate to overseas firms doing business with other overseas firms, and few of the firms involved are based in the region, let alone in Australia or New Zealand. This makes it difficult for students to identify with the issues involved. In this text there are a large number of new cases written from the perspective of firms in the region and at least two international marketing highlights are included in each chapter, most of which relate to Australian or New Zealand firms. In addition, concepts are illustrated by anecdotes relating to experiences of managers undertaking international business activities in the region.

The writing of the fourth edition was preceded by a rigorous review of the third edition by academics at 14 universities in Australia which were engaged in the teaching of international marketing. A consensus of their views is reflected in a number of changes in the fourth edition. The structure of the book has also been modified. After the introductory chapter, which explores what international marketing is, the book is divided into five parts each of which has an introduction. The linking between the parts is reflected in the figure below which connects analysis with planning, planning with strategy, and strategy with implementation. The fifth part is devoted to contemporary issues in international marketing.

## STRUCTURE OF THE BOOK

**Part A** covers international environmental analysis and contains chapters on the various environmental variables that impact on international marketing. These include economic and financial variables, social and cultural, political and legal and (unlike most texts) information and contemporary variables in the international environment such as terrorism, disease, ethics and environmentalism.

**Part B** covers international planning and commences with a chapter on researching overseas markets. This is followed by a chapter in which selecting and entering foreign markets is discussed. This part concludes with a chapter on planning for international marketing.

**Part C** is devoted to strategic considerations in international marketing with a particular focus on devising marketing strategies for the region. Chapters cover the gaining of competitive advantage, creating international marketing strategies, issues involved in globalisation and the formation of relationships, networks and strategic alliances. The chapters in this part have been further refined to increase their international focus.

**Part D** relates to international implementation and considers ways in which each of the marketing mix variables need to be modified when doing business overseas. Included in this part are chapters on modifying products and services for overseas markets, promoting and advertising overseas, pricing for profit and effective international distribution.

**Part E** covers contemporary challenges in international marketing, detailed discussion of which is rarely found in international marketing texts. Chapters are devoted to the impact of international trade

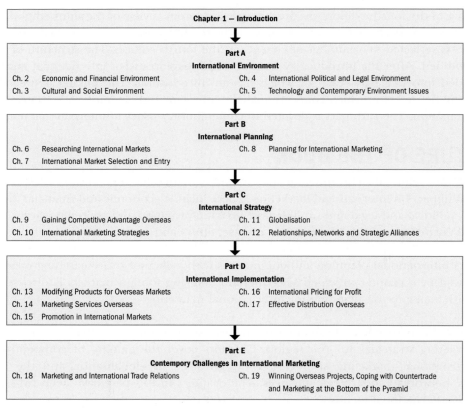

Chapter 1 — Introduction

Part A
International Environment

| Ch. 2 | Economic and Financial Environment | Ch. 4 | International Political and Legal Environment |
| Ch. 3 | Cultural and Social Environment | Ch. 5 | Technology and Contemporary Environment Issues |

Part B
International Planning

| Ch. 6 | Researching International Markets | Ch. 8 | Planning for International Marketing |
| Ch. 7 | International Market Selection and Entry | | |

Part C
International Strategy

| Ch. 9 | Gaining Competitive Advantage Overseas | Ch. 11 | Globalisation |
| Ch. 10 | International Marketing Strategies | Ch. 12 | Relationships, Networks and Strategic Alliances |

Part D
International Implementation

| Ch. 13 | Modifying Products for Overseas Markets | Ch. 16 | International Pricing for Profit |
| Ch. 14 | Marketing Services Overseas | Ch. 17 | Effective Distribution Overseas |
| Ch. 15 | Promotion in International Markets | | |

Part E
Contempory Challenges in International Marketing

| Ch. 18 | Marketing and International Trade Relations | Ch. 19 | Winning Overseas Projects, Coping with Countertrade and Marketing at the Bottom of the Pyramid |

relations on the marketing activities of firms overseas and business overseas, specific issues involved in winning project work in other countries, the significance and operation of countertrade and marketing to those at the bottom of the pyramid.

At the end of each chapter there are a number of discussion questions which can be used either for self-testing or for examination purposes. Moreover, the structure of the chapters—the introductory paragraphs, the international marketing highlights, the anecdotes and the new case studies—help to bring the real world of international marketing from an Asia–Pacific perspective directly into the classroom.

Because this fourth edition has been considerably restructured and augmented it contains much more material than is needed for a basic unit in international marketing. This allows the instructor to select those aspects that suit the course requirements and to use the remainder of the book as additional reading for students. The structure of the book is such that, through the selection of different parts or chapters, it can be used as a tertiary text at different levels. The book can be used as (1) a basic text for international marketing, (2) an advanced text for international marketing management or (3) a text for contemporary issues in international marketing.

**Basic international marketing text** Those proposing to use the book for this purpose might consider the combination of Chapter 1 (The Rationale for International Marketing) with Chapter 2 (Appreciating the International Economic and Financial Environment), Chapter 3 (Catering for the Cultural and Social Environment), Chapter 4 (Avoiding the Pitfalls of the International Political and Legal Environment) and Chapter 5 (The Technology Environment and Contemporary Environmental Variables) from Part A; Chapter 6 (Researching International Markets) and Chapter 8 (Planning for International Marketing) from Part B; Chapter 13 (Modifying Products for Overseas Markets), Chapter 15 (Promotion in International Marketing), Chapter 16 (International Pricing for Profit) and Chapter 17 (Effective Distribution Overseas) from Part D.

**International marketing management text** Those proposing to use the book as an international marketing management text may consider the combination of  Chapter 1 (The Rational for International Marketing) with Chapter 6 (Researching International Markets) and Chapter 8 (Planning for International Marketing) from Part B; Chapter 9 (Gaining Competitive Advantage), Chapter 10 (International Competitive Marketing Strategies), Chapter 11 (Globalisation) and Chapter 12 (Relationships, Networks and Strategic Alliances) from Part C; Chapter 13 (Modifying Products for Overseas Markets), Chapter 15 (Promotion in International Markets), Chapter 16 (International Pricing for Profit) and Chapter 17 (Effective Distribution Overseas) from Part D. Students could also be required to familiarise themselves with the content of Part B as part of their background reading.

**Contemporary issues in international marketing text** Those proposing to use the book for a contemporary international marketing unit as a follow-on to one of the above units may consider a combination of Chapter 5 (The Technology Environment and Contemporary Environmental Variables) from Part A; Chapter 7 (International Market Selection) from Part B; Chapter 12 (Relationships,

Networks and Strategic Alliances) from Part C; Chapter 14 (Marketing Services Overseas) from Part D; Chapter 18 (Incorporating International Trade Relations into Overseas Marketing) and Chapter 19 (Contemporary International Marketing Issues) from Part E.

Other changes in this fourth edition include having at the end of each of the five parts a longer 'end of part' case which covers issues addressed in all chapters in that part. Many of the examples used previously have been replaced with more recent illustrations; statistics have also been updated and a chapter on the internet has now been replaced with an expanded discussion at the end of each chapter of the significance of the internet as far as the contents of that chapter are concerned.

The focus on Asia has been retained. However, in a number of instances where theories of international marketing are discussed there is a focus on the fact that theories developed on the basis of research in Western developed countries need to be viewed with circumspection before they can be applied to emerging markets, most of which are in developing rather than developed countries. More examples of doing business in countries outside Asia have been included to reflect better the changing market conditions faced by Australian and New Zealand firms in the international domain due to the enlargement of the European Union and the signing of an increased number of free trade agreements by Australia and New Zealand.

## SUPPLEMENTARY MATERIALS

This text is supported by a range of supplementary learning and teaching aids:

- Instructor's Manual—includes chapter overviews, chapter outlines and suggested teaching strategies.
- PowerPoint slides—for each chapter a series of PowerPoint slides has been developed to follow the structure of the text.
- Test item file—contains a large bank of questions for use in exams or exercises.
- Website—contains additional case studies and student-focused learning material.

Information Sources—this invaluable reference for students containing details on where to find information on all the topics in the book has been updated and upon popular request placed onto the website to enable the content to be updated continually.

We gratefully acknowledge the following contributors for their work on the supplementary material that accompanies the text: Dr Susan Dann, Consultant (PowerPoint and TestBank); Dr Geoff Fripp, University of Sydney (Companion Website); and Dr Marilyn Healy, Queensland University of Technology (Instructor's Manual)

All supplements are available to adopters of the text—for details please contact your Pearson Education representative or your local Pearson Education office.

# ACKNOWLEDGEMENTS

No book is solely the work of its authors. Many reviewers at other universities provided valuable comments and suggestions. We are indebted to the following colleagues:

| | |
|---|---|
| Kathleen Griffiths | Royal Melbourne Institute of Technology |
| Campbell Jeffery | University of Ballarat |
| Linda Hall | University of Tasmania |
| Bharati Singh | University of Queensland |
| Clare D'Souza | La Trobe University |
| Joe Williams | Flinders University |
| Tony Pecotich | University of Western Australia |
| Diane Slade | Edith Cowan University |
| Vanessa Ratten | Queensland University of Technology |
| Paul Harrison | Deakin University |
| Rob Hecker | University of Tasmania |
| Ho Yin Wong | Central Queensland University |
| Mike Willis | Monash University |

We would also like to thank all the reviewers of previous editions of this book.

Special thanks go to academics and international marketing practitioners throughout Australia and New Zealand who contributed their time and expertise in providing the case studies that are a feature of this text. They are:

| | |
|---|---|
| Peter Moore | Director, Interstrat Corporation, Europe |
| Greg Walton | Victoria University of Wellington |
| John Kweh | University of South Australia |
| Justin Cohen | University of South Australia |
| Jan Charbonneau | Massey University |
| Al Marshall | ACU National |
| Hongzhi Gao | University of Otago |
| John Knight | University of Otago |
| Mike Willis | Monash University |

| Troy Heffernan | University of Plymouth |
| Marcelle Foundling | Charles Sturt University |
| Bradley Mitchell | Inveratek Group Ltd |
| Joe Williams | Flinders University |
| Susan Dann | Consultant |

Special thanks also go to Sebastien Vaccari, Wisitta Gray, Jun Wen Chen, Darek Chrabowski, Anke Peter, Danielle Lawson, Mary Pugh, Chloe Savage, Tina Slattery and Trevor Morgan for their invaluable contributions to the case studies for this edition.

The authors would particularly like to acknowledge the contribution of Kaylene Bailey of the University of Western Sydney for her patience in 'polishing' the diagrams and tables. The authors also thank Peter Moore of Interstrat Corporation for his assistance with International Highlights and sourcing of new material in several of the chapters.

We also owe a great debt to the people at Pearson Education Australia who helped develop this book, in particular to Paul Burgess, Louise Cavander and Katie Millar. It is their guidance, support and skill at managing the authors that has resulted in the finished product in which these acknowledgements appear.

# ABOUT THE AUTHORS

**Professor Richard Fletcher** is Professor of Marketing at the University of Western Sydney (UWS). From 2003 to 2006 he was also Head of the School of Marketing and International Business. Professor Fletcher holds a Master of Arts by Research from the University of Sydney, a Master of Commerce in Marketing from the University of New South Wales, and a Doctorate in Philosophy in International Marketing from the University of Technology, Sydney (UTS). During the time he spent at the University of Technology, Sydney prior to taking up his current appointment, he lectured in Marketing and International Marketing at both the graduate and undergraduate levels and created five new international marketing subjects not previously offered in Australia. He is the principal author of the text *International E-Business Marketing* along with J. Bell and R. McNaughton published by Thomson, UK.

Richard's research interests are countertrade, internationalisation, networking, ethical issues, cultural impacts and the problems of marketing to emerging markets. His research has been published in *Industrial Marketing Management*, the *European Journal of Marketing*, the *Journal of Global Business*, the *International Business Review*, the *Australasian Marketing Journal*, the *Journal of International Marketing and Exporting* and the *Journal of Communication Management*. It also appears in several books of case studies and readings in international marketing as well as in the form of chapters in a further six books of scholarly articles.

He is a fellow of both the international think tank IC2 and the Academy of Marketing Science and he is a member of the executive of the Australian and New Zealand Marketing Academy (ANZMAC). He is on the editorial board of the US *Journal of Industrial Marketing Management*. He is also a member of the European Marketing Academy (EMAC), the UK Academy of Marketing (UKAM), the Academy of International Business (AIB), the Australian and New Zealand Academy of International Business (ANZIBA) the Industrial Marketing and Purchasing Group (IMP) and the Australian Institute of Export.

Prior to becoming an academic, Richard was an Australian Trade Commissioner with 25 years' experience in representing Australia's commercial interests overseas, in New Delhi, Bombay, San Francisco, Jakarta, Tehran, Libya, Los Angeles and Bangkok. During that period he organised major Australian trade promotions in seven overseas cities, managed several trade missions, led two trade missions to Vietnam in the late 1980s and participated in bilateral trade negotiations with various countries on behalf of Australia on a number of occasions.

**Professor Linden Brown** was Adjunct Professor of Marketing and Director of the Market Strategy and Information Technology (M*SAT) Group at the University of Technology, Sydney, from 1995 to 2005. He was Visiting Professor at INSEAD, France, in 1999 and Visiting Professor at Cranfield University, England, from 2000 to 2002. Professor Brown is one of Australia's leading consultants and academics.

His first degree, in Accounting and Economics, was followed by a PhD in Marketing at the University of New South Wales. He has lectured in marketing at a number of Australian universities, including the Melbourne Graduate School of Management, Sydney Graduate School of Management and Public Policy, Royal Melbourne Institute of Technology, the University of New South Wales and the University of Technology, Sydney.

Professor Brown has published twelve books, the most recent being *Marketing, 7th edition*, co-authored with Philip Kotler, Stewart Adam, Suzan Burton and Gary Armstrong, published in 2007. His most recent published articles and working papers are in the field of marketing excellence and market culture, related to business transformation and competitive strategy.

As a business practitioner, Professor Brown was co-founder of an international transportation company and has been a director and owner of small businesses in the printing and food marketing areas. He also has extensive experience as a marketing consultant in a range of industries, including computer products and services, telecommunications, finance, retailing, hotels, building products, steel and minerals, and the education industry.

Professor Brown has designed and conducted executive development programs in strategic marketing for many Australian and international corporations over the past 20 years. He is particularly experienced in the use of marketing software tools for individual and team learning. Since 1994 much of his work has been in China as well as other Asian countries such as Taiwan, Japan, Malaysia and the Philippines. In the past four years he has been conducting many of his activities in North America.

He is founder of Interstrat, which has provided strategic marketing services to multinational companies since its incorporation in 1988. In 2007 he co-founded a new company in the US, MarketCulture Strategies, whose mission is to assist mid-sized and large companies to embed a market-oriented culture.

# ADDITIONAL CASES ON THE WEBSITE

ADDITIONAL CASES ON THE WEBSITE

# INTRODUCTION

# THE RATIONALE FOR INTERNATIONAL MARKETING

## LearningObjectives

**After reading this chapter you should be able to:**

- appreciate the position and interests of individual countries such as Australia and New Zealand in international trade and how one country's situation can differ from that of other countries;

- recognise the diversity of stakeholders in the international marketing scene;

- assess the driving and restraining forces that underlie the international marketing imperative;

- recognise the various approaches being adopted and evaluate the various classification systems that apply in international marketing;

- identify underlying concepts of international marketing;

- appreciate the beneficial role of international marketing in firms' overall marketing activity;

- assess, from the firm's perspective, the application of the 'wheel of international marketing'; and

- recognise the importance of global trade and the role that marketing plays.

# The next generation of mega markets

As markets in developed countries become saturated, for many products, firms are increasingly looking to the less-developed markets as potential sources of income. Whereas several years ago these markets accounted for 20% of gross world product, now they account for more than half (on a purchasing power parity basis). They account for 40% of world exports, consume half the world's energy and hold 70% of the world's foreign exchange reserves (Gittins, 2007). However, this growth in wealth is far less evenly spread throughout society than is the case in developed countries.

Figure 1.1 shows that overseas markets can be divided into developed, emerging and developing. If market size is a consideration, then on the basis of multiplying average income by population the bottom of the pyramid (i.e. developing markets) represents a larger potential than do the developed markets.

To date, most firms when expanding from trade with developed markets have focused on emerging markets and many have pursued the same segments in these markets as they have in their more traditional markets. This is evidenced by their focus on the growing middle class in emerging markets which appear to offer potential because they are growing fast, and are engaged in market liberalisation, privatisation and modernisation. They have young populations, are receptive to technology

leapfrogging, have low competitive intensity and are less regulated. In many of these markets family companies dominate the commercial scene.

Below these markets of promise is another stratum of markets usually described as developing or low-income markets. These are often referred to as markets at the bottom of the pyramid (BOP). This is the lowest strata of markets as depicted in Figure 1.1. In these markets different approaches will be required as Western-style patterns of economic development are unlikely to take place. Marketing strategies will need to be based on leveraging the existing strengths of these markets rather than addressing their weaknesses with Western-derived approaches. This will involve developing relationships with non-traditional partners; working with local interests to create customised solutions; and developing local capacity.

Increasingly, major multinational companies such as LG Electronics are realising that when operating at this level in developing countries, non-traditional marketing methods are necessary in order to both reach and satisfy the BOP market. In India, LG Electronics offers free first aid and clean drinking water at popular religious events even though it does not sell its products on such occasions. However, when its mobile vans go to the villages again, its logo is already familiar to the villagers and, as a result, access for its salespeople is easier. It also has petrol pump owners displaying its products and tractor dealers acting as its sub-dealers, and it

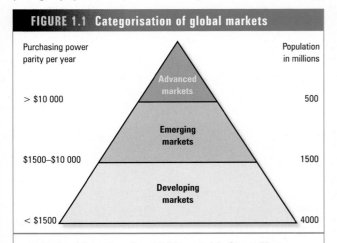

**FIGURE 1.1  Categorisation of global markets**

| Purchasing power parity per year | | Population in millions |
| --- | --- | --- |
| | Advanced markets | |
| > $10 000 | | 500 |
| | Emerging markets | |
| $1500–$10 000 | | 1500 |
| | Developing markets | |
| < $1500 | | 4000 |

**SOURCE:** *Adaptation of a model presented by Stuart Hart, Kenan-Flagler Business School, at the World Business Council for Sustainable Development, Johannesburg, 2002.*

parks its mobile vans near where people congregate, to carry out demonstrations and directly take orders.

In the process of tapping these markets, it will be necessary to address issues such as the large informal economy that exists and which is not recorded in official statistics; the lack of enforcement of the rule of law as exemplified in lack of protection for intellectual property; political instability, government interference, bureaucracy and bribery; and the need to develop separate marketing approaches for the wealthy, the middle class and the poor.

Business models that have evolved from within such markets, like the Grameen Bank and its offshoots in Bangladesh (where customers have become entrepreneurs)

and the Wao microbank in Papua-New Guinea, and techniques espoused by a select band of transnational companies such as Unilever illustrate how such markets can be tapped in their own terms. In the case of Unilever, its Indian subsidiary, Hindustan Lever Ltd (HLL), uses a wide variety of partners to deliver its products and requires its managers to live in villages so they can develop empathy and understanding of their customers. HLL provides opportunities and training to local entrepreneurs and experiments with new types of distribution involving selling via local performers and village street theatres. These business models point up the need to adapt each element of the marketing mix to reach and motivate BOP consumers.

**SOURCES:** *Adapted from London, T. and Hart, S.L. (2004), 'Reinventing strategies for emerging markets beyond the traditional model',* Journal of International Business Studies, *Vol. 35, pp. 350–70;* Financial Times *(2004),* Special Report on Business and Development, *24 June; Cavusgil, S.T. (2004), 'The promise of emerging markets', invited lecture, 1 November, University of Western Sydney; Kotler, P., Keller, K.L., Ang, S.H., Leong, S.M. and Tan, C.T. (2006)* Marketing Management: An Asian Perspective, *4th edn, Pearson Prentice Hall, Singapore, p. 247; and Fletcher, R. (2006) 'International marketing at the bottom of the pyramid–a three country study',* Proceedings of the Meeting of the Consortium for International Marketing and Research, *Istanbul, 27–30 May.*

# INTRODUCTION

While many US texts in international marketing currently being used in Australasia focus on the activities of the transnational firm and the merits of a global as opposed to a local approach to international marketing, such approaches are not always relevant to firms in the Australasian region, apart from alerting them to the nature of the international competitive environment in which they are likely to operate. This is because the region has spawned only a limited number of global firms. Exporters in the region can be classified for the most part as:

• indigenous small- and medium-scale exporters (SMEs); or

• local subsidiaries of transnational firms.

A global or transnational approach to international marketing is not an operating strategy for the first category of firms above and is only partially appropriate to the second category. With regard to the first group, globalisation is only a reality as far as potential competitors in both the domestic and the international markets are concerned. With the second category, executives in these subsidiaries are preoccupied with balancing the demands of the transnational corporation with the requirements of the local market and the regulations that circumscribe activities in that market. For these reasons this book is written primarily from the perspective of firms in the above categories rather than from the perspective of the global or transnational firm. Although globalisation and its manifestations are covered in the book, such coverage is intended to sensitise Australasian firms to future trends and the underlying forces, which may have an impact on their future international competitiveness. Table 1.1 shows how the world's top 500 firms are distributed between countries/blocs.

During the six-year period, there has been a shift away from the US and Japan in favour of Europe and the large emerging markets such as China, India and Mexico.

| TABLE 1.1 | The world's 500 largest multinational enterprises (MNEs) by country/region, 2000 and 2006 |

| Country/bloc | Number of MNEs 2000 | Number of MNEs 2006 |
| --- | --- | --- |
| United States | 185 | 170 |
| European Union | 141 | 163 |
| Japan | 104 | 70 |
| China | 12 | 20 |
| Canada | 15 | 14 |
| South Korea | 11 | 12 |
| Switzerland | 11 | 12 |
| Australia | 7 | 8 |
| India | 1 | 6 |
| Mexico | 2 | 5 |
| Russia | 2 | 5 |
| Brazil | 3 | 4 |
| Taiwan | – | 3 |
| Norway | 2 | 2 |
| Malaysia | 1 | 1 |
| Saudi Arabia | – | 1 |
| Singapore | 1 | 1 |
| South Africa | 1 | – |
| Thailand | – | 1 |
| Turkey | – | 1 |
| Venezuela | 1 | 1 |
| *Total* | 500 | 500 |

**SOURCE:** Fortune, *24 April 2006.*

# THE NEW INTERNATIONAL MARKETING ENVIRONMENT

Today we are faced with shrinking communications in a situation where information is power. At the click of a mouse we can access data about both threats and opportunities that arise from activities overseas over which we have little control. Gone are the days where we can rely on our national government to protect us from the threats posed by international competitors. Technology is making size far less important than was formerly the case and small firms from strange countries can bob up overnight as competitors in the domestic market. By contrast, we can now compete in overseas markets previously closed to us on account of size and scale economies. Technology is also causing size-related communications infrastructure to be bypassed as exemplified by developing countries abandoning plans to invest in land-based communications in favour of satellite technology as illustrated by 16.09% of China's population having mobile phones resulting in over 300 million mobile phone users (*Infoworld*, 22 January 2007). For those on the move, the communications revolution means that wireless applications protocol (WAP) technology makes online shopping available via the mobile phone, and the global system for mobile communications technology (GSM) facilitates locating customers wherever they might be in the world and sending them instant promotional messages.

The international trading scene is also going through major changes which affect the ability to access overseas markets. In the 1990s a new world trade order, embodied in the creation of the World Trade Organization (WTO), which would address issues of agriculture, services, investment and intellectual property, caused a certain euphoria. In recent years disillusionment has set in as the WTO has been no more successful than its predecessor, the General Agreement on Tariffs and Trade (GATT), in solving problems of market access. The focus has now shifted towards bilateral trade agreements. Being outside major world trading blocs such as the European Union and the North American Free Trade Area, Australia and New Zealand have been embracing bilateral arrangements as evidenced in the case of Australia in free trade agreements with Singapore, Thailand and the USA. Full details of this new thrust in international trade relations are provided in Chapter 18.

Increasingly firms are having to focus not just on the interests of their shareholders, but also on the interests of a broad range of other stakeholders located anywhere in the world, any one of whom could adversely affect operations either directly or via withdrawal of support or via damage to the firm's image or reputation. Figure 1.2 shows a typical spread

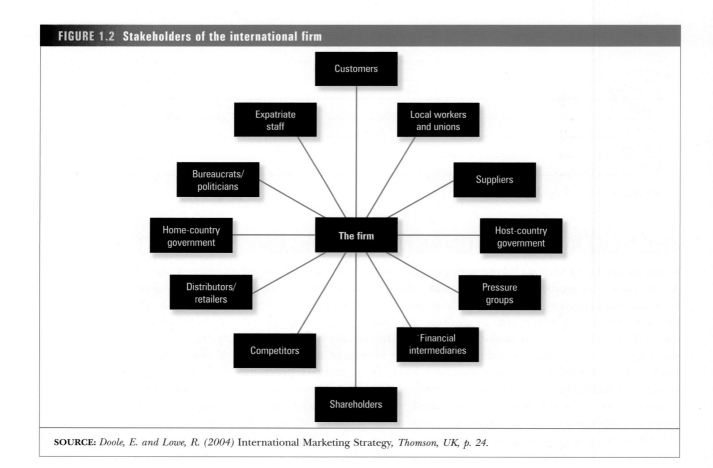

**FIGURE 1.2 Stakeholders of the international firm**

**SOURCE:** *Doole, E. and Lowe, R. (2004)* International Marketing Strategy, *Thomson, UK, p. 24.*

of stakeholders whose interests the firm needs to take into account when it operates across national borders.

This in turn leads to the concept of holistic marketing. Holistic marketing recognises that in marketing, everything matters, whether it be consumers, employees, other companies, competition, government and society as a whole and that a broad integrated perspective is necessary. Kotler et al. (2006, pp. 17–21) claim that holistic marketing involves:

- relationship marketing—building satisfying relationships with key parties;

- integrated marketing—integrated programs that create, communicate and deliver value for customers;

- internal marketing—ensuring that all in the company are driven by a recognition of the need to serve customers well; and

- social responsibility marketing—taking into account the broader concerns and the ethical, environmental, political, legal and social context of marketing programs.

The above approach, which leads to a sense of corporate social responsibility, is very important in international marketing where increasing attention needs to be paid to its three elements of first, *product use*—a focus on the contribution of products to assisting the wellbeing and quality of life of the society; secondly, *business practice*—a focus on good corporate governance and environmental sensitivity, and thirdly, *distribution of profits*—which should be done both equitably and in a manner that represents a just return to the host community (Warhurst 2001).

## 1.1 INTERNATIONAL HIGHLIGHT

# Times—they are a'changing and marketing must keep pace

Historically Australia's greatest export and wealth creator, especially until the 1960s, was wool. Even just 16 years ago, Australia had more than 180 million sheep and a wool clip worth more than A$5 billion—but not any more. Prices for wool have fallen since the abandonment of the Wool Reserve Price Scheme in 1991 and farmers have diversified into other crops. Internationally the demand for wool has shrunk from 5.25% of world fibre production in 1990 to 2.1% in 2004, reflecting changes in consumer taste. Even though China now buys 60% of Australia's wool, in fact Chinese consumers prefer cotton. If it is to survive, the wool industry needs marketing—marketing directed not to buyers of wool, but marketing directed to buyers of the products made from wool. The focus needs to be on what buyers need in terms of those end-use applications in which wool could be involved. This requires the development of products from wool to meet their wishes—be it the fabric or the garment made from the fabric. Generic promotion of wool is now a thing of the past and the international marketing of this commodity and Australian icon needs to focus on the current generation of consumers and use their cult figures, such as Elle McPherson and Greg Norman, to reach them. Such an approach will mandate partnerships with designers, manufacturers and retailers around the world. As an example, US fashion houses are now being involved in the promotion of wool with Saks focusing on women's wear and Dillards (329 department stores) on men's wear made from wool.

**SOURCE:** *Adapted from* Sydney Morning Herald, *23–24 September 2006, pp. 25, 30–1.*

# What is international marketing?

All of us live in an international marketplace. As you read this book you may be sitting in a chair purchased from IKEA and imported from Scandinavia, and on your desk you may have a PC with a US brand, but manufactured in Korea. The software may be designed in Bangalore, India, and the video recorder for screening the recommended international marketing film may be a Panasonic made in Malaysia. The book itself, while written in Australia, may have been printed in Singapore. What a contrast to 150 years ago when students sitting at their desks would be surrounded by items all of which came from their own countries and in most cases from within a 120 km radius.

International marketing is the process of planning and undertaking transactions across national boundaries that involve exchange. Its forms range from exporting to licensing to joint ventures to wholly owned acquisitions to management contracts. Because the transaction takes place across national boundaries, the international marketer is subject to a different set of macro-environmental factors and constraints deriving from different political systems, legal frameworks, cultural norms and economic circumstances.

Given these difficulties and differences, why undertake international marketing? The answer lies in the forces that both drive and restrain involvement in international markets.

## DRIVING FORCES

The first of these forces is that of market needs. These needs transcend national boundaries and exist in many countries. International marketing is about catering to these needs. However, often in international marketing these needs are created by promotion. The advertising campaign may focus on a global appeal, but is adapted to the specific requirements of each culture. The marketing of diamonds by De Beers is an example of this. It promotes diamonds to announce an engagement in Japan where giving an engagement ring is not a traditional custom. In so doing, it is capitalising on the fact that the emotions that surround the engagement are universal and these can be harnessed to a new want—that of celebrating an engagement with a diamond ring.

A second driving force is that of technology. It is a universal, uniform and consistent factor that crosses national boundaries as everyone aspires to the latest technology. Of itself, technology knows no cultural boundaries—only in its application does culture come into play. When this happens the modification is not in the technology, but rather in its application. If a company knows how to manage technology in one country it has experience that is relevant to the rest of the world. News Corporation was well placed to succeed with its takeover of Fox Broadcasting in the USA in that it could draw on its experience in creating and managing a network of radio and TV stations in Australia.

Cost is another driving force. Economies of scale deriving from supplying more markets than just Australia or New Zealand can drive down research, engineering, design, creative and production costs. The cost pressure is becoming more and more intense when new products increasingly involve major investment and extended periods for development. The pharmaceutical industry is an example. It typically costs between A$70 million and A$150 million to develop a new product from scratch in this industry and the average development period is about eight years. Rarely can these development costs be recovered from one national market alone, which is why such products are usually launched on a worldwide basis.

Government can be another driving force via the creation of policies and assistance measures that facilitate international involvement and the creation of standards that are compatible with those in other countries.

Communication has been revolutionised by the changes in information technology. New innovations become known throughout the world more rapidly than was previously the case and, as a result, everyone wants the latest product. The information revolution has also spawned media that overlap national borders, and global media have emerged. Customers in one country are increasingly exposed to messages about products that do not originate in that country. Figure 1.3 illustrates the forces that influence standardisation versus adaptation in international marketing.

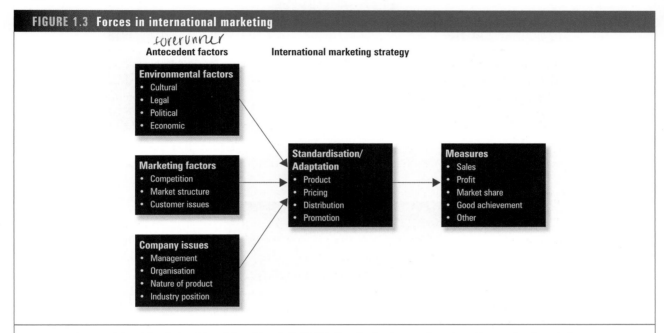

**FIGURE 1.3 Forces in international marketing**

forerunner

**SOURCE:** *Reprinted from Theodosiou, M. and Leonidou, L.C. (2003) 'Standardisation vs adaptation of international marketing strategy; an integrated assessment of the empirical research',* International Business Review, *Vol. 12, p. 143. Copyright 2003 with permission from Elsevier.*

## RESTRAINING FORCES

The first of the restraining forces is to do with differences between national markets. Usually the differences are sufficiently pronounced to require adaptation of at least some elements of the marketing mix to suit local conditions. They may be a function of economic development, the political system, legal requirements and cultural norms.

In addition, most countries implement some form of control over entry and access to their market. In part these controls are driven by a desire to maintain national sovereignty and in part to protect national values, local vested interests and domestic companies. This is achieved by both tariff and non-tariff barriers. With the progressive reduction of the former as a result of the activities of the WTO, non-tariff barriers are becoming increasingly important as a control mechanism. Controls also apply to investment, acquisition by foreign interests, franchising and licensing.

Another restraining force is that of actual or perceived risk. Cavusgil (2004) categorises these as commercial risks, cross-cultural risks, country risks (political and legal) and financial risks, as shown in Figure 1.4. A final restraining force is that of myopia on the part of some managers, often due to ethnocentric attitudes.

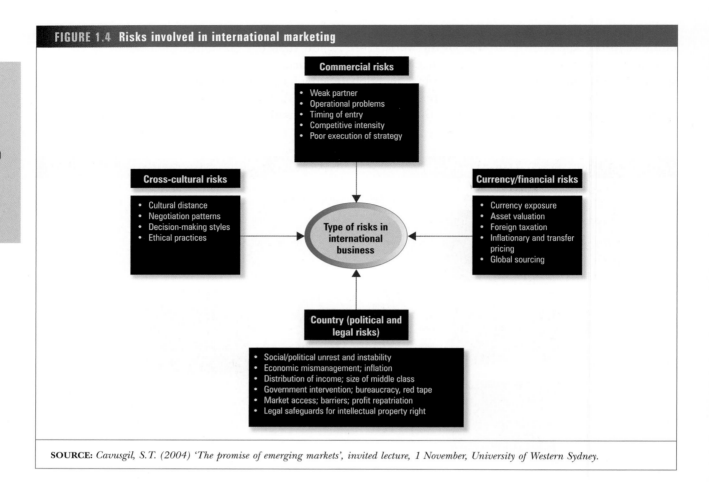

**FIGURE 1.4  Risks involved in international marketing**

**Commercial risks**
- Weak partner
- Operational problems
- Timing of entry
- Competitive intensity
- Poor execution of strategy

**Cross-cultural risks**
- Cultural distance
- Negotiation patterns
- Decision-making styles
- Ethical practices

**Type of risks in international business**

**Currency/financial risks**
- Currency exposure
- Asset valuation
- Foreign taxation
- Inflationary and transfer pricing
- Global sourcing

**Country (political and legal risks)**
- Social/political unrest and instability
- Economic mismanagement; inflation
- Distribution of income; size of middle class
- Government intervention; bureaucracy, red tape
- Market access; barriers; profit repatriation
- Legal safeguards for intellectual property right

**SOURCE:** *Cavusgil, S.T. (2004) 'The promise of emerging markets', invited lecture, 1 November, University of Western Sydney.*

## RATIONALE

In the immediate post-war period the ratio of world trade (i.e. cross-border trade) to total trade was much less than 10%. By the late 1980s this ratio had doubled, and at the end of the 20th century hovered around 35%. World trade in manufactured goods now represents more than 35% of total output with more than 50% of this being intracompany transfers. Overall, the expansion of world trade over the last 50 years has been above 7% per annum, far outpacing world economic growth during that period. As a result of the continued expansion of world trade, there is an inescapable network of global linkages that bind countries, institutions and individuals closer together. A currency crisis in Thailand affects its Asian neighbours and its trading partners in North Asia before adversely affecting countries in the developed world such as Australia. In a similar way, acts of war such as the invasion of Lebanon by Israel, and acts of terrorism such as the destruction of the World Trade Center in New York can have an impact on oil prices, stock markets, trade and travel throughout the world. Underlying the growth of the international economy since World War II are a number of factors. The most important of these are discussed below.

**Change in management orientation** Perlmutter (1995) developed a typology whereby firms could be classified according to the orientation of their management, as follows:

- An *ethnocentric orientation* is underpinned by the belief that the home country is superior and that the approach used in the home country should be applied to every other country. This leads to the view that the products of the home country can be sold anywhere without adaptation and that foreign operations are secondary or subordinate to domestic ones, and, from a manufacturing perspective, foreign markets are mostly viewed as an opportunity to dispose of surplus domestic production.

- A *polycentric orientation* is the opposite of ethnocentrism and reflects the approach that each country is different and that no country is necessarily inferior to another. Therefore the home country approach is viewed as largely irrelevant and, to be successful, products must be specifically tailored to the differences in each overseas country. This leads to the view that each overseas subsidiary should develop its own unique business and marketing approaches.

- *Regiocentric orientation* views the region as the market, and integrated strategies are developed for the region taking into account both the similarities and differences between the home market and the region. The world outside the region may be viewed from either an ethnocentric or polycentric standpoint.

- *Geocentric orientation* involves a world marketing strategy based on the recognition that countries have both similarities and differences. The entire world is viewed as a market and a strategy developed accordingly. It represents a synthesis of the ethnocentric and polycentric approaches and seeks to operate a global approach that is able to respond to local needs and wants.

An increasing number of companies that began with an ethnocentric orientation and then moved to a polycentric orientation have now adopted a regiocentric or geocentric orientation in response to changing circumstances in the international marketplace.

**International monetary framework** The rapid growth in trade and investment has created a need for greater liquidity to facilitate the trading of goods and services between nations. Until 1969 exchange rates were fixed, but since that time they have been allowed to fluctuate. International liquidity has been augmented by the International Monetary Fund (IMF) enabling its members to use special drawing rights (SDRs) in settling transactions involving reserves. This has overcome the limits on expanding liquidity imposed by earlier reliance on gold and foreign exchange.

**The world trading system** Following World War II nations did not want to return to the discriminatory trading practices of the 1920s and 1930s. The General Agreement on Tariffs and Trade (GATT) was born and the operations of this body did result in a lowering of the tariff barriers for industrial products. In 1996, following the conclusion of the Uruguay Round of the GATT negotiations, the WTO replaced the GATT. The WTO is now in the process of addressing other issues which stand in the way of a more liberal world trade system, such as non-tariff barriers, barriers to trade in agricultural products, freeing up services trade and issues related to investment.

Recent decades have been characterised by the emergence of an increasing number of regional trade groupings such as the ASEAN Free Trade Area and NAFTA. These trade blocs are posing a threat to those outside and nations are rushing to join blocs lest they be commercially disadvantaged as a result. Regional trade groupings (RTGs) vary in terms of the degree of national sovereignty surrendered—from the European Union at one extreme to the looser arrangement of the Asia-Pacific Economic Cooperation (APEC) at the other. Although a number of these RTGs were formed because of the perceived shortcomings of GATT, the extent to which such RTGs can co-exist with the WTO has yet to be determined.

Since 1945 the world has remained free of global conflicts and this has assisted the growth of the international economy. The passing of the Cold War has further accelerated this process, as conflicts now are more likely to be local rather than global. The Australian and New Zealand economies have experienced a period of strong economic growth and the resulting market opportunities have stimulated the movement of their firms offshore. This internationalisation has also improved the reception given to foreign firms operating in both markets with a consequent reduction in barriers to firms selling to or investing in Australia and New Zealand.

**Communications and transport** The time taken to transport goods and the cost of the goods have fallen considerably over recent decades. This has been due to the use of containers and larger vessels, as well as improved waterside efficiency, electronic data interchange (EDI) and rationalisation of shipping services. The jet aeroplane has made face-to-face meetings in international business easier and cheaper while the ability to transmit data electronically has improved the ease and reduced the cost of staying in touch with overseas customers and representatives and facilitated the management of diverse operations around the globe.

**Technology** Owing to technologies such as the world wide web, never before has it been so easy to gather, analyse and disseminate information. Products can be produced more quickly and obtained less expensively from sources around the world. Advances in technology allow firms to operate in 'market space' rather than the 'marketplace' by keeping the content while changing the context of the transaction. A newspaper, for example, can be distributed globally online, rather than delivered house to house, enabling unprecedented expansion in the ability to reach new customer groups. The burgeoning level of global investment means that an increasing number of Australians and New Zealanders are working for companies owned by non-Australian or New Zealand interests. This global interdependence is not stable, but continually changes as firms realign their international involvement. The pace of technology innovation grows faster each year, spurred on by the increasing speed of transmission of ideas across national boundaries.

# APPROACHES TO INTERNATIONAL MARKETING

There are a number of different approaches to international marketing. These are based on increasing forms of involvement or commitment. They reflect the fact that since World War II the international trading environment has become more complex and the interdependencies between firms in different countries are much greater. The first of these approaches classifies firms in terms of management approach to international involvement.

## From domestic to transnational

In this approach, firms are considered in terms of their orientation. The firm can operate as a domestic entity and in the past could be quite successful operating within the Australian or New Zealand markets. Export marketing is the first stage in the firm exploring opportunities outside the home country. By leveraging its experience in the domestic market, the firm exports its products overseas. This may involve a separate strategy to produce specifically for an overseas market or it may be the result of an attempt to dispose of surplus production or utilise excess production capacity. International marketing extends international involvement further, and usually includes a greater commitment of resources to the overseas market. For example, instead of relying on an intermediary overseas, the firm may establish its own direct representation in the overseas country. A further stage of involvement is operating on a multinational basis. This stage involves creating programs specifically for each overseas market that take into account the differences and unique circumstances of each country. Finally, global or transnational marketing focuses upon leveraging the global assets of the firm by taking what is unique and different in each country in which it operates and combining the unique features to create the most globally competitive offering. The transnational firm does not have a centre from which decisions are dictated to operations elsewhere, but rather the various operations operate relatively autonomously. They are connected to each other in the interests of dissemination of information and global rationalisation.

## From indirect exporting to foreign direct investment

In this approach, firms are classified according to the nature of their involvement in export-led or outward-driven international activities. This is based on the fact that initially firms may not export on a direct basis, but rather through an export intermediary (either an export merchant who takes title to the goods, or an export agent who receives a commission). From the perspective of the Australian or New Zealand firm, the sale is akin to a domestic one as little extra effort is involved because the goods are destined for overseas. The next stage is that the firm exports directly, but appoints an agent to represent its interests in the overseas market. This is the most common form of international involvement for small and medium-sized Australian exporters. In this case the agent receives a commission for arranging the distribution and sale of the products. Should the firm feel a loss of control over the marketing of its products in the overseas market because this is left to the agent, it can take the further step of establishing its own sales office in the market. This office is used to manage the distribution network necessary to get the goods to the final customer. It may be that tariff or non-tariff barriers either prohibit or make direct selling of the product from either Australia or New Zealand uneconomic.

## From an export focus to a holistic focus

The approaches previously discussed are based on the assumption that the domain of international marketing is restricted to outward-driven international activities. This view does not match the reality of international business, as the international involvement of firms can also be driven by inward activities such as importing. The stages of outward international involvement can be paralleled when international involvement is inward driven. In this situation, initially the firm imports through an agent based in Australia. Following this it imports direct from overseas. Then it may establish a buying office overseas as major Australian retailers such as David Jones Ltd have done. The next stage of international involvement may require manufacturing the foreign product in Australia or New Zealand under licence or becoming the franchisee for an overseas operation in Australia or New Zealand. The final stage could be foreign direct investment in the supplying country to produce goods for sale in the Australian or New Zealand markets so as to retain a competitive edge.

The reality of international business today is that outward and inward international activities do not operate in isolation from each other, but are frequently linked. This linkage is manifested in two ways. In the first, an outward activity can lead to an inward activity and vice versa. This happens when the Australian licensee of a US firm is given the rights to license manufacture of the product in New Zealand, or when the Australian franchisor gives the rights to its New Zealand franchisee to extend the franchise to the Cook Islands. The second type of linkage derives from more complicated forms of international involvement in which inward-driven international activities are directly dependent on outward-driven activities and vice versa. Strategic alliances, programs of cooperative manufacture, outsourcing and countertrade are examples of growing international business practices in which inward and outward international activities are linked to each other. The international marketer needs to take this linkage into account and adopt a holistic rather than an outward-driven approach to international marketing.

# CONCEPTS UNDERLYING INTERNATIONAL MARKETING

There are a number of concepts that provide a rationale for involvement in international activities. These may have an economic rationale, such as comparative advantage or internalisation of activities; a marketing rationale, such as extending the life of the product; or an information rationale, based on extending the networks of relationships in which the firm is involved.

## Comparative advantage

The theory of comparative advantage argues that a country can gain from international trade even if it has a disadvantage in production of all goods, or even if it is better than other countries at the production of all goods. The theory is based on the notion that a country should focus on what it does best rather than trying to produce everything. The following two-country/two-product model illustrates the concept. The two countries are the USA and Australia, both of which produce apples and oranges. There is no money involved and there is no difference in the Australian and the US product. Figure 1.5 illustrates that with any production mix between (A) and (E) total production is less at these production mixes than when there is concentration of production on the product in which each country has the greatest competitive advantage. For the USA it is oranges, whereas for Australia it is apples. To calculate this comparative advantage it is necessary to establish the production ratios for the two products. From a US perspective this is 1.25 (100/80) for apples and 3.0 (60/20) for oranges. From an Australian perspective, this is 0.80 (80/100) for apples and 0.33 (20/60) for oranges. Comparing what each country can produce under conditions of total specialisation, Australia has a comparative advantage in apples whereas the USA has a comparative advantage in oranges.

There are limits to the concept of comparative advantage. Even in the above example where the products offered are undifferentiated, seasonality should be taken into account. The production season for apples in Australia is the reverse of the production season in the USA with the result that Australian apples are available when prices are at their highest in the USA.

## Product life cycle extension

A well-known paradigm in marketing is that of the product life cycle. This states that products proceed through stages in their life from their inception to their abandonment. These stages are usually labelled 'introduction', 'growth', 'maturity' and 'decline'. This paradigm is specific to a market. Given the differences between the Australian and overseas markets, especially as far as levels of economic development are concerned, it is often the case that a product that has reached maturity in Australia may be at an introductory or growth stage in a specific

## FIGURE 1.5 Comparative advantage—an example

### 1. Production possibilities of United States and Australia (1000 production units)

| | Before specialisation and trade (000 bushells) | | | |
| | United States | | Australia | |
| Use of production units or production possibilities | Apples | Oranges | Apples | Oranges |
| --- | --- | --- | --- | --- |
| A 1000 in apples, 0 in oranges | 100 | 0 | 80 | 0 |
| B 750 in apples, 250 in oranges | 75 | 15 | 60 | 5 |
| C 500 in apples, 500 in oranges | 50 | 30 | 40* | 10* |
| D 250 in apples, 750 in oranges | 25* | 45* | 20 | 15 |
| E 0 in apples, 1000 in oranges | 0 | 60 | 0 | 20 |

*Production in isolation.

### 2. Production and consumption after total specialisation and trade

| | United States | | | Australia | | |
| | | Trades: Imports (+) | | | Trades: Imports (+) | |
| | Produces | Exports(–) | Consumes | Produces | Exports(–) | Consumes |
| --- | --- | --- | --- | --- | --- | --- |
| Apples (000 bushells) | 0 | +30 | 30 | 80 | –30 | 50 |
| Oranges (000 bushells) | 60 | –12 | 48 | 0 | +12 | 12 |

Trading price 30/12 = 2.5 apples = 1 orange
12/30 = 4 oranges = 1 apple

**SOURCE:** *Adapted from Keegan, W.J., Warren, J. and Green, M.C. (1995)* Global Marketing Management, *p. 12. Reproduced with permission of Pearson Education, Inc., Upper Saddle River, NJ.*

overseas market. As a result, the life of a product in the Australian market can be extended, by exporting it to an overseas market where the 'decline' stage has not yet been reached.

A related concept is that of the product trade cycle, which incorporates the life cycle of markets. This concept proposes that the relationship between product and market proceeds through four stages. Initially the product is exported to the overseas market; then production commences in that overseas market; that market in turn exports to nearby markets; finally, because of rising production costs, it is no longer worthwhile producing it in Australia and the overseas market begins supplying the Australian firm. From a macro perspective, high-income, mass-producing countries, such as the USA and to a lesser extent Australia, were initially exporters of many basic manufactures such as textiles and clothing, but ultimately became importers. A second tier of developing countries initially imported the product before becoming exporters. Then a third tier of less-developed countries initially imported, then began manufacture and finally exhibited the same trend from importing to exporting. The shift to low-cost production sources is only inevitable if the product remains the same. Continual product innovation can halt this process because it results in a different product with a different life cycle.

Figure 1.6 illustrates how countries at different stages of development move from importing to manufacturing to exporting, then to importing. It also shows that product life cycle—whether the product is new, mature or has become a standardised product—has an impact on the product trade cycle.

The evolution of the VCR illustrates the product trade cycle model. In the mid-1970s Japanese companies such as Sony and JVC produced VCRs for the Japanese market and for export. Customers overseas were buying Japanese-made goods even if they carried local brand names such as RCA. When the product category entered the growth phase, South Korean companies such as Goldstar and Samsung entered the international market in competition with Japan with a cheaper product due to their lower labour and other costs. When the product reached the mature phase, Japanese producers shifted production to low-cost producers in other countries such as Malaysia, Indonesia and Thailand.

SOURCE: *Keegan, W.J. and Green, M.C. (2003) Global Marketing, 3rd edn, Prentice Hall International Inc., p. 432.*

Underlying the above model is the assumption that the product originates in the advanced country, then trickles down to developing countries and then to less-developed countries (as illustrated in Figure 1.7). This concept, however, may not reflect the behaviour of all firms, especially those that wish to introduce the product into all markets simultaneously, as is the case with many 'born global' companies. This 'shower' approach recognises that we live in a global village where market opportunities may emerge simultaneously on a regional or global basis.

## Internalisation

As firms consider their involvement in international activities they are faced with either committing large resources so as to exercise the same degree of control over what happens to their product overseas as they achieve in the domestic market, or committing fewer resources by relinquishing some control to others such as agents. The exercise of control involves the firm in internalising activities in the overseas market. This usually requires it to replicate its Australian or New Zealand operation in the overseas market in terms of activity, management and control. By internalising overseas activities within the firm, a number of problems frequently encountered in international marketing can be avoided. These include search and negotiating costs, protection of the firm's reputation, costs of contracts being broken and buyer uncertainty as to quality and maintenance of quality. Other problems that may be reduced by internalisation are:

- the management of the relationship with the overseas government;
- control over purchases and conditions of sale overseas;
- consistency in the volume and content of promotional activities in the overseas market;
- control over marketing outlets in the other country; and
- integration of activities in the overseas country with activities in third-country markets as well as in the home country.

## Relationships and networks

The growing involvement of Australian and New Zealand business with Asia has led to the realisation that the tangible elements and the financial attractiveness of an offering in overseas markets may not be the main determinants of the purchasing decision. International marketing is perceived as more risky than marketing within Australia or New Zealand. If the reasons for this are analysed, perceived risk is due to the parties to the transaction being unfamiliar with each other. The establishment of relationships becomes important in

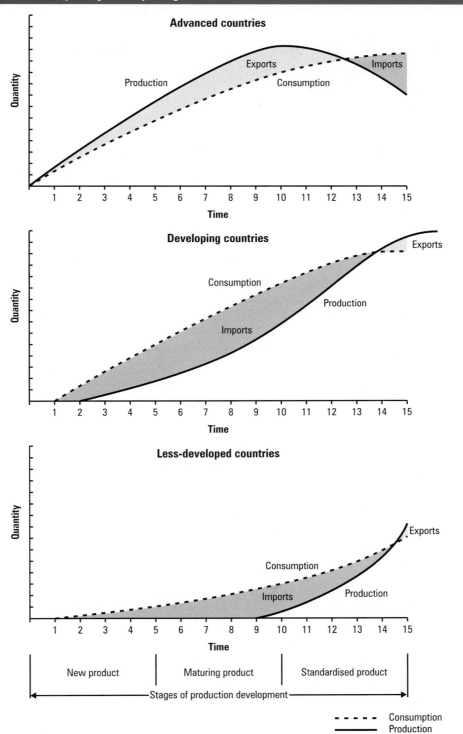

**FIGURE 1.6 Comparison of exporting and importing between countries**

Advanced countries

Developing countries

Less-developed countries

Stages of production development

New product · Maturing product · Standardised product

- - - - Consumption
———— Production

**SOURCE:** *Keegan, W.J. and Green, M.C. (2003)* Global Marketing, *3rd edn, Prentice Hall International Inc., NJ, p. 433.*

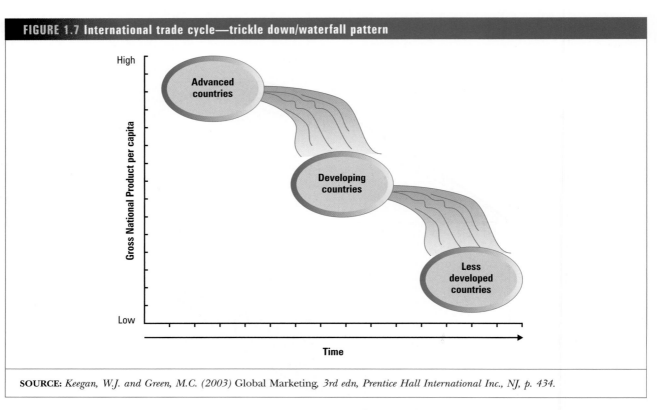

**FIGURE 1.7 International trade cycle—trickle down/waterfall pattern**

**SOURCE:** *Keegan, W.J. and Green, M.C. (2003)* Global Marketing, *3rd edn, Prentice Hall International Inc., NJ, p. 434.*

reducing this perceived risk. In the Australian environment for example, firms operate as members of an established network of relationships and the competitive position of the firm is as dependent on the contributions of other partners in the network as it is on the firm's own activities.

Effective international marketing is often a matter of linking the local network of which the firm is a part to an overseas network in such a way that network members derive advantage from their relationship with members of the other network. When searching for agents to represent them or joint venture partners overseas, the Australian or New Zealand firm needs to study the network with which the other party is involved. The reasons for doing this include ensuring the compatibility of aspirations and effectiveness of reach, otherwise the new relationship is unlikely to deliver the anticipated benefits to the Australian or New Zealand firm.

# THE WHEEL OF INTERNATIONAL MARKETING

## The hub

The hub of the wheel in this analogy consists of the marketing mix variables—product, price, promotion and distribution (see Figure 1.8). These variables, which lie at the core of any marketing operation whether it be domestic or international, can be controlled by the firm. Products vary in terms of usage patterns, stage in the life cycle and the extent to which they are capable of being standardised as opposed to the degree to which they are sensitive to customer demands. Pricing varies according to whether it is determined by the marketplace or can be established on a cost-plus basis. This may be contingent on whether the strategy of

**FIGURE 1.8  International marketing task**

**SOURCE:** *Adapted from Cateora, P.R. and Graham, J.L. (2005)* International Marketing, *McGraw Hill Irwin, Ohio, p. 10.*

the firm is short-term gain or long-term market share. Promotion can vary according to the relative importance of advertising, personal selling, trade promotion or public relations in the promotion mix for the product. Finally, distribution varies according to the willingness to accept risk as opposed to a desire to have control over the product from factory to final consumer. In international marketing, these variables will need modifying to take account of uncontrollable variables in both the local and overseas markets.

## The spokes

The spokes of the wheel connect the hub to the rim and affect the relationship between the hub and the rim. The spokes in this analogy are akin to regulations on exporting that are usually imposed by governments—for commercial, economic, technological, political and legal reasons. These regulations can be commercially motivated and driven by a desire to protect the interests of domestic industry. An example is the ban that existed for many years in Australia on the export of Merino sheep. Regulations may be driven by a desire to protect the country's image in the international marketplace. These are exemplified by export inspection requirements. Although usually on agricultural products, they can apply to manufactures. Table 1.2 illustrates areas where export regulations apply in Australia. Lack of such requirements can have major repercussions on international trade as the UK recently experienced in its trade relations with the EU because of 'mad cow' and foot-and-mouth disease in its livestock. Regulations may be imposed for economic reasons, such as balance of payments problems. Developing countries often ban their firms from accepting countertrade

**TABLE 1.2**    **Australian export regulations**

| Commodity | Authority |
|---|---|
| Primary products (excluding minerals), animals and marine life | Department of Agriculture, Fisheries and Forestry<br>Ph: 02 6272 3933  web: <www.affa.gov.au> |
| Animal furs and skins, live animals (native), wildlife and products derived from it, native flora and fauna, and any animal named under the Convention of International Trade in Endangered Species (CITES) | Department of the Environment & Water Resources<br>Ph: 02 6274 1111  web: <www.environment.gov.au><br><br>Department of the Environment & Water Resources, Biodiversity Group<br>Ph: 02 6274 1111  web: <www.environment.gov.au/biodiversity> |
| Fruit and vegetables, grain, live animals (non-native) and animal products, plant and plant products, foodstuffs and animal products, certain woodchips and sawlogs | Australian Quarantine and Inspection Service<br>Ph: 1800 020 504<br>web: <www.aqis.gov.au> |
| Heritage items (including Australian works of art, artefacts, coins, stamps, collector banknotes, precious stones, minerals, fossils, items of national significance) | Australian Heritage Council<br>Ph: 02 6274 1111<br>web: <www.ahc.gov.au> |

SOURCE: <*www.austrade.gov.au*>.

for products which are readily saleable overseas for free foreign exchange. Regulations are also imposed for security reasons particularly when a country does not want its defence technology to end up in the hands of nations it perceives as a threat to them. Allied to this are regulations imposed for political reasons such as embargoes on trading with a specific country due to either United Nations' sanctions (as with North Korea) or national prohibitions such as the ban on US companies trading with Vietnam until 1996 (under the US *Trading With The Enemy Act*). Finally, restrictions may be due to legal agreements entered into between nations to control the degree to which each will compete with the other in each country's domestic market. The operation of the US *Meat Import Law* with respect to Australia is an example.

## The rim

The rim cushions the impact of the bicycle on the road and, in this analogy, is akin to cushioning the impact of domestic marketing approaches on the international marketplace. The rim can be summed up in one word—'sensitivity'. The main areas requiring sensitivity are the economic, financial, legal, political, social, cultural, infrastructure and technology areas and the country's international agreements and obligations. All the marketing mix variables at the hub of the wheel need to be substantially modified to take the above environmental factors into account if international business is to be successful. The extent of the modification will vary according to the nature of the product and the extent of the psychic distance between that market and Australia or New Zealand.

## The importance of world trade

The increasing importance of global linkages is reflected in the growing importance of international trade. As the 1997–98 Asian currency crisis illustrated, it is more and more difficult to isolate domestic economic activity from international market events. Decisions that were once considered in the domestic domain are now being modified by influences from abroad and tailored to take into account global market forces. A reflection of the above is the change over recent decades in the pattern of diplomacy between nations. Whereas historically the main thrust of diplomacy has been on political relationships between countries, now commercial relationships are given equal importance. This trend is likely to continue due to absence of global conflicts and the cessation of the Cold War. Achieving access for products, overcoming impediments to business and solving trade disputes is accounting for an increasing percentage of the efforts of Australian and New Zealand diplomatic missions overseas.

The composition of international trade itself has been changing. In general, trade in primary commodities has declined while that of manufactures has risen. International trade in services has risen fastest of all.

## The dilemma of definition

With the advent of globalisation there are a confusing number of terms used to describe firms that operate across national boundaries. Often three terms are used interchangeably. The three most common terms are:

- *global companies*—they produce for the world market and production occurs where it can be done cheapest. Such firms aim for standardised high volume production and seek experience-curve benefits and location economies. They endeavour to coordinate their activities across markets and integrate these activities into their overall planning by subsidising activities in some markets with resources generated in others.

- *transnational companies (multinationals)*—they produce goods and services or manage investments in more than one country and blend the market specific approach with standardised production methods. They transfer this distinctive competence while responding to pressures for local responsiveness.

- *multi-domestic companies*—although they aim for maximum local responsiveness they are willing to customise both their product offering and market strategy to different local conditions. They do well in situations requiring strong local responsiveness and weak pressure for cost reductions.

## THE GLOBAL MARKETING ENVIRONMENT

Marketing is often about perception and the same is true of international marketing. Global portrayals of situations do not accurately reflect how issues and opportunities are viewed from the standpoint of a particular country.

While a regular map of the world shows both Australia and New Zealand at the bottom of the world underneath Asia, a map drawn from the perspective of these countries, with them at the centre of the world (Figure 1.9), creates a different picture and one more reflective of how Australian and New Zealand businesses view other nations.

A review of Australia's patterns of imports, exports, services trade and major trading partners highlights Australia's position in the international trading environment (see Tables 1.3 and 1.4). Australia's position in global trade is that in 2004 it was the 27th largest exporting nation and the 19th largest importing nation (Department of Foreign Affairs and Trade 2006, pp. 12, 14).

## FIGURE 1.9 Map of the world from an Australasian business perspective

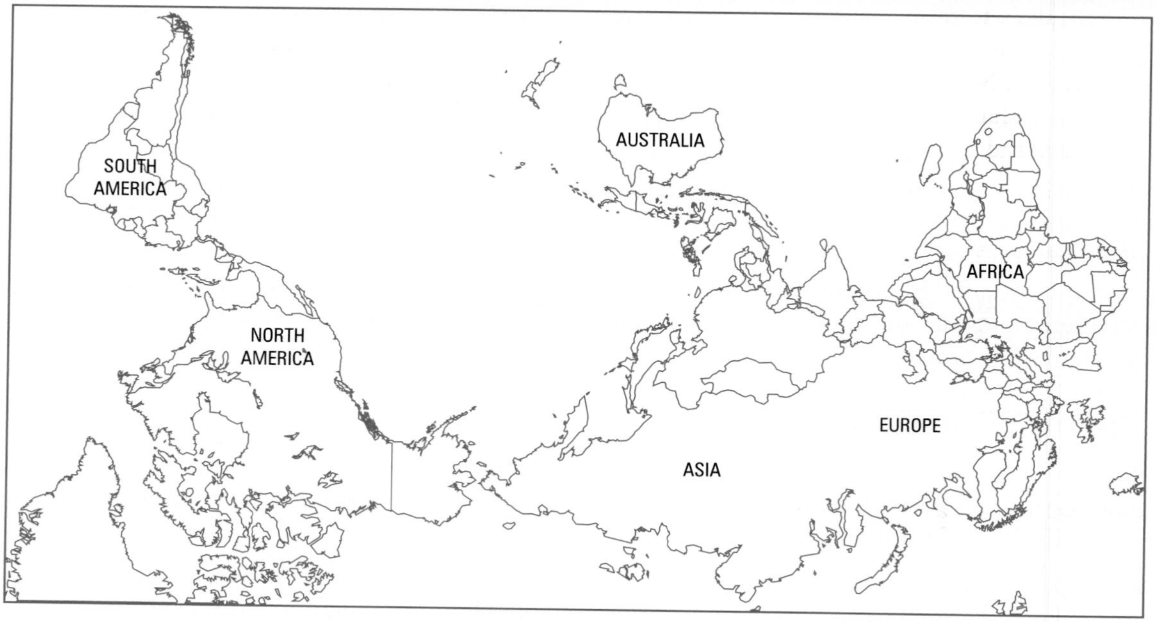

## TABLE 1.3 Australia's top 10 export markets, 2005 (A$ billion)

|  |  | Goods[a] | Services[b] | Total[c] | Share |
|---|---|---|---|---|---|
| 1 | Japan | 28.3 | 3.2 | 31.5 | 17.9% |
| 2 | China | 16.0 | 2.4 | 18.4 | 10.5% |
| 3 | United States | 9.3 | 4.5 | 13.7 | 7.8% |
| 4 | Republic of Korea | 10.9 | 1.2 | 12.1 | 6.9% |
| 5 | New Zealand | 9.0 | 2.7 | 11.7 | 6.6% |
| 6 | United Kingdom | 5.0 | 4.2 | 9.2 | 5.2% |
| 7 | India | 7.0 | 0.9 | 7.9 | 4.5% |
| 8 | Singapore | 4.0 | 2.4 | 6.4 | 3.6% |
| 9 | Taiwan | 5.5 | 0.4 | 5.9 | 3.4% |
| 10 | Thailand | 4.1 | 0.5 | 4.7 | 2.6% |
| Total exports | | 138.7 | 37.1 | 175.8 | 100.0% |
| Of which: | APEC | 102.0 | 21.8 | 123.9 | 70.4% |
|  | ASEAN | 15.9 | 5.1 | 21.0 | 12.0% |
|  | EU25 | 14.9 | 7.8 | 22.7 | 12.9% |
|  | ECD | 75.6 | 20.5 | 96.2 | 54.7% |

(a) Recorded trade basis   (b) Balance of payments basis   (c) Total may not sum due to rounding

**SOURCE:** *Department of Foreign Affairs and Trade (2006)* Trade at a Glance, *p. 13.* Copyright Commonwealth of Australia, reproduced with permission.

# Major export activity

In 2005 Australia's trade in goods and services was valued at A\$373 billion. Of this figure, exports were worth A\$176 billion with the largest customers being Japan, China, the USA, Republic of Korea, New Zealand, the UK, India, Singapore, Taiwan and Thailand. Since 2000, there has been a sharp increase in exports to both China and India, reflecting the economic growth of industrial activities in these countries.

Traditionally, Australia's exports were agricultural products and, for the first three decades following World War II, minerals and energy products. Although these continue to be the mainstay of Australia's export activity, their significance is decreasing and the export

**TABLE 1.4    Australia's leading exports (goods and services), 2005**

| Export type[a] | (A\$ billion) |
|---|---|
| Coal | 21.8 |
| Iron ore | 11.0 |
| Personal travel (excl education related)[b] | 10.9 |
| Education services [c] | 7.5 |
| Crude petroleum | 6.3 |
| Non-monetary gold | 5.8 |
| Beef[d] | 4.7 |
| Aluminium ores and alumina | 4.7 |
| Aluminium | 4.4 |
| Passenger services | 4.1 |
| Natural gas | 3.7 |
| Other transportation services[e] | 3.3 |
| Professional and business services[f] | 3.2 |
| Passenger motor vehicles | 3.1 |
| Wheat | 3.0 |
| Medicines (incl. veterinary) | 2.9 |
| Wine | 2.8 |
| Refined Petroleum | 2.8 |
| Copper ores | 2.4 |
| Wool | 2.3 |
| Total Exports | 176.7 |

(a) Goods on recorded trade basis, services on balance of payments basis
(b) Inbound tourists mainly for recreational purposes
(c) Includes education-related travel and other education services (which have been estimated for 2005)
(d) Fresh, chilled or frozen
(e) Other transportation services cover a range of services provided in ports and airports, such as cargo handling, counter and baggage services. Also included in this category are agents' fees associated with passenger and freight transportation
(f) Includes services such as architecture, legal, accounting and engineering

**SOURCE:** *Department of Foreign Affairs and Trade (2006)* Trade at a Glance, *p. 4.* Copyright Commonwealth of Australia, reproduced with permission.

of manufactures, both simply and elaborately transformed, has become increasingly significant. Exports now account for nearly one-quarter of all economic growth. In the next decade it is anticipated that knowledge-intensive exports, such as biotechnology and software, will become increasingly important. Table 1.5 shows Australia's top 10 two-way trading partners in 2005.

## Major import activity

In 2005 Australia's imports were worth A$194 billion and the largest sources of supply were the USA, China, Japan, Singapore, United Kingdom, Germany, New Zealand, Malaysia, France and Thailand. Traditionally, a majority of Australian imports were more sophisticated manufactures. Although this pattern continues, in recent years imports have increasingly included less sophisticated manufactures that can be produced more cheaply in countries other than Australia, particularly in Asia.

## Trade in services

In line with the global pattern, services are accounting for a growing percentage of international trade for both Australia and New Zealand. Australia's balance of trade in services, which used to be negative, for the first time achieved a surplus in 1995–96 due to increases in tourism, international education, computer software and other advanced industries. In 2005 services exports were valued at A$37 billion.

| TABLE 1.5 | Australia's top 10 two-way trading partners, 2005 (A$ billion) | | | | |
|---|---|---|---|---|---|
| | | Goods[a] | Services[b] | Total[c] | Share |
| 1 | Japan | 45.4 | 5.2 | 50.6 | 13.6% |
| 2 | United States | 30.7 | 10.9 | 41.5 | 11.2% |
| 3 | China | 37.4 | 3.6 | 41.0 | 11.1% |
| 4 | United Kingdom | 11.2 | 8.6 | 19.8 | 5.3% |
| 5 | New Zealand | 14.4 | 4.8 | 19.2 | 5.2% |
| 6 | Singapore | 12.7 | 5.2 | 17.8 | 4.8% |
| 7 | Republic of Korea | 16.1 | 1.5 | 17.6 | 4.7% |
| 8 | Germany | 10.1 | 2.2 | 12.3 | 3.3% |
| 9 | Malaysia | 8.6 | 1.9 | 10.5 | 2.8% |
| 10 | Thailand | 8.9 | 1.4 | 10.3 | 2.8% |
| Total exports | | 294.5 | 75.8 | 370.3 | 100.0% |
| Of which: | APEC | 210.8 | 42.9 | 253.6 | 68.3% |
| | ASEAN | 43.9 | 11.4 | 55.3 | 14.9% |
| | EU25 | 51.0 | 17.2 | 68.2 | 18.4% |
| | ECD | 165.6 | 42.6 | 208.2 | 56.1% |

(a) Recorded trade basis   (b) Balance of payments basis   (c) Total may not sum due to rounding

**SOURCE:** *Department of Foreign Affairs and Trade (2006)* Trade at a Glance, *p. 11*. Copyright Commonwealth of Australia, reproduced with permission.

# Australian–Asian trade

The trading interrelationship between Australia and its Asian neighbours is a substantial one as indicated by the percentage of Australia's overall imports and exports accounted for by Australia's trade with each country. Although Australians accept the need for an increasing trade involvement in Asia, there needs to be more of an emotional commitment to the region. This commitment should involve a greater democratisation of Australia's cultural and political institutions to reflect more adequately both our focus on Asia and the multicultural nature of Australia in decision making. Many business opportunities in the 1970s and 1980s were wasted because of a historical affinity for Europe and the USA. Although this affinity has diminished, more needs to be done to invest in a future that embraces Asia. It needs to be appreciated that the potential for increased business from Asian development has not gone unnoticed by other countries. If Australia is not to be 'beaten to the punch' in its own backyard, it needs to maintain its Asian focus and not be discouraged by current problems in the Asian region.

## 1.2 INTERNATIONAL HIGHLIGHT

# International marketing goes sky-high

International marketing in the new millennium will increasingly involve sourcing from as well as selling to a multitude of organisations in a number of different countries. This is illustrated in the case of the 550–800 seat Airbus A380 due to come into service in late 2007. Inaugural customers for this double-decker aircraft, apart from European airlines belonging to countries in the Airbus consortium, include Singapore Airlines, Emirates and Qantas. As the illustration shows, parts for this aircraft will come not only from European suppliers in the UK, France, Germany, Belgium and Spain, but also from the US, Japan and Australia. In addition there are indirect sources of supply as occurs when Australian bauxite is converted into alumina that is shipped to Texas for conversion into aluminium ingots. The ingots are then rolled into 6 tonne, 35 metre wing pieces that are shipped to North Wales where they are changed into aircraft wings. In many cases, there is an interdependency between inaugural customers and sources of supply, with the promise of the latter being a factor in the selection of the aircraft by the nation's airline. A new aircraft is in fact a global project regardless of where its final assembly occurs and this situation is replicated in a number of other industries. This global nature of such projects is reflected in the A380 where responsibilities are:

- France—assembly, wing box construction;

- Germany—fuselage, rudder;

| | |
|---|---|
| France | |
| Germany | |
| UK | |
| Belgium | |
| Spain | |
| Rolls Royce (UK) and Engine Alliance (US) | |

**OTHER BASES INCLUDE:**

**AUSTRALIA**

**Sydney:** Wing tip and wingtip fence

**JAPAN**

Vertical fin edges, cargo doors

- United Kingdom—wings, wing ribs, engines;

- Belgium—wing components;

- Spain—forward and rear belly fairings;

- United States—engines;

- Australia—wing tips and wing tip fences;

- Japan—vertical fin edges, cargo doors.

**SOURCE:** *Adapted from Rochfort, S. (2005) 'Crowds in the clouds', Sydney Morning Herald, 22–23 January, p. 39.*

# The impact of the internet on international marketing

Adoption of the internet has been faster than the adoption of any other technology in history. The number of people having access to the internet grew from 2.3 million in 1995 to 934 million in 2004 (CIA 2007). This means that approximately 15% of the world's population are now online. Table 1.6 shows the internet access situation for countries in 2004.

| TABLE 1.5 | Top 15 countries in terms of internet access, 2004 | | |
|---|---|---|---|
| **Country** | **Population** | **Internet** | **% online** |
| Total | 6 302 309 691 | 934 million | 14.8 |
| **Rank** | | | |
| 1 United States | 290 342 554 | 185.5 | 63.9 |
| 2 China | 1 286 975 468 | 99.8 | 7.8 |
| 3 Japan | 127 214 499 | 78.1 | 61.4 |
| 4 Germany | 82 398 326 | 41.9 | 50.8 |
| 5 India* | 1 065 070 607 | 37.0 | 3.5 |
| 6 United Kingdom | 60 094 648 | 33.1 | 55.1 |
| 7 Korea, South | 48 289 037 | 31.7 | 65.6 |
| 8 France | 60 180 529 | 25.5 | 42.4 |
| 9 Italy | 57 998 353 | 25.5 | 44.0 |
| 10 Brazil | 182 032 604 | 22.3 | 7.7 |
| 11 Russia | 144 526 278 | 21.2 | 14.7 |
| 12 Canada | 32 207 113 | 20.5 | 63.7 |
| 13 Mexico* | 104 959 594 | 13.9 | 13.2 |
| 14 Australia | 19 731 984 | 13.0 | 66.0 |
| 15 Indonesia* | 238 452 952 | 12.9 | 5.4 |
| **Share of total** | **60.3%** | **70.1%** | |

*New to list in 2004

**SOURCE:** *Hanson, W. and Kalyanam, K. (2007)* Internet Marketing and eCommerce, *Thomson South-Western Publishing, Mason, USA, p. 14. Reprinted with permission of South-Western, a division of Thomson Learning: <www.thomsonrights.com>. Fax 800 730-2215.*

The adoption has been fastest in countries with a high gross domestic product (GDP) and in countries where English is the first language or a widely spoken second language. However, the dominance of the US in internet adoption is disappearing as shown in Figure 1.10 and now both the Asia–Pacific region and Europe each have a larger percentage of the world's internet users than does the US.

The web is an alternative to 'real world' environments, not a simulation of one. Success requires trust between vendor and customer and security issues still hamper the operation of electronic business.

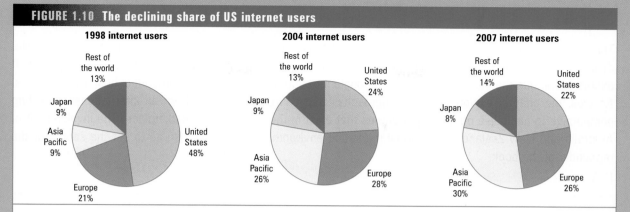

**FIGURE 1.10  The declining share of US internet users**

**1998 internet users**

- Rest of the world 13%
- Japan 9%
- Asia Pacific 9%
- Europe 21%
- United States 48%

**2004 internet users**

- Rest of the world 13%
- United States 24%
- Japan 9%
- Asia Pacific 26%
- Europe 28%

**2007 internet users**

- Rest of the world 14%
- United States 22%
- Japan 8%
- Asia Pacific 30%
- Europe 26%

SOURCE: *Hanson, W. and Kalyanam, K. (2007)* Internet Marketing and eCommerce, *Thomson South-Western Publishing, Mason, USA, p. 14. Reprinted with permission of South-Western, a division of Thomson Learning: <www.thomsonrights.com>. Fax 800 730-2215.*

The explosion of electronic business does call into question a number of fundamental principles in international marketing. These include:

- **barriers to internationalisation by small and medium exporters (SMEs)**—with the world wide web, size is no longer a barrier to the same extent as it has traditionally been;

- **incremental internationalisation**—with the world wide web, firms do not have to internationalise by moving from elementary modes of international behaviour to more advanced modes of international behaviour to the same extent;

- **need for overseas intermediaries**—with the world wide web, it is easier to locate overseas customers and deal directly with them rather than deal through overseas agents and distributors; and

- **country screening**—with the world wide web, firms do not have to approach international business by moving from countries they are familiar with to more unfamiliar countries. This is because information is more readily available on the internet and the medium is more interactive.

The internet's low-cost communication ability allows firms with limited capital to become global marketers at an early stage of their development because the internet connection can significantly enhance communication with overseas customers, suppliers, agents and distributors. Peterson et al. (1997) argue that, as a marketing channel, the internet has the following characteristics:

- an ability to store vast amounts of information inexpensively at different virtual locations;

- the ability to be a powerful and inexpensive means of searching, organising and disseminating such information;

- interactivity and the ability to provide information on demand;

- the ability to provide perceptual experiences superior to the printed catalogue;

- the facility to serve as a physical distribution medium for certain goods such as software; and

- relatively low entry and establishment costs for sellers.

# SUMMARY

This chapter introduces students to the reasons for undertaking international marketing and describes the dynamics of the international business environment in which the international marketer must operate. It examines various theories underlying the rationale for becoming involved in international business activities. As well, the chapter explores various approaches that can be undertaken from an international marketing perspective to capitalise on the opportunities that exist in the international marketplace. The involvement of Australia and New Zealand in the global marketing environment is reviewed so as to set the scene for the remainder of the book.

---

## ETHICS ISSUE

Increasingly, social issues are influencing success in international marketing. Many of these social issues involve ethical considerations, which relate to all aspects of international marketing. Because of this, rather than have a separate chapter on ethical issues, at the end of each chapter there is an ethical issue for the student to consider, relating to the subject matter of the chapter. Following an ethical scenario in each case, a question is posed requiring the student to consider their position on the issue. This is designed to sensitise the student to the importance of ethical considerations in international marketing.

---

## Websites

**Airbus Industries** http://www.airbus.com/en
**Austrade** http://austrade.gov.au
**CIA (2007)** *The World Factbook* https://www.cia.gov/cia/publications/factbook/index.html
**Department of Foreign Affairs and Trade—trade at a glance** http://www.dfat.gov.au/trade/taag/index
*Economist* http://www.economist.com/
**International Business Forum** http://www.ibf.com/
**Organisation for Economic Co-operation and Development (OECD)** http://www.oecd.org/home/
**United Nations Conference on Trade and Development (UNCTAD)**
  http://www.unctad.org/Templates/StartPage.asp?intItemID=2068
**World Bank** http://www.worldbank.org/

## Discussion questions

1  To what extent is a global approach to international marketing appropriate to firms in Australia or New Zealand?

2  Do the driving forces always outweigh the restraining forces in ensuring the attractiveness of international marketing to the Australian or New Zealand firm?

3  Why is it necessary to adopt a holistic approach to international marketing?

4  Discuss the theory of comparative advantage and its limitations as an explanation for international trade.

5 Compare the product life cycle with the product trade cycle as explanations for involvement in international marketing.

6 In what ways do uncontrollable factors in the local environment affect the application of marketing mix variables overseas?

7 Comment on recent trends in Australia's or New Zealand's international trade performance and prepare a prognosis for the direction of international marketing in the second decade of the new millennium.

# REFERENCES

Cateora, P.R. and Graham, J.L. (2005) *International Marketing*, McGraw-Hill Irwin, Columbus, Ohio.

Cavusgil, S.T. (2004) 'The promise of emerging markets', invited lecture, 1 November, University of Western Sydney.

CIA (2007) *The World Factbook*, <https://www.cia.gov/cia/publications/factbook/index.html>.

Department of Foreign Affairs and Trade (2006) *Trade at a Glance, 2006*, Department of Foreign Affairs and Trade, Canberra.

Doole, E. and Lowe, R. (2004) *International Marketing Strategy*, Thomson, UK.

*Export*, June 2007, p. 23.

*Financial Times* (2004) 'Special report on business and development', 24 June.

Fletcher, R. (2006) 'International Marketing at the Bottom of the Pyramid—a three country study', *Proceedings of the Conference of the Centre for International Marketing and Research (CIMAR)*, Istanbul, 27–30 May.

*Fortune*, 24 April 2006.

Gittins, R. (2007) 'The shock of the new economic order', *Sydney Morning Herald*, 3–4 May, p. 45.

Hanson, W. and Kalyanam, K. (2007) *Internet Marketing and eCommerce*, Thomson South Western Publishing, Mason, USA.

*Infoworld*, <http://www.infoworld.com/article/07/01/22/HNchinamobilesubscribers_1.html> 22 January 2007.

Keegan, W.J. and Green, M.C. (2003) *Global Marketing*, 3rd edn, Prentice Hall, Englewood Cliffs, NJ.

Keegan, W.J., Warren, J. and Green, M.C. (1995) *Global Marketing Management*, Pearson Education, Inc., Upper Saddle River, NJ.

Kotler, P., Keller, K.L., Ang, S.H., Leong, S.M. and Tan, C.T. (2006) *Marketing Management: An Asian Perspective*, 4th edn, Pearson Prentice Hall, Singapore.

London, T. and Hart, S.L. (2004), 'Reinventing strategies for emerging markets; beyond the transnational model', *Journal of International Business Studies*, Vol. 35, pp. 350–70.

Perlmutter, H.V. (1995) in Bartlett, C.A. and Ghoshal, S. (eds) *Transnational Management*, Irwin, Chicago.

Peterson, R.A., Balasubramanian, S. and Bronnenberg, B.J. (1997) 'Exploring the implications of the Internet for international marketing', *Journal of the Academy of Marketing Science*, Vol. 25, Issue 4, pp. 329–46.

Rochfort, S. (2005),' Crowds in the clouds', *Sydney Morning Herald*, 22–23 January, p. 39.

Theodosiou, M. and Leonidou, L.C. (2003) 'Standardisation vs adaptation of international marketing strategy: an integrative assessment of the empirical research', *International Business Review*, Vol. 12, pp. 141–71.

'Times—they are a'changing and marketing must keep pace', *Sydney Morning Herald* (2006), 23–24 September.

Warhurst, A. (2001) 'Corporate citizenship and corporate social investment: drivers of tri-sector partnerships', *Journal of Corporate Citizenship*, Spring, pp. 57–73.

# '42 Below'—the excitement of 'start-up', new products, new markets, innovation and creative promotion

Greg Walton, School of Marketing and International Business, Victoria University of Wellington, New Zealand

The economies of Australia and New Zealand are rift with small-to-medium-sized enterprises (SMEs). This simply reflects the entrepreneurial spirit of managers in these countries. New Zealand's Ministry of Economic Development estimates SMEs with fewer than 20 staff make up some 96% of all businesses in New Zealand and 86% of these have fewer than five staff (<http://www.med.govt.nz>). An increasing amount of academic research and published literature is focusing on SME internationalisation. If there is a gap in this research at all it is in the area devoted to the 'pre-internationalisation' and 'early internationalisation' stages of firm internationalisation—hence the importance of early chapters in texts like this devoted to important considerations to understanding, ultimately, the international competitiveness of the early stages of firm export activity. This understanding by both students and managers is especially important when we consider the emerging characteristics of 'new to export' firms. SMEs are often characterised by entrepreneurial management that sees the firm's growth pathway internationalising early, rather than a more conventional approach to business growth by developing the domestic market first, then going offshore (usually to psychically close countries first). 'Start up' and 'born global' firms add to this mix and to the increasing need for new understandings about readiness to go offshore and building international competitiveness.

What it lacks in size, 42 Below Ltd more than makes up for with its entrepreneurial approach and creativity, increasing exports of its super premium vodka and other beverages to NZ$9.6 million in 2006, up 30% on the previous year.

42 Below produces award-winning spirits and spring water that are uniquely New Zealand. Established in the late 1990s by advertising executive and now company CEO Geoff Ross, it started exporting in 2003 and today its products are sold in the top bars around the world. Significantly, says commercial manager Andrew Steel, export sales surpassed domestic for the first time in 2005 (full year).

The company's original product is the country's only super premium vodka, '42 Below', a brand that is 'unashamedly New Zealand', says Mr Steel.

*We have created the cleanest vodka because we have one of the purest water supplies in the world and we are the most awarded vodka in the world because of our pristine environment.*

There are two ways a firm can grow—organic growth (sell more of what it makes) and growth by acquisition. 42 Below is still a small firm (albeit with dynamic entrepreneurial management) and growth by acquisition may be some time in the future yet. So organic growth is the key for the firm, regardless of whether it becomes an object of acquisition itself. But how? Growth can also occur (or be planned for) by two strategic growth paths—new product development (NPD) and new market development (NMD). This is often a choice, one or the other. Factors such as the nature of the product, demand function, experience and skills of management, and the nature of both the market and the marketing help to determine which pathway is more appropriate for management to take the firm. Some academics would advocate only choosing NPD or NMD and, only when satisfying its 'now' (current products in current markets), when 'market penetration' strategies are no longer contributing to growth. 42 Below is so ambitious it is doing both NPD and NMD at the same time.

42 Below 'extended its line' to include four varietal flavours—feijoa, Manuka honey, passion fruit and kiwifruit. Product innovation has also seen the introduction of South Gin (another award-winning product), Stil Vodka, Tahiti Dark Rum, Seven Tiki Rum and 420 Water.

Operating on a shoestring budget and up against some big international brands, the small New Zealand company has had to be a bit maverick in order to make its mark in a very competitive market.

42 Below knows what business it is in—consumer food and beverage and specifically, discerning alcohol segments with its vodka line of products. It determines both the markets (geographical) and the segments it chooses to compete in.

42 Below has a market entry approach that is not conventional. The conventional market entry for a food and beverage provider is by first appointing a distributor or agent via agreement/contract. This is typical entry level exporting. 42 Below does it differently. It enters a new market by targeting a specific segment of the retail market—the most influential bar in the city. A team of brand ambassadors, typically expatriate Kiwis passionate about the brand, then sell 42 Below to every top bar and restaurant in the targeted area. 'It's a matter of convincing bar owners to give the vodka with the most unique story a go', says Mr Steel. Whereas most spirit brands tend to market themselves directly to the end consumer, 42 Below targets bar owners and bartenders, initially with its super premium vodka, introducing other products once the relationship is established. 'We're not afraid to make comparisons between our brand and others, we're very confident and we've won enough gold medals to back us up', says Mr Steel.

Unusual for a relatively 'new to export' firm is this 'sales office' approach to market entry. Expatriate Kiwis provide the sales and after-sales servicing function to this retail segment. This market entry mechanism is equivalent to transferring the sales function to an in-market partner short of being a wholly owned function. The fuller marketing function remains in New Zealand. Once traction has been gained in the market 42 Below adopts a more conventional market development approach and seeks importer/distributors to take the brand to the next level, allowing 42 Below to reduce its own costs and gain the benefit of a larger, more experienced local partner.

As a 'consumer good' 42 Below must understand product decisions. Product positioning and branding decisions are critical to capture the minds, hearts and wallets of a firm's target audience. A product that does not have a clear position in the customer's mind consequently stands for nothing in a marketplace with many substitutes. 42 Below has positioned its premium product with a set of product attributes that are different to that of substitutes, including long-standing substitutes with high brand awareness. It's quirky and, importantly, memorable:

'Every year the boffins from some institute that measure "air purity" come on down and set up their instruments. And every year they tell us the same thing: "Your air is still the best and sets a benchmark for purity". Not only is this cool for the scientists that get a free trip to our ski slopes, it's cool for us as well . . .'

*If you were going to choose the perfect environment to make the world's most perfect vodka, you'd have to pick New Zealand. The water is clear and sweet, the air holds a natural standard for purity, and hardly anyone is French . . . (<http://www.42below.com/enter.sm>)*

London's Ritz hotel celebrated its centenary last year and nominated 42 Below as its cocktails supplier. 'You'd expect a special 100 year birthday cocktail at one of the world's best known hotels to attract a premium price and The Ritz 100 does just that, retailing for NZ$50 in the hotel's bar.'

42 Below chief vodka bloke Geoff Ross says the selection of 42 Below Pure shows the New Zealand brand is being recognised in all the right places: 'It's great to see an iconic British brand such as The Ritz choosing a vodka from the colonies to celebrate its centenary. This is colonialism in reverse—our vodka is laying claim to home territory in the most renowned of the empire's establishments. It shows Kiwis should never be daunted about taking their brands to the world stage'.

Education is another key tool in 42 Below's arsenal to engender brand loyalty. It holds regular Vodka Universities for bartenders and the annual Cocktail World Cup in Queenstown, New Zealand, where competing teams of elite bar tenders from around the world fight it out to make the most original 42 Below-based cocktail. This activity is an example of conventional promotional strategy. It is designed to build brand awareness and encourage 'influencer' buy-in. Having fun is clearly an element of the firm and involving key stakeholders like its customer group (bar tenders) is a part of the promotional/ communications mix and an important statement in firm and product positioning.

The company increased total sales to $15.8 million in 2006 and Mr Steel says that growth is coming from increasing sales in existing markets, in particular the UK and USA, and expansion into new, developing markets in Asia and the rest of Europe. Sales are also growing strongly in its important home markets, New Zealand and Australia. 'Expansion into new export markets is costly and in the beginning it means investing a lot of money', cautions Mr Steel. 'It's a risk and you have to be very careful about where you choose to put your product. But the reward is a huge audience and the great feedback we get from the rest of the world.'

In order to take advantage of the direct channels to markets it has created, 42 Below is expanding its product portfolio. 'In this way we believe we can continue to grow while protecting ourselves from cyclical or faddish changes in the market', explains Mr Steel.

As an entrepreneurial company it encourages staff to take sensible risks: 'In order to stay on top of that risk, we constantly monitor the situation in each of our markets. This also allows us to react quickly and effectively, minimising negative effects and maximising opportunities'.

42 Below has 25 staff in its Auckland office, the heart of its marketing and product innovation, and its offshore Brand Ambassadors. Bottling and distribution are outsourced. The company listed on the New Zealand Stock Exchange in October 2003 and in late 2006 liquor giant Bacardi offered to buy it.

'That's a fantastic development for the brand; it will give us access to their global distribution network and put some real muscle behind the company', says Mr Steel. 'They want to help us grow and stay true to what the company is now.' He says a challenge will be to grow carefully to make sure 42 Below does not lose its strengths: 'It's very important to us to stay fresh. To make sure we don't rest on our laurels, to stay slightly hungry. We treat exporting like warfare; we never hold our position, we are always advancing, because if you're not going forward you're going backwards. We're getting out there and hammering it'.

## Bibliography

<http://www.42below.com>.
New Zealand Trade and Enterprise,
<http://www.nzte.govt.nz/section/14606/16256.aspx>.

## Questions

1 What can be said about 42 Below's motivations to internationalise?
2 What indicators of firm 'readiness to internationalise' or compete successfully are evident in this case study? What elements of these indicators appear to have more emphasis?
3 What model is appropriate to consider the strategic growth paths open to 42 Below? Discuss.

4 What factors lend to a broad geographical spread of markets and a firm being successful in serving them all? Conversely, what factors lend to market concentration? Considering these factors what should 42 Below do?

5 How should we go about assessing how 'internationally competitive' 42 Below is?

6 Explain the value of an international marketing plan.

7 What tactical marketing considerations (marketing mix elements) should 42 Below consider?

# PART A

# ENVIRONMENTAL ANALYSIS OF INTERNATIONAL MARKETS

An analysis of what makes marketing overseas different from marketing domestically is an essential first step in the internationalisation process of the firm. This requires a study of the way a number of factors operate in the international domain. The world is characterised by different economic systems (Chapter 2) and different economic climates in individual countries. Financial systems also differ from country to country, as do the financial instruments available in each country to the international marketer. In addition, levels of facilitation in your own country for international business expansion also differ as between countries. Cultures (Chapter 3) vary from international market to international market and a knowledge of underlying cultural differences leads to cultural sensitivity, without which most overseas activities are doomed to failure. This cultural sensitivity is essential when negotiating overseas, and strategies for effective negotiation need to be developed. A study as to how political systems differ (Chapter 4) is also required, as is an appreciation of the role of government in each country as both a facilitator and inhibitor of foreign international business involvement. Legal systems differ markedly from country to country, as does the application of law, the interpretation of law and degree of evasion of the law. For international marketers, knowledge of how the law might influence each element of the marketing mix is necessary. With the stakeholder approach replacing the shareholder approach to business, there are a number of contemporary international marketing variables (Chapter 5) that must be factored into any evaluation of location and mode of foreign market involvement. These include technology, attitude towards innovation, ethics, environmentalism, terrorism, health, infrastructure, consumerism, climate and geography. Analysis of these variables in the environment of international marketing provides the building blocks for international involvement.

# CHAPTER 2

# APPRECIATING THE INTERNATIONAL ECONOMIC AND FINANCIAL ENVIRONMENT

## LearningObjectives

**After reading this chapter you should be able to:**

■ identify ways of segmenting the global economic environment and appreciate the ways in which countries differ from each other in terms of global variables;

■ recognise that consumption patterns have an important effect on demand in overseas markets;

■ measure international markets so as to predict likely outcomes of involvement;

■ analyse the role of international bodies in regulating the international business environment;

■ appreciate how the international financial system operates;

■ recognise how foreign exchange variations influence the successful undertaking of international business;

■ establish alternative strategies when faced with recession in an overseas market; and

■ identify the role of aid in international business opportunities.

# Big can be beautiful

Recent years have seen a dramatic change in the economic situation of various markets. Countries such as China and India are now being viewed as economic powerhouses of the future. Boosted by transnational firms seeking economies via outsourcing offshore, a rapidly expanding middle class has emerged in these markets; their sheer numbers make them an attractive segment for firms in developed countries to target. Both China and India have benefited from the trend towards outsourcing in the 'West' and cities where outsourcing activities took off, such as Dalien in China and Bangalore in India, are being emulated by others in both countries. In addition, as discussed in Chapter 1, the number of wealthy people in these markets is increasing and for many products there is growing potential among the poor at 'the bottom of the pyramid' in both India and China.

The potential is further illustrated by the fact that China's GDP is growing at around 9% per annum and its annual trade surplus exceeds US$100 billion a year (*Guardian*, 28 August 2006). One consequence of this growth is the rapidly increasing trade deficit many developed countries have with China. Wal-Mart in the USA, for example, sourced US$12 billion worth of goods from China and estimate their purchases from this source will rise to US$30 billion by 2005. Chrysler Corporation uses China as its benchmark in making sourcing decisions and French retailer Carrefour buys stock worth more than US$3.5 million a year from China.

Less well documented is India's dramatic economic growth on the back of its booming IT sector. India's potential is underscored by the fact that its economy is growing at more than 8% per year and 40% of its population

is under 20 years. In future years, while in Western countries populations are ageing and leaving the workforce, in India large numbers will be entering the workforce. India's growth in international trade is facilitated by the widespread use of English, which has particularly caused a growth in the service sector in areas such as call centres.

The case of Cookie Man illustrates how even small firms might take advantage of this potential. This Australian firm commenced establishing franchised outlets in India in 2000. These were targeted at India's middle class, which the firm estimates as numbering being between 150 and 200 million and which is not only increasing in numbers, but also embracing Western concepts, styles and consumerism, according to managing director, Peter Elligett. Cookie Man now has a total of 20 stores in India, five stores in Chennai and five in Bangalore, four in Bombay, three in Hyderabad and three in New Delhi. His experiences in India have convinced Peter Elligett of the need to employ the right indigenous staff who will understand better the highly complex business environment in that country and who are 'plugged in' to the family networks that dominate the business landscape.

**SOURCES:** *Adapted from Kaul, R. (2004) 'Not such a sticky wicket',* Export, *May; Cavusgil, S.T. (2004) 'The promise of emerging markets', invited lecture, 1 November, University of Western Sydney;* Time Magazine, *3 July 2006, pp. 18–26; Asia Inc, July/August 2006, pp. 106–7,* Guardian, *28 August 2006; and* Far East Economic Review, *21 March 2007.*

# INTRODUCTION

Over the last 50 years one of the most profound changes in the international environment has been the advent of globalisation. No longer can nations operate in isolation within their boundaries as they are now inextricably linked to the rest of the world. Global markets and global competitors have replaced local markets and local competitors. Tariff and non-tariff barriers have fallen, and nations are increasingly entering into free trade arrangements with other countries, so that trade flows more freely and regional or national advantages can be maximised. This global trend applies not only to the current economic environment but also to the current financial environment. Foreign exchange trading, international financial management and the international financial system have all felt the winds of change due to globalisation.

# THE ECONOMIC ENVIRONMENT

The global economic environment is unpredictable, as the events since 2001 in Asia and the Middle East have shown. When downturns occur, consumer confidence is shaken and the potential for foreign products is affected. This happened during the 1997–98 Asian currency crisis. Now in most Asian countries the economic situation appears to have improved. Table 2.1 provides growth figures based on real GDP for a number of Asian countries for the period 2001–05 and estimations (indicated by *) for 2006 and 2007.

| TABLE 2.1 | Asian development outlook 2006—country-by-country growth and forecasts | | | | | | |
|---|---|---|---|---|---|---|---|
| | (% age change from a year earlier) | | | | | | |
| Growth rate of GDP (% per year) | 2001 | 2002 | 2003 | 2004 | 2005 | 2006* | 2007* |
| *East Asia* | 5.1 | 7.4 | 7.1 | 8.3 | 7.7 | 7.7 | 7.1 |
| China, Peoples Republic of | 8.3 | 9.1 | 10.0 | 10.1 | 9.9 | 9.5 | 8.8 |
| Hong Kong, China | 0.6 | 1.8 | 3.2 | 8.6 | 7.3 | 5.5 | 5.0 |
| Korea, Republic of | 3.8 | 7.0 | 3.1 | 4.6 | 4.0 | 5.1 | 4.9 |
| Taipei, China | −2.2 | 4.2 | 3.4 | 6.1 | 4.1 | 4.4 | 4.0 |
| *South Asia* | 5.1 | 3.7 | 7.7 | 7.2 | 7.8 | 7.3 | 7.5 |
| India | 5.8 | 3.8 | 8.5 | 7.5 | 8.1 | 7.6 | 7.8 |
| Pakistan | 1.8 | 3.1 | 4.8 | 6.4 | 8.4 | 6.2 | 7.3 |
| *South-East Asia* | 1.9 | 4.7 | 5.3 | 6.3 | 5.5 | 5.5 | 5.7 |
| Indonesia | 3.8 | 4.3 | 5.0 | 4.9 | 5.6 | 5.4 | 6.0 |
| Malaysia | 0.3 | 4.4 | 5.4 | 7.1 | 5.3 | 5.5 | 5.8 |
| Philippines | 1.8 | 4.4 | 4.5 | 6.0 | 5.1 | 5.0 | 5.3 |
| Singapore | −2.3 | 4.0 | 2.9 | 8.7 | 6.4 | 3.1 | 4.6 |
| Thailand | 2.2 | 5.3 | 7.0 | 6.2 | 4.5 | 4.7 | 5.5 |
| Vietnam | 6.9 | 7.1 | 7.3 | 7.8 | 8.4 | 7.8 | 8.0 |

**SOURCE:** *Adapted from 'Asia development outlook 2006–country by country growth forecasts', <http://www.adb.org/Media/Articles/2006>, accessed 12 December 2006. Reproduced with permission.*

Until the events of late 1997, and more recently of 11 September 2001, it could be said that the global economy was growing strongly and was continuing on a path started at the beginning of the decade. Since 1990 developing economies had grown at about twice the rate of the industrialised economies (according to the International Monetary Fund (IMF)), Latin America had been largely free of debt and the end of the Cold War had brought the economies of Russia and Eastern Europe into the market-driven environment of mainstream international business. Also, China's casting off of the shackles of a closed economy was hailed as an event of major importance. The pace of globalisation has increased rapidly, facilitated by the revolution in communications. Transnational companies employ approximately 10% of non-agricultural workers worldwide and nearly 20% in developed countries. A major feature of the global marketing environment is the diversity of economic environments. The characteristics of each need to be appreciated if international marketing efforts are to be successful. There is available a substantial body of data which provides economic profiles on a country-by-country basis. This data is published by country sources, regional or economic grouping sources (European Union, OECD) and world sources. Included in the latter is the United Nations, the statistical year books and monthly statistical reports of which provide data on items such as gross national product, gross domestic product, consumption, investment, government expenditure, production figures, imports, exports and demographics. The *United Nations Statistical Yearbook* contains information on agriculture, mining, manufacturing, energy output and consumption, internal and external trade, transportation, wages and prices, health, housing, education and communication. To facilitate comparison all data is provided in US$. However, the way data is collected results in information from many developing countries being incomplete. Therefore some of this data should be treated as indicative because it may be understated.

## The global economic scene

### RECENT TRENDS

Keegan and Green (2005, p. 46) comment that the most profound change in the world economy in the last 50 years is the emergence of global markets and global competitors who have steadily replaced local competitors. This change in the last two decades has been accompanied by a reduction in tariffs and, to a lesser extent, in non-tariff barriers. This means that the extent to which local firms are subject to import competition has increased. They attribute this to five factors:

1   Capital movements rather than trade are now the driving force in the world economy. Whereas world trade is running at US$9.2 trillion a year, the London Foreign Exchange Market turns over US$450 billion each working day.

2   Production is no longer directly linked to employment. Although employment in manufacturing has declined, production continues to grow.

3   The world economy has more impact on economic outcomes within a country than the nation state.

4   The contest between capitalism and socialism is over, with the economies of socialist countries becoming increasingly market oriented.

5   The growth of e-commerce diminishes the importance of national barriers and forces companies to re-evaluate their business models.

These five factors have rendered former classifications of countries according to their economic system less relevant than was formerly the case.

## ECONOMIC SYSTEMS

Since World War II, countries have been classified according to their economic system. They were classified as one of three systems:

- *Market allocation system*: This system relies on the consumer to allocate resources. It is consumer choice that decides what is produced and by whom. It is the purchase decisions and purchase intentions on which producers in turn base their plans.

- *Command allocation*: In this system, resources are allocated by government planners who determine in advance the number and specifications of each item to be produced. Under the command system, consumers are free to spend their money on whatever is available. However, the decision as to what will be available is determined by the state's planners.

- *Mixed system*: In reality, there are no pure market allocation or command allocation systems as all market systems have a command sector (such as government regulation and involvement in production of some items) and all command systems have a market sector (e.g. when the country's government-owned airlines seek business overseas).

Because government is involved in all economic systems, classifications such as the above are a matter of degree. There is an overall trend throughout the world for the government to be less involved in economic participation. This is apparent in the move in both developed and developing countries towards the privatisation of government enterprises. Although there is a strong trend for command economies to move towards a market allocation system, this will be a slow process.

### 2.1 INTERNATIONAL HIGHLIGHT

## Putting the puff into Proton

Malaysia under Mahatir was a prime example of government in a free enterprise economy endeavouring to stimulate economic development by initiating and continuing to be involved in command activities. This involvement included the north–south freeway which cut travel time by two thirds and the Pelapas seaport located close to Singapore so as to challenge that country's maritime supremacy. Not so successful were the Petronas Towers (until recently the world's tallest buildings) which have never been completely occupied, its involvement in Malaysian Airlines which caused them to fly unprofitable routes for political reasons and the national automobile, the Proton, whose manufacture was 'kick-started' with a raft of subsidies in 1985. Mahatir's successor, Abdullah Badawi, has decided that the Proton must stand on its own two feet without subsidies from the public purse as otherwise it will have no incentive to upgrade quality and become globally competitive. As a stimulus, Badawi is signing free-trade agreements that allow more imports of foreign cars. Today Proton's market share is 40% with profits of US$7.6 million compared with 60% and profits of US$113 million in 2003.

**SOURCE:** *Adapted from* Fortune Magazine, *10 July 2006, pp. 29–31.*

# ECONOMIC STRUCTURE

As an alternative to classifying countries according to their economic system, it is possible to classify them according to their economic structure. This classification reflects the relative dominance in the economy of the country of the following:

- *Agriculture*: Agriculture includes crop growing, hunting, fishing, grazing and forestry. Generally countries dependent on agriculture are among the economically poorer ones. The importance of agriculture to the wealth of nations has steadily declined in all countries.

- *Industry*: This group comprises mining, manufacturing, construction, electricity, communications infrastructure and gas. Industrial activity by low-income countries is more at the level of simply transformed manufactures, such as steel drums and extruded plastic products. The activity of middle-income and industrialised countries is more in the direction of elaborately transformed manufactures, such as computer-driven machine tools and telecommunications equipment. Within this classification, a distinction may be drawn between countries dependent on 'smokestack' (i.e. mature) industries and those dependent on high-tech industries.

- *Services*: This involves all other forms of economic activity. It accounts for an increasing percentage of employment in all countries and is the fastest growing area of economic activity in all except most low-income countries.

There are some problems with classifying countries in terms of economic structure. This is because within an economic sector operations vary widely between countries. For instance, broad-acre grain farming in Australia has little in common with subsistence rice farming in the Philippines. The same is true of labour-intensive operations in the textile industry of low-income countries compared with capital-intensive high-tech manufacturing of telecommunications equipment in Australia. An alternative classification is that based on stages of market development.

# STAGES OF MARKET DEVELOPMENT

This involves grouping countries according to GNP per capita. Table 2.2 shows four groupings of countries on this basis.

The stage of market development and the economic structure of countries act as an important reference point for the timing of investment by foreign corporations. Australian companies need to consider possible discontinuities in economic growth in terms of contingency plans for unexpected 'hiccoughs'.

1 *High-income countries*: Apart from several oil-rich nations, countries in this category reflect sustained economic growth. Sometimes referred to as post-industrial countries, this group is heavily dependent on services for income generation, is involved in information processing, places a premium on knowledge as a critical resource and has an orientation towards the future. In these countries, new product development is a potent force for innovation and creativity. Countries in this category include the USA, Japan and Sweden.

2 *Upper middle-income countries*: These are industrialising countries that in Asia are referred to as 'tigers', such as Singapore, Taiwan and Korea. The percentage of the population engaged in agriculture is small as people move to the cities and work in industrial or service sectors. Both wage rates and literacy are on the rise in these countries and they

| TABLE 2.2 | Stages of market development | | | |
|---|---|---|---|---|
| Income group by per capita GNP | 2003 GNP ($ millions) | 2003 GNP per capita ($) | % of world GNP | 2003 population (millions) |
| *High-income countries* GNP per capita > $9266 | 27 370 922 | 28 396 | 80.8 | 964 |
| *Upper middle-income countries* GNP per capita > $2995 but ≤ $9266 | 2 750 743 | 4723 | 8.1 | 582 |
| *Lower middle-income countries* GNP per capita > $755 but ≤ $2995 | 2 642 056 | 1245 | 7.8 | 2106 |
| *Low-income countries* GNP per capita ≤ $755 | 1 107 982 | 434 | 3.2 | 2554 |

SOURCE: *Keegan, W.J. and Green, M.C. (2005)* Global Marketing, *4th edn, Prentice Hall, NJ, p. 58. Reproduced with permission of Pearson Education Inc, Upper Saddle River, NJ.*

are formidable competitors with the high-income countries. Their economic growth tends to be export led.

3 *Lower middle-income countries*: These countries are at an early stage of industrialisation. Their industrial output supplies their growing domestic markets with basic items such as processed foods, batteries, tyres, textiles and building materials. They are also competitive producers for export of mature products that are standardised in nature and labour intensive, such as clothing. Examples are to be found in Vietnam and the Philippines in South-East Asia.

4 *Low-income countries*: These countries are characterised by dependence on agriculture with very basic, if any, manufacturing activity. They tend to have high birth rates, heavy reliance on foreign aid and low literacy, and are often characterised by political unrest. Examples of such countries abound in Africa and Central America, such as Ethiopia, Sudan and Nicaragua.

## OLD, NEW AND TRANSITION ECONOMIES

A final classification format is based on the nature of the economy rather than on national boundaries:

- *old economies*: Here the focus is on product, share of market, production, pyramid management and targeting consumers.

- *new economies*: The business priority in the new economy is for information and success is measured by revenue. The leading function is IT rather than production and the management structure is flat with vendors being the sales target.

- *transition economies*: These markets of opportunity are based on knowledge and success is measured in profits rather than market share or revenue. The leading function is marketing and the management structure is team oriented. Customers are the sales target (Ettenberg 2002).

Knowledge as to how countries are categorised in economic terms is important for the international marketer. This is because it indicates the type and level of demand for various products in that country, the likely level of infrastructure that exists within the country and

## 2.2 INTERNATIONAL HIGHLIGHT

# End trade barriers to cut poverty

Roughly one-fifth of the world's population lives on less that one dollar a day. The United Nation's millennium summit of 2000 pledged to halve the percentage of people living in these conditions by 2015. Probably no single change would make a greater contribution to fulfilling that pledge than fully opening the markets of the prosperous countries to the goods produced by poor ones. At present, farmers in poor countries not only have to compete against subsidised food exports, but they also face high import barriers. In addition, the more value developing countries add to their products by processing them, the higher the tariffs they face. In Japan and the EU for instance, fully processed food products face tariffs twice as high as those on products in the first stage of processing. In effect, the already industrialised countries, while preaching the virtues of free and fair trade, practise protectionist policies that actively discourage poor countries from developing their own industries. Even in these conditions, developing countries' annual export earnings are more than US$1500 billion. The minimum net gain if barriers were removed would be more than US$100 billion a year—more than twice the amount of annual aid flows. Over time, as producers adjust to the new export opportunities, the gain could be much greater. In addition, these opportunities would attract an increased flow of foreign direct investment to the developing countries which currently is only US$200 billion a year. In fact, the 49 least developed countries—home to more than 10% of the world's population—are missing out almost entirely on global trade and investment. Between them, they receive only US$12 billion in annual aid flows, only US$25 billion in export earnings and a paltry US$5 billion in foreign direct investment.

**SOURCE:** *Annan, K. 'End trade barriers to cut poverty', Irish Times, 9 March 2001, p. 6.*

the degree to which marketing is needed or allowed in that country. Apart from knowing the classification into which the country falls, it is also necessary for the international marketer to appreciate how that country conducts its international trade.

# International trade

## INTERNATIONAL ECONOMIC ENVIRONMENT

Historically many countries, including Australia, have been dominated by a desire to protect domestic industry from foreign competition. Prior to Federation, the colony of Victoria was protectionist and the colony of New South Wales wanted free trade. One of the obstacles to Federation in the last decades of the 19th century was how to resolve the protection versus free-trade debate between the colonies.

Protectionism includes both tariff and non-tariff barriers. Typical non-tariff barriers include import licensing (controls over the volume of imports), tariff quotas (limits on the quantity that may be imported at a specific tariff after which a higher tariff applies), quarantine restrictions (although intended to provide protection from diseases, these are often used as a protectionist measure) and standards (these often act as a barrier to entry due to their complexities and costs of conformity).

There have been many attempts to regulate the international economic environment in the interests of freeing up trade between countries. The most noteworthy activity in this connection was the formation of the General Agreement on Tariffs and Trade (GATT) in 1948. This body was replaced by the World Trade Organization (WTO).

Australian electrical items cannot be sold in the USA without Underwriters Laboratories Approval. This involves shipping a number of units to the USA for testing, which takes a considerable period of time and is very costly. As a result, few Australian electrical items are sold in the USA.

**The World Trade Organization (WTO)** Formed in 1994, the WTO involves 149 countries (as at 16 October 2006). It was an outcome of the GATT Uruguay Round of negotiations. The GATT established guidelines for the conduct of international trade and provided a forum for the negotiation of multilateral reductions in tariffs and non-tariff barriers. The members of its successor body, the WTO, account for in excess of 80% of world trade. Its central tenet is that the treatment accorded by one member to another must be accorded to all members and that there shall be no discrimination in treatment. Every member is to treat every other member as a 'most favoured nation'. Associated with this is the 'no new preference rule' whereby one country shall not accord a new preferential arrangement to any other country. Members are required to consult with each other concerning trade problems and the agreement provides a framework for negotiation. Rules also prohibit the placing of quantitative restrictions on goods entering your own country except for balance of payments reasons. This exception is often abused. A mechanism was also provided for resolving trade disputes. In 1974 there was a significant departure from this when a scheme was devised for assisting the less-developed countries with a 'generalised scheme on preferences'. Developed countries such as Australia were authorised to give products from such countries a margin of preference through a lower import duty, so that they could compete more effectively in developed country markets and improve their economic wellbeing.

Despite agriculture being raised in successive rounds of discussions in the GATT, efficient agriculture-producing nations such as Australia and New Zealand felt they were disadvantaged because the GATT failed to address their complaints. These complaints centred on claims that they were unfairly treated by the agricultural protectionism of industrial nations. This protectionism was exemplified in the Common Agricultural Policy of the EU and the Grain Enhancement Program of the USA. In addition, although the GATT had regulated trade in manufactures, it had not addressed investment or the fastest growing trade sector of services, or associated problems such as intellectual property rights. At the conclusion of the last GATT round of talks in Uruguay, the GATT was replaced by the WTO. The WTO is endeavouring to address the shortcomings of the GATT through a broadening of its coverage of international trade to include agriculture, investment (Trade Related Investment Measures) and intellectual property (Trade Related Aspects of Intellectual Property Rights). Its effectiveness in these new areas is yet to be determined.

Successive Australian and New Zealand governments have supported multilateral forums, such as the GATT and now the WTO, as vehicles for raising trade problems. This is because, for smaller countries with limited clout, the WTO offers a better chance of overcoming a barrier than does bilateral negotiation with a specific country. In bilateral negotiations it is necessary to give a concession in return, which is not the case in multilateral negotiations.

The second form of regulation of the international economic environment is in many respects a reaction to the perceived failure of the multilateral system to address the concerns of individual countries. Many nations felt that their concerns could be more effectively addressed by economic integration between like-minded countries.

**Economic integration** Since the end of World War II there has been a move towards economic integration. Nations are doing on a macro level what firms are doing on a micro level—banding together to improve their competitive position. Integration can take a variety of forms. These can be categorised as:

* *preferential trading arrangements*: Participants reduce most restraints to trade between themselves, but retain barriers to trade with countries that are not party to the arrangement. Earlier relationships between Australia and New Zealand fell into this category.

* *free-trade areas*: This is a more formal version of the above and is the loosest form of economic integration which entails no loss of national sovereignty. It involves the removal of all restraints to trade between members, although occasionally exceptions are made for certain products. The US–Canada agreement of 1989 and the European Free Trade Area of 1960 are examples. A more recent example is the successor of the US–Canada Agreement—the North American Free Trade Area (NAFTA) of 1994, which involved the addition of Mexico.

* *customs unions*: As in a free-trade area, the members dismantle the barriers to trade in goods and services between themselves. In addition, a common trade policy is established with respect to non-members. Usually this is a common external tariff whereby all imports are subject to the same tariff on products entering any member country. A well-known example is the one between Belgium, the Netherlands and Luxembourg of 1921.

* *common markets*: These combine the characteristics of a customs union with the elimination of barriers against the movement of labour and capital between member countries. It also removes all non-tariff barriers to the free exchange of goods and services.

* *economic unions*: This involves freeing the movement of goods, services, capital and people so that not only the product but also the factors of production can move freely across borders. Under an economic union, members endeavour to harmonise monetary policies, taxation and government spending. Ideally this could lead to a common currency and fixed exchange rates. Various forms are compared in Table 2.3.

Within the Asian region there is the ASEAN Free Trade Area that has expanded from the original six ASEAN members (Singapore, Malaysia, Thailand, Indonesia, the Philippines and Brunei) to include Vietnam, Laos, Cambodia and Myanmar. In addition, there is a looser grouping initiated by Australia in 1989 called APEC (Asia–Pacific Economic Co-operation). Originally this was to be a consultative body along the lines of the OECD (Organisation for Economic Co-operation and Development). It is now moving more towards becoming a free-trade area. It includes the ASEAN nations, Australia, New Zealand, Canada, the USA, Japan, South Korea, Chile, Mexico, China, Papua New Guinea, Hong Kong, Peru, Russia and Chinese Taipei and is viewed as a possible counterbalance to the EU and NAFTA.

Economic integration poses challenges for the international marketer. In the first place the Australian or New Zealand exporter is now faced with supplying a larger market as goods going to one country can easily move to another within the economic grouping. This is facilitated by harmonisation of standards and tariffs within that grouping. Forms of economic integration have implications for the appointment of representatives. For instance, does the firm appoint agents and distributors in each country or appoint an agent

| TABLE 2.3 | Forms of regional economic integration | | | |
|---|---|---|---|---|
| Stage of integration | Elimination of tariffs and quotas among members | Common tariff and quota system | Elimination of restrictions on factor movements | Harmonisation and unification of economic and social policies and institutions |
| Free-trade area | Yes | No | No | No |
| Customs union | Yes | Yes | No | No |
| Common market | Yes | Yes | Yes | No |
| Economic union | Yes | Yes | Yes | Yes |

SOURCE: *Keegan, W.J. and Green, M.C. (2005)* Global Marketing, *4th edn, Prentice Hall, NJ, p. 86.*

in one and distributors in each of the others? Regional trade groupings impact on foreign direct investment. The manufacturing operation established in one country is able to supply not only the market where the goods are manufactured, but also markets in member countries as there are no tariff or non-tariff impediments to entry. On the other hand, economic groupings also increase competition, as domestic competitors are firms that can be based anywhere in the economic grouping, not just in the country where manufacture takes place.

In the early 1990s during the GATT Uruguay Round, many countries lost faith in the ability of the multilateral body to solve world trade problems and reverted to bilateral or regional trade arrangements. This trend was reversed in the second half of the decade with the euphoria surrounding the creation of the WTO. However, following the failure of the WTO meeting in Seattle in December 1999 to address world trade problems in a meaningful way, countries are again turning to bilateral arrangements and regional trade agreements. A more complete discussion of international trade relations issues is in Chapter 18.

## TRADE PATTERNS

Trade patterns are usually measured in terms of a country's balance of payments, which is a record of transactions between the residents of one country and those of all other countries. It represents the difference between receipts from foreign countries on the one hand and payments to them on the other. As the name implies, the overall total of these transactions must be in balance. Within the balance of payments account, any given category, such as merchandise trade, services and capital movements, can either be positive or negative. The balance of payments is divided into:

- *current account*: the record of merchandise and services traded as well as gifts and aid transactions between countries; and

- *capital account*: direct investment, portfolio investment, short- and long-term capital flows.

A surplus or deficit in the current account will be compensated for by an entry in the capital account so that balance is achieved. The *balance of trade* is the relationship between merchandise imports and exports. It may be that within the current account an unfavourable balance of trade is compensated for by a favourable trading position in services.

## CONSUMPTION PATTERNS

Both income and population have an impact on consumption patterns. Availability and statistics on such patterns vary widely between countries due to differences in sophistication and recency of data collection. Engel's law states that as income rises above a certain minimum, expenditure on food as a percentage of total income decreases. United Nations surveys have proved this by contrasting developed with developing countries. The share of income spent on necessities provides an indication as to how much consumers are likely to spend on other purchases. D'Andrea et al. (2003) found that that while spending on consumer goods accounts for 30–35% of total average spending in emerging markets, among the lower socioeconomic groups it accounts for between 50 and 75% with the lowest strata claiming to spend nearly all their income on consumer goods. The nature of this other spending can be significant. In countries where the tendency is to rent accommodation rather than own a home, disposable income levels are likely to be greater. Countries where the level of savings is high, for example Japan, will also exhibit different consumption patterns.

Another issue is the percentage of potential buyers or households already owning a product. In general, product saturation levels increase as per capita national income increases. For example, in countries where average income is high, the market for whitegoods is more likely to be saturated and is mostly a replacement market. In countries where income is low, regardless of need the majority of people cannot afford whitegoods. Consumption patterns are important for the international marketer because they influence the nature of demand in the overseas market.

**Merchandise trade** Since the end of World War II merchandise trade has grown at a faster rate than world production and it is the high-income countries that are responsible for more than 80% of imports and exports of merchandise. Of these countries, North America, Japan and Western Europe account for approximately two-thirds of world imports and exports. Australia accounts for about 1.0% and is regarded as a middle-ranking trading nation.

**Services trade** This is the fastest growing sector in international trade. Statistics, however, are not as accurate for services as for merchandise trade. Evasion in payment for services can be a problem as illustrated by the increasing international focus on enforcing international copyright and patent laws. The growth in services trade is one explanation for the increasing disparity in world trade between the developed and the developing nations. This is due to services involving intellectual capital. This is influenced by education levels and research expenditure that tends to be higher in developed nations.

## TRADING ENVIRONMENT

The trading environment governs what firms can and cannot do when they go offshore. Trading environments are regulated by government. Most governments wish to control the international flow of trade into and out of their countries. In this they are motivated by:

- *financial issues* such as generating revenue from import duties and sale of import licences;
- *security issues* such as the sale of ingredients for chemical weapons manufacture to potentially hostile countries, or developing local industries so that the country can be self-supporting in times of conflict;
- *safety issues* such as importing defective aircraft parts from sources not approved by the original equipment manufacturer;

- *health issues* such as avoiding the entry of non-AIDS-tested plasma, anthrax, etc.; and most commonly

- *protectionist issues* designed to safeguard domestic industry from import competition.

Barriers to entering an overseas market can be divided into structural (natural) barriers or strategic barriers (ones that have been deliberately contrived to keep goods out and inhibit the free flow of trade). Structural barriers include economies of scale which favour established competitors, capital costs of market entry and switching costs for buyers. The strategic barriers to the free flow of trade can be divided into tariff and non-tariff barriers.

Tariff barriers usually operate as a tax on imports to make them less attractive to buyers. They can be imposed for either revenue or protectionist reasons. Tariffs can be either by value (ad valorem) or by volume (specific) or a combination of both. The way the tariff is applied influences its impact. In the 1990s a significant percentage of Australian wine imported into Thailand suffered a disadvantage compared to French wine, even though the product from both countries was liable for the same tariff rates. This was because the duty was levied both by value (per cent) and by volume (baht per litre). The Australian wine, which was largely sold in wine casks, faced the same impost as bottled French wine when duty was levied by volume although its price was considerably less. During successive rounds of bilateral trade talks between Australia and Thailand, Australia argued that the way duty was assessed discriminated against Australian wine.

There are occasional cases where tariffs are imposed on exports. This can be for revenue reasons. As an example, duties were applied to the exports of some Australian resources that were in short supply in the 1960s. Tariffs on exports can also be imposed when pressure is applied by another country seeking to protect its producers from an excess of import competition, as happened in the case of Brazilian frozen orange juice concentrate entering the US market. With tariffs there is no limit as to the volume that can be imported provided the duty is paid, whereas with quotas the volume is controlled. The resulting restrictions on supply can force up prices and profit margins may also increase due to restrictions on supply. This happened with Japanese cars in the USA in the 1980s.

Non-tariff barriers include all other means of limiting trade between countries. Quotas may be mandated by the government or voluntarily agreed to under threat of mandated quotas, as was the case above with the Japanese automobiles entering the US market. The semi-conductor industry in the USA and the textile industry in Australia are examples of how quotas have been used to restrict local demand by forcing up prices. Recent years have seen a general lowering of tariff barriers throughout the world. This has been the case not only with developed countries, but also with a number of developing countries in the Asia–Pacific region.

Other non-tariff barriers can include government procurement restraints. An example is the 'Buy Australian' policy of the Australian government. Limitations on trade between countries can also apply to exports as well as imports. Boycotts are another example. Examples of boycotts include the previous Australian embargo on trading with South Africa, United Nations' sanctions against North Korea and the US *Trading with the Enemy Act* which until 1994 prevented US firms doing business with Vietnam.

A factor in the international trading environment is the growth of foreign direct investment (FDI). This has recently grown faster than that of other economic indicators such as world production, capital formation and trade. This global expansion of investment is driven by more than 60 000 transnational corporations with more than 800 000 overseas affiliates. Developed countries remain the prime recipients of FDI, accounting for more than 75% of global inflows, and most of this investment takes the form of mergers and acquisitions. In 2000, inflows into developed countries increased by 21% to just above US$1 trillion. By contrast, inflows of FDI into developing countries declined for the second year in a row (19%) and only amounted to US$240 billion (United Nations 2001, p. 1).

## Measuring markets

There are a number of different ways of assessing the size of the market in different countries. They include income, population, quality of life, infrastructure, debt and resources. These can affect the attractiveness of a market from an export or investment viewpoint in different ways.

### INCOME

Countries are often classified according to levels of income and measured by annual Gross National Product (GNP) per head (see Table 2.2). The extent to which income varies between countries influences the ability of the country to fund future development. The degree to which average levels of personal income vary between countries also affects the ability of people to buy consumer goods. Income is a most important indicator of potential for a vast range of industrial and consumer goods. Income is usually measured and compared across countries in terms of GNP per capita and this is treated as a measure of purchasing power. However, it is only an approximate indicator because usage rates vary between countries and this may have an impact on affordability. In addition, variations between currencies can distort real income and standard of living figures. As a consequence, a consistent measure of real value needs to be applied to reflect the relative differences in the volumes of goods produced and purchased. The use of 'purchasing power parities' achieves this objective by showing how many units of currency are needed to buy in country A what one unit of currency will buy in country B. In effect this takes into account that prices tend to be lower in poorer countries. The difference between market price and purchasing power parity estimates of income is pronounced in the case of developing countries like China and India. One reflection of this notion of purchasing power parity is to take a commonly consumed product and compare its prices. This has been done for the 'Big Mac' hamburger and the comparisons are shown in Table 2.4.

### POPULATION

People make a market. For basic and essential products the more people there are, the larger the size of the market. The significance of population size decreases with the sophistication of the product or service offered, as a person's hierarchy of needs becomes more important in determining what is purchased. The size of individual country markets varies from the largest—such as China and India, each with in excess of one billion people—downwards. In predicting future trends in overseas markets it is also useful to take into account population growth rates. Generally speaking, there tends to be a negative correlation between stage of development and population growth rates, with the less-developed countries having higher growth rates than developed countries. There are exceptions to this, such as in China where the earlier government-imposed one-child policy has substantially lowered population growth. Distribution of the population is significant. This distribution can be in terms of both age and location:

**TABLE 2.4** **The hamburger standard**

| | | Big Mac prices In local currency | in dollars | Implied PPP* of the dollar | Actual 31/01/07 exchange rate | Under (−)/over (+) valuation against the dollar, % |
|---|---|---|---|---|---|---|
| United States | $ | 3.22 | 3.22 | | | |
| Argentina | Peso | 8.25 | 2.65 | 2.5621 | 3.10875 | −17.583859 |
| Australia | A$ | 3.45 | 2.67 | 1.0714 | 1.29099 | −17.0072 |
| Brazil | Real | 6.4 | 3.01 | 1.9876 | 2.12525 | −6.47794 |
| Britain | £ | 1.99 | 3.90 | 1.6181 | 1.9574 | 20.96975 |
| Canada | C$ | 3.63 | 3.08 | 1.1273 | 1.1804 | −4.496 |
| Chile | Peso | 1670 | 3.07 | 518.6335 | 544.45 | −4.74175 |
| China | Yuan | 11 | 1.41 | 3.4161 | 7.7739 | −56.0562 |
| Colombia | Peso | 6900 | 3.06 | 2142.8571 | 2253.525 | −4.91088 |
| Costa Rica | Colones | 1130 | 2.18 | 350.9317 | 519.075 | −32.3929 |
| Czech Republic | Koruna | 52.1 | 2.41 | 16.1801 | 21.64955 | −25.2635 |
| Denmark | DK | 27.75 | 4.84 | 8.6180 | 5.7381 | 50.1893 |
| Egypt | Pound | 9.09 | 1.60 | 2.8230 | 5.697 | −50.4479 |
| Estonia | Kroon | 30 | 2.49 | 9.3168 | 12.04085 | −22.6237 |
| Euro Area | € | 2.94 | 3.82 | 1.0952 | 1.29945 | 18.64543 |
| Hong Kong | HK$ | 12 | 1.54 | 3.7267 | 7.80905 | −52.2771 |
| Hungary | Forint | 590 | 3.00 | 183.2298 | 196.841 | −6.91481 |
| Iceland | Kronur | 509 | 7.44 | 158.0745 | 68.445 | 130.9512 |
| Indonesia | Rupiah | 15 900 | 1.75 | 4937.8882 | 9100 | −45.7375 |
| Japan | Yen | 280 | 2.31 | 86.9565 | 120.96 | −28.1113 |
| Latvia | Lats | 1.35 | 2.52 | 0.4193 | 0.53585 | −21.759 |
| Lithuania | Litas | 6.5 | 2.45 | 2.0186 | 2.65715 | −24.0301 |
| Malaysia | Ringgit | 5.5 | 1.57 | 1.7081 | 3.5005 | −51.2048 |
| Mexico | Peso | 29 | 2.66 | 9.0062 | 10.8894 | −17.2938 |
| New Zealand | NZ$ | 4.6 | 3.16 | 1.4286 | 1.454968 | −1.81424 |
| Norway | Kroner | 41.5 | 6.63 | 12.8882 | 6.2632 | 105.7766 |
| Pakistan | Rupee | 140 | 2.31 | 43.4783 | 60.725 | −28.4014 |
| Paraguay | Guarani | 10 000 | 1.90 | 3105.5901 | 5250 | −40.8459 |
| Peru | New Sol | 9.5 | 2.97 | 2.9503 | 3.1975 | −7.73071 |
| Philippines | Peso | 85 | 1.74 | 26.3975 | 48.9 | −46.0174 |
| Poland | Zloty | 6.9 | 2.29 | 2.1429 | 3.01115 | −28.8359 |
| Russia | Rouble | 49 | 1.85 | 15.2174 | 26.50575 | −42.5883 |
| Saudi Arabia | Riyal | 9 | 2.40 | 2.7950 | 3.7507 | −25.4797 |
| Singapore | S$ | 3.6 | 2.34 | 1.1180 | 1.53655 | −27.2388 |
| Slovakia | Crown | 57.98 | 2.13 | 18.0062 | 27.1909 | −33.7785 |
| South Africa | Rand | 15.5 | 2.14 | 4.8137 | 7.25375 | −33.639 |
| South Korea | Won | 2900 | 3.08 | 900.6211 | 941.5 | −4.34189 |
| Sri Lanka | Rupee | 190 | 1.75 | 59.0062 | 108.585 | −45.659 |
| Sweden | SKr | 32 | 4.59 | 9.9379 | 6.96755 | 42.63103 |
| Switzerland | SFr | 6.3 | 5.05 | 1.9565 | 1.2478 | 56.7977 |
| Taiwan | NT$ | 75 | 2.28 | 23.2919 | 32.927 | −29.2619 |
| Thailand | Baht | 62 | 1.78 | 19.2547 | 34.74 | −44.575 |
| Turkey | lire | 4.55 | 3.22 | 1.4130 | 1.41 | 0.10935 |
| UAE | Dirhams | 10 | 2.72 | 3.1056 | 3.6728 | −15.4435 |
| Ukraine | Hryvnia | 9 | 1.71 | 2.7950 | 5.269 | −46.9533 |
| Uruguay | Peso | 55 | 2.17 | 17.0807 | 25.328 | −32.5618 |
| Venezuela | Bolivar | 6800 | 1.58 | 2111.8012 | 4306.854 | −50.9665 |

*Purchasing power parity.

**SOURCE:** © The Economist Newspaper Limited, *London, 30 January 2007.*

- *Age*: People at different stages of life have different needs. Increases and decreases in the percentage of the population in specific age groups are related to demand for particular products and services. In the developing world, the distribution towards younger people creates a different demand pattern from that in the developed world where the population distribution is towards older people whose needs and willingness to adopt new ideas and products differ. Acording to the Australian Bureau of Statistics in 2003, 12.8% of the Australian population was over 65 and it is estimated this figure could rise to 25% by 2050. By comparison, in Turkey, only 5% are over 65. The distribution pattern in Asia is markedly different. For example, in Vietnam the average age is much younger compared with Japan where there has been a significant ageing of the population during recent decades.

- *Location*: In some countries, for example many developing countries, the population is relatively evenly dispersed but in other countries, such as Australia and New Zealand, it tends to be mostly concentrated in a limited number of urban areas. Australia is the world's most urbanised nation with 86% of its population living in urban areas. In the more-developed countries in Asia there is also a strong trend towards urbanisation as people move from the country to cities in search of employment. The degree of urbanisation and the movement from country to city are measures of significance to marketers. This is because in many developing countries there are usually wide differences in standards of living between country and city. China is a case in point. In addition, the patterns of consumption of urban dwellers in different countries are more likely to be similar than those of urban and rural dwellers within the same country. Because globalisation of tastes is more apparent in cities, products targeted at urban consumers may require less modification than those targeted at rural consumers whose tastes are more likely to be traditional. The location of the population also assists in identifying pockets of purchasing power as well as the cost of researching the market or targeting market segments overseas.

Within large markets there are many submarkets that may be more appropriate for Australian or New Zealand firms, given likely limited resources and ability to supply. It is important to define carefully the specific market to be targeted.

> Frequently when Australian businesspeople visit the USA they are overwhelmed by the size of its market. They tend to tell Australian Trade Commissioners in the USA that if they could obtain 1% of the US market they would be very happy. Unfortunately they do not focus on which 1% of the market they wish to target or devise specific strategies to secure that specific 1%.

## PHYSICAL QUALITY OF LIFE

Economic advancement usually is accompanied by a price tag. This aspect is increasingly being taken into account as evidenced by the requirement for environmental impact statements to accompany development proposals. While wealthy countries have the luxury of being able to trade off development for quality of life, this luxury eludes many less-developed countries whose citizens have little option other than to trade away quality of life today in order to improve the lives of their children tomorrow. The Physical Quality of Life Index is a measure of the level of welfare in a country and takes into account life expectancy, infant mortality and adult literacy rates. Together these three factors constitute a social indicator that provides a measure over time of how individual countries are advancing in terms of the quality of life enjoyed by their citizens. This issue is further explored in Chapter 11 in the context of the macro aspects of globalisation.

## INFRASTRUCTURE

Infrastructure generally refers to facilities and services necessary for the functioning of the economy and includes energy supplies, transport and communications, and commercial and financial services. It is often the engine of development, as witnessed by railroad development in Australia in the 19th century. The availability and nature of infrastructure are important when marketing in other countries. It can also affect the capability of a country to export its resources. For instance, investment in infrastructure was necessary for landlocked Laos to export electricity to Thailand, now Laos's largest foreign exchange earner. Infrastructure can also have an impact on the ability of Australian firms to supply overseas markets. For example, all Australia's sugar exports are in bulk and unless the overseas market has installed bulk receiving facilities Australia cannot supply sugar to that market. Not only does infrastructure influence physical distribution, but infrastructural elements such as availability and cost of water and power also affect the ability to operate, and the cost of operating, in specific areas. Infrastructure also affects the ability to communicate messages to potential customers (the availability and quality of advertising agencies and market research operations) and the ability to finance activities (communications, banking and financial networks). The internet is an example of a rapidly expanding communications technology that relies for its effectiveness on infrastructure being available to the customer. Table 2.5 shows internet usage comparable to population in different continents.

## DEBT

Another indicator of economic difference between countries is their level of indebtedness. As illustrated by the Asian currency crisis of 1997, this has an impact on a country's ability to borrow to finance development (especially physical infrastructure), its attractiveness as a market, the extent to which foreign exchange is freely available and the likelihood of being paid. In many developing countries, interest on debt consumes a major percentage of export receipts. It can lead to debt crises and countries engaging in barter or other forms of countertrade.

## RESOURCES

Resource endowment varies from country to country and traditionally was an indicator of relative prosperity as reflected in commodity exports. In some cases the wealth of a country is almost totally dependent on a single resource (e.g. Libyan dependence on oil). In other cases the resource leads to other resource-related activity (e.g. water leading to rice production in Thailand). In some instances the resource is geography, as happens when a country like Singapore lies across a strategic trade route that leads to entrepôt activities. Resources that shape economic activity can also be a matter of geography. An example is the affect of topography on Australia's river systems. In this case the rivers rise in the Great Dividing Range and irrigate a narrow coastal strip before flowing out to the sea. Climate can also influence how a firm's product offering is received. For example, snow skis have limited

| TABLE 2.5 | World internet usage and population statistics (percentages do not exactly total 100% due to rounding errors) |

| World region | Population (2005 est.) | Population (% of world) | Internet usage (latest data) | Usage growth (2000–05) | Penetration (% of population) | World users (%) |
|---|---|---|---|---|---|---|
| Africa | 900 465 411 | 14.0 | 13 468 600 | 198.3 | 1.5 | 1.5 |
| Asia | 3 612 363 165 | 56.3 | 302 257 003 | 164.4 | 8.4 | 34.0 |
| Europe | 730 991 138 | 11.4 | 259 653 144 | 151.9 | 35.5 | 29.2 |
| Middle East | 259 499 772 | 4.0 | 19 370 700 | 266.5 | 7.5 | 2.2 |
| North America | 328 387 059 | 5.1 | 221 437 647 | 104.9 | 67.4 | 24.9 |
| Latin America/Caribbean | 546 917 192 | 8.5 | 56 224 957 | 211.2 | 10.3 | 6.3 |
| Oceania/Australia | 33 443 448 | 0.5 | 16 269 080 | 113.5 | 48.6 | 1.8 |
| World total | 6 412 067 185 | 100.0 | 888 681 131 | 146.2 | 13.9 | 100.0 |

*Notes*: (1) Internet usage and world population statistics were updated on 24 March 2005. (2) Demographic (population) numbers are based on data contained in the world-gazetteer website. (3) Internet usage information comes from data published by Nielsen/NetRatings, by the International Telecommunications Union, by local NICs (newly industrialised countries) and by other reliable sources.

appeal in Indonesia. Another resource-related issue is the source and diversity of a nation's export income. The greater the spread, the better the cushion against an economic downturn in a particular activity. On the other hand, in order to influence prices in an area the country needs to be a major world supplier in that field, as is the case with Australian coal and New Zealand lamb. Many less-developed economies are monocultures in which one industrial or resource sector dominates the economy and often their opportunities are circumscribed by world prices for a product or activity over which they may have little influence.

## Marketing implications

Although the most common relative measure of different markets is GNP, other measures which may influence a market's attractiveness include the level of unemployment, consumer prices, level of productivity, trends in foreign trade, nature of balance of payments, exchange rate movements, the level of country indebtedness, foreign currency reserves and government management of the economy. The international marketer needs to monitor the economic environment on both a global and individual country basis. This enables the targeting of specific markets, assessment of the best means of entering those markets, determination of the potential in those markets, evaluation of the best combination of marketing mix elements and estimation of future prospects. The economic environment should be carefully considered when preparing plans and strategies for involvement in a country.

This is because it has an impact on the volume and nature of demand, the most appropriate form of market entry, the ability to compete in that market, the way products are to be delivered to customers in that market and which segment of the market should receive most attention.

# THE FINANCIAL ENVIRONMENT

The financial environment is the second major environmental influence discussed in this chapter. While the discussion of the economic environment primarily related to the economic situation within countries and regions, the following discussion of the financial environment primarily relates to the circumstances that affect relations and marketing opportunities between countries. Particular issues to be covered in this connection include foreign exchange, financial management and the international financial system.

## Foreign exchange issues

By its very nature, exporting does not usually occur unless money changes hands and as a consequence exporters need to address the issue of foreign currency. While it is possible to quote in and insist on being paid in A$ or NZ$, unless you have an eagerly sought after product, this is unlikely to be acceptable to the overseas buyer. The foreign exchange market is a market for currencies through which the currency of one country is exchanged for the currency of another country. Participants in the market include banks, governments, speculators, individuals and firms. The price of one currency in terms of another is the rate of exchange. As with many forms of financial trading, rates quoted can be either at the present time (known as the spot market rate) or at some time in the future, such as 30, 60 or 90 days hence (known as the forward market rate). There is considerable gambling on rates, similar to the futures market for commodities or shares. This enables firms to hedge against a variation in the exchange rate and to negotiate a forward market rate that applies on the date on which receipt of payment is expected. In this situation likely gains from a movement in the exchange rate are sacrificed to ensure protection from possible loss if the exchange rate moves the other way. Forward contracts for unstable currencies are very expensive and are not always available for lesser known or less frequently traded currencies. Underlying the forecasting of exchange rates is the previously discussed concept of purchasing power parity. This is based on the notion that a change in relationship between price levels in two different countries requires an adjustment in the exchange rate to offset the difference in price levels.

### SETTING OF EXCHANGE RATES

Exchange rates may be linked to a single currency, pegged to a basket of currencies, determined by cooperative arrangements, based on some other form of managed float or allowed to float independently. For decades the US dollar has been treated as a 'reserve' currency in international trade, but recently its role as a reserve currency is being challenged by the euro.

### DYNAMICS

One problem that faces all people involved in international business is the risk that between the time a sale is agreed upon and the time payment is received the exchange rate may have changed. When this happens the amount received in the currency quoted by the seller will be different from that which was expected when the contract was entered into. It could be that a major devaluation of the currency in the buying country occurred, as happened in Thailand in the last six months of 1997, or that there was a shift in the rate which, although small, had the effect of eroding the profit to be made on the transaction. An example of this is illustrated in Table 2.6.

### FORECASTING

There are a number of factors that influence the forecasting of exchange rates in addition to the purchasing power parity of a country. The most important ones are economic and political.

| TABLE 2.6 | Example of foreign exchange impact | | | | |

**Monthly contract: US$10 000**
**Cost of goods to marketer: A$7500**

| Date | Exchange rate | Revenue (A$) | Cost (A$) | Net income (A$) |
|------|---------------|--------------|-----------|-----------------|
| 15 September | US$1 = A$0.80 | 8000 | 7500 | 500 |
| 15 October | US$1 = A$0.75 | 7500 | 7500 | – |
| 15 November | US$1 = A$0.70 | 7000 | 7500 | (500) |

**Economic factors** The economic factors are as follows:

- Policy and performance can create a rate of growth higher than the world average. When this happens the exchange value of a country's currency will increase.

- Real interest rates (nominal interest rate minus the rate of inflation) compared to the world average will also have an impact. If the rate is higher it will attract capital from overseas and create a demand for the country's currency.

- The importance of the currency in the world's financial system. If a currency is desirable, like the US dollar, and included in baskets of currencies and held by individuals and institutions as a form of wealth in countries overseas, it is less susceptible to fluctuation. Also, the spread between buying and selling rates for this currency is likely to be less.

**Political factors** Political factors are important in the value attributed to a currency. Political factors include the philosophy of the party in power, the stability of governments, the nature of the underpinning of power (such as the role of the King in Thailand), sources of impending change (suppression of popular alternatives as in Myanmar) and the nature of the government.

The freewheeling flow of capital around the global village is forcing a rethink of long-held exchange rate theories according to Ross Gittins. Whereas previously exchange rate movements were explained by what was happening to a country's trade, now it is explained by what is happening to a country's capital inflow. Billions of dollars in hot money are now roaming the world in search of the highest returns. The idea that exchange rates move according to the current account deficit no longer stacks up. The concept that exchange rates move according to the differential between Australia's interest rates and those in the other country does not explain why the A$, which most economists consider is 'worth' US 65 cents, only had an exchange value of US 49 cents in late March 2001 compared with an exchange rate of US 84 cents in August 2006. With free floating exchange rates, Australia's currency is at the mercy of global currency traders whose speculative activities call into question various economic explanations of exchange rate movements. Most of the foreign exchange movements are about speculation and the amounts involved are about forty to sixty times the value of real trade.

**SOURCES:** *Adapted from World Bank (2001) 'World development indicators 2002'*, Sydney Morning Herald, *24 March 2001, p. 46; and Saul, J.R. (2005)* The Collapse of Globalism and the Reinvention of the World, *Viking-Penguin Books, London, pp. 20–1.*

## MANAGING FOREIGN EXCHANGE RISK

When a firm undertakes transactions in foreign currencies the firm runs the risk of losses or gains from a change in the value of the currency involved. This exposure takes three forms:

1  *transaction exposure*: the effect of outstanding contracts involving overseas countries on the likely receipts of the firm;

2  *translation exposure*: the effect of translating results of overseas activities in the currency of the home country; and

3  *economic exposure*: the impact on the forward movement of the exchange rate arising from economic circumstances in the overseas market. An example of exposure is the effect on the economies of various countries in South and South-East Asia due to the tsunami crisis of 26 December 2004.

Various strategies can be employed to reduce exposure to foreign exchange risk. These include modifying the risk. An example would be to borrow funds in the country with which the firm already has exposure so that the possible loss on foreign exchange is matched by profits when paying off that loan. Alternatively, risk modification can occur by shifting the risk by purchasing options and/or futures (hedging). Whereas options give the right to buy or sell currency at a nominated price up until a specified date, futures are usually longer term and for larger values. They involve the right to buy an amount of a nominated currency at some future time at a specified price. Another way to reduce exposure to foreign exchange risk is to purchase and sell currency in different markets so as to profit from unwarranted differences in rates (arbitrage). The challenges involved in managing exchange rate risk can be seen in the international removals industry in International Highlight 2.3.

---

### 2.3 INTERNATIONAL HIGHLIGHT

# OSS—managing exchange rate risks

Overseas Shipping Services (OSS) is an Australian-based international removalist involved in shipping household furniture and personal goods throughout the world. It has a very strong presence in Asian markets, especially Hong Kong, Malaysia, Thailand, Singapore and Indonesia. Strong Asian immigration into Australia, as well as Asian families and students returning home, has encouraged a significant two-way market in the movement of personal household goods.

At any moment in time OSS owes money to its overseas agents (resulting from prepaid exports to the end overseas destination) and it is owed money when overseas agents accept full payment from clients; this also covers OSS disbursements for clearance and delivery in Australia. Depending upon the balance of export and import business between different countries, OSS may owe money or may be owed by its overseas agents. Multiple exchange rate risk is a fact of life for OSS.

The financial crisis in Asia in late 1997 and in 1998 forced OSS to increase radically its frequency of reconciliation of accounts with its overseas agents as the premiums of forward exchange cover increased dramatically for several Asian currencies.

---

Governments also intervene in free-floating foreign exchange markets. The motive for intervention is to support or depress the price of their own or other currencies, to dampen fluctuations in exchange rates or to manipulate the value of the currency for political or economic reasons. Sometimes governments attempt to discourage their nationals from importing by making the domestic currency more expensive in comparison with the currencies of major import sources. In Australia, such intervention usually takes the form of the Reserve Bank buying or selling the Australian dollar or other currencies or gold.

A decade after the Asian financial crisis of 1997, finance ministers from ASEAN together with those from China, Japan and South Korea have agreed to pool part of their burgeoning foreign exchange reserves to avoid a repeat of that crisis. This will replace the current bilateral emergency currency-swap system.

**SOURCE:** Sunday Nation, *Bangkok, 6 May 2007, p. 1A.*

## MULTIPLE EXCHANGE RATES

When there is a difference between the official rate of exchange for a currency and what people think it is worth, a black market for the currency is likely to develop, as existed in India for years prior to 1994. Often this situation is caused because the exchange rate is set by the government for political or balance of payments reasons and is not allowed to float according to demand or supply. When the situation gets out of hand the government may give partial recognition to the problem by setting a different exchange rate for transactions by specific sectors such as a special rate for tourists visiting the country. On other occasions the situation arises because the currency is pegged to a basket of other currencies and moves in step with them. If the relative weighting accorded to currencies in the basket does not reflect the relative market value of those currencies, then the float is skewed and the exchange rate does not reflect the market value of the currency.

In Vietnam in the late 1980s there were three exchange rates for the local currency – the dong. There was the official rate of 6.5 to the US$, a tourist rate of 12 to the US$, and an illegal black market rate of 300 to the US$.

# Financial management

The discussion of financial management focuses on sources of funds and types of financial risks likely to be encountered in the international marketplace.

## SOURCES OF FUNDS

In many cases it is necessary for firms in Australia or New Zealand to assist their customers abroad with financing. In countries where finance is a problem it is often the case that the attractiveness of the financial terms will outweigh the price. The more attractive the finance (measured in terms of the rate of interest and/or the grace period and/or the length of the loan), the greater the chance of winning the business. Some of the more common sources of finance are banks, government and factoring.

**Banks** Banks may be located in Australia or in other countries. They provide trade financing depending on their commercial relationship with the exporter, the nature of the transaction, the perceived risk of the country of the borrower and the availability of export insurance to reduce the risk. These institutions usually finance first-rate credit risks only. Often this means that banks do not insure transactions in promising or newly emerging markets. The increasing level of debt in the developing world and the lack of conformity by these countries to accepted 'Western' financial practices has increased the reluctance of the banking sector to finance transactions involving such countries.

Another factor may be the nature of the bank's overseas network. This may consist of a series of relationships with correspondent banks. A stage of increased overseas involvement is for the bank to establish representative offices in the more promising overseas markets either from the perspective of servicing its Australian customers that seek offshore involvement or attracting new customers. The most resource-intensive form of bank involvement is acquiring equity in banks in other countries. This may increase the likelihood of the bank financing transactions in those countries. The ANZ Bank, for example, purchased the UK National and Grindlays Bank which had extensive branch operations in the Indian subcontinent and Africa. During the time the ANZ Bank owned this operation, it was more informed about the reality of doing business and getting paid in countries in these areas.

Not all banking systems are the same. Islamic banking differs in that the collection of interest (riba) is prohibited under (shariah) law. Islamic law (morabaha), however, does allow a seller to resell an item at a higher price than it was purchased for, as long as there are two separate transactions. Instead of lender–borrower-based relationships as encountered in Western banking, there is a trade relationship. Although they look and feel like a loan transaction, the substance of the contractual relationship is different. Other popular banking instruments in the Arab world focus on profit sharing where profit and risk are shared between the parties (mudaraba and mosharaka).

In emerging markets, 'people's banks' are being established to serve those at the 'bottom of the pyramid' (see Chapter 1) and mobilise small unit savings in a manner that relates to the needs of the poor and underprivileged—often with the aim of assisting them to become small-scale entrepreneurs. Examples of this are the Wao microbank in Papua-New Guinea and the Grameen Bank in Bangladesh. This latter bank was established in 1976 to enable the poor, especially women, to start up small businesses without collateral. The bank now serves 6.1 million borrowers and has spawned a number of similar institutions in other countries.

**Government** When the risks are not commercially insurable or the government decides that it is in the national interest to fund a sale to a country that has a high credit risk, then it may extend the loan itself or underwrite a loan extended by a commercial institution. Official assistance can take the form of either a loan or a guarantee. In the latter case governments often mix aid with credit to offer a blended loan. As Letovsky (1990) points out, this has resulted in an export credit war in which countries try to outdo each other in offering concessional loans so as to improve the chances of their firms winning overseas business. This often occurs with major projects. An example in the Australian context was the Development Import Finance Facility that operated until 1996. The principal Australian government body that finances international business transactions is the Export Finance Insurance Corporation (EFIC). It provides both guarantees and loans (commercial and aid assisted) as well as other products. These indirectly influence export financing, such as political risk insurance, overseas investment insurance, performance bonds and working capital guarantees. EFIC rates countries in terms of non-payment risk. Their rating of countries is from 1 (most creditworthy) to 5 (least creditworthy).

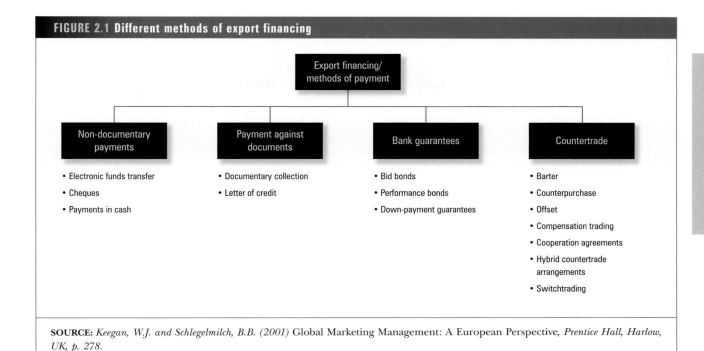

**FIGURE 2.1 Different methods of export financing**

Export financing/
methods of payment

Non-documentary payments
- Electronic funds transfer
- Cheques
- Payments in cash

Payment against documents
- Documentary collection
- Letter of credit

Bank guarantees
- Bid bonds
- Performance bonds
- Down-payment guarantees

Countertrade
- Barter
- Counterpurchase
- Offset
- Compensation trading
- Cooperation agreements
- Hybrid countertrade arrangements
- Switchtrading

**SOURCE:** *Keegan, W.J. and Schlegelmilch, B.B. (2001)* Global Marketing Management: A European Perspective, *Prentice Hall, Harlow, UK, p. 278.*

**Forfeiting and factoring** With forfeiting, the importer provides the exporter at the time of shipment with a promissory note, which the exporter then sells at a discount for cash. With factoring, the factoring house purchases the cash. Where the exporter is still liable for buyer default the discount is modest, but where the factoring house accepts liability the discount tends to be large. Figure 2.1 summarises different methods of payment and export financing in terms of whether they are short term or middle/long term. The countertrade option is discussed in greater detail in Chapter 19.

## TYPES OF FINANCIAL RISK

There are a number of different sources of financial risk. Knowledge of these can assist in reducing or managing risk. Overseas political, commercial and economic developments can quickly render the most careful financial judgements irrelevant. In addition, changes in the structure or ownership of the overseas party with whom the transaction is being undertaken can also have an unanticipated impact.

- *Commercial risk*: Commercial defaults usually result from changes to personnel in the firm, loss of a key customer by the buyer, the buyer encountering unexpected financial problems or the buyer being threatened with a takeover bid. Slow payment by the buyer's other customers, such as government instrumentalities, or natural disasters, such as an earthquake, can also result in commercial default. While all these sources of change exist in the domestic market, lack of direct involvement in the overseas market as well as geographic and psychic distance make the risks more difficult to anticipate when exporting overseas.

- *Political risk*: This is beyond the control of either the Australian seller or the overseas buyer. Often this is caused by the buyer wishing to pay, but the government of the host

Many countries have bodies established by their governments to provide a range of export and investment financing services. Australia's Export Credit agency, EFIC assists Australia's exports and overseas investments and at 30 June 2006 had an exposure of A$3 billion across 32 countries predominantly for the support of Australian exports and investments. Its core business is in providing finance, finance guarantees, insurance and bonding facilities. Recently it launched new initiatives to assist small and medium-sized enterprises (SMEs), such as the US$50 million bonding facility, to help SME exporters take advantage of the opportunities arising from the Free Trade Agreement with the US. They are also coming up with a new working capital facility that will assist banks extend additional finance to SME exporters.

country delaying the approval to remit funds for balance of payments reasons. Other political risks include war, revolution, changes in official policy, cancellation of projects, change in the political party in power and expropriation of firms in the host country.

- *Foreign exchange risk*: Fluctuating exchange rates influence how much is actually received in Australian dollars. As discussed previously, there are various mechanisms to minimise this form of risk, but, as these affect the cost of the transaction, the charges for minimising foreign exchange risk need to be factored into the price.

## COPING WITH RECESSION

The Asian currency crisis of a decade ago and the Japanese economic recession that began in the late 1990s illustrate the need for international marketers to have available plans to cope with recession. These can be short term and driven by the need to provide shareholders with continuous dividends or long term, driven by the desire to cater for customer needs in the market encountering recession. Kotabe and Helsen (2000) propose eight strategies as follows:

1 *Pull out*. Although a short-term, easy option, it does have long-term consequences, particularly in Asian countries where long-term, trustworthy relationships are an integral element of the business scene. Retail firms such as J.C. Penny and Wal-Mart, which left Indonesia when its currency crisis occurred, will find it very difficult to enter that market again.

2 *Emphasise a product's value*. Despite the recession, middle-class consumers in Asian markets will want to maintain their current lifestyle. In tough times they will need reassurance that the products previously purchased without much thought now represent value for money. This might be achieved by emphasising the quality of the product. This tactic was adopted by Proctor and Gamble for its range of shampoos in Hong Kong.

3 *Change the product mix*. The firm can shift the product mix offered in the market experiencing recession by pushing the relatively inexpensive elements of the range while de-emphasising the more expensive elements. Burberry, the UK men's clothing retailer, replaced its expensive jackets with its range of T-shirts in the windows of its Asian outlets during the currency crisis.

4 *Repackage the goods*. So that loyal customers will keep buying the product in times of difficulty, the product can be offered in smaller packs at more affordable prices, as was the case with Unilever's Magnum ice cream and its range of detergents.

5 *Maintain stricter inventory*. This involves not only reducing unnecessary inventory, but also improving product assortment by offering only what the customers in the market

experiencing recession actually want. In Kuala Lumpur, IKEA, the Swedish furniture retailer, has not restocked slow-moving items.

6 *Look outside the region for expansion opportunities.* Lower labour costs and cheaper Asian currencies mean that plants in countries experiencing recession have a competitive cost advantage as sources of supply to other markets. Having your own plants in such markets focus on supplying international markets rather than the local market may be a strategy for coping with recession.

7 *Increase advertising in the region.* A fall in exchange rates and recession will mean that it is much cheaper to advertise in markets experiencing downturn. This, coupled with historical evidence that it is a mistake to cut advertising during a recession, suggests that advertising should be increased.

8 *Increase local procurement.* Currency variations will make local sourcing cheaper than imported sourcing and this provides the opportunity for re-evaluating local sources of supply for inputs so as to improve competitiveness. Increasing local procurement offers greater protection against fluctuating exchange rates.

# The international financial system

## BACKGROUND

Towards the end of World War II the allied powers met to determine an international financial framework that would facilitate post-war reconstruction. This meeting resulted in the Bretton Woods Agreement that established:

- a world lending body—the International Bank for Reconstruction and Development (also known as the World Bank);
- a body to oversee the management of the international financial system and manage currency adjustments—the International Monetary Fund (IMF); and
- a system whereby exchange rates were to be pegged to the US dollar. Nations agreed to maintain exchange rates to within ±1% of the fixed rate. The US dollar was defined in terms of its gold value and convertibility into gold.

This system collapsed in 1971 due to mounting US balance of payments deficits. With reserves of US$11 billion in gold, and US$47 billion of dollars held by foreign interests, there was no way the USA could redeem dollars for gold if called upon to do so. The world moved to a foreign exchange market system. In effect this meant that currencies were free to fluctuate and foreign exchange rates were subject to demand and supply. The rates could be 'officially' influenced by governments intervening in the market by buying or selling their own currency, if they wished to reduce or increase its value in terms of other currencies.

## INTERNATIONAL MONETARY FUND

The International Monetary Fund (IMF) is an international organisation that has 184 countries as members (as of 16 October 2006) compared with less than 50 when it was founded in 1945. The IMF has six objectives:

1 To promote international cooperation among members on international monetary issues.

2 To facilitate the balanced growth of international trade and contribute to high levels of real income, employment and production.

3   To promote exchange stability and orderly exchange arrangements and avoid competitive currency devaluation.

4   To foster a multilateral system of payments and transfers, and eliminate exchange restrictions.

5   To make financial resources available to members.

6   To seek a reduction of imbalances in payments.

Following the collapse in 1971 of the system established by the Bretton Woods Agreement, the IMF created a system of Special Drawing Rights (SDRs) to supplement both the dollar and gold as reserves. SDRs, often referred to as 'paper gold', represent an average base of value derived from the value of a group of the most important currencies. SDRs are allocated by the IMF to each member country on the basis of various factors including share of gross world product and share of world trade. When members encounter balance of payments difficulties they can exchange SDRs for currency held by other countries. The creation of SDRs has increased liquidity in the international business environment and some international contracts are written in SDRs to reduce exposure to foreign exchange rate fluctuations. SDRs play an important role by providing short-term financing to governments trying to clear current accounts deficits. Governments are able to do this because control over SDRs enables governments to operate as short-term lenders.

The IMF's lending capacity in recent years has led to a broadening of its role. Increasingly, the IMF operates as a financial consultant to governments of countries in financial difficulty. It organises a package of financial assistance measures for such countries, but these are usually conditional on the country undertaking a package of financial remedies. In the case of the Asian currency crisis, in part this was due to pressure on nations to expose themselves to unfettered capital inflows regardless of their ability to absorb them. When a country encounters problems, typical IMF demands are to cut government expenditure, establish realistic exchange rates, reduce growth in money supply, curtail government subsidies and prepare an active program to stimulate exports. These measures are based on Western economic rationalism and not on Asian relationship-oriented approaches to business. Because of this there is often resentment towards the IMF and consequent claims that its conditions for assistance infringe national sovereignty. In response to criticism the IMF has created a special fund (US$8.4 billion) to help the poorest of the less-developed countries. This fund extends loans at concessional interest rates for up to 10 years.

The Thai currency was devalued in July 1997. The IMF became involved in structuring a rescue package and Thailand agreed to a number of measures including A$3.9 billion sale of state enterprises. However, two finance ministers resigned in succession after failing to get government support for tax increases sufficient to match IMF demands. When the Thai baht went into 'free fall' in October 1997, the IMF became involved in restructuring the rescue package. Because of the size of the necessary package, the IMF sought assistance from other countries. This assistance in Australia's case took the form of increasing its holdings of baht by A$1 billion. The conditions imposed by the IMF, although accepted by Thailand, contributed to political instability resulting in a change in government in November 1997.

The IMF was formed at a time of financial regulation and fixed exchange rates. In a current environment of floating exchange rates and financial deregulation, the IMF is having to reappraise its approach in order to ensure its continued relevancy.

## THE WORLD BANK

The World Bank is owned by 184 member countries (as at 16 October 2006) and has traditionally operated as a development bank channelling technical assistance and finance to developing countries. The primary focus of its lending program until recently has been on project financing for economic and social infrastructure. Although some of its financing is provided by developed countries, most is raised on international capital markets. As a consequence most of its loans are made at near commercial rates. Its loans are usually repayable over 15 to 20 years with a grace period of three to five years. Each loan must be made to or guaranteed by the recipient country. Because poorer countries cannot afford to pay high rates of interest concessional finance is provided to them through the World Bank's subsidiary, the International Development Association. Another subsidiary provides funds for private sector investment projects—the International Finance Corporation.

In more recent years the World Bank has been under pressure, particularly from the USA, to move away from project financing towards activities that foster deregulation and more market-driven economic policies. On a number of occasions the USA has used its power of veto in the World Bank to impose on other countries its view of the world. This is regarded by many as being contrary to the spirit of a truly multilateral organisation.

> From the time the Socialist Republic of Vietnam was created in 1972 until US recognition in 1994, the World Bank was unable to fund development projects in that country despite the fact that a majority of the world's nations such as Australia had long since recognised the regime. It was the US power of veto which enabled it to stop World Bank assistance to Vietnam and resulted in the strange situation whereby the United Nations Development Program funded feasibility studies in Vietnam against the day when the World Bank would be allowed to fund feasible projects.

## INTERNATIONAL AID

The motives underlying aid vary. It is given for political, financial and altruistic reasons:

* *Political*: The purpose in this case is to increase the dependency of a regime in another country on the nation giving the aid, such as Australian aid to Papua New Guinea, or as a means of improving relationships between the donor and recipient nations, such as Australian aid to Indonesia.

* *Financial*: This is designed to assist firms in donor countries to achieve increased business in the overseas country. It may be direct, as happens when aid is used to provide concessional interest rates on loans for commercial projects overseas. It may be indirect, as happens when the aid is used to fund Australian-built projects or supply Australian products so as to demonstrate to the recipient country the quality of Australian products, services and improve Australia's image as a source of supply.

* *Altruistic*: Until the early 1980s this was the primary motive behind most Australian aid. The view was held that the recipient country knew best what it needed and that aid should have no strings attached. Goods supplied were not necessarily of Australian origin. As most other countries were using their aid as a 'bait' for commercial purchases, Australian policy over recent years has become more commercial in approach, but still varies according to whichever political party is in power in Canberra.

Aid can be either a grant (gift) or a loan (usually at non-commercial interest rates and repayment periods). It can also come from different sources:

* *Multilateral aid* is extended by agencies such as the World Bank and the Asian Development Bank. These are bodies that extend concessional loans to their poorer members. Such aid is altruistic and tendering procedures involve a balance of decision making between the relevant agency in the recipient country and the experts in the bank responsible for development assistance to that country. These procedures are transparent and are designed to ensure that the bidder with the most appropriate offer and price is selected.

* *Bilateral aid* is that given by one country to another. It usually has strings attached and is motivated by political and economic considerations. Projects to be financed or products/services to be provided are usually worked out in advance in talks between the two countries and often in the context of political or trade talks. The only exception occurs when there is an unanticipated event, such as the tsunami disaster of 26 December 2004 in countries bordering the Andaman sea, where one country seeks special help from another in times of need.

* *Non-government aid* is mostly extended by charitable bodies such as the Red Cross, Save the Children Fund or Freedom from Hunger campaign. Non-government aid can be offered on a country basis or on a global basis.

The flow of aid from the developed to the developing world has slackened somewhat as developed countries are finding it more difficult to balance their budgets. A UN resolution in the 1970s that each developed country should aim to give 1% of its GDP in aid was modified to 0.75% in the 1980s to reflect attainability and reality. The percentage of GNP given in aid by developed countries has fallen further in the 1990s with a decrease in availability of long-term, low-interest loans offered on a bilateral basis. Australian aid was reduced by the incoming Liberal–National Party Coalition government in 1996. In particular, the Development Import Finance Facility, whereby aid funds were used to provide concessional interest rates on loans associated with commercial projects in overseas markets, was withdrawn.

A major problem with aid, whether it be motivated by altruistic or commercial considerations, is the involvement of the government of the recipient country. Leading UK economist Lord Peter Bauer has pointed out that often the governments of developing countries use aid to advance their political objectives or the individual objectives of the ministers responsible for the activity concerned, rather than to advance the welfare of the people. In countries where political divisions are on racial or religious grounds, aid can be used to advance the interests of one race or religion to the detriment of the other. This can backfire on the country giving the aid, cause negative publicity for the firms involved in the execution of the project and engender criticism of the country providing the aid for violating global norms such as human rights and protection of the environment. The Three Gorges Project in China, involving massive relocation of population, resulted in criticism of the Snowy Mountains Engineering Corporation of Australia for its involvement.

## Marketing implications

The international financial system regulates financial transactions and provides opportunities for international business. Mechanisms exist for assessing and minimising financial risks involved in international business. International bodies operate so as to facilitate the country's management of its international financial exposure and also to assist the less advantaged nations. They do this in case the financial problems of such nations cause recession or depression throughout the world. This is a reason why the IMF insisted that Indonesia in 1998 fully comply with its recommendations, rather than take the soft option of linking the rupiah to the US dollar.

The international marketer needs to know the sources of funds when doing business overseas. If the funds are aid funds, payment may come from another country, from a multilateral agency or even from your own government. The international marketer also needs to monitor the financial situation in the economy of the overseas country. The financial state of the overseas economy provides an indication as to the likely stability of the exchange rate, the availability of funds and the cost of funds. All these factors affect the attractiveness of the overseas market as well as the short- and long-term risks of involvement.

## The internet and the international economic environment

The internet has affected or has the potential to affect most aspects of modern life. It has led to digital 'haves' and 'have nots', especially as far as international trade is concerned. Issues that underlie this situation include:

- **Innovation versus control**—Innovation takes place when it ruptures a stable structure. It prospers when demand is strong, when there is a stable investment climate and when infrastructure exists. However, innovation threatens the status quo and attracts the attention of regulators including the taxation authorities. The internet is an example of a technology that has evolved at such a rapid rate that it is one step ahead of the regulators. The challenge for governments is to create regulation that is technology neutral and development supportive. Governments vary substantially in this respect.

- **Entrepreneurial versus social benefits**—Although entrepreneurial activities associated with international e-business may be good for individual business interests, they need to be reconciled with macro issues which are the responsibility of governments, such as the right to privacy, social justice, security and the public good.

- **'Bricks' versus 'clicks'**—The focus when implementing the internet in international marketing should be on e-enabling traditional internet business rather than on creating a parallel way of undertaking such business. This can be achieved despite the fact that that 'clicks' requires a different focus as far as business development is concerned. This is because the products are often e-based, e-facilitated and digitally deliverable.

**SOURCE:** *Badrinath (2001), p. 5.*

It is necessary to strike a balance as far as the above three aspects are concerned. This balance will depend on the state of e-readiness of the country with which it is proposed to do business electronically. E-facilitated trade should not be viewed as an alternative to traditional international trade because technology is a tool and it is up to the user to make the most effective use of this new tool called the internet.

The internet is rapidly developing as an international trading medium and its spread is likely to be in four waves. An appreciation of these waves is necessary in order to assess the appropriateness of trading with potential overseas trading partners via the internet.

The first wave began in 1993 and basically involved North America and some Nordic countries. It evolved from an educational tool to a vehicle for corporate communications and transactions. The following are the characteristics of first-wave societies:

- advanced information societies;
- a marked clustering of information technology, telecommunications and content industries;
- very high levels of internet usage; and
- close cooperation on information technology issues between government, business and the general community to create national competitive strength—based on information technology.

The second wave began in 1996 and involved northern Europe, North-East Asia, Israel, Singapore, Hong Kong, Australia and New Zealand. It is distinguished from the first wave only by the slower, large-scale commercial uptake of the internet. The extent of these countries' development as information societies differs according to the type of information society these countries wish to create. Some countries, like the UK and Germany, are virtually indistinguishable from first-wave countries while others lag behind in policy development and levels of online penetration. Based on the number of internet hosts per person, Australia is further ahead than Canada; Japan lies well behind Australia; and Spain, Italy and Korea lag well behind Japan. One factor could be the abundance of software in English and paucity in Japanese, Korean and some European languages. There are local factors at work influencing internet uptake, such as the attachment of large firms in North Asia to existing EDI networks and the impact of their existing systems, like Minitel in France (a free service with text and email capabilities delivered by France Telecom to 17 million households). Second-wave countries differ in their objectives for embracing e-business. Some see it as improving international commercial advantage and as a vehicle for accessing diverse new content and cultural enrichment. Others, while attracted by the international commercial advantages, wish to limit the social and political influence of the medium. (An example is Singapore, where a broadband intranet offering rich locally oriented content operates at the highest speeds available in the world, but where licensed ISPs regulate content provided from outside the system.)

The third wave began in 1998 and involved the use of the internet by business and social elites in a number of the more developed of the developing countries in South and South-East Asia, Latin America, the Pacific Islands and the Middle East. Increasing local language content, improved telecommunications infrastructure and greater foreign participation in both manufacturing and telecommunications are increasing the rate of internet adoption. As this gathers momentum the internet will eventually cease to be a US-centric technology and become more of a global tool for trade with a majority of users living outside the USA. This is evidenced in the slowing growth in internet use in the developed world, the rapid growth in East Asia and Latin America where users are from narrow commercial and political elites interested in business rather than personal applications, and the rapid increase in internet hosts in a small number of transition economies such as Brazil, the Czech Republic, Thailand and the United Arab Emirates (Department of Foreign Affairs and Trade 1999, p. 100). This category of countries has little in common, apart from a desire to improve competitiveness using advanced technology. Many of their governments are often downplaying social, moral and political aspects of the internet in the interest of accessing online business benefits and reducing the gap between internet 'haves' and their situation as internet 'have-nots'. Their focus is on specific business benefits reflecting their economic circumstances and not on technology, simply because it replaces labour. The transition to an information economy for most third-wave countries will be difficult because there are major development problems, such as shortage of skills and capital and a large number of competing priorities; there are often serious deficiencies in telecommunications infrastructure which are capital intensive to remedy; and internet adoption problems encountered by countries in wave two will be intensified because business environments are geared to traditional forms of transaction and change is slow. Examples include the requirement in the Philippines that credit card transactions must be validated by a written signature, and the combination in Russia of endemic credit card fraud and lack of any legal basis for online trade.

The fourth and final wave is only starting to become apparent and involves the least developed of the developing countries. This delay is due to:

- the lack of infrastructure to support significant internet commerce; and
- governments shunning the internet on political grounds.

Some of these countries, however, are interested in promoting online commodity trade because most of their exports are commodity related. In addition, in countries where the internet has been declared illegal, cross-border online trade is used to get around the restrictions. Due to the prevalence of poverty, the information society is an abstract issue for most of these countries, which are more concerned with feeding the population and reducing disease by provision of clean water. In these countries, internet security is a problem and the necessary infrastructure often non-existent. Purchasing a computer is affordable only for a small elite because it costs between 10 and 15 times the average annual wage. Also, connecting to an ISP is astronomically expensive; in Bangladesh, 20 hours of access a month costs more than twice the average annual income (Department of Foreign Affairs and Trade 1999, p. 121). Some governments ban ISPs and the use of international phone lines to access them. Myanmar requires all faxes and modems not used in teaching or business to be registered with the government. In Laos the government screens the internet content available to subscribers, censors information exchanged and approves each person, business and piece of equipment connected to the internet.

# SUMMARY

From the perspective of the Australian firm the economic and financial condition of overseas markets influences the likelihood of undertaking profitable business with the countries involved. It influences selection of markets, the likely form of involvement in the selected market and whether the involvement should be long term or short term in the first instance. Also of relevance is the degree to which the country is involved in the international financial system, how its performance is rated and the degree to which it is economically stable and its currency subject to exchange rate volatility.

# ETHICS ISSUE

Your agent in Thailand has unearthed an opportunity to supply the same compressor kits to a customer in Myanmar as you are currently supplying to Thailand for both civilian and military uses. Payment would be in Thai baht and not in kyats. It is not possible to sell these kits in Myanmar as their import is banned due to a shortage of foreign exchange. In addition, the customer operates in the Golden Triangle region, in an area over which the central government has little control. Shipment would be via Bangkok and your Thai agent would be the consignee. You understand that your agent would arrange for the compressor kits to be smuggled across the border into Myanmar.

*If you were the Australian manufacturer of the compressor kits would you pursue this business? What factors would you take into account in assessing this business opportunity?*

## Websites

**Asian Development Bank** http://www.adb.org/media/articles
**Dr Ed Yardeni's Economics Network** http://www.yardeni.com/
*Economist* http://www.economist.com/
**General Agreement on Trade in Services (GATS)** http://www.wto.org/english/tratop_e/serv_e/serv_e.htm
**Global Edge** http://globaledge.msu.edu/
**International Monetary Fund** http://www.imf.org/
**International Monetary Fund (IMF)—country information** http://www.imf.org/external/country/index.htm
**Mondaq** http://www.mondaq.com/
**Proton Motors Berhad** http://www.proton.com
**TDC Trade—country risk profiles** http://www.tdctrade.com/countryrisk/index.htm
**TDC Trade—market profiles** http://www.tdctrade.com/mktprof/
**TradePort—country profiles** http://tradeport.org/countries/index.html
**World Bank Indicators** http://www.worldbank.org/data
**World Trade Organization** http://www.wto.org/english/info_e/site_e.htm

## Discussion questions

1   Apart from those mentioned in the chapter, what are the new emerging global trends likely to influence the global economic scene in the first decade of the 21st century?

2   Classification of countries according to economic criteria is often a way of assessing their likely potential as markets. Discuss the merits of classification by economic system, by economic structure or by stage of development.

3   A number of criteria can be used to measure overseas markets. Which is most relevant for Australian or New Zealand suppliers of:

(a)  basic consumer goods?

(b)  luxury consumer goods?

(c) industrial products?

(d) environmentally friendly products?

(e) infrastructure projects?

(f) mining equipment?

4 Are regional trade groupings more effective the greater the extent to which national sovereignty is ceded to the group, as happens in an economic union? How would you rate the effectiveness of APEC in this context?

5 Discuss the role of the International Monetary Fund in enforcing financially responsible behaviour on the nations of the world. Is there a better alternative?

6 What were the economic and financial causes of the Asian crisis of late 1997? Why did Australia become heavily involved in the IMF rescue packages in the face of claims that such assistance would disproportionately go to wealthy elites rather than benefit the population in general?

7 What are the most common forms of financial risk involved in doing business overseas? What ways exist of minimising this financial risk for Australian or New Zealand firms?

# References

Annan, K. (2001) 'End trade barriers to cut poverty', *Irish Times*, 9 March, p. 6.

'Asia development outlook 2006—country by country growth forecasts', <http://www.adb.org/Media/> Articles/2006, accessed 12 December 2006.

*Asia Inc*, July/August 2006.

Badrinath, R. (2001) 'Playing @ the digital game', *International Trade Forum*, Issue 1, p. 4.

Cavusgil, S.T. (2004) 'The promise of emerging markets', invited lecture, 1 November, University of Western Sydney.

D'Andrea, G., Stengel, A. and Goebel-Crystal, A. (2003) '*Crear valor par los consumidores emergentes*', *Harvard Business Review*, Edicion Amplida, Latin America, October.

Department of Foreign Affairs and Trade (1999) *Creating a Clearway on the New Silk Road: International Business and Policy Trends in Internet Commerce*, Commonwealth of Australia, Canberra.

*Economist*, 30 January 2007.

Ettenberg, E. (2002) *The Next Economy–Will You Know Where Your Customers Are?*, Tata McGraw-Hill, New Delhi.

*Far East Economic Review*, 21 March 2007.

*Guardian*, 28 August 2006.

Kaul, R. (2004) 'Not such a sticky wicket', *Export*, May.

*Fortune Magazine*, 10 July 2006, pp. 29–31.

Keegan, W.J. and Green, M.C. (2005) *Global Marketing*, 4th edn, Prentice Hall, Englewood Cliffs, NJ.

Keegan, W.J. and Schlegelmilch, B.B. (2001) *Global Marketing Management: A European Perspective*, Prentice Hall, Harlow, UK, p. 278.

Kotabe, M. and Helsen, K. (2000) *Global Marketing Management Update 2000*, John Wiley and Sons, New York.

Letovsky, R. (1990) 'The export finance wars', *Columbia Journal for World Business*, Spring/Summer, pp. 25–34.

Saul, J.R. (2005) *The Collapse of Globalism and the Reinvention of the World*, Viking-Penguin Books, London.

*Sunday Nation*, 'Asean Plus 3 agree to pool fourex resources', 6 May 2007, p. 117.

*Time*, 3 July 2006.

United Nations (2001) *World Investment Report, Promoting Linkages*, p. 1.

World Bank (2001) 'World development indicators 2002', *Sydney Morning Herald*, 24 March, p. 46.

## go online

Go online to <www.pearsoned.com.au/fletcher> to find more case studies.

# CASE STUDY 2

# Tourism New South Wales's experience in marketing tourism during the aftermath of the Asian financial crisis

**Wisitta Gray and Richard Fletcher**

*International services marketing often involves the 'exported item' being delivered in the country doing the exporting as with medicine and education. The case that follows illustrates this aspect of international services marketing.*

## INTRODUCTION

Tourism New South Wales is a state government agency the role of which is to market and develop the state as a leading tourism destination. Tourism being the biggest and fastest growing industry in New South Wales, the agency is committed to maximising the benefits from tourism and spreading them to every region of the state. Tourism is central to the state's economic growth; for example in 1998–99 it supported at least 240 000 full-time and part-time employment positions in New South Wales. The industry currently generates $20 billion in income per year, around 10% of the state's economy.

The state of New South Wales (NSW) promotes itself as one of Australia's most exciting, beautiful and culturally rich states. It is a well-known tourist destination that offers a range of attractions with an emphasis on its cultural landscape, beautiful weather, flora and fauna. The capital, Sydney, is promoted as the gateway to NSW. Tourism New South Wales encourages visitors to experience and explore the state through its regular marketing and promotional programs.

## PRE-CRISIS PERIOD

Prior to the Asian financial crisis most Asian countries were enjoying an average annual growth rate of around 10% in the period 1990–96. The rapid economic growth created a larger middle class who were able to undertake foreign travel. Australia's tourism industry enjoyed the growing trend in inbound tourism from Asia during this period.

The Tourism Forecasting Council was optimistic and projected the growth to continue into the 21st century. Optimism about the growth created a surge of interest in tourism investment in Australia.

## THE CRISIS

The Asian financial crisis was regarded as one of the world's worst economic calamities. It started in July 1997 with the devaluation of the Thai currency which, by December, had fallen 40% in value against the US dollar. Indonesia appeared to be the worst hit, with its currency falling 70% in value against the US dollar. To make things worse, the crisis coincided with severe drought and forest burning in some parts of the region.

## THE IMPACT OF THE CRISIS ON AUSTRALIAN TOURISM

The Australian tourism industry became alarmed at the effect of the crisis in December 1997 when inbound tourism from Korea fell dramatically. Airline traffic suffered and as demand fell Qantas

| TABLE 1 | International visitors to Australia, by country of residence, 1996–2006 |

| | 1996 | 1997 | 1998 | 1999 | 2006 |
|---|---|---|---|---|---|
| Japan | 766 600 | 766 000 | 704 400 | 662 500 | 681 000 |
| Hong Kong | 137 600 | 136 600 | 130 400 | 127 900 | 155 900 |
| Singapore | 185 900 | 201 300 | 215 600 | 234 100 | 259 600 |
| Malaysia | 118 200 | 125 800 | 101 800 | 126 500 | 161 200 |
| Indonesia | 129 900 | 138 200 | 82 600 | 82 400 | 82 600 |
| Taiwan | 144 800 | 138 900 | 135 100 | 133 600 | 109 900 |
| Thailand | 80 500 | 61 800 | 44 600 | 55 700 | 76 200 |
| Korea | 216 200 | 220 500 | 62 300 | 100 100 | 244 900 |
| China | 52 300 | 63 800 | 73 300 | 87 500 | 280 200 |

**SOURCES:** *Bureau of Tourism Research (1999)* International Visitors in Australia, *Bureau of Tourism Research, Canberra; and Australian Bureau of Statistics (2006)* Overseas Arrivals and Departures, *Cat. No. 3401.0, Commonwealth of Australia, Canberra.*

| FIGURE 1 International visitors to Australia, by country of residence, 1996–99 |

**SOURCE:** *Bureau of Tourism Research (1999)* International Visitors in Australia, *Bureau of Tourism Research, Canberra.*

and Ansett airlines started suspending services in January 1998.

In the first quarter of 1998 Asian arrivals were down 32% compared to the same quarter in 1997. However, the fall in the value of the Australian dollar in the first quarter of 1998 resulted in an increase in arrivals from Europe (9.1%) and America (14.9%). This appears to have resulted in the belief that the reduced value of the dollar increased Australian's competitiveness in the non-Asian markets.

At the beginning of 1999 a closer analysis

| TABLE 2 | International visitors to NSW, by country of residence, 1996–2006 | | | | |
|---------|--------|--------|--------|--------|--------|
| | **1996** | **1997** | **1998** | **1999** | **2006** |
| Japan | 562 400 | 529 900 | 429 196 | 396 200 | 256 786 |
| Hong Kong | 102 400 | 9 900 | 81 963 | 90 000 | 79 898 |
| Singapore | 69 900 | 72 500 | 64 440 | 77 900 | 69 979 |
| Malaysia | 48 900 | 57 700 | 38 342 | 50 300 | 40 472 |
| Indonesia | 71 100 | 79 800 | 32 720 | 36 200 | 28 134 |
| Taiwan | 120 600 | 117 100 | 101 025 | 90 800 | 40 976 |
| Thailand | 52 000 | 38 600 | 20 774 | 37 700 | 33 755 |
| Korea | 167 400 | 16 900 | 49 600 | 86 500 | 200 012 |
| China | 48 200 | 48 500 | 56 940 | 75 700 | 226 690 |

**SOURCES:** *Bureau of Tourism Research (1999)* International Visitors in Australia, *Bureau of Tourism Research, Canberra;* <http://www.tourism.nsw.gov.au>, *under 'research'; and Australian Bureau of Statistics (2006)* Overseas Arrivals and Departures, *Cat. No. 3401.0, Commonwealth of Australia, Canberra.*

revealed the significance of the decline in all the key Asian markets. The fall in inbound tourism from Korea was 72%, Indonesia 40%, Thailand 28%, Malaysia 19% and Japan 8%.

## THE IMPACT OF THE CRISIS ON TOURISM NSW

The number of visitors from Korea and Hong Kong were alarmingly low at the end of 1997. Both fell by 90% from the previous year. Although the number of Hong Kong visitors recovered in 1998, to be closer to the 1996 figure, there was little increase in Korean visitors with the number being still close to the low 1997 figure. One of the state's key markets, Japan, also dwindled in numbers, by 6% in 1997, 19% in 1998 and 8% in 1999. This added to the overall decrease in numbers of visitors from Asia between 1997 and 1998. Countries such as Korea, Indonesia, Malaysia and Thailand, which were badly affected during the crisis, appeared to have held up well in 1999.

NSW is one of the most popular Australian states for international visitors. In 1999 visitors to NSW made up 63% of the total international visitors to Australia. Asia represents a very important market to NSW; nearly 40% of all NSW's visitors come from Asia.

## TOURISM NEW SOUTH WALES'S RESPONSE TO THE CRISIS

The initial response to the crisis by Tourism New South Wales was one of concern but not alarm. The crisis was identified early on, as a result of industry contacts and commentary by Tourism New South Wales's regional officers in the affected areas. The extent of the problem became more apparent when government statistics on inbound tourism became available. By that time, several media sources had been painting a bleak picture of the entire Asian-based tourism industry, creating hysteria within the travel and tourism industry as a whole.

Tourism New South Wales conducted its own analysis on the nature and extent of the crisis, and how it affected the travel and tourism industry on a country-by-country basis. It monitored the news reports for accuracy and, at senior levels, disseminated information through the press to paint a more comprehensive picture of what was happening. Its goal was to revive confidence and calm down the hysteria generated through some speculative and biased reports. At lower levels in the organisation, regular meetings with key industry contacts were held to discuss the issues in more detail, as well as media and conference presentations.

The key elements of the response were as follows:

- analysis and interpretation of anecdotal and statistical information;
- dissemination of information to industry;
- providing leadership in terms of how the NSW industry should respond; and
- providing forecasts which projected the nature and extent of the recovery in all markets.

In addition, many tactical decisions on marketing expenditure were made. For example, a large proportion of the budget allocated to the Asian region was diverted to other key growth markets such as the USA and Europe. Careful marketing investment decisions in Asia were also made on the basis of analysis of which markets would recover first. For example, marketing was undertaken in the markets that showed evidence of rebound, to ensure that NSW did not lose presence and awareness in those markets.

## THE OUTCOME

Tourism New South Wales managed to minimise the reduction in flow of total visitors to the state through careful management of the crisis. It succeeded in defusing the industry hysteria and ensured that the industry was adequately informed. The information it provided gave the industry directions on how to conduct its short- and medium-term strategy in response to the crisis. Most importantly, the industry did not abandon the region entirely, which could have led to a very damaging loss of face and presence in many of the markets in question.

## Bibliography

Australian Bureau of Statistics (2006) *Overseas Arrivals and Departures*, Cat. No. 3401.0, Commonwealth of Australia, Canberra.

Bureau of Tourism Research (1999) *International Visitors in Australia*, Bureau of Tourism Research, Canberra.

Cassedy, K. (1991) *Crisis Management Planning in the Travel and Tourism Industry: A Study of Three Destination Cases and a Crisis Management Planning Manual*, Pacific Asia Travel Association.

Henderson, J.C. (1999) 'Managing the Asian financial crisis: tourist attractions in Singapore', *Journal of Travel Research*, Vol. 38, No. 2, pp. 177–81.

<http://www.tourism.nsw.gov.au, under 'research'>.

Prideau, B. (1998) 'The impact of the Asian financial crisis on bilateral Indonesian–Australian tourism', in Gunawan, M.P. (ed.) *Pariwisata Indonesia Menuju Keputusan Yang Lebih Baik*, Vol. 2, Bandung Institute of Technology, Bandung, Indonesia.

Prideau, B. (1999) 'The Asian financial crisis—the Australian dimension', in *Tourism and Hospitality: Delighting the Senses*, Proceedings of the 9th Australian Tourism and Hospitality Research Conference, Bureau of Tourism Research, Canberra, pp. 287–97.

Prideau, B. and Witt, S.F. (2000) 'The impact of the Asian financial crisis on Australian tourism', *Asia Pacific Journal of Tourism Research*, Vol. 5, No. 1, pp. 1–7.

Richer, L.K. (1999) 'After political turmoil: the lessons of rebuilding tourism in three Asian countries', *Journal of Travel Research*, Vol. 38, No. 1, pp. 41–5.

Tourism New South Wales (1999) *Annual Report 1998/1999*.

## Questions

1 Do you think the measures taken by Tourism New South Wales were effective in helping the travel and tourism industry in general?

2 How will the approach differ for the Asian countries affected by the crisis?

3 The travel and tourism industry is often exposed to uncertainty, risk and disaster. How important is it to incorporate crisis management in an organisation's strategic business plans?

4 The unexpected can happen to any overseas market or group of markets. What should international strategic marketing plans incorporate to reduce damage from unforeseen contingencies?

# 3

**CHAPTER**

# CATERING FOR THE CULTURAL AND SOCIAL ENVIRONMENT OF INTERNATIONAL BUSINESS

## LearningObjectives

**After reading this chapter you should be able to:**

- appreciate the impact of culture on international marketing;

- apply key cultural concepts when evaluating international marketing situations;

- evaluate the ways in which cultural differences impede international communication;

- undertake cross-cultural analysis and comparison; and

- recognise the need for cultural sensitivity when preparing for and conducting international negotiations.

# Creating favourable conditions—*feng shui*

**M**arketers in Asia have come to recognise that the supernatural attracts many Asians. Many folklores, taboos and superstitious and religious connotations of colours, numbers and symbols exist in Asia today. *Feng shui* is a particularly good example of this and is widely applied in Chinese culture, as well as in Japan and Vietnam.

*Feng shui* means 'wind and water'; it refers to the ancient art of geomancy—a calculated assessment of the most favourable conditions for any venture. A key focus of *feng shui* is its emphasis on the shape of mountains and the direction of water flows. It is believed that people's destiny could be enhanced if there is a correct alignment of the environment's *chi* (invisible energy) with the human *chi*. Thus *feng shui* involves the art of placing things, ranging from orientation of a building to the furnishing of the interiors, to influence the *chi* of a site. The philosophy maintains that excellent living conditions contribute to good health, which in turn leads to success and prosperity.

Some general guidelines for *feng shui* include where the front door of a business should face for a favourable orientation. For law firms, medical centres and shipping firms it should face north or east, while for accounting, finance, architectural and banking firms it should face north-west or south-east. North and south-east facing is appropriate for saloons and retail stores. In addition to having *feng shui* the building must also face the water and be flanked by the mountains, but this should not block the view of the mountain spirits, which is why many Hong Kong offices have see-through lobbies and even holes like the building pictured, to keep the spirits happy.

Sharp angles give off bad *feng shui*. The Gateway building in Singapore has two triangular towers, its sharp edges and jutting points giving off bad luck. The Gateway tries to compensate for this by having a north-east–south-east facing frontage; the building's sharp edges thus slice

through oncoming winds to reduce their power.

*Feng shui* also incorporates numerology, which means addresses and opening dates must be chosen with care. The numbers 2, 5, 6, 8, 9 and 10 are deemed lucky (especially 8, which connotes wealth), but not 4, which connotes death. It is no accident that the Summer Olympics in Beijing are scheduled to open on 8/8/08 at 8 pm or that one of the authors of this book was able to buy his house in Sydney at a more reasonable price when the potential Chinese buyer withdrew from the sale after the local council refused to allow the previous owner to change the number from 4 to 6A.

*Feng shui* is big business in Asia. A company which consults an expert geomancer, and publicises it, signals to its customers and employees that it cares for their prosperity and wellbeing. Western firms in the Asian region have also come to adopt *feng shui* as they have adapted their business practices to the Asian culture. As more financial institutions like ANZ and AXA turn their attention beyond serving Western firms in Asia to targeting local firms they will need to adapt to *feng shui*. To be proactive Australian firms may consult an expert geomancer and, with appropriate cultural sensitivity, communicate this to customers and prospects as well as those in government and elsewhere who influence decisions.

**SOURCE:** *Adapted from Kotler, P., Keller, K.L., Ang, S.H., Leong, S.M. and Tan, C.T. (2006)* Marketing Management: An Asian Perspective, *Prentice Hall, Singapore, pp. 612–13; and other sources.*

# INTRODUCTION

The focus on globalisation can lead to the assumption that rapid developments in communication and rising incomes will result in a common culture worldwide. However, this does not mean that the product is viewed the same way by consumers in all cultures, even with global brands that are available in a multitude of countries. Knowledge of the culture is essential to understanding the meaning attributed by customers to firms' international marketing efforts. Whether buyers accept or reject a marketing offering will be determined to a large extent by the cultural factors influencing their cognitive, affective and connotative behaviour. Often, culturally determined preferences or reactions to a foreigner's approach will override what Australians and New Zealanders think is rational economic decision making. To understand this behaviour and its impact on the decision maker the subtleties and dynamics of culture must be understood. However, the concept of culture is undergoing change as expanding networks of interpersonal communication, stimulated by the growth of sophisticated communications technology, have altered the traditional static territorial notions of culture and caused greater interchange and linkages between cultural groups (see Craig and Douglas 2006, p. 323).

## DEFINITION OF CULTURE

Culture is the glue that binds groups together. However, defining culture has always been difficult. Over 50 years ago Kroeber and Kluckholn (1952) found 164 definitions of culture. Some of the common characteristics of these definitions are that:

- culture is prescriptive in that it prescribes those forms of behaviour that are acceptable to people in a specific community;

- culture is learned, because people are not born with a culture, but are born into a culture. The norms of the culture are acquired as people are raised in and exposed to the culture;

- culture is dynamic, because not only does it influence our behaviour but, in turn, our behaviour influences the culture reflecting its interactive nature; and

- culture is subjective, because people attribute meaning to issues on a subjective basis and these subjective meanings develop within the context of the culture.

From the above, there appear to be two broad dimensions of culture—first, that it is learned and, second, that it is shared. Therefore any definition needs to be broad enough to distinguish members of one group from those of another. Two such definitions are from Fletcher (1979): 'Culture is the total way of life in a society'; and Hofstede (1980): 'Culture is the collective programming of the mind'. Craig and Douglas (2006, p. 324) argue that culture has three elements: language and communications systems, material culture and artefacts, and values and belief systems. These will be elaborated upon in more detail later in the chapter.

## THE IMPACT OF CULTURE ON INTERNATIONAL MARKETING

Culture is integral to the marketing concept, which is based on satisfaction of wants and needs of potential buyers. Not only does culture condition these wants and needs, but it also influences the way messages about the ability of the product or service to satisfy the wants or needs are received and interpreted. This is even more so in international marketing where cultures differ markedly from those in Australia and New Zealand. Culture pervades all elements of the marketing mix—product, pricing, promotion and distribution—and the acceptability of each of these elements will be judged in the context of the culture to which they are targeted.

# Culturally related factors which influence marketing

When considering culture in the context of international marketing, the following factors should be taken into account.

## KNOWLEDGE

Knowledge of another culture can be either factual or interpretative. Factual knowledge conveys meaning which appears straightforward about a culture. However, a fact may assume additional significance when interpreted within the context of a specific culture. For example, an Australian wishing to do business in Indonesia and Malaysia would need to recognise that, while business activities in both countries are largely controlled by the Chinese community, there are some differences. In Malaysia, this community makes up a larger percentage of the population and is subject to more government constraints because of the official policy to encourage the economic advancement of the Malay portion of the population. In Indonesia, by contrast, the Chinese business community has very close links to government, and in its businesses there are usually powerful Indonesian political figures on the boards of directors of Chinese-owned firms. Issues of this kind may influence decisions like the appointment of an agent or the selection of joint venture partners.

Interpretative knowledge is based on feelings and intuition and is often influenced by past experiences. It can be erroneous if evaluated according to norms or behaviours in the home country. One way of acquiring such knowledge is to develop empathy for the host culture by associating with people from that country.

## SENSITIVITY

Cultural sensitivity involves being aware of the nuances of the different culture, being empathetic with it and viewing it objectively rather than subjectively. It begins with an acceptance that other cultures in themselves are not right or wrong and one culture is not inferior to another but, rather, is different. Being culturally sensitive will reduce disharmony, alleviate aggravation, improve communication and pave the way for long-term international business relationships. Associated with cultural sensitivity is the need for the international marketing executive to evaluate the relevance of the cultural assumptions on which assessments are based, especially when those assumptions are embedded in the marketing executive's own culture.

## COLLECTIVISM

Whereas in Western societies decisions are generally made by individual consumers, this is not the case in all cultures, especially in many Asian cultures. There, collectivism plays a greater role in decision making than individualism, because of the strength of family ties, strong affinity with the group to which the individual belongs and sensitivity to the wishes of other members of the network. This behaviour stems from the broad definition of the family in Asian cultures, which is more extended than in Western cultures. Often such behaviour is not reflective of the will of the individual, but rather of a consensus or compromise between the individual and members of the extended family.

## SOCIAL CONVENTIONS

These reflect the culture and have an influence on effective marketing practices in the overseas country. Many of these are related to eating—specifically the number of meals per day, time taken to eat the meal, the composition of each meal, the time at which the meal is eaten, the degree to which the meal is a social occasion as opposed to a functional occasion, who prepares the meal and how it is served. These social conventions would be important background to a marketer of food. Culturally influenced social conventions apply to the marketing of most consumer goods and services, but apply to a lesser extent to the marketing of industrial products. Such conventions also apply to occasions that generate or restrict expenditure, such as weddings, New Year celebrations and Ramadan in the Islamic world.

## COGNITIVE STYLES

The extent to which consumers are loyal to products varies between cultures. In countries like Australia it is assumed that consumers are less loyal to products, as evidenced by switching from one brand to another to test their benefits. In many Asian countries consumers are more loyal and less inclined to switch brands on the basis of price or benefit comparison.

One of the issues in marketing is the degree of customer involvement in the purchase decision, with products being classified as high or low involvement. The nature of involvement in purchase decisions varies between cultural groups. In China the overall level of consumer involvement is less than in Australia when the product is for private consumption, with the focus being more on the physical functions of the product rather than on the relationship between its price and quality. However, the opposite is the case when the product is purchased for its social symbolic value, as it would be when it is intended as a gift. This is because the item is likely to be interpreted by the recipient as a measure of status, gratitude or approval.

The perception of risk is another culturally influenced cognitive variable. This is both in terms of extent and in terms of relative importance attributed to the various elements of risk—be they physical, financial or social. People in some cultures, such as those in Africa, may be more susceptible to physical risk due to infrastructure or health inadequacies and seek reliability and protection when making a purchase. In other cultures, such as Australia, people may consider financial risk more important and are more likely to be concerned with cost in relation to value and affordability. People in Asian cultures, however, are more likely to feel most threatened by social risk and tend to be more concerned with whether the purchase might cause a loss of status in the eyes of their family or network.

# Cultural universals

Although there are clear differences, there are also universal tendencies in all cultures. These relate to the physical world, such as the desire to look beautiful or keep track of time; the social environment, such as the desire to cooperate, to be a member of a group or to differentiate according to status; and the emotional setting, such as courtship, religious observance or mourning.

Marketing can be targeted at these cultural universals, although the way these universals are reflected in each culture will need to be taken into account because they are likely to differ. Cohen (1996) studied the cultural universals of right and left and explored how, throughout history, right has tended to be associated with good or superior and left with bad or inferior. This has its origins in the fact that because most people are right-handed, left-handedness acquires negative connotations. Although this right–left symbolism originates in physiology, it manifests itself through culture and is extremely deep rooted. Cohen argues that, by recognising the enduring nature of right–left symbolism and the way it is manifested in different cultures, marketers can avoid making blunders in their international promotional activities.

# Elements of culture

In order to understand customers in the overseas market it is necessary to be aware of their cultural heritage. Appreciating the intricacies of the culture is imperative in order to be effective in a foreign market. It should also be borne in mind that cultural differences are a matter of difference rather than exotica—culture exists in Melbourne, Moscow and Manchester just as it does among the Australian Aborigines, the New Zealand Maoris, the Arctic Eskimos and the Navajo Indians. To understand the significance for marketing of cultural differences in an overseas market it is necessary to study the elements of culture carefully. These influences include the material, social, religious, aesthetic and linguistic.

## MATERIAL CULTURE

Material culture consists of both technology and economics. The former relates to the techniques used to produce material goods. Certain skills related to an industrial society which are taken for granted in Australia and New Zealand, such as an ability to read forms of measurement and gauges, do not widely exist in some other cultures which are agrarian based. In some cultures with a higher technology orientation, preventative maintenance is the norm, whereas in some other societies, such as in Libya, cars are driven until they grind to a halt.

Economic culture relates to the level of demand: what kinds of products are sought; how these goods are produced; how they get paid for and how they get to the buyer. Included are associated infrastructure needs, such as availability of electricity to operate refrigerators and affordability in relation to the purchasing power of local incomes, such as refrigerators being viewed as necessities rather than luxury items. Also included are the size and nature of average accommodation because this may influence the physical size of the refrigerator that will be sought. In Japan, for example, apartments are very small and communications links congested. This is likely to mean that in Japan the demand will be for small refrigerators that will fit into small apartments and can be delivered without being damaged.

One of the trappings of western consumerism is the widespread use of credit cards. The banking research and advisory firm, Lafferty Group, see little chance that the loss by Chinese banks on credit cards of US$84 million in 2005 is likely to be reversed as there is in China a very high proportion of unprofitable customers from the bank's perspective because of a cultural reluctance by Chinese to do other than pay off each month their total credit card bill.

**SOURCE:** *Adapted from Wighton, D. (2006) 'Gloomy forecast for China credit card profits',* Financial Times, *5 July, p. 17.*

## SOCIAL INSTITUTIONS

These are the spine of the cultural process because they link the individual to the group. They include family, educational providers, political parties and social organisations. They are concerned with the way people relate to each other, how they achieve harmony in their relations with each other, how they govern themselves and how, in the process, they create norms for acceptable behaviour in the culture. These institutions generally provide rewards for conforming to rules. Roles performed and status within the society are influenced by the social institutions. Because of this and the impact of social institutions on values, behaviour and lifestyle, the nature of social institutions in the culture should be catered for when marketing to that culture.

## RELATIONS WITH THE UNIVERSE

In Judeo-Christian scripture there is a separation between church and state which explains why these scriptures are silent on matters of trade and commerce. Islam is different and the prophet Muhammad, who was a trader, viewed religion and commerce as intertwined and the deals in the souk were a metaphor for the contract between God and the faithful. The business model Muhammad preached was very much in the laissez-faire tradition and prices set were the will of God. This may explain why, despite other difficulties, there are no differences between Arab nations and the West regarding free-market economics.

**SOURCE:** *Adapted from Glain, S. (2006) 'Islam in office',* Newsweek, *3–10 July, pp. 34–5.*

Symbolic and sacred elements form the link between the material and the metaphysical worlds. Belief systems, such as those embodied in religion or superstition, affect the value systems of a society in which legal, political and economic precepts are often based. Religion is one of the most sensitive elements of culture. It influences people's habits, the foods they eat, their perceptions of what is moral and immoral, the products they buy and the way they view life. Failure to appreciate fully a religion's significance in a specific culture can easily cause the marketer to give offence, as the following examples illustrate.

There are between 800 million and 1.2 billion people in the world who embrace Islam, yet major international companies often unintentionally offend Muslims. A recent incident involved the French fashion house of Chanel, which unwittingly desecrated the Koran by embroidering verses from the sacred book of Islam on several dresses shown in its summer collections. The designer said he took the design, which was aesthetically pleasing to him, from a book on India's Taj Mahal and that he was unaware of its meaning. Another incident involved a boycott of Danish firms by millions of Muslims, causing an 85% drop in Danish dairy exports to the Islamic world. This boycott was triggered when a Danish newspaper, Jyllanda-Posten, published 12 cartoons about the prophet Muhammad, including one in which the founder of Islam was shown wearing a turban shaped like a bomb.

**SOURCES:** *Adapted from* Wall Street Journal, *21 January 1994, p. 97; and 'Cartoon sees dairy exports drop 85%',* New Zealand Herald, *22 April 2006, p. C4.*

The same religion may have a different impact on business customs and practices in different countries. This is because there are other factors in the environment that modify the impact of religion. While Islam is the predominant religion in both Malaysia and Saudi Arabia, its influence on business is much less in the former than in the latter.

What we in Australia and New Zealand might view as superstition plays an important role in the belief systems of some cultures. To be dismissive of practices based on superstition because they are disregarded in Australia or New Zealand is a certain way to give offence. Cutting the air with a knife to get protection from thunder and lightning (Thailand), sacrificing an animal to drive spirits away (Malaysia) and basing actions and decisions on predictions as to whether the day or time is auspicious (China) should be taken seriously by the foreign marketer.

While religion has an influence on culture in most countries, its impact is likely to be deeper in developing country markets and affect business practices to a greater extent than in developed countries.

## AESTHETICS

Art, folklore, music, drama and dance all have a role in interpreting symbolic meanings in each culture. These aesthetic manifestations point up the uniqueness of a culture and need to be incorporated in marketing approaches to customers in that culture so as to enhance the appeal of and identification with the message. An appreciation of aesthetic values will improve the appeal of the product and its packaging as well as its promotional effectiveness.

## LANGUAGE

Language that members of a culture learn as they are raised shapes their view of the world and their social behaviour. Languages differ in the way they convey meaning, the precision of the message, the degree to which things are implied as opposed to specified and the extent to which meaning is conveyed by verbal as opposed to non-verbal cues. Because of the influence of culture, simple translation from English into another language rarely conveys the meaning accurately. Culture determines the meaning attributable to words. A house means something different to an Aboriginal person living on a reserve than it does to someone living on Sydney's North Shore. When marketing in other countries it is important to be aware of the meaning attributable to words in the language of that culture as well as to appreciate the role of idiomatic expressions in that language in conveying meaning. When translating from a foreign language into English, literal translation can yield hilarious results as the following collection of 'bloopers' show (Kelly 1990).

- The lift is being fixed for the next day. During that time we regret that you will be unbearable. (*Romania*)

- You are invited to take advantage of the chambermaid. (*Japan*)

- Because of the impropriety of entertaining guests of the opposite sex in the bedroom, it is suggested that the lobby be used for this purpose. (*Switzerland*)

- If this is your first visit to the USSR, you are welcome to it. (*Russia*)

- Ladies are requested not to have children in the bar. (*Norway*)

- The manager has personally passed all the water served here. (*Mexico*)

- Drop your trousers here for the best results. (*Thailand*)

- Ladies have fits upstairs. (*Hong Kong*)
- We take your bags and send them in all directions. (*Denmark*)
- Please do not feed the animals. If you have any suitable food, please give it to the guard on duty. (*Hungary*)

---

**3.1 INTERNATIONAL HIGHLIGHT**

## Multiculturalism is an asset

Australia traditionally has, by comparison with most of its overseas competitors, been linguistically impoverished. This is due to lack of common borders and an immigration focus until the 1940s on persons of Anglo-Saxon origin.

No longer is this the case. Australia in its overseas promotion features its multiculturalism. This multiculturalism is reflected in 3 million Australians (15% of the population) speaking a language other than English in the home, 1 million being fluent in another European language and 900 000 speaking a major Asian language. Not only does this help Australia's export effort, but Australian Government bodies such as Invest Australia use these figures in promoting Australia offshore as a location for investment or regional headquarters.

**SOURCE:** *Invest Australia advertisement in* Economist, *24 April 2004, p. 26.*

---

## Expressions of culture

Culture is expressed in a number of ways through symbols, heroes and rituals:

- *Symbols* are words, gestures, objects or pictures that carry a particular meaning recognisable only by those who are members of the culture. Jargon, dress, clothing and hairstyles, and certain products fall into this category. Symbols are the most superficial element of culture because they are easily developed, often borrowed from other cultures and quickly disappear.

- *Heroes* are people who, whether alive or dead, possess qualities that are highly prized in a particular culture and serve as models to emulate.

- *Rituals* are collective activities that are an essential element of social activities within a culture. Ceremonies, ways of greeting and even sporting events are rituals for those involved.

Symbols, heroes and rituals are all categorised as practices as they result in people behaving in certain ways, either directly or via emulation. However, at the core of culture are *values*, which may be considered as tendencies to prefer certain states of affairs over others. Usually, values embody contrasts such as evil versus good, ugly versus beautiful and irrational versus rational. Values are usually the first things people learn, but this learning is implicit rather than conscious. Figure 3.1 illustrates this.

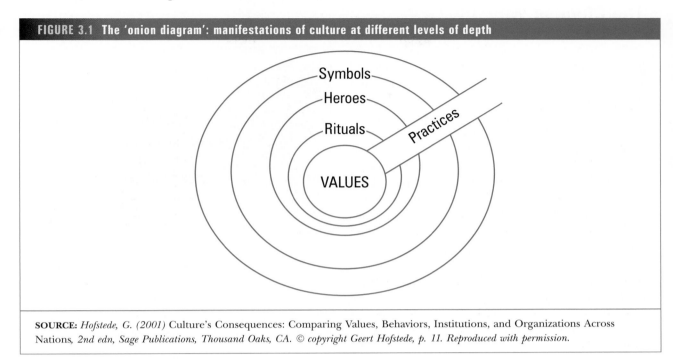

**FIGURE 3.1  The 'onion diagram': manifestations of culture at different levels of depth**

Symbols
Heroes
Rituals
Practices
VALUES

**SOURCE:** *Hofstede, G. (2001) Culture's Consequences: Comparing Values, Behaviors, Institutions, and Organizations Across Nations, 2nd edn, Sage Publications, Thousand Oaks, CA. © copyright Geert Hofstede, p. 11. Reproduced with permission.*

## Culture as a collective fingerprint

Culture is a mark of identity not of superiority. Elements of culture will have a different impact on different aspects of the marketing program. Furthermore, although culture itself is dynamic in nature and constantly changing, it contains elements that are resistant to change.

These must be understood so that the marketer will appreciate those aspects of the culture that might cause resistance to changes that the new product offering might generate. Culture is a total picture, although made up of different elements, and it cannot be separated into parts and be completely understood. It is not possible to select the best elements from each culture and arrive at an ideal combination. This is illustrated in the following joke:

> Heaven is where the cooks are French, the mechanics are German, the policemen are English, the lovers are Italian and it is all organised by the Swiss. Hell is where the policemen are German, the mechanics are French, the cooks are English, the lovers are Swiss, and it is all organised by the Italians.

## Levels at which culture operates

Culture operates at various levels, each having an influence on negotiating or undertaking business overseas. To this point, the discussion has related to personal cultural differences. Culture also operates at the global, national, organisational and group levels. These levels are

## 3.2 INTERNATIONAL HIGHLIGHT

# The Chinese way

China now represents Ericsson's largest market for telecommunications network equipment and services, displacing the USA as number one market at the end of 1997. This has occurred for many reasons—one important reason is that Ericsson understands the Chinese way.

When a 'Chinese-experienced' Australian executive was calling on a large telecom customer in regional China he received a number of criticisms from the senior Chinese management team about Ericsson's service. In fact, it was suggested that an unfavourable report might be sent to the board, which in China is constituted of senior government officials. Instead of attempting to counter the criticisms, he agreed with all of them and explained how Ericsson, with the client's help, could overcome the problems. He understood that Chinese managers who criticise and question are really asking for help and solutions that can be sold internally and passed onto their superiors as a means of maintaining

confidence. By seeking to cooperate and find solutions, rather than the Western penchant for debating the issues, he gave them a means of taking the relationship forward. After several discussions and banquets his, and Ericsson's, relationship with his Chinese clients was stronger than before.

shown in Figure 3.2. However, culture is a multi-layered construct at all levels from the global to the individual and, when shared by individuals who belong in the same cultural context, it becomes a shared value that characterises the aggregated unit, be it group, organisation or nation; hence the 'top-down' and 'bottom-up' approach illustrated in Figure 3.2.

## GLOBAL LEVEL

Global culture is created by global networks and global institutions that cross national and cultural borders. Such cultures need to adopt common rules and procedures and have a common frame of reference for communicating across cultural borders. Given the dominance of Western multinational corporations, the principle values in a global cultural context are often based on a free market economy and on democracy.

## NATIONAL LEVEL

The national culture affects dealings with governments and is reflected in the values on which laws and institutions are based. National culture also influences the way the law is applied. This explains why in some cultures nepotism and cronyism can result in transgressors evading punishment and the tacit acceptance of some forms of bribery. One example of national culture is the insistence on the use of the national language as opposed to the most commonly spoken language among a group. The use of Malay in those Malaysian cities where Chinese dominate is an example. Other examples include observance of hierarchical order as in Thailand; power being vested in certain elements in the community such as in the

**FIGURE 3.2 The different layers of culture**

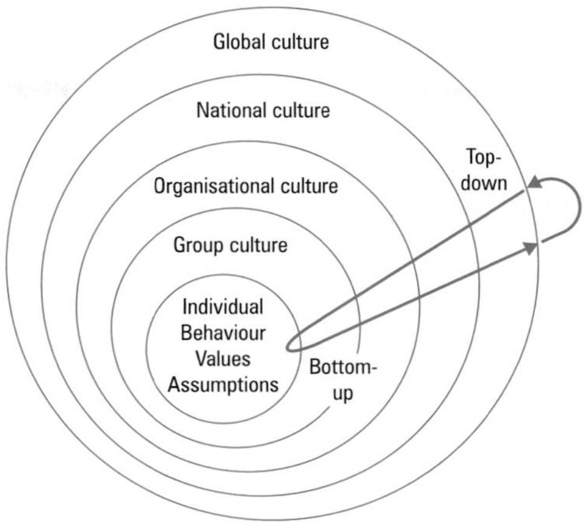

SOURCE: *Leung, K., Bhagat, R.S., Buchan, N.R, Erez, M. and Gibson, C.B. (2006) 'Culture and international business: recent advances and their implications for future research',* Journal of International Business Studies, *Vol. 36, pp. 357–78.*

Philippines where power resides among a handful of families; and religion dominating national life as happens with Islam in Saudi Arabia. National culture is also manifested in close relationships between business and government as happens in Japanese business life.

> Prior to both the conclusion of the GATT Uruguay Round in 1994 and trade relations pressure from USA and Australia, the rice market in Japan was closed to imports in response to pressure by Japanese rice farmers. This same close relationship between agriculture and government has subsequently led to rice imported into Japan being stored and used for aid to other countries or diverted into industrial uses where its origin is concealed so that Japanese palates will not be exposed to foreign rice.

An interesting concept was developed by Keillor et al. (1995) and Keillor and Hult (1999) called the National Identity Scale (NATID). This scale identifies the importance placed by a nation or culture on its uniqueness and the specific elements that define that uniqueness. The scale measures national identity along four dimensions—national heritage, cultural homogeneity, belief system and consumer ethnocentrism.

Finally, national culture influences the degree to which the practice in the society is to depend on law as opposed to trust, when business dealings are involved.

## INDUSTRY LEVEL

Culture influences negotiations with industry. Industry culture is reflected in the values and norms governing the activities performed by the industry in the other country. Manifestations of industry culture include credit policy, as exemplified in the issue of usury in Islamic nations, and attitudes to the environment, as seen in a number of Asian countries where concrete wins out over trees (e.g. Taiwan). It is also manifested in business relationships as indicated by the degree to which such relationships are confined to the transaction or extend beyond it, and the importance of trust in the particular industry or profession. This can be seen in norms of negotiation (the norm is to cement deals with a handshake) and in the acceptance of 'kickbacks' in the industry, as is the case in some countries where medical specialists give gifts to general practitioners who refer patients to them.

### ORGANISATIONAL LEVEL

Organisational culture influences negotiations with firms as opposed to individuals and is exemplified in the entering into of alliances or the arranging of takeovers. Organisational culture is reflected in the basic pattern of assumptions developed by the firm. These include its code of ethics and its attitude to employees. For example, in many Asian countries the employer is considered to be responsible for the welfare of the employee and their family, whereas in Australia and New Zealand employees tend to be regarded as expendable, short-term resources. Another manifestation of organisational culture is reflected in the relationships between managers and staff. This is exemplified in the authoritarian relationship that operates in Japan compared with the egalitarian relationship that applies in Australia, and in approaches to problem solving, which is a group activity in many Asian cultures but an individual responsibility in Australia and New Zealand. Decision-making style is also a manifestation of organisational culture. It varies markedly between countries. In Japan, decision making tends to be by consensus of those likely to be involved in implementing the decision. In Australia and New Zealand by contrast, decision making tends to be undertaken by senior managers and imposed on those below. Some manifestations of organisational culture are visible, such as the practice in Japan of starting the workday by singing the company song, and some are tacit, such as codes of company behaviour for personnel. In some transnational organisations (e.g. IBM), organisational culture can be very powerful and can reduce the effects of national, industry or personal cultures.

Hofstede (2001) found that at the national level cultural differences reside more in values and less in practices, and at the organisational level cultural differences reside more in practices and less in values. At the occupational level the balance is even, as shown in Figure 3.3.

## CULTURAL CONCEPTS AND CULTURAL DIFFERENCES

In order to be able to understand how culture can influence firms' international marketing activities, an understanding of key cultural concepts is necessary, as well as how cultural differences manifest themselves in the overseas business environment.

## Key cultural concepts

The following four concepts are important to understanding the impact of culture on international marketing.

### MASLOW'S HIERARCHY OF NEEDS

A basic model for understanding the wants and needs of consumers, Maslow's model has been used by international marketers to appreciate how consumers in different countries behave in response to cultural stimuli. Maslow (1964) argues that the needs of the individual form a

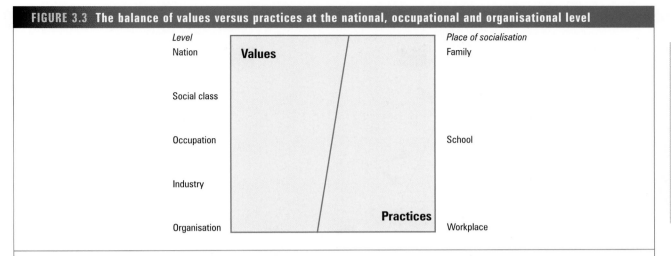

**FIGURE 3.3** The balance of values versus practices at the national, occupational and organisational level

SOURCE: *Hofstede, G. (2001)* Culture's Consequences: Comparing Values, Behaviors, Institutions, and Organizations Across Nations, *2nd edn, Sage Publications, Thousand Oaks, CA. © Geert Hofstede, p. 394. Reproduced with permission.*

hierarchy from basic physiological needs (hunger, thirst), to safety needs (security, protection), to social needs (sense of belonging, love), to esteem needs (self-esteem, recognition, status), to higher order self-actualisation needs (self-development, realisation). Lower-order needs in the hierarchy such as hunger tend to be satisfied first and higher-order needs such as those related to self-esteem tend to be satisfied last. Although culture can have an impact on needs at all levels, its impact tends to be greater where higher-order needs are involved—needs involving emotion and cognition. This aspect requires research in the specific overseas market, as there may be cases where lower-order needs are not always satisfied first. Examples occur when people go without food in order to buy drugs or cigarettes, or forgo food in order to buy a refrigerator because owning a refrigerator increases social status and self-esteem in the local culture. In some societies, higher-order needs are encouraged at the expense of lower-order needs: Hinduism, for example, encourages self-realisation by focusing on acts that will improve an individual's position in the incarnations that follow rather than in that individual's present existence. Figure 3.4 shows a comparison of hierarchy of needs based on research in Western and Asian countries. The research indicates that both the specific needs and their rank order can vary between cultures.

## SELF-REFERENCE CRITERION

Often, perception of the needs of the overseas market is blocked by our own cultural experience. The tendency is to evaluate the overseas situation in terms of experience in Australia or New Zealand and this also is the basis used for evaluating and interpreting others in the negotiation situation. In short, the self-reference criterion (SRC) is the cultural baggage that the businessperson takes overseas. Many years ago, Lee (1966) developed a four-step systematic framework for reducing this myopic approach, which can be adapted to the Australian or New Zealand situation as follows:

1 Define the problem or goal in terms of Australian or New Zealand cultural norms, habits and traits.

2 Define the problem or goal in terms of the cultural norms, habits or traits in the overseas market.

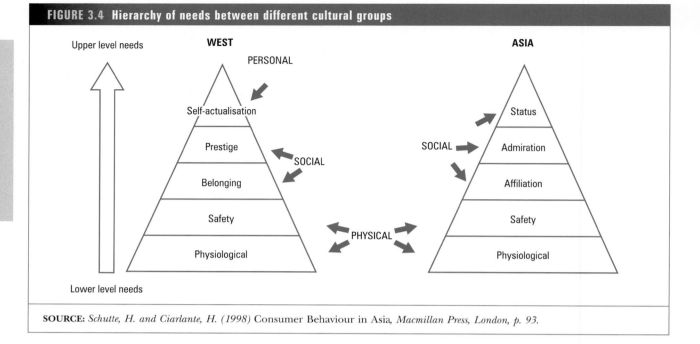

**FIGURE 3.4 Hierarchy of needs between different cultural groups**

SOURCE: *Schutte, H. and Ciarlante, H. (1998)* Consumer Behaviour in Asia, *Macmillan Press, London, p. 93.*

3 Isolate the SRC element in the problem and examine it carefully to see how it complicates the problem and its interpretation.

4 Redefine the problem without the SRC influence and proceed to solve the problem in the foreign market or negotiation.

## CONTEXT AND CULTURE

Both verbal and non-verbal cues and messages are necessary to establish the full meaning of a communication. People in different cultures interpret verbal and non-verbal cues differently and this can be due to the influence of context in the culture. Cultures can be classified according to where they fall on a continuum between high- and low-context cultures.

A high-context culture is one where what is said conveys only a limited portion of the meaning, which must also be interpreted in terms of how it is being said, where it is being said and the body language of the speaker. In high-context cultures, much of the message will be implied in the context of the communication and is influenced by the background and basic values of the communicator. Thailand is an example of a country tending towards a high-context culture. In a low-context culture, messages are mostly explicit and the words convey most of the meaning in the communication. The impact of non-verbal cues on intended meaning is far less and the status of the speaker is less important in interpretation of meaning. Australia tends towards being a low-context culture. Figure 3.5 (adapted from Hall 1976) illustrates where certain countries fall along a continuum from low- to high-context cultures.

Context influences most of the cultural variables in international marketing, as shown in Table 3.1.

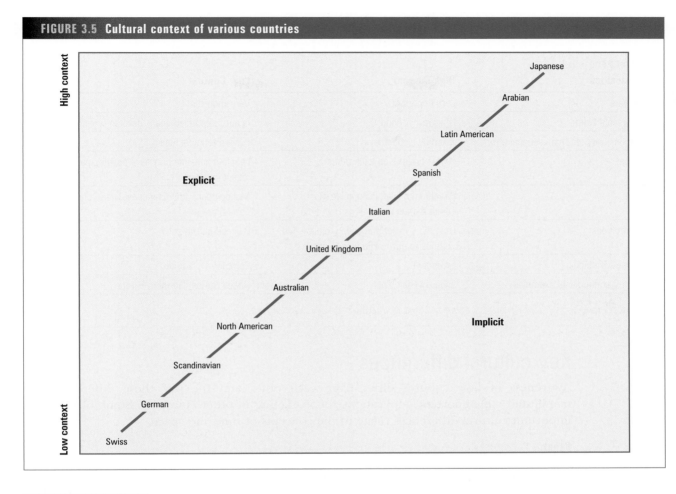

**FIGURE 3.5  Cultural context of various countries**

## PSYCHIC DISTANCE

Psychic distance, a perceptual concept, is a reflection of a range of environmental variables that differentiate an overseas market from one in Australia or New Zealand. The variables include linguistic, commercial, ethical, educational, political, developmental and cultural factors. Culture is the most important element of psychic distance because it is a product of many elements that are culturally influenced, such as belief systems, language barriers, differing attitudes to business, levels of education, material standards, infrastructure shortcomings and patterns of behaviour. As a consequence, cultural distance is often used as a surrogate measure of psychic distance. Psychic distance is a measure of how far a country is perceived to be away from your own country in terms of a mental aggregation of the above factors. It is also a measure of how different the country is when compared to your own. Psychic distance acts to impede communication and understanding and can cause executives to prefer to deal with countries which are closer to their country in psychic distance terms. This may not always be desirable as often opportunities are greater in countries which are distant than in those closer to their country or New Zealand. Table 3.2, patterned after the work of Hofstede and Bond (1988) and Hofstede (1994) and based on cultural elements, provides an estimate of the psychic distance of various countries from Australia.

| TABLE 3.1 | Impact of context on cultural dimensions | |
|---|---|---|
| **Factors and Dimensions** | **High Context** | **Low Context** |
| Lawyers | Less important | Very important |
| A person's word | Is his or her bond | Is not to be relied upon; 'get it in writing' |
| Responsibility for organisational error | Taken by highest level | Pushed to lowest level |
| Space | People breathe on each other | People maintain a bubble of private space and resent intrusions |
| Time | Polychronic: everything in life must be dealt with in terms of its own time | Monochronic: time is money; linear: one thing at a time |
| Negotiations | Lengthy: a major purpose is to allow the parties to get to know each other | Proceed quickly |
| Competitive bidding | Infrequent | Common |
| Country and regional examples | Japan, Middle East | United States, Northern Europe |

**SOURCE:** *Keegan, W.J. and Green M.S. (2006)* Global Marketing, *4th edn, Prentice Hall, NJ, p. 133.*

# Key cultural differences

Awareness of how cultures differ from each other and the way these differences are manifested has important implications for marketing in other countries. Some of the most important cultural differences relate to the concepts of time and space.

## TIME

Attitude towards time is one of the most important areas where cultures differ. Most marketing concepts, such as the product life cycle, sales forecasting and new product launches, are time-based. However, although formally most cultures adopt a common model of time—the clock—assumptions about time are very deep-seated and vary from culture to culture. Because of this it is often necessary to allow a longer period of time to transact business in Asian countries than would be the case in Australia, New Zealand or the USA.

The relationship of time and business decision making also varies from culture to culture. In some, the time required to reach a decision is directly proportional to the importance attached to the decision. To try to hurry the decision-making process is likely to be counterproductive, as it can in the eyes of the other party diminish the importance the businessperson attaches to the proposal.

Temporal orientation is based on the Western assumption that time can have a past, present and future. To classify cultures according to whether they are oriented to past, present or future is to apply a notion of time that is not basic to many cultures. As an example, the Japanese are not time-based, but rather have a view of time in which the future is viewed as a natural extension of the past.

Figure 3.6 illustrates this perception, which the Japanese refer to as the makimono time pattern.

Another dimension of time is the difference between monochronic and polychronic time. In the former, time is linear, having a beginning and an end. It usually operates on the basis

| TABLE 3.2 | Index of psychic distance ratings of countries from Australia | | | | |
|---|---|---|---|---|---|
| **Country** | **Index** | **Country** | **Index** | **Country** | **Index** |
| United States | 0.1 | Sweden | 8.8 | Mexico | 17.6 |
| Great Britain | 0.6 | Argentina | 9.2 | Greece | 18.0 |
| Canada | 0.6 | Iran | 9.3 | Indonesia | 18.3 |
| New Zealand | 0.7 | India | 9.7 | Singapore | 19.3 |
| Switzerland | 1.5 | Kenya | 12.2 | Korea | 20.3 |
| Germany | 1.7 | Zimbabwe | 12.2 | Taiwan | 20.4 |
| Ireland | 1.7 | Tanzania | 12.2 | Hong Kong | 20.5 |
| South Africa | 2.0 | Rwanda | 12.2 | Chile | 20.7 |
| Italy | 2.2 | Brazil | 12.3 | Portugal | 21.9 |
| Finland | 4.7 | Turkey | 13.6 | Yugoslavia | 21.9 |
| Netherlands | 5.5 | Japan | 15.2 | Peru | 23.3 |
| Belgium | 6.1 | Philippines | 15.7 | Colombia | 23.5 |
| France | 6.1 | Russia | 16.0 | Malaysia | 23.6 |
| Austria | 6.3 | Nigeria | 16.3 | Costa Rica | 25.0 |
| Israel | 7.1 | Ghana | 16.3 | Venezuela | 26.2 |
| Denmark | 7.3 | Uruguay | 16.4 | Ecuador | 27.4 |
| Norway | 7.4 | Thailand | 16.5 | China | 29.2 |
| Spain | 8.6 | Pakistan | 17.3 | Panama | 31.4 |

*Note:* A high index number for a country indicates that the country is further away from Australia in terms of psychic distance. It also indicates that the higher the index number of a country with which a firm does business, the less the extent to which psychic distance is perceived by that firm as a barrier to undertaking international business.

**SOURCE:** *Fletcher, R. and Bohn, J. (1998) 'The impact of psychic distance on the internationalisation of the Australian firm', Journal of Global Marketing, Vol. 12, No. 2, pp. 56–7.*

of doing one thing at a time and adhering to schedules. In polychronic time, time is cyclic and people using this perception are likely to do several things at the same moment, change schedules and seldom view time as being wasted. In polychronic time the completion of a human transaction is more highly regarded than keeping to a schedule. Examples of the differences in time and space can be seen in International Highlight 3.3.

## SPACE

An important cultural manifestation relates to space. Space can be both physical and abstract. Physical space refers to a location such as a town or an office as well as personal proximity. In the Western business environment, space often denotes status, as reflected in the size of a person's office and its location. This is often not the case in other cultures.

Differences in attitudes to space can also be seen in matters of personal proximity. In Australia there are three degrees of personal proximity—intimate, 0 to 45 cm; personal, 45 cm to 1 metre; social, 1 metre to 2 metres. The size of these zones vary from culture to culture.

In Japanese cultural time, the past flows continuously towards the present and also the present is firmly linked to the future. In philosophical terms, we might say that the past and the future exist simultaneously in the present.

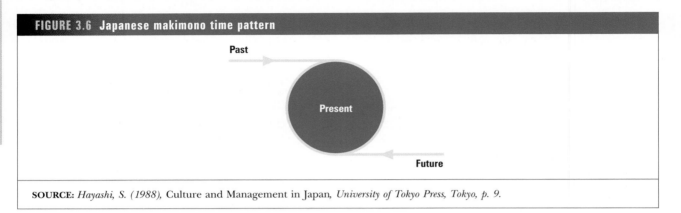

**FIGURE 3.6 Japanese makimono time pattern**

Past

Present

Future

**SOURCE:** *Hayashi, S. (1988),* Culture and Management in Japan, *University of Tokyo Press, Tokyo, p. 9.*

Cultures differ as to who is allowed to enter each zone and what is considered an adequate sensory exchange within each zone.

Abstract space refers to a grouping of people based on common characteristics such as profession, education or religion. Abstract space gives rise to a number of issues. These include whether people are considered insiders or outsiders, the rights and obligations for group members, the extent to which outsiders can become insiders and how this might be achieved. This cultural concept is also reflected in language. For example, the word for foreigners in Japanese (*gai-jin*) means 'those from outside'.

## LANGUAGE

This is another manifestation of cultural difference. The nature of discourse differs between cultures: people in some cultures, who for example put the justification first followed by the main point, whereas people in other countries, such as in Australia, put the main point first and the justification afterwards. The degree of precision versus ambiguity with which language conveys meaning also varies and is linked to the issue raised earlier of high- versus low-context cultures. The frequent problem encountered by Australian businesspeople in Asia as to whether 'yes' means 'yes' or merely 'I hear what you are saying' (as in Japan) is an example. Some languages are tonal and this affects meaning. For example, there are five tones in Thai and the same sound can have a number of different meanings depending on the tone used. The same is true of Mandarin where there are four different tonal levels. Scripts also differ: whereas many languages use a script involving individual letters which when joined together form a word, other languages such as Mandarin or Japanese are ideographic and based on symbols, each of which represents a concept rather than a letter.

Different cultures vary also in the way meaning is conveyed, such as the way things are said, the pitch of voice, what is left unsaid and inferred, gestures when speaking and loquaciousness versus brevity. In some languages such as Indonesian there are a number of words for 'you' that vary according to the status of the person speaking and the status of the person spoken to. Associated with this is the number of words to denote honorifics and the frequency of the use of honorifics, indicating the degree to which hierarchy is the norm in

# Differences in time and space

## TIME

When an Australian businessperson proceeds overseas it is within a time frame, and usually involves reference points fixed in time.

An Australian business executive had planned a first visit to Indonesia. He intended to fly to Jakarta on Sunday evening, have a series of meetings on the Monday and leave for the UK on the Tuesday morning. Via fax, he has arranged five appointments on the Monday based on the number of outside appointments he could comfortably make in his headquarter city of Adelaide. His first appointment in Jakarta is at 9.30 am on the Monday and although he is on time he is kept waiting. When he is finally ushered in to see the Indonesian government official at 10.15 am, his annoyance at the delay is reflected in his facial expression. As a consequence the business discussion is strained because of this reflection of annoyance—heightened by the knowledge that not only will he be late for subsequent appointments but now he is unlikely to be able to keep the remaining four appointments before the close of business hours at 4 pm. Unaware of the customs of the country, the Australian business person did not realise that the person he has been waiting to meet considers that to tell his earlier visitor his time was up was far ruder than to keep his next visitor waiting 45 minutes.

Polychronic time, in which several things are done at the same time and schedules change, is a common experience in some cultures.

The tendency in some cultures to do several things at the same time can be rather disconcerting for Australians. Australia's senior diplomatic representative in Libya had frequent occasion to meet cabinet ministers (Heads of the Peoples' Bureaux) in their offices. He was used to the Western notion that an appointment set aside a span of time exclusively for a 'one on one' discussion about matters of mutual interest. This practice did not operate in Libya, where inevitably on being ushered into the minister's office he discovered there were a number of other people in the room and conversations were being conducted with a number of people simultaneously. Even on the occasion where the discussion just involved the minister and himself, it was likely to be interrupted by relatives or members of the minister's kin group, all of whom had immediate right of access without prior appointment and the right to command immediate attention to their problems.

## SPACE

An Australian managing director with a large office in a corner position in a building with a view over Sydney Harbour is inclined to judge the seniority of those executives he meets overseas by the size and location of their offices. When the executive visits Korea he finds things very different. He arrives for an appointment with a senior executive from one of the *chaebol* (e.g. Lucky Goldstar, Hyundai, Samsung or Daewoo). He is confronted with a room of 50 people all labouring away at desks of the same size and is surprised when the receptionist goes to a person at a desk in the centre of the room to announce the visitor's arrival. This person escorts the visitor to an interview room, causing the Australian to wonder if he has been fobbed off with a junior clerk. The norm in Korea is for the executive to work in the midst of those they supervise rather than separate from them. To evaluate a person's importance in an overseas country in terms of your own norms for office space and location can lead to serious misinterpretation of the status of the individual.

The space dimension also applies to 'personal space'. Australian businessmen visiting Iran on occasion feel their masculinity is under threat. Apart from the custom of males in this part of the world greeting each other by kissing on both cheeks, social distance is considerably less than in Australia and Iranians complain that the Australian executives keep 'running away from us'.

the culture. It is also important that a businessperson visiting a different culture inquires as to the style and basics of the language. This is because it is likely that those contacted in the other culture, although able to speak English, will apply the thought patterns of their language when interpreting what is said.

There are four ways of writing Japanese and each has a different image and effect. The four ways are *kanji*, which is a multi-stroke ideogram; *hiragana* or *katakana*, which are simplified one- or two-stroke methods of representing the sounds of Japanese syllables; and *romaji*, which is Roman letters used to spell out 'Japanised' English. When used in advertising, for example, kanji gives a stiff, formal impression, hiragana imparts soft, delicate and often feminine mood, and katakana is used to express foreign words that have been 'Japanised' in pronunciation and impart a crisp, direct feeling to the advertising copy.

## FAMILIARITY

Cultural differences are also reflected in familiarity and friendship patterns. These vary as far as the speed with which friendships are formed, superficiality, the obligation friendship imposes and motivation for the friendship. In many cultures, friendships are not based on business opportunism as is often the case in Australia, and are not formed quickly. In these cultures, once friendships are formed they are much deeper, last longer and involve a real obligation to assist in times of need.

## CONSUMPTION PATTERNS

These are reflected in different views of material possessions and dress. In many cultures power is symbolised by material possessions and these are likely to be prominently displayed. Some years ago in India, when refrigerators were a status symbol in middle-class homes, refrigerators were likely to be given pride of place in the living room. In some countries, admiring possessions can be a mistake as the other party feels obligated to give the item to you. Mead (1990, p. 151) recounts the following example:

An Australian manager made the mistake of admiring his Arab host's new silk tie. The man immediately took it off and insisted that his guest should have it. The Australian was only able to get out of this difficult situation by accepting the tie graciously, but adding that if he wore it he would no longer be able to see it; therefore he preferred that his friend should take it back on loan to wear whenever he wished, in order that its new owner might then have a better opportunity to enjoy it.

Another manifestation of differing cultural approaches towards material possessions is the habit in some cultures of bluntly demanding to know how much you earn and how much things cost—issues which in Australia and New Zealand are regarded as somewhat private.

Dress also can be an expression of cultural difference. Often, what is considered formal and informal dress differs. In Indonesia, formal dress is a long-sleeved batik shirt rather than a suit, and in India the more formal alternative to a suit may be a Nehru jacket or even a homespun dhoti. In some hierarchical societies, such as Thailand, formal dress may be a uniform with indications of rank. Uniforms are worn not only by the military but also by officers in the public service. The tendency of Westerners to dress informally in tropical countries is often not followed by the business community in that country. They, despite the climate, wear shirts and ties and expect foreign visitors to do the same. The Australian or New Zealand business visitor needs to dress for each occasion at the level of formality expected of that person as an outsider. Whether the visitor adopts local or their own dress is an issue to be ascertained in advance lest the visitor be inappropriately dressed on the one hand or appear patronising on the other.

Differences in consumption patterns can influence the product offered and the way it is promoted in the overseas market. The culture in which a person lives affects consumption patterns and also the meaning attached to certain products. When promoting the product to a new culture it is easier to appeal initially to existing cultural requirements or expectations than to try to change them. Product promotion must be sensitive to the basic values of the country and the differences in the patterns of consumption. For example, promoting a 'do-it-yourself' timesaving device in a country with widespread unemployment may not only be pointless, but could also lead to unfavourable criticism. The independence movement in India owed much of its popular appeal to Gandhi's encouragement that people should spin their own cloth in the home instead of relying on imported, machine-made fabric from Great Britain.

## BUSINESS CUSTOMS

An example of the many business customs and practices that are culturally influenced is that of bribery. The degree to which this is practised varies substantially from country to country, as does the degree to which it is tacitly accepted. This applies to both the concept of bribery and the form the bribery takes. In some countries, minor bribery such as 'tea money' is accepted as an inescapable cost of doing business, whereas in others it is totally unacceptable. This is discussed in more detail in Chapter 5.

Figure 3.7 is a cross-cultural comparison grid using each of the key cultural variables. In the first column briefly detail the practice in Australia or New Zealand. In the second column note the practice in the selected overseas market, and in the third column describe the appropriate course of action or behaviour modification that should be undertaken. This will heighten cultural sensitivity when approaching the overseas market.

# CULTURE AND COMMUNICATION

## Verbal communication

Although the differences in verbal communication between countries are immediately obvious to global marketers (Egyptians speak Arabic and Australians speak English), some of the subtleties may not be. Although Arabic is spoken throughout the Middle East, it differs from country to country in accent, vocabulary, origin of technical terms and intonation. These label the speaker in terms of association or origin and may influence the attitude towards the foreign person when attempting to speak the language of the other party.

When an Australian diplomat was posted to Libya his wife commenced intensive study of Arabic in the months preceding their departure. On arrival in Tripoli her attempts to speak Arabic were greeted with strange looks and on occasion outright rudeness or deliberate lack of comprehension. Later she learnt that she spoke the Egyptian form of Arabic (due to her teacher in Australia being originally from Egypt). This was unacceptable to the Libyans as the border between the two countries was closed, Egyptians were viewed as lax in their observance of Islam and the Libyan leader, Colonel Gadaffi, referred to the country as 'the defeated Egyptian regime'.

**FIGURE 3.7  Comparison grid**

| Variable | Attitude in Australia | Attitude in overseas country | Modification required |
|---|---|---|---|
| Control over destiny | | | |
| Time | | | |
| Process vs task approach | | | |
| Status and relationships | | | |
| Technology orientation | | | |
| Space | | | |
| Language | | | |
| Business practices | | | |

People interpret their world through language. The more important an item is in daily life, the more words are used to describe it and the more shades of meaning are attached to it. In the same way that many Eskimo groups have a variety of words to define the subtle differences in snow, so Australians have a broad vocabulary relating to automobiles. In communicating the benefits of an automobile to an Eskimo, the shades of meaning used in promotion in Australia are likely to be viewed as unnecessary and irrelevant.

Verbal communication differs from one culture to another. It differs not only in terms of language but also in terms of the relative importance of the variables involved—of who, what, how, where, when and why. A message is less likely to persuade when it does not reflect these variables in a manner appropriate to the culture of the recipient of the message. More specifically it involves:

- *who communicates the message and to whom*—cultures vary as to the degree in which people are free to communicate with each other. This may be due to hierarchy, status consciousness or others acting as gatekeepers.

- *what message is communicated*—this is often determined by the function of the office held and the need to manage personal relationships. What is considered relevant varies by culture with some interpreting relevance widely and others narrowly defining relevance as immediately applying to the situation.

- *how the message is communicated*—this involves choosing the channel (spoken or written) and the mode (face to face or phone). This will vary according to the channels available in a culture and factors such as speed, formality, legality and seniority.

- *where the message is communicated*—cultures vary in terms of whether certain types of messages must be conveyed in a formal setting (e.g. the manager's office) or an informal setting (whenever the occasion permits) and whether those messages conveyed in informal settings carry less weight than those communicated in more formal settings.

- *when the message is communicated*—some messages are communicated without warning, such as via email, and some at regular times such as at scheduled meetings. The acceptability of random versus scheduled conveying of messages varies between cultures.

- *why the message is communicated*—although messages may be intended to inform or persuade, the relative weighting accorded to their motivation varies. In socialist countries, for example, the intention of advertising is more to inform than to persuade.

## Non-verbal communication

It is not unusual when dealing with different cultures to receive contradictory signals and not to know what to believe or whom to trust. Care should be taken to spot non-verbal signals as these can supplement the verbal signals to yield a more accurate picture of reality. In general, if there is a contradiction in the message conveyed between the verbal and the non-verbal signals, the non-verbal signal should be carefully considered as 'body language' is hard to fake. Morris (1978) developed a scale of non-verbal signals to be observed by the marketer. The most important of these are:

- *body stress signals*—perspiration, licking of lips, raising pitch of voice indicate stress;

- *lower body signals*—foot tapping, frequent crossing and uncrossing of knees can indicate impatience;

- *body posture signals*—body sagging or slumping can indicate boredom;

- *random gestures*—these can either confirm or contradict the verbal message, e.g. movements of the hands; and

- *facial expressions*—are these consistent with other non-verbal signals and with the verbal message?

## Cultural adaptation and communication

Adaptation is an important concept in international marketing. This involves affirmative acceptance rather than just tolerance for a different culture. It does not mean that executives must forsake their own ways and totally conform to the other culture—rather that they become aware of local customs and are willing to accommodate those differences that cause misunderstanding. Cateora and Graham (2005, p. 125) list 10 basic criteria for adaptation: open tolerance; flexibility; humility; justice/fairness; adjustability to varying tempos; curiosity/interest; knowledge of the country; liking for others; ability to command respect; and ability to integrate oneself into the environment.

In order to apply these criteria of adaptation most effectively it is important to understand business customs in terms of the following categories:

- *Imperatives*: These are customs that must be accommodated and conformed to if business relationships are to be successful. They vary from culture to culture and involve differing degrees of friendship, human relations and trust. Removal of your shoes before entering the home of a Thai businessperson is an example of a cultural imperative.

- *Options*: Conforming to optional customs will enhance chances of a successful commercial outcome but is not mandatory. The Middle Eastern custom of male businessmen kissing each other on both cheeks is not expected of an Australian. However, if he is sure of its appropriateness in context, this gesture by an Australian indicates sensitivity to the culture, which is likely to be interpreted as a gesture of good will.

- *Exclusives*: These are customs in which an outsider may not participate. A foreigner is not welcome to participate but must be able to recognise them, because failure to do so is certain to give offence. Often these customs may be associated with religion. One such example would be a person performing religious rituals belonging to faith to which they are not an adherent.

An ability on the part of the businessperson to perceive when they are dealing with a cultural imperative, a cultural option or a cultural exclusive, and the nuances associated with each in a particular culture, is likely to have a positive impact on cross-cultural communication.

Cultural adaptation implies a willingness to be open towards other cultures. Thomas Friedman (2006), in his book *The World is Flat*, argues that the degree to which a country is open to foreign influences and ideas—namely, globalisation—will influence the extent to which the country will prosper in today's world, and that cultures that are open and willing to change will have a major advantage. He argues that the concept of openness should be added to the list of cross-cultural variables against which countries are compared.

# CROSS-CULTURAL COMPARISONS

## Bilateral comparisons

Much of the research into this aspect has involved comparing two countries. Examples of research where Australia is a participating country are Isackson (1980) and Chau and Fletcher (1990).

Isackson found that although Australia and the USA are regarded as being very similar in cultural background there were significant differences in cultural attitudes and these affected business behaviour. He found that, compared with Australians, Americans viewed management as more crucial than technical superiority, and personal time was viewed as less important and should be subordinated to work where necessary. He also found that in the USA negotiation should be undertaken by a powerful individual in the firm rather than by a committee, that loyalty was not as important and authority should be questioned, and that maintenance of good relations should be subordinated to achieving profitable results.

The Chau and Fletcher study included members of both the Thai-Australia Chamber of Commerce and the Australia-Thai Chamber of Commerce. Compared with Australians, Thais were more conscious of saving face and of the need to repay obligations. They were more inclined to favour consensus decision making, loyalty in business dealings, operating through networks and harmony in business, and were more risk averse. Contrary to the Australian approach of work in order to live, the Thai approach was one of live in order to work.

An analysis of the Australia–Japan coal negotiations highlights culturally influenced differences in negotiation techniques as follows:

- When Australian negotiating teams go offshore their members tend to pursue self-interest and operate as individuals first and as members of a team second. This enabled the Japanese to break down quickly the Australian bargaining position by finalising a negotiated price with one team member. This established the price point and reduced the negotiating position of the other members of the Australian team.

- Australians tend to reject authority and distance themselves from government. When they criticise the Australian government and its officials overseas they may reduce their own credibility. This is because businesspeople in most Asian countries accept rather than reject authority and they use it in negotiation.

- In most Asian countries formality is a state of mind and a reflection of the correct order of things. Hierarchy is inescapable and is respected. The Australian individualistic approach with its aggressive egalitarianism is viewed in many parts of Asia as an ill-disciplined affront to notions of order and formality.

- Whereas in Australia the person takes over the function, in many parts of Asia the function takes over the person. In Japan the role of the leader of the delegation is known and the person appointed as leader conforms to the norms expected of the role. By contrast, the Australian businessperson uses their personality and abilities to be a more effective leader by modifying the leader's role to reflect personality and attributes.

## Global comparisons

There are two researchers whose work deserves comment in this connection: Hofstede and Trompenaars.

### HOFSTEDE

The most comprehensive attempt to measure cultural differences on a global basis was by Hofstede (1980). He undertook a global survey of employees of IBM[1] and came up with four underlying dimensions of culture—power distance, uncertainty avoidance, individualism/collectivism and masculine/feminine. Subsequently, his work with Bond (Hofstede and Bond 1988) caused a fifth dimension to be added—long-term/short-term orientation. Table 3.3 (p. 102) shows where various countries lie in terms of each dimension.

- *Power distance.* This is the degree to which less powerful people in a culture accept the existence of inequality and the unequal distribution of power as a normal situation. Although inequality exists in most cultures the degree to which it is accepted varies from one culture to another. In Table 3.3 countries with a low power distance incline towards 0 and those with a high power distance incline towards 100. This figure places Austria as the lowest country in terms of power distance and Malaysia as the highest. This reflects the egalitarian nature of New Zealand society compared with the Philippines society where inequality is accepted and where a handful of families control most of the wealth.

- *Uncertainty avoidance.* This is the extent to which people in a culture feel threatened by uncertain or unknown situations. They are nervous of situations that they consider unstructured, unclear or unpredictable. People in cultures that are low in uncertainty avoidance tend to be more willing to take risks and are more relaxed, whereas those

[1] 116 000 surveys from over 88 000 employees from 72 countries (reduced to 40 countries that had more than 50 responses each) at IBM between 1967 and 1969 and then between 1971 and 1973. He later expanded the data base with 10 additional countries and three regions (Bradley et al. 2006).

from cultures with a high score on uncertainty avoidance are more focused on welfare and consensus. A low score is evidence of a strong desire to avoid uncertainty and the people from such cultures tend to be aggressive, intolerant and emotional. Table 3.3 shows a wide range of uncertainty avoidance from a very low rating for Singapore through to a very high rating for Japan.

- *Individualism/collectivism.* This reflects the extent to which people in a culture look after their own interests and those of their immediate family, and where ties are loose. The collectivist dimension reflects the extent to which people in a culture are members of a group and group needs should be subordinated to individual desires. Membership of the group confers status and plugs the individual into a network, but in exchange for this the group expects permanent loyalty of its members. In Table 3.3 cultures with a high degree of collectivism tend towards 0 and those with a high degree of individualism tend towards 100. This figure shows that Venezuela is the most collectivist of societies and the USA the most individualist.

- *Masculine/feminine.* Cultures use the biological differences between the sexes to define different social roles for men and women. This is reflected in masculine cultures stressing material success and assertiveness and feminine cultures stressing quality of life and caring for the weak. In Table 3.3 cultures with a high degree of focus on feminine values tend towards 0 and those with a high degree of focus on masculine values tend towards 100. In this figure, Sweden with its tradition of social welfare is shown to be the most feminine and Japan the most masculine of countries.

While Hofstede's work provides a useful insight into factors underlying differences between cultures and a global basis for comparison, there are some qualifications. The study was conducted entirely within a single organisation—Hofstede's sample consisted of IBM executives in each country. It is well known that IBM has a strong corporate culture and it is possible that this corporate culture could mask some of the differences between countries. The second relates to the fact that the actual survey was conducted in the late 1970s and since that time there have been changes within individual countries and a rise in the globalisation of world trade. The third qualification relates to the dimensions of national culture found by Hofstede. These are largely Western dimensions and may not be appropriate measures of cultural differences in some Asian countries. In these cultures, a qualification such as collectivism does not necessarily exclude its opposite of individualism. Furthermore, the search for truth may be irrelevant in cultures whose members believe there is no such concept as a single truth. In such cultures in Asia, uncertainty avoidance may have only limited meaning. This raises the issue of whether there are other dimensions that might have been overlooked because they are not important in Western cultures. Hofstede recognised this latter shortcoming and in subsequent research with Bond from the Chinese University of Hong Kong, he arrived at a fifth dimension which was initially labelled Confucian Dynamism and subsequently long-term versus short-term orientation.

- *Long-term versus short-term orientation:* This is the extent to which cultures exhibit a pragmatic, future-oriented perspective as opposed to a historic short-term point of view. Cultures having a long-term orientation reflect the values of thrift, perseverance, concern for proper ways of doing things, building market share rather than chasing immediate returns to shareholders, respect for tradition, fulfilling social obligations and a focus on causing others to gain rather than lose face in business dealings. In Table 3.3 cultures with a short-term orientation tend towards 0 and those with a long-term orientation tend towards 100 or more. This figure shows that Spain and the Philippines are most likely to have a short-term orientation whereas the country with the greatest tendency to have a long-term approach is Hong Kong. In the 2001 edition of his basic work, Hofstede argues that there is a relationship between long-term versus short-term orientation and marginal propensity to save, with savings propensity being greatest in cultures with a long-term orientation.

## TROMPENAARS

Another attempt to measure cultural differences on a global basis was by Trompenaars. Unlike Hofstede, the research by Trompenaars involved 30 companies (not one), and 75% of interviews were with management and 25% with general administrative staff (rather than 100% with managers) (Trompenaars and Hampden-Turner 1997). Trompenaars arrived at five dimensions as follows:

- *Universalism versus particularism.* For the universalist what is good and right can be applied everywhere whereas for the particularist the obligations imposed by relationships are more important than general rules.

- *Individualism versus communitarianism.* This is similar to the Hofstede dimension of individualism versus collectivism and is a matter of whether people consider themselves as individuals first or feel obliged to follow group desires.

- *Neutral versus affective.* In affective cultures expression of emotion is viewed as natural whereas in neutral cultures expression of emotion is repressed to give the impression of objectivity and 'being in control'.

- *Specific versus diffuse.* People in specific cultures get straight to the point whereas people in diffuse cultures discuss business only after relationships have been established. Should involvement in the contract or activity be confined to that contract or activity or should the 'whole' person be involved? In part this dimension approximates that of high context versus low context.

- *Achievement versus ascription.* In the achievement culture status derives from your own achievements whereas in ascribing cultures status comes from age, gender, kinship, education, connections, etc.

The scores for each of these dimensions are shown in Table 3.3 for a representative selection of countries with a high score supporting the first of the pair in the dichotomy (e.g. universalism) and a low score supporting the second of the pair (e.g. particularism). Four of these five dimensions are different from those of Hofstede although, yet again, they measure Western values. Furthermore the sample was based on upper-level participants in management training programs. The approaches of Hofstede and Trompenaars can be described as etic approaches (see Chapter 6), which categorise countries according to their fit with a number of alleged cultural discriminators. The problem with these etic studies is that they do not reflect the fact that culture can be both dynamic and stable.

In clustering, it is the practice to seek within-cluster similarity and between-cluster difference. Table 3.3 provides evidence that the clustering of countries by Ronen and Shenkar (1985) based on language, religion, race and economic development is supported by Hofstede's cultural dimensions. However, this does not appear to apply to the same extent with Trompenaar's cultural dimensions as there is less within-cluster similarity.

## TABLE 3.3 Clustering of countries on the basis of cultural similarities

| Cluster | Hofstede dimensions | | | | | Trompennars dimensions | | | | |
|---|---|---|---|---|---|---|---|---|---|---|
| | Power Distance | Uncertainty Avoidance | Individualism Collectivism | Masculinity Feminity | Long term Short term | Universalism Particularism | Individualism Communitarianism | Neutral Affective | Diffuse Specific | Achievement Ascription |
| **Near eastern** | | | | | | | | | | |
| Turkey | 66 | 85 | 37 | 45 | | | | | | |
| Iran | 59 | 59 | 41 | 43 | | | | | | |
| Greece | 60 | 112 | 35 | 57 | | 61 | 46 | 38 | 67 | 79 |
| **Nordic** | | | | | | | | | | |
| Sweden | 31 | 29 | 71 | 5 | 33 | 92 | 60 | 46 | 91 | 87 |
| Denmark | 18 | 23 | 74 | 16 | 46 | | 67 | 34 | 89 | 92 |
| Norway | 31 | 50 | 69 | 8 | 44 | | 54 | 39 | 80 | 94 |
| Finland | 33 | 59 | 63 | 26 | 41 | | 64 | | 89 | 89 |
| **Germanic** | | | | | | | | | | |
| Austria | 11 | 70 | 55 | 79 | 31 | | | 59 | 65 | 51 |
| Germany | 35 | 65 | 67 | 66 | 31 | 87 | 53 | 35 | 83 | 74 |
| Switzerland | 34 | 58 | 68 | 70 | 40 | 97 | 66 | 32 | 90 | 73 |
| **Anglo** | | | | | | | | | | |
| South Africa | 49 | 49 | 65 | 63 | | | | | | |
| UK | 35 | 35 | 89 | 66 | 25 | 91 | 61 | 45 | 88 | 89 |
| Australia | 36 | 51 | 90 | 61 | 31 | 91 | 63 | 48 | 78 | 86 |
| New Zealand | 22 | 49 | 79 | 58 | 30 | | | 69 | 70 | 86 |
| Ireland | 28 | 35 | 70 | 68 | 43 | 92 | 50 | 29 | 84 | 94 |
| Canada | 39 | 48 | 80 | 52 | 23 | 93 | 71 | 49 | 87 | 87 |
| USA | 40 | 46 | 91 | 62 | 29 | 93 | 69 | 43 | 82 | 87 |
| **Latin European** | | | | | | | | | | |
| Portugal | 63 | 104 | 27 | 31 | 30 | | 44 | 47 | 73 | 86 |
| Spain | 57 | 86 | 51 | 42 | 19 | 75 | 63 | 19 | 71 | 82 |
| Italy | 50 | 75 | 76 | 70 | 34 | | 52 | 33 | | 80 |
| Belgium | 65 | 94 | 75 | 54 | 38 | | 57 | 41 | 83 | 72 |
| France | 68 | 86 | 71 | 43 | 39 | 73 | 41 | 30 | 88 | 83 |
| **Latin American** | | | | | | | | | | |
| Colombia | 67 | 80 | 13 | 64 | | | | | | |
| Peru | 64 | 87 | 16 | 42 | | | | | | |
| Mexico | 81 | 82 | 30 | 69 | | 64 | 32 | 41 | 70 | 81 |
| Chile | 63 | 86 | 23 | 28 | | | | | | |
| Venezuela | 81 | 76 | 12 | 73 | | 32 | 53 | 20 | 52 | |
| Argentina | 49 | 86 | 46 | 56 | | 69 | | 28 | | 69 |
| **Far Eastern** | | | | | | | | | | |
| Thailand | 64 | 64 | 20 | 34 | 56 | | | 38 | 69 | 57 |
| Taiwan | 58 | 69 | 17 | 45 | 87 | | | | | |
| Indonesia | 78 | 48 | 14 | 46 | | 57 | 44 | 55 | 58 | |
| Singapore | 74 | 8 | 20 | 48 | 48 | 69 | 42 | 48 | 58 | 79 |

| TABLE 3.3 | Clustering of countries on the basis of cultural similarities *(continued)* |

| | Hofstede dimensions | | | | | Trompennars dimensions | | | | |
|---|---|---|---|---|---|---|---|---|---|---|
| Cluster | Power Distance | Uncertainty Avoidance | Individualism Collectivism | Masculinity Feminity | Long term Short term | Universalism Particularism | Individualism Communitarianism | Neutral Affective | Diffuse Specific | Achievement Ascription |
| Vietnam | 70 | 30 | 20 | 40 | 80 | | | | | |
| Philippines | 94 | 44 | 32 | 64 | 19 | 40 | | 23 | 78 | 62 |
| Malaysia | 104 | 36 | 26 | 50 | | | 45 | 30 | 72 | |
| Hong Kong | 68 | 29 | 25 | 57 | 96 | | | 64 | 73 | 58 |
| **Arab** | 80 | 68 | 38 | 53 | | | | | | |
| Oman | | | | | | | | 19 | 78 | 53 |
| Kuwait | | | | | | | | 15 | 47 | 50 |
| UAE | | | | | | | | 48 | 76 | |
| Bahrain | | | | | | | | 24 | 63 | 67 |
| **Independent** | | | | | | | | | | |
| Brazil | 69 | 76 | 38 | 49 | 65 | 79 | 40 | 40 | 77 | 70 |
| Japan | 54 | 92 | 46 | 95 | 80 | 68 | 39 | 74 | 71 | 79 |
| India | 77 | 40 | 48 | 56 | 61 | 54 | 37 | 51 | 66 | 57 |
| Israel | 13 | 81 | 54 | 47 | | | 89 | 38 | 75 | |

**SOURCES:** *This table is based on research into clusters of countries by Ronen and Shenkar (1985) and illustrated by scores on cultural variables in countries in this clustering by Hofstede (2001) and Trompenaars and Hampden-Turner (1997).*

## ETIC VERSUS EMIC APPROACH

Many would share the view expressed by Abosag et al. (2002) that, although these underlying dimensions of culture have some limitations and may not explain all behaviours in a specific market, they still constitute the best framework available for comparing cultural behaviours in a business context. However, the etic approach is based on the notion that underlying cultural differences between nations are a set of variables that can be applied uniformly and which cover all dimensions of difference between one culture and another. This is questionable, as these studies were all undertaken before the 1990s revolution in cross-border communication, the accelerated movement of peoples between countries, the rising level of globalisation and the information revolution led by the internet. This raises the issue of whether Hofstede's and Trompenaar's resulting dimensions are as relevant in the new millennium as when they were originally developed.

These approaches were also derived from large-scale surveys based on Western cultural values and evaluated according to Western interpretation of measurement descriptors (i.e. very high; high; somewhat high; neither high nor low; somewhat low; low; very low). It is likely that the resulting measures do not account for the reluctance of people in many cultures to provide information, to give accurate answers as opposed to what they think you would like to hear, or express definite opinions (see Chapter 6 for a more in-depth discussion of this issue). In such circumstances, can the resulting scores truly reflect the extent of difference on these variables between respondents in one culture compared to another? The implied assumption in these studies that all cultural variance can be explained by these dimensions ignores the possibility that there might be dimensions that are unique to a particular culture or group of cultures.

For the most part, advocates of the etic approach identify cultural boundaries with political (i.e. geographic) ones. Although beguilingly convenient, such an approach ignores the fact that a number of different ethnic groups can exist within a political boundary (e.g. Malay, Chinese and Indian in Malaysia), that ethnic groups may flow across political borders (Chinese in South-East Asia; Kurds in Iran, Iraq and Turkey); and that within a political boundary there can be distinctive cultural groups as evidenced by the increasing multiculturalism in Australia and the growing rural–urban divide in many developing Asian countries. Aligning cultural groups with national boundaries therefore provides a questionable basis for predicting cultural variables that may need to be taken into account in developing relationships with parties in emerging markets. Furthermore, cultures that originally developed relative to resources in one location now draw from different resources in multiple locations which are linked together by improvements in communications technology. Table 3.4, which is derived from later work by Hofstede, shows differences on his cultural dimensions within a country based on linguistic divisions.

Even within a country there can be differences between rural and urban and between upper/middle and lower classes as far as culture is concerned. This is due to the upper/middle class and urban groups being more exposed to 'Western' cultural values via education and greater media exposure. There can also be cultural differences from one region of a country to another as pointed out by Hu (1994) with respect the regional characteristics of Chinese people:

- Beijing people are straightforward.

- Shanghai people are clever.

- Tianjin people are capable and seasoned.

**TABLE 3.4**    **Index scores by language area for multilingual countries**

| Country and part | Power distance index | Uncertainty avoidance | Individualism index | Masculinity index | Long-term orientation index |
|---|---|---|---|---|---|
| Belgium total | 65 | 94 | 75 | 54 | |
| Dutch speakers | 61 | 97 | 78 | 43 | |
| French speakers | 67 | 93 | 72 | 60 | |
| Switzerland total | 34 | 58 | 68 | 70 | |
| German speakers | 26 | 56 | 69 | 72 | |
| French speakers | 70 | 70 | 64 | 58 | |
| Yugoslavia total | 76 | 88 | 27 | 21 | |
| Croatia (Zagreb) | 73 | 80 | 33 | 40 | |
| Serbia (Belgrade) | 86 | 92 | 25 | 43 | |
| Slovenia (Ljubljana) | 71 | 88 | 27 | 19 | |
| Canada total | 39 | 48 | 80 | 52 | 23 |
| French speakers | 54 | 60 | 73 | 45 | 30 |
| Australian total | 36 | 51 | 90 | 61 | 31 |
| Aborigines | 80 | 128 | 89 | 22 | −10 |

**SOURCE:** *Hofstede, G. (2001)* Culture's Consequences: Comparing Values, Behaviors, Institutions, and Organizations Across Nations, *2nd edn, Sage Publications, Thousand Oaks, CA, p. 501.*

- The people of Guandong, Zhejiang and Anhui are decisive and full of strategems.

- Fujian people are honest and sedate.

- Shandong people are forthright and generous.

- The people of Liaoning, Jilin and Heilongjiang are reasonable and loyal.

- The people of Henan, Hebei, Hunan and Hubei are open and direct.

- The people of Sichuan, Shannxi, Jiangxi and Shanxi are upright.

- Those in Yunnan, Hianan, Guanxi, Guizhou and Qinhai always behave in an unhurried manner.

- The people of Inner Mongolia, Xinjiang and Tibet are warm-hearted, but dubious.

An alternative way of addressing cultural differences is the emic approach. Unlike the etic approach, which seeks dimensions of cultural variability, the emic approach is culture-specific. It endeavours to identify the idiosyncrasies of individual cultures in order to understand the effective negotiating behaviours to employ when dealing with executives. It recognises that some important values are culture specific. As an example, in Rokeach's often-cited list of values that were derived from 'Western' cultures, there are two important Asian cultural values that are omitted—thrift and perseverance (de Mooij 2005).

Advocates of this emic approach such as Fang (1999) argue that an emic approach is necessary in order to discover the indigenous cultural values that underlie people's behaviour. Examples of Chinese emic values include *guanxi* (relationships), *mianzi* (prestige, face), *renquing* (favour) and *bao* (reciprocity), all of which are interrelated to each other (Fletcher and Fang 2006). Fang (1999, p. 67) modelled the business culture of China on the basis of three forces—the People's Republic of China condition, Confucianism and 'Chinese strategems'. Although developed to describe Chinese culture, this framework can be applied to any culture to uncover its idiosyncrasies and the three forces might be described in a more general way as local situation, social conventions/belief systems and negotiation strategy.

Tolerance of ambiguity is another cultural factor that can complicate relationships between Asian and Western organisations. This characteristic, which can lead to accusations of unreliability and deception, is sometimes included with Hofstede's variable of uncertainty avoidance. It differs in that it reflects the common situation in many Asian cultures where a strong tendency towards one extreme of a bipolar dimension (such as individualism) does not preclude its opposite (collectivism). Examples are:

- In Chinese society, *guanxi* and reliance on networks is indicative of collectivism whereas the focus on family and money-oriented behaviour reflects individualism.

- Asian cultures are characterised by a situation-accepting orientation (Leung 1992) and people react in a flexible manner. They accept uncertainty and disorder as natural phenomena (Lamposki and Emden 1996) and cope with situations on an individual or communal basis as circumstances require.

- Cultures in Asia are generally high context. Because meaning is contextual the degree of commitment is likely to be qualified by the context and this often creates ambiguity. This results in differences in meanings attached to positives and negatives being different from that in the West (e.g. does 'yes' mean 'yes' or merely 'I hear what you are saying'?).

- The *ying–yang* principle. This simultaneously results in elements of both the female (water, weak, dark, soft, passive) and the male (fire, strong, bright, hard, active) being present in a situation.

# Social aspects of the conduct of international marketing

There are two social aspects that deserve mention.

## SOCIAL SENSITIVITY

As well as being culturally sensitive the international marketer should also be socially sensitive. People in other countries are likely to react with more warmth towards foreigners who have taken the time and trouble to learn about the history, the geography, the religious underpinnings, the current political situation and the economic circumstances of the country with which they are seeking to do business. Furthermore, they appreciate efforts to learn their language even though the knowledge acquired might be rudimentary. Social sensitivity helps the international marketer recognise in advance any sensitive issues that are likely to be encountered and facilitates appreciating and adjusting to business practices that differ from Western norms. Finally, such sensitivity will lead to an improved perception of opportunities in the market as well as assist in identifying likely future constraints and how they might best be managed.

## GOOD CORPORATE CITIZENSHIP

The term 'corporate citizenship' is commonly used to describe the relationship of the firm with its various stakeholders. These are different in international marketing and include individuals, firms, groupings and governments in the overseas country. Prior to its merger with Billiton, BHP, the Australian multinational, described its approach to corporate citizenship as highly valuing its employees, the environment and its host communities; and constantly striving to improve these valued relationships (Zarkada-Fraser et al. 1999).

According to Maignan (1997), corporate citizenship consists of:

- *economic citizenship*—corporations should be productive and profitable while at the same time meeting consumer needs;

- *legal citizenship*—corporations should fulfil their economic mission within a legal framework;

- *ethical citizenship*—corporations should follow socially established moral standards; and

- *discretionary citizenship*—corporations should become actively involved in the betterment of the local communities in which they operate. Such activities are assumed voluntarily and do not produce a direct tangible benefit to the firm.

It is the discretionary element that can often make the difference in the award of contracts by governments in overseas countries. Firms that actively seek to employ locals in management, search out local sources of raw materials and other inputs, appoint locals of influence to the local directorship of the subsidiary or joint venture and create opportunity for local shareholding are demonstrating good corporate citizenship. A proactive policy of good corporate citizenship will offset criticism of the firm as a 'foreigner' and head off nationalistic antagonism, especially in developing countries.

Firms that are not socially sensitive or do not try to be good corporate citizens when operating in or dealing with an overseas country are likely to encounter 'push-back'. This occurs when one or more categories of local stakeholders oppose the activities of the foreign firm (often via local and/or global media). As an example, 70% of the 60 000 Chinese surveyed were opposed to the locating of a Starbucks café in the Forbidden City in Beijing due to likely damage to the cultural heritage and the atmosphere of this location (White et al. 2003).

# CULTURE AND INTERNATIONAL NEGOTIATION

International negotiation requires familiarity with both the broader environment of the country in which the negotiation is to take place and the specific setting for the conduct of the actual negotiations. These in turn will have a direct bearing on the negotiation process. Factors in the negotiation environment include the variety of laws that apply, as each party is likely to be subject to different laws; the political climate in the country of each party and the overall political relationships between the countries of the parties involved; the ability to transfer funds from one country to another and the likely fluctuations in exchange rates; the extent of government controls and bureaucracy; the degree of overall instability and change in both governments and government regulations; ideological differences as far as business customs and practices are concerned; external stakeholders who have a vested interest in the outcome of the negotiations; and finally cultural differences, which will be explored in depth later in the chapter.

Factors in the immediate negotiation setting include the relative bargaining power of the negotiators and the extent of mutual dependence of the parties on each other; the level of conflict underlying the negotiations and the extent to which the parties are likely to agree on key points; the relationship between the negotiators before and during the negotiations, especially the degree of trust; what is the desired outcome of the negotiations, for example profit or technology transfer; the immediate impact on the stakeholders; and finally the style of the negotiations which in turn is likely to be influenced by the cultural baggage of the negotiators. Cellich and Jain (2004) have modelled the above in terms of the impact of both the environment and the setting of the negotiation on the actual international negotiation process.

According to Cellich and Jain (2004), the environment in which the negotiations take place can have the following features:

* instability and change;
* foreign government control and bureaucracy;
* currency and foreign exchange fluctuation;
* political pluralism;
* legal pluralism;
* external stakeholders;
* differences in ideology; and
* differences in culture.

The setting of the actual negotiation is likely to be characterised by:

* underlying levels of conflict;
* relationships between negotiators (both before and during the negotiation);
* the desired outcome of the negotiation by each party;
* the style of negotiation;
* the impact of immediate stakeholders; and
* the relative bargaining power of the negotiators.

Factors in both the negotiation environment and the setting of the negotiation are likely to influence the process of the negotiation, and in particular:

- pre-negotiation planning;
- initiating the negotiation and making the first move;
- the negotiating price;
- winding down the negotiations; and
- undertaking re-negotiation.

Culture needs to be taken into account both when preparing for international negotiations and when conducting negotiations overseas. In negotiation, there are usually two types of goals at stake:

1  *substance goals*—concerned with outcomes related to the content of issues involved; and

2  *relationship goals*—concerned with outcomes related to how well people involved in the negotiations can work with each other once the negotiations are concluded.

Many negotiations result in a sacrifice of relationships, due to a focus on short-term gains, as the parties become preoccupied with substance goals and self-interest. However, effective negotiation takes place when both substance issues are resolved and working relationships are maintained or improved.

## Background to negotiation

All aspects of business activity involve negotiation. It is involved when introducing a product/service to the market; when selling a product/service; when taking steps to ensure that the customer is satisfied; and when endeavouring to secure reorders. In international business, negotiation is more complicated because the environment into which the product/service is being sold is different from the domestic market, especially in terms of the different cultural norms that apply. Cultural norms can critically affect the outcome of negotiations and many Australian firms have lost significant business overseas because of cultural insensitivity on the part of those sent abroad to negotiate business on their behalf.

## The environment of international negotiation

Underlying all international negotiations is the iceberg principle (Figure 3.8). Just as the *Titanic* sank because the part of the iceberg it hit that was above the surface of the ocean was small and the portion below the surface was very large, so in international negotiations that which is obvious and on the surface is limited and that which underlies the motives and statements of the other party is substantial. Failure to appreciate what lies below the surface can either sink the negotiation or result in an unfavourable outcome. If unfavourable outcomes are to be avoided, then the underlying concerns, interests and needs of the other party should be researched, as should the impact of cultural differences.

It is also necessary to guard against facile comparisons of differences between countries. As an example, *Sydney Morning Herald*, 2 April 1994, contained the headline: 'Chirpy Australians lift world gloom over future'. This was followed by an article that included the following table of responses to a question that asked whether in five years' time the world will be better, worse or about the same. These responses resulted from surveys conducted by leading newspapers in five countries.

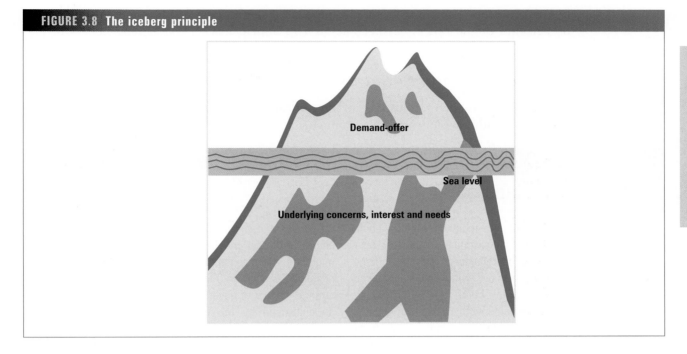

**FIGURE 3.8  The iceberg principle**

Often cross-national comparisons are not soundly based in terms of the behavioural differences between nationalities and to assume that other countries can be compared with Australia in terms of Australian norms is erroneous. Interpretation of the article and its table needs to take the following into account:

- Australians tend to be optimistic by nature as reflected in the saying 'She'll be right';
- Americans' egos drive them to postulate positive outcomes;
- Germans tend to be conservative in their judgements;
- Japanese have difficulty in saying 'no'; and
- British tend to be pessimistic.

It should be remembered that people view negotiations through the 'eyes' of their own culture and carry this 'baggage' with them into international negotiations. The significance of culture to the conduct of the negotiation is not that it defines the outcome of the negotiation, but rather that it influences the process of the negotiation and the underlying strategy of the bargaining. For example, is it the cultural norm to offer a 'take it or leave it' price or is it the norm to ask for more than you expect to receive and for the other party to offer less than they would expect you to accept, and for both parties to inch towards a

|  | Better | Worse | Same |
|---|---|---|---|
| Australia | 21% | 43% | 32% |
| US | 19% | 40% | 36% |
| Germany | 18% | 44% | 32% |
| Japan | 16% | 23% | 56% |
| Britain | 13% | 42% | 39% |

mutually acceptable figure during the process of negotiation? Understanding the cultural background of the other party enables you to anticipate likely bargaining behaviour and respond with confidence.

## Culture and the conduct of negotiations

There are a number of culturally influenced factors that need to be kept in mind when negotiating with people from other countries.

---

**3.4 INTERNATIONAL HIGHLIGHT**

## A bull in the china shop

Qantas and Telstra have much in common—both were former government utilities now answerable to shareholders, both have large consumer businesses with well recognised brands and both have been forced by government policy to compete with rivals—but what a difference in effectiveness! Whereas Qantas, led by its understated CEO Geoff Dixon, has excellent relations with Canberra that undoubtedly played a part in the refusal by the Australian government to allow Singapore Airlines to fly the lucrative Pacific route from Sydney to Los Angeles, despite the likely upsurge in tourism revenues, Telstra with its US-born CEO, Sol Trujillo, and imported US executive team ('the four amigos') confronts and criticises the federal government at every turn, generating irreparable damage to the company's image with shareholders as its share price declines and new share offerings go on the market at prices less that current shareholders paid for their existing shares. Although criticising the government in the media might be an acceptable tactic in the US, it causes a negative reaction in Australia where there is a much stronger history of government involvement in commerce, as evidenced by the creation of statutory marketing corporations for agricultural products and a well-developed antipathy towards people from other countries 'telling us what we should do'. Trujillo seems to lack sensitivity in this connection or appreciate the strength of passive resistance his 'bullying' engenders on the part of the federal government or its regulator, the Australian Competition and Consumer Commission. Even in so called 'free-enterprise' economies, government is a force to be reckoned with and a culturally sensitive approach towards government is essential as, even in the US, government is elected by the people as the voice of the people.

**SOURCE:** *Adapted from Sexton, E. and Coultan, M. (2006) 'Sol destroying'*, Sydney Morning Herald, *12–13 August 2006, p. 27.*

---

### DIFFERENT APPROACHES TO THINKING

Thought processes differ between cultures and this is manifested in the way both parties reach agreement. An understanding as to how both parties think through problems will facilitate the planning of an appropriate negotiation strategy.

### SELF-ESTEEM AND 'FACE'

These are of differing degrees of importance to various cultures. In most Asian cultures causing a person to lose face is unforgivable. In these circumstances it is essential in negotiation that the other party is allowed to win some points so as to save face and maintain self-esteem.

A linked issue is that of relationships. When relationships between an inferior and a superior are involved it is important not to criticise or humiliate the superior in front of the subordinate. Relationships could involve membership of a particular caste, position in

In Chinese culture there are two kinds of 'face'—'lian' which is associated with personal behaviour and the way it is viewed within the society and ' mianzi' which is the prestige accorded through success and outward show. Face influences the behaviour of consumers in China in the following ways:

- Refer to others: Chinese refer to others for their opinions and in so doing, give them their 'mianzi'. This results in their heeding the advice of opinion leaders so as to appear to behave like the majority.

- Ostentatious living: This reflects 'mianzi' .Chinese are sensitive to their position in the social network and anxious to preserve their social standing. This influences them to purchase items, focus on brand names and engage in activities that enhance their social standing.

- Fewer complaints: Chinese are less likely to complain when dissatisfied with a purchase as this would cause the party that sold the goods to lose his 'lian'.

- Reject comparative advertising: This reflects 'mianzi' as it is considered an insult to the moral character of the advertised brand.

- In negotiation: Chinese cover up mistakes made rather than seizing on them for advantage as this protects the 'lian' of the other party. This is also why Chinese usually use a mediator during the negotiations so as to protect their prestige.

SOURCE: *Adapted from Kotler, P., Keller, K.L., Ang, S.H., Leong, S.M. and Tan, C.T. (2006),* Marketing Management: An Asian Perspective*, Prentice Hall, Singapore, p. 185.*

the social hierarchy or links to powerbrokers or royalty. These linkages should be understood so as to avoid giving offence and so as to understand the value of the network that the negotiation outcome might link the firm to.

## VALUE SYSTEMS

It is desirable to appreciate the aspects that are valued in the culture from which the other party comes. Human behaviour largely depends on values and attitudes as these determine what is considered to be 'right' or 'wrong', what is considered important and what is considered to be desirable. Heritage, history and traditions that are valued provide indicators as to which aspects of the Australian proposal are most likely to appeal to the other side.

## APPROPRIATE DEGREE OF FORMALITY

It is useful to ascertain in advance whether the other party would prefer negotiations to be conducted on a formal or an informal basis. While a casual inquiry might elicit the response 'informal', this may not be what the other party really wants. The Australian assumption of informality is not shared by many other cultures.

## HARMONY AND EMOTION

In many cultures (like Japan) harmony is highly valued and anything which disturbs it is frowned upon. When negotiating with people from cultures in which harmony is valued, it is wise not to sour the negotiation with excessive displays of emotionalism or become involved in a confrontation. If agreement cannot be reached it is always advisable to 'leave the door open'.

## CHANGE

In societies that have undergone major change, there is likely to be a conflict between traditional values underlying business behaviour and those that are expected to apply in the changed environment. This is particularly the case with societies that have been or are currently in the process of transition from a socialist to a market economy. Pashtenko and Ahmed (2004), in discussing negotiation in Russia, point out that today's typical Russian, while being infused with a traditional distrust of foreigners, and existing in a society redolent with symbols of the former USSR, is now told that the diminished significance of his country is a preferable state of affairs. 'Where there was once a community that he believed would take care of his needs throughout his life, there is now an assembly of people who he is now competing against. Similarly, the subservience and anonymity that had been taught for centuries has now been replaced with self-advancement and individuality. Anonymity meant security; now anonymity equates to failure' (Pashtenko and Ahmed 2004, p. 259).

# Preparing for international negotiation

Success in international negotiations requires considerable research and advance planning. Of particular importance are the development of a strategy, choosing the correct negotiating team and researching the context in which the negotiations will take place.

## STRATEGY

Developing a strategy which is culturally sensitive is a prerequisite for successful negotiation. A decision should be reached in advance in general terms as to whether the Australian team should go out of its way to meet the expectations of the other side, whether it should make no accommodation whatsoever, or whether it should aim for a compromise between the two extremes. In general, when planning a negotiation strategy Australians and New Zealanders should try to be themselves, avoid compromising personal integrity, be willing to modify their behaviour to make others feel comfortable and show respect while being firm but friendly. The approach to negotiation should, to the degree appropriate to the culture, reflect respect for age, respect for tradition, respect for government and/or authority, reflect an understanding of inequality and the reasons for it, and show respect for education and recognition of local titles and symbols of rank.

## COMPOSITION OF THE NEGOTIATING TEAM

The following aspects, many of which can have cultural implications, should be borne in mind:

* *Numbers*: The number of people in the team should be matched to the number in the other negotiating team. Although this can be expensive when discussions are held outside Australia or New Zealand, so can mistakes due to having a smaller team that becomes exhausted from overwork. It is advisable to have a sufficient number in the team so that members can occasionally be given a day off.

* *Status*: There should be a matching of the members of each team in terms of status. This facilitates harmony and an ability to enter into commitments without reference 'back home'. It also conveys the impression that the Australian or New Zealand side is treating the negotiations as important.

* *Interpreter*: With the permission of the other side, an interpreter should be included as a member of the Australian or New Zealand team. This enables the team to acquire a

more accurate understanding of the views and sensitivities of the other side, and misunderstandings due to translation mistakes or imprecision of meaning are less likely to occur.

- *Tasks*: These should be defined in advance for each member of the negotiating team so that each member knows their role and members do not get in each other's way or inadvertently contradict each other, either in public or in private. Examples of possible roles are leader, negotiator, strategist, recorder, technical expert, sales expert, production expert or financial adviser.

- *Deployment*: Use the junior members of the team to argue over unpleasant details and test how far the other party will concede, while keeping the more senior people to smooth over ruffled feathers, to resolve minor disputes and sign the final agreement.

## RESEARCHING THE CONTEXT OF NEGOTIATIONS

In undertaking this research it is necessary to seek not only information which confirms currently held ideas as to the appropriate negotiation approach, but also to seek out information which might contradict these assumptions:

- *The other negotiating team:* There is a need to research the likely composition of the negotiation team of the other party and the background of their team members so as to establish biases or likely areas of common experience or interest. It is also advisable to ascertain the planned location of discussions and whether there will be adequate and secure communications facilities available in case, during negotiations, it is necessary to refer an issue to head office. It is useful to ascertain the need for the Australian or New Zealand team to provide either interpreters capable of translating what is being said as it is being said and/or translators to translate written documents and records of discussion. Although the other side might offer to provide interpreters/translators at their expense, there is always the doubt as to whether they will provide the Australian or New Zealand team with a full and correct message if they are paid by the other party. Often the nuance of what is said or the accumulated context of the conversation is more important than the actual words. Researching in advance the degree of authority the members of the other negotiating team have to make decisions is also useful. Another issue is who will be the decision maker regarding the topic under discussion and whether that decision maker is likely to be a member of the team. If any important decision makers are not team members, it is useful to find out how they might be contacted and to extend hospitality to them if this is culturally acceptable. Finally it is desirable to establish what is likely to happen to the other party if negotiations are unsuccessful. Knowing how badly they want a successful outcome can strengthen the negotiating hand of the Australian or New Zealand delegation.

- *The competition*: It is also advisable to research which competitors are likely to be in the overseas market. This research should include their strengths and weaknesses, whether they have done business in the market before, how their performance was judged and whether they were viewed as being culturally sensitive in their approach. Included in this appraisal should be an analysis of the influence exerted by the competitor's government, the connections and influence these competitors are able to bring to bear and the competitor's connections in the market. The availability or otherwise of attractive competitors impacts on the strength of the Australian or New Zealand negotiating position.

- *The Australian or New Zealand organisation*: It should be clearly established at the outset how badly the Australian or New Zealand firm wants this overseas business. Whether the contract is to be viewed as a 'one-off' event or the start of a long-term relationship with that market or as a vehicle to obtain a foothold in that market also needs to be decided. In this connection, it is necessary to determine the minimum acceptable package that can be agreed to in relation to each of the above strategies.

- *Alternative approaches*: It is useful to work out in advance a contingency plan if the original basis for negotiation proves unworkable. Such a plan could include an alternative approach that yields competitive advantage in a different way (e.g. offer a price in relation to usage so that, to the customer, the purchase becomes a variable as opposed to a fixed cost). Another alternative is to study all the elements of the offer so as to determine which elements are the most attractive to the other side. Then as a fall-back position offer the most unique of these elements (e.g. the packet-switching expertise elements of a digital trunk network project). This could be costed on the basis of offering the element direct or as part of a consortium or to the successful bidder in the event of failure to win the contract.

## Stages in international negotiation

An understanding of the various stages through which international negotiations proceed will assist in deciding which strategies to pursue at each stage. The strategy most useful at the beginning of negotiations may be inappropriate as negotiations proceed. There are five major stages in most international negotiations.

### PRE-NEGOTIATION STAGE

At this stage, it is necessary to work out the composition of the negotiation team and to formulate objectives and strategies. It is also necessary to conduct a preliminary analysis of the context of the negotiations, attempt an initial definition of likely problem areas, assess the position likely to be adopted by the other side and develop a desired agenda. Failure to prepare properly is likely to result in lack of commitment to a specific position and a willingness to grant concessions unnecessarily or too early in the negotiation. This stage also involves establishing rapport with members of the other team and the length of this stage is likely to be influenced by whether the other party comes from a low-context or high-context culture.

### OPENING STAGE

During the second stage, the negotiating teams begin 'to get down to business' as opposed to conversation designed to build trust. The appropriate level of formality needs to be considered as does the exchange of name cards and any associated formalities (as in Japan). At this stage it is desirable to check that both sides have common understandings as to the topic of the negotiations, what has been previously agreed to and how the relationship has developed to date. This exchange of information relating to the topics to be discussed is likely to take longer when the other party comes from a culture characterised by decision making by consensus. This is because more information will be required and many more people in the organisation represented by the other team will need to be provided with information.

### BARGAINING STAGE

This third stage is one in which the previously developed negotiation strategy needs to be applied. This is the stage where it is necessary to decide whether a broad agreement is negotiated first (such as intent to enter into a joint venture) or whether each aspect is negotiated individually for incorporation in a final agreement (such as human resource issues, financial issues and technology exchange issues). Another aspect for consideration at this stage is the speed with which negotiations should be conducted. North Americans, in keeping with their 'time is money' approach, value a speedy approach, whereas in many Asian countries the time devoted to negotiations is a reflection of the importance attached to the subject matter. To rush the negotiation in these circumstances is to send a signal to the other party that the issue is regarded as being of limited importance. In some cultures, negotiations are characterised by frequent restating of the position and in some circumstances this may be a deliberate ploy to give the party time to think. The bargaining stage is likely to be shorter in cases where the earlier stages have been protracted. At this stage, tactics are also important, as is knowledge as to what the other party considers acceptable behaviour. In some cultures aggressive tactics are likely to be met with silence, changing the subject or by withdrawal from negotiations.

## CONCESSION AND AGREEMENT STAGE

Complications at this stage often arise from contrasting styles of negotiation. Issues, such as volatility versus patience and trying to hurry resolution versus indifference to the time it takes to reach agreement, can be very important in reaching a mutually satisfying outcome. The norm of the other party in agreeing to concessions is also important: are concessions made progressively throughout the negotiations or only during the latter stages of the bargaining? The issue of the nature of contracts is applicable at this stage. In high-context cultures formal contracts are disliked whereas in low-context cultures they are sought because they provide the negotiators with feelings of comfort and security. A final factor at this stage is how each party views the negotiation in terms of total relationship and whether both parties view it in the same way. Is the negotiation regarded as a single event or as part of an ongoing long-term relationship?

## POST-NEGOTIATION STAGE

The final stage is where cognitive dissonance can set in and the parties question whether they made the right decisions and whether they are satisfied with the negotiated arrangement. In the interests of good relations and future business, it is good tactics after the deal has been concluded to give the other party an extra concession that they did not expect to receive. At the post-negotiation stage, another tactic common in some cultures, such as in India, is the practice of 'nibbling'—making further demands after the terms of the deal have been finalised. One way of handling this is to ask that the additional request be put in writing so that it can receive formal consideration when the agreement next comes up for review.

# The atmosphere of international negotiations

Atmosphere is very important in the conduct of negotiations in all countries but this is especially the case with high-context cultures. The atmosphere that prevails during the course of negotiations can have a positive or negative impact on the outcome. It is likely to be affected by a number of factors.

## DEGREE OF MUTUAL ORIENTATION

This will be a matter of whether both sides have the same view of the purpose of the negotiation and wish to achieve a mutually beneficial outcome. This mutuality of orientation is likely to be greater if both parties seek a 'win–win' outcome and view the exchange between them as improving the possibility of attaining their specific goals as opposed to maximising their own advantage by exploiting the other party.

## FEELINGS TOWARD THE OTHER PARTY

The atmosphere of negotiations will be conducive to a successful outcome if both parties trust each other, if there is a genuine willingness to cooperate, if there is a strong commitment to the relationship and if each side makes a genuine attempt to understand each other's motives and circumstances.

## OPENNESS VERSUS SECRECY

This factor will also impact on atmosphere and is often a reflection of differences in cultural values. Countries differ according to their tendency to be cautious in assessments on the one hand and to be open as opposed to secretive on the other. This ranges from Anglo-Saxon countries being transparent and optimistic at one end of the spectrum to the less-developed Latin countries being secretive and conservative on the other.

## WILLINGNESS TO MAKE CULTURAL ADJUSTMENTS

This is often a matter of the position of the party in the negotiation and whether one party has a greater need to achieve a result than the other. In general, the greatest degree of cultural adjustment in the negotiation situation should be made by the seller rather than the buyer, by the party to the transaction with the least power and by the party which wants a successful outcome the most.

## BATNA

One alternative for consideration is the best alternative to a negotiated agreement (BATNA). There is a BATNA for any issue. A BATNA should be acceptable to all parties. Often the potential for a BATNA to resolve disputed issues in a negotiation is overlooked as negotiators tend to be too focused on their predetermined strategies for the negotiation.

# The internet, culture and negotiation

Culture affects the way information is used, the credibility attached to information and the degree of trust exhibited in the internet as a medium for information. The internet is more culturally geared to the US cultural norms of anti-government, individualism, populism and egalitarianism. This means that some people in other countries will consider that US culture is embedded in the internet and this will lead to resistance to internet use in cultures that are different from the USA. One of the characteristics of the internet is its global reach. This means that to be effective e-marketers must address the diversity of the consumer's global culture. This is because nations and subcultures within nations differ from each other on various cultural dimensions. Those that appear to apply to internet adoption and usage are as follows.

## Cultural dimensions

### TIME

The internet is regarded as a medium that saves time because of its interactivity, ability to consummate a sale and the speed of its information exchanges. This means that it will be valued in cultures where 'time is money' and punctuality is prized. In cultures that adopt a more relaxed approach to time and where time is subordinated to creating or maintaining relationships, the timeliness of the internet is not likely to be valued as much. In societies where the focus is on the past (e.g. Iran), innovations like the internet are not as likely to be as prized as in societies like, for example, the USA where the focus is on the present or on the future.

### MATERIALISM

Because of its association with 'Americanness', the internet is regarded in many countries as being associated with materialism and the dollar, rather than quality of life or improvement in the welfare of the average citizen. The association of the internet with transnational companies endeavouring to become global firms reinforces this perception. The internet is regarded as being a vehicle for achieving these aspirations. The adoption of the internet in societies that are critical of materialism may be delayed because of this association.

### TECHNICAL ORIENTATION

Technical orientation is a dimension along which countries differ. The internet is strongly associated with new technology. Countries that are not strong in new technology creation may be countries that are not innovators or early adopters as far as diffusion of innovation is concerned. Such countries are less likely to invest funds in embracing the internet because of its association with new technology.

### LANGUAGE

In its structure, content and form language manifests the culture of those who speak it. This is reflected in word order, grammatical structure, number of words used to indicate shades of meaning, discourse analysis (where the emphasis comes in the sentence), and specificity versus vagueness of meaning. As the internet is specific rather than contextual and is associated with the American direct style of communication rather than with oblique styles of communication, its adoption in some countries may be delayed because its directness could lead to giving offence.

## BUSINESS CUSTOMS AND PRACTICES

Cultures vary in terms of acceptable business customs and practices. In some cultures these are specific and transparent while in others they are opaque, providing room to manoeuvre, to repay favours and to provide a commercial return in circumstances where regulations eliminate the incentive. Because of the transparency of the internet and the traceability of internet transactions, people in cultures where business customs and practices are opaque and negotiable may be more reluctant to adopt the technology than people in cultures where business activities are more transparent. This is particularly the case where bribery is common or a significant percentage of international trade flows through unofficial channels.

## Cultural concepts and the internet

There are a number of underlying cultural concepts that impact on the influence of culture on international marketing.

### HIGH VERSUS LOW CONTEXT

It would seem that low-context countries are more likely to adopt the internet than high-context countries. This may be because the internet is not contextual and internet messages convey all the intended meaning. This has led Fock (2000) to propose that the communication behaviour of internet visitors from high-context cultures will be different from that of visitors from low-context cultures and that perceptions of web messages by web visitors from high-context cultures will also be different from the perceptions of messages by visitors from low-context cultures.

### PSYCHIC DISTANCE

A comparison of degree of a country's psychic distance from Australia (see Table 3.2) with rates of internet adoption (see Chapter 2, Table 2.5) provides some indication that psychic similarity with Australia is linked to a higher rate of internet adoption. There is some logic to this because Australia is close to the USA in psychic distance terms and internet uptake in Australia has been extremely high in world terms. There are some exceptions to this conclusion, which lead to it being tentative; for example Singapore, although psychically distant from Australia, has a very high rate of internet adoption. Some people such as Ng (2004) argue that psychic distance may not be as important a factor for internet users as for others. This is because it facilitates the firm communicating with all markets simultaneously regardless of cultural, commercial or economic differences.

### ETHNOCENTRISM

Perlmutter (1995) developed a typology whereby firms could be classified according to the orientation of their management as still ethnocentric, polycentric, regiocentric or geocentric. Some researchers have found that ethnocentrism is related to a reluctance to adopt the internet. Wheeler (1998) found that Islamic societies in the developing world reject technology associated with the Western world as imperialistic, morally corrupt and harmful to local identity. She found that Kuwaiti companies do not use the internet for business deals, but they do use it to reinforce local identity or spread Islamic conservatism.

## Culture and global comparisons of internet adoption

With regard to Hofstede's dimensions, while logically it would seem that strong uncertainty avoidance would be correlated with internet adoption, there is no evidence for this and Park (2000) found the opposite.

Similarly, there would appear to be a logical connection between low power distance and internet adoption as the internet provides a facility for people to access information regardless of status. While Hofstede's classification of countries supports this proposed relationship, Park's research does not.

There appears, however, to be a correlation between individualism and adoption of the internet. Collectivist cultures put considerable pressure on members to conform to one another and this pressure for conformity and uniformity in collective cultures is not conducive to adoption of the internet where diversity and different viewpoints are encouraged. This forgoing would suggest that individualistic cultures are more likely to use the internet than collectivist cultures. Hofstede's classification of countries on this dimension tends to support the above suggestion. In addition, Park (2000) found that individualistic cultures are more prone to adopt the internet than collectivist cultures. This he attributes to the autonomy, freedom and optimal flexibility that the internet provides.

Finally, it could be argued that the internet is more compatible with feminine cultures where inter-dependence, interrelationships with other people and caring for other people are valued. This suggests that feminine cultures are more likely to adopt the internet than masculine cultures. Hofstede's classification of countries on this dimension provides some support for this proposition although there are some exceptions, such as Sweden, the Philippines and Japan. Park (2000) found strong support for the argument that feminine cultures were more likely to use the internet than were masculine cultures. This he attributes to the fact that people in feminine cultures enjoy the anonymity that the internet provides to avoid gender or ethnic identity.

One answer to the problems and differences associated with culture is to design ethnic portals, if the ethnic market is large enough. The reach of such portals will not necessarily be confined to a country but to the ethnic group wherever they may be. Given the increasingly mobile nature of the global workforce, especially professionals, this could be an advantage; for example United Airlines could promote round trips to Kuala Lumpur for Malaysians worldwide using a Malaysian portal (Park 2000, p. 2).

In designing ethnic portals for markets which are worthwhile in terms of numbers or purchasing power, it is necessary to take the host country's culturally influenced preferences into account. Proctor and Gamble has designed country-specific localised websites of a different style and content, targeted at the ethnic audience for each of its major markets, for example Brazil (<http://www.procter.com.br/pg/index.html>), China (<http://www.pg.com.cn>) and Germany (<http://www.procterundgamble.de>).

# Summary

Cultural sensitivity is a critical aspect of doing business overseas and is particularly important in the conduct of international negotiations. There are a number of culturally related factors that influence marketing overseas as well as various characteristics of culture itself, which manifest themselves in different ways from market to market. Cultural sensitivity requires an understanding of the way cultural differences affect communication, awareness of the elements of culture which are likely to have the greatest impact and a knowledge of the way culture operates at different levels—national, industry, organisation and personal.

There are a number of key cultural concepts that assist in classifying cultures in broad terms and these are reflected in the way culture manifests itself in international business settings. Included in these are time, space, language, familiarity and consumption patterns. The way in which culture is communicated can be both verbal and non-verbal and operating in a different culture will require some degree of adaptation. Cross-cultural comparisons, be they on a global or bilateral basis, highlight patterns of cultural difference and their implications for management. The work of Hofstede and Trompenaars in this connection needs to be considered in depth for the insights it can bring to an appreciation of the implications of cultural differences for marketing overseas. Social sensitivity and good corporate citizenship also play a role in successful international involvement. Cultural signposts abound in both planning for and undertaking international negotiations and apply differently at each stage of the negotiation process. Successful negotiation from a cultural perspective requires careful research, development of a strategy and management of the conduct of negotiations. Finally, the impact of culture on the atmosphere of negotiations is important as are the different negotiation styles adopted by people from different cultural backgrounds.

## ETHICS ISSUE

Your company, which makes small pumps, has been barred from entering the market in a large Asian country because of the collusive efforts of the local pump manufacturers. Your firm could expect to increase profits by A$5 million from sales in that market if the ban on your supplying the market were lifted. Last week a businessman from that Asian country contacted your management and stated he could smooth the way for the company to sell in his country for an inducement of A$500 000.

*You are the international marketing manager for the company and have visited the country on a number of occasions and have some familiarity with the cultural norms and business practices that prevail there. Your board has sought your advice as to whether the inducement should be paid, the legality of doing so and, if payment is recommended, how this might be handled.*

## Websites

Business culture guides http://www.executiveplanet.com
Cultural diversity http://www.takingitglobal.org/themes/diversity/home.html
Global Edge—country insights http://globaledge.msu.edu/countryInsights/

## Discussion questions

1   To what extent are cultural factors which impact on domestic marketing of greater importance when marketing overseas?

2   Why, when doing business in other countries, is it important to analyse the impact of culture at the national, the industry and the firm levels as well as at the personal level?

3   Discuss how you would compensate for the self-reference criterion when marketing in Vietnam.

4   Illustrate the difference between high-context cultures and low-context cultures by comparing China with Germany.

5   Why is time so important as a cultural variable when doing business overseas? How would you take this variable into account during your first visit to Myanmar? What are the likely consequences if you don't?

6  Describe the ways in which cultural differences can act to impede communication between businesspeople of different nationality.

7  What are the shortcomings of Hofstede's criteria for assessing cultural differences on a global basis? Do you consider that his fifth factor adequately caters for the underlying differences between Asian and Western cultural values?

8  Why is it necessary to prepare comprehensively for international negotiations? Prepare a list of issues you would research before leaving Australia or New Zealand.

9  As the newly appointed international marketing manager, you are taking over relationships in the firm's two most important markets of West Java and northern California. You will shortly leave to visit both markets to negotiate a long-term contract. How would the approach you would adopt at each stage of the negotiation process differ between the two regions?

# References

Abosag, I., Tynan, C. and Lewis, C. (2002) 'Relationship marketing: the interaction of cultural value dimensions', *Academy of Marketing Annual Conference*, 2–5 July, Nottingham Business School.

Bradley, L.K., Lowe, K.B. and Gibson, C.B. (2006) 'A quarter century of cultures consequences: a review of empirical research incorporating Hofstede's cultural values framework', *Journal of International Business Studies*, Vol. 37, pp. 285–320.

'Cartoon sees dairy exports drop 85%', *New Zealand Herald*, 22 April 2006, p. C4.

Cateora, P.R. and Graham, J.L. (2005) *International Marketing*, 12th edn, Mc Graw-Hill Irwin, New York.

Cellich, C. and Jain, S.C. (2004) *Global Business Negotiations: A Practical Guide*, Thomson South Western, Mason, USA.

Chau, R. and Fletcher, R. (1990) 'Australia–Thai cultural study', unpublished report, University of Technology, Sydney.

Cohen, J. (1996) 'The search for universal symbols: the case of right and left', in Manrai, L.A. and Manrai A.K. *Global Perspectives in Cross-cultural and Cross-national Consumer Research*, Haworth Press Inc., New York.

Craig, C.S. and Douglas, S.P. (2006) 'Beyond national culture: implications of cultural dynamics for consumer research', *International Marketing Review*, Vol. 23, No. 3, pp. 322–42.

De Mooij, M. (2005) *Global Marketing and Advertising–Understanding Cultural Paradoxes*, Sage Publications, Thousand Oaks, California.

*Economist*, 24 April 2004, p. 26.

Fang, T. (1999) *Chinese Business Negotiating Style*, Sage Publications, Thousand Oaks, California.

Fletcher, R. (1979) 'Don't let culture cripple your prospects', *Forum*, October–December, pp. 17–21.

Fletcher, R. and Bohn, J. (1998) 'The impact of psychic distance on the internationalisation of the Australian firm', *Journal of Global Marketing*, Vol. 12, No. 2.

Fletcher, R. and Fang, T. (2006) 'Assessing the impact of culture on relationship creation and network formation in emerging Asian markets', *European Journal of Marketing*, Vol. 40, No. 3/4, pp. 430–46.

Fock, H. (2000) 'Cultural influences on marketing communication on the World Wide Web', *Proceedings of the Multi-cultural Marketing Conference*, 17–20 September, Hong Kong Academy of Marketing Science.

Friedman, T. (2006) *The World is Flat–a Brief History of the 21st century*, Farrer, Strauss and Giroux, New York.

Glain, S. (2006) 'Islam in office', *Newsweek*, 3–10 July, pp. 34–5.

Hall, E.T. (1976) *Beyond Culture*, Anchor Press/Doubleday, New York.

Hayashi, S. (1988) *Culture and Management in Japan*, University of Tokyo Press, Tokyo, p. 9.

Hofstede, G. (1980) *Culture's Consequences: International Differences in Work-related Values*, Sage, Beverly Hills, CA.

Hofstede, G. (1991) *Culture and Organisations*, HarperCollins, London, p. 5.

Hofstede, G. (1994) 'The business of international business is culture', *International Business Review*, Vol. 3, No. 1, pp. 1–14.

Hofstede, G. (2001) *Culture's Consequences: Comparing Values, Behaviors, Institutions, and Organizations Across Nations*, 2nd edn, Sage Publications, Thousand Oaks, CA.

Hofstede, G. and Bond, M.H. (1988) 'The Confucious connection: from cultural roots to economic growth', *Organizational Dynamics*, Vol. 16, No. 4, pp. 4–21.

Hu, W. (1994) 'China's social custom and traditions in business relations', in Reuvid , J. (ed.) *Doing Business with China*, Kogan Page, London, pp. 234–41.

Isackson, J. (1980) 'Differences in cultural and business patterns between Australia and the United States', unpublished paper, San Francisco Institute for Management Development.

Keegan, W.J. and Green, M.S. (2006) *Global Marketing*, 4th edn, Prentice Hall, NJ.

Keillor, B.D. and Hult, G.T.M. (1999) 'A five country study of national identity: implications for international marketing research and practice', *International Marketing Review*, Vol. 16, pp. 65–82.

Keillor, B.D., Hult, G.T.M., Erffmeyer, R.G. and Babakus, E. (1995) 'NATID: the development and application of a national identity measure for use in international marketing', *Journal of International Marketing*, Vol. 4, pp. 57–73.

Kelly, M. (1990) *The Milwaukee Journal*, 25 November, p. H5.

Kotler, P., Keller, K.L., Ang, S.H., Leong, S.M. and Tan, C.T. (2006), *Marketing Management: An Asian Perspective*, Prentice Hall, Singapore, pp. 612–13.

Kroeber, A.L. and Kluckholn, C. (1952) 'Culture: a critical review of concepts and definitions', *Anthropological Paper No. 4*, Peabody Museum, Cambridge, MA.

Lamposki, K. and Emden, J.B. (1996) *Igniting Innovation: Inspiring Organizations by Managing Creativity*, John Wiley, New York.

Lee, J .A. (1966) 'Cultural analysis in overseas operations', *Harvard Business Review*, March/April, pp. 106–14.

Leung, K. (1992) 'Decision making', in Westwood, R.I. (ed.), *Organizational Behavior: Southeast Asian Perspectives*, Longman, Hong Kong, pp. 343–61.

Leung, K., Bhagat, R.S., Buchan, N.R., Erez, M. and Gibson, C.B. (2006) 'Culture and international business: recent advances and their implications for future research', *Journal of International Business Studies*, Vol. 36, pp. 357–78.

Maignan, S. (1997) 'Antecedents and benefits of corporate citizenship: a comparison of US and French businesses', PhD thesis, University of Memphis, Tampa.

Maslow, A.H. (1964) 'A theory of human motivation', in Levitt H.J. and Pondy L.R. (eds), *Readings in Managerial Psychology*, University of Chicago Press, Chicago, pp. 6–24.

Mead, R. (1990) *Cross-Cultural Management Communication*, John Wiley, Chichester, p. 151.

Morris, D. (1978) *Man Watching*, Triad, Granada.

Ng, L.N. (2004) 'International market selection behaviour: a study of New Zealand exporters', unpublished MCom thesis, Victoria University, Wellington.

Park, H. (2000) 'A cross-cultural analysis of internet connectivity', *Journal of Current Research in Global Business*, Fall, pp. 97–107.

Pashtenko, V.H. and Ahmed, Z.U. (2004) 'An institutional theory perspective on negotiating with foreign principals: a case study of joint venture executives in Russia', in Ogunmokun, G. and Gabbay, R. (eds), *International Business and Cross Cultural Marketing: Contemporary Research in Selected Countries*, Academic Press International, Nedlands, Western Australia.

Perlmutter, H.V. (1995) 'The tortuous evolution of the multinational corporation', in Bartlett, C.A. and Ghoshal, S. (eds) *Transnational Management*, Irwin, Chicago.

Ronen, S. and Shenkar, O. (1985) 'Clustering countries on attitude dimensions: a review and synthesis', *Academy of Management Review*, Vol. 10, No. 3, pp. 435–54.

Schutte, H. and Ciarlante, H. (1998) *Consumer Behaviour in Asia*, Macmillan, London, p. 93.

Sexton, E. and Coultan, M. (2006) 'Sol destroying', *Sydney Morning Herald*, 12–13 August 2006, p. 27.

Trompenaars, F. and Hampden-Turner, C. (1997) *Riding the Waves of Culture: Understanding Cultural Diversity in Business*, 2nd edn, Nicholas Brealey Publishing, London.

*Wall Street Journal*, 21 January 1994, p. 97.

Wheeler, D.L. (1998) 'Global culture or culture clash: new information technologies in the Islamic world—a view from Kuwait', *Communication Research*, Vol. 25, No. 4, pp. 359–77.

White, M., Haire, J., Rex, J. and King, J. (2003) 'Managing stakeholder "push-back", an exploratory study into dealing with negative cross-cultural communication in a global environment', Conference of the Australia–New Zealand Marketing Academy, Adelaide, 1–3 December, University of South Australia.

Wighton, D. (2006) 'Gloomy forecast for China credit card profits', *Financial Times*, 5 July, p. 17.

Zarkada-Fraser, A., Kusku, F. and Fraser, C. (1999) 'Can corporate citizenship measures be culturally transferable?', *Proceedings of the 1999 Annual Conference of the Australia–New Zealand International Business Academy,* Australian Centre for International Business, University of New South Wales.

**go online**

Go online to <www.pearsoned.com.au/fletcher> to find more cases.

# CASE STUDY 3

# Hong Kong Disneyland: when big business meets *feng shui*, superstition and numerology

John Kweh, School of Marketing, University of South Australia and Justin Cohen, Ehrenberg-Bass Institute for Marketing Science, University of South Australia

## BACKGROUND

Disney, one of the world's most recognised brands, launched its most recent theme park in Hong Kong in 2005. Hong Kong Disneyland, the fifth theme park globally, was created to service the Hong Kong market, but more strategically to reach the rapidly growing Chinese market. Hong Kong Disneyland is located on Lantau Island, 10 minutes from the Hong Kong International airport and 30 minutes from the city via the subway (Holson 2005).

The theme park is a joint venture between the Walt Disney Co. and the Hong Kong Special Administrative Region (HKSAR) government (Landreth 2005). The theme park is Disney's smallest at 745 hectares, but still consists of four distinct entertainment arenas: Main Street USA, Fantasyland, Adventureland and Tomorrowland. Hong Kong Disneyland is based on the Anaheim, California original (Landreth 2005).

Hong Kong has been chosen as the stepping-stone into the vast Chinese market as most Chinese have not grown up with Disney (Miller

2007). Another theme park in Shanghai is tentatively planned for 2010. Hong Kong, a capitalist economy where English is prevalent, maintains a sound legal and judiciary system and good corporate governance (Fong 1995). Thus Hong Kong has been an ideal choice for many corporations to launch into China. PricewaterhouseCoopers predicts a 25.2% rise in Chinese entertainment and media spending through to 2009, making China the fastest growing market for entertainment in Asia (Landreth 2005). This can be attributed to the rapid growth of the middle class in China, compounded with the reinvestment of money by overseas Chinese in their now-flourishing country.

## MICKEY MOUSE GOES GLOBAL

In 1983, Tokyo Disneyland was launched in Japan with a huge success. This seemed to bode well for Disney because it cloned its American theme park and reproduced it in Tokyo. Unfortunately, this proved to be a false sense of security for its overseas expansion. Disney next set its sights on a market and culture much closer to home.

Its next project was Euro Disney, launched in Paris in 1992. Cultural sensitivity issues marred EuroDisneyland (now known as Disneyland Paris) from the first day. Disney was accused of ignoring French culture and criticised for exporting American imperialism in its European venture (Brennan 2004) The issues regarding language, alcohol consumption and pricing of tickets and merchandise damaged the Disney brand (Brennan 2004). Euro Disney received negative publicity and headlines such as 'Disney is cultural Chernobyl' ('The horns of a dilemma', *Economist*,

November 1992). There were continuous protests from French farmers because of the French government's acquisition of farmland for the Disney theme park (Anonymous 1998). Workers resisted the Disney management style and dress code (Anonymous 1998).

These incidents made Disney aware that venturing into non-American markets could be extremely complex due to cultural differences. This outcome startled Disney. How could a copy-cat launch of their product in an Eastern country with vast cultural differences succeed, but yet fail immensely in a Western European market?

Disney had global recognition and an association with fun and family, but senior managers and strategists now understood that they needed to truly understand the cultures of their host nations.

## THE FRENCH REVOLUTION: LEARNING TO BREAK BREAD OR BAGUETTES

In order to reach a balance between Disney tradition and French culture, Stephen Burke, the then vice president in charge of park operations and marketing at EuroDisney made a number of changes to retain Disney's image while still adapting to the French culture. First, the name EuroDisney was changed to a more nationalistic Paris Disneyland, so that the French would be more receptive to it (Anonymous 1998).

Burke's strategies to retain Disney's image included:

- focusing on hiring an outgoing and friendly Disney cast;
- increased training;
- the placement of additional Disney characters throughout the park.

Burke's strategies to adapt Disney to the French culture included:

- removing the ban on alcohol in the theme park;
- lowering the corporate Disney premium on admission, merchandise, hotels and food;
- relaxing Disney's hierarchical management structure;

- cutting managerial staff by almost 1000 in order to flatten management and empower the employees (Anonymous 1998).

## DISNEY FOLLOWS MULAN HOME

Disney had one great success and one great failure in its international expansion. Its next launch had to succeed at all costs. This time Disney was prepared for a long planning period. Disney now knew that it must consider the various cultural nuances and sensitivities of its host nation. The design of Hong Kong Disneyland took into account Chinese cultural aspects and planners went to great lengths to ensure that it was well received by the local Hong Kong population and their projected mainland Chinese visitors (Fowler and Marr 2005). Hong Kong Disneyland focused on three core markets: Hong Kong residents, visitors from the southern part of China and visitors from South-East Asian markets (Emmons 2001). Table 1 clearly shows the value of these three markets, but most importantly the rapid rise in visitors to Hong Kong from mainland China. Although people from Hong Kong live with cutting edge technology, superstition still plays a vital part in their culture. Numbers and *feng shui* are taken seriously in all aspects of everyday life and business.

## FENG SHUI, SUPERSTITION AND NUMEROLOGY

Hobson (1994) discussed the influence of *feng shui* on the Asian hospitality industry. It has been noted that the location, interior and exterior of the building are important factors to be considered. Rossbach (1984) stated that the Chinese see a link between humanity and the earth whereby everything is interconnected and needs to be in balance. Buildings and other structures need to blend into the landscape to ensure that there is a good flow of energy or 'qi'. The five elements of *feng shui* (water, wood, fire, earth and metal) have been incorporated into the Hong Kong Disneyland design (see Figure 1). Tom Morris, chief designer, said, 'Regarding feng shui, the thing that is most visible is the heavy usage of water in the park' ('Disney uses feng shui to build Mickey's new kingdom in

| TABLE 1 | Visitor arrivals to Hong Kong by country/territory of residence | | |
|---|---|---|---|
| | | | Visitors ('000) |
| Country/territory of residence | 2001 | 2005 | 2006 |
| The mainland of China | 4 449 | 12 541 | 13 591 |
| Taiwan | 2 419 | 2 131 | 2 177 |
| South & Southeast Asia | 1 747 | 2 413 | 2 660 |
| North Asia | 1 762 | 1 853 | 2 030 |
| The Americas | 1 259 | 1 565 | 1 631 |
| Europe, Africa & the Middle East | 1 171 | 1 726 | 1 917 |
| Macao | 532 | 510 | 578 |
| Australia, New Zealand & South Pacific | 387 | 620 | 668 |
| Total | 13 725 | 23 359 | 25 251 |
| | (+5.1) | (+7.1) | (+8.1) |

**SOURCE:** *Census and Statistics Department (2007)* Hong Kong in Figures, Census and Statistics Department, *Hong Kong Special Administrative Region.*

**FIGURE 1   The five elements of *feng shui* and how they interact**

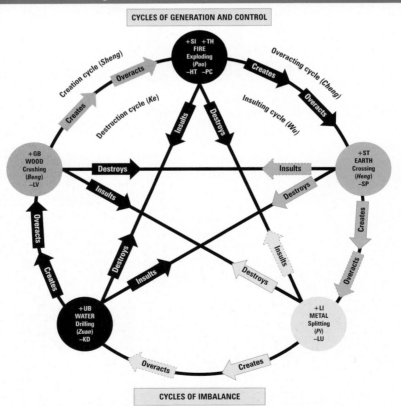

**SOURCE:** *<http://en.wikipedia.org/wiki/Image:FiveElementsCycleBalanceImbalance.jpg>.*

Hong Kong' 2005). The Chinese, in many cases, would attribute business failure to bad *feng shui*—hence few dare to ignore it.

The fundamental *feng shui* principle is to create harmony between humanity and the earth. *Feng shui* principles have been adopted in the placement, orientation and design of the park. A geomancer, a *feng shui* specialist, was consulted before the construction of the theme park began (Miller 2007). *Feng shui* practices at Hong Kong Disneyland are prevalent. The main entrance gate of the theme park was shifted 12 degrees to maximise good energy flow (Holson 2005). Ritual incense burning was customary upon the completion of each building (Holson 2005).

Boulders have been placed throughout the theme park to represent stability. A bend was also created in the walkway from the train station; this was believed to ensure that good fortune does not flow out the back of the park (Holson 2005). To ensure a balance of the five elements of *feng shui*, some areas have been designated as 'no fire zones' (Lee 2005). This meant that Disney had to ensure that there were no kitchens in these areas (Lee 2005).

The theme park has no fourth floor as the number 'four' sounds the same as the word 'death' in Cantonese and Mandarin and is considered unlucky (Yardley 2006). On the other hand, the number eight, considered lucky, is used extensively (Yardley 2006). It signifies prosperity and wealth. For example, the main ballroom of one of the hotels is 888 square feet (Ho 2006). There are 2238 crystal lotuses that decorate one of the restaurants. When one pronounces the number '2238' in Cantonese, the sound strongly mimics the Chinese phrase for 'becoming wealthy with ease' ('Disney uses feng shui to build Mickey's new kingdom in Hong Kong' 2005). Numbers play an important role in Chinese culture and it is no coincidence that the Summer Olympics in Beijing are scheduled to open on 8/8/8 at 8 p.m. (Yardley 2006). Hong Kong Disneyland opened on 12 September 2005, at exactly 1 p.m., a date and time believed to be most auspicious according to the Chinese Almanac (Miller 2007).

Apart from lucky numbers, the Chinese love the colour red due to its symbolic representation of prosperity; that is why it is seen throughout the theme park. Chinese taboo and superstition have been taken into consideration as well. Certain merchandise is not sold in the park. Clocks are nowhere to be seen because giving a clock as a gift is strictly forbidden in Chinese culture—it is a bad omen and insinuates that one will go to a funeral. Green hats are also not on sale. This is because a man wearing a green hat symbolises that his partner has committed adultery ('Disney uses feng shui to build Mickey's new kingdom in Hong Kong' 2005).

Besides *feng shui*, many adaptations have been made to better suit Chinese visitors. Its employees are culturally diverse and many speak a number of languages. Hong Kong Disneyland is officially trilingual with English and two dialects of Chinese (Mandarin and Cantonese), which are used in all signage and audio-recorded messages (Einhorn 2005). Euro Disneyland on the other hand had an English-only policy for staff when it first opened (Brennan 2004).

Chinese food is also abundant in the theme park. Although Western food such as hotdogs, hamburgers and candyfloss is served, lots of local delicacies can be enjoyed as well. Don't be surprised to come across soy sauce chicken wings or black sesame ice cream!

Disney has now launched its theme parks in three international markets. Each experience has been unique. Tokyo Disneyland was clearly beginner's luck. Paris Disneyland proved to be one of the company's biggest blunders. Changes have been made, but the Paris operation has never yielded their projected returns. Hong Kong Disneyland is truly a marriage of East and West. Thus far, the venture has been successful, but time will tell. Disney has looked to the past to secure its future.

## Bibliography

Anonymous (1998) 'Balancing tensions: Stephen Burke', *MIT Sloan Management Review*, Vol. 40, No. 1, p. 27.

Brennan, Y.M. (2004) 'When Mickey loses face: recontextualization, semantic fit, and the semiotics of foreignness', *Academy of Management Review*, Vol. 29, No. 4, pp. 583–616.

Census and Statistics Department (2007) *Hong Kong in Figures*, Census and Statistics Department, Hong Kong Special Administrative Region.

'Disney uses feng shui to build Mickey's new kingdom in Hong Kong' (2005), <http://english.sina.com/taiwan_hk/1/2005/0907/45097.html>, accessed 27 April.

Einhorn, B. (2005) 'Disney's not-so-magic new kingdom', Business Week Online.

Emmons, N. (2001) 'Disney tradition to carry on at Hong Kong park', *Amusement Business*, Vol. 113, No. 3, p. 1.

Fong, A. (1995) 'Points: the future looks bright for China and Hong Kong', *Columbia Journal of Business*, Vol. 30, No. 2, pp. 61–62.

Fowler, G.A. and Marr, M. (2005) 'Disney's China play', *Wall Street Journal* (Eastern Edition), Vol. 245, No. 117, pp. B1–B7.

Ho, D. (2006) 'Hong Kong Disneyland—it's a small world', <http://www.brandchannel.com/features_profile.asp?pr_id=269>, accessed 20 April 2007.

Hobson, J.S.P. (1994) 'Feng shui: its impacts on the Asian hospitality industry', *International Journal of Contemporary Hospitality Management*, Vol. 6, No. 6, pp. 21–26.

Holson, L.M. (2005) 'Disney bows to feng shui', *International Herald Tribune Business*, <http://www.iht.com/articles/2005/04/24/business/disney.php>, accessed 25 April 2007.

'Hong Kong Disneyland: the Magic Kingdom meets the Middle Kingdom', <http://www.china-connections.net/Articles/1ed/DisneylandHK.htm>, accessed 27 April 2007.

Landreth, J. (2005) 'Mouse meets Mao', *Amusement Business*, Vol. 117, No. 9.

Lee, M. (2005) 'East meets west: Hong Kong park is a classic Disney with an Asian accent', *USA Today*, <http://www.usatoday.com/travel/destinations/2005-07-07-hong-kong-disney_x.htm>, accessed 25 April 2007.

Miller, P.M. (2007) 'Disneyland in Hong Kong', *China Business Review*, Vol. 34, No. 1, pp. 31–33.

Rossbach, S. (1984) *Feng Shui*, Rider, London.

'The horns of a dilemma' (1992) *Economist*, Vol. 325, No. 7787, p. 80.

Yardley, J. (2006) 'Numbers game in China', *International Herald Tribune: Asia-Pacific*, <http://www.iht.com/articles/2006/07/04/news/plates.php>, accessed 25 April 2007.

## Questions

1 Discuss the elements of culture that have been addressed in this case study.
2 What did Disney learn from its mistakes in Paris?
3 How did Disney embrace Chinese culture with its Hong Kong venture?
4 What cultural issues would arise if Disney chose Dubai for its next theme park?

## Photo credit

Hong Kong Disneyland © Kim Morgan.

# CHAPTER 4

# AVOIDING THE PITFALLS OF THE INTERNATIONAL POLITICAL AND LEGAL ENVIRONMENT

## LearningObjectives

**After reading this chapter you should be able to:**

■ appreciate the functions of government in terms of its effect on international marketing;

■ identify those aspects of the local political-legal environment that affect a firm's international marketing;

■ recognise those aspects of the political-legal environment in the overseas country that will affect the risk of operating in that country;

■ determine which options are available to minimise political-legal risk;

■ calculate how the legal environment in an overseas market influences each element of the marketing mix;

■ appreciate the increasing dilemma in international marketing regarding the protection of intellectual property;

■ assess the way legal systems differ and the effect of these differences on the drawing up of contracts and the resolving of disputes; and

■ identify the ways in which the impact of national laws might be minimised in the international environment.

# A conflict of interest

Embargoes are a fact of life in international trade, but are inevitably a result of politics rather than economics. Increasingly, embargoes hurt the domestic populations of the countries subject to the embargo, which in turn raises humanitarian issues and allegations that they cause starvation and the spread of disease. For this reason, foodstuffs and medicines are often exempt from embargoes and, in the case of Iraq, this was recognised in the United National Food for Oil Program. However, this type of special consideration in turn creates the risk that the regime involved may try to use these loopholes in the embargo to assist their military objectives. This is what happened with the Saddam Hussein regime in Iraq, and both the Australian Wheat Board (AWB) and New Zealand's dairy giant Fonterra knowingly paid 'incentives' to intermediaries of the Iraq regime (AWB to a Jordanian company, Alia, and Fonterra to a Vietnamese intermediary) so as to retain their position as major suppliers in their respective product categories to Iraq. In the case of AWB this was to protect a relationship going back 50 years. Under the Food for Oil Program, the AWB had shipped US$3 billion of wheat to Iraq involving 'kick-backs' to the regime varying from 10 to 19% and totalling US$300 million paid as trucking fees to Alia. With the fall of Iraq in 2003, AWB contracts detailing these payments to Alia fell into the hands of the powerful US Wheat Lobby whose attempts to break into the Iraq market had been relatively unsuccessful.

Australian stakeholders in this situation, apart from the

AWB, include wheat farmers who wished to retain their lucrative major international market and be compensated by long-term sales for the US$480 million debt the AWB forgave Iraq at the request of the Australian government and its ministers, who had a vested political interest in maintaining a pre-eminent position in the Iraq market in the face of US and Canadian competition. A similar set of circumstances would apply in the case of the New Zealand dairy industry although, unlike the Cole inquiry into the actions of the AWB, no commission was set up in New Zealand to investigate the actions of Fonterra. One outcome of this issue is the way both countries are now perceived in terms of corruption. Whereas in 2003, New Zealand was rated by Transparency International as the third least corrupt country and Australia the eighth, ratings for 2006 show these rankings as having fallen for both New Zealand and Australia.

**SOURCES:** *Adapted from Overington, C. (2006), 'Aid to the enemy',* Australian, *21–22 January, pp. 17, 22; Marr, D. and Wilkinson, M. (2006) 'This worries me',* Sydney Morning Herald, *25–26 March, p. 32; and O'Sullivan, F. (2006) 'Kiwis avoid harsh light of independent scrutiny',* New Zealand Herald, *15 April, p. A25. Image from AFP Photo/Sabah Arar.*

# INTRODUCTION

The political and legal risks faced in foreign markets are considerable. These risks are a major factor in deciding whether or not to enter a market and, if the decision is taken to enter, what form the entry should take. Although the exporter may be plagued by government 'red tape', the investor is faced with a host of government laws and regulations which all increase the risk of doing business in the overseas country. In addition to the politics and laws of both the home and host countries, the international marketer must consider the global political and legal environment. Political issues usually lead to laws and regulations, and consequently political and legal issues in the international marketplace are often intertwined.

The national political environment is affected by a number of variables that form the context of all political activity. These include ideology, the economic system and the strength of nationalism. It is in the interests of international firms to monitor continually their activities in a market in relation to these variables because they contain the underlying forces that influence the degree of political risk. The major actor in the political arena in most countries is the national government. However, there are also state and regional governments. Often Australian and New Zealand firms make the mistake of courting the national government only in order to win the project or gain investment approval. In the process they ignore local government bodies in whose area the project will be undertaken or new plant located. To secure effective implementation as well as approval it is necessary to court all levels of government.

This is illustrated by the case of Myanmar (Burma) where on the one hand there is a central government controlled by the military and on the other a dozen resistance armies formed among ethnic minorities such as the Shan, the Karen, the Karenni and the Kachin. It is in areas controlled by these groups that many resources for the future development of the nation, such as natural gas, lie. As such development cannot take place without foreign investment, potential investors face the prospect of dealing with two different regimes.

**SOURCE:** *Adapted from McDonald, H. (2006) 'Burma's hard reign',* Sydney Morning Herald, *18–19 November, p. 29.*

# THE ROLE OF GOVERNMENT IN INTERNATIONAL MARKETING

## Different types of national governments

Knowledge of the various forms of government is useful in making an appraisal of the political environment for the firm. Forms of government are democracy, monarchy and dictatorship, as distinct from capitalism, communism and socialism, which are economic systems characterised by varying degrees of market orientation (see Chapter 2). You can classify government as either open (e.g. parliamentary governments) or closed (e.g. absolutist regimes such as dictatorships).

### PARLIAMENTARY GOVERNMENTS

This form of government consults with citizens at periodic intervals to ascertain their wishes and preferences. Policies are intended to reflect the desires of the majority and opportunity is provided for the population to take an active role in the formulation of these policies. Most industrialised nations can be classified as parliamentary democracies. Such forms of government can include monarchies provided they are constitutional such as in Britain (and hence Australia) or Thailand. The number of political parties in such governments may vary and some governments are made up of coalitions of parties rather than one party.

## ABSOLUTIST GOVERNMENTS

These dictate government policy without considering citizens' needs or opinions. Often these are to be found in newly independent countries undergoing some form of political transition. Absolute monarchs are comparatively rare, although dictatorships are not. Dictatorships need not involve one person, but can involve a group such as the military in Myanmar. Many governments in communist states are absolutist because, although they have elections, no alternatives to party candidates appear on the ballot paper.

### 4.1 INTERNATIONAL HIGHLIGHT

## Rising dragon still sees red

It is an increasing misconception that former communist countries now pursuing market economies behave as the Western developed economies they are striving to emulate. This emulation is only skin deep and below the surface these countries continue to exhibit ways of behaving and thinking that reflect their socialist past. In many of these economies, a significant percentage of business is still conducted by State Owned Enterprises (SOEs) and State Trading Companies (STCs) whose approach to business is in sharp contrast with that of the private sector. While the private sector has burgeoned in the cities as evidenced by the Australian designed 24 storey A$670 million Friendship Mansion retail complex in Beijing, the situation in the towns and villages is still reflective of the communist era. In China, it is a gross oversimplification to say Marxism-Leninism has been abandoned for capitalism as the Communist Party is still the ruling party and has a major impact on rules and regulations, according to Tom Gorman, founder and chairman of *Fortune China* magazine. Currently there is a balancing act in China between economic growth and the Marxist philosophical code. This is seen in the desire of government to corporatise rather than privatise state owned companies so that the state continues to own and control them—they can compete commercially, but be hauled into line when they stray from the need to be used as an instrument of government policy. As a consequence, China can best be described as a socialist market economy rather than as a market economy.

**SOURCE:** *Needham, K. (2006) 'Rising dragon still sees red',* Sydney Morning Herald, *7–8 October 2006, pp. 23 and 31.*

## OTHER GOVERNMENTS

Most governments fall between these two extremes. Some monarchies and dictatorships have parliamentary elections (Saudi Arabia and South Korea); others hold elections, but the results are suspect because of government involvement in voting fraud (the Philippines under Marcos and Zimbabwe under Mugabe); and others hold elections, but ignore the results (Myanmar).

## The role of government in the economy

Government involvement in the economy presents commercial opportunities for Australian and New Zealand firms where government undertakings are the purchasers. Governments can also provide targets for lobbying activity when governments are regulating access by a foreign firm into their market. Further, governments can be solicited by overseas firms when

Thailand is a constitutional monarchy and elections mostly result in governments formed by a coalition of parties. In most ministries responsible for awarding government contracts such as communications, the usual practice is to have a minister and two deputy ministers. Each has responsibility for a specific area and each represents a different party in the coalition government. When bidding on a project involving the ministry, it is important for the Australian and New Zealand businessperson to ascertain which minister has responsibility for the project. It is likely that this responsibility will be used to repay favours owed (which influences with whom the businessperson should collaborate) or indirectly generate funds for the party.

a government is facilitating foreign involvement in its market via investment incentives, free-trade zones and the like.

## PARTICIPATOR

An extreme form of involvement is the state trading company (STC) which is a common feature of the commercial environment in current and former communist countries. A lesser form of involvement is the Australian and New Zealand situation of control over the marketing of agricultural products by statutory marketing authorities established by government and commercial interests. Although in many cases, these have been partly or wholly privatised, government can still influence their operations due to the background and composition of the boards of these corporations. In almost all countries there are commercial activities undertaken by the government, especially in areas related to transport, infrastructure, defence, health, education and public welfare. In some of these, government will be the sole customer, as in the case of water and sewerage and in others it will be an important customer as with airlines. Government ownership may preclude foreigners selling a competing product (e.g. the Thai Tobacco Monopoly) or owning an operation making a competing product. There is, however, a trend for governments to reduce their involvement in commercial undertakings, via privatisation including in those instrumentalities that deliver public services. Often this reduced involvement is driven by a need to sell off public sector enterprises in order to balance the budget as in Australia or because of rising costs of public sector activities.

It is important for the Australian business person to establish the degree of government participation in the area of activity of interest in the overseas market. This is because selling to a government is quite different from selling to the private sector. In addition, the pace of privatisation in the country should also be considered because the government-controlled activity of today may be the privatised activity of tomorrow.

Public servants in most countries, by comparison with employees in the private sector, have security of employment, are not financially accountable for their actions and tend to be remunerated (and promoted) on the basis of responsibility exercised rather than efficiency or achieving savings. These issues should be borne in mind when selling to public servants overseas because they affect what they will consider to be appealing about the offer.

In dealing with government officials overseas it is important to discover their real needs. Apart from macro interests, such as promoting economic development, expanding the tax base and providing national security, public servants are also likely to be concerned with how the deal will affect their ministry, the political party in power, their political patron and their own power and status.

Another reason why it is important to establish in advance the extent of government involvement in procurement is that there may be preferential arrangements with other countries when government purchases are involved. As an example, the *Australia–New Zealand Government Procurement Act* of 1991 provides that companies in Australia will be accorded the same treatment as New Zealand firms as far as New Zealand government procurement is concerned, and vice versa.

For further information on selling to overseas governments, see Chapter 19 where winning project business overseas is discussed in detail, as such business mostly involves dealing with government bodies.

## FACILITATOR

Governments can facilitate international marketing via export incentives. These can range from remission of taxes paid (as with rebate of payroll taxes), the provision of tax deductions in relation to the volume of exports generated and grants to offset promotional expenditure overseas. This latter form of incentive is exemplified in Australia's Export Market Development Grants Scheme, which allows firms in the SME sector to claim as tax deductions expenses above A$15 000 incurred in promoting overseas. As the definition of eligible expenditure can include overseas representatives and export consultants, governments offering export incentives are often accused of subsidising exports, which is contrary to the principles of the World Trade Organization. New Zealand has the New Zealand Enterprise Development Grants Program which has both a Capability Building Component (EDG-CB) and a Market Development Component (EDG-MB).

Government can also operate as a facilitator to overseas business. Governments often attract new foreign investment and technology by providing a range of concessions such as tax holidays, duty-free import privileges, subsidised rent for factory sites, concessional loans or grants and discounted power and utility charges. Governments can also set up export processing zones to attract overseas manufacturing activity to generate exports. Examples are the Northern Territory Trade Development Zone and Subic Bay in the Philippines.

For many years Kodak supplied film to South-East Asian markets from its plant in Melbourne. As part of a worldwide rationalisation of manufacturing activities in 1990, Kodak was seriously considering closing its Australian manufacturing operation due to the 35% corporate tax in Australia compared with the 13% in Brazil, the country to which operations would be transferred. The Australian manufacturing plant happened to be located in the electorate of the then Minister for Industry, Commerce and Technology. Ensuing negotiations resulted in Kodak receiving a grant of A$36 million over three years from the Australian government to retain their manufacturing facility in Melbourne and increase the level of export activity from that plant to A$1 billion over the three years. Kodak Australia became one of the most efficient groups in the Kodak organisation as well as one of the research centres for the international group. Kodak's exports had risen to A$600 million by 1996. However on 16 September 2004 Kodak announced that it was shutting its Australian plant by November allegedly because of technology change—digital cameras had caused a global slump in the demand for film.

Situations such as the above can create a precedent. In 2004 Mitsubishi threatened to close at least one of its two car plants in Australia. The federal government then engaged in talks with Mitsibishi Japan to ascertain what incentives would be necessary to avoid these plant closures.

# REGULATOR

Government regulatory activities are often tied in with government planning activities. It is not only current and former Centrally Planned Economies that have five-year plans. Such plans exist in many developing countries and are the basis for economic development activities and funding, including aid. In many Asian countries powerful government planning bodies exist, like Bappenas in Indonesia and the National Economic and Social Development Board in Thailand. Australian and New Zealand businesspeople should study the five-year plans because they indicate not only present priorities but the direction of likely future economic, welfare, industrial and infrastructure development. From these national plans come decisions as to how these priorities will be funded. Funding from within the country is usually by taxation. Some of the means of raising taxes, for example import duties, licensing fees and tax liabilities, have an impact on foreign firms operating in the country. Governments also regulate in terms of setting mandatory standards and by imposing conditions for the repatriation of profits, dividends and royalties, as well as imposing rules covering foreign exchange and by setting exchange rates.

There are several other areas where the government acts as a regulator and which affect Australian and New Zealand firms doing business overseas:

- Governments impose a variety of taxes on business in the Australian and New Zealand markets. Many of these are hidden in the prices firms pay for their inputs and may be levied by state or municipal governments rather than the federal government. They all have the effect of raising costs of products sold overseas and hence they have an impact on the competitive position of the Australian or New Zealand product unless government refunds these taxes when the goods are exported. Payroll tax, road and haulage taxes, inspection fees, duty on imported components are just a few of these taxes.

- Governments impose embargoes on dealing with certain other countries. Sometimes these are applied by most countries and approved by the United Nations, such as the embargo on trading with North Korea introduced in October 2006. In other cases these are imposed by one country alone such as the US embargo on dealing with Cuba. Embargoes distort the free flow of trade in goods, services and ideas and are imposed for political rather than for economic reasons. When embargoes are implemented, they hurt not only the receiving country, but often the firms doing business with that country. Embargoes imposed by governments, especially if directed by one country against another rather than multilaterally, do not usually succeed. This is because evasion is possible using devices such as countertrade or dealing through intermediaries based in countries that do not subscribe to the embargo.

Boycotts are another form of restriction on trade and have come into prominence with conflicts in the Middle East. Arab nations have developed a blacklist of companies that trade

When US President Bill Clinton lifted the US embargo on Vietnam on 4 February 1994 it was estimated that the move would create about A$5.7 billion of business for US firms. Australia and other countries such as France and Japan were likely to be disadvantaged by the US move. This was because they had for a number of years supplied Vietnam with goods that Vietnam might otherwise have sourced from the USA and established joint ventures in Vietnam whose overseas partners might otherwise have been US companies.

## 4.2 INTERNATIONAL HIGHLIGHT

# The sting of sanctions

The effect of sanctions is dramatically illustrated when examining the case of Libya. Following the alleged downing by Libya of a Pan-Am aircraft over Scotland more than a decade ago, the USA imposed sanctions on Libya and encouraged many other countries to do the same. At the same time it banned its firms from engagement with Libya and this caused major economic difficulties, especially as a number of US firms played a major role in extracting the country's oil. It was the economic toll of these sanctions that caused Libya to commence *rapprochement* with the West. This involved Libya paying compensation of US$14 million to the family of each passenger in the downed Pan-Am aircraft and also opening to public scrutiny its earlier activities involving moves to create an atomic bomb and weapons of mass destruction. In November 2004 Libya agreed to abandon its activities to establish a plant for the enrichment of uranium.

with Israel. The USA in turn has created a series of measures to prevent US firms complying with the Arab boycott. Boycotts can put Australian and New Zealand firms in a difficult position if they are already trading with Israel on the one hand or substantially owned by US interests on the other. This issue can become very complex as the following example shows:

> The Clinton administration decided to defer trade sanctions against the French oil firm Total over a US$2 billion gas deal with Iran. It held off on trade sanctions in order to avoid a trade war with the European Union. Under the *Iran-Libya Sanctions Act* of 1996, the administration was expected to impose trade sanctions against any company that invests more than US$40 million in Iran or US$20 million in Libya.

Actions such as the above are controversial as they raise questions of intruding on national sovereignty:

- Governments impose export control measures that are designed to deny or delay the acquisition of strategically important goods by current or potential enemies. In some cases exports are controlled by legislation as with the US *Trading with the Enemy Act* or the *Munitions Control Act*. In other cases control is by bureaucratic approval as in Australia where the export of certain items requires the approval of the Department of Foreign Affairs and Trade. With Australia's procurement of defence equipment from the USA the procurement is actually a 'foreign military sale' by the US government rather than an acquisition direct from the equipment manufacturer.

- Governments impose controls on imports. Often such controls are imposed for balance of payments reasons. Imports may also be banned in order to foster the development of domestic industries. Not only does this affect the Australian exporter but, if the Australian firm is manufacturing in the overseas country imposing the controls, the efficiency of the Australian operation is threatened. This is because the import controls deny the firm access to the cheapest or best quality sources of inputs. A final reason for import controls is that certain goods are considered dangerous or environmentally unsuitable (such as toxic waste), regarded as a health threat (for example, tobacco products) or viewed as being unacceptable on religious grounds. Alcoholic drinks in many Islamic countries, such as Libya and Saudi Arabia, are forbidden due to religious beliefs.

• Joint ventures come under particular scrutiny in countries such as China. Since the first joint ventures in the early 1980s in China, the political process has played a decisive role in their success. Political appointees to the boards of companies such as Hewlett-Packard, one of the very early foreign companies in China, have acted as an important link to the political process. Although this has relaxed somewhat in the late 1990s, Australian and New Zealand businesses need to be aware of these factors and the complex web of politics and government networks before embarking on investment activities.

## POLITICAL APPROACHES IN INTERNATIONAL MARKETING

As the marketing concept evolved in the USA, it tends to be practised most rigorously in countries that are close in ideological terms to that country. Although marketing has no ideology of its own, the way marketing functions are performed varies according to the ideological environment. Marketing managers are a product of their own countries and the underlying ideologies in them. Therefore marketing can operate effectively in countries that are different from Australia and New Zealand although the way in which it operates will differ. This is apparent in the former Centrally Planned Economies that are rapidly adopting a market orientation.

One approach that has an impact on marketing is that of nationalism. A basic and pervasive force, nationalism is present to a degree in all countries. In Australia, for example, it underlies the Republican debate. For many firms venturing offshore, nationalism can be a source of problems. Where nationalism is high, foreign firms tend to be regarded with suspicion and their products are discriminated against. In such circumstances foreign firms are targeted for rigorous scrutiny and control and at worst the assets of the foreign firm can be expropriated.

Often nationalist pressure builds up when people consider a foreign government is interfering in the affairs of their own country. The USA has often caused such manifestations of nationalism when it has applied pressure on other countries to liberalise their import regime for products, especially in the agricultural sector. Examples include pressure on Japan to liberalise rice imports and on the European Union to reduce grain and dairy subsidies.

## POLITICAL STABILITY AND RISK

This is a key concern for the international marketer. Political stability does not mean an absence of change as all markets are continually changing. Rather, political stability means that change should be gradual and non-violent. From a marketing perspective, the change should be such that it has a minimum adverse effect on business activities in the country. In this connection it is necessary to be cautious of labels applied to political change. The perspective held in Australia about political change in Thailand is one of upheaval accompanied by violence, because many of these changes in Thailand are described in the media as coups. For foreign business activities, a coup in Thailand usually means less change in the commercial environment than that which occurs in Australia when there is a change in the party in power (say, from Labor to the Liberal–National coalition).

To assess political stability in a target overseas market an Australian firm should be aware of indicators of political instability. These indicators include:

- the degree of social unrest that is caused by underlying conditions, such as economic hardship, internal dissension and racial, religious and ideological differences;

- the frequency of changes in the regime because these can mean changes in the attitude towards business if the new body in power has a different socioeconomic approach or a different degree of nationalism;

- the extent to which the country is divided culturally and/or ethnically as political borders often contain separate national groups (as in the former Yugoslavia);

- religious division, such as that witnessed in India and Lebanon; and

- linguistic diversity such as Tamil and Sinhalese in Sri Lanka.

The attack on the World Trade Center and the Pentagon on 11 September 2001 was a blow to the collective ego of the USA. It launched the so-called 'war on terrorism' which has resulted in the fabric of US democracy being deeply dented in the interests of political expediency. On 18 October 2006, US President George W. Bush approved legislation that endorsed rendition (the torturing of political prisoners in third countries) and their trial by military tribunals instead of by civil courts in the US. Other overreactions, such as incarceration without trial, denial of access to lawyers for large numbers of prisoners at Guantanamo Bay and human rights abuses in US-run jails in Iraq, have caused the USA to lose its high moral status as the protector of global democracy.

# Sources of political instability

## POLITICAL SOVEREIGNTY

Concerns about political sovereignty lead nations to try to exert control over foreign-owned enterprises operating within their borders. The rules evolve and are predictable. Many less-developed countries impose restrictions on foreign business in order to protect their political independence from foreign economic domination and also the position of local firms in the domestic market. A common form of protection is an increase in taxes payable by foreign corporations. Issues of political sovereignty are mostly encountered in dealings with developing nations.

## POLITICAL CONFLICT

Political conflict can be categorised as turmoil, internal war and conspiracy. Turmoil is generally an unanticipated upheaval on a major scale against a regime, such as the overthrow of the Shah of Iran. Internal war is organised violence on a large scale against a government, such as that which has occurred recently in Sudan and Afghanistan. Conspiracy is an instant planned act of violence against those in power, such as the assassination of Egypt's President Sadat. Political change does not always lead to a less favourable business climate in the long term although the climate may be adversely affected during the period of conflict. This is especially the case if the new government is more favourably disposed towards foreign enterprise than the previous one. (This happened when Suharto replaced Soekarno as President in Indonesia.) In addition, political conflict does not always lead to political risk as the example of Thailand cited earlier shows. Therefore, Australian and New Zealand businesspeople should analyse each occurrence of political conflict and assess whether it is likely to have an impact on their current or proposed business activities in the selected country. This appraisal may cause the firm to change its mode of involvement in the market, for example from a greenfields investment to licensing, rather than totally withdrawing from that market. Political conflict can have direct effects on the foreign firm, such as damage to property, strikes and/or kidnapping of expatriate executives. It can also have indirect effects, such as shortage of inputs, removal of staff to serve in the military and new controls on the firm's operations.

## POLITICAL INTERVENTION

Political intervention occurs when decisions by government(s) in the host country force the foreign firm to change its strategies, policies or operations. Usually this involves governments intervening in the operation of the firm to further their own interests. In many countries, power is exerted by a number of vested interests, many of which see foreign investment as a tempting target. The situation is particularly evident in cases where the foreign plant is located in a regional area where the local government has a degree of autonomy and imposes its own regulations on the firm in addition to those imposed by the central government. Sometimes such intervention can take the form of dictating membership of the board of the joint venture. It can involve making purchases from specified sources mandatory, charging special local taxes and insisting on the right to vet employees so that jobs in the firm can be used to pay off political debts or relationship obligations. Intervention can be more extreme and involve either expropriation or domestication.

*Expropriation* is the official seizure of a foreigner's property in an overseas country on the excuse that the property seized is to be used in the public interest. This is recognised in international law as a right of a sovereign state, provided the foreign party is given adequate compensation. Expropriation has several distinct forms. Nationalisation refers to the transfer of a total industry to public control, regardless of nationality of ownership. Confiscation is expropriation without compensation. In recent times the incidence of expropriation has reduced because, with the reduction in aid, less-developed countries need to attract technology to create an industrial base for survival, and expropriation discourages foreign investment (which is the chief source of technology transfer). On the other hand, there continue to be instances of appropriation for ideological reasons as is the case with white-owned property in Zimbabwe—an action that sends a negative message to potential foreign investors.

*Domestication* is a process by which controls and restrictions placed on the overseas firm gradually reduce the influence of the foreign firm in the operation of the company. These conditions may have been spelled out as part of the original approval or may have since been instituted by government fiat. Domestication is less radical than expropriation because it allows the foreign party to continue to operate in the country. It takes several forms. It can include gradual transfer of ownership to nationals and promotion of a large number of employees of the country to high levels of management as well as ensuring more decision making power vested in national employees. It also may include products being manufactured locally as opposed to being imported or assembled, and the introduction of specific export regulations which restrict the export activities of the foreign partner.

# Nature of political risk

Political risk varies considerably from country to country. Countries that have a track record of stability and consistency are perceived to be lower in political risk than those that do not. Taking the previous discussion into account, there are three main types of political risk:

1 *general instability risk,* which is risk due to internal threats such as revolution or external threats to the government such as invasion;

2 *ownership risk,* which is risk to property and the lives of the expatriate employees; *operating risk,* which is interference in the ongoing operations of the company overseas; and

3 *transfer risk,* which occurs when the firm is prevented from moving funds between countries or back home, for example repatriation of profits, capital and dividends.

According to Hadjikhani and Hakansson (1996):

> *Sometimes political risk can arise from the actions of a fellow national company. As an example, when Bofors of Sweden was accused of unethical involvement with Prime Minister Rajiv Gandhi and his Congress Party, other Swedish firms operating in India were affected to differing degrees.*

## Assessment

Because political risk is so pervasive, especially in developing countries, its assessment is increasingly important. Political risk assessment is necessary to identify the countries of today which may become the Irans or Afghanistans of tomorrow, so that firms can protect themselves by minimising their exposure; it may reveal countries which are currently politically unstable; it can identify those countries which were considered a bad risk in the past, but which are now less risky; finally it can help identify those countries that, although politically risky at present, are not so risky as to be excluded from consideration. These countries have a potential for risk that needs to be taken into account when planning entry strategy and involvement.

Jain (1996) offers four methods for determining political risk:

1 *The grand tour*: An executive team visits the country in which investment is being considered following the conduct of market research. A first-hand appraisal involving meetings with government officials and local businesses will yield information as to the likely level of political risk. This can be misleading, however, because those contacted usually represent the establishment and not the sources of future political risk.

2 *The old hand*: This method employs an expert on the country as a consultant. Usually such people are educators, former diplomats or trade commissioners, local political figures or business identities. Not only will the capability and experience of the consultant be a determinant of the accuracy of the resulting report, but if the person is not a national the quality will be affected by how recent the consultant's experience is of the country. If, on the other hand, the consultant is a national the quality of the report may be influenced by the breadth of the consultant's network of local contacts.

3 *The Delphi technique*: This technique involves asking a group of experts on the country to share their opinions independently. Opinions are scored on various aspects of potential political risk in a manner that will produce a statistical distribution of opinion. The experts are then shown the resulting distribution and given the opportunity to modify

their opinion on each aspect. This process may be repeated several times and a decision made on the basis of the final round.

4   *Quantitative methods*: The most common method for measuring political risk is discriminant analysis. This involves developing a mathematical relationship between a series of quantifiable factors in order to predict the likelihood of certain events, through the collection of different forms of data and expert interpretation of results.

There are a number of political risk assessment indices published by bodies such as the Economist Intelligence Unit which are updated at regular intervals. Frost & Sullivan (<http://www.frost.com>), using a worldwide panel of experts, compiles 18-month forecasts of regime stability, restrictions on international business activity and controls on trade and economic policy for 85 countries. These forecasts develop general measures of risk not related to the specific situation of the firm.

Any appraisal of a firm's exposure to political risk in an overseas country should at least cover four factors—general political environment, product, external and company:

1   *General political environment factors*: This takes into account the general nature of the political situation in the overseas country (see Fisher et al. 2006, p. 129):

- Is the country a democracy or dictatorship?

- Does the government rely on the free market or on itself to allocate resources?

- Are the customers for the products or services to be offered in the public or the private sector and, if the latter, is there a policy of preferment for local firms?

- When changing policies, does the government rely on the rule of law or act arbitrarily?

- How stable is the existing government and does political change result in major changes to economic policies?

2   *Product-related factors*: These include an assessment of whether the product is a likely topic of political debate in terms of a number of questions:

- What is the effect of adequate supply on the country's security or welfare?

- Is the product a critical input for other industries?

- Is the product socially or politically sensitive, as with food and drugs?

- Does the product have national defence significance, as with uranium?

3   *External factors*: These include the following considerations:

- the state of relations between the government of Australia or New Zealand and the government of the other country;

- the size of the Australian or New Zealand firm because the larger it is the more threatening it may appear to be; and

- the extent to which the firm has visibility as a foreign business—the larger its visibility, the greater its vulnerability.

4   *Company factors*: These factors include:

- the general reputation of the firm overseas as a good corporate citizen;

- the extent of past contributions by the firm to the welfare and development of the host country; and

- the extent to which operations in the country have been localised.

There are a number of published political risk guides that assess various countries in terms of risk factors such as frustration of contracts, unfair calling of performance bonds and confiscation of foreign assets. The rate to insure against the risk is given for each of these factors and, in the case of contract frustration, information is often provided as to the waiting period before the contract is deemed to have been frustrated.

A preliminary indication of assessed political risk attributed to a country can be obtained from the LIBOR (London Interbank) rate. This is the interest rate charged for loans between banks. Borrowers from a country with a high risk of default must expect to pay a high premium. The premium is a reasonable indication of risk since it reflects a lender's assessment of a country in terms of its debt level and payment history.

## The trade-off

There is often a trade-off between perceived political instability on the one hand and growth prospects on the other. Nowhere is this more likely to occur than in the Arab world. This is a diverse region and there are differences between the Gulf Arabs, the North African Arabs and the East Mediterranean Arabs. Despite changes since the mid-1980s in social, cultural and economic conditions, the Arab world is still associated with a lack of attractiveness from a political perspective. This is due to the Middle East peace process, the rise of Islamic fundamentalism and the instability of regimes pursuing economic, but not political liberalisation (Trimeche 2004). This can be off-putting to foreign firms, especially when nations in the region (with the exception of Tunisia) all have suffered either war, internal unrest or serious border disputes (Beshara 1999).

# MANAGING THE OVERSEAS POLITICAL ENVIRONMENT

A company involved in dealing with an overseas nation can take a number of measures to minimise potential political problems.

## Company behaviour

Firms can adopt a deliberate policy of political neutrality and convey the impression that its interests in the country are solely economic. Companies should also be conscious as to which political labels are acceptable and which are not because use of the wrong label can denote political sympathy for a particular group.

Companies should ensure that they combine investment projects with civic projects. If the firm has its manufacturing operation in a town, it should examine ways of becoming a major benefactor in that town by supporting education, health and community projects that will benefit its local workforce. Contributions to local infrastructure development are likely to benefit not only the community, but also the company.

If the policies of the country could cause offence in either the Australian market or in other markets with which the company is involved, it may be necessary for the firm wholly or partially to disengage itself from a country. This is especially the case if that country is the target of sanctions as was the case with South Africa during the apartheid regime.

Another risk-minimisation activity includes lobbying by the firm to influence political decisions. In the public arena publicity to focus on the benefits the firm's operation is bringing to the country can be a useful risk-minimisation strategy. Finally, just as embassies monitor what the political opposition in a country is doing, so foreign firms should also be aware of the likely impact on their operations of the policies espoused by those who might

## 4.3 INTERNATIONAL HIGHLIGHT

# China punishes firms over use of the term 'Taiwan'

China has threatened to punish Japan's Matsushita Communications Industrial Co. for making mobile phones that refer to Taiwan as a country. Its Panasonic brand of mobile phones includes the Republic of China in an electronic list of country codes. The Republic of China is the Taiwan government's designation for the island, a name Beijing rejects because it regards Taiwan as its own territory, although the two have been divided for more than five decades following civil war.

A spokesperson for China's Ministry of Information Industry said that Matsushita may have to cease assembly of mobile phones at its Chinese joint venture. The impending ban is likely to cover all five models of mobile phones the firm makes in China. Matsushita's Beijing operation, which has the capacity to make two million mobile phones a year, accounts for a fraction of the company's global output. However, getting on China's bad side helped drive down the price of Matsushita's shares on the Tokyo stock exchange by 7.9%.

**SOURCE:** *Adapted from* Wall Street Journal, *Europe, 7–8 September 2001, p. 7.*

form alternative governments. Such monitoring is likely to reduce surprises from political upheavals in the country.

Above all, firms should display political sensitivity in their dealings involving overseas countries. This applies both to the use of country names (see International Highlight 4.3) and to names used for geographical features.

Both Iran and Iraq lay claim to the gulf of water that separates them. While the Iranians refer to it as the Persian Gulf (the name used by the United Nations), the Iraqis refer to it as the Arabian Gulf. In dealing with either country, using an inappropriate term on official documents, such as export labels or contracts, can cause serious difficulties for the business involved as well as for the firm's local partners or representatives.

In a similar fashion, it is unwise to categorise people who are located adjacent to each other in the same way. Despite geographical proximity and some cultural similarity, Arabs and Persians are completely separate peoples and resent being misidentified or grouped together. Arabs are of Semitic background and are originally from the Arabian peninsula and the Levant. Their language belongs to the same family as Aramaic and Hebrew. Persians are ethnically Caucasian and their language, Farsi, is of Indo-European origin.

**SOURCE:** *Adapted from the Department of Foreign Affairs and Trade (2000)* Accessing Middle-East Growth: Business Opportunities in the Arabian Peninsula and Iran, *East Asia Analytical Unit, Department of Foreign Affairs and Trade, Commonwealth of Australia, Canberra, p. 53.*

## Home government actions

Actions by the Australian or New Zealand governments or their representatives towards an overseas country can both enhance or retard the position of their firms in that country. Giving aid to countries such as Indonesia, providing financial rescue packages as in propping up the Thai baht or according diplomatic recognition as in the case of Vietnam in 1972 are examples of Australian government actions that can enhance commercial prospects and reduce the likelihood of political problems for Australian companies.

Criticising the leaders of countries can cause problems for firms. For example, when Prime Minister Keating accused Malaysian Prime Minister Mahatir in 1995 of being 'recalcitrant' it may have contributed to the failure of Transfield Corporation to win a major contract to supply patrol boats to the Malaysian navy. Problems can also be caused by the failure of government to control criticism in the media of actions by other countries. This difficulty is compounded when the media involved is owned by the government, as is the case with the Australian Broadcasting Corporation (ABC). In many nations government-run media act as the official mouthpiece for government policy. Such nations find it hard to believe that criticism by the ABC does not reflect the views of the Australian government.

## Contribution to the host country

Firms that set out to be good corporate citizens of the host country are more likely to evade the consequences of political upheaval and minimise potential political risk. Good corporate citizens stimulate the local economy by linking their commercial activities to the host nation's economic interests and planned developments—buying local products whenever possible, forming alliances or joint ventures with local firms, establishing training programs for local employees and demonstrably upgrading technology levels. Using the operation to generate exports, recruiting locals to occupy senior management positions and converting the firm from a private to a public company by listing on the local stock exchange are additional ways of minimising political risk.

Increasingly, Chinese firms are both investing in and taking action to protect their position in Australia. When their son was kidnapped in Sydney, the Liu family from Shanghai was able to produce several pages listing their investments in Australia, to prove they could pay the ransom if needed. Included in this list was the building housing the headquarters of the New South Wales Police. Chinese entrepreneurs also protect their position in Australia by making donations to political parties as is the case with the Shimao Property Group which in 2002–03 was the largest individual donor to the NSW Branch of the Australian Labor Party.

## Localisation of operations

The greater the local ownership of an operation, the less likely it will be subject to political risk. Pressure to indigenise operations can come not only from political upheaval, but also from the established government changing its foreign investment policy, as happened in India in 1973. When a country for political reasons demands that foreign firms reduce their ownership and surrender equity to local interests, the firm has to decide on the degree of its disengagement. In their article, 'Foreign ownership: when hosts change the rules', Encarnation and Vachani (1985) offer four alternative courses of action for the company:

1  leave the country altogether (like IBM in India);

2  totally indigenise operations so it becomes a local company (like Colgate-Palmolive in India);

3  negotiate an arrangement under the new law (like Ciba-Geigy in India); or

4  take pre-emptive action in advance of announced changes. Phased indigenisation is one such action and may enable the firm to benefit from a range of investment incentives.

Another is to generate sizeable exports to step up the host government's dependency on the operation.

## Globalisation

Firms that set up operations overseas may have operations in other countries and aspire to rationalise their operations globally. This may cause political problems because there can be a divergence between maximising returns to their shareholders on the one hand and being a good corporate citizen of the countries in which they are operating on the other. Often these conflicts in interest cause problems in the company's relationship with the government of the host country. One frequent example of this is in the area of taxation. In order to minimise taxation liability on a global basis, firms structure international operations so that via transfer pricing the majority of profits are brought to account in the lowest tax regime countries in which the firm operates. This results in the host country not receiving the full tax revenue on the real profits earned as a result of activities undertaken within its boundaries.

Other problems arise when the firm wishes to reduce costs by standardising its product, pricing, promotion and distribution strategies on a global basis. This can create political problems, for example when the standardisation contravenes regulations in the host country. The issue has become more complicated with the global spread of communication through global or regional media and the internet, because now national governments are less able to control messages received within their national borders.

## Political risk insurance

In addition to actions to reduce risk and to avoid risk, Australian firms can shift risk by insuring against it. Although this can be done through private insurers, the main agency in Australia is the government-operated Export Finance Insurance Corporation (EFIC). This was set up to insure against those risks of exporting and investing overseas not normally covered by commercial insurers, one of which is political risk. The premiums for political risk will vary according to: (a) the country concerned; and (b) whether the company insures all its overseas transactions with EFIC as opposed to only the risky ones. A range of politically induced risks can be insured against, including currency inconvertibility, expropriation of assets and loss/damage due to war, revolution or insurrection.

## Marketing implications—political

The international marketer should carefully examine the political climate in an overseas market before making a commitment to that country because the political situation may not be compatible with profitable business. Political sovereignty, desire by the government to assert its authority and internal or external political conflict all threaten profitable business. The history of intervention by the governments of the country in foreign business activities should be studied, as should the form of such intervention. An analysis of political risk should be undertaken which covers the form of government, its stability, competence in economic management, frequency of changes in policy towards foreign investment and the nature of the relationship between the government and its people. An indication of general country risk should be obtained from a risk-monitoring agency and then risk-assessment techniques applied to cater for the individual circumstances of the firm in the specific overseas market.

## Political winds of change

Prior to the 1979 Iranian revolution, the Shah n Shah (King of Kings) appeared firmly entrenched and operated from the Niavarin Palace guiding the destiny of his people. The 2500th anniversary of the Persian civilisation had been celebrated at Persepolis a few years before with international fanfare. Coffers flush with relatively new-found oil wealth, the Shah was spurring on the country's economic development by creating alternative sources of export income against the day the oil dried up. Imports were flooding the country, creating port congestion of up to nine months. US President Carter, in Tehran several months before the revolution took place, did not foresee it and on that occasion praised Iran under the leadership of the Shah as 'an island of stability in one of the more troubled areas of the world'. At that time US political assessment agencies rated Iran as a low political risk. Australia, along with other countries, was courting the regime. A stream of cabinet ministers and officials visited Tehran at every opportunity pursuing trade opportunities. The Australian commercial sector treated Iran as the most important country in the Middle East. The Australian Meat Board had its regional headquarters in the capital and with government support and financial backing (from the Export Finance and Insurance Corporation), a multimillion dollar consortium was established (AUSTIRAN) to revolutionise trade between the two countries.

Two years later the Shah was gone; the ministers so assiduously cultivated by Australian businesspeople and officials had been shot or had fled; AUSTIRAN was an unfulfilled dream; and Australian operations had either retreated to Australia or re-established their Middle East presence in other countries. Why did no one foresee the Islamic revolution? Western nations were caught short, but could it have been foreseen? Changes of this kind are usually the product of a slow build-up of internal pressure that is triggered by some event. Were there signs that everyone ignored?

In 2004, 25 years after the Iranian revolution, Iran was dubbed 'The Mideast's Model Economy' by the conservative US magazine, *BusinessWeek*. Those who fled overseas were moving back, internet users numbered 1.3 million, 3.4 million Iranians owned mobile phones, GDP growth had exceeded 5% for the previous four years, foreign exchange reserves were over US$35 billion, its 69 million people made it the largest market in the region and 60% of its population were not born when the revolution occurred. The constraints of Islamic fundamentalism had relaxed, politicians were increasingly concerned about economics and the business climate continued to improve. Gradually, the government is opening the country to the outside world and the pressures of the global economy. The case of Iran reflects that politics are continually changing and reading them the wrong way at a point in time can adversely affect your chances of business in the overseas market in the future.

**SOURCE:** *Adapted from 'The Mideast's model economy', BusinessWeek, 24 May 2004, pp. 30–3.*

## The internet and the international political environment

While the internet empowers customers, it enables sellers to have unfettered access to information related to customers' preferences and buying profiles. This raises the issue of the right to privacy of citizens of a country and the ability of governments to control its citizens and control what happens economically within its borders. The approach to protection of privacy versus commercialisation of data about people varies from country to country. Whereas, in general, Americans see privacy as a commodity and the issue one of control over property rights, Europeans tend to view privacy as an inalienable human right that should not be traded in the marketplace.

The internet can threaten national sovereignty and political stability by providing a vehicle for minority groups within a national boundary to advance the cause of self-determination. With the advent of the internet, the national government no longer has complete control over the media or the content of messages disseminated within its borders. Related to this is the issue of free speech. Whereas in the marketplace governments have the power to regulate forms of speech the content of which is regarded as reprehensible or offensive to national wellbeing, the new information infrastructure diminishes this control because, to date, censorship of the internet has not proved possible. The internet also makes it more difficult for governments to regulate national commerce in the interests of the economic wellbeing and safety of its citizens. How can governments license service providers such as doctors and lawyers who practise globally over the internet?

Governments also collect taxes and duties and control capital flows into and out of their geographical jurisdiction. The internet has increased the level of interference of external parties in these areas and facilitated evasion of the economic rents governments levy on external entities and transnational corporations in the national interest. Governments face a problem in regulating and levying taxes on internet transactions because these might adversely influence national competitiveness due to the effects on knowledge diffusion, investment flows and cost–price structures of industries compared to other nations. Whereas in the international marketplace issues are addressed by public choice, with a focus on how firms in host countries might raise protectionist barriers against foreign firms, in 'marketspace' local firms will seek from government regulations that will give them advantages over other countries in attracting internet companies. The emphasis shifts from protecting what you have to attracting what you do not.

The Australian government has been addressing the need for rules to regulate e-commerce on both a national and an international basis. It sees the need for both unfettered markets on the one hand and non-restrictive ground rules on the other.

# THE LEGAL ENVIRONMENT

## 4.5 INTERNATIONAL HIGHLIGHT

## China's legal and arbitration systems

The Chinese legal system is still developing and Chinese courts do not use the Anglo-American common law tradition of following precedent and requiring publication of cases. Responsible ministries determine, interpret and supervise relevant regulations and many judicial judgements are difficult to enforce due to a property rights regime that is still developing and the lack of an effective enforcement mechanism. As a consequence of these factors, foreigners cannot rely on Chinese courts for prompt and predictable

**4.5 INTERNATIONAL HIGHLIGHT** *(continued)*

resolution of disputes or contract judgement. Because of these circumstances, most foreign businesses in China do not generally favour resolving commercial disputes through the courts, but rather via arbitration. The China International Economic Trade Arbitration Commission is the main body used for Sino-foreign dispute resolution in China. Another arbitration body is the Beijing Arbitration Commission. Enforcing awards remains a challenge as, under local law, foreign-related awards can only be challenged on procedural grounds, not on substantive grounds as with domestic awards. Enforcement remains problematic due to local protectionism and the lack of experience of local courts in dealing with international legal matters.

**SOURCE:** *East Asia Analytical Unit (2005),* Unlocking China's Services Sector, *Department of Foreign Affairs and Trade, Canberra. Copyright Commonwealth of Australia, reproduced with permission.*

## Introduction

International trade involves two or more countries and usually two or more legal systems. Hence the legal complexities are greater with international trade than they are with domestic trade. The Australian international business executive does not need to be aware of the detail of the law as it applies in each overseas market. Rather, the executive needs to be sensitive to the broad principles of law as it applies to doing business abroad and the way the law varies in implementation between different countries. Such sensitivity will alert the executive as to legal pitfalls and when to seek legal advice if entering into transactions or if faced with specific issues.

It is important to appreciate that there is no single uniform commercial law which governs foreign business transactions. Although the lack of such law and the need for it has been commented upon in different forums, nothing of importance has resulted. As a consequence marketers have to operate under different legal systems whenever they venture offshore. The legal environment for international business consists primarily of the laws and courts of the many nations in the world. These national systems vary in philosophy and practice, and each nation maintains a court system that is independent of those in every other nation. The differences between legal systems and the laws in various countries affect the practice of international marketing in many ways.

**4.6 INTERNATIONAL HIGHLIGHT**

## When is a contract legal?

n 1977 the Australian media carried extensive critical reports of the Japanese evading payment on a long-term contract for the supply of sugar from Australia. Frequent attempts were made by officials of both the Australian and Queensland governments to resolve the issue and eventually the dispute escalated to the stage where ministers became involved. When the stand-off resulted in 30 ships carrying 230 000 tonnes of sugar lying unloaded at Yokohama Bay, the Australian and Japanese prime ministers intervened and a solution was reached. At the heart of the dispute were differing views as to what constituted a contract and the obligations associated with it.

By way of background, in 1974 the international price of sugar escalated from US$143 per tonne to a record level of US$650 by October. In December, a long-term contract (five years) was entered into between the Australian sugar industry represented by CSR and the Japanese sugar refining industry represented by Mitsui and Mitsubishi. This contract involved the supply of Australian sugar at stg 229 per tonne at a time when the equivalent international price was stg 400 per tonne. Australian sugar growers used the security of the long-term contract to acquire more land for the growing of the sugar to meet the requirements of the contract. The long-term contract was supported by an exchange of letters between the governments of both countries. Almost immediately after the signing of the contract, the world price for sugar began to fall and by July 1975 was stg 130 per tonne. The Japanese refiners, faced with growing inventories, stagnant demand and escalating deficits, wanted the long-term contract immediately reviewed in line with the provision in the contract that 'both contractors shall re-examine the operation and continuity of this contract at least once a year'.

Although the Australian parties were willing to review the contract, they believed that any review should not occur until the contract had been operating for two years. In addition, they believed that the situation of the Japanese refiners was largely due to their excess capacity and inefficiencies. Hence the Australian parties required as a condition of agreeing to a review of the contract that there be some rationalisation of the Japanese sugar refining industry so as to avoid a repeat of the current situation. They suggested that this could be achieved by the removal of the sugar import duty and commodity tax. The Japanese viewed these suggestions as interference and rejected the Australian offer. Despite several minor compromises by each side, the dispute dragged on. CSR then engineered the involvement of the Australian government on the basis that the contract had been supported by an exchange of letters between the two governments. In addition they increased the pressure on the Japanese by holding a series of press conferences to present the Australian side of the argument. This further upset the Japanese government who considered that the matter should be treated on a commercial basis and resolved between the contracting parties.

The Japanese approach in demanding a renegotiation of the contract was in accordance with their norms of behaviour which accepted that if a contract could no longer be adhered to without suffering being caused due to changed circumstances, then the other party was obliged to agree to renegotiate the contract. This position led the Japanese sugar refiners to cancel the long-term contract and reject the sugar. Following the intervention of Prime Ministers Tanaka and Fraser, the dispute was eventually resolved in 1977 by a lower price being agreed to with the offset of a new contract involving an increased tonnage. The dispute had at its heart a different view of the law of contracts.

Reviewing the issue some 25 years later, sugar trade between Japan and Australia continues and the outcome illustrates the wisdom of 'not closing the door' whatever your perceived wrongs and rights might be. The Japanese government never fully implemented the reform of the sugar refining industry. A more recent analysis of the issue by Welch and Wilkinson (2004) argues that the case illustrates three types of political activity that firms might take:

- policy making—by becoming insiders via regular working parties with Japanese officials, CSR was able to engage in information exchange and influence Japanese decision making to its benefit and to the disadvantage of its competitors;

- policy learning—this was the result of the experiential knowledge CSR gained from having to identify decision makers, understand how policy was made, keep abreast of policy changes and become involved in related networks;

- international diplomacy—CSR became actively involved in the operation of multilateral agreements, such as the Commonwealth Sugar Agreement (CSA) and the International Sugar Agreement (ISA), as well as in the negotiation of bilateral arrangements such as that with Japan.

# DIFFERING LEGAL SYSTEMS AND JURISDICTIONS

In the global economy there are a variety of legal systems and diversity in the application of laws. In Asia many governments have neglected laws, regulations and property rights that control the excesses of capitalism. This has caused crippling of the financial and banking system resulting in intervention by the International Money Fund as happened with the Asian currency crisis of 1997.

The two most common are based on common law and civil law. Therefore the foreign marketer must be aware of both the legal system which operates in the overseas market and the specific laws impinging on business activities and marketing practice.

# Legal systems

## COMMON LAW

This operates in the UK, Canada, the USA and many of the former colonies and dominions of the UK including Australia and New Zealand. It is based on tradition, past practices, legal precedent and interpretation via court decisions. The interpretation of what the law means on a specific subject is influenced by previous decisions of the courts as well by usage and custom. If there is no precedent common law requires the court to make a decision that in effect creates a new law. Under common law commercial disputes are subject to laws that apply to all matters, regardless of whether civil or commercial. This is because under common law there is no specific recognition of commercial problems as such.

## CODE LAW

Code law derives from Roman law and is found in most countries where common law is not used. It is based on an all-inclusive system of written rules (codes) of law. The legal system is generally divided into three separate codes—civil, commercial and criminal. Because of its 'catch all' provisions, code law is considered to be complete and caters for most contingencies. As an example, the commercial code governing contracts is made inclusive via a clause to the effect that 'a person performing a contract shall do so in conformity with good faith as determined by custom and good morals'. Under code law the commercial code is given precedence over other codes when matters of business are involved. With code law the courts adopt precedents to fit the case thereby allowing marketers a better idea of the judgement likely to be rendered.

## ISLAMIC LAW

Islamic law is based on the Koran and is applied by Islamic countries in varying degrees. It encompasses religious duties and obligations and also the secular aspect of law, especially relating to human acts. An example is the right of relatives to determine punishment, as was the case in the 1997 trial of two British nurses for the alleged murder of an Australian colleague in Saudi Arabia. It defines a complete system of social and economic behaviour with the overriding objective of social justice. It is often applied in conjunction with code or common law. In Islamic societies aspects of law can influence the nature of economic development. Inheritance law makes it difficult to keep property intact over generations and has led to the creation of small partnerships whose limited economic viability has discouraged efficient organisational structures. Furthermore, the system of Waqf (an incorporated trust to fund a service in perpetuity as with the operation of a school) has resulted in public services not being provided by the state and this in turn has inhibited the 'rule of law'.

## OTHER LEGAL CODES

Included in this group are tribal or indigenous laws such as traditional Aboriginal or Maori law and socialist laws based on the tenets of Marxism. These laws are rarely applied by themselves. They are usually applied in conjunction with the prevailing common or civil code of law.

The reality is that the legal system in most countries is a blend of different legal systems. Even in common law countries there are examples of code law such as the Uniform Commercial Code in the USA. In Afghanistan the legal system is a blend of Islamic and indigenous law and in Sri Lanka the legal system is a blend of indigenous and common law. The following is a comparison of the two most common systems:

- *industrial property rights*: under common law ownership is established by use, whereas under code law ownership is determined by registration;

- *performance of contract*: under common law impossibility of performance does not excuse compliance with contract provisions unless caused by 'an act of God'. Under code law impossibility of performance is an acceptable excuse whether due to the elements, natural causes or unfavourable human acts;

- *interpretation of contract*: this can differ as seen in the Australia–Japan sugar dispute (see International Highlight 4.6). Whereas to Australians operating under common law the contract was a binding obligation, to the Japanese the contract was a piece of paper that operated as a memorandum of an understanding reached between buyer and seller. According to the Japanese Commercial Code article 415, 'if performance has become impossible for any cause for which the obligor is responsible, the obligee may sue and recover damages. If the obligor is not responsible for the impossibility, the other party cannot claim damages.'

Countries differ not only in terms of legal systems, but also in the degree to which the law is applied on an equitable basis and the extent to which commercial disputes are settled by the courts or by arbitration/negotiation. Furthermore, once a decision has been made, countries vary in the extent to which such awards are enforceable. International Highlight 4.5 illustrated this in respect of China.

The arrest, on arrival in Abu Dhabi, of three Australian first-class passengers travelling on Ethiad Airlines in May 2007 highlights the issue of globalisation versus national sovereignty. In this case, behaviour which would be judged by most authorities in Western countries as a minor transgression was deemed by authorities in Abu Dhabi to be immoral and liable for extreme penalties. Allegedly the passengers became rowdy, abusive and made disparaging remarks to female cabin attendants when their expectations of first-class service were not met by the airline. This resulted in a complaint by airline staff to the authorities who promptly threw them into jail where they remained for 10 days before being deported back to Australia. Ethiad, which is endeavouring to become a global airline and which had only recently commenced services to Australia, will, as a consequence of the publicity surrounding the incident, find passengers in Western countries reluctant to fly an airline that applies the stringent laws of its home country to passengers who transgress its norms of acceptable behaviour. This raises the issue of whose laws should apply in cases of this kind—the laws of the originating country, the laws of the destination country, the laws of the country of which the passenger is a citizen or the laws of the intermediate stop at which the passengers are removed from the aircraft. Possibly there is a need for an international body of law to apply in situations of this kind.

## International law

International law grows out of the agreement of two or more nations and implies a desire to lessen differences in the way countries treat legal problems. Generally, international law minimises the range of differences between national laws, for example international patent agreements. Traditionally, international law has only been concerned with relations between nations with a principal focus on political and military issues. However, the coverage in recent years has become much broader and now can include international trade and investment, taxation, labour relations, intellectual property and the environment. Whereas only nations used to be recognised as subjects for international law, today international organisations and their agencies are also covered. International law is reflected in the determinations of multilateral bodies such as the World Trade Organization and the United Nations. Probably the most important attempt to promote harmonisation of international trade law was the establishment of the United Nations Commission on International Trade Law (UNICITRAL). It has produced a set of rules governing arbitration (1976); a Convention on the Carriage of Goods by Sea (1987); a Convention on Contracts for the International Sale of Goods (1980); and a Model Law on International Commercial Arbitration (1985). Increasingly, the determinations of regional bodies such as ASEAN have led to the creation of laws applied on a regional basis. Within the European Union, for example, one of the essential requirements for integration has been the harmonisation of laws of member states affecting international business. Once such harmonisation is achieved one common law is applied to the member states.

With both multilateral and regional bodies, after agreement is reached on issues that are to be binding upon their members, it is up to individual national governments to legislate the issue into their domestic law. For this reason, even when agreement is reached on matters to be covered by international law, implementation will vary widely between signatories. As a consequence there is no such thing as international law for business activities, only the application of domestic law to international disputes. The need for a larger body of international law is likely to grow due to increasing problems in the area of protection of intellectual property and the information revolution, rendering international boundaries of decreasing relevance. Another problem can arise when a bilateral agreement between two countries is alleged to be in conflict with international law. This is illustrated by the Timor Gap Treaty between Australia and Indonesia.

As of 2004, there were 191 member countries in the United Nations, but only 56 of them recognised the jurisdiction of the International Court of Justice—Australia does and Indonesia does not. Australia, in a case brought to the court by Portugal, defended its right to join Indonesia in developing the oil resource in the Timor Sea. Portugal's challenge rested on the view that the Timor Gap Treaty between Australia and Indonesia was illegal because the United Nations had not recognised Indonesia's sovereignty over East Timor. Under the terms of their 1989 treaty Australia and Indonesia agreed to develop jointly oil and gas in the Timor Sea and share the revenue. Since the independence of East Timor jurisdictional aspects of the issue have changed, especially because East Timor is looking to use the oil reserves to underwrite its future national development. In the resulting negotiations the issue of legal boundaries was tempered with arguments of natural justice. The matter was resolved in September 2004 by a compromise arrangement whereby Australia did not renounce its sovereignty over the disputed area, but agreed to a revenue sharing deal that would give East Timor A$5 billion in tax and royalty payments from the massive natural gas project. Without the security of such an arrangement the consortium to develop the resource was threatening to pull out of the Greater Sunrise Project.

Underlying disputes such as the above as well as the dispute between Malaysia and Indonesia over their maritime boundary, are new found riches such as oil and natural gas.

# Legal jurisdiction

A common legal problem in international business is determining which country's laws apply in the event of a dispute. This is decided according to whether the country is nominated in the jurisdictional clause in the contract, where the contract was entered into or where the provisions of the contract are to be carried out. As the last two can differ, it is important to have a specific jurisdictional clause included in the contract so as to avoid the problem of determining jurisdiction after a dispute has arisen.

Where a jurisdiction is nominated, as in the state of New South Wales, the law of that jurisdiction is likely to apply regardless of where the suit is filed. Where no jurisdiction is nominated, then the suit is likely to be heard in either the country where the contract was entered into or the country where the provisions of the contract are to be carried out. This can become the subject of dispute.

Jurisdiction can be further complicated when different sets of laws are alleged to apply, for example where:

- the practice of international law conflicts with national law (as with the Law of Japan);

- one nation endeavours to impose its laws on another, for example when the USA attempts to enforce its Anti-Trust Legislation extraterritorially; or

- businesspeople operating in an overseas country are required to conform to the laws of their country of citizenship. For example, there have been many US attempts to enforce the *Foreign Corrupt Practices Act* in matters of bribery.

Due to the above, when operating offshore a businessperson can at the one time be subject to two or more sets of law, depending on the number of countries involved.

The USA argues that where foreign transactions have a substantial effect on US commerce they are subject to US law regardless of where they take place. Australia rejects this approach as far as government and the private sector are concerned. The USA tried to apply anti-trust action worldwide in the case of uranium, directed at preventing Australian producers continuing discussions with non-US producers with the object of stabilising prices. Australia enacted legislation to curtail this interference in 1976 and 1979 and influenced the signing of a bilateral Anti-Trust Agreement between Australia and the USA in 1982.

Even within an overseas country the Australian or New Zealand businessperson may be subject to federal, state and municipal laws and regulations. The degree to which these overlap is often a function of the development of law within the country and the extent to which it can be enforced. For instance in some developing countries the central government has only token control over some regional areas within the national boundaries.

# Legal risk

Legal risk is the likelihood of unfavourable outcomes due to legal uncertainties. It can arise from non-compliance with laws and regulations; from changes in laws and regulations; from failure to protect the firm's legal rights and interests; from contractual and non-contractual liabilities and from disputes and litigation (Frick 2006). As is evident from the above, there is in many instances an overlap between legal risks and political risks with one often giving rise to the other.

# LAW AND THE MARKETING MIX OVERSEAS

The law as it applies to commercial activities varies between countries even when the countries operate under the same legal system. This situation complicates the creation of a common marketing plan for implementation in several countries at the same time. The laws governing each element of the marketing mix vary between countries.

## Product

Both the physical and chemical aspects of a product are affected by laws seeking to protect consumers. Such laws may prescribe standards for purity, safety and performance. In Australia it is an offence to use lead-based paint on children's toys. Even where countries have laws covering the same issue the standards to which the product must conform can vary. Permissible crowd numbers for theme park rides considered safe in Queensland would not be acceptable in the USA. Because nations differ in rigorousness or even the existence of standards, it is often necessary for a country to impose quarantine controls or ban products from certain countries of origin. There have been cases of children's toys imported into Australia being stuffed with soiled hospital bandages. There can also be instances where the regulations and laws applying to imports have been imposed more to protect the domestic industry than the health and safety of Australian citizens, for example the 180-day quarantine period applied to some cheeses from Europe!

Laws also apply to packaging and may specify the type of outer packaging material and the nature of the container. Labelling regulations differ markedly between countries and even within a country. There is a lack of uniformity in labelling regulations between the states in Australia, but there is usually a legal basis for such regulations as in the case of the *Pure Foods Act*. Labelling requirements may decree that the ingredients be specified, the packing or expiry date be shown, the volume of the contents be in metric or imperial measure and the name and address of the manufacturer and/or importer be shown. Even the size of print for each piece of information is often prescribed.

## Price

The free-market system does not operate in many countries and national health laws and government price controls can have a significant impact on the prices that may be charged in an overseas market. Generally, price controls are motivated by a desire to protect consumers' interests or control inflation. These are the primary roles of the Australian Competition and Consumer Commission (ACCC). Other laws relating to pricing may be motivated by a desire to ensure price competition in the market. These laws cover areas such as retail price maintenance, action to discriminate against competitors, limitations of licensing and franchising agreements and collusive action in setting prices, whether directly or indirectly, via mechanisms such as discriminatory rebates. In some countries the prices of essential commodities are controlled, as are some non-essential items.

Other laws that affect pricing include those relating to dumping (selling goods below current domestic value in the country of origin) and transfer pricing (undervaluing the price of product exported from an overseas operation to another division of the firm so as to avoid/minimise tax payable in the country of manufacture). Also in this category are laws that relate to the size of the profit margin included in the price. Price is also affected by taxes such as sales tax, value-added tax, import tax and port tax.

## Distribution

There are laws in most countries covering physical distribution of products. These relate to shipping, such as the use of Australian-registered vessels in the Australian coastal trade, and rights of carriage by air and sea. Regulation of airline services between Australia and overseas markets ('bilaterals') operate in the international airline industry and various liabilities for loss and damage to cargo by air or sea apply. Distribution channel activities are also subject to different laws from country to country and the techniques permitted in one country are often prohibited in another, for example door-to-door selling is not permitted in France. Exclusive distribution arrangements may also be prohibited and from time to time this aspect has been scrutinised in Australia such as occurred in the *Newsagents Case* before the Trade Practices Commission in 1978. In some countries, such as Libya, agents are banned and in others the law decrees whom a foreign firm may employ as its agent or distributor. In many current and former Centrally Planned Economies, a foreign firm must use the state-owned national import/export company for the product category. This is especially relevant for Australian firms doing business in South-East Asia where regulations in some countries like Indonesia prescribe that the agency firm must be local rather than European or Chinese. Finally, many countries have regulations regarding the conditions under which a foreign firm might terminate a local agency arrangement.

## Promotion

Promotion is a highly regulated element of the marketing mix in many countries. Most nations try to protect their members against deceptive, misleading or fraudulent marketing practices. Societies also try to regulate advertising in terms of propriety and taste. For example, nudity in advertising is relatively common in Australia whereas it is illegal in Saudi Arabia and India. Some of the more frequent areas of regulation are:

- *Trade descriptions*: Legislation in this connection seeks to bar statements which are deceptive or quotations from testimonials which are not wholly factual.

- *Prohibitions on advertising certain products*: Typical products are contraceptives, tobacco products, alcohol and drugs. In some countries the prohibition is total and in others qualifying statements are mandatory (e.g. the message on cigarette packets that cigarette smoking is harmful to health).

- *Prohibitions on using certain words and expressions*: Some words or expressions that might be misinterpreted by the consumer are prohibited (e.g. the ban on using a region to describe a wine (e.g. Burgundy) unless the wine is produced in that region).

- *Limitation on extent of promotional expenditure*: This is likely to be more of a problem in socialist and developing economies either on philosophical grounds or because of a feeling that promotional expenditure reduces the affordability of the product/service. The issue was raised in Australia in 1977 in *the Colgate-Palmolive Case* before the Prices Justification Tribunal.

- *Content and style of advertisement*: The degree of permissible advertising puffery and the use of comparatives and superlatives in describing products and offers varies between countries.

- *Other promotional elements*: These are subject to different laws in various countries and include the use of premiums (cash-off or cash-back offers), contests, vending machines and catalogue sales.

## Extraterritorial application of law

Marketing mix variables can be affected by extraterritorial application of law. This occurs when one country endeavours to apply its national law outside its boundaries. This can mean that overseas operations or subsidiaries are also subject to the law of the home country as well as that of the host country. This can upset the host country that views this as a violation of its sovereignty. Examples occur when subsidiaries are prevented from trading with a country because of an embargo imposed by the home government, when the provisions of the home government's anti-corruption legislation is enforced on the subsidiary or when the home country's anti-trust legislation is applied to the overseas operation. The USA becomes involved in many international trade disputes because of its insistence on extraterritorial application of its laws.

> The ANZ Bank has stopped lending to those of its customers that wish to trade with 12 countries on the US 'black list', after discovering it had inadvertently breached US economic sanctions by undertaking to finance deals with such countries in US dollars. The cases involve around US$50 million of transactions in American currency with countries such as Iran, Sudan and Cuba. As a result of its exposure in this connection, the ANZ Bank has decided not to finance transactions in any currency with these countries for fear of further allegations of complicity to circumvent the US sanctions law.
>
> **SOURCE:** *Adapted from* Sydney Morning Herald, *7 February 2007, p. 19.*

## THE IMPACT OF LAW ON INTERNATIONAL OPERATIONS

Three additional areas in which the firm faces problems due to the application of different laws between countries are in relation to the environment, human resources and intellectual property. All these issues influence the operating of an office or a manufacturing concern in an overseas country, although legal issues relating to intellectual property can also affect firms merely exporting to the foreign market.

## Environment

Environmental consciousness is an increasing focus of attention, both within countries and in multilateral forums. Therefore, not only are there laws in individual countries relating to environmental issues, but there is an increasing prospect of a body of international law on this subject. Accelerating this process is the growing consciousness that environmental problems cross national boundaries, as evidenced by the not infrequent forest fires in Indonesia and Malaysia which it is claimed cause substantial health problems in neighbouring countries such as Thailand and the Philippines. Global conferences on the environment are now almost an annual event and some countries are facing an ethical dilemma. Do countries accept internationally agreed targets for aspects such as greenhouse gas emissions knowing that there is no possibility of their reaching these targets, or do they, like Australia, refuse to agree to the targets and incur strident criticism from the international community?

Environmental laws relating to packaging include material used, recycling and the extent to which packaging is wasteful of resources. Visual pollution such as advertising billboards is also a problem. Environmental laws also govern noise pollution and the requirement to indicate the level of energy consumption (as with refrigerators in Australia). In Germany, green marketing legislation is increasingly requiring the manufacturer to accept legal responsibility for the collection and recycling of packaging materials associated with the product. The European Union has now issued a global packaging directive to its members (which is less stringent than the German requirement).

# Human resources

When operating in an overseas market the Australian or New Zealand firm will be involved in employing locals. This will mean conforming to the labour laws of the overseas country and accepting employment conditions different from those that operate in your own country. In addition, the firm will be involved in abiding by local laws regarding the employment of expatriate staff, the conditions under which they can enter the country and the length of time they can remain. Also, the Australian or New Zealand firm will have to conform to laws and expectations for training locals to replace expatriate managers as required by the country's investment legislation. A final issue results from the fact that in many overseas countries, such as Saudi Arabia, there is a dearth of unskilled local labour. This then requires the employment of guest workers who are usually covered by employment laws that are different from those applying to nationals of the country.

Lack of sensitivity to this issue can be very costly as Mitsubishi found out when its US subsidiary was forced to pay A\$58 million in compensation to 289 female employees because its Japanese managers took no action to stop sexual harassment on the shop floor of its US plant. Mitsubishi tolerated practices at its US plant which were acceptable in Japan, but not in the USA. In addition, the company was reluctant to interfere with supervisor–employee relations in another country. After vehemently protesting the charges the company then adopted a more conciliatory tone, admitting to problems involving sexual harassment that required correction.

# Intellectual property protection

The ability to create and manage knowledge assets is a source of competitive advantage for firms in industrialised nations. The protection of such knowledge assets in the form of intellectual property through either withholding it from the public domain or securing the rights to its use is a very important issue in international marketing.

The main devices to protect intellectual property are:

- *patents*: these provide the holder with a legal monopoly on the patented technology for a specified extended period (usually from 15 to 21 years depending on the country);

- *copyrights*: these protect original literary, musical, artistic, dramatic and some other intellectual works. This protection can last from 50 to 95 years depending on the country;

- *trademarks*: these distinguish one product or service from another and are used to prevent others from offering a product/service with a mark that might cause confusion as illustrated in the case of Starbucks/Starbuck discussed later in this chapter.

As far as patents are concerned, Australian or New Zealand firms venturing into the US or European markets need to be aware that in those markets, there is a culture of aggressive use and enforcement of patents as they are regarded not only as a mechanism for the protection of intellectual property rights, but also as a source of value for the firm.

Different rules apply in different countries and the protection that Australian companies may take for granted does not apply everywhere. The international protection of patents, copyright, trademarks, design, trade secrets and plant variety rights is inadequate and has recently attracted increased attention because of piracy of computer software. Often the costs of registration in a country may outweigh the benefits, especially if this is a preventative

> At the first ASEAN Trade Fair in Australia, held in Sydney in 1978, one of the exhibitors from Singapore exhibited gold-plated orchids that were sold in Singapore under the brand name 'Rhisis'. An Australian entrepreneur visited the Fair and claimed he had registered the trademark and brand name in Australia. His threat of litigation resulted in Myer & Co cancelling its order. Investigation revealed that although neither company had actually obtained registration, the application from the Australian entrepreneur had been received by the patent office one week prior to receipt of the application from the Singapore firm.

measure designed to forestall future competition. Even if registration is proceeded with on this basis, a careful check of the local legislation and its interpretation is required lest prior use outweighs prior registration.

The fact of filing for protection requires that the party filing demonstrates the uniqueness of the intellectual property. This can mean that in order to justify protection the item's unique properties must be revealed. This can lead to creating the competition that the seeking of protection was intended to avoid. For example, an Australian firm may find that its logo or brand name has already been registered in the overseas country, in which case it is likely to have to buy back the rights of use from the holder in that market. Registration in one country often does not give protection in another unless both Australia and the other country are parties to the same international convention on intellectual property, for example the Paris Convention, the Madrid Arrangement or the Inter-American Convention. The expense of filing for protection in a number of countries has belatedly caused the USA to consider signing the Madrid Protocol of 1995. This would involve a single enforcement and registration agency called the World Intellectual Property Organisation (WIPO). A US company could file one application with the US Patent and Trademark Office and obtain a single registration valid through WIPO in all participating nations.

From an Australian perspective the main copyright infringement problems in foreign markets relate to book publishing, music recording, film and video production and computer software. The main offending countries tend to be the Philippines, Thailand, Malaysia, China, India and South Korea. Counterfeiting of patents, trademarks and design mostly relates to agricultural products, veterinary chemicals, pharmaceutical products, automotive parts and manufactured goods in general. The main offending countries in this tend to be Indonesia, Brazil, the Philippines, Taiwan and Thailand. Australia has benefited from actions by offending countries to take a more serious stand on respecting copyright. China has enacted copyright legislation; Indonesia has been more serious about enforcing copyright law and has enacted a patent law; South Korea and Malaysia have joined international copyright conventions; and Singapore enacted legislation to protect Australian copyright works.

The Uruguay Round of the GATT addressed intellectual property for the first time in its closing stages (1992–94) and the resulting World Trade Organization embodies a code covering intellectual property—Trade in Intellectual Property (TRIPS)—which contains comprehensive new rules to protect intellectual property and to govern disputes. All but the poorest countries had until 2006 to implement TRIPS. Despite this, firms still face a threat as far as intellectual property is concerned when they venture offshore to countries with a weak institutional system for protection of intellectual property.

This can be illustrated in the case of China. China is a country whose culture does not contain a strong tradition embodying the need to protect intellectual property rights. Historically, imitation of literary or artistic works from the past was a scholarly and respectable activity. However, this cultural inclination to revere the past and promote its reproduction is at odds with the enforcement of property rights of the work being imitated.

In addition, during the communist era the underlying concept of returning all wealth to the people militated against preserving an individual's ownership rights in intellectual property. As a result foreign firms are reluctant to license sensitive technology in China except to firms in which they have direct ownership.

The Chinese government has somewhat belatedly recognised that this issue is a stumbling block to attracting foreign direct investment and has taken some measures to strengthen enforcement of intellectual property laws. However, in so doing there is a further problem in that there are fundamental differences between Chinese and Western interpretations of both the definition and purpose of licensing technology. In the first instance, regulations in China are based on technology transfer rather than technology licensing. The Chinese are uncomfortable with the notion of a licence as a temporary right to use a technology, and they view it as an instalment sale with the licensee gaining full rights to the technology at the end of the term of the licence. As far as purpose is concerned, the Chinese partner wants the technology to boost its profitability in the short term whereas the foreign party sees the licensing of the technology as a way of gaining access to China's market. The above illustrates that an understanding of the reasons underlying prevailing practice towards the protection of intellectual property is essential when deciding on the entry strategy to be adopted in overseas countries, especially in Asia.

When faced with a different philosophy regarding the protection of intellectual property, the Australian firm will have to devise measures to protect itself from piracy by divulging only some elements of its design uniqueness as the following example highlights.

Incat of Tasmania, a dominant player in the world market for catamaran-style seagoing ferries, in 1996 entered into a joint venture with its former Hong Kong licensee, AFAI High Performance Ships Ltd (AFAI), for construction of its 'K-class' catamarans at a shipyard at Panyu in Southern China. Under the arrangement Incat was responsible for the design of the vessel and the supply of major machinery and prefabricated components, such as engines, generators, water jets, electronics and seats. It was also obliged to provide technical assistance with respect to building techniques and technology for the K-class vessels. AFAI was responsible for supplying the labour to build the hull and for managing the construction of the vessel and the yard. Incat had no equity interest in the Chinese shipyard. Despite the well-known threat to intellectual property when manufacturing in China, Incat did not engage in conventional modes of asset protection such as registering patents or designs. It did, however, ensure protection of its intellectual assets by arranging that only limited disclosure of its proprietary knowledge took place. This was achieved because its joint venture agreement did not require the Australian firm to provide its partner with the background research upon which the data and technological information are based, nor did they need to provide details of the principles underlying the design features of Incat's vessels. Such principles are critical when making alterations to a design to accommodate requests for customisation.

**SOURCE:** *Adapted from McGaughey S.L., Liesch, P.W. and Poulson, D. (2000) 'An unconventional approach to intellectual property protection',* Journal of World Business, *Vol. 35, No. 1, pp. 1–20.*

Another form of piracy is *brand piracy*. The incidence of this is increasing with the emphasis on global brands. This applies not only for goods but also for services, especially those that are franchised on a global basis. This form of piracy can occur:

• when the global brand or logo is applied to a product with which it has no connection (e.g. the Lacoste crocodile being sewn onto fake garments in some Asian countries);

• by modifying the brand name or logo so that although it is different the overseas consumer is misled into believing it is the same (e.g. Coalgate for Colgate).

The misrepresentation of Starbucks shown in the photo below illustrates this point. The use of brand names similar to those of famous foreign brands is common in China. Lax laws and poor enforcement make it difficult for foreign firms to do much about this although Starbucks Corporation of Seattle has taken legal action against at least one Chinese firm in order to protect its name. Often political and legal risks are difficult to separate. Figure 4.1 (below) shows the factors that result in a reduction of risk when doing business overseas.

(AAP Photo/Greg Baker)

## Reducing the impact

There are a number of ways in which an Australian or New Zealand firm can reduce the impact of foreign laws on its international activities.

**FIGURE 4.1 Factors affecting the risk in marketing overseas**

**HOST COUNTRY FACTORS**
- Political stability
- Infrastructure
- Legal restrictions
- Sanctions

**HOME COUNTRY FACTORS**
- Reciprocal agreements
- Legal restrictions
- Sanctions/disputes

**INTERNATIONAL LEGAL FACTORS**
- World Trade Organization
- United Nations rulings
- Sanctions

**POLITICAL RISK ANALYSIS**
- Economic, social factors
- Assess political vulnerability
- Import/export regulations
- Incentives/impediments for FDI

**SOURCE:** *Bradley, F. (2004)* International Marketing Strategy, *4th edn, Prentice Hall, Harlow, UK, p. 132. Reproduced with permission of Pearson Education Ltd.*

## 4.7 INTERNATIONAL HIGHLIGHT

# Drug giants told to reveal secrets

Pharmaceutical companies claim that protection of their patents is necessary because of the huge research and development costs they have incurred in bringing new drugs to market. This might seem reasonable, except for the fact that usually these expenses have been recovered in prices charged for drugs in developed country markets, resulting in the need to recover only marginal costs in developing country markets. Critics of pharmaceutical companies also point out that prices are inflated because the industry spends huge amounts on marketing (especially to prescribing doctors) and that their alleged research and development (R&D) outlays often exceed their actual R&D outlays because much of the ground breaking research involved was undertaken by government-funded scientists. For a number of years developing countries have been complaining about the high prices being charged in their domain by multinational pharmaceutical manufacturers for life-saving drugs. Whenever 'copycat' drugs appear in these markets the drug companies lobby their domestic governments to pressure the developing countries to remove the 'copycat' pharmaceuticals from the market under threat of sanctions or withdrawal of preferences. This poses an ethical dilemma. On the one hand the government is being asked to protect intellectual property, but on the other hand to condemn those people (often in the millions), who can only afford the 'copycat' item, to a life of misery and eventual death. This issue gained prominence in South Africa several years ago with respect to

AIDS drugs. Given the spread of AIDS on the African continent, the government of South Africa legislated to allow it to import cheap versions of medicines. Thirty-nine drug companies have challenged this law in Pretoria and the court has demanded that the multinational pharmaceutical firms reveal closely guarded details of their business practices, including their pricing policies. In addition, international public pressure has resulted in parent governments of some of these multinationals (the USA, Germany as well as the EU and the WTO) backing South Africa's right to introduce the law and calling on the industry to drop the case. More recently the issue flared up again in India where GlaxoSmithKline challenged the right of local firms such as Cipta to manufacture the generic AIDS antiretroviral combination drug, Duvoir. GlaxoSmithKline is arguing that now India has signed TRIPS (the multilateral intellectual property rights agreement), Duvoir should be banned despite it having been introduced to the market before India signed the TRIPS. Meanwhile, courts in other emerging markets such as Thailand are ruling that drug companies can be held liable for injury to HIV/AIDS patients if companies restrict availability of drugs through pricing policies. In that case, the drug company Bristol-Myers Squibb agreed to an out of court settlement in which it dedicated the patent on the drug DDI to the people of Thailand. The Thai government's pharmaceutical organisation is now arranging to produce the drug for one-tenth of the price being charged by Bristol-Myers Squibb.

SOURCES: *Adapted from Crispin, S. (2004) 'A heathy precedent',* Far Eastern Economic Review, *15 July, pp. 50–1; Williams, D. (2005) 'Big pharma syndrome',* Time, *September, p. 47; and Pepper, D. (2006) 'Patently unfair',* Fortune, *18 September, p. 27.*

## TRANSFER PRICING

Transfer pricing involves the firm setting the prices at which they transfer products, technologies or services to their affiliates in other countries. If the price is set artificially high, then the profit earned in the overseas country is reduced, as is the amount of tax payable. As a result, greater profits are earned by the parent company. This is especially the case when affairs are arranged so that, via use of transfer pricing, most profits accrue in those countries where the rate of taxation is least. In recent years there has been increasing attention by governments to this practice as they are missing out on tax revenue due to them from operations conducted within their jurisdiction. The Australian Taxation Office is endeavouring to crack down on this practice, but it is not always easy to prove that the intent behind the setting of the transfer price was tax evasion. Increasingly firms are being asked to prove that the transaction is truly 'arm's length'. Australian companies with overseas affiliates will need to give greater attention to non-arm's-length transactions to ensure that efforts to achieve profit maximisation on a global basis do not expose the firm to charges of tax evasion.

## INTERNATIONAL COUNTERTRADE

Countertrade involves the linking of an import and an export transaction in a conditional way and is fully discussed in Chapter 19. Because goods supplied are either fully or partly paid for with other goods or services rather than with cash, one of the negotiating issues in such transactions is what value to place on the goods bought and the goods sold. The undervaluing or overvaluing of goods can influence the profit attributable to the transaction. As a result, countertrade can be used to avoid taxes, to evade anti-dumping legislation and to evade agreements on international prices.

## DUMPING

Dumping involves selling products in an overseas market below cost or below domestic prices. Dumping is prohibited by the WTO via its Anti-Dumping Code. Difficulties arise because, although it is prohibited in international marketing, it is a common practice in domestic marketing. Dumping in domestic marketing is reflected in the 'loss leader' technique that is aimed at seizing market share, injuring competitors and increasing the degree of control of the market. During recent years there have been an increasing number of complaints and government investigations into dumping, both in Australia and overseas. Imports of textiles, clothing and footwear into Australia have attracted attention in this connection. On occasion, government export incentives such as the Australian Export Development Grants Scheme can give rise to dumping charges overseas (as happened with BHP in the USA). It has been alleged that the incentives are factored into the prices charged in the overseas markets enabling products to be sold in the overseas market below current domestic value in the country of origin.

# CONTRACTS AND DISPUTE RESOLUTION

When faced with a dispute in international business that cannot be settled by informal negotiation between the parties there are three possible avenues for settlement. These are conciliation, arbitration or litigation.

## Conciliation

This is the best approach if at all possible because it is least likely to close the door on future business. Sometimes it may be necessary to seek the intervention of a third party to convey to each side the views of the other side and clear up misunderstandings that might have arisen. Often Australian or New Zealand Trade Commissioners can assist in this connection. In countries such as China, where business is largely based on trust and relationships, conciliation is preferred. In Asia this often takes the form of the third party shuttling back and forth between the disputants trying to negotiate a solution. This 'shuttle' conciliation does save face for both parties in the dispute.

# Arbitration

Many international contracts contain a clause requiring both parties to submit to arbitration before embarking on litigation. When arbitration is formal the disputing parties usually present their cases to a panel of respected persons who will referee, determine the merits of the case and make a judgement that both sides agree to honour. Coddington (1994) summarises the advantages of arbitration as follows:

- arbitration conventions, such as the New York Convention to which almost 90 countries are signatories, increase the ability of parties to enforce judgements;
- arbitration hearings are usually held in private and sensitive matters remain confidential to the parties concerned;
- arbitration is likely to be quicker than litigation;
- the parties can choose the 'judges' who become members of the arbitration panel; and
- unlike a court judgement, an arbitration judgement is unlikely to be appealed and more likely to be treated as final.

A number of formal arbitration organisations exist, such as the International Chamber of Commerce. In the case of this body, each party selects one person from an approved list to argue their case and the Chamber appoints a third member, who is usually a distinguished legal figure, to arbitrate. Success of arbitration often depends on the willingness of both parties to accept the arbitrator's rulings because not all countries have the necessary statutes to enforce arbitration determinations.

# Litigation

This should be used only as a last resort. It is an approach whose victories are often spurious and it involves large costs, delays and aggravation that generally exceed the benefit obtained. On occasion, the threat of litigation is sufficient to bring about a settlement. Other disadvantages of litigation are that:

- it usually closes the door on future business;
- it can create a poor image and damage public relations;
- there is the risk of unfair treatment at the hands of a foreign court;
- there may be difficulty in collecting the judgement; and
- there is considerable opportunity cost—time and funds tied up in bringing legal action.

During the latter part of the negotiations in 1977 to settle the previously mentioned sugar dispute between Australia and Japan, Koichiro Ejiri, Executive Managing Director of Mitsui & Co., provided the following insight as to the Japanese view on how the negotiations might have been better handled:

- it is necessary to settle these problems one by one by exercising a pragmatic and calm attitude, without becoming too nervous;
- it is desirable that the communications media be more careful in their reporting and try to avoid unnecessary confusion;
- sometimes governmental interventions bring about sensational media news, therefore much care should be exercised in this regard;

- sometimes negotiators are led to believe that some parties to the contract may have worked to bring about governmental intervention; and

- it is necessary to establish and expand common grounds between the sellers and buyers based on the spirit of the partnership between the two parties.

## Marketing implications—legal

While the international marketer is not expected to be a legal expert, it is necessary that there be an awareness of those areas where international law might impinge on international marketing activities. It is also necessary for the international marketer to be aware of differences in legal practices between Australia and New Zealand and the market in which it proposes to do business.

In many countries there is a difference between what the law says and what people actually do. This needs to be understood, as do the underlying reasons for this situation. As an example, many laws that operate in developing countries were introduced during, or were based on laws of, the colonial era and may be unsuitable, irrelevant or impractical in contemporary circumstances.

Not only do legal systems differ from overseas market to overseas market, but the interpretation of laws also differs between countries following the same legal system. In some countries the law is absolute and once it has been broken is modified via its interpretation, and in other countries the law has some flexibility, but once broken its interpretation is rigid. To transact business successfully in overseas markets the Australian or New Zealand international marketer needs to be sensitive to the legal differences between Australia or New Zealand and the foreign markets.

Table 4.1 provides examples of country risk ratings as produced by the PRS Group who publish an international country risk guide.

| TABLE 4.1 | Political and legal risk of doing business overseas—country risk ratings for selected countries, January 2005 |

| Country | Current Ratings | | | | Forecasts | | | |
|---|---|---|---|---|---|---|---|---|
| | | | | | One year | | Five year | |
| | Political risk | Financial risk | Economic risk | Current | Worst case | Best case | Worst case | Best case |
| 1 Norway | 88.0 | 48.5 | 48.0 | 92.3 | 91.0 | 94.5 | 83.5 | 94.8 |
| 2 Switzerland | 89.0 | 48.5 | 45.0 | 91.3 | 87.8 | 92.5 | 83.5 | 93.3 |
| 3 Singapore | 84.0 | 45.5 | 50.0 | 89.8 | 85.5 | 91.8 | 77.0 | 93.5 |
| 4 Finland | 93.5 | 37.0 | 44.5 | 87.5 | 83.5 | 89.0 | 77.3 | 90.3 |
| 5 Austria | 88.5 | 42.5 | 44.0 | 85.5 | 82.5 | 88.5 | 79.5 | 89.8 |
| 6 Japan | 83.0 | 46.5 | 40.5 | 85.0 | 81.5 | 87.0 | 76.5 | 90.0 |
| 7 Sweden | 91.5 | 40.5 | 44.0 | 88.0 | 84.0 | 89.5 | 80.0 | 91.3 |
| 8 Canada | 86.0 | 43.0 | 44.0 | 86.5 | 83.5 | 88.3 | 78.0 | 90.5 |
| 9 United Kingdom | 84.0 | 32.5 | 39.5 | 78.0 | 75.5 | 81.8 | 73.3 | 85.8 |
| 10 Belgium | 84.0 | 41.5 | 42.5 | 84.0 | 89.0 | 86.8 | 79.8 | 88.8 |
| 11 Taiwan | 77.0 | 47.0 | 43.5 | 83.8 | 78.8 | 86.3 | 68.8 | 89.8 |
| 12 Netherlands | 86.5 | 41.0 | 41.5 | 84.5 | 83.5 | 87.3 | 78.8 | 91.0 |

*continued*

| TABLE 4.1 | Political and legal risk of doing business overseas—country risk ratings for selected countries, January 2005 *(continued)* | | | | | | | |
|---|---|---|---|---|---|---|---|---|
| 13  Germany | 81.5 | 35.0 | 41.0 | 78.8 | 76.3 | 81.5 | 72.3 | 85.5 |
| 14  France | 76.5 | 34.5 | 40.0 | 75.5 | 72.8 | 77.3 | 69.3 | 84.3 |
| 15  South Korea | 77.5 | 43.5 | 44.0 | 82.5 | 77.3 | 84.3 | 72.3 | 83.3 |
| 16  Australia | 89.0 | 35.5 | 41.5 | 83.0 | 79.0 | 83.0 | 74.5 | 87.5 |
| 17  Spain | 80.5 | 38.5 | 39.5 | 79.3 | 75.5 | 80.3 | 72.0 | 84.8 |
| 18  China | 68.5 | 44.5 | 38.0 | 75.5 | 73.0 | 77.8 | 62.8 | 81.8 |
| 19  United States | 82.5 | 32.5 | 39.0 | 77.0 | 72.8 | 79.8 | 72.0 | 83.5 |
| 20  Chile | 79.0 | 39.0 | 42.0 | 80.0 | 75.0 | 80.5 | 68.0 | 83.0 |
| 21  Russia | 68.0 | 44.5 | 42.5 | 77.5 | 74.0 | 79.0 | 63.3 | 84.3 |
| 22  Croatia | 76.0 | 37.0 | 36.0 | 74.5 | 66.5 | 73.5 | 64.0 | 75.0 |
| 23  Mexico | 74.0 | 39.5 | 37.5 | 75.5 | 72.8 | 78.5 | 65.0 | 82.5 |
| 24  South Africa | 71.0 | 41.0 | 35.5 | 73.8 | 70.5 | 76.0 | 64.3 | 80.3 |
| 25  Ukraine | 60.0 | 40.0 | 39.0 | 69.5 | 65.0 | 74.0 | 59.5 | 78.3 |
| 26  India | 63.5 | 44.0 | 36.0 | 71.8 | 68.8 | 74.5 | 63.8 | 77.5 |
| 27  Brazil | 66.5 | 35.0 | 38.0 | 69.8 | 65.8 | 73.0 | 59.3 | 80.3 |
| 28  Myanmar | 46.5 | 39.5 | 32.0 | 59.0 | 55.0 | 65.1 | 48.3 | 76.3 |
| 29  Venezuela | 51.5 | 37.0 | 36.0 | 62.3 | 60.5 | 71.5 | 54.3 | 79.3 |
| 30  Somalia | 25.0 | 33.0 | 28.5 | 43.3 | 40.3 | 51.3 | 36.8 | 61.8 |

*Note*: Lower scores represent higher risk (highest risk = 1, lowest risk = 100).

**SOURCE:** *PRS Group (2005)*, International Country Risk Guide, © *January, East Syracuse, NY 13057. Reproduced with permission.*

# The internet and the legal environment of doing business offshore

Global computer-based communications cut across territorial boundaries undermining the feasibility of applying laws based on geographic borders. New boundaries have arisen based on screens and passwords that separate the virtual world from the real world. This new boundary defines a distinct cyberspace that some would argue needs its own laws and legal institutions. These will have to cater for new phenomena that have no clear parallel in the real world and, in the process, define legal personhood and property rights, resolve disputes and establish a convention as to value in the international virtual marketplace. Furthermore, because of the speed and borderless nature of the internet, this new law will have to cater for multiple jurisdictions, often simultaneously. It must accommodate persons who exist in cyberspace only in the form of an email address. internet business will increasingly be scrutinised by authorities in different countries and, with the growth in international e-business, the volume of international disputes is likely to escalate. Recent examples include copyright infringement (e.g. *Playboy*, Sega), trademark infringement, buyer and seller being located in different legal jurisdictions (e.g. who is liable for taxes and where has value been added?), intellectual property (e.g. website design, site ownership), violation of privacy, breach of regulations on promotion (e.g. whose regulations govern internet sweepstakes?) and cyber squatting (who owns the site domain name?). Solving the above issues is complicated because the laws that govern the internet are still ill defined and in many cases nonexistent. internet development moves faster than traditional lawmakers are used to. It is debatable whether the laws that apply in the international domain to bricks-and-mortar businesses will work for online commerce because many of the former were enacted at a time of slow-moving trains, not high-speed computers. E-business adds a new level of complexity to international business law and raises issues as to what constitutes a contract in cyberspace, international tax harmonisation and enforcement for online transactions and disparagement, defamation and consumer protection for online customers. Finally, there is a view in many developed countries that, because the internet is new, it is too early for governments to become involved in regulating it, lest in the process its growth becomes stifled. The consequence is that a firm using the internet in international business may face multiple and contradictory national laws applying to the same transaction.

# Summary

Figure 4.2 provides a summary of the way in which the international political and legal environment impacts on Australian firms doing business overseas.

## ETHICS ISSUE

The US government continues to castigate China over its human rights record. The Australian government publicly disagrees with the US position. This would have been unthinkable at the start of the 1990 decade. Do changes in position on alleged human rights abuses in Asian countries reflect the fact that Australia is now driven more by trade than by human rights? Does it signify that if Australia wants to convince its neighbours that it wants to be part of the region, it is prepared to turn a blind eye to morally questionable behaviours in the region so as to protect its business interests there? At a time when world pressure is increasingly focusing on human rights and when developing nations are being encouraged by bodies such as the United Nations to address human rights abuses, is Australia's current approach in the long-term interests of its commercial sector?

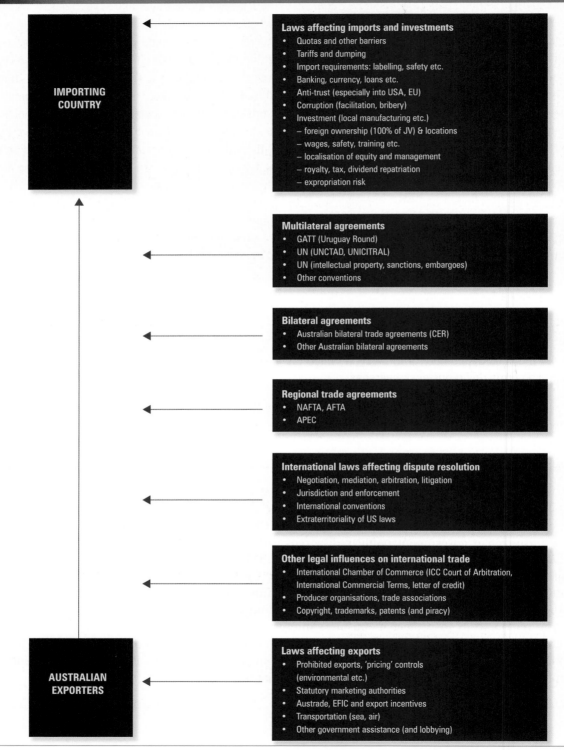

**FIGURE 4.2  Factors in the international and political environment affecting Australian business activities overseas**

IMPORTING COUNTRY

**Laws affecting imports and investments**
- Quotas and other barriers
- Tariffs and dumping
- Import requirements: labelling, safety etc.
- Banking, currency, loans etc.
- Anti-trust (especially into USA, EU)
- Corruption (facilitation, bribery)
- Investment (local manufacturing etc.)
- – foreign ownership (100% of JV) & locations
  - – wages, safety, training etc.
  - – localisation of equity and management
  - – royalty, tax, dividend repatriation
  - – expropriation risk

**Multilateral agreements**
- GATT (Uruguay Round)
- UN (UNCTAD, UNICITRAL)
- UN (intellectual property, sanctions, embargoes)
- Other conventions

**Bilateral agreements**
- Australian bilateral trade agreements (CER)
- Other Australian bilateral agreements

**Regional trade agreements**
- NAFTA, AFTA
- APEC

**International laws affecting dispute resolution**
- Negotiation, mediation, arbitration, litigation
- Jurisdiction and enforcement
- International conventions
- Extraterritoriality of US laws

**Other legal influences on international trade**
- International Chamber of Commerce (ICC Court of Arbitration, International Commercial Terms, letter of credit)
- Producer organisations, trade associations
- Copyright, trademarks, patents (and piracy)

AUSTRALIAN EXPORTERS

**Laws affecting exports**
- Prohibited exports, 'pricing' controls (environmental etc.)
- Statutory marketing authorities
- Austrade, EFIC and export incentives
- Transportation (sea, air)
- Other government assistance (and lobbying)

**SOURCE:** *Coddington, I. (1994) 'Supplementary notes on the political and legal environment', University of Technology Sydney.*

# Websites

Australian Wheat Board http://www.awb.com.au
Center for Strategic & International Studies http://www.csis.org/
Country data—political risk services http://www.prsgroup.com/CountryData.aspx
CSR http://www.csr.com.au
Department of Foreign Affairs and Trade http://www.dfat.gov.au/
eMarket Services http://www.emarketservices.com
Fonterra http://www.fonterra.com
Frost and Sullivan http://frost.com
International trade law http://www2.spfo.unibo.it/spolfo/TRADE.htm
Islamic and Middle Eastern law materials http://www.soas.ac.uk/Centres/IslamicLaw/Materials.html
Islamic law http://www.usc.edu/dept/MSA/law/
Political risk, economic risk and financial risk http://www.duke.edu/~charvey/Country_risk/pol/pol.htm
Public Entity Risk Institute http://www.riskinstitute.org/
United Nations Commission on Trade Law (UNICITRAL) http://www.unicitral.com
World Intellectual Property Organization (WIPO) http://www.wipo.int

# Discussion questions

1  How can firms maximise the opportunities offered when foreign governments act as facilitators of involvement?

2  How can firms minimise the inconvenience to their international operations when foreign governments act as regulators of international commercial involvement within their borders?

3  What are the key differences between various forms of political instability?

4  Discuss how you would evaluate the degree of political risk your fibreboard plant in Indonesia is likely to face at the present time.

5  What steps can you take to minimise political risk in the countries in which your firm is presently involved?

6  To what extent did the Australia–Japan sugar dispute reflect a clash of legal systems as opposed to a clash of cultures?

7  Discuss the circumstances in which international law can clash with national law as far as commercial matters are concerned. Will globalisation ever create a situation where international law will take precedence over national law?

9  Comment on circumstances where national law can frustrate global marketing strategy and the potential savings that can result from globalisation.

10  Under what circumstances would it be worthwhile to file for protection of intellectual property in an overseas market?

11  When is it preferable to arbitrate as opposed to conciliate on the one hand and litigate on the other?

# References

Beshara, M. (1999) *Globalisation and the Middle East: Growing or Growing Apart?*, Policy Brief, Middle East Institute, Washington.

Bradley, F. (2004) *International Marketing Strategy*, 4th edn, Prentice Hall, Harlow, UK, p. 132.

Coddington, Ian (1994) 'Supplementary notes on the political and legal environment', University of Technology, Sydney.

Crispin, S. (2004) 'A heathy precedent', *Far Eastern Economic Review*, 15 July, pp. 50–1.

Department of Foreign Affairs and Trade (2000) *Accessing Middle-East Growth: Business Opportunities in the Arabian Peninsula and Iran*, East Asia Analytical Unit, Department of Foreign Affairs and Trade, Commonwealth of Australia, Canberra, p. 53.

East Asia Analytical Unit (2005) *Unlocking China's Services Sector*, Department of Foreign Affairs and Trade, Canberra.

Encarnation, D.J. and Vachani, S. (1985) 'Foreign ownership: when hosts change the rules', *Harvard Business Review*, September–October, pp. 152–60.

Fisher, G., Hughes, R., Griffin, R. and Pustay, M. (2006) *International Business: Managing in the Asia–Pacific*, Pearson Education Australia, Frenchs Forest, NSW.

Frick, H. (2006) 'Identification, assessment, treatment and monitoring of legal risk in foreign direct investments: a multiple case study approach for Australian investments in Chile', unpublished PhD thesis, University of Queensland.

Hadjikhani, Amjad and Hakansson, Hakan (1996) 'Political actions in business networks: a Swedish case', *International Journal of Research in Marketing*, Vol. 13, pp. 431–47.

Jain, S. (1996) *International Marketing Management*, 5th edn, South Western College Publishing, Cincinnati, Ohio.

John, D. (2007) 'ANZ refuses loans that defy US trade bans', *Sydney Morning Herald*, 7 February, p. 19.

Marr, D. and Wilkinson, M. (2006) 'This worries me', *Sydney Morning Herald*, 25–26 March, p. 32.

McDonald, H. (2006) 'Burma's hard reign', *Sydney Morning Herald*, 18–19 November 2006, p. 29.

McGaughey, S.L., Liesch, P.W. and Poulson, D. (2000) 'An unconventional approach to intellectual property protection: the case of an Australian firm transferring shipbuilding technologies to China', *Journal of World Business*, Vol. 35, No. 1, pp. 1–20.

Needham, K. (2006) 'Rising dragon still sees red' *Sydney Morning Herald*, 7–8 October, pp. 23 and 31.

O'Sullivan, F. (2006) 'Kiwis avoid harsh light of independent scrutiny', *New Zealand Herald*, 15 April, p. A25

Overington, C. (2006), 'Aid to the enemy', *Australian*, 21–22 January 2006, pp. 17, 22.

Pepper, D. (2006) 'Patently unfair', *Fortune*, 18 September, p. 27.

PRS Group (2005) *International Country Risk Guide*, January, East Syracuse, NY.

*Sydney Morning Herald*, 7 February 2007.

'The Mideast's model economy', *BusinessWeek*, 24 May 2004, pp. 30–3.

Trimeche, M. (2004) 'International marketing and exporting to the Arab world', in Ogunmokun, G. and Gabbay, R. (eds) *International Business and Cross Cultural Marketing: Contemporary Research in Selected Countries*, Academic Press International, Perth, pp. 61–77.

*Wall Street Journal* (Europe), 7–8 September 2001, p. 7.

Welch, C. and Wilkinson, I. (2004) 'The political embeddedness of international business networks', *International Marketing Review*, Vol. 21, No. 2, pp. 216–31.

Williams, D. (2005) 'Big pharma syndrome', *Time*, September, p. 47.

## go online

Go online to <www.pearsoned.com.au/fletcher> to find more case studies.

# 'So where the bloody hell are you?': Tourism Australia faces off with British and Canadian legislation

**Jan Charbonneau, Massey University**

*We've bought you a beer . . .*
*And we've had the camels shampooed . . .*
*We've saved you a spot on the beach . . .*
*And we've got the sharks out of the pool . . . so . . ?*

Iconic Australian images of Uluru, Sydney Opera House, Great Barrier Reef and the sun setting on a Western Australian beach coupled with iconic Australian slang—getting the 'roos off the green'—and iconic Australian humour—driving a ute down a long dusty road to open the 'front gate'—what better way for Tourism Australia to encourage overseas visitors to come Down Under and swell the coffers of Australia's multi-billion dollar tourism industry? And who better than Lara Bingle in a bikini to ask visitors, 'Where the bloody hell are you?'

Before Tourism Australia committed $180 million for this international advertisement campaign, launched by tourism minister Fran Bailey in early 2006, it did its homework. It knew that Australia was viewed as one of the most desirable tourist vacation spots but was often seen as a 'can wait' destination. Tourism Australia wanted to 'cut through' the advertising from other 'desirable' tourist destinations and convince tourists that coming Down Under just couldn't wait any longer.

While $180 million may sound like a lot of money, it was simply not enough to allow Tourism Australia to develop individualised advertisements with unique messages and creative executions for each country (adaptation). To make its $180 million stretch as far as possible, Tourism Australia chose to go with a standardised advertisement that would play around the world, with only minor adjustments for local language. Besides the obvious cost savings, such standard-ised advertising would allow Tourism Australia to communicate the same basic message to all potential tourists, regardless of their home country. To do this effectively however, it needed to ensure that its message and creative execution was interpreted in the same way by potential tourists, regardless of home country.

To that end, it invested over $6 million in researching international markets, including conducting focus groups with more than 47 000 people in key markets including the United States, United Kingdom, China and Japan. The results showed the campaign grabbed attention, with one Japanese participant commenting, 'Bloody hell

. . . the more I hear it the more I like it'. It was viewed as distinctively Australian and authentic with an American participant commenting 'Definitely Aussie. It's something they would say and is unique' and a participant from the UK noting, 'It's Aussie . . . cheeky, laid back, forthright'. Participants in all key markets saw the ad as representing a genuine invitation—'Australians want us there—it's real' (UK); understood the message—'Bloody hell just means you should come' (Korea); and challenged their perceptions about the diversity of tourist experiences on offer—'didn't know there was so much to do' (USA).

If so many potential tourists liked and understood the ads, why were they initially banned in the UK, partially banned and then edited in Canada, and changed for Asian markets? And why did Tourism Australia and the Australian government care so much?

The latter is easy to answer. Overseas tourists contribute over $17 billion a year or over 10% of annual export earnings. British tourists represent the largest share, with over 700 000 visitors spending almost $3.5 billion dollars annually. So attracting tourists is big business.

In terms of the Asian markets, Tourism Australia realised that 'Where the bloody hell are you?' would probably be offensive to many Asian tourists, despite reactions in the focus groups. The slogan was changed from the outset to 'Where are you?' for the Japanese, Korean, Thai and Singaporean markets. The reaction in the UK and Canada was not anticipated, however, catching Tourism Australia off guard and forcing tourism minister Fran Bailey and bikini girl Lara Bingle to make a quick trip to London to sort it out. The issue in the UK was the use of the word 'bloody'. The Canadians had no problem with 'bloody'; they took offence at 'hell' and a half-full glass of beer!

So, what was the problem with 'bloody'—a term used quite widely in British humour and everyday conversation? And why did the Canadians, who are known to drink the occasional beer while watching hockey, object? In both instances, Tourism Australia ran afoul of government regulations, industry self-regulation or a combination of the two.

In the United Kingdom, all UK-based broadcasters must be licensed under the *Broadcasting Act 1990*, with the licences granted by Ofcom, the agency responsible for regulating communication under the *Communications Act 2003*. One of the conditions of continued holding of the licence is that broadcasters ensure advertising complies with applicable advertising codes. Ofcom has delegated the creation and enforcement of advertising codes to the Committee of Advertising Practice (CAP), an industry association that is part of the Advertising Standards Authority (ASA), itself an industry association. Television advertising must comply with the Television Advertising Standards Code, administered by the Broadcast Committee of Advertising Practice Ltd (BCAP). The Broadcast Advertising Clearance Centre (BACC) vets and pre-approves all television advertising and the Advertising Standards Authority (Broadcast) Ltd adjudicates viewer complaints. While administration and enforcement has been delegated to industry associations, many functioning as limited liability companies, ultimately it is the *Broadcasting Act 1990* and the *Communications Act 2003*, which dictates what can and cannot appear on UK television screens. If this sounds complicated, it is—especially so for offshore advertisers who must comply with all codes and regulations, same as their domestic counterparts, if they want their advertisements to be aired.

In March 2006, the BACC imposed a ban on the advertisement, requiring that the word 'bloody' be removed. Following meetings with tourism minister Bailey and Lara Bingle, the ban was removed with the BACC giving the advertisement an 'ex-kids' restriction to ensure it was not scheduled during programs specifically aimed at children and also restricted its showing around religious programming. However, 36 viewers complained to the Advertising Standards Authority about the 'swearing', claiming they found the term 'bloody' offensive and were concerned that children might see the advertisement. During the complaint investigation process, the BACC referred to the focus group research conducted by Tourism Australia and the Advertising Standards

Agency's own research on offensive words where 'bloody' was relatively low at #27, after 'crap' and before 'God'. M&C Saatchi, the advertising agency responsible for creating the ad, said the use of 'bloody' had to be viewed in the context of the ad, which used everyday Australian language that would be judged as harmless and inoffensive by most.

In the end, the advertisement was found to breach the Television Advertising Standards Code rules concerning social, moral and psychological harm to children but not rules concerning offensiveness. It was ordered that the advertisement could no longer air before 9 p.m.

Was this the end of the story in the UK? No . . . next came the posters, appearing on billboards on major motorways. Three posters were created as a joint effort between Tourism Australia and Qantas. One showed the Sydney Opera House at night with information about special Qantas fares and the tagline 'We've switched on the lights. And the champagne is on board. So where the bloody hell are you?' In early 2007, 32 complaints were received by the ASA with complainants again finding the 'swearing' offensive and concerned about potential exposure of children. Tourism Australia argued the posters targeted an older, more informed audience, were not placed near community based facilities such as schools, and that no offence was intended, just a hospitable welcome. The ASA found the posters breached rules concerning responsibility and children in the British Code of Advertising, Sales Promotion and Direct Marketing, which covers all non-broadcast advertising such as outdoor and cinema. The ASA believed parents were entitled to expect that poster advertising would not endorse or encourage swearing. In March 2007, Tourism Australia was ordered to remove all posters and refrain from using 'swear' words in future posters.

The Canadians, on the other hand, had no problem with the use of 'bloody': they objected to 'hell'. In March 2006, the Canadian Broadcasting Corporation, Canada's national broadcaster, banned running the ads during family programming such as Sunday evening's high-rating

*Wonderful World of Disney* and monitored audience reaction to the advertisement run during other programming. Telecaster, the organisation that vets advertisements for Canada's private broadcasters, cleared the use of 'hell', but warned private broadcasters that the advertisement contained 'objectionable language' and they should schedule accordingly. The Television Bureau of Canada which operates Telecaster felt the main issue was potential exposure of children to the word 'hell'.

So far, so good. No 'hell' during family programming, but okay for adult programming. But now the real problem—that half-full glass of beer and whether it complied with the Canadian Radio-television and Telecommunications Commission's (CRTC) Code for Broadcast Advertising of Alcoholic Beverages.

The CRTC is the independent public authority that regulates broadcasting under the *Broadcasting Act 1991*, reporting to Parliament through the Minister of Canadian Heritage. The CRTC licences television broadcasters and adjudicates complaints concerning television broadcast standards. Like the UK, a condition of continued holding of a Canadian broadcasting licence is compliance with all applicable CRTC codes. So in Canada, like the UK, ultimately it is the *Broadcasting Act 1991* that will dictate what can and cannot be aired on Canadian television screens.

Advertising Standards Canada (ASC) is the advertising industry's self-regulatory body, enforcing compliance with its member initiated Canadian Code of Advertising Standards. The ASC also pre-clears advertisements to ensure they adhere to all applicable legislation, regulations and CRTC and sectoral codes. Canadian broadcasters rely on this pre-clearance and will only air advertisements with an ASC pre-clearance number. Canada's private broadcasters also look to Telecaster for additional vetting.

So how does all this apply to a half-full glass of beer in an outback pub? The CRTC code prohibits, for example, alcohol advertising that attempts to influence purchase, implies social acceptance can be acquired through consumption or that alcohol is necessary for enjoyment of life.

Telecaster took particular issue with the implied consumption of unbranded alcohol, seeing, from its perspective, the now half-empty glass as a prop for mood setting, contrary to the Code. The end result was that the opening shot of the beer ended up on the editing room floor. No offer of Aussie beer for potential Canadian visitors!

Throughout, Tourism Australia tried to put a positive spin on the UK and Canadian bans with then managing director, Scott Morrison, referring to them as a 'marketer's dream', generating incalculable word of mouth and driving traffic to their website <http://www.wherethebloodyhellareyou>.com where the full advertisement could be viewed. Newspapers had a field day and parodies appeared on YouTube. Tourism minister Fran Bailey first questioned the Brits' sense of humour and then the Canadians', commenting 'Canada lags behind Americans, Brits and even Germans in the sense of humour stakes'. She extended an invitation to both British and Canadian regulators to come to Australia and she'd shout the beer to say thanks for the free publicity.

While Fran Bailey joked publicly, her emergency trip to the UK to meet with regulators and government officials told the real story. At stake was a $180 million dollar campaign directed at assisting a critically important sector of the economy. In the final analysis, it did not matter how harmless and stereotypically 'Aussie' the advertisement was. What mattered was whether it complied with domestic legislation and industry self-regulation in the markets in which it aired.

So was the advertisement a success? According to statistics released in March 2007, tourist spending increased by $1.8 billion in 2006. This increase, however, was mainly due to longer stays and increased spending as actual numbers of tourists decreased slightly. Although the tourists who came stayed longer and spent more, Tourism Australia is still asking tourists who view Australia as a 'can wait' destination . . .'Where the bloody hell are you?'.

## Bibliography

'Aussie ad meets more resistance', *Globe and Mail*, 23 March 2006, accessed online.

'Bingle ad rakes in extra $1.8 billion', *The Age*, 8 March 2007, <http://www.smh.com.au/news/travel/bingle-ad-rakes-in-extra-18-billion/2007/03/08/1173166848974.html>.

'Bloody hell! Australia's new tourism campaign banned in U.K.', 10 March 2006, <http://Bloomberg.com>.

Boswell, R. (2006) 'Canadian regulator takes fizz from Aussie ad', *Vancouver Sun*, 24 March.

'Brit ban on "bloody" ad "incredibly ludicrous"', *Sydney Morning Herald*, 28 March 2007, <http://www.smh.com.au/news/travel/bloody-ad-ban-incredibly-ludicrous/2007/03/28/1174761533507.html>.

'Brits lift bloody hell ad ban', *Sydney Morning Herald*, 18 March 2006, <http://www.smh.com.au/news/national/brits-lift-bloody-hell-ad-ban/2006/03/18/1142582557678.html>.

'Have a beer on Australia? No thanks, says Canada', *Reuters*, 22 March 2006, <http://english.people.com.cn/200603/23/eng20060323_252856.html>.

Industry Tourism and Resources, media releases 'So where the bloody hell are you?' 23 February 2006 and 'New ad campaign already cutting through', 27 February 2006.

## Questions

1 Advertisers only need to be aware of applicable media laws in any given foreign market. Do you agree?

2 M&C Saatchi would have checked applicable legislation during the creation of the advertisement. Tourism Australia tested viewer reactions through its focus group research. With all this research, why did the advertisement cause such problems in the UK and Canada?

3 The tourism minister referred to the CRTC code as 'some sort of quirky Canadian regulation'. Does her opinion matter?

4 Standardisation is attractive to companies and organisations operating in a number of different markets due to economies of scale. However, as this case illustrates, standardisation may not always be appropriate. Given the financial constraints under which Tourism Australia operates, discuss which elements of the promotional campaign might be standardised and which must be localised.

5 In 2006, New Zealand's Advertising Standards

Complaint Board received 71 complaints concerning a Hyundai advertisement depicting a toddler driving its Santa Fe 4WD. Australia's Advertising Standards Board received more than 80 complaints about the same advertisement. What would you expect to be the findings of the two industry associations?

# CHAPTER 5

# THE TECHNOLOGY ENVIRONMENT AND CONTEMPORARY ENVIRONMENTAL VARIABLES

## LearningObjectives

**After reading this chapter you should be able to:**

- identify the key elements and drivers underlying the information technology revolution;

- determine how firms are capitalising on the information and technology environment to expand internationally;

- evaluate the significance of the international diffusion of innovation processes and the role of end-users;

- appreciate the impact of terrorism on the conduct of international marketing;

- recognise how health-related issues can affect operations in an overseas market;

- identify ways in which climate and geography affect consumers in other countries;

- manage the ethical dilemmas that confront international marketers, especially in emerging markets; and

- appreciate the opportunities and constraints created by increasing global environmental consciousness.

# Global Skype entrepreneur

Globalisation for small and medium-sized Australian and New Zealand companies until now was synonymous with time zones, poor communications with their suppliers and resellers and increasing costs of frequent interactions.

Many companies are expanding to other countries and need a way to keep their international offices and agents not just connected but an integral part of the enterprise.

Just as corporations such as Coles Myer and General Motor's–Holden require their worldwide suppliers to have closer connections with them, so too small businesses require the people they do business with to have ways of interactively communicating. That doesn't just mean email. In the future, small and medium-sized businesses as well as larger companies will be required to integrate easily with both supply and sales channels.

VoIP (Voice over Internet Protocol), along with unified messaging, provides one of the new low-cost means for the needed collaboration and interactivity. VoIP technology is creating a milestone in the telecommunications industry just as dramatic as the invention of the telephone. Consumers connected to broadband internet services can download free software and make computer-based voice calls anywhere in the world at no cost (apart from their monthly broadband subscription fees).

Now myriad new service providers enable small and mid-sized businesses to have a global presence at a fraction of traditional telephony costs. The best known and most rapidly expanding is Skype, with a total of more than 8 million registered users in 2007.

Skype is a peer-to-peer internet telephony network founded by the entrepreneurs Niklas Zennström and Janus Friis, who also founded the famous file sharing application, Kazaa. Skype competes with open VoIP protocols such as SIP, IAX, and H.323. The Skype group, acquired by eBay in October 2005, is headquartered in Luxembourg, with offices in London, Tallinn and Prague.

Since its launch Skype has experienced rapid growth in both popular usage and software development for both its free and paid services. The Skype communications system is notable for its broad range of features, including free voice and video conferencing and its ability to use a peer-to-peer (decentralised) platform. Small companies can now have call centres, call forwarding, local numbers and free call numbers at a fraction of their traditional cost. All is needed for the success is for the business to have access to the internet. Businesses can shave up to 95% off their international and local costs using this type of system.

What about people who don't have Skype? They can use a service called 'SkypeOut'. They use a credit card to open an account, then use a dial-pad to call a regular land line. The rates are significantly less expensive than those charged by incumbent telephone companies. Finally, you may wonder how people who don't have Skype can contact you. For $50 Australian a year, you can have a landline phone number that connects with your account.

This is one example of how technology is changing the international marketing environment.

# INTRODUCTION

The world has changed since 11 September 2001. The subsequent wars in Afghanistan and Iraq and ongoing conflicts in various parts of the Middle East, Africa and the former Soviet Union reflect increased the danger and security risks inherent in the international marketing environment. The next US presidential election as well as the Australian federal election will also be fought on the issue of terrorism as well as a range of domestic issues, including health, environmentalism, outsourcing of jobs to low-cost countries and innovation.

These issues are mirrored in countries around the world and their various attitudes and policies have an impact on the decision by a company to set up and invest in particular countries and how it goes about doing it.

One of the biggest business drivers for international marketing still remains technology, which creates opportunities for entry to new markets. A range of new technologies affecting communication, health, security and manufacturing will have an impact on international marketing in the next decade.

Environmental variables such as health, pollution and conservation, and terrorism are playing an increasing role; however, they also provide both opportunities and restrictions for international marketers. A hotly contested political and public debate has yet to be resolved, regarding whether anything should be done about global warming, and what could be cost-effectively done to reduce or reverse future warming, or to deal with the expected consequences. Most national governments have signed and ratified the Kyoto Protocol aimed at combating global warming. (See the list of Kyoto Protocol signatories at <http://en.wikipedia.org/wiki/List_of_Kyoto_Protocol_signatories>.) These issues are also influencing exporters' attitudes to travel and to the overseas countries targeted as market growth opportunities. Ethics remain a challenge for international marketers as they interact with a variety of cultures with different religions, beliefs and value structures.

# TECHNOLOGY

Technology is still the most dramatic force transforming the international environment. From biotechnology to computer technology we have seen a vast array of technological innovations in just the last 10 years. New technologies have an impact upon or replace older ones: the motor car hurt the railways, television challenged the cinemas and communications affected the airline industry. In each case a level of substitution has occurred. More recently, as security risks have increased and the quality of video-conferencing and other email-style communications has improved while its costs have fallen, businesspeople have reassessed their 'real' need to travel. This decision has caused a consequent reduction in business travel for various purposes. This is visible on some domestic and international airline carriers which have reduced the number of business class seats in their planes. Also the cost of travel with all additional levies (such as fuel, security and environmental levies) have affected this greatly. As environments change new technologies create new markets and opportunities, but also pose a threat to those old technologies and industries that might be tied to them.

Scientists today are working on new products and services in communications, robotics, miniature electronics, solar energy applications, biological cloning, voice-activated and voice-controlled computers and dispensing machines, and myriad other applications. Our interactions with company's service centres are taking on a different view. Voice recognition cuts costs and allows the primary point of contact to be anywhere in the world. Companies in the computer industry like Dell, telecommunications companies like Nokia and Ericsson and banks have already used this technology to significantly cut costs. These companies spend large portions of their budgets as they move to make customer service fully automated in a few years' time.

Some industries like telecommunications, as discussed above, are being revolutionised by information technology. In this industry the emergence of high speed internet and software applications capable of delivering VoIP (Voice over Internet Protocol) using a computer allow users to talk bypassing some if not all of the traditional telephony company's services. As a result the number of new players offering services at the fraction of the cost charged by the traditional players is growing steadily. It is now possible to have your long-distance calls supplied to you by a company like Vonage or Skype, which have their business base in the USA and the Europe respectively.

Airlines are also riding on the crest of the technology wave. Paper airline tickets, once the industry standard, are disappearing fast. The International Air Transport Association (IATA) aims to issue only electronic tickets by the end of 2007, shifting paper tickets into the history books. The US airlines are leading the world in terms of e-ticketing and going electronic.

IATA sees the potential savings by going to electronic ticketing at around $3 billion a year globally. On average, an airline spends $10 to process a paper ticket, compared with $1 to process an electronic ticket. Electronic tickets also encourage self check-in, which saves airlines money.

Already at Northwest Airlines, travellers who prefer paper tickets must pay an additional $50 fee as a discouragement of such practices. At airlines such as Northwest only 2% of tickets are paper (<http://www.iata.org/workgroups/etwg.htm>, accessed 10 March 2007; *Sydney Morning Herald*, 'Paper airline tickets on the way out', 1 March 2007, <http://www.smh. com.au/news/travel/paper-airline-tickets-on-the-way-out/2007/03/01/1172338752660.html>, accessed 10 March 2007).

Of the many technologies that will have an impact on international marketers in the fields of conservation, health, transportation, manufacturing and service, the pervading technology will be to do with information.

Broadband infrastructure has rapidly penetrated businesses and households, more than any previous infrastructure, and goes well beyond transporting goods and services to *creating, developing, moving and delivering* them—thus transforming all parts of society.

The next section looks at how different technology infrastructure developments have transformed the business environment, with emphasis on the current revolution based on information and communication.

## INFRASTRUCTURE DEVELOPMENT AND ECONOMIC HISTORY—'TECHNO-ECONOMIC PARADIGMS'

Economic history dating from the Industrial Revolution in the late 18th century to the present day is typically classified through economic business cycles.

1st—Early mechanisation (1770s to 1840s)

2nd—Steam power and railway (1830s to 1890s)

3rd—Electrical and heavy engineering (1880s to 1940s)

4th—Fordist mass production (1930s to 1990s)

5th—Information and communication (1980s to 2015?)

6th—Information omnipresence (2010–35) These are depicted in Figure 5.1.

Figure 5.1 outlines the *techno-economic paradigms* with their associated key technology resources and infrastructure developments. Each techno-economic paradigm has a cycle of between 60 to 70 years, with 10 years in an emergent phase in a previous paradigm and 10 years in a declining phase in a subsequent paradigm. To date this pattern has pointed to a period of about 40 to 50 years when the paradigm is dominant. The transition periods are typically times when major structural crises and adjustments have occurred throughout the international economy. We have identified a 6th paradigm, still based on information, but involving the embedding of networks and linkages on a global basis built on low-cost communication which is starting to build momentum in 2007.

Freeman and Perez (1988), who undertook a review of these changes, contend that the diffusion of the key technologies and resources associated with each of these techno-economic paradigms radically transformed international markets at the macro country and industry levels and the micro business and individual levels with all-encompassing outcomes, including:

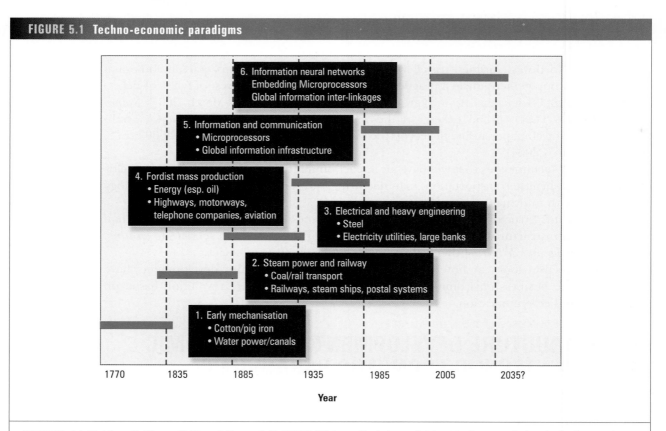

**FIGURE 5.1 Techno-economic paradigms**

**SOURCE:** *Adapted from Pattinson, H.M. and Brown, L.R. (1996) 'Metamorphosis in marketspace–paths to new industries in the emerging electronic marketing environment',* Irish Marketing Review, *Vol. 9, p. 56.*

- emergence of new industries based on the key technologies and resources;
- effective solutions to the limitations of previous techno-economic paradigms;
- new infrastructure both at the national and international levels;
- countries gaining technological and economic leadership positions from the application of key technologies and resources associated with the new paradigm;
- significant changes in spatial distribution and distance between associated production factors (including land, labour and capital sources) and market locations (marketplaces and customers);
- shifts in population density and urbanisation;
- radical changes in organisational forms associated with firms in new industries;
- new approaches to national and international regulation;
- new training and education systems;
- new services linked to the techno-economic paradigm;
- new innovative entrepreneurs.

These changes are occurring at a chaotic pace in the newer transforming market economies of China, India, Russia and Eastern European countries like Bulgaria and Romania—the latter gaining entry to the European Union in 2007.

## Information and communication: the fifth techno-economic paradigm

The current fifth techno-economic paradigm is driven by the microprocessor and to date new infrastructure development can be divided into two phases. In the first phase, a number of 'carrier branches' based on the microprocessor have emerged and evolved into new or redefined industries. These branches include:

- computer systems;
- computer operating systems and software;
- telecommunications equipment and optical fibres;
- satellites;
- consumer and professional electronics;
- robotics, flexible manufacturing systems;
- electronic networks;
- information content providers; and
- information technology services.

In the second phase, all the 'carrier branch' industries are converging into a new information-based infrastructure that is capable of providing most forms of data—text, sound and images—through the requisite functions of generation, processing, storage and transmission.

The new phone devices that are providing this capability in 2007 are described in International Highlight 5.1.

# Is it a phone?

The convergence of technology has spawned a growing variety of multifunction devices for consumers and businesses. Consider the mobile phone. The days when a mobile phone was just for talking are long gone. Now it is a mini digital entertainment centre that includes a phone as just one of its features.

Apple is trying to make our global interactions even more seamless. The Apple iPhone is not just a phone—it is a phone, music player, video player, internet device, and camera all in one—like its Apple iPod Nano and iPod video cousins.

Apple's visionary founder, Steve Jobs, has such a strong belief in this new creation that he is predicting iPhone sales to reach over 10 million units by 2008.

Despite the phone's revolutionary features, its strongest feature is its redefinition of how calls are made.

'We want to reinvent the phone,' Jobs said. 'What's the killer app? The killer app is making calls. It's amazing how hard it is to make calls on phones. We want you to use contacts like never before.'

A visual voice-mail feature allows users to skip directly to voice mails they want to hear. An easy-to-use conference call feature lets users connect two calls with one touch of the screen. Text messaging on the iPhone is similar to iChat, with user dialogue encased in bubbles and with the familiar iChat sounds, and a touch keyboard appears below for entering text.

The iPhone uses its Wi-Fi and EDGE capabilities to automatically connect to the internet. Internet connectivity includes HTML-capable email that works with any IMAP or POP3 email service. Jobs also announced that Yahoo will offer free push email—similar to the email system on a Blackberry—to all iPhone customers.

With the phone's extensive features it will be possible to redefine how, how often and for how much the phone calls will be made.

Skype Technologies provides software that can be downloaded free. With an internet connection users will be able to call millions of other Skype users around the world for free. Calling internationally to any regular phone amounts to a small number of cents per minute.

**SOURCES:** *Based on <http://www.apple.com/iphone/>; Sparks, J.D. (2007) 'Europe's Apple attack', Newsweek, 5 March, p. 47; and Rosenbush, S. (2004) 'Net calls: there's lots to like', BusinessWeek, 8 November, p. 122. Image © 2007 Apple Inc.*

## THE INFORMATION REVOLUTION AND THE INTERNET

Access points to the new infrastructure include telephone networks, commercial online services, satellite and broadcast television, cable networks, cellular networks, established corporate proprietary and open networks. The internet is emerging as the fulcrum for the information infrastructure as it connects increasingly diverse networks. For example, the use of the internet for telephone calls noted above, referred to as VoIP, is about to revolutionise the telecom industry as companies position themselves to provide telephone network services at lower prices and with additional features that will cannibalise their traditional long-distance toll call businesses. Some of the incumbent telcos are still not taking this service seriously. But at the same time, the penetration of high-speed internet access in businesses and households is very high in most developed countries around the world and is gathering momentum in the developing countries of the Asian region. The Republic of Korea is an example of a country that has transformed its telecommunications and broadband infrastructures. This transformation is described in detail in Kelly, Gray and Minges (2003) and Hazlett (2004).

## The global network

Businesses embracing the concept of the 'globally networked business' enable dissemination of the corporate information infrastructure to all key constituencies, leveraging the network for competitive advantage. The globally networked business is an open and collaborative environment that eliminates the traditional barriers to business relationships and across geographies, allowing diverse constituents to access information, resources and services in the most efficient and advantageous manner. Organisations are embracing three key areas of the networked enterprise:

1  *e-learning*: E-learning is changing the way people around the world provide and receive education, information and training. By eliminating the barriers of time and distance, e-learning provides accountability, accessibility and opportunity to people and organisations around the world. E-learning is all about providing people with access to the learning anytime, anywhere and often at the user's own pace. International companies like HSBC Bank have adopted e-learning so that basic knowledge and information is available to staff worldwide as and when required by users.

2  *internet commerce*: Internet commerce, a key component of the globally networked business model, provides a company's customers and its partners with end-to-end solutions to conduct sales transactions. The myriad internet commerce applications accessed through such networks help users place and manage orders for the company's products and services. The software applications streamline processes and deliver enhanced productivity, improved service, worldwide around-the-clock availability and faster access to a wider range of useful information. As an example, Australian company, Orica, has developed its Chemnet Division to provide chemical products and services to its markets in Australia and Asia.

3  *customer support*: The globally networked business model opens the corporate information infrastructure, enabling the creation of innovative support offerings. Support applications provide customers with all the information they need to be successful. Removing the traditional barriers and re-engineering the information dissemination process allow new standards in business relationships to emerge, ensuring mutual benefits.

This exploding growth of electronic networks and commerce has implications for the adoption and diffusion of innovations and presents both opportunities and challenges for international marketers.

International marketers need to understand how these new technology applications can create international market potential. Some observers believe that the global spread of the new information infrastructure will have dramatic structural impacts on many industries. Many companies and industries already exhibit this globalisation due to investment requirements for research and development and the convergence and reshaping of industries. Industry convergence and the need for global alliances is occurring with media, publishing, entertainment and communication. Industries like pharmaceuticals, finance, telecommunications and airlines are becoming increasingly global as country standards become international and deregulation occurs. Also, a growing proportion of business customers and consumers are buying from global sources, particularly as electronic commerce and internet access rapidly increase. However, smaller geoeconomic regions, such as Silicon Valley in Southern California, Southern China, the Kansai region in Japan or Penang in Malaysia, may be more effective at developing stronger economic couplings within a global economic environment.

Naisbitt's 'Mind Set' (Naisbitt 2006) points towards strongly integrated global economic and information systems, but with many small 'units' driving the economy. These units include much smaller geoeconomic states, small to medium-sized enterprises, and units formed across borders based on common interests. The smaller units will emphasise their differences within the global economy.

At the other end of the spectrum, Sheth and Sisodia (2002) have proposed 'The Rule of Three', where three firms, one from each 'Triad' group, will dominate in many global industries. The Triad refers to the three economic regions of Europe (particularly the European Union), North America and Japan—regarded as the powerhouses of the world economy. Following Sheth and Sisodia's analysis, the three Triads as integrated units will exercise increasing market power over the next 10 years. However, at the Asian end of the triad, to Japan should now be added Korea, China and India.

Whether global markets evolve into many small corporations, or three large dominant ones, most firms operating within the Triad markets will have to compete in a global market or face strong business pressures from global competitors—all with significant grounding in the new information infrastructure.

However, future global industry analysis based on a *unidimensional* spectrum with many or few firms may prove to be myopic, because the new information infrastructure will be a driving force for convergence from quite diverse backgrounds. Examples of industries where the breakdown of boundaries is occurring are the pharmaceutical industry and the cosmetics industry, hotels and hospitals, banking and insurance, media companies and telecommunications companies—and this is only the start of many different possible combinations.

As firms become more information based and service oriented they may run headlong into firms from other industries that have taken control of the basic transaction or information systems required to drive future growth within the former firm's industry.

Alternatively, firms that are augmenting their physical products toward information-based service offerings may find themselves forming strategic alliances with firms that may be in completely different industries—and even then the resultant virtual organisation may be in a new industry. For instance, alliances between some of Australia's energy authorities and telecommunications and computer players will form new industries to address new markets based around information. (Relationships, networks and strategic alliances are analysed in Chapter 12.)

The challenge for strategic thinking posed by globalisation is not just the *unidimensional* convergence within an industry, but the requirement to focus on *multidimensional* industry convergence. This requires lateral thinking to determine not only the sources of convergence, but the new or redefining industries that will emerge as a result.

Industry transformation in a global economy connected to a powerful information infrastructure will flow through to business transformation in organisational communication, technology infrastructure, organisation structure and market orientation.

# THE NEW INFORMATION INFRASTRUCTURE

The evolution of this new information infrastructure to 2007 has resulted in a much more interconnected world. Now many of the technological constraints associated with the new infrastructure have been overcome and high-quality broadband access via optical fibre, microwave systems or satellites is available to almost all businesses and well over half of the population of the countries of the European Union, USA and Canada, Japan, Hong Kong, Singapore, Taiwan, South Korea, Australia and New Zealand. Significant business numbers and population segments also have similar services in Eastern Europe, Mexico, Brazil, Argentina, Chile, Uruguay, Venezuela, India, Indonesia, Thailand, Malaysia and South Africa.

## Implications for international marketing

There are many implications for marketers in this new and increasingly global information-rich environment. Business customers and consumers have much quicker and more widespread access to business intelligence, company products and services, prices, new innovative concepts and potentially higher levels of service. In this knowledge age, the focus is on considerations such as growth, adding value, creating wealth and exceeding customer expectations. Knowledge is the main source of value and power in the modern economy—technology is the manifestation of that knowledge into something that is tangible and has the potential to be the centrepiece of a firm's competitive advantage. For example, Interstrat, an Australian-based marketing consultancy servicing transnational corporations based in North America, uses its technological knowledge of online diagnostic tools and tests to add value for the marketing communities within its clients' organisations. The greater the knowledge and technological intensity of a business's product offerings, the more likely it can create differentiated value in international markets (Bradley 2005, pp. 37–9).

The power of information is shifting from producers to consumers. Governments are having less influence than global corporations. Customers are expecting and demanding more. They are much more knowledgeable.

Australian and New Zealand firms can use information and communication technologies to access and service markets that previously were considered too remote or too expensive to address. They need to become lead users of these technologies to create added value for their overseas customers and consolidate relationships already established. Countries such as Singapore, South Korea, Malaysia and Taiwan are already well advanced and committed to the use of information technology. As the IT infrastructure develops in other Asian countries, Australian and New Zealand firms can take a lead in supporting their products and services with appropriate technology.

## International diffusion of innovation

The diffusion and adoption of technologies and products in overseas markets is a key element of the technological environment analysis. For example, Australia has a high propensity for acceptance and rapid diffusion of new technologies and new product concepts. Measuring this propensity is one way researchers can assess an overseas country's likely acceptance rate of new technologies and products. Some of the new technologies that are showing potential in 2007 will directly influence health and manufacturing. (See International Highlight 5.2.) The international diffusion of innovation is assisted by the introduction of global standards—an activity being pursued by the International Standards Association (ISO) based in Geneva.

The first set of global standards was the ISO 9000 series relating to standardised systems and procedures for manufacturing that included all activities of firms and embraced quality systems, control of designs and documents, purchasing activities, control of process inspection and testing, storage, packaging and delivery, quality audits, training and surveys and other responsibilities of management. Initially this applied within the European Union (EU), but spread globally as unless non-EU firms conformed to these standards they could not sell their products in the EU. The second tranche of standards was the ISO 14000 series relating to environmental management. These were based on a market-driven approach to environmental protection that encourages business to self-regulate their activities so that they can demonstrate to environmentally conscious customers worldwide that they are making environmental improvements to both production and the way they do business.

---

**5.2 INTERNATIONAL HIGHLIGHT**

# What's next—from brain boosters to a factory in the home!

## SMART DRUGS BOOST THE MEMORY AND SLOW DOWN THE AGEING PROCESS

Alzheimer's disease afflicts millions of elderly people around the world. In the USA alone more than $100 billion was spent in 2006 on the care and treatment of those suffering from this illness. Canadian pharmaceutical firm Neurochem completed Phase III clinical trials of a drug called Alzhelmed in February 2007. Eli Lilly and Novartis are also in the field. A separate group of companies is developing memory-enhancing drugs for healthy people. US-based Cephalon has been very successful with its Provigil—a drug for alertness and sleep disorders. These and other 'anti-ageing' drugs will have a negative impact on the demand for nursing homes and the assisted-care industry while creating opportunities for biopharma companies and related service industries.

## TECHNOLOGY TO CHANGE MANUFACTURING

Manufacturers have traditionally adopted a business model focused on mass production, labour specialisation and centralised assembly. However, consumers are now looking for customised solutions and as a consequence of this manufacturers have had to grapple with the notion of mass customisation—providing individualised products or services for each customer.

Printable mechatronics has the potential to offer consumers far greater product variety, while eliminating the need for factories. Research teams at MIT and UC Berkeley are adapting inkjet printing technology to build ready to use products in the home.

To replace a lost TV remote control, a consumer would download digital plans from the internet and use a home mechatronic printer to squirt out, one layer at a time, a new remote control using cartridges filled with polymer and other materials.

The business opportunities for international marketers are now in the product design companies, inkjet technology companies and CAD (computer-aided design) software companies.

**SOURCES:** *See <http://www.neurochem.com> and <http://www.cephalon.com>; Zachary, G.P. (2004) 'Brain boosters',* Business 2.0, *September, pp. 85–6; and Maier, M. (2004) 'A factory in every home',* Business 2.0, *September, p. 85.*

---

Diffusion refers to the movement of new products to and within overseas markets so that they are available to customers in those markets. For example the iridium mobile phone was designed to access satellite technology to provide communication from Mount Everest to the South Pole. But this narrow positioning and its high cost of usage, as well as its bulky size, confined it to a very small niche market and insufficient revenue for success. It is only in 2007, many years after its initial launch, that it is finding wider acceptance in markets around the world (see <http://www.iridium.com>).

The lesson to be learned from this experience indicates how major time lags in diffusion impact on the costs and viability of a business. It also indicates how vested interests, having sunk investment monies into existing technologies, take action to reduce or delay the competitive threat of the new technology.

The diffusion process is characterised both by production lag-time, which elapses between initial output of a product and the commencement of its production in the foreign market, and by market lag-time, which elapses between the initial marketing of a product and its introduction into a specific overseas market. With market lag, there are differences in the extent of the lag between different types of products.

Typically the adoption process involves a number of stages, such as awareness, interest, evaluation, trial and adoption. Figure 5.2 shows the classic sequence of *adopter categories* from innovators, representing about the first 2.5% of a potential market, through to the laggards at 16%. This is based on a process of diffusion of a product, service or idea throughout a defined market or community.

The propensity of customers to adopt new products varies considerably from overseas market to overseas market and is a matter of differences in cultural lifestyle, strategic opinion leadership, economic environment and communication. In addition, the classification of consumers into innovators, early adopters, late adopters and laggards will also be affected by the following variables.

This classic sequence varies markedly from country to country as people from different countries have a different willingness to adopt or try something that is not new. Steenkamp (2002) researched this in relation to packaged goods in Europe and found different patterns of diffusion in different countries. Table 5.1 shows the relative proportions of innovators, early majority, late majority and laggards for these goods in different countries.

The late adopters in Australia might fall into the early-adopter category in some Asian countries for certain products or services.

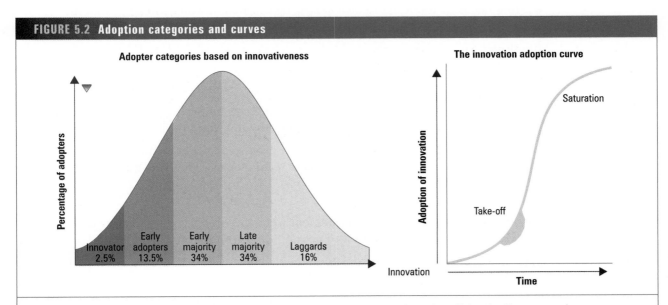

**FIGURE 5.2  Adoption categories and curves**

**SOURCE:** *Klopfenstein, B. (1998)* Diffusion of Innovations on the Web, *Bowling Green State University, Department of Communications, Bowling Green, OH.*

| TABLE 5.1 | Diffusion of innovations and culture | | | |
|---|---|---|---|---|
| | Innovators (%) | Early majority (%) | Late majority (%) | Laggards (%) |
| World | 16.0 | 34.0 | 34.0 | 16.0 |
| UK | 23.8 | 43.4 | 26.4 | 6.4 |
| France | 15.1 | 25.5 | 35.6 | 23.8 |
| Germany | 16.8 | 26.1 | 34.2 | 22.9 |
| Spain | 8.9 | 34.1 | 43.9 | 13.1 |
| Italy | 13.4 | 30.8 | 41.0 | 14.8 |
| *Correlation coefficients*[i] | | | | |
| IDV | 0.75 | | −0.74 | |
| UAI | −0.83 | | 0.83 | |

[i]IDV refers to the individualism/collectivism dimension (0–100) with 100 denoting high individualism; UAI refers to the dimension of uncertainty avoidance (0–100) with 100 denoting low uncertainty avoidance.

**SOURCE:** *Steenkamp, J-B. (2002) 'Global consumers', presentation of a working paper at Tilburg University, 17 November, Tilburg University, Tilburg, The Netherlands.*

What makes an innovation *successful*? Innovation diffusion theorists have identified *five critical characteristics* that may work as accelerators or inhibitors. It is important to note that these are not *requirements* for a successful innovation, but their presence or absence tends to affect the rate at which the new technology or new products are adopted.

1 *Relative advantage*—Is the innovation better than the status quo? Will people *perceive* it as better? If not, the innovation will not spread quickly, if at all.

2 *Compatibility*—refers to the innovation's fit with the market's past experiences and existing needs. If it doesn't fit *both of these criteria* well, it won't spread as rapidly.

3 *Complexity*—How difficult is the innovation to understand and apply? The more difficult, the slower the adoption process.

4 *Trialability*—Can people 'try out' the innovation first? Or must they commit to it all at once? If the latter applies, people will be far more cautious about adopting it.

5 *Observability*—How visible are the results of using this innovation? If markets adopt it, can the difference be discerned by others? If not, the innovation will spread at a slower rate.

A modification of life cycle theory has been proposed as the Technology Adoption Cycle for discontinuous innovations based on new technologies. The 'landscape' of this cycle is shown in Figure 5.3.

The cycle divides into six zones, which are described as:

1 *the early market*—a time of great excitement when customers are technology enthusiasts and visionaries looking to be first to get on board with the new paradigm;

2 *the chasm*—a time of great despair, when the early market's interest wanes, but the mainstream market is still not comfortable with the immaturity of the solutions available;

3 *the bowling alley*—a period of niche-based adoption in advance of the general marketplace, driven by compelling customer needs and the willingness of vendors to craft niche-specific whole products;

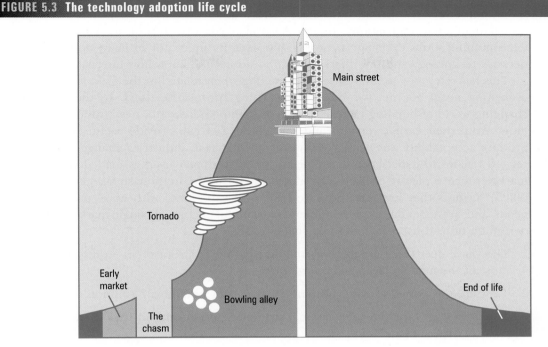

**FIGURE 5.3  The technology adoption life cycle**

Main street

Tornado

Early market

The chasm

Bowling alley

End of life

**SOURCE:** *Moore, G. A. (1995)* Inside the Tornado: Marketing Strategies from Silicon Valley's Cutting Edge, *Harper Business, New York, p. 25.*

4  *the tornado*—a period of mass-market adoption, when the general marketplace switches over to the new infrastructure paradigm;

5  *main street*—a period of aftermarket development, when the base infrastructure has been deployed and the goal now is to flesh out its potential;

6  *end of life*—which can come all too soon in high-tech products because of the semiconductor engine driving price/performance to unheard of levels, enabling wholly new paradigms to come to market and supplant the leaders who themselves had only just arrived.

Experience with high-tech products highlights the discontinuities occurring at different stages of the life cycle—particularly 'the chasm', when acceptance does not take place, and 'the bowling alley', which involves niche-specific solutions that need to be progressively broadened to appeal to a wider marketplace. Successful broadening of the conditions for general purpose solutions encourages the pragmatist to adopt the product or service resulting in 'the tornado' of rapid market growth.

This is a major challenge in developing overseas markets and Australian firms can gain insight in a particular industry and market if they can identify lead users.

## LEAD USERS

It is frequently assumed that technological and product innovations are developed by technology or product manufacturers. von Hippel (2005) shows that for industrial markets the innovation process is distributed across users, manufacturers and suppliers. In some areas, such as scientific instruments, Herstatt and von Hippel (1992) have shown that users of innovations were the prime innovators. These users were also the primary instigators of diffusion of their innovations. In the Australian context, Telstra, as a user of Ericsson's telecommunications exchange networks, has been an innovator in many applications of the network technology and now markets its innovations and know-how internationally.

This has relevance to international marketing when related to the task of researching and evaluating needs for new products by analysing prospective users. In the relatively slow-changing world of building materials, such as steel or fibreboard, new products do not differ much from their earlier versions and the typical user can provide useful feedback on new product acceptability and appeal. However, in high-tech industries change is so rapid that related real-world experience and visualisation of ordinary users is inadequate in helping a marketer form a picture of likely acceptance and diffusion. In these situations Eric von Hippel (2005) suggests that *lead users* do have real-world experience with novel product or service needs and are essential to development of a useful picture through market research. The definition of lead users includes two characteristics:

1  They have needs that are general in a market, but confront them months or years before most of the marketplace encounters them.

2  They are positioned to gain substantial benefits by obtaining a solution to those needs.

The advantages for the international marketer of focusing on lead users in a particular overseas market are threefold:

1  they are users whose present strong needs are likely to become general in a market in the future;

2  they can serve as a need-forecasting benchmark for market research; and

3  they can provide new product concept and design data to manufacturers because of their own attempts to satisfy their needs.

As Herstatt and von Hippel (1992) found in a lead user study of 'low-tech' industrial products, joint development of new product concepts by a manufacturer with lead users can reduce the costs of development and enhance success.

The challenge of today's high-tech environment for many marketers is to identify lead users in their targeted overseas markets as an input in the adoption and diffusion processes. In any event, Moore (2005) contends, great companies need to innovate and find lead users at every phase of their evolution.

## CONTEMPORARY FACTORS IN THE INTERNATIONAL MARKETING ENVIRONMENT

Managers, especially those from developed nations, tend to seek predictability when including new markets in their plans for expanding their international marketing activities. While there is an element of unpredictability in all the environmental variables of international marketing, recently several variables have come into prominence where predictability is elusive. There is a widespread perception that, due to these variables, international marketing involves a greater degree of risk than was formerly the case. There are already many forms of risk inherent in traditional variables in international marketing. These traditional sources of risk can be summarised as follows:

- economic risk—the likelihood that a change in a nation's economic circumstances will cause major changes in the business environment in that country;

- market risk—the likelihood of unanticipated movements in prices, exchange rates and interest rates in a country which affect the profitability of doing business with that country;

- political risk—changes in the political scene that cause major changes in a country's business environment as happened in Ukraine after the Soviet Union breakdown. As a result of the 'orange revolution' of 2005, Ukraine distanced itself from Russia as its traditional political and ideological allay. This later resulted in the dispute with Russia over Russian's energy (oil and gas) supplies. Ukrainian refineries and energy companies now have to pay higher rates for energy as dictated by Russia; this influences its competitive capabilities and directly affects the Ukrainian population and their disposable income—already one of the lowest in the Europe. These risks can take two forms: (1) extra-legal risk, which involves activities that violate existing international laws or regulations, such as war or revolution, as well as major changes in public sector competition and government interference in commercial activities of foreign people, and (2) legal-government risk events, which harm a firm, but are permissible within the existing legal system in a country, such as expropriation, nationalisation, and restriction on remittance of profits, capital and dividends;

- legal risk—the likelihood of unfavourable outcomes due to legal uncertainties (Frick 2006). These may be due to differing legal systems and variance in the application of existing laws; and

- technology risk—this may arise when existing technology used by a firm is rendered obsolete by new technologies available to the overseas market or when existing sophisticated technology is inappropriate for an overseas country because of its stage of development, affordability or lack of necessary infrastructure.

The risk inherent in many contemporary variables in the international marketing environment requires that international marketing managers make allowance in their international planning for the potential chaos that can ensue from these unforeseen contingencies. The need for such contingency planning is particularly evident with contemporary variables such as terrorism and health scares. Other contemporary variables such as climate and geography, consumerism, infrastructure endowment, environmentalism and ethics are more predictable, but there is considerable uncertainty that arises due to differences between rhetoric and application of laws in developing countries with these variables. Contemporary environmental factors in international marketing include a number of issues that need to be taken into account in the context of adopting a stakeholder as opposed to a shareholder approach as part of applying a philosophy of corporate social responsibility in dealing with these activities. This can be a 'win–win' scenario, as demonstrated by the change in sponsorship approach of the global transport firm TNT. This firm operates transport services in 64 countries and when international disasters occur, as with the tsunami of 2004, they become heavily involved in transporting relief supplies. Recently they replaced sponsorship of sport with sponsorship of the World Food Program on a worldwide basis.

## Terrorism

Terrorism has a negative impact on the outlook and attitudes of people around the world and has contributed to fluctuations and uncertainty in the global economy. It has affected retailing, insurance, entertainment, commercial aviation, other forms of transport, petrol prices and many other industries as well as the military, government bodies and postal services. The impact of terrorism can be psychological when it discourages foreign direct investment. This can be crippling to a country such as Indonesia that is already suffering from a severe flight of capital. There is also the inconvenience factor, exemplified by the fact that entry to the USA at any major airport now includes fingerprinting, a photograph, scanning of passport, reference to a database of 'suspect' people, substantial questioning as to the purpose of visit, length of stay, accommodation arrangements, company employer, role in company and other background information—all of which act as a disincentive for tourists to visit the USA.

The impact of terrorism can be direct as when the Australian manager of a contract catering firm in Cambodia was shot, or indirect as occurs when investors are frightened away from a market because of terrorist threats. Consciousness of terrorism as an environmental variable has increased markedly since the attacks on the World Trade Center in New York on 11 September 2001. The IMF estimates this event caused the loss of output in the US worth US$75 billion p.a. and an increase in spending on security by the transport sector (Department of Foreign Affairs and Trade 2004). Penn et al. (2003) found that the impact of terrorism on transport and tourism from one country to another was markedly different, as reflected in Table 5.2.

Enderwick (2001) categorises the impact of terrorism as follows:

- primary impacts—these are most likely to be on 'frontline' industries such as airlines and tourism;

- secondary impacts—these will be experienced in increased insurance rates, transport charges, security expenditures and investment;

- response-generated impacts—these will be reflected in government spending, defence spending, slowdown in implementing reforms, reduction in growth rates, oil prices and migration;

- longer-term impacts—these will cause an increase in the overall level of instability and uncertainty, slowdown in the pace of globalisation, increased levels of personal security

**TABLE 5.2    Impact of terrorism on productivity and output**

| Economy | Productivity | Output of airline, tourism and hospitality industries |
|---|---|---|
| The world economy | −0.50 | −7.5 |
| United States of America | −0.30 | −8.0 |
| Japan | −0.25 | −6.0 |
| European Union | −0.60 | −6.0 |
| East Asia | −0.60 | −6.0 |
| ASEAN | −0.80 | −10.0 |
| Other Asia | −0.80 | −12.0 |
| The rest of the world | −0.90 | −9.0 |
| Australia | −0.25 | −5.0 |

and the formation of geopolitical alliances. The Department of Foreign Affairs and Trade (2003) categorises the economic costs of terrorism as follows:

– It is a major threat to regional economic prospects due to the greater costs imposed by terrorism.

– It creates uncertainty, reduces confidence, increases risks and hence insurance costs, reduces investment flows and disrupts international trade.

– Due to their greater dependence on trade and capital inflows it impacts hardest on developing countries.

For certain industries terrorism can be good business. Apart from the obvious effect on producers of defence equipment, there has been a huge positive impact on the security industry, which now provides products and services for personal safety and public safety that only a few years ago did not exist. Firms such as Kroll (intelligence gathering, investigation and security) and Halliburton (engineering and construction) thrive in risky environments. In the case of the latter, Iraq is contributing one-third of its revenues (about US$1.7 billion), although 42 of its workers have died in the region. Mining firms have also found that dangerous places can be highly profitable as unexploited mineral deposits are increasingly to be found in politically unstable countries and/or regions where government is unable to exercise law and order and terrorism is rife. As recent events in Iraq show, the military is increasingly outsourcing activities that it used to perform itself to private contractors (for instance, Halliburton subsidiary Kellog, Brown and Root was feeding 130 000 troops a day in July 2004) and the contractors themselves have become targets of terrorism.

**SOURCE:** *Adapted from* Economist, *12 August 2004.*

International marketers need to evaluate the risks of operating in various countries and also becoming associated with activities which could make the employees or agents of their company a target for terrorism. At the same time, there is potential to tap into these markets as far as personal goods and services are concerned as there is now a rapidly growing demand to provide safety, screening and security for civilians around the world.

## Health-related issues

These fall into two broad categories. The first relates to animals and the second to humans. These are not always separate as recent occurrences show and animal disease can be threatening to humans.

Some recent examples of *animal-related* health issues include the outbreak of SARS (severe acute respiratory syndrome) in China and other parts of Asia in 2003 and an upsurge of mad cow disease (CJD) in Europe in 2001. Events of this kind often cause closure of tourist sites to prevent the spread of disease as happened when Northern Ireland's premier tourist attraction, the Giant's Causeway (among others), was closed in 2001 as a result of mad cow disease, with substantial loss of tourism revenue. As a result of this disease in Europe, McDonald's and Burger King changed their product emphasis away from beef and 'big macs' to 'chicken wings' and 'bacon treats' (Schmidt and Hollensen 2006, p. 9). These events also cause the slaughter of large numbers of animals and a ban on the export of animal products, with a negative impact on the balance of trade. SARS also affected humans, and at the height of the SARS outbreak in China in mid-2003 machines were lying idle because the foreign technicians needed to fix them would not travel to China due to the perceived risk to their health. A consequence of mad cow disease was that Australia has for several years had a virtual monopoly in supplying beef to Japan at prices some 25% higher than before the emergence of the disease in 2001. The consequent distortion in world trade in beef resulted in Canada not exporting beef to the US and the US not exporting beef to Japan.

A more recent scare and one that does not respect national boundaries is avian bird flu which since 1997 has travelled steadily west across Asia. The current outbreak, which began in 2003, most seriously affected South-East Asia. but there are fears that this flu, which kills both birds and humans, will spread further.

**SOURCE:** *Adapted from Forman, C. (2005) 'Should the US be scared?', Time, 17 October, pp. 17–20; and Jack, A. (2006) 'WHO seeks data on avian flu treatment',* Financial Times, *30 May, p. 4.*

With regard to *human-related* health issues AIDS is the best known in this category, and it overstrains the capacity of health services, affects the availability of labour and significantly reduces GNP and hence the attractiveness of the overseas market. Human health scares increase the risk and costs of operating in a market, with some industries being more affected than others. This certainly has been the situation in Africa. In the case of AIDS, more than 20 million people have died and it threatens major emerging markets such as India and China. More than half the new HIV infections hit people under 25. This is the market that global media operations such as MTV target. This company is leading the fight against AIDS in the belief that if left unchecked AIDS will kill off its audience (Gunther 2004, p. 30). Such has been the impact of AIDs in Africa that in some countries, such as Zimbabwe, children are often the decision makers (in households with sick parents).

Health is a major issue worldwide—it involves not only the problem of diseases such as AIDS discussed above but also malnutrition in the underdeveloped countries of Africa and the cost of health in the ageing populations of the West. The trends appear to be unfavourable and have an impact on international marketing decisions. The growth in demand for organic foods in Australia, North America and other Western markets is in response to the consumer perception that disease and obesity come from manufactured and chemically enhanced food. Texas-based Wholefoods is a rapidly growing supermarket chain specialising in organic products and is tapping this trend in the North American and UK markets. It also provides a whole range of food products for people with certain types of food intolerances.

A preoccupation with health is becoming increasingly important in markets such as Japan, according to Cameron (2004), where consumers want information down to the last detail about food products, including the name of the farmer, the paddock, how it was grown and when it was harvested. These details can be implanted in bar codes, which consumers of the future will be able to scan for themselves. With bird flu, mad cow disease, mercury in fish, industrial accidents and the use of artificial agents in food production, consumers are becoming increasingly fussy as to what they consume. In a country like Japan, which imports over 60% of what it eats, such concern needs to be taken seriously by international suppliers of foodstuffs, particularly as consumers will pay premium prices for foods accompanied by detailed information regarding its antecedents.

For international marketers these trends present threats and opportunities and for countries like Australia provide direction for food growers, manufacturers and marketers on how to enter these new markets. As significant exporters of fish, meat, dairy and agricultural products both New Zealand and Australia have a lot to gain—and to lose!

## Geography and climate

Often terms that classify nations broadly according to their geographic location, such as 'east versus west' or 'north–south dialogue', are bandied around. Underlying such classifications is the assumption that location influences the extent of wealth versus poverty, democracy versus autocracy, etc. Sheth (2002) has suggested that it is climate that underlies such categorisations and illustrates this with examples of how climate influences differences in culture and consumption. If this is the case then climate is an important variable for the international marketer to consider when assessing whether there is a possibility of successfully marketing the product or service in an overseas country.

Climate is the antecedent of cultural and genetic differences. As a consequence trade patterns historically have tended to flow from colder to warmer climates such as from the USA to Mexico, from Russia to Mediterranean Europe and from Northern China to South-East Asia. Patterns of economic integration also reflect this trend, as evidenced by recent accessions by countries close to the equator to established regional trade groupings (e.g. the expansion of the EU in 2004 from 10 to 25 members—mostly south-eastern and Mediterranean countries—and moves by Central and South American nations to join the North American Free Trade Area). Within large nations the differences in climate are alleged to be responsible for different patterns of consumption and behaviour as with the distinction between north and south Indians, northern and southern Europeans and Mandarin and Cantonese in China.

Sheth (2002) illustrates the impacts of climate in terms of differences in foods and beverages, clothing and shoes, shelter and cultural differences. Figure 5.4 provides a summary of these impacts.

As far as food and beverage differences are concerned, in climates away from the equator

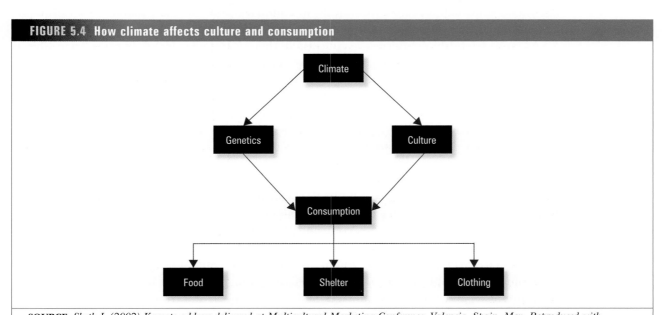

**FIGURE 5.4  How climate affects culture and consumption**

**SOURCE:** *Sheth J. (2002) Keynote address delivered at Multicultural Marketing Conference, Valencia, Spain, May. Reproduced with permission from the author.*

the main source of energy is animal fat and the human gene has adapted to this. In climates close to the equator the main source of energy is lentils and the adaptation of the body to this is reflected in the narrower veins of inhabitants of these areas.

Whereas in desert and tropical climates the preference is for spicy foods, in arctic and temperate climates the preference is for non-spicy foods.

With clothing and footwear, animals are used for clothing away from the equator and this accounts for the predominance of wool and leather. Closer to the equator, vegetation is used for clothing and the dominant materials are cotton and linen. Climate has an influence on footwear as preference changes from boots and shoes in colder climates to sandals and thongs or jandles in warmer climates. In addition, with clothing there is a move from multi-layer garments to single-layer garments as you move closer to the equator.

A similar pattern is reflected in differences in shelter. Away from the equator, wood and stone are used and roofs are pitched. Closer to the equator, building materials tend to be clay and brick and the roofs are flatter. Climate also influences the nature of family living. In colder climates the indoors and outdoors are segregated so as to keep out the cold whereas in warmer climates indoors and outdoors are blended.

Sheth (2002) argues that climatic differences underlie many cultural manifestations in international marketing. Weather influences attitude to punctuality. Because in colder climates the window of opportunity is narrower due to the weather and there is less time available for the conduct of business, punctuality is stressed and time is treated as an economic asset. Closer to the equator the reverse is the case: stress levels are lower and cultures are said to be more 'laid back'. As far as the space dimension of culture is concerned, those in colder climates tend to be more territorial and protective of their space and are nervous of close proximity even when having a conversation. By contrast, those from warmer climates are more inclined to share space, engage in communal living and be closer in their personal proximity. Climate also has an effect on innovation. Because in colder climates resources are fewer and resource extraction is more difficult, innovation historically has commenced in such areas before moving to countries closer to the equator. As an example, the Industrial Revolution began in nations with colder climates.

As far as friendship patterns are concerned, there is a similar trend. Because friendship is not as valued in colder climates there is a greater reliance on laws and contracts, whereas the reverse is the case closer to the equator where friendship is more valued and network membership and verbal agreements rather than contracts are relied upon. Sheth claims that this also explains the low-context/high-context difference between those situated in colder as opposed to warmer climates and cites the greater use of non-verbal cues in the latter as evidence. Other differences are greater uncertainty avoidance in colder climates due to lack of resources, a win–lose attitude in negotiation in colder climates as opposed to a greater win–win attitude in warmer climates as people in the latter tend to place a higher value on social gain. Finally, Sheth explains individualism versus collectivism on the basis that further from the equator performance is assessed on an individual basis and self-achievement praised, whereas closer to the equator it is contribution to the group that is rewarded and loyalty to family, firm and society that is praised.

Although exceptions can be found to the above generalisations and although with increasing mobility of peoples these generalisations might need to be modified, the under-lying premises and their consequences should be kept in mind not only when evaluating prospects and necessary product modifications in an overseas market, but also when contemplating acquiring, managing or establishing an operation in another country.

# Consumerism

This is an organised movement of citizens (often supported by government) to improve the rights and power of buyers in relation to sellers (Kotler et al. 2006, p. 98). It is necessary for international marketers to factor into their overseas market assessments the extent to which this is a powerful force in the selected overseas market as consumer watchdog groups can exert a powerful influence on both perception of the brand and business activities in the market. If consumerism is a factor, then the views expressed need to be taken into account.

Consumerism is strong in many developed countries like Australia and New Zealand. In Australia, the Australian Consumers Association tests thousands of products, advocates safety standards and often is instrumental in having changes made to the law to protect consumers. They publicise the results of their tests via their magazine *Choice*. As an example of consumerism, in Australia there is growing concern at the levels of obesity which is generally regarded as being caused by the consumption of fast foods. Firms in this category are responding, not only via public relations campaigns but also by offering products alleged to be healthier.

# Infrastructure endowment

The availability of an adequate infrastructure will have an impact on both the costs of servicing an overseas market and the feasibility of carrying out activities in the market, as well as on the feasibility of different ways of entering that market. The adequacy of ports, airports and domestic transport links, be they road or rail, will affect costs and even the possibility of doing business, as happens when ports are congested and clearance delays extend for months.

The availability and adequacy of inputs in a foreign country such as power and water can influence what you can sell (e.g. electric refrigerators when there are frequent interruptions to electricity supply), and the costs of operating in a market (e.g. the need to sink your own bore wells or install your own power generators in cases where water flow is infrequent or polluted and/or electricity is not available or 'brown outs' are a common occurrence).

Infrastructure endowment also affects the ability to communicate and costs of doing so. Specifically, this depends on the state of telephony and the adequacy of the local IT structure to handle internet communication.

# Environmentalism

Environmentalists around the world are becoming global in their operations and scope, with organisations like Greenpeace leading the way and creating awareness of ecological mismanagement and disasters and their impact on the environment. The impacts of acid rain, global warming, deforestation, mining and urban infringement on the ecological system are being reported on TV networks like CNN, Discovery Channel and Animal Planet and consumer awareness of the pollution effects is increasing. Governments are trying to coordinate efforts to slow down these effects, but only with partial success.

However, in Europe the green consumer movement is large, with some countries considered leaders in environmental awareness. For instance, 80% of German consumers are prepared to pay premiums for household products that can be recycled and are non-damaging to the environment. In France 50% of consumers will pay a premium for supermarket products that are perceived to be environmentally friendly (Hollenson 2004, pp. 481–2). These markets vary in size in different countries, and they represent opportunities for the Australian and New Zealand international marketer to provide innovative packaging and product solutions that will gain a niche in these market places.

Concern for environmental issues is increasing and according to Howard (1998) this is due to:

- greater public awareness following publicity given to environmental disasters;
- increased national and local government regulations over actions likely to affect the environment;
- greater awareness on the part of multinational enterprise (MNE) stakeholders of actions by such firms affecting the environment;
- increased awareness by MNEs that environmental actions will have an impact on their being perceived as good corporate citizens in the countries in which they operate; and
- almost every major international conference becoming a target for protest by environmental activists as happened at the G20 summit held in Melbourne in November 2006.

In the Australian and New Zealand markets, environmentalism increasingly is a factor marketers have to take into account as far as both their aspirations and their corporate image are concerned. The press seizes on examples of firms abusing the environment or wasting scarce resources, and oil spills, toxic chemical overflow from tailings dams, acid rain, pollution, wasteful timber logging and burning of forests are headline news. In Australia it is argued that we can afford to pay more to protect the environment, but this is a hard argument to justify in emerging markets that are desperate for growth at any cost. The issue of growth versus the environment has been around a long time. In the 1800s Malthus argued that finite land and resources could not support continued population growth. Over a century later Schumpeter argued that this was wrong and that technical innovation could extend economic output and hence the ability to support more people. In 1972 the Club of Rome modelled known resource reserves and argued that these were insufficient and that the world faced hunger and economic dislocation in the future. The oil crises of the 1970s showed, however, how improved resource management and utilisation could stretch reserves of resources.

Although the growth versus environment debate continues, due to increased attention paid to environmentalism during recent decades it has become an issue that is increasingly focused upon in international trade relations. This is because in part developing countries are using it as a lever to extract concessions from developed countries. They argue that their straightened economic circumstances prevent them adopting environmentally friendly practices and force them to become the dumping ground for environmental excesses such as toxic waste from developed countries. The developing countries also suffer from greenhouse gas emissions and the hole in the ozone layer caused by industrialisation and the fascination with the motor car (which they cannot afford) in Western, developed nations.

The growth versus environmentalism debate creates an international trade relations dilemma. The World Trade Organization (WTO) has as one of its aims improving living standards by fostering the growth of world trade. However, measures to protect the environment can distort the natural flow of trade, which is contrary to the principles of the WTO. This happens when these measures are not transparent, when they are used as a protectionist device or when they contravene another WTO code of practice (e.g. technically the noise tax on passengers using Sydney's airport contravenes the WTO (formerly GATT) Subsidies Code). An example of this dilemma occurred when the USA banned tuna imports from Mexico because Mexico failed to meet US standards for protecting dolphins. This was overturned by the GATT because it violated GATT rules on distorting trade. In an attempt to address this conflict, the Doha round of WTO negotiations is attempting to strike a balance between WTO rules and specific trade obligations as set out in various multilateral environment agreements.

However, since the late 1980s, because the WTO and its predecessor the GATT had little success in addressing environmental issues, multinational agreements referred to above have been entered into on specific environmental issues and global environmental conferences are now held at regular intervals. The specific agreements include the Montreal Protocol (1989), which in order to protect the ozone layer endeavoured to impose trade restrictions on nations unwilling to reduce the use and production of ozone-depleting chemicals, and the Basel Convention (1992) on the control and transportation of hazardous wastes and their disposal. Several multinational environmental conferences have been held:

- 1992 Rio Earth Summit;
- 1995 Berlin Summit;
- 1997 Kyoto Summit;
- 1998 Buenos Aires Conference; and the
- 2002 Johannesburg World Summit on Sustainable Development.

The positive aspects of these conferences have been the focusing of attention on a wide range of environmental issues including sustainable development, global warming, carbon dioxide levels, emission targets, climate change and, at Johannesburg, the anti-globalisation movement. In the case of the Kyoto Summit, there was widespread agreement to reduce emissions by at least 5% below 1990 levels by 2012.

Under the Kyoto protocol's 'Clean Development Mechanism', companies in industrial nations can identify sources of greenhouse gas emissions in a developing country, finance a project to reduce those emissions and claim an emissions reduction credit, which they can either offset against the emissions they create elsewhere or sell to others. The trading in these so called 'carbon credits' is rapidly increasing and recently the World Bank and 11 utilities, banks and trading firms, put together the largest greenhouse gas emissions trade to date, which will result in two Chinese chemical companies reducing emissions equivalent to 19 million tons of carbon dioxide a year.

SOURCE: *Adapted from Fialka, J. J. (2006) 'Beijing to be the beneficiary of giant emissions trade',* Wall Street Journal Asia, *30 August, p. 1.*

The negative aspects were the continuing polarisation between the developing ('have nots') and developed ('haves') countries based on the conflicting demands between economic growth and protecting the environment, countries agreeing to motions, but having no intention or ability to implement the measures agreed to, and resolutions full of good intentions but few specifics for implementation or enforcement.

Australia's image at these conferences has suffered because in the last decade it has gone from being in the middle of the list of nations generating pollution to be near the top. This is because other countries have (allegedly) reduced their pollution levels. Also, since it (unlike New Zealand and another 140 countries) refused to ratify the Kyoto Protocol in 1997 on reducing greenhouse gas emissions on the grounds of its special position due to its dependence on fossil fuels, it has incurred criticism of its attitude towards environmentalism at succeeding world environmental meetings. In October 2004 Russia announced formal approval of the Kyoto Protocol on greenhouse gas emissions. This was likely due to President Putin wanting European support for his country's admission into the WTO. However, with other countries such as Australia and the USA refusing to sign on and developing country polluters such as Brazil, India, Indonesia and China not being required to reduce emissions before 2012, the Russian acceptance may not make much difference to global pollution levels or to actual reduction of pollution levels within Russia itself. Pollution from the developing world is certain to rise with increasing industrialisation, especially in countries like China and India. According to the World Bank, China is home to 16 of the world's 20 most polluted cities and pollution and environmental degradation is costing the country US$170 billion annually (*Economist*, 21 August 2004, p. 11).

The Indonesian coastal town of Sidoarjo is being inundated by 25 000 cubic metres a day of noxious mud as a result of a drilling mishap in an oil well operated by a subsidiary of the powerful Bakri Group. This has caused closure of factories, treatment of 900 people for respiratory ailments and the relocation of 5000 villagers. The Bakri Group is a major family conglomerate with influential connections to government. It has a majority ownership in the oil well and strong links to the drilling contractor involved. Initially, Bakri argued that the mud flow was caused by an earthquake 300 kilometres away, but now it is offering some compensation to the affected people. It is now alleged that the fault was caused by negligence on the part of the drilling contractor who failed to install preventative casing deeply enough.

**SOURCE:** *Adapted from Donnan, S. (2006) 'Mudflow raises questions over Indonesian business',* Financial Times, *5 July, p. 7.*

The future of environmentalism will continue to be characterised by conflict between scientific desirability and political reality, between free trade and environmental issues, and its use as a protectionist device as other trade barriers come down.

## ENVIRONMENTALISM AS A THREAT

For the international marketer environmentalism is a minefield that must be addressed directly and not left to one's overseas agent or joint venture partner. If something goes wrong it will be the foreign firm that is held accountable (as in the case of Union Carbide at Bhopal), not the local business partner. The foreign firm will receive the adverse publicity and this may injure its reputation and business prospects, not only in the country where the problem occurs but also in other overseas markets and possibly in its home market. This may cause it to be blacklisted for future projects in those countries as well as for projects funded by multilateral aid agencies such as the World Bank. This is because the local business person may not have the same environmental standards; powerbrokers in the capital cities in developing countries (e.g. Port Moresby) may not be affected by environmental consequences in the location of the operation (e.g. Ok Tedi); and the local partner may have 'called in favours' or paid a bribe to secure the investment approval in full knowledge of its environmental consequences.

Unfortunately, foreign firms also 'cop the flack' because historically they have tended to operate in pollution-prone or hazard-prone sectors of industry overseas. In addition, they have often transferred environmentally sensitive activities to countries that impose the least costly environmental restrictions (e.g. the Japanese *sogo shosha*), they have dumped unproven or outdated products on developing markets (e.g. the USA exporting to developing countries large volumes of pesticides and pharmaceuticals not allowed for sale in the USA) and they have operated plants in other countries where safety standards and employment conditions are substantially inferior to those in the home country (e.g. Nike).

The other side of the coin is that the Australian or New Zealand firm can find itself in a situation where it can only make a profit in the overseas market if it does not conform to the environmental practices expected of a good corporate citizen. In all likelihood, there will be competitors which do not conform to such standards and the rationale will be offered that developing countries cannot afford the extra costs of conforming to the environmental standards of developed countries, so why should the Australian or New Zealand firm do so in that market?

## ENVIRONMENTALISM AS AN OPPORTUNITY

There is an increasing global segment that values environmentalism and this segment has an increasing political constituency (e.g. the Australian Greens political party). Targeting this segment can take the form of creating new products for global distribution that are environmentally friendly (e.g. the Body Shop, long-life bank notes) or that contain environmentally friendly inputs (e.g. solar energy driven) and provide services to cater to the environmentally conscious (e.g. ecotourism).

Recently the major Australian bank Westpac capitalised on environmentalism as an opportunity via an advertising campaign on television extolling the virtues of the 'Equator Principles' whereby 10 major international banks had agreed not to fund projects causing pollution, and making the point that the only Australian bank in this group was Westpac.

This segment can also be reached by modifying existing products to appeal to the environmentally conscious—changing the ingredients, the packaging and the promotion. Then there are opportunities caused by environmental pollution itself. International opportunities here can lie in products and technology that will reduce future environmental problems or will clean up existing environmental problems and consultancy services to advise overseas operations on how to avoid environmental problems. Research has shown that environmentally conscious consumers are more likely to:

- sacrifice general comfort for environmental gain;

- take the environmental crisis seriously;

- believe the task of saving the environment rests with individuals and not just governments;

- pay more for 'green' products; and

spend more time locating 'green' products (Pickett et al. 1993).

Opportunities will be further enhanced as it is realised that environmental sensitivity is not so much a cost of undertaking international business, but a catalyst for constant innovation and wealth creation.

Recently L'Oreal SA, the world's largest cosmetics company, agreed to pay US$1.14 billion for Body Shop International, a 30-year-old UK manufacturer of natural beauty products. This illustrates that environmental consciousness can become a commercial opportunity. One of the underlying principles of its founder, Anita Roddick, was 'commerce with conscience', as reflected in the firm's policy of community trade on the one hand (buying natural ingredients from communities around the world, so as to reduce poverty) and opposition to testing products on animals (which eventually caused the European Union to introduce legislation in this connection). The niche market developed by Roddick involved a network across 55 countries exceeding 2000 stores.

**SOURCE:** *Adapted from Kartajaya, H. (2006) 'Sellout? It's the Body Shop's selling point', Asia Inc, July–August, p. 19.*

---

**FIGURE 5.5  Types of environmental strategies**

|  |  | Value creation approach | |
|---|---|---|---|
|  |  | *Benefit enhancement for customers* | *Cost reduction* |
| **Change orientation** | *Proactive* | Green product Innovation (major modification) | Pollution prevention Beyond compliance |
|  |  | *1* \| *2* | |
|  |  | *3* \| *4* | |
|  | *Accommodative* | Green product Differentiation (minor modification) | Pollution prevention Compliance |

**SOURCE:** *Starik, M., Throop, G.M., Doody, J.M. and Joyce, M.E. (1996) 'Growing an environmental strategy', Business Strategy and Environment, Vol. 5, p. 17. Copyright John Wiley and Sons Ltd. Reproduced with permission.*

---

Figure 5.5 shows different types of environmental strategies for the marketer. In this figure the horizontal axis represents providing value to those customers concerned with environmental issues and the vertical axis represents the willingness of the firm to make changes to accommodate such concerns.

## Ethics

Companies operating in a number of different countries are likely to be subject to different local ethical standards which in turn may be different from those that operate in the domestic market. It is in emerging markets that the issue of ethics crops up most frequently. This is true of markets in the former Soviet bloc as well as those in the Third World. In both cases, this is due to governments in these countries neglecting the laws, regulations and property rights that control the excesses of capitalism, according to Ham (2004).

Corruption is the major but not the only ethical issue in international marketing. Research by Collins and Uhlenbruck (2004) found that with government corruption in India there was a considerable difference between the stated perceptions of corruption and the practice of engaging in corrupt activities. They found that corruption was an institution that all firms,

# Companies tiptoe through Indonesia's political minefields

The New Orleans based company Freeport is hard pressed to reap the full benefits from its Grasberg mine in Indonesia's Irian Jaya province. This year, the firm expects to sell 1.3 billion pounds of copper, down from 1.5 billion pounds in 2005. This fall is due to a number of setbacks in developing one of the world's most promising resources. Included in these setbacks have been:

• A blockade by illegal miners shut down the Grasberg pit for a period in February;

• Indonesian nationalists have called for Freeport's contract to be either renewed or cancelled;

• Environmentalists are pressuring the Indonesian Government over Freeport's mining practices;

• Freeport is being accused of corruption over paying officers in Indonesia's military to provide security services at the mine;

• This corruption allegation has resulted in investigations into the company's activities being carried out by both the US Justice Department and the US Securities and Exchange Commission;

• The situation is causing Freeport difficulty in raising capital from the world's financial community who are increasingly worried about political risk in Indonesia; and

• New exploration to expand the capacity of Grasberg has ceased because of the uncertain regulatory environment in Indonesia.

**SOURCE:** *Adapted from 'Companies tiptoe through Indonesia's political minefields',* Financial Times, *26 May 2006, p. 3; and Freed, J. (2006) 'Ethics test miner's mettle',* Sydney Morning Herald, *1–2 April, p. 30.*

both domestic and foreign, needed to take into account when making strategic management decisions. They also found that the closer the relationships between business executives and government officials, the greater the likelihood of corruption. Another example is the case of an Australian marketing author entering into an arrangement with a Chinese academic for publication of his text for the Chinese market. This involved a committee of people in China who needed to agree on publication arrangements, distribution, translation, ownership, payment and other logistics. It became clear after several meetings and discussions that the different members of the committee had entirely different views of property ownership rights based on a different set of values. International marketers face these issues constantly. Different cultures and value systems directly influence the behaviour of consumers and managers and these need to be understood by international marketers along with the constraints imposed on their own behaviour by corporate ethics and personal values. In this book each chapter addresses an ethical issue that is commonly faced by international marketers.

To the traditional marketing concept of satisfying customer's wants and needs at a profit is added the dimension of ethical and corporate responsibility. International marketing is vulnerable to ethical considerations on many fronts. It can involve advertising where the ethical issue can be misrepresentation, personal selling where the ethical issue can be bribery and market research where the ethical issue can be invasive questioning or breach of confidence. In the international domain ethical considerations are more complex because different criteria apply in different countries as to what is acceptable ethical behaviour and what is not. Also the degree to which ethical norms are enforced will vary not only between countries but also within the one country depending on who has engaged in the unethical practice. A working definition of ethics is 'culturally based assumptions as to what is right or wrong'. Ethical misbehaviour can take many forms, including bribery, smuggling, child labour, intellectual piracy, coercion, conflict of interest, environmental degradation, paternalism/nepotism, abuse of safety standards and the manufacture of defective or harmful goods.

The problem is particularly acute in emerging markets that, while offering the greatest opportunities for growth in many activities on the one hand, are also as a group the most corrupt on the other. Although corruption is not the only manifestation of ethical misbehaviour, it is the most prominent. In essence, the problem faced by many Australian and New Zealand firms when they venture offshore is whether they can handle non-Western cultures that pay lip service to Western notions of ethics, but practise traditional modes of conducting business. The international marketer needs to be aware of these differences and also of the laws regarding ethical behaviours that operate in both the home country and the host country. Where ethics are concerned the marketer is likely to be confronted by two sets of laws and two sets of behaviours when transacting business overseas. The marketer may also be confronted by the laws of a third party as happens when the subsidiary of a US firm operating as a corporate citizen in Australia is bound by the US *Foreign Corrupt Practices Act* regarding its business dealings in Asia. This Act makes it illegal for companies to pay bribes to foreign officials, candidates or political parties. Although ethical misbehaviour occurs in developed countries, the greatest offenders are likely to be found among the emerging markets. Figure 5.6 shows the relative corruption ratings of various emerging markets, with a high score indicating a relative absence of corruption and a low score indicating a high degree of corruption. In the wider table from which this data was extracted New Zealand at 9.5 and Australia at 8.8 were shown as being relatively free of corruption, but the rating of Australia has fallen following the AWB bribery issue discussed in Chapter 4. The corruption rating for all countries in 2006 can be found at <http://www.transparency.org/pressreleases_archive/2003/2003.10.07.cpi.en.html>.

Views of correct ethical behaviour differ according to whether the person holds a:

- *relativist perspective*—what is ethical is determined by the host culture, for example bribery is OK because it is customary in the host country; or a

- *utilitarian perspective*—what is ethical is that which delivers the greatest benefit to the greatest number of people; for example, bribery is acceptable because it leads to contracts that create employment; or a

- *universalist perspective*—there is a universal set of acceptable ethical behaviours that should be applied to the conduct of business wherever it occurs; for example bribery is unacceptable under any circumstances.

The problem with the relativist perspective is that consumers in the developing world are not as likely to be as well informed as their counterparts in developed countries; there is less regulation of the marketplace; and many of the developing countries do not have well-developed democratic institutions. The problem with the utilitarian perspective is that it is usually short term and can be detrimental in the longer term. The problem with the universalist perspective is that it assumes that one culture (Western) has the right to define ethical behaviour for the whole world. This raises the issue of whether this perspective is appropriate in an environment of increasing globalisation and whether corporate codes of conduct, such as the Moral Authority of Transnational Corporate Codes, or ethical watch-dogs, such as Transparency International, really work. Are such bodies effective or are they another example of the West imposing its values on the East?

The best solution to the dilemma may well lie between the relativist and universalist perspectives. If 1 is the relativist perspective and 5 is the universalist perspective, then the

## FIGURE 5.6  Corruption perception index of major emerging markets

| Country rank | Country | CPI 2003 score | Surveys used | Standard deviation | High–low range |
|---|---|---|---|---|---|
| 5 | Singapore | 9.4 | 12 | 0.1 | 9.2–9.5 |
| 14 | Hong Kong | 8 | 11 | 1.1 | 5.6–9.3 |
| 20 | Chile | 7.4 | 12 | 0.9 | 5.6–8.8 |
| 21 | Israel | 7 | 12 | 0.9 | 5.6–8.1 |
| 37 | Malaysia | 5.2 | 10 | 1.2 | 3.6–8.0 |
| 40 | Hungary | 4.8 | 13 | 0.6 | 4.0–5.6 |
| 48 | South Africa | 4.4 | 12 | 0.6 | 3.6–5.5 |
| 50 | South Korea | 4.3 | 12 | 1 | 2.0–5.6 |
| 54 | Czech Republic | 3.9 | 12 | 0.9 | 2.6–5.6 |
| 59 | Colombia | 3.7 | 11 | 0.5 | 2.7–4.4 |
| | Peru | 3.7 | 9 | 0.6 | 2.7–4.9 |
| 64 | Mexico | 3.6 | 12 | 0.6 | 2.4–4.9 |
| | Poland | 3.6 | 14 | 1.1 | 2.4–5.6 |
| 66 | China | 3.4 | 13 | 1 | 2.0–5.5 |
| 70 | Egypt | 3.3 | 9 | 1.3 | 1.8–5.3 |
| | Thailand | 3.3 | 13 | 0.9 | 1.4–4.4 |
| 77 | Turkey | 3.1 | 14 | 0.9 | 1.8–5.4 |
| 83 | India | 2.8 | 14 | 0.4 | 2.1–3.6 |
| 86 | Russia | 2.7 | 16 | 0.8 | 1.4–4.9 |
| 92 | Argentina | 2.5 | 12 | 0.5 | 1.6–3.2 |
| | Philippines | 2.5 | 12 | 0.5 | 1.6–3.6 |
| 100 | Venezuela | 2.4 | 12 | 0.5 | 1.4–3.1 |
| 122 | Indonesia | 1.9 | 13 | 0.5 | 0.7–2.9 |

*Notes*: CPI score relates to perceptions of the degree of corruption as seen by businesspeople, academics and risk analysts, and ranges between 10 (highly clean) and 0 (highly corrupt).

'Surveys used' refers to the number of surveys that assessed a country's performance. A total of 17 surveys were used from 13 independent institutions, and at least three surveys were required for a country to be included in the CPI.

'Standard deviation' indicates differences in the values of the sources: the greater the standard deviation, the greater the differences of perceptions of a country among the sources.

High–low range provides the highest and lowest values of the different sources.

**SOURCE:** Transparency International, Corruption Perceptions Index, 2003, *<http://www.transparency.org/layout/set/print/policy_research/surveys_indices>. Copyright 2006. Transparency International: the global coalition against corruption. Used with permission. For more information, visit <http://www.transparency.org>.*

'win–win' position is likely to be at neither extreme. Taking the hypothetical example of paying a bribe, with:

1   a local party who says direct bribes are necessary;

2   direct bribery modified by global standards;

3   paying unavoidable bribes indirectly via your agent;

4   observing global standards but making facilitation payments if unavoidable;

5   under no circumstances, paying any inducement

then the win–win zone is 2, 3 or 4.

This kind of pragmatism is reflected in the decision by the change in the US *Foreign Corrupt Practices Act* to exempt facilitation payments and the Australian practice of allowing small bribes paid overseas to be tax deductible. The ethical validity of the latter is questionable as facilitation payments paid in Australia are not tax deductible.

Ethical behaviours differ from country to country because of:

- *popular attachments to governments*—if people respect the government they are less likely to break its laws in pursuit of individual gain. This is offered as an explanation as to why democracies in general are less corrupt than absolutist regimes;

- *popular customs*—in many countries, gift giving is the norm in business and is treated as an expression of friendship. While it may be argued that although the gift is trifling, the feeling is profound, it can easily degenerate into a situation where the more generous the gift, the more profound the feeling;

- *level of economic development*—low levels of economic development intensify the role of government as a source of jobs and benefits. As economic development in such countries increases, government contracts become larger and the scope for incentives to secure the contract increases;

- *relative size of the public sector*—as it grows, more aspects of life come under its control and with new rules come new opportunities and incentives to break them;

- *low income for public servants*—this creates an unwritten convention that, as the government cannot afford to pay its public servants properly, the cost of employing them should be shared between the government on the one hand and those who benefit from the service provided on the other. An example of this is payment of 'tea money' to the public servant to speed up the approval process or a facilitation payment to have a container cleared from the wharf in reasonable time;

- *obscure political and legal environments*—poorly defined property rights, investment procedures and accounting standards all provide scope for questionable ethical practices. This tends to be exacerbated when the regime in power is unstable or does not exercise control over the whole country;

- *high level of government control and state ownership*—this enables politicians and bureaucrats to appropriate legal rights unto themselves and use their positions for personal enrichment or to raise funds for political election campaigns.

Attempts by world bodies such as the WTO and regional bodies such as NAFTA, the EU and ASEAN to impose ethical standards on their members have encountered difficulties because of different ethical practices by some members (e.g. Mexico in NAFTA). Disaffected countries in these circumstances are likely to argue that efforts to impose Western-derived ethical standards are impinging on their national sovereignty. It is anticipated that global ethical standards will improve due to the information revolution, increasing levels of transparency, the extension of democracy, greater internationalisation of the media and the increase in the numbers in the middle class as a bridge between the 'haves' and the 'have nots'. This would be true if ethical breaches were rare in developed Western countries. Unfortunately, this is not the case, as evidenced by the Australian firm James Hardie Pty Ltd restructuring its affairs in a legal manner so that, by incorporating the organisation in the Netherlands, it was able to reduce the amount of compensation payable to large numbers of people dying from asbestosis due to its manufacturing processes and the contaminants in the fibre board it produced. A chorus of public outrage eventually caused the firm to make a more adequate provision for compensation to victims of this disease.

An ethical behaviour, often confused with corruption, that Australian and New Zealand firms find hard to cope with is cronyism. This is found in social networks characterised by complex, indirect and mutually reinforcing social exchanges, according to Khatri et al. (2006). In the reciprocal exchange involved, there is a particular favour based on the relationship with an implicit unspecified return obligation. Nepotism is an example of cronyism, but is confined to family.

## 5.4 INTERNATIONAL HIGHLIGHT

# It takes two to tango

Corruption indices and the like rate countries in terms of the likelihood of bribes being requested in order to secure contracts. These, however, ignore rating multinational firms in terms of their willingness to offer bribes. Recently, the head of the Organization of American States resigned amid accusations that he received bribes while he was President of Costa Rica. Little coverage has been given to the French telecommunications giant Alcatel, which allegedly offered the bribe. Alcatel reportedly paid politicians of all factions when negotiating a US$149 million mobile phone contract in 2001 and another US$109 million for a fixed phone line contract in 2002. Much of the bribe money went from the company account at ABN Amro bank in Holland to ABN Amro in New York and from there to the International Bank of Miami.

More recently, Total Oil became the subject of investigation over dubious payments in both Russia and Iraq. Such actions are in violation of the 1999 OECD convention that requires countries (including France) to enact laws prohibiting their countries from bribing foreign officials. In every corruption scandal there is a hand that gives and a hand that receives and, unless governments adhere to international treaties that require them to crack down on corporations caught bribing foreign officials, attempts to eliminate corruption in international trade will prove futile.

**SOURCE:** *Adapted from Openheimer, A. (2004) 'OAS scandal's other side–corporate corruption',* Miami Herald, *10 October, p. 18A.*

Ethical issues, however, are not confined to corruption. One area of increasing focus is that of manufacture offshore in countries where costs are low because workers are exploited and local labour regulations ignored. While Nike is well known in this connection, it is only one of many firms from Western countries that 'turn a blind eye' to activities in offshore plants which, when they become known, damage the global image of the organisation. With the increasing tendency to outsource manufacture and services supply to other countries, international marketers need to be sensitive to this issue lest practices in one country damage their reputation in others.

Other ethical issues that involve taking advantage of different rules and standards, the absence of rules or standards or the lack of enforcement of existing rules and standards in other countries, include polluting the environment (which caused BHP Billiton to eventually abandon its Ok Tedi mine in Papua New Guinea), selling products offshore that do not meet standards in the home country and producing unsafe products by economising on the quality of inputs or components.

In many cases it will be necessary for the international marketer to research in advance of entry, whether it is possible to enter an overseas market without compromising internal business conduct standards as far as corruption and other ethical issues are concerned.

A report by Nike on its 700 factories shows that there are cases of abusive treatment in more than a quarter of its Asian plants. Such abuse involves denying workers access to drinking water, not allowing them one day off in 7, requiring them to work more than 60 hours a week and punishing them if they refuse to work overtime. Nike found it was paying below minimum wages in 25% of its factories.

**SOURCE:** Sydney Morning Herald, *16–17 April 2005, p. 17.*

# The internet and the contemporary environment

The internet environment has created a level of immediacy that provides access to real-time information from literally millions of information sources globally. We can access government, corporate and market information through sophisticated search engines at any time to gain information relevant to operating in international markets. At the same time our computers can be accessed by global 'hackers' if our corporate or personal firewalls are insufficient to block out 'intruders'. The internet provides significant opportunities for SMEs.

It reduces the competitive advantages of scale economies making it easier for small companies to compete internationally. Advertising costs, formerly a barrier to overseas marketing, have reduced as the web makes it possible to reach a global audience at low cost.

The role of traditional intermediaries is changing as the internet connects producers directly with end-users. Price differentials between customers and between countries are narrowed as consumers become more price aware. The web can act as an efficient low-cost medium for conducting worldwide market research—gaining customer feedback, tracking customer behaviour and establishing virtual communities. In summary, the internet is providing SMEs with low-cost access to global markets by reducing the barriers to internationalisation commonly experienced by small companies.

In 2008 the internet is reaching a new stage. Futurists suggest that instead of you having to find information or entertainment, the web will find you and provide exactly what you want or need at that moment—the network becomes a butler. This requires meshing with new technologies such as Wi-Fi wireless broadband connections, the Global Positioning System (GPS) and radio frequency identification tags (RFID). These technologies are becoming a network of networks enabled by powerful new devices and databases, all interlinked and communicating with each other. This is becoming a fundamental 'world network' on which companies can build services that will find you and provide consumer or business services and products, unprompted, to meet your needs depending on where you are and what you are doing.

The web also affects contemporary environmental variables. Taking the example of terrorism, there is the phenomenon of cyberterrorism, which is a terrorist attack that both uses and targets computer systems, especially those that control national infrastructure such as water, power and communications. This terrorism can take several forms, the most likely of which is via the introduction of a virus or worm. Both the likelihood of such terrorism and the extent of damage possible will influence the attractiveness of an overseas market.

SOURCES: *Wildstrom, S.H. (2007) 'Juicing up Home Networks',* BusinessWeek, *5 February, p. 22; and Maney, K. (2004) 'Next big thing: the Web as your servant',* USA Today, *1–3 October, pp. 1–2A.*

# Summary

The information and technology revolution in the new century is transforming the international business environment. Access to information and to the purchase of services and certain products via internet or intranet systems provides the opportunity for Australian and New Zealand businesses instantly to reach and be reached by overseas customers and prospects connected to these systems. This provides potential market penetration and speed of a totally different dimension from traditional marketplace activities. Technology is now playing a central role in the international marketing environment as we see new technologies revolutionising sectors like health, manufacturing, communications and the electronics in the home.

The adoption and diffusion processes of new products, services and technologies need to be viewed in the light of this revolution. The identification of lead users in overseas markets is a particular challenge and opportunity for Australian and New Zealand firms. An understanding of how relevant industry structures are changing, globally and in country and regional markets, is an important aspect in reviewing the information and technology environment.

Contemporary variables that affect the international marketer's decisions also include health, geography, consumerism, infrastructure, environmentalism, terrorism and ethics, which add to the challenge of creating opportunities by firms in the changing international marketplace.

## ETHICS ISSUE

Emergence of a 'world network' has the potential to pre-empt your needs by acting as a butler and seeking you out with a solution to a particular need at a moment in time. This could be a travel butler that changes your flight booking and notifies your partner of a late arrival home after it detects that you are stuck in traffic and will miss your flight.

*Are there ethical issues associated with these kinds of services? What kinds of services and situations could raise ethical concerns?*

# Websites

**3M** http://www.3m.com
**Adobe** http://www.adobe.com
**Animal Planet** http:animal.discovery.com/
**Cephalon** http://www.cephalon.com
**CNN** http://www.cnn.com
**Design Graphics Warehouse** http://dgwarehouse.com
**Discovery Channel** http://www.discovery.com
**Ericsson** http://www.ericsson.com
**Getty Images** http://www.gettyimages.com
**GPS** http://www.gpsworld.com
**Greenpeace** http://www.greenpeace.org
**Halliburton** http://www.halliburton.com
**HP** http://www.hp.com
**Imation** http://www.imation.com
**Kroll** http://www.kroll.com
**Merck** http://www.merck.com
**Microsoft** http://www.microsoft.com
**Motorola** http://www.motorola.com
**Neurochem** http://www.neurochem.com
**Nokia** http://www.nokia.com
**Novartis** http://www.novartis.com
**Oracle** http://www.oracle.com
**Packet8** http://www.packet8.net
**RFID** http://www.rfid.com
**Rim Blackberry** http://www.blackberry.com
**Roche** http://www.roche.com
**Skype** http://www.skype.com
**Telstra** http://www.telstra.com
**Transparency International** http://www.transparency.org/publications
**Warren and Brown Technologies** http://www.warrenandbrown.com.au
**World Trade Organization** http://www.wto.org

# Discussion questions

1   What are the technology drivers of the fifth techno-economic paradigm?

2   Using International Highlight 5.1 as a reference point, discuss how new technology supporting iPhone and its competitors is changing the way people live and work in the international business environment.

3   Look at the websites of HSBC Bank and Qantas, and evaluate them in terms of potential for attracting international business.

4   How do lead users play a part in the adoption and diffusion of a new technology, product or service? Give an example.

5   What are the likely impacts of technological change, globalisation and information technology on industry structures—globally and in local country markets?

6  What trends in health and fitness provide opportunities for Australian or New Zealand organisations in the international market?

7  What are the impacts of terrorism on the opportunities for Australian or New Zealand businesses in international markets? Provide examples of these impacts.

8  How might global warming provide overseas opportunities for Australian and New Zealand businesses?

9  The internet is entering a new phase as part of a bigger 'world network'. What are the implications for Australian firms wanting to use this network to access world markets?

## References

Apple <http://www.apple.com/iphone/>.

Bradley, F. (2005) *International Marketing Strategy*, 5th edn, Financial Times Prentice Hall, Harlow, UK.

Cameron, D. (2004) 'Japanese hungry to know where their food has been', *Sydney Morning Herald*, 25–26 September.

Collins, J. and Uhlenbruck, K. (2004) 'How firms respond to government corruption: insights from India', presented at the Academy of International Business Conference, Stockholm, 10–13 July.

'Companies tiptoe through Indonesia's political minefields', *Financial Times*, 26 May 2006, p. 3.

Department of Foreign Affairs and Trade (2003) 'Economic costs of terrorism', Global Issues Brief, Report 01/2003, Economic Analytical Unit, Department of Foreign Affairs and Trade.

Department of Foreign Affairs and Trade (2004) 'Combating terrorism in the transport sector—economic costs and benefits', Economic Analytical Unit, Department of Foreign Affairs and Trade, Canberra.

Donnan, S. (2006) 'Mudflow raises questions over Indonesian business', *Financial Times*, 5 July, p. 7.

*Economist*, 21 August 2004, p. 11.

Enderwick, P. (2001) 'Terrorism and the international business environment', *AIB Insights*, special electronic issue, available at <http://www.aibworld.com>.

Fialka, J.J. (2006) 'Beijing to be the beneficiary of giant emissions trade', *Wall Street Journal Asia*, 30 August, p. 1.

Forman, C. (2005) 'Should the US be scared?', *Time*, 17 October, pp. 17–20.

Freed, J. (2006) 'Ethics test miner's mettle', *Sydney Morning Herald*, 1–2 April, p. 30.

Freeman, C. and Perez, C. (1988) 'Structural crises of adjustment, business cycles and investment behaviour', in Dosi, G., Freeman, C., Nelson, R., Silverberg, G. and Soete, L. (eds) *Technical Change and Economic Theory*, Pinter, London, summary of section on Keynes (pp. 41–5) and Samuelson (p. 45).

Frick, H. (2006) 'Identification, Assessment, Treatment and Monitoring of Legal Risk in Foreign Direct Investments: A multiple case study approach for Australian investments in Chile', an unpublished PhD thesis, *University of Queensland*.

Gunther, M. (2004) 'A crisis business can't ignore', *Fortune*, 6 September, p. 30.

Ham, P. (2004) 'Beware the dragon', *Export*, August–September, p. 10.

Hazlett, T.W. (2004) 'Broadband miracle', *Wall Street Journal*, 26 August.

Herstatt, C. and von Hippel, E. (1992) 'From experience: developing new product concepts via the lead user method: a case study in a "low tech" field', *Journal of Product Innovation Management*, Vol. 9, pp. 200–12.

Hollensen, S. (2004) *Global Marketing–A Decision-Oriented Approach*, Financial Times Prentice Hall, Harlow, UK.

Howard, E. (1998) 'Keeping ahead of Green regulators', Marketing Global Management, Part 10, *Financial Times*.

IATA <http://www.iata.org/workgroups/etwg.htm>, accessed 10 March 2007.

Jack, A. (2006) 'WHO seeks data on avian flu treatment', *Financial Times*, 30 May, p. 4.

Kartajaya, H. (2006) 'Sellout? It's the Body Shop's selling point', *Asia Inc*, July–August, p. 19.

Kelly, T., Gray, V. and Minges, M. (2003) *Broadband Korea: Case Summary*, International Telecommunication Union, March 2003, pp. 1–3.

Khatri, N., Toang, E.W.K. and Bigley, T.M. (2006) 'Cronyism: a cross-cultural analysis', *Journal of International Business Studies*, Vol. 37, pp. 61–75.

Klopfenstein, B. (1998) *Diffusion of Innovations on the Web*, Bowling Green State University, Department of Communications, Bowling Green, OH.

Kotler, P., Keller, K.L., Ang, S.H., Leong, S.M. and Chin, T.T. (2006) *Marketing Management: An Asian Perspective*, 4th edn, Pearson Prentice Hall, Singapore.

Maier, M. (2004) 'A factory in every home', *Business 2.0*, September, pp. 85–6.

Maney, K. (2004) 'Next big thing: the Web as your servant', *USA Today*, 1–3 October, pp. 1–2A.

Moore, G.A. (1995) *Inside the Tornado: Marketing Strategies from Silicon Valley's Cutting Edge*, Harper Business, New York, p. 25.

Moore, G.A. (2005) *Dealing with Darwin: How Great Companies Innovate at Every Phase of their Evolution*, Penguin Books Limited, London, Chapter 2, pp. 15–28.

Naisbitt, J. (2006) *Mind Set: Reset your Thinking and See the Future*, HarperCollins, New York.

Openheimer, A. (2004) 'OAS scandal's other side—corporate corruption', *Miami Herald*, 10 October, p. 18A.

'Paper airline tickets on the way out', *Sydney Morning Herald*, 1 March 2007, <http://www.smh.com.au/news/travel/paper-airline-tickets-on-the-way-out/2007/03/01/1172338752660.html>, accessed 10 March 2007.

Pattinson, H.M. and Brown L.R. (1996) 'Metamorphosis in marketspace—paths to new industries in the emerging electronic marketing environment', *Irish Marketing Review*, Vol. 9, p. 56.

Penn, J.Y., Buetre, B. and Tran, Q.T. (2003) *Economic Costs of Terrorism–An Illustration of the Impact of Lower Productivity Growth on World Economic Activity using GTEM*, Australian Bureau of Agricultural and Resources Economics, Commonwealth of Australia, Canberra.

Pickett, G.M., Cangun, N. and Grove, S.J. (1993) 'Is there a general conserving consumer? A public policy concern', *Journal of Public Policy and Marketing*, Vol. 12, No. 2, pp. 234–43.

Rosenbush, S. (2004) 'Net calls: there's lots to like', *BusinessWeek*, 8 November, p. 122.

Schmidt, M.J. and Hollensen, S. (2006) *Marketing Research: An International Approach*, Financial Times Prentice Hall, Harlow, UK.

Sheth, J. (2002) Keynote address delivered at Multicultural Marketing Conference, Valencia, Spain, May.

Sheth, J. and Sisodia, R. (2002) *The Rule of Three: Surviving and Thriving in Competitive Markets*, The Free Press, New York.

Sparks, J.D. (2007) 'Europe's Apple attack', *Newsweek*, 5 March, p. 47.

Starik, M., Throop, G.M., Doody, J.M. and Joyce, M.E. (1996) 'Growing an environmental strategy', *Business Strategy and Environment*, Vol. 5, pp. 12–21.

Steenkamp, J-B. (2002) 'Global consumers', Presentation of a working paper at Tilburg University, 17 November, Tilburg University, Tilburg, The Netherlands.

*Sydney Morning Herald*, 16–17 April 2005, p. 17.

von Hippel, E. (2005) '*Democratizing Innovation*', MIT Press, Cambridge, Mass., Chapter 2, pp. 19–32.

Wildstrom, S.H. (2007) 'Juicing up home networks', *BusinessWeek*, 5 February, p. 22.

Zachary, G.P. (2004) 'Brain boosters', *Business 2.0*, September, pp. 85–6.

## go online

Go online to <www.pearsoned.com.au/fletcher> to find more case studies.

# CASE STUDY 5

# The dilemma of live sheep exports

**Jun Wen Chen and Richard Fletcher**

*Until the events of late 1997, and more recently of 11 September 2001, it could be said that the global economy was growing strongly and was continuing on a path commenced at the beginning of the decade. Since 1990 developing economies had grown at about twice the rate of the industrialised economies (according to the IMF), Latin America had been largely free of debt and the end of the Cold War had brought the economies of Russia and Eastern Europe into the market-driven.*

## INTRODUCTION

Samex is an Australian-based company that exports meat products around the world. It operates a processing facility in Western Australia and also exports live product as required. The company has a strategy of identifying new markets and then developing products to enter these markets. This means having different international business strategies according to the export market. Along with product development, this also includes market entry and distribution strategies.

The live sheep export trade was one area that Samex had developed over the years, but it had been under attack for many years because of ethical issues associated with the trade. Live sheep were sought by some important customers in the Middle East who preferred to process the meat themselves. Problems with this arose when pressure groups attacked the trade as unethical. This was made worse when the Egyptian government refused to accept a shipment of live sheep because it claimed the sheep were in poor condition.

Samex has had to re-establish its market in the live sheep trade and make sure any ethical issues are dealt with. This case study looks at the issues Samex had to deal with as it developed a market in the United Arab Emirates (UAE), and how international marketing must be adjusted according to the particular situation. International trade usually involves dealing with many different separate issues, but this case study examines how culture, ethics, and distribution must sometimes

work together if the trade is going to be successful.

## MIDDLE EAST MARKET

Middle East countries have shown a preference for importing live sheep that can then be processed according to local culture. The demand for fresh sheep meat has been increasing over recent years as the Middle East has become more affluent and has demanded the ability to handle its food in line with Islamic religious beliefs (MLA 2007). In other words, there is a consumer demand for a different type of product to that which is usually exported, and this demand is supported by arguments that the product must be processed locally or it will not be suitable for the market.

The information in Table 1 shows how the value of live sheep exports has steadily increased since 1994 to reach over 5.8 million sheep by 2003, but sharply decreased in 2004 and 2005, due to the

| **TABLE 1** | **Australian live sheep exports 1994–2005** | | | |
|---|---|---|---|---|
| **Year** | **Number of sheep ('000)** | **Gross weight ('000 tonnes)** | **Gross value ($'000)** | **Unit value ($)** |
| 1994–95 | 5697.0 | 290.2 | 184 291 | 32.35 |
| 1995–96 | 5879.9 | 296.9 | 226 913 | 38.59 |
| 1996–97 | 5237.2 | 269.8 | 189 944 | 36.27 |
| 1997–98 | 4961.1 | 256.0 | 193 266 | 38.96 |
| 1998–99 | 4958.7 | 254.9 | 181 671 | 36.64 |
| 1999–2000 | 4858.6 | 243.3 | 180 345 | 37.12 |
| 2000–01 | 5936.0 | 283.6 | 257 661 | 43.41 |
| 2001–02 | 6443.2 | 318.0 | 391 705 | 60.79 |
| 2002–03 | 5843.2 | 273.0 | 408 235 | 69.87 |
| 2003–04 | 3842.7 | 188.2 | 266 457 | 69.34 |
| 2004–05 | 3233.2 | 166.1 | 206 678 | 63.92 |

**SOURCE:** *Australian Bureau of Statistics* Year Book Australia, 2004, *<http://www.abs.gov.au>*.

sales to Saudi Arabia, once Australia's largest market, being suspended in August 2003 after a row that saw 58 000 live sheep stranded at sea when Saudi officials rejected them on health grounds.

It should also be noted that behind these export figures is an extensive and sophisticated infrastructure that supports the industry, which gives many sheep farmers a reliable and consistent market. Live sheep exports are therefore very important to some parts of rural Australia.

## HOFSTEDE'S CULTURAL DIMENSIONS

One way of understanding how culture might influence business and work is through Hofstede's cultural dimensions covering the basic categories of:

- power distance–shows how much distance there is between people within a society or how much inequalities were highlighted;
- individualism versus collectivism–shows the relationship between the individual and the society, whether individualism is valued or whether the collective is emphasised;
- uncertainty avoidance–shows the extent to which a culture avoids ambiguous or risky situations;

- masculinity versus femininity–shows what gender roles are more important in the culture (Hill 1997, pp. 86–7).

When these dimensions are applied to Arab countries the significant features are that there is a high level of power distance and uncertainty avoidance (Geert Hofstede 2007). In practical terms this means Arab societies are more likely to have clearly defined levels of society that people do not usually cross; there is very little upward mobility. Along with this they are highly rule-oriented, with many laws and systems of control that reduce uncertainty (ITIM 2003). In a society such as this it is important to deal with those who have the power because it is only those with power who will be able to move and act relatively freely throughout the society.

## CHANNEL MEMBER SELECTION

The interesting lesson that can be learned from Hofstede's dimensions is the way they can have an impact on the selection of and relationships between channel members. It is possible to follow the guidelines developed by Usunier (1996, pp. 353–4) to see that a high level of uncertainty avoidance might mean that prospective business partners would be looking for someone with a solid reputation and who might also be able to give a guarantee that they can deliver or perform as specified. Along with this, high power distance business partners might prefer face-to-face contact with the owner or senior member of a business, and also want all business to go through them.

When Samex applied this to the UAE, the first aspect was that it should connect with a customer, distributor or partner who had authority over a wide region. An important part of this was that the partner might be insulted if Samex also tried to establish business relationships in areas that the UAE channel member had its own business. For example, if Samex wanted to enter the Saudi Arabian market and the UAE partner already managed the Saudi Arabian market for a number of other suppliers, then the UAE partner would assume that they would also handle this business for Samex.

## RETAIL CONCENTRATION

There are also distribution considerations when exporting to the Middle East. The different languages and cultures mean that products might require different packaging before they are suitable for the Middle East market. It is also necessary to consider the retail concentration to determine how far the company can reach with its marketing strategy. The Middle East in general does not have a highly concentrated retail sector, and this can make it difficult for exporters to reach the consumers in the market unless there are a number of intermediaries in place.

## CHANNEL LENGTH

Samex had to be prepared to develop longer channels than might have been necessary in other markets. The fragmented Middle East retail system made it much too expensive for the company to try to contact retailers directly. Along with this, the Middle East retail market relies on wholesalers to move products into particular areas, so it was the task of the company to consider how it was going to connect with these wholesalers.

The selection of the UAE as an export destination was based on the ability of the UAE to act as a base for the rest of the Middle East. According to Kizirian and Taha (2004), six of the 15 major meat processing plants in the Middle East are located in the UAE. The output from these processing plants includes burger patties, minced meats, pastrami and beef mortadella, and these products are then marketed around the region. The importance of this for an Australian food exporter to the region can be seen in the Department of Foreign Affairs and Trade's (2004) advice that the best way for food products to enter Saudi Arabia, for example, is through the UAE. A company such as Samex needs to locate an agent in the UAE with a view to that agent also operating as a convenient distribution channel into other countries in the region, such as Saudi Arabia.

## PRODUCT DEVELOPMENT

One of the important components of developing international markets is the way that each of those markets might have different requirements that need to be met. Samex caters to a range of different markets including Asia, South America and the Middle East. The development of the Middle East export market, in particular to Egypt and the United Arab Emirates (UAE), opened up opportunities for a different marketing mix to be applied.

The company had to consider the needs of its Middle East customers and what the company had to do to make sure its products were attractive to this market. The example of the UAE shows that some parts of the Middle East are wealthy enough to import various products from around the world. However, exporting food products to an Islamic country such as the UAE must be done after considering the differences in dietary practices. It was for this reason that Samex became committed to live sheep exports rather to try to develop a market for its processed meat products.

## PRESSURE GROUPS

One of the problems facing Samex when it makes decisions about its international business operations is the way pressure groups can influence the outcomes of any decisions. It is understood that pressure groups can have a lot of influence, and have become much more vocal over recent years (Lee and Carter 2005). Pressure groups such as

Animals Australia have in recent years undertaken investigations and provided evidence of the animal welfare problems both on ships and in the destination countries. The Animals Australia website includes a section entitled 'The Death Files' which provides sheep mortalities on ships over the past several decades. The Animals Australia website also includes information about the reasons why animal welfare groups oppose long-distance transport.

Table 2, taken from Animals Australia's (2007) website, is interesting in that it shows that the improvements that have been implemented to the live sheep trade have resulted in lower mortality rates in recent years.

## ETHICAL TREATMENT OF LIVE SHEEP

The other issue that Samex had to deal with was how to negotiate with its UAE customer regarding the ethical treatment of the sheep after the customer had taken delivery of them. Nations or cultures can have their own approach to ethical perceptions and behaviour, and these result in different types of business outcomes. A lesson from this is how far a company should go in accepting the ethical standards that exist in the host or destination company and how much they should implement the ethics from their home country. In this case there were powerful business reasons why Samex had to convince its UAE customer to change the way it treated the sheep because this would affect the ability of Samex to continue to supply the product.

Two sets of circumstances helped Samex convince the UAE customer that it should adapt to a way of treating the sheep that was different from what they usually did. The first was that the pressure to change was not just coming from the Australian live sheep industry, but also from other suppliers such as New Zealand where there were also concerns about the ethical issues associated with the trade. The second circumstance was the excellent reputation that Australia had for the quality of its livestock and how much better this was than livestock from other countries. This can be seen in the *Farmers Guardian* (2002) report about how foot and mouth disease was a constant threat to the supply of sheep exports from Britain.

| TABLE 2 | Live sheep export deaths 1981–2005 | | |
|---|---|---|---|
| Year | Total exported | Deaths | % mortality |
| 1981 | 4 357 345 | 102 630 | 2.36 |
| 1982 | 5 787 660 | 129 233 | 2.23 |
| 1983 | 6 127 916 | 126 046 | 2.06 |
| 1984 | 6 537 387 | 132 821 | 2.03 |
| 1985 | 7 088 209 | 133 990 | 1.89 |
| 1986 | 6 557 410 | 127 515 | 1.94 |
| 1987 | 8 439 069 | 138 543 | 1.64 |
| 1988 | 7 013 427 | 120 962 | 1.72 |
| 1989 | 5 116 343 | 110 085 | 2.15 |
| 1990 | 4 153 703 | 81 607 | 1.96 |
| 1991 | 3 972 000 | 83 226 | 2.10 |
| 1992 | 4 583 938 | 137 432 | 2.99 |
| 1993 | 5 108 722 | 129 414 | 2.53 |
| 1994 | 5 458 746 | 109 000 | 2.00 |
| 1995 | 5 784 207 | 98 654 | 1.95 |
| 1996 | 5 593 465 | 152 930 | 2.79 |
| 1997 | 5 122 981 | 68 136 | 1.33 |
| 1998 | 4 928 965 | 75 413 | 1.53 |
| 1999 | 5 051 772 | 67 693 | 1.34 |
| 2000 | 5 436 202 | 71 214 | 1.31 |
| 2001 | 6 712 332 | 84 575 | 1.26 |
| 2002 | 5 943 557 | 73 700 | 1.24 |
| 2003 | 4 546 211 | 45 462 | 1.00 |
| 2004 | 3 292 949 | 24 697 | 0.75 |
| 2005 | 4 101 094 | 38 960 | 0.95 |

**SOURCE:** *Compiled by Animals Australia Inc.*

## SELECTED DUBAI PARTNER

The UAE customer operates a feedlot at Jebel Ali near Dubai and uses this as the central point to distribute the sheep and other livestock to its slaughterhouses and butchers or direct to markets around the region. The facility has been designed to ensure the welfare of the sheep can

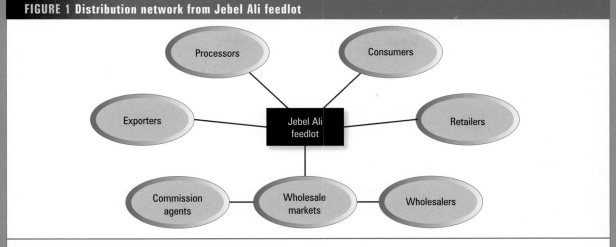

**FIGURE 1 Distribution network from Jebel Ali feedlot**

SOURCE: <*http://en.wikipedia.org/wiki/Image:FiveElementsCycleBalanceImbalance.jpg*>.

be maintained at levels acceptable to the general public in the exporting countries so as to minimise any ethical issues that arise from the trade. The development of this feedlot to international standards represents a change in the way Samex usually did business because it had to maintain an interest in its product even after the product had been delivered to the customer in the UAE. The move into active exporting of live sheep was been viewed as a separate and distinct business from the domestic business Samex traditionally undertook.

The UAE customer based in Jebel Ali was the centre of a distribution network that could reach much of the Middle East. Figure 1 shows the way that product could be move along the marketing channel in different ways once it reached the Jebel Ali feedlot. It would have been very difficult for Samex to access this network in full unless it connected with a local customer in the way it did. Having a central customer was an effective way for Samex to deal with ethical issues even after the product had been delivered.

## CONCLUSION

The case study has demonstrated a number of important lessons regarding international trade. The main overall lesson has been the importance of culture and ethics in developing distribution, channel length and exclusivity strategies. The live sheep trade in particular arouses a lot of opposition because of certain ethical issues that are raised. Some of these ethical concerns are unfounded, but it is still necessary to deal with them to make sure the trade can survive. Samex has worked hard developing a Middle East customer who is willing to follow international guidelines in the treatment of sheep rather than its own traditional approach to sheep management. The lesson from this is that sometimes it is necessary for the destination country to adapt to an external ethical framework rather than the international business making concessions. Culture, ethics, and distribution all work together in international trade, usually in hidden ways, but in this case of Samex's live sheep exports to the Middle East the cultural and ethical components become equally important.

### Bibliography

Animal Liberation (2007), 'Live exports', <http://www.animalliberation.org.au/livexport2.php>, accessed 21 April 2007.

Animals Australia (2007), 'Live animal export: indefensible', <http://liveexport_indefensible.com/facts/death_files.htm>, accessed 7 July 2007.

Department of Foreign Affairs and Trade (2004), *Doing Business with Saudi Arabia*, <http://www.dfat.gov.

au/publications/business_saudi_arabia/doing_ business_saudi.html>, accessed 21 April 2007.

*Farmers Guardian* (2002), 'Lamb exports under threat', 29 November, p. 1.

Geert Hofstede™ Cultural Dimensions (2007), <http:// www.geert-hofstede.com/hofstede_arab_ world.shtml>, accessed 28 April 2007.

Hill, C. (1997), *International Business: Competing in the Global Marketplace*, Irwin, Chicago.

ITIM (2003), 'Geert Hofstede™ Cultural Dimensions', <http://www.geert-hofstede.com/hofstede_arab_ world.shtml>, accessed 21 April 2007.

Kizirian, H. and Taha, M. (2004), 'That's desert (dessert) food processing', <http://www.fas.usda.gov/info/ agexporter/1998/Sept%201998/thats.html>, accessed 21 April 2007.

Lee, K. and Carter, S. (2005), *Global Marketing Management*, Oxford University Press, Oxford.

MLA (2007), 'Live export overview', Meat & Livestock Australia, <http://www.mla.com.au/TopicHierarchy/ InformationCentre/IndustryOverview/LiveExport Industry/Live+export+verview.htm>, accessed 21 April 2007.

Usunier, J. (1996), *Marketing Across Cultures*, 2nd edn, Prentice Hall, London.

## Questions

1 How do Hofstede's cultural dimensions affect channel length and channel member selection?
2 What decisions did Samex have to make regarding product development for the Middle East market?
3 Do you think that an international business should be concerned about ethical issues in the destination country or just accept that things are done differently in different countries?
4 What is the best way to resolve ethical issues that emerge in international trade?

## go online

Go online to <www.pearsoned.com.au/fletcher> to find more case studies.

# CASE STUDY A

# From 0 to 100 in 3 years 4 months: Shangri-La, Sydney

**Dr Troy Heffernan, University of Plymouth, UK and Marcelle Foundling, Charles Sturt University, Australia**

*You cannot transport a culture, but you can indeed translate it; that is, take into account and adapt to the local environment (Giovanni Angelini, CEO and managing director of Shangri-La Hotels and Resorts (Hamdi 2006)).*

## INTRODUCTION

The Hong Kong-based Shangri-La Hotels and Resorts is the largest Asian-based deluxe hotel group in the region. The name 'Shangri-La' and company philosophy, 'Shangri-La hospitality from caring people', were inspired by James Hilton's legendary novel, *Lost Horizon*. The novel's mythical paradise perfectly encapsulates the ideal of genuine serenity and service for which Shangri-La Hotels and Resorts has come to be recognised. 'Shangri-La Care' is a living culture within the group, strongly supported by the top management and continuously cascaded through the organisation.

In July 2003, the group took control of its first Australian property, Shangri-La Hotel Sydney (formerly ANA Harbour Grand Hotel) as part of a global expansion strategy. Of the 49 Shangri-La hotels worldwide, 37 are owned by the group through Hong Kong-listed Shangri-La, Asia. The Sydney venture represents a shift away from the owner-operator strategy of previous years as it leased the property. The company recognises that greater expansion opportunities are available through lease, joint venture or management contracts, but such projects threaten control over the quality of the Shangri-La brand. In this context, success in Sydney has far-reaching implications for success of the group. The struggles with cultural adaptation and adjustments to organisational processes will provide a springboard for organisational learning and inform the group's expansion into other non-Asian locations.

Located in the heart of the historic Rocks district, Shangri-La, Sydney is most famous for its sensational views of Sydney Harbour and twin

icons the Harbour Bridge and Opera House. In March 2005 an A$37 million refurbishment was completed, incorporating guest rooms, public areas, restaurants and bars and setting a new citywide benchmark for accommodation, food and beverage products and service.

Performance figures showed rapid improvement under the new management and have been continuing to improve over the last 3 years 4 months. A competitor analysis carried out by ANA Harbour Grand Hotel showed it was ranked fourth against the other major luxury hotels in Sydney in 2001 and third in 2002. In July 2003 Shangri-La, Sydney was ranked fourth against its competitors (Four Seasons, Westin, Sheraton and Intercontinental) in occupancy ranking, third for average revenue per day and third for revenue share index. By December 2005 and December 2006 year-to-date figures showed that Shangri-La was ranked number one over all these key indicators.

As further recognition of Shangri-La's success, the hotel received seven industry awards in 2005. In 2006 it won Best Luxury Accommodation, NSW Tourism Awards; Australian Hotels Association

Deluxe Hotel of the Year; and Australian Hotels Association Most Creative Marketing Campaign. The hotel was also voted One of the Top 20 Overseas Business Hotels, Conde Nast Traveller (UK) 2006–07, demonstrating Shangri-La's growing international reputation.

Shangri-La went from '0 to 100', from arriving to number one, in the Sydney deluxe hotel market in a short period of time. However, the transition has not been easy, with a number of challenging cultural and operational issues that needed to be addressed.

## SHANGRI-LA ARRIVES . . . SLOWLY SLOWLY

On his arrival at Shangri-La, Sydney, the general manager, Michael Cottan articulated a clear vision to his team:

*We are going to be the number one hotel in two years!*

The realisation of this vision meant facing some key challenges unique to the Australian environment and new for the Shangri-La group's singularly Asian experience of hotel management. To the general manager's frustration, and contrary to expectations, he found that the process actually took 3 years 4 months.

Some of the key issues faced by Shangri-La in the 'early days' included:

- *the property*: This was the most pressing issue. Until the major refurbishment could be undertaken in 2004, the initial re-branding needed to be supported by soft changes, such as physical signage and bed linen, that could be accomplished quickly.

- *re-branding*: Shangri-La considers itself to be the market leader in Asia yet the brand image in Australia and North America is relatively low. This meant Sydney represented an important stage of the global strategy.

- *human resource issues*: ANA employees were firmly entrenched in the hotel and the new management made a commitment to its new employees that Shangri-La was not going to come in and get rid of people. The staffing issue had two major implications. First, the change to a highly customer-responsive culture

would be difficult without the ability to employ new staff endowed with the necessary service-oriented attitude characteristic of the Shangri-La brand (Bettencourt, Gwinner and Meuter 2001). The second implication was the practical obstacle to attaining the high levels of customer service with only half the number of staff available than would normally be present in an Asian hotel.

- *national culture*: Aside from the differences between the organisational cultures of ANA and Shangri-La, the new management was facing its first foray into a Western culture, which formed an interesting overlay to all the above challenges. How would Australians interpret the brand? Could this environment really deliver the standard and style of service that Shangri-La was used to delivering? The lack of experience with working in a Western environment meant there was not a lot of experience to fall back on.

So what is 'Shangri-La'? And how do you inspire employees to realise the vision when they already feel they are providing a high level of service?

The following section describes how Shangri-La responded to the above organisational, industrial and cultural issues and analyses how it successfully navigated its way from 0 to 100 (from start-up to market leader on revenue per room for the deluxe segment of the hotel market in Sydney), albeit a little more slowly than was first anticipated.

## CULTURAL STRUGGLES (1)—BUILDING A CUSTOMER-RESPONSIVE ORGANISATIONAL CULTURE

The Shangri-La group's defining feature is based on its philosophy, 'Shangri-La hospitality from caring people'. Appendix A describes in detail the guiding principles of 'Shangri-La hospitality' and how employees are socialised into the culture through the extensive training programs offered. A number of significant challenges had to be faced in order to develop the Shangri-La culture. This next section identifies why Shangri-La, Sydney can be considered a customer-responsive organisation and follows with a discussion of the obstacles encountered in building this culture.

The organisational culture of Shangri-La can be understood as a customer-responsive culture. Some key variables identified in the marketing literature as being routinely evident in customer-responsive cultures have been developed at Shangri-La, Sydney. An important one of these is staff attitudes (Bettencourt and Gwinner 1996). Shangri-La 'hires for attitude, trains for skills'. Appendix A demonstrates that training constitutes a serious investment—Shangri La spends about 1% of its total labour costs on training. Further, successful customer-responsive cultures have employees who are conscientious about pleasing the customer and willing to work outside their normal job requirements to satisfy a customer's needs. For example, when the door-person greets a guest and finds out some information they pass that information on to other members of the front office team.

Shangri-La, Sydney largely succeeded in building a customer-responsive culture, but change was slower than initially anticipated due to restraining forces such staff turnover, inappropriate training styles, low staffing levels and the complex legislative environment of the Australian workplace. These restraining forces will now be discussed.

## STAFF TURNOVER

Shangri-La, Sydney has one of the lowest staff turnover rates in the industry, but the issue is a pressing one in countries such as Australia where work in the hospitality industry is not generally considered as a career move. The group seeks to retain high-calibre employees by helping them achieve their personal and career goals. The general manager has had little success in lowering the level of turnover due to the nature of the labour force, which consists of a large number of part-time and casual staff.

## TRAINING STYLES

Shangri-La invests heavily in training (as described in Appendix A), and this forms the core of the socialisation process. The training programs were also highly standardised across the group, a fact which jarred with the Australian employees who questioned the length of the training and the style of the videos used in training sessions. The human resources manager has had to eliminate the culturally inappropriate content of the courses and make them shorter. The basis of some of this resistance to the training styles of the Asian parent company can be explained by differences in national culture, discussed later in this case.

## STAFFING LEVELS

It is an ongoing frustration for all staff that they are expected to perform the same tasks in the same way as in Asian hotels, but with almost half the number of staffing hours available. On average the Shangri-La hotels in Asia have twice the number of employees than the Sydney operation. This is largely due to the differences in costs associated with salaries. Shangri-La, Sydney needed to adjust systems and apply for exceptions to policies and procedures in order to adjust to its staffing levels.

The composition of the workforce in the Australian hotel industry is also different to that in Asian countries. Research suggests that up to two-thirds of hospitality employment in Australia is characterised as non-standard (combining part-time and casual) and around half is on a casual basis (Timo and Davidson 2005), whereas the staff in other locations would be predominantly full-time. This has important implications for training outcomes, motivation and cultural change.

## LAWS AND LEGISLATION

Australia's industrial relations framework has undergone substantial change since the 1980s, including award restructuring and enterprise bargaining in line with the federal government's efficiency principles (Knox 2006). However, Australia's institutionalised industrial-relations framework, and the practices and attitudes associated with it, are still very much a part of present-day management–employee relationships. The labour market is characterised by more centralised, formalised processes, based significantly on legal adversary relationships, than what is likely to be found in other countries (Lewis,

Morkel and Stockport 1999). Job demarcation rules are of particular significance for an organisation building a customer-responsive culture. With restrictive workplace legislation, it is very hard to get people to be flexible. The general manager highlighted this as one of the biggest learning experiences:

> . . . the general laws, legislation and issues here around labour force rules are also quite different to Asia. You can pretty well do what you want in Asia to a certain degree. Every country has certain regulations but nothing even gets close to the environment of work legislation [in Australia].

## CULTURAL STRUGGLES (2)—ASIAN VERSUS AUSTRALIAN VALUES

Psychic distance refers to a measure of how far a country is perceived to be away from Australia in terms of cultural elements such as belief systems, language barriers, and different attitudes to business, material standards and patterns of behaviour (Fletcher and Bohn 1998). The index of psychic distance ratings of countries from Australia shows that China (the country of origin of the Shangri-La group) has the second largest psychic distance (29.2) of the countries listed (Fletcher and Bohn 1998). Further, other Asian countries where Shangri-La operates also have high psychic distance, for example Hong Kong (psychic distance of 20.5), and Singapore (psychic distance of 19.3). Research has shown that 'the success of a relationship marketing strategy is heavily dependent on levels of psychic distance' (Conway and Swift 2000, p. 1391) and as highlighted, the psychic distance between Australia and China is very high. Consequently, culture should have an impact on the operations and dealings Shangri-La, Sydney has with head office, and when dealing with the whole concept of operating in a new culture.

The most obvious and by far the most important focal point of psychic distance that needed to be resolved quickly was the belief system associated with what 'good service' embodied. 'Asian hospitality' is at the heart of the Shangri-La brand and rests on the core values of respect, courtesy, sincerity, helpfulness and humility. Australians are certainly capable of behaving in this manner, but these are not the first qualities likely to come to mind when describing the value systems that underlie Australian culture. When asked which of these values were the most challenging to instil, one manager identified 'sincerity' and 'humility' as the most difficult:

> Sincerity because some people see this as a job on the side while they're studying. It's not their career. Sometimes it becomes very robotic, that style of service. It's not innate to genuinely want to be here for the customer.

This was reiterated by another manager who noted that humility was not an attitude that came naturally to many Australians:

> Being in Australia we've had a slightly different form of hospitality. I think we're not quite as humble as the Asian style of hospitality. Even though we are serving people we can tend to be a little bit proud.

'Asian hospitality' has now become 'Shangri-La' hospitality according to company documents. This change is reflective of the new cultural mix that incorporates the strengths and weaknesses of the employees in a new location and Shangri-La's willingness to adapt to new markets. Although Australians find humility a challenge they can actually be strong in such service aspects as flexibility, empowerment and anticipation of customer needs.

It can be observed that whenever a challenge has arisen, Shangri-La has responded by listening carefully and responding flexibly without compromising its core values. Maintaining core values requires a deeper understanding of what constitutes national cultural values of each Shangri-La location. Using Hofstede's (1980) framework as a guide some important differences between the value systems of Asia and Australia were identified:

- *Social orientation*: Shangri-La is a very family-focused company; this comes from the Malaysian–Chinese family side of the company that is still very much involved. The family culture encourages regular social activities for all staff, but when such functions are run in Australia staff members are unlikely to enjoy the bonding experience.

A humorous example of differing values of

group identification was played out as Shangri-La head office directed staff to learn a company song. The human resources manager reported that the staff in Asia were very proud of this song about peace, serenity and paradise as it represented the company. She accurately anticipated that the song would be far too 'gooey and lovey-dovey' to inflict on Australians who would most likely greet it with derision. Fortunately the song was dropped from the training program before it was imposed on the incredulous Australian staff.

- *Planning and attention to detail*: Shangri-La, in its administrative style, typifies the great deal of formal attention generally given to processes in Chinese organisations to ensure that there are significant levels of certainty (Shanks et al. 2000). It is this attention to detail and systems that has been a sometimes tedious challenge for the Australian employees, yet at the same time ensures consistency of quality.

- *Humility*: this is a core value at Shangri-La, yet in a strongly egalitarian country such as Australia humility can almost seem like servility. Australians are typically casual, not tending to treat people differently even when there are great differences in age or social standing (Mackay 1993). A few staff noted that they felt they were expected to look up to the guests in a way that they did not feel comfortable about. They are willing to offer service, but view the guest as very much their equal no matter what their social standing is.

There is also ongoing discomfort noted amongst some staff members with the reinforcement of hierarchical relationships within the culture of Shangri-La management. Some employees note that managers maintain distance from staff below them and are unlikely to engage directly with frontline employees.

The disregard for power differentials has, however, been turned to advantage by the sales and marketing team, who are unafraid of approaching prospective clients to carve out new markets. They have greater confidence than the Asian sales teams to prospect assertively for influential clients.

- *Goal orientation*: Australia exhibits moderately aggressive goal behaviour. Chinese culture presents a paradox, with research suggesting that the Chinese attitude when directed at activities aimed at achieving something such as material goods could be seen to be supportive of aggressive goal behaviour. Taoist and Confucian values, on the other hand, emphasise harmony, simplicity and the rejection of self-assertiveness and competition, which would be associated with passive goal orientation. The paradox became evident in some comments:

*This is going to contradict slightly, but it is a very Americanised Asian culture. It was all these kind of programs, our core values, and all those sort of things. Very American based in terms of the actual structure of the training and modules but the flavour is Asian.*

While the feminine goal orientation may be appropriate with regard to service the more aggressive style of the Australian sales force is certainly valued.

## THE MARKETING FUNCTION AT SHANGRI-LA, SYDNEY

A key factor that has contributed to its success is the core values instilled at Shangri-La, Sydney. These core values are firmly underlined by the clear market orientation that runs through the whole organisation. Market orientation is the basis of the marketing discipline; it refers to the implementation of the marketing concept, the cornerstone of marketing theory (Kohli and Jaworski 1990). A definition of market orientation is 'the organization wide generation of market intelligence pertaining to current and future customer needs, dissemination of the intelligence across departments, and organization wide responsiveness to it' (Kohli and Jaworski 1990, p. 6).

It was reported that under ANA and in the early months of the transition the hotel did have good service. But Shangri-La's strategic vision was not merely to adjust individual elements—it was to alter the structure, systems and values of the hotel such that the *gestalt* of market orientation was realised. Shangri-La, Sydney creates value for its guests by increasing the benefits to them in relation to their costs. This was exemplified by the growth in the corporate segment resulting from a strategy of bundling services rather than cutting rates. The hotel decreases the guests' costs in relation to what they are buying by providing a unique style of service that is difficult to replicate. Training programs are developed and adapted according to feedback from customers. For example, regular and high-status customers like to be recognised, so the front office staff have instituted a program whereby frequent guests are invited to be photographed so that next time they visit staff will recognise them and address them by name. There is a high level of commitment to return custom, and guest recovery is the basis of one Shangri-La's compulsory training programs.

The effort to create superior value for the customer is evident throughout all the company's systems and processes. Inventory, revenue, bookings, check-in and customer service systems are being upgraded constantly to make use of the latest technology to create customer value. The company is diligent in removing obstacles to coordination. One example of this is the call diversion system. When the phone bookings are overloaded they are automatically bounced through to Kuala Lumpur so that no customer is discouraged by unanswered calls.

Helping to build the market orientation of Shangri-La, Sydney was the marketing function. This played a pivotal role in the success of Shangri-La, Sydney. The Shangri-La has been proactive in strategic and tactical areas of marketing. Four areas of marketing are critical in the success of Shangri-La. These are (1) the service encounter; (2) branding; (3) systems innovation; (4) target marketing. Further, a major driver of their success is the repeat business they generate from key customers. The Shangri-La, Sydney has achieved a 38% return guest ratio for the business segment and a 22% return guest ratio for total guest numbers. Further, the lifetime value of a key customer to the whole Shangri-La group is estimated at US$120 000. Consequently, the importance of getting the marketing 'right' so customers will return is critical.

## (1) The service encounter

The service encounter with consumers is a critical part of the overall marketing mix for hotels, particularly hotels that are in the deluxe segment of the market. Shangri-La hospitality has been successfully embedded in the corporate culture and is communicated to the customer through the marketing activities. Marketing in particular needs to match this culture as the 'mystique' of Shangri-La may be as much to do with shaping and reaffirming guests' perceptions of the Shangri-La experience as it is to do with developing any specific staff behaviours.

## (2) Branding

*They associate the brand with Audrey Hepburn. She [the Shangri-La] is refined, she's beautiful and really the only subtle difference is that she's Asian.*

The development of the Shangri-La brand has been successful, given the short period of time the product has been in the market. A number of factors have helped build the brand over this period of time, including:

- *labelling the hotel*: The Shangri-La building holds a prominent position on the Sydney city skyline, thus allowing for a high level of exposure.

- *integrated marketing communications*: The majority of the marketing messages disseminated by Shangri-La have been seen as being 'on brand'—that is, telling the one story.

- *service levels*: Service has been a key ingredient in building the brand.

- *aggressive public relations and advertising campaigns*: Shangri-La has used public relations and advertising assertively to disseminate the brand message in the marketplace.

- *price integrity*: Shangri-La was seen not to reduce its room rates to the extent of other competitors in the deluxe segment of the hotel market in Sydney. Consequently, this has limited the diluting effects that large discounts can have on the brand, particularly with competitors at the premium end of a market.

### (3) Systems innovation

Although Shangri-La service levels are a key component of its success, the face-to-face element of the interaction is only one part of the experience. Systems that allow quality service to be delivered are needed. This is another area where it is evident that the marketing activities of the hotel are well integrated throughout the organisation. Systems that allow for the staff to better meet service levels have been implemented. This is critical at Shangri-La, Sydney compared to a number of other Shangri-La hotels throughout Asia due to the low staffing levels in Sydney that make it particularly vulnerable to service shortfalls.

### (4) Target marketing (the corporate market)

The seasonal fluctuation in demand was a weakness that Shangri-La turned into an opportunity by reducing dependence on the leisure market and assertively seeking corporate accounts. This strategy has paid dividends for Shangri-La with demand now more evenly spread over the year. The way in which this was achieved was also an important element in the success of Shangri-La. Rather than engage in rate-cutting competition that would damage the brand Shangri-La followed a value-added approach. They won over accounts by identifying the specific needs of the corporate customer and bundling services to satisfy those needs, for example internet facilities for specific groups.

All these marketing activities required that a central question of international marketing be addressed—to what extent should an international firm standardise its marketing mix when entering other countries? Like many international firms Shangri-La Hotels and Resorts seems to adopt a two-step process: it standardises some elements of the marketing mix such as brand name, product design and positioning, and then local managers are called upon to critique the marketing strategies and develop plans to implement customised

elements of the marketing mix. There is clearly a high degree of control of the brand that is exercised centrally, yet examples such as dropping of the word 'dominance' from the corporate mission statement indicate a willingness to respond to varying conditions.

The journey from 0 to 100 has not been an easy one, but the cultural blend exemplified by Shangri-La, Sydney has provided much valuable learning for the larger organisation as it seeks out new markets and ventures into new socio-cultural environments.

## APPENDIX A    FROM GOOD TO GREAT— TRAINING IS KEY AT SHANGRI-LA

*'Great hotels are made by great employees, not by crystal chandeliers or expensive carpets.' This strongly held belief at Shangri-La Hotels and Resorts translates to a firm commitment to employee development. Such dedication will be increasingly important as the group's workforce grows from 28 000 to an expected 50 000 by 2010.*

*The process begins with careful selection–staff are 'hired for attitude, trained for skills'–providing a fertile foundation for the Shangri-La philosophies to be embraced. Shangri-La then invests heavily in training– perhaps more than any other hotel group–with intensive, ongoing coaching for all staff at 50 hotels and resorts.*

*The group then retains its high calibre staff by creating an environment whereby employees may achieve their personal and career goals; Shangri-La has one of the lowest staff turnover rates in the industry.*

*The group's defining feature is its exceptional and warm hospitality, as defined by its philosophy 'Shangri-La Hospitality from Caring People'. All staff undergo the 'Shangri-La Care' training program within six months of joining the group.*

*The program is designed to develop a consistent Shangri-La style of service to deliver a superior guest experience and build brand loyalty. Respect, courtesy, sincerity, helpfulness and humility are all core values of the training. Under the umbrella theme 'Shangri-La Care . . . The Shangri-La Way,' the program is divided into four modules: Shangri-La Care 1–'Shangri-La hospitality from caring people', Shangri-La Care 2– 'Delighting customers', Shangri-La Care 3–'Recover to gain loyalty' and Shangri-La Care 4–'Taking ownership'.*

*The four modules of Shangri-La Care focus on the*

*group's mission: 'delighting customers each and every time', part of Shangri-La's Guiding Principles.*

*Shangri-La Care is a living culture within the group, strongly supported by top management and continuously cascaded through the organisation. All hotels are required to allocate a specific budget for [staff] training and development, and the hotels' general managers are responsible for ensuring that all the allocated funds are spent year after year.*

### Training in China

*A focal region for training programs is China as Shangri-La [expects to] expand its portfolio of 21 hotels there to more than 30 by 2008, requiring its current China workforce to increase by nearly 9000 employees, of which 20% will be at managerial levels.*

*In December 2004, the group opened the Shangri-La Academy, Beijing. The Academy offers a number of certificate programs and a diploma program open to both existing Shangri-La employees [and] public students. The certificate programs [cover the] culinary arts, food and beverage service, front office, housekeeping, laundry, engineering, training and development, and human resources management. All the courses have an institutional learning component and sequential on-the-the-job training in the hotels. To date, the Academy has trained more than 770 students, with a total of 2000 graduates expected by 2008.*

### Creating a 'STAR' sales force

*Shangri-La Hotels and Resorts launched a proprietary sales and marketing training program in 2005–'STAR' (Shangri-La Training for Aggressive Revenues). More than US$3 million will be spent over four years to STAR-train 2000 sales and marketing employees in hotels and worldwide sales offices. The first tailor-made sales education program for Shangri-La, STAR incorporates the essence of Shangri-La's corporate culture in teaching essential selling skills, negotiation, strategic sales management, sales leadership and motivation skills.*

### Learning online

*E-learning courses for management staff were launched with eCornell in April 2005. There are 57 online courses available in five areas: human resources management, management essentials, hospitality and food service management, strategic management and financial management. Three thousand spaces for employees will be offered over the [period 2006 to 2011].*

### Training 'on the road'

*The Shangri-La group established the Mobile Learning Centre in 2003, which offers a wide variety of leadership and management programs conducted by in-house and external trainers in different hubs in strategic locations. This provides employees continuous learning opportunities within the group.*

*Hong Kong-based Shangri-La Hotels and Resorts, Asia–Pacific's leading luxury hotel group, currently manages 50 hotels under the five-star Shangri-La and four-star Traders brands, with a rooms inventory of over 24 000. The group has over 40 projects under development in Canada, mainland China, France, India, Japan, Macau, Maldives, Philippines, Qatar, Seychelles, Thailand, United Arab Emirates, United Kingdom and the United States.*

**SOURCE:** *Shangri-La Hotels and Resorts Press Release, 16 February 2006, <http://www.shangri-la.com/>, accessed 10 February, 2007.*

## Bibliography

Beilharz, P. (2001) 'Australian civilization and its discontents', *Thesis Eleven*, Vol. 64, p. 65.

Bettencourt, L.A. and Gwinner, K. (1996) 'Customization of the service experience: the role of the frontline employee', *International Journal of Service Industry Management*, Vol. 7, No. 2, pp. 3–20.

Bettencourt, L.A., Gwinner, K.P. and Meuter, M.L. (2001) 'A comparison of attitude, personality, and knowledge predictors of service-oriented organizational citizenship behaviors', *Journal of Applied Psychology*, Vol. 86, No. 1, pp. 29–41.

Conway, T. and Swift, J.S. (2000) 'International relationship marketing—the importance of psychic distance', *Journal of Marketing*, Vol. 34, No. 12, pp. 1391–414.

Cushman, D.P. and King, S.S. (1985) 'National and organizational cultures in conflict resolution: Japan, the United Sates, and Yugoslavia', in Gudycunst, W.B., Stewart, L.P. and Ting-Toomey, S. (eds) *Communication, Culture, and Organizational Processes*, Sage Publications, Beverly Hills, CA.

Fletcher, R. and Bohn, J. (1998) 'The impact of psychic distance on the internationalisation of the Australian firm', *Journal of Global Marketing*, Vol. 12, No. 2, pp. 47–68.

Hamdi, R. (2006) 'Guardian of an expanding Shangri-La', *Ehotelier*, 1 June, <http://www.ehotelier.com/browse/news_more.php?id=A8457_0_11_0_M>, accessed 7 February 2007.

Hartline, M.D., Maxham III, J.G. and McKee, D.O. (2000) 'Corridors of influence in the dissemination of customer-oriented strategy to customer contact service employees', *Journal of Marketing*, Vol. 64, No. 2, pp. 35–50.

Hofstede, G. (1980) *Culture's Consequences: International Differences in Work-related Values*, Sage, Beverly Hills.

Hofstede, G. (1984) 'The cultural relativity of the quality of life concept', *Academy of Management Review*, Vol. 9, No. 3, pp. 389–98.

Hofstede, G. (1991) *Cultures and Organizations: Software of the Mind*, McGraw-Hill, London.

Hofstede, G. (1994) 'The business of international business is culture', *International Business Review*, Vol. 3, No. 1, p. 1.

Hofstede, G. and Bond, M.H. (1988) 'The Confucius connection: from cultural roots to economic growth source', *Organizational Dynamics*, Vol. 16, pp. 4–21.

Jusdanis, G. (1995) 'Beyond national culture?' *Boundary*, Vol. 22, pp. 23–59.

Knox, A. (2006) 'The differential effects of regulatory reform: evidence from the Australian luxury hotel industry' *Journal of Industrial Relations*, Vol. 48, No. 4, pp. 453–74.

Kohli, A.K. and Jaworski, B.J. (1990) 'Market orientation: the construct, research propositions, and managerial implications', *Journal of Marketing*, Vol. 54, April, pp. 1–18.

Lewis, G., Morkel, A. and Stockport, G. (1999) 'Australia and New Zealand's economic heritage', in Lewis, G., Morkel, A., Hubbard, G., Davenport, S. and Stockport, G. (eds), *Australian and New Zealand Strategic Management: Concepts, Context and Cases*, 2nd edn, Prentice Hall Australia, Sydney.

Mackay, H. (1993) *Reinventing Australia: the Mind and Mood of Australia in the 90s*, Angus and Robertson, Pymble, NSW.

Ruekert, R.W. (1992) 'Developing a market orientation: an organizational strategy perspective', *International Research in Marketing*, Vol. 9, pp. 225–45.

Schudson, M. (1994) 'Culture and the integration of national societies', *International Social Science Journal*, Vol. 46, pp. 63–81.

Shangri-La Hotels and Resorts Press Release, 16 February 2006, <http://www.shangri-la.com/>, accessed 10 February 2007.

Shanks, G., Parr, A., Hu, B., Corbitt, B., Thanasankit, T. and Seddon, P. (2000) 'Differences in critical success factors in ERP systems implementation in Australia and China: a cultural analysis', 8th European Conference on Information Systems.

Timo, N. and Davidson, M. (2005) 'A survey of employee relations practices and demographics of MNC chain and domestic luxury hotels in Australia', *Employee Relations*, Vol. 27, No. 2, pp. 175–92.

Wallace, A.F.C. (1970) *Culture and Personality*, Random House, New York.

## Questions

1 How did the Shangri-La, Sydney go from 'a new kid on the block' to the top hotel in the deluxe hotel segment of the market in 3 years 4 months?

2 Identify and explain the cultural issues that the Shangri-La, Sydney faced in their first years of operation. Use Hofstede's (1980) work into cultural dimensions to identify possible cultural differences between the head office of Shangri-La in China and Shangri-La, Sydney.

3 Customer service employees perform a critical role in the successful running of a deluxe hotel. In relation to the employment of customer focused staff, what differences exist between the economic structures of the Shangri-La's traditional markets (Asia) and the economic structure of Australia? How did management attempt to reduce the impact of this difference?

4 Mr Cottan, the general manager of Shangri-La, Sydney, had previously worked in Shangri-La hotels in Asia. He found that there was a marked difference in labour laws and industrial relations between countries in Asia and Australia. Identify any of these differences highlighted in the case. How did they affect the operations of the business?

## Photo credit

Image courtesy of Shangri-La Hotel, Sydney.

# PART B

# INTERNATIONAL MARKET PLANNING PROCESS

Completion of the analysis of the international marketing environment in Part A should be followed by preparation of detailed plans for proposed international involvement. The first step is to undertake a program of detailed market research (Chapter 6). The objectives of the research need to be carefully spelt out and the stages of the research program articulated. This is then followed by a program for accumulating secondary data and then undertaking the primary research program, taking into account the constraints on data gathering and accuracy in the overseas markets. Issues relating to interpreting such data need to be considered, as does the ability to compare data from one overseas market to another. The next stage of the planning process is that of selection of those overseas markets (Chapter 7) likely to offer the greatest prospects for the firm. A screening process needs to be established whereby markets are progressively listed and eliminated from your consideration set according to criteria external to the firm and both policy and strategic considerations within the firm. Once overseas markets have been decided upon the form of overseas involvement most appropriate to the market and the circumstances of the firm needs to be established. This will involve a trade-off between commitment of resources and consequent risk on the one hand and desire to control what happens to your offering, product, service or intellectual property in the overseas market on the other. The final step in the planning process is the preparation of a marketing plan (Chapter 8) for each of the selected overseas markets. This plan should follow a predetermined structure and focus on both short-term goals and long-term objectives, as well as contain a mechanism for progressive review and updating as required.

# CHAPTER 6

# RESEARCHING INTERNATIONAL MARKETS

## LearningObjectives

**After reading this chapter you should be able to:**

- appreciate the role of market research in international marketing;

- discuss the research process as it applies to international marketing;

- identify sources of secondary data and secondary data issues in international marketing;

- recognise the differences between domestic and international market research;

- assess issues in emerging markets that affect the utility of market research;

- describe the techniques for conducting primary research overseas;

- appreciate the relative merits of qualitative and quantitative research in international marketing; and

- recognise the role and limitations of government agencies in providing information and export assistance.

# International marketing research—oranges or lemons?

Should the international business executive undertake market research to ascertain what people want and then design a product to suit their needs, or should the executive take an existing product and use market research to ascertain which group of customers find the offering appealing and then concentrate efforts on that group? The first approach, which many would argue represents marketing in its purest form, assumes that people know what they want, are able to articulate this and that what they say they want actually drives their decision making when confronted with a choice.

Almost half a century ago Ford designed a car from scratch based on market research as to what people wanted in their ideal car. The Ford Edsell was a lemon that few wanted and was dropped. In the early 1990s Toyota sent a group of engineers and designers to Southern California to observe how women get into, out of and operate their vehicles. They found that women having long fingernails encountered difficulty in opening doors and operating knobs on the dashboard. Based on their observations, the Toyota engineers and designers redesigned some aspects of both the exterior and interior of Toyota automobiles intended for sale in the USA.

More recently, Volvo went further and had an all-female team design a new model car following market research amongst potential female customers. The research found that women wanted a car that needed little maintenance and was easy to park. Named YCC (Your Car Concept), it embodies gull-wing doors, has low emissions, only requires oil changes every 50 000 kilometres, is coated with paint that has properties akin to a non-stick frying pan so that it repels dirt, and has a sensor that determines in advance whether a parallel parking space is sufficient for the vehicle. Research shows that half of Volvo buyers are women and women currently have a say in about 80% of vehicle purchases in the USA. The next stage of the project is to exhibit the prototype at New York's auto show to obtain a reaction from American consumers.

**SOURCES:** *Adapted from Czinkota, M.R. and Kotabe, M. (1994) 'Product development the Japanese way', in Czinkota, M. and Ronkainen, I.* International Marketing Strategy, *Dryden Press, Fort Worth, pp. 285–91; and Job, A. (2004) 'Female team designs new Volvo',* Auto Insides Report, Detroit News, *3 March. Image courtesy of Volvo Car Corporation.*

# INTRODUCTION

A study of blunders in international marketing leads to the conclusion that most could have been avoided if the manager had known more about the overseas market. As firms push the boundaries of geography in pursuit of international opportunities they need to collect information from an increasingly diverse range of markets. Information is the key element in developing successful international marketing strategies, and the information needed ranges from general data for assessing market opportunities to specific information to make decisions about product, promotion, distribution and price. Although most Australian and New Zealand managers appreciate the need for marketing research in the domestic market, few accord the same priority to market research when they consider entering and operating in overseas markets. This requires them to not only collect information in a cost-effective manner, but also to be able to predict responses to unfamiliar stimuli and then use the results to develop an effective international marketing strategy. Major mistakes occur in overseas marketing because the firm and its managers do not adequately understand the overseas business environment. This is particularly so with small and medium-sized firms (SMEs), which often conduct no research before they enter an overseas market and, once there, make decisions regarding the marketing mix elements following a subjective assessment of the situation and discontinue any research undertaken once they have entered the market. Unfortunately, many Australian and New Zealand firms either do not believe that international market research is worthwhile or they consider that, given the potential for business, such research is not warranted in cost or human resources terms. As the international marketplace is more complex than the domestic market and information is critical for informed decision making, the need to conduct market research in overseas countries is at least as great, if not greater, than is the case in Australia and New Zealand. What such firms overlook is that international market research is an aid to decision making. It helps reduce the risk of decisions taken in a climate of environmental uncertainty and lack of knowledge of international markets. It assists the international marketer to focus strategic thinking on the needs of the marketplace rather than on the product.

Some of the more common causes of failure in overseas markets are due to not undertaking market research in advance of entry and include not understanding why the preference for a local product was entrenched, projecting research based on large cities as representative of the total population in countries that are predominantly rural, not appreciating local preference for products in a particular form and not recognising that the same product might serve a different function in different countries.

## INFORMATION NEEDS FOR INTERNATIONAL MARKETING

According to Craig and Douglas (2005, p. 11), information needs will vary according to the firm's experience and prior degree of involvement in international marketing. At the initial phase of involvement in international marketing, research will be needed to assess opportunities and establish the most appropriate mode of entry into different countries (see Chapter 7). Once the entry decision has been made, each area of the marketing mix needs research. After experience in international marketing has been gained, research will be required to improve resource allocation across markets of involvement and achieve synergies through integration and coordination of international strategies. Information is needed for initial market entry, for planning how to approach the overseas market and for rationalising activities across international markets:

- *Information for initial market entry*: In the first place, a firm requires information on the general business climate in overseas markets of interest and will cover the issues raised in Chapters 2 to 5 of this book. It is only by gathering information on the business environment that the most attractive market opportunities can be isolated and appropriate modes of entry established. In the second place information relating to the specific product or service being offered, such as sales potential, market growth, competitive situation and structure of the market, is needed with respect to the overseas markets.

- *Information for how to approach the overseas market*: This involves testing all elements of the marketing mix for the product or service in the selected overseas markets and checking the degree to which modifications in each are likely to be required. Research in this connection will establish how changing positioning or modifying products is likely to broaden the customer base or increase market penetration. Promotional themes and advertising copy, as well as packaging, will need to be tested, especially as far as cultural sensitivity issues are concerned. Price sensitivity, as well as distribution expectations and alternatives, will need to be explored.

- *Information for rationalising activities across international markets*: Secondary data that helped guide entry decisions is now needed to monitor change in the overseas environments in which the firm is operating. The firm requires information to enable it to manage its global portfolio of involvements, optimise activities on the one hand and spread risk over both the short and long term on the other. The firm will also need to establish an information structure so that its operations in one country can exchange information with its operations in another. It needs to gather information on items like consumer tastes across all markets so that it can group commonalities and spot emerging trends.

# INTERNATIONAL RESEARCH DECISIONS

The main difference between domestic and international market research is that the latter is much broader in scope due to higher levels of uncertainty.

The types of studies required for international marketing relate to the market and the marketing mix variables of product, promotion, price and distribution. They involve decisions about:

1 whether to 'go international';

2 which overseas markets to enter;

3 whether to enter, leave or expand activities in an overseas market;

4 whether to add, delete or modify products in an overseas market;

5 how to determine the appropriateness of promotional activities such as copy design, media selection and sales compensation in an overseas market;

6 how to assess the relationship between price and demand and resultant profitability of operating in an overseas market; and

7 how to ascertain distribution channels in and the logistics of getting products to consumers in an overseas market.

For each of the above, more specific research tasks can be established. Using the variable of 'market' as an example, the marketing decisions to be taken and the intelligence that needs to be gathered would be as follows.

- *Go international or concentrate on the domestic market?* Assess the global market demand and the firm's likely share in view of local and international competition, and compare these to opportunities in the Australian or New Zealand market.

- *Which markets to enter?* Rank world markets according to potential, local competition and political situation.

- *How to enter target markets?* Ascertain the size of the market, international trade barriers, transport costs to and within the chosen market, strength of local competition, government regulations affecting imports and investment and political stability.

- *How to market in the selected market?* Gather intelligence on buyer behaviour, competitive practices, distribution channels, promotional media, pricing practices and government regulations.

Figure 6.1 shows a decision support system that can be applied when making major international marketing decisions.

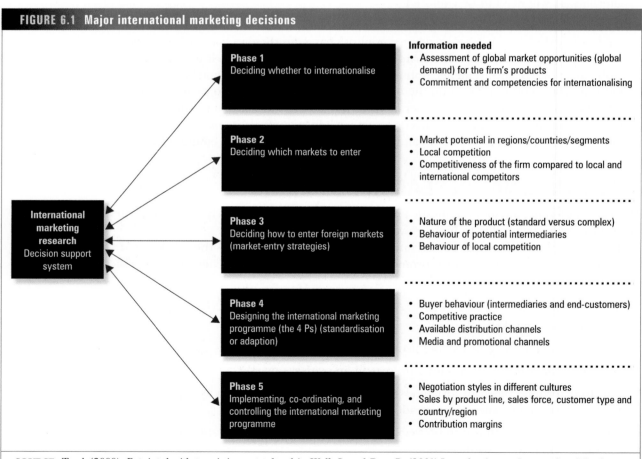

**FIGURE 6.1 Major international marketing decisions**

**International marketing research**
Decision support system

**Phase 1**
Deciding whether to internationalise

**Information needed**
- Assessment of global market opportunities (global demand) for the firm's products
- Commitment and competencies for internationalising

**Phase 2**
Deciding which markets to enter

- Market potential in regions/countries/segments
- Local competition
- Competitiveness of the firm compared to local and international competitors

**Phase 3**
Deciding how to enter foreign markets (market-entry strategies)

- Nature of the product (standard versus complex)
- Behaviour of potential intermediaries
- Behaviour of local competition

**Phase 4**
Designing the international marketing programme (the 4 Ps) (standardisation or adaption)

- Buyer behaviour (intermediaries and end-customers)
- Competitive practice
- Available distribution channels
- Media and promotional channels

**Phase 5**
Implementing, co-ordinating, and controlling the international marketing programme

- Negotiation styles in different cultures
- Sales by product line, sales force, customer type and country/region
- Contribution margins

**SOURCE:** *Tayeb (2000). Reprinted with permission; reproduced in Wall, S. and Rees, B. (2001)* Introduction to International Business, *Financial Times Prentice Hall, Harlow, UK.*

While the above could in most instances apply equally to domestic and international market research, they are being applied in a different environment. Because overseas environments are so different from that with which the firm is already familiar in Australia or New Zealand, international market research is more complex than domestic market research. The four major differences are the different parameters involved, the new environments in which research will be undertaken, the increased number of factors involved and the broader definition of competition.

When doing research in other countries the firm must cope with parameters not found when carrying out research in Australia or New Zealand. Some of these are import duties, foreign currencies which fluctuate relative to our dollar and logistics, such as port facilities. Information must be obtained on these as they influence business decisions. In addition, the way a firm may be required to operate in another country, such as via a joint venture or a licensing arrangement, may require extra information for business decisions than is the case in the domestic market. Market research conducted overseas will need to include this information.

When going overseas firms are exposed to a different environment in which many of the assumptions that guided their decision making in Australia or New Zealand are unlikely to apply. These assumptions will need changing to take into account the culture, politics, economics, stability, language and social structure of the other country. Additional areas where information will need to be obtained include legal regulations and enforcement effectiveness, as well as the level of technology in the society. Assumptions made on the basis of operations in Australia or New Zealand will need to be re-evaluated. Information gathered in international market research must include issues that reflect the differences in the overseas environment. Such information is essential if the manager is to begin to appreciate the different structures, type of regulations and different patterns of operating which govern business activities in other countries.

Not only are the factors to be taken into account when operating offshore different, but they are also more numerous. This is particularly the case when entering or operating in more than one overseas market. Apart from the number of factors that need to be researched, the interaction between them requires study and this adds to the complexity of international market research.

Cultural bias is a critical factor in designing and interpreting research in international marketing. This is because it typically involves researchers from one culture undertaking research in a different cultural environment. As this cultural bias may occur in communication between the researcher and the respondent, it is often necessary to arrange for the data to be gathered by a local in the overseas market.

Finally, when operating in another country firms expose themselves to a broader range of competition than is the case in the domestic market:

- the competition is likely to be from local firms which receive some form of government protection or preference and from other suppliers of imported products; and

- it is likely to come from substitute products or other products with a similar end-use application. As an example, devices that are labour saving in Australia face competition from cheap manual labour when marketed in India.

For this reason international research should determine the breadth and nature of competition in the overseas market.

## 6.1 INTERNATIONAL HIGHLIGHT

# Common international research mistakes

nformation about international markets and the conditions that operate in them is essential if firms are to develop effective strategies to enter and develop business in those markets. This information is critical if mistakes are to be avoided and market research is necessary to obtain such information. Mistakes commonly occur because:

- *The need for research was ignored.* An Australian firm ascertained that tomato sauce was not available in Japan. Anxious to be the first into that market with tomato sauce, the firm shipped a large quantity to Japan. The product was not purchased because Japanese people prefer soy-based products. Market research before market entry would have avoided this mistake.

- *Market research was inadequate.* Kentucky Fried Chicken entered the Brazilian market with the aim of eventually opening 100 stores. Sales from the initial store in Sao Paulo were disappointing. In deciding to enter the market, KFC had not researched all sources of competition. Street corner vendors sold low-priced charcoal grilled chicken virtually everywhere and this chicken was more appealing to local tastes than the KFC offering.

- *Market research was misdirected.* An Australian soft drink company conducted research in Indonesia to establish market potential. For cost reasons, it confined its research to urban areas, yet used the results to predict how the entire Indonesian population would react

to the product. Based on the research, the results of which were encouraging, the company established large bottling and distribution facilities throughout Indonesia. Unfortunately, there were major differences between urban and rural Indonesia. Sales proved to be disappointing as the product was purchased primarily by urban middle-class Indonesians, tourists and visitors.

- *Failure to appreciate cultural differences.* Coffee and its preparation are important in the life of the typical French household. Chase and Sanborn found considerable resistance when it attempted to enter the French market with its instant coffee. French consumers rejected the concept of instant coffee as it did not provide the ritual of coffee preparation that they viewed as inseparable from coffee. Prior marketing research would have alerted Chase and Sanborn to how deeply ingrained in the French culture was the ceremonial aspect of coffee preparation.

**SOURCE:** *Craig, C.S., Douglas, S.P. and Flaherty, T.B. (2000) 'Information access and internationalisation–the internet and consumer behaviour in international markets',* Proceedings of the eCommerce and Global Business Forum, *17–19 May, Santa Cruz, CA, Anderson Consulting Institute for Strategic Change.*

## Costs of international marketing research

The cost of undertaking market research overseas is often higher than anticipated based on experience in the domestic market, as the factors to be researched are more numerous. This cost escalation is also due to the need for exploratory research so as to become familiar with unfamiliar markets. These costs may act as a barrier to SMEs undertaking market research, but the downside is that the costs of *not* undertaking the research in terms of failed marketing activities can be greater than the costs of the research itself. Research tends to be concentrated in major industrialised nations with 79% being spent in Europe and North America (Craig and Douglas 2005, p. 95). Although research expenditure is less in the developing countries, it is none the less necessary as, despite the difficulties of undertaking research in such markets, these are more difficult markets where mistakes are more likely due to this lack of familiarity. Costs of research in various country markets are shown in Table 6.1.

**TABLE 6.1** **Marketing research project price indices, 2005**

| Country | Average cost (US$) | Country | Average cost (US$) |
| --- | --- | --- | --- |
| Japan | 216 | Malaysia | 76 |
| Australia | 184 | Mexico | 68 |
| UK | 182 | Philippines | 66 |
| France | 172 | Venezuela | 64 |
| USA | 171 | Czech Rep | 63 |
| Canada | 163 | Hungary | 63 |
| South Africa | 157 | Poland | 60 |
| Germany | 149 | Slovak Republic | 59 |
| Netherlands, The | 149 | China, PR of | 57 |
| Switzerland | 146 | Indonesia | 53 |
| Belgium | 145 | Argentina | 51 |
| Denmark | 139 | Cyprus | 50 |
| Norway | 138 | Estonia | 50 |
| Italy | 137 | Croatia | 47 |
| Austria | 122 | Russian Federation | 47 |
| Sweden | 121 | Peru | 45 |
| Finland | 117 | Egypt | 44 |
| Spain | 110 | Colombia | 43 |
| Korea | 106 | Latvia | 43 |
| Hong Kong | 102 | Ukraine | 37 |
| Greece | 93 | Vietnam | 37 |
| Portugal | 89 | Romania | 36 |
| Brazil | 87 | Bulgaria | 35 |
| Slovenia | 87 | India | 35 |
| UAE | 87 | Ecuador | 27 |
| Turkey | 77 | | |

**SOURCE:** *Adapted from* ESOMAR *Prices Study 2005. The European Society for Opinion and Marketing Research, Amsterdam. Permission for using this material has been granted by The European Society for Opinion and Marketing Research, J.J. Viottastraat 29, 1071 JP Amsterdam, The Netherlands. © 2006.*

## Stages

Figure 6.2 shows a number of stages to be undertaken when preparing a market research plan for international markets. In the first place it is necessary to identify the problem to be researched. Some familiarity with both the overseas market and the underlying strategy of the firm's involvement is necessary because if the problem is not properly identified the data gathered may not be useful. It is also necessary to determine what information is likely to be needed and set research objectives that are achievable and commercially justifiable.

The next stage is to select the research design and this will involve drawing up time scales and allocating resources to carry out the research. This stage will also involve selecting a research design that will minimise the problems of collecting and comparing data between countries to ensure reliability. At this stage, issues such as quantitative as opposed to qualitative data collection will need to be considered. The collection of data is then undertaken. This may be on the basis of secondary sources, primary data gathering or a combination involving gathering secondary data first and then undertaking primary research to verify or add to it. If primary data collection is involved, a decision as to method will be required (telephone, mail, personal interview or focus groups).

Intertwined with this stage is the next stage of interpreting the data. Interpretation involves an awareness of the biases that can creep in, such as respondent bias and researcher bias, as well as the comparability of data. The interpretation needs to take account of both the objectives of the research and the needs of the company commissioning the research.

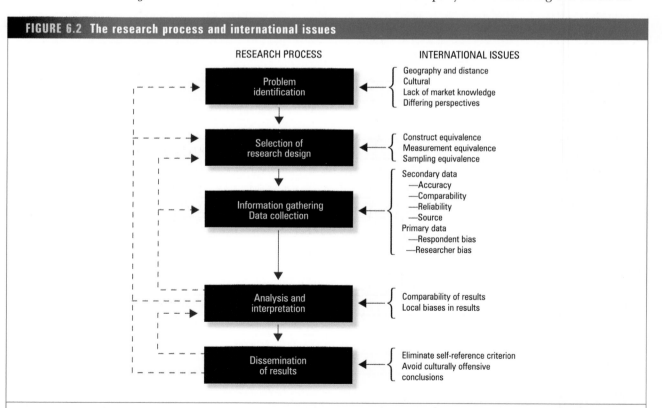

**FIGURE 6.2  The research process and international issues**

RESEARCH PROCESS — INTERNATIONAL ISSUES

Problem identification
- Geography and distance
- Cultural
- Lack of market knowledge
- Differing perspectives

Selection of research design
- Construct equivalence
- Measurement equivalence
- Sampling equivalence

Information gathering Data collection
- Secondary data
  —Accuracy
  —Comparability
  —Reliability
  —Source
- Primary data
  —Respondent bias
  —Researcher bias

Analysis and interpretation
- Comparability of results
- Local biases in results

Dissemination of results
- Eliminate self-reference criterion
- Avoid culturally offensive conclusions

**SOURCE:** *Adapted from Toyne, B. and Walters, P.G. (1993)* Global Marketing Management: A Strategic Perspective, *2nd edn, Allyn and Bacon, Boston, p. 366. Reprinted with permission of Pearson Education Inc., Upper Saddle River, NJ.*

The final stage is to disseminate the results, which involves summarising the findings and preparing the research report. This requires ensuring that the findings are communicated to all those people in the company influencing decisions on matters covered by the report. A discussion of these stages will occupy much of this chapter.

# THE INTERNATIONAL RESEARCH PROCESS

## Issues

There are a number of general issues that need to be kept in mind when engaging in international market research. These relate to selection of markets and comparability of results.

If market research is being used to decide which overseas market to enter, then the research should consider the issue of degree of stability of the market. This is because there may be a need for a trade-off between stable markets with low returns on the one hand and less stable markets with higher rates of return on the other. Such research will need to include the source of the instability and whether any political instability affects the stability of the commercial environment, the stability of the economy and the stability of the currency. The issue of psychic distance (see Chapter 3) also affects the selection of markets and the research needs to cover language influence and cultural differences so as to ascertain whether the perceived psychic distance is a real barrier. Research should also ascertain the legal restraints in the overseas country on carrying out research and the cost of research in relation to the apparent size of the market.

Comparability of results can be affected by the nature of the language in which the data is collected (this is discussed further later in this chapter). Languages vary in their degree of precision with which meaning is conveyed. Answers to a questionnaire couched in a precise language, such as German, may give a different result to answers to a questionnaire couched in a language that tends to be imprecise in meaning, such as Thai. The use to which products are put is another variable affecting comparability, as is the method by which they are sold. As an example, bananas are sold by number in Germany whereas in the UK they are sold by weight. To ensure comparability it is important that the same segment be researched in each market and that allowance be made for any differences in socioeconomic conditions. Socio-economic conditions affecting comparability include affordability, social class, educational levels and family composition issues. If the data source is secondary, then another issue is the reliability of statistics available in the foreign market. In general, the accuracy of secondary data increases as the level of economic development increases. Another issue relates to the privacy of data; there has been an increase in the number of laws to protect privacy worldwide and this can affect the conduct of market research in overseas countries. Finally, comparability can be affected by the difference in the marketing environment between countries, as figures from research in socialist countries may reflect different conditions from figures based on research in a market-oriented country.

## The process

The international research process involves defining the problem, developing a research plan, collecting data, interpreting data and summarising the findings in a research report. Before undertaking international market research it is useful to ask the following questions:

1   What information is needed and what will happen to the information when obtained?

2   From where can the information be obtained?

3   Why is the information needed?

4   When is the information required?

5   What is the information worth in dollar terms?

6   What is the likely cost of not getting the information?

The answers to these questions will influence the approach to be adopted in the research process.

## STAGE 1: PROBLEM IDENTIFICATION

At the problem-identification stage the following need to be established: the decision makers, the objectives of the research, possible courses of action to obtain the information and the consequences of each alternative course of action. In international marketing, those who design the research and those whose decision making is the subject of the research are geographically separated. Because of this it is often difficult for the researcher to arrive at a well-defined understanding of the research problem.

This leads to two areas of difficulty in formulating the research problem to be investigated. The first relates to the cultural norms and values of the party commissioning the research. Known as the self-reference criterion (see Chapter 3), this refers to people's tendency to view the overseas situation in terms of their own background. To avoid mistakes due to the self-reference criterion, it is necessary to isolate the influence of the self-reference criterion and view the research problem from the perspective of the foreign parties involved.

The second problem area is lack of familiarity with the foreign environment to be investigated. Lack of familiarity can lead to false assumptions and poorly defined research problems. This can be overcome by some preliminary research into the general conditions in the overseas market. For many markets there exist omnibus surveys conducted by market research agencies. These are conducted at regular intervals, contain a large number of consumer-related questions and are administered to a very large sample of consumers. Subscription to such surveys where available can assist in avoiding some mistakes at the problem formulation stage.

## STAGE 2: RESEARCH DESIGN

This refers to the framework for studying the issue to be researched. Its purpose is to ensure that the study is relevant to the problem and that it employs effective procedures. Researchers need to be familiar with problems that are unique to conducting research within and across countries and cultural groups. Three issues that are critical when designing this research are construct equivalence, measurement equivalence and sample equivalence.

**Construct equivalence** Basic concepts such as beauty, youth, sex appeal and wealth are often used in market research questionnaires where the motivation for buying products is related to self-image or social values. Although these are seemingly universal concepts, their meaning can vary from country to country. Construct equivalence is concerned with whether both researcher and the subjects of the research view a particular phenomenon or concept in the same way. Problems arise due to social, cultural, economic or political differences; perspectives may be neither identical nor equivalent.

This difference in perspectives can influence *functional equivalence*. This relates to the function served by an action as a result of which differing interpretations might be placed on an activity in cross-cultural research. As an example, in Asia shopping is often undertaken by servants, in Europe it is considered a social activity, whereas in Australia or New Zealand it tends to be regarded as a chore.

The difference in perspectives may also affect *conceptual equivalence*. This refers to the concepts used by the researcher to identify an activity. Difficulties arise because many concepts are culture bound and are not equivalent when applied across national boundaries. This influences the selection of terms to use in the research instrument or the words used to grade or measure the responses. As an example, what is considered reliable in one country may not be considered reliable in another because the experience of the consumer with the product category may have been different. Reliable might mean something quite different to a car owner in Germany where sales of Mercedes-Benz and BMW vehicles are high, compared with a car owner in India used to, say, the locally produced Hindustan Ambassador of 1950s design.

Difference in perspectives influences *definitional equivalence*. Definitional equivalence relates to the categories used by the researcher to group data. Examples include the different meanings given by people from different cultures to classes of products, roles performed by families and inclusions in occupational categories. For example, in Australia businesspeople are accorded relatively high status, but in other countries where status is based on education or caste this may not be the case. Sometimes businesspeople come from a despised minority group, as is the case with the Chinese in Indonesia.

Difference in perspectives influences on *temporal equivalence*. In international marketing temporal equivalence cannot be assured by simultaneous measurement because seasonal, religious, cultural, political and economic factors can intervene. For example, gift-giving seasons do not coincide between countries and they are often influenced by religion, for example, Hanuka in Israel, Ramadan in Iran and Christmas in Australia. As well reverse seasons between the northern and southern hemispheres affect research in areas such as fashion clothing.

Finally, difference in perspectives can be affected by *market structure equivalence*. In different countries there will be differences in the level of awareness of products and the availability of products. Aspects of market structure causing these differences are the nature of distribution channels in the overseas country, the advertising coverage in the market, the availability of product substitutes and the intensity of competition. There is a world of difference between the market structure in Vietnam and that in Australia or New Zealand.

**Measurement equivalence** This deals with the methods used by the researcher to collect and categorise information. A method of measurement that works well in one culture may fail in another, and special care is needed if the reliability and validity of measurements taken in different countries are to be assured, so that the results can be compared. A distinction is necessary between two kinds of measuring instruments: etic and emic.

The *etic approach* to research uses general cultural variables such as individualism versus collectivism, and cultures are compared in terms of these variables. Therefore, etic instruments are those that are culturally universal and, when translated, can be used in other cultures. Each measurement in the instrument, however, will need to be tested in advance of use to ensure that it does not contain any cultural biases. Etic instruments are very difficult to create and are not often used.

The *emic approach* to research takes the idiosyncratic traits of each culture to explore actual business behaviour in a culture. Therefore, emic instruments are tests constructed to study a phenomenon in one culture only. When the emic approach is used, country-specific instruments have to be created for each country involved in the research in order to ensure comparability of results. When developing emic instruments to measure the same phenomenon between different overseas markets, it is necessary to ensure gradation, translation and scale equivalence.

**Gradation equivalence** This refers to equivalence in the units of measurement used in the research instrument. While it is normal to ensure equivalence in monetary and physical measurements such as volume, it is also necessary to aim for equivalence in items such as product grades, procedures, safety standards, quality and similar issues that vary from country to country. Perceptual cues also vary from country to country as is illustrated in the following:

> *The colour green has positive associations in Muslim countries due to it being the colour of Islam. As an example, in Libya Gaddafi's treatise on global reform is known as the 'Green Book', and the focal point for popular rallies in support of Gaddafi in Tripoli is called 'Green Square'. By contrast, in some Asian countries green is associated with disease because of its connection with dense, green, humid jungles.*

**Translation equivalence** This applies to both verbal and non-verbal language. Context, whether high context, where much is implied, or low context, where most of the meaning is stated, will influence translations because expectations will differ. For example, in high-context cultures more meaning may be conveyed in non-verbal ways such as by gestures. Differences in idiom and in rendering an exact translation of the intended meaning create problems in obtaining the specific information that is desired. Languages differ in how precisely they convey meaning and the number of words used to indicate shades of meaning. Differences also occur in the degree to which meaning is asserted as, for example, when 'yes' means 'definite agreement' or merely that the person is listening, and 'no' means 'definitely not' as opposed to 'I will need to think further about it'. Usunier (2005, p. 196) points out that translation equivalence may be further divided into lexical equivalence, idiomatic equivalence, grammatical equivalence and experiential equivalence. To this might be added character equivalence.

1  *Lexical equivalence* refers to whether the translations in dictionaries exactly match. If the English dictionary gives the word for 'hot' in French as *chaud* does the French dictionary give the English word for *chaud* as 'hot'?

2  *Idiomatic equivalence* relates to a linguistic usage that is natural to a native speaker. In this case the equivalence is not in the words, but in a different phrase to convey the intended meaning.

3  *Grammatical equivalence* deals with the ordering of words and the construction of sentences. Whereas English proceeds in an active way, with the subject followed by the verb and then the circumstances, many other languages such as Japanese start by explaining the circumstances before dealing with the subject or the action. This can result in sentences that are much longer than those in English.

4  *Experiential equivalence* is about what the word means to a reader/listener in terms of their experience. Translated terms should refer to real items and real experiences, which are familiar to the cultures involved in both languages. As an example, languages used by those living in hot countries are likely to have a number of words for degrees of heat and few words for degrees of cold whereas the reverse applies to those living in very cold countries.

5   *Character equivalence* arises because different languages are written in different scripts. In English and most European languages meaning is conveyed by letters making words and words forming a sentence to convey meaning. In many Asian languages such as Chinese or Japanese meaning is conveyed by ideographs which are word pictures, each one of which has meaning which needs to be translated as a phrase. Translation can be complicated because these ideographs can be highly contextual.

The difficulties that can arise from translation equivalence were highlighted at the 1994 UN World Conference on Population Development in Cairo:

> At this conference the Americans raised the concept of 'reproductive health'. This was translated into German as the equivalent of 'health of propagation' and into Arabic as 'spouses take a break from each other after childbirth'. The equivalent in Russian became 'the whole family goes on holiday' and in Mandarin as 'a holiday at the farm'.

A number of techniques are available to overcome the problems of translation equivalence. The most commonly used is back translation, which involves having the questions translated from English into the target country's language by one translator. The translated questions in the other language are then translated back into English by another translator. A second technique is parallel blind translation, which involves a number of translators translating the questions from English into the other language independently of each other. The translations are then compared and discrepancies resolved. Another technique is the random probe approach whereby several probe questions are included in both the English and translated versions to ensure that the respondents understand the questions in the same way.

Scale equivalence   When developing an instrument for collecting data it is important not only to ensure that the same scale is used in each questionnaire, but that the meanings that respondents attach to each point in the scale are the same. Many questionnaires employ a version of a Likert scale. In countries like Australia and New Zealand these have five or seven points, whereas in other countries such as Germany there may be 10 points. This is important when comparing secondary data and other research between countries. Another problem area is differences between countries in the weight attached to respondent scores. The relative importance placed on scale values can vary, as can the interpretation of values given. In countries where people tend to be definite there is more likely to be a spread of responses across the spectrum of the scale compared to countries where people are more equivocal and responses cluster around the midpoint.

The problem is even more complicated when conducting research in developing countries or in developed countries among underprivileged groups. This can be overcome as illustrated in the pictorial scales (see Figure 6.3) employed in a survey of Aboriginal health. Devices used in these scales included different-sized circles and climbing a hill.

Research by Sood (1989) involved translating nine scale terms into Arabic, Chinese, Farsi, French, German, Korean and Spanish and asking respondents to place values on the translated items.

The average values of the translated terms were then compared with the average value of the English terms to see whether there was a measurement equivalency problem. Sood found significant differences in the way measurement terms were interpreted between countries and concluded that intuitively developed rating scales, even with careful translations, resulted in poor comparability in research results.

**FIGURE 6.3  Extracts from a questionnaire used in a study of Aboriginal health**

**Does eating SUGAR cause diabetes? (Tick one circle or dot)**

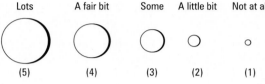

| Lots | A fair bit | Some | A little bit | Not at all |
|------|-----------|------|-------------|------------|
| (5) | (4) | (3) | (2) | (1) |

**How WELL are most people in your community? (Tick one circle or dot)**

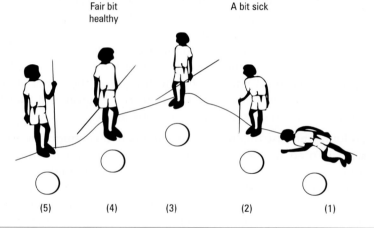

Fair bit healthy          A bit sick

| (5) | (4) | (3) | (2) | (1) |

**SOURCE:** *Spark, R. (1999) 'Developing health promotion methods in remote Aboriginal communities', PhD thesis, Curtin University of Technology, Perth.*

**Sample equivalence** Because of social, cultural, economic and political differences there are unique problems in international marketing which are not found in domestic marketing. The first relates to identifying and making operational equivalent population samples to test in two or more countries. While it is possible to define a population for research by using externally imposed criteria (e.g. location, income, age or education), comparison and equivalence will be affected by internally generated criteria (e.g. personality and psychological characteristics). External definitions of population such as income classification ignore the fact that the same income group may have different lifestyles in different countries. Furthermore, internal definitions could result in inclusion of people in one country with a high interest in the product and inclusion in another country of people with a low interest, as it cannot be assumed that either externally imposed or internally generated population definitions are comparable.

The second problem area in sampling equivalence concerns the scope and representative nature of the sample. It is necessary to select comparable samples from each population in the research. Often this is expensive and time consuming and some markets may not warrant the expense of obtaining truly representative samples. Here it may be necessary to sacrifice representativeness of the samples in order to enhance the comparability of selected variables in the survey instrument.

## STAGE 3: COLLECTION OF DATA

There are two ways of gathering data for undertaking research into overseas markets. One method involves collecting from the overseas market data specifically related to the purpose

---

### 6.2 INTERNATIONAL HIGHLIGHT

# Market research issues in Russia and China

With official statistics hopelessly outdated or incomplete, Russian marketers are turning to the private sector for market information. Official statistics don't count the rapid growth of small companies in the service sector that are hiding from the tax authorities. These are listed, however, in the figures for new company registrations, which exceed 300 000. However, a private research agency, Mobile, estimates that only 8000 of the above companies actually advertise their activities or do business. The difference between the two figures reflects the legal fiction that managers use to hide from taxation. Mobile analyses real commercial activities in the absence of reliable official statistics, by devising ways of tracking sales, surveying dealers and checking claims against how much they advertise, the prices they publish and the amount of electricity they consume. For example, media advertising provides a vast database of offers to sell; these offers are then checked against price lists, sample surveys of sales figures and media circulation figures. It is believed that in Russia there is a mathematical relationship between advertising volume, turnover and profitability. By tracking advertising in the media every 36 hours, Mobile claims it can reliably pinpoint changes in buying and selling patterns in Russia. Despite smuggling and other unofficial commercial activities, using indirect measures and surrogate indicators enables private sector research firms to provide reasonably accurate secondary data on the market.

The fact that the last census was conducted in 1988, along with infrastructure being in disrepair and the country having long-held traditions of secrecy, obtaining a representative sample for the purposes of conducting national research in Russia is a nightmare. The absence of telephones in many parts of the country precludes telephone polls and requires data to be gathered using personal interviews, which are both time consuming and expensive. According to Vsevolod Vilchek, director of sociological research for Russia's public television channel, obtaining a representative nationwide sample of 3000 people to poll is an impossibility and attempts to do so fail by a wide margin of error. On average, he stated, 15% of people approached to participate in a poll refused to participate, and many people do not know how to answer questions. If difficult questions are posed you cannot count on people telling you what they actually think. A question about attitude to privatisation is likely to yield a positive response of 20%, a negative response of 30% and a 'don't know'-type response of 50%. This is due to people not understanding what the word 'privatisation' means.

In the case of China, conducting national research is hampered by problems in defining the sample frame, of proportionately very small sample sizes, difficulty in framing questions so that the meaning is appropriate and accurate when translated, very low response rates, and over-simplification of responses, especially when Likert scales are employed.

SOURCES: *Adapted from Helmer, J. (1997)* Business Review Weekly, *9 June, p. 32; Hoffman, D. (1996) 'Russian voters' poll position: fear, uncertainty',* The Washington Post, *23 May, p. A3; and Newman, P., Minghua, J. and Ibrahim, N. (2001) 'The meaning of the brand to the young educated Beijing consumer: a comparison between local and foreign fashion goods',* Proceedings of the Conference of the Academy of Marketing, *Cardiff, July, University of Cardiff.*

of the study. This is referred to as primary data. The other method is to check on what has already been gathered for other purposes and what information is already available. This is secondary data. Usually secondary data is obtained before the collection of primary data is undertaken. as secondary data might obviate the need for primary data or reduce the number of areas for which primary data needs to be gathered. For this reason we discuss secondary data first.

### Secondary data

***Sources*** Often referred to as preliminary desk research, much of the secondary data on overseas markets can be gathered in Australia or New Zealand. Sources of such information can be internal to the firm or external to the firm. Sources internal to the firm include sales records, agents' reports and distributors' purchases/sales; when analysed these can provide valuable information, especially when split by country. This data can provide a good indication of which market niches in each country are likely to be most profitable and should be the focus of increased attention. Analysis can be undertaken by market segment as well as by channel of distribution. Where a company uses various distribution channels it is often possible using internal data sources to ascertain the profitability and effectiveness of each channel type. Historical data relating to the effect on sales of changes in price in each market enables the prediction of the likely effect of varying the price as a marketing strategy. In a similar way, the effect and appropriateness of various types of promotion in each market can be estimated.

Sources external to the firm can vary from general information readily available from public libraries and the like to more specialised and costly sources such as consultancy reports. The internet is also an increasingly valuable source of data. Cost, as opposed to quality, will also be a criterion affecting the use of these external sources of information.

Specifically external sources can involve a study of export statistics in the home market, a study of export statistics of other countries with which a firm is likely to be competing in the target market overseas, and finally a study of the export statistics in the target market itself. The home market study is likely to indicate whether exports are taking place already, where the exports are going, the volume and value of these exports and whether there is a seasonal pattern. The study of other countries may reveal comparative export prices, competitive export quantities, the magnitude of import trade to the markets in which a firm has an interest and any seasonal trends. The study of the target market is likely to show the key sources of supply, the volume by source of supply and values on a cost, insurance and freight (CIF) basis by source of supply, enabling a firm to assess its level of competitiveness (Noonan 2000, pp. 37–9).

There are seven major sources of secondary data related to doing business overseas. In the case of firms in Australia, these are:

1 *international agencies*: The United Nations, the World Bank, the International Monetary Fund and the Asian Development Bank gather a wide variety of economic and social information on different countries. This information is publicly available. It suffers from the drawback of being supplied by each member country, which may use different criteria for collecting and classifying the information, and from being dated, because it takes time to collect and analyse information from all around the world.

2 *Australian government*: The Department of Foreign Affairs and Trade and the trade promotion body Austrade are the main federal government agencies that supply information on overseas markets. Other government departments can supply

information on overseas markets in the areas of their specialisation—such departments being those responsible for primary industry, energy, defence, education and transport.

3 *Australian consulting firms*: Many consulting firms, including accounting firms, specialise in services for Australian firms overseas. Some firms such as PricewaterhouseCoopers will conduct original research for a fee and issue newsletters on specific markets, produce information about various countries in material such as 'Guide to the Market in . . .', and may continuously track, analyse and forecast economic and business conditions in a number of countries.

4 *Australian government overseas representatives*: Australian trade commissioners can, in the area for which they are responsible, provide updates on market conditions and a general background on the market. They can undertake more detailed research on the market for the firm's product or service for a fee. Information can also be obtained from embassy and consular officials as well as the overseas representatives of other government departments. In some overseas markets state governments have representatives who will assist firms from their state with information on market conditions.

5 *databases*: Electronic databases provide international marketing information and updates on international trade statistics. Online databases, such as the internet, link computer users worldwide and allow firms to find out about international developments in their field of interest. The interactive nature of the medium enables firms to discuss the information provided so as to check and improve its relevance to their needs.

6 *other commercial interests*: Other organisations which provide information to Australian firms on international conditions and opportunities include the Australian Business Chamber, chambers of manufactures such as the Australian Chamber of Commerce and Industry, and industry associations such as the Metal Trades Export Group. Australian banks through their network of representative offices and correspondent banks overseas can also provide their clients with overseas market information, as can legal firms such as Freehills.

7 *miscellaneous sources*: These include business libraries, university libraries, brokerage houses, legal firms and accounting firms.

Information will be of different degrees of importance as shown in Figure 6.4, which illustrates the results of a survey conducted in countries in the Asia–Pacific region. As shown in Table 6.2, in different countries various sources of secondary data have different degrees of importance. This needs to be kept in mind when gathering data.

**Problems with secondary data** Unfortunately, much of the secondary data available in Australia and New Zealand is not available in many countries with which Australian and New Zealand firms wish to trade. In some countries data gathering is only of recent origin. Although the situation is improving through the efforts of the United Nations and other multilateral bodies, there are still problems in cross-country comparison of secondary data. These problems relate to availability, age, accuracy, reliability and comparability:

• *Availability of data*: In overseas markets there is a paucity of data available for many areas of interest. Detailed data on numbers of manufacturers, wholesalers and retailers is not available in many developing countries because there are no government agencies that collect such data on a regular basis. In these circumstances it is necessary to commission private agencies to supply secondary data, as in the Russian example mentioned in International Highlight 6.2.

**TABLE 6.2**    The most used sources of information by country, by rank of importance

| Japan | Singapore | Taiwan |
|---|---|---|
| Customers | Government | Customers |
| Government | Political contacts | In-house surveys |
| In-house surveys | In-house surveys | Competitors |
| Personal contacts | Customers | Government |
| Local surveys | Business contacts | Personal contacts |
| **South Korea** | **Hong Kong** | **China** |
| Customers | Customers | Customers |
| In-house surveys | Personal contacts | Political contacts |
| Personal contacts | In-house surveys | Newspapers |
| Business contacts | Trade associations | Personal contacts |
| Political contacts | Magazines | Magazines |
|  | Business contacts |  |
| **Indonesia** | **Philippines** | **Malaysia** |
| Customers | Personal contacts | Customers |
| Competitors | Customers | Personal contacts |
| Personal contacts | Local and international surveys | In-house surveys |
| Business contacts | Business contacts | Competitors |
|  |  | Trade associations |
|  |  | Local surveys |
| **Thailand** | **Vietnam** |  |
| Personal contacts | Trade associations |  |
| Customers | Personal contacts |  |
| Business contacts |  |  |
| Competitors |  |  |

*Note*: Only sources which, on average, are used substantially, a lot or heavily are reported.

**SOURCE:** *Lassere, P. (1997), in Doole, I. and Lowe, P. (eds)* International Marketing Strategy: Contemporary Readings, *Thomson Business Press, London, Chapter 7.*

- *Age of data*: The desired data might be available but, because it was collected some years previously, it is outdated. Many countries collect data on a much less frequent basis than is the case in Australia or New Zealand and difficulties comparing overseas data for example with Australian data occur, when data in Australia is collected every four years and in the other country it could be only every 10 years.

- *Accuracy of data*: Problems arise in this connection because the definition used for certain indicators varies across countries, and the quality of the information becomes compromised by the mechanisms that were used to collect it. Whereas in developed countries data collection mechanisms are sophisticated, in developing countries this is not the case due to lack of resources and skills.

- *Reliability of data*: Official statistics in some countries are not reliable: the data might have been selectively collected for statistical purposes; may be overly optimistic to reflect national pride; or may be incomplete because it does not reflect a sizeable 'black' economy.

- *Comparability of data*: As mentioned, the factors above make it difficult to compare data between countries. Another factor contributing to comparability problems with secondary data is the manner in which the data is collected. In some developing countries, especially where literacy is a problem, data can be estimated rather than accurately gathered, and very frequently data is reported in categories that are too broad to be compared with classifications which apply in developed countries, such as Australia and New Zealand.

To check whether the secondary data can be relied upon it is useful to ascertain, for each data source, who collected the data and whether there was any party that might benefit from the data being misrepresented. Other issues to inquire about include the purpose of having the data collected, how the data was collected and whether the data is consistent with other, related factors. As an example of consistency checking, data on the sale of infant formula could be compared with the number of women of child-bearing age and with birth rates.

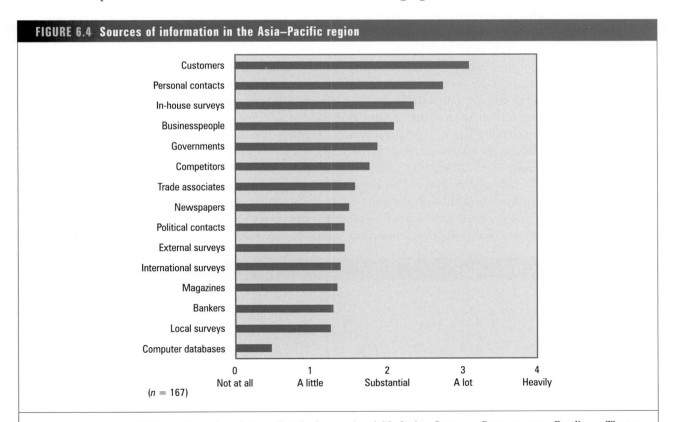

**FIGURE 6.4  Sources of information in the Asia–Pacific region**

(n = 167)

**SOURCE:** *Lassere, P. (1997), in Doole, I. and Lowe, P. (eds)* International Marketing Strategy: Contemporary Readings, *Thomson Business Press, London, Chapter 7.*

When confronted by contradictory information one possibility is triangulation—the obtaining of information on the same item from at least three different sources to check if there are any reasons for the contradiction. In the case of wine such triangulation might reveal that the import figures for Singapore were by value and those for Thailand were by volume, or that one country categorised all sparkling wine as champagne, while another categorised as champagne only that sparkling wine which originated in the Champagne region of France.

**Primary data** Primary research is undertaken to fill specific needs for information. Although the research may be undertaken by an agency rather than the firm because it is being carried out for a specific purpose, it is different from secondary research, which cannot supply the answers to specific questions.

Different environments, attitudes and market conditions add to the complexity of conducting primary market research in other countries. Furthermore, collecting primary research is expensive in terms of both money and time and therefore care is necessary in designing the research to ensure that it is conducted economically and that the effort is justified in terms of the costs involved. It can take one of two basic forms—quantitative or qualitative data collection.

*Quantitative techniques* Quantitative techniques involve gathering data from a large, representative group of respondents. They are usually conducted at a distance from the firm and its personnel, for example by mail or the internet, and creation of the questionnaire, data gathering, data retrieval and data analysis are undertaken at different times.

The most common instrument for the gathering of primary data in international marketing is the questionnaire. Preparation of questionnaires for administration overseas requires care both with wording and sequencing of questions so as to ensure that results from one country can be compared with results from another. (The elements to be considered in this connection were discussed earlier in this chapter.) When difficulties arise in ensuring that concepts will be rated the same way across different countries, it may be necessary to use pictures rather than words, as in Figure 6.5.

In selecting the sample from which to collect the data, a sampling plan should be drawn up addressing issues such as: What is the target population? How many people should be surveyed? How should the prospective respondents be chosen from the target population? Usually, a larger sample will be required from heterogeneous countries such as India than will be required from more homogeneous countries such as Thailand.

When preparing the sampling plan it is necessary to decide how prospective respondents are to be contacted. Data collection methods can vary from mail to telephone to personal

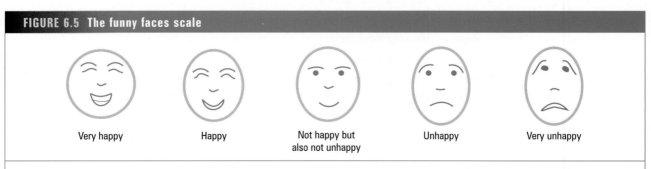

**FIGURE 6.5 The funny faces scale**

Very happy    Happy    Not happy but also not unhappy    Unhappy    Very unhappy

**SOURCE:** *Corder, C.K. (1978) 'Problems and pitfalls in conducting market research in Africa', in Gelb, B. (ed.) Marketing Expansion in a Shrinking World, Proceedings of American Marketing Association Business Conference, Chicago, pp. 86–90.*

interviews, for example shopping intercepts. The use of these methods varies from country to country as illustrated in Table 6.3 and the custom of the country regarding methods of data collection needs to be taken into account.

Questionnaire design should take account of format, content and wording so as to achieve both cultural sensitivity and a low non-response rate:

- *Question format*: Questions can be structured or unstructured. The latter, being open-ended questions, capture a greater amount of in-depth information, but increase the potential for interviewer bias. Another issue to be taken into account is that some societies prefer indirect questions and others have no problem with direct questions. Sensitivity to this issue is important to reduce the non-response factor. A typical example relates to age. Should the question be phrased: 'How old are you?' or 'In what year were you born?'?

- *Question content*: Content influences willingness to respond. Information available to respondents may vary because of different education levels and access to different communication infrastructure. Questions should also be adapted to societal restraints such as tax evasion and the black economy. Where these constraints apply questions must be asked indirectly lest the respondent feels that a truthful answer will end up in the office of the tax commissioner or lead to a charge of black-market activity.

- *Question wording*: The potential for misunderstanding spoken or written words should be reduced by careful attention to the influence of language and culture on the design of questions. Words used should be simple rather than complex, unambiguous rather than ambiguous and, where culturally acceptable, the questions should be couched in specific terms.

Using a badly designed data-gathering instrument in international marketing will yield poor results. For this reason any instrument should always be pre-tested, preferably with a sample drawn from the population it is intended to survey.

***Qualitative techniques*** Qualitative data gathering, on the other hand, helps to create a holistic overview of the research problem by gathering in-depth information. Fewer respondents but a larger number of variables tend to be involved in qualitative research. These techniques are

| TABLE 6.3 | Comparison of European data collection methods | | | | |
| --- | --- | --- | --- | --- | --- |
| | France (%) | Netherlands (%) | Sweden (%) | Switzerland (%) | UK (%) |
| Mail | 4 | 33 | 23 | 8 | 9 |
| Telephone | 15 | 18 | 44 | 21 | 16 |
| Central location/streets | 52 | 37 | – | – | – |
| Home/work | – | – | 8 | 44 | 54 |
| Groups | 13 | – | 5 | 6 | 11 |
| Depth interviews | 12 | 12 | 2 | 8 | – |
| Secondary | 4 | – | 4 | 8 | – |

**SOURCE:** *Demby, E.H. (1990) 'ESOMAR urges changes in reporting demographics, issues worldwide report',* Marketing News, *8 January, p. 24. Reprinted with permission of the American Marketing Association.*

characterised by proximity between the researcher and the respondent, with data retrieval and data analysis usually being undertaken by the same person (the interviewer).

Qualitative techniques include interviews, focus groups, observation and Delphi studies:

* *Interviews*: These constitute the primary form of research when visiting an overseas market. If the interviews are with knowledgeable or influential people they can be a major source of information because opinions expressed are a result of that person analysing a variety of other opinions and sources of information. However, because of the risk of bias the objective of the interview should be to gather in-depth information as opposed to a wide variety of material.

* *Focus groups*: These are a popular form of exploratory research in international marketing. Focus groups consist of small groups of potential customers, usually between eight and 12 people, facilitated by a professional moderator. A free-ranging discussion takes place around a series of predetermined topics. In an international setting the moderator needs to be familiar with the local language and patterns of social interaction; for example, people from some cultures such as Japan are more reluctant to offer criticism than are people from cultures such as Hong Kong. In countries where non-verbal language is important the moderator needs to be skilled at interpreting the degree to which body language adds to meaning.

* *Observation*: In international marketing, observation can shed light on issues not previously understood or practices not previously encountered. Observation is useful when researching how consumers in different countries actually behave and for this reason it can be obtrusive or unobtrusive. Problems can arise with unobtrusive observation when people discover that their behaviour has been observed and become resentful.

* *Delphi studies*: These are a technique for aggregating the views of a number of experts who cannot come together physically. These experts are people who are very knowledgeable about a particular issue as opposed to the general interviewee who has limited knowledge only. Participants are asked to identify major issues relating to the topic, rank their statements according to importance and give a rationale for their ranking. The aggregated responses are then returned to all participants, who are asked to indicate their agreement or disagreement with the aggregate ranking. Repetition of this process occurs until a degree of consensus has been achieved. Using mail, email or fax, the opinions of informed individuals can be obtained at a reasonable cost, despite their being separated by large distances.

***Comparing quantitative with qualitative techniques*** The relative merits of each technique are summarised in Table 6.4.

There are a number of factors that need to be taken into account in determining whether to undertake quantitative or qualitative research in a specific international market. These are the sources of the information, the issues involved and the techniques most appropriate to the specific market.

***Sources*** An Australian or New Zealand firm can obtain primary research by visiting the overseas market and checking at first hand the impressions formed as a result of the secondary research undertaken back home or commissioned from the overseas market. Participation in trade missions can be a useful way of gathering primary data. Another way is to visit the overseas market at the time of a major trade display of products in the firm's area of expertise. The show itself provides a useful venue for gathering information on competitive offerings, the state of development of the market and likely reaction to the product to be offered. The most common source of primary research for a firm is for it to commission a firm in the overseas market to undertake specific research on its behalf. Such research is usually intended to obtain answers to questions that are directly related to the firm's decision making with respect to that market.

*Issues* A large number of issues need to be considered when conducting or evaluating primary market research. These include:

* *the ability to communicate opinions*: The respondent's ability to express attitudes about an item depends on their ability to recognise the usefulness or value of the item or concept. Opinions and attitudes are difficult to form if the respondent is unfamiliar with the concept or the item is not widely used in the community. The more complex the concept, the more difficult it is to design research to elicit useful opinions about it.

* *willingness to respond*: Culture may influence this in two ways. In the first place culture can influence who in the household expresses opinions to outsiders. In Muslim countries this is generally the male in the household and a male interviewer is not allowed to interview a female. In the second place there may be a reluctance to tell

| TABLE 6.4 | Quantitative versus qualitative research |

| Comparison dimension | Quantitative research (e.g. a postal questionnaire) | Qualitative research (e.g. a focus group interview or the case method) |
|---|---|---|
| Objective | To quantify the data and generalise the results from the sample to the population of interest | To gain an initial and qualitative understanding of the underlying reasons and motives |
| Type of research | Descriptive and/or causal | Exploratory |
| Flexibility in research design | Low (as a result of a standardised and structured questionnaire: one-way communication) | High (as a result of the personal interview, where the interviewer can change questions during the interview: two-way communication) |
| Sample size | Large | Small |
| Choice of respondents | Representative sample of the population | Persons with considerable knowledge of the problem (key informants) |
| Information per respondent | Low | High |
| Data analysis | Statistical summary | Subjective, interpretative |
| Ability to replicate with same result | High | Low |
| Interviewer requirements | No special skills required | Special skills required (an understanding of the interaction between interviewer and respondent) |
| Time consumption during the research | Design phase: high (formulation of questions must be correct) Analysis phase: low (the answers to the questions can be coded) | Design phase: low (no 'exact' questions are required before the interview) Analysis phase: high (as a result of many 'soft' data) |

**SOURCE:** *Hollensen, S. (2004) Global Marketing: A Decision-oriented Approach, 3rd edn, Prentice Hall, London, p. 144.*

interviewers what the respondent actually thinks or to reveal the actual situation. This may be due to secrecy reasons such as covering up tax evasion or fear of the state.

- *sampling*: As was evident from the Russian example at the beginning of the chapter, sampling in field surveys can be problematic in undertaking primary research in many countries. The types of problems encountered in drawing up a random sample can include no officially recognised census, lack of other listings that can serve as a sampling frame, inaccurate or out-of-date telephone directories and no accurate maps of population centres from which cluster samples can be taken.

- *language and comprehension*: Differences in idiom and difficulty in arriving at an exact translation create problems in obtaining the specific information sought and in interpreting a respondent's answers. This is because equivalent concepts rarely exist in all languages. Literacy can also be a problem in developing countries where literacy rates are low and written questionnaires are largely irrelevant. Within a country, there can be a number of different languages and dialects (as is the case in India where, for example, different languages are spoken in each of the four southernmost states). This can influence the conduct of primary research.

- *respondent bias*: This can include social biases, such as telling the interviewer what it is believed the interviewer wants to hear; social desirability biases as exemplified by giving answers that are considered to reflect desirable social status or educational levels; and topic biases which result from some topics being taboo in some cultures (as with sex in India).

- *non-response bias*: Often this is a matter of reluctance to answer personal questions or questions on particular topics. It can also be a matter of members of some cultures being more reluctant than members of other cultures to respond to market research questions. As a consequence, non-response rates vary substantially between countries.

- *interaction bias*: Many primary research studies require interaction between researcher and respondent. This can be influenced by the location where the interaction occurs and whether there are others present when the interaction occurs. In the first instance the formality of the location may influence the formality of the response because responses to interviews conducted in a home may be more relaxed and forthcoming than responses to interviews conducted in an office or in a rented interview room. In the second instance when others are present the interviewee may be more inclined to provide a socially acceptable response rather than a response reflecting what is actually felt. Another source of bias is difference in social status between interviewer and interviewee, which can inhibit expression of frank opinions. Few countries are as egalitarian as Australia or New Zealand and social class differences are more pervasive in most other countries.

The problems of conducting primary research overseas are compounded when emerging markets are involved.

**Techniques** Cultural and individual preferences vary substantially between nations. These are important for determining the most appropriate research technique to use. Executives in countries such as Australia usually prefer to collect large amounts of data through surveys so that the data can be manipulated statistically. Executives in other countries such as Japan prefer to gather research through visits to dealers and other channel members and match this with hard secondary data, such as statistics on sales, imports and inventory levels. Techniques for gathering primary research can vary according to whether the data is to be collected in a real-world or controlled environment. Surveys are an example of the former, whereas focus groups are an example of the latter. Also influencing the selection of the technique for gathering primary data will be the extent to which the data to be gathered is subjective or objective and the degree to which it is to be structured or unstructured. Subjective, unstructured data is more likely to be collected by qualitative research whereas objective, structured data is more likely to be collected by quantitative research. Table 6.5 contains a comparison of survey methods used in international marketing research.

## STAGE 4: ANALYSIS AND INTERPRETATION OF DATA

In research the same situation can be interpreted in different ways, as the following indicates:

> There's a story told about difficult markets along the following lines. Two shoe company salesmen get the nod to open the first international sales territories. Joe goes to Zimara and Bob to Didyuri Doo. After one week, Joe sends a cable back to headquarters that reads: 'Coming home tomorrow. No possibilities in Zimara. The natives don't wear shoes'. Bob isn't heard from in the first week, nor in the second. Because Didyuri Doo was so remote, people at HQ began to worry. In the third week a cable arrived which said: 'Fantastic sales opportunity! Natives are all barefoot. Everyone here needs shoes!'
>
> SOURCE: Adapted from Zhan, S.E. (2000) 'Penetrating difficult markets', World Trade, January, pp. 84–6.

Many issues must be taken into consideration at this stage, ranging from cultural interpretations to different concepts of the product in various countries. As an example, in Australia beer is considered to be an alcoholic beverage, whereas in southern Europe it is regarded as a soft drink. This relates to comparability of data collected in different cultural contexts. Affecting comparability is how reliable the data is likely to be. This can be a matter

**TABLE 6.5  A comparative evaluation of survey methods for use in international marketing research**

| Criteria | Telephone | Personal | Mail |
|---|---|---|---|
| High sample control | + | + | − |
| Difficulty in locating respondents at home | + | − | + |
| Inaccessibility of homes | + | − | + |
| Unavailability of a large pool of trained interviewers | + | − | + |
| Large population in rural areas | − | + | − |
| Unavailability of current telephone directory | − | + | − |
| Unavailability of mailing lists | + | + | − |
| Low penetration of telephones | − | + | − |
| Lack of efficient postal system | + | + | − |
| Low level of literacy | − | + | − |
| Face-to-face communication culture | − | + | − |

Note: + denotes an advantage; − denotes a disadvantage.

SOURCE: Doole, I. and Lowe, R. (2004) International Marketing Strategy: Analysis, Development and Implementation, 4th edn, Thomson Learning, London, p. 125.

of accessibility on the one hand and quality on the other. Accessibility of information varies from one country to another. Factors affecting accessibility can be the stage of development of the country, its market research infrastructure, the extent of freedom and dissemination of information and the degree to which the political regime is democratic or authoritarian. Comparability is also influenced by the quality of information available as this also varies between countries. It can vary in terms of reliability, detail and whether it is short or long term.

Interpretation of research results in international marketing requires a degree of scepticism because the data has been collected under varying circumstances that can result in errors in both collection and analysis. Substantial biases in answers to questions on attitude, for example, can arise because of cultural differences. If researchers wish to compare answers given to the same question by respondents from two culturally distinct environments, they may need either to standardise or normalise the data before interpreting it (see Craig and Douglas 2005, Chapters 7–9). Standardisation involves taking the questionnaire scale and setting the mean answer for each respondent at zero. Differences from that mean are then expressed in terms of standard deviations. Normalisation occurs when differences are expressed in terms of deviation from the country's or cultural group's mean. Interpretation of data gathered on an international basis also involves a high degree of cultural sensitivity because of selective perception due to cultural biases. This can be minimised by ensuring that at least one of the people interpreting the data from a particular country is either from that country or is well acquainted with business customs and practices in that country.

Interpretation of statistics also requires consideration of purchasing power parity (PPP). This refers to a method of comparing the size of economies using international price comparisons to reflect the domestic purchasing power of the local currency. This is more accurate than the traditional method of comparing countries' Gross National Products (GNPs) via converting to US dollars by applying the official exchange rate to the local currency. This traditional approach does not reflect the fact that prices of services and other non-traded goods tend to be much lower in developing countries. As a consequence, PPP measures of developing economies are frequently higher than estimates based on exchange rate calculations. This is illustrated in Table 6.6.

## STAGE 5: DISSEMINATION OF INFORMATION/PREPARATION OF THE RESEARCH REPORT

In preparing the final report it is important to comment on the reliability as well as on any limitations relating to the facts as presented. The report should:

- identify the sources of the data because different sources of data justify differing degrees of confidence;

- where appropriate, identify by name and title those interviewed as this enables the recipient of the report to assess the value of the information it contains;

- simplify statistical computations so as to facilitate understanding by the recipient, and fully explain the way the data was obtained; and

- spell out alternative courses of action resulting from the research so that management is able to make an informed decision.

Finally, international marketing research is not just confined to establishing a market for a product or service. It may be specifically directed to understanding an overseas market and how it operates, so that a specific segment of that market can be targeted. This is illustrated in the Ogilvy BrandConsult example from China.

| TABLE 6.6 | Top 10 and bottom 10 countries based on per capita income |

| | Population (millions) 2002 | GNP per capita | | PPP estimates of GNP per capita | |
|---|---|---|---|---|---|
| | | Dollars 2002 | Rank | Dollars 2002 | Rank |
| *Low-income economies* | | | | | |
| Burundi | 7 | 100 | 201 | 630 | 199 |
| Congo Dem. Rep | 52 | 100 | 201 | 630 | 199 |
| Ethiopia | 67 | 100 | 199 | 780 | 196 |
| Guinea-Bissau | 1 | 130 | 198 | 680 | 197 |
| Liberia | 3 | 140 | 197 | – | – |
| Sierra Leone | 5 | 140 | 197 | 500 | 201 |
| Malawi | 11 | 160 | 195 | 570 | 200 |
| Niger | 11 | 180 | 194 | 800 | 195 |
| Tajikistan | 6 | 180 | 194 | 930 | 194 |
| Eritrea | 4 | 190 | 192 | 1040 | 193 |
| *High-income economies* | | | | | |
| Austria | 8 | 23 860 | 10 | 28 910 | 5 |
| Finland | 5 | 23 890 | 9 | 26 160 | 9 |
| Hong Kong | 7 | 24 690 | 8 | 27 490 | 6 |
| United Kingdom | 59 | 25 510 | 7 | 26 580 | 8 |
| Sweden | 9 | 25 970 | 6 | 25 820 | 10 |
| Denmark | 5 | 30 260 | 5 | 30 600 | 4 |
| Japan | 127 | 34 010 | 4 | 27 380 | 7 |
| United States | 288 | 35 400 | 3 | 36 110 | 2 |
| Switzerland | 7 | 36 170 | 2 | 31 840 | 3 |
| Norway | 5 | 38 730 | 1 | 36 690 | 1 |

**SOURCE:** 'World Bank development indicators, 2004', in Craig, C.S. and Douglas, S.P. (2005) International Marketing Research, 3rd edn, John Wiley & Sons, p. 6. © 2005 John Wiley & Sons Limited. Reproduced with permission.

Ogilvy BrandConsult, a recently established marketing advisory firm, has researched China's middle class through a study of brand buying behaviour. They established four key segments within the marketplace. These were 'seekers', or those considered to be leading social change, 'adapters', or those who follow the seekers but wish the pace of change to slow somewhat, 'tolerators', who struggle physically and emotionally with the new system, and 'resisters', the most traditional members of the middle class, who tend to adopt new opinions and behaviours slowly.

# Other issues

Some final issues in international market research for consideration include undertaking international research in developing countries and new techniques for market research that have recently been developed in advanced countries, managing the international research process and undertaking test market activities.

## RESEARCH IN DEVELOPING COUNTRIES

The lack of sampling resources and the obstacles encountered when sampling a poor, mobile and illiterate population prevented the sampling of large segments of the Egyptian population. This forced researchers to abandon more precise sampling techniques, in favour of a more realistically obtained convenience sample consisting of 500 consumers living in Cairo in the summer of 1990. The test instrument was hand delivered due to the lack of a reliable postal service. The sample, with a response rate of 67%, was skewed in favour of educated and professional consumers. Although the above did not result in a proportionate representative sample, it was acceptable to the researchers in the circumstances. This was because poorer people are more reluctant both to form and express opinions, tend to be negative towards market research and are more inclined to be biased towards issues that are socially sensitive. Due to the hardship they face because of economic circumstances, the cost of reaching poorer areas and respondents with low education is prohibitively expensive and such respondents have a general mistrust of strangers, obstructing the conduct of market research (Al-Khatib et al. 1995).

In some of these countries, low levels of telephone ownership and poor communications infrastructure make telephone surveys impractical. According to Craig and Douglas (2005), telephone connections vary from 106 per 1000 in Thailand to 36 per 1000 in Indonesia. Cellular phone ownership is also low in these countries. However, in some developing countries such as South Africa and Venezuela, low levels of landline telephone ownership are compensated for by high levels of mobile phone ownership. Because in most developing countries mail and phone surveys are not practical, personal interviewing is usually used. This has the advantage of low wage costs, making it cheaper than other forms of data gathering. Personal interviewing also overcomes the frequently encountered difficulties in such countries of illiteracy and lack of reliable mailing lists.

## NEW INTERNATIONAL RESEARCH TECHNIQUES

Most of the techniques in the preceding section obtain information on how people say they behave, which may well be different to how people actually behave. There is often a difference between people's stated intention and what exit surveys reveal. Some of the new techniques focus on how people actually behave.

**The internet** The internet is a vehicle for quick, low-cost research. It is useful in international market research as it is 'borderless'. Not only does it provide access to large amounts of secondary data, but it is increasingly being used as a vehicle for primary research. It can take a number of forms, all of which can be used to gather market research in the international domain, but whose potential yet remains to be fully exploited:

- *online surveys*: these are often sent as attachments to emails and completed/returned electronically;

- *bulletin boards*: visitors can post questions and responses on these;

Japanese companies tend to be sceptical about Western-style market research using consumer surveys asking questions that try to identify traits so as to predict future behaviour. Researchers in Japan find out what they need by travelling around and visiting retailers who stock their products. They want information that is context-specific rather than context-free and they want data that is directly relevant to the way buyers have used or will use specific products. When Japanese companies conduct surveys, they interview consumers who have actually purchased or used a product and avoid scrutinising an undifferentiated mass public to learn about attitudes and values.

SOURCE: *Adapted from De Mooij, M. (2004)* Consumer Behaviour and Culture—Consequences for Global Marketing and Advertising, *Sage Publications, Thousand Oaks, California, p. 200.*

- *chat groups*: these are virtual discussion groups that hold online conversations on specific topics;
- *visitor tracking*: servers automatically collect vast amounts of information on the behaviour of visitors to the site;
- *Focus groups*: participants in these online groups are selected because they meet the selected criteria of interest to the firm;
- *cookies*: these are the devices that collect information on visitors to the site and their use in some countries may be restricted for privacy reasons.

Related to the above is data warehousing and data mining. Data warehousing contains a series of integrated databases designed to support decision making. They contain large amounts of information on customers from sources internal to the firm, from the customer and from third sources such as government, credit bureaux and market research firms. The data can range from behavioural preferences to lifestyle information to records obtained from transactions entered into. The process of exploring databases involves data mining. This is the process of using information technology to uncover previously unknown patterns of behaviour with a focus on discovering consumer's buying patterns so as to help marketers make better decisions. Data mining is often used to classify customers into specific segments.

**Omnibus surveys** A major barrier to the conduct of primary research in overseas markets is often lack of familiarity with the market. Omnibus surveys are a preliminary form of primary research that can in part address this issue and which can be followed by primary research initiated by the firm. Research agencies in overseas countries, such as ACNielsen, regularly administer surveys to a large panel of consumers and allow clients to include their own specific questions in these larger surveys. Omnibus surveys are relatively inexpensive as costs are averaged across a large number of clients and are useful when you desire to ask a small number of important questions across a large number of respondents (see <http://asiapacific.acnielsen.com>).

**Scanner data** Recent years have seen an increasing use of various forms of scanner data as a vehicle for international market research and comparison between markets in developed countries. Most non-durable consumer goods are sold with a barcode to facilitate scanning at the point of sale. Scanner data is collected more frequently than other forms of data gathering, is more accurate, enables shifts in sales volume and market shares to be spotted quickly and can be used as the basis for an automatic order to replenish stocks. In countries like Japan, where scanner data has met with some resistance, consumer panels are used. There are two approaches to these. One is to issue members of the panel with an ID card to use when checking out at the cash register so that purchasing information is entered every time the panel member shops. The other method is to provide the panel member with a scanner so that the member scans all purchases made on returning home after shopping.

Another advanced form of data gathering for market research purposes is to use 'people meters' to track TV programs as they are watched and then correlate viewing behaviour with purchase transactions. Referred to as single-source data, this approach allows companies to gauge the effectiveness of their advertising.

The use of these technologies in cross-country comparisons in consumer research is at present confined to the more developed countries—even then, comparability is patchy due to the reluctance by retailers to release their scanner data for competitive reasons and the uneven use of these new technologies.

## MANAGING INTERNATIONAL RESEARCH

This involves two aspects: the selection of a research agency and coordination of global research activities.

**Selecting a market research agency** There are three choices. The first is to select a research agency based in the geographical area. In all developed countries and in many developing countries such agencies exist. The need to use a local agency varies from mandatory in countries such as China, where closeness to the market and an understanding of how to cope with government 'red tape' is essential, to optional in countries such as New Zealand.

The second option is to select a research firm that specialises in the industry of which the Australian or New Zealand firm is a member. These firms are more likely to understand research issues peculiar to the industry and may have undertaken multi-country research studies for the industry or have undertaken individual studies for the industry in other countries.

The third alternative is to hire a firm that is either a multinational agency operating in many countries or has alliances with agencies in other countries. Such agencies rely on branches and/or associates in all developed countries and in many developing countries, but the client deals with only one office located in Australia. Examples of firms with extensive networks of offices overseas are SRG International of New York, ACNielsen of Chicago and to a lesser extent Frank Small and Associates of Sydney (who are strong in Asia). By using them for surveys, interviews and analyses, clients avoid the hassle of managing research projects from a distance, not to mention the headaches over cultural differences and translation into the other language.

**Coordination and management of market research** International marketing research may need to be carried out both at headquarters and in the host country. Marketing research at headquarters is useful for short-term planning and strategy formulation, whereas marketing research in host countries is necessary for tactics to achieve goals, short-term market planning and day-to-day activities. Marketing information is important at all levels of the organisation and it is important that a balance be achieved between centralising functions at headquarters in the interests of achieving economies and devolving responsibility to the regional or national levels so that the research has a 'local look and feel'.

As can be seen from Table 6.7, costs of various forms of market research vary widely from country to country and this is illustrated by benchmarking other countries in relation to Western Europe or the USA. For example, using Western Europe as a cost benchmark (i.e. 100), usage and attitude studies for various countries ranged from a high of 181 in Japan to a low of 13 in India.

## TABLE 6.7 — Cross-country comparison for market research studies

### Usage and attitude survey

|  | | |
|---|---|---|
| Western Europe (SwFrs 40 800) | 100 | |
| North America | 220 | |
|   USA | | 234 |
|   Canada | | 202 |
| Japan | 181 | |
| Australia | 136 | |
| Central/South America | 100 | |
|   Brazil | | 114 |
|   Argentina | | 105 |
|   Mexico | | 92 |
|   Colombia/Chile/Venezuela | | 67 |
| South Africa | 102 | |
| Middle East | 96 | |
|   Saudi Arabia | | 106 |
|   UAE | | 84 |
| Pacific Rim | 87 | |
|   Hong Kong | | 140 |
|   Indonesia | | 63 |
|   Taiwan/South Korea | | 92 |
| Eastern Europe | 61 | |
|   Hungary | | 48 |
|   Czechoslovakia | | 65 |
|   Poland | | 62 |
|   Russia | | 81 |
| North Africa | 50 | |
|   Egypt | | 49 |
| Turkey | 45 | |
| India | 13 | |

### Telephone tracking study

|  | |
|---|---|
| USA (SwFrs 36 120) | 100 |
| Canada | 106 |
| Japan | 103 |
| USA | 100 |
| Australia | 80 |
| Taiwan | 78 |
| Brazil | 59 |
| Hong Kong | 48 |
| South Africa | 47 |
| Argentina | 34 |
| Hungary | 27 |
| Turkey | 26 |

### In-home product test

|  | | |
|---|---|---|
| Western Europe (SwFrs 12 750) | 100 | |
| North America | 318 | |
|   USA | | 283 |
|   Canada | | 362 |
| Japan | 297 | |
| Central/South America | 190 | |
|   Brazil | | 225 |
|   Mexico | | 150 |
| South Africa | 188 | |
| Australia | 157 | |
| Middle East | 151 | |
|   Saudi Arabia | | 165 |
|   UAE | | 129 |
| Pacific Rim | 144 | |
|   Hong Kong | | 152 |
|   Indonesia | | 73 |
|   Taiwan/S Korea | | 187 |
| Eastern Europe | 119 | |
|   Hungary | | 94 |
|   Czechoslovakia | | 111 |
|   Poland | | 127 |
|   Russia | | 155 |
| North Africa | 100 | |
|   Egypt | | 102 |
| Turkey | 77 | |
| India | 25 | |

### For group discussions

|  | | |
|---|---|---|
| Western Europe (SwFrs 15 061) | 100 | |
| Japan | 194 | |
| North America | 129 | |
|   USA | | 135 |
|   Canada | | 115 |
| Pacific Rim | 90 | |
|   Hong Kong | | 92 |
|   Indonesia | | 53 |
|   Taiwan/S Korea | | 133 |
| Central/South America | 82 | |
|   Brazil | | 107 |
|   Argentina | | 53 |
|   Colombia/Chile/Venezuela | | 51 |
|   Mexico | | 83 |
| Australia | 74 | |
| Middle East | 70 | |
|   Saudi Arabia | | 72 |
|   UAE | | 69 |
| South Africa | 51 | |
| Eastern Europe | 50 | |
|   Hungary | | 51 |
|   Czechoslovakia | | 53 |
|   Poland | | 48 |
|   Russia | | 45 |
| North Africa | 33 | |
|   Egypt | | 32 |
| Turkey | 51 | |
| India | 17 | |

SOURCE: ESOMAR. *The European Society for Opinion and Marketing Research, Amsterdam. Permission for using this material has been granted by The European Society for Opinion and Marketing Research, J.J. Viottastraat 29, 1071 JP Amsterdam, The Netherlands.*

Given this variation in cost, the issue arises as to the desirability of coordinating cross-country market research. Coordination facilitates cross-country comparison of results and also provides the benefits of timeliness, cost savings, centralisation of communication and quality control. The degree of coordination depends on the conflicting demands of users of the market research. Headquarters tends to favour standardised data collection, sampling procedures and survey instruments, whereas local users tend to favour country-customised research that takes into account the peculiarities of their local environment. The ideal approach should embody both the etic and emic approaches referred to earlier in the chapter. If coordination is attempted, then all user groups should be involved and multi-country research should make some provision for particular circumstances of specific countries. It can do this by adding some country-specific items to the standardised questionnaires.

## TEST MARKETING

Should a 'go–no go' decision to launch into an international market be made on the basis of market research or should the firm do what is commonly done in Australia and New Zealand and conduct a field experiment otherwise known as a test market? Test marketing allows the firm to test the entire marketing program for the offering, including its positioning strategy, its pricing, its distribution, its advertising, its branding and its packaging. A test market operation overseas is advisable if the decision to proceed would involve new capital investment in production facilities in Australia or New Zealand. In such a case, using existing excess capacity, the firm could supply a test market location overseas with product so as to assess its sales potential, the reception to the planned promotional strategy, the degree of price elasticity, and to analyse ways of achieving cost-effective distribution.

The test market selected should be a microcosm of the larger market that would be targeted if the test market is successful. This means that it should reflect the same characteristics of demographics, lifestyles, economics and culturally influenced behaviours. It should also reflect the same commercial impediments, incentives and media availability as the larger market. In Australia a city that has similar characteristics to the average for Australia as a whole is often selected for test market purposes. One such city is Newcastle, NSW.

In developed countries locating a test market city is possible because test marketing is a well-established practice. In developing countries, especially where there is a wide gulf in socioeconomic conditions between rural and urban areas, as in Thailand, test market locations may not be available. One possibility is to launch in one location and, if results are promising, progressively roll out the launch to other locations. This can be within a country: for example in the USA you could use San Diego as a test market, then roll out the launch to the rest of California and, if this is satisfactory, extend the launch nationwide. This can be done on a country-by-country basis within a geographic region. Using ASEAN as an example, the initial test market could be Singapore, followed by Malaysia, then Thailand, the Philippines and Indonesia. The weakness of this approach is that these markets differ from each other and the Singapore results may not be an accurate predictor of acceptance of the product in Thailand.

Many firms skip the test market stage when marketing internationally because they consider that, having announced their intention to introduce their product into a market, if they do not do so in all areas their competitors may launch nationally and pre-empt them. Test market operations are costly and the results may be misleading if the conditions in the test market cannot be replicated in the wider market should the product eventually go to a national or a regional launch.

# GOVERNMENT EXPORT ASSISTANCE WITH INTERNATIONAL MARKETING RESEARCH

For many firms the government is a vital element in their researching the potential of and entering overseas markets. The government can assist with export promotion, which Seringhaus (1986, p. 55) defines as 'all public policy measures that actually or potentially assist exporting activity either from a firm, industry or national perspective'. Government assistance is provided to improve the firm's competitive position overseas and in the process enhance a nation's competitiveness. From the firm's perspective export promotion measures create a pro-exporting attitude, facilitate dealing with specific export problems and assist in making exporting a positive experience for the firm. The level and type of assistance a government can provide is restricted by the WTO with the result that for the most part government assistance is restricted to 'back-up' services. Assistance differs between countries depending on national trade policy and the prevailing view towards government intervention in the business sector. Some countries have a pure government export promotion organisation (e.g. Austrade in Australia or New Zealand Trade and Enterprise in New Zealand), whereas others have privately funded bodies (e.g. Austria). Government export promotion programs provide both indirect and direct assistance as illustrated in Figure 6.6.

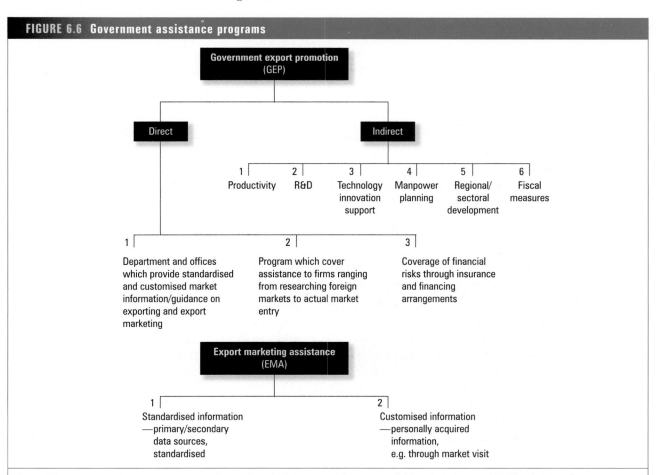

**FIGURE 6.6** Government assistance programs

**SOURCE:** *Diamantopoulos, A., Schegelmilch, B.B. and Katy Tse, K.Y. (1993) 'Understanding the role of export marketing assistance: empirical evidence and research needs',* European Journal of Marketing, *Vol. 27, No. 4, p. 6.*

Indirect measures, although not specifically designed for export, can generate export benefits via enhancing future competitiveness. They include assistance to firms to improve their productivity, research and development incentives, support to firms to create and employ innovative technology, assistance with manpower planning, incentives for undertaking activities in specific regions or industry sectors and fiscal measures such as tax and investment incentives.

Direct measures are intended to enhance the firm's export competitiveness. They include the activities of government departments that supply standardised and customised market information and give advice on exporting in general and export marketing in particular; programs that provide assistance to firms extending from awareness to market entry; and programs that cover firms' financial risks through insurance and financial arrangements.

The focus of all programs is on exporting and as such does not reflect the reality of current international business, which involves varied forms of international involvement including licensing, franchising, strategic alliances, overseas investment, cooperative manufacture and countertrade. Given that inward and outward international activities are often interdependent, governments in future may need to adopt a less restrictive approach towards assistance for encouragement of international involvement. Evidence from the literature is that these programs do not provide the incentive for internationalisation, but are of assistance once firms have decided to 'go international'; the information provided is inadequate for the needs of smaller firms; and it is practical and financial assistance that is considered to be the most useful.

# The internet and international market research

The internet as a data collection vehicle was discussed earlier in this chapter. The internet is a significant tool for international market research and an increasing percentage of market surveys are being conducted using the internet as it is regarded as more cost efficient, because data can be obtained more quickly and at lower cost than other methods. The internet extends both the depth and the breadth of the search process because, in addition to company sites, consumers can access product category sites, retailer sites and consumer-dominated sites (e.g. bulletin boards and chat rooms). With the internet, the initiative in the search process shifts to the consumer, resulting in topic-focused rather than sequential, process-oriented searches.

The information environment on the internet differs from that in the marketplace in that, due to most sites being located in Western countries, internet sites in general reflect the conventions and symbols of Western culture. As a result there may be difficulty in the interpretation and retention of information where communication crosses cultural and linguistic boundaries. Specific areas of concern are:

- *Language*: There is predominance in the use of English on the internet (57% of users are English speakers). This implies that non-English-speakers have access to a much more limited range of information, although there are signs that a global internet vocabulary is starting to emerge. Using other languages is impeded by some having a number of spoken dialects (e.g. Mandarin is the written form of Chinese, but there are many spoken forms) and meaning conveyed in the spoken form in some languages varies by tonality.

- *information misinterpretation*: Because there are no filters on accessing internet information there is greater scope for misinterpretation and miscommunication of messages on the internet, especially by non-English-speaking or non-Western consumers.

- *information credibility*: As 'word of mouse' replaces 'word of mouth', it is much more difficult to assess the objectivity or biases of the presenter of the information.

- *product cues*: On the internet, consumers are faced with a truncated set of cues and an absence of sensory cues. This leads to a greater reliance on objective cues such as price and product description. The latter can be termed 'digital' cues because they can be conveyed on the internet, whereas the former can be considered as 'non-digital' cues.

- *sampling*: Internet users do not represent the general population at large as they tend to be both better off and better educated.

Market research often has as its major focus the understanding of consumer behaviour. In traditional marketplace models cultural factors are viewed as key factors in explaining geographic variations in behaviour. However, these factors play a much smaller role in 'virtual' markets. There, a cyber-culture dominates and local culture acts as a contingency variable that mediates behaviour. Compounding the situation is that access to information can be acquired in one geographic sphere that is totally separate from the geographic sphere in which the resulting transaction will occur. Some related international issues for market research are:

- diffusion of innovation: geographic proximity will no longer be as important as the internet provides a vehicle not only to rapidly communicate the latest developments but also as a conduit to deliver them;

- complexity of evaluations: consumers now have to evaluate stimuli and make choices based on heterogeneous and often unfamiliar cues (e.g. does the hotel stars-rating system mean the same in all countries?);

- country of origin effect: the role of national culture in the formation of values and behavioural norms is likely to decline in importance. This will occur as consumers, via the internet, become exposed to stimuli from other countries. As they become more global in outlook, country of origin becomes less salient as a cue; and opinion leaders—models focusing on the role of personal influence—are no longer likely to apply to the same extent. With the proliferation of chat rooms, bulletin boards, etc., the role of such influence becomes more diffuse and depersonalised.

With the internet the degree of consumer involvement in the purchase process becomes less and the distinction between high- and low-involvement goods also becomes less meaningful. Another factor is that the consumer who uses the internet is different from the consumer who does not (in terms of demographics and innovation adoption). This has implications for international market segmentation.

# Summary

Although undertaking market research overseas is fraught with more difficulties than in Australia or New Zealand and available information on which to base decisions is far less perfect, international market research is necessary to ascertain whether a market for the product does exist and, if so, how that market should be approached. It is a useful vehicle for learning in advance what changes need to be made to the product, what pricing strategy should be adopted, how best use can be made of the available media and which channels of distribution are likely to prove most effective. When carrying out market research overseas considerable care is necessary to ensure that at each stage of the research process differences between Australia/New Zealand and the overseas market are recognised and compensated for. If this does not happen, in all probability the research results will be irrelevant because there will be no basis for comparison. Not only must these differences be taken into account when collecting secondary and primary data, but also when analysing and interpreting the data. Despite the fact that international market research is complex and at times frustrating, it does reduce uncertainty and provide a better basis for informed decision making as far as commitment of resources to international activities is concerned. In the process, firms should take maximum advantage of government assistance programs, especially as far as provision of information and facilitation of the conducting of primary research is concerned.

## ETHICS ISSUE

You are the export manager of a major Australian pump producer that has been exporting small quantities of pumps to Indonesia for years. Sales have not grown with the market. For the last year you have been endeavouring to persuade your managing director that a manufacturing operation in Indonesia would give the firm a major share of what has been both an expanding market and a source of cheaper pumps as a hedge against competition in the Australian market from Taiwanese imports. In order to strengthen your argument, and without the knowledge of your managing director, you commissioned primary research on current and future prospects in Indonesia for your firm's pumps. Today two reports arrive on your desk. One was from the Jakarta office of Frank Small and Associates advising that in the short term there would be a severe downturn in the Indonesian market for pumps because of the flow-on effect of the currency crisis. In the longer term and within five years the market would recover and expand. The other report was from your Indonesian agent advising that representatives of the only other firm in the world with your advanced technology, US-based 'Pumps R Us', had recently been in Jakarta talking with the Indonesian Investment Promotion Authority (BKPM) about incentives for establishing a manufacturing operation in Bandung to supply the Asia–Pacific region.

*Given the conservative approach of your managing director, if you were the export manager would you show the Frank Small report to him?*

# Websites

ACNielsen http://acnielsen.com
Austrade http://www.austrade.gov.au
Brint business research interests http://www.brint.com/interest.html
Department of Foreign Affairs and Trade http://www.dfat.gov.au
European Society for Opinion and Market Research (ESOMAR) http://www.esomar.org
Frank Small & Associates (Melbourne) http://www.marketsdirectory.com/tmdintn/1196n.htm
Global Business Web http://www.globalbusinessweb.com/
KFC http://www.kfc.com.au
Market research http://www.knowthis.com/research
Mercedes-Benz http://www.mercedes-benz.com
New Zealand Trade and Enterprise http://www.nzte.govt.nz
Ogilvy Brandconsult http://www.ogilvypr.com.au/brand
PricewaterhouseCoopers http://www.pwcglobal.com
Roy Morgan http://www.roymorgan.com.au
TradePort—market research http://tradeport.org
US Department of Commerce http://www.stat-usa.gov
Web resources for international trade http://www.fita.org/webindex

# Discussion questions

1   What are the factors that cause market research overseas to differ from market research in Australia or New Zealand?

2   Outline the stages in an international market research plan.

3   Why is the issue of equivalence a major problem in cross-cultural market research?

4   Do the suggested techniques overcome all the problems of translation equivalence?

5   Which sources of secondary data are more important for industrial than for consumer goods?

6   Discuss the problem of cross-comparison of secondary data between countries.

7   What are the main areas of bias in primary research overseas and how would you compensate for these?

8   Under what circumstances is qualitative research preferable to quantitative research in the international environment?

9   What criteria would you apply in selecting an overseas test market location?

# References

Al-Khatib, J.A., Dobie, K. and Vitell, S.J. (1995) 'Consumer ethics in developing countries: an empirical investigation', in N. Delener (ed.) *Ethical Issues in International Marketing*, International Business Press, New York.

Corder, C.K. (1978) 'Problems and pitfalls in conducting market research in Africa', in Gelb, B. (ed.) 'Marketing expansion in a shrinking world', AMA, *Proceedings of American Marketing Association Business Conference*, Chicago, pp. 86–90.

Craig, C.S. and Douglas, S.P. (2005) *International Marketing Research*, 3rd edn, John Wiley and Sons, Chichester, UK.

Craig, C.S., Douglas, S.P. and Flaherty, T.B. (2000) 'Information access and internationalisation—the Internet and consumer behaviour in international markets', *Proceedings of the eCommerce and Global Business Forum*, 17–19 May, Santa Cruz, CA, Anderson Consulting Institute for Strategic Change.

Czinkota, M.R. and Kotabe, M. (1994) 'Product development the Japanese way', in M. Czinkota and I. Ronkainen, *International Marketing Strategy*, Dryden Press, Fort Worth, pp. 285–91.

Demby, E.H. (1990) 'ESOMAR urges changes in reporting demographics, issues worldwide report', *Marketing News*, 8 January, p. 24.

De Mooij, M. (2004) *Consumer Behaviour and Culture–Consequences for Global Marketing and Advertising*, Sage Publications, Thousand Oaks, California.

Diamantopoulos, A., Schegelmilch, B.B. and Katy Tse, K.Y. (1993) 'Understanding the role of export marketing assistance: empirical evidence and research needs', *European Journal of Marketing*, Vol. 27, No. 4, pp. 5–18.

Doole, I. and Lowe, P. (eds) (1997) *International Marketing Strategy: Contemporary Readings*, Thomson Business Press, London.

Doole, I. and Lowe, R. (2004) *International Marketing Strategy: Analysis, Development and Implementation*, 4th edn, Thomson Business Press, London.

ESOMAR. The European Society for Opinion and Marketing Research, J.J. Viottastraat 29, 1071 JP Amsterdam, The Netherlands.

Helmer, J. (1997) *Business Review Weekly*, 9 June, p. 32.

Hoffman, D. (1996) 'Russian voters' poll position: fear, uncertainty', *The Washington Post*, 23 May, p. A31.

Hollensen, S. (2004) *Global Marketing: A Decision-Oriented Approach*, 3rd edn, Financial Times Prentice Hall, Harlow, UK.

Job, A. (2004) 'Female team designs new Volvo', Auto Insides Report, *Detroit News*, 3 March.

Lassere, P. (1997), in Doole, I. and Lowe, P. (eds) *International Marketing Strategy: Contemporary Readings*, Thomson Business Press, London, Chapter 7.

Newman, P., Minghua, J. and Ibrahim, N. (2001) 'The meaning of the brand to the young educated Beijing consumer: a comparison between local and foreign fashion goods', *Proceedings of the Conference of the Academy of Marketing*, Cardiff, July, University of Cardiff.

Noonan, C. (2000) *Export Marketing: A Practical Guide to Opening and Expanding Markets Overseas*, Butterworth Heinemann, Oxford.

Seringhaus, F.H.R. (1986) 'The impact of government export marketing assistance', *International Marketing Review*, Vol. 3, No. 2, pp. 55–66.

Sood, J. (1989) 'Equivalent measurement in international market research: is it really a problem?', *Journal of International Consumer Marketing*, Vol. 2, No. 2, pp. 25–41.

Spark, R. (1999) 'Developing health promotion methods in remote Aboriginal communities', PhD thesis, Curtin University of Technology, Perth.

Toyne, B. and Walters, P.G. (1993) *Global Marketing Management: A Strategic Perspective*, 2nd edn, Allyn and Bacon, Boston.

Usunier, J-C. (2005) *Marketing Across Cultures*, 4th edn, Financial Times Prentice Hall, London.

Wall, S. and Rees, B. (2001) *Introduction to International Business*, Financial Times Prentice Hall, Harlow, UK.

Zhan, S.E. (2000) 'Penetrating difficult markets', *World Trade*, January, pp. 84–6.

## go online

Go online to <www.pearsoned.com.au/fletcher> to find more case studies.

CASE STUDY 6

# Market opportunities for Australian furniture in Asia

**Al Marshall, ACU National**

## THE BRAND AND ITS DOMESTIC MARKET

Moda Milano Mobili is a medium-sized manufacturer of finely crafted leather and timber furniture. The company specialises in living room sofas, chairs and dining room chairs, using Australian cowhide. It also manufactures a range of complementary coffee tables, side tables and dining room tables using Australian native timbers. The product lines are based on contemporary designs with simple clear flowing lines, rather than on more traditional designs with more detailing.

The in-house designer Max Paolo (who is also part-owner of the business) takes his inspiration for the sofa, chair and table designs from European designs, especially contemporary Italian designs. Max regularly visits stores like the Design Warehouse, Aero and Space, as well as reading magazines like *Architectural Digest*, *Wallpaper* and *Italian Vogue*.

In the Australian domestic market, Moda Milano Mobili furniture retails through a range of independently owned furniture stores in Sydney, Melbourne, Brisbane and Adelaide. The company does not own its own outlets since it is principally a manufacturer. Max Paolo and his business

partners perceive the company's core competencies to be its commitment to Italian style design, using good quality Australian materials, and quality manufacturing, using their own skilled furniture craftsmen.

The furniture is positioned at the higher quality and higher priced end of the market, and the outlets it supplies in each of Australia's four biggest cities are noted for furniture and household accessories that are not mass produced, and for their higher level of personalised customer service.

Neither the products lines nor the retail outlets that they are distributed through compete with Freedom Furniture, IKEA, Dare or Oz Design, despite these brands also marketing themselves on their 'design'. At the same time Moda Milano Mobili furniture is considerably less expensive (and less exclusive) than the furniture retailed through brands like the Design Warehouse, Aero and Space. In terms of the design and the price points Moda Milano Mobili competes most directly with the furniture in retail brands like the Sydney-based Nick Scali (<http://www.nickscali.com.au>).

The typical Moda Milano Mobili furniture purchaser is white collar professional in their 30s or early 40s, with a higher income and who lives in an inner city suburb in an apartment, terrace or town house. They typically do not have children or only have one child, and they travel overseas relatively frequently and appreciate good (particularly European) design, as well as fine craftsmanship, using Australian sourced materials.

## OPTIONS FOR FUTURE GROWTH

Max Paolo and his business partners at their recent marketing meetings have been discussing options to ensure the future growth of the business. These all require the hiring of more craftsmen and expanding the factory in order to produce more sofas, chairs and tables (both living and dining) for the domestic market, or for an overseas market, or for a mixture of both. In terms of Ansoff's four growth matrix model they are principally interested in market penetration and market development (Kotler et al. 2004). They are less interested in product development or diversification.

By expanding production Max and his partners believe that they can attain greater economies of scale. The furniture factory currently operates below its optimal capacity and, by producing more, the fixed costs can be held constant while the variable costs per unit produced can be reduced. In order to finance such an expansion, and to hire the quality craftsmen that are so central to their quality positioning, they need to convince their bank (Westpac) that they have a viable plan to sell the additional furniture that would be produced. Securing a loan from the bank would require them to submit a business plan for Moda Milano Mobili containing extensive details on how they plan to ensure future sales in the furniture market.

Options that they have discussed include appointing more retail distributors in Sydney, Melbourne, Brisbane and Adelaide; encouraging the existing distributors to carry more of their stock; appointing distributors in other Australian cities, like Perth, Canberra, and Hobart; and appointing distributors overseas in booming markets like the People's Republic of China, Hong Kong, Taiwan or South Korea.

The other business partners are less keen on this last option, which they perceive as inherently more risky and problematic from a business point of view than some of the other options. They are unsure if Westpac would be prepared to lend them the money to finance the factory expansion in the first place, let alone be prepared to finance a foray into foreign markets. International marketing is perceived as inherently more risky and resource intensive by many organisations contemplating overseas expansion.

## THE CASE FOR THE OVERSEAS OPTION

Max Paolo had proposed the overseas distributor idea at the last meeting, and has built what he considers a strong case for this option to be put on the table along with the other domestic expansion options.

Points in his argument include the fast economic growth rate and rising purchasing power in markets like China, growing Westernisation in consumer preferences and product consumption, more sophisticated market structures relating to logistics (transportation and storage in particular), an increasingly sophisticated and well-travelled middle to upper-middle class in all these countries (the perceived target market), established and frequent shipping between Australia and north-east Asian markets, the rapid growth in trade between China and Australia in many manufactured product categories (including imports of furniture, so why not exports?), the possibility of a free trade agreement with China in the future doing away with any formal furniture import barriers in the latter's market, and the robust nature and rapid recovery of economies like South Korea's following the Asian financial crisis in the late 1990s.

One of Max's final points made to his fellow business partners was to cite IKEA, the Swedish furniture and household accessories retailer, which has a presence in many markets around the world and which reputedly appeals to a distinct demographic and psychographic segment of consumers that exists in many markets around the world. Max pointed out that a consumer shopping for IKEA products in an IKEA store in Vancouver allegedly shares many traits and behaviours with a consumer shopping in an IKEA store in Singapore or in Stockholm. Max argued that, just as there appears to be international demand for inexpensively priced Swedish designed furniture, so too there may be an international demand for up-market Italian inspired furniture design in leather and natural timbers.

He also cited Freedom Furniture, which as part of its growth strategies some time ago expanded into an overseas market (New Zealand) with apparent success, and which as early as the mid to late 1980s was contemplating international expansion. Furthermore, he pointed out that Moda Milano Mobili would not be assuming nearly as much risk as Freedom Furniture, since its business model does not involve retailing, and full control over quality and materials used could be maintained, since production of the furniture would remain in Australia. Organisations are attracted to marketing their products overseas by a range of 'pull' (for example, factors like the growth rate of overseas markets and the purchasing power in overseas markets) and 'push' (for example, factors like slow economic growth in the domestic market, or too much competition in the domestic market) reasons, and Max principally cited a number of the 'pull' reasons.

## QUESTIONS RAISED BY THE OVERSEAS OPTION

Against this, Max suspected that his argument might raise more questions among his business partners. He was in fact correct, with one of the partners immediately pointing out that while IKEA is successful in many markets around the world this was not really a very good guide to the likely success of Moda Milano Mobili in international markets since the globally successful IKEA products are of a different style, quality, and pricing and do not use premium quality raw materials (rather, they typically are sourced at the lowest possible cost from suppliers in developing countries). Furthermore they are retailed through a radically different retail model than Moda Milano Mobili would use (assuming that retail distributors similar to the ones uses in Australia exist in the identified potential markets).

The same business partner also argued that while Freedom Furniture has expanded to markets like New Zealand this had been a far less ambitious endeavour than Max was advocating. The culture and lifestyle in New Zealand, and more specifically furniture tastes, are very similar to those in Australia, and the costs of shipping bulky furniture products would be far less than they would be with far more distant north-east Asian markets.

Another business partner who seemed less sceptical at the meeting simply questioned if the middle to upper-middle class in countries like China and South Korea are likely to place a high importance on design aesthetics in their furniture evaluation and purchasing criteria. This would be important, she argued, since the furniture would be produced in a high cost country, and the landed cost in South Korea, for instance, would make the furniture non-competitive in price relative to locally manufactured furniture, or furniture from other low cost input countries. She argued that it would therefore have to differentiate itself and sell on the basis of its Italian-inspired design. Max added that the Australian cowhide from which the sofas and chairs are constructed and the Australian native timbers from which the complementary tables are constructed would help to differentiate Moda Milano Mobili's product lines further.

What he did not share with the others is the moot question as to whether Australian leathers and native timbers are sought after in these markets (assuming that they are even known). Often research data on overseas markets does not exist or it exists in a form that is not directly useful. On the positive side Max floated the idea that being 'Made in Australia' might be a selling point among north-east Asia's social-status-conscious middle and upper-middle classes. Against this, one of the business partners pointed out that the status-conscious target market might in fact prefer to buy imported Italian-style furniture from the original sources, rather than from the Antipodes, particularly if Moda Milano Mobili's furniture ended up at similar prices in retail outlets in Shanghai for instance as furniture from furniture design companies in Milan. Intuition has a role to play in assessing overseas markets, in the absence of reliable qualitative or quantitative data.

Perhaps more fundamentally, the partners all questioned whether Italian-style furniture is likely to be appreciated and sought after in these markets (is there market demand?). Maybe the target market might prefer contemporary design interpretations of Chinese, Korean, and even Japanese furniture. There are distinctive traditions of furniture design and craftsmanship in the region, and people might feel more comfortable owning furniture with more of a connection to their own cultural past. Reflecting this, the level of market demand for Moda Milano Mobili's style of furniture might be quite low. Primary and secondary data collection can assist in evaluating the aggregate level of market demand.

One concern that Max himself has is that 'classic' reproduction and contemporary Italian-style furniture (a lot of it in leather fabrics) is produced in markets like China. Max is aware of this since it is imported into Australia from China, and is available through discount furniture importers like Glicks (<http://www.glicksfurniture. com.au>) and Matt Blatt (<http://www.mattblatt. com.au>). Max hypothesises that it may also be readily available in China and other countries in the region, at a price much lower than Moda

Milano Mobili's Australian-made furniture, which has much higher cost labour and raw material inputs.

Against this, on the positive side, if this furniture is available in retail outlets in China and possibly in neighbouring countries, this at least indicates that some consumers in these markets have a taste for Italian-inspired contemporary furniture.

This last meeting had ended with Max being tasked to investigate this option of overseas expansion for the company, and to report back to the next planning meeting with a recommendation backed by sound research as to whether this option was worthy of being kept on the table. The research in turn could be used to assemble the business plan for Westpac, if the international option is chosen.

## Bibliography

Kotler, P., Brown, L., Adam, S. and Armstrong, G. (2004) *Marketing*, 6th edn, Pearson Prentice Hall, Sydney.

## Questions

1  List the macro environmental factors and the micro environmental factors (using PESTEL as your organisational tool for the former and Porter's five forces model as your organisational tool for the latter) likely to be required in a furniture market opportunity assessment.

2  Identify the types of services provided by Austrade (<http://www.austrade.gov.au>) for potential exporters like Moda Milano Mobili. Identify other governmental or quasi-governmental or business organisations in Australia likely to provide assistance to potential exporters like Moda Milano Mobili. Briefly describe the services that they provide.

3  What role might exploratory field trips to cities like Shanghai, Beijing, Hong Kong, Taipei and Seoul be able to play, and what types of data could be collected on such a field trip? Is this data more likely to be qualitative or quantitative in nature? How might such data contribute to the decision whether to enter these markets?

4  If more than one of the overseas markets to be investigated appears to offer market potential for Moda Milano Mobili, what are the most important internal and market factors that would need to be reviewed in order to choose one market? Do these factors require additional information to be collected, or would Max and his business partners already have this available (either prior to their overseas market investigation or as a result of this investigation)?

CHAPTER 7

# INTERNATIONAL MARKET SELECTION AND ENTRY

## LearningObjectives

**After reading this chapter you should be able to:**

■ identify the different problems faced by firms in international business when selecting an overseas market;

■ assess a country's attractiveness in terms of its potential, its membership of trading blocs, its competitive intensity and its entry barriers;

■ create a portfolio of the most attractive overseas markets to enter given the circumstances of the firm and the potential offered by the market;

■ recognise the different available modes for entering an overseas market and the advantages and disadvantages of each;

■ appreciate the relative merits of different theories of internationalisation; and

■ adopt a holistic view of the way the internationalisation of a firm influences selection of entry mode in terms of inward-driven, outward-driven or linked forms.

# Australian small business exporting successes

Care began manufacturing childcare products in the 1970s and started exporting in 1992, with special focus on Asia. Their Australian businesses Britax, Selleys and Riversun have each achieved considerable success in the export market. Britax 'Safe-N-Sound' child restraints, prams and strollers now sell in Korea, Malaysia, Singapore and Hong Kong. Britax sees its success tied to world-class product safety attributes and selection of distributors in each country which have strong relationships with government, retail chains, industry associations and the media. Commitment by Britax to customer education programs through advertising and seminars supports its export growth path.

Selleys, famous for 'do it yourself' (DIY) home handyman products in Australia, has export sales of more than $20 million from its business in Asia. However, in most Asian countries the DIY concept does not exist so Selleys focused its attention on car-care polishes and washes and supplying the needs of tradespeople. Selleys predicts a 20% per annum growth rate in its export business and has its eyes firmly fixed on Asian markets.

Permo–Drive is a success story in the making. In 1998, three Australian engineers had an idea for a fuel saving device for heavy vehicles that would cut fuel consumption on vehicles that frequently stop-start, by up to 37%. However, following the successful testing of the prototype, it was

estimated that it would take at least seven years to commercialise. Permo–Drive then gained the jump on larger firms such as Ford when the United States Army decided to fund further testing of the device that it sees as vital for its fleet of trucks, which is among the largest in the world. A prospectus has been issued with the aim of raising $20 million to achieve commercialisation. The NSW Local Government Superannuation Scheme's Regional Development Trust has already agreed to contribute $11 million.

# INTRODUCTION

Whether the firm is experienced or new to international business, two of the most critical questions involved in the decision to go offshore and which have an impact on the resulting profitability of international involvement are:

1 Which of the vast range of markets overseas should the firm enter?

2 What mode should the involvement in the selected market take?

As far as market selection is concerned, this is complicated by changes in the international business environment. These changes, involving the formation of regional trade groupings, the creation of strategic alliances between firms and the exponential spread of information technology, are resulting in a breaking down of barriers between countries and the need to view the world as a global entity rather than as a series of national markets. As a consequence, choosing the most appropriate international market to enter has become more difficult. As markets can now stretch across national boundaries, geographic segmentation may no longer be an appropriate basis for market selection. While this may be true for large or transnational firms, most Australian firms are small to medium sized and, when they venture offshore, are still likely to do so on a country-by-country basis. For such firms it is useful to have a systematic procedure for selecting individual markets to enter.

Decisions as to the form of market entry (such as exporting, joint ventures or franchising) logically follow the decision as to the most appropriate market to enter. However, market selection and entry are linked because the attractiveness of markets is influenced by the strategic thrust of the corporation, competitive action in those markets and government regulation relating to the permissible forms of foreign entry. For example, a ban on the import of automobiles into the Myanmar market may mean that a joint venture is the only viable entry mode. This may make the market unattractive to a firm without the resources to establish a joint venture or to a firm whose international strategy is focused around export rather than investment overseas. Deciding on the most appropriate form of market entry involves understanding each of the various modes available and the conditions under which one mode might be more suitable than another.

## OVERSEAS MARKET SELECTION

Selecting an overseas market can affect the other activities of an Australian or New Zealand firm. This is because the outcome may influence the profitability of the firm in its domestic as well as in its other overseas markets. Not only will this have an impact on overall profits, but it might also affect other areas such as its global reputation. This is illustrated in situations like the impact on the Union Carbide Corporation following the Bhopal calamity; the security of a firm's intellectual property (in countries where intellectual piracy is common); and the physical risk to its personnel (in countries like Iraq or Cambodia).

Underpinning the selection of markets to enter should be a strategic orientation that treats market entry selection as part of the firm's overall strategy, linked both to its resource base and distinctive competence on the one hand and its position in relation to competitors on the other.

In isolating the markets that offer the greatest potential it is necessary to take the situation of the firm and the circumstances of the overseas markets into account. In doing so, the characteristics of the individual markets, as well as the extent to which one overseas market is integrated with another, need to be considered. Where there is an integrated group of overseas markets, entering one may facilitate subsequent or simultaneous entry into others.

In addition to balancing the firm's strategic orientation with the characteristics of the overseas market(s), market entry decisions should also take into account:

- the structure of the global industry of which the firm is a part—consideration of the structure of the industry recognises that, in whatever it does, the firm is part of a network and the strengths deriving from that network can affect the decision as to which market to enter; and

- the strategy of current or potential global competitors—the inclusion of competitor strategy recognises that markets are dynamic and the fact of entering an overseas market is likely in many instances to provoke a competitive reaction, either from firms in that market or from firms in other countries.

Selection of overseas markets involves comparison. This can be difficult because the quality of data varies from country to country. Although the expansion of global databases and international online services has helped comparison, difficulties remain because of differences between countries in both recency and rigour of data collection. These limitations make a structured approach to overseas market selection desirable.

There are various approaches to market selection and these have different implications for small and medium-sized as opposed to large firms. The first approach focuses on whether to enter overseas markets on an incremental basis (this entails moving from one to another only after establishing a presence in the first) or whether to enter a number of overseas markets simultaneously and, on the basis of experience, decide on which markets to concentrate. The advantages of incremental entry are that it enables the firm to gain experience at a measured pace, requires the commitment of fewer resources and involves less risk in terms of exposure. However, this approach involves greater competitive risk as competitors may leapfrog the firm into other markets. For instance, after seeing what an Australian or New Zealand firm is doing successfully in Thailand, competitors may move immediately into Malaysia, Indonesia and the Philippines, which were potential target markets for the firm following its establishing a presence in Thailand. The incremental approach may also preclude achieving economies of scale and result in a haphazard approach to entering additional overseas markets. On the other hand, the simultaneous entry approach does enable the firm to acquire overseas experience rapidly, facilitates achieving economies of scale in overseas activities and is likely to prevent pre-emption by competitors in other markets. Offsetting these advantages is the fact that it is a resource-intensive strategy and one that entails higher operating risk.

The second approach to overseas market entry focuses on whether a concentrated as opposed to a diversified approach should be adopted. If a firm decides to concentrate its resources in a limited number of markets, it is likely to have a more focused effort, encounter reduced operating risks and costs, and benefit from economies of scale in exploiting information and acquiring experience. On the other hand, it will have 'all its eggs in one basket' and if something happens to the selected markets (such as the events in the former Centrally Planned Economies 1989–91 or the Asian currency crisis of 1997–98) the firm is in an exposed position. In addition, this approach leaves the firm largely ignorant about potential in the rest of the world. A diversified strategy spreads both risk exposure and broadens knowledge of potential in a variety of markets, as well as offering greater strategic flexibility. It can, however, result in the firm spreading itself too thinly, may affect its ability to be competitive as economies of scale prove elusive and may require greater management resources at the firm's headquarters.

# SCREENING FOR MARKET SELECTION

## Analysing the attractiveness of individual markets

The purpose of screening is to enable the firm to arrive at a portfolio of attractive overseas markets. An example of this approach is that of the Australian Trade Commission (Austrade) in 1990, which compared the attractiveness of the overseas market with the competitiveness of the Australian firm in order to decide the merit of entering the specific overseas market.

The *first element*, which relates to the overseas market, involves rating:

- the characteristics of the market (e.g. growth of and sensitivity to imports, degree of market segmentation, extent of customer concentration, sensitivity to quality and performance characteristics, availability of close substitutes);

- the competitive conditions (e.g. concentration of domestic industry, other exporters, complexity of the distribution system, threat of new entrants—both domestic and foreign);

- the financial and economic conditions (e.g. industry pricing practices, usual payment terms, currency parities, import tariffs and charges, need for concessional finance, foreign exchange conditions); and

- the legislative and sociopolitical conditions (e.g. political stability, trade legislation, consumer and environmental laws, registration and licensing requirements, cultural affinity, foreign investment legislation, labour laws and employment norms, intellectual property protection)

for the category of products/services to be offered by the Australian firm.

The *second element*, which relates to the Australian firm, involves rating:

- management characteristics (e.g. adequacy of management resources, involvement in international contracts and alliances, degree of institutional support);

- marketing characteristics (volume of market intelligence, effectiveness of the distribution network, pricing approaches, advertising and promotion capabilities);

- technology attributes (e.g. product design and development, investment in technology, customer service and support expectations, breadth of product line); and

- production-related competencies (e.g. cost competitiveness, scale of operation, consistency of quality, logistics capabilities, control over inputs, packaging and labelling requirements)

in terms of potential competitiveness in the overseas market.

As a result of the ratings of individual characteristics on both export market attractiveness and the firm's competitiveness, an overall assessment of both aspects is arrived at from which the suitability of entering the overseas market can be determined. Countries that rated high for the firm on both export market attractiveness and competitiveness would constitute a portfolio of attractive markets for the firm to consider entering.

A major Australian wine producer, such as Southcorp, in evaluating overseas markets to enter, might undertake the above exercise and arrive at the following five markets—California, Western Canada, Wales, Denmark and Singapore. This selection may be based on its capacity to supply, its ability to fund increments to current production, its willingness to modify the product and the suitability of such markets for a standard marketing approach. It could also be influenced by characteristics of the overseas market such as the level of wine consumption, a willingness to try overseas products and the relative absence of tariff and non-tariff barriers.

# A screening approach

The above, which involves an analysis of each country, is time consuming and may be beyond the management resources of many small and medium-sized Australian or New Zealand firms (SMEs). Hollensen (2004, pp. 225–7) advocates a filtering approach that has two stages. The first is preliminary screening, which looks at countries in terms of the risk in the business environment. Countries that pass this scrutiny are then subject to stage 2, which involves 'fine-grained' scrutiny based on combining the attractiveness of the market with the competitive strength of the firm. Although less work intensive than preparing analyses for each country, it still involves a detailed analysis of many markets—a task that is likely to be beyond the resources of many SMEs.

An alternative approach might involve commencing the selection procedure by considering all markets in the world and then filtering markets in relation to a succession of criteria. Unsuitable markets are progressively eliminated from consideration. The result is likely to be a small group or cluster of markets that offers the greatest potential for the firm. As the selection procedure moves from stage to stage a greater degree of analysis is likely to be required. As a consequence most effort is put into studying those markets that are likely to offer the most promise in relation to the characteristics of the firm and the opportunities of the market.

The approach to progressive screening described below and shown in Figure 7.1 is a modified version of that developed by Toyne and Walters (1993). It is made up of five stages. The first three can be described as preliminary screening and the last two as 'fine-grained' screening.

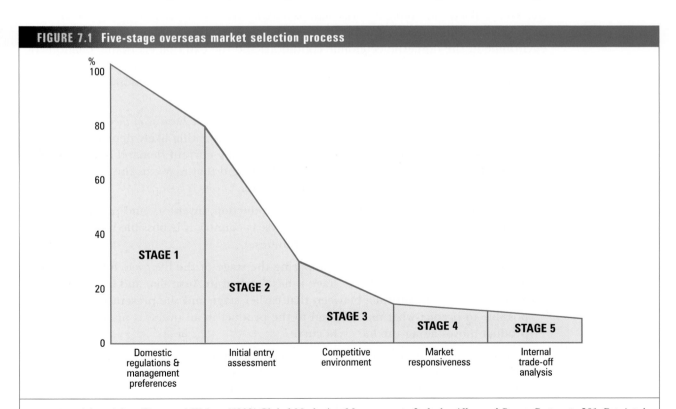

**FIGURE 7.1  Five-stage overseas market selection process**

**SOURCE:** *Adapted from Toyne and Walters (1993)* Global Marketing Management, *2nd edn, Allyn and Bacon, Boston, p. 301. Reprinted with permission of Pearson Education Inc., Upper Saddle River, NJ.*

## STAGE 1

Stage 1 involves answering the following questions relating to domestic considerations:

* *Question 1: Which overseas markets are of no interest to the firm regardless of their apparent potential?* This issue, although seeming irrational, affects market selection. It is often due to the prejudice or preference of the senior executives. For example, an unhappy holiday experience in India may result in a refusal by a CEO to contemplate exporting to that country.

* *Question 2: Which remaining overseas markets should be excluded because of regulations initiated by or involving support of the Australian or New Zealand government?* These regulations may be political, such as the former embargo on trading with Iraq, defence-related (export of defence equipment allowed to friendly countries only) or have economic/protectionist motives (restrictions on the export of Merino sheep).

At the conclusion of this portion of the analysis it is likely that around 20% of world markets can be excluded from further consideration.

## STAGE 2

Stage 2 involves answering the following questions relating to macroenvironmental factors in overseas markets and an initial assessment of general prospects. The second step, described as 'initial entry assessment', screens out economically unattractive markets.

* *Question 3: Which remaining overseas markets have the least attractive political and social environments?* This question can be assessed by considering the political and economic environment, the domestic economic conditions and the external economic relations of the country. At this stage of the analysis economic considerations could also be included, such as the ease with which profits can be repatriated, freedom to convert local currency and the volatility of the exchange rate.

* *Question 4: Which remaining overseas markets are least attractive because of their nature and potential size?* There are a number of simple ways for estimating likely demand sufficient for a screening activity. These not only involve assessing current demand but also likely future demand as well as untapped or unfilled demand that may exist in a particular market. Some of the more common techniques are:

  – *demand pattern analysis*: By analysing local production, inventory and patterns of international trade for a product in an overseas country it is possible to estimate consumption trends and market opportunities.

  – *international product life cycle*: By comparing the stage of the life cycle for the product in the overseas market with the stage it has reached in Australia, and by reflecting on what happened in Australia between that earlier stage and the present one, it is possible to predict what may happen to the product in an overseas market as the product moves along the life cycle curve.

  – *income elasticity measurements*: This is the relationship between change in demand for a product divided by the change in income. This measure can be used for predicting change in likely quantity demanded for a particular product category.

  – *proxy and multiple factor indices*: When information about the product in the overseas market is unavailable it is possible to estimate likely demand using demand patterns for another product or service that are correlated with demand for the firm's own product/service. For example, electrification of villages will be associated with demand for refrigerators. A multiple factor index involves two or more proxy variables believed to correlate with demand for the product.

This second stage of the analysis may indicate that demand for the product/service may not exist in a further 50% of world markets.

## STAGE 3

By stage 3 only about 30% of world markets remain. In this stage and the next the more expensive and time-consuming elements of evaluation are applied to the remaining limited number of countries offering potential. During this phase it is important to answer the following questions relating to the likely competitive environment in the overseas market:

- *Question 5: Which remaining overseas markets have substantial barriers to products from Australia or New Zealand to protect domestic industry or to enable them to conform to trade relations arrangements with other countries?* These barriers may relate to entry, exit and the marketplace. Entry barriers can be both tariff and non-tariff (e.g. quotas, quarantine or standards). Such barriers also include aspects that impinge on the form of overseas market entry, such as regulations relating to local content and ownership. Exit barriers may relate to repatriation of profits, dividends and capital, taxation issues and technology transfer. Marketplace barriers can include access to skilled personnel, availability of warehouse space, transportation, allocation of critical inputs such as power and water and control over prices. These barriers may take different forms all of which would serve to rule out markets from further consideration. This is reflected in the composition of the markets in Japan and China. In the former, the main barrier is the complex and multilayered distribution system which underpins a major sector of business activity and generates significant employment. In China, by contrast, the tariff and non-tariff barriers are a continuing legacy of the previous regime, designed to create a climate for the development of indigenous industry. Although the barriers are being lowered in both countries, they still continue to operate as a substantial impediment to Australian or New Zealand firms wishing to enter these markets.

- *Question 6: Which remaining overseas markets should be avoided because competitors (both domestic and foreign) are already well entrenched in them?* This will require some knowledge as to whether the competitors are local, Australian/New Zealand or foreign, and how they will react to entry into their markets. With each competitor or potential competitor knowledge as to relative strengths and weaknesses in relation to a firm's operation helps establish whether a market should be excluded because of potential competitive reaction. There are a number of competitive strategies which might influence selection of markets. These include entering a market so as to pre-empt the entry of others, entering a market in which there are already competitors and confronting them, and entering a market where large competitors do not exist. The latter strategy might be designed both to build up share of market and gain experience for attacking more competitive markets in other countries at a later stage.

This third stage of the analysis is likely to screen out a further 15% of countries.

## STAGE 4

Stage 4 and subsequent stages represent a more fine-grained screening where the firm's competitive advantages and distinctive competencies in specific overseas markets are taken into account (Hollensen 2004, pp. 225–6). This stage involves answering the following questions relating to the degree to which markets are unlikely to respond to, or prohibit, certain market activities:

- *Question 7: Which remaining overseas markets are not large enough to justify the marketing effort that will be necessary to gain a satisfactory market share?* This requires an assessment as to what share of the total market in the country the firm can reasonably expect to obtain, given domestic and other foreign competition and affordability of the product. In cases where demand is not sufficient to justify risk or the costs of entry the market should be excluded from further consideration.

- *Question 8: Which remaining overseas markets are unlikely to respond to those marketing activities which are considered necessary to establish the product/service in the marketplace effectively?* What will need to be determined is whether the market allows or prevents the firm achieving its objectives. These may be couched in terms of product (e.g. achievement of brand identity and product line extension) and in terms of pricing (e.g. such as the ability to achieve acceptable levels of return on investment and match changes in competitors' pricing). The market will also need to be assessed in terms of whether the firm will be able to achieve its objectives in promotion (e.g. securing media coverage, optimising salesforce effectiveness and attaining advertising objectives), plus its objectives in distribution (e.g. achievement of coverage, building up appropriate inventory levels and the ability to modify the channel when this becomes necessary).

- *Question 9: Which remaining overseas markets prohibit the form of presence that your firm considers optimal and can afford when entering a new overseas market?* The answers to previous questions and the firm's preferred way of operating overseas may indicate the form of market presence that would be most appropriate for each market. It is necessary to establish whether the desired form is permissible (because some may not be allowed), and whether those forms which are allowed are likely to be profitable. If the company always operates overseas via licensing its technology and the government limits the size of the allowable licensing fee, then the attractiveness of the market may be questionable. Before the reforms of the Indian economy in 1993 the Indian government restricted royalty payments to 3% maximum, taxable at 50% yielding 1.5% net. Most Australian and New Zealand firms found this figure unattractive.

- *Question 10: Which remaining overseas markets are unattractive because of costs and problems of reaching them from Australia/New Zealand?* Answering this question involves ensuring that reasonable logistics links exist both between Australia or New Zealand and the overseas market and within the overseas market. The impact of the cost of logistics on both the ability to compete and satisfy demand also needs to be considered. Also relevant in selecting a market is whether these links are reliable and timely: that delivery can be relied upon; that the time taken for goods to reach the destination does not adversely affect the ability to compete; and that the goods arrive in an acceptable condition.

Completion of this fourth stage of the analysis is likely to exclude another 10% of countries.

## STAGE 5

The fifth stage involves eliminating markets because of internal trade-offs. At this point it is likely that around 5% of markets remain for consideration. It may be useful to create a weighting system that reflects the goals of the firm and perceived importance to the firm of circumstances in the overseas market. This weighting could then be applied to answers to the final two questions. Appraising the remaining countries in relation to these final questions is likely to result in only a few markets being contemplated for entry. This step involves answers to the following questions:

- *Question 11: Which remaining overseas markets are no longer attractive because of the extent to which resources need to be committed and changes need to be made to existing company resources?* Some of the remaining markets may require more resources than others. Trade-offs are likely: first, between markets which require more resources and those which require less in terms of the anticipated pay-off; and, second, between resource requirements of specific overseas markets and using those same resources to expand activities in the Australian or New Zealand markets.

- *Question 12: Do any of the markets still under consideration fail to meet the company's objectives or match its competitive advantages?* This last question recognises that market attractiveness does not exist independently of a firm's competitive strategy. The process by which the remaining markets have been arrived at should mean that the answer is 'no'. However, it is useful to pose a check question of this type at the conclusion of the screening process.

With the several remaining markets having promise, no final decision should be made until these markets have been visited by a responsible executive to see whether the impressions of potential are justified. It is only then that they should be ranked in order of attractiveness.

# MARKET SELECTION IN THE NEW MILLENNIUM

A detailed screening approach to market selection such as the above is particularly relevant for firms at an early stage of international involvement. Although many of the same selection criteria apply, a screening approach will be less relevant for firms already active overseas that wish to expand their involvement.

In the new millennium it is increasingly likely that, for the experienced firm, international market selection will be influenced by strategic objectives, such as establishing a competitive position, transferring risk and rating market investment against profitability. Although international market selection will still require a 'fit' between the requirements of the prospective markets and the firm's competencies, these markets may not parallel geographic boundaries and may be a result of cultural or ethnic similarities. According to Walton and Ashill (2001) there may be a need for change in the traditional patterns of international market selection to cater for a world 'that values choice, speed, information, collaboration, market convergence, business cost reduction and increased consumer value'. Their research also suggests that, in the future, international market selection will be increasingly influenced by the desire to select the right partner and the need to transfer risk to other markets in order to even out your risk exposure between countries. It will also be influenced by the desire to capitalise on the potential of e-commerce in overseas markets and the need to gain insider status in emerging regional trading blocs.

Experienced exporters may be driven by different considerations when selecting subsequent markets to enter. Two studies illustrate this: Brewer (2001) found that experienced Australian firms seek out new country markets on the basis of expected commercial returns; Clark and Pugh (2001) found that UK-based multinationals, in selecting further markets to enter, were more likely to be influenced by the affluence of the market than by its size, and by the extent of geographical separation rather than by its cultural distance.

The approach of Cavusgil et al. (2004) is relevant to the experienced exporter. This approach commences with clustering markets on the basis of structural similarities, then ranking markets in terms of their size and overall attractiveness and finally combining these two approaches to arrive at a clustering of countries based on both macro similarities and market potential. Using exploratory factor analysis, Cavusgil et al. (2004) clustered countries into groups based on the five variables of infrastructure, economic wellbeing, standard of living, size of market and dynamism of the market. Table 7.1 shows the resulting clusters of countries.

However, grouping countries on the basis of macroeconomic potential does not necessarily result in a grouping on the basis of market potential, which is important if the firm is to obtain synergistic benefits from the clustering of countries. These researchers then developed an index of market potential and overall attractiveness (see <http://globaledge.msu.edu/resourceDesk/mpi.asp>). This index is made up of eight dimensions, and Table 7.2 shows 89 countries on an individual basis in terms of these variables and provides an overall market potential score for each country. This has been constructed as a flexible online tool and managers can vary the assigned weights to cater for the unique circumstances of their own industry.

The experienced firm has a choice of using either the cluster approach or the individual country market potential approach to assess attractiveness. A firm that wishes to standardise its strategy and product offerings across a number of markets should focus on the clustering approach, which is more likely to reveal structural similarities between markets. However, a firm wishing to identify the best market to enter should adopt the ranking approach as a means of determining the several countries that deserve the most attention. Cavusgil et al. (2004) recommend combining both approaches as clustering provides an indication of structurally similar groups of countries but it does not indicate relative market potential, and ranking identifies the most attractive markets, but it does not provide information on the similarities and differences between them. They combine the two approaches and Table 7.3 shows a new clustering of countries when market potential is taken into account.

## The nation state and market selection

Most firms for convenience use the country as the key variable is selecting overseas markets. However, with the reduction in trade barriers, the rise in the number of bilateral and regional trade agreements, the increase in the size of various diaspora and the growth of multiculturalism, the nation state is a less reliable delineator of overseas markets today than was formerly the case. This is because different groups can exist within the same country or specific groups can exist across a number of contiguous political borders. As examples, if the Malaysian market is the target, then is the market that of the Malays, the Chinese or the Indians or all three? If there is a product to be exported of specific appeal to the Kurdish community, this market group is likely to span a number of countries including Turkey, Iraq and Lebanon. If a manufacturer of Lebanese pita bread ovens in Australia wishes to export overseas, should the target be Lebanon or Lebanese communities in the US, or Canada, or New Zealand or other parts of the Middle East? Possibly the exporter might use one of the Lebanese diaspora groups as a test market before trying to enter Lebanon itself. The above suggests that ethnicity rather than the nation state may be an attractive variable to use when selecting overseas markets to enter. Pires and Stanton (2005) describe ethnicity as a shared identity or similarity of a group of people based on common characteristics.

**TABLE 7.1** **Clusters of countries**

| Cluster 1 | Rank | Cluster 4 | Rank | Cluster 6 | Rank | Cluster 7 | Rank |
|---|---|---|---|---|---|---|---|
| Mozambique | 59 | Mexico | 34 | Singapore | 4 | Japan | 3 |
| Senegal | 81 | Thailand | 47 | Ireland | 5 | Germany | 7 |
| Bangladesh | 85 | Georgia | 49 | Korea, South | 17 | United Kingdom | 7 |
| Yemen | 87 | Turkey | 49 | Spain | 17 | Belgium | 9 |
| Nepal | 88 | Philippines | 52 | Chile | 25 | Netherlands | 11 |
| Kenya | 88 | Peru | 55 | Portugal | 25 | Hong Kong | 12 |
| | | Jordan | 58 | Estonia | 28 | France | 14 |
| **Cluster 2** | **Rank** | Albania | 61 | Slovenia | 29 | Denmark | 16 |
| South Africa | 47 | Armenia | 61 | UAE | 31 | Switzerland | 17 |
| Egypt | 65 | Ukraine | 61 | Greece | 32 | Austria | 22 |
| Honduras | 65 | Azerbaijan | 70 | Czech Republic | 34 | Italy | 22 |
| Morocco | 65 | Sri Lanka | 70 | Hungary | 34 | Israel | 24 |
| Ghana | 76 | Moldova | 73 | Poland | 34 | | |
| Indonesia | 76 | Belarus | 76 | Costa Rica | 38 | **Cluster 8** | **Rank** |
| Algeria | 80 | Mongolia | 81 | Latvia | 39 | Canada | 1 |
| Nigeria | 84 | | | Lithuania | 44 | Australia | 6 |
| Pakistan | 86 | **Cluster 5** | **Rank** | Panama | 46 | Finland | 9 |
| | | Russia | 27 | | | Sweden | 12 |
| | | Brazil | 29 | | | Norway | 15 |
| **Cluster 3** | **Rank** | Argentina | 39 | | | New Zealand | 20 |
| Malaysia | 33 | Uruguay | 41 | | | | |
| Slovak Republic | 41 | Kuwait | 43 | | | | |
| Dominican Rep. | 54 | Croatia | 44 | | | **Cluster 9** | **Rank** |
| Tunisia | 57 | Bolivia | 49 | | | China | 2 |
| Vietnam | 76 | Saudi Arabia | 53 | | | India | 21 |
| Syria | 83 | El Salvador | 55 | | | | |
| | | Venezuela | 60 | | | | |
| | | Colombia | 61 | | | | |
| | | Bulgaria | 65 | | | | |
| | | Guatemala | 65 | | | | |
| | | Paraguay | 70 | | | | |
| | | Ecuador | 74 | | | | |
| | | Romania | 74 | | | | |

**SOURCE:** *Cavusgil, S.T., Kiyak, T. and Yeniyurt, S. (2004) 'Complementary approaches to preliminary foreign market opportunity assessment: country clustering and country ranking',* Industrial Marketing Management, *Vol. 33, p. 612. Copyright Elsevier 2004.*

**TABLE 7.2**   Market potential indicators and overall market attractiveness index

| | Market size | | Market growth | | Market intensity | | Infrastructure | | Market receptivity | | Free market structure | | Country risk | | Overall market potential | |
|---|---|---|---|---|---|---|---|---|---|---|---|---|---|---|---|---|
| | Index | Rank | Index | Rank | Index | Rank | Index | Rank | Index | Rank | Index | Rank | Index | Rank | Index | Rank |
| Canada | 24 | 8 | 23 | 72 | 87 | 11 | 85 | 4 | 70 | 2 | 93 | 8 | 88 | 14 | 100 | 1 |
| China | 100 | 1 | 60 | 13 | 18 | 81 | 16 | 57 | 3 | 80 | 16 | 86 | 49 | 32 | 91 | 2 |
| Japan | 53 | 3 | 23 | 72 | 86 | 12 | 60 | 12 | 4 | 76 | 80 | 25 | 88 | 14 | 90 | 3 |
| Singapore | 2 | 48 | 47 | 29 | 94 | 4 | 40 | 27 | 100 | 1 | 70 | 36 | 89 | 12 | 87 | 4 |
| Ireland | 1 | 62 | 87 | 3 | 74 | 21 | 55 | 18 | 45 | 4 | 97 | 2 | 90 | 11 | 83 | 5 |
| Australia | 10 | 18 | 39 | 42 | 89 | 8 | 100 | 1 | 9 | 51 | 96 | 4 | 86 | 16 | 76 | 6 |
| Germany | 31 | 5 | 11 | 85 | 90 | 7 | 56 | 16 | 10 | 47 | 87 | 14 | 91 | 9 | 75 | 7 |
| United Kingdom | 21 | 9 | 24 | 69 | 89 | 8 | 67 | 8 | 12 | 35 | 92 | 10 | 91 | 9 | 75 | 7 |
| Belgium | 5 | 30 | 38 | 46 | 100 | 1 | 57 | 14 | 36 | 6 | 87 | 14 | 89 | 12 | 73 | 9 |
| Finland | 3 | 38 | 53 | 21 | 75 | 20 | 98 | 2 | 11 | 40 | 94 | 7 | 92 | 5 | 73 | 9 |
| Netherlands | 6 | 27 | 26 | 65 | 92 | 5 | 65 | 9 | 31 | 7 | 97 | 2 | 93 | 4 | 72 | 11 |
| Hong Kong | 2 | 48 | 24 | 69 | 96 | 3 | 42 | 24 | 65 | 3 | 83 | 18 | 76 | 22 | 70 | 12 |
| Sweden | 7 | 24 | 34 | 51 | 85 | 13 | 79 | 5 | 16 | 18 | 92 | 10 | 92 | 5 | 70 | 12 |
| France | 25 | 7 | 22 | 77 | 80 | 18 | 60 | 12 | 8 | 56 | 74 | 31 | 92 | 5 | 69 | 14 |
| Norway | 5 | 30 | 28 | 60 | 89 | 8 | 86 | 3 | 12 | 35 | 84 | 17 | 96 | 2 | 67 | 15 |
| Denmark | 2 | 48 | 23 | 72 | 92 | 5 | 77 | 6 | 11 | 40 | 95 | 5 | 95 | 3 | 64 | 16 |
| Korea, South | 14 | 13 | 70 | 8 | 72 | 25 | 40 | 27 | 16 | 18 | 75 | 29 | 51 | 31 | 63 | 17 |
| Spain | 12 | 14 | 54 | 19 | 74 | 21 | 44 | 22 | 7 | 61 | 83 | 18 | 86 | 16 | 63 | 17 |
| Switzerland | 3 | 38 | 15 | 80 | 82 | 15 | 65 | 9 | 23 | 9 | 95 | 5 | 100 | 1 | 63 | 17 |
| New Zealand | 2 | 48 | 28 | 60 | 81 | 16 | 72 | 7 | 12 | 35 | 100 | 1 | 82 | 19 | 61 | 20 |
| India | 58 | 2 | 56 | 17 | 14 | 83 | 5 | 83 | 1 | 86 | 48 | 63 | 41 | 42 | 60 | 21 |
| Italy | 15 | 11 | 24 | 69 | 73 | 23 | 48 | 19 | 6 | 66 | 82 | 20 | 85 | 18 | 58 | 22 |
| Austria | 3 | 38 | 28 | 60 | 76 | 19 | 56 | 16 | 15 | 23 | 91 | 12 | 92 | 5 | 58 | 22 |
| Israel | 2 | 48 | 51 | 27 | 84 | 14 | 36 | 30 | 23 | 9 | 71 | 35 | 64 | 26 | 55 | 24 |
| Chile | 3 | 38 | 88 | 2 | 64 | 28 | 21 | 48 | 8 | 56 | 88 | 13 | 54 | 29 | 54 | 25 |
| Portugal | 3 | 38 | 60 | 13 | 60 | 30 | 37 | 29 | 9 | 51 | 87 | 14 | 81 | 20 | 54 | 25 |
| Russia | 47 | 4 | 29 | 57 | 56 | 34 | 26 | 39 | 9 | 51 | 25 | 81 | 18 | 68 | 51 | 27 |
| Estonia | 1 | 62 | 35 | 50 | 52 | 37 | 64 | 11 | 25 | 8 | 93 | 8 | 47 | 36 | 50 | 28 |
| Brazil | 31 | 5 | 41 | 38 | 58 | 32 | 26 | 39 | 1 | 86 | 54 | 49 | 30 | 53 | 48 | 29 |
| Slovenia | 1 | 62 | 68 | 9 | 52 | 37 | 35 | 31 | 16 | 18 | 66 | 42 | 67 | 25 | 48 | 29 |
| United Arab Emirates | 2 | 48 | 47 | 29 | 81 | 16 | 22 | 45 | 22 | 11 | 54 | 49 | 74 | 23 | 47 | 31 |
| Greece | 3 | 38 | 48 | 28 | 57 | 33 | 43 | 23 | 5 | 70 | 68 | 41 | 78 | 21 | 46 | 32 |
| Malaysia | 4 | 34 | 64 | 12 | 43 | 51 | 19 | 52 | 40 | 5 | 38 | 71 | 48 | 34 | 43 | 33 |
| Mexico | 17 | 10 | 23 | 72 | 55 | 35 | 18 | 54 | 18 | 15 | 62 | 44 | 49 | 32 | 42 | 34 |
| Poland | 9 | 19 | 45 | 34 | 49 | 42 | 33 | 32 | 6 | 66 | 74 | 31 | 48 | 34 | 42 | 34 |
| Czech Republic | 4 | 34 | 12 | 84 | 63 | 29 | 46 | 21 | 20 | 12 | 81 | 23 | 52 | 30 | 42 | 34 |
| Hungary | 2 | 48 | 22 | 77 | 53 | 36 | 47 | 20 | 16 | 18 | 81 | 23 | 62 | 27 | 42 | 34 |
| Costa Rica | 1 | 62 | 68 | 9 | 38 | 60 | 22 | 45 | 20 | 12 | 75 | 29 | 36 | 49 | 40 | 38 |
| Argentina | 8 | 21 | 41 | 38 | 73 | 23 | 28 | 37 | 1 | 86 | 79 | 27 | 26 | 58 | 39 | 39 |
| Latvia | 1 | 62 | 32 | 55 | 48 | 44 | 57 | 14 | 15 | 23 | 79 | 27 | 38 | 47 | 39 | 39 |
| Slovak Republic | 2 | 48 | 38 | 46 | 47 | 47 | 41 | 25 | 19 | 14 | 70 | 36 | 40 | 43 | 38 | 41 |
| Uruguay | 1 | 62 | 39 | 42 | 68 | 26 | 33 | 32 | 4 | 76 | 82 | 20 | 44 | 38 | 38 | 41 |
| Kuwait | 2 | 48 | 4 | 88 | 98 | 2 | 30 | 36 | 15 | 23 | 49 | 60 | 69 | 24 | 37 | 43 |
| Croatia | 1 | 62 | 68 | 9 | 42 | 53 | 26 | 39 | 12 | 35 | 52 | 54 | 40 | 43 | 34 | 44 |
| Lithuania | 1 | 62 | 28 | 60 | 49 | 42 | 41 | 25 | 12 | 35 | 82 | 20 | 36 | 49 | 34 | 44 |
| Panama | 1 | 62 | 52 | 24 | 39 | 58 | 16 | 57 | 15 | 23 | 74 | 31 | 39 | 45 | 33 | 46 |
| South Africa | 11 | 15 | 26 | 65 | 40 | 55 | 20 | 49 | 5 | 70 | 70 | 36 | 45 | 37 | 32 | 47 |

| TABLE 7.2 | Market potential indicators and overall market attractiveness index *(continued)* |
|-----------|-----------------------------------------------------------------------------------|

| | Market size | | Market growth | | Market intensity | | Infrastructure | | Market receptivity | | Free market structure | | Country risk | | Overall market potential | |
|---|---|---|---|---|---|---|---|---|---|---|---|---|---|---|---|---|
| | Index | Rank | Index | Rank | Index | Rank | Index | Rank | Index | Rank | Index | Rank | Index | Rank | Index | Rank |
| Thailand | 5 | 30 | 52 | 24 | 15 | 82 | 14 | 62 | 15 | 23 | 73 | 34 | 44 | 38 | 32 | 47 |
| Turkey | 11 | 15 | 52 | 24 | 52 | 37 | 23 | 44 | 5 | 70 | 36 | 74 | 26 | 58 | 31 | 49 |
| Georgia | 1 | 62 | 100 | 1 | 36 | 64 | 27 | 38 | 9 | 51 | 39 | 69 | 2 | 88 | 31 | 49 |
| Bolivia | 1 | 62 | 72 | 6 | 37 | 61 | 19 | 52 | 4 | 76 | 70 | 36 | 20 | 64 | 31 | 49 |
| Philippines | 8 | 21 | 39 | 42 | 37 | 61 | 8 | 75 | 15 | 23 | 61 | 46 | 39 | 45 | 30 | 52 |
| Saudi Arabia | 7 | 24 | 26 | 65 | 67 | 27 | 20 | 49 | 11 | 40 | 24 | 83 | 58 | 28 | 29 | 53 |
| Dominican Republic | 1 | 62 | 55 | 18 | 44 | 50 | 8 | 75 | 13 | 32 | 64 | 43 | 24 | 60 | 28 | 54 |
| Peru | 3 | 38 | 46 | 31 | 48 | 44 | 11 | 65 | 2 | 84 | 69 | 40 | 30 | 53 | 27 | 55 |
| El Salvador | 1 | 62 | 43 | 35 | 30 | 69 | 15 | 61 | 10 | 47 | 80 | 25 | 34 | 51 | 27 | 55 |
| Tunisia | 1 | 62 | 53 | 21 | 45 | 49 | 11 | 65 | 11 | 40 | 39 | 69 | 44 | 38 | 26 | 57 |
| Jordan | 1 | 62 | 29 | 57 | 48 | 44 | 9 | 74 | 15 | 23 | 54 | 49 | 30 | 53 | 22 | 58 |
| Mozambique | 1 | 62 | 85 | 4 | 19 | 79 | 1 | 87 | 4 | 76 | 51 | 57 | 8 | 79 | 21 | 59 |
| Venezuala | 6 | 27 | 23 | 72 | 59 | 31 | 17 | 56 | 5 | 70 | 34 | 76 | 28 | 56 | 20 | 60 |
| Ukraine | 11 | 15 | 13 | 81 | 43 | 51 | 32 | 34 | 14 | 31 | 26 | 80 | 8 | 79 | 19 | 61 |
| Albania | 1 | 62 | 84 | 5 | 24 | 74 | 10 | 70 | 3 | 80 | 38 | 71 | 3 | 86 | 19 | 61 |
| Colombia | 6 | 27 | 11 | 85 | 51 | 40 | 20 | 49 | 3 | 80 | 51 | 57 | 32 | 52 | 19 | 61 |
| Armenia | 1 | 62 | 43 | 35 | 42 | 53 | 16 | 57 | 8 | 56 | 54 | 49 | 9 | 78 | 19 | 61 |
| Egypt | 7 | 24 | 46 | 31 | 27 | 71 | 12 | 64 | 3 | 80 | 24 | 83 | 38 | 47 | 18 | 65 |
| Morocco | 3 | 38 | 29 | 57 | 34 | 67 | 10 | 70 | 7 | 61 | 43 | 68 | 42 | 41 | 18 | 65 |
| Bulgaria | 3 | 38 | 1 | 89 | 47 | 47 | 32 | 34 | 13 | 32 | 52 | 54 | 27 | 57 | 18 | 65 |
| Honduras | 1 | 62 | 37 | 48 | 30 | 69 | 11 | 65 | 18 | 15 | 53 | 53 | 17 | 69 | 18 | 65 |
| Guatemala | 1 | 62 | 53 | 21 | 24 | 74 | 4 | 84 | 6 | 66 | 56 | 47 | 24 | 60 | 18 | 65 |
| Azerbaijian | 1 | 62 | 59 | 15 | 34 | 67 | 11 | 65 | 11 | 40 | 25 | 81 | 11 | 76 | 17 | 70 |
| Paraguay | 2 | 48 | 34 | 51 | 36 | 64 | 13 | 63 | 7 | 61 | 50 | 59 | 20 | 64 | 17 | 70 |
| Sri Lanka | 1 | 62 | 54 | 19 | 12 | 85 | 7 | 78 | 10 | 47 | 56 | 47 | 20 | 64 | 17 | 70 |
| Moldova | 1 | 62 | 37 | 48 | 26 | 72 | 25 | 42 | 16 | 18 | 49 | 60 | 3 | 86 | 16 | 73 |
| Ecuador | 2 | 48 | 33 | 53 | 40 | 55 | 16 | 57 | 8 | 56 | 47 | 65 | 8 | 79 | 15 | 74 |
| Romania | 4 | 34 | 13 | 81 | 39 | 58 | 22 | 45 | 7 | 61 | 49 | 60 | 22 | 62 | 15 | 74 |
| Belarus | 2 | 48 | 41 | 38 | 51 | 40 | 24 | 43 | 18 | 15 | 3 | 88 | 1 | 89 | 14 | 76 |
| Vietnam | 3 | 38 | 72 | 6 | 7 | 88 | 7 | 78 | 13 | 32 | 10 | 87 | 22 | 62 | 14 | 76 |
| Indonesia | 15 | 11 | 13 | 81 | 23 | 76 | 8 | 75 | 7 | 61 | 45 | 66 | 13 | 75 | 14 | 76 |
| Ghana | 1 | 62 | 39 | 42 | 20 | 78 | 7 | 78 | 11 | 40 | 52 | 54 | 15 | 73 | 14 | 76 |
| Algeria | 4 | 34 | 31 | 56 | 40 | 55 | 10 | 70 | 5 | 70 | 34 | 76 | 20 | 64 | 13 | 80 |
| Senegal | 1 | 62 | 40 | 41 | 25 | 73 | 4 | 84 | 9 | 51 | 48 | 63 | 11 | 76 | 12 | 81 |
| Mongolia | 1 | 62 | 8 | 87 | 37 | 61 | 18 | 54 | 15 | 23 | 62 | 44 | 6 | 84 | 12 | 81 |
| Syria | 2 | 48 | 58 | 16 | 35 | 66 | 10 | 70 | 8 | 56 | 1 | 89 | 17 | 69 | 11 | 83 |
| Nigeria | 8 | 21 | 26 | 65 | 22 | 77 | 6 | 81 | 10 | 47 | 35 | 75 | 6 | 84 | 10 | 84 |
| Bangladesh | 5 | 30 | 46 | 31 | 9 | 86 | 1 | 87 | 1 | 86 | 37 | 73 | 17 | 69 | 9 | 85 |
| Pakistan | 9 | 19 | 28 | 60 | 19 | 79 | 6 | 81 | 2 | 84 | 29 | 79 | 14 | 74 | 8 | 86 |
| Yemen | 1 | 62 | 43 | 35 | 9 | 86 | 11 | 65 | 11 | 40 | 20 | 85 | 8 | 79 | 5 | 87 |
| Kenya | 2 | 48 | 18 | 79 | 14 | 83 | 3 | 86 | 6 | 66 | 32 | 78 | 16 | 72 | 1 | 88 |
| Nepal | 1 | 62 | 33 | 53 | 1 | 89 | 1 | 87 | 5 | 70 | 44 | 67 | 8 | 79 | 1 | 88 |

**SOURCE:** *Cavusgil, S.T., Kiyak, T. and Yeniyurt, S. (2004) 'Complementary approaches to preliminary foreign market opportunity assessment: country clustering and country ranking',* Industrial Marketing Management, *Vol. 33, p. 613. Copyright Elsevier 2004.*

**TABLE 7.3**    **A combination of country clusters and market potential rankings**

| Cluster 1 | Cluster 2 | Cluster 3 | Cluster 4 | Cluster 5 | Cluster 6 | Cluster 7 | Cluster 8 | Cluster 9 | Cluster 10 |
|---|---|---|---|---|---|---|---|---|---|
| Bangladesh | Algeria | Dominican Rep. | Albania | Argentina | Chile | Austria | Australia | China | USA |
| Kenya | Egypt | Malaysia | Armenia | Bolivia | Costa Rica | Belgium | Canada | India | |
| Mozambique | Ghana | Slovak Republic | Azerbaijan | Brazil | Czech Republic | Denmark | Finland | | |
| Nepal | Honduras | Syria | Belarus | Bulgaria | Estonia | France | New Zealand | | |
| Senegal | Indonesia | Tunisia | Georgia | Colombia | Greece | Germany | Norway | | |
| Yemen | Morocco | Vietnam | Jordan | Croatia | Hungary | Hong Kong | Sweden | | |
| | Nigeria | | Mexico | Ecuador | Ireland | Israel | | | |
| | Pakistan | | Moldova | El Salvador | Korea, South | Italy | | | |
| | South Africa | | Mongolia | Guatemala | Latvia | Japan | | | |
| | | | Peru | Kuwait | Lithuania | Netherlands | | | |
| | | | Philippines | Paraguay | Panama | Switzerland | | | |
| | | | Sri Lanka | Romania | Poland | United Kingdom | | | |
| | | | Thailand | Russia | Portugal | | | | |
| | | | Turkey | Saudi Arabia | Singapore | | | | |
| | | | Ukraine | Uruguay | Slovenia | | | | |
| | | | | Venezuela | Spain | | | | |
| | | | | | UAE | | | | |

**SOURCE:** *Cavusgil, S.T., Kiyak, T. and Yeniyurt, S. (2004) 'Complementary approaches to preliminary foreign market opportunity assessment: country clustering and country ranking',* Industrial Marketing Management, *Vol. 33, p. 615. Copyright Elsevier 2004.*

# The internet and foreign market selection

Whereas market selection prior to the introduction of the internet was based on country, with the advent of the internet this may no longer be the case. This is because with e-business marketing, the internet has created a cyber-marketplace structured around internet access and commonality of interests and consumption needs. The internet is rapidly changing the significance of national boundaries in defining market areas. No longer do businesses have to be structured around political boundaries. The attractiveness of markets will more likely now be rated in terms of ease of internet access, influenced by both infrastructure (personal computers and telephone access) and language. Consumers without internet access will be restricted to information from traditional sources and will have a more limited range of product offerings. As internet access is unlikely to be available in the least developed of the developing countries, this factor will make them less attractive as markets for those firms using the internet as a marketing vehicle. On the other hand, consumers with internet access in geographically isolated or distant markets can become linked into the global market structure. This will be of particular benefit to them. Market selection will also be influenced because the internet establishes direct channels of communication between exporters and importers and reduces the need for intermediaries, such as overseas agents. In some cases, however, reintermediation occurs and traditional intermediaries are replaced by cyber-intermediaries (e.g. search engines) that perform matching functions.

# MODES OF ENTERING FOREIGN MARKETS

Having identified promising overseas markets the next issue is the mode of entry that is most appropriate for the markets selected. Although this is treated as a separate decision to market selection, it is often directly related because of a preference by the firm for a specific mode of entry. Hollensen (2004, p. 273) points out that, whereas for most SMEs market entry represents a critical first step, for established firms the problem is not how to enter the new market but rather how to exploit new opportunities within the context of their existing international operations. Modes of entry can be divided into those that aim to sell the product and those that aim to transfer know-how to the host country. Further discussion of various modes of entry as they relate to effective distribution overseas can be found in Chapter 17.

## Export-based entry

These forms for entry are driven by a desire to sell either a product/service or technology overseas with the minimum commitment of resources.

### INDIRECT EXPORTING

Indirect exporting refers to the use of agencies in the home country to get the product into the foreign market. Indirect export agencies can be subdivided into export agents, who receive a commission for exporting goods produced by firms, and export merchants, who buy the goods from the manufacturer and subsequently export them. In addition, firms can export using specific agencies established to market overseas products in their category. This is often referred to as cooperative exporting. Cooperative exporting has long been a feature of the export of agricultural products from Australia and not only takes the form of cooperative associations but also of statutory corporations set up by state or federal governments which involve government, trading and grower representatives. Examples are the Australian Meat and Livestock Corporation (now Meat and Livestock Australia), the Australian Wheat Board, and the Australian Dairy Corporation (now Dairy Australia). To varying degrees these bodies set conditions and influence or control the export of the product category. Another form of indirect exporting is that of piggybacking, whereby an inexperienced exporter uses the facilities of an experienced exporter to enter and market products into an overseas market.

This can be initiated by government, for example when a government trade promotion agency initiates a 'foster firm' scheme for inexperienced exporters. It can also be encouraged by the private sector, for example when an industry group such as the Australian Business Chamber or the Metal Trades Export Group of Australia encourages those members that are successful in international business to seek opportunities overseas for newer and smaller members. The history of BHP Billiton provides one example of indirect exporting—for many years as BHP it exported its steel products through Australian export agents such as Brown and Dureau, Heine Bros and Gollin and Co.

## DIRECT EXPORTING

In this case the firm itself contacts the buyers overseas and either sells direct to the end-user or arranges for firms in the target market to act as agents and/or distributors for their products. The firm establishes its own export sales organisation which becomes responsible for all marketing activities in respect of overseas sales. This group identifies potential markets and segments and is involved in export documentation, shipping and planning both strategy and marketing activities in the overseas market. Although direct export entails a greater commitment of resources, it enables the firm to exercise more control over the conditions under which its products are sold. For many small and medium-sized firms, direct exporting is the dominant form of foreign market involvement. Another variant that is becoming increasingly important, especially with the advent of the internet, is direct marketing. This is proving to be a very useful entry mode for small firms and firms initially entering a new overseas market.

Typical Australian examples are to be found among exporters of swimwear, wine and food products such as export award winners Aussiebum, Palandri Wines, Bundaberg Brewed Drinks and Maggie Beer. For other examples see International Highlight 7.1.

## ESTABLISHING A SALES OFFICE IN THE OVERSEAS MARKET

Whereas direct exporting involves appointing a non-employee in the overseas market to represent the firm and set up a network of distributors, establishing a sales office in the overseas market represents a further commitment of resources beyond what is entailed in the usual form of direct exporting. Establishing a sales office in the overseas market also enables a greater measure of control over what happens to the product in that market. The office controls not only the selling of the product or service, but also its promotional program. This refinement enables the firm to set up and control its own distribution channels.

When Barbeques Galore of Australia first entered the US market it established a sales office in Los Angeles. This served as the base for expansion horizontally into other areas of the USA and vertically into speciality retailing.

## LICENSING

Licensing enables a firm to earn overseas income from its technical innovations, its brand, its corporate image or its other proprietary assets without engaging in either manufacturing or marketing overseas. It usually involves an 'upfront' payment for the transfer of know-how and a royalty linked to volume produced and sold in the overseas market. Exclusive licences grant the other party sole rights within a specific geographic area whereas non-exclusive licences do not grant the other party sole access to a market. Cross-licensing occurs when firms exchange intangible assets, such as know-how or technology, with each other, often as a means of reducing research and development costs.

Although there is a minimal commitment of resources involved, this form of market entry

## 7.1 INTERNATIONAL HIGHLIGHT

# The lure of Asia

Now, as never before, Australian companies have turned to Asia for their future growth prospects. Asia is the new frontier. TNT started warehouse-management operations in 1995 in Thailand, Indonesia and China. Mining apart, CRA is undertaking exploration for gold and copper in Laos, following its gold and coalfields in Indonesia. BHP Billiton is developing wide-ranging steel, petroleum and minerals operations in several Asian countries. The Commonwealth Bank of Australia (CBA) and Bank International Indonesia (BII) are working on a 50–50 joint venture bank in Indonesia. The CBA plans to focus on corporate, commercial and multinational Indonesian customers as well as the more than 300 Australian firms doing business in Indonesia.

CSR is representative of this growing crop of Australian companies moving to Asia, where they see rates of return well in excess of those achievable in their own country. CSR, originally known for sugar, started diversifying into building and construction materials in the 1930s. It is one of Australia's oldest companies (founded in 1855) and also has a 25% interest in Australia's second-largest aluminium smelter at Tomago. Annual revenues are A$2 billion a year and the firm had 4500 employees as at March 2004. In the late 1980s CSR targeted the USA by purchasing several companies in the building materials industry—in 1996 it acquired three more American building materials companies. During this time its Asian business was not a key priority. CSR's entry into Asia goes back to the 1970s when it started selling sugar to agents in a variety of countries. One of its early agents, Robert Kuok, a Malaysian sugar and property entrepreneur, bought 25% of CSR's Asia operations in 1995. Kuok has wide-ranging interests covering media, commodity trading and property development. He is well connected with senior business and government leaders in Hong Kong, mainland China, Malaysia and Singapore. CSR foresees plasterboard made in Beijing, fibreboard assembled in its Hunan province factory and door components made in its Malaysian facilities not only being sold to those markets but also exported to Australia and New Zealand.

CSR has two key objectives for Asia:

1  to develop significant, profitable integrated building materials businesses in high-growth Asian markets; and

2  to export existing and new value-added products as a means of developing markets prior to establishing manufacturing facilities.

The challenges faced by these firms and many more seeking to enter new markets are addressed in this chapter.

**SOURCES:** Chow, L. (1996) 'Go north: like many Australian firms, CSR sees its future in Asia', Far Eastern Economic Review, 29 August; Banker (1996) 'Aussies find Asian partners', Vol. 146, Issue 845, July, p. 77; and CSR, <http://www.csr.com.au>.

provides limited return especially in cases where the licensee does not fully develop the potential that the market has to offer. A further disadvantage is that licensing agreements are usually for a fixed term, during the course of which the firm is prevented from entering the market directly. In addition, there is a risk that licensing might lead to 'cloning a competitor' should the licensee export to other markets in competition with the licensor or continue to manufacture the product after the expiration of the licensing period. However, with an increasing number of countries accepting the new World Trade Organization regime on intellectual property protection this risk is diminishing. A final problem occurs when the licensee produces substandard products under the company's brand and the firm's global image suffers as a result.

Australian firms that have achieved considerable success using this mode are the Orbital Engine Company, the Wiggles and Done Art. The orbital engine, invented by Ralph Sarich, was licensed to the two major US outboard marine engine manufacturers Mercury Marine and Johnson Matthey, and the designs of Done Art were licensed to firms in the USA, Japan, Singapore and Mexico. (See also the progress of the Orbital Engine Company in International Highlight 7.2.)

## FRANCHISING

Whereas international licensing usually applies to products, in the services industry the variant of international franchising is becoming increasingly common, especially in the global expansion of hotel and fast-food chains. The franchisor gives the franchisee the right to undertake business in a specified manner under the franchisor's name in return for a royalty payment that usually takes the form of a fee or a percentage of sales. Many of the advantages and disadvantages that apply to licensing apply to franchising. In particular, one of the problems of international expansion in both the retail and hospitality sectors is the cost of purchasing or renting sites and this responsibility is usually that of the franchisee. Franchising is also important where contact with customers and the well-managed operation of the business is critical to success. The franchisor can lay down guidelines for this interface to ensure a uniform projection and include in the franchising agreement penalties or threat of abrogation of contract for non-compliance. Successful franchising involves the establishment of performance standards and mechanisms for monitoring and control. Because of this, franchising can often be more resource intensive than licensing.

Australian examples include Sheridan Sheets franchised in the USA, Singapore and Japan, Sweathog garments franchised in the UK, Ozemail which franchised its internet phone and fax service in Hong Kong and Coca-Cola Amatil, which used franchising as a way of entering the Chinese and East European markets.

Sumo Salad began in 2003 and expanded rapidly to three company owned outlets in Australia. Then franchising was used to expand further in Australia and, as of early 2007, the firm had 20 outlets across five Australian states. Franchising was used as a vehicle for international expansion and Sumo's first venture was in Dubai in the United Arab Emirates. A master franchisee was appointed and now there are seven franchised outlets in the United Arab Emirates. The firm has faced a learning curve due to different cultural requirements—with their popular Caesar salad, it was necessary to replace pork bacon pieces with veal bacon pieces. Once the Emirates have been fully developed, the firm plans to franchise the concept in the UK and New Zealand.

SOURCE: *Adapted from 'Salad days', Export, 1 September 2005, p. 12.*

## Manufacturing-based entry

Often referred to as direct foreign investment (DFI), this can take a number of forms, varying from limited equity involvement to total ownership of the overseas operation.

## JOINT VENTURE

The most common form of manufacturing-based entry into overseas markets for Australian firms is that of the joint venture. This is because Asia is the target of many such firms and the governments of many Asian countries have foreign investment laws that mandate some local equity in any investment in their country. Joint ventures are a means of the firm limiting its equity exposure in an overseas market and can provide a vehicle for entering markets where the economic systems and marketing environments are so different that it is necessary to have a local partner in order to be successful.

Where the object of the joint venture is the building of a major infrastructure project, a number of foreign firms might be involved in a consortium together with local interests from either or both the public and the private sectors. The Australian firm of CMPS&F was involved with the government in water supply projects in Indonesia, and Signet Engineering of Western Australia was involved with private sector interests in a gold-processing plant in Chile. When the manufacture of products is involved the more common form of joint venture is that between an Australian and a local firm. The Australian firm brings to the joint venture technology and production expertise while the local partner provides access to the distribution network as well as familiarity with the local marketing environment. This is what happened when Kirby Refrigeration formed a joint venture with the Simakulthorn Company in Thailand in the early 1980s for the manufacture of refrigeration compressors. Selecting the 'right' joint venture partner is often a problem—Kirby Refrigeration solved this by locating a partner in Thailand that was also a family company with a similar set of values.

As a mode of entry, joint ventures reduce the capital and other resource commitment that is required, involve a spreading of risk and result in access to contacts and expertise in penetration of the local market. The main disadvantages are the risk of conflict between the Australian firm and its joint venture partner, problems of communication and management when different cultures are involved and the fact that the Australian firm has only partial control. Because of this, joint ventures are likely to have a limited lifespan unless the partners can develop an agreed corporate mission and agree on a common strategy and mode of governance.

---

### 7.2 INTERNATIONAL HIGHLIGHT

## Australian technology finds its niche

The Orbital Engine Company (OEC) has had a chequered history. Ralph Sarich's first revolutionary new orbital engine design failed to deliver the licence fees and royalties originally targeted. It has had a number of false starts, including the design of the Maleo, intended to be Indonesia's second national car and intended to be unveiled in 1998. The Maleo was to be a small four-door, front-wheel-drive sedan with Orbital's 1.2 litre, three-cylinder, direct-injection two-stroke engine. The design rights and patents were held by Melbourne's Millard Design. However, due to political upheaval in Indonesia, it never got off the ground.

By 2002, Orbital's technology was being used on a number of products around the world, including Mercury Marine's Optimax and Tohatsu TLDI outboard engines. Also Bombardier Sea-Doo GTX-DI and RX-DI personal watercraft use Orbital's technology. In the scooter market, Italy's Aprilia have released the 50 cc DITCH scooter with widespread distribution throughout continental Europe, the United Kingdom and the United States. In China, Sundiro Motorcycles have released their 50 cc HI-Jeter scooter into the market and early this year Peugeot Motorcycles also introduced its 'TSDI' 50 cc scooter. These niche markets are providing the basis for Orbital to build overseas markets for its unique technology.

---

## ACQUISITION

This involves entering an overseas market by acquiring an existing company. It is an entry technique often employed by multinational firms that are cash rich; however, it is often beyond the resources of small and medium-sized firms. Acquiring an existing operation enables rapid entry into the overseas market in that it usually provides an established distribution channel and existing customer base. It is a desirable strategy in cases where the industry is highly competitive or where there are substantial entry barriers for a new entrant. Such a move requires considerable research lest the equipment is outdated, the assets of the company are overvalued, labour laws inhibit change and increased productivity or the intellectual assets of the firm cannot be protected. Many of Australia's larger corporations like ANZ, Pacific Dunlop, CSR and BHP Billiton have adopted this approach.

## GREENFIELD OPERATION

This occurs where a firm decides to build its own manufacturing plant in an overseas country using its own funds. This is an attractive entry option if there are no suitable firms to acquire or the firm needs to establish its own operation because of technology or logistics considerations. It enables firms to use the latest production technologies while selecting the most attractive locations in terms of labour costs, local taxes, land prices and transportation. Firms wishing to rationalise their operations on a global basis are more likely to find this the most attractive entry option despite the costs in terms of capital and management. A typical Australian example is the decision by the Ansell Division of Pacific Dunlop to establish a factory in Thailand to produce rubber gloves and balloons.

# Relationship-based entry

These forms of entry are more reliant on the creation of relationships than those discussed previously. They occur where a considerable degree of cooperation is necessary in order to achieve success. This is because the level of resource commitment by the Australian firm is usually modest and both parties to the transaction have a mutual stake in the outcome.

## CONTRACT MANUFACTURING

In this case the firm contracts the production to a local manufacturer but retains control over the marketing of the product. It is a strategy suitable in circumstances where the overseas market does not justify establishing a manufacturing operation and where there are high barriers to imports. It requires little investment and is a relatively quick way of entering an overseas market. Because brand name and company reputation are involved, it does require the exercise of quality control by the Australian or New Zealand firm so that the contract manufacturer meets the firm's quality and delivery standards. Contract manufacture can also include cooperative manufacture. This is becoming an increasingly common feature of global business. It entails either various parts being produced in differing countries, as in the Boeing example below, or different functions being carried out in differing countries. For example, Fujitsu and NEC now conduct R&D in one country, component manufacture in another, assembly in a third and servicing in a fourth.

Originally, Boeing aircraft were made entirely in the United States. Today however, Boeing sources fuselages from Japan, rudders from Australia, landing gear doors from Northern Ireland, wing tip assemblies from Korea and wing flaps from Italy. In part this contract manufacturing was caused by pressure from governments of these countries to give their firms business; this is discussed in detail in Chapter 19. Contracting manufacture offshore has involved Boeing in purchasing physical assets and/or traded stock of these foreign suppliers as a means of securing decision making power in supplier organisations and ensuring quality control.

## OFFSHORING

Related to the above is the rapidly expanding technique of offshoring. This involves the relocation to another country of business processes that were previously undertaken by the firm itself. Offshoring can either relate to production or to services. According to Wikipedia (2007), China is now the prominent destination for production offshoring and India for services offshoring. For many firms, offshoring is a form of market entry that increases their international experience and enables them to retain their cost competitiveness as is the case with Blundstone boots. For larger firms offshoring often involves hiving off some elements of their value chain previously undertaken in Australia or New Zealand in the interests of retaining global competitiveness. Firms in this category include Qantas Airways and the ANZ Banking Group.

> In India, the existence of a well-educated, English-speaking workforce and the growing availability of broadband internet connections have resulted in companies in developed countries outsourcing to Indian firms tasks such as medical record transcription, technical writing and tax return preparation in addition to call centre operation.

## STRATEGIC ALLIANCES

Although this term is sometimes used in a broader context as a market entry strategy, strategic alliances refer to collaborations between firms in various countries to exchange or share some value-creating activities. The firms involved might be competitors in the Australian or New Zealand markets which see collaboration as being necessary in order to enter and compete in an overseas market. Alternatively, the strategic alliance may be between a group of firms the activities of which complement each other. These strategic alliances can involve joint R&D, shared manufacturing (as is common in the automotive industry), the use of common distribution channels or any other activities in the value chain. In distribution alliances the members all agree to use an existing distribution network. The Star Alliance between an increasing number of airlines including United Airlines, SAS, Air Canada, Lufthansa, Air New Zealand, Austrian Airlines, South African Airways, ANA, Singapore Airlines and Thai International is an example of such an alliance, involving pooling of route information, common access to frequent flyer programs and sharing of passenger traffic on certain routes using code share flights. Strategic alliances are discussed in greater detail in Chapter 12.

> As Thailand emerges as a regional automotive manufacturing hub, Bendix, Australia's leading manufacturer and supplier of automotive and industrial brakes, is expanding its Thai operation. At the peak of the Asian currency crisis it invested A$7 million in a new manufacturing plant at Rayong. The plant, producing brake linings for passenger cars and small trucks, opened in September 1998. Already it exports more than 20% of its production to other South-East Asian markets. Bendix (Thailand) has increased production levels and improved productivity by investing a further A$5 million in a new distribution system that allows for direct selling to domestic buyers rather than through intermediaries. Bendix (Thailand) uses strategic alliances with local Thai firms to maximise local content and leverage costs and efficiencies. While it is cooperating with local Thai foreign joint ventures in a localisation program, at the same time it is building on successful partnerships in Australia with AAT, General Motors–Holden, BMW and Toyota.

## COUNTERTRADE

Countertrade involves the linking of an import and an export transaction in a conditional manner. It includes barter, counterpurchase, buy back, offsets and debt exchange, all of which can result in a firm entering an overseas market. In countertrade there is a mutually dependent relationship between buyer and seller and this is discussed in detail in Chapter 19.

Australian examples include a barter deal between Hancock Mining and Romania involving Australian coal and Romanian machinery; a counterpurchase deal between Elders Countertrade and the Trading Corporation of Bangladesh involving the exchange of nominated goods over a fixed term; a buy-back deal involving Bulk Materials Coal Handling and Coalimex of Vietnam for the rehabilitation of a coal washery; and an offsets arrangement between the Royal Australian Air Force and McDonnell Douglas (now a division of Boeing Corporation) for the supply of F/A-18 aircraft.

## OTHER ENTRY MODES

These include management contracts, undertaking turn-key projects and build, operate and transfer arrangements. As these mostly relate to the winning of projects overseas, they are discussed in more detail in Chapter 19.

# The 'born global' phenomenon

Some firms begin their international involvement with the view that in order to survive they will from inception or shortly thereafter have to cater for international markets. Categorised as 'born globals' their overseas entry modes are often dictated by the circumstances of the industry to which they belong, as was the case with Whittle Programming, a Melbourne-based company. Knight et al. (2001) claim that in small isolated economies such as New Zealand a large percentage of firms have had to go international from inception, and these include traditional as well as knowledge-intensive industries. 'Born globals' are usually created by people who are entrepreneurial and have extensive international personal and business networks. Whereas in many Western countries the decision to 'go global' from inception is part of the firm's strategic intent, in many emerging markets this is not the case and the 'born global' firm is a result of accident or circumstance.

Bluefish444 produces video capture cards for the broadcast industry. Because the broadcast industry in Australia is very small, export has been crucial to the firm since its inception and exports make up 99% of its business. The company now exports to any country that has TV, with Europe and the US being the largest export markets.

SOURCE: *Adapted from 'Bluefish444'*, Dynamic Export, *December/January 2007, p. 20.*

# Evaluation of entry modes

In viewing these modes of market entry it is important to recognise that they involve a trade-off between degree of control on the one hand and commitment of resources on the other. This trade-off exists between forms of exporting. For instance, with indirect exporting commitment of resources is minimal and the degree of control non-existent, whereas with direct exporting more resources are required but there is more control over what happens to the product/service and how it is represented. A similar trade-off applies to contractual forms when comparing licensing the manufacture of a product with entering into a joint venture. Even within the category of wholly owned subsidiaries, buying out an established operation involves less commitment of management resources but less control. This is because employees who do things a different way are inherited. In a greenfield operation building the organisation from scratch will absorb considerable management time, but will result in an operation that will be totally controlled by the firm from the start. The latter will operate according to the way the firm usually does business in Australia or New Zealand. In addition, it can be argued that moving from one group of modes to another, such as from export to contractual to wholly owned subsidiaries, also involves the same trade-off between resources and control. Motivation and situation are other factors in market-entry decision making. The issue of risk is also a major factor in the decision as to which entry mode to adopt. Choe and Jin (2004) found that whereas before the Asian currency crisis foreign firms preferred to establish new ventures overseas from scratch (i.e. greenfield operations) in Korea, after the crisis the preference was for entry via acquisition.

# THEORIES OF MARKET ENTRY

Considerable research has been undertaken into the factors that cause firms to manufacture in the overseas country rather than export to it. Two theoretical approaches are summarised below. (Full details can be found in the references at the end of this chapter.)

## Dunning's eclectic paradigm

Dunning (see Brouthers et al. 1996) argues that entry modes are influenced by OLI (ownership, location, internalisation). The paradigm has its origin in the concept that different countries have different factor endowments (they are endowed with different combinations of the various factors of production) that could be mobile or immobile across national boundaries. The more uneven the geographic distribution of factor endowments, the greater the likelihood of production taking place in the overseas country. The second concept underlying the paradigm is that of market failure, which arises because different countries have distinct political and economic institutions. Market failures can be structural (barriers to entry, government intervention) or transactional (economies of scale, risk, etc.). This theory is relevant to explaining not only the location of economic activities across national boundaries, but also the division of those activities between multinational and uni-national firms. The *OLI paradigm* (see Figure 7.2) describes the degree to which the firm has advantages due to its:

* *ownership.* Is it sufficient to offset the costs of operating in a foreign environment? In order for a firm of one nationality to compete with those of another by producing in the latter's country, it must possess advantages specific to the nature and/or nationality of its ownership. These advantages can take the form of asset advantages and transaction advantages.

* *location.* Is it more advantageous for the firm to exploit its assets through manufacture overseas than via export from its home market? Location advantages are benefits that arise from a company performing certain operations in a specific location driven by lower labour costs, tax incentives, proximity to state of the art research, etc.

* *internalisation.* Is it more profitable to capitalise on its unique assets by foreign direct investment than selling the rights to their use via licensing arrangements? In other words, is it more beneficial for a company to make direct use of its competitive advantage in a foreign country rather than to sell it or lease it to someone else?

The appropriateness of this OLI paradigm is likely to vary according to the selected form of market entry. Pinto et al. (2001) found that, as far as the financial services sector was concerned, the OLI advantages were greatest when the firm used acquisition as its market entry mode and least effective when it set up a wholly owned subsidiary.

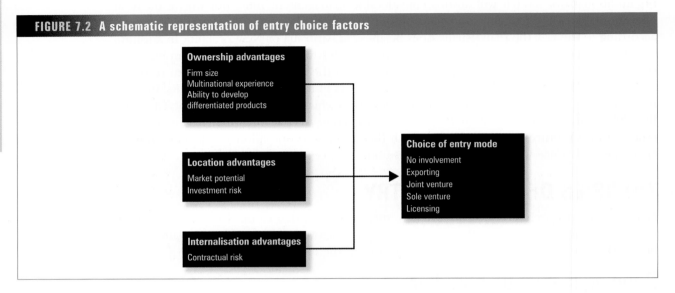

**FIGURE 7.2  A schematic representation of entry choice factors**

## Williamson's transaction cost approach

In an article by Anderson and Gatignon (1986) *Williamson's 'transaction cost approach'* is used to argue that the foreign entry mode selected should be that which maximises long-run efficiency measured in terms of the risk-adjusted rate of return on investment. It is suggested that control is the most important determinant of risk and return and that high-control entry modes (e.g. wholly owned subsidiaries) increase return on the one hand and risk on the other. By contrast, low-control modes (e.g. licensing) involve less commitment of resources but also have lower returns. The authors postulate that the extent to which the chosen entry mode should provide control is a function of:

- transaction-specific assets including specialised physical or human investments such as proprietary processes or products at an early stage of the product life cycle;

- external uncertainty reflecting unpredictability in the chosen overseas market due to economic and political factors;

- internal uncertainty related to difficulties in exercising control over the agent in the overseas market due to lack of experience, culture and linguistic knowledge and familiarity with business customs and practices; and

- free-riding potential, which refers to the agent's ability to exploit the relationship for personal advantage, for example by degrading the brand name or by taking on the line to neutralise its competitive impact.

On the above basis, high-control modes of entering foreign markets should be chosen when the firm possesses transaction-specific assets, when external uncertainty is high, when it is difficult to control the agent's performance and when there is considerable opportunity for agents to take advantage of the relationship.

# INFORMATION FOR MARKET ENTRY AND EXPANSION

The information necessary to enable decisions to be made as to the nature of involvement in a specific overseas market can be categorised according to whether it relates to factors internal or external to the firm.

## Factors internal to the firm

The characteristics of management and the characteristics of the firm can affect decisions made about both the form of market entry and the form of expansion.

### MANAGEMENT CHARACTERISTICS

One of the often-overlooked resources that firms can use to improve their prospects for successful entry to overseas markets is the previous international exposure of its executives. Research in Australia (Barrett 1986; Fletcher 1996) has shown that country of birth, years spent overseas and frequency of overseas business trips have a positive impact on the executive's willingness to engage in international activities. Given the increasing number of Australian or New Zealand executives with ethnic backgrounds, leveraging this resource should be investigated in the context of deciding which markets to enter and the form of entry. Other relevant characteristics of managers influencing overseas expansion decisions are planning orientation, knowledge of different cultures and business practices, experience with international transactions, adoption of a strategic approach to international business, espousal of a marketing orientation and willingness to take a long-term view of international involvement.

These characteristics influence the management objectives of the firm. They often influence the trade-off between resources committed and control of overseas activities discussed earlier in this chapter. Another issue, important in the Australian and New Zealand contexts, is the source of the firm's management objectives. Many firms operating in both countries and involved in international activities are wholly or partially foreign owned. While they are allowed to operate worldwide or within the Asia–Pacific region, they are usually required to conform to corporate policy laid down by headquarters in the USA, such as Detroit for automobile manufacturers, or in the UK, such as Port Sunlight for detergents. These policies often prescribe the mode of overseas entry and constrain the overseas activities of the Australian and New Zealand subsidiaries in the interest of the firm's global operations.

### FIRM'S CHARACTERISTICS

Research in Australia has found that international involvement is affected by:

- the problems of competing in the domestic market (especially with competitors that enjoy economies of scale due to international activities);
- the willingness to commit resources to overseas activities;
- the nature of the domestic market for the firm's products and excess capacity within the firm;
- the ability of the firm to make the necessary resources available for market entry and expansion;
- the extent to which products are high-tech; and
- the size of the firm (Fletcher 1996).

# Factors external to the firm

Factors external to the firm can influence the form of market entry which is most appropriate for the firm. They can act as either incentives or impediments to international involvement. They include the international nature and attractiveness of the product category, receipt of unsolicited export orders, reversal of seasons between Australia/New Zealand and the overseas market, the overall potential of the selected overseas market, government regulations and trade barriers (including embargoes and less obvious barriers, such as deliberate administrative delays, local-content requirements) and assistance offered by the Australian/New Zealand governments and other external bodies, in both Australia/New Zealand and overseas markets. Relevant information may be available from secondary data sources in both countries (e.g. United Nations publications, Austrade, Department of Foreign Affairs and Trade, international organisations such as the Asian Development Bank, and computerised data banks). Primary research agencies, such as Dun and Bradstreet, ACNielsen and Accenture (formerly Andersen Consulting), conduct valuable firm-specific studies.

## NATURE AND ATTRACTIVENESS OF THE PRODUCT CATEGORY

The physical characteristics of the product, such as its weight, value, perishability and composition, will influence where to locate its production. When the product incorporates such assets as a high level of technology or a well-known brand name, management may be reluctant to participate in operations overseas where it loses control over the production process. For this reason the nature of the product category can be a very important determinant of entry mode especially when deciding between licensing/franchising on the one hand and direct manufacture overseas on the other.

## THE POTENTIAL OF THE OVERSEAS MARKET

The greater the potential of the overseas market, the more likely it is that the firm will be willing to commit resources to market entry and development. Potential can be a matter of the size of the market, maturity for the product category involved and the growth rate in the market. As previously discussed, the more advanced stages of entry involve a greater commitment of resources; therefore the greater the potential, the more likely it is that the firm may engage in a more advanced stage of activity in that market. Potential, however, can be negatively affected by political and environmental risk. If these factors are high in the overseas market, participation in that market is likely to involve a lesser commitment of resources. Another factor influencing the form of entry is accessibility to the market from Australia or New Zealand. If the market is difficult or expensive to access this may result in some form of manufacturing in that market rather than export to it.

Another external factor to consider is marketing infrastructure. A number of questions are relevant:

- Is the general attitude in the market towards marketing positive (as in Singapore) or negative (as in North Korea)?

- Do the marketing intermediaries that a company is used to exist in the overseas market, such as advertising agencies, market research agencies or media buying groups?

- Do the media on which the company's domestic marketing is based exist in the overseas market? If so, are they available to the firm and viable for the marketing of its product in the selected overseas market?

The answers to these questions may influence whether the firm engages in a mode of entry where it is responsible for marketing or whether it engages in a mode of entry where responsibility for marketing is left to a local party.

## GOVERNMENT REGULATIONS AND TRADE BARRIERS

There are situations where government regulations prevent imports into a market, restrict manufacture of a product category to local firms or only permit manufacture in less attractive geographical locations in that market. The Thai government, for example, will provide investment incentives only for foreign firms prepared to locate manufacturing facilities outside Bangkok. The attractiveness of these incentives varies according to the extent to which the facility is located in areas accorded high priority in terms of Thailand's industrialisation and economic development plans. Hence the form of entry may be prescribed by the host government. Trade barriers such as tariff and non-tariff barriers like import quotas, quarantine barriers and mandatory local standards may also influence the form of entry.

An indirect trade barrier of increasing importance is environmentalism. The trade-off between need for foreign exchange and industrial development on the one hand and the degree to which environmental regulations are enforced on the other varies from country to country. Criticism of international firms engaging in environmentally damaging activities, even when allowed by the host country, is likely to increase and could affect decisions to become involved in a particular market. This issue has recently been highlighted in the growing debate concerning the Three Gorges Project in China. Environmental considerations can therefore affect the cost of various forms of market entry and the decisions between contractual forms of entry and wholly owned subsidiaries. Even with a contractual form of entry, if something goes wrong it is likely that the foreign firm, rather than the local partner, will be both criticised and pursued in the courts for compensation. (The Union Carbide Corporation and the Bhopal calamity in India is a case in point.)

Allied to government regulation is involvement of a target country in a regional trade grouping. This is a factor of increasing relevance in today's international business environment. The individual country's market may not be large enough to justify an entry mode other than export. However, membership of a regional trade grouping aiming for a common external fiscal boundary and free trade/industrial rationalisation among its members may make contractual or wholly owned subsidiary modes much more attractive. This is because insider status in one country enables access to all the others. An Australian manufacturer of automotive steering equipment for the after-market may consider that the demand in Malaysia would not warrant manufacture in that country. However, Malaysia's membership of ASEAN and the creation of the ASEAN Free Trade Area means that products the Australian firm might manufacture in Malaysia would receive either preferential or duty-free entry into Indonesia, Singapore, Brunei, the Philippines, Thailand and Vietnam. As the demand in ASEAN is many times that in Malaysia, manufacture in Malaysia to supply ASEAN becomes a more viable option.

## ASSISTANCE FROM GOVERNMENT AND OTHER BODIES

The nature of assistance available from your own government may influence choice of entry mode. In general, Australian government assistance is focused mostly on export and to a lesser extent on establishing joint ventures overseas. It is unlikely to be available for relationship-based entry forms. Assistance available from other bodies in Australia may also influence the mode of entry. The Australian Business Chamber, for example, facilitates relationship formation between parties in Australia and overseas. Incentives offered by governments of overseas countries also have an influence on entry mode. If an overseas country has an attractive package of investment incentives, an Australian or New Zealand firm may elect to establish a joint venture in the overseas market rather than export to it. The Thai Board of Investment maintained an office in Sydney for a number of years for the purpose of attracting investment by Australian and New Zealand firms in Thailand and used it to promote the range of investment incentives offered. It was these incentives which prompted James N. Kirby to enter into a joint venture in Thailand to produce refrigeration compressors.

# APPROACHES TO INTERNATIONALISATION

An examination of what has been written about selecting an overseas market and the best way of entering an overseas market indicates that most studies have focused on the novice exporter. However, even the novice will learn by experience and become more adventurous by, first, entering difficult but potentially more rewarding markets and, second, by attempting new entry modes involving greater commitment of resources and control over the operation. The larger firm, already knowledgeable about international activities, will also learn by experience and increase its degree of internationalisation. An understanding of the process by which firms increase their international involvement is necessary.

Internationalisation has usually been depicted as an incremental or sequential process of limited commitment in the face of uncertainty. However, according to Rosenzweig and Shaner (2000) a number of major changes in recent years—ranging from deregulation of industry to newly emerging markets, to the revolution in information technology—have changed the pattern of internationalisation. As a result, firms face lower barriers to international growth and more firms which are smaller and limited in resources can expand internationally. This has meant a surge in international activities requiring firms to internationalise more rapidly than in the past and adopt both sequential and non-sequential approaches. The various approaches to internationalisation are as follows.

## Sequential approaches

### STAGES APPROACHES

The earliest group of theories to explain this process were the so-called 'stages approaches'— firms started with the mode of entry which required the least commitment of resources and with experience gradually increased their commitment of resources to international activities. Typical of these approaches were those of Bilkey and Tesar (1977), based on the theory of diffusion of innovation; Cavusgil (1980), based on progressive reduction of uncertainty; and Reid (1981), who argued that firms moved from awareness (of export potential) to intention (to begin doing something about exporting) to trial (attempt exporting) to evaluation (of the results of initial exporting) to acceptance (of exporting as a good thing). These theories, summarised in Fletcher (2001), were somewhat static, although logical.

### LEARNING APPROACHES

A second group of theories applied learning theory and recognised that internationalisation is a dynamic process. They focused more on an evolutionary, sequential build-up of foreign commitments over time and recognised the role that psychic distance can play in the process. For instance, firms commence their overseas involvement in nearby markets that are most similar to the market in Australia and, as they learn more about the export process, become willing to try markets that are more distant in terms of cultural background, political system and economic circumstance. Typical of this group of theories of internationalisation was that of Johanson and Weidersheim-Paul (see summary in Fletcher 2001), who argued that from a position of no export activity firms first exported via an intermediary and then on a direct basis. This often involved establishing a sales subsidiary in the overseas market. This stage could be followed by some form of production overseas.

Both the above theories are incremental and imply that firms repeat the process in all markets, rather than apply their experience in one market when entering another by using an entry mode requiring a greater commitment of resources. Research in Australia by Brewer (2001) indicates that, whereas psychic distance is likely to influence the choice of overseas markets by new or novice exporters, it is less the case with experienced or mature exporters whose decision as to which overseas market to enter is more likely to be influenced by overall market attractiveness, likely competitive position in the market and information about conditions in the market.

# Non-sequential approaches

## CONTINGENCY APPROACHES

A third group of theories of internationalisation are based on contingency theory, whereby the firm evaluates and responds to an opportunity as it occurs, regardless of whether the market is close in psychic distance terms or whether an advanced mode of entry is required. Exponents of this approach (Okoroafo 1990) argue that factors internal to the firm as well as external situations or opportunities will cause firms to leapfrog stages and select the one that is the most appropriate for the overseas market. This situation also occurs when firms choose initially to enter overseas markets that are very different using forms of market entry that are also different. Cuervo-Cazurra (2004) argues that the ability to do so will depend on firms' ability to manage complexity and diversity, their ease in being able to transfer and employ resources across countries and their acquisition of resources through alliances with foreign firms.

## NETWORK APPROACHES

The fourth group of approaches is based on the network paradigm that emphasises the role of linkages and relationships in the internationalisation process (see Chapter 12). The approach here is that firms become involved in international activities by establishing linkages with networks in other countries. The network of the exporting firm in Australia, including those firms which provide inputs and facilitate the activities of the firm, becomes linked to the network of the buying firm in the overseas country, including those firms which distribute, service and on-sell the product. Using this approach Johanson and Mattsson (1988) describe modes of entry in terms of the position established in overseas networks as:

• *international extension*—entering a network overseas that is new to the firm;

• *international penetration*—consolidating and building upon a position already established in an overseas network; and

• *international integration*—coordinating the positions already occupied in networks in different countries.

These authors believe that the degree of internationalisation of the firm in terms of the nature of its product network should be compared with the degree of internationalisation of the market in terms of the national network for the product in the selected country. They arrive at four categories of firm:

1 *early starter*—firms in this category often begin exporting to nearby markets using agents so as to take advantage of positions in the market occupied by firms in the network in that country;

2 *lonely international*—because this firm has considerable international experience and because the overseas market is not highly internationalised, this firm is likely to experience little difficulty in entering the network in that country;

3 *late starter*—this firm may be 'pulled' into becoming involved in the overseas country by members of its network in Australia such as customers or suppliers. Being 'pulled', it may become involved in a more advanced stage of internationalisation and/or in markets perceived to be more psychically distant;

4 *international among others*—firms in this category can easily use their position in the overseas network in one country as a way of entering networks in other countries. For example, they may use production capacity in one to supply another.

The network approach caters for the current dynamic situation in international marketing whereby internationalisation not only involves outward-driven activities but also inward-driven activities, as well as activities in which import and export transactions are linked and mutually dependent. As such, because of its focus on the need for buyers (importers) and sellers (exporters) to build up knowledge about each other, it is the only approach with a capacity to cater for more advanced forms of overseas market entry, such as strategic alliances, cooperative manufacture and countertrade.

### 7.3 INTERNATIONAL HIGHLIGHT

## International production networks

A key factor in trade dynamism in ASEAN and some other Asian economies has been the development of international production networks. As manufactured products are becoming more technologically sophisticated, their production involves an increasing number of stages. These production stages can be decoupled and farmed out to a network of geographically dispersed locations to take advantage of lower costs. This cross-border multi-staged production process has been facilitated by major improvements in transportation, coordination and communication technologies and the liberalisation of trade and investment regimes.

While production fragmentation has been frequently used in consumer goods like garments, footwear and toys for decades, it is now being applied more intensively in electronics, communications technology products and transport equipment. Production sharing also includes services as well as goods. Service activities that have been outsourced include the provision of call-centre support and back-end business process operations like data entry, payroll management, accounting and bookkeeping, transcription (both medical and legal) and IT related services such as web hosting and network and server management.

**SOURCE:** *Adapted from Department of Foreign Affairs and Trade (2006),* ASEAN: Building an Economic Community, *p. 65.*

# A HOLISTIC VIEW OF INTERNATIONALISATION

Fletcher (2001) looked at market entry modes in a broader way in an endeavour to consider what actually happens to firms when entering markets overseas as opposed to theories built around what firms should do. His research is based on a definition of internationalisation developed by Welch and Luostarinen (1988)—it is 'the process of increasing involvement in international operations'.

The research endeavours to accommodate recent trends in the international business environment such as the information super highway, rising fixed costs, shorter product life cycles and converging consumer tastes. These trends have resulted in more complex forms of international behaviour which are imposing an increasing requirement for global cooperation in order for firms to be globally competitive.

A broader approach to market entry is necessary. This is illustrated in Figure 7.3. Firms can enter markets which are highly relationship dependent via both inward and outward activities. As with outward activities, inward activities can occur as a series of stages involving increasing commitment of resources. Alternatively, they may be the result of experience, with each activity being incremental to the previous one and influenced by the learning that has taken place. Further, they may be the result of contingencies in either the firm or the overseas market, or be the result of relationships arising out of connections with an overseas network. Figure 7.3 shows the modes of both outward-driven and inward-driven entry in overseas markets, and Figure 7.4 shows that internationalisation is about more than just exporting.

Figure 7.3 also shows that, in addition to outward and inward modes of entry, there is a third category of linked forms of entry into overseas markets. In the case of countertrade the linkage of outward and inward forms is conditional. It is often either a condition of doing business directly mandated by a government or the direct result of a set of conditions created by government, such as the non-availability of foreign exchange. Given that countertrade is estimated to account for about 15% of world trade, this form of overseas market entry should not be ignored. Also, strategic alliances are becoming increasingly popular due to a desire to achieve economies of scale, reduce R&D costs and overcome protectionism. These alliances are intended to improve international competitiveness by serving customers in a global environment, bringing products to market more quickly, introducing products into several countries simultaneously, lowering costs by focusing on core competencies and reducing promotion costs by marketing under one brand. Such alliances are built upon entering overseas markets, cooperating with a party in that market and gaining competitive strength by becoming involved with that firm's network. Cooperative manufacture and offshoring also involve parties in two countries in a mutual endeavour, the success of which is dependent on delivering benefits to both parties.

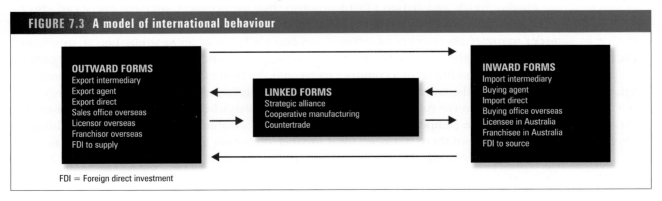

**FIGURE 7.3 A model of international behaviour**

**OUTWARD FORMS**
Export intermediary
Export agent
Export direct
Sales office overseas
Licensor overseas
Franchisor overseas
FDI to supply

**LINKED FORMS**
Strategic alliance
Cooperative manufacturing
Countertrade

**INWARD FORMS**
Import intermediary
Buying agent
Import direct
Buying office overseas
Licensee in Australia
Franchisee in Australia
FDI to source

FDI = Foreign direct investment

## FIGURE 7.4 Internationalisation is more than just exporting

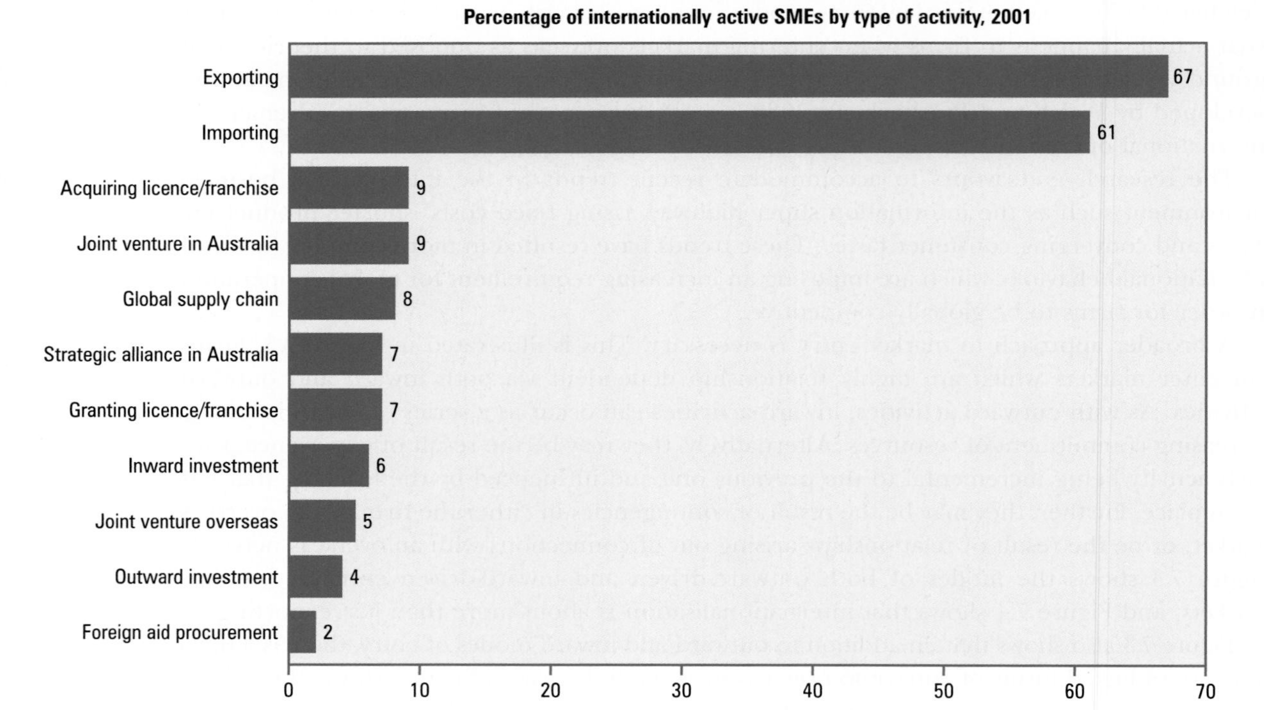

**Percentage of internationally active SMEs by type of activity, 2001**

|  |  |
|---|---|
| Exporting | 67 |
| Importing | 61 |
| Acquiring licence/franchise | 9 |
| Joint venture in Australia | 9 |
| Global supply chain | 8 |
| Strategic alliance in Australia | 7 |
| Granting licence/franchise | 7 |
| Inward investment | 6 |
| Joint venture overseas | 5 |
| Outward investment | 4 |
| Foreign aid procurement | 2 |

**SOURCE:** Yellow Pages Business Index, *May 2001.*

Another reality of international marketing is that outward- or export-led involvement can often lead to inward- or import-led involvement and vice versa. This happens, for example, when the licensee in Australia is given the rights to license manufacture of the product in another country such as New Zealand, or when the Australian joint venture partner is allowed to set up manufacturing operations in South-East Asia. This interconnectedness between inward and outward forms of internationalisation is illustrated in Figure 7.5.

Finally, Welch and Benito (1996) propose that, on occasion, overseas entry can also be associated with exit from an overseas market—either exiting from one form of involvement in order to undertake another or exiting from one market in order to strengthen an established position in another. They refer to this as de-internationalisation. It can occur when political or economic conditions in a country change and the firm exits but re-enters when conditions improve, as is the case with the history of IBM's involvement in India. This is analogous to what happens in the Australian or New Zealand markets when firms rationalise, downsize and refocus on core competencies, all in the interest of greater market share or profitability. In view of the above there is a need for a broader definition of internationalisation than those previously discussed. One such definition is that by Calof and Beamish (1995): 'Internationalisation is the process of adapting firms' operations to international environments'.

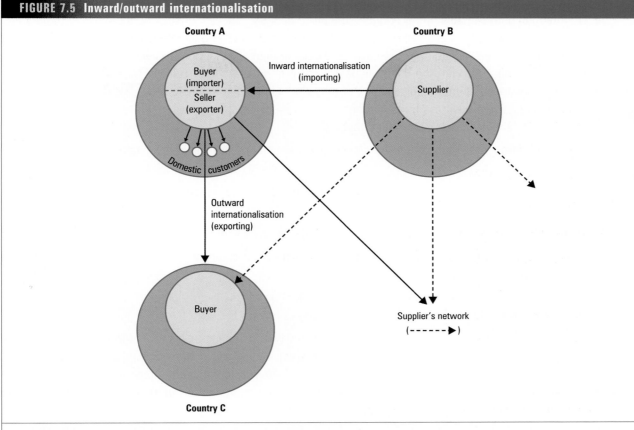

**FIGURE 7.5  Inward/outward internationalisation**

Country A

Buyer
(importer)

Seller
(exporter)

Domestic customers

Inward internationalisation
(importing)

Outward
internationalisation
(exporting)

Country B

Supplier

Supplier's network
(- - - - - ▶)

Country C

Buyer

**SOURCE:** *Hollensen, S. (2004)* Global Marketing: A Decision-Oriented Approach, *Prentice Hall, UK, p. 39.*

# The internet and foreign market entry

When marketing using the internet the availability of the necessary infrastructure in a country will influence the form of market entry. Infrastructure availability may not be the same in all countries and the existing infrastructure prior to the introduction of the internet will influence how the internet develops in that country (e.g. Europe's advanced digital phone infrastructure will result in greater use of mobile phones for accessing the internet). E-business firms can internationalise only by dealing with countries that are internet enabled and use the internet. A country with a large percentage of the population using the internet is more attractive as a market for e-business firms to enter. Global technology parity involves availability of both computers and accessible telecommunications services in a country. E-business firms cannot implement an internationalisation strategy in countries where this parity in technology is absent. The higher the level of technology parity a country exhibits, the faster the e-business firm is able to move into it.

Another factor influencing the form of entry when the internet is involved is the extent to which there is legal protection of intellectual property rights in a given country. The lack of such protection is detrimental to e-business firms since the core competencies of such firms are centred on know-how and the development of patent and software technology. The better the legal protection, the more rapidly the e-business firm will move into a country. As with the internationalisation of traditional firms, cultural distance is significant for determining the speed of internationalisation of e-business firms. For example, language and the need to use it properly may delay e-business firms in preparing their websites and portals.

Research by Zhao and Du (2000) found that:

- e-business firms were much more likely to enter markets that were culturally distant than were traditional firms;

- e-business firms began international activities much sooner after establishment (on average 2.71 years) than traditional firms (21 years);

- e-business firms entered a larger number of foreign markets a year (3.62) than did traditional firms (1.60);

- the internationalisation of e-business firms was neither incremental nor sequential but rather a function of acquired knowledge; and

- high degrees of technological parity and legal protection of intellectual property rights were necessary preconditions for the internationalisation of e-business firms.

Because of the internet's characteristics of interactivity and speedy access to information, a knowledge of overseas markets is acquired more quickly in marketspace than in the marketplace and, as a result, internet-driven internationalisation is more likely to follow a contingency process of responding to opportunities as they occur. The relevance of the incremental approach to internationalisation is called into question by the explosion of international business activity on the world wide web, particularly as technology now exists to provide small and medium-sized enterprises with a low-cost gateway to international markets.

# Summary

Selecting an overseas market is one of the most difficult decisions to be undertaken by the international marketing executive. This is because selecting the wrong market can not only be costly in profit terms but also result in management disenchantment with any future involvement in international operations. The difference between the novice and the experienced firm is a matter of accumulated international experience; both need to adopt a systematic approach to market selection, taking the circumstances of the firm and the circumstances of the market into account. The form of market entry is another issue which merits careful consideration because some modes, while requiring greater commitment of resources, also allow a greater degree of control and have the potential for greater profitability. In selecting the mode and form of involvement current business issues such as the information revolution, the linking of networks, the operations of the transnational firm and regional trade groupings need to be taken into account. A more holistic view of market entry should be adopted catering for inward, outward and linked forms of international behaviour.

## ETHICS ISSUE

Your company has a large amount of capital tied up in manufacturing plant for milling grains. Australia has recently introduced environmental protection legislation to come into force 12 months hence. This will make this equipment unusable because it gives off more dust than the new legislation allows. Although this machinery will be written off, the company wishes to dispose of it as profitably as possible. You have been advised that potentially profitable opportunities exist to establish joint venture milling operations in Vietnam and Laos. Research also indicates that there is no environmental protection legislation in these countries or restriction on the supply of second-hand milling equipment provided a joint venture is being established.

*You are the international marketing manager for the company and the board has called for recommendations for disposing of the firm's current milling machinery with minimum loss. Would you recommend entering into a joint venture in either Vietnam or Laos?*

## Websites

Barbecues Galore http://www.bbqgalore.com
Bendix http://www.bendix.com
'Capture the flag' http://www.exporter.com
CSR http://www.csr.com.au
Foreign Trade Online http://www.foreign-trade.com
New Zealand government web pages http://www.govt.nz
Orbital Engine Company http://www.orbeng.com
Selleys http://www.selleys.com.au
Star Alliance http://www.staralliance.com
Union Carbide Corporation http://www.unioncarbide.com
US International Trade Administration trade development home page http://ita.doc. gov/td/td_home
World Trade Organization http://www.wto.org

## Discussion questions

1 Discuss the pros and cons of:

(a) simultaneous versus incremental entry into international markets;

(b) concentrated versus diversified market entry strategies.

2 (a) Take a product you are familiar with and which has not previously been sold overseas and apply a selection procedure to arrive at the three most promising markets for the overseas product.

(b) Take a product you are familiar with and which is already being sold in several overseas markets, and apply a selection procedure to arrive at the three most promising markets that could be considered when expanding overseas business for the product.

(c) What different factors would you consider in the case of a product never exported compared with the one already exported to several countries?

3 What factors would you consider if you were an Australian or New Zealand manufacturer of catamarans in choosing between Mexico, Indonesia and Japan as the next country to enter?

4 What would be the advantages and disadvantages of licensing the manufacture of your product overseas as opposed to manufacture under a joint venture arrangement?

5 What aspects of an overseas market might cause you to settle on an entry mode which gives you less control over how your product is marketed but requires less investment of resources?

6 Because it is located in the southern hemisphere Australia's and New Zealand's fruit-growing industry has a counter-seasonal advantage in many northern hemisphere markets. What entry mode would be most suitable in view of possible trade barriers in some of these markets?

7 It is often argued that theories of international marketing should be based on a process approach (i.e. what actually happens) rather than on a structured approach (using a predetermined model to explain or predict what should happen). Which of the approaches to internationalisation most closely follows the process approach and why?

8 (a) In what circumstances would you enter an overseas market via an inward form of international involvement?

(b) When should you contemplate a linked form of market entry and how do you ensure that the relationship is beneficial to both parties?

# References

Anderson, E. and Gatignon, H. (1986) 'Modes of foreign entry: a transaction cost analysis and propositions', *Journal of International Business Studies*, Vol. 17, No. 3, pp. 1–26.

'Aussies find Asian partners', *Banker* (1996) Vol. 146, No. 845, July, p. 77.

Australian Trade Commission (1990) 'Austrade User Guide', Sydney.

Barrett, N.J. (1986) 'A study of the internationalisation of Australian manufacturing firms', unpublished PhD thesis, University of New South Wales.

Bilkey, W.J. and Tesar, G. (1977) 'The export behaviour of smaller-sized Wisconsin manufacturing firms', *Journal of International Business Studies*, Spring/Summer, pp. 93–8.

'Bluefish444', *Dynamic Export* (2007), December/January, p. 20.

Brewer, P. (2001) 'International market selection: developing a model from Australian case studies', *International Business Review*, Vol. 10, No. 2, pp. 155–74.

Brouthers, K.D., Brouthers, L.E. and Werner, S. (1996) 'Dunning's Eclectic Theory and the smaller firm: the impact of ownership and locational advantages on the choice of entry modes in the computer software industry', *International Business Review*, Vol. 5, No. 4, pp. 377–94.

Calof, J.C. and Beamish, P.W. (1995) 'Adapting to international markets: explaining internationalization', *International Business Review*, Vol. 4, No. 2, pp. 115–31.

Cavusgil, S.T. (1980) 'On the internationalisation process of firms', *European Research*, Vol. 8, No. 6, pp. 273–81.

Cavusgil, S.T., Kiyak, T. and Yeniyurt, S. (2004) 'Complementary approaches to preliminary foreign market opportunity assessment: country clustering and country ranking', *Industrial Marketing Management*, Vol. 33, pp. 607–17.

Choe, S. and Jin, C. (2004) 'The Asian crisis and inward FDI in Korea: the choice between acquisition and greenfield investment', presented at the Academy of International Business Conference, Stockholm, 10–13 July.

Chow, L. (1996) 'Go north: like many Australian firms, CSR sees its future in Asia', *Far Eastern Economic Review*, 29 August.

Clark, T. and Pugh, D.S. (2001) 'Foreign country priorities in the internationalisation process: a measured and an exploratory test of British firms', *International Business Review*, Vol. 10, pp. 285–303.

CSR (2004) <http://www.csr.com.au>.

Cuervo-Cazurra, A. (2004) 'Explaining the non-sequential internationalisation across countries', paper presented at the 46th Annual Meeting of the Academy of International Business, Stockholm, 10–13 July.

Department of Foreign Affairs and Trade (2006) *ASEAN: Building an Economic Community*, Economic Analytical Unit, Department of Foreign Affairs and Trade, Canberra.

East Asia Analytical Unit (2000) *Transforming Thailand–Choices for the New Millennium*, Department of Foreign Affairs and Trade, Canberra.

Fletcher, R. (1996) 'Countertrade and the internationalisation of the Australian firm', PhD thesis, University of Technology, Sydney.

Fletcher, R. (2001) 'A holistic view of internationalisation', *International Business Review*, Vol. 10, pp. 25–49.

Hollensen, S. (2004) *Global Marketing–A Decision-Oriented Approach*, Financial Times Prentice Hall, Harlow, UK.

Johanson, J. and Mattsson, L-G. (1988) 'Internationalisation in industrial systems—a network approach', Reprint Series, No. 1, Department of Business Administration, University of Upsalla, in N. Hood and J-E. Vahlne (eds), *Strategies in Global Competition*, Croom Helm, New York.

Johanson, J. and Wiedersheim-Paul, F. (1975) 'The internationalisation of the firm: four Swedish cases', *Journal of Management Studies*, Vol. 12, No. 3, pp. 305–22.

Knight, J., Bell, J. and McNaughton, R. (2001) 'The 'born-global' phenomenon: a rebirth of an old concept', in Jones, M.V. and Dimitratos, P. (eds), *Researching New Frontiers: Proceedings of the McGill Conference on International Entrepreneurship*, University of Strathclyde, 21–23 September.

Okoroafo, S. (1990) 'An assessment of critical entry factors affecting modes of entry substitution patterns in foreign product markets', *Journal of Global Marketing*, Vol. 3, No. 3, pp. 87–104.

Pinto, J.C., Shaw, V. and Fahrhangmehr, M. (2001) 'Foreign market entry modes in the financial services sector: an empirical testing of Dunning's Eclectic Model', *Proceedings of the European Marketing Academy Conference*, Bergen, 8–11 May, Norges Handelshoyskole.

Pires, G.D. and Stanton, P.J. (2005) *Ethnic Marketing: Accepting the Challenge of Cultural Diversity*, Thomson Learning, London.

Reid, S.D. (1981) 'The decision-maker and export entry and expansion', *Journal of International Business Studies*, Vol. 12, No. 2, pp. 101–12.

Rosenzweig, P.M. and Shaner, J.L. (2000) 'Internationalisation reconsidered: new imperatives for successful growth', *Proceedings of the Annual Meeting of the Academy of International Business*, 17–20 November, Phoenix, AZ, Thunderbird University.

'Salad days', *Export* (2005) 1 September, p. 12.

Toyne, B. and Walters, P.G.P. (1993) *Global Marketing Management*, 2nd edn, Allyn and Bacon, Boston, Chapter 9.

Walton, G. and Ashill, N. (2001) 'International market selection: challenging the status quo', *Proceedings of the Conference of the Academy of Marketing*, Cardiff, 1–4 July, University of Cardiff.

Welch, L.S. and Benito, G.R.G. (1996) 'De-internationalisation', Working Paper 5/96, Department of Marketing, University of Western Sydney, Nepean.

Welch, L.S. and Luostarinen, R.K. (1988) 'Internationalisation: evolution of a concept', *Journal of General Management*, Vol. 14, No. 2, pp. 34–55.

Wikipedia (2007) <http://en.wikipedia.org/wiki/Offshoring>, accessed 22 January.

*Yellow Pages Business Index*, May 2001.

Zhao, J.H. and Du, J. (2000) 'Electronic commerce and international business: a new test of internationalisation theory', *Proceedings of the e-Commerce and Global Business Forum*, Santa Cruz, CA, 17–19 May, Anderson Consulting Institute for Strategic Change.

## go online

Go online to <www.pearsoned.com.au/fletcher> to find more case studies.

# International market selection: balancing opportunity and risk

**Hongzhi Gao, Department of Marketing, University of Otago and John Knight, Department of Marketing, University of Otago**

*(This case is based on a real-life company. In order to protect confidentiality, names of the company and people mentioned in the company have been changed.)*

## BACKGROUND

Craig Technology is a New Zealand-based, small-to-medium-sized enterprise (SME). Despite its small size, the company is recognised as a global leader in the design and building of automated assembly lines for appliance manufacturers. The company is 'born global' and has a strong export focus such that 98% of the company's total sales were from export in 2006. Both growth and survival for the company rely on the reinforcement of existing markets and the exploration of new markets.

Craig Technology's staff are proud of their expertise in this specialised area as well as their strong financial position over the years. According to the annual reports:

> We must rank as one of the country's most conservative listed companies, with no debt, substantial short-term cash investments, and no intangibles in its balance sheet.
>
> To ensure continued growth, Craig Technology is dedicated to providing innovative, state of the art, quality solutions to our customers. Our plans include undertaking selected research and development in key areas that will assist the company to keep ahead of the competition in our appliance and automation sectors where we have leadership positions.

The management of the company acknowledged the importance of trade skills and marketing initiatives in the continuing success of the company, but according to them it is the creativity and innovative abilities of their technical staff which gives Craig Technology the leading edge. A shareholder of the company commented: 'they are composed of a bunch of engineers but prove to do very well in the international marketing arena'.

Craig Technology has remained in a buoyant position in North American and South American markets for more than a decade. However, the senior management has started to realise that these traditional markets are being challenged by the economic recession of the USA, and the new marketing initiatives in Europe and Asia in the late 1990s. One of these major challenges is to manage the dynamics of the global market. The company has also faced challenges from the impact that a high New Zealand exchange rate has had on its exports since 2002. The company's strategy has been to increase its business in both geographic expansion within the appliance industry and diversification into non-appliance industries.

This case demonstrates how Craig Technology made selections between different overseas markets at different stages of maturity, and became committed to a developing market, China. Further, the case shows how the company chose a direct exporting strategy instead of other market entry modes to enter foreign markets.

## INCREMENTAL SELECTION OF FOREIGN MARKETS

In 1999, in order to adapt to the changes in the global market, Craig Technology established a base in the UK to enable it to increase its marketing throughout Europe. The former managing director stepped down from this position to concentrate on the European market, residing in London. The company successfully secured its first substantial contract in Poland in 2000. It then anticipated Europe would develop into a major source of work in the future. However, the biggest challenge for Craig Technology is the competition from direct suppliers in Italy and Spain for the same type of equipment.

Apart from the European market, the company also considered opportunities in the fast-growing Asian market. The company first commissioned an Otago MBA student, a Chinese national, Mr Han, to conduct a market research report on China. From this exploratory research, the company acknowledged the existence of considerable market opportunities in Asia. It also knew from this research that innovation and technology consciousness are Craig Technology's dominant competitive advantages in China. The most significant advantage of Chinese manufacturers is the low labour cost. Craig Technology was therefore in the advantageous position to fill this void. Despite the potential of the Chinese market, the company was not sure if Chinese manufacturers could afford to buy New Zealand equipment. Furthermore, it was concerned that anything it provided might get copied. A general attitude of the company towards China was that it would be desirable but scary. It wanted to open Chinese markets but did not know how to do it. However, it was well aware of the advantages of being 'first mover' in the fast-growing market of China.

In its feedback to Mr Han's report, Craig Technology indicated that it was not ready to tap into Chinese markets yet, in view of its commitment to the European market at the time. In response to this, Mr Han made a simple request: 'Please come to China with me'. When Mr Han showed the marketing team of Craig Technology around in China, their attitudes towards Chinese markets changed. When they visited a production line that one appliance manufacturer imported from Japan, the Craig Technology managers were astonished by the advanced state of the product line. The appliance industry in China is just in the _growth_ stage in the product life circle (Fletcher and Brown 2005, pp. 13–17). This industry in China is attracting highly educated people. The new generation of management has international visions and knows how to interact with foreign businesses in a professional way. This is in sharp contrast to the old-fashioned manufacturing equipment used by some North American manufacturers. In North America, the white-ware industry appeared to have conservative attitudes towards the up-to-date technologies Craig Technology could provide. This is because the white-ware industry in North America is in the _decline_ stage in the product life cycle.

Mr Han volunteered to promote Craig Technology in China, using his personal relationships to contact big manufacturers. Through the introduction of his classmate in middle school, Mr Han got to know a marketing manager of one big appliance manufacturer. Through this link, he finally met the CEO of the Chinese company. In 1999, Craig sold one automated line to this Chinese manufacturer. The wholesale process was not nearly as difficult as Craig Technology thought it would be. It made money from the Chinese market even before it had made a full commitment. After Mr Han facilitated this sale, he became employed half-time by Craig Technology. This success in the Chinese market came earlier than the company ever expected.

In 2000, global sales of Craig Technology continued going up. However, the North American market had significantly slowed. Its marketing activities in Europe continued unabated during the year and achieved a significant potential customer base. The company expected to be able to build upon this base in this very large market.

## SIMULTANEOUS SELECTION OF EUROPEAN AND CHINESE MARKETS

In 2001, the slowing North American economy had a continuing impact on the sales of Craig

Technology in the market. Due to heavy reliance on the North American market, the company was forced to reduce the workforce. After more than a year's exploration of the European market, the company realised its European market had lagged behind China. Despite this, it believed that it was still important to maintain and build customer relationships in Europe.

After placing its major focus on Europe for the preceding two years, the company finally determined to establish a sales presence within China in 2001. The company set up a branch office in Shanghai, responsible for all marketing activities in respect of sales. The manager of the Shanghai office is the former Otago MBA student, Mr Han. The company also considered other entry modes such as licensing and joint ventures. There is a risk for licensing as it may lead to 'cloning a competitor' (Fletcher and Brown 2005, pp. 266–70). This is of major concern for Craig Technology in China. Joint ventures provide access to the distribution network as well as familiarity with the local marketing environment. But the motive of a Chinese partner is obviously to acquire technology and production expertise from Craig Technology. In addition, selecting the right joint venture partner is often a problem. Craig Technology had great concerns about potential cultural conflict in joint ventures. Establishing the Shanghai branch office has granted the company more control over activities in China. Based on many years' experience in overseas markets, the company believed setting up its own marketing team would be the most effective way for operating in overseas markets. However, all the manufacturing and engineering decisions are still taken from the New Zealand headquarters to protect their core technology.

According to the Chinese marketing manager of Craig Technology, the key for working with big Chinese companies is to find key decision makers (there are always changes of personnel occurring in these positions). Of course, identifying key decision makers requires facilitation from some *guanxi* (insiders in the organisations who are in a position to help outsiders). The secret is to get to know when the top-level management in the client companies are planning a new project. This information is normally confidential. Therefore, a marketer in China has to have the ability to get access to small circles of decision makers to get first hand information. In order to do this, a marketing manager has to have *ren mai* (multiple levels of interconnected relationships) in the industry. A marketing manager has to keep frequent contacts with senior management of Chinese appliance manufacturers at the personal level. Developing contacts with government officials can also have noticeable influence on securing and implementing projects. All these have been well achieved by the marketing manager of Craig Technology in China in a relative short period of time.

In 2002, after more than two years' downturn in Northern American markets, the company achieved record levels of sales and this cemented the company's position as a supplier of choice for major American white-ware appliance manufacturers such as Whirlpool. Market analysis indicated that the surge of demand from the North American market was driven by economic recovery factors combined with the emergence of niche markets for higher cost 'fashion' products. However, a significant trend seen was that American white-ware manufacturers faced strong competition from Chinese competitors in both domestic and export markets. The continuous growth of the Chinese economy and the success of Chinese appliance manufacturers such as Haier in overseas markets made the management of Craig Technology realise that Chinese markets have greater long-term potential than even their conventional market in the USA.

During the 2002 year, a second assembly line was designed, constructed and shipped to a customer in China. The installation, commissioning and sign-off was successfully completed, further cementing their relationship with the Chinese client and furthering the company's reputation and credibility within the Chinese market. However, one major hindering factor for the company's operation in China is the threat from piracy in China, which is not an issue in Western markets. The company determined to take all the necessary care and measures to protect its technology from being copied in China. Yet it is also aware that, to be successful, a foreign entrant in China has to bring in some valuable technology and expertise to enable Chinese counterparts to participate in international competition.

## READJUSTING THE GLOBAL STRATEGY

In 2003–05, the company set its major priority as improving profitability through efficiency and cost reduction programs. The strategic move was indicated from the recent appointment of a new general manager to focus on operational management alongside the chief executive who continued to focus on international markets and product design in 2005. Tapping into Chinese markets also provided the company with the opportunity of offshore outsourcing.

The company put its effort of research and development into diversifying into non-appliance industries including meat-processing automation. The new position for the company is described as 'a niche, specialised supplier of design and build systems'.

In the appliance industry, the company still focuses on China. Although the company has secured a big project in Turkey, some attached conditions, including finance support and a tight deadline, have increased the developmental cost and reduced the profitability of the project. After the establishment of the Shanghai office in China, the company has achieved some success in securing orders, but it did not meet the original expectations from the company at the start. However, the company takes a long-term view in Chinese markets. The company has adopted different criteria for performance evaluation in China. Apart from the evaluation of sales performance, the management has also attached importance to setting up vital business connections and accumulation of local market knowledge. Having flexibility in performance evaluation criteria has helped the company gain a firm foothold in the market. It is important to note that if the company had evaluated the China office purely on the basis of sales performance it would have probably ended up withdrawing from the market already.

## Bibliography

Ambler, T. and Styles, C. (2000) 'The future of relational research in international marketing: constructs and conduits', *International Marketing Review*, Vol. 17, No. 6, pp. 492–508.

Fletcher, R. and Brown, L. (2005) *International Marketing: An Asia–Pacific Perspective*, 3rd edn, Pearson Prentice Hall, Sydney.

Miles, R.E. and Snow, C.C. (1978) *Organizational Strategy, Structure and Process*, McGraw-Hill, New York.

Parnell, J.A. and Wright, P. (1993) 'Generic strategy and performance: an empirical test of the Miles and Snow typology', *British Journal of Management*, Vol. 4, No. 2, pp. 29–36.

Shoham, A., Evangelista, F. and Albaum, G. (2002) 'Strategic firm type and export performance' *International Marketing Review*, Vol. 19, No. 3, pp. 236–58.

## Questions

1  How did management preferences and product life cycle influence the selection of overseas markets?

2  What are the differences between a 'survival' or 'defender' strategy compared to 'first mover' or 'prospector' strategy? Discuss the strategic orientation that drove Craig Technology to choose overseas markets.

3  Craig Technology's selection of the European market and the Chinese market can be envisaged as a simultaneous process. Discuss the strategic reasons for this process instead of incremental selection.

4  How did personal relationships and *ren mai* in the industry facilitate the entrance of Craig Technology into Chinese markets?

5  Discuss the market entry modes available to Craig Technology with respect to the changing market environment.

6  What short-term and long-term benefits exist for a foreign entrant in the Chinese market? Discuss the strategic implications for Craig Technology.

# PLANNING FOR INTERNATIONAL MARKETING

## LearningObjectives

**After reading this chapter you should be able to:**

- describe the strategic marketing planning process and the role of scenario planning;

- explain the steps involved in the international marketing planning process;

- develop an international marketing plan;

- illustrate the challenges to effective international marketing planning; and

- discuss the requirements for practical international marketing planning.

# Nudie, anyone?

Tim Pethick decided to leave a high-paying executive position in the UK and return to Australia for a less hectic life. While overseas Tim had developed a taste for fresh fruit juice without preservatives and so started a quest to find a similar product back home. He couldn't find any. Frustrated, Tim decided to make the juice himself.

In 2002 the juice bar phenomenon hit Australia: Boost Juice, Squeeze and Viva to name a few. Tim observed that there was a niche in the juice market for a preservative-free bottled juice at a premium price compared with the regular bottle juice, but cheaper than the juice bar alternative. In 2003 he launched Nudie juice and by 2004 the sales figures were $12 million.

Part of the Nudie brand's success has been the planning and the marketing of the product. It has been a word-of-mouth success story. The company is now recognised as the 10th most influential brand in the Asia–Pacific region, and has developed this standing without the use of advertising, preferring word-of-mouth, gimmicks and customer contact. In fact it is the Nudie language and sense of humour in its packaging and promotions that has helped it strengthen its relationship with 'Nudie addicts' and attract new customers. This loyalty was rewarded when its main factory burnt down and had to be rebuilt in 2004.

Tim described his mindset thus: 'You really need to think like a consumer. They want real fruit juice product, not a reconstituted mix. Low growth comes from lack of

innovation'. This innovative thinking has developed the Nudie products from just juices to smoothies, ice-cream and now soups.

Nudie now exports to New Zealand, Singapore and Hong Kong. New forms of communication have helped with the promotion of the Nudie brand: SMS-ing, point of sale materials and an interactive website. Tim wants to build the Nudie brand to the status of a company like Virgin and, given the huge support from Nudie addicts and the culture it is creating, he is well on the way. However, the next steps for Nudie will require an international marketing planning process of the type described in this chapter.

**SOURCES:** *Ross, E. and Holland A. (2004)* 100 Great Businesses and the Minds behind Them, *Random House Australia, Sydney, p. 212;* <http://www.marketingmag.com.au/index.php?option=com_content&task=view&id=645&Itemid=0>, *accessed 19 February 2007; and* <http://www.abc.net.au/catapult/stories/s1259696.htm>, *accessed 19 February 2007.*

# INTRODUCTION

The competitive and rapidly changing environment of 2008 and beyond has prompted most Australian firms pursuing overseas opportunities to use strategic market planning to identify, tap and profit from international markets. Successful companies periodically evaluate their market environments in order to assess changes in their opportunities and threats. External and internal environmental changes frequently require them to modify their objectives and sometimes change direction. As discussed in earlier chapters, changes in government regulations, emergence of new competitors, the introduction of new technology and the opening of new markets can change the way in which an Australian firm does business overseas. As they gain experience, develop new competencies and add more resources, firms change their objectives and sometimes their mission.

Strategic market planning in international markets is essentially a way of thinking and a mode of acting. In terms of thinking it challenges international marketers to be constantly sensitive to changes and assess the implications for marketing. In terms of acting, marketers need to be flexible and responsive in the way they plan for and manage the firm's resources and capabilities.

Toyne and Walters (1993, p. 51) provide a useful definition of strategic market planning:

*Strategic market planning is the systematic and periodic process used by managers to examine the environments in which their company competes, the opportunities and threats they face, the goals and objectives to be achieved, and the products and services offered in order to maintain a viable fit between their company's capabilities and resources and the threats and opportunities that arise from a changing environment. Its purpose is to identify and develop a corporate purpose, objectives and goals, and plans of action that effectively relate the company, its businesses, and functional areas to their relevant environments and that enables the company to profitably exploit future marketplace opportunities in which it is likely to enjoy a competitive advantage.*

In this chapter the foundation for effective strategic market planning is laid using an adaptation of a successful Australian firm's overseas marketing plan and by exploring the challenges and practical requirements for effective international marketing planning. The context and process of international marketing planning are discussed first.

## THE CONTEXT OF INTERNATIONAL STRATEGIC MARKET PLANNING

During the 1990s companies began adopting strategic market planning processes that were more flexible and more externally focused by comparison with earlier rigid, internally focused and historically based systems. However, the early years of the new century are reflecting industry convergences, such as banking and insurance and computers and communications, which are transforming industries and changing their global competitive structures. The focus of strategic market planning in the future will be on balancing and matching internal and external drivers, building core competencies, competing as part of 'virtual' networks involving alliance structures and building business value through customer value creation.

There are a number of inputs into the international market planning process as illustrated in Figure 8.1. On the one hand, these relate to the resources of the firm. These are the material resources, the managerial resources, the firm's competitive advantages and its network connections. On the other hand the inputs to the international market planning process also relate to the environment in which the firm operates. The environment can be that in the domestic market, in the selected overseas market, in the regions in which both the home and host countries are located and the global environment. These inputs influence international planning at the company level (plans related to shareholders and returns on their investment), at the business level (plans related to profit, investment and expansion) and at the marketing level (plans related to specific markets, share of market and allocation of marketing activities between markets). As shown in Figure 8.1, the above lead to marketing plans for effective international involvement. The steps proposed by many authors in the international marketing literature are embodied in the outline in Figure 8.2. It includes terms such as *mission*, *vision* and *strategy*, which are now widely used, frequently with different meanings. The notes at the end of this chapter give a definition of strategic terms as a reference point.

However, the need for flexibility, quick response and agility with resources and competencies has led to a resurgence in the process of scenario planning as a means of painting pictures of plausible futures that firms may have to face. This is particularly relevant to international marketers where unexpected changes can open up opportunities or close down markets.

Many leading international organisations, such as Shell, Ericsson and Fujitsu-ICL, as well as international government institutions like the IMF, undertake scenario planning because of the uncertainty of future operating environments.

No single outcome can be accurately forecast in times of turbulence, rapid change and convergence. Scenario planning is therefore becoming an essential capability for managing in this present environment (van der Heijden 1996). The essential steps in scenario planning are outlined below:

- *familiarisation*–understanding the organisation, key stakeholders, their needs and expectations;

- *discovery*–gaining an understanding of current trends and events and anticipating possible future discontinuities in the international environment;

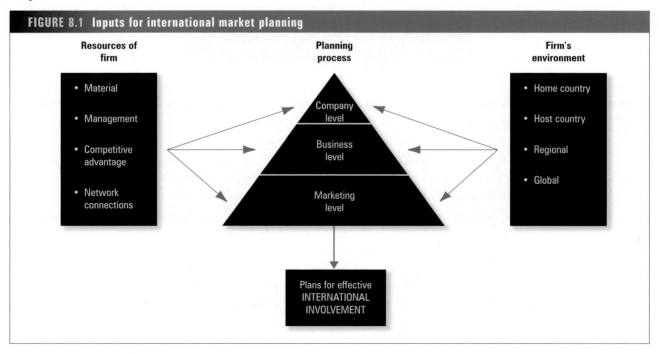

**FIGURE 8.1  Inputs for international market planning**

## FIGURE 8.2 Classic strategic planning sequence

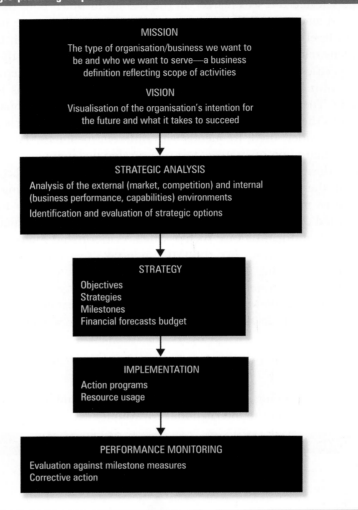

**MISSION**
The type of organisation/business we want to be and who we want to serve—a business definition reflecting scope of activities

**VISION**
Visualisation of the organisation's intention for the future and what it takes to succeed

**STRATEGIC ANALYSIS**
Analysis of the external (market, competition) and internal (business performance, capabilities) environments
Identification and evaluation of strategic options

**STRATEGY**
Objectives
Strategies
Milestones
Financial forecasts budget

**IMPLEMENTATION**
Action programs
Resource usage

**PERFORMANCE MONITORING**
Evaluation against milestone measures
Corrective action

**SOURCE:** *Brown, L. (1997)* Competitive Marketing Strategy, *2nd edn, Nelson ITP, p. 17. Copyright L. Brown. Reproduced with permission of the author.*

- *scenario building*—developing and progressively upgrading a range of scenarios that reflect events, patterns and discontinuities. These factors together form possible operating environments of the future relevant to targeted overseas markets;

- *action and integration*—developing appropriate business and marketing strategies that enable the organisation to operate effectively within the scenarios generated. This phase also includes coming to terms with managing the migration; that is, blending the emerging business with the existing business. This may involve closer integration of a company's international and domestic business operations. The most critical part of this phase is to manage the expectations of the key internal and external stakeholders of the organisation.

The significance of scenarios is that each has different implications for marketing strategies in terms of what customers value and where the business value is in the changing value chain. In turn, they imply quite different investments, strategies, alliance partners and people capabilities for success and ongoing growth.

The international marketer's task is to be on the leading edge of the industry in target markets as they develop. This will involve a number of components:

- progressive scenario development which portrays realistic operating environments of the future, globally and in target markets;

- integrated business and marketing strategies which exploit the opportunities and identify the threats in the emerging scenarios;

- ensuring the process of change is driven by customer considerations rather than technology and internal processes; and

- ensuring that cultural and organisational changes are planned and managed effectively to provide international capability.

The challenge is to understand future operating scenarios so that international business and marketing strategies can be progressively developed and implemented. International marketers need to manage the existing overseas business while progressively integrating new market opportunities presented by change. The core requirement in this challenge is to develop an effective international marketing capability so that Australian and New Zealand businesses develop products and services which satisfy the changing needs of target international markets in such a way as to meet financial objectives and shareholder value expectations.

# STEPS IN THE INTERNATIONAL MARKETING PLANNING PROCESS

There are clearly defined steps in the international marketing planning process and the development of a marketing plan. In this section a real marketing plan of an Australian firm (disguised by name and modified for confidentiality) is used to illustrate the planning elements, a similar process as that outlined in Figure 8.2. It comprises situation analysis, including SWOT, an evaluation of alternative marketing strategies, objectives and marketing strategy including the marketing mix and economic evaluation. This type of planning may focus on one country or a region such as two or three countries in an economic zone. In the example that follows the marketing plan is for a new operation comprising a sales office in another country. It is focused at the marketing level and indicates plans for international involvement in that country as depicted in Figure 8.1.

CASE EXAMPLE 8.1

### THE FURNITURE REMOVALS INDUSTRY

The moving industry in Australia and in most Western countries is large and fragmented. It has many different sectors covering household furniture moving within cities and towns, states, across the country and movements internationally. Office removals are a significant sector in the capital cities. Consignments range from small items of

baggage to specialised movement of antiques and expensive office equipment to full households of furniture and personal belongings.

A complex network of moving companies, local and interstate carriers, specialist storage depots and international shipping companies and airlines operates to move items from origin to destination. Throughout Australia there are several hundred companies that coordinate the movement of furniture and household goods. Grace Movers is the largest national removalist and is the recognised leader in the eastern states while having a strong presence in other states and territories. The two main national competitors to Grace are locally based Wridgeways and Allied Pickfords, a subsidiary of UK-based Pickfords. Each state and region has well-established local removalists such as Amos in Sydney and K.L. Kent in Melbourne. These large businesses with fleets of trucks, regional depots and sophisticated storage and loading facilities contrast with the hundreds of owner-drivers with a fleet of one or two vehicles doing local moves.

The international moving sector has additional dimensions such as shipping documentation, containerisation for international movements, bond facilities and customs procedures in Australia and other countries. These different requirements from local moving have led the national movers to establish separate international divisions to deal specifically with overseas movements. Also a number of companies have set up specifically to service this sector of the market.

The product offering of the international movers includes the movement of furniture, household items, baggage and personal effects from a dwelling in one country to a location in another. This encompasses movement from Australia to another country, referred to as exports, or from an overseas country to Australia, denoted as imports. The services provided in this overall offering are listed below:

- *export from Australia*: components include pick-up, packing, transportation, storage, shipping, insurance, documentation, clearance at destination port by overseas agent, delivery to home, unpacking and removal of empty boxes and rubbish;

- *import to Australia*: components include pick-up, packing and transportation to Australia, clearance through customs, storage, delivery to the home in Australia, unpacking and removal of empty boxes and rubbish.

A number of separate service packages can be provided such as:

- storage, awaiting shipment or delivery;

- consignment to destination port for client-reorganised clearance (export);

- completion of documentation for client;

- organised clearance in Australia (import);

- consignment door to door involving the full range of removalist services.

The overall service has a physical component, which includes the packing of items in boxes, trunks, cartons and containers for security and protection against damage.

Modes of transportation to and from Australia are shipping and air transport. With the exception of the Australia–New Zealand link, air transport involves a very large premium in return for speed of delivery. To frequently serviced areas such as Europe, the UK, Japan and west coast USA, furniture movement occurs within a three- to six-week period. Frequent services operate within the Asian region and movements take from two to three weeks. Less frequently serviced ports may take three or even four months for movement of goods.

## EXPORT MARKET CHARACTERISTICS

The market is segmented by direction of flow (export or import), country of origin and destination, customer (who pays) and the size of the consignment. Export market segments are as follows:

- The largest market is made up of Britons moving to the UK for a minimum two-year period.

- The next significant sector is composed of ethnic groups, being mainly Greek, Italian and Maltese. The market also includes Australians moving overseas for an extended period.

- A much smaller segment is made up of Northern Europeans, North Americans and minority groups such as Asians, Israelis and South Americans.

- The corporate market is a major sector composed of large multinational mining, manufacturing and services corporations transferring executives between countries.

- The government market segment includes contract arrangements with the Australian government and foreign embassies for the storage and movement of public servants' household effects.

- Another form of segmentation is in terms of the size of job and the packing requirements. A specific feature of the ethnic markets is that of self-packing. Traditionally, the non-ethnic markets have packed personal effects only, leaving the packing of breakable items and furniture to the moving company.

- There are some small segments that require highly

specialised packing of items having great value, such as antique furniture and musical equipment.

## IMPORT MARKET CHARACTERISTICS

The same segments apply in the import market as in the export market. In addition, segmentation occurs on an overseas source country basis with specific reference to the overseas agents in each country. The main sources of supply of import business are:

- *household-paid moves*: Britain, Greece, Italy, the countries of former Yugoslavia, Malta, New Zealand, South Africa, Hong Kong, Malaysia and Singapore;
- *corporate moves*: USA, Japan, Hong Kong, UK and Europe.

The market can also be segmented on the basis of moving industry structure in overseas countries. For instance, the American international moving industry is dominated by a small number of large companies which consolidate the moves of small moving companies and control the exports and imports of the industry. Close alignment with one of these large movers is necessary to receive any consignments from the USA. The South African industry is similar. The EU countries, however, have moving industries composed of a few large companies and many small ones. Hong Kong and Singapore are dominated by three or four companies. If an Australian mover does not have its own overseas office and depot it relies for its imports on links with these overseas movers.

## THE EXPORT/IMPORT LINK

Where two-way traffic exists between two countries the main method of deriving supports is through reciprocation. In the British and European markets reciprocal arrangements are agreed between the Australian removalist and their overseas agent, and consignments flow accordingly. Where there is a one-way flow, as with Hong Kong and South Africa in the late eighties and into the nineties, the movers in those countries chose their Australian agents on the basis of service and clearance rates.

## METHODS OF OBTAINING BUSINESS

The main method of securing export business is by referral and through inquiries from *Yellow Pages* advertising. Only Grace Movers has engaged in consistent media advertising to maintain its market position. Wridgeways and Pickfords have periodic media campaigns.

All large, long-established movers are members of the national and international industry associations. These hold annual conferences and provide a venue for keeping contact and preserving industry standards and methods. To be a member of the 'club' is to be accepted as a legitimate operator in the market. None of the small removalists is a member of the international association.

## THE ENTRY OF FAST FORWARD REMOVALS

Fast Forward Removals (FFR) entered the international removals market in Sydney in 1985 and started operations in Melbourne in 1990. At that time this segment was dominated by Grace Movers, 'The Professionals', with around 40% of the national market (both export and import). Other significant companies were Wridgeways (Sydney-based) and Downards (Melbourne-based). FFR quickly became established in servicing the ethnic markets, in particular the Greek, Italian and Asian communities.

By 2007 FFR dominated the ethnic markets and employed 50 people in Sydney and 30 in Melbourne, as well as a large group of owner–driver contractors. It had obtained reciprocal arrangements with Greek, Italian and Asian agents who consigned household removals from their respective countries to FFR in Australia, thus providing an import market to FFR. It had also developed the skills of operating in a very price-sensitive marketplace.

It had evaluated various overseas markets to determine the potential for expanding its import business—Hong Kong, Britain, Southern Europe and the USA. In all markets except the USA it had very strong relationships with overseas agents which provided a steady stream of import business. It now wanted to strengthen its imports business by establishing a presence in the USA, a market with great potential for the movement of executives and their families to Australia, but a market in which FFR was weak.

## SITUATION ANALYSIS

The starting point for any international marketing plan is to engage in a detailed situation analysis covering the overall business environment, market analysis, competitor analysis, the organisation's resources and capabilities, and a SWOT analysis.

### Business environment

The following is a summary of the key aspects of the business environment that will have an impact on FFR's operations in the USA.

### Social and cultural factors

In the USA business is conducted differently from the way it is conducted in Australia: the Americans tend to approach business in an aggressive, sales-oriented way; frequently relationships are transitory; while open and frank in terms of their sales approach, it is not always easy to penetrate the surface; and business is also often approached with much persistence and dedication, typical of the American entrepreneurial spirit and work commitment. Americans like Australians and see them as people with whom they have a lot in common. However, America, like most countries in the northern hemisphere, considers Australia to be a country that is not 'top of the American mind'. Americans think 'big' in terms of doing business in line with the size of their market and the mass market volume culture that exists for most products and services provided in the US marketplace.

### Technological factors

Advances in communications technology will have an impact on client communication, customer service and potential new services in this industry and are available to all players at relatively low cost. Technology available for storage and logistics is unlikely to have significant impact in terms of change in this industry in the next three years.

### Political and legal factors

The political environment in the USA has polarised voters and many Americans are looking at alternative countries like Canada as a place to reside. This is expected to make Australia a more attractive place to live and work for Americans. The legal environment is expected to affect this industry through stricter documentation and delays in wharf clearances due to tighter security.

### Demographics

The biggest group of international travellers are located on the west and east coasts of the USA. The major cities of California as well as New York, Boston, Philadelphia and Chicago are large centres of multinational corporations and mobile executives.

### Economic factors

The USA has experienced mixed economic conditions in different parts of the country since 11 September 2001. Commitments to defence spending, homeland security and its foreign policies will continue to place burdens on the US economy over the next few years. In 2007 the US economy was experiencing slow growth.

### Market analysis

### The product market

FFR's international moving services will be similar to those offered by its US-based competitors—removal quotations, packing, storage, shipment, relocation advice. In the USA FFR will be operating in the international relocation market in which relocation agents offer a much wider range of services including advice on housing, schooling and services relevant to all of the challenges faced by relocating executives and their families.

### Market characteristics and forecasts

Americans live in a service-oriented society with all of the modern-day conveniences and they typically expect a high level of service. The corporate market of relocating executives expects top service and companies are prepared to pay for it. This will vary from large multinational corporations that continuously relocate their executives around the world to SMEs in which budgets are smaller and executive relocation occurs sporadically.

### Distribution and pricing trends

The relocation industry in the USA is dominated by a few large van lines which consolidate the shipments of hundreds of small local moving companies. It is an industry of specialisation in which businesses focus on a specific service and geographic location. The industry is very price competitive as commoditisation has occurred and prices and margins are continually under pressure due to low barriers to entry and exit.

### Positioning

The relocation service is a 'trust' business as individuals part with their most valuable belongings and hope that they will arrive at the destination undamaged and on time. FFR will need to establish trust as well as a differential value in the minds of its target market.

### Market segments and needs

The two main segments for the service are citizens that are relocating privately and executives that are being relocated by their companies.

Different marketing mixes are required for both the private citizen and the corporate executive. The private citizen will be influenced by referrals that imply trust, perceived service quality, price, reliability and flexibility of the mover. Price will be a more important factor than for the corporate executive (for whom the company pays), who will be focused on reputation, full range of services, perception of customer 'care', quality and reliability.

### Competitor analysis

FFR would be competing against both small and large firms that are well established in the relocation business. These competitors will have local knowledge, specialised expertise and many will have a long-standing track record of success. A large number of competitors operate in each of the main cities of the USA. In San Francisco and San Jose, which bound the Silicon Valley corridor in the 'Bay area', a potential target market for FFR, a long list can be found on the web from a Google search.

### Organisational resources and capabilities
#### Financial capabilities

FFR is a small to medium-sized, family-owned business with financial limitations. But its profit growth in recent years has given it a strong financial foundation. FFR's Australian-based business is strong and it has the financial resources to fund a highly focused US expansion in one geographic area of the USA. The previous three financial years FFR has achieved a net profit in excess of $500 000. However, it has a small management team and will be stretched by relocating a senior executive to head up the American business and it will be operating on a limited budget.

#### Research capabilities

Much of the research required for setting up in the USA will come from external assistance. FFR has made contact with the Australian Trade Commission in San Francisco and will be taking advantage of its available databases and experience. Austrade has also compiled a detailed guide for doing business in California with a list of organisations that can assist—legal, accounting, finance and information.

#### Capacity

FFR will need to establish outsourcing arrangements and alliances to create the capacity required to handle the potential business if it is successful. This will take several months to arrange a full capability in providing moving and relocation services.

#### Management skills

One of FFR's limitations is the lack of international market experience of its senior managers. It plans to use the government assistance programs to make up skill deficiencies.

#### Promotional materials

FFR already maintains point-of-sale materials and other promotional materials in the Australian market. It will need new material for use in export markets such as the USA.

### SWOT analysis

Analysis of the situation supported by detailed information (usually contained in appendices to the plan) enables executives to develop an assessment of company strengths, weakness, opportunities and threats. To be useful, these should be a short list of key factors which need to be used to advantage or addressed in the plan. The SWOT summary for FFR is noted below:

* *Strengths*: innovative, flexible, responsive, knowledgeable on Australian conditions and relocation environment, experience in the physical moving process;

* *Weaknesses*: financial, management, general resources, lack of connections and knowledge of the US market;

* *Opportunities*: the US market has large potential for future revenue and profit; alliances with other relocation service providers can widen its services for its existing Australian market as well as its new marketplace;

* *Threats:* many established and expert competitors, lack of understanding and experience of the legal and cultural environment in the USA.

# Evaluation of alternative marketing strategies

Formulation and evaluation of marketing strategies requires a clear and detailed understanding of the overseas market's segmentation structure and the opportunities for valued differentiation and unique positioning. Segmentation should be founded first on need differences between customer groups which then may be reflected in particular positioning strategies. Sometimes need differences are mirrored by different demographics, geographic locations and distribution channels.

# SEGMENTING INTERNATIONAL MARKETS

Few companies have the resources to operate in all, or even most, of the countries around the world. Although some large companies, such as Coca-Cola, Nestlé and Ericsson, sell products in more than 150 countries, most Australian firms focus on a much smaller set. Operating in several countries presents new challenges. The different countries of the world, even those that are close together, can vary dramatically in their economic, cultural and political make-up. Thus, just as they do within their domestic markets, international firms need to group their world markets into segments with distinct buying needs and behaviours.

Companies can segment international markets using one or a combination of several variables. They can segment by geographic location, grouping countries by regions such as South-East Asia, Western Europe, North America, the Middle East or Africa. In fact, countries in many regions already have organised themselves geographically into market groups or free trade areas, discussed in Chapter 18. These associations reduce trade barriers between member countries, creating larger and more homogeneous markets.

Geographic segmentation assumes that nations close to one another will have many common traits and behaviours. Although this is often the case, there are many exceptions. For example, although the USA and Canada have much in common, both differ culturally and economically from neighbouring Mexico. Even within a region, consumers can differ widely. For example, until recently many international marketers thought that all Asian countries were the same. However, Indonesia is no more like the Philippines than Italy is like Sweden.

World markets can be segmented on the basis of economic factors. For example, countries might be grouped by population income levels or by their overall level of economic development. Some countries, such as the so-called Group of Eight—the USA, Britain, France, Germany, Japan, Canada, Russia and Italy—have established, highly industrialised economies. Other countries have newly industrialised or developing economies (Singapore, Taiwan, South Korea, Brazil and Mexico). Still others are less developed (China and India). A country's economic structure shapes its population's product and service needs and therefore the marketing opportunities it offers.

Countries can be segmented by political and legal factors such as the type and stability of government, receptivity to foreign firms, monetary regulations and the amount of bureaucracy. Such factors can play a crucial role in a company's choice of which countries to enter and how. Cultural factors also can be used, grouping markets according to common languages, religions, values and attitudes, customs and behavioural patterns.

Segmenting international markets on the basis of geographic, economic, political, cultural and other factors assumes that segments should consist of clusters of countries. However, many companies use a different approach, called intermarket segmentation. Using this approach, they form segments of consumers who have similar needs and buying behaviour even though they are located in different countries. For example, brand icons like Louis Vuitton target the world's affluent, regardless of their country. And Coca-Cola uses ads filled with kids, sports and rock music to target the world's teenagers.

Similarly, an agricultural chemicals manufacturer like Incitec (owned by Orica), based in Queensland, might focus on small farmers in a variety of developing countries: whether from Thailand or Indonesia or Kenya or India small farmers have common needs and behaviour patterns. Most of them till the land using bullock carts and have very little cash to buy agricultural inputs. They lack the education to appreciate fully the value of using fertiliser and depend on government help for such things as seeds, pesticides and fertiliser. They acquire farming needs from local suppliers and rely on word of mouth to learn and accept new things and ideas. Thus, even though these farmers are in different countries, perhaps continents apart, and even though they speak different languages and have different cultural backgrounds, they may represent a homogeneous market segment.

## EMERGING BASES OF GLOBAL SEGMENTATION

Global market segmentation can be defined as country groups, or individual consumer groups across countries, that contain potential customers with homogenous attributes and similar buying behaviour.

Countries can be segmented by diffusion patterns. Some countries are fast adopters of a product, like Australia is with consumer electronics, while others require a long period to adopt a product. In response to this a business could launch its products in countries that are innovators and later in those countries that are imitators or lag countries. So instead of using macro-variables to classify countries a firm could segment on the basis of new product diffusion patterns. Usually diffusion patterns in countries differ by product, as shown in Figure 8.3, which illustrates the order and grouping of countries according to adoption–diffusion (Kumar et al. 1998).

Consumers in lag countries may learn from the product experience of lead countries, resulting in a faster diffusion rate in lag markets. So lag countries that show strong learning ties with lead countries would indicate a sequential entry strategy that speeds up the diffusion in lag countries.

The maxim of 'think globally, act locally' also applies to market segmentation. Having identified and grouped countries according to adoption and diffusion patterns, it is important to look at local differences. Here a multidimensional segmentation approach is useful and more feasible for planning strategy and executing tactics. A segmentation scheme that accounts for the three dimensions—*needs*, *means* and *desires*—is particularly useful in international marketing. For example, a potential buyer in Japan may *need* a reliable vehicle to carry two adults and one child, may have the *means* to afford a vehicle in the $20 000–$25 000 range and *desire* unique styling. Another buyer may have the *need* for a vehicle to carry small loads, the *means* to spend $10 000–$15 000 and the *desire* for a working vehicle image (Neal and Wurst 2001). These emerging forms of segmentation provide further options for the international marketer to understand market potential better and plan marketing strategy.

## FIGURE 8.3  Segments based on diffusion patterns

### Product categories

| Segment | DVD player | Video cameras | Mobile phones | Personal computers |
|---------|------------|---------------|---------------|--------------------|
| 1 | Germany, UK, France | Belgium, Denmark, Spain | Sweden, Norway | Germany, UK, France |
| 2 | Spain, Austria, Finland | Russia, Hungary, Austria | Finland, France | Norway, Austria |
| 3 | Poland, Greece, Swizerland | Germany, UK, France | Germany, UK, Italy, Hungary | Poland, Italy, Hungary |

**SOURCE:** *Adapted from Kumar, V., Ganesh, J. and Echambadi, R. (1998) 'Cross-national diffusion research: what do we know and how certain are we?',* Journal of Product Innovation Management, *Vol. 15, No. 33, pp. 255–68.*

# MARKET POSITIONING FOR INTERNATIONAL MARKETS

Once a company has decided which segments of the market it will enter it must decide which 'positions' it wants to occupy in those segments.

**What is market positioning?** Product position is the way the product's important attributes are defined by consumers—the place the product occupies in consumers' minds relative to competing products. Thus, Porsche is positioned as an elite performance sports car, BMW is positioned on prestige and 'sheer driving pleasure', Mercedes and Lexus are positioned on luxury, Holden Commodore is positioned as Australia's own car, Nissan is positioned on reliability and Subaru is positioned on value for money. Van Pham (2006) conducted a study of products originating from 18 countries and identified country of origin and country of assembly as important positioning attributes.

Consumers are overloaded with information about products and services. They cannot re-evaluate products every time they make a buying decision. To simplify buying decision making they organise products into categories—they 'position' products, services and companies in their minds. A product's position is the complex set of perceptions, impressions and feelings that consumers hold for the product compared with competing products. The international marketer should plan positions that will give their firm's products the greatest advantage in selected target markets, and then design marketing mixes to create the planned positions. International Highlight 8.1 shows the integral link between segment selection and market positioning and the importance of international marketing planning in achieving a desired future position.

**Positioning strategies** Marketers can follow several positioning strategies (Rangan et al. 1992). These can be best illustrated with reference to well-known world brands. They can position their products on specific product attributes—Daihatsu advertises its low price; Saab and Peugeot promote on the basis of performance. Products can be positioned on the needs they fill or on the benefits they offer—Colgate Fluorigard toothpaste reduces cavities; Aim tastes good. Or products can be positioned according to usage occasions—in the summer Gatorade can be positioned as a beverage for replacing athletes' body fluids; in the winter it can be positioned as the drink to use when the doctor recommends plenty of liquids. Another approach is to position the product for certain classes of users—Johnson & Johnson improved the market share for its baby shampoo by repositioning the product as one for adults who wash their hair frequently and need a gentle shampoo—they even added a variant with conditioner to reinforce this point.

A product can also be positioned directly against a competitor. For example, in advertisements for its printers Lexmark has at times directly compared its products with Hewlett-Packard. It even supplies printer consumables like toner cartridges specifically for HP printers, thus aligning itself very closely with the market leader. In its famous 'We're number two, so we try harder' campaign, Avis successfully positioned itself against the larger Hertz.

Finally, the product can be positioned for different product classes. For example, some margarines are positioned against butter, others against cooking oils. Camay hand soap is positioned with bath oils rather than with soap. Marketers often use a combination of these positioning strategies. Thus, Johnson & Johnson's Affinity shampoo is positioned as a hair conditioner for women over 40 (product class and user). It is important to understand that these positionings can differ in different cultures due to history, indigenous competitive entries and cultural context.

***Choosing and implementing a positioning strategy*** Some firms find it easy to choose their positioning strategy. For example, a firm that is well known for quality in certain segments

# *Pecunia non olet*—or does it? (Latin for 'money does not smell')

Think carefully about your international success—failure is coming to your neighbourhood.

In his song 'Get Your Mind Right Mami', American rapper Jay Z extols the benefits of drinking Belvedere Polish vodka, known in the USA as 'Belve'. In the West this vodka is considered a luxury good. For this product positioning the manufacturer paid the rapper, hoping for an increase in sales. In the meantime, with the same rapper, the French champagne manufacturer Cristal is embroiled in a bitter battle to shake off the association with his type of clientele. As a result sales of this luxury champagne have significantly diminished in the world of 'hip-hop'.

A good marketing effort and planning becomes paramount in the international arena if any brand is to build a longer lasting and profitable presence, and avoid bad positioning.

International manufacturers of luxury goods are trying to sever their connections and prefer lower profits but maintenance of their status, rather than elevated popularity amongst what they consider to be 'less desired social classes'.

The American agency Brandstand calculated that last year alone Cristal champagne was one of the names most sung about, alongside Mercedes Benz, Louis Vuitton and Cadillac. At the Golden Globe party alone, in excess of two million dollars worth of Cristal champagne was consumed. However, as a result of this 'marketing success' many corporations are turning away from Cristal, not wanting to create associations with the rap scene. Cristal is stretching its public relations muscle to the fullest, believing that its brand is losing its premium status.

The result of bad association was clearly evident with the Burberry clothing icon. Its profits have risen for many years by as much as 38%. But in 2001, instead of celebrating their marketing planning success the corporate board was close to a nervous breakdown. Put simply, Burberry had become the preferred brand for hooligans and gangs. Although these gang members could not afford a coat in the famous checked pattern, they could quite easily afford accessories such as baseball caps. An extreme case of bad association happened in the British town of Sunderland where gangsters called themselves the 'Burberry Boys' and, wearing Burberry baseball caps, attacked Turkish immigrants. This bad association and extensive press coverage of this incident resulted in immediate withdrawal from sales of low-cost accessories. This situation had never been envisaged in Burberry's marketing planning and positioning strategy.

A similar move was executed by the French Connection UK, 'FCUK', which now is seen as a cheap and distasteful brand. In 2005 its sales plummeted, and now FCUK is on the brink of bankruptcy. But clients do not have to come from an 'undesirable' group to create problems for luxury brands—there could be simply too many customers. This is exactly what Louis Vuitton (LV) faced. For the past few years this brand became very visible and a desired brand of clothing and accessories. In Japan, for example, almost 50% of young Japanese women aspired to and then purchased an LV handbag. As a result LV saw its brand losing its prestige status and thus its market positioning. This was coupled with the growing counterfeit production and sales of aspirational brands in South-East Asian 'flea markets'. Now LV says that, as a part of their newly forged marketing planning strategy, no longer will money be the key obstacle in purchasing LV bag. Now LV asks potential new clients for references from existing clients before they can 'sign up' as clients. Another result is that many genuine clients are walking away from them, not only from fear that someone will judge them to be wearing a 'fake' item, but also because when they pay tens of thousands of dollars for an item, they want it to remain elite.

In a different industry, premium home builders in USA and Europe are now more frequently selecting 'desirable' applicants as acceptable potential apartment buyers for prestige buildings. Now the selection criteria include occupation, heritage, marital status, and even as far as the type of a car owned.

Companies need to think carefully when expanding both physically and through brand positioning, as the sales success can cost them dearly in their local and global markets.

SOURCES: <http://www.wprost.pl/tygodnik/?I=1243>, accessed 15 March 2007; <http://www.burberry.com; http://www.belvederevodka.com>; and <http://www.news.bbc.co.uk/1/low/entertainment/5086482.stm>.

will usually go for this position in an overseas market segment if it sees enough buyers seeking quality. But, in many cases, two or more firms will go after the same position. Then, each will have to find other ways to set itself apart, such as promising 'high quality for a lower cost' or 'high quality with more technical service'. That is, each firm must differentiate its offer by building a unique bundle of competitive advantages that appeal to a substantial group within the segment.

A simplified summary of the issues relating to segmentation and positioning as well as marketing mix strategy alternatives for Fast Forward Removals is provided in Case Example 8.2. In this example the firm is focusing just on one country market—the USA.

---

CASE EXAMPLE 8.2

### ALTERNATIVE MARKET ENTRY STRATEGIES

There are three basic types of successful patterns for entry into the US relocation market:

1 using a US agent and developing reciprocation agreement on Australian–US removals between the two countries. This is what FFR currently does in other overseas locations;

2 setting up a US sales office and aligning with other companies in the industry to provide a range of moving and relocation services;

3 setting up a US business with all its own facilities to provide services to the market.

The last option is not available to FFR in the short term simply because of insufficient financial and management resources. Setting up a US sales office and a network of service providers is the preferred option.

### ALTERNATIVE TARGET MARKET AND SEGMENTATION STRATEGY

The two main international removal markets are the corporate market and the consumer (self-paid) market. There are many subsegments within each market with different value requirements and purchasing behaviour. There are also different geographic markets within the USA which FFR will need to decide upon as targets. The most appropriate segmentation form for FFR will be determined by current market structure, scope of operations and changing consumer needs. After an evaluation of the alternatives and the attractiveness of different segments the company has decided to locate its sales office in Silicon Valley, California,

to target initially the relocation market of private citizens and executives and their companies currently located in the 'Bay' area of San Francisco.

### ALTERNATIVE POSITIONING STRATEGY

The positioning strategy will need to be chosen according to the specific target market selected and will differ according to the existing established competitors' positionings. Once selected it will need to be focused and consistent for relevant targets due to FFR's limited resources and scope.

### ALTERNATIVE MARKETING MIX STRATEGIES

• *Distribution*: FFR has to consider alternative sales channels to its target market. Should it look for one or two large channels to market or a large number of small agents to access customers or should it go direct to end customers?

• *Price*: The price structure will depend on the type of sales channel used, whether through intermediaries or direct to end customers.

• *Product*: Alternative service ranges can be considered, from a narrow range of removal services to a full range of relocation services.

• *Promotion*: The company will need to reassess its promotional strategies, communication media and materials for the US market. The quality and form of communication will depend on the target market selected. FFR will need to determine its priorities in terms of awareness creation and positioning communications.

# Corporate objectives

A firm's corporate objectives usually include a mission statement and objectives reflecting financial growth, new business and new markets. As far as possible these should be measurable so that progress can be assessed over time. FFR's mission statement and objectives can be found in Case Example 8.3.

---

## CASE EXAMPLE 8.3

### MISSION STATEMENT

FFR's mission is to provide a worry-free, high-quality moving service for people wanting to relocate internationally, at competitive prices, to its customers' complete satisfaction, while providing its staff with a safe, healthy and fulfilling working environment.

### CORPORATE OBJECTIVES

The major objectives to be achieved by FFR in the next three years include:

- successful development of the US market as a springboard for development in other international markets;

- sales increase of 20% per annum, through the market share growth of selected Australian market segments and the development of the US import market through its US base;

- net profit to increase from 10% to 12% of sales in 2008 and 2009.

### CORPORATE STRATEGY

The broad corporate strategies suggest how the corporate objectives will be achieved:

- *Development of international import markets*: Management and marketing resources will be added to support focused market strategies through new sales offices first in the USA then in other targeted overseas markets.

- *Steady sales growth*: An improved aggressive marketing strategy for export and import markets will include the development and implementation of relevant promotional materials for foreign markets, improved and more direct sales force efforts, development of new alliance partners and ongoing investigation and further development of overseas markets.

- *Net profit increase*: The combined strategies of sales growth, capacity utilisation, productivity improvements and gross margin maintenance will result in profit increases to achieve objectives.

---

# Marketing objectives and strategy

Marketing objectives and strategy may address all the firm's markets or focus on individual priority markets. In Case Example 8.4 the objectives and strategy focus on FFR's American market. This includes marketing objectives, target markets, positioning and the marketing mix.

---

## CASE EXAMPLE 8.4

### MARKETING OBJECTIVES

The fragmented nature of the US market and the large number of competitive suppliers suggest realistic marketing objectives as follows:

- achieve brand awareness in the target market of 5% at end of year 1, 10% at end of year 2 and 15% at the end of year 3;

- achieve market share of the targeted US–Australia removal market of 1% at end of year 1, 3% at end of year 2 and 5% at the end of year 3;

- gain two new Silicon Valley-based large corporate customers by the end of year 1, five large corporate customers by year 2 and 10 large corporate customers by year 3.

## TARGET MARKETS

FFR has chosen to target large multinational companies with head offices or large branch offices located in the Silicon Valley area of California. Primary targets would be corporations like Hewlett-Packard, IBM, Apple, Oracle, Cisco, Dell and ChevronTexaco. Secondary targets would be identified Australian companies operating in the 'Bay' area.

Research shows that there are more than 100 large multinationals with head offices or large branch offices in the targeted geographic area.

## MARKET POSITIONING

FFR positioning will be to 'provide a fast, efficient, knowledgeable moving service to Australia providing a full range of relocation services'. Its service will target the quality- and service-sensitive corporate market.

## MARKETING MIX

The marketing mix strategy for the US market will require some new services to be provided by new alliance partners to be established by FFR:

- *Product*: The service range includes the normal full service removal plus relocation advice provided by an aligned relocation specialist operating in the USA and Australia. A new innovative service will be provided by FFR using the internet to advise which household items the consumer may want to sell before leaving the USA and the cost of replacing them in Australia.

- *Distribution*: The company will use direct selling as its sale channel to the large multinationals as well as alignment with a locally based relocation specialist to gain entry to the corporate human resource departments of its target customers.

- *Pricing*: FFR aims to position its comparative price at the middle of the price range to appear to be competitively priced. Additional services such as its internet service will be priced separately as an add-on service, but at an attractive price positioned around the savings from sale and repurchase of household items.

- *Promotion*: Promotion of its US–Australia service includes:

  - qualified sales calls working with aligned relocation specialist and leads gained from membership of Australian-American Association in San Francisco;

  - participating in relevant industry forums to connect with other complementary service providers in the relocation and removal market;

  - advertising in targeted trade magazines that reach the human resource managers of multinationals in the 'Bay' area;

  - attending relevant San Francisco area Austrade functions to make contact with Australian businesses in the region;

  - creating a promotional video showing Sydney and Melbourne FFR stores, bond facilities and vehicles as well as location views of living conditions in Australia.

The promotional strategy needs to be dynamic and flexible responding to the changing level of experience in the US market.

# Economic evaluation

An economic evaluation of an international marketing strategy includes planning assumptions underpinning the logic of the plan, sales and costs forecasts, break-even analysis and sensitivity analysis to establish financial benchmarks and consequences of alternative possible outcomes. A summary of these is provided in Case Example 8.5 for illustrative purposes for Fast Forward Removals relevant to the US market. Detailed financial analysis would normally be contained in an appendix to the marketing plan.

# Implementation and control

## ACTION PLANS FOR IMPLEMENTATION

**Action program** Marketing strategies should be turned into specific action programs that answer the following questions: What will be done? When will it be done? Who is responsible

## PLANNING ASSUMPTIONS

- Growth in the US–Australia relocation market will continue at the same rate as the previous two years.

- There will be no new revolutionary technologies or products in the next three years.

- Sales forecasts for pessimistic, realistic and optimistic volumes are relevant to the current economic conditions and competitive structure.

- Profit and loss forecasts are based on costs and margins ratios for the current financial year ending 2006–07, and include all relevant costs for entry into the US market.

- Staff can be added and trained in the USA within three months of initial demand increase.

## FORECAST SALES AND COSTS

From research conducted the following points have arisen:

- The initial FFR sales office will be staffed by a manager/salesperson supported by a logistics person, and a quotation salesperson. This three-person team will be supported by outsourced services providing office administration, legal and accounting.

- It is unlikely FFR will generate substantial sales from its entry into the market in the first year, as the product and promotional materials will need to be diffused and contacts made. It is also expected that the sales cycle to gain a new corporate customer could be as long as six months.

- Market share is likely to be low for some time until the market becomes aware of the FFR brand and services and adopts them; and

- US sales are subjective estimates based on business and market research. Below are the profit forecasts for the first three years of operation in the US market.

| Profit (Loss) | Pessimistic | Likely | Optimistic |
|---|---|---|---|
| First year | ($100 000) | ($50 000) | $50 000 |
| Second year | ($0) | $50 000 | $100 000 |
| Third year | $50 000 | $250 000 | $500 000 |

## BREAK-EVEN ANALYSIS

It is expected that a minimum of $300 000 will be spent initially in entering the US market. This cost includes travel, promotional materials, wages and other costs. Calculations result in at least $750 000 in sales needed to break even. This falls between the likely and optimistic sales positions. Many of the costs will be incurred in initially entering the market, and the second year of trading will have lower costs and increased sales. Analysis confirms that entry into the US market requires a long-term financial commitment.

## SENSITIVITY ANALYSIS

Sensitivity analysis provides 'what if' scenarios based on possible change in variables affecting revenues and costs. Some of the volatile variables to be tested include currency fluctuations, product prices, sales variations and competitor impacts on market share.

Other factors affecting sales and profit sensitivity are supply delays, loss of an alliance partner, and changes in economic conditions affecting relocation. Contingency plans will need to be developed to deal with any of these situations.

---

for doing it? How much will it cost? For example, the international marketer may regard sales promotion as a key strategy for winning market share. A sales promotion action plan should be drawn up to outline special offers and their dates, trade shows entered, new point-of-purchase displays and other promotions. The action plan shows when activities will be started, reviewed and completed.

**Budgets** Action plans allow the manager to make a supporting marketing budget that is essentially a projected profit and loss statement (statement of financial performance). For revenues, it shows the forecasted number of units that would be sold and the average net price. On the expense side, it shows the cost of production, distribution and marketing. The difference is the projected profit. Senior management will review the budget and either approve or modify it. Once approved, the budget is the basis for materials buying, production scheduling, personnel planning and marketing operations.

**Marketing implementation** Planning good strategies is only a start toward successful marketing. A brilliant marketing strategy counts for little if the company fails to implement it properly. Marketing implementation is the process that turns marketing strategies and plans into marketing actions in order to accomplish strategic marketing objectives. Implementation involves day-to-day, month-to-month activities that put the marketing plan to work effectively. Whereas marketing planning addresses the what and why of marketing activities, implementation addresses the who, where, when and how.

Successful implementation depends on several key elements. First, it requires an action program that pulls all the people and activities together. Second, the company's formal organisational structure plays an important role in implementing its international marketing strategy. For instance, James Hardie Industries (JHI) is organised to operate in two main regions—the Asia–Pacific and North America. New international markets in the Asia–Pacific region are explored by a marketing network team made up of people from Australia, New Zealand and the Philippines. The infrastructure of JHI is much larger in the USA and international marketing opportunities in Europe and Latin America are initially explored from the USA before on-the-ground marketing people are placed in targeted countries. The corporate centre at Mission Viejo, California, guides and integrates the marketing strategies of the regions with overall corporate priorities and strategies. However, the structure used by JHI may not be right for other firms, and many have to change their structures as their strategies and situations change.

The company's decision and reward systems—operating procedures that guide planning, budgeting, compensation and other activities—also affect implementation. For example, if a company compensates managers for short-run results they will have little incentive to work toward long-run objectives. Effective implementation also requires careful human resources planning. At all levels, the company must fill its structure and systems with people who have the needed skills, motivation and personal characteristics. In recent years more and more companies have recognised that long-run human resources planning can give the company a strong competitive advantage. An international marketing plan will need to be supported by a commitment to training and development of required international experience. One of the constraints confronting TransGrid, a Sydney-based engineering consultancy, was the perception by prospective clients in various Asian markets of its limited international experience.

Finally, to be successfully implemented the firm's marketing strategies must fit with its company culture. Company culture is a system of values and beliefs shared by people in an organisation—the company's collective identity and meaning. International marketing strategies that do not fit in with the company's culture will be difficult to implement. Because company culture is so hard to change, companies usually design strategies that fit their current cultures rather than trying to change their styles and cultures to fit new strategies. However, the speed of change today may force companies to be more market focused, leading many more to tackle the big challenge of culture change.

A case in point is the current transformation of Apple from a specialist computer company to achieve its new positioning as a consumer electronics business.

## MONITORING OF ACTION PLAN

**Marketing control** Many surprises occur during the implementation of marketing plans requiring the international marketer to practise ongoing marketing control. This involves evaluating the results of marketing strategies and plans and taking corrective action to ensure that objectives are attained. Performance in the marketplace is measured against objectives and the causes of any differences between expected and actual performance are evaluated. Corrective action to close the gaps between objectives and results may require changing the marketing action programs or even changing the objectives.

The purpose of control is to ensure that the company achieves the sales, profits and other objectives set out in its international marketing plan (see Case Example 8.6).

---

**CASE EXAMPLE 8.6**

### CONTROL MECHANISMS

Fast Forward Removals has developed detailed action plans supporting all elements of the marketing mix including the timing of market entry activities, distributor appointments and shipping schedules to penetrate the US market. An initial export marketing organisation structure has been established with sufficient people and resources to action its international marketing plan.

Performance measures and monitoring systems have been specifically designed to assist the export division to manage the new export business and control activities and expenses. These details are contained in appendices to the plan with a one- to two-page summary of important milestones included in the main planning document.

---

## CHALLENGES TO INTERNATIONAL MARKETING PLANNING

Several weaknesses in international marketing planning are common among Australian companies attempting market expansion overseas.

Many international marketing plans lack market reality. International marketing managers and product managers are frequently too removed from the overseas marketplace to maintain a handle on what is really happening in fast-changing environments. This can be rectified with a commitment to extracting timely and relevant market information and use of appropriate interpretive tools. However, often this is hard to get in Asian countries and it is necessary to maintain an ongoing on-the-spot presence. Nothing beats face-to-face contact with intermediate and end customers. For instance, the James Hardie marketing manager for Latin America, based in Southern California, made more than 15 visits to talk to distributors and customers in a six-month period to keep in touch with the fast-changing events and markets in that region.

International marketing plans are often not integrated into the overall strategies of the business and corporate hierarchy. This is because of lack of clear vision or understanding at various levels of the strategic priorities about how various product initiatives and functional strategies fit. Where there is a lot of planning done at each level there can be misunderstanding to the point where each level prepares a full plan with either different or conflicting plans, where one level's vision is translated to another level's objectives and then to a lower level's tasks or operations. This can be resolved with a clear strategic planning framework providing a logical fit for the initiatives at various levels. The framework provided earlier in this chapter is a useful starting point.

There is often a lack of financial integration with international marketing at the business strategy level. This is because the disciplines of financial analysis and marketing analysis have not been effectively brought together to develop business strategies. Financial analysts too frequently do not understand market realities and uncertainties, while marketing analysts have limited experience in evaluating the financial impacts of proposed international marketing strategies.

Too much emphasis is given to 'the plan' document rather than the international marketing planning process. Stories abound of plans evaluated on the basis of size or weight ('It must weigh at least 5 kilos to pass the test!'), coloured pictures or politically correct contents ('That's what I want to hear!'). An international marketing plan should be concise, clear and directional and weigh 5 grams, not 5 kilos.

Team involvement in the international marketing planning process is often lacking. Again, too much emphasis on the 'the plan' document occurs without attention to the process. In the end a plan developed but not implemented due to lack of support or understanding is a waste of resources. Those who need to support the plan in terms of resource allocation or through implementation roles need to be 'involved' and 'own' it in a commitment sense. This problem is endemic in organisations where objectives and priorities are unclear or conflicting divisional objectives are allowed to continue unresolved.

Traditional strategic planning does not take sufficient account of the role of key external relationships in improving competitive position. Strong relationships with key suppliers, distributors and alliance partners may lead to higher quality products and services and superior distribution/delivery systems.

A series of systematic interrelated steps is crucial in effectively formulating and implementing international marketing strategies. This reduces the risk of leaving out key issues and people, and highlights the assumptions upon which strategies are based and resources committed. The example of Fast Forward Removals provides a detailed illustration.

In reality, organisations adopt a hybrid of management systems depending upon their size, diversity, position in the market and rate and type of external change. However, a generic series of steps in formulating and implementing international marketing strategies applies to all. The five steps discussed early in this chapter (see Figure 8.2) suggest a sequential process. In practice, the sequence will depend upon the organisation's current position in the market. For instance, a business's mission and vision may be well established and may require little development or review. If this is the case they will act as the foundation from which other steps emanate. Alternatively, a company may become lost in a sea of change and need to establish its mission. It would do this through strategic analysis and a review of its broad objectives against reality.

The challenge is to develop proactive strategies in the light of expected changes and adaptive strategies to confront unexpected changes.

Many of these challenges are faced by Nudie as it expands its export operations to South-East Asia, described in the opening part of this chapter, and also for The Wiggles, whose planned US market entry is described in International Highlight 8.2. As their success was achieved in the USA, the overall vision and strategy changed.

# PRACTICAL INTERNATIONAL MARKETING PLANNING

Developing international marketing strategies and plans often involves trade-offs in practice. The history of the firm, the relative importance of international markets, its competitive position and market trends in its home market all play a part and influence the approach taken. Three areas need to be considered: the starting point for international marketing planning, the inclusion of creative insight and the influence of management aspirations.

## 8.2 INTERNATIONAL HIGHLIGHT

# How to wiggle your way into new markets

Since their inception in 1991 The Wiggles have grown to become by far Australia's most successful children's entertainment group. With three of the original four band members having studied early childhood development at Sydney's Macquarie University, the group has managed to develop a unique style of entertainment using song, dance and the development of a number of characters such as 'Dorothy the Dinosaur'.

Much of their success has been due to their educationally sound practices which appeal to many parents wanting their children to be entertained but also to learn and develop. In addition to the content, the distinctive coloured skivvies that each of the band members wears has left a lasting impression on the children and provided a distinctive look.

This unique value proposition has allowed The Wiggles to also develop a following in overseas markets. Their approach has led them to three tours a year of the USA and two tours to the UK over the past 16 years.

The Wiggles originally worked with Gaffney International Licensing to launch their licensed products in Australia and overseas. In 1997 the group embarked on a movie venture, a follow-on to a number of successful video releases, as a way to gain more exposure in international markets. In fact if successful this would provide access to millions of children worldwide. The movie and videos turned out to be very successful extensions of their albums and songs but what became apparent was that live performances were the real drivers of word-of-mouth and that a local live presence would be necessary.

With this in mind The Wiggles' success in the US market started with an initial trip in 1998 to test the waters and perform at Disneyland and other amusement parks. While at one of their shows they were spotted by Hit Entertainment (home of *Bob the Builder, Barney* and other hit children's shows) who subsequently signed them up for video and music distribution in the USA.

Over the next few years The Wiggles' songs breached the

top 10 Amazon best selling list several times as The Wiggles momentum built. By the end of 2002 they had sold more than two and half million videos and albums and had just begun a season of shows running on the Disney channel which provided access to 79 million homes across the country.

The next steps for The Wiggles and their promoters Hit Entertainment are to capitalise on the lucrative merchandising markets as well as develop cross-promotional activities, such as point of sale in the Disney outlets to penetrate the US market further.

The Wiggles provide a fascinating example of how a great value proposition that is carefully targeted to a segment in one geographic market can be a fantastic success in other similar markets around the world. The Wiggles, with help from their business advisers and careful planning, developed the right strategy to wiggle into the biggest developed market of all.

The Wiggles have now developed a business that includes video, music, TV rights, live performances, franchises, Wiggly Play Centres and a 'Wiggles World' within the Dreamworld theme park on the Gold Coast in Queensland, as well as Wiggles Worlds in three Six Flags theme parks in the USA with more parks to roll out in the coming years.

In 2007 their sales of DVDs and videos alone was 22 million units. Sales of albums reached 5 million worldwide. According to *BRW* The Wiggles topped the list as the richest Australian entertainers in 2005 and 2006.

**SOURCES:** Urban, R., 'Wake up Jeff here comes Wiggles World', <http://www.smh.com.au/news/Arts/Wake-up-Jeff-here-comes-Wiggles-World/2005/04/12/1113251626812.html>, accessed 19 February 2007; 'Getting into the export driver's seat–the Wiggles', <http://www.theaustralian.news.com.au/story/0,20867,20599315-5000920,00.html>; <http://www.thewiggles.com.au/country/usa/usatour.html>, accessed 14 December 2004; McCormick, M. (2002) 'Wiggles working their way Into US', Billboard, Vol. 114, No. 6, p. 49; and Fitzgerald, M. (1997) 'Conquering the kids', Time Australia, Issue 51, p. 68. Image © 2007 The Wiggles Pty Ltd.

# Market-based and product-based planning

These are two approaches to practical marketing planning. The *market-based* approach proposed in this chapter is one which starts with an analysis of consumer needs. The service or product is then designed or adapted to those needs, and the strategies and marketing mix plans are developed accordingly.

This approach is most appropriate when a new product is being developed or the intention is to modify or adapt an existing product in line with overseas market needs. Positioning is a key consideration in the development of the marketing strategy and plans for the new product or service.

The *product/service-based* approach is the one which is most frequently encountered in practice. For example, it is not at all unusual to be facing the situation of 'a product searching for an overseas customer'. This situation also applies when the organisation's skills are limited (e.g. in the case of a personal services organisation such as a consultancy).

The international marketing planning approach in this case is to identify the target market segments as clearly as possible and to find these segments. The planning task is to develop appropriate programs (distribution, pricing and communications) to reach these segments and supply them as effectively and profitably as possible (market penetration). There will be an emphasis on tactical planning. Alternatively (or additionally) it may be necessary to identify segments which are currently not catered for (market development). However, in this case other organisations in the industry may be offering a similar service or product and all may be aiming at the same segment(s). Therefore, competition may be extreme and it may not be possible to supply to those segment(s) profitably.

The product/service-based approach should therefore be considered as a possible short-term planning and international marketing management approach, with a market-based approach being required in the longer term.

# Incorporating creative insight

One common reason or excuse given for not planning is that *the formality of carrying out the tasks and/or following a prescribed structure stifles creativity*. The challenge for the planner is to incorporate the creative insight and to identify a new or better way of doing international business.

There are ways of encouraging creativity. One approach is to question all key assertions and recommendations. Another is to discuss these areas with people with a different perspective, such as management staff or a consultant. It also helps to allow enough time in writing the plan to be able to reflect on and mull over the findings and conclusions. Leaving the writing of a report to the last minute and producing it in a rush is not conducive to creative thought.

Although lateral thinking is valuable it is not enough to base the plan on one idea which at first sight might appear to be brilliant. The idea or insight must be relevant and capable of being put into practice. It must enhance and strengthen other marketing mix elements and help to achieve the chosen objectives. It is therefore necessary to have a sound marketing analysis and clear objectives to provide the basis for evaluating the creative insight.

# The importance of management aspirations

The role of a chief executive is important in all organisations and is vital in small ones. Their personal aspirations, attitudes and expectations greatly influence the objectives, direction and activities of the organisation. Similarly, senior executives may have great influence in these important areas in the international marketing plan.

It is important for the marketing planner to understand these personal attitudes and aspirations, and to identify what drives the key influencers in the organisation. An international marketing plan which ignores this aspect may well be rejected as not 'fitting in' with the organisation. For example, the key executive(s) may have aspirations and expectations regarding the positioning and image of the organisation's product or service which are not matched by the view held by the consumer or customer in the firm's foreign markets.

The planner's task is first to take the time and effort to identify the key decision makers in the organisation and to understand their personal and management aspirations. The planner must then either make the executives understand the realities of the marketplace which may be unpalatable to them, or help the executives do the things they want to do as well as possible—if the marketplace allows this. Note that this situation is similar to the product-based approach to planning described above.

In the same vein, it is important for the international marketer to be familiar with the 'political' attitudes and factors within the organisation. These may result in some activities being accepted and others rejected. The achievability of a plan will therefore depend on these internal political influences and on minimising, avoiding or successfully countering conflict in this area.

## The internet and planning

Whether we are operating our SME in London, San Francisco, Hong Kong, Sydney or the Bahamas, the help of an international financial institution for business finance is essential for those businesses operating in several countries.

HSBC, the London-based international bank (<http://www.hsbc.com/>), has more than 5000 offices in 79 countries. However, much more than that it is one of the few banks that provide a seamless service for SMEs to conduct their banking globally. It provides a global internet-accessed service which enables SMEs to view all their bank accounts together, no matter in which country those accounts have been established, transfer funds between accounts of different currencies, conduct share trades on all the major stock markets and provide funding from Australia in US dollars and UK pounds at local country interest rates. This information and funding service enables SMEs to more efficiently engage in international financial planning and the resourcing of international marketing activities.

# Summary

Planning and strategy for international marketing follows a series of steps and processes which are practised by most successful international marketing firms. These include a systematic and detailed analysis of the external market environment and the internal capabilities of the firm, a clear understanding of alternatives, concise, measurable and well-communicated objectives and well thought-out marketing strategies supported by time-phased action plans and resource allocation. Financial evaluation leading to forecasts and budgets form the basis for monitoring performance and taking action to keep the business on target.

Tools such as scenario planning are now being used to build flexibility into both company response and planning processes and provide a context for international marketing planning.

The centrepiece of all international marketing planning should be detailed market analysis incorporating actionable market segmentation targets. Different approaches to segmentation should be evaluated before a segmentation scheme is settled upon. This leads to alternative choices for market positioning in the targeted overseas markets. An important part of planning for international markets is sales and cost forecasting, break-even and sensitivity analysis and a thorough evaluation of the financial consequences of missing sales targets.

The many practical issues to be considered in international marketing planning include the implementation of action plans, the management aspirations of the company, the extent to which the plan can be market based as distinct from product based and the integration of the plan with the rest of the business and its competencies.

## Definitions of strategic terms

*Action plan*: A division of the overall plan into implementable pieces of work along with all the other information (how, what, when, where, why, who) that a person being given accountability for the task will need in order to do the task and get the desired result.

*Mission*: The organisation's purpose statement.

*Objective*: A statement of what is going to be achieved, stated in a measurable (numeric) and time-specific way.

*Strategic planning*: A systematic methodology for charting the 'big issue' future of an organisation.

*Strategy*: A statement of how an objective is going to be achieved. One objective may have several strategies associated with its achievement. Strategies can cascade in hierarchies from a grand strategy, the overall 'means by which', down through successive layers to very specific 'means by which' statements. This is the hardest part, the least understood and potentially the most fruitful area.

*Vision*: A word picture of a desirable future state for an organisation in sufficient detail that readers can unambiguously understand and picture that future themselves.

SOURCE: *Adapted from Davies, M. (1995) 'Learning at work', unpublished paper, Robertson, Queensland.*

## ETHICS ISSUE

The international division of your company of which you are the manager has had several unsuccessful attempts at penetrating several Asian markets. Your board has asked you to submit a new international marketing plan. You know that this must show break-even results in year 1 and profit from year 2 onwards for it to be acceptable to the board or otherwise they will close your division resulting in the loss of your position and the jobs of your staff. Your investigations of the Asian markets clearly show that China is by far the best prospect for your company's products but the experience of almost all companies entering the Chinese market shows that break even is usually not possible until three or four years of operations in that market. You are firmly convinced that your company will achieve very large profits and sales in the Chinese market in the long term. As you are the only executive with international experience and your reputation is excellent with all the board members they will accept your recommendation.

***Would you fudge the figures to show profitability in the short term to save your division and your job from extinction? Or would you present a realistic plan showing losses in the short term and profits in the long term?***

## Websites

**Austrade** http://www.austrade.gov.au
**Avis** http://www.avis.com
**Colgate-Palmolive** vhttp://www.colgate.com
**Ericsson** http://www.ericsson.com.au
**Export Finance and Insurance Corporation** http://www.efic.gov.au
**Fujitsu** http://www.fujitsu.com.au
**Hertz** http://www.hertz.com.au
**Hewlett-Packard** http://www.hp.com
**HSBC** http://www.hsbc.com
**International Monetary Fund (IMF)** http://www.imf.org
**James Hardie Industries** http://www.jameshardie.com
**Japan External Trade Organization (JETRO)** http://www.jetro.go.jp
**Johnson & Johnson** http://www.jnj.com
**Lexmark** http://www.lexmark.com
**Matsushita Electric Industrial Co., Ltd** http://www.panasonic.net/index.html
**Motorola** http://www.motorola.com/
**Nokia** http://www.nokia.com.au
**Panasonic** http://www.panasonic.com.au
**Philips** http://www.philips.com
**Samsung** http://www.samsung.com.au
**Shell** http://www.shell.com/home/Framework?siteId=au-en
**TransGrid** http://www.tg.nsw.gov.au
**World Bank** http://www.worldbank.org

# Discussion questions

1   What is scenario planning? Under what conditions is it useful? How important do you think scenario planning is as a context for international marketing planning?

2   Which part of the international marketing plan do you believe is most important? Why?

3   What are the most important factors in segmenting international markets?

4   Discuss the concept of market positioning. How do Australian or New Zealand firms position their companies or products in overseas markets?

5   What are the major challenges faced by marketers in developing and implementing international marketing plans?

6   What are the practical internal issues to be addressed by marketers when developing an international marketing plan?

7   Airlines are considered to be truly global/international businesses. Visit the websites of Lufthansa, Qantas (or Air New Zealand) and another airline of your choice. Analyse their websites taking a perspective of an international (non-English-speaking) traveller and analyse which one of these websites is mostly geared to service such needs. What strategy should Qantas or Air New Zealand adopt to expand its international business?

8   What role can the internet play in facilitating the planning for international marketing?

# References

Brown, L. (1997) *Competitive Marketing Strategy*, 2nd edn, Nelson ITP, Melbourne.

Davies, M. (1995) 'Learning at work', unpublished paper, Robertson, Queensland.

Fitzgerald, M. (1997) 'Conquering the kids', *Time Australia*, No. 51, p. 68.

'Getting into the export driver's seat—the Wiggles', <http://www.theaustralian.news.com.au/story/0,20867,20599315-5000920,00.html>.

Howarth, B. (2003) 'Bells and whistles on the move', *Business Review Weekly*, 24 April, p. 74.

<http://www.abc.net.au/catapult/stories/s1259696.htm>, accessed 19 February 2007.

<http://www.marketingmag.com.au/index.php?option=com_content&task=view&id=645&Itemid=0>, accessed 19 February 2007.

<http://www.thewiggles.com.au/country/usa/usatour.html>, accessed 14 December 2004.

Kumar, V., Ganesh, J. and Echambadi, R. (1998) 'Cross-national diffusion research: what do we know and how certain are we?', *Journal of Product Innovation Management*, Vol. 15, No. 3, pp. 255–68.

McCormick, M. (2002) 'Wiggles working their way Into US', *Billboard*, Vol. 114, No. 6, p. 49.

Neal, W.D. and Wurst, J. (2001) 'Advances in market segmentation', *Marketing Research*, Vol. 13, pp. 14–19.

Rangan, V.K., Moriaty, R. and Swartz, G. (1992) 'Segmenting customers in mature industrial markets', *Journal of Marketing*, October, pp. 72–82.

Ross, E. and Holland A. (2004) *100 Great Businesses and the Minds behind Them*, Random House Australia, Sydney, p. 212.

Terpstra, V. and Sarathy, R. (1994) *International Marketing*, Dryden Press, New York.

Toyne, B. and Walters, P. (1993) *Global Marketing Management: A Strategic Perspective*, Allyn and Bacon, Division of Simon & Schuster Inc., Boston.

Urban, R., 'Wake up Jeff here comes Wiggles World', <http://www.smh.com.au/news/Arts/Wake-up-Jeff-here-comes-Wiggles-World/2005/04/12/1113251626812.html>, accessed 19 February 2007.

van der Heijden, K. (1996) *Scenarios: The Art of Strategic Conversation*, John Wiley, Chichester, England.

Van Pham, K.-Q. (2006), 'Strategic offshoring from a decomposed COO's perspective: a cross-regional study of four product categories', *Journal of American Academy of Business*, Vol. 8, No. 2, p. 59–66.

**go online**

Go online to <www.pearsoned.com.au/fletcher> to find more case studies.

CASE STUDY 8

# Planning your approach to capturing the Japanese market

**Darek Chrabowski and Richard Fletcher**

## INTRODUCTION

A challenge that many Australian and international firms face is how to create a competitive advantage in the intended target market. There are many models or theories available for firms to adopt and implement in their business practices in order to gain that competitive advantage. This case explores the challenge facing AMPM Pty Limited and how it is overcoming the challenge and entering a growing market in Japan—the air purifying market.

The air purifying market in Japan is a growing market with demand increasing at a rapid pace. Products that service the air purifying market worldwide are respirators which are segmented into three types: from high technical respirators (half-face respirators and full-face respirators) to low technical respirators (disposable respirators).

This case study demonstrates the changes and challenges that occur to the value chain's primary activities and support activities when new product development is undertaken in a global firm.

## BACKGROUND

AMPM Pty Limited lies within the personal protective equipment industry which services the safety industry. AMPM Pty Limited offers 10 000 items of personal protection and hazard detection equipment. These include gloves, spectacles, hard hats, ear plugs and muffs, protective clothing (including rainwear), harnesses and lanyards, as well as specialised self-contained breathing apparatus, respirators and sophisticated gas detection equipment. AMPM Pty Limited manufactures or sources locally around 60% of its product.

AMPM Pty Limited's parent is AMPM, with headquarters located in Chicago, Illinois, USA. A

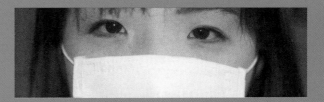

publicly held company, AMPM stock is traded over the NYSE. AMPM has manufacturing operations on five continents and more than 30 international locations which help protect lives in more than 140 countries.

AMPM Pty Limited manufactures safety equipment which it sells through distributors who onsell to end consumers. AMPM Pty Limited has 45 years' experience in the safety industry and has introduced many new and innovative products in order to remain ahead of competition in Australia. It is this business practice that has led AMPM Pty Limited to introduce innovative products to overseas markets and increase export sales, taking advantage of the Australian government's incentive of utilising the export market development grant. Currently AMPM Pty Limited is registered under the Textile Clothing & Footwear (TCF) Strategic Investment Program (SIP) offered through AusIndustry, which is an Australian government initiative. This has seen AMPM Pty Limited export innovative products to overseas markets.

## VALUE CHAIN

The value chain is made up of primary activities: inbound logistics, operations, outbound logistics, marketing and sales and service (Fletcher and Brown, 2005, p. 481). These activities are primarily concerned with the creation and delivery of the product. Whereas support activities of firm infrastructure, human resource management, technology development and procurement (Fletcher and Brown, 2005, p. 481) are not directly linked to the creation of the product, they may increase the efficiency or the effectiveness of the creation of the product. The value chain is aimed at the activities that take place in a business, but it is rare that a firm will undertake all the primary and secondary activities itself. A more recent trend is the firm outsourcing certain activities in order to gain value and a competitive advantage not only in the domestic market but also in the international markets the firm chooses to enter.

## DEVELOPING AN INTERNATIONAL VALUE CHAIN WITHIN A GLOBAL FIRM

In global firms it is not unusual for parent companies to identify which subsidiaries or affiliates possess capabilities in different activities of the value chain. Subsidiaries can identify a need in a market for a certain product or service, but they accept that they do not possess all the elements of the value chain necessary to create value and gain a competitive advantage. In order to overcome this challenge and not miss the opportunities that exist in their market they source assistance from either the parent or an affiliate company in order to satisfy the needs of the market, create value and gain a competitive advantage. In the case of AMPM Pty Limited, AMPM Japan and AMPM (the parent company), AMPM Japan identified the need of the growing trend of half-face respirators required in the Japanese market. It accepted that its value chain could not satisfy this need, and sourced assistance from the parent company, AMPM. AMPM could not satisfy these needs due to other projects and the sourcing of materials necessary for new product development. Research was conducted on which of its manufacturing subsidiaries could undertake this new product development and supply AMPM Japan with this new product. AMPM Pty Limited was chosen due to its manufacturing capabilities, innovation, supply base, geographic location to Japan and experience. AMPM Pty Limited did in fact produce a half-face respirator that satisfied local

market demands, but the problem faced was that the half-face respirator did not fit the average Japanese consumer due to the facial differences of Western and Asian people, in particular the size and position of the nose piece on the half-face respirator.

This new product development saw the value chain dissected between three firms. AMPM Japan took the position as leader of the project team and its primary activities were marketing and sales. AMPM Pty Limited's primary activities were inbound logistics, operations and outbound logistics; its support activities were technology development and procurement. The support activities of firm infrastructure and human resource management were split between AMPM, AMPM Pty Limited and AMPM Japan, and AMPM Japan and AMPM Pty Limited respectively. The primary activity of service was also split between AMPM Japan and AMPM Pty Limited. Figure 1 depicts the break up of the value chain in regard to the new product development.

The firm infrastructure was split as the general management of the new product development was being led by AMPM Japan, with the financing of the new product development the responsibility of the parent company, AMPM. The planning management and quality management of the new product development were the responsibility of AMPM Pty Limited. Splitting support activities and primary activities allows for problems to creep into the new product development, as the parent company and subsidiaries did not see eye to eye on certain elements of the project.

## PROBLEMS WITH AN INTERNATIONAL VALUE CHAIN WITHIN A GLOBAL FIRM

When problems begin to occur in a value chain, especially one this complex, the value and competitive advantage that the value chain offers diminish. The first problem that occurred with the new product development began with the support activity of technology development that saw AMPM Pty Limited design a half-face respirator with the specifications of average Japanese facial features and that complied with Australian standards in order to control the quality of the product domes-

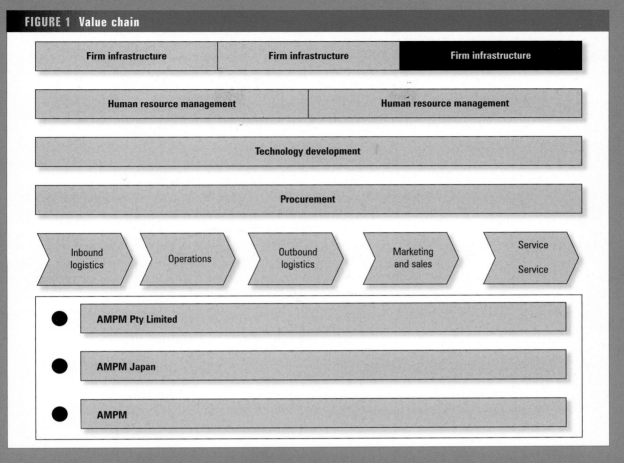

**FIGURE 1  Value chain**

| Firm infrastructure | Firm infrastructure | Firm infrastructure |

| Human resource management | Human resource management |

Technology development

Procurement

| Inbound logistics | Operations | Outbound logistics | Marketing and sales | Service Service |

● AMPM Pty Limited

● AMPM Japan

● AMPM

tically. A sample was sent to AMPM Japan for their perusal and feedback on the product. A month went by before feedback was received, during which time other projects were required to take a backseat. This time lapse is indicative of a Japanese cultural tendency to be long-term oriented, and its feedback of the sample was that AMPM Pty Limited rushed the design and manufacture, which reflects the Western culture of being short-term oriented and searching for short-term success. AMPM Japan relayed the message that its specifications of the design of the product were not followed, which is indicative of low-context cultures, whereas AMPM Pty Limited followed the exact specifications word for word and not the implied message, as evidenced in high-context cultures. AMPM Japan also requested in its feedback that the product comply with Japanese standards, which are much lower than Australian standards, meaning that AMPM Pty Limited faced

problems testing the quality of the product. The timeframe for the finalisation of the new product development was continually extended, frustrating AMPM (the parent company), and as a result the cost of the product development rose, resulting in AMPM pulling the financing and requesting that AMPM Japan fund the product development. This is another example of Western cultures being short-term oriented. This action placed pressure on AMPM Japan to source funding which delayed the project further. This further delay cost AMPM Pty Limited more as it was storing raw materials specifically for the project, taking up space in its warehouse that could have been used for other product storage. AMPM Japan sourced funding and sent a consultant to Australia to oversee the redesign of the product. Redesign of the project began according to AMPM Japan's feedback and was based on Japanese standards with the input of the Japanese consultant—this also became a problem due to the language barrier. Frustration began to grow between AMPM Pty Limited and AMPM Japan due to the time lost and time taken to accept the new product.

## OUTCOME

After redesigning commenced and the feedback, Japanese standards and language barrier were overcome, AMPM Pty Limited finally produced some samples. These samples were sent to AMPM Japan and were accepted after a short period. Full production is expected to be underway shortly with the first order waiting to be received. This case study depicts only a few of the problems that can occur when using a value chain within a global firm for new product development, specifically when different cultures are involved. This new product development was intended to create value not only for AMPM Japan but for the global group. Creating value for a global group is difficult as it was AMPM's intention to utilise certain

subsidiaries around the world to create a value chain that would not only create value but would also create a competitive advantage for AMPM Japan in the Japanese market.

## CONCLUSION

When utilising or undertaking to use a value chain within a global firm it is important to understand that cultures play an important role in creating a successful value chain that creates value and a competitive advantage. Even though the above three companies fall under one group, consideration must be made for the cultures that not only exist in the country where the business is located but consideration must be made on the culture that exists within the business as well. Business practices and cultures vary from country to country and must be considered when undertaking new product development, especially when primary activities and support activities of the value chain are detached.

### Bibliography

Fletcher, R. and Brown L. (2005) *International Marketing: an Asia-Pacific Perspective*, Pearson Prentice Hall, Sydney.
<http://www.valuebasedmanagement.net/methods_porter_value_chain.html>, accessed 13th April 2007.

### Acknowledgements

The authors of this case study are thankful to a certain person who cannot be named for their time spent giving interviews and precious insights. Please note that the company name was changed for protection reasons.

### Questions

1  When a firm outsources a primary activity of the value chain does its level of control decrease?
2  Do the support activities dictate primary activities of the value chain?
3  Should the support activities be split up between firms as seen in the case study, particularly in firm infrastructure?
4  Could the value chain be more effective if the affiliates and parent company possessed the same or similar culture?

## go online

Go online to <www.pearsoned.com.au/fletcher> to find more case studies.

# Crisis management in international markets: 'least said, soonest mended?'

John Knight, Department of Marketing, University of Otago and Bradley Mitchell, Inveratek Group Ltd

## BACKGROUND

An inevitable reality of doing business in the modern world is that crises recognise no boundaries (Fink 1986). A crisis management strategy needs to be part of the overall corporate strategy of any company operating internationally. Our chaotic times have led to some spectacular commercial crises. Sometimes these have been of companies' own making through carelessness. A well-known example is the action of McDonald's in promoting its sponsorship of the 1994 football World Cup by printing the flags of all competing nations on disposable packaging: the name of Allah is on the Saudi flag, and deep offence was caused by the fact that this was to be thrown away with the packaging (Starrett 1995). At other times crises have been caused by events completely outside of the control of the company. Examples of the latter include the deliberate product tampering of Tylenol products, leading to deaths by poisoning in the USA, and the massive product recall of Coca-Cola products in Belgium resulting from what appears to be a case of mass hysteria (Johnson and Peppas 2003). Furthermore, companies in the midst of a crisis may not be able to

control the behaviour of others, but with proper planning and management the negative effects of a crisis can be mitigated, or even turned to one's advantage (Meyers 1986, Burnett 1998). This case provides a very interesting demonstration of how world events, seemingly completely unrelated to the international marketing environment that a company is operating in, can very quickly do enormous damage to that company's fortunes. In addition, the case demonstrates how adequate crisis management plans can be used to defuse a highly volatile situation. Bad choices by politicians and/or company executives can have consequences of unthinkable proportions in the volatile age we live in!

Formed in October 2001, Fonterra is one of the top six dairy companies in the world by turnover according to Rabobank ratings (Fonterra 2007). It is New Zealand's largest company, co-operatively owned by more than 11 600 New Zealand dairy farmers. Fonterra is the world's leading international trader of dairy products, accounting for more than a third of all international dairy trade. New Zealand dairy farmers have long been renowned for producing quality milk more efficiently than anyone else in the world, due in part to climatic conditions favouring year-round grass growth, but also to development over many decades of innovative production and processing methods. According to Fonterra's website (<http://www.fonterra.com>):

> Fonterra's global supply chain stretches from 13 000 farms in New Zealand to customers and consumers in 140 countries, with some of the best known dairy brands, world leading manufacturing sites, quality and cost marketing and distribution with seamless integration from cow to customer.

Fonterra has extended its international reach with manufacturing at 29 sites in New Zealand and also at 35 sites in other countries throughout the Americas, Asia (particularly China), Europe, and Australia. The company has pursued an aggressive policy of acquisitions and joint ventures, including among its partners such giant dairy companies as Arla of Denmark, Bonlac Foods of Australia, Dairy America, Dairy Farmers of America, and Swiss-based Nestlé, with whom Fonterra has a joint venture operating in Ecuador, Colombia, Brazil, Argentina and Venezuela. Fonterra has wholly-owned subsidiaries operating in important dairy markets such as Mexico, where it has the largest share of the $1.3 billion cheese market. In Chile, Fonterra has a 50% market share of the liquid milk and yoghurt market through its Soprole brand, which has been a market leader in Chile for 50 years. In the Middle East, also, Fonterra has developed important markets— particularly in Saudi Arabia, Algeria, Egypt, the United Arab Emirates, Iran, Jordan and Syria. By 2006 these Middle Eastern markets were accounting for more than NZ$1 billion of its total turnover of approximately NZ$12.3 billion, and were viewed by the company as a very significant and lucrative part of its global business. New Zealand exports to the Middle East have ballooned over the past decade as the United Arab Emirates in particular experience spectacular economic growth, which has significantly boosted its trade profile with New Zealand. Fonterra's dairy products make up approximately 90% of this export effort in the Middle East.

How quickly this could all be put at risk by events completely outside the control of this company! The simple mechanism by which this threat arose was a decision by the editors of three foreign-owned newspapers in New Zealand to publish material to demonstrate the strength of the editors' views about the importance of 'freedom of the press'.

## THE MUHAMMAD CARTOONS CRISIS

Initially, the crisis had nothing whatever to do with New Zealand, nor with Fonterra. It began when a Danish newspaper, the *Jyllands-Posten*, invited cartoonists to contribute cartoons that depicted the Islamic prophet, Muhammad. The newspaper announced that the reason for this publication was to contribute to an ongoing debate regarding news media criticism of matters concerning Islam. Twelve editorial cartoons were printed on 30 September 2005 (they can be viewed at <http://en.wikipedia.org/wiki/Jyllands-Posten_Muhammad_cartoons_controversy>).

Perhaps the most inflammatory was a depiction of Muhammad with a bomb in his turban. Danish Muslim organisations, who objected to the depictions, rapidly organised public protests to raise awareness of the issue. Critics of the cartoons argued that they were blasphemous of the Muslim faith and were intended to humiliate a Danish minority. Within Muslim communities, there have been varying views regarding depiction of Muhammad. Shiite Muslims have been generally tolerant of pictorial representations, whereas Sunni Muslims have generally forbidden any pictorial representation of Muhammad, believing that this constitutes blasphemy. In Muslim societies generally, insulting the prophet Muhammad is regarded as the gravest of all crimes, even warranting a death sentence in some communities.

Flemming Rose, the culture editor of *Jyllands-Posten*, claimed:

> The modern, secular society is rejected by some Muslims. They demand a special position, insisting on special consideration of their own religious feelings. It is incompatible with contemporary democracy and freedom of speech, where you must be ready to put up with insults, mockery and ridicule. It is certainly not always attractive and nice to look at, and it does not mean that religious feelings should be made fun of at any price, but that is of minor importance in the present context. We are on our way to a slippery slope where no-one can tell how self-censorship will end.

*Jyllands-Posten, 30 September 2005*

Having received petitions from Danish Imams, ambassadors from 11 Islamic countries complained to the Danish prime minister, Anders Fogh Rasmussen, requesting a meeting with him and urging him to:

*Take all those responsible to task under law of the land.*

The Danish prime minister declined to meet them, and replied that the Danish government had no means by which it could influence the press. However, Danish law prohibits blasphemous or discriminatory actions. So it was up to the aggrieved party to take the matter to court if it so wished.

The refusal of the prime minister to meet the ambassadors has been criticised subsequently by the Danish Opposition and 22 Danish former ambassadors.

The Muhammad cartoons controversy received only minor media attention outside of Denmark during 2005. Egyptian newspaper *El Fagr* reprinted six of the cartoons on 17 October 2005, together with an article strongly condemning them. However, towards the end of 2005 and in January 2006 major European newspapers in Norway, the Netherlands, Germany, Belgium and France reprinted them, and as the controversy spread newspapers in other countries followed suit. Notable for not printing them were newspapers in the USA, UK and Australia where the stories were covered without the pictures. (Of possible relevance is that these three countries were all involved in the war against Iraq).

In interesting contrast to the consistent refusal of the Danish government to give in to demands that it apologise for the publication of the cartoons and introduce censorship, Norwegian foreign minister Jonas Gahr Støre, a leading member of prime minister Jens Stoltenberg's Workers' Party, wrote the following e-mail to Norwegian embassies that had a security problem during the controversy to use in their external communications:

*I am sorry that the publication of a few cartoons in the Norwegian paper Magazinet has caused unrest among Muslims. I fully understand that these drawings are seen to give offence by Muslims worldwide. Islam is a spiritual reference point for a large part of the world. Your faith has the right to be respected by us. The cartoons in the Christian paper Magazinet are not constructive in building the bridges which are necessary between people with different religious and ethnic backgrounds. Instead they contribute to suspicion and unnecessary conflict. Let it be clear that the Norwegian government condemns every expression or act which expresses contempt for people on the basis of their religion or ethnic origin.*

*Norway has always supported UN efforts to combat religious intolerance, and we consider these efforts to be essential for preventing distrust and conflicts between people. Tolerance, mutual respect and dialogue are fundamental values both in Norwegian society and in our foreign policy. Freedom of expression is a universally recognised human right and one of the mainstays of Norwegian society. This also entails tolerance for views that are not shared by everyone.*
*(<http://www.brusselsjournal.com/node/722>)*

In late January a consumer boycott of Danish products was organised in Saudi Arabia, Kuwait and other Middle Eastern countries, in particular targeting products of Danish dairy giant, Arla. Supermarkets began displaying signs saying that Danish goods had been taken off the shelves, such as (translated from Arabic):

*To our dear customers: As a result of mockery towards The Prophet (Peace Be Upon Him), Al Tamimi Markets announces its boycott of all kinds of Danish Products.*
*Guaranteed! You will not find Danish products on our shelves!*

On 5 February the Danish and Norwegian embassies in Damascus, Syria were set ablaze and in Beirut, Lebanon, the Danish embassy was set on fire, causing one death. Altogether, 139 people were killed in protests, mainly in Nigeria, Libya, Pakistan and Afghanistan. Several death threats and reward offers were made for killing the cartoonists responsible, resulting in them going into hiding. Boycotts were to prove costly for many Danish interests. Estimates for the total impact on the Danish economy are in the hundreds of millions of dollars. Danish dairy giant Arla, which had been operating in the Middle East for over 40 years and is in no way connected to *Jyllands-Posten*, was losing 1.3 million euros per day at the height of the boycott in early February 2006. By mid-February, the boycott had spread to include Saudi Arabia, Kuwait, the United Arab Emirates, Qatar, Yemen, Lebanon, Morocco, Egypt and Sudan. Arla had closed its factory in Riyadh. This was devastating for a company which, having planned to double sales to the region over the next five years, had targeted the Middle East as a valuable export market and had moved some of its production plants from Denmark to Saudi Arabia.

Fonterra was placed in an interesting position as the boycott began to affect Arla. In order to distance itself from Arla, Fonterra published advertisements in Middle Eastern newspapers emphasising the New Zealand origins of its Anchor brand milk powders, but otherwise avoiding reference to the controversy. On the one hand, Fonterra saw that the misfortune befalling a major competitor in Middle Eastern markets had the potential to provide a gap for them to fill. But on the other hand, Fonterra and Arla are involved in a major joint venture, based in the UK, to co-distribute Fonterra's Anchor butter and Arla's Lurpak butter, which are the number one and two brands in the UK butter market. Furthermore, Arla is a significant customer for Fonterra, buying commodity ingredients from Fonterra to incorporate in some of its own products. Therefore, Fonterra did not want to be seen to be taking advantage of the situation facing its business partner. According to a Fonterra executive:

> We did pick up some market share but it wasn't something that we went out to compete for in a negative way towards Arla. We would be better off having the gap in the market and other customers wanting to buy more of Fonterra's products.

As events unfolded, this was probably a fortunate viewpoint for Fonterra to adopt.

## CONTROVERSY SPREADS TO NEW ZEALAND

On 3 February 2006 the editor of a major daily newspaper in New Zealand gave advance notice of intention of publishing the cartoons, presumably to gauge the intensity of the adverse reaction within New Zealand. Despite prime minister Helen Clark urging them not to do so, and exporting companies and organisations expressing outrage, the editor of Wellington newspaper *The Dominion Post* and two other newspapers (all three owned by Australian-owned company Fairfax) decided to publish the cartoons out of solidarity with editors elsewhere in the world. (Fortunately for Australian exporters, Fairfax-owned newspapers in Australia chose not to do so.)

As rumblings of a boycott of New Zealand products emanated from the Middle East region, exporters—especially Fonterra—realised they had a potential crisis on their hands. The company activated their crisis management team, comprising their most senior managers, and placed the issue at the top of the agenda. They decided at an early stage to avoid any public comment, either in New Zealand or in foreign markets. The objective was to avoid inflaming the controversy in any way, and to hope that the issue would 'blow over' as quickly as possible. The main emphasis was placed on reassuring business partners in the Middle East that Fonterra did not condone the publishing of the cartoons and is respectful of all religions. The long-standing personal relationships that the company (and its predecessor, the New Zealand Dairy Board) had built up with distribution channel members were seen as the key to riding out the storm.

By 8 February 2006, the Iranian government had set up a committee to look at possibly annulling trade deals with countries that had published the cartoons, threatening over $100 million worth of New Zealand exports. Politicians in Jordan called for trade worth $70 million with New Zealand to be cancelled. New Zealand prime minister Helen Clark made public statements deploring the actions of the newspaper editors, and indicating that the New Zealand government did not condone publication of the cartoons in New Zealand. New Zealand-based Muslim groups began drafting letters to the governments of 52 Muslim countries urging them not to boycott New Zealand goods.

By 9 February New Zealand diplomats in Muslim countries were put on high alert against a possible backlash, as a majority of members of the Jordanian parliament supported a petition to act against New Zealand. New Zealand's annual meat trade with Jordan was worth approximately NZ$32 million. Meat and Wool New Zealand urged companies whose exports to Islamic countries were affected to seek legal redress against the newspapers concerned. Trade negotiations minister Jim Sutton said that by upsetting Muslim nations, the newspaper publishers put the nation's economy at risk. Observers noted that Australia would stand to benefit from any boycott of New Zealand exports and called for Australian publisher Fairfax to be held accountable.

By 21 February, Arla was indicating that it might have to withdraw completely from the Middle East, its second-largest market. It made a public statement indicating that it considered the printing of the cartoons to be a very, very bad idea. Losses thus far amounted to US$20 million, and if the boycott were to continue throughout the year, Denmark's economy would stand to lose US$2.6 billion. Leaders from the Muslim world were quoted as saying that Denmark had not taken enough action over the cartoons. Arla first revoked, then reinstated, its sponsorship logo on the shirts of the Danish national football team ahead of a match against the Israeli national team in Tel Aviv, reflecting the uncertainty of Danish companies as to how to respond to the public relations nightmare. The Confederation of Danish Industries urged its members to be quiet and cautious, and to avoid advertising at the time. Interestingly, Danish companies that do not have to face consumers directly, such as Maersk shipping company, appeared to escape repercussions. Conversely, the Kuwaiti Danish Dairy Company, which had severed links with Denmark some 20 years before, saw its sales plummet 95% just because of its misleading name.

Fonterra's policy of avoiding public comment, while reassuring distribution channel contacts, continued throughout this turbulent period. The company made statements available to sales staff in foreign markets, saying that Fonterra is respectful of all religions, and that it does not support the position taken by three of New Zealand's many newspapers. However, the purpose of these statements was to inform sales staff as to how to deal with their business customers, rather than to communicate with end consumers. One part of the organisation took a somewhat independent stance, perhaps without the prior knowledge of the crisis management team. A full-page advertisement appeared in a Saudi Arabian newspaper, emphasising that cultural sensitivity is the basis of Fonterra's products, that the products themselves are manufactured according to Muslim practices and that Fonterra is a trustworthy company. It seems likely that this was a decision taken by a manager in the Saudi Arabian office, rather than at head office in New Zealand, reflecting the difficulty of ensuring a uniform response in a far-flung operation in a time of crisis. Furthermore, the decision could well have been influenced by the fact that Arla had instigated an advertisement offensive in a number of Saudi Arabian newspapers.

By April 2006 retailers across the Middle East were beginning to restock Arla's products, although uptake was slow, with only 20% of pre-boycott sales being recorded by the end of May. Market recovery proved slow despite Arla investing heavily in advertising campaigns in selected markets such as Algeria. However, by March 2007 Arla Chairman Knud Erik Jensen was able to say, 'We're back in the Middle East and expect to return to previous levels of sales by the end of 2007'.

A Fonterra executive, reflecting on the handling of the controversy after the event, made the following assessments:

- Despite the potential damage that New Zealand exporters, and Fonterra in particular, were exposed to, the situation never threatened to get out of hand and develop into a full-blown crisis for Fonterra.

- Fonterra's close business relationships in Middle Eastern countries meant that staff were well-informed and able to quietly reassure business customers. Communication with gatekeepers in the distribution channel— wholesalers, distributors, retail buyers—was seen as the top priority.

- Domestic media articles stating that New Zealand exporters stood to lose hundreds of millions of dollars seemed to be largely the assessment of creative journalists, rather than based on industry assessments.

- Fonterra's crisis management approach consisted of avoiding public comment as far as possible:

  *We were not going to get involved in a media stoush.*

- Condemning the cartoons publicly and highlighting the independence of the news media in New Zealand would only have drawn unwanted attention.

- The intensity of the crisis for Danish exporters was in large part due to the cartoons having been originally published in that country—republishing them later in other countries was not seen as quite so serious (and, as already mentioned, an Egyptian newspaper also published them).

- The strident defence of the freedom of the press and right to publish in the Danish media, and the refusal of the Danish government to apologise, seems likely to have greatly intensified the crisis for Denmark and Danish companies.

- In contrast, the New Zealand government publicly condemned the publishing of the cartoons, emphasising that New Zealand's efforts to build relationships with Islamic countries and reinforce New Zealand's

| TABLE 2 | New Zealand exports to Middle East in millions of NZ dollars | | |
|---|---|---|---|
| | **2004** | **2005** | **2006** |
| Saudi Arabia | 326 | 379 | 411 |
| United Arab Emirates | 136 | 160 | 222 |
| Algeria | 107 | 135 | 214 |
| Iran | 90 | 76 | 122 |
| Egypt | 91 | 114 | 156 |
| Jordan | 21 | 62 | 61 |
| Total Middle East | 1045 | 1186 | 1555 |

reputation as a peaceful and understanding nation were starting to bear fruit.

- In addition to public statements by New Zealand politicians for the benefit of the news media, it seems likely that Ministry of Foreign Affairs personnel were active behind the scenes, reassuring counterparts in Muslim countries and using relationships built up over many years.

New Zealand trade statistics (<http://www.stats.govt.nz>) indicate that exports to the Middle East region continued to increase year by year through 2005 and 2006 as shown in Table 1.

## Bibliography

Burnett, J. (1998) 'A strategic response to managing crises', *Public Relations Review*, Vol. 24, No. 4, pp. 475–88.

'Danish business feels the pain of cartoon boycotts', MiddleEastOnline, <http://www.middle-east-online.com/ENGLISH/business/?id=15795>, accessed 20 February 2006.

Fink, S. (1986) *Crisis Management: Planning for the Inevitable*, American Management Association, New York.

Fonterra (2007) <http://www.fonterra.com/>.

Johnson, V. and Peppas, S. (2003) 'Crisis management in Belgium: the case of Coca-Cola', *Corporate Communications,* Vol. 8, No. 1, pp. 18–22.

Knight, J., Holdsworth, D. and Mather, D. (2007) 'Country-of-origin and choice of food imports: an in-depth study of European distribution channel gatekeepers', *Journal of International Business Studies*, Vol. 38, No. 1, pp. 107–25.

Meyers, G. (1986) *When It hits the Fan: Managing the Nine Crises of Business*, Houghton Mifflin Co, Boston.

Starrett, G. (1995) 'The political economy of religious commodities in Cairo', *American Anthropologist*, Vol. 97, No. 1, pp. 51–68.

## Questions

1  (a)  Identify the key elements that led to the intensity of feeling expressed about the cartoons crisis from the point of view of:
   (i)   Danish imams and the wider Danish Muslim community;
   (ii)  Sunni Muslims and Shiite Muslims—which countries would be expected to react most

strongly, based on differing religious perspectives?

(iii) the Danish government, the Norwegian government, the New Zealand government;

(iv) the Danish news media; news media in other countries, including New Zealand and Australia.

(b) Where does 'freedom of the press' end, and what responsibility does the press have?

2 Identify the key elements of a successful crisis management response, illustrated by this case. Consider the different responses of Danish, Norwegian, and New Zealand companies and governments, and analyse the extent to which these different responses contributed to:

(a) the intensity of the reaction against particular companies and embassies;

(b) defusing of the situation.

3 What are the pros and cons of a company maintaining a strong country association for its brands in international markets? Could it be that Fonterra was to some extent insulated from the crisis because New Zealand is a small country a long way away from Middle Eastern markets, and 'slipped beneath the radar' in terms of being a target for consumer reaction? What factors associated with country of origin seem most likely to be important in regard to exported food products? Consider this from the perspective of end-consumers, and also from the perspective of food distribution channel members who have been referred to as 'gatekeepers of consumer choice' (Knight et al. 2007).

4 What does the case illustrate about the interconnectedness of international companies operating in foreign markets? Competitors in some markets may be partners or business clients in another. Consider the various interrelationships between Fonterra and Arla in different countries.

5 This case could provide a basis for a debate in which individual students, or groups of students, assume the role of one of the protagonists in the crisis.

# PART C

# INTERNATIONAL MARKET STRATEGY

The preparation of the marketing plan needs to be followed by the creation of strategies to achieve the objectives articulated in the international marketing plan. This process begins with the application of various marketing strategies to the international marketing environment that the firm is likely to encounter in its chosen overseas market. Selecting the most appropriate segment in that market needs to be carefully undertaken as does creative positioning of one's offering in that segment. Such strategy development is essential in order to gain competitive advantage (Chapter 9) and will require not only identification of competitors and their relative strengths and weaknesses but also strategies to confront, bypass or ignore them. An analysis of the value chain in which the firm is embedded is also necessary so as to establish for each market the value chain elements in which the firm has the greatest competitive advantage. An understanding of likely competitor reaction (Chapter 10) to one's entry or expansion of activities in the market is necessary. Strategies need to be developed to minimise threat from competitors such as formation of strategic alliances and acquisition of 'insider status' in that market. Given the trend towards globalisation (Chapter 11), the firm needs to establish whether its approach to international involvement will be local or global, and the extent of standardisation as opposed to differentiation of its offerings for each overseas market and between its domestic and its overseas markets. An appreciation of both the micro advantages and macro disadvantages of globalisation needs to be considered in the context of the firm's international strategic development. The aspect of gaining insider status in foreign markets raises the issue of relationships and networks (Chapter 12). The creation of networks of relationships, both within each overseas market and between overseas markets, needs to be explored as in many parts of the world networks are more powerful determinants of business than the specific advantages of the offering. In this connection, entering into strategic alliances is often essential. Careful thinking about underlying strategic issues will ensure that the implementation of the international marketing plan will cater for consequences likely to be encountered and accord with the overall objectives of the company.

# GAINING INTERNATIONAL COMPETITIVE ADVANTAGE

## LearningObjectives

**After reading this chapter you should be able to:**

■ identify the key elements and drivers of national advantage that contribute to competitive advantage of an industry;

■ determine the relevant bases of competitive advantage at the firm level and how they relate to generic competitive strategies in overseas markets;

■ evaluate the significance of an industry value chain and how customer value can be created overseas through restructuring it;

■ conduct a systematic step-by-step process of competitive analysis in order to determine a firm's international competitiveness and most relevant positioning; and

■ follow a process of competitive intelligence gathering with particular reference to the internet as an information channel.

# Casella finds a blue ocean in the 'red' US wine market

In the US wine industry, conventional strategic thinking resulted in companies overdelivering on prestige and quality of wine at a price point. This meant that costs were increased as wine makers increased the complexity of their wines (ageing them for longer, using better oak storage, etc.) in order to win awards and pursue increased levels of prestige.

Casella Wines, an Australian winery, redefined the problem of the wine industry by looking across alternatives and specifically defining a new problem statement: how to make a fun non-traditional wine that is easy to drink for everyone. Casella looked at the alternatives of beer, spirits and ready-to-drink cocktails which made up three times the sales of wine and found that Americans saw wine as a turnoff relative to these alternatives. American consumers saw the industry as intimidating and pretentious and the complexity of the wine's taste created flavour challenges for the average consumer even through it was a key basis for competition.

With this key insight Casella Wines was ready to redraw the strategic profile of the US wine industry. In order to achieve this they turned to what Kim and Mauborgne (2005) describe as a four-actions framework:

1  Which of the factors that the industry takes for granted should be eliminated?

2  Which factors should be reduced well below the industry's standard?

3  Which factors should be raised above the industry standard?

4  Which factors should be created that the industry has never offered?

By using this framework Casella Wines created a wine [yellow tail] whose strategic profile broke away from the competition and created a 'blue ocean'. Casella did not position wine in the traditional way, rather they positioned it as a social drink accessible to everyone, beer drinkers, cocktail drinkers and other non-wine drinkers. Within two

years [yellow tail] became the number one imported wine in the USA and by 2003 it was the number one red wine, even outstripping Californian labels.

Casella Wines applied all four actions—eliminate, reduce, raise and create—to unlock uncontested marketspace in the US wine market.

By looking at the alternatives to wine Casella Wines created three new factors in the US wine industry—easy drinking, easy to select, and fun and adventure—as well as eliminating or reducing everything else. The [yellow tail] brand reduced the range by producing just a red and a white wine initially. They also reduced the prestige of the wine by leveraging the Australian cultural characteristics of laid-back, fun and adventurous. By providing this additional value, Casella was able to raise its pricing above the budget wines to more than double a jug of wine.

Through the [yellow tail] brand Casella Wines was able to deliver additional value to its customers and at the same time reduce its costs to deliver that value. Also, Casella has been unaffected by competitors and has been able to grow the US wine market. This value innovation is the essence of blue ocean strategy.

**SOURCE:** *Kim, W.C. and Mauborgne, R. (2005)* Blue Ocean Strategy: How to Create Uncontested Market Space and Make the Competition Irrelevant, *Boston, Harvard Business School Press. Image courtesy of Anson Smart.*

# INTRODUCTION

Until recent decades, society was conditioned by a scarcity mindset which emanated from the industrial age when the focus was on managing scarce resources. In the current knowledge age however, the focus in developed countries is on abundance due to new technologies, enhanced international competition and product parity in consumer and industrial goods markets. Firms now have to focus on adding value and exceeding customer expectations. In these circumstances, the greater the knowledge content and technology intensity of the firm's output, the greater the likelihood that a firm will have a competitive advantage in international markets. The product in which the competitive advantage is embodied can either be exported or alternatively the technology involved can be licensed to an overseas firm or incorporated in a joint venture arrangement with a firm in another country (Bradley 2002, p. 37).

This chapter discusses the elements underlying international competitive advantage and explores generic strategies relevant to firms conducting business internationally. The value chain concept is examined as a tool to help companies identify opportunities for competitive advantage in overseas markets. This leads into discussion of a process for analysing steps in competitor analysis ending with a brief overview of the internet as an intelligence gathering tool.

*Competitive advantage* is defined as an advantage gained over competitors by offering customers greater perceived value, either through lower prices or by delivering more benefits that justify higher prices. If a company can position itself as providing superior perceived value to its selected overseas markets—and deliver it to customer expectations—it gains competitive advantage.

Competitive advantage is closely related to the idea of international competitiveness. This is relevant at both country and firm levels. International competitiveness at a national level is based on superior productivity performance. It is associated with rising living standards and the country's ability to stay ahead technologically and commercially in those product markets that contribute to a bigger share of world consumption and added value.

Competitiveness for the firm is closely related to its ability to increase sales, margins and profits in the overseas markets in which it chooses to compete—and its capability to defend its market position as new waves of competitive offers emerge (Bradley 2002, p. 77). Several frameworks have been developed to analyse both national and firm competitive advantage.

## NATIONAL COMPETITIVE ADVANTAGE

Analysis of competitive advantage by international marketing managers primarily focuses on the firm's competitive advantage. However, this usually is conditioned in part by *a nation's competitive advantage*. For example, Australia's natural advantages in primary and extractive industries have resulted in it being a significant producer and trader of agricultural and raw material commodities. Its developed advantages in higher education have resulted in it having a significant export industry targeted to Asia for tertiary education.

Michael Porter, in *The Competitive Advantage of Nations* (1990, p. 71), suggests that the determinants of national advantage for an industry are fourfold:

1  *factor conditions*: the nation's position in factors of production, such as skilled labour or infrastructure, necessary to compete in a given industry;

2  *demand conditions*: the nature of home demand for the industry's product or service;

3  *related and supporting industries*: the presence or absence in the nation of supplier industries and related industries that are internationally competitive;

4  *firm strategy, structure and rivalry*: the conditions in the nation governing how companies are created, organised and managed, and the nature of domestic rivalry.

Porter's model, shown as Figure 9.1, also includes government influences and chance events. These latter elements are regarded as important influences rather than determinants.

Strong relationships between the four determinants and the two influencers over time foster national competitive advantage in various industries. For each of the determinants, Porter identifies some of the influencing factors that strengthen its contribution to national advantage for an industry.

## Influences on factor creation

*   A cluster of domestic rivals stimulates factor creation.

*   Perceived national challenges stimulate factor creation.

*   Home demand influences priorities for factor-creating investments.

*   Related and supporting industries create or stimulate the creation of transferable factors.

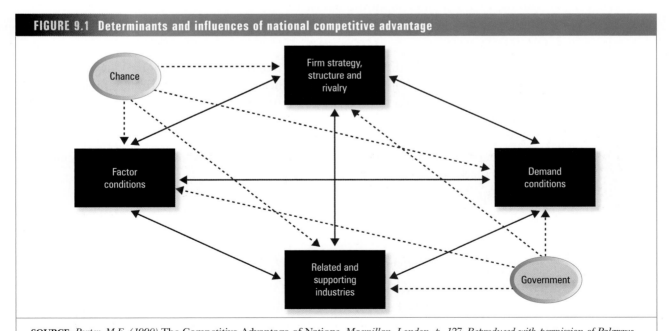

**FIGURE 9.1  Determinants and influences of national competitive advantage**

**SOURCE:** *Porter, M.E. (1990)* The Competitive Advantage of Nations, *Macmillan, London, p. 127. Reproduced with permission of Palgrave.*

# Influences on home demand conditions

- Intense rivalry increases home demand and makes it more sophisticated.
- A group of rivals builds a national image and recognition as an important competitor.
- Sophisticated factor-creating mechanisms attract foreign experts and participation by foreign firms that pull through the nation's products.
- The image of world-class related and supporting industries spills over to benefit an industry.
- Internationally successful industries producing complementary products pull through foreign demand for the industry's product.

# Influences on development of related and supporting industries

- Specialised factor pools are transferable to related and supporting industries.
- A group of domestic rivals encourages the formation of more specialised suppliers as well as related industries.
- Large or growing home demand stimulates the growth and deepening of supplier industries.

# Influences on firm strategy, structure and domestic rivalry

- Factor abundance or specialised factor-creating mechanisms spawn new entrants.
- Early product penetration feeds entry.
- New entrants emerge from related and supporting industries.
- World-class users enter supplying industries.

# Governments

Governments can significantly influence the determinants of national advantage mainly through the creation and implementation of policies. Australian government policies provide incentives for exporting in both marketing and research and development activities by firms. Examples of such policies may include:

- education and training;
- infrastructure industry regulation (e.g. telecommunications, media, transport, utilities, financial services);
- industry-specific regulation;
- purchasing and procurement;
- industry investment and assistance;
- foreign investment guidelines; and
- foreign affairs and military policies.

However, Porter (1990) believes that government cannot create competitive advantage in itself and therefore is not a determinant of competitive advantage, but it can reinforce present underlying determinants of competitive advantage.

# Chance events

Chance events are occurrences that have little to do with circumstances in a nation and are often largely outside the power of firms and national governments to influence. Chance events are important because they create discontinuities that allow shifts in competitive position. Examples of such chance events include:

- acts of pure invention;

- major technological discontinuities;

- discontinuities in input costs such as oil supply/price shocks;

- significant shifts in world financial markets or exchange rates such as the 1997 Asian crisis;

- surges of world or regional demand;

- political decisions by foreign governments; and

- wars.

By conducting analysis of this type in the firm's home country and the countries of its major competitors, a context is established for evaluating the company's competitive advantage. Ketels (2006) provides a review of research conducted using this model and identifies further priorities for work to be done.

The Australian wine industry reflects many of the positive elements in each of the four determinants, making it now an industry with significant national competitive advantage. Related industries such as cheese manufacture are supporting the international image of Australia as a world-class wine supplier.

Porter's diamond model is mainly used to explain the sources of national competitive advantage in industrialised nations. Its application is limited when explaining the levels of activity and changes in the economies of developing countries as it ignores the greater importance that human variables play in such economies of workers, politicians/bureaucrats, entrepreneurs and professionals. There have been several applications of this model to both developing and developed nations and to industries in regions. Chobanyan and Leigh (2006) used the diamond model application to Armenia, a developing economy, while Stone and Ranchhod (2006) used it to explain the competitive advantage of USA and the UK. Bowen and Leinbach (2006) analysed the competitive advantage in global production networks with reference to air freight services and the electronics industry in South-East Asia.

Moon et al. (1998) criticise Porter's approach to the competitive advantage of nations on the grounds that it ignores the fact that, in economies that are open to world trade, national competitive advantage derives from international as well as domestic activities. Each of the elements of Porter's diamond will be influenced to a greater or lesser extent by international involvement and therefore, they argue, national competitive advantage is a combination of the domestic and the international diamond as illustrated in Figure 9.2.

The '*double diamond*' approach overcomes the shortcoming that Porter does not include in his analysis of national competitive advantage foreign activities, such as the ability to attract foreign capital and investment (inbound foreign direct investment (FDI)) and the ability to access cheap labour resources in other countries (outbound FDI). By contrast, Porter views national competitive advantage in the context of a strategy of concentrating activities in the home country and serving the world from this base. Such an approach has an export focus and does not take into account national competitiveness deriving from more advanced forms

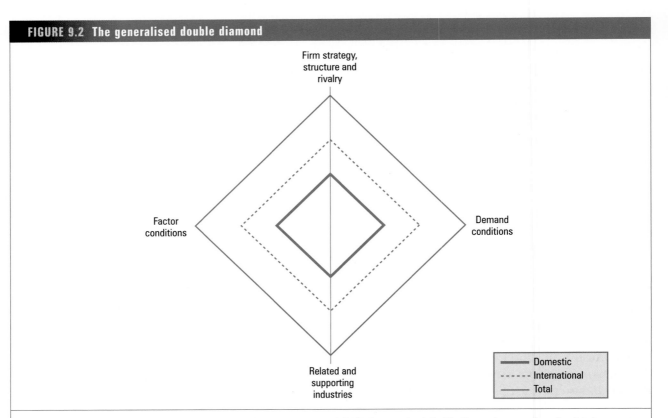

**FIGURE 9.2 The generalised double diamond**

Firm strategy, structure and rivalry

Factor conditions

Demand conditions

Related and supporting industries

Domestic
International
Total

of international involvement such as strategic alliances. Moon et al. (1998) argue that this oversight has led Porter to underestimate the national competitive advantage of countries like Singapore whose success has been due both to inbound and outbound FDI. Multinational activities are also important in explaining South Korea's competitiveness.

Double diamonds for both Singapore and South Korea are shown in Figures 9.3 and 9.4. Singapore's success has been magnified through international activities in all four points of the diamond with a strong driver being international demand conditions. South Korea's success has been enhanced by foreign activities supporting three of the four points of the diamond.

An element of national competitive advantage that operates despite the move towards globalisation is that of location. Although logically the role of location should have diminished because of the advent of a more open global market, faster transportation and the revolution in communications, in many industries localisation as reflected in clusters of firms in a specific region remains. Clusters can be considered as geographic concentrations of interconnected companies and institutions in a particular field. Porter (1998) argues that clusters were previously based on input costs and now they are based on knowledge, relationships and motivation. They can also extend downstream to customers and laterally to manufacturers of complementary products, as well as involving other stakeholders, such as universities and government. Figure 9.5 illustrates the California wine cluster.

**FIGURE 9.3  The double diamond for Singapore**

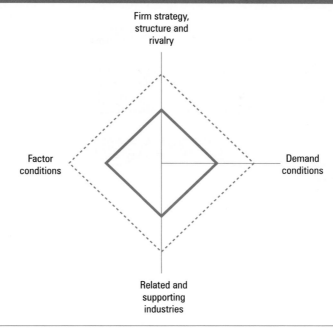

SOURCE: *Reprinted from Moon, H.C., Rugman, A.M. and Verbeke, A. (1998) 'A generalised double diamond approach to the global competitiveness of Korea and Singapore', International Business Review, Vol. 7, pp. 135–150. Copyright 1998 with permission from Elsevier.*

**FIGURE 9.4  The double diamond for South Korea**

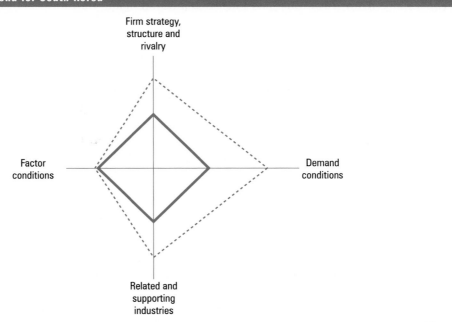

SOURCE: *Reprinted from Moon, H.C., Rugman, A.M. and Verbeke, A. (1998) 'A generalised double diamond approach to the global competitiveness of Korea and Singapore', International Business Review, Vol. 7, pp. 135–150. Copyright 1998 with permission from Elsevier.*

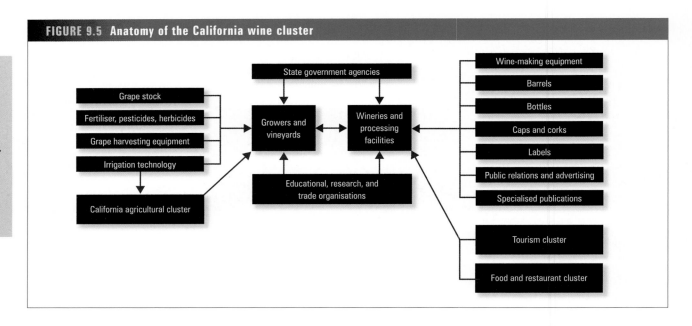

FIGURE 9.5 Anatomy of the California wine cluster

Clusters are critical to international competitive advantage in that they result in better access to employees and suppliers and lower transaction costs, provide access to specialised information, create complementarities that enhance a customer's overall experience and facilitate access to institutions and public goods. They also drive the direction and pace of innovation because members of a cluster have a better feel for the market than isolated competitors, are able to be flexible and respond to changed circumstances rapidly and operate in an environment conducive to innovation and transmission of new ideas. Furthermore, there is a within-cluster stimulus of constant comparison with competitors, suppliers and peers. Finally, clusters stimulate the formation of new businesses due to synergies leading to innovation, the ability to spot gaps and opportunities and lower barriers to entry (Porter 1998).

# COMPETITIVE ADVANTAGE AND GENERIC STRATEGIES

The concepts of competitive advantage and competitive strategy at the firm level are closely related. Competitive advantage refers to the basis upon which a firm competes in its target overseas markets. Competitive strategy refers to how it competes.

## Basic competitive strategies

More than two decades ago Michael Porter (1980) suggested three winning basic competitive positioning strategies that companies can follow:

- *overall cost leadership*: Here the company works hard to achieve the lowest costs of production and distribution so that it can price lower than its competitors and win a large market share. The Warehouse in New Zealand and Harvey Norman in Australia, now operating internationally, are leading retail practitioners of this strategy.

- *differentiation*: Here the company concentrates on creating a highly differentiated product line and marketing program so that it comes across as the class leader in the industry. Most customers would prefer to own this brand if its price is not too high. In

Australia, ICI, now called Orica, follows this strategy in its explosives business which is expanding rapidly in overseas markets through acquisition and market growth strategies.

• *focus*: Here the company focuses its effort on serving a few market segments well rather than going after the whole market. Furniture removalists Overseas Shipping Services focus only on the international removals sector of the market, and within that it dominates the Asian and English market segments for two-way movement of goods.

Companies that pursue a clear strategy—one of the above—are likely to perform well. The firm that carries out that strategy best will make the most profits. But firms that do not pursue a clear strategy—middle-of-the-roaders—do the worst. Middle-of-the-roaders try to be good on all strategic counts, but end up being not very good at anything.

These generic strategies may change over time for an individual company. For example, Figure 9.6 shows the competitive path taken internationally by Japanese car manufacturers such as Toyota and Honda. Extending from their domestic market they produced low-cost/low-price products with little differentiation. As volume grew and market coverage widened in their various Asian and American markets they improved quality and brand image and widened their ranges. While Toyota has remained in the mass market, it appears that Honda has moved to a focus strategy with high differentiation in many of its markets. It seems that over the past few years the South Korean manufacturers are taking a similar approach to the Japanese earlier, in particular in the consumer electronics market with brands such as LG and Samsung moving from cost leadership positions to ones that are putting real pressure on the traditional differentiation leaders in this category—Sony and Panasonic. In fact Samsung has recently surpassed Sony in terms of market capitalisation making it the largest consumer electronics company in the world (Moon 2004; Foroohar and Lee 2004). In many sectors, South Korea's role as a cost leader is being replaced by China, illustrating that there is often a relationship between international competitive strategy and the stage of development.

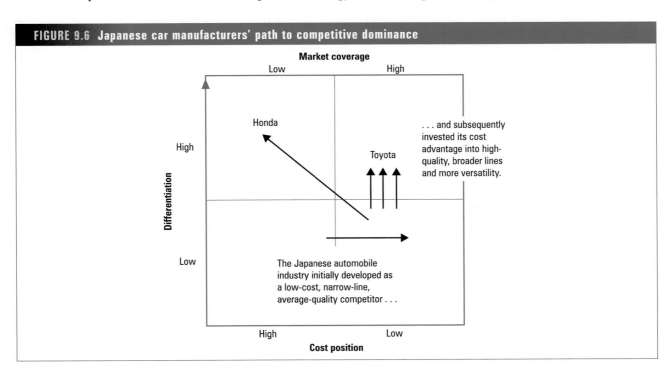

**FIGURE 9.6  Japanese car manufacturers' path to competitive dominance**

Market coverage

Low — High

Differentiation: High — Low

Honda

Toyota

. . . and subsequently invested its cost advantage into high-quality, broader lines and more versatility.

The Japanese automobile industry initially developed as a low-cost, narrow-line, average-quality competitor . . .

High — Low

**Cost position**

Subsequently, two marketing consultants, Michael Treacy and Fred Wiersema (1995), offered an alternative classification of competitive marketing strategies. They suggested that companies gain leadership positions by delivering superior value to their customers. Companies can develop any of three competitive advantages—called *value disciplines*—for delivering superior customer value:

- *operational excellence*: Here the company provides superior value by leading its industry in price and convenience. It works to reduce costs and to create a lean and efficient value delivery system. It serves customers who want reliable, good-quality products or services, but who want them cheaply and easily. Examples include Kmart, with its discount concept extended to New Zealand, and computer company Dell.

- *customer intimacy*: In this case the company provides superior value by precisely segmenting its markets and then tailoring its products or services to match exactly the needs of targeted customers. It builds detailed customer databases for segmenting and targeting, and empowers its marketing people to respond quickly to customer needs. It serves customers who are willing to pay a premium to get precisely what they want, and it will do almost anything to build long-term customer loyalty and to capture the customer's 'lifetime' value. Different but outstanding examples of this are the campaigns developed and implemented by the major consulting firms to win large government and corporate consultancy contracts.

- *product leadership*: The company provides superior value by offering a continuous stream of leading-edge products or services that make their own and competing products obsolete. It is open to new ideas, relentlessly pursues new solutions and works to reduce cycle times so that it can get new products to market quickly. It serves customers who want state-of-the-art products and services, regardless of the costs in terms of price or inconvenience. Examples include Cisco, Porsche and Sony.

Some companies successfully pursue more than one value discipline at the same time. For example, Federal Express and Amazon.com excel at both operational excellence and customer intimacy. However, such companies are rare—few firms can be the best at more than one of these disciplines. By trying to be good at all of the value disciplines a company usually ends up being best at none.

Treacy and Wiersema (1995) have found that leading companies operating internationally focus on and excel at a single value discipline, while meeting industry standards on the other two. They design their entire value delivery system to single-mindedly support the chosen discipline. For example, Lexmark knows that customer intimacy and product leadership are important in overseas markets. Compared with other low-cost suppliers of printers such as Oki (<http://www.okiprinters.com.au>), it offers very good customer service and an excellent product assortment. Still, it offers less customer service and less depth in its product assortment than Canon or Hewlett-Packard, which pursue customer intimacy or product leadership strategies. Instead, it focuses obsessively on operational excellence—on reducing costs and streamlining its order-to-delivery process in order to make it convenient for customers in various countries to buy just the right products at the lowest prices.

Australian companies targeting Asian markets such as Penfolds Wines and Macquarie Bank need to consider closely the cultural differences between countries when positioning their value proposition. While in most Asian markets customer intimacy is highly valued because of the importance of family, friends and connections in doing business, foreign businesses need to focus on different aspects of the other value disciplines. For example, in

China and South Korea negotiation is firmly focused on price, meaning that low costs and operational efficiency become important elements for doing business profitably. (Wiederhecker 2007). However, for many products and services sold to buyers in Japan and Singapore product quality is important. Therefore we see that premium brands such as European cars or Swiss watch makers are excelling in these markets (see Sanchanta 2006).

Classifying competitive advantage in terms of value disciplines is appealing. It defines competitive advantage and marketing strategy in terms of the single-minded pursuit of delivering value to customers. It recognises that management must align every aspect of the company with the chosen value discipline—from its culture, to its organisation structure, to its operating and management systems and processes.

## VALUE INNOVATION

Kim and Mauborgne (2005) propose another approach to competitive advantage and strategy, which they call value innovation. This involves creating significant leaps in value for both the company and its customers in a manner that makes rivals obsolete and creates an uncontested marketspace.

In so many markets competition is fierce and companies compete for market share in what Kim and Mauborgne describe as a 'red ocean' or bloodbath of competitive activity—contesting the same marketspace with fiercely competitive matching strategies in a hyper-competitive environment. Their book, *Blue Ocean Strategy*, provides a methodology for analysing, creating and capturing new market opportunities. The book uses the 'blue ocean' analogy to describe uncontested and typically undefined market opportunities and describes the markets most companies compete in as 'red oceans' due to the fierce competitive rivalry that exists in most markets today (Kim and Mauborgne 2005).

The authors studied 150 strategic moves spanning 100+ years across more than 30 industries and found that the most successful strategies were built around the concept they call value innovation, which involves creating significant leaps in value for both the company and its customers in a manner which makes rivals obsolete. In generic strategy terms this means being able to achieve both significant differential advantage as well as substantial cost advantage through innovation in value to customers and value to the business.

In order for a company to create a blue ocean strategy the authors suggest six principles. These six principles can be categorised into two groups. The first group is formulation principles and includes:

* reconstructing market boundaries;
* focusing on the big picture (rather than on the numbers);
* reaching beyond the current demand; and
* getting the strategic sequence correct.

The second group is that of execution principles and includes:

* overcoming major hurdles within the organisation; and
* building a program for execution into the chosen strategy.

The US wine market and Casella Wines provide the basis for one example used by the authors to explain the blue ocean strategy process. The USA is the third largest consumer of wine worldwide and is an intensely competitive market with local wines from California, Oregon, Washington and New York competing with European, Australian and South

American wines. With all of this competition the number of wines available to the consumer has exploded; however, the demand levels have remained fairly stagnant resulting in much consolidation at the producer and retailer levels of the value chain. Conventional wisdom would suggest this industry is hardly attractive, so how do the incumbents make the right strategic moves to break out of this increasingly unattractive set of market conditions? The authors suggest first detailing the bases of competition on a strategy canvas. In this example, pricing, packaging, advertising, ageing of wine, prestige, complexity of wine taste and range of wine varieties make up the key bases of competition. When current offerings are mapped against these bases, two value lines emerge, a budget wine line-up and a premium wine line-up. The budget wines are low priced and offer low levels of benefits, while the premium wines are more expensive and follow a classic differentiation strategy. These competitive groupings mean that it is very difficult to set a company on a strong profitable growth track as it will not work to benchmark competitors and try to out-compete them by offering a little more for a little less. The authors suggest that market research is not the answer either as their research suggested that customers can barely imagine how to create an uncontested marketspace and usually suggest they want more for less based on the most common industry offers.

In order for a company to make a strategic shift in these circumstances it must change its focus from competitors to alternatives and from customers to non-customers of the existing industry.

The next step is to work out how value is transferred along an interconnected chain of channel players to end customers.

## VALUE CHAIN ANALYSIS

Firms create value for their customers by the activities they perform. The *value chain* is a tool to disaggregate a business into strategically relevant activities that create value. The value chain concept identifies the functions within the firm that create value. This enables identification of the source of competitive advantage on both costs and differentiation. A business gains competitive advantage by performing these activities more cheaply or better than its competitors. Its value chain is part of a larger stream of strategic activities carried out by other members of the channel—suppliers, distributors and customers. It is necessary to understand the links in the chain that provide customer value to be able to restructure the offer or the industry to the firm's advantage. Figure 9.7 illustrates the value chain. Value chains exist at each level of a distribution channel and value is created by the linkages between players in an industry as value is transferred towards the end-buyer. Together these value chains constitute the value system whereby the value chain of the suppliers of your inputs is linked to your value chain and your value chain is linked to the value chain of your distributors which in turn is linked to the value chains of the buyers served by your distributors.

The concept is summarised below.

- The value chain examines all activities a business performs by disaggregating functions into discrete but interrelated activities from which value stems.

- Examination of the value chain allows understanding of the behaviour of costs within a business and existing and potential sources of differentiation.

- Value activities are the physically and technologically distinct activities a business performs, the discrete building blocks of competitive advantage. There are primary value activities and support activities.

## FIGURE 9.7 The value chain

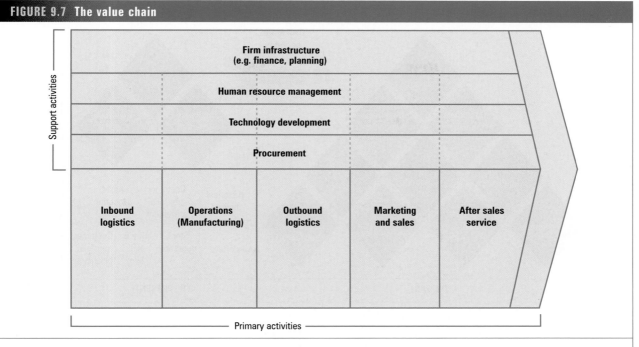

SOURCE: *Porter, M.E. (1990)* The Competitive Advantage of Nations, *Macmillan, London, p. 41. Reproduced with permission of Palgrave.*

Often the keys to competitive advantage are the links or relationships between activities in the value chain. For instance, vertical linkages between buyers, suppliers and ensuing channel activities can lower costs or enhance differentiation.

A firm's competitive scope is a source of competitive advantage because it affects the value chain. This may be in terms of segment scope, the range of products and buyers; geographic scope, the range of regions; vertical scope, the extent of integration; or industry scope, the range of related industries (Brown 1997). Further analysis of value chain linkages can be found in Donlon (2007).

Changes in and convergence of information and communication technologies are restructuring traditional value chains in particular industries. An example is the unbundling of broker services in the financial sector shown in Figure 9.8. The emerging value chain in this and other industries promises to restructure those industries and redistribute value among different components and players in the value chain. For example, the international banking system now helps tourists by the use of globally linked services such as CIRUS where travellers can now access cash via an ATM in Beijing rather than take travellers cheques and incur the cost, time and inconvenience associated with setup and encashment. Similarly, the ANZ Bank can service many of its Australian company customers' needs in Indonesia through electronic interconnection rather than through an extensive branch network. The impacts of these changes are very significant in terms of how value is delivered and which companies and networks of businesses deliver it. There will be irrevocable shifts in retailing and distribution and elimination of intermediaries, rapid shifts in market share and significant leaps forward in mass customisation. International Highlight 9.1 illustrates how the time and place location of buyers is becoming less relevant. Overseas buyers are accessing a company's products and services in an increasingly similar way to domestic customers.

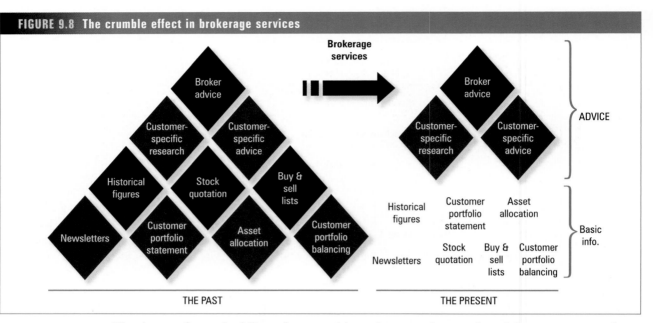

**FIGURE 9.8  The crumble effect in brokerage services**

THE PAST

THE PRESENT

The issue of sustainability of competitive advantage is questioned by some researchers. D'Aveni (1994) identifies a form of competitive intensity referred to as hyper-competition, in which competitors continually match each other's advantages in a continually unstable environment. No competitor is able to sustain an advantage. D'Aveni claims that many industries reflect this situation and the quest for sustainable competitive advantage is untenable. He proposes that companies seek small advantages on an ongoing basis as competition escalates from cost and quality to timing and know-how through to market strongholds and 'deep pockets' (large resources). D'Aveni presents a framework for creating disruption as a means of continually holding small advantages in the firm's chosen markets. This has implications for Australian firms operating in overseas markets as local and international competitors continually match strategies. SMEC, the Australian-based international engineering consulting firm, operates in Asia, Europe and North America. A recent comment by a senior executive indicates that as soon as tenders for international jobs are decided on by the customer, it can be expected that any innovations will be matched by competitors in the next tender process.

The value chain concept when applied to many corporations tends to focus on linear relationships within the chain. There is considerable emphasis on improving service and relationships that are next in line in the chain. The notion that the next person in the value chain is also your customer is strongly emphasised. There can be problems if the whole chain is not improved within the context of supplying demonstrable customer value to the ultimate customer.

There is some evidence to suggest that as organisations become more involved in alliance structures and participate in the new electronic infrastructure, value creation is likely to be a multidimensional activity. Tapscott et al. (2000) paint a scene of value webs, where customer value may be created, collected and delivered within a multidimensional environment of inter-connected businesses. Leaders are using technology to enable broader collaboration within their companies and with external partners. For example, Eli Lilly has set up the web-based InnoCentive to create a talent pool of more than 50 000 scientists in 150 countries. Eli Lilly posts R&D problems on the site, and any scientist with the expertise can tackle them. The success rate has been far higher than in-house performance—at one-sixth the in-house cost. Similarly, P&G has devoted an entire division to collaborate along the value chain with external partners on new

## 9.1 INTERNATIONAL HIGHLIGHT

# Value chains in disarray

### THE TRAVEL AND TOURISM VALUE CHAIN

It has long been recognised that tourists buy destinations, not transport. Accordingly, the airlines and travel operators market the benefits of the destination. Travel agents have traditionally been the key point of sale and service. Now an increasing number of travellers are bypassing both airlines and travel agents to organise their international travel—using the internet as the purchasing channel for airline, hotel and tours.

### FINANCIAL SERVICES

In the banking industry the development of credit cards, then automatic teller machines and then home banking services enhances the accessibility of services to customers and has implications for the branch banking networks. The firms that lead these innovations are able to restructure the industry to their advantage.

Not only are value chains restructuring in this sector but cross-border competition in the banking industry is increasing as the functionality of virtual networks like the internet is creating new fields of competition. The National Australia Bank (NAB) and the ANZ are reallocating capital to develop new positions in the financial services value chain so as to meet the challenge of new competitors that have much lower overhead structures and operating costs. This is being done to protect their domestic markets and to tap new opportunities in overseas markets. For example, the NAB can now provide foreign exchange accounts for businesses that typically would have had to establish banking arrangements with foreign banks, particularly in the USA and Canada. This service allows Australian firms that operate internationally to receive and hold foreign currencies in NAB accounts.

### THE MUSIC INDUSTRY'S VALUE CHAINS— DISINTERMEDIATION

The distribution of music has undergone a number of dramatic changes in the past five years. In particular, demand for digital music has soared due to new software which enables the easy digitisation of consumers' current CD collections, and the introduction of new digital music players and, in particular, Apple's success in convincing the music industry to allow it to sell digital music online via its iTunes service, which was launched in 2003 have dramatically changed the way music is purchased. The digitisation of music poses a number of challenges for the music industry as it unbundles many of its offerings, allowing consumers to purchase by the song rather than by the album, and it has the potential to reduce the revenue and profits available to members of the industry via the ease of sharing and copying of music in digital form. However, the greater challenges lie with the traditional retailers of music such as HMV and Virgin, which have the most to lose from online availability. These companies need to find ways to continue to provide value and relevance as the digital world accelerates.

### CONVERGENCE OF COMMUNICATIONS, MEDIA AND COMPUTER VALUE CHAINS

The rapid trend towards the merging of tele-communications, media and computerisation creates options for the location of computer power in the communications terminal or in the telephone (communications) exchange. If Telstra can provide better solutions for customers from the exchange rather than from terminal hardware it may secure a strategic advantage. Understanding the value chain of the user and the benefits desired is vital. But if computer manufacturers, software firms and telecommunications equipment suppliers are able to provide better solutions to customers through their equipment they will become dominant players. We are seeing moves by Nokia and others to create wireless web devices that go well beyond the current capabilities of mobile phones.

**SOURCE:** *Anon (2004) 'Music's brighter future', Economist, 30 October, p. 71.*

products and technologies. Management at P&G says that half of all new P&G products should originate outside of the company. The company's 'Mr. Clean Magic Eraser', a fast-selling household cleaning tool, was developed in collaboration with IDEO, a product design firm. The next phase will be to translate its success in international markets beyond the USA.

This concept of collaboration and its different forms is explored in more detail in Chapter 12.

## COMPETITOR ANALYSIS

To plan effective competitive marketing strategies the company needs to find out all it can about its competitors both domestically and overseas. It must constantly compare its products, prices, channels and promotion with those of close competitors. In this way the company can find areas of potential competitive advantage and disadvantage. And it can launch more effective marketing campaigns against its competitors and prepare stronger defences against competitors' actions.

But what do companies need to know about their competitors? They need to answer the following: Who are our competitors? What are their objectives? What are their strategies? What are their strengths and weaknesses? What are their reaction patterns? Figure 9.9 shows the major steps in analysing competitors.

## Identifying the company's competitors

Normally it would seem an easy task for a company to identify its competitors. Qantas knows that Singapore Airlines is a major international competitor especially in the Asian region. Adidas knows that it competes with Nike and Dell with HP. At the narrowest level, a company can define its competitors as other companies offering a similar product or service to the same customers at similar prices. Thus, Holden might see Ford as a major competitor, but not Audi or Honda.

But companies actually face a much wider range of competitors. The company might define competitors as all firms making the same product or class of products. Thus, Holden would see itself as competing against all other car makers for targeted export markets. Even more broadly, competitors might include all companies making products that supply the same service. Here Holden would see itself competing against not only other car makers but also companies that make trucks, motorcycles or even bicycles. This is particularly true in some of the Asian developing countries, like China and Vietnam and in the countries where the social scene is changing in the light of the energy and pollution crisis. Finally, and still more broadly, competitors might include all companies that compete for the same consumer dollars. Here Holden would see itself competing with companies that sell major consumer durables, new

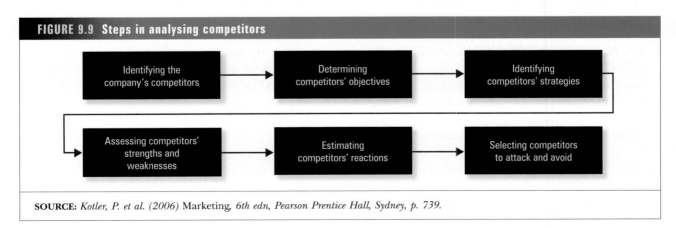

**FIGURE 9.9  Steps in analysing competitors**

Identifying the company's competitors → Determining competitors' objectives → Identifying competitors' strategies → Assessing competitors' strengths and weaknesses → Estimating competitors' reactions → Selecting competitors to attack and avoid

**SOURCE:** *Kotler, P. et al. (2006)* Marketing, *6th edn, Pearson Prentice Hall, Sydney, p. 739.*

homes, overseas holidays. Again, in countries like the Philippines, Thailand and Malaysia and the less developed former Soviet Union countries such as Ukraine, Georgia and Belarus for many, the choice may be between buying a new car or buying an apartment.

Companies must avoid 'competitor myopia'. A company is more likely to be 'buried' by its latent competitors than its current ones. For example, Kodak, in its film business, has been worrying about the growing competition from Fuji, the Japanese filmmaker. But Kodak faces a much greater threat from the recent advances in digital imaging technology. Digital cameras sold by Canon and Sony take video, and still pictures that can be shown on a variety of display units such as TV sets, Data Projectors, and other Plasma and LCD units and then turned into hard copy and later erased. What greater threat is there to a film business than a digital camera? However, there are also opportunities if Kodak understands the entire value chain and how it is changing.

Companies can identify their competitors from the industry point of view. They might see themselves as being in the food industry, the travel industry or the biotechnology industry. A company must understand the competitive patterns in its industry if it hopes to be an effective 'player' in that industry. Michael Porter (1980) suggests that five major forces drive industry competition. These are shown in Figure 9.10. He proposes that the structure of the industry itself, its suppliers and its buyers have a major influence on the evolution of the industry and its profit potential. The threat of substitutes and new entrants also influences the appropriate strategies to be adopted. These parties exert differing levels of power and act as forces which shape the evolution of the industry, control the competitive balance and influence the profit potential.

## Industry structure and competitive forces

Industry structure is not static. Major or minor changes may be occurring at any point in time. Some industries may be undergoing structural change or convergence with other industries.

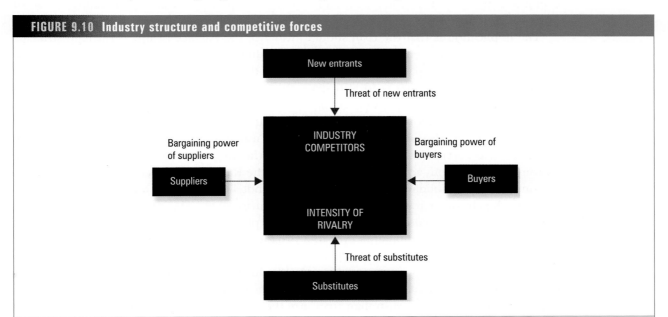

**FIGURE 9.10  Industry structure and competitive forces**

Hence, definition of the relevant industry is important for structural analysis purposes. From an airline's perspective, is the relevant industry 'leisure air travel' or is it 'tourist holidays'? The latter implies that the industry includes accommodation as well as travel.

Since much of the competition revolves around holiday packages in this market, through alliances or networks of airlines, hotels, coaches and resorts, the 'tourist holidays' definition may be more appropriate.

Porter (2001) has reinterpreted his model in the light of the internet's influences on industry structure. The following observations are made in relation to each competitive force, which can have both positive and negative impacts on a competitor's position:

- *New entrants*: there are reduced barriers to entry because the internet reduces the need for a salesforce, access to distribution channels and physical assets.

- *Substitutes*: there are additional new substitution threats and potential market expansion from online retailers offering a wide range of products and services.

- *Suppliers*: the internet provides a channel for suppliers to end-users as well as enabling procurement processes that can standardise products and reduce differentiation.

- *Buyers*: the internet improves bargaining power, through wider choice, and reduces switching costs.

- *Rivalry of competitors*: the internet migrates competition to price by reducing differences between competitors as well as widening the geographic market, increasing the number of competitors.

In any industry, a small number of factors will be relevant. Analysis of industry structure using this model provides an assessment of the strength of competitive position of industry competitors as a group, and this in turn reflects on the individual industry competitor. It is useful also to assess the sustainability of a firm's competitive advantage including those of pure dot.com businesses.

The implication is that the firm should influence the balance of forces through strategic moves, thereby strengthening the firm's position. Alternatively, the strategist might reposition the firm so that its capabilities provide the best defence against the array of competitive forces. A further approach is to anticipate shifts in the factors underlying the forces and respond to them, thus exploiting change by choosing a strategy appropriate to the new competitive balance before competitors recognise it.

Companies can also identify competitors from a market point of view. Here they define competitors as companies that are trying to satisfy the same customer need or serve the same customer group. From an industry point of view, the Radisson hotel chain in Asia might see its competition as Holiday Inn and other four-star hotel chains. From a market point of view, however, the customer really wants 'shelter and nourishment'. This need can be satisfied by a large range of accommodation houses and eating places. In general, the market concept of competition opens the company's eyes to a broader set of actual and potential competitors. This leads to better long-run market planning.

The key to identifying competitors is to link industry and market analysis by mapping out product/market segments. This will reveal that in many Asian country markets the most important competitors to Australian firms are the local companies. In Japan, the interlinked ownerships of the conglomerates create barriers to entry to many markets. The local support by consumers of home-grown companies in South Korea and Thailand, particularly in tough economic times, squeezes out foreign competitors.

# Determining competitors' objectives

Having identified the main competitors, the international marketer now asks: What does each competitor seek in this marketplace? What drives each competitor's behaviour?

The marketer might at first assume that all competitors will want to maximise their profits and will choose their actions accordingly. But companies differ in the emphasis they put on short-term versus long-term profits. And some competitors might be oriented toward *satisficing* rather than *maximising* profits. They have target profit goals and are satisfied with achieving them, even if more profits could have been produced by other strategies. Many competitors, like Daewoo based in South Korea, adopt price penetration strategies to build market share in the Asian region, with profit as a secondary consideration.

Thus, marketers must look beyond competitors' profit goals. Each competitor has a mix of objectives, each with differing importance. The company wants to know the relative importance that a competitor places on current profitability, market share growth, cash flow, technological leadership, service leadership and other goals. Knowing a competitor's mix of objectives reveals whether the competitor is satisfied with its current situation and how it might react to different competitive actions. For example, a company that pursues low-cost leadership will react much more strongly to a competitor's cost-reducing manufacturing breakthrough than to the same competitor's increase in advertising.

A company also must monitor its competitors' objectives for various product/market segments. If the company finds that a competitor has discovered a new segment, this might be an opportunity. If it finds that competitors plan new moves into segments now served by the company, it will be forewarned and, hopefully, forearmed.

# Identifying competitors' strategies

The more that one firm's strategy resembles another firm's strategy, the more the two firms compete. In most industries the competitors can be sorted into groups that pursue different strategies. A strategic group is a group of firms in an industry following the same or a similar strategy in a given target market. For example, in the car market in Japan Toyota and Mazda belong to the same strategic group. Each produces a full line of medium-priced cars supported by good service. Mercedes and BMW, on the other hand, belong to a different strategic group. They produce a narrow line of very high quality cars, offer a high level of service and charge a premium price. Similarly, Nissan doesn't make any of its own minicars, which keeps production costs low, analysts say. Through a manufacturing agreement, Nissan rebrands Suzuki's Alto model as a Pino, outfitting it with Nissan accessories, handbag hooks, fancier seat cushions and other features (Chozick 2007).

Some important insights emerge from strategic group identification. For example, if a company enters one of the groups the members of that group become its key competitors. Thus, if a company like Ford enters the first group against Toyota and Mazda in Japan, it can succeed only if it develops some strategic advantages over these large local competitors.

Although competition is most intense within a strategic group, there is also rivalry between groups. First, some of the strategic groups may appeal to overlapping customer segments. For example, no matter what their strategy all major car manufacturers will go after the semi-sports car segment. Second, the customers may not see much difference in the offers of different groups—they may see little difference in quality between Honda and BMW. Finally, members of one strategic group might expand into new strategy segments. Thus, Toyota's premium-quality, premium-priced Lexus is designed to compete with BMW and Mercedes.

The company needs to look at all of the dimensions that identify strategic groups within the industry. It needs to know each competitor's product quality, features and mix; customer services; pricing policy; distribution coverage; salesforce strategy; and advertising and sales promotion programs. It must also study the details of each competitor's R&D, manufacturing, purchasing, financial and other strategies.

## Assessing competitors' strengths and weaknesses

Marketers need to assess carefully each competitor's strengths and weaknesses in order to answer the critical question: What can our competitors do? As a first step, companies can gather data on each competitor's goals, strategies and performance over the last few years. Admittedly, some of this information will be hard to obtain. For example, business products companies find it hard to estimate competitors' market shares because they do not have the same syndicated data services that are available to consumer packaged-goods companies. This is so, particularly in emerging markets like China, India and Indonesia.

Companies normally learn about their competitors' strengths and weaknesses through secondary data, personal experience and hearsay. They also can conduct primary marketing research with customers, suppliers and dealers. Recently, a growing number of companies have turned to benchmarking, comparing the company's products and processes to those of competitors or leading firms in other industries to find ways to improve quality and performance. Benchmarking has become a powerful tool for increasing a company's competitiveness (Larreche 1998).

## Estimating competitors' reactions

Next, the company wants to know: What will our competitors do? A competitor's objectives, strategies and strengths and weaknesses go a long way towards explaining its likely actions, as well as its likely reactions to company moves, such as price cuts, promotion increases or new product introductions. In addition, each competitor has a certain philosophy of doing business, a certain internal culture and guiding beliefs. International marketers need a deep understanding of a given competitor's mentality if they want to anticipate how the competitor will act or react.

Each competitor reacts differently. Some do not react quickly or strongly to a competitor's move. They may feel their customers are loyal; they may be slow in noticing the move; they may lack the funds to react. Some competitors react only to certain types of moves and not to others. They might always respond strongly to price cuts in order to signal that these will never succeed. But they might not respond at all to increased advertising, believing this to be less threatening. Other competitors react swiftly and strongly to any action. Thus, the local beer icons in countries in the Asian region do not let a new beer come easily into the market. Many firms avoid direct competition with the local brand and look for easier prey, knowing that it will react fiercely if challenged. Finally, some competitors show no predictable reaction pattern. They might or might not react on a given occasion, and there is no way to foresee what they will do based on their economics, history or anything else.

In some industries, competitors live in relative harmony; in others they fight constantly. Knowing how major competitors react gives the company clues on how best to attack.

## Selecting competitors to attack and avoid

A company has already largely selected its major competitors through prior decisions on customer targets, distribution channels and marketing mix strategy in its overseas market.

## 9.2 INTERNATIONAL HIGHLIGHT

# Aromababy—natural baby skincare all the rage!

Catherine Arfi is the CEO of the now well known Aromababy range—a completely natural and organic baby skincare range. Aromababy is now becoming increasingly popular in the US with leading celebrities promoting the products on their children.

Catherine began working on the product range in 1994 from her home office in Victoria after having been involved in the body care and beauty industry for some years. It was when Catherine was pregnant with her first child that she discovered the opportunity for natural baby skincare products.

Catherine explained her exploration for baby skincare: 'I had the idea to make totally natural baby care because I knew the existing products all had a heavy chemical component'.

This idea has proven to be a very popular one with Aromababy a market leader in skincare for babies in Australia and now exporting its product range to the Middle East, parts of Asia and Europe, UK and the US.

Aromababy has been embraced by the health professional community and is being used in some hospitals on newborns. It is a premium priced product because it uses certified organic ingredients and has to undergo significant testing in laboratories before being released for sale. The high price tag of some of the products has not hindered Aromababy's sales and it has helped to position the product in some countries like Japan as the product of choice. The organic positioning and the packaging with the price position is making this product attractive to markets that have a low birth rate and where parents are willing to pay a premium for products for their children.

Catherine Arfi continues to augment her product range and now has a new range called Pure Spa Baby. With celebrities like Sarah Jessica Parker and Tara Reid promoting Aromababy it certainly is a great success story of a small Australian company in the highly competitive cosmetics industry.

SOURCES: *'Natural care makes baby's bottom line'*, <http://www.austrade.gov.au>, accessed 19 February 2007; *'Exporting cosmetics to Asia'*, <http://www.austrade.gov.au/ArticleDocuments/1418/Export-Cosmetics-Asia.pdf.aspx>, accessed 19 February 2007; and <http://www.aromababy.com>, accessed 19 February 2007.

These decisions define the strategic group to which the company belongs. Management must now decide which competitors to compete against most vigorously. The company can focus on one of several classes of competitors.

## STRONG OR WEAK COMPETITORS

Most companies prefer to aim their shots at their weak competitors. This requires fewer resources and less time. But in the process the firm may gain little. The argument could be made that the firm also should compete with strong competitors in order to sharpen its abilities. Furthermore, even strong competitors have some weaknesses, and succeeding against them often provides greater returns.

A useful tool for assessing competitor strengths and weaknesses is customer value analysis. The aim of customer value analysis is to determine the benefits that target customers' values and how customers rate the relative value of various competitors' offers. In conducting a customer value analysis, the company first identifies the major attributes that customers value and the importance customers place on these attributes. Next, it assesses the company's and its competitors' performance on the valued attributes. The key to gaining competitive advantage is to take each customer segment and examine how the company's offer compares to that of its major competitor. If the company's offer exceeds the competitor's offer on all important attributes, the company can charge a higher price and earn higher profits or it can charge the same price and gain more market share. But if the company is seen as performing at a lower level than its major competitor on some important attributes, it must invest in strengthening those attributes or finding other important attributes where it can build a lead on the competitor. A detailed process for conducting customer value analysis and developing value maps is found in Best (2006).

## CLOSE OR DISTANT COMPETITORS

Most companies will compete with competitors who resemble them most. Thus, Toyota competes more against Ford than against Jaguar. At the same time the company may want to avoid trying to 'destroy' a close competitor. For example, in the late 1990s an American competitor, believing that Australian-based Burns Philp was trying to destroy its position, moved aggressively against it in the US market with great success. Due to continuing losses Burns Philp has had to sell a number of its businesses to survive and focus on a core business with a few key markets.

## 'WELL-BEHAVED' OR 'DISRUPTIVE' COMPETITORS

A company really needs and benefits from competitors. The existence of competitors results in several strategic benefits. Competitors may help increase total demand. They may share the costs of market and product development and help to legitimise new technologies. They may serve less attractive segments or lead to more product differentiation.

However, a company may not view all its competitors as beneficial. An industry often contains 'well-behaved' competitors and 'disruptive' competitors. Well-behaved competitors play by the rules of the industry. They favour a stable and healthy industry, set reasonable prices in relation to costs, motivate others to lower costs or improve differentiation and accept reasonable levels of market share and profits. Disruptive competitors break the rules. They try to buy share rather than earn it, take large risks and in general shake up the industry. For example, Qantas finds Air New Zealand to be a well-behaved competitor on the US route because it plays by the rules and attempts to set its fares sensibly. But both airlines found US carrier Northwest Airlines a disruptive competitor because it destabilised the profitability of this route through continual heavy price discounting and extensive promotional schemes. Subsequent to a price war, Northwest withdrew from the Australia–US route. A company might be smart to support well-behaved competitors, aiming its attacks at disruptive competitors.

The implication is that 'well-behaved' companies would like to shape an industry that consists of well-behaved competitors only. Through careful licensing, selective retaliation and coalitions, they can shape the industry so that the competitors behave rationally and harmoniously, follow the rules, try to earn market share rather than buy it and differentiate to compete less directly. These Western notions of behaviour need to be seen within the context of the varying cultures of Asia. What might be seen as disruptive by Australian firms might be normal practice in Taiwan or South Korea.

# OBTAINING COMPETITIVE INTELLIGENCE

The main types of information that companies need about their competitors have been described. This information must be collected, interpreted, distributed and used. The cost in money and time of gathering competitive intelligence is high, and the company must design its competitive intelligence system in a cost-effective way.

The competitive intelligence system first identifies the vital types of competitive information and the best sources of this information. Then, the system continuously collects information from the field (salesforce, channels, suppliers, market research firms and trade associations) and from published data (government publications, speeches, articles). Next the system checks the information for validity and reliability, interprets it and organises it in an appropriate way. Finally, it sends key information to relevant decision makers and responds to inquiries from managers about competitors. Hewlett-Packard has developed this kind of system and advertises central access points through its intranet to managers all over the world.

With this system, company managers will receive timely information about competitors in the form of phone calls, bulletins, newsletters and reports. In addition, managers can connect with the system when they need an interpretation of a competitor's sudden move, when they want to know a competitor's weaknesses and strengths, or when they need to know how a competitor will respond to a planned company move.

Smaller companies that cannot afford to set up formal competitive intelligence offices can assign specific executives to watch specific competitors. Thus, a manager who used to work for a competitor might follow that competitor closely—they would be the 'in-house expert' on that competitor. Any manager needing to know the thinking of a given competitor contacts the assigned in-house expert.

The internet represents a useful channel for the international marketer to obtain up-to-date competitive information quickly. Using a search engine like Yahoo! or Google the starting point would be the competitor's website. This will provide information on products, services, positioning, availability and often pricing. By 'digging' through the website, recent press releases and announcements of new products, financial results and company objectives can often be found. The next step may be to visit the industry association website which may include proceedings of industry conferences, press releases about the major players' strategies and intentions and articles on companies and the industry. This may be followed by visiting the websites of leading business magazines which record interviews and write stories about specific companies. This may include *The Australian Financial Review*, *Business Review Weekly*, *National Business Review*, *Far Eastern Economic Review*, *International Business Week* and *Fortune* magazine. Channel 9's 'Sunday' program provides transcripts of their interviews with business leaders. ABI INFORM is an Australian database, accessible immediately within the university system. It provides a source of articles, case studies and books that may be relevant to particular companies and industries for providing competitive intelligence.

Information of this kind is continually expanding worldwide and is a source of competitive information accessible via the internet.

## LEVERAGING CAPABILITIES

Having identified and evaluated its major competitors, the company must now design competitive marketing strategies that will best position its offer against competitors' offers and give the company the strongest possible competitive advantage. But what marketing strategies might the company use? Which ones are best for a particular company, or for the company's different divisions and products?

No one strategy is best for all companies. Each company must determine what makes the most sense given its position in its overseas market and its objectives, opportunities and resources. Even within a company, different strategies may be required for different businesses or products. International marketers also need to determine how the firm's capabilities can be leveraged in overseas markets. One approach is to build networks to extend the value chain by using alliance partners. (Alliance strategies and their implications are discussed in Chapter 12.) Another strategy for leveraging capabilities is the use of electronic commerce and electronic marketing as a means of reducing costs, increasing customer access and extending market reach.

# The internet and competitive advantage

## Major effects of electronic business

The major effects of electronic business on international competitiveness are outlined below.

### SHIFTS IN IMPORTANT STRATEGIC DIMENSIONS

With e-commerce, price and quality are no longer the only determinants of a firm's competitiveness. Fast delivery and customisation are also important factors—factors for which customers are willing to pay a premium. E-business, combined with flexible production systems such as computer integrated manufacturing, flexible manufacturing systems and just-in-time inventories makes mass customisation possible by compressing the time it takes firms to deliver products/services to customers.

### COMPRESSED VALUE CHAIN

Not only do some of the traditional elements in the chain disappear with e-business, but also sharing demand information throughout the value chain helps plan and control upstream activities based on future demand that has already occurred downstream. In the process, excessive inventory and backorders are reduced. Online ordering and the real-time transfer of ordering information to the manufacturer significantly shorten lead times to meet customer demands.

### GLOBALISATION OF MARKETS

No longer is producing the best product or service in a country a guarantee of success, as the market is also accessible by foreign competitors. To be competitive it is necessary to create a product or service that is attractive to global customers and at the same time is customised to specific needs in a country. No longer is it feasible for country-specific units of multinational firms to act independently from each other. To do so means that they are unable to coordinate operations between different countries or carry separate stocks for different countries and, as a consequence, they end up with a poor matching between customer demand and warehouse inventory.

### OUTSOURCING AS A STRATEGIC WEAPON

E-commerce makes it convenient and efficient to share information among different firms in the value chain through the use of electronic data interchange (EDI) and the internet. This facilitates firms outsourcing activities. Outsourcing can take the form of activities that provide little added value if done internally (e.g. bookkeeping, maintenance), activities that cannot be done due to lack of resources (e.g. R&D, logistics), and activities that can be done better by other firms (e.g. advertising).

### GLOBALISATION OF THE SUPPLY NETWORK

International business traditionally has been inefficient and time consuming because of the wide areas to cover and long lead times. E-business has compressed time and distance and therefore it becomes feasible for firms to overcome national boundaries and multinational activities can be executed with the efficiencies of domestic operations. As an example, Dell computers have taken the opportunity to build a worldwide network of suppliers and customers into a virtual corporation, providing what customers want in a fast and efficient manner. Furthermore, with e-commerce, firms no longer have to confine sources of supply to domestic suppliers. A supply network on a global scale is one of the most important sources of a firm's competitiveness. This is shown in Figure 9.11.

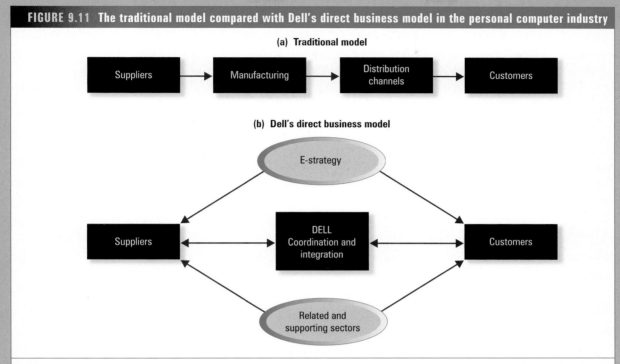

**FIGURE 9.11** The traditional model compared with Dell's direct business model in the personal computer industry

**(a) Traditional model**

Suppliers → Manufacturing → Distribution channels → Customers

**(b) Dell's direct business model**

E-strategy

Suppliers ← DELL Coordination and integration → Customers

Related and supporting sectors

SOURCE: *Cho, D.S., Moon, H.C. and Park, J. (2000) 'Competitiveness impacts of electronic commerce: supply chain management perspective', in e-Commerce and Global Business Forum, 2000, Andersen Institute for Strategic Change.*

## COMPETITIVENESS AND E-BUSINESS

Theories of competitive advantage need to be modified to take account of the impact of the internet. As an example, Porter (1990) modelled the factors causing nations to gain competitive advantage in certain industries and drew conclusions as to the implications for company strategies and national economies. His model had four determinants—factor conditions, demand conditions, related and supporting industries, and firm strategy, structure and rivalry. In addition, he included two variables external to the firm, those of government and chance.

He emphasised domestic rivalry and geographic concentration. With e-business, firms cannot restrict rivalry to the domestic scene and geographic concentration in the home country is less important. For factor conditions and demand conditions there are a number of upstream and downstream activities in the value chain to be taken into account as well as the existence of intermediaries. The possibilities in e-business of deconstruction of the value chain and of disintermediation of agents will change the businesses in the chain that are related to factor conditions and demand conditions.

In addition, the elements of domestic rivalry and the geographic concentration of related and supporting industries are both less important in e-business where geographic restriction to a certain area in a country is not very important in an increasingly digital environment. Porter largely ignored the role of human factors.

These are very important in e-business because the competitiveness of an organisation can be a function of the computerised capabilities of its members. As far as factors in Porter's original diamond are concerned, according to Cho et al. (2000) e-business requires their modification as explained below.

## FACTOR CONDITIONS

Porter's focus on domestic resources is not applicable in the internet age. This is because the internet, combined with an international logistics infrastructure and trade-related deregulation, enables companies to produce goods in foreign countries; that is, countries where it is most cost efficient to produce and then distribute goods to the global market, or to source low-cost high-quality parts from foreign countries for incorporation into domestic production.

## RELATED AND SUPPORTING CONDITIONS

Firms no longer have to rely on domestic-related and supporting industries because globalisation offers the opportunity to use foreign-related and supporting industries such as international logistics or communication services.

## DEMAND CONDITIONS

With e-commerce, firms can sell their products/services to customers in the global market. They can also customise goods/services to every customer's needs to a greater extent.

## STRUCTURE, STRATEGY AND RIVALRY

With e-commerce, through the integration of online ordering, real-time transfer of order information throughout the value chain and an efficient logistics system, a firm can get closer to both suppliers and customers so as to maximise its value to both parties.

# Summary

Success as an overseas marketer is determined in large part by the design and implementation of an effective marketing strategy. The foundation for strategy is built on a careful assessment of a firm's competitive advantage in its targeted overseas markets, its relevant generic strategies and an understanding of the value chain leading into overseas markets and how they are changing.

A useful starting point is to assess the competitive advantage of an industry from a national standpoint. This requires a detailed assessment of the home country national advantage using a framework similar to that developed by Michael Porter. A similar assessment could be done for the home country national advantages of major competitors and also that of the target overseas country market. The next level of assessment is a consideration of relevant competitive advantage options and generic strategies at the firm level. This decision is particularly important because it involves investment commitments to the relevant value model underlying the desired competitive advantage. Related to this analysis is an understanding of the industry value chain and how it is changing in relation to the creation and delivery of customer value.

In order to conduct this analysis realistically it is necessary to follow a process of competitive analysis that attempts to factor in the strategic intent and current strategies of the firm's most important competitors in its overseas market. A systematic analysis of competitors—both current and likely future competitors—forms the basis for the firm's positioning in its targeted international markets. In order to carry out these evaluations the firm needs to collect wide-ranging information about competitors. This process is becoming facilitated by a much greater level of electronic interconnection and use of such information channels as the internet.

---

## ETHICS ISSUE

Your firm is losing sales in an important overseas market as a result of the entry of a new international competitor. In a matter of months it will be necessary to pull out of the country if the trend continues.

A loyal customer has obtained a copy of your competitor's detailed marketing strategy, price book and action programs for the next year. The customer offers you the document to help you out.

**What would you do?**

---

## Websites

**BRW** http://www.brw.com.au
**CEA Technologies Pty Ltd** http://www.cea.com.au
**CSL Limited** http://www.csl.com.au
**Dell Australia** http://www.dell.com.au
**Ericsson** http://www.ericsson.com
**FedEx** http://www.fedex.com
**Honda** http://www.honda.com.au
**Kmart** http://www.kmart.com.au
**Lexmark** http://www.lexmark.com
**Orica** http://www.orica.com.au
**Toyota Australia** http://www.toyota.com.au

## Discussion questions

1 Map out in broad terms the Australian or New Zealand pharmaceutical industry using Porter's model of national competitive advantage.

2 Clarify the distinction between product leadership, operational excellence and customer intimacy as a basis for competitive advantage.

3 Describe three companies operating in overseas markets that appear to conform to each of the three distinctive advantages outlined in Question 2.

4 Select an Australian or New Zealand company doing business overseas and explain how its generic strategy has changed over time with reference to Porter's framework.

5 What does it mean to have a 'blue ocean' strategy based on value innovation? Provide an example of one Australian or New Zealand company that is adopting this in overseas markets.

6 How has the internet affected competitive advantage for Australian or New Zealand exporters? Provide an example of a company that has been able to use this to advantage.

7 Describe how the value chain has changed in the international music industry.

8 What are the steps involved in systematically conducting competitive analysis?

9 Qantas competes aggressively with Singapore Airlines on the 'kangaroo route' between Sydney and London. Conduct a competitive analysis of Singapore Airlines and suggest how Qantas should position itself on this route.

# References

Anon (2004) 'Music's brighter future', *Economist*, Vol. 373, Issue 8399, p. 71.

Best, R. (2006) *Market Based Management*, 4th edn, Prentice Hall, Englewood Cliffs, NJ, Chapter 4.

Bowen, J.T. Jr, Leinbach, T.R. (2006) 'Competitive advantage in global production networks: air freight services and the electronics industry in southeast Asia'. *Economic Geography*, Vol. 82, No. 2, pp. 150–53.

Bradley, F. (2002) *International Marketing Strategy*, 4th edn, Financial Times Prentice Hall, Harlow, UK.

Brown, L.R. (1997) *Competitive Marketing Strategy*, 3rd edn, ITP Nelson, Melbourne.

Cho, D.S., Moon, H.C. and Park, J. (2000) 'Competitiveness impacts of electronic commerce: supply chain management perspective', in e-Commerce and Global Business Forum, Andersen Institute for Strategic Change, Santa Cruz, CA.

Chobanyan, A. and Leigh, L. (2006) 'The competitive advantages of nations; applying the "Diamond" model to Armenia', *International Journal of Emerging Markets*, Vol. 1, No. 2, p. 147.

Chozick, A. (2007) 'Nissan's pitch for mini-car: accessorize it; pino is secondary in spots that woo young women', *Wall Street Journal* (Eastern edition), 30 March, p. B.3.

D'Aveni, R.A. (1994) *Hyper-Competition: Managing the Dynamics of Strategic Manouvering*, The Free Press, New York.

Donlon, J.P. (2007) 'Ensuring a healthy value chain', *Chief Executive*, March, p. 34.

'Exporting cosmetics to Asia', <http://www.austrade.gov.au/ArticleDocuments/1418/Export-Cosmetics-Asia.pdf.aspx>, accessed 19 February 2007.

Foroohar, R. and Lee, B. J. (2004) 'Masters of the digital age', *Newsweek*, Vol. 144, Issue 16, p. E10.

<http://www.aromababy.com>, accessed 19 February 2007.

Ketels, C.H.M. (2006). 'Michael Porter's competitiveness framework—recent learnings and new research priorities', *Journal of Industry, Competition and Trade*, Vol. 6, No. 2, p. 115.

Kim, W.C. and Mauborgne, R. (2005), *Blue Ocean Strategy: How to Create Uncontested Market Space and Make the Competition Irrelevant*, Harvard Business School Press, Boston.

Kotler, P., Brown, L., Adam, S., Burton S. and Armstrong, G. (2006) *Marketing*, 7th edn, Pearson Prentice Hall, Sydney.

Larreche, J.C. (1998) *Report on Competitive Fitness of Global Firms*, Pitmann Publishing, London.

Moon, H.C., Rugman, A.M. and Verbeke, A. (1998) 'A generalised double diamond approach to the global competitiveness of Korea and Singapore', *International Business Review*, Vol. 7, pp. 135–50.

Moon, I. (2004), 'Samsung inside?', *BusinessWeek*, 25 October, p. 58.

'Natural care makes baby's bottom line', <http://www.austrade.gov.au>, accessed 19 February 2007.

Porter, M.E. (1980) *Competitive Strategy: Techniques for Analysing Industries and Competitors*, The Free Press, New York.

Porter, M.E. (1990) *The Competitive Advantage of Nations*, Macmillan, London.

Porter, M.E. (1998) 'Clusters and the new economics of competition', *Harvard Business Review*, November–December, pp. 77–90.

Porter, M.E. (2001) 'Strategy and the internet', *Harvard Business Review*, March, pp. 63–78.

Sanchanta, M. (2006) 'Youngsters display a yen for exclusive stuff', *Financial Times*, 5 June, p. 3.

Stone, H.B.J. and Ranchhod, A. (2006) 'Competitive advantage of a nation in the global arena: a quantitative advancement to Porter's diamond applied to the UK, USA and BRIC nations', *Strategic Change*, Vol. 15, No. 6, p. 283.

Tapscott, D., Ticoll, D. and Lowy, A. (2000), *Digital Capital*, Harvard Business School Press, Boston, MA.

Treacy, M. and Wiersema, F. (1995) *The Discipline of Market Leaders*, Knowledge Exchange Santa Monica, CA.

Wiederhecker, A.( 2007) 'Chinese hang onto opulent dreams', *Financial Times*, April 14, p. 8.

**go online**

Go online to <www.pearsoned.com.au/fletcher> to find more case studies.

CASE STUDY 9

# Opus International Consultants—an internationally competitive company

Greg Walton, School of Marketing and International Business, Victoria University of Wellington, New Zealand

Opus International Consultants has come a long way from its parental origins—the Ministry of Works and Development—to become the country's leading engineering, architecture, planning and property management consultancy, achieving record revenue of NZ$255 million in 2006, of which about 20% was derived from exports.

Based in Wellington and with offices in Australia, Canada, New Zealand and the UK, Opus provides innovative and specialist services to a wide range of public and private sector clients on a diverse range of projects. These include, for example, asset management of thousands of kilometres of New Zealand's and Western Australia's highways and road networks, underwater structural engineering investigation work on major bridges on the River Thames and infrastructure upgrading for the London Underground in the UK.

Dr Kevin Thompson, Chief Executive for Opus, says the skills and capability the company have developed over decades working in New Zealand have been instrumental in building the business internationally. A key strength is its road asset management capability, a niche in which he says New Zealand is regarded as a world leader.

'With a population of just over four million, New Zealand is a relatively small global economy, but its transport infrastructure is relatively large because of its geography', he says. 'We've had to get quite smart over the years in the ways we manage transport assets and we've developed many innovative techniques which we are now successfully taking offshore.

'We particularly chose the three "established" overseas countries we operate in as they are

*Dr Kevin Thompson, CEO, Opus.*

recognising the benefits of good asset management, compared to the developing world where the key focus is on first constructing nsew infrastructure', says Dr Thompson. 'Selecting English-speaking, culturally attuned countries was made on the basis that we needed to make exporting our services as easy as possible, given we had an expectation that simply building a foreign foothold was going to be difficult.'

Companies increasingly define the markets they supply to in terms of customer attributes. This contemporary thinking transcends conventional market definition in terms of the country market. Opus operates in many country markets that are both 'psychically close' and 'psychically distant' to their home country. Yet, they have made a concerted decision that at least in the immediate future markets are those that are 'culturally attuned' and 'easy'. There is no doubt commercial objectives that include financial performance in markets have determined market selection and development. Indeed, market criteria would include the importance of a higher level 'asset management' principle that is beyond more elementary infrastructure development—road building. The decision to focus on fewer markets (market concentration) is based on the relationship between ROI, market share and marginal return from a market penetration strategy.

Some of the high profile international projects Opus is currently involved in are the upgrading of the London Underground Piccadilly Line stations, including the preservation of many heritage sites; specialist water management services in Western Australia; and advice for the Trans-Canada Expressway development and the British Columbia highway privatisation program.

Opus has increased export revenue from $12 million in 2003 to more than $46 million in 2006 (see Figure 1), and Dr Thompson says it is the international business opportunities that will help the company achieve its target of at least doubling its size between 2001 and 2007. 'Transit New Zealand, which is responsible for New Zealand's state highway network, is our largest single client, while the New Zealand local authority community is our largest client group. Work for local authorities and departments of transportation dominate our activity in Australia, Canada and the UK', he says.

Opus is also planning to become a publicly listed company by the end of 2007 and Dr Thompson says this will further accelerate its growth.

All firms need to ask themselves what business they are in. This business discipline is critical to make business decisions that revolve around such fundamentals like 'what products do we produce?' and 'what do our customers look like, where are they and how do we reach them?'. This understanding is also crucial to make business expansion decisions like, 'do we concentrate on a few markets or do we widely diversify?'. Opus has been widely diversified in many markets spanning Asia, the Middle East and the markets stated above with a diverse range of projects. Strategic decisions have been taken in recent times. Opus has determined that its customer groups are concentrated in few segments akin to its competencies, yet these segments reside in widely diverse geographical country markets. This might normally lead to a market selection and development strategy that is diversified. Opus has determined to focus on few segments in a few country markets. Importantly, to address this question Opus has referred again to its understanding of the business it is in.

Ayal and Zif (1979) were early researchers who helped managers determine a market expansion strategy. This decision framework is akin to the 'what business are you in?'. They suggested criteria to determine whether a firm should be

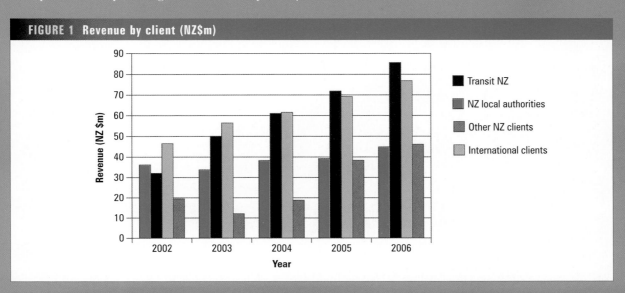

**FIGURE 1  Revenue by client (NZ$m)**

Legend:
- Transit NZ
- NZ local authorities
- Other NZ clients
- International clients

widely spread in markets and segments or more narrowly focused. Criteria for determining which strategy is appropriate for a firm are spread over four categories—company factors, product factors, market factors and marketing factors. Opus has determined that its 'engineering, architecture, planning and property management consultancy' expertise has high repeat consumption value in a few markets, high value sales, high customer loyalty, long competitive lead time, high market growth rate in mature markets, and is in the middle of the product cycle.

Notwithstanding, this decision to concentrate on some segments in few country markets is commensurate with Opus's capacity to produce product and adequately supply its chosen segments and country markets. Opus has determined the relative cost of wide diversification compared to building solid relationships in fewer markets with high repeat sales.

Currently Opus is focused on expanding its business in existing markets through a strategy of organic growth and, more importantly, through a program of mergers and acquisitions with locally-based businesses, leveraging off its local knowledge, skills and market recognition. 'We see acquisition as an excellent way of expanding, so long as we select the right companies, ensuring that both the business and its values are appropriately aligned with Opus', says Dr Thompson.

Presently Opus has over 1800 staff in four countries, operating through 58-offices, including 300 staff in 18 offices throughout Australia, Canada and the UK. 'One of our key strengths is our "local office" model', explains Dr Thompson. 'Based on its success in New Zealand, we're applying this model internationally, operating multiple, small, locally focused offices, where similar competitors have typically only one to two large, impersonal offices. Each Opus office has a large degree of delegated authority and clients know and appreciate that they are working with local people at a local office with the ability to "make things happen". At the same time they know each office is backed by the global network that Opus provides and this gives them an added sense of security.'

Technology is critical to the smooth running of the Opus network, as is personal contact. Senior managers regularly move across international borders and meet with clients. 'Nothing beats this face-to-face contact', says Dr Thompson. 'Without trying to sound clichéd, Opus is very much about its people and we put a lot of effort into that. We've got to; our people are our particular strength and our marketing point of difference.'

Dr Thompson's advice to would-be New Zealand exporters is to focus on a niche where you do really well and find a business model that is transportable and repeatable. Also ensure that there is sufficient support and systems behind it 'back home' to make it work, and that you understand the cultural 'minutiae' of the country you are targeting. 'That's what Opus has done', he says. 'While we face ongoing challenges, from acquisitions to fluctuating currencies, there is also a huge potential for us globally.'

## Bibliography

Ayal, I and Zif, J (1979) 'Market expansion strategies in multinational marketing', *Journal of Marketing*, Vol. 43, No. 2, pp. 84–94.

New Zealand Trade and Enterprise, <http://www.nzte.govt.nz/section/14606/16249.aspx>.

## Questions

1 What academic model would be useful to understand how Opus began building its capability and core competencies? Explain.

2 International competitive advantage begins with understanding a firm's positioning relative to other suppliers. What can be said about the perceived value that Opus provides its customers (compared with purchase price) against the relative costs of its competitors producing, delivering/transferring similar expertise?

3 What is competitive advantage and in what areas do you think Opus has competitive advantage in?

4 What competitive analysis framework would be useful to examine Opus's international competitiveness? Explain.

5 Describe the link between competitive advantage and market entry strategy and mode (entry mechanism).

# CHAPTER 10

# INTERNATIONAL STRATEGIES

## LearningObjectives

**After reading this chapter you should be able to:**

■ assess the competitive position of a firm in an overseas market;

■ identify the characteristics of a dominant competitive position and strategies used by international firms to consolidate dominance;

■ examine alternative offensive and defensive marketing strategies adopted in overseas markets; and

■ evaluate strategies of market leaders, challengers, followers and niche specialists in overseas markets.

# How to create a new international market with a new product . . . the Apple iPod strategy

Consider the Apple story in terms of what it takes to succeed and dominate an international marketplace. Apple was not the first company to introduce a digital music player to the market. In fact, the demand for iPods after the product's initial launch in late 2001 was not impressive—about 376 000 devices were sold worldwide in its first full year. Aside from its sleek design, there was not much to differentiate the iPod from other music players like Creative and Rio, which had pioneered this market. Also, the launch of the iTunes online store in April 2003 seemed at first to be a non-event. There were other services competing in the market for music downloads, as well as the illegal music-sharing networks.

Industry observers believed in 2003 that iPod and iTunes were both competing in a crowded segment for music players and downloads. However, no one company had a position in both markets—here Apple had a clear start against all other competitors. About 100 million iPod sales and two billion iTunes downloads later, Apple dominates this international market because it was the first to recognise the consumer need for an all-in-one integrated music player, download and music-management system. In 2007 Apple controlled about 75% of the combined market for digital music players and legal music downloads.

Steve Jobs, the CEO of Apple Computer, proclaimed the iPod as 'the Walkman of the 21st century' at the November 2004 launch of the latest flavour of iPod—the Red and Black U2 edition. Since the iPod's introduction in 2001, Apple has dominated the sales of digital music players. Apple took a two-pronged approach that focused on the product itself and the means to use it. In designing the iPod, Apple decided to take a different approach from current offerings in the market; these are based on flash memory, which has only low music storage capacity. Instead, Apple signed an agreement with Toshiba to take all its supply of a new small-format hard drive, which would allow consumers to store thousands of songs rather than 100 or 200 at the most from

competing manufacturers. The second piece of the strategy lay in convincing the music industry to allow Apple to sell music online. Once it was convinced, the Apple iTunes store was born. With these two foundations in place the iPod has established itself as an 'iconic' product in popular culture.

Not only has Apple achieved enormous success with the iPod, but the product has also served as a launch platform for Apple to move beyond the computer industry and into the consumer electronics and entertainment industries. This is an industry which many of the large IT vendors such as Microsoft, Dell and HP are looking to enter to capture increased profits as demand for the emerging digital home solution increases.

Apple has certainly played all its cards right to date, but its success has many industry observers recalling a similar situation in Apple's history—one that did not play out as well for Apple. The early battle for the personal computer market saw Apple competing with IBM and a little-known software vendor called Microsoft. At that time Apple lost out in terms of market share due to Microsoft's ability to set the industry standards. Given that Apple has gone down the proprietary route again (Apple's music file format is only compatible with the iPod and the iTunes website only sells music in this format), will it fall victim to the same attack from Microsoft? Certainly Bill Gates (CEO of Microsoft) thinks so; while Microsoft has been working on digital music formats for some time it has really only started to go into overdrive recently after seeing Apple's success. Microsoft has been busy gaining support for its Windows media format from vendors like Dell and Samsung as well as enlisting support from the competing online music suppliers—Napster, America Online and RealNetworks.

How did a company like Apple come from seemingly nowhere to beat the traditional music hardware vendors like Sony? Sony, you would have thought, would be the most likely producer of such a breakthrough portable music device. However, it has been unable to release itself from its own music production heritage. Sony owns one of the largest record labels in the world and so has spent much of its time trying to reduce the expansion of the MP3 digital music format popularised by the Napster file-swapping services of the late 1990s.

Meanwhile, Apple is looking to expand its lead in the market and recently introduced the iPod mini—a smaller version of the original iPod—to capture share against the lower-cost flash memory card players. It also introduced the iPod photo model that allows the iPod to display photos as well as play music. Each of these moves are stoking the fire of the market and pushing Apple further into the lead. The challenge for Apple going forward will be working out the international marketing strategies it should implement to defend and increase its dominance. Competitors have since launched substitute products, but the advantage of being the first mover, coupled with strong brand relevance, has enabled Apple to defend its market position.

In 2006 Apple said it sold more than 21 million iPods in the quarter ended 30 December, up 50% from the 14 million it sold a year earlier. It was reported in April 2007 that it had sold 100 million iPods since November 2001. The company achieved US$3.43 billion in sales from the device, accounting for nearly half of Apple's total revenue. One of the biggest gains for Apple is the level of profitability where its gross profit margin grew to 31.2% in 2006, up from 27.2% in 2005.

SOURCES: *Hansell, S. (2004) 'Gates vs. jobs: the rematch',* New York Times, *Sunday Business, 14 November, Sunday Late Edition, Section 3, p. 1; Salkever A. (2004) 'A bitter apple replay?',* BusinessWeek Online, *14 October, accessed 16 November 2004; 'Shareholder scoreboard (a special report 2007): performance of 1,000 major U.S. companies compared with their peers in 75 industry groups; finding tomorrow's winners today: try firms with fresh perspectives: companies that depart from the conventional wisdom in defining their markets may deliver strong returns',* Wall Street Journal *(Eastern edition), 26 February, p. R.4; and <http://www.sfgate.com/cgi-bin/article.cgi?file=/c/a/2007/04/10/BUGH4P5FKS1.DTL>, accessed 10 April 2007. Image supplied by Apple Pty Ltd.*

# INTRODUCTION

The purpose of this chapter is to identify the key dimensions of competitive position and provide a framework for evaluating relevant marketing strategies to be adopted in overseas markets.

Would the marketing strategy for overseas markets relevant to one airline be relevant to another? Would the strategic options be the same? No; each firm's situation is distinct. Each marketplace is unique. Firms competing in a given target market will, at any point in time, differ in their objectives and resources. Some firms will be large, others small. Some will have many resources, others will be strapped for funds. Some will be old and established, others new and fresh. Some will strive for rapid market share growth, others for long-term profits. And the firms will occupy different competitive positions in the target market. The competitive position in an overseas market that a firm holds at a point in time directly dictates the ability of that firm to cater for the needs of the market and, ultimately, to achieve its corporate objectives. If a firm does not have this ability it must develop a competitive position that offers it. A firm's current position in an overseas market will determine, in part, what alternative positions are available to it and the relevant options for strategy.

This chapter examines a variety of competitive dimensions in which a business holds a 'position' in its industry. This is examined with reference to a firm's position in an overseas market. Competitive position is not a precise or fixed point. It describes the relationship a company has with a market relative to its competitors in that market. It is measured in both quantitative and qualitative terms on a number of important dimensions. The relative position on each of these dimensions, when combined together, make up a business's overall competitive position.

# COMPONENTS OF AN INTERNATIONAL MARKETING STRATEGY

The global economy today is shaped by two major forces. The first is the increasing political and economic convergence of markets due to the increasing number of trade blocs and bilateral free trade agreements between countries; this mandates that firms need to adopt flexible marketing strategies in specific markets in order to retain a competitive position. The second of these forces is that of technology—more specifically, improvements in communication technologies resulting in low-cost communications which have opened markets to new customers around the world.

In this new environment there are four basic components of an effective international marketing strategy. These are (Fisher et al. 2006):

* *distinctive competence*: This is what a firm does well in comparison to its competitors. It can reside in a number of areas of the value chain, such as leading edge technology, efficient distribution networks, well-recognised brands and better organisational practices.

* *scope of operations*: This relates to where the firm intends to conduct its business. Scope can be specified in terms of geographical region, product specialisations or market niches.

* *resource deployment*: This involves the allocation of resources between international markets in which the firm has an interest or a presence. It may be specified in terms of product, geography or both.

* *synergy*: This requires a focus on how the different elements of the business, both domestic and overseas, can benefit each other. The aim of synergy is to arrive at a situation where the whole is greater than the sum of the parts.

# SEGMENTATION, TARGETING AND POSITIONING

The above constitute the STP approach, which assists international marketing managers to design a product line that appeals to the market, select communication messages that will have the greatest appeal, select media that will have maximum impact and time launches to capitalise on periods of greatest market responsiveness (Hollensen 2006). Figure 10.1 illustrates the six steps in this process.

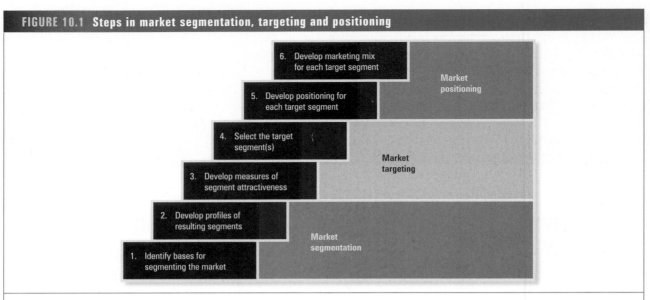

**FIGURE 10.1  Steps in market segmentation, targeting and positioning**

6. Develop marketing mix for each target segment

5. Develop positioning for each target segment

Market positioning

4. Select the target segment(s)

3. Develop measures of segment attractiveness

Market targeting

2. Develop profiles of resulting segments

1. Identify bases for segmenting the market

Market segmentation

**SOURCE:** *Kotler, P., Adam, S., Brown, L. and Armstrong, G. (2006)* Principles of Marketing, *3rd edn, Pearson Education Australia, Sydney, p. 217.*

# Global market segmentation

## SEGMENTATION SCENARIOS

These can be global segments, regional segments or unique segments:

- Global segments are segments that transcend national boundaries and are universal in that customers have the same needs. Examples of global segments are consumers that patronise airport shops, middle class teenagers, and cyberphiles. Commonality of needs is high for travel products and hi-tech consumer durables.

- Regional segments are based on circumstances where similarity of customer needs and preferences exists at a regional rather than at a global level. Although there may be similarities within the region, there will still be differences between regions.

- Unique segments exist when customer needs and preferences differ from one country to another. Unlike the case with global or regional segments where an undifferentiated marketing strategy can yield economies of scale, in these segments a differentiated marketing strategy is required.

## BASES FOR SEGMENTATION

An initial step in market segmentation is deciding on the criteria to be used to segment the country markets. The main criteria in international marketing are:

- *demographic segmentation*: This is based on measurable characteristics of the population, such as age, income, gender, education and occupation. A number of global demographic trends are responsible to an extent for global market segments. These trends are fewer married couples, smaller families, changing roles of women, ageing of populations and higher incomes/living standards.

- *behavioural segmentation*: This is based on groups of people behaving or responding in a similar manner. Behavioural segmentation criteria include degree of brand/supplier loyalty, usage rate, willingness to try new products and benefits sought.

- *lifestyle segmentation*: This is based on grouping consumers in terms of their attitudes, opinions and core values. Advertising agencies often segment on this basis. One example is Roper Starch Worldwide which argues that there are six global value segments: strivers (23%); devouts (22%); altruists (18%); intimates (15%); fun seekers (12%) and creatives (10%) (Kotabe et al. 2005, p. 238).

- *ethnicity-based segmentation*: This is based on the fact that in many countries such as Australia, Canada and the USA there are many ethnic groups, all of which have preferences that reflect to some extent their country of origin. Often it is necessary to have marketing campaigns specifically pitched at specific ethnic segments.

# Targeting

After estimating the overseas market using one or more of the above segmentation criteria, it is necessary to assess the attractiveness of the identified segments. This will involve assessing whether the segment is large enough for the company to make a profit. If not, then does the same segment exist in a number of countries, as profit may result from targeting the same segment in several countries which collectively constitute a worthwhile market? The targeting decision also relates to which overseas markets to pursue as well as which segments to seek out.

# Positioning

This is the act of differentiating a brand in the customer's mind in comparison with the competitive offerings in terms of attributes and benefits. Developing a positioning statement often involves creating a unique selling proposition. In international marketing this can mean battling for the customer's attention not just within a specific country but across the globe within the same market segment. Kotabe et al. (2005) list the stages in developing an international positioning strategy as follows:

- Identify the set of competing products or brands so as to establish the competitive frame.

- Determine the current perceptions of consumers about the product/brand and the competitive offerings.

- Develop possible positioning themes.

- Screen positioning alternatives to select the most appealing.

- Develop a marketing mix strategy for the selected overseas market(s) that will implement the chosen positioning strategy.

- At regular intervals monitor the effectiveness of the selected positioning strategy.

A uniform positioning strategy across international markets may not always work because of the impact of environmental variables such as culture, politics, economics and the law. This will also be influenced by whether you are targeting the same segment in a number of countries. This may lead to alternatives as follows:

- uniform positioning theme/universal segment;

- uniform positioning theme/different segments;

- different positioning themes/universal segment;
- different positioning themes/different segments.

Ryanair has developed a positioning as Europe's leading discount airline. The challenge for discounters, particularly in the airline industry, is to remain financially viable. Ryanair's positioning is reinforced by the fact that a quarter of its seats are free (with the exception of taxes and fees). But passengers pay for checked baggage, bus rides to its out-of-the-way airports, on-board snacks and water. Flight attendants sell digital cameras and iPocket MP3 players on-board with the promise of cellphone service and gaming to come. Ryanair sells more than 98% of its tickets online and you can buy insurance, hotel rooms and car rentals through its site—all aimed at keeping costs low and generating profitable additional revenue (Capell 2006).

# COMPETITIVE POSITION MODEL

There is considerable overlap in the international business strategy and marketing literature in the use of the terms 'position' and 'positioning', mainly because there are many positions that a firm may hold on different criteria. The position the firm holds on each of these shows only part of the picture. A full view of the firm, taking account of all aspects of its competitive environment, is needed to form a sound basis for international marketing strategy development.

In broad terms, competitive position is assessed on those dimensions that affect overseas market performance, namely sales revenue, market share and brand/company image, and on profit performance—investment levels, costs, margins, prices and productivity—which can be evaluated against important competitors. Brown (1997) proposed that competitive position is an amalgam of several key dimensions: the firm's industry and market structure, the firm's overall strategic position, its position in the marketplace and its resource position. These dimensions are classified as structural, strategic, market and resources.

A business's relative strength or weakness in each of these dimensions provides a portrait of its overseas competitive position and will indicate areas of vulnerability and potential strategies for improvement. The overall competitive position model proposed by Brown is depicted in Figure 10.2.

This model provides a framework for assessing the relative dominance of a business in a defined overseas market or industry in terms of its competitive position from which competitive marketing strategies may be evaluated and developed.

Different overseas competitive positions may be strong or weak. Each position has its advantages and disadvantages—its opportunities and threats. However, some positions are more vulnerable to erosion than others. A full and objective assessment of overseas competitive position indicates a range of options for the future; these can be formulated as competitive marketing strategies.

Brown's model suggests that a firm should examine its position on each of the four dimensions and develop strategies to strengthen it in targeted overseas markets. Elements of each dimension are summarised.

## Structural position

This includes an evaluation of *industry structure*, as outlined in Porter's five forces model shown in Chapter 9, Figure 9.10, *market share structure*, which identifies the spread of market share among the key players from monopoly structure to fragmented shareholdings, and the *firm's share position*—including dominance or non-dominance of the market. These three

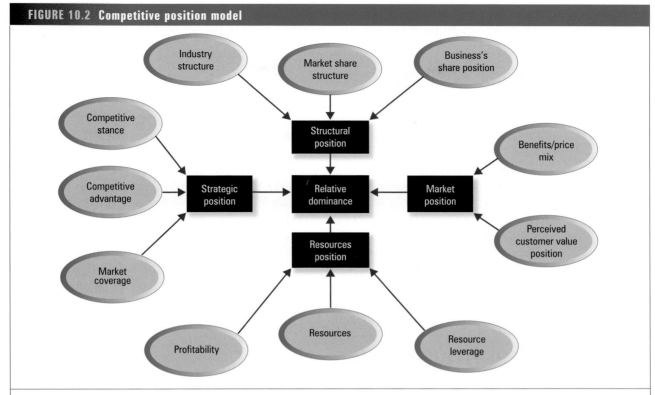

**FIGURE 10.2 Competitive position model**

SOURCE: *Brown, L.R. (1997)* Competitive Marketing Strategy, *2nd edn, ITP Nelson, Melbourne. p. 77. Copyright L. Brown. Reproduced with permission of the author.*

factors together provide a view of the firm's structural position and indicate both future opportunities and threats.

## INDUSTRY STRUCTURE LEVEL

Through innovation, technological change, alliance formation, acquisitions and direct competitive strategies the firm may act to change the balance of forces in the industry or restructure it to its advantage. Australia's Cash Converters has adopted an innovative franchising strategy in Britain and France to restructure the industry in those markets.

## MARKET SHARE STRUCTURE

Competitor acquisitions and exit, innovation and decline of traditional leaders may result in market share restructure. This may be part of a direct strategy to strengthen the firm's position. AXA purchased several insurance companies around the world (including National Mutual in Australia) and Australian Ansell Limited (formerly known as Pacific Dunlop Limited) acquired companies around the world such as Unimil in Poland. These are examples of restructuring of market share structure related to overseas markets.

## FIRM'S SHARE POSITION

Competitive marketing strategies targeting specific competitors may be adopted to improve competitive position, moving from non-dominance to a dominant share level. SingTel has been acquiring new firms, opening up new markets in the telecommunications arena both to establish and improve its competitive position in emerging markets. In July 2001 it acquired Cable & Wireless Optus, Australia's second largest carrier, for $17.2 billion.

## Strategic position

A firm's *strategic position* is reflected in the way in which it has addressed its markets to counter competitive forces and create competitive advantage. Strategic position is composed of three elements, each of which has arisen as a result of the way the firm has operated in the past. These are competitive stance, competitive advantage and market coverage.

Analysis of a firm's strategic position may reveal opportunities to strengthen its competitive position. Sometimes this may occur as a result of external changes in market dynamics or in competitors' strategies. Usually it will be necessary for the firm to adopt innovative competitive strategies. It can affect its strategic position at three levels. For example in a US$1.25 billion acquisition of the IBM computer-making business in 2005, Chinese computer manufacturer Lenovo substantially strengthened its strategic position. This gave Lenovo the ability to enter new markets, increase its technological know-how and benefit from economies of scale. In 2006 Lenovo had a 35% market share of PCs sold in China—mostly through stores to consumers and small businesses. Outside China, it has almost 5% share—mostly with large corporations (Hamm and Roberts 2006).

## COMPETITIVE STANCE

This reflects the roles firms play in the overseas target market—that of leading, challenging, following or niching. Moves from follower to challenger to market leader will strengthen a firm's position. Similarly, a niche specialist may adopt strategies to move itself to challenger or leader. The airline market is an example. In the British holiday package market for air travel to Australia, Qantas could be considered the market leader, challenged by British Airways. Singapore Airlines might be considered a follower in the leisure market, mainly focusing on business passengers. Several other international airlines with flights from Europe to Australia account for niche markets within the British leisure marketplace.

The competitive stance of innovator or follower is determined by the extent and timing of the introduction of new products. Competitors frequently take a deliberate decision on whether to be an innovator or a follower and structure their research and development functions and marketing departments accordingly. The advantages of being first into a market are well known, but the risks can be high and the costs of failure great. Long-term competitive position is strengthened by a record of successful innovations.

For the business-class passenger travelling in Asia and between Asia and Europe, Singapore Airlines has created an image of innovation with its lead moves of the newest aircraft fleet, on-board telephone and entertainment services and its personalised cabin service.

The market leader has the position of being first in the customer's mind. This, in the long term, is supported by the highest market share. In some markets there are two or even three leaders. This characterises joint leadership. Other positions in the market are the high-share challenger, who poses a serious threat to the market leader. The *market follower* position is a stance in which the firm attempts to follow the innovative moves being made by the market leader. The remaining positions belong to specialists who focus on market niches.

# COMPETITIVE ADVANTAGE

Several moves are possible depending on starting position:

- from undifferentiated to low cost or differentiated;
- from low cost to differentiated as product leader or in terms of customer intimacy; or
- from differentiated to low cost and high differentiation in product or customer relationship terms.

The basis of competitive advantage—product leadership, operational excellence and customer intimacy—was examined in Chapter 9, as was the concept of market coverage and focus. Both of these elements are relevant to assessing a firm's strategic position in its overseas market.

# MARKET COVERAGE

Moves from an unfocused to a focused position may be one option to strengthen strategic position. Another option is to extend market coverage.

An example in the international airline industry is Richard Branson's Virgin Airlines. Its early strategy of charter flights and low-cost trans-Atlantic travel has now changed to differentiation through service. Customer intimacy is reflected in the availability of passenger massage services on long flights between Europe and Asia.

Orange's 2006 mobile telephony entry into the Polish market has repeated its initial strategy of low-cost telephony. Its entry into the Poland was through acquisition of existing distribution and infrastructure assets held by local carrier, Idea. This in turn made Orange a third force in the market.

Virgin Blue's entry into Australia in 2001 has repeated its initial strategy of low-cost air travel. Its entry into the Asia–Pacific market through Virgin Atlantic's access to India, China and South Korea has been supplemented by code-sharing arrangements with Malaysian Airlines and Singapore Airlines.

## Market position

Market position refers to the relevant market's recognition and perception of a firm's position in the market—what it stands for and what its offerings provide relative to its competitors' offerings. For example, in the customer relationship management (CRM) software market, Siebel is perceived to be the industry leader (the standards setter) in the provision of relevant packages of good-quality, reliable CRM software supported by accessible after-sales service. Companies and their products become positioned in the market's collective mind on a variety of intangible and functional dimensions which are used by customers to distinguish them and assess *customer perceived value*. When international business travellers decide which airline to fly, frequently the differences in value come down to the perceived quality of the airport club lounge, the speed of luggage recovery and the attitude towards customer care taken by cabin staff.

Perceptions of quality, range, availability, image and other relevant dimensions can be measured for competing firms. A firm can use positioning studies to focus its attention on what target customers believe to be important in order to improve areas of perceived relative weakness and consolidate perceived advantages. This type of analysis provides direction to improve or reinforce market positioning in line with customer perceptions of value.

The strongest market position is one in which a firm offers superior perceived value in terms of the *benefits/price mix*, relative to its competitors. It is possible to have viable market positions in an overseas market in upmarket or downmarket positions, providing the benefits/price mix is superior for the relevant market segment. The Japanese penchant for cars reveals a popularity of very broad offerings, from Mercedes-Benz through to bottom of the range Toyotas.

## Resources position

The *profitability* and *resources* elements of competitive position are internal to the company, but should be assessed in relation to competitors' profitability and resources. It flags the company's ability or otherwise to fund and continue support for its strategy in relation to competitors. In overseas markets *resource leverage* through alliance and business partners extend the Australian firm's capability to reach and service different market segments.

Elements such as cost structure, specific skills, responsiveness and other internal characteristics that affect success in the industry also form elements of competitive position. Frequently, as part of a competitive strategy, a business must act on costs, know-how or factors that make the company more market responsive to enable it to improve its competitive position. Many of a firm's unique resources are intangible—human (the motivation and capability of its employees), organisational (the way its structure enables it to respond to customer demands), cultural (the values and ethics embedded by leadership that either appeal to or turn away customers) and relational (its network of suppliers and customers—a subject discussed in more detail in Chapter 12 (Bradley 2005).

The complete competitive position model shown as Figure 10.2 recognises the interrelationships between the dimensions of competitive position. Many of these relationships are revealed in strategic analysis of the PIMS database. Analysis of the database primarily of American and European firms reveals that high market share is correlated with high profitability, high customer value is correlated with high profitability, and high product quality is associated with price premium positioning and high return on investment. Businesses with market shares above 40% were found to earn an average return on investment three times that of those with shares under 10%. The importance of share varies between industries and market situations. The higher sales volume allows the dominant firm economies of scale and learning curve effects, which can translate into lower costs. Often the strong market position and leading brands owned by the dominant firm enable it to maintain higher price levels and control market price sensitivity (Buzzell et al. 1975). These types of empirical interrelationships and the development of strategic thinking in the literature suggest that a few common profiles of competitive position are prevalent and stand out as fairly clear positions from the almost infinite number of variations of competitive position that exist. More information on the PIMS study is available at <http://www.pimsonline.com>.

## THE DOMINANT LEADER IN OVERSEAS MARKETS

The distinguishing feature of the dominant firm is that it holds a significantly higher market share than its nearest competitor in its overseas market. In the short to medium term this competitive position can be almost unassailable. This is particularly so when there are effective barriers to entry of overseas markets, as has been the case in Japan, the competition is fragmented and no other firm holds a position such that it could mount an effective challenge to the leadership position.

No dominant firm is invulnerable in the long term, however. Strategies must be based on an understanding of the areas of vulnerability as well as the sources of strength. The central objective of the dominant firm is to maintain or even strengthen its future competitive position in both its current overseas market or in any redefined future market.

> Cochlear Australia has reinforced its position as a world leader in the market for hearing implants with its recent acquisition of Sweden's Entific Medical Systems. Cochlear already holds 65% of the key US market in implants for the profoundly deaf, so the acquisition of the Swedish firm enables it to diversify its product base by addressing other forms of deafness.
>
> **SOURCE:** *Evans, M. (2005) 'Cochlear buys into Sweden',* Sydney Morning Herald, *5–6 March 2005, p. 47.*

Very few firms are dominant in all their overseas markets. Even Ericsson, which has operated for decades in many overseas markets, is not dominant in all its markets. For example, its dominance in the fixed telephone exchange market in China is not matched in Japan. Its dominance in the Hong Kong mobile market, with more than 60% of total mobile phones, is not carried across into the Indonesian market. Microsoft software, Intel microchips and Hewlett-Packard (HP) printers are among the few examples of worldwide dominance. But even here there are some markets like Japan in which these companies have a challenger or niche position. For the Australian firm it is more realistic to think of dominance in a niche in perhaps one overseas country market or a region comprising two or three country markets.

The dominant firm has many advantages that place it in an enviable position. These include the ability to manage the market and the competition and, ultimately, to generate higher levels of profitability. This is, however, more limited in overseas markets where political considerations and community factors constrain super-profits resulting from dominance.

The dominant firm usually has the highest market credibility and acceptance. Product or service users see it as a company that can be trusted. This provides the opportunity to manage the flow and timing of new products, their penetration levels and the associated withdrawal of obsolete ones. While not absolute, it does give the dominant firm a measure of 'management' of the market, depending upon its level of dominance. Within the overseas markets for international beer brands, Heineken has highest market credibility.

The dominant firm also has the opportunity to influence competitive evolution significantly. As noted earlier, the current dominance of Microsoft with its Windows operating system and its application programs such as Microsoft Office enable it to direct the evolution of the market and manage its competitors. Microsoft has managed to form alliances with potentially threatening competitors such as Apple and Oracle and it uses market penetration strategies to keep other competitors, such as Lotus (owned by IBM), relatively small. It also faces ongoing court cases with the US anti-trust authorities in its competitive battles in a range of IT and internet-related markets. However, even Microsoft is not immune to the growth of the Linux operating system—an open source operating system for computers which is gaining credence and penetration within large companies for certain types of applications. For example, HP has introduced for companies wanting to manage their printing environment a dedicated print server using the Linux operating system as a means of avoiding the high licence fees that would be incurred if the Microsoft operating system had been used.

# THE DOMINANT FIRM PROFILE

Figure 10.3 shows the characteristic profile of the firm with a dominant competitive position. Variations of this profile exist across each of the elements of competitive position although strength in each is essential for a dominant position.

## Structural position and strategic position

The market share structure position is one of individual dominance. The dominant firm has a significantly higher market share than the nearest competitor. Share structure may be one of monopoly dominance as reflected in Ericsson's Hong Kong market, with a 60% market share dominance. Alternatively, it may be one of duopoly dominance, such as the basic telecommunications networks in which the telecoms in Australia and New Zealand each have a large share advantage over their respective competitors—Optus (now owned by SingTel) and Clear Communications (now owned by BT—British Telecom). The danger for dominant firms lies with the erosion of their share by new entrants and substitutes, as well as existing rivals, to a level where individual dominance is lost.

The dominant firm is usually a market leader, a position that has historically been built by being first in the customer's mind: Kraft is synonymous with cheese, Colgate with toothpaste, Sony with consumer electronics and Apple with iPod. A dominant firm may periodically have a follower stance. This occurs when the dominant firm allows a smaller rival to offer innovative products and initiate change in a market. A stance of being a continuous follower will erode the dominant firm's competitive position and provide a platform from which the smaller firm can launch an attack.

One of the few Australian companies that approaches dominance in some overseas markets is BHP Billiton. This has occurred through its minerals exploration and acquisition strategies, which have made it a major player in copper and petroleum.

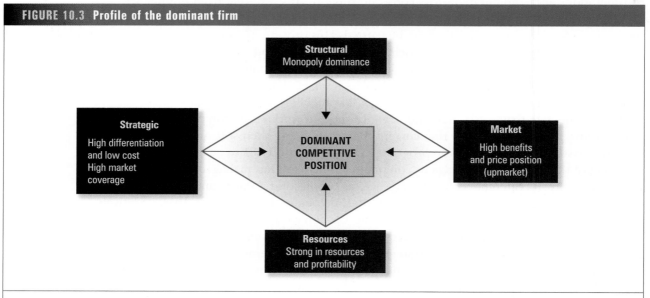

**FIGURE 10.3  Profile of the dominant firm**

**SOURCE:** *Brown, L.R. (1997)* Competitive Marketing Strategy, *2nd edn, ITP Nelson, Melbourne. Copyright L. Brown. Reproduced with permission of the author.*

The strongest dominant firms achieve a competitive advantage on both the cost and differentiation dimensions in mainstream markets. Dominant firms may have a differentiated position with relatively low costs.

A dominant firm must also have wide coverage of the main market segments to achieve the critical mass necessary for share leadership. A focus position may be necessary in a low-segmentation market where there are similar or differentiated product offerings. The main danger to a dominant firm is to become unfocused and spread resource support too thinly. This erosion of position is usually accompanied by a declining market share.

## Market position and resources position

Dominant firms attain their position by offering superior customer value. This may be in the form of high perceived benefits and high cost or high perceived benefits with low cost. *Yellow Pages* has an upmarket position because it offers customers superior value among their advertising alternatives.

Some dominant firms achieve a strong market position with a high-benefits/low-price position. Philips holds this position over Sony in the European market for LCD screens. It offers superior value by combining high product quality with a low price in the face of many low-price alternatives. However, outside its dominant markets, it has niche positions in most of its overseas markets. The main danger to dominant firms is a drift towards inferior customer value represented by moving down-market into a weak position.

The individual dominant firm has a relatively large resource base and usually earns higher levels of profit. Productivity levels, as reflected in cost structures and output levels, need management to maintain advantage relative to competitors. Dominant firms will usually have a strong group of alliances in overseas markets to create resource leverage.

## STRATEGIES FOR THE INTERNATIONAL DOMINANT FIRM

Australian firms seeking dominance of overseas markets are most likely to achieve this in either of two ways. One strategy is to focus on one overseas market. Kmart Australia adopted this strategy with its entry into the New Zealand discount department store market. A full account of its strategy is described in Brown (1997, pp. 408–17). A second approach is to identify a specialised market with global potential and seek to dominate it. This has been achieved by several high-tech Australian firms in the biotech area.

A much smaller Australian firm now dominates the world market in a specialised area. Cochlear is a publicly listed company on the Australian Stock Exchange and sells its Nucleus cochlear ear implant system in over 70 countries; it now dominates this market worldwide. The story of its journey to dominance is described in International Highlight 11.5 in Chapter 11.

The dominant firm must, above all else, focus on maintaining and strengthening its position of dominance in its core market. Regardless of the substantive elements of the strategy it must establish and reinforce a market leadership position while managing the competitive balance and taking heed of its obligations to the market:

- *Reinforce market perceptions*: The dominant leader should reinforce its positioning as the standard—Coca-Cola's themes from 'the real thing' to 'always Coca-Cola' and Xerox's reinforcement of 'we invented the product' maintain the positioning of being the original. The leader may need to adopt strategies to improve the product, its service or its distribution, but the focus should be on reinforcing the leader positioning in the overseas market's collective mind (Ries and Trout 1986a).

• *Manage the market*: A dominant firm has the greatest ability to manage the market and the competition by investment in new initiatives. These enable it to maintain its market influence and its profit and cash to contain the activities of its competitors. Just as the size of a dominant leader's share should be considered and managed in relation to profit and risk, so it should manage the market share levels of individual competitors. This may require strategies to limit the market share growth of some competitors while enhancing the market share growth of others. Market leaders have the opportunity of shaping the competition in the market by targeting the strategies they adopt. Costs, risks and protection should be considered when formulating competitor targeted strategies.

• *Market and competitive obligations*: The dominant firm must be aware of the social, economic and political obligations that accompany its advantageous position—a company that acquires a very high market share exposes itself to risks that its smaller competitors do not encounter. With the dominant position comes an obligation to guard against misuse of its position and to avoid behaviour that reduces the level of competition to the extent it allows it to make 'unfair' profits. Competitors, consumers and overseas governmental authorities are more likely to take certain actions against high-share companies than against small-share ones. Microsoft is a case in point.

# Offensive and defensive strategies

The character of dominant firms' strategies may be either offensive or defensive. Offensive moves are those strategic changes the market leader initiates. They are threatening to competitors when the objective is to take market share and undermine their positions through a frontal attack on selected competitors' markets. Alternatively, they are nonthreatening when they are designed to improve volume and profitability in the market as a whole.

*Offensive strategies* include:

• product, packaging and service innovations;

• development of new market segments;

• redefinition of the market to broaden its scope and position products more closely against broad substitutes;

• market development through product variety and distribution strategies to increase usage and widen availability; and

• international expansion to reduce the impact of global competitors.

*Defensive strategies* include:

• blocking competitors by brand-for-brand matching, distribution coverage and price strategies to reduce their market share and profit potential;

• pre-emption of a competitor's action by being first with a new product or distribution system; and

• use of government regulations, tariffs, import quotas or court actions to increase a competitor's cost or deny a market base.

In practice, dominant firms adopt both offensive and defensive strategies to strengthen and protect their leadership position. The strategies for competing in Asia should be related

## 10.1 INTERNATIONAL HIGHLIGHT

## Harvey Norman moves into Asia, Eastern Europe and the UK

Harvey Norman entered Singapore in October 1999 when Harvey Norman Ossia, a joint venture between Harvey Norman Singapore (60%) and Ossia International (40%), bought just over 50% of the publicly listed Singapore electronics retailer, Pertama Holdings. It effectively acquired six electronics stores in Singapore operating under the Pertama brand name. In January 2001 it acquired a further eight Electric City outlets and immediately rebranded all 14 stores Harvey Norman. The company had two major challenges:

1   creating brand awareness, recognition and positioning— to be done with an aggressive media advertising campaign; and

2   being profitable in a price-sensitive, highly competitive retail market—to be done by increasing margins and prices with the value proposition of interest-free loans for purchasers and extended warranties.

In December 2003 Harvey Norman opened its first store in Malaysia, which, if it proves successful, paves the way for a possible move into India and China. During 2002 Harvey Norman also launched a store in Slovenia, which was treated as an R&D project to understand European consumers better with the intention of launching further stores in the immediate region. By the end of 2004 Harvey Norman had established two stores in Ireland as a foundation to build on its strategy of penetrating the UK. These moves all have the same requirement—establishing a desirable and profitable competitive position in each overseas market.

Gerry Harvey has a really down-to-earth persona. He is someone who prefers the suburbs to exclusive neighbourhoods in Sydney and a beer to champagne. He pays himself only a modest salary. At 22 he opened his first store in 1961, and now he has over 470 franchises and 175 stores with an annual turn over in excess of $240 million. This franchise model is a tough business to survive in. Up to 60% of franchisees are quickly weeded out due to poor performance, but the top franchisees make over $1 million a year. Harvey brought to Australia the 'superstore' concept— a stand-alone store with plenty of parking, selling couches alongside computer goods.

Harvey's latest challenge is to keep the business growing. He is acquiring new businesses including Domayne (high quality interiors) and Rebel Sport, and is now looking into India and China as new markets in which the Harvey Norman brand can grow. He has also made his wife Katie Page the new managing director of the company, to build and expand the business, while he enjoys tending to breeding race horses.

SOURCES: Hannen, M. (2001) 'Harvey Norman widens its global ambitions', Business Review Weekly, *9 March, pp. 40–1;* <http://www.harveynorman.com.au/html/investor/investor.asp>, *accessed 26 June 2001; the 2004 company profile on the Harvey Norman corporate website,* <http://www.harveynorman.com.au/html/investor/docs/view/CompanyProfileSept04.pdf>, *accessed 30 November 2004;* Ross, E. and Holland, A. (2004) 100 Great Businesses and the Minds Behind Them, *Random House Australia, pp. 119–22; Chessell, J. 'Harvey still has big dreams for his empire',* <http://www.smh.com.au/articles/2004/09/01/10939389957555.hmtl?from=storylhs>; *and* <http://www.harveynorman.com.au/site/01/html/corp/companyprofile.htm>, *accessed 25 April 2007.*

to the current experience that many firms have had with the growing group of Asian-based competitors. This is discussed in more detail in Chapter 11.

## Built to last

Drawing from a research project of 18 exceptional and long-lasting international companies, Collins and Porras (1994) tried to identify what made them different and able to sustain long-term dominance in their markets. These included General Electric, 3M, Walt Disney, Hewlett-Packard, Proctor and Gamble, Motorola, Sony, Merck and Boeing. They identify two key principles as internal drivers of those firms that are built to last. First, it is of critical importance to preserve and protect its core ideology. Core ideology goes beyond making money. For 3M it is respect for individual initiative and for Boeing it is being on the leading edge of innovation—being pioneers. Second, there is a relentless drive for progress. This means urging continual change, pushing continual movement towards goals and improvement, expanding the number and variety of possibilities and being prepared to implement radical change consistent with the firm's core ideology (Collins and Porras 1994).

Many longstanding Australian and New Zealand exporters, particularly of agricultural products, apply these two principles. Radical changes have occurred in the product development and export of fruit, fish and horticultural products to meet the different market needs of Japan, North America and Europe.

We now look at specific marketing strategies that are available to market leaders, challengers, followers and nichers. These classifications often do not apply to a whole company, but only to its position in a specific industry or in a specific overseas market. In fact, it is likely that an Australian firm may be market leader in Australia or New Zealand, but a challenger, follower or nicher in other overseas countries.

# STRATEGIES FOR INTERNATIONAL MARKET LEADERSHIP

Most overseas markets contain an acknowledged market leader. It usually leads the other firms in price changes, new product introductions, distribution coverage and promotion spending. The market leader may or may not be admired or respected, but other firms concede its leadership position. The leader is a focal point for competitors, a company to challenge, imitate or avoid. Some of the best-known international market leaders are Toyota (cars), Kodak (photography), Dell (computers), Microsoft (software), Cadbury Schweppes (chocolate confectionery), Nokia (mobile phones), Coca-Cola (soft drinks), McDonald's (fast food), Gillette (razor blades) and Rolex (watches).

A study by Wiersema (2001) of strategies by the new market leaders in today's international environment indicates that leaders have elevated customer focus to a new level around four key mindsets:

1  create a larger-than-life market presence by ensuring recognition;

2  seek out customers that extend their capabilities;

3  ensure customers understand the full value of their offerings; and

4  be bold in everything they do.

These companies, measured as leaders in terms of sales growth and market value, include some of the major world corporations like Cisco, Wal-Mart Stores and Nokia. But they also include lesser known international marketers like Taiwan Semiconductor Manufacturing Company, Murata Manufacturing Company (a Japanese electronic components firm) and Medtronic Inc. (a world leader in medical technology and treatments for chronic diseases).

The profile of a market leader position is similar to that of the dominant competitor profile, shown again as Figure 10.4. In this section the relevant strategies for a market leader in an overseas market are described. They include both offensive and defensive strategies noted in the previous section.

Market leader strategies require action on three fronts: (1) the firm must find ways to expand total demand; (2) the firm must protect its current market share through good defensive and offensive actions; and (3) the firm may try to expand its market share further, even if market size remains constant.

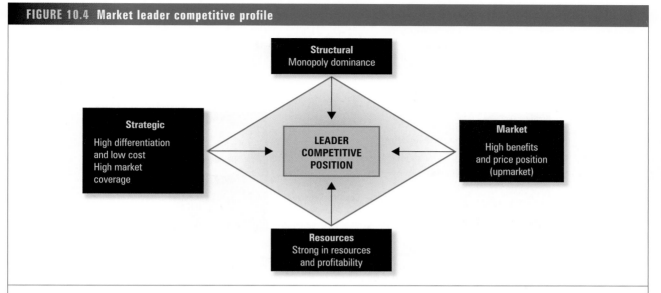

**FIGURE 10.4 Market leader competitive profile**

## Expanding the total market

The leading firm normally gains the most when the total market expands. If we make more mobile phone calls, Nokia stands to gain the most in the Asia–Pacific markets because it sells more than 20% of the region's mobile phones. If Nokia can convince us to make calls, or make calls on more occasions, it will benefit greatly. In general, the market leader should look for new users, new uses and more usage of its products.

## Protecting market share

While trying to expand total market size, the market leader should also constantly protect its current business in its overseas market against competitor attacks. Coca-Cola must constantly guard against Pepsi; Gillette against Bic; Kodak against Fuji; and McDonald's against Hungry Jack's and KFC. These battles are occurring in most of their international markets.

What can the market leader do to protect its position? First, it must prevent or fix weaknesses that provide opportunities for competitors. It needs to keep its costs down and its prices in line with the value the customers see in the brand. The leader should 'plug holes' so that competitors do not jump in. But the best defence is a good offence, and the best response is continuous innovation. The leader refuses to be content with the way things are and leads the industry in new products, customer services, distribution effectiveness and cost cutting. It keeps increasing its competitive effectiveness and value to customers. It takes the offensive, sets the pace and exploits competitors' weaknesses.

Increased competition in recent years has sparked management's interest in models of military warfare (Ries and Trout 1986b, Boar 1993, Thompson and Strickland 1998, Trout 2004). Leader companies have been advised to protect their market positions with competitive strategies patterned after successful military defence strategies. Six defence strategies that a market leader can use are shown in Figure 10.5:

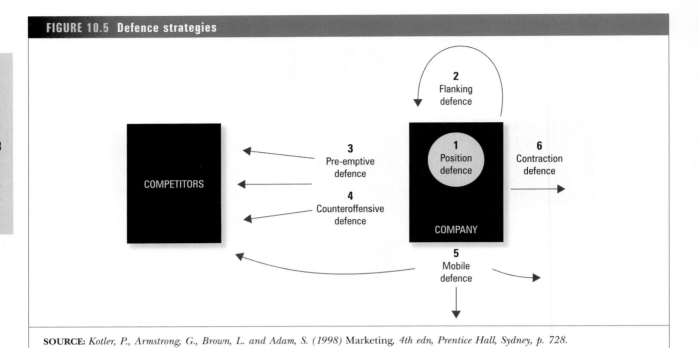

**FIGURE 10.5  Defence strategies**

SOURCE: *Kotler, P., Armstrong, G., Brown, L. and Adam, S. (1998)* Marketing, *4th edn, Prentice Hall, Sydney, p. 728.*

- *Position defence*: The most basic defence is a position defence in which a company builds fortifications around its current position. But simply defending your current position or products rarely works. Even such lasting brands as Coca-Cola and Panadol cannot be relied upon to supply all future growth and profitability for their companies. These brands must be improved and adapted to changing conditions, and new brands must be developed. Today, Coca-Cola, in spite of producing more than one-third of America's soft drinks, is aggressively extending its beverage lines and penetrating developing Asian markets, and has diversified into desalinisation equipment and plastics.

- *Flanking defence*: When guarding its overall position, the market leader should closely watch its weaker flanks. Smart competitors will normally attack the company's weaknesses. Thus, the Japanese successfully entered the small car market because car makers left a gaping hole in that submarket. Using a flanking defence, the company carefully checks its flanks and protects the more vulnerable areas.

- *Pre-emptive defence*: The leader can launch a more aggressive pre-emptive defence, striking competitors before they can move against the company. A pre-emptive defence assumes that prevention is better than cure.

- *Counteroffensive defence*: When a market leader is attacked, despite its flanking or pre-emptive efforts, it can launch a counteroffensive defence. When Fuji attacked Kodak in the Asian film markets, Kodak counterattacked by dramatically increasing its promotion and introducing several innovative new film products. Sometimes companies hold off for a while before countering. This may seem a dangerous game of 'wait and see', but there are often good reasons for not rushing in. By waiting, the company can more fully understand the competitor's offence and perhaps find a gap through which a successful counteroffensive can be launched.

- *Mobile defence*: A mobile defence involves more than aggressively defending a current market position. The leader stretches to new markets that can serve as future bases for defence and offence. Through market broadening, the company shifts its focus from the current product to the broader underlying consumer need. For example, James Hardie redefined its focus from 'fibre cement walls' to 'decorative room covering' (including walls and ceilings) and expanded into related businesses that were balanced for growth and defence in its US market. Market diversification into unrelated industries is the other alternative for generating 'strategic depth'. When Australian tobacco companies W.D.&H.O. Wills (part of Amatil) and Philip Morris faced growing curbs on cigarette smoking, they moved quickly into new consumer products industries: Amatil moved into soft drinks and Philip Morris moved into the wine industry. Both now have strong positions in overseas markets emanating from these Australian moves.

- *Contraction defence*: Australian companies may find that they cannot easily defend positions in a large number of overseas markets. Their resources are spread too thinly and competitors are nibbling away on several fronts. The best action then appears to be a contraction defence (or strategic withdrawal). The company gives up weaker positions and concentrates its resources on stronger ones. Currently several Australian firms are withdrawing from Indonesia because of extreme price competition and economic conditions.

## Expanding market share

Market leaders can also grow by increasing their market shares further. In many markets small market-share increases result in very large sales increases. For example, in large markets, such as financial services and telecommunications, a 1% increase in market share translates into millions of dollars profit. This also applies to smaller markets in which premium price segments exist.

For example, Mercedes holds only a small share of the total car market, but it earns a high profit because it is a high-share company in its luxury car segment. And it has achieved this high share in its served market because it does other things right, such as producing high quality vehicles, giving good service and holding down its costs as well as reinforcing an image of prestige. Mercedes has been very successful at the top end of most of Asia's marketplaces. Mercedes vehicles are widely used to transport senior government officials, visiting dignitaries and high-profile entertainers.

Companies must not think, however, that gaining increased market share automatically improves profitability. Much depends on their strategies for gaining an increased market share. Many high-share companies endure low profitability, and many low-share companies enjoy high profitability. The cost of buying a higher market share may far exceed the returns. Higher market shares tend to produce higher profits only when unit costs fall with increased market share or when the company offers a superior quality product and charges a premium price that more than covers the cost of offering higher quality.

The financial risks associated with Australian firms attempting to become market leaders in overseas markets must be weighed against the potential for market-share gains.

# STRATEGIES FOR THE INTERNATIONAL CHALLENGER

Firms that are second, third or lower in an overseas market are sometimes quite large, such as the Macquarie Bank operating in the European and American markets. These challengers can adopt one of two competitive strategies. They can attack the leader and other competitors in an aggressive bid for more market share (market challengers). Or they can play along with competitors and not rock the boat (market followers). Figure 10.6 shows the competitive position profile of market challengers.

## Defining the strategic objective and competitor

A market challenger must first define its strategic objective. Most market challengers seek to increase their profitability by increasing their market shares. But the strategic objective chosen depends on the competitor. In most cases the company can choose which competitors to challenge.

The challenger can attack the market leader, a high-risk but potentially high-gain strategy that makes good sense if the leader is not serving the market well. This can be a dangerous strategy for Australian companies targeting overseas markets, particularly in Asia. Political factors and interlinked loyalty for the indigenous country supplier or brand are important constraining factors. Carlton United Beverages with its Foster's brand has found it difficult to beat indigenous beer brands in Japan, the Philippines and China. To succeed with such an attack a company must have some sustainable competitive advantage over the leader—a cost advantage leading to lower prices or the ability to provide better value at a premium price. In the construction equipment industry, Komatsu successfully challenged Caterpillar by offering the same quality at much lower prices. When attacking the leader a challenger must also find a way to minimise the leader's response. Otherwise its gains may be short-lived (Porter 1985).

The challenger can avoid the leader and instead attack firms its own size, or smaller local

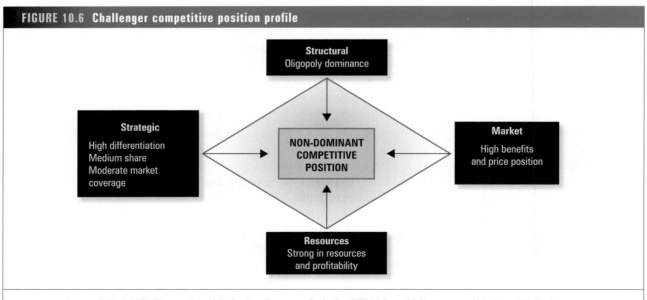

**FIGURE 10.6 Challenger competitive position profile**

**Structural**
Oligopoly dominance

**Strategic**
High differentiation
Medium share
Moderate market
coverage

**NON-DOMINANT
COMPETITIVE
POSITION**

**Market**
High benefits
and price position

**Resources**
Strong in resources
and profitability

**SOURCE:** *Brown, L.R. (1997) Competitive Marketing Strategy, 2nd edn, ITP Nelson, Melbourne, p. 181, Copyright L. Brown. Reproduced with permission of the author.*

and regional firms. Many of these firms are underfinanced and will not be serving their customers well. Several of the major international beer companies grew to their present size not by attacking large competitors, but by absorbing small local or regional competitors.

Thus, the challenger's strategic objective depends on which competitor it chooses to attack. If the company goes after the market leader, its objective may be to wrest a certain market share. Bic knows that it can't topple Gillette in the razor market—it simply wants a larger share. Or the challenger's goal might be to take over market leadership. Dell entered the personal computer market late, as a challenger, but quickly became an important challenger to Compaq in overseas markets with its direct marketing and distribution strategy. If the company goes after a small local company its objective may be to put that company out of business or buy it to gain a base in the overseas market. The important point remains: the company must choose its opponents carefully and have a clearly defined and attainable objective.

# Choosing an attack strategy

How can the market challenger best attack the chosen competitor and achieve its strategic objectives? Five possible attack strategies are shown in Figure 10.7. When considering these strategies the firm must continually keep in mind the political and regulatory conditions of the overseas country and the established distributor and end-customer loyalties entrenched in many markets.

## FRONTAL ATTACK

In a full-frontal attack the challenger matches the competitor's product, advertising, price and distribution efforts. It attacks the competitor's strengths rather than its weaknesses. The outcome depends on who has the greater strength and endurance. Even substantial resources may not be enough to challenge successfully a firmly entrenched and resourceful competitor. Consider the task of Adidas and Reebok in tackling the global market leader Nike, outlined in International Highlight 10.2.

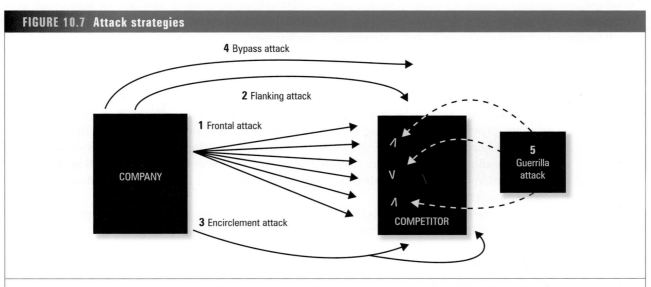

**FIGURE 10.7 Attack strategies**

**SOURCE:** *Kotler, P., Armstrong, G., Brown, L. and Adam, S. (1998)* Marketing, *4th edn, Prentice Hall, Sydney, p. 731.*

# Adidas and Reebok challenge Nike

Adidas has not always been in the position of a challenger. Twenty years ago, it was the undisputed, long standing 'king' of the sports shoe market. But share started to drop as Reebok and Nike tapped into the trend for fashion trainers. By 1987, Reebok boosted its presence and market position by focusing on the growing niche of aerobics and had become the world leader in this category with sales of US$1.38 billion, with Nike close behind as a challenger. Only a year later, Nike stepped out of the aerobics niche and became the market leader, and has steadily widened the gap between Adidas and Reebok ever since. Reebok dropped back into third place behind Adidas.

Now Adidas is working to narrow the gap with Nike. It has acquired Reebok as the means of closing the gap with Nike by attacking it in its key markets, using Reebok's large presence in the US as a springboard for the attack of Nike in its home market.

The combination of the world's number two and three sporting goods companies has a significant challenge to catch Nike, which holds a 31% share of the lucrative sporting footwear market in the USA. Together, Adidas and Reebok account for US$10.78 billion in sales and US$473 million in net profits. Nike's annual revenue of US $13.28 billion and US $946 million in net profits makes it a powerful number one competitor.

If the combined force of Adidas and Reebok is to compete head on with Nike, they must work out how the Reebok brand will mesh and complement Adidas. The success will depend on the level of cost savings and distribution synergies achieved and the effect of this merger on the consumer's minds.

Adidas is a brand with a strong heritage, but it also has a niche position. In recent years, it has tried to become more fashionable and widen its brand domain; Nike has done so successfully. Now Adidas can go back to its core focus of being the 'most authentic' sporting company, while positioning Reebok as the fashion/lifestyle brand.

Some industry branding experts are already warning that Adidas could end up cannibalising market share with its acquisition of Reebok if the two brands are not given a sufficiently different positioning. If the product portfolio is managed well, it could see Nike struggling to maintain its current position and profitability.

There is little doubt that Adidas, even combined with Reebok, faces a big task wresting market leadership from Nike. This industry leader not only controls 28% of the global footwear market, but has become a serious competitor in the areas such as football, swimwear and other niches. It has also survived potential disasters, such as the 'sweatshop' controversy of the 1990s.

For Adidas the challenge can be best summarised in Nike's Atlanta Olympics advertising, 'You don't win silver; you lose gold'.

**SOURCE:** *Turner, C. (2005) 'Adidas's challenge: Adidas jumps for the title' Marketing Week, 11 August, p. 22.*

SMEC, the Snowy Mountains Engineering Corporation, operates in many overseas markets providing engineering consultancy services and project management services. It competes head-to-head with larger firms from Europe and the USA for projects in developing countries and the Asian region. Each major project can be considered a frontal attack on the other tenderers for the job. SMEC is a very successful, strong international challenger in these overseas markets.

If the market challenger has fewer resources or less resource leverage than the competitor a frontal attack makes little sense.

## FLANKING ATTACK

Rather than attacking head-on the challenger can launch a flanking attack. The competitor often concentrates its resources to protect its strongest positions, but it usually has some weaker flanks. By attacking these weak spots the challenger can concentrate its strength against the competitor's weakness. Flank attacks make good sense when the company has fewer resources than the competitor. Another flanking strategy is to find gaps that are not being filled by the industry's products, fill them and develop them into strong segments.

Comalco, one of Australia's largest aluminium producers, sells 65% of its output in the Asian region—30% to Japan, 12% to South Korea and 23% to other Asian countries including Taiwan and Indonesia. The 1997 financial and economic crisis in Asia reduced volumes and prices and Comalco redirected some of its aluminium into Europe and the USA to maintain overall sales volume. This move put Comalco in a challenger position against other big world producers that have traditionally focused on the European and American markets (Howarth 1998).

Consider the recent move by Kodak—a risky new strategy to build printers and sell ink at low prices, undercutting Hewlett-Packard's immensely profitable inkjet cartridge business. It plans to make its money from the printers and operate at very low margins on cartridges. This is the reverse of Hewlett-Packard's strategy (Hamm 2007; Bulkeley 2007).

## ENCIRCLEMENT ATTACK

An encirclement attack involves attacking from all directions so that the competitor must protect its front, sides and rear at the same time. The encirclement strategy makes sense when the challenger has superior resources and believes that it can quickly break the competitor's hold on the market. An example is Seiko's attack on the watch market. For several years Seiko has been gaining distribution in every major watch outlet and overwhelming competitors with its variety of constantly changing models. In most of Asia's markets it offers more than 500 models, but its marketing clout is backed by the 2300 models it makes and sells worldwide.

## BYPASS ATTACK

A bypass attack is an indirect strategy. The challenger bypasses the competitor and targets easier markets. The bypass strategy can involve diversifying into unrelated products, moving into new geographical markets or leapfrogging into new technologies to replace existing products. Technological leapfrogging is a bypass strategy used often in high-technology industries. Instead of copying the competitor's product and mounting a costly frontal attack the challenger patiently develops the next technology. When satisfied with its superiority it launches an attack where it has an advantage. Thus, Minolta toppled Canon from the lead in the 35-millimetre SLR camera market when it introduced its technologically advanced auto-focusing Maxxum camera. Canon's market share dropped towards 20% while Minolta's zoomed past 30%. It took Canon three years to introduce a matching technology. A multitude of entries into the digital camera market is enabling new players to this market like Sony and Hewlett-Packard to bypass traditional leaders like Kodak.

## GUERRILLA ATTACK

A guerrilla attack is another option available to market challengers, especially the smaller or poorly financed challenger. The challenger makes small, periodic attacks to harass and demoralise the competitor, hoping eventually to establish permanent footholds. It might use selective price cuts, executive raids, intense promotional outbursts or assorted legal actions. Normally, guerrilla actions are taken by smaller firms against larger ones. But continuous guerrilla campaigns can be expensive and they must eventually be followed by a stronger attack if the challenger wishes to 'beat' the competitor.

# STRATEGIES FOR THE INTERNATIONAL FOLLOWER

Not all runner-up companies will challenge the market leader. The effort to draw away the leader's customers is never taken lightly by the leader. If the challenger's lure is lower prices, improved service or additional product features, the leader can quickly match these to defuse the attack. The leader probably has more staying power in an all-out battle. A hard fight might leave both firms weakened. Thus, the challenger must think twice before attacking. Therefore, many firms prefer to follow rather than attack the leader. Figure 10.8 shows the competitive position profile of a follower.

A follower can gain many advantages. The market leader often bears the huge expenses involved with developing new products and markets, expanding distribution channels and informing and educating the market. The reward for all this work and risk is normally market leadership. The market follower, on the other hand, can learn from the leader's experience and copy or improve on the leader's products and marketing programs, usually at a much lower investment. Although the follower probably will not overtake the leader, it can often be as profitable (Haines et al. 1989).

The follower is a major target of attack by challengers. Therefore the market follower must keep its manufacturing costs low and its product quality and services high. It must also enter new markets as they open up. Following is not the same as being passive or existing as a carbon copy of the leader. The follower must define a growth path, but one that does not provoke competitive retaliation.

The market-follower firms fall into one of three broad types: the *cloner*, the *imitator* and the *adapter*. The *cloner* closely copies the leader's products, distribution, advertising and other marketing moves. The cloner attempts to live off the market leader's investments. The *imitator* copies some things from the leader, but maintains some differentiation in terms of packaging, advertising, pricing and other factors. The leader doesn't mind the imitator as long as the

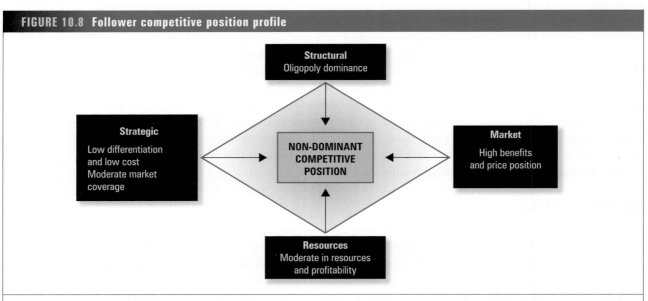

**FIGURE 10.8  Follower competitive position profile**

**Structural**
Oligopoly dominance

**Strategic**
Low differentiation
and low cost
Moderate market
coverage

**NON-DOMINANT
COMPETITIVE
POSITION**

**Market**
High benefits
and price position

**Resources**
Moderate in resources
and profitability

**SOURCE:** *Brown, L.R. (1997) Competitive Marketing Strategy, 2nd edn, ITP Nelson, Melbourne, p. 241. Copyright L. Brown. Reproduced with permission of the author.*

imitator does not attack aggressively. The imitator may even help the leader avoid accusations of monopoly. Finally, the *adapter* builds on the leader's products and marketing programs, often improving them. The adapter may choose to sell to different markets to avoid direct confrontation with the leader. But often the adapter grows into a future challenger, as many Japanese firms have done after adapting and improving products developed elsewhere.

The firm adopting a follower strategy is quite content to remain a number two or three company. The objective is to position the firm and its products as viable alternatives to the market leader, leaving the market leader with the responsibility for market development and expansion.

The risks associated with innovation and the development of new products can be reduced by being a close follower. D'Aveni (1994) refers to one study that reports that 60% of successful patented innovations were imitated within an average of four years, and the imitating firm's development costs were at least 35% less than the innovator.

Of course, the true follower firm is not interested in challenging the dominant firm, often out of fear of disrupting the competitive balance and causing the dominant firm to take a more offensive stance. Dominant firms are often happy to allow a follower firm to operate as a means of maintaining the existing market share structure.

Some firms take a market-follower position as a first step in challenging the market leader. This is a strategy adopted by Japanese companies in most industries in which they compete. Follower companies are able to learn from the product and marketing mistakes of the leaders and develop a product and overall market offer that is better suited to the needs of the market. Development costs are reduced by reverse engineering; the follower firm then focuses on improving process technology to reduce the costs of production, often resulting in a significant cost advantage. This then forms the base for a more direct, frontal attack on the market leader.

Consider the strategies of Acer, the Taiwan-based PC maker described in International Highlight 10.3.

D'Aveni (1994) suggests the following follower strategies:

- *Imitation*: offer the same product at a lower price. This strategy requires lower manufacturing costs, reduced research and development costs and lower marketing expenditure;

- *Adding features*: offer additional features that differentiate the product in a manner that is relevant to the market;

- *Stripping down*: eliminate features to provide a more basic product at a lower price;

- *Flanking*: strip down and/or add features to develop a product suited to smaller market segments. Schnaars (1994) proposes a two-step imitation process. Following the innovation, the first step occurs when an imitator enters the market with a much better product or another party offers virtually the same product but at a lower price. The second-step imitation occurs when a much later entrant to the market comes in with a much lower price.

Several examples of this two-stage process can be found. Pocket calculators were pioneered by a number of small assemblers of electronic components. The large integrated circuit manufacturers moved in quickly when they saw the market grow, and forced out the small assemblers. As calculators began to appeal to the mass market beyond engineering and scientific usage, Asian manufacturers mobilised low-cost mass production and took the volume

## 10.3 INTERNATIONAL HIGHLIGHT

# Here comes a racer called Acer

t's a good thing that the president of Acer likes lots of coffee and lots of air travel. This company president shuttles continuously between his hometown Milano (Milan) in Italy and headquarters in Taiwan. But currently it seems Acer is also performing on a caffeine high. It is perceived in the marketplace as a fast follower that is starting to challenge the number three player, Lenovo, which gained its strong market position after its purchase of IBM's PC division.

The challenge to replace Lenovo as the number three PC maker is not just about prestige, but also market share, revenue and economies of scale. Latest industry projections acknowledge that the PC competitive arena will be reduced to just a few large players. Therefore getting bigger for Acer is a survival issue. Analysts estimate that the industry will shrink even further and only the top-three players will generate sustainable profitability. Credit Suisse estimated that in 2006 Acer had sales of US$11.1 billion and profits of US$338 million.

Acer is moving from a follower strategy to a typical challenger, producing PCs cheaper and with added features compared to its rivals. Simply, it gives its customers a favourable price-versus-benefits package. This strategy seems to be working, with sales nearly doubling since 2003.

But this growth had its impact on profit margins, which declined to 2%—less than half that of HP or Dell.

To keep the momentum going, Acer needs to expand beyond its stronghold position in Europe where it holds the market leader position in laptops and number three market share overall with other electronic peripherals. Now Acer is focusing on China, where it is number nine. Over the financial year 2005–06 Acer reduced costs even further by revamping its operation, almost halving its head count and outsourcing its distribution.

Acer also has a follower position in the USA, where currently it holds just 1.8% of the market. According to IDC research the company sells notebooks mainly to small businesses, but it lacks the credibility needed by large corporate customers. However, this is a typical competitive stance that market followers and challengers need to overcome. Acer has raised its profile in the US market by adopting a focused strategy and gaining consumers over the past two years through deals at Wal-Mart, CompUSA, and Circuit City. This will ultimately raise its profile with big companies. Acer is also working on brand recognition and brand-positioning strategies which it hopes to improve by generating more of a presence in US retail shops.

SOURCES: *Einhorn, B. and Kharif, O. (2007) 'A racer called Acer; Look out, Lenovo. The world's No. 4 computer maker is gaining on you', BusinessWeek, 29 January, p. 48; and Hamm, S. and Roberts, D. (2006) 'China's first global capitalist', BusinessWeek, 11 December, pp. 52–8.*

market at low prices. A similar pattern occurred with digital watches, although the Swiss manufacturers came back to appeal to certain 'style' segments, but left the volume low-price versions to Asian suppliers. Microwave ovens were pioneered by American firms who were later challenged by Japanese companies at lower prices. This was followed by South Korean-dominated manufacturers, with lower costs and able to sell at much lower prices to supply the mass market.

Market leaders and other innovating firms will not remain idle while a follower firm piggybacks its development initiatives. The distinction between challenger and follower strategies is very fine. The follower that aims to outperform the market leader is in effect mounting a challenge and should be prepared for the competitive consequences!

# STRATEGIES FOR THE INTERNATIONAL NICHE FIRM

Almost every overseas market includes firms that specialise in serving market niches. Instead of pursuing the whole market, or even large segments of the market, these firms target segments within segments, or niches. This is particularly true of Australian firms because of their limited resources. But smaller divisions of larger firms may also pursue niching strategies. The competitive position profile of a niche player is shown in Figure 10.9.

The main point is that firms with low shares of the total market can be highly profitable through smart niching. International Highlight 10.4 illustrates the focus taken by one Australian firm.

Marketing strategy theory very often focuses on the means to penetrate a market rapidly using the support of high-level marketing expenditures in advertising, sales effort and promotion. The high profile of leading marketers, such as McDonald's, Toyota and Coca-Cola, and their enormous promotional budgets reinforces this view. Many companies, however, adopt quite different marketing strategies that aim to establish a presence in a market and then develop gradual but progressive growth. Most of these companies are relatively small in both financial resources and staff, although many medium-sized and even large companies in industrial markets and service industries adopt this marketing approach. For example, in terms of niche operations the ANZ Bank identified the credit card market overseas as a good entry point for establishing retail operations.

An infiltration strategy is based on a slow but increasing rate of sales and market-share growth and supported by a commensurate build-up of marketing effort. Once a position is established this is consolidated and nurtured while the momentum for the development of a larger market-share base builds slowly. This is contrasted with the rapid penetration strategy in which a company aims, through sheer force, to snatch market share from the existing competitors.

The essence of the infiltration strategy is that it has relatively low market impact and aims to attract minimal attention from the competition in the market. The positioning of the

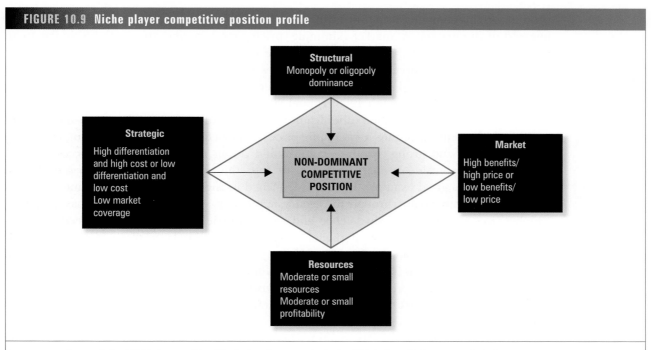

**FIGURE 10.9  Niche player competitive position profile**

**Structural**
Monopoly or oligopoly dominance

**Strategic**
High differentiation and high cost or low differentiation and low cost
Low market coverage

**NON-DOMINANT COMPETITIVE POSITION**

**Market**
High benefits/ high price or low benefits/ low price

**Resources**
Moderate or small resources
Moderate or small profitability

**SOURCE:** *Brown, L.R. (1997)* Competitive Marketing Strategy, *2nd edn, ITP Nelson, Melbourne, p. 316. Copyright L. Brown. Reproduced with permission of the author.*

## 10.4 INTERNATIONAL HIGHLIGHT

# Taking marketing to the USA

Interstrat is an example of a niche specialist that has successfully moved its operations and customer base from Australia to North America. Interstrat began operations in Sydney in 1988 offering marketing skills workshops to Australian companies. It was established to bridge the marketing knowledge and capability gaps among Australian and multinational organisations and offered a wide range of services. During the nineties it expanded its reach to the Asia–Pacific region, conducting marketing training programs for transnational companies in China, Japan, Singapore and the Philippines. In 2000 it obtained its first global contract with a large US-based global corporation by first providing programs in its Asia–Pacific region, followed by programs in North America. This required a highly customised approach in one specialist area of marketing skills development, which was used as a base for developing other highly customised and specialised offerings. Its unique blend of online and offline delivery, supported by proprietory software tools for on-the-job use by marketers in applied marketing decision making, has enabled it slowly to add to its customer base. The use of client referrals and test sites has been a key element of its marketing strategy to establish credibility and add new clients at a rate consistent with its ability to deliver. Its strategy of narrowing its service range and specialising in a specific niche—of marketing skill areas and specific industries—enabled it to establish a viable competitive position in a specialised field in a very large potential market for its services.

By 2007 Interstrat's infiltration strategy was providing steady growth in sales and profitability from North American-based transnational corporations, and it had a small network of marketing professionals based in the USA, Australasia and Europe.

**SOURCE:** *Interview with Christopher Brown, CEO, Interstrat Corporation, 20 March 2007.*

product or the company using an infiltration strategy may range from the premium to the low end of the market. A 'market skimming' pricing strategy may appear to be similar to an infiltration strategy, but this represents only one variant.

Studies of highly successful small companies have found that in almost all cases these companies innovated and niched within a larger market rather than going after the whole market (Clifford and Cavanagh 1988; Hamel 2000).

These studies have also found other features shared by successful smaller companies—that is, offering high value, charging a premium price supported by soundly based but innovative business models and strong corporate cultures and visions. Most of Australia's successful long-term exporters, outside primary industry, fit into this category. Melbourne-based Poltech International is a good example. In 2001 it launched its high-tech traffic infringement systems and solutions into Spain through an agency agreement with Etel 88, which has preferred supplier access to the Spanish defence and civil industries. Poltech's digital speed camera—Lasercam—combines the latest in digital image capture with laser speed detection and is completely portable. Poltech also does business in Taiwan, Hong Kong, Brazil and the Netherlands. Poltech now has major business operations in the USA as well as Australia (Poltech International Limited profile, <http://www.business.com/directory/retail_and_consumer_services/consumer_electronics/poltech_international_limited/ profile/>, accessed 8 December 2004).

Why is niching profitable? The main reason is that the market nicher ends up knowing the target customer group so well that it meets its needs better than other firms that casually sell to this niche. As a result, the nicher can charge a substantial mark-up over costs because of the added value; whereas the mass marketer achieves high volume, the nicher achieves high margins.

Nichers try to find one or more market niches that are safe and profitable. An ideal market niche is big enough to be profitable and has growth potential. It is one that the firm can serve effectively. Perhaps most importantly, the niche is of little interest to major competitors. And the firm can build the skills and customer goodwill to defend itself against an attacking major competitor as the niche grows and becomes more attractive.

The key idea in 'nichemanship' is specialisation. The firm must specialise along market, customer, product or marketing mix lines. There are several specialist roles open to a market nicher:

- *End-use specialist*: The firm specialises in serving one type of end-use customer. For example, a law firm can specialise in the criminal, civil or business law markets.

- *Vertical-level specialist*: The firm specialises at some level of the production/distribution cycle. For example, a copper firm may concentrate on producing raw copper, copper components or finished copper products.

- *Customer-size specialist*: The firm concentrates on selling either to small, medium or large customers. Many nichers specialise in serving small customers who are neglected by the majors.

- *Specific customer specialist*: The firm limits its selling to one or a few major customers. Australian point-of-sale technology specialist Keycorp Ltd, which has successfully sold terminals to banks, is now taking its EFTPOS terminals into Europe. By adopting new payment technologies such as the Mondex scheme and smart-card systems from Visa and MasterCard it is in a good position to succeed with this specific customer target.

- *Geographical specialist*: The firm sells only in a certain locality, region or area of the world. For example, English retail giant Tesco has targeted Eastern Europe as a high priority international market. Its hypermarkets in the western part of Poland are set to give it a strong position to develop further in the emerging volume markets of Eastern Europe and Russia.

- *Product or feature specialist*: The firm specialises in producing a certain product, product line or product feature. For instance, within the laboratory equipment industry are firms that produce only microscopes or, even more narrowly, only lenses for microscopes. Food is another area of product specialisation. Oporto started in the Sydney suburb of Bondi in 1986, offering high-quality chicken burgers. From this first outlet the company now has more than 72 stores in Australia and New Zealand and is planning to expand its franchises to the UK (<www.hospitalitymagazine.com.au/articles/d6/0c0296d6.asp>, accessed 8 December 2004).

- *Quality–price specialist*: The firm operates at the low or high end of the market. For example, Hewlett-Packard specialises in the high-quality, high-price end of the hand calculator market.

- *Service specialist*: The firm offers one or more customised services for a specific market not available from other firms. An example is Sydney-based company Easynet, the services of which are designed specifically for small business and in-home customers. Its focus is to offer all customers extremely fast, full-featured internet connection, of a standard normally available only under private contract to large corporations or at premium prices. For businesses it offers high data-rate capacity available at budget prices.

Niching carries a major risk in that the market niche may dry up or be attacked. That is why many companies practise multiple niching. By developing two or more niches, the company increases its chances of survival. Even some large firms prefer a multiple-niche strategy to serving the total market. One large law firm has developed a national reputation in the three areas of mergers and acquisitions, bankruptcies and prospectus development, and does little else.

## THE ASIAN APPROACH TO STRATEGY

The above analysis of various strategies for international marketing follows the Western prescriptive approach where planning cascades in sequential steps from the broad mission statement to specific objectives. It usually involves firms matching their strengths and weaknesses against opportunities and threats in overseas markets in a search for competitive advantage. The Western approach involves setting a goal and actions being geared towards achieving that goal.

The Asian approach involves a series of experimental steps and once one step is achieved strategies will be developed for achieving the next step. There is less of a distinction between developing the strategy and the implementation. Described by El Kahal (2001, p. 198) in the case of Japanese firms as 'intuitive incrementalism', it involves experience-based learning, which accelerates implementation and progressive adjustment to strategy. This approach does not preclude long-term planning as evidenced by companies such as Sony. However, it does enable firms when faced with uncertainty in foreign markets to operate on a trial and error basis rather than to be locked into grand schemes and formal planning techniques (El Kahal 2001, p. 197).

## The internet and international marketing strategies

Australia's oldest mint, the 108-year-old Perth Mint (established 1899), was established by the government to produce sovereigns for the dominions and colonial governments of the British Empire. It no longer produces Australian or other currencies and its main business now is to produce collectors' and investment coins. For its excellent work in 2000 it received a 'Mint of Honour' at the World Money Fair in Basel, Switzerland. The Perth Mint is currently taking on an expansion initiative, and e-commerce and the internet have opened up new international market frontiers and customer service possibilities.

Perth Mint sees itself as a marketing-department-driven organisation constantly looking for new opportunities to add value and new sales. The Perth Mint's management sees new technologies as enablers to extend its core business well beyond the Australian market.

Initial establishment of the website (the Perth Mint was one of the first mints to establish a website) enabled it to be perceived in the marketplace as an innovative business around the world. Initially the website (launched in early 1997) had around 16 000 page impressions per month and was used purely as an informative medium with no transactional capabilities. Current website capabilities enable Perth Mint to be truly competitive in the global/international business arena. Its customers now see Perth Mint as an innovative company with fully functioning e-commerce facilities and well-integrated delivery systems. Its IT infrastructure is similar to that in the banking sector—after all, they are dealing with precious currencies! Sometimes too much security or user-unfriendly security systems can restrict sales; however, Perth Mint is different because its website customer focus specifications were jointly developed by its IT and marketing departments. The benefits of this interdepartmental collaboration are clearly visible. Now, the website not only attracts new customers, but, by being a fully integrated system, it looks after its existing customers. The purchasers' orders and inventories are updated in the real time; this makes sure that the Perth Mint's existing customers will remain loyal.

Customers can now track their delivery route, select their courier and provide online feedback. Instead of customers from overseas markets calling the company and asking, 'Where is my order?' they can now track it themselves. For overseas customers it means a reduction in overseas calls and greater convenience when they follow up on their order status; for the Perth Mint it means a much smaller call centre. This is a win–win situation achieved with the help of the internet. Now the customer is in control of their order.

Perth Mint considers itself as an e-business organisation that can deal with demanding and empowered customers. Perth Mint has really 'coined' the term 'global marketing company'.

**SOURCE:** *Adapted from the Perth Mint, <http://www.perthmint.com.au/default.aspx>, accessed 23 April 2007.*

# Summary

International competitive marketing strategies are closely related to a firm's competitive position. Firms holding a dominant position usually have available a wider range of strategic alternatives than those in follower or niche positions. Also, firms starting out will be constrained by their resources, access to markets and the challenge of creating a competitive position in international markets.

The wide range of strategies relevant to the different competitive positions of dominance, market leadership, challenger, follower and niche specialist indicates the need for careful assessment and selection followed by creative implementation by the international marketer.

Although some Australian firms have been able to become market leaders or strong challengers in specific overseas markets, most opportunities exist for niche players. Consequently, Australian firms must master the strategies needed to succeed as specialists in an end-use, specific customer, specific geographical area, product or service. When linked to electronic commerce—a subject discussed in detail in Chapter 18— Australian firms have the potential to lead many of the international niche markets of the future.

# ETHICS ISSUE

Your company is a major exporter of flu vaccines to the USA. Your main competition is a new vaccine supplier from the UK. You have unconfirmed reports of contaminated vaccines uncovered in the competitor's plant. Knowing the US focus on security you know that a rumour, whether true or unfounded, would halt your competitor's market penetration.

***Would you actively spread this rumour?***

## Websites

**AMP** http://www.amp.com.au
**Apple Computers** http://www.apple.com
*Australian Financial Review* http://www.afr.com.au
**AXA** http://www.axa.com
**BHP Billiton** http://www.bhpbilliton.com
**British Airways** http://www.britishairways.com
**Cadbury** http://www.cadbury.com.au
*Cash Converters* http://www.cashconverters.com.au
**Comalco** http://www.comalco.com.au
**Easy Internet Services** http://www.easynet.net.au
**Ericsson** http://www.ericsson.com
**Hewlett-Packard** http://www.hp.com.au
**IndymacBank** http://www.imb.com
**Keycorp Limited** http://www.keycorp.net
**Lion Nathan** http://www.lion-nathan.co.nz
**Microsoft** http://www.microsoft.com
**Philippines Airlines** http://www.philippineairlines.com
**Singapore Airlines** http://www.singaporeair.com
**SingTel** http://www.singtel.com
**Sony Corporation** http://www.sony.com
**Tall Women's Clothing** http://www.tallwomensclothing.com
**Toyota** http://www.toyota.com.au
**Virgin Atlantic Airways Limited** http://www.virgin-atlantic.com

## Discussion questions

1 Evaluate the position of Nokia in one of its overseas markets, using Brown's competitive position model.

2 Identify the competitive positions of four players in the international airline passenger market. Describe their strategies and make inferences about their possible future competitive positions.

3 Apple iPod leads the digital music market worldwide. Describe its offensive and defensive strategies.

4 Identify an Australian or New Zealand firm that is a market leader in one or more overseas markets. Summarise its strategies in those markets and compare them with typical market leader strategies.

5 Identify an Australian or New Zealand firm that is a challenger or follower in its overseas markets. Examine its strategies in relation to typical strategies adopted by challengers and followers.

6 What types of niche strategies are relevant to Australian or New Zealand firms? Describe these strategies and give examples of firms using them.

7 Describe a niche strategy adopted by an Australian or New Zealand exporter. Suggest how its strategies could be improved.

8 Describe the international marketing strategy of one well-known Australian or New Zealand company and how it has succeeded.

# References

'Adidas's challenge: Adidas jumps for the title', *Marketing Week*, 11 August 2005, p. 22.

Bloom, P.N. and Kotler, P. (1975) 'Strategies for high market share companies', *Harvard Business Review*, November–December, pp. 63–72.

Boar, B. (1993) *The Art of Strategic Planning for Information Technology*, John Wiley and Sons, New York.

Bradley, F. (2005) *International Marketing Strategy*, 5th edn, Financial Times Prentice Hall, London, Chapter 2.

Brown, L.R. (1997) *Competitive Marketing Strategy*, 2nd edn, ITP Nelson, Melbourne.

Bulkeley, W.M. (2007) 'Kodak's strategy for first printer—cheaper cartridges', *Wall Street Journal* (Eastern edition), 6 February, p. B.1.

Buzzell, R.D., Gale, B.T. and Sultan, R.G.M. (1975) 'Market share—a key to profitability', *Harvard Business Review*, January–February, pp. 97–106.

Capell, K. (2006), 'Wal-Mart with Wings', *BusinessWeek*, 26 November, pp. 44–5.

Chessell, J. 'Harvey still has big dreams for his empire', <http://www.smh.com.au/articles/2004/09/01/10939389957555.hmtl?from=storylhs>.

Clifford, D.K. and Cavanagh, R.E. (1988) *The Winning Performance: How America's High-growth Mid-size Companies Succeed*, Bantam Books, New York, p. 36.

Collins, J.C. and Porras, J.I. (1994) *Built to Last: Successful Habits of Visionary Companies*, Harper Books, New York.

D'Aveni, R.A. (1994) *Hyper-Competition: Managing the Dynamics of Strategic Manouvering*, The Free Press, New York.

Einhorn, B. and Kharif, O. (2007) 'A racer called Acer; Look out, Lenovo. The world's No. 4 computer maker is gaining on you', *BusinessWeek*, 29 January, p. 48.

El Kahal, S. (2001) *Business in Asia–Pacific: Text and Cases*, Oxford University Press, Oxford.

Evans, M. (2005) 'Cochlear buys into Sweden', *Sydney Morning Herald*, 16–17 April, p. 17.

Fisher, G., Hughes, R., Griffin, R. and Pustay, M. (2006) *International Business*, 3rd edn, Pearson Education Australia, Sydney.

Haines, D.W., Chandran, R. and Parkhe, A. (1989) 'Winning by being first to market . . . or last?', *Journal of Consumer Marketing*, pp. 63–9.

Hamel, G. (2000) *Leading the Revolution*, Harvard Business School Press, Boston, Chapter 3.

Hamm, S. (2007) 'Kodak's Moment of Truth', *BusinessWeek*, 19 February, pp. 42–5.

Hamm, S. and Roberts, D. (2006) 'China's first global capitalist', *BusinessWeek*, 11 December, pp. 52–8.

Hannen, M. (2001) 'Harvey Norman widens its global ambitions', *Business Review Weekly*, 9 March, pp. 40–1.

Hansell, S. (2004) 'Gates vs. Jobs: the rematch', *New York Times*, Sunday Business, 14 November, Sunday Late Edition, Section 3, p. 1.

Hollensen, S. (2006) *Marketing Planning*, McGraw Hill Education, Maidenhead, UK.

Howarth, I. (1998) 'Comalco looks to a strong '98 despite Asia', *Australian Financial Review*, p. 20.

<http://www.harveynorman.com.au>.

<http://www.hospitalitymagazine.com.au>, accessed 8 December 2004.

<http://www.sfgate.com/cgi-bin/article.cgi?file=/c/a/2007/04/10/BUGH4P5FKS1.DTL>, accessed 10 April 2007.

Kotabe, M., Peloso, A., Gregory, G., Noble, G., MacArthur, W., Neal, C., Reige, A. and Helsen, K. (2005) *International Marketing: An Asia Pacific Focus*, John Wiley and Sons, Milton, Qld.

Kotler, P., Adam, S., Brown, L. and Armstrong, G. (2006) *Principles of Marketing*, 3rd edn, Pearson Prentice Hall, Frenchs Forest NSW.

Kotler, P., Armstrong, G., Brown, L. and Adam, S. (1998) *Marketing*, 4th edn, Prentice Hall, Sydney.

Perth Mint, <http://www.perthmint.com.au/default.aspx>, accessed 23 April 2007.

Poltech International Limited profile <http://www.business.com/directory/retail_and_consumer_services/consumer_electronics/poltech_international_limited/ profile/>, accessed 8 December 2004.

Porter, M. (1985) 'How to attack the industry leader', *Fortune*, pp. 153–66.

Reis, A. and Trout, J. (1986a) *Positioning: The Battle for your Mind*, McGraw-Hill, New York.

Reis, A. and Trout, J. (1986b) *Marketing Warfare*, McGraw-Hill, New York, pp. 55–66.

Ross, E. and Holland, A. (2004) *100 Great Businesses and the Minds Behind Them*, Random House Australia, pp. 119–22.

Salkever A. (2004) 'A bitter apple replay?', *BusinessWeek Online*, 14 October, accessed 16 November 2004.

Schnaars, S.P. (1994) *Managing Imitation Strategies: How Later Entrants Seize Markets from Pioneers*, The Free Press, New York, p. 216.

'Shareholder scoreboard (a special report 2007): performance of 1,000 major U.S. companies compared with their peers in 75 industry groups; finding tomorrow's winners today: try firms with fresh perspectives: companies that depart from the conventional wisdom in defining their markets may deliver strong returns', *Wall Street Journal* (Eastern edition), 26 February, p. R.4.

Thomas, I. (1998) 'Exit signs light up for Asian airlines', *The Australian Financial Review*, 29 June, p. 3.

Thompson, A.A. and Strickland, A.J. (1998) *Strategic Management: Concepts and Cases*, 10th edn, Irwin McGraw-Hill, Boston.

Trout, J. (2004) *Trout on Strategy: Capturing Mindshare, Conquering Markets*, McGraw-Hill, New York, pp. 63–70.

Turner, C. (2005) 'Adidas's challenge: Adidas jumps for the title', *Marketing Week*, 11 August, p. 22.

Wiersema, F. (2001) *The New Market Leaders: Who's Winning and How in the Battle for Customers*, The Free Press, New York, pp. 63–4.

**go online**

Go online to <www.pearsoned.com.au/fletcher> to find more case studies.

# CASE STUDY 10

## Contract manufacturing: an efficient internationalisation strategy for Dry-Treat

**Anke Peter and Richard Fletcher**

### INTRODUCTION

Many Australian firms are small to medium-sized companies catering to small niche markets. As the Australian market with a population of 21 million people is a relatively small market, these Australian firms are forced to open up overseas markets and engage in export activities. The Australian Bureau of Statistics reported that in the year 1997–98, 77% of all exporting companies were small businesses with less than 20 employees (Australian Bureau of Statistics 2000). However, small companies usually have only limited human and financial resources. Therefore, the internationalisation process constitutes a challenge for these small and specialised companies. Entering foreign markets is a very complex business activity as a complete new macro environment with different legal regulations, a differing political and economic situation and a different culture have to be understood correctly by the foreign company. Furthermore, they have to adapt to the characteristics of the overseas environment and need to incorporate it into their international marketing strategy. In addition, the overseas market might be defined in a different way to the domestic market and the Australian company might be operating in a new market segment with a different kind of competitors to those in their original home market. For small companies in particular, that focus on a niche market segment in this internationalisation process is on the one hand indispensable in order to remain profitable, but on the other hand more risky as it has only limited resources to cope with the challenging new market environment.

This is also the case for Dry-Treat, a developer of high quality chemical sealers for various porous

surfaces like natural stone, tiles and pavers. The company has 10 employees in total and is 100% equity financed. Even though the company is small, it manages to compete against well-established multinational companies, mainly from the USA and Europe, in the chemical surface protection industry. This is possible through its internationalisation strategy via contract manufacturing, which allows it to focus on its core competencies, which lie in the developing and marketing of high-quality sealing products. In comparison, Dry-Treat's main competitors all produce their chemical surface protectors and cleaners in-house. The small Australian company recognised that it is more profitable and less risky for it to find new markets for its existing products than to develop new products for existing markets. Hence, Dry-Treat differentiates itself substantially from its international competition, which in general have in-house production facilities and develop new products in order to further penetrate their existing markets.

The following case study analyses the circumstances that encouraged Dry-Treat to engage in contract manufacturing in the US market and then examines some advantages and disadvantages deriving from contract manufacturing. Furthermore, how this internationalisation strategy allows Dry-Treat to focus on its core competences through value chain orientation is outlined.

## BACKGROUND

Dry-Treat, with its 10 employees, is a small Australian developer of premium chemical protective sealers and cleaners for natural stone, tiles and pavers, based in Sydney. The company was founded in 1991 and today serves an international customer base originating from more than 20 countries. Dry-Treat stresses that its products are premium quality surface sealers. Therefore, it employs engineers who continuously improve the quality of the Dry-Treat product range. The small Australian company has no production facilities itself, but cooperates with contract manufacturers in Rydalmere (Australia), Charlotte (USA) and Miehlen (Germany), which produce, label and package the products and are furthermore responsible for quality control on behalf of Dry-Treat. The manufacturers then ship the sealers and cleaners to contract warehouses from where they are allocated to Dry-Treat's distributors which buy the commodities in bulk and sell them to retailers. In order to emphasise the high quality of its products Dry-Treat issues 15 year-warranties if its products are applied by a Dry-Treat Accredited Applicator. The special characteristics of the Dry Treat sealers are that, first, surfaces treated with Dry-Treat products do not change their natural colour and, second, after the application of a Dry-Treat sealer on a porous mineral surface, any cleaner can be used without causing any damage to the surface, as the sealers provide an in-depth protection.

## DRY-TREAT IN THE USA

When Dry-Treat started exporting its high quality chemical sealers to the US market in 2003, it first wanted to explore the market and find out if there was a demand for its products and if it would be able to establish itself in this big market. Being a complete newcomer, it knew little about this market, the market's characteristics and the

demand for its products. Therefore it used a test market strategy to conduct a field experiment and research the US market directly. Dry-Treat selected Long Beach in California as a location to rent warehouse space. Long Beach is the other major port, in addition to Los Angeles, in the Southern California region for handling freight from the Pacific Rim. Unsure whether the US market was suitable for its first-class penetrating sealers, Dry-Treat decided to initially ship its products from Australia. It dispatched 10 pallets of goods with a net worth of A\$100 000, from Sydney to Long Beach, California and stored them in a warehouse before dispatching them to customers all over America. However, this direct exporting raised some problems for Dry-Treat (see Table 1).

Overall, the shipment of products to the US was very costly and time-consuming for Dry-Treat. Even though the market entry via direct exporting seemed at first to involve fewer outlays and lower risk, the costs exceeded the turnover considerably. One incident, where Dry-Treat had to fly products from Sydney to Florida in order to meet the customer's needs, caused Dry-Treat to engage in contract manufacturing with a US company just six months after shipping the first products from Sydney to Long Beach.

The main reasons to engage in contract manufacturing were to reduce costs related to transportation, reduce lead times and thereby increase the responsiveness to customer needs while focusing on Dry-Treat's core competencies, which were the developing and marketing of premium surface sealers by optimising its value chain activities. Furthermore, the contract manufacturer in the US could support Dry-Treat in successfully adapting the product to the new market. Being a new player in the market Dry-Treat was not sure what products to make and in what quantities. Cooperating with a contract manufacturer in the US helped it to plan more efficiently and to make better forecasts since holding a buffer stock was not necessary.

## CONTRACT MANUFACTURING

Contract manufacturing is considered as a fast, relation-based market entry mode that requires

| TABLE 1 | Dry-Treat's main problems resulting from directly exporting to the USA |
|---------|---------------------------------------------------------------------|

| Type of problem | Impact on Dry-Treat |
|-----------------|---------------------|
| Shipping time is approx. eight weeks. | • For eight weeks the capital is tied up in the shipment which for a small company like Dry-Treat is a long time as it is unable to generate profits from the products while they are being transported.<br>• Very long lead times make it impossible to react flexibly and quickly to urgent orders. This is a considerable disadvantage when starting to establish a product in a new overseas market. |
| Dry-Treats solvents-based products are classified as flammable goods. | • The shipping company needs to employ trained staff, accredited by the government and familiar with the handling of flammable chemicals. This further increased the costs for Dry-Treat.<br>• The warehouse in the USA needs to be specialised in handling hazardous goods: it is time- and cost-intensive to find such a location. |
| Customs clearance/import duties | • Customs clearance costs as well as import duties are payable when the freight arrives in Long Beach. |
| Long dispatch times from the warehouse in Long Beach | • Long Beach turned out to be an unfavourable location for a warehouse, as Dry-Treat had some of its first customers in Florida and on the US East Coast. |

very low investment on the part of the Australian firm. According to Clark (2004), this form of market entry is becoming more popular as about 42% of all global manufacturing activities are outsourced, mainly for cost reasons. This is also the case for Dry-Treat. However, in marketing theory it is often stated that contract manufacturing is practised to benefit from cheaper labour costs in offshore countries (Kotabe and Helsen 2001). However, for Dry-Treat the transportation costs and related import barriers like customs clearance and duties were the drivers that made

direct exporting from Australia inefficient. Table 2 outlines the major advantages and disadvantages contract manufacturing has for Dry-Treat.

However, contract manufacturing allows Dry-Treat to not only save costs, but also to increase its value chain orientation by focusing on its sustainable competitive advantages. The Australian company retains all marketing and product development activities, which are the company's core competencies. However in order to reduce any disadvantages, it is important for Dry-Treat to establish good and trustworthy relationships with

| TABLE 2 | Contract manufacturing and the consequences for Dry-Treat |
|---------|-----------------------------------------------------------|

| Advantages | Disadvantages |
|------------|---------------|
| Increased financial independence; capital no longer tied up for eight weeks | Secrecy of formulation is at risk as the contract manufacturer needs to be provided with the formulation; threat of educating a future competitor |
| Reduced transportation costs | Some raw materials that are unavailable in the USA still need to be imported from Australia in order to maintain the premium quality |
| Higher replenishment speed and responsiveness to customer demand | No influence on the contract manufacturer's production schedule |
| More time and resources to focus on development and marketing of the premium sealers | Quality control is difficult; this has an impact on the brand management |

its contract manufacturer so that in particular the high quality level of the Dry-Treat product range can be maintained as well as an ability to flexibly respond to demand alterations. As suggested by Kotabe and Helsen (2001) it is therefore beneficial to integrate the contract manufacturer into Dry-Treat's business activities. This can be achieved through value chain orientation and the integration of the contract manufacturer's value chain into Dry-Treat's value chain system.

## VALUE CHAIN

As mentioned before, contract manufacturing results on the one hand in a considerable reduction of transportation costs for Dry-Treat, and on the other hand the ability of management to focus on the development and marketing of its premium sealers. While this approach enables Dry-Treat to concentrate on continuously improving its products and optimising its marketing and after-sale service activities, including the training

and briefing of its distributors, dealers and applicators, it also adds value and improves the perceived benefit to the customer.

Figure 1 shows Dry-Treat's current value chain where the outsourced manufacturing activities are highlighted in grey and the main activities constituting Dry-Treat's core competencies are displayed in dark blue (marketing and sales, after-sale service and technology development). Inbound and outbound logistics are mainly exercised by the contract manufacturer; however, Dry-Treat exports some essential ingredients from Australia (part of the inbound logistics) and might assist in the managing of the product delivery to distributors and dealers (outbound logistics). Therefore, the shared logistics activities have two colours, grey and light blue. All other activities performed and organised by Dry-Treat are highlighted in light blue.

As stated by Cavinato (1989) contract manufacturing is 'the management of entire commercial relationships' (p. 16) and for Dry-Treat this means

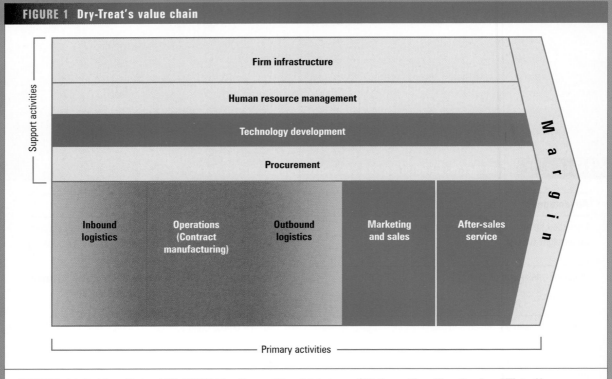

**FIGURE 1  Dry-Treat's value chain**

SOURCE: *Adapted from Porter, M.E. (1998)* The Competitive Advantage of Nations, *Macmillan, London, UK, p. 41.*

to manage timing, locations, quality, customer service and order information flows in an efficient and optimal way. This can only be beneficial for all parties when they have an integrated value chain system where the activities of each individual player in this complete system are well coordinated. Figure 2 illustrates Dry-Treat's value chain system where the value chains of the contract manufacturer are an integral part of Dry-Treat's value chain. However, it is also obvious that only the whole value chain system, consisting of supplier value chains, channel value chains from Dry-Treat's distributors, dealers and applicators as well as the buyer value chains, needs to be integrated and coordinated so that Dry-Treat can focus on its core competency, which is the development and marketing of first-class surface sealers.

But how does this minimise the disadvantages deriving from contract manufacturing? By focusing on the continuous improvement on its products, it will be difficult for Dry-Treat's contract manufacturer's to imitate Dry-Treat and to offer products of a similarly high quality. Furthermore, by establishing a strong brand through extensive marketing activities and customer relationship management as part of the after-sale service activities, the customers will appreciate the added values Dry-Treat products and services provide. In addition, the integration of the contract manufacturer's value chain into Dry-Treat's value chain system increases the commitment and loyalty between the two parties.

As a consequence, it should be easier for the two parties to agree upon quality standards and production schedules.

## CONCLUSION

In conclusion, it can be argued that for Dry-Treat contract manufacturing is not only a way to reduce costs, but also a management strategy that helps to focus on what it can do best: the development and marketing of premium stone surface sealers. The combination of contract manufacturing and value chain orientation reduces Dry-Treat's costs and risk considerably while at the same time increases its responsiveness to the needs of the US market. Furthermore, this internationalisation strategy will help the Australian sealant developer to further improve its competitive advantage as it can focus all its resources on these activities. Thus, the company creates and increases the value it adds for its customers. However, it is crucial to optimise the coordination among all players in Dry-Treat's value chain system and to be aware of the interdependencies of all involved parties. In order to achieve this optimised coordination, communication is indispensable. Dry-Treat's managing director points out that this form of internationalisation works well for the Australian company only through the usage and support of ICT, in particular email and internet communication, which makes it easy to cooperate across national borders and time-zones.

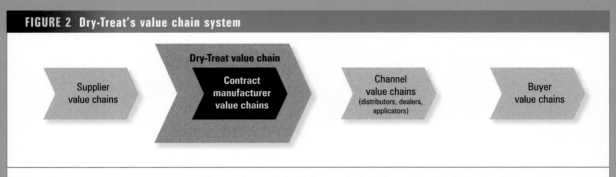

FIGURE 2 Dry-Treat's value chain system

SOURCE: Adapted from Porter, M.E. (1998) The Competitive Advantage of Nations, Macmillan, London, UK, p. 43.

## Bibliography

Australian Bureau of Statistics (2000) 'A portrait of Australian Exporters – A report based on the Business Longitudinal Survey.' Australian Bureau of Statistics, Canberra.

Cavinato, J.L. (1989) 'The logistics of contract manufacturing', *International Journal of Physical Distribution & Logistics Management*, Vol. 19, No. 1, pp. 13–20.

Clark, R. (2004) 'The real cost of outsourcing'. America's Network, 108 (7), p. 32–35.

Dry-Treat (2007) <http://www.drytreat.com>.

Kotabe, M. and Helsen, K. (2001) *Global Marketing Management*, 2nd edn, John Wiley & Sons, Inc., New York, USA.

Porter, M.E. (1998) *The Competitive Advantage of Nations*, Macmillan, London, UK.

## Questions

1  Can you imagine other, more efficient and less costly ways for Dry-Treat to enter the US market?

2  What could Dry-Treat do in order to reduce or completely eliminate the disadvantages resulting from contract manufacturing?

3  With regards to the Value Chain, do you think Dry-Treat should outsource other activities? Justify your decision.

4  Discussion: Contract manufacturing is often associated with big multinational companies that outsource their manufacturing activities to low-wage countries like India, China, Russia and the Philippines. However, Dry-Treat has contract manufacturers in Australia, Germany and the USA—definitely not cheap labour countries. Why would it be inefficient for Dry-Treat to cooperate with companies in low-wage countries? Can you think of other industries that might apply a similar strategy? What are the advantages of this strategy?

## Photo credit

Image reproduced with permission from Dry-Treat Pty Ltd.

# CHAPTER 11

# GLOBALISATION

## LearningObjectives

**After reading this chapter you should be able to:**

- evaluate the forces of globalisation and the underlying philosophy of globalism;

- assess the motivations of globalisation and Yip's three-stage process;

- identify the elements relevant to global planning;

- examine basic global competitive strategy profiles and the pitfalls of global marketing;

- appreciate perceptions of globalisation from a macro perspective; and

- explore the rise of Asian competitors and their activities in regional and global market development.

# Australia and the global automotive industry

The Australian automotive sector generates sales close to A$20 billion and employs around 70 000 people. This sector is made up of foreign and local companies and is Australia's sixth largest export earner. In 2005, exports totalled A$5.1 billion, comprising vehicles exports of A$3.5 billion and components of A$1.6 billion.

Why is it that overseas-owned automobile manufacturers with operations in Australia are increasingly using their plants in Australia to supply markets in other countries rather than supply such markets from their country of headquarters? They do so in an endeavour to compete on a global basis and achieve global economies of scale. This requires them to manufacture specific models in specific countries or locate various elements of their value chain in different countries. Often, the requirement to modify or produce a model to suit Australian conditions makes that model particularly suitable for an overseas market where conditions approximate those in Australia such as climate, terrain and road conditions.

The case of the Toyota Manufacturing Company of Australia (TCMA) is revealing in this connection. The Australian-built Camry is one of the largest-selling cars in the Middle East and in 2003 TCMA shipped 62 000 cars to Saudi Arabia, the United Arab Emirates, Kuwait, Oman, Bahrain and Qatar, valued at A$1.4 billion. The Middle East market has played a pivotal role in Toyota's globalisation plan and currently TCMA is Toyota's fourth largest offshore exporter worldwide. Australian plants of other automobile manufacturers are often used to supply models to cater for niche markets overseas.

That is the case with General Motors, where its Australian division, Holden, is in the process of supplying 18 000 Monaro coupés badged as Pontiac GTs to the US market. Holden began exporting in 1954 and its exports rose steadily until they reached a peak of 40 000 units in 1973. Then exports rapidly fell and averaged less than 10 000 units a year until 1979 when they rose again each year and in 2004 52 372 units were shipped overseas. As an outcome of GM rationalisation between manufacturing locations, Holden has won access for its large rear-wheel-drive vehicles to a number of export markets such as the USA, Middle East, UK, South Africa and Brazil.

It is, however, in the value chain area that Holden play their greatest role in the globalisation of General Motors (GM). Here some 70% of the output of the firm's V6 engine plant in Victoria is exported to GM plants in other countries—a trade valued at A$450 million a year. In the components area globalisation is evident in sourcing on a global basis: 'If you buy a BMW Z sports car assembled in the US, it will have an instrument panel made by Siemens VDO in Melbourne. If you buy a Mercedes Benz, you will get Australian-made seat and front suspension mechanisms. And if you buy any GM product worldwide, it will have steering components and technology from A.E. Bishop in Sydney' (Rennick 2004, p. 25).

Holden will benefit from the introduction by GM of a single global manufacturing system (GMS). This will involve using the Commodore platform and basic engineering structure as the basis for very different cars designed for different markets. The GMS gives the company greater flexibility to manufacture this model in different plants and to move manufacturing from one plant to another to cater for fluctuations in demand.

Globalisation also operates the other way and in the case of Holden its Barina and Astra models are not produced in Australia, but instead are manufactured in the Opel plant in Belgium.

---

**SOURCES:** *Adapted from* Age, *10 March 2007, 'Australia's car industry needs a jump start', <http://www.theage.com.au>, accessed 19 March 2007; Austrade, <http://www.austrade.gov.au/Automotive-overview-/default.aspx>, accessed 25 March 2007; King, P. (2004) 'Altona's ships of the desert',* Australian, *20 April, p. 23; Cooper, C. (2004) 'Revving up for action',* Export, *May, pp. 24–7; Department of Foreign Affairs and Trade (2005)* Australia and the United States—Trade and the Multinationals in a New Era, *Department of Foreign Affairs and Trade, Canberra, p. 25; Roberts, P. (2005) 'Holden leads GM's global shift',* Australian Financial Review, *10 March, p. 69; and Department of Foreign Affairs and Trade (2003)* The Big End of Town and Australia's Trading Interests, *Department of Foreign Affairs and Trade, Canberra, p. 45. Image supplied by Toyota Australia.*

# INTRODUCTION

In a Harvard Business Review article, Holt et al. (2004) argue that when a brand is marketed around the world the fact that it is a global brand gives it both an aura of excellence and a set of obligations. Herein lies the dilemma of globalisation. From a micro or firms' perspective globalisation can offer considerable benefits; from a macro or consumer perspective questions are increasingly being asked as to what are the real benefits. In their global brands study (1500 urban consumers in 41 countries aged between 20 and 35) these researchers found that with global brands 44% of brand preference was explained by the quality signal (if it is a global brand, it must be good), 12% by the global myth (buying a global brand identifies you as a citizen of the world) and 8% by social responsibility (global firms are more likely in their actions and operations to address global issues such as environmentalism and child labour).

Very few Australian companies have developed a powerful global brand. Although similar in size and the level of consumer preference Swiss companies, Nestlé and Novatis, originating in a country of eight million people, were able to create such global presence (for the top 100 brands see *BusinessWeek*, <http://bwnt.businessweek.com/brand/2006>, accessed 19 March 2007). Australian companies have been reticent and slow to develop a global presence. Few have managed to develop international leadership in their industries. One exception is News Corp. Another, BHP, merged with Billiton in 2001 to become a global resources company. Also, Billabong has become a global brand leader in its niche area. Foster's Brewing is focusing on developing world beer and wine brands.

It is in the context of 'being a very small fish in a big pond' that globalisation is to be viewed from Australia and New Zealand. However, it is also necessary to understand globalisation in terms of what global competitors are doing and the impact they can have on Australian firms in their overseas markets.

The world is becoming increasingly globally linked in terms of migration of production, technology, capital, people, information and business. Some businesses have been operating globally for many years. Qantas, Kodak and Nestlé are examples. However, in recent times the pace of business globalisation has increased at an exponential rate. Now much smaller companies are achieving global reach in a shorter period of time. For example, Lexmark, which started business in 1991 with an alliance with IBM to market printers, operates in the large markets of Europe, the USA and Asia–Pacific and represents a serious challenge to Hewlett-Packard's printer business. As markets and companies become global they face a variety of different competitive situations. One organisation may need to adopt all the strategies discussed in Chapters 9, 10 and 12—sometimes simultaneously across a range of different markets and certainly over time as its competitive position changes. Strategies will include greenfields development, alliances in some markets, acquisitions in others and a variety of offensive and defensive moves in both new and existing markets. Strategy becomes increasingly complex and multidimensional, a mosaic of different strategies in different markets—a kind of 'global chess' tied together by an overall global mentality and strategy.

This chapter looks at globalisation from an Australasian perspective. It presents a framework for looking at global strategy. It also identifies the benefits and costs of globalisation and the steps involved in moving to a global marketing program. Global firms wield tremendous power and some of them are larger in terms of capitalisation than many nations, as illustrated in Table 11.1.

# GLOBALISATION

## What is globalisation?

*Globalisation* is the process by which firms operate on a global basis, organising their structure, capabilities, resources and people in such a way as to address the world as one market. The objective in its purest sense is to serve the global market by maximising the capabilities and advantages that individual countries have to offer—manufacturing productivity, R&D capability, market access, attractive interest rates and marketing experience. Strategic decisions are not taken from any particular country's perspective, there is no nationality bias in senior management and globalisation involves ongoing global searches for technology, people and alliance partners from which global competitive advantage can be achieved. In practice, this is not absolute but a matter of degree. For instance, Nestlé's operations around the world are influenced by the founding culture emanating from Switzerland, as are those of eBay flowing from Silicon Valley and Nokia originating from Finland.

## Globalism trends

Myriad forces are coming together and triggering the globalisation of industries, companies and individuals. These forces include the reduction in barriers to trade and investment, market liberalisation and privatisation, the integration of world financial markets and improvements in transportation, communications and information technology. Trade blocs are forming which are consolidating market regions such as the triad of Europe, North America and Japan and the regions of Asia–Pacific, Southern Africa and Latin America. Global communications and media are bringing information, services, cultures and brands to all corners of the world. Industries, such as finance, computers, telecommunications and media, have become global. The demise of the English-based Barings Bank in 1995 (through transactions to the Japanese stock exchange controlled in Singapore) illustrates the inter-connectedness of the finance industry. This was first demonstrated with such force in the October 1987 stock market crash. The speed and impact of financial markets' 'tornado' effect on Indonesia, Malaysia, Thailand and South Korea in 1997 demonstrates this again. The slowdown of the US economy and the demise of many of the fledgling dot.coms in 2000 and 2001 reverberated around the world. The impact of the strengthening Euro currency and devaluation of the US dollar in 2004–07 affected the Australian and New Zealand economies as well as having an impact on the ability of EU countries to export to the USA.

## TABLE 11.1 World's 100 largest economic entities

| Rank | Entity | | Value US$billion | Rank | Entity | | Value US$billion |
|---|---|---|---|---|---|---|---|
| 1 | USA | | 13 245 | 51 | MALAYSIA | | 151 |
| 2 | JAPAN | | 4 367 | 52 | CHILE | | 145 |
| 3 | GERMANY | | 2 897 | 53 | CZECH REPUBLIC | | 142 |
| 4 | CHINA | | 2 630 | 54 | ISRAEL | | 140 |
| 5 | UK | | 2 374 | 55 | ING Group | (Netherlands/US) | 138 |
| 6 | FRANCE | | 2 232 | 56 | COLOMBIA | | 135 |
| 7 | ITALY | | 1 853 | 57 | SINGAPORE | | 132 |
| 8 | CANADA | | 1 269 | 58 | Citigroup | | 131 |
| 9 | SPAIN | | 1 226 | 59 | AXA | (France/US) | 130 |
| 10 | BRAZIL | | 1 068 | 60 | PAKISTAN | | 129 |
| 11 | RUSSIA | | 979 | 61 | ROMANIA | | 122 |
| 12 | SOUTH KOREA | | 888 | 62 | PHILIPPINES | | 117 |
| 13 | INDIA | | 887 | 63 | NIGERIA | | 115 |
| 14 | MEXICO | | 840 | 64 | ALGERIA | | 114 |
| 15 | AUSTRALIA | | 755 | 65 | HUNGARY | | 114 |
| 16 | NETHERLANDS | | 663 | 66 | Fortis | (Europe/US) | 112 |
| 17 | BELGIUM | | 394 | 67 | Credit Agricole | (France) | 111 |
| 18 | TURKEY | | 392 | 68 | American Intn'l Group (US) | | 109 |
| 19 | SWEDEN | | 385 | 69 | EGYPT | | 107 |
| 20 | SWITZERLAND | | 377 | 70 | UKRAINE | | 106 |
| 21 | INDONESIA | | 364 | 71 | NEW ZEALAND | | 103 |
| 22 | REPUBLIC OF CHINA TAIWAN | | 365 | 72 | Assicurazioni Gen | (Italy) | 101 |
| 23 | SAUDI ARABIA | | 349 | 73 | Siemens | (Germany) | 100 |
| 24 | Exxon Mobil | (US) | 340 | 74 | Sinopec | (China) | 99 |
| 25 | POLAND | | 339 | 75 | KUWAIT | | 96 |
| 26 | NORWAY | | 335 | 76 | Nippon T&T | (Japan) | 95 |
| 27 | AUSTRIA | | 322 | 77 | Carrefour | (France) | 94 |
| 28 | Wal-Mart Stores | (US) | 316 | 78 | HSBC Holdings | (UK) | 93 |
| 29 | GREECE | | 308 | 79 | PERU | | 93 |
| 30 | Royal Dutch Shell | (UK/Netherlands) | 307 | 80 | Eni | (Italy) | 93 |
| 31 | DENMARK | | 277 | 81 | Aviva | (UK) | 93 |
| 32 | BP | (UK) | 268 | 82 | IBM | (US) | 91 |
| 33 | SOUTH AFRICA | | 255 | 83 | McKesson | (US) | 88 |
| 34 | IRELAND | | 222 | 84 | Honda Motor | (Japan) | 88 |
| 35 | ARGENTINA | | 213 | 85 | State Grid | (China) | 87 |
| 36 | IRAN | | 212 | 86 | Hewlett-Packard | (US) | 87 |
| 37 | FINLAND | | 211 | 87 | BNP Paribas | (France) | 86 |
| 38 | THAILAND | | 206 | 88 | PDVSA | (Venezuela) | 86 |
| 39 | PORTUGAL | | 195 | 89 | UBS | (Switzerland) | 85 |
| 40 | General motors | (US) | 193 | 90 | Bank of America | (US) | 84 |
| 41 | HONG KONG PRC | | 190 | 91 | Hitachi | (Japan) | 84 |
| 42 | Chevron | (US) | 189 | 92 | China National Petrol | (China) | 84 |
| 43 | Daimler Chrysler | (Germany) | 186 | 93 | Pemex | (Mexico) | 83 |
| 44 | Toyota Motor | (Japan) | 186 | 94 | Nissan Motor | Japan | 83 |
| 45 | VENEZUELA | | 182 | 95 | Berkshire Hathaway | (US) | 82 |
| 46 | Ford Motor | (US) | 177 | 96 | Home Depot | (US) | 82 |
| 47 | UAE | | 168 | 97 | Valero Energy | (US) | 81 |
| 48 | Conoco Phillips | (US) | 167 | 98 | J.P.Morgan Chase | (US) | 80 |
| 49 | General Electric | (US) | 157 | 99 | Samsung Electronics | (Korea) | 79 |
| 50 | Total | (France) | 152 | 100 | Matsushita Electric | (Japan) | 79 |

**SOURCES:** *Figures on country GDP 2006 taken from International Monetary Fund as cited on <http://en.wikipedia.org/List_of_countries_by_GDP>, accessed 17 August 2007; and revenues of companies 2006 taken from Fortune Global 500 figures as cited on <http://money.cnn.com/magazines/fortune/global500/2006/full_list>, accessed 17/8/2007.*

A growing number of companies around the world are looking at their business in a global context. For some this means considering the company's markets and operations together within an integrated framework. For others it means standardising products and marketing programs, and rationalising research, development and production to create global economies of scale with tactical product/service marketing done on a country-by-country basis. For a growing number of firms it means transformation from domestic or multinational players to a single global entity operating seamlessly anywhere in the world. BHP Billiton, the Australian-headquartered minerals and resources group, and Fletcher Challenge, the diversified New Zealand-based resources and building products company, are both undergoing this transformation.

Nokia has already become a global company. Its mobile products division operates as a world business. New products are rolled out worldwide in months rather than years. Manufacturing has been consolidated into fewer plants, operations have been standardised so production can be moved from place to place rapidly. Human resource policies are standardised to facilitate personnel transfers. The same can be said for Sony.

Global advertising is consolidated through fewer agencies that design world campaigns and adaptation to local markets (Moss Kanter 1994; Nelson and Paek 2007).

The massive global advertising, promotion and publicity campaign by Apple promoting its iPhone in 2007 simultaneously around the world illustrates the speed of market penetration that can be achieved in multiple markets.

A global strategy means that a company competes on the basis of its entire combination of competencies, infrastructure and products in all its markets, rather than on a country-by-country basis (De Mooij 2003). To do this effectively requires integration of activities and communication between managers in different countries. Implementing the company's global strategy requires less bureaucracy, flatter organisational structures, effective and quick communication and a clear understanding in each market area of the corporate vision. Toyota is a company that has been able to achieve this in the car industry—see International Highlight 11.1.

In the previously mentioned global brands survey Holt et al. (2004) segmented consumers on the basis of whether they were global citizens (55%—they care about how the firm behaves regarding the environment and other issues), global dreamers (23% readily accept the global myth and see themselves as global citizens), anti-globals (13%—try to avoid buying trans-nationals products and are sceptical of claims by global companies) and global agnostics (8%—do not see anything special about a global brand compared to a local brand).

Such segments are important for firms operating on a global basis and the size of these segments vary from country to country as shown in Figure 11.1.

## Globalism as a philosophy

Globalism is a philosophy based on an integrated, standardised world where people buy, sell and share common products, services and ideas.

McLuhan's observation in 1967 (see McLuhan et al. 2001) that electronic media would re-create the world into a global village was a significant articulation of the premise that media in the form of television and radio would stimulate cultural convergence around the world.

Gradually this premise was applied to marketing strategy. More than 30 years ago Robert Buzzell questioned which elements of multinational marketing strategy could be standardised. He pointed out that various benefits could arise from standardisation, including significant cost savings, consistency with customers, improved planning and control and the exploitation of more good ideas (Buzzell 1968).

## 11.1 INTERNATIONAL HIGHLIGHT

# Toyota—a visionary car company acting on global trends

I t is hard to believe that General Motors (GM) and Toyota were on par in developmental work on hybrid cars. A decade ago both makers developed a process for production of hybrids. GM pioneered the first prototype. However, this new technology has proven to be so expensive that hybrid cars could only be sold at a considerable loss. American car makers did not see any sense in manufacturing cars at a loss, yet Toyota's vision of the future was committed to R&D to design technologies and vehicles to meet future motoring and environmental needs.

Toyota initially sold its Prius model at a loss in all markets. But today it is starting to yield profits. Public opinion, crude oil prices, environmental issues and reducing disposable income is strengthening Toyota's position.

Toyota's success lies in its philosophy of continuous improvement and its consistent positioning of durability and reliability. The process of continuous improvement and driving costs out of business allows Toyota to make a significantly higher profit margin than its American counterparts. According to Automotive Lease Guide USA, Japanese cars have a higher resale value (52% of new car price for Toyota compared to 43% for General Motors).

The success of Toyota lies in its long-term vision compared with the short-term reactionary tactics implemented by its rivals. Whereas US makers continue to produce petrol-gobbling SUVs, pickups, 4WDs and family vans that have bigger and more powerful engines, Japanese makers have been focusing on the total cost of ownership. This focus has paid off in the light of the ongoing oil supply and price fluctuation and the perceived environmental impacts on global pollution and climate. Few automakers have a better environmental position than Toyota and no car has a more 'green' credibility than Prius.

As at November 2006 Toyota became number two car maker in the world in terms of sales and the prognosis is that by the end of 2007 it will become number one.

The lesson from this story of a visionary giant is that international marketers need to go beyond the traditional mantra of acting globally but thinking locally, to a commitment to long-term global trends.

**SOURCES:** *Welch, D. (2007) 'Why Toyota is afraid of being number one',* BusinessWeek, *5 March, pp. 42–50; <http://www.toyota.com>; <http://www.toyota.com/prius/>; <http://www.lexus.com/>; and <http://www.gm.com/>.*

In 1983 Theodore Levitt presented a world with globalised markets where 'global companies will systematically shape the vectors of technology and globalisation into its great strategic fecundity' (Levitt 1983, p. 204). He concluded that the world is being driven by technology toward a converging commonality making communication, transport and travel available to all. Most people are interested in the things they have discovered or seen via the new technologies. Globalism had entered the mindset of the international marketing strategist (Bauer et al. 2005).

Kenichi Ohmae (1985, 1989a, 1989b, 1995) suggests that on a political map boundaries between countries may be clear, but a competitive map showing flows of financial and trading activity have transcended those boundaries. This is occurring through an ever speedier flow of information.

Hamel and Prahalad's *Competing for the Future* (1994) is a culmination of global business strategy grounded on strategic intent that typically searches for global dominance through the development and leverage of global core competencies.

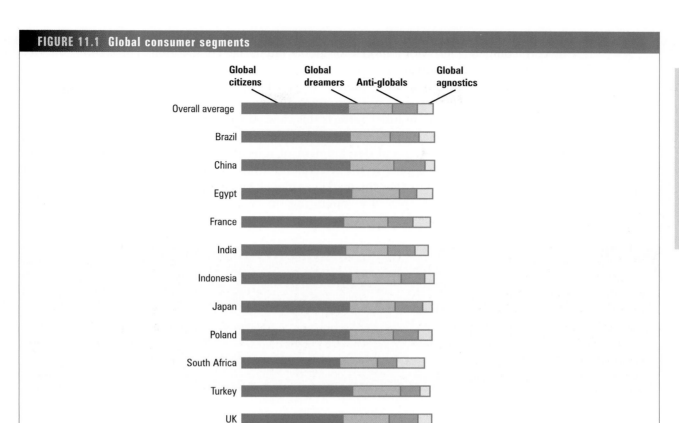

**FIGURE 11.1 Global consumer segments**

Global citizens Global dreamers Anti-globals Global agnostics

Overall average
Brazil
China
Egypt
France
India
Indonesia
Japan
Poland
South Africa
Turkey
UK
US

0% 20% 40% 60% 80% 100%

**Percentage of respondents who fit into each consumer segment**

**SOURCE:** *Holt, D.B., Quelch, J.A. and Taylor, E.T. (2004) 'How global brands compete',* Harvard Business Review, *September, p. 73.*

Organisations should view strategic intent as being the underlying component of their strategic foundation. Hamel and Prahalad refer to this as a strategic architecture capstone. This strategic architecture aims at pointing organisations to a desired future position, however the strategic intent provides the fuel for the journey. The fuel is needed for both emotional and intellectual areas within the organisation. Thus strategic architecture is seen as the brain and strategic intent is the heart of the organisation.

Hamel and Prahalad (1994) contend that core competencies for a firm must pass three tests:

1 *customer value*: a core competency must make a disproportionate contribution to customer-perceived value;

2 *competitor differentiation*: to qualify as a core competency a capability must be competitively unique;

3 *extendability*: core competencies must be the gateways to tomorrow's markets.

Hamel and Prahalad reinforce the global strategy framework of strategic intent supported by core competencies, with a model for global multistage competition. Throughout the first decade of the 2000s globalism has been embraced by a growing group of business strategists and developed to the point where there is a distinct sphere of global business strategy thought and application.

The financial services industry reflects this view. Australia's biggest fund managers such as MLC have taken their expertise into international markets. The NAB and ANZ banks have moved through acquisition and development of international banking networks to become more global. The same applies to the telecommunications industry. Nortel, British Telecom, AT&T and a host of others view the market as global. Smaller players like Telstra and Telecom (NZ) understand that they are operating in a part of an interconnected global telecommunications industry.

Often globalisation is regarded as synonymous with Americanisation because most of the world's global firms originated there. However, A.T. Kearney has developed a Globalisation Index which uses as measures of globalisation foreign trade, internet use, international telephone traffic and number of international visitors. Notably it excludes a nation's cultural impact on the rest of the world. The top 15 globalised countries according to the A.T. Kearney Globalisation Index for 2005 were Singapore, Ireland, Switzerland, United States, Netherlands, Canada, Denmark, Sweden, Austria, Finland, New Zealand, United Kingdom, Australia, Norway, Czech Republic.

## MOTIVATIONS FOR GLOBALISATION

Companies that operate in global industries, where their strategic positions in specific markets are strongly affected by their overall global positions, must think and act globally. Thus, car firms must organise globally if they are to gain purchasing, manufacturing, financial and marketing advantages. Firms in a global industry must compete on a worldwide basis if they are to succeed.

Any of several factors might draw a company into the global arena. Global competitors might attack the company's domestic market by offering better products or lower prices. The company might want to counterattack these competitors in their home markets to tie up their resources. Or the company might discover foreign markets that present higher profit opportunities than the domestic market. The company's domestic market might be shrinking or the company might need an enlarged customer base in order to achieve economies of scale. Or it might want to reduce its dependence on any one market so as to reduce its risk. Finally, the company's customers might be expanding overseas and require international servicing. This applies particularly to the Australian banking and financial services sector. ANZ, Westpac, CBA and NAB are all in the process of globalisation.

Before going into foreign markets the company must weigh several risks and answer many questions about its ability to operate globally. Can the company learn to understand the preferences and buyer behaviour of consumers in other countries? Can it offer competitively attractive products? Will it be able to adapt to another country's business cultures and be able to deal effectively with foreign nationals? Do the company's managers have the necessary international experience? Has management considered the impact of foreign regulations and political environments? These questions have been discussed in detail in earlier chapters.

There are many reasons motivating firms to go global. Three reasons apply to most firms. The first is competition and customers—in many industries, competitors can access customers almost anywhere. In contrast, many customers that are going global want their key suppliers to be there to service them. Second, technology evolves at different speeds in different countries. As a major driver of change and competitive advantage, it is no longer sufficient to source technologies from one country only. Ghemawat (2007) sees this as one of the central challenges of a global strategy.

If a business is located close to leading-edge technology development, it is likely to be closer to the early adopters phase of new markets (as discussed in relation to lead users in Chapter 5). Third, economies of doing business are changing in terms of cost of funds, cost of labour, availability of specialised skills and opportunities for standardisation. As an example, manufacturing advantages for textiles moved from Australia to Hong Kong, then Taiwan, South Korea and Mauritius, then to China. A global approach enables the firm to plan for and respond to these changes in relation to both the costs and quality of its inputs.

Another driver of globalisation is the need to tie up sources of supply of key raw materials and inputs as well as diversify locations of operation. India's second largest steel maker, Tata Steel, plans to buy coalmines in Australia, Indonesia, Mozambique and possibly New Zealand so as to triple its annual steel production to 15 million tonnes. Its purchase of Natsteel Asia in 2004 gave it steel plants in Thailand, Malaysia, Philippines, Australia, Vietnam and China (Wong 2005).

Yip (2003) classifies the drivers of globalisation under four headings:

1 *market drivers*: These include rising expectations, converging per capita incomes, convergence of lifestyles and tastes, increasing travel, establishment of more world brands, emergence of global market segments (e.g. teenagers), the push to have global advertising campaigns and the internet.

2 *cost drivers*: These include the push for economies of scale, accelerating technological innovation, advances in transportation, transferring operations to newly industrialising countries in search of lower labour costs and the increasing cost of product development relative to the market life of the product.

3 *government drivers*: These include the reduction in trade barriers, the formation of more regional trade groupings, privatisation of government businesses and the reduction in the number of state-dominated economies.

4 *competitive drivers*: These include the continuing expansion in world trade, increasing levels of foreign ownership, more companies seeking to operate on a global as opposed to a national basis and the formation of global strategic alliances.

## 'Glocalisation'

Forces for global integration and market responsiveness of both small and medium-sized enterprises (SMEs) and large-scale enterprises show them moving towards similar 'glocal' strategies—'think global, act local', as shown in Figure 11.2.

Sheth and Parvatiyar (2001) and Segal-Horn (2002) suggest that the major forces for global integration can be identified in seven forces:

1 *Removal of trade barriers (deregulation)*: The removal of historical barriers, including both tariffs and non-tariff barriers, which typically imposed obstacles to generating trade across borders has reduced the time cost and other complexities involved in these transactions.

FIGURE 11.2  The global integration/marketing responsiveness grid: the future orientation of LSEs and SMEs

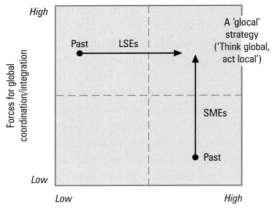

SOURCE: *Hollensen, S. (2004)* Global Marketing: A Decision-Oriented Approach, *3rd edn, Financial Times Prentice Hall, p. 14; see also Vignali, C. and Mattiacci, A. (2004) 'The typical products within food "glocalisation": The makings of a twenty-first century industry',* British Food Journal, *Vol. 106, No. 10/11, p. 703.*

## 11.2 INTERNATIONAL HIGHLIGHT

# Pitching globally, selling locally

In a climate of terrorism, anti-Western sentiment and street protests on anti-globalisation, global firms have to go out of their way to identify with local interests in the countries in which they operate. In Saudi Arabia, the Big Mac is marketed as a McArabia and in Indonesia, McDonald's licensees decorate their premises with green flags and play religious music to enhance their Islamic affiliation. Often this requires adaptation of the product to local tastes such as the Chicken Maharaja Mac in India and the Teriyaki Burger in Japan. Through advertising, global firms such as Coca-Cola stress local identification and adjust messages to highlight local relevance as with 'Everyone and everything crazy for Argentina' and 'Everyone and everything crazy for Paraguay'. Many firms that do not localise pay the price. Wal-mart incurred two years of losses in Korea and sold its 16 stores to local retail group, Shinsegae. Wal-mart also pulled out of India at a loss of 1.5 billion dollars, not able to satisfy Indian tastes and cost perceptions despite what was believed to be a sizeable middle class market. Wal-mart sold its operations to the German Metro chain, which believes that it can appeal more closely to Indian consumers' needs. Another global retail group, Carrefour, has pulled out of the Korean market and sold its 32 stores to local fashion retailer, E.Land. In both cases these overseas retailers applied so-called global standards to the Korean market without understanding the needs of Korean customers. In many of these markets it is the local firms that dominate rather than global firms. Whereas in Korea, Coca-Cola has a 20% market share, local bottler Lotte Chilsung has 40%.

SOURCES: *Adapted from Altman, D. (2006) 'Selling globally, pitching locally',* International Herald Tribune, *31 May, p. 13;* Financial Times, *5 February 2004, p. 20; Jung-a, S. (2006) 'Big boys reel from Korean culture shock',* Financial Times, *26 May, p. 20; and Sridharan, R. (2007) 'Local adaptation is the key in retail business'* Business Today *(New Delhi), February 25, p. 154.*

2 *Global accounts/customer*: As customers become more global and rationalise their purchasing arrangements they demand more from their suppliers, in particular global pricing, worldwide-service-level agreements or standardised product offerings.

3 *Relationship management/network organisation*: A global marketplace requires global reach, and to gain this reach and reduce market uncertainties it is necessary for many companies to partner and form alliances or networks.

4 *Standardised worldwide technology*: World demand for technology products was originally dominated by government and defence sectors of the leading economies before trickling down to consumer applications. However, the desire by manufacturers to gain scale in production has meant that increasingly products are produced for a worldwide market and homogeneity in demand across nations is increasing as a result.

5 *Worldwide markets*: These markets are developing due to an increased reliance on worldwide demographics. For example, if a marketer had a product for teenagers it would be relatively easy now to develop a worldwide strategy to target this market globally and set up market coverage measures and other marketing metrics accordingly.

6 *'Global village'*: This terms refers to the fact that the world's population shares commonly recognised cultural symbols. The business result of this is that similar products can be sold to similar customer segments around the world and the potential for the worldwide convergence of markets which we are seeing with brands like Coca-Cola and Nike.

7 *Worldwide communication*: The internet and email technologies are opening up markets to even the smallest of businesses as people can access products online from many different countries around the world.

These authors (see Hollensen 2004, p. 15) also suggest that there are countervailing forces for market responsiveness that fall into three areas:

1 *Cultural differences*: Cultural diversity continues and is reflected in differences in personal values and the practice of marketing and business in different cultures. In places like Australia and Canada, which have highly diverse cultural groups, the practice of 'local' marketing has a strong presence.

2 *Regionalism/protectionism*: Regional clusters of countries into groups such as the European Union, ASEAN and NAFTA have created regional trading blocs which act as a blockage to globalisation.

3 *Deglobalisation trends*: Demonstrations at world trade conferences and current movements in Arab countries indicate that there could be a return to old values, which could promote barriers to further globalisation.

## Characteristics of the global firm

Early pioneers in global thinking, Daniels and Frost, in a paper entitled 'On becoming a global corporation' (1988), developed a typology for the global firm, the highlights of which are as follows. The global firm:

• has a business concept rather than a geographic concept with a focus on how you do business rather than where you do business;

• is decentralised rather than centralised and is willing to do business in any location and does not worry about centralising activities in a particular location;

- adopts a holistic view of its operation and believes that any part of the business should reflect the whole of the business (i.e. its genetic code). The firm has shared values, attitudes and beliefs that are evident wherever it chooses to do business, and are apparent to its stakeholders;

- consciously eliminates the isolation that precludes the sharing of information and deliberately lowers the boundaries between members of its value chain;

- builds trust between members of the organisation and the networks in which the elements of the organisation are embedded so as to speed up communication and decision making and overcome the 'not invented here' syndrome;

- goes out of its way to be a good corporate citizen in the countries in which it operates, and caters to local tastes without sacrificing economies of scale;

- operates as a coordinator among members of its network of companies rather than as a controller. This enables the amplification and interpretation of communications and facilitates the sharing of experiences;

- actively works to remove duplication of facilities and achieve economies of scale by leveraging knowledge. This is reflected in its pursuing outsourcing;

- encourages horizontal communication within the group from one level to another (e.g. from the product manager for ice-cream in Australia to the product manager for ice-cream in India), rather than vertical communication from operating level up to CEO (e.g. in Australia) to CEO (e.g. in India) then down to operating level in the other country;

- understands the worldwide economics of the businesses in which it is involved and engages in cross-subsidisation between areas of activity as required with a focus on long-term financial rewards rather than short-term gains.

## Global or multinational?

One of the most vigorous debates in international marketing is the preference for multinational or global marketing. For the strategist this debate raises many key questions including:

- Which approach provides a better picture for developing future competitive position—an aggregation of several national and industry competitive position models or a model that starts with an overall global competitive position?

- Which elements of the marketing mix or aspects of the value chain can be effectively standardised or modified to service global customer sets?

- Which external or environmental variables (such as economical, political, legal and cultural variables) require analysis that goes below a global perspective to a regional or national level?

- What is the impact of global telecommunications, media and computing on the development of effective international competitive marketing strategy?

- How does a multinational firm convert to a global company?

- Is true globalisation really ever possible—or even desirable?

The issues relevant to the standardisation versus adaptation debate are discussed in Chapter 13. Although the issue has been vigorously debated there is increasing recognition that a global strategy can possess sufficient flexibility to have a standardised business strategy and yet still market and deliver products adapted for many different markets. Quelch and Hoff (1986) developed a Global Marketing Planning Matrix accommodating both standardisation and adaptation (see also Brock and Birkinshaw (2004), pp. 5–10). This matrix is presented in Figure 11.3

Now companies do not just need to debate over whether they are going to standardise their products or customise their products for the potential global market. There is a new manufacturing technique that, with the help of the internet and advanced machinery technology, will allow individual customers to design their own products. It's called mass customisation and is now a serious competitive issue in the global marketplace. The companies that are involved in mass customisation are instantly global because they use interactive websites to reach global customers. McDonald's is embarking on a bold new digital strategy, which is described in International Highlight 11.3.

### FIGURE 11.3 Global planning matrix

| | | ADAPTATION | | STANDARDISATION | |
|---|---|---|---|---|---|
| | | FULL | PARTIAL | FULL | PARTIAL |
| **Business functions** | Research and development | | | | |
| | Finance and accounting | | | | |
| | Manufacturing | | | | |
| | Procurement | | | | |
| | Marketing | | | | |
| **Products** | Low cultural grounding High economies or efficiencies | | | | |
| | High cultural grounding High economies or efficiencies | | | | |
| | High cultural grounding Low economies or efficiencies | | | | |
| **Marketing mix elements** | Product design | | | | |
| | Brand name | | | | |
| | Product positioning | | | | |
| | Packaging | | | | |
| | Advertising theme | | | | |
| | Pricing | | | | |
| | Advertising copy | | | | |
| | Distribution | | | | |
| | Sales promotion | | | | |
| | Customer service | | | | |
| **Countries** Region 1 | Country A | | | | |
| | Country B | | | | |
| | Country C | | | | |
| Region 2 | Country D | | | | |
| | Country E | | | | |

**SOURCE:** *Adapted from Quelch, J.A. and Hoff, E.J. (1986) 'Customizing global marketing',* Harvard Business Review, *May–June, in P. Barnevik and R. Moss Kanter* Global Strategies—Insights from the World's Leading Thinkers, *Harvard Business School Publishing, Boston, MA, p. 181.*

# M stands for 'Wired Arches'

McDonald's is launching a global strategy aimed at positioning McDonald's as the world's most innovative digital marketer. McDonald's executives have taken a decision to be at the forefront of the changes happening to its target market, who now wants to be engaged in new, interactive and 'fun' ways.

To achieve this position McDonald's had to go beyond its existing agency suppliers operating in local or geographic markets and appoint one global communications supplier. The AKQA agency has sealed this bid with McDonald's.

McDonald's strategy is to focus on embracing multiple digital platforms such as web and mobile. The aim of this global digital strategy is to build strong consumer relationships ensuring that consistent, compelling consumer experiences are delivered worldwide.

McDonald's knows that the selection of one global supplier should not and must not affect local advertising accounts in specific countries for dealing with local idiosyncrasies as part of its 'glocal' marketing philosophy. Being a global brand requires developing a global digital strategy and uniform platforms to enable consistency and integration for the brand across the world. The appointment of a single global digital marketing agency demonstrates the brand's commitment to taking a leadership position.

Although McDonald's operates on the global marketing stage, digital platforms for communicating globally with target customers are still relatively new. This strategy is in addition to local country strategies and must be executed seamlessly so as not to alienate or hinder growth in specific country markets. Global communication is planned to work as a more holistic and integrated approach to meeting customer needs.

There are several challenges facing McDonald's global digital communication strategy:

1  Despite being one of the most recognised brands in the world, according to Nielsen NetRatings, McDonald's global online audience is estimated to be only around 1.9 million people—about 0.6% of the world's active internet population. Currently McDonald's is viewed as a major multinational brand, but is currently ranked in 974th place amongst the most popular online brands in the world. Market analysts recognise that there's a huge gap between where McDonald's is in the minds of consumers compared with the company's existing online efforts. McDonald's challenge is to understand how it can use the online space and online technologies to engage and interact with consumers being currently targeted by traditional media.

2  Another challenge inhibiting the brand is the widening spectrum of regulations around advertising to children. McDonald's faces advertising restrictions in some of its international markets in terms of how and how often it targets children using traditional media.

3  This, combined with serious issues about fast food and obesity, and with political and environmental issues, poses significant problems for its online global strategy bid. McDonald's aims at making sure that people will associate McDonald's not with 'junk food', but with nutritional options on the menu.

5  At Nielsen-NetRatings, McDonald's is categorised as a corporate site and the global site (<http://www.mcdonalds.com>) serves as a landing page, with corporate information and links to its local country sites. Since users are 'not going to go online to buy a hamburger' it will need to look at other ways to engage the audience.

McDonald's online strategy commitment is being supported by a marked increase in online marketing spending. It has already increased its online investment significantly. For example, promotion for 'Pirates of the Caribbean' proved very successful and helped boost the brand's unique audience from 1.7 million in January 2006 to 5.3 million in July 2006. An immediate result of this integrated digital media push made McDonald's the seventh-fastest growing brand online in 2006. But the challenge is whether the brand will find ways to maintain this growth and position. With over 30 000 restaurants around the globe, there is an opportunity to embed the digital strategy to be much more integrated and connected around those restaurants and while it might be in the form of promotional content, or entertainment, this new technology can also enhance the whole ordering experience.

**SOURCE:** *Adapted from Long, D. (2006) 'McDonald's unveils digital strategy revolution',* Marketing Week, *December, p. 15.*

# Global strategy framework

Every industry has aspects that are global or potentially global—global meaning that there are inter-country connections. A strategy is global to the extent that it is integrated across countries. This does not equate with any one element, such as global manufacturing or standardised global products. A global strategy is a flexible combination of many elements. Yip (2003) suggests that a *total global strategy* usually has three separate steps or components:

- *Step one* is the development of a core strategy, which is the basis of the firm's competitive advantage.

- *Step two* involves the internationalisation of the strategy through expansion of activities and adaptation of the core strategy to several country markets.

- *Step three* integrates the strategy across countries. At this stage globalisation is achieved. This involves managing for worldwide business leverage and competitive advantage. Yip's (2003) framework for global strategy is shown as Figure 11.4.

Industry globalisation drivers that reflect underlying market, cost, government and competitive conditions create the potential for a business to achieve the benefits of a global strategy. This occurs if the business can set global strategy levers such as market coverage, standardised products and global marketing appropriately relative to the industry drivers and relative to the position and resources of the business and the parent company. The company's ability to implement a global strategy determines how substantial are the benefits to be achieved. The global strategy will also determine how the organisation should be structured and managed.

Globalisation strategy is multidimensional, requiring choices along at least five strategic dimensions:

1 *Market participation* relates to the choice of country markets and the level of activity in these countries.

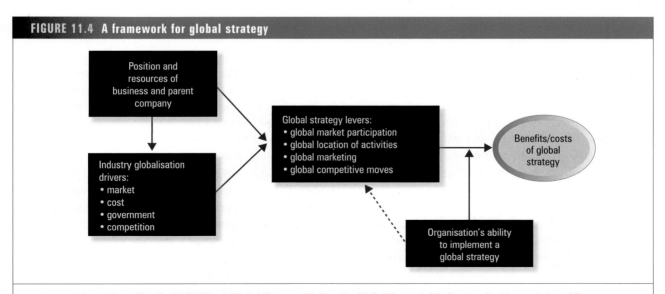

**FIGURE 11.4 A framework for global strategy**

**SOURCE:** *Adapted from Yip, G. (2003)* Total Global Strategy II, *Prentice Hall, NJ, pp. 1–29. Reprinted with permission of Pearson Education Inc., Upper Saddle River, NJ.*

# Global market of one—customisation by global companies spreads

At the forefront of the mass customisation revolution are companies like Dell Computers (<http://www.dell.com>). Since 1996 a significant portion of Dell's business has come from people who visit its website to customise their made-to-order PCs. Despite the technology companies' downturn in 2001, Dell still maintained relatively strong profitability. Dell's initial focus was to cater for the business market or those purchasing their second computer. The thinking was that online customisation required the customer to know at least some basic requirements for their 'to be configured' PC. Also, typical business users in most cases have their own IT departments, which look after fine-tuning their company's hardware to its organisational needs. Therefore, if a problem arose with their company's PC, in most cases they would solve the problem on their own before consulting Dell. As a result the servicing costs of Dell were kept to a minimum. In recent times Dell has shifted its focus towards the home computer market and has also broadened its range of offerings to business. During 2003 Dell entered the printer market in partnership with companies like Lexmark and Samsung and it has made an immediate impact, capturing more than 3% of the inkjet market and upwards of 14% of the all-in-one market, demonstrating that its direct-customer-focused approach is very powerful (Park and Gross 2004). The home market became increasingly a stronger focus for Dell in 2004 and the company has a belief that the digital home concept that has been promising to take off for a number of years is finally a viable consumer solution (Thomas et al. 2003).

As of 2007, Dell has moved to take advantage of the digital household trend, by expanding into plasma screens, projectors, TVs, MP3 players and portable hand-held PCs, software, networking, and gaming and hardware accessories. In effect, Dell has become a 'one stop shop' for general computing needs.

A late entrant to online customisation was HP (<http://www.hp.com>). Its bricks-and-mortar business and global alliances hindered its initial push to online customisation. However, HP succeeded in convincing both its distribution partners and customers about the benefits of online customisation. Even Apple has entered the game, lifting sagging fortunes with their build-to-order store. The advent of the mass customisation model also enabled small players/resellers such as Harris Technology (<http://www.ht.com.au>) to become customisation players by adopting the Dell model and configuring budget computers for their customers.

The challenge presented by this new customisation model is one of the reasons why businesses not traditionally organised in this manner have found it very difficult to compete profitably. In fact in December 2004 IBM announced the sale of its PC business to Lenovo (a Chinese-owned hardware maker and seller) as it had become more of a liability than an asset due to the aggressive competition in this market brought on by, in particular, Dell's customisation/direct approach (Poletti and Takahashi 2004; see also 'Business: bold fusion; face value', *Economist*, 17 Feb 2007, p. 74).

As customers become more empowered in the computer industry they can also apply the same principle to cars. Car manufacturers, such as Daimler Chrysler (Mercedes-Benz), Ford and BMW, use their websites to stimulate demand for their products. These companies allow customers to configure their own car, make the order online, select the nearest dealer for pick up and then trace their car being built and its current transit location.

Another example of mass customisation has developed in the clothing industry. The Interactive Custom Clothes Company (<http://www.ic3d.com>), launched in 2002, offers a wide array of made-to-measure men's and women's jeans that give customers a plethora of choices—including style, fit and fabrics. This business was even praised for its innovation by top designers at the Italian Gucci brand such as Tom Ford, who said that 'the company who can adapt and can customise will be the success of the decade'. Customers can even choose the colour of rivets and pocket labels for an individualised fit. The costs of the jeans vary from $65 for denim up to $250 for silk velvet. The measurements and specifications sent by the customer are placed into a computer intelligence system, which generates a pattern to the customer's size. The information is then downloaded and entered into an industrial cutter, which takes 42 seconds to cut the pieces of cloth needed to make the pair of jeans. They are then sent onto a sewing shop and shipped to the customer in about a week. Levi Strauss & Co. (<http://www.levis.com>) has also been offering its Personal Pair customised women's jeans.

As consumers become more aware of the products and services offered in the global marketplace, companies will need to be able to give each individual exactly what they want, because, if they can't, other, more advanced companies will. Most of us are probably using customisation tools every day—examples are My Yahoo!, MySchwab and My Bank.

**SOURCES:** *Mathieson (1998) 'Market of one: mass customization meets the net',* E Business, *June; James, D. (1999) 'New ease of production makes the pursuit of mass rather critical',* Business Review Weekly, *15 March, <http://www.brw.com.au/newsadmin/stories/brw/19990315/ 1552.htm>, accessed 20 June 2001; and Brady, D., Kerwin, K., Welch, D. and Lee, L. (2001) 'Customising for the masses',* BusinessWeek, *20 March, <http://www.businessweek.com>, accessed 30 June 2001.*

2 *Product/service standardisation* involves the extent to which standardisation or differentiation exists in each country.

3 *Location of value-adding activities* requires choices of location of each of those activities in the business's value chain from R&D to service backup.

4 *Marketing* involves choices about worldwide use of brand names, advertising, sales strategies and service.

5 *Competitive moves* relate to the extent to which moves in specific countries form part of a global competitive strategy.

The benefits and drawbacks of global strategy need to be evaluated by Australian firms in this situation. International Highlight 11.5 reflects the success achieved by one outstanding Australian company—Cochlear.

In summary, the benefits of global strategy fall into the four areas of cost reduction, improved quality of products and programs, enhanced customer preference and increased competitive leverage.

Drawbacks generally lie in standardisation of products, services and processes, which may not meet the needs of a specific country's customers well. Also, competitive positions may substantially differ between countries, making some strategies much less effective in specific countries than in other countries. Management and coordination costs may also be significant through the creation of additional overheads and reporting requirements.

A company that fails to globalise when its competitors do or when it faces global competition in its domestic market may face financial hardship.

However, globalisation of an industry can be used to advantage, as we see in the transformation of Foster's Brewing Group (International Highlight 11.6).

The key goal of any international strategy is to manage the fundamental differences that emerge when looking at the borders of markets. Executives often neglect to exploit market, product and production discrepancies, focusing instead on the tensions between standardisation and localisation. According to Ghemawat (2007), there are three effective responses to the challenges of globalisation. These responses are shown in Figure 11.5. This framework, which is called the AAA, looks at three distinctive types of international strategy.

Through the use of adaptation, companies look for ways to boost revenues and market share by maximising their local relevance. Through aggregation, companies attempt to deliver economies of scale by creating regional, or occasionally global, operations. Through arbitrage, businesses exploit discrepancies between local, national or regional markets.

## 11.5 INTERNATIONAL HIGHLIGHT

# 'The ears have it'

With the exception of a few very large Australian firms, the opportunities for Australian companies to globalise and adopt global strategies is confined to focusing on narrow niche products and markets-businesses that are highly specialised in their expertise and activities. This has been achieved to with some success by high-technology Australian firms in the biotechnology area.

The Australian star in this sector is Sydney-based Cochlear, which now dominates world markets in its specialised area. In 1998 Cochlear Ltd gained US regulatory approval for its most advanced ear implant system, the Nucleus 24 system—an implant in the cochlea, which is a shell-shaped part of the inner ear. Cochlear Ltd then had the opportunity to sell implants to over 200 000 severely hearing-impaired Americans—100 times the total number of Nucleus 24 implants sold worldwide to June 1998. The hearing-aid manufacturer has had its system approved by most other countries. Cochlear Ltd's implant had an estimated 70% share of the global market in 1998. By 2001, there were 31 500 Cochlear Nucleus implants worldwide, a sales revenue of $144 million and profit of $20 million in 2000. By mid-2002 Cochlear Ltd had 60–65% of global sales, Advanced Bionics (a US company) had 30%, which included nearly half of the North American market, and Med-El (an Australian firm) had 5–10% with its main focus on Europe. Total worldwide market sales in 2001–02 were around $400 million. Cochlear Ltd's sales were $256 million for 2001–02 with an after-tax profit of just over $40 million.

Since that time Cochlear Ltd's vision of being the global leader in innovative implantable hearing solutions has become a reality. Cochlear Ltd implant unit sales grew 11.9% in the first half of 2004–05 but accelerated to 20.0% in the second half, helped by the release of its next generation Nucleus Freedom cochlear implant system. This system provides the best hearing performance available. This effort has resulted in Nucleus Freedom offering the next step in cochlear implant technology and being a platform for future innovations. In anticipation of the Nucleus Freedom launch, detailed market research was conducted in multiple markets. This helped identify key messages that would resonate with customers and provided facts for marketing decisions. During the year, marketing resources were rebalanced between corporate marketing and regional marketing as well as rebalancing the focus between recipients and professionals (rather than solely healthcare professionals). Net profit after tax grew by 48.3% over the previous year to $54.5 million in 2005.

For its 2006 financial year revenue grew by 30% over 2005 to $452 million and net profit after-tax was $80 million. Sales revenue in 2006 increased 50% in the Americas, 35% in Europe and 7% in the Asia–Pacific region. Global market share of Cochlear Ltd implants was estimated at 70% in 2006.

Cochlear Ltd is a textbook case of globalisation for a technology company.

SOURCES: *Hensrud, D.D. (2003) 'Can you hear me now?', Fortune, 17 March p. 142; Quinlivan, B. (2002) 'Cochlear's chance', Business Review Weekly, 8–14 August, p. 38; Field, N. (1998) 'US approval is music to cochl-ears', Australian Financial Review, 29 June, p. 25; <http://www.cochlear.com/Corporate/Investor/AnnualReport2005/ed04_president/pres01_report.htm> (annual report for year ending June 2005); and <http://www.cochlear.com/Corp/Investor/190.asp> (annual report for year ending June 2006 and half-year report for 2006–07 at December 2006).*

Companies do so by locating different parts of the supply chain in different places—for instance, call centres in India, factories in China, and retail shops in western USA (Ghemawat 2007).

# BASIC COMPETITIVE STRATEGY PROFILES

Most of the basic competitive strategy profiles described in Chapter 10 apply in a global context. Also, the *built to last* characteristics proposed by Collins and Porras (1994) should be considered and the research findings of Treacy and Wiersema (1995) on market leaders apply.

**11.6** INTERNATIONAL HIGHLIGHT

# A different global brew from Foster's

The purchase of Beringer Wine Estates of California has transformed Foster's Group Ltd from an Australian brewer into an international beverage company. Foster's acquired Beringer at a time when there were moves towards rationalisation of the Australian wine industry so that there would be fewer, bigger producers with the scale to handle a big export business and supply multinational retailers. Faced with the prospect of growth levels in the beer business of somewhere between inflation and 5% in financial year 2000–01, Foster's set out to find another growth engine for the company. Growth through acquisition of a foreign brewer was considered but, according to CEO Kukkel, the countries Foster's would be comfortable entering had mature beer markets and, with those having the right growth profile for beer, either the country risk or the currency risk was unacceptable to the firm. Any new acquisition was to be overseas. With 90% of company earnings and assets in Australia, Foster's wanted to spread its geographic risk. The transformation of Foster's into a global beverage business is even more remarkable considering that it only entered the wine business in 1996 with the purchase of Mildara-Blass. In 2007, Foster's also will expand through international partnerships in new geographic markets such as Finland, Spain, Germany, France, Italy, Scandinavia, Russia and the USA. The biggest threat now is oversupply in the North American wine markets and where stringent government regulations inhibit the company's growth.

**SOURCE:** *Anonymous (2006),* Foster's Group: 2006 Company Profile Edition 2: Company Dossier, *Just-Drinks, Bromsgrove, pp. 1–3.*

---

**FIGURE 11.5  The AAA framework**

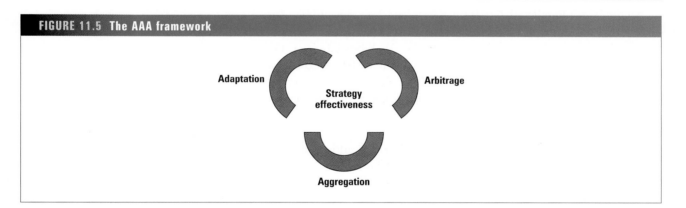

---

# Global leader strategy

*Innovator in technologies, products and markets with high global share and wide country market coverage.*

Microsoft, Cisco, Coca-Cola, Intel, Sony and Nokia are clear global leaders in their respective markets. Each adopts aggressive global strategies designed to be ahead of competitors in new expanding markets. Intel and Sony lead in their respective technologies. Microsoft, through a range of alliances with computer makers, dominates the operating systems and application software for PCs. Coca-Cola's focus on brand management, world-wide coverage and intensive distribution and advertising makes it the leading and most profitable soft drink company in the world. Nokia's brand positioning segmentation and product line strategy has made it a global leader in mobile phone handsets and GPS systems. Cisco dominates the supply of routers and equipment associated with the internet and strengthened its position via acquisition of Linksys.

# Global challenger strategy 1

*Frontal or encirclement attack on the leader in all markets with increasing country market coverage and high global share, but less than the leader.*

Komatsu is a major threat to Caterpillar's leadership, as is Pepsi's challenge to Coca-Cola in many of its major markets. News Corporation is a challenger in many of its media markets around the world—film, television, newspapers and cable and satellite networks.

# Global challenger strategy 2

*Flanking or bypassing world leader with increasing country market coverage and high global share, but less than the leader.*

Domino's challenge to Pizza Hut and Toyota's challenge to Ford involve strategies to map out new geographic markets in which the leaders are weak.

# Global follower strategy

*Rapid imitation of leader or challenger with moderate country market coverage and emphasis on price-sensitive markets. The result is overall moderate share with high shares in selected country markets.*

Examples include LG, Daewoo and Sanyo.

# Global niche strategy 1

*Rapid penetration of narrow market segments by selective targeting of country markets and a small share of the overall market.*

Examples include BMW, Toshiba (laptops), Georgio Armani (clothes), Ecco (shoes) and IKEA (furniture). Many Australian firms now have the potential for a global niche strategy from day one using the internet as the primary penetration vehicle. The NetMen Corp is an Argentine-based corporate logo, brochure and web design company that does all of its business via the internet. It adopts a low price strategy to generate high volume sales (see <http://www.thenetmencorp.com/>). This model is relevant to Australian and New Zealand companies operating in web design and online communication strategies.

# Global niche strategy 2

*Infiltration, slow penetration of selected narrow markets with focus on selected country markets and a low share of the overall market.*

Many of Australasia's food products fall into this category—wine, cheese, beer and dairy products. New Zealand-based boutique wine company Cloudy Bay has infiltrated a large number of overseas markets with its distinctly flavoured sauvignon blanc and chardonnay. United Milk Limited and Lactos, both based in Tasmania, have infiltrated many of the dairy milk and cheese markets around the world.

# Global collaborator strategy

*Innovator in research and development of technologies, products and markets, sets standards and shares them with other firms. This shows small or moderate country market shares, but high shares when all strategic 'standards users' are included.*

For example, Hewlett-Packard sells many of its competitors' products to provide its customers with tailored solutions in its 'network systems' division. Volkswagen provides its components to Skoda (Czech-based maker auto brand) and Audi to Seat (the Spanish-based car maker). Sony provides Trinitron screens to PC vendors as well as for sale in its own products. Other companies generating sales and share growth through collaboration are Philips and Canon.

# THE PITFALLS OF GLOBAL MARKETING

Although the global strategy may be right, the pitfalls of global marketing lie in implementation. This may involve a combination of vertical integration, joint ventures and alliances depending upon regulatory, competitive and market conditions in target countries. Global niche strategies particularly are likely to require alliance arrangements as a means of leveraging resources. There are several critical success factors to be considered to avoid the pitfalls in global marketing.

Key success factors are both external and internal. External factors relate to market, competitive, regulatory and industry conditions, which provide opportunities in world markets for a profitable fit to the company's competencies. These external factors must be considered in the context of future conditions. For instance, major world car manufacturers competed for the contract to produce the 'Chinese People's Car' on the basis of expected growth in purchasing power and progressive deregulation of this massive market.

However, many of the success factors are internal. First, they involve attitude. People in the company must perceive it as a global operation treating the world as one market and the competitors as global. Second, the company must develop global strategic capability. This requires information processing capability including development of systems for tracking political changes, technological innovation, threatening competitive moves having global significance and analytical sophistication of managers. Probably the greatest challenges involve the development and understanding of a shared vision and corporate culture and identity by people in different countries and divisions which can be translated into managing innovation and strategic change. Global teams working on R&D, new product rollouts and common service strategies need to facilitate coordination across functions and countries. This is a major challenge for even the most experienced global companies. This was the case for the American car makers such as General Motors that launched its premium brands of Cadillac. As at the first quarter of 2007 it was still struggling to penetrate the European market where preference remains for smaller cars and local brands that are more appealing to European economic and road conditions ('US car icons struggle to cross Atlantic', *Marketing Week*, 30 November 2006, p. 8).

## Issues

A number of issues and questions need to be looked at by marketers in the context of implementation of global marketing.

*Can a global marketing approach embrace both:*

1 *positioning the same product differently in each national market? or*

2 *positioning the product the same way in each national market, but modifying the product to meet the needs of each market?*

The answer to this is: think global—act local.

*Global marketing implies some form of standardisation.* Is the potential for standardisation (with respect to any or all of the marketing mix) greater for certain types of products than it is for others?

*Global marketing implies that world wants are becoming homogenised*, and proponents point to global customer segments and global brands targeted to those segments. Are these products of general appeal or are they products targeted to a relatively restricted, upscale international customer segment?

*Global marketing implies that customers behave the same way in different countries.* Do the same market segments exist in all countries and, if so, are they of the same significance? Alternatively, are similarities in customer behaviour restricted to a relatively limited number of target segments while for the most part there are substantial differences between countries? Chung (2005) investigated cross-market standardisation experience in the European Union and Gehrt and Shim (2003) reviewed segmentation in the Japanese snackfood market compared with other markets.

*Global marketing implies a universal preference for low price at acceptable quality.* However, what does this mean for:

- the drivers of brand preference?
- the impact of government subsidies/duties on a price positioning strategy?
- a standardised low price being 'overpriced' in some countries and 'underpriced' in others?

*Global marketing implies economies of scale.* How far is this moderated by technological developments and demand differences, which require more tailored marketing mix approaches?

*Global marketing may not take into account external constraints* such as:

- government and trade restrictions;
- the nature of marketing infrastructure in each country;
- interdependencies with resource markets, like availability of raw materials or low-cost skilled labour;
- the competitive situation in each market.

# GLOBALISATION FROM A MACRO PERSPECTIVE

The previous discussion has focused solely on globalisation from the perspective of the firm—that is, a micro perspective. Such a perspective implies that globalisation is inevitable, it is the way of the future and it will dictate a nation's future economic policies. US texts on international marketing, usually written from the perspective of transnational firms, put a positive spin on it, as do writers such as Friedman (2005). They argue it is inevitable for reasons as varied as rising fixed costs, the rapid dissemination of information, the need to increase expenditure on R&D to bring new products to market, the rapid dispersion of technology, shortening product life cycles, converging consumer tastes and the increased value being placed by the share market on brand equity.

In such an environment globalisation is essential from a profit perspective because it facilitates serving customers on a global basis by bringing products to market more quickly, being able to introduce products into several countries simultaneously and reducing promotion costs by having a single brand. Such a micro perspective on globalisation leads to it being viewed in terms of profitability considerations only. Firms, however, have many stakeholders other than their shareholders and it is relevant to view globalisation in the context of other stakeholders as well, in view of the pervasive effect it is alleged to have on the lives we all lead. From a macro perspective, the spin on globalisation does not appear to be as positive. This is particularly so since the attacks on the New York World Trade Center and the Pentagon on 11 September 2001, and there has been a fundamental questioning of the value and benefits of globalisation. The reality of globalisation is that it has created a number of 'hot spots' in the world such as Bangalore, India (Yee 2007; Merchant 2006). These hot spots attract most of the investment and entrepreneurial energy, but leave vast regions embedded further in the poverty trap to which this globalisation has contributed. Countries are beginning to question the appropriateness of open border policies at one level and at another, the benefits provided by free trade, both of which are elements of globalisation. Figure 11.6 by Korten (1999) illustrates this.

In Figure 11.6 the *top line* represents the rapid growth since 1980 in financial assets as measured by stock market capitalisation. The *second line* shows the rise in GDP, being the market value of output of goods and services that bring about growth in corporate profits and thence in share prices. As can be seen, GDP growth has not been as rapid as that in financial assets. The *third line* shows net beneficial output when GDP is discounted to allow for expenditures on products harmful to society, defence expenditures and depreciation. The net beneficial output since 1980 has in fact declined. The *fourth line* relates to living capital. Globalisation has a number of social costs, for example when rationalisation by transnational firms results in unemployment in a location. Therefore when these social costs which include resource depletion, social fragmentation and environmental degradation are taken into account, living capital has substantially declined during the two decades when globalisation has rapidly risen. Korten's analysis indicates that a macro perspective on globalisation is different from the micro perspective. This issue can be explored at the sociocultural level, the economic/financial level, the political/legal level and the technological level.

## Sociocultural level

Australia is a multicultural nation. However, globalisation promotes homogeneity of culture, not the celebration of diverse individuality as with multiculturalism. Each country has its

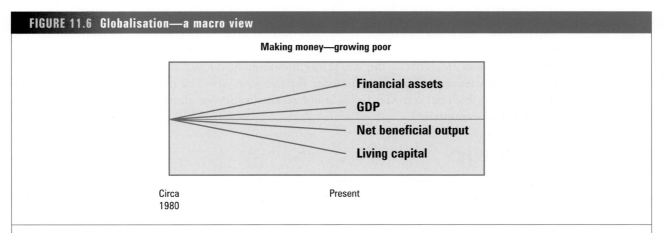

**FIGURE 11.6 Globalisation—a macro view**

Making money—growing poor

Financial assets

GDP

Net beneficial output

Living capital

Circa 1980

Present

**SOURCE:** *Korten, D.C. (1999) 'The dark side of globalisation: financial and corporate rule',* Proceedings of the Annual Meeting of the Academy of International Business, *Charleston, SC, 22–24 November. Reproduced with permission of David Korten.*

national icons, many of which take the form of brands or companies. Globalisation causes a loss of such icons as when successful local firms are acquired by transnational companies (TNCs), as happened when Arnott's Biscuits was taken over by Campbell's Soups of the USA. The loss of such icons has an impact on cultural identity. Also, globalisation often results in importing the cultural baggage of other nations. This is exacerbated when the content of the local media is dominated by overseas interests. In these circumstances globalisation can be synonymous with Americanisation, with consequent reduction of Australian cultural identity.

## Economic/financial level

Research shows that, overall, TNCs do not create employment in other countries or shift production away from developed to developing countries (Martin and Schumann 1997). Although the top 500 firms in the world account for 25% of global production, they only account for 0.1% of the global workforce. Globalisation is accentuating wealth divisions in many societies throughout the world (Stiglitz 2006). This is evidenced in higher salaries paid to chief executive officers (a trend led by TNCs), by an expanding gap between salaries paid in commercial/technical sectors and those paid in the social service/education sectors, and by urban areas becoming richer and rural areas poorer. TNCs are able to exert influence on governments by shifting or threatening to shift capital from one country to another. This is illustrated in the case of Kodak threatening to withdraw its operations from Australia. The above calls into question the practice in many countries, such as Australia, of using taxpayers' funds to attract TNCs to establish subsidiaries in their country and give them benefits not accorded to local firms.

## Political/legal level

Globalisation calls into question the democratic process as it exposes countries to influences by 'non-elected' bodies such as the World Trade Organization and the International Monetary Fund. These are bodies, however, that are subject to influence by countries from whom the majority of TNCs come. Furthermore, there is opportunity for 'non-elected' TNCs to influence the deliberations of local governments via lobbying and contributions to party campaign funds. This could result in an eventual change in the focus of local governments from looking after the citizens that elect it to protecting the interests of the TNCs that fund it. Globalisation can also become an excuse to impose Western norms on other countries, such as those relating to employment, worker safety and human rights. TNCs are able to evade national laws, as they relate to various elements of the marketing mix. Finally, do global firms make a contribution to host countries sufficient to compensate for the costs of social dislocation caused when the dictates of their global activities bring about rationalisation or elimination of a local operation in an overseas country?

## Technology

TNCs often supply outmoded plant and equipment when they invest overseas. The development of the motor vehicle industries in India and Iran were retarded for years when UK firm Leyland shipped the Morris Isis plant to India to build the Hindustan Ambassador, and Hillman shipped the Hillman Hunter plant to Iran to build the Peykan. TNCs often ship products banned for sale on health or safety grounds in the home country to developing countries. Finally, TNCs can use their power to challenge intellectual property protection at the national level if it suits their commercial convenience (see International Highlight 11.7).

---

**11.7 INTERNATIONAL HIGHLIGHT**

# Globalisation and the offshoring of jobs

Globalisation no longer only involves the offshoring of unskilled jobs to lower labour cost countries, but increasingly also involves the offshoring of middle income white-collar positions. People in professions that have been long considered free from international competition, such as accountants, lawyers, financial advisors, health care and IT professionals, face lay-offs and erosion of conditions as developing nations perform increasingly sophisticated offshore work. Forrester Research estimates that 3 million US jobs and 1.5 million European jobs will move offshore in the next 10 years. In Australia, as the business environment becomes even more competitive, major corporations such as Qantas, Telstra, Woolworths and the Commonwealth Bank have already engaged in major offshoring programs involving white-collar jobs. According to the OECD, one in five of Australia's 1 million jobs could be offshored if cost alone was the criterion.

**SOURCES:** *Adapted from Ernsberger, R. (2005) 'The Big Squeeze', Newsweek, 30 May 2005, pp. 40–3; Sydney Morning Herald, 21 August 2006, p. 2; Ahlawat, S.S. and Ahlawat, S. (2006) 'Competing in the global knowledge economy: implications for business education', Journal of American Academy of Business, Vol. 8, No. 1, pp. 101–6; and Boland, V., Johnson, J., Kuper, S., Luce, E. and Ward, E. (2006) 'Luck in the middle. Once synonymous with stability and affluence, the middle classes in the developed world are being hit hard by a tide of globalisation', Financial Times, 16 December, p. 18.*

When the impact of globalisation on the marketing mix is considered, further macro issues come to light. As countries such as Australia and New Zealand have few global firms, it is appropriate to consider how relevant it is to such countries. Certainly, as has been pointed out, SMEs in these countries have to compete with global firms in international markets and in their own markets; and they have to compete with the subsidiaries of global firms. Yet is globalisation as relevant to firms in these countries as it is to firms in countries that have spawned most of the world's transnational companies? This proposition is discussed in relation to each element of the marketing mix in Australasia below:

- *Product*: There is a problem regarding standards. Whose standards for a product should apply? Should they be the standards drawn up in Australia or New Zealand or global standards reflecting the interests of TNCs, whose home governments lobby international trade forums such as the World Trade Organization? Globalisation can retard innovation within a country. With rationalisation of activities between countries in which the TNC operates, it might be decided to have all R&D for the firm undertaken outside Australasia. Another product-related problem with globalisation is that the country of origin and national identity of products become masked. Products previously actually made in Australasia may no longer be manufactured there due to globalisation, yet the illusion of local manufacture is created by phrases such as 'designed in', 'assembled in', 'fabricated in', etc.

- *Promotion*: With globalisation, messages are increasingly received from sources outside the country. Such promotional messages may not be sensitive to either the culture or social circumstances of the country and may arouse the ire of the elected government of that country because that government has less control over the messages its citizens receive. This is particularly the case when the offending messages beamed from outside the country breach local government regulations on promotion and advertising. China has expressed concern at this and the fact that the messages received may have a destabilising effect on its regime especially by making its citizens discontented because they cannot have what people have in other countries. Global firms are increasingly promoting themselves by sponsoring global events, such as the soccer World Cup, which can have the effect of diverting sponsorship from local to global events to the detriment of local sporting and cultural groups, and possibly of local firms.

- *Pricing*: Corporate citizens of any country should pay a reasonable economic rent for operating in that country. Globalisation has resulted in some TNCs evading their responsibilities in this connection, with the result that the taxation burden falls more heavily on local firms. Financial engineering and operation of the global money market facilitates such evasion. Some global firms avoid their taxation obligations via transfer pricing as discussed in Chapter 16. Global firms are able to set the prices to be charged in Australia and New Zealand by reference to their global strategy and not by reference to the Australian or New Zealand markets. In implementation of this global pricing approach they may evade local government-imposed price controls and regulations by dumping, price fixing and price discrimination. As a consequence of their operation in the Australasian market, foreign government laws regarding competitive pricing are imposed on subsidiaries of TNCs (e.g. the US *Anti-Trust Act*).

- *Distribution*: In general, because of the power they wield, when TNCs enter a country they may take over control of established channels or reduce the number of stages in such channels, thus creating intermediary unemployment. When they set up their own intermediary operations these are often less amenable to local government control. The same applies to physical distribution and global firms now account for an increasing percentage of transport and the charges that are set for it. In cases where TNCs control distribution channels in a country the government of that country is likely to encounter greater difficulty in tracking and taxing the distribution of goods.

An understanding of the macro aspects of globalisation is essential when implementing a firm's global strategy in overseas markets. It sensitises managers to how such globalisation efforts might be perceived at the local level. It enables an assessment of the likelihood that the local government might engage in defensive intervention and impose regulations on the operation of the global firm's subsidiary, or offensive intervention such as nationalisation of the operation of the global firm's local subsidiary.

## THE GROWTH OF ASIAN COMPETITORS

Like Australia and New Zealand, few Asian corporations (other than a number in Japan and South Korea) are global. However, there are many companies within the region that are in the process of becoming more global. Many Australasian businesses venturing into Asian markets are finding that their toughest competitors are not other Western multinationals or Japanese companies, but lesser-known Asian companies based in other Asian countries. These Asian competitors are using quite different strategies. Although the strategies differ by industry, home country and company culture, Williamson (1997) reports there are eight strategies that have been identified as general rules to be studied by any company intending on competing successfully within Asian markets. These strategies are being consistently applied by Asian firms today and are summarised below.

# 1. It's always best to be a first mover

Emerging multinationals believe that it is better to be the first in a market and enjoy the first pick of partners, sites and resources, as well as being able to establish products and brands cheaply, before the marketing channels become cluttered with competing offers. They believe that although some mistakes will be made in the first instance, the advantages of being the first mover will allow the company to fix these mistakes with time to recover before other competitors can take the dominant position.

To justify the early entry into markets, many Asian companies imagine the worst-case scenarios of entering a new market or industry. If they believe they can weather the worst-case scenario then the worst will pass and the upside will develop as time goes on. This first mover approach has seen many Asian companies entering frontier Asian markets, such as Cambodia, Myanmar and Vietnam, well before Western companies do. For example, in 2001 Taiwanese companies' cumulative investment in Vietnam was higher than all the European Union countries' investments in Vietnam combined and more than double the total investment of either Japan or the USA.

# 2. Control the bottlenecks

Bottlenecks occur when propriety technologies, specialised skills, distribution networks and resources are limited. Many Asian companies have been investing in these areas to take control of the bottlenecks and also influence their competitors' volume growth and cost structures. This leverage has been especially great in the emerging markets that grow rapidly.

Taiwan's Acer company is using this approach in the personal computer business. There has been a mass of entrants into this market, with new competitors moving into the assembling of new computers. This has caused a severe bottleneck in other links in the value chain of the industry: in sourcing key component technologies, manufacturing key components at high volumes, brand building, logistics and channel management. Acer's strategy is to invest in these bottlenecks through global brand building, advanced logistic and distribution systems and highly efficient design and manufacture of key components.

# 3. Build walled cities

At the core of most of the large emerging multinationals are 'walled cities'—one or more industries in which the company holds a dominant position. Some examples are the Indonesian company Salim Group which dominates Indonesia's cement industry, controls more than 60% of flour milling and has approximately 85% of the noodle market. Charoen Pokphand of Thailand controls more than 50% of large-scale production of animal feed in Thailand.

These walled cities provide protection against competitive attack, often with the aid of governments, with exclusive licences or concessions granted for these companies. Walled cities also provide a reliable source of cashflow that can be used for investment in international expansion.

Traditionally, walled cities were found in the company's home country, as with the examples mentioned above; however, now some emerging Asian multinationals intend to build walled cities in pan-Asian product segments. For example, the Salim Group plans to build a pan-Asian and ultimately global position in the oleochemicals industry. This move involves having plants in the Philippines, Batam Island off Singapore, China and Malaysia, as well as the acquisition of 50% of an Australian producer of oleochemicals and an interest in a producer in Germany. These actions are motivated by more than just market share motives; they come from the desire 'to be the head of a chicken, [rather] than the tail of a cow'. Dominance in large segments is preferable; however, growth through dominance in multiple smaller segments (the head of the chicken) is always considered better than being a follower in a large business driven by others (the tail of the cow).

## 4. Bring market transactions in-house

Asian nations have poorly developed markets for inputs (e.g. raw materials and energy) and services (e.g. distribution, logistics and financing) which reflect Asian companies preference for controlling the sources of supply, distribution and ancillary services. This has been a powerful force behind vertical integration in Asia and the formation of conglomerates.

One example is Formosa Plastics in Taiwan. It is vertically integrated in the polyvinyl chloride (PVC) plastics industry, from basic feedstocks right through to finished goods. As for conglomerates, the empire of Robert Kuok, a Chinese Malaysian entrepreneur, is a good example. The empire extends into areas as diverse as sugar plantations, tin mining, TV broadcasting and newspaper publishing.

In 2001 Jiang Miankeng was the most influential person shaping technology in China. He organised private funding to launch China Netcom in 1999 to compete with a new broadband network against former monopoly China Telecom. He also partnered with Taiwanese billionaire Winston Wong to build semiconductor plants in Shanghai (Lee-Young 2001).

Emerging Asian multinationals actively seek involvement in upstream and downstream industries, while Western corporations are outsourcing non-core activities. Asian companies in contrast take comfort in knowing they control their sources of supply. This also helps them to build strong trusting relationships, which is often bolstered by cross-shareholdings and family or ethnic ties. This is also reflected in more cross-border Asian alliances.

## 5. Leverage your host government's goals

Asian governments will give monopoly rights, concessions and protection to companies whose goals are aligned with theirs. Asian governments believe that regulations to steer their country's goals and growth in the right direction are needed.

One of Asia's goals is to reduce the migration from the rural areas into the city by increasing employment opportunities in the country regions. Chareon Pokphand's successful entry into the poultry business was due to the improved income opportunities from this business in country areas. This is also the reason for Chareon Pokphand's welcomed expansion into 80 other regions in China. The message is clear: making the government your silent partner is an important part of the new Asian game.

## 6. Encourage company networks and information sharing

In Asian companies the extended family is the core of the cooperative business network. This means that many companies are run like family dynasties, often under a powerful patriarch. From this system has sprung the extended networked organisations that rely on continual information sharing among all their business units. The flow of information is two-way which serves as a strong competitive advantage for those companies in the family as they have access to technology and market intelligence, which is relatively hard to come by in Asian countries. Acer is one company that takes a networked approach.

## 7. Commercialise on others' inventions

Western companies' lead in technological advancement was out of reach of Asian companies a decade ago. Today the gap between leading technological companies in the USA or Japan and Asia has closed. Many Asian companies are now developing direct links, via partnerships, investment or alliances, with companies on the technological cutting edge.

The emerging Asian competitors excel at bringing technologies, pioneered by cutting-edge technology companies, into development and production at very low costs. Samsung in South Korea and Creative Technology in Singapore are examples of this.

## 8. Rewrite the rules

The most common way Western companies have entered Asian markets in the past is by joint ventures with Asian companies, where the Western company usually held more power and gained much more from the partnership through connections with local distribution and political networks. Asian companies have now grown and they have also begun to rewrite the ways in which joint ventures are formed and managed, which presents Western companies with yet another challenge when entering the Asian markets of today.

The emerging Asian multinationals have built up strong finances, resources, systems and technical skills. This means they want much more from their partnerships with Western companies. They are looking for companies that provide them with more resources and partners that give them access to other profitable markets. They want equal partnerships or partnerships that see them as the lead player.

## The internet and globalisation

The internet has stimulated globalisation because it advantages countries with leading technology such as the USA from which a majority of global firms emanate. The drivers of internet demand are communications (email and information) and commerce. The enablers of such demand are access, security and bandwidth and these require significant investment—investment which global firms may be best able to provide.

Jupiter Communications (see Plumley 2000, p. 19) depicts the evolution of e-commerce from domestic to global as shown in Figure 11.7.

Globalisation is likely to be influenced by a number of factors in the e-business environment:

- *Global integration*: This is driven by supply-based pressures. There is no evidence that e-business has removed the underlying pressures impacting upon business in the global environment—environmental, technological, economic and cultural. These are still there. but they impact in a different way due to e-business, for example, there is a cultural preference for cash over credit in India and China, and there is weak protection of intellectual property rights for information given over the internet.
- *Local responsiveness*: This is driven by demand-based pressures. These can be expected to evolve as

consumer access widens and if the promise that technology changes the nature of the relationship between customer and producer proves true. Extraneous factors may operate—the reason why online shopping in Europe is more successful than in Australia or the USA is because retail opening hours are much shorter.

- *Transaction completeness*: This is driven by contracting pressures to outsource as many non-core activities as possible. The internet facilitates this. Given the fewer complications with international commodity trade, this has proved amenable to internet trading and is reflected in internet auctions replacing global commodity exchanges.

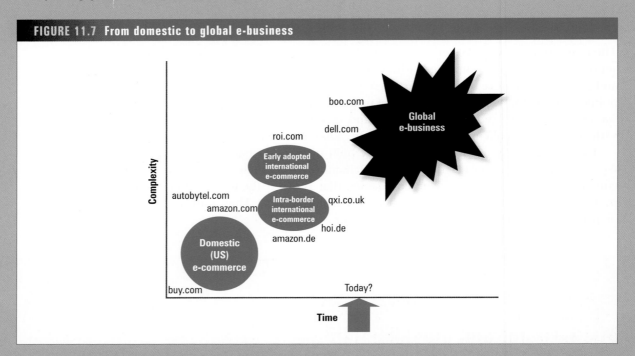

FIGURE 11.7  From domestic to global e-business

# Summary

Products, markets, companies and lifestyles are becoming more global as people travel and communication links provide real-time reporting of events. This is particularly common in sport and is exemplified by the soccer World Cup final won by Italy in 2006. Hundreds of millions watched on television, global sponsors advertised, players became household names in all corners of the globe and the soccer culture with all its associated products took another step towards full globalisation.

For companies to take advantage of these trends they need to develop a global philosophy and think of the world as one marketplace. However, for almost all businesses the steps to globalism are progressive, the risks and capability limitations act as constraints and economic shocks such as those experienced after the attacks on New York and the Pentagon on 11 September 2001 provide setbacks.

The issue of standardised versus adapted product offerings continues to be assessed by most companies, but the move towards mass customisation is changing the economies of adaptation.

A global strategy framework assists firms in assessing the external factors, internal capabilities and the benefits and costs of global strategies. This is reviewed in the light of different competitive strategies—global leaders, challengers, followers, nichers and global collaborators.

There are many successful Asian companies becoming more global. Australian and New Zealand firms can learn from their experiences when developing global strategies.

---

## ETHICS ISSUE

You are the international marketing manager of a trading company based in Monte Carlo. You trade globally in top brand merchandise, sourcing products from global manufacturers and selling to retail chains in Europe, Japan, the USA, South-East Asia and Australia. You are aware of a ruling by the European Court of Justice in Luxembourg outlawing the distribution of upmarket brands to discount chains in Europe without the prior agreement of manufacturers. You are also aware that your main competitor disregards this ruling and sells at a discount in the so-called 'grey' market from its Asian base.

Large European discount chains have approached you, being outside the EU, to supply top brand products to them at a discount without the agreement of manufacturers.

*These potential deals would launch your business into the big league and also ensure lucrative business in the USA. Despite its illegality the size of these deals are tempting. What would you do?*

---

# Websites

AMP http://www.amp.com.au
ANCA Proprietary Ltd http://www.anca.com/
ANZ New Zealand http://www.anz.com/nz
BHP Billiton http://www.bhpbilliton.com.au
*BRW* Inside Business http://www.brw.com.au
BT http://www.bt.co.uk
*BusinessWeek Online* http://www.businessweek.com
Compaq products information site, hosted on the HP site http://www.hp.com
Dell http://www.dell.com
Dick Smith Electronics http://www.dse.com.au
ECSI International http://www.ecsinstitute.org
Exxon http://www.exxon.com
Foster's Group Ltd http://www.fosters.com.au
Gateway http://www.gateway.com
Harris Technology http://www.ht.com.au
IBM htpp://www.ibm.com
Interactive Customer Clothes Company http://www.ic3d.com
James Hardie Industries http://www.jameshardie.com.au
McDonald's http://www.mcdonalds.com
McGraw-Hill Primis Custom Printing http://www.primisonline.com

Microsoft http://www.microsoft.com
NAB http://www.nab.com.au
Nokia Australia http://www.nokia.com.au
Nortel Networks http://www.nortel.com
Telstra http://www.telstra.com
Visa http://www.visa.com
Vodafone United Kingdom http://online.vodafone.co.uk
Westpac http://www.westpac.com.au

## Discussion questions

1  List the main factors driving businesses towards globalisation.

2  What are the main inhibitors to operating a global business?

3  How does the philosophy of globalism differ from multinational marketing?

4  What are the main management motivations for going global?

5  How valid is the step-by-step internationalisation process in a world in which some new businesses gain immediate global access through the internet?

6  What challenges do Australian or New Zealand firms have in attempting to globalise their operations?

7  Using a specific industry like consumer electronics or the car industry, select a leading company to focus upon. Describe their global strategy.

8  Describe the strategy of an Australasian firm that seems to fit the profile of a global niche player.

9  Explain one or more of the eight strategies suggested in competing in Asian markets against Asian country competitors. Identify examples of Australian or New Zealand firms adopting these strategies.

10  What macro issues are emerging in the debate on globalisation?

## References

Ahlawat, S.S. and Ahlawat, S. (2006) 'Competing in the global knowledge economy: implications for business education', *Journal of American Academy of Business*, Vol. 8, No. 1, pp. 101–6.

Altman, D. (2006) 'Selling globally, pitching locally', *International Herald Tribune*, 31 May, p. 13.

Austrade, <http://www.austrade.gov.au/Automotive-overview-/default.aspx>, accessed 25 March 2007.

'Australia's car industry needs a jump start', *Age*, 10 March 2007, theage.com.au, accessed 19 March 2007.

Bauer, H.H., Reichardt, T., Barnes, S.J. and Neumann, M.M. (2005) 'Driving consumer acceptance of mobile marketing: a theoretical framework and empirical study', *Journal Of Electronic Commerce Research*, Vol. 6, No. 3, pp. 181–92.

Boland, V., Johnson, J., Kuper, S., Luce, E. and Ward, E. (2006) 'Luck in the middle. Once synonymous with stability and affluence, the middle classes in the developed world are being hit hard by a tide of globalisation', *Financial Times*, 16 December, p. 18.

Brady, D., Kerwin, K., Welch, D. and Lee, L. (2001) 'Customising for the masses', *BusinessWeek*, 20 March, <www.businessweek.com>, accessed 30 June 2001.

'Business: bold fusion; face value', *Economist*, 17 February 2007, p. 74.

*BusinessWeek*, http://bwnt.businessweek.com/brand/2006, accessed 19 March 2007.

Brock, D.M. and Birkinshaw, J. (2004) 'Multinational strategy and structure: a review and research agenda', *Management International Review*, Vol. 44, pp. 5–10.

Buzzell, R.D. (1968) 'Can you standardise multinational marketing?', *Harvard Business Review*, November, pp. 103–7.

Chung, H.F.L. (2005) 'An investigation of crossmarket standardisation strategies: Experiences in the European Union', *European Journal of Marketing*, Vol. 39, No. 11/12, pp. 1345–71.

Collins, J.C. and Porras, J.I. (1994) *Built to Last: Successful Habits of Visionary Companies*, Harper Business, New York.

Cooper, C. (2004) 'Revving up for action', *Export*, May, pp. 24–7.

Daniels, J.L. and Frost, N.C. (1988) 'On becoming a global corporation', *Stage by Stage*, Nolan, Norton & Co., One Cranberry Hill, MA.

De Mooij, M. (2003) 'Convergence and divergence in consumer behaviour: Implications for global advertising' *International Journal of Advertising*, Vol. 22, Part 2, pp. 183–202.

Department of Foreign Affairs and Trade (2003) *The Big End of Town and Australia's Trading Interests*, Department of Foreign Affairs and Trade, Canberra.

Department of Foreign Affairs and Trade (2005) *Australia and the United States–Trade and the Multinationals in a New Era*, Department of Foreign Affairs and Trade, Canberra, p. 25.

Ernsberger, R. (2005) 'The Big Squeeze', *Newsweek*, 30 May, pp. 40–4.

Field, N. (1998) 'US approval is music to cochl-ears', *Australian Financial Review*, 29 June, p. 25.

Friedman, T. (2005) *The World is Flat–the Globalised World in the Twenty-first Century*, Penguin Books, London.

Gehrt, K.C. and Shim, S. (2003) 'Situational segmentation in the international marketplace: The Japanese snack market' *International Marketing Review*, Vol. 20, No. 2, pp. 180–96.

Ghemawat, P. (2007) 'Managing differences: the central challenge of global strategy', *Harvard Business Review*, Vol. 85, No. 3, p. 58.

Hamel, G. and Prahalad, C.K. (1994) *Competing for the Future*, Harvard Business School Press, Boston.

Hensrud, D.D. (2003) 'Can you hear me now?', *Fortune*, 17 March, p. 142.

Hollensen, S. (2004) *Global Marketing: A Decision-Oriented Approach*, 3rd edn, Financial Times Prentice Hall, London, pp. 14–15.

Holt, D.B., Quelch, J.A. and Taylor, E.T. (2004) 'How global brands compete', *Harvard Business Review*, September, pp. 68–76.

<http://www.cochlear.com/Corporate/Investor/AnnualReport2005/ed04_president/pres01_report.htm> (annual report for year ending June 2005).

<http://www.cochlear.com/Corp/Investor/190.asp> (annual report for year ending June 2006 and half-year report for 2006–07 at December 2006).

James, D. (1999) 'New ease of production makes the pursuit of mass rather critical', *Business Review Weekly*, 15 March, <http://www.brw.com.au/newsadmin/stories/brw/19990315/1 552.htm>, accessed 20 June 2001.

Jung-a, S. (2006) 'Big boys reel from Korean culture shock', *Financial Times*, 26 May, p. 20.

King, P. (2004) 'Altona's ships of the desert', *Australian*, 20 April, p. 23.

Kohler, A. (1998) 'The imperative of globalisation', *Australian Financial Review Online*, 7 July, <http://www.afr.com.au/content/980707/news/news8.html>.

Korten, D.C. (1999) 'The dark side of globalisation: financial and corporate rule', *Proceedings of the Annual Meeting of the Academy of International Business*, Charleston, SC, 22–4 November.

Lee-Young, J. (2001) 'The Digital Prince of China', *The Industry Standard*, pp. 38–9.

Levitt, T. (1983) 'The globalization of markets', *Harvard Business Review*, May–June, in C.A. Montgomery, and M.E. Porter (1991) *Strategy–Seeking and Securing Competitive Advantage*, Harvard Business School Publishing, Boston, MA, p. 204.

Long, D. (2006) 'McDonald's unveils digital strategy revolution', *Marketing Week*, December, p. 15.

McLuhan, M., Fiore, Q. and Agel, J. (2001) *The Medium is the Message*, Gingko Press, Inc., Carte Maderia, California.

Martin, H.P. and Schumann, H. (1997) *The Global Trap*, Zed Books, London.

Mathieson, R. (1998) 'Market of one: mass customization meets the net', *E-Business*, 20, <http://www.hp.com/Ebusiness/index_m_customization.html>, accessed 13 May 2000.

Merchant, K. (2006) 'IBM to invest 6bn dollars in India technology', *Financial Times*, 7 June, p. 27.

Moss Kanter, R. (1994) 'Afterword: What thinking global really means', *Global Strategies: Insights from the World's Leading Thinkers*, Harvard Business Review Book Series, Boston, MA.

Nelson, M.R. and Paek, H.-J. (2007) 'A content analysis of advertising in a global magazine across seven countries; Implications for global advertising strategies', *International Marketing Review*, Vol. 24, Issue 1, p. 64.

Ohmae, K. (1985) *Triad Power*, The Free Press, New York.

Ohmae, K. (1989a) 'Managing in a borderless world', *Harvard Business Review*, May–June, in C.A. Montgomery and M.E. Porter (1991) *Strategy–Seeking and Securing Competitive Advantage*, Harvard Business School Publishing, Boston, MA, p. 206.

Ohmae, K. (1989b) 'The global logic of strategic alliances', *Harvard Business Review*, March–April, in Barnevik, P. and Kanter, R.M. (1994) *Global Strategies–Insights from the World's Leading Thinkers*, Harvard Business Review Book Series, Boston, MA, p. 109.

Ohmae, K. (1995) *The End of The Nation State,* HarperCollins, London, p. 80.

Park, A. and Gross, N.D. (2004) 'You're getting a printer', *BusinessWeek*, 19 April, p. 87.

Plumley, D.J. (2000) *Global eCommerce: The Market, Challenges and Opportunities*, Browne Global Solutions, January.

Poletti, T. and Takahashi, D. (2004) 'IBM prepares to sell remaining PC business', *San Jose Mercury News*, 4 December.

Quelch, J.A. and Hoff, E.J. (1986) 'Customizing global marketing', *Harvard Business Review,* May–June, in P. Barnevik and R. Moss Kanter *Global Strategies–Insights from the World's Leading Thinkers*, Harvard Business School Publishing, Boston, MA, p. 181.

Quinlivan, B. (2002) 'Cochlear's chance', *Business Review Weekly*, 8–14 August, p. 38.

Rennick, K. *Export*, May 2004, p. 25.

Roberts, P. (2005) 'Holden leads GM's global shift', *Australian Financial Review*, 10 March, p. 69.

Segal-Horn, S. (2002) 'Global firms: heroes or villains? How and why companies globalize', *European Business Journal*, Vol. 14, No. 1, pp. 8–19.

Sheth, J.N. and Parvatiyar, A. (2001) 'The anecdotes and consequences of integrated global marketing', *International Marketing Review*, Vol. 18, No. 1, pp. 16–29.

Sridharan, R. (2007) 'Local adaptation is the key in retail business', *Business Today* (New Delhi), 25 February, p. 154.

Stiglitz, J. (2006) 'Social Justice and Global Trade', *Far Eastern Economic Review*, Vol. 169, No. 2, pp. 18–22.

*Sydney Morning Herald* (2001) 31 March, p. 32.

*Sydney Morning Herald* (2006) 21 August, p. 2.

Thomas, C., Booth Oda, Y. and Sekiguichi, T. (2003) 'Dell wants your home', *Time*, Vol. 162, No. 14, p. 48.

Treacy, M. and Wiersema, F. (1995) *The Discipline of Market Leaders*, Addison Wesley, Reading, pp. 31–41.

'US car icons struggle to cross Atlantic', *Marketing Week*, 30 November 2006, p. 8.

Vignali, C. and Alberto Mattiacci, M. (2004),'The typical products within food "glocalisation": The makings of a twenty-first century industry', *British Food Journal*, Vol. 106, No. 10/11, p. 703.

Welch, D. (2007), 'Why Toyota is afraid of being number one' *BusinessWeek*, 5 March, pp. 42–50.

Williamson, P.J. (1997) 'Asia's new competitive game', *Harvard Business Review*, September–October, pp. 55–67.

Wong, C.P. (2005) 'Indian steelmaker eyes Australian mines', *Sydney Morning Herald*, 10 March, p. 28.

Yee, A. (2007) 'Cisco gives billion-dollar endorsement to India', *Financial Times*, 26 Jan, p. 2.

Yip, G. (2003) *Total Global Strategy II*, Prentice Hall, Upper Saddle River, NJ, pp. 1–29.

**go online**

Go online to <www.pearsoned.com.au/fletcher> to find more case studies.

# Global website strategy in an international business*

**Danielle Lawson and Richard Fletcher**

According to Roy Morgan research (<www.roymorgan.com/news/internet-releases>) over 5 million Australians are online daily and the internet ranked either first or second as the medium most useful for making key decisions across all audiences. A government survey found that on a monthly basis 1.9 million Australians researched a product prior to purchase. This research tells us that consumers have changed, the way they interact with products and brands has changed and the media landscape has changed, so Australian marketing platforms must now integrate the web.

This case study outlines a website unification project for a global security firm with interests in Australia. This project was designed to review the current website situations for the business and blend them into a unified global approach.

## COMPANY BACKGROUND

The Australian security firm, Aus-Sec, became part of a global corporation when the Australian firm was bought ought by US interests that operated in a wide range of industry sectors, including security, where their global security and fire prevention division traded under the name of Entrystop.

Entrystop was formed by the amalgamation of two separate security divisions of the US conglomerate: Comsec, which catered for commercial security, and Firesec, which catered for fire detection and fire prevention security protection. Entrystop's products and services include fire prevention, detection and extinguishment as well as physical and electronic security. Entrystop had a turnover of US$3.5 billion and employed 45 000 people worldwide.

The former security divisions of the US

conglomerate had strong brand names with loyal customers. In order to serve a broader market and in recognition of existing market positions, these and other brands have been maintained by Entrystop. The company does not go to market as Entrystop, although companies now refer to themselves as being a part of Entrystop Fire and Security in literature and other promotional material.

Under Comsec (the security side) the business provides integration, installation, monitoring and service of intruder alarms, access control and video surveillance systems. It also provides alarm response and security personnel services as well as cash logistics and some physical security in niche markets.

Under Firesec (the fire safety side) the company manufactures various fire detection, suppression and fire fighting products. It also provides the integration, installation and service of fire detection and fixed suppression systems in addition to the manufacture and service of portable fire extinguishers.

Entrystop has retained and expanded both the Comsec and Firesec brands. For ease and clarity, this case study will focus solely on the website unification project from the perspective of the Comsec business.

* Names have been changed for reasons of confidentiality.

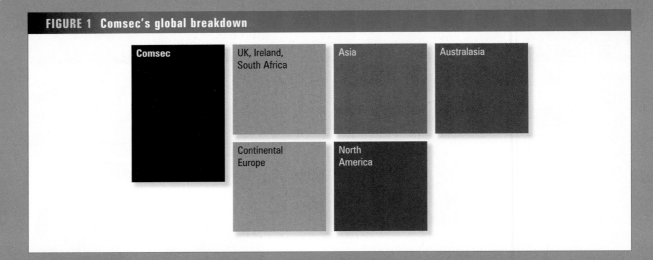

**FIGURE 1 Comsec's global breakdown**

Comsec

UK, Ireland, South Africa

Asia

Australasia

Continental Europe

North America

## THE INTERNET AND GLOBAL BUSINESS STRATEGY

Historically the Comsec website has not been used for online sales, but a website need not achieve online sales to successfully influence profits.

Many customers use the web to search for information prior to making an offline purchase. Consumers will travel from site to site seeking information, making comparisons or seeking consumer reviews. Therefore, marketers need to consider the purpose of a company's website from the perspective of why your customers should use it, then use technology to add value for the customer and deliver service they cannot get elsewhere. Otherwise, why should a customer visit the Comsec site? Comsec cannot rely on customers to remember to visit its site—it has more important things to do!

As today's customers become increasingly adept at gathering information on the web, the job of marketers becomes more challenging. Comsec needed to ensure prospects not only visit the website but repeatedly return to it—in essence, become loyal online visitors as well as repeat offline customers.

Existing multi-national corporations such as Comsec tend to adopt what Quelch and Klein (1996) term the 'information to transaction' model, meaning the main purpose of the website is to offer information to address the needs of existing customers, as opposed to the 'transaction to information' model used by many start-up companies,

which begin with the transaction and use the medium to build brand image and secure repeat orders (Fletcher, Bell and McNaughton 2004, p. 42).

In Australia the Comsec website portrays all Comsec business units and outlines product and service information to the 16 000 unique visitors the site receives per month. The site follows the 'information to transaction' model pictured in Figure 2. Many customers gather information from various security company websites and then make their decision to contact a specific company in order to find out more details and obtain quotations on specific services or products. The Comsec website is used as a contact point for potential customers and customer service for existing customers. It also has customer interactive functions, such as an online bill pay facilities, flash virtual security demonstration and an online archival browser for existing customers.

The website unification project undertaken by Comsec served to reduce costs across the global company, while maximising local level customer service.

## PROJECT BACKGROUND AND APPROACH

At present Comsec, Firesec and their affiliated companies have more than 100 separate websites, each with their own look and feel, layout and navigation. Additionally, each site is built, hosted and maintained separately, therefore resulting in redundant costs and inefficiencies.

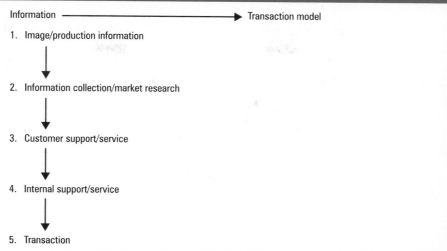

**FIGURE 2  Evolutionary paths of a website—existing multinational corporation**

Information ⟶ Transaction model

1. Image/production information

2. Information collection/market research

3. Customer support/service

4. Internal support/service

5. Transaction

**SOURCE:** *Fletcher, R., Bell, J. and McNaughton, R.B. (2004),* International E-Business Marketing, *Thomson Learning, London, p. 43.*

Entrystop identified an opportunity to standardise the layout and navigation of sites of member companies in order to support a consistent global brand image for Entrystop. The concept of a single international website has been proven by other divisions of the US conglomerate that have realised the benefits of lower costs in web-development, hosting and support, as well as better brand image and control.

The unified websites will provide company information for all key stakeholders of the combined Entrystop companies. The intent of this project was to allow Comsec, Firesec and other brands to clearly convey their position as part of the Entrystop family.

When this project was embarked on, several marketing and communications objectives were outlined:

- Establish an Entrystop corporate site, a global brand site and local brand sites, which are geared to customers in a particular geographic market.

- Develop consistency amongst the sites so that customers who drill up to corporate level from the local brand site or vice versa feel a sense of continuity.

- Sites will be sufficiently different to reflect the different audiences as well as to give distinct visual treatments to separate brands.

As the project spanned several countries a uniform approach was needed to ensure that the needs and wants of all countries were heard and addressed. A web-council was formed consisting of 14 members from across the Entrystop businesses and world headquarters.

The council was developed to provide cross-functional and cross-business representation to ensure that the website developed met the key requirements of the collective businesses. The web-council met on a regular basis and provided direct input into all key decisions regarding the project. The web-council was responsible for evaluating and ensuring the website structure and design met the requirements of the business.

Key responsibilities of the web-council were discussed and communicated to the team:

- Provide worldwide and cross functional representation.

- Provide feedback and guidance on design, navigation and content.

- Serve as advocates of the project.

- Identify content management resources within the regions.

### Target audiences

A marketer normally starts with a clear target audience in mind. The audience may be potential buyers or current users, those who make the buying decision or those who influence it. The audience may be individuals, groups, special publics or the general public. The target audience will heavily affect the marketer's decision on what will be said, how it will be said, when it will be said, where it will be said and who will say it.

In a Roy Morgan intention study (<www.roy morgan.com/news/internet-releases>) 50% of Australian marketers said that the web would be a vital component of their company marketing strategy over the next three years, while 59% believed it was an effective medium to build brand awareness and 61% agreed that it allows them to efficiently reach their target audience.

Entrystop realised the advantage of the web for targeting various audiences and providing information. Therefore the target audiences for the new websites were broken down by both corporate level and local level audiences.

The target audiences for the Entrystop corporate site are media and investors and the target audiences for the global and local sites are:

- new customers looking for product information for use in their local country;

- new customers looking for information on the strength of Entrystop's global brands;

- existing customers;

- Entrystop, Comsec, Firesec and other employees of the US conglomerate looking for product information in cases where they were not familiar with the type of product;

- consulting or specifying engineers looking for a solution to a specific problem;

- retail customers looking for product information or where to buy a product;

- job seekers.

Each region was asked to outline the region's use cases. This activity was undertaken to ensure that the design and functionality of the new website supported each region as needed.

## CONCLUSION AND RECOMMENDATIONS

With the consumer ever changing and becoming more internet savvy, Entrystop needed to address the way Comsec was communicating with customers and other publics, the brand image it is portraying and ensure that the website positions Comsec as the market leader in terms of security and fire safety, not only in the Australasian region but globally.

The website unification project was the result of months of analysis and design to ensure that the objectives of the project were met and exceeded. The primary purpose of the website unification project lay in cost reduction for the Entrystop group of companies. Although this is a valid business reason, care needed to be taken to ensure that, despite cost reduction through the use of a content management system, strong controls and processes were in place to ensure that from a global branding perspective the company is maintaining its image across all new websites.

The content management system opens up new doors for Comsec in terms of using the internet as a marketing tool rather that a transactional tool, as it has been historically used. Comsec has never used the internet as a component of an integrated marketing strategy and placing the control of content at the local business level will allow business units that are proactive to take advantage of the popularity of the Comsec website and use it as a promotional tool to consumers.

As the extent of this project covered several companies and spanned the globe, the decision to employ the services of a design agency ensured that Comsec was working with a company with high levels of expertise to ensure that the result was in line with the complex needs of this project. The web-council ensured that the project maintained high levels of visibility across the business and that all requirements for the Comsec business were addressed in the design and navigation of the website.

Overall the approach taken for this project has been beneficial and was managed well. From start to completion this has been a long-term project, and much research, analysis and strategy have been incorporated to ensure that the project objectives are met at a local and global level.

## Bibliography

Camilleri, R. and Tassi, E. (2006) 'Building customer loyalty with content-rich website', *Marketing Magazine*, April.

Fletcher, R., Bell, J. and McNaughton, R.B. (2004), *International E-Business Marketing*, Thomson Learning, London.

Fradkin, M. (2003) 'Which search engine strategy is right for your business?', *Marketing Magazine*, May.

Marovitch, S. (2005) 'Road testing automotive websites', *Marketing Magazine*, July.

Marovitch, S. (2006) 'Analysing online—Part One', *Marketing Magazine*, December/January.

Marovitch, S. (2006) 'Analysing online—Part Two', *Marketing Magazine*, February.

Quelch, J.A. and Klein, L.R. (1996) 'The internet and international marketing', *Sloan Management Review*, Spring, pp. 60–75.

Roy Morgan Research <http://www.roymorgan.com/news/internet-releases>.

## Questions

1 Do you think Entrystop took the right approach in standardising the branding of the website on an international scale? Should it localise?
2 What key factors make the difference in the success of an international website?
3 Looking at internet business models, what approach do you think Entrystop took?
4 How important is search engine strategy in a website?

# CHAPTER 12

# RELATIONSHIPS, NETWORKS AND STRATEGIC ALLIANCES

## LearningObjectives

**After reading this chapter you should be able to:**

- understand the elements of relationship marketing in the international domain;

- explain the network paradigm and the central role of relationships;

- describe different types of strategic alliances in international business;

- outline the elements used to model how industries transform and develop;

- illustrate alliances that have been formed by market leaders, challengers, followers and niche market specialists; and

- discuss the factors relevant to the success and failure of alliance relationships.

# Collaborative networks in the international marketplace

Collaborative networks (CNs) manifest in a large variety of forms, including virtual organisations, virtual enterprises, dynamic supply chains, professional virtual communities and collaborative virtual laboratories. During the last five years various forms of CNs have emerged. Some examples are described below:

- *dynamic virtual organisation*: a virtual organisation (VO) established for a short time to respond to a competitive market opportunity that typically has a short life cycle. It dissolves when the short-term purpose of the VO is achieved;

- *virtual enterprise* (VE): a temporary alliance of enterprises that join their forces to share skills or core competencies and resources to better respond to market or business opportunities. VE success relies on strongly supported networks managed by elaborate computer networks;

- *extended enterprise*: a concept typically applied to an organisation in which a dominant enterprise 'extends' its boundaries to all or some of its suppliers;

- *virtual organisation* (VO): this structure is somewhat similar to a VE. It comprises a set of (legally) independent organisations that share resources and skills to achieve its goal. A VE is a particular case of VO;

- *VO breeding environment* (VBE): represents an association (known as a cluster) of organisations and their related supporting institutions that have both the capability and the will to cooperate with each other through the establishment of a 'base' long-term cooperation agreement and interoperable infrastructure. When a business opportunity is identified by one member (acting as a broker), a subset of these organisations can be selected to form a VE/VO.

Collaborative networks in the international domain can be horizontal or vertical. Horizontal networks consist of firms producing similar products or services banding together to be able to offer the quantity sought by the overseas customer, to be able to offer products of comparable quality or to pool resources so as to be able to make a promotional impact on the overseas market. In these cases, often the individual brand is relegated to second place in favour of the collective identity. Examples abound as with the Ayrshire knitwear manufacturers from that region in Scotland, the SSMG AB small manufacturing subcontractors in northern Sweden and the Joint Action Group of hay exporters in Australia.

Vertical networks comprise firms that contribute different expertise to a collaborative endeavour and these are often found in the marketing of projects overseas (see Chapter 19). The members of these networks, each of whom supplies different elements of the value chain, can be from the same country and this enables the marketing of the joint endeavour overseas as the 'Australian' bid as with the China Grain Handling Project. Alternatively, they can be from different countries, in which case the network formed for the occasion is often described as a consortium, as with the bid for a light rail project in Bangkok involving Leighton Holdings of Australia and two European partners.

CNs are important strategic initiatives in the international marketplace.

**SOURCES:** *Camarinha-Matos, L.M. and Afsarmanesh, H. (eds) (2004)* Collaborative Networked Organizations—A Research Agenda for Emerging Business Models, *Kluwer Academic Publishers, Boston; Snyder, D.P. (2005), 'Extra-preneurship: reinventing enterprise for the information age',* Futurist, *Vol. 39, No. 4, pp. 47–53; Bohman, H., Boter, H. and Tesar, G. (2003) 'Beyond networking: a case study of rigorous cooperation among SMEs',* Proceedings of the 19th Annual IMP Conference, *University of Lugano, 4–6 September; and Welch, D., Welch, L., Wilkinson, I.F. and Young, L.C. (1998) 'The importance of networks in export promotion: policy issues',* Journal of International Marketing, *Vol. 6, No. 4, pp. 66–82.*

# INTRODUCTION

Successful Australian international marketers have realised the vital role of marketing relationships, collaborative networks and strategic alliances in their ability to expand their businesses overseas. For example, to develop and sustain profitable business in the Indian Ocean island of Mauritius it is essential for the Australian firm to develop alliances and close relationships with at least one of three dominant companies—Rogers & Co. Limited, Island Blyth and Harel Mallac & Co. Limited. This will ensure access to hotels, supermarkets, sugar plantations, textile manufacturers, travel services, consulting and almost the entire import/export industry. Cross-directorships occur on the boards of all three companies as well as the Mauritius Commercial Bank—the dominant financial institution. A close personal relationship with just one senior director is enough to get access to this market. Close connections exist between all important government agencies and the political hierarchy. These three companies have close connections with South Africa and other African markets and can provide a gateway for the Australian or New Zealand firm into African markets. This example provides a microcosm of the important elements in alliance strategies, which are discussed in this chapter.

It is important for the Australian or New Zealand firm to see itself as part of a competitive network of interrelated firms bound together by relationships of mutual benefit. It is also important to see the emerging opportunities of information technology linkages creating 'virtual' organisations. This new form of organisation is made up of alliances held together by relationships between players and linked together by electronic communication and information networks. When viewed holistically it is possible to see how industries are becoming transformed. Alliance strategies incorporating these elements can create competitive advantage—whether for leaders, challengers, followers or niche market specialists. This chapter begins with an overview of networks, relationships and strategic alliances.

## 12.1 INTERNATIONAL HIGHLIGHT

# The new relationship marketing perspective

Once upon a time . . .
. . . in a village in ancient China there was a young rice merchant, Ming Hua. He was one of six rice merchants in that village. He was sitting in his store waiting for customers, but business was not good. One day Ming Hua realised that he had to think more about the villagers and their desires, and not just distribute rice to those who came into his store. He understood that he had to provide villagers with more value and something different from what the other merchants offered them. He decided to develop a record of his customers' eating habits and ordering periods and to start to deliver rice to them.

To begin with, Ming Hua walked around the village and knocked on his customers' doors asking:

- how many members were there in the household;

- how many bowls of rice did they cook on any given day; and

- the size of the rice jar of the household.

Then he offered every customer:

- free home delivery; and

- a service to replenish the rice jar of the household at regular intervals.

By establishing these records and developing these new services, Ming Hua managed to create more extensive and deeper relationships with the villagers, first with his old customers, then with other villagers. Eventually the size of his business increased and he had to employ more people.

Ming Hua spent his time visiting villagers and handling the contacts with his suppliers, a limited number of rice farmers whom he knew well.

The above story illustrates how Ming Hua, the simple rice merchant, through using what today would be called a relationship marketing strategy, changed his role from a transaction-oriented channel member to a value-enhancing relationship manager, thus creating a competitive advantage over rivals who continued to employ a traditional strategy. He included three typical tactical elements of a relationship strategy:

1   the seeking of direct contacts with customers and other stakeholders such as rice farmers;

2   the building up of a database covering necessary information about customers and others; and

3   the development of a customer-oriented service system.

It is possible also to distinguish three strategic elements of a typical relationship marketing approach:

1   redefinition of the business as a service business and the key competitive element as service competition; that is competing with a total service, not just the sale of rice;

2   looking at the organisation from a process management perspective and not from a functional perspective—i.e. managing the process of creating value for the villagers; and

3   establishing partnerships and a network to handle the whole service process—i.e. close contacts with well-known rice farmers.

**SOURCES:** *Gronroos, C. (1996) 'Relationship marketing logic',* Asia–Australia Marketing Journal, *Vol. 4, No. 1, pp. 7–18; see also Lawrence, M. (2006) 'Keys to global relationships',* Baylor Business Review, *Vol. 24, No. 2, p. 8.*

# RELATIONSHIPS AND NETWORKS

There is a marketing genre that emphasises the role of relationships and networks in international marketing as opposed to the more traditional marketing management approach. This traditional approach focuses on exchange and views transactions as discrete one-off events. The relationship approach is based on the view that exchanges take place in the context of ongoing relationships between the parties in the marketplace. Such exchanges involve collaboration rather than competition. The contrast between the exchange perspective and the relationship perspective is illustrated in Figure 12.1. This shows that whereas with the exchange approach the focus is on the outcome and the distribution of value, with the relationship approach the focus in on process and the creation of value.

It is also important to understand the implications of relationships and networks on the internet for e-business.

Ching and Ellis (2006) have found that business transactions established in unregulated cybermarkets are invested with similar expectations regarding cooperative relationships and behaviours to the 'physical' marketplace.

In once-off exchanges little information is shared, the partners remain detached, and the threat of opportunism runs high. With repeated interactions expectations shift from opportunism to relationship. Exchange parties are better placed to evaluate satisfaction with past behaviours and are more likely to commit to transacting with the same party over the long run, therefore establishing trusted relationships and networks.

As transactions increase in volume and longevity, social and emotional aspects surface and the underlying basis for exchange becomes more relational.

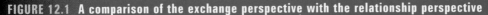

**FIGURE 12.1  A comparison of the exchange perspective with the relationship perspective**

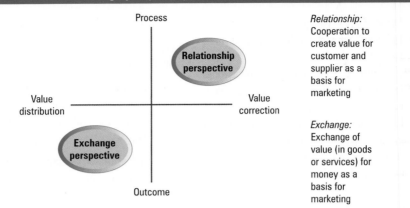

Process

**Relationship perspective**

Value distribution

Value correction

**Exchange perspective**

Outcome

*Relationship:*
Cooperation to create value for customer and supplier as a basis for marketing

*Exchange:*
Exchange of value (in goods or services) for money as a basis for marketing

**SOURCE:** *Sheth, J.N. and Parvatiyar, A. (1995) 'The evolution of relationship marketing',* International Business Review, *Vol. 4, No. 4, 397–418. Reproduced with permission from the authors.*

This new genre of relationship marketing, which had its origins in Europe (especially Scandinavia), is especially relevant when doing business in Asia where business has been conducted for centuries based on relationships as epitomised in concepts such as guanxi ('inside' connections, reciprocal obligations and personal ties). Although there is an element of opportunistic advantage in relationship marketing, there is usually a background of personal liking, trust and loyalty. Relationships are important in Western countries, but they are even more important when marketing in Asia. The difference is reflected in the fact that whereas in the West performance drives relationships, in Asia relationships drive performance. The importance attached to relationship marketing in many Asian countries has its origins in colonisation, which created an unwillingness by those who were native inhabitants to trust non-native inhabitants and an aversion to taking risks, leading to reliance on those they know, trust and with whom they have reciprocal obligations, be they family, relatives or friends. As a consequence the Asian business style is to emphasise personal relationships, whereas the Western business style is to emphasise corporate relationships.

Healy et al. (2001) explored the linkage between relationship marketing and networks. They arrived at the following classification.

An increasing number of firms recognise the importance of satisfying and retaining their international customers. Satisfied customers are the firm's 'relationship capital'. Those seeking to acquire the firm would not only have to pay for the brand name and the tangible assets, but also for this customer base, i.e. for the firm's relationship capital. Reichheld (1996) argues that the value of this capital is influenced by the following:

- Acquiring new customers can cost five times as much as the cost of retaining an existing customer.

- The average company loses 10% of its customers each year.

- A 5% defection rate reduction can increase profits for a firm from between 25% to 85% depending on the industry.

- The profit rate per customer increases the longer the firm retains that customer.

Relationship marketing involves a dyadic buyer–seller relationship that tends to ignore the role of other elements in the distribution channel and the role of other stakeholders—it is only concerned with the focal relationship.

Neo-relationship marketing, although still dyadic, goes beyond the relationship between buyer and seller and includes all marketing relationships aimed at ensuring success. It includes both focal and connected relationships.

The common element in the above is that of interdependent relationships rather than of one-off transactions:

- Relationships have substance in that they must be recognised; they need to be managed; they can be a solution to a problem; they may involve a technical content in that they can result in the linking of production processes of two different firms; and they have a social content in that they involve trust, commitment and power.

- Relationships are assets in that they optimise the time spent and activities undertaken by both parties (e.g. if one party trusts the other they do not need to spend time checking on credentials or pre-qualification); they provide access to the resources and skills of the other party; and they allow division of tasks between the parties,

- Relationships have disadvantages on the other hand in that they restrict the firm's autonomy, they require resources to manage, and the future of the firm can become dependent on others over whom the firm has no control.

Commitment to continue and develop a relationship is affected by many factors. Morgan and Hunt (1994) suggest these include trust, relationship benefits, shared values and relationship termination costs. An investigation of 136 international business relationships by Holm et al. (1996) shows that relationship profitability is directly affected by relationship commitment and indirectly through commitment by business network connections. They found that the relationship development process needs to be coordinated with ongoing processes in other connected relationships of the partners. Cooperative relationships such as formal alliances are more likely to be successful if the partners can bring their business networks into the alliance.

Network theories are more complex structures involving all elements that directly or indirectly influence a transaction and cater for the situation where international marketing can occur by the linking of a network in one country with a network in another. Relationships are connected to each other and form part of the firm's wider network. The consequent network is likely to have the following characteristics:

- reciprocity—contributions of each party are not expected to be in balance for each specific transaction, but rather over the total relationship;

- interdependence—the parties are knowledgeable about each other and draw on this information when solving problems;

- loose coupling—while the network does not involve formal legal obligations it does provide a reasonably stable framework for interaction and communication;

- power—this is used to exploit the interdependencies that exist in the network; and

- boundedness—because the network in which a firm is embedded in its own country becomes linked to the network of the importer or partner in the other country and that network in turn is linked to other networks, it is difficult to place a boundary around networks.

## 12.2 INTERNATIONAL HIGHLIGHT

# Telstra in Vietnam

Of all Western countries, Australia was the first to normalise relations with Vietnam and did so in 1972, two years before the end of the Vietnam War. One of the results was that by 1995 Australia's foreign investment in Vietnam was the highest of any Western nation, with 30 of its major corporations operating in that country.

Telstra's relationship with Vietnam began almost by accident when in 1986 OTC (Overseas Telecommunication Commission now part of Telstra), which became its overseas carrier arm, sought permission to put undersea cables in Vietnamese waters. Staff working on the project realised that an opportunity existed to link Vietnamese in Australia with Vietnam on a direct basis rather than calls being routed via Moscow, which made the calls both expensive and unsatisfactory in terms of quality. A Business Cooperation Contract was signed between OTC and the Vietnam Posts and Telegraph Department (VNPT), involving OTC supplying a 'Standard A' earth station located in Ho Chi Minh City valued at US$8.5 million, the costs of which were to be recovered by each party receiving 50% of the revenue from the traffic between Australia and Vietnam. Demand for the service rapidly outstripped the capacity of the station and a much larger one was installed in Ho Chi Minh City; the existing one was then transferred to Hanoi, involving a US$66 million investment by OTC, also on a revenue-sharing basis. The initial

move by OTC involved a 'leap of faith' which the Vietnamese reciprocated by building on the relationship between Telstra and VNPT so that by 1993 the value of the business cooperation and revenue-sharing partnership contracts was worth US$200 million. Subsequent involvement included international gateway exchanges, an optical fibre cable linking Vietnam with Thailand and Hong Kong and provision of domestic networks. By 1995, the relationship from Telstra's perspective was generating in excess of A$100 million in revenues per year. In its approach to developing business in Vietnam, Telstra pursued a relationship-building approach, the essential elements of which were:

- respect for the hierarchy implied in Vietnamese social and organisational structures;

- pragmatic instead of hard-line style of negotiation;

- providing technology and skills relevant to the circumstances in Vietnam;

- the training of Vietnamese employees and giving them broader international experiences;

- a willingness at an early stage in the relationship to allow decisions to be made locally rather than by HQ in Australia; and

- ensuring there was a close affinity between its activities and Australia's aims in its relationship with Vietnam.

**SOURCES:** *Stace, D. (1997) Reaching Out From Down Under, McGraw-Hill Australia, Roseville, NSW; and recollections of one of the authors, who was the Senior Trade Commissioner responsible for Australia's trade with Vietnam during Telstra's initial entry stages.*

A simple illustration of the operation of networks in international marketing is provided in Figure 12.2, which illustrates a hypothetical transaction between an Australian exporter of two horse power engines and a Malaysian manufacturer of pumps.

At the centre of the network approach is the concept of relationships, which infers interdependence, a medium- to long-term time horizon and the need for exporters and importers or alliance partners to develop knowledge about each other. This enables the firm both to export its products and gain access to resources such as an overseas salesforce and important market information. The network model shown in Figure 12.3 depicts the interdependence between actors, resources and activities. The network concept of actors carrying out activities that transform resources takes place in an atmosphere that encompasses the attitudes of the players towards each other and the relationship.

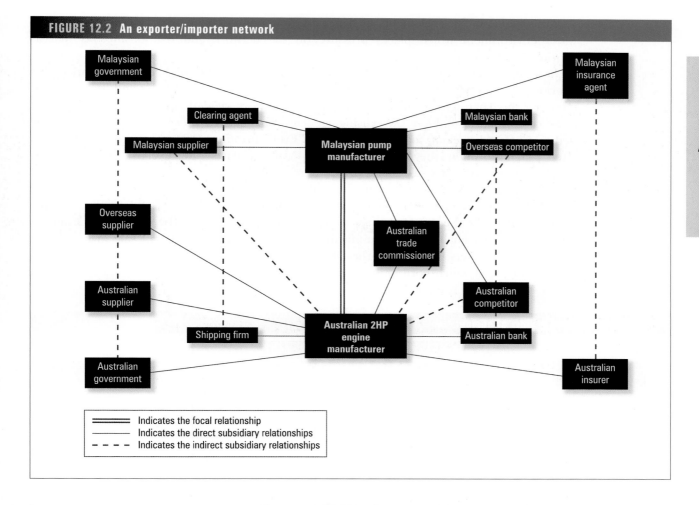

**FIGURE 12.2  An exporter/importer network**

Malaysian government

Malaysian insurance agent

Clearing agent

Malaysian bank

Malaysian supplier

**Malaysian pump manufacturer**

Overseas competitor

Overseas supplier

Australian trade commissioner

Australian supplier

Australian competitor

Shipping firm

**Australian 2HP engine manufacturer**

Australian bank

Australian government

Australian insurer

Indicates the focal relationship
Indicates the direct subsidiary relationships
Indicates the indirect subsidiary relationships

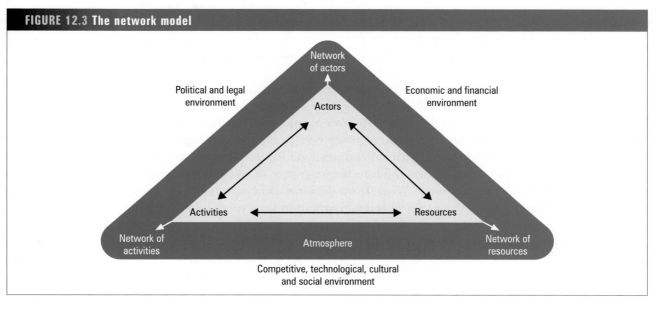

**FIGURE 12.3  The network model**

Network of actors

Political and legal environment

Economic and financial environment

Actors

Activities

Resources

Network of activities

Atmosphere

Network of resources

Competitive, technological, cultural and social environment

Atmosphere includes elements such as trust, power and dependency. This all occurs in the wider environment which places pressure on the network and relationships as well as providing opportunities.

In an international marketing context competition usually occurs between networks. This is evident in the export market for cars when comparing Ford Australia and Toyota Japan targeting the Thai market. Figure 12.4 reflects a network view of competition in which raw material and parts suppliers, advertising agencies, car manufacturers and dealers are closely tied to a network seeking to obtain customers. Even customers become part of that network after purchase when they return for car servicing, parts and exercise of warranties. Globalisation of this industry is at a stage where different elements of the value chain, R&D, manufacture, distribution and sales, are centred on locations and skills bases that exhibit world's best practice and competence in these functions. These form part of the multiple networks that take the product range to its end-user markets. It is the total network and its interlinkages that enable a car manufacturer to compete at the point of sale in its various international markets, such that rather than Ford Australia competing with Toyota Japan, it is the network in which Ford Australia is embedded that is competing with the network in which Toyota Japan is embedded.

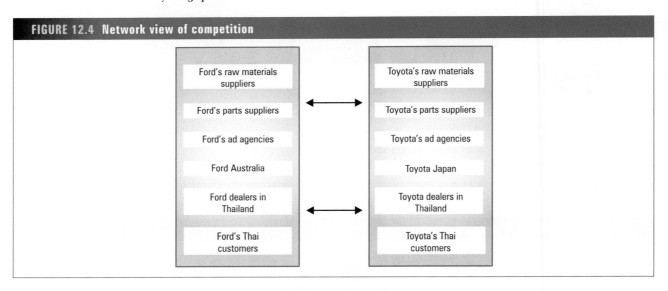

**FIGURE 12.4  Network view of competition**

Ford's raw materials suppliers

Ford's parts suppliers

Ford's ad agencies

Ford Australia

Ford dealers in Thailand

Ford's Thai customers

Toyota's raw materials suppliers

Toyota's parts suppliers

Toyota's ad agencies

Toyota Japan

Toyota dealers in Thailand

Toyota's Thai customers

Hence, an international network can be thought of as a process of building relationships with other firms to create the necessary infrastructure for effective competition in overseas markets. These networks change over time with changes in the environment and the atmosphere between actors. Fletcher (1996) explored changes in the Australian–overseas networks within the context of countertrade in the Vietnamese coal and seafood industries. These and other studies indicate the relevance of network competition in an international marketing environment. When firms decide to develop alliance agreements networks become more formalised, usually with the intention of cementing longer-term relationships.

# STRATEGIC ALLIANCES

International strategic alliances are the fastest growing form of international activity. In international marketing, they often involve a linking of the inward and outward flows of international activity (see Chapter 7). When such alliances involve partners in both developed and developing countries, the partner in the developed country gains access to a new market and faces fewer difficulties because the partner has insider status in that market, and the partner in the developing country gains from the transfer of expertise in marketing, management, production, technology and financial engineering. Strategic alliances involve a cooperative linkage of two or more otherwise independent organisations with the aim of achieving competitive advantage due to the resulting synergies.

## Theories underlying strategic alliances

There are five theoretical explanations for strategic alliances:

1 *Transaction cost*: Firms form strategic alliances in order to minimise costs and risks. Strategic alliances represent a vehicle for the firm to internalise all necessary processes and bring them under its control thereby reducing uncertainty.

2 *Resource dependence*: Few firms are self-sufficient in all the resources they need and must depend on other firms for important resources. Strategic alliances provide a way for the firm to access such resources and in times of shortage access them on a priority basis and at a reasonable cost.

3 *Organisational learning*: Whereas specific knowledge can be transferred (by licensing, for example), tacit knowledge is embedded in the individual and can only be transferred by working alongside the individual. Strategic alliances enable the firm to acquire both forms of knowledge as they involve cooperative interaction as opposed to legal transfer.

4 *Relationship marketing*: Firms should form strong relationships with both customers and suppliers so as to provide superior value to the customers. Strategic alliances provide an effective way of doing this.

5 *Strategic behaviour*: Firms will form strategic alliances if they believe that such alliances will better enable them to meet their strategic objectives and maximise profits. Each of the above theories reflects differing motivations for entering into strategic alliances and some theories will explain a specific strategic alliance better than others.

## The nature of strategic alliances

Strategic alliances are partnerships between firms. The strategic alliance partners contractually pool, exchange or integrate business resources for mutual gain. They remain separate businesses and aim to learn and acquire technologies, products, skills and knowledge from each other that would not otherwise be available to them or their competitors (Lei and Slocum 1992). The inexorable move to alliances has been expressed this way: 'Globalisation mandates alliances, makes them absolutely essential to strategy. Uncomfortable perhaps—but that's the way it is. Like it or not, the simultaneous developments that go under the name of globalisation make alliances—entente—necessary' (Ohmae 1989). The main advantage to a firm is the ability to operate beyond its own capabilities, as evidenced in airlines joining 'One World' or 'Star Alliance'. The factors driving the increased prevalence of strategic alliances include:

• moving into new markets;

• filling knowledge gaps;

- pooling to gain operational economies;
- building complementary resource capabilities; and
- speeding up new product introduction (time-based competition).

Strategic alliances are now viewed as a more effective diversification strategy than the traditional conglomerate approach. Human relationships between alliance members are a major influence on the development and maintenance of strategic alliances, especially for senior management. The drivers of international strategic alliances can be internal or external.

Companies need to combine competencies to enable them to have a strong global position in future markets. For instance, BHP Billiton is increasingly linked through electronic data interchange (EDI) with its alliance partners, suppliers and customers overseas, as are Ansell Limited and CSR. Also, the online division of the Australian Business Chamber has been set up to provide its 3500 small business members with an electronic connection service to link them with their domestic and overseas partners. These developing electronic networks add a new dimension to the concept of networks and have brought about new organisational forms with new alliance partners.

Strategic alliances can result in further international involvement for the company in the future. The Australian locomotive builder United Goninan entered into a strategic alliance with General Electric and Mitsubishi for the design and building of locomotives in Australia. This provided the Australian firm with a niche capability that it could exploit in international markets. In 2000, General Electric approached United Goninan to assist in the manufacture of lightweight locomotives for several Asian markets in which they were active but which were new to the Australian firm (Thailand, Indonesia and China). The design was undertaken by United Goninan and drive components were supplied by the other alliance partners.

**SOURCE:** *Jack, R. (2006) 'The impact of service embeddedness and inseparability on the firm's entry mode decisions', unpublished PhD thesis, Monash University, p. 169.*

## Internal drivers

Internal drivers of strategic alliances are reflected in the value chain as shown in Chapter 9, Figure 9.7. With internal drivers the strategic linkages in the value chain can be either;

- vertical—these are alliances across different levels and are designed to improve the product offering. They can include distribution or outsourcing arrangements and customer–supplier relationships; or
- horizontal—these can be within individual elements of the value chains so as to reduce investment or access markets.

By contrast with vertical alliances, horizontal alliances are usually driven by the desire to achieve economies. The linkages can be either in support activities (e.g. human resource management as with Boeing and Lockheed sharing staff; technology development as with Airbus Industries; procurement as with cooperative buying arrangements between retail chains); or in primary activities (e.g. logistics as with code sharing by airlines; manufacturing as with model sharing between Ford and Mazda; and in marketing/sales).

# External drivers

External drivers of strategic alliances are related to competitive threat or advantage. They may be motivated by a desire to tie up sources of inputs, to obtain insider status in overseas markets, to improve chances of securing government business, to be more acceptable to government in an overseas market or to access low-cost product for marketing back in Australia.

# The ways strategic alliances operate

Strategic alliances can be classified according to whether they are market-related, technology or development related, risk reducing or growth enhancing and related to achieving economies of scale. This is shown in Table 12.1.

By contrast, Table 12.2 provides a classification of alliances based on different kinds of strategies and relationships (Stafford 1994). The letters A to I in Table 12.2 indicate the different combinations of strategies and relationships. An example of a cooperative alliance between competitors can be seen with reference to the Boeing-Lockheed alliance illustrated in International Highlight 12.3.

International Highlight 12.4 shows the importance of alliances for entry into new markets, particularly new markets like China, where establishment of a strong competitive position can take many years and frequently decades.

| TABLE 12.1 | Objectives of strategic alliances |
| --- | --- |
| **Goals** | **Subgoals** |
| Market related | • increasing marketing opportunities and abilities<br>• overcoming obstacles or making use of the advantages of commercial, political and economic integrations<br>• satisfying ever-growing ecological requirements<br>• enriching the offer of products and services by adding or complementing product lines<br>• taking over leading market shares and maintaining existing ones<br>• conquering market niches in emerging markets<br>• responding to growing competition |
| Technology and development | • joining R&D capacities or sharing increasing R&D costs and investments in technology<br>• adapting to emerging innovations and general and technological advancement<br>• joining and exchanging know-how experiences and information<br>• reducing the time needed for the introduction of new products<br>• setting global standards |
| Reducing risks and increasing internal strength | • dividing and dispersing risks<br>• defence against risky or undesired takeovers<br>• increasing internal strength by learning from others<br>• enhancing growth with early links |
| Achieving economies of scale and rationalising operation | • economies of scope<br>• economies of scale<br>• dislocation of individual business functions |

| TABLE 12.2 | Cooperative strategies relationships | | |
|---|---|---|---|
| Corporate strategies | Contract | Creative joint venture | Acquisitive joint venture |
| Hand over | A | B | C |
| Trade | D | E | F |
| Pool | G | H | I |

**Strategy definitions**

*Hand over*: one-way transfer of a resource or chain activity, where one partner literally hands over to the other.
*Trade*: two-way exchange between partners trading complementary outputs or value chain activities with one another.
*Pool*: partners share the same value chain activity or common resource.

**Relationships definitions**

*Contracts*: non-equity agreements specifying the cooperative contributions and powers of each partner.
*Creative joint ventures*: partners contribute resources to the formation of a new separate subsidiary, jointly owned by the partners.
*Acquisitive joint venture*: one partner acquires partial interest of the other, and the partners work together with joint management teams and joint-owned assets.

**SOURCE:** *Adapted from Stafford, E.R. (1994) 'Using co-operative strategies to make alliances work'*, Long Range Planning, *pp. 65–7.*

## 12.3 INTERNATIONAL HIGHLIGHT

# How two fierce rivals find a 'soft-spot' to be friends again!

In January 2007 Lockheed Martin Corp. and Boeing Co. formed a strategic alliance to help the Federal Aviation Administration modernise its air-traffic control system. This could further open up possibilities to modernise and make compliant other nations' traffic management systems. As the USA follows in modernising its air traffic system by 2025, two of the world's largest aerospace companies are joining hands, in part to encourage faster progress and ultimately strengthening their market position.

This is paramount, especially since US air traffic is expected to double or even triple over the next two decades. This next-generation traffic-management system will guarantee safety for passengers and yield greater efficiency for airlines and airports. So it is unsurprising that Boeing's Air Traffic Management Unit agreed to form a 'strategic alliance' with Lockheed Martin's Transportation and Security Unit on every ATC (Air-Traffic Control) contract that may emerge in the next five years.

The alliance does not constitute a joint venture, but Boeing has a huge stake in this major endeavour because it wants to sell new commercial aircraft without having congestion and delays that may eventually inhibit sales. Lockheed Martin, as the supplier of ground-based ATC systems to 12 nations and handling 60% of the world's air traffic, has an interest in seeing that its system is not substituted by competition.

Together Boeing, the Chicago airplane and aerospace manufacturer, and Lockheed, the Bethesda, Maryland, defence contractor, plan to offer a strategic traffic-management solution that connects satellites, surface operations, and new cockpit technology in aircraft. This alliance will fence out other aerospace and avionics companies that are expected to compete for air-traffic management contracts.

It is noteworthy that a similar partnership, the Air Traffic Alliance, was formed in 2002 by EADS, Airbus and Thales. Their objective is to accelerate ATC modernisation in Europe. These allied partners are the drivers behind Sesar (the Single European Sky Air Traffic Management (ATM) Research Program). Sesar is run by a broad-based industry team mandated to define Europe's ATC.

**12.3 INTERNATIONAL HIGHLIGHT** *(continued)*

Moreover, both companies will also work on expanding operational trials of the type that they have been participating in together, such as the tailored arrivals with United Airlines 777s at San Francisco International Airport. Boeing being so closely involved in this system will make its planes more appealing than the Airbus, since it will reduce traffic control delays for their planes. It is common knowledge that airlines generate revenues when their planes are in the air going from destination A to destination B, but not circling around the airports. It is estimated that, due to delays, IATC airlines loose on average 73 hours of flying time per plane (this is the equivalent of almost four flights from Sydney to London).

However, the biggest ATC contract in the USA now up for tender is the one for which both of the aerospace heavyweights will not be on the same side. Lockheed Martin has already secured its partners to work on the FAA's Automatic Dependent Surveillance Broadcast contract. Boeing is already engaged as advisor to the US government, so it cannot join the team. Additionally, both companies are required to continue to honour all of their existing agreements with other companies with which they are teamed on various ATC projects. As it can be seen, strategic alliances are formed for specific purposes, and do not exclude these allied companies from fiercely competing on other projects. Based on the industry dynamics and future corporate visions, this is a textbook case of the true nature of strategic alliances.

**SOURCES:** *Hughes, D. (2007) 'ATC Allies: Boeing and Lockheed Martin partner on ATC contracts',* Aviation Week & Space Technology, *29 January, p. 42; and Lockheed Martin Corp. (2007) 'Alliance set up with Boeing for air-traffic control deals',* Wall Street Journal *(Eastern edition), January 23.*

**12.4 INTERNATIONAL HIGHLIGHT**

# Old players drive into new markets

Both European and US markets are showing signs of saturation and decline for the major global car makers. The car industry also faces reshuffle, with the Asian automaker Toyota moving to become the largest car maker in the world.

As a result of this competitive position Europeans and Americans are seeking growth in other international markets, especially South-East Asia. Western companies are seeking relevant alliance partners to serve these markets. There are several reasons for seeking a South-East Asian alliance:

- *Volume*: For GM the rapid moves to increase production and sales in Asia would help to hinder Toyota's challenge to GM's reign of over 60 years as the world's number one car maker. Already through its joint ventures, GM sold over 877 000 cars in China last year, compared with just over 277 000 vehicles sold by Toyota.

- *Labour costs*: European and US car makers have shifted jobs in high-wage countries into lower-cost areas in order to be able to compete on price in highly price-sensitive and feature-rich markets. In Shanghai, for example, the total cost to the company of wages and benefits for workers assembling GM Buick Excelle compact cars is around US$9 an hour, compared with more than US$60 for the wage and benefit costs of hourly workers in the USA. This is a huge saving to the bottom line.

- *Production speed*: The Shanghai-GM factory outsources most of its subcomponent assembly work and other support jobs to contractors, who are paid around 30% less than the standard Asian GM wage rate. Additionally, absenteeism is at only 1%, and the average car requires 15 hours of labour to build, on the same level as the best-performing GM plants in North America.

- *Distribution*: Both GM and Volkswagen have a minimal presence in South-East Asia. Both are struggling to expand in Asia and are seeking strategic alliances, mainly for market distribution access rather than production facilities.

For the European makers and US makers it seems that there is finally an attractive strategic alliance partner. Set up in 1983 as an icon of Malaysian self-reliance in heavy industry, Proton used to rely on protection in the form of high tariffs on foreign cars. But unfortunately for Proton, tariffs have now come down under a regional free trade pact and as a consequence Proton faces an uncertain future.

Proton's passenger car sales in Malaysia fell 11% to an all-time low of 490 000 units in 2006. Proton has been struggling to match its Japanese and South Korean rivals and its market share fell to 32% last year, down from 40% in 2005 and nearly 70% six years ago. Proton reported a loss of 281.5 million Malaysian ringgit (US$80 million) during the last three months of 2006 due to higher component costs and lower sales. Analysts expect a loss of 360 million Malaysian ringgit for the financial year ending in June 2007.

Volkswagen has been one of four global car makers (the other three being GM, Chrysler and Peugeot) negotiating a strategic alliance with Proton. This will consist of half-ownership and management control of its manufacturing plant. The Malaysian government initially set the end of March 2007 as interim deadline to bring in a foreign partner to help prop up the company, but at the time of writing they are talking about selling the brand.

The Proton purchase would complement Volkswagen's (VW) plants in China, its Skoda factory in India and another planned for India. Volkswagen sees the fast-growing South-East Asian region as a big gap in its expansive Asian strategy. In 2006, sales in the region accounted for less than 7% of VW's sales.

The alliance would make VW a formidable force in this region and enable it to export cars back to Europe at a fraction of the European production cost. This strategic alliance with VW would give Proton access to the German company's technology and would bring greater economies of scale in operations, purchasing and research and development.

VW is interested in buying Proton because it has large, modern production facilities that would serve as a manufacturing base in South-East Asia, where VW lacks a presence. Proton's dealer network would provide access to the region's largest passenger car market.

Time will tell which of the large Western car makers will leave the most bargaining chips on the table to consummate this lucrative access deal to the Asian markets.

SOURCES: *Bream, R. and Burton, J. (2006), 'Peugeot and Proton study possible strategic alliance',* Financial Times *(Asia edition), 19 September, p. 15; Shameen, A. (2007) 'Volkswagen nears Proton deal',* Financial Times, *19 March, p. 27; and Burton, J. (2007) 'Malaysian government keen to sell Proton',* Financial Times *(UK edition), 3 April, p. 28.*

## Selecting strategic alliance partners

The selecting of a partner for a strategic alliance requires much thought and care. It requires that the following should be taken into account:

- company goals and objectives,
- the needs of the customer such as speed of service, frequency of contact and long-term development of relationships;
- the nature of the product or service such as its complexity, the need for maintenance, requirement for customisation, the length of the purchase cycle, its position on the experience curve and the intellectual property content;
- the resources of the firm—financial, managerial, marketing; and
- government issues such as political stability in the country of the alliance partner and the need for connections at government levels to achieve commercial objectives.

Research by Jack (2006) found that there is general agreement that strategic alliances between partners from culturally similar backgrounds have a greater chance of success than alliances between partners from widely different cultural backgrounds.

There is a life cycle for strategic alliances as shown in Figure 12.5 and partner selection occurs at the inception stage. The criteria to be applied will vary in terms of importance from nation to nation and as a result the criteria you apply to selecting an alliance partner overseas may not be the same as that partner applies when selecting you.

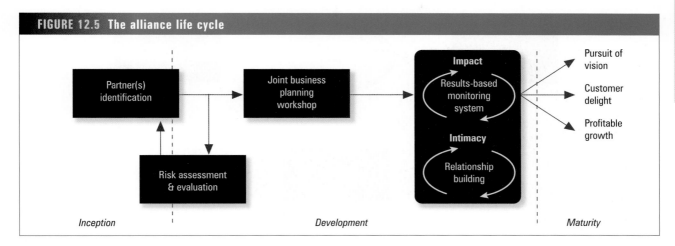

FIGURE 12.5 The alliance life cycle

## ALLIANCE STRATEGIES FOR CREATING COMPETITIVE ADVANTAGE

While the particular market may be the focus of attention, if the context is global the firm will need to consider alliances with firms in the same or related industries so as to create an appropriate alliance network strategy. In an alliance network the firm must consider the overall strategy of the group of which it is a part. The basis of competitive advantage and market coverage needs to be looked at from the alliance network's viewpoint.

## Market leader alliance strategies

If the intent is to achieve leadership rapidly in the new overseas market and to have a major impact, the firm needs to develop a network of alliances that can quickly deliver innovative products and services with appropriate support. The alliance network must be planned with foresight to include additional or different players as the market evolves and as competition responds to the new entrant. The strategy should contain the following elements:

- focus on mainstream markets;
- resource leverage for rapid penetration entry;
- positioning to take the high and middle end of the market; and
- integration of alliance partners into a seamless organisation to deliver the offer.

In Australia, Qantas has formed a range of alliance relationships through its One World membership to deliver worldwide passenger travel. A simplified picture of Qantas's alliance network is shown in Figure 12.6.

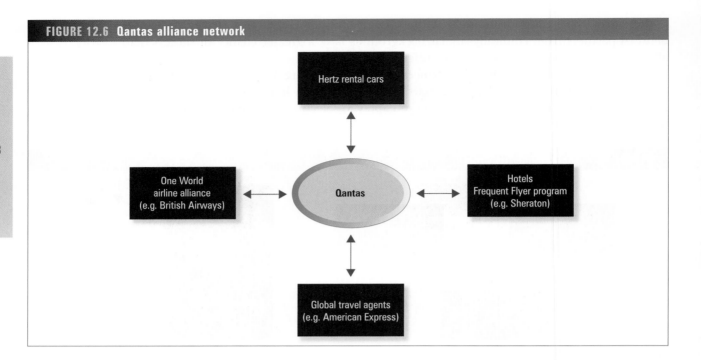

**FIGURE 12.6 Qantas alliance network**

## Alliance strategies for challengers and followers

To be a major threat it is necessary to design a challenger alliance network with sufficient resource leverage to have a major impact on the market. Market entry may be narrowly focused on key market segments or focused on broader market coverage. The specific strategy will be determined in part by the strength of incumbent competitors. The principles discussed in Chapter 10 on challenger and follower strategies apply.

Followers usually rely for their success on speed of implementation and lower costs. Here the alliance network requires the following elements:

- an alliance configuration of small units;
- communication lines and relationships, enabling rapid decision making and implementation;
- low-cost structures;
- a well-organised competitive intelligence system, providing early information on competition developments and initiatives; and
- competencies in imitating and improving products, services, delivery processes and customer communications.

The alliance network of Singapore Airlines, which has followed Qantas into global airline travel markets, is shown in part in Figure 12.7.

The Star Alliance, which is the catalyst for Singapore Airlines' multi-airline alliance network, was formed in May 1997 by six regional airlines and now has 14 airline members. Singapore Airlines formalised its participation in April 1999 and became part of the IT (information technology) infrastructure that enables customers to use an agent from any alliance member to help them plan a series of flights across all alliance airlines. The alliance

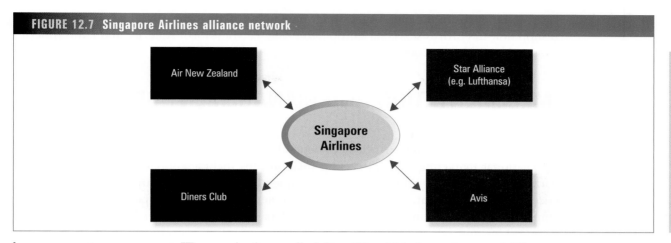

**FIGURE 12.7 Singapore Airlines alliance network**

Air New Zealand

Star Alliance (e.g. Lufthansa)

Singapore Airlines

Diners Club

Avis

has a separate, permanent IT organisation, called Star IT, which is made up of IT team members from the alliance airlines and works to ensure that the alliance's strategy is compatible with each individual company's objectives. It has a variety of ongoing global IT projects, all involving Star Alliance airlines covering reservations, departure control and frequent flyer programs. In the Asia–Pacific region the airline alliances are becoming even closer as Singapore Airlines seeks to acquire a larger equity share of Air New Zealand, which in turn has absorbed some regional airlines (Chung 2000). Such alliances need to be fluid as travellers are becoming more and more selective for their locations and seeking alliance partners to take them to previously 'unchartered' or more exotic locations. As a result Star Alliance is on a continuous lookout for new, value-adding partners and is prepared to let go of non-performing partners (Knibb 2007; Sanchanta 2007).

## Alliance strategies for niche specialists

Chapter 10 discussed appropriate strategies for niche specialists. The alliance network for new market entry should be composed of partners that specialise in various parts of the value chain relevant to the target market—product or service supply, specialised distribution, specialised customer communication and specialised support services.

Bishop Steering Technology Limited is an example of an Australian niche specialist developing alliances to grow its business overseas. It is becoming a leader in automotive steering gear technology.

In July 1998 Bishop signed a joint venture agreement with Mercedes-Benz to create BMB Steering Innovation to manufacture Bishop's patented variable ratios steering racks. In September 2000 Bishop signed an agreement with Robert Bosch GMBH for the Bishop torque and angle sensor.

Bishop is continually forging offshore business alliances in research and development and it has licensed its intellectual property to the major global suppliers of automotive steering gears—bringing in multimillion dollar revenues. Bishop's commitment to ongoing research and development has been the core strategy behind its success. The group holds over 350 patents and patent applications. Last year, Bishop technology was incorporated in over 11 million passenger cars, 20% of the total manufactured worldwide. It has signed a deal with Japanese NSK, the world's leading supplier of electric power steering. Now Bishop technology will be used in the fastest growing car makes such as Toyota and Honda as well as Mercedes-Benz, Audi, BMW, Ford, Saab and Peugeot.

This highly focused niche strategy built on a network of alliances has been very successful. Bishop now has offices servicing Europe, the Asia–Pacific, North America and Latin America (Austrade 2000; Grey 2005).

# IMPLEMENTATION AND MANAGEMENT OF STRATEGIC ALLIANCES

Ultimately, successful overseas alliances depend upon the relational exchanges that occur in international marketing. The marketing relationships include supplier partnerships, lateral partnerships involving competitors and frequently governments, buyer partnerships that encompass intermediate and ultimate customers, and internal partnerships involving employees, business units and functional departments. The effectiveness of all these partnerships and relationships will determine the overall effectiveness and longevity of the network and the alliance strategy.

Research into international business relationships by Holm et al. (1996) points to some of the causes of implementation problems. They suggest that the strategic fit between alliance partners is brought about by the relationship development process. For the most part, the process leading up to formal agreement is conducted by top management, whereas the process of implementation is dealt with by middle management. The relative understandings and commitments of the different management levels can be quite different. Relationship commitment is affected by positive factors such as trust, acquiescence and relationship benefits, as well as negative influences like propensity to leave and uncertainty. It is no wonder that this web of interrelationships causes difficulties in alliances in practice.

The implementation of strategic alliances can be difficult and time consuming, particularly cross-cultural alliances. The failure rate is high. Most strategic alliances do not seem to have lived up to initial management expectations over time. One study suggests that seven out of ten joint ventures fail to meet either partner's management expectations (Stafford 1994). The challenges and obstacles to strategic alliances may be summarised as:

- autonomy of alliance members;

- forward momentum;

- focus on the external environment;

- politicking—internal agendas that may go against alliance development;

- commitment to change and innovation;

- learning—desire and commitment to learning about each other;

- people—having the best people committed to the alliance;

- 'black box'—fear of giving away something; and

- culture.

Studies on the matching of partners have led to the following observations about the success of strategic alliances (Lorange et al. 1992):

- ventures tend to be more successful where partners are homogeneous;

- ventures are less successful where neither partner has products, services, assets or experience related to its venture; and

- ventures last longer between partners of similar cultures, asset sizes and venturing experience levels.

The high levels of management energy required to initiate, develop and maintain alliances with a substantial number of members is a major challenge. This is a special problem for management of the alliance founder or alliance deal driver. It is particularly pertinent with the alliances developed by Rupert Murdoch of News Corporation with John Malone of TCI, America's largest cable operator. Their surfeit of alliances in the last few years have shaped media programming and entertainment content not only in the USA, but worldwide. The big joint ventures include Fox Liberty Networks LLC, Fox Family Worldwide Inc. and United Video Satellite Group (Chenoweth 1998).

In relation to the management of people in a virtual organisation, Handy (1995) suggests seven elements of trust are critical success factors. These include:

- don't place blind trust in everyone;

- trust needs boundaries;

- trust demands learning;

- trust requires toughness, especially when wrong matches are made;

- trust includes component parts which must bond to goals of the whole virtual organisation;

- trust still requires 'touch' or physical face-to-face contact throughout the virtual organisation, although this may not be in the conventional workplace environment; and

- trust requires a multiplicity of strong leaders in the virtual organisation.

A final issue is that of terminating strategic alliances because successful strategic alliance management involves knowing when to end it. Often this can be planned for from the inception stage, especially when the alliance is to be terminated by development into a merger or an acquisition by one party of the other.

Not so easy to plan for is termination by 'walking away'. This, however, may be easy if the alliance was formed for the purpose of undertaking a specific project and at the conclusion of the project there are no further benefits to be gained from continuing the alliance. The issues outlined above point towards a complex set of human behaviours that may make or break the formation and development of strategic alliances.

## 12.5 INTERNATIONAL HIGHLIGHT

# Clustering

One of the more recent phenomena of international marketing is the clustering of companies, their suppliers and their services industries in the one location. Underpinning such clusters are the concepts of relationships, networks and strategic alliances, which yield synergies that enable firms in the cluster to create global competitive advantage. Examples of such clusters are software firms in Bangalore, India; telemarketing firms in Omaha, Nebraska; and wool garment knitters in Ayrshire, Scotland. Clusters are localised aggregations of people, infrastructure and capital that together develop a world trading industry capability. An increasing number of clusters are emerging in Australia, as with horse breeding in the Hunter Valley, wine in the Barossa and McLaren Vale regions in South Australia, and aluminium and ferromanganese processing at Bell Bay in Tasmania.

SOURCE: *Adapted from James, D. and Thomson, J. (2003) 'Why togetherness works', Business Review Weekly, 31 July–6 August, pp. 42–6.*

# The internet and relationships, networks and strategic alliances

Underlying relationships, networks and alliances in the international electronic environment is the concept of the rational as opposed to the biological person. Because the biological person acts on their feelings, it is the biological person that underlies relationships and networks (Ambler and Styles 2000). On the other hand, the internet is based on rationality. This raises the question as to whether there is a future for relationships in the internet age. Although the internet is based on rationality, does it entirely do away with both memory and affect? While there may appear to be an apparent inconsistency between e-business and relationships, it will be argued that relationships, networks and alliances have a definite role in international e-business.

## Relationships in marketspace

Information technology (IT) has altered social exchange in the interaction process. This has led to relationships becoming more impersonal and more formalised as the relationship atmosphere has changed. However, businesses still need to interact, albeit in different ways, as interactions remain at the heart of successful relationships and successful relationships are fundamental to successful business. Figure 12.8 shows typical applications of IT and how they have replaced situations where face-to-face activities were formerly involved.

The virtual organisation is a collection of business units in which people and work processes from the business units interact intensively in order to perform work that benefits all. They enable organisational and/or personal competencies to be brought together when needed and disbanded when no longer needed. They mirror the fluidity of the global marketplace. The virtual corporation assesses all marketing activities across the entire global value chain in order to 'virtually vertically integrate' across a 'web of companies'.

These marketing relationships can be characterised as virtual when a significant amount of activity between relationship partners occurs outside their organisational domains and therefore in a non-'face-to-face' context. The management orientation will need to go beyond the command and control model and focus on cooperation as a basis for the interaction. These virtual relationships/organisations will develop a culture and identity of their own. This will be apart and distinct from those of the two parent organisations.

The importance of trust in e-business is high. The physical separation of buyer and seller, the physical separation of the buyers and the merchandise, and the perceived insecurity of the internet all challenge

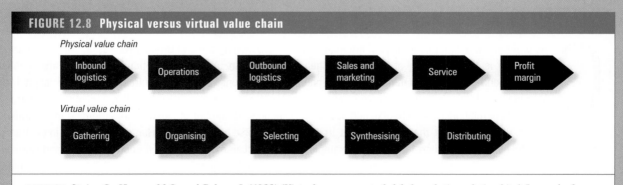

**FIGURE 12.8 Physical versus virtual value chain**

*Physical value chain*

Inbound logistics → Operations → Outbound logistics → Sales and marketing → Service → Profit margin

*Virtual value chain*

Gathering → Organising → Selecting → Synthesising → Distributing

**SOURCE:** *Speier, C., Harvey, M.G. and Palmer, J. (1988) 'Virtual management of global marketing relationships'*, Journal of World Business, *Vol. 33, No. 3, p. 266. Copyright 1998, with permission of Elsevier.*

marketers to find new ways to initiate and develop relationships with their customers. When there is no personal face-to-face contact between seller and customer, building and maintaining trust are more difficult to achieve. This is particularly relevant when doing business in Asia where trust is an important element of a relationship.

Indicators of trust are twofold—experience-based and cue-based. Experience-based indicators are the result of an exchange that has taken place, whereas cue-based indicators occur prior to the exchange and create trust by the customer in advance of the purchase. E-business marketers therefore should focus on providing cues to potential customers or business partners so that they trust the company sufficiently to engage in the initial transaction.

In cue-based trust, the cues, which may serve as indicators of trustworthiness, may consist of return policies, name recognition, the professional look of the website, a privacy and security policy, availability of company address and phone number for alternative ordering procedures, and references and testimonials from existing customers.

## Networks in marketspace

According to Poon and Jevons (1997) the internet provides small business with the opportunity to share information and experiences. This can lead to collaboration such as the sharing of customer orders or a number of small firms jointly bidding on a large project. Because the internet is a virtual borderless platform on which suppliers, customers, competitors and network partners can interact, it enables the formation and maintenance of business network links that would otherwise be prohibited by barriers such as distance, time and limited resources. Networks involve establishing linkages both upstream and downstream with networks in other countries to facilitate efficiencies in the transnational value chain. This requires efficient and continually evolving communication between the various members of the network. The internet can facilitate this because of the instantaneous way it communicates over both geographical and psychic distances. However, although the internet does allow freer and easier flow of communication, it does not replace the need for personal relationship building, especially in cultures that are high context in character such as Thailand or Japan (Bengtsson, Boter and Vanyushyn 2007).

## Strategic alliances in marketspace

Inkpen and Currall (2000) argue that alliances driven by the internet will operate under different assumptions and create substantially different management challenges to those in traditional global alliances. Traditional alliances, because of their coordination and competitive costs, tend to be transitional. Many smaller firms shy away from alliances because of the complexities associated with both forming and terminating them.

By comparison, the internet will dissolve many of the constraints of time and geography and make it possible for organisations to connect and collaborate across borders. In the internet economy, alliances will become easier both to create and terminate, and location and size will become less critical as variables. The classic market entry form of a bricks-and-mortar joint venture will decline in relevance as firms discover that relationships can be easily and efficiently established electronically. Personal interactions, which are expensive and time consuming, offer the prospect of being largely replaced by electronic interchanges. However, during the alliance formation stage face-to-face interaction is still likely to be critical. As the alliance develops and matures, electronic interactions between the partners may be sufficient to maintain the alliance. Although foreign market entry alliances will still be formed, the internet is likely to shift the focus of the objective in alliance formation away from market entry towards the achievement of strategic efficiency. In addition, firms will be able to access overseas markets that were previously beyond their reach.

# Summary

Companies today are unable to dominate any technology, business or market region alone. They need to develop networks of strategic alliances that provide access to technologies, new products and new markets. These alliance arrangements encompass both a variety of strategies and relationships.

The convergence of telecommunications, computers, software and media industries has resulted in a new information infrastructure—the most public embodiment being the internet. In response, new organisations are being created to take advantage of those opportunities—'virtual' organisations, which involve linkages and alliances by companies in pursuit of common objectives and markets.

Many industries are undergoing transformation due to the impact of electronic communication structures and the formation of alliance networks. An industry transformation model incorporating electronic information infrastructure, industry structure and alliance structure helps us describe the key elements relevant to the development of marketing strategies. Alliance strategies for market leaders, challengers, followers and niche specialists are considered in terms of creating competitive advantage.

Finally, the organisation must consider the requirements of common objectives, cultures and trust required to implement and maintain successful alliance strategies.

## ETHICS ISSUE

Your company has just signed a very important alliance with a distributor in a foreign country. The distributor dominates the market area relevant to your company's products and has all of the right government and industry connections to introduce your products very successfully.

You have been told by the senior marketing executive of your alliance partner firm that it is essential to provide 'monetary benefits' to a number of government officials and industry facilitators; these include wharf personnel, customs and transport companies. This is to ensure minimal 'red tape' and disruption to the flow of your products through to customers.

You believe these to be bribes and know that your firm will turn a 'blind eye' to this issue, even though bribes are illegal in the foreign country.

***How would you handle this?***

## Websites

Air New Zealand http://airnz.co.nz
Ansell Limited http://Ansell.com/company/index
AT&T http://www.att.com
Austar http://www.austar.com.au
Austrade http://www.austrade.gov.au
Australian Financial Review htpp://www.afr.com.au
Avis http:// www.avis.com.au

BHP Billiton http://www.bhpbilliton.com
Bigblue Internet http://www.bigblueinteractive.com
Bishop Technology Group http://www.aebishop.com
Bosch http://www.bosch.com
Compuserve http://www.compuserve.com
CSR http://www.csr.com.au
Ford http://ford.com.au
Fox http://fox.com
Galileo (A Cendant Company) http://galileo.com
Hertz http://www.hertz.com.au
HM—Harel Mallac http://www.harelmallac.com
ITV http://www.itv.com
Kodak http://wwwau.kodak.com
Mauritius Commercial Bank http://www.mcb.co.mu
Mercedes-Benz http://www.mercedesbenz.com
Morgan Hunt http://www.morganhunt.com
News Corporation http://www.newscorp.com.au
OSS World Wide Movers http://www.ossworldwidemovers.com
Ozemail http://www.ozemail.com.au
Philips http://www.philips.com
Qantas—The Spirit of Australia http://www.qantas.com.au
Radisson—hotels and resorts http://www.radisson.com
Rochester Housing Authority http://www.rha.com
Sabre Holdings http://www.sabre-holdings.com
SEGA http://www.sega.com
Singapore Airlines http://www.singaporeair.com
Star Alliance http://www.staralliance.com
TD Waterhouse http://www.tdwaterhouse.ca
Time Warner http://www.aoltimewarner.com
Toshiba http://www.toshiba.co.uk
Toyota http://www.toyota.com
wine.com http://www.wine.com/

## Discussion questions

1 Given the experience of limited success of many alliance partnerships, why do so many companies develop alliance networks?

2 Describe the network concept and its key elements. Outline an example of network-based competition in a specific industry or between two competitors.

3 Why is it that information is creating new business? Give examples of some new products or businesses which are purely information based and are selling internationally.

4 Traditional industry structure analysis (discussed in Chapter 9) is being augmented by analysis of alliance structure and electronic infrastructures. How do these additional elements (i.e. alliances and electronic infrastructure) create added value in international markets? Use an example to illustrate.

5   Identify an Australian or New Zealand company adopting a niche strategy with its overseas business. Outline its alliance partners and relationship network.

6   What do you consider are the main factors needed to ensure longevity of alliances in overseas markets?

7   By accessing the internet go to the home page of Qantas, Singapore Airlines and Air New Zealand and study their services and linkages with other websites. From this study, see if you can identify their main alliance partners.

8   Identify an Australian or New Zealand company that is part of an alliance network that is challenging the leaders in an overseas market. Draw up the alliance network to illustrate.

## References

Ambler, T. and Styles, C. (2000) *The Silk Road to International Marketing: Profit and Passion in Global Business*, Pearson Education, London.

Austrade (2000) 'Commonwealth Bank Small to Medium Manufacturer Export Award, 2000 national finalist', <http://www.austrade.gov.au>, accessed 29 June 2001.

Bengtsson, M, Boter, H. and Vanyushyn, V. (2007) 'Integrating the Internet and marketing operations', *International Small Business* Journal, Vol. 25, No. 1, p. 27.

Bohman, H., Boter, H. and Tesar, G. (2003) 'Beyond networking: a case study of rigorous cooperation among SMEs', *Proceedings of the 19th Annual IMP Conference*, University of Lugano, 4–6 September.

Bream, R. and Burton, J. (2006) 'Peugeot and Proton study possible strategic alliance', *Financial Times* (Asia edition), 19 September, p. 15.

Burton, J. (2007) 'Malaysian government keen to sell Proton', *Financial Times* (UK edition), 3 April, p. 28.

Camarinha-Matos, L.M. and Afsarmanesh, H. (eds) (2004) *Collaborative Networked Organizations–A Research Agenda for Emerging Business Models*, Kluwer Academic Publishers, Boston.

Chenoweth, N. (1998) 'The big dealers', *Australian Financial Review*, 27–28 June, pp. 22–3.

Ching, H.L. and Ellis, P. (2006) 'Does relationship marketing exist in cyberspace?', *Management International Review*, Vol. 46, No. 5, p. 557.

Chung, D. (2000) 'Reaching for the stars', *MIS Australia*, May, pp. 43–7.

Davidow, W.H. and Malone, M.S. (1992) *The Virtual Corporation*, HarperCollins, New York.

Fletcher, R. (1996) 'Network theory and countertrade transactions', *International Business Review*, Vol. 5, No. 2, p. 169.

Grey, B. (2005) 'Strategy for success in manufacturing', presentation at the The National Manufacturing Summit, 13 December 2005, http://www.nationalmanufacturing.org/downloads/Presentations/Case Study_Bishop_BruceGrey.pdf), accessed 24 May 2007.

Gronroos, C. (1996) 'Relationship marketing logic', *Asia–Australia Marketing Journal*, Vol. 4, No. 1, pp. 7–18.

Handy, C. (1995) 'Trust and the virtual organisation', *Harvard Business Review*, May–June, pp. 44–8.

Healy, M., Hastings, K., Brown, L. and Gardiner, M. (2001) 'The old, the new and the complicated: a trilogy of marketing relationships', *European Journal of Marketing*, Vol. 35, Nos 1/2, pp. 182–93.

Holm, D., Eriksson, K. and Johanson, J. (1996) 'Business networks and cooperation in international business relationships', *Journal of International Business Studies*, Special Issue, pp. 1033–53.

Hughes, D. (2007) 'ATC Allies: Boeing and Lockheed Martin Partner on ATC contracts; Boeing and Lockheed Martin partner to bid on air traffic control contracts', *Aviation Week & Space Technology*, 29 January, Vol. 166, No. 5, p. 42.

Inkpen, A. and Currall, S.C. (2000) 'Joint venture trust: interpersonal, intergroup and interfirm levels', in De Rond, M. and Faulkner, D. (eds) *Cooperative Strategies: Economic, Business and Organizational Issues*, Oxford University Press, Oxford, pp. 324–40.

Jack, R. (2006) 'The impact of service embeddedness and inseparability on the firm's entry mode decisions', unpublished PhD thesis, Monash University.

James, D. and Thomson, J. (2003) 'Why togetherness works', *Business Review Weekly*, 31 July–6 August, pp. 42–6.

Knibb, D. (2007) 'Star scrambles to fill Latin network void left by Varig', *Airline Business*, Vol. 23, No. 2, p. 16.

Lawrence, M. (2006) 'Keys to global relationships', *Baylor Business Review*, Vol. 24, No. 2, p. 8.

Lei, D. and Slocum, J.W. (1992) 'Global strategy, competence-building and strategic alliances', *California Management Review*, Vol. 35, No. 1, pp. 81–97.

Lockheed Martin Corp. (2007) 'Alliance set up with Boeing for air-traffic control deals', *Wall Street Journal* (Eastern edition), 23 January.

Lorange, P., Roos, J. and Bronn, P.S. (1992) 'Building successful strategic alliances', *Long Range Planning*, Vol. 8, No. 4, pp. 10–17.

Morgan, R. and Hunt, S. (1994) 'The commitment-trust theory of relationship marketing', *Journal of Marketing*, Vol. 58, No. 3, pp. 28–38.

Ohmae, K. (1989) 'The global logic of strategic alliances', *Harvard Business Review*, March–April, in Barnevik, P. and Kanter, R.M. (eds) (1994) *Global Strategies: Insights from the World's Leading Thinkers*, Harvard Business School Press, Boston, p. 109.

Poon, S. and Jevons, C. (1997) 'Internet-enabled international marketing: a small business network perspective', *Journal of Marketing Management*, Vol. 13, pp. 29–41.

Reichheld, F.F. (1996) *The Loyalty Effect*, Harvard Business School Press, Boston.

Sanchanta, M. (2007) 'JAL makes more room to win back customers' world view', *Financial Times* (Asia edition), 16 January, p. 16.

Shameen, A. (2007) 'Volkswagen nears Proton deal', *Financial Times*, 19 March, p. 27.

Sheth, J.N. and Parvatiyar, A. (1995) 'The evolution of relationship marketing', *International Business Review*, Vol. 4, No. 4, pp. 397–418.

Snyder, D.P. (2005) 'Extra-preneurship: reinventing enterprise for the Information Age' *Futurist*, Vol. 39, No. 4, pp. 47–53.

Speier, C., Harvey, M.G. and Palmer, J. (1988) 'Virtual management of global marketing relationships', *Journal of World Business*, Vol. 33, No. 3, p. 266.

Stace, D. (1997) *Reaching Out from Down Under; Building Competence for Global Markets*, McGraw-Hill Australia, Roseville.

Stafford, E.R. (1994) 'Using co-operative strategies to make alliances work', *Long Range Planning*, June, Figure 1 and pp. 65–7.

Welch, D., Welch, L., Wilkinson, I.F. and Young, L.C. (1998) 'The importance of networks in export promotion: policy issues', *Journal of International Marketing*, Vol. 6, No. 4, pp. 66–82.

## go online

Go online to <www.pearsoned.com.au/fletcher> to find more case studies.

# Into the world of *guanxi* relationships—a study of success, failure and decline

**Dr Mike Willis, Senior Lecturer in Marketing, Monash University**

*Until the events of late 1997, and more recently of 11 September 2001, it could be said that the global economy was growing strongly and was continuing on a path commenced at the beginning of the decade. Since 1990 developing economies had grown at about twice the rate of the industrialised economies (according to the IMF), Latin America had been largely free of debt and the end of the Cold War had brought the economies of Russia and Eastern Europe into the market-driven.*

## INTRODUCTION

China is one of the largest markets in the world and it seems that almost everybody wants to be there. With over one billion seemingly insatiable customers, this massive country is a beacon for businesses who want a chunk of this gigantic and endlessly fascinating powerhouse of an economy. One of the key areas of doing business in China is the issue of relationships—and there has been much written about *guanxi* relationships, which are complex, reciprocal and formed for mutual and usually long-term benefit. Many authors have suggested that foreign businesspeople need to form such relationships to navigate China. This case study discusses what these relationships really meant for one large service organisation.

complex, difficult and multilayered, and companies need to know this to succeed.

## CONTEXT

This case study documents what one Australian education provider found when it entered the China market to set up a higher education joint venture for the delivery of courses, training programs, exchanges, seminars and consultancy activities. The group involved the international manager, a consultant, a project person and two academic staff. The project failed and then succeeded—for some time—because of a single issue—that of the formation and maintenance of *guanxi* (deep-level, mutual relationships) with key Chinese hosts. The world of relationship formation at a *guanxi* level, in China, proved to be

## THE TRADITIONAL VIEW OF *GUANXI* RELATIONSHIPS

Traditionally, *guanxi* relationships have been depicted as being deeply felt, encompassing and enduring relationships based on long-term mutual benefits for the two or more people involved in the relationship (Wong and Leung 2001). If one has a *guanxi* relationship, one might expect to have a deep friend for life, and it is upon this basis that one can undertake a range of social and business activities and projects in an environment of complete trust (Punnett and Yu 1991). In many situations and contexts in China, a *guanxi* relationship is the foundation stone of business and social life

(Morgan and Hunt 1994; Willis 2006). A true *guanxi* relationship encompassed aspects of trust, empathy, respect, mutual benefit, commitment (affective and cognitive) amongst other aspects and attributes (MacInnes 1993). *Guanxi* certainly remains complex, diffuse and pervasive (Lee 2005). But what this organisation found was a very different world of *guanxi* relationships.

## WHAT HAPPENED

The company went through four stages of the project.

The first was what could be called *naïve and enthusiastic*. During this phase, company representatives discussed their proposed ideas with their Chinese hosts (in Beijing), signed a few documents, went to banquets, had fun, and enjoyed the sights and sounds of China. It all seemed easy, but somehow vague.

The second was what could be termed a *vague feeling of unease*, and during this phase, the group started to feel that the project, which had been mapped out in the most general of detail on paper, was not actually going anywhere. Specifics were never discussed, and the concept remained just that—a concept. There was a vague yet tangible sense that the project was almost on hold, somehow superficial and generalised in its detail and conceptual in its profile. A sense of lethargy and apathy started to creep into discussions. This was within six weeks of the negotiations starting.

The third stage was what one could perhaps term *disillusionment*. There was now a feeling (this was week seven, but the timeframe does not really matter), that the project would never actually happen. Gradually it seemed that it was being whittled down to a most basic and general sort of relationship with the Chinese side. What had started off as a large, bold and complex project involving a wide range of activities had now drifted into perhaps a few exchanges and a number of Chinese students studying in Australia—the concept of a joint venture campus in China had seemed to vanish. The Chinese hosts now seemed even more elliptical and guarded. There was a sense of an opportunity lost, but no one knew quite why.

*Paranoia* well describes the next stage of this project. The staff now started to hold late night dinners (without the Chinese) in which they discussed the fact that the whole project had always been a chimera anyway, that they were right (and their hosts were wrong), and that it had always been a dream. It was 'them' and not 'us' was the tenor of the conversations. One person hopped on a plane and went home, direct and fast. The happy and friendly Chinese hosts seemed to pick up on the vibes and became even more guarded and elusive. There were little arguments about money, profits, who was right and who was wrong. Oddly, no one could put a finger on what had actually gone wrong, or when or how. But it was no longer fun and it was now suddenly stressful and frustrating. As one person said, it was if the group had suddenly realised that they were not on some kind of holiday, but were actually in a very different country with a very different culture. One person even started to avoid going out of his hotel. There was a very real sense of being dislocated from China, unable, now, to understand it at all.

The next step was *retreat* (not at all unusual in these situations) and now the group went back to Australia to regroup, blame others and ponder what had happened. At that time the author was able to interview them and also their Chinese hosts who commented that this was usual and normal because 99% of joint ventures failed anyway. They knew what was wrong—no proper sense of relationship had been formed between the two sides, but they could not really say this so directly to the Australians because there was no relationship so they could not to be so direct. 'Let it all go' was the general view of things in China.

The next stage was unusual, and it was not the death of the project (as one might have expected and which is common in the situation and context) but what one could term *realistic reassessment*; this occurred because the Australians called in a consultant to help them out—after all, they knew something wrong but they were just not quite sure what it was (and who to blame). What they found was that there had been no relationship formed, no sense of bonding between themselves and the Chinese, so the project had never had a true, emotional and affective basis to develop in any shape or form. They did not understand that the true basis for a project in China was an emotional relationship, not just facts and figures, plans and documents. These meant little if the emotional core was not there. They had remained outsiders, never insiders, and were always kept distant and in a sense distrusted. They used terms such as 'our side' rather than 'all of us' and they had never shown their hosts their true, human and emotional side. To them, business was business, but to the Chinese, business is people. The gap was enormous, and there had been no connections.

The next step was *regrouping and trying again*. The same group went back to China and this time found a different partner (this time in Southern China) and they were able to form and maintain a range of *guanxi* relationships which did form the basis upon which all doors were opened and a joint venture program could be established. However, not all the Australians achieved this goal so there was some change in personnel over time as the group settled into a new manner and way of doing business—working on emotions, feelings, trust, empathy and respect rather than a more basic and fundamental 'business is business', black and white orientation. Those who felt at home in China, who developed genuine friendships with their Chinese hosts and who took the time to appreciate the real nature of China (and never judged it by Western standards) were most successful.

The final stage of the project should have been *maturity* and long-term success but as it happened this was not the case. The original core group of foreigners (Australians) who had set up and managed the business in the first few years splintered and drifted away from the project, and their roles were taken over by people who were less passionate and committed to the project and who did not developed the same level of *guanxi* relationships. Gradually, barriers appeared and the core of the joint venture, a world of openness, directness, humour and genuine empathy was replaced by a relationship context which became more guarded 'us and them', and far less open. Within three years the project had faded and fragmented and gone beyond repair. What the original group of people knew had not been followed through—and once those deep-level and complex relationships had been dissipated the alliance was barely a shell of its former self. Passion had been replaced by routine, empathy by distrust and enthusiasm by a sense of disillusioned apathy. The project was no more.

## WHAT THE FOREIGN SERVICE PROVIDER FOUND IN CHINA

Additional comments made by staff were as follows:

1 There were a *range* of *guanxi* and related relationships observable in business situations in China. Not all *guanxi* relationships were deeply felt and complex in nature—some were basic and less detailed. Others were based around a particular context or situation, but to develop and maintain a successful Sino-foreign joint venture it was desirable to develop a complex, deeply felt and multilayered relationship so that each side could be open, frank and trusting with each other. These sorts of relationships took a great degree of time and commitment—and being there—in China. Many foreigners believed they had a *guanxi* relationship, but did not. This was a trap.

2 There were types of business relationships other than the *guanxi* context and definition. Not all relationships were *guanxi*-like in nature and the company identified two others—*basic friends* (where people knew colleagues enough to say 'hello' and 'goodbye') and *working colleagues* (where people developed a working relationship in an office situation). These relationships were common in a joint venture. They were entirely appropriate, but to manage a successful alliance, it was crucial to have a range of proper and detailed *guanxi* relationships amongst key leaders.

3 *Guanxi* relationships, particularly of a committed intense kind, developed in a range of stages—sometimes! *Guanxi* relationships

tended to develop in at least four stages. Time was not an issue here—a relationship could be developed quickly or slowly. This was an issue of intuition as much as anything. The initial stage was a formative one where the two sides were guarded, formal and wary. The second was where the *guanxi* relationship started to flower and at this stage the two sides became more open, direct and trusting. The third stage was where the relationship had matured into a proper and deeply *guanxi* relationship and it was *only then* that the two sides could be open, direct, trusting, and able to manage a business relationship in a genuine and truthful manner (many company staff never developed relationships at this level). The fourth and final stage was maintenance where the two sides both had to work hard to maintain and nurture their relationships. This was a real problem and challenge when distance was involved, not to mention issues of cross-cultural behaviour.

4  Not all *guanxi* relationships covered business and social life. A traditional view of *guanxi* relationships was that they tended to cover social and business life—that is, in an encompassing and almost holistic manner—but this was not always the case. The company found that some relationships covered only a social context whereas others did move into a business environment. The idea that *guanxi* relationships were inclusive was not always found to be the case. This caused some degree of consternation and confusion.

5  *Guanxi* relationships could extend to cover more than two people. *Guanxi* relationships were usually perceived to be formed between two people as a deeply abiding and encompassing relationship, but sometimes this relationship could be extended to include a range of other people on the Chinese side. These networks (which often included a large number of people) formed what could be called the informal structure of an alliance on the Chinese side. Some networks were hierarchical (where one person had power

over others), horizontal (where most, if not all, had equal power), uneven (where one or more people had more power than others) and partly invisible (where some people uninvolved in a network were not made known to others— this was an issue of power, control and status). In short, there was a variety of personal networks and a foreigner tended to be connected to a network through only one person, not always aware that others were often involved. To be successful, it was necessary (and not always easy) to identify which networks had power and which did not, and exercise relationship development with those who had status, power and the ability to make an alliance successful. This was one of the key challenges facing this and other companies in a Chinese situation and context. Foreigners remained naïve about this issue.

6  All relationships and particularly *guanxi* relationships needed to be maintained and worked on over time. Every day, the managers said, new problems, issues and stresses would test their relationships and this volatile, demanding and at times frustrating aspect of *guanxi* relationships needed to be recognised. Some problems were cross-cultural in nature, some were quite specific (such as those about a project, or money), and others were just misunderstandings.

## CONCLUSION

Staff from this university organisation felt that one of the most vital aspects to long-term business success was to develop, nurture and maintain a network of key *guanxi* relationships and to understand them in a wide and more complex context. They felt that:

If key managerial staff were not able to form *guanxi* relationships in the true sense of the term they could not develop a successful business in China.

If these relationships were not formed within a reasonable period of time (say, a month or two), it was not possible to form them later on.

Maintaining these relationships over time was

just as important as forming them in the first place, but often they neglected to put in the time and effort later on—say, in the second year of the alliance.

It was important to understand that underneath the key *guanxi* relationships there was a range of more basic relationships and associated network issues which were part of a normal joint venture, but this was often overlooked.

If they did not recognise the role of *guanxi* relationships in wider networks they tended to remain somewhat confused and outside the real world Chinese business.

The managers sometimes felt a sense of tension between their *guanxi* relationships in China and home office back in Australia—the difference perhaps in 'thinking Chinese and thinking Australian'. This had to be handled, which it often was not. A *guanxi*-driven joint venture could actually be 'killed' by an angry parent company completely unable to understand the cultural dynamics of China.

## Bibliography

Lee, T.Y. (2005) 'Development of management philosophy for Chinese business environment', *Management Decision*, Vol. 43, No. 4, pp. 542–50.

MacInnes, G. (1993) '*Guanxi* or contract: a way to understand and predict conflict between Chinese and Western senior managers in China based joint ventures', in McCarty, D. and Hilde, S. (eds), *Research on Multidimensional Business Management and Internationalisation of Chinese Enterprises*, Nanjing University, Nanjing, pp. 345–51.

Morgan, R. and Hunt, S. (1994) 'The commitment-trust theory of relationship marketing', *Journal of Marketing*, Vol. 58 (July), pp. 20–38.

Punnett, B. and Yu, P. (1991) 'Attitudes toward doing business with the PRC', in Shenkar, O. (ed.), *Organisation and Management in China, 1979–1990*, M.E. Sharpe, Inc. Armonk, New York.

Willis, M. (2006) 'Chinese cultural values and their applicability to successful Sino foreign educational alliances', *Journal of Teaching in International Business*, Vol. 17, No. 3, p. 5.

Wong, Y.H., and Leung, T. (2001) *Guanxi: Relationship Marketing in a Chinese Context,* Haworth Press, New York.

## Questions

1  What are some of the steps one should take to develop and mould a *guanxi* relationship in China?

2  In what sense can some of the lower level relationships be useful in a strategic alliance or joint venture context in China, or indeed in another country where relationships form the core of business success?

3  If a company insists that it is only interested in managing its China activities at a distance and in a simplistic manner, what steps can a marketer take to encourage them to adopt a more complex and committed view of the market and its human dynamics?

4  Are there perhaps cases where a 'great company' can actually enter a country like China and do business successfully—perhaps on the basis of its brand, image or other aspects of its 'offer' *without* worrying about human relationships and aspects of *guanxi*?

## Photo credit

Image reproduced with kind permission of Louise Cavander.

## go online

Go online to <www.pearsoned.com.au/fletcher> to find more case studies.

# Turning tradition into export success

### Joe Williams, Flinders Business School, Flinders University

## BACKGROUND

Beerenberg Farm is located at the end of the main street in one of South Australia's major historic locations—Hahndorf in the Adelaide Hills. The town was founded in the 1830s by German immigrants and it remains, and proudly displays, its German heritage to this day.

The German settlers were hard-working and community-minded. They founded businesses, farms, community services such as schools and hospitals and they took part in local government. One of these industrious newcomers was Johann Christian Paech who arrived in 1839 and established a farm in a place he named 'Paechtown'—now renamed Beerenberg, which is German for Berry Hill.

Over the years the farm grew and the fertile land yielded support for a variety of crops, for a herd of prize Charolais cows and for a wonderful rose garden. Nothing was wasted. As an example, Carol Paech's serene rose garden yields the petals from which is made rose petal jam—one of the more special products made on site and one which gives the 'Farm-made' boast such a proud cachet.

Although Beerenberg Farm prospered as a farm it wasn't until 1971 that the first commercial batch of strawberry jam was made. For years afterwards Grant Paech—a graduate of Roseworthy Agricultural College in 1960—made and sold strawberry jam and strawberry punnets from the back of his truck in the Adelaide Produce Market. He later added cherries, plums, quinces, figs, sweet corn, gherkins and chillies to the product range. These are still processed on the farm into jams, chutneys, pickles, sauces and marinades.

## ENTER THE PREMIER

This story would probably have continued as a farm success story only if it were not for the then premier of South Australia, Mr (now Dr) John Bannon. It was 1985. Mr Bannon had been to Europe and the UK on a typical premier's visit to boost his state's exports. It was a successful trip for the premier, but on his Qantas flight home he received a shock. With his breakfast tray of cereal, fruit, coffee and toast was—wait for it—Scottish jam. On an Australian airline. Mr Bannon was shocked to the core.

When premiers return home after an overseas sales promotion, they face up to the media. On this day when he was asked how his trip had gone, the premier replied, 'Very well but for one thing. On the plane home—a Qantas plane—I was served Scottish jam from a company called Baxters. Don't we make jam in South Australia? Can't we supply Qantas with local produce? Surely there's a producer out there who can compete with Scottish jam?'

Indeed there was. Grant Paech was having his mid-morning coffee and scones and spreading his own, farm-made Beerenberg jam as he heard the premier's plea. He tells the story:

*I couldn't believe I was listening to the premier asking if anyone in South Australia could compete against the overseas product. We'd never thought of ourselves as players in the international market. Nor had we thought*

*we could replace what we saw as much bigger, much more sophisticated operations with our home-made range.*

*Anyway, my wife, Carol, and I thought we would see what could happen. I rang the government and was put through to the person in charge of the consulting division of the Small Business Corporation. He was as intrigued as I was by the possibilities and he came up to see us the next day.*

*We sat down and talked and decided as a first step to see what Qantas would say if we told them that, yes, we did make jam and, yes, we were interested in taking on this Scottish-made product.*

This was the start of Beerenberg's move into export. Long discussions unearthed lots of questions:

*Why would we want to go into export? Isn't the local market big enough for us? We don't even have significant exposure in our home state, so shouldn't we aim for expansion inter-state first?*

*Can we expand our production sufficiently to meet any export demand we create? Where do we source the fruit? The jars? The labels?*

*Can we divert production away from the domestic market to export? Away from our range of fruits and chutneys to export jam?*

*What makes us think we can take on Baxters? Don't they have the airlines sewn up? Don't they produce quality products at acceptable prices? Even if we displace them, why do we think we will retain this new business? Won't other producers see what we've done and develop a similar competitive attack on us?*

*More importantly, what competitive advantages do we have? Are they sustainable? Are they sufficient?*

These and many other questions were discussed and debated over the next few weeks. All the while Carol and Grant held to the belief that their quality product was more than a match for any overseas jam. It was this belief that sustained the Beerenberg export effort.

## COMPETITIVE ADVANTAGE

Without competitive advantages no business can survive in export markets. Grant Paech knew this intuitively. He also knew that he could list some clear advantages for his business. They included:

- a bias towards Australian products by Australian consumers—this consumer ethnocentrism (Grant did not use this term) was thought to extend to Qantas's decision-making as well;
- the fact that his products were genuine farm-made products;
- the quality ingredients leading to a quality taste;
- the current highly satisfied market;
- the exclusive range.

This was all very well—for the Australian market. But what about export markets? There the need was different. Airlines, for example, do not want to serve jam in 380 gram jars. Imagine the mess, to say nothing of the hygiene issues of lots of passengers dipping their knives into communal jars. The same would apply to international hotels. The product would have to be modified to suit new markets.

Modifications cost money and the government came to the party. Applications were made to Austrade under various schemes to aid new and growing exporters. Grants were made by Austrade for upgrading the bottling line and for developing new products wanted by airlines and international hotels.

The state government also helped with a 99-year loan for new equipment and for the recruitment of a key human resource—a savvy export manager. This appointment was a resounding success with the appointee, John Fry, acting as the export manager for 20 years until his retirement in mid-2007.

At this point, Grant introduced a system for information and control of the export effort. He called it the Management Group. It comprised Grant and Carol, John Fry as export director (who, usefully, was also a qualified accountant), the man from the Small Business Corporation and one of the senior consultants engaged *pro tem* by the SBC. The Management Group met monthly and developed plans, assessed progress and got down to the detailed work of product development, market research and performance management. The system was so successful it is still in place 20 years after its introduction.

## PRODUCT MODIFICATIONS

As we have seen, the target market was international airlines and top of the range international hotels. The product had to be modified for these institutional buyers. With the help of government funds and by dipping into its own reserves, Beerenberg took the risk.

New 28-gram jars were developed with, for those days, innovative 'security' seals which, once the jar was opened, showed clearly that the single-use product had been used. So there were no more unsightly, and possibly unhealthy, opened jars that had been used by others. This was just what the hotels and airlines wanted.

Additionally, the market asked for single-serve, 14-gram, plastic portions. These were also developed.

## THE TRIAL

Developing new products, even with government assistance, is a risky business. Funds have to be found, designers have to be engaged and briefed, existing clients and production concerns have to be passed on to staff and new fruit has to be grown on site or sourced elsewhere.

All of this has to be done under a cloud of uncertainty. Will the market respond positively? Will the airlines buy? Will the hotels buy? Will the industry readily admit one more competitor?

The best that the buyers could offer Grant Paech was a trial run of his product. Grant Paech is a very prudent man and knew this was a big risk. A family and business round-table determined that this was indeed a big opportunity and that it was based on experience, quality product and a market that seemed able to sustain a new entrant. The green light was given to develop the product and go for a trial market run.

## EXPORT PROBLEMS

The market offered opportunities with retail outlets along with the corporate buyers. This was a new issue—it was one thing dealing with airlines and hotel chains but retail outlets require regular overseas trips and the appointment and management of agents. Once Grant Paech realised that the core airline and hotel markets also needed to be serviced in this way, the decision to supplement the core markets was an easy one to make. Retail products would be added to the export effort.

Appointing agents was a key issue. Grant explains how this was done:

*For every new target country you have to go to a food exhibition. Austrade helps with this. You pay your fee and the organisers give you a booth which you stock and make it look attractive. You send a pallet of samples and you go for four or five days. You have a translator for the booth and you must have someone from the company who knows the business backwards.*

*Then you stand back and deal with the would-be agents. That's quite a problem. They all want to sell your product in their home markets. They all profess to be excellent salespeople with ethical approaches to business and with your best interests at heart.*

*The best way to deal with them is to let things cool down. Ask them a lot of questions. Check their references and their performance claims. They want to wine and dine you, but you resist that unless it amounts to a cultural snub.*

Grant says of the problems arise at these shows or in dealing with agents:

*Beware of the would-be agent who wants to use his connection with you to enhance his prospect of emigrating to Australia.*

*Also, just because you have a translator with you doesn't mean you won't have language difficulties. I remember when we were in Glasgow. Of course, we hadn't bothered with a translator and we couldn't understand a word the Scots were saying. I went back to my hotel room with an awful headache.*

More serious problems can arise with contractual disagreements. 'We had a dispute with a Malaysian agent', remembered Grant. 'It lasted for ages. The agent was clever in that he would ring us to tell us his side of the dispute but he usually got us to commit our side of the dispute to a fax or email. So he had written evidence of any concessions we'd made, but we had no hard evidence of where he had transgressed. We could have forced the issue but our Australian lawyer told us I would have to go to Kuala Lumpur to plead my case in court and that would cost a lot just for local legal representation. In the end we reached an amicable settlement. This is the only such dispute we've had in 20 years, so we're quite proud of that.'

> *We've had people order samples on consignment and not pay us. We stopped that very early. If you want a pallet of samples now, you pay up front. We had a Nigerian importer who told us he wanted to buy 10 containers of goods per month, which is a huge amount. He asked us for a sample consignment and for the money to get the sample through customs, then he'd place his orders for a container per month. We declined this offer.*
>
> *All in all, it's been reasonably pain free. We've stuck by our payment up-front policy. And we're loyal to our customers. The strong Australian dollar hurt us at times but our local sales kept us solvent. There have been lots of times where our export markets have been very important, so having both export and domestic markets has certainly helped grow our business.*

## THE FUTURE

What is in the future for Beerenberg? Grant has retired from full-time management and the family has stepped into his and Carol's shoes. Son Robert now manages the farm and son Anthony, after earning an MBA in Perth, is managing director.

A new company-owned warehouse in Adelaide's north now caters for Beerenberg's distribution as well as that of several other companies in the expanded Beerenberg group.

Beerenberg is now merely one supplier to a range of company-owned food processors.

Alliances and take-overs of other food producers have proved to be beneficial over the years. Beerenberg has acquired other small jam makers, other brands, other distributors and other labels. Grant keeps an eye on this part of the business as Anthony and Robert run the main game.

The aim of the next few years is to steadily expand the export markets. Exports currently account for over 25% of the company's A$12 million turnover and this is expected to remain even as sales within Australia increase. The Beerenberg brand is well known in South Australia, but not quite as prominent elsewhere in Australia; this will change in the next few years. The current 25 or so countries to which Beerenberg exports will still be served, but sales in each of these markets are primed for growth. New hotel chains are being built in emerging markets, and new airline routes are opening. Beerenberg intends to supply these with its flagship export production.

The final word should come from the Beerenberg founder who, despite national recognition and increasing export prowess and success has always kept his feet on the ground:

> *We have local clients like Coles and Woolworth's who sell to Australian customers. We always put these at the top of our production priorities. Exporting is great—but you must look after your local customers first.*

For further information see Beerenberg's website <http://www.beerenberg.com.au>.

## Questions

1   To what extent has the 'Australian-ness' of Beerenberg helped to expand this business?
2   There is no mention in this case of Beerenberg doing any competitor analysis or of assessing the industry structure. Are these significant defects in the attempt to win and retain a foothold in export markets?
3   Entering new export markets can be done in many ways. Was Grant Paech's way the best?
4   Can an SME that has never exported make it under its own steam?

# PART

D

# INTERNATIONAL MARKETING IMPLEMENTATION

Having taken the strategic aspects of the planned international marketing activity into account, it is necessary to implement the plan. Decisions must be taken regarding the basic marketing mix variables as they might apply in an international context. As far as product (Chapter 13) is concerned, the extent to which modifications will be needed in each overseas market must be established and evaluated in terms of affordability versus market potential. The end-use application in the selected overseas market must be established at an early stage as this may differ from the application in the domestic market or other foreign markets. Also for consideration are expectations as to quality and durability of the packaging and the different requirements for industrial products compared to consumer goods. Issues in international and global branding are also covered in this chapter although these apply to both goods and services. If it is a service (Chapter 14) that is being marketed overseas, special circumstances will apply, such as whether the service will be delivered in the overseas market or in the home country as with tourism and education. Attention will need to be given to the fact that, because service delivery is people-dependent, cultural variables play a major role is securing both initial and repeat business. As far as promotion is concerned (Chapter 15), the degree of marketing orientation in the foreign market will play a role in local decision making. The relative emphasis on individual forms of promotion varies from country to country as does the requirement to modify the content of each form of promotion and the availability of specific media. The setting of price (Chapter 16) in overseas markets can be a 'make or break' variable in international marketing. Decisions need to be taken as to whether cost recovery will be on a full cost or marginal cost basis and a price-setting methodology adopted based on an evaluation of alternatives such as cost-plus versus marketplace pricing. In overseas markets, the distribution channel (Chapter 17) tends to be longer than in domestic markets. Managing intermediaries offshore requires both cultural sensitivity and patience. The logistics aspect of distribution also requires consideration, as costs of getting goods to the overseas market can cause the offer to be uncompetitive. Accessibility to markets, availability of transport modes and value in relation to bulk are other issues for consideration. Failure to carefully consider issues relating to implementation can adversely affect the appeal of your offering to the offshore customer.

# 13 CHAPTER

# MODIFYING PRODUCTS FOR OVERSEAS MARKETS

## Learning Objectives

**After reading this chapter you should be able to:**

- determine how products spread to overseas markets and what influences their adoption by consumers in other countries;

- develop specific strategies for marketing products offshore;

- know when to tailor products to suit the needs of customers in overseas markets;

- appreciate which aspects of the product are likely to require modification for overseas markets;

- ascertain when it will be necessary to develop a new product specifically for an overseas market;

- recognise how the international marketing of industrial products differs from that of consumer goods;

- develop an awareness of the complexities of branding and packaging products in the international marketplace; and

- create strategies to cater for different packaging requirements in overseas markets.

# Wining over the Europeans

HUNTER VALLEY Wine Country

Since the beginning of the 1990s Australian wines have been selling overseas in huge volumes and in the year 2004–05 the volume of wine shipped grew by 15% to 670 million litres and the value of exports by 9% to A$2.7 billion (<http://www.abs.gov.au/AUSTATS>, accessed 25 January 2006). Although in part this is due to European winemakers, such as Veuve Cliquot and Moët et Chandon, establishing operations or buying equity in Australian vineyards, it has also been due to Australian winemakers modifying the product, packaging and labelling to suit European requirements. According to British wine master Jasper Morris, whereas others just made wines first and tried to sell them, the Australians worked out what the European consumer wanted and at what price, and then came up with a suitable offering. Critical in this process was Australia agreeing to European Community demands. These were that Australian winemakers stop using the names of European winemaking regions (e.g. Champagne, Burgundy, Moselle and Chablis) on their products and conform to European regulations as to the percentage of a variety that can be in a blend before the wine can be called by its varietal name. This marketing challenge has resulted in an upsurge in the use of Australian regional names of wine-growing areas and Europeans are now asking for Coonawarra Pinot Noir and Hunter Valley Semillon.

# INTRODUCTION

Even if a product is successful in Australia or New Zealand there is no guarantee that it will be successful when exported to other countries. In the overseas market, as in the Australian or New Zealand market, a marketer must always establish local needs and then take them into account. Although some products have universal appeal and require little change before being offered overseas, other products have narrower appeal and must be modified before being offered to buyers in other countries. In general, it is easier and cheaper to modify a product than it is to try to change a consumer's preference. Often this most basic of marketing concepts is ignored in international marketing.

This is even more often the case when the firm becomes involved in operations offshore rather than simply exporting to overseas countries. When the firm ventures offshore it is faced with a need to reappraise its domestic marketing strategies so as to take into account the differing circumstances of the overseas markets and the changes such international involvement will make to the total strategic approach of the firm. International involvement will require a redefinition of the business, a leveraging of the existing capabilities of the firm and a reappraisal of the firm in relation to its competitors—not only domestic, but also foreign. Such a reappraisal will involve adopting a different approach to segmenting the market and a different strategy when positioning the product or service.

# THE PRODUCT

## What is a product?

A product is a collection of attributes—physical, service or symbolic—which yield satisfaction to the buyer or end-user. Products can be further defined in relation to the different marketplaces in which they are found:

* local products have potential in only one market;
* international products have potential to be extended from the domestic market to a number of overseas markets;
* multinational products are products offered to many international markets, but which are adapted to suit the needs of each market; and
* global products are designed to meet the needs of market segments that are the same the world over.

A product is often considered in a narrow sense as something tangible that can be described in terms of its shape, dimensions, colour and form. This misconception also occurs in international marketing and many people have the idea that it is only physical products that can be exported. The reality is that intangible products (often called services) can be exported. Two of Australia's largest earners of export income, tourism and education, are intangible products. In many instances the actual offering to an overseas market consists of both a tangible and an intangible product, the totality of which is useful or satisfying to the buyer.

Kotler et al. (2006) believe that this utility or satisfaction can be best appreciated by categorising the elements of a product into the core benefit, the basic product, the expected product, the augmented product and the potential product, all of which may need changing when venturing overseas. The *core benefit* consists of the fundamental benefit or service that the customer is really buying. The *basic product* is the item actually purchased and its functional features. The *expected product* is the attributes and conditions that the buyer expects to receive when purchasing the item and may also include the styling, the packaging, the quality, the brand name and the trademark. The *augmented product* consists of items that exceed customer expectation and may also involve repair and maintenance, installation, instruction book, delivery, warranty, spare parts and credit facilities. Finally, there is the *potential product*, which embraces the possible augmentations and transformations that the product might undergo in the future (e.g. the possibility to add more memory to a computer).

Each of these elements may need modification when the product is offered to buyers in other countries. Such modification may be required for:

* competitive reasons (e.g. when someone else has registered the brand name);

* for legal reasons (e.g. when the manufacturer is required to show weights and volume in imperial measure);

* for linguistic reasons (e.g. when dealing with a bilingual market, such as Canada, where instructions must be in both French and English);

* for fiscal reasons, so as to qualify for a lower rate of duty due to the changed product being eligible for a different tariff classification;

* for cultural reasons (e.g. when the colour of packaging needs to be changed because it denotes the colour of death);

* for economic reasons (e.g. when consumers in the market cannot afford the product in its Australian or New Zealand form); and

* political reasons, such as government regulation on the way firearms are described and sold.

An Australian manufacturer of tanning lotions directed at the women's market will need to do a radical rethink when contemplating prospects in Asia and come up with a different product for changing skin colour. While Westerners tan to appear attractive, Asians purchase products that promise to lighten the skin. Research has shown that over 38% of women in countries such as Hong Kong, Taiwan, Malaysia, Korea and the Philippines use skin-whitening products and that most men in these countries find women with fair complexions more attractive. In South-East Asia light skin has historically indicated aristocracy, wealth, nobility and status whereas dark skin is associated with those who worked in the fields, as only the rich could afford to remain indoors.

**SOURCE:** *Adapted from Kotler, P., Keller, K.L., Ang, S.H., Leong, S.M. and Tan, C.T. (2006)* Marketing Management—an Asian Perspective, *Pearson Prentice Hall, Singapore, p. 179.*

# INTERNATIONAL PRODUCT STRATEGIES

## Product diffusion and adoption in overseas markets

Diffusion refers to the movement of new products to and in overseas markets so that they are available to customers in those markets. Typically the adoption process involves a number of stages—awareness, interest, evaluation, trial and adoption. The propensity of consumers to adopt new products varies considerably from overseas market to overseas market (see Chapter 5).

Although there is no shortage of new ideas, few are successful in commercial terms. According to Ambler and Styles (2000), of the 20 000 new products that appeared on US supermarket shelves in 1994 only 10% were on sale two years later. They argue that the majority of innovations are incremental and, for the most part, marketers develop what already exists by appreciating customer needs, seeing what is available and filling the gap between.

While the international marketer may be in the fortunate position of seeing which products survive being launched locally before deciding which ones should be launched in other countries, this is becoming increasingly impractical as product life cycles shorten, the costs of bringing new products to market escalates and global competition intensifies. Increasingly, international marketers need to be involved at the birth, if not at the conception, of new products. Their presence enables a reduced possibility of failure by ensuring that issues are addressed, such as how the innovation compares with those coming from other countries (as products involving overseas innovations could be future competitors in the domestic market) and what problems were encountered when products embodying these innovations were launched in other countries. According to Ambler and Styles (2000), the international manager can adopt three strategies for cross-fertilising innovation:

- *passive*–encourage various national units in the organisation to learn from each other. The international manager cross-fertilises the ideas, but contributes nothing of his or her own;

- *pacemaking*–the international manager creates a portfolio of the best innovations available throughout the organisation and uses incentives such as research funding to persuade other divisions of the company to adopt them; and

- *participative*–in cases where the global market demands a global product, the international manager becomes actively involved in forming/leading an international task force to come up with the desired global innovation.

In order to do business in overseas markets it is necessary to make changes in both business attitude and strategic posture. It may be necessary to redefine the business in which the firm is engaged, leverage the core competencies or expertise of the firm so as to achieve economies of scope and redefine the competitive approach that the firm will adopt when doing business in the overseas market.

## Redefining the business

Businesses tend to be defined in terms of the benefits they provide to the customer, the segments of the market they occupy, the technology they employ, the nature of the value chain in which they are involved, the stage in the life cycle of the product they market and the form of their involvement in the market. Each of these factors can change when the firm ventures offshore and, as a result, there is likely to be a need to redefine the business when going overseas.

### CUSTOMER BENEFITS

Consumers around the world have many different needs and will perceive products as satisfying these needs to differing degrees. While some of these needs are basic and universal, such as the desire to improve living standards, people's ability to satisfy these needs is not universal. The economic, political and social structure of a country affects the ability of consumers to satisfy their needs and the methods they use to do so. As a consequence, the same product will offer different benefits to customers in different countries. For example, in Australia outboard engines are overwhelmingly used on pleasure boats, whereas in Indonesia outboard engines are predominantly used on small commercial vessels. As a result, the definition of the firm's business for outboard marine engines in Indonesia would be very different from the definition of that same business in Australia.

Customer benefits will also vary according to whether the product is regarded in the overseas market as a low-involvement or high-involvement purchase. What might be a low-involvement purchase in one country can be a high-involvement purchase in another, especially where there are differences in standards of living between the two countries.

The degree of difference between brands can also vary between countries depending on the benefits the item is perceived to confer and the availability of choice between brands in the specific overseas market.

## CUSTOMER SEGMENTS

Entering or expanding activities in an overseas market may result in the firm targeting different segments from those targeted in the home market. Unilever, a transnational company, markets the same brand of products in different markets and often the product serves different segments in one market as opposed to another. For instance, Domestos is a remover of bathroom plaque in Australia, whereas in Germany it is a general purpose cleaner. For Unilever, the definition of its Domestos business would be different in Australia from what it is in Germany. As a consequence, while the manufacturer might initially think that it is offering the same standard product in different countries, consumers may impose a differentiation of their own on the product and the uses to which it is put. Frequently this is due to the availability of other products in the same category in the overseas market.

## TECHNOLOGY

The technologies that are used in Australia may be either too sophisticated or too unsophisticated for various overseas markets. The appropriateness of different technologies will be a matter of levels of education, availability of infrastructure, the R&D environment, the cultural attitude towards innovation and the relative cost of various factors of production. As an example, in a country where labour is very cheap the attractiveness of labour-saving technology is not as significant as in countries where labour is expensive. Also, in countries where the average skill levels of labour are low the ability to sell products whose application requires skill is likely to be somewhat restricted.

Another issue is the social cost associated with the importation of high-tech products. Will the costs of associated social dislocation such as unemployment and resettlement be greater than the benefits resulting from the technology? Even if they are less, will there be an unacceptable political cost? This issue of appropriateness can affect how the business is defined in a particular overseas market.

## VALUE CHAIN

Production is defined as value-creating activity. Figure 9.7 in Chapter 9 illustrates the structure of the value chain in which the typical firm is involved. Added value is achieved by converting inputs of lesser worth into outputs of greater worth. There are going to be many elements in the chain that are perceived by the customer to offer value over which the firm has little direct control.

Elements of the *value chain* may lie at the input end (e.g. raw materials, delivery, infrastructure support such as power, water and gas) and also the output end (e.g. warehousing, performance of intermediaries, servicing and warranty performance and transport facilities and infrastructure). The degree to which the firm can participate in the value chain in an overseas country in the same manner as it does in Australia or New Zealand will be affected by the existence and relative efficiency/cost of elements of the value chain in that country. If the opportunities for participating in the value chain in the foreign market are restricted, then the firm has to decide whether to become directly involved in elements of the value chain in that country which back home in Australia or New Zealand it leaves to other suppliers. An alternative is to supply elements of the value chain from affiliates or subsidiaries in other countries, as happens when transnational companies undertake a global rationalisation of activities. The current trend to international outsourcing and offshoring is a manifestation of this. The degree to which it is possible to replicate the Australian situation in the overseas market as far as the value chain is concerned will influence how the business is defined with respect to that particular market.

## NEW PRODUCT DEVELOPMENT PROCESSES IN ASIA

As is discussed in Chapter 16, Japanese firms have traditionally approached cost issues in a way that yields substantial savings. They begin with market research and product characteristics as do Western companies. At the next stage the processes differ and in Japan the planned selling price minus the desired profit is calculated, resulting in a figure that represents the targeted cost ceiling. Negotiations between the various divisions of the firm and value-chain members take place so that this targeted cost ceiling can be achieved. Once this cost ceiling has been agreed upon, then manufacturing begins, followed by a plan of continuous cost reduction so as to retain competitive advantage in the face of competitor reaction to the products entry to the market. In Western countries, according to Keegan and Green (2005, p. 369), cost is usually determined after (not before) design, engineering and marketing decisions have been made.

## PRODUCT LIFE CYCLE

This aspect influences how the business is defined in the overseas market. The theory of product life cycle argues that, like people, products have a life and move through stages from introduction to growth, to maturity to saturation, and, finally, to decline. As is shown in Figure 13.1, the stages in the product life cycle and its overall spread may vary from one national market to another.

In Asian markets the innovation stage tends to be shorter, the growth stage longer and the maturity stage considerably shorter as customers rapidly abandon the product as others do so. Allegedly this is due to:

• attempts to avoid uncertainty;

• a pronounced tendency towards collectivism;

• referral as a common method of expanding product trial.

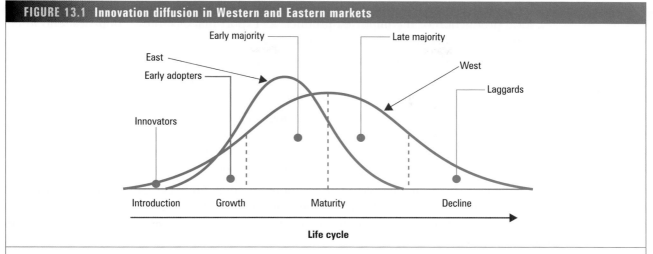

**FIGURE 13.1  Innovation diffusion in Western and Eastern markets**

SOURCE: *Bradley, F. (2004) International Marketing Strategy, 4th edn, Financial Times Prentice Hall, Harlow, UK. © 2004, Pearson Education Limited.*

The international product life cycle (briefly commented on in Chapter 1) describes this process as related to the spread of products across national boundaries. Products that are at a decline stage in the Australian or New Zealand markets may have their overall life extended if they can be marketed in a country where the product is not known or where, if it is known, it has not yet reached the decline stage. Conversely, an Australian or New Zealand firm with a product at the growth stage, and believing it is ripe for export, needs to avoid overseas markets where that same product class is at the decline stage.

Bicycles are an example of a product that is at different stages of the product life cycle in different countries. Whereas in industrialised countries such as Australia or New Zealand, bicycles are at a decline stage of the market, in the late 1980s they were at a growth stage in Vietnam and are now at a mature stage following the recent and rapid introduction of motor scooters. In the late 1950s and early 1960s British motor car producers launched two models which did not prove popular in the UK market and rapidly reached the decline stage. These were the Morris Isis and the Hillman Hunter. The life cycle of both models was extended in terms of contributing to company profitability by their manufacture being licensed to overseas countries without a domestic automobile industry. Manufacture of the Morris Isis was licensed in India as the Hindustan Ambassador and manufacture of the Hillman Hunter was licensed in Iran as the Peykan.

Onkvisit and Shaw (1983) developed a five-stage description of the international product life cycle:

1  *Local innovation*: The firm in developed countries such as Australia or New Zealand has developed an innovation because consumers are relatively affluent and have relatively unlimited wants.

2  *Overseas innovation*: With the domestic market saturated, firms look to overseas markets to expand sales and profits. Initially the products tend to go to markets where the psychic distance is least. In the case of Australia these are likely to be New Zealand, the UK, Canada, the USA and Singapore.

3 *Maturity*: Growing demand in advanced nations provides the stimulus for firms to start local production of the imported product. As export markets, these countries tend to be replaced by other markets further down the development scale.

4 *Worldwide imitation*: The innovating nation runs out of new export markets as the product is produced in many countries. Economies of scale suffer and costs in Australia/New Zealand rise as export markets dry up.

5 *Reversal*: Other countries with the technology and cheaper labour costs are more efficient producers than the innovating country and these countries commence supplying the innovating country, which ceases production. The last imitators now are able to undersell manufacturers in the Australian and New Zealand markets.

There are many examples of the international product life cycle. The textile, clothing and footwear industries illustrate the involvement of the low-income developing countries and the automotive industry the involvement of the middle-income developing countries. (This issue was explored in Chapter 1.)

In the example of Kirby Refrigeration (below), it can be seen how the five stages of the cycle can apply to a firm. In this case the firm's international involvement moved through five distinct stages:

1 manufacture in Australia based on technology licensed from overseas;

2 commence exporting the product to nearby markets with the permission of the licensee;

3 commence production overseas;

4 products from the overseas operation become increasingly competitive in world markets;

5 products from the overseas operation are imported into Australia.

Kirby Refrigeration of Milperra, NSW, was originally a licensee of Tecumseh of the USA for the manufacture of refrigeration compressors in Australia. Then it exported to countries in South-East Asia including Thailand. Subsequently Kirby established a joint venture manufacturing operation in Thailand known as Kulthorn-Kirby, Thailand. The Thai company not only supplied the Thai market but also other overseas markets and now supplies compressor kits to the original US licensee, Tecumseh. Kirby no longer produces compressors in Australia and imports almost all its requirements from Kulthorn-Kirby. Several years ago it was acquired by Lennox of the USA and the refrigeration division now trades as Heatcraft Australia. The definition of its business in Thailand would be substantially different now to what it was 25 years ago.

## Leveraging capabilities

When considering the direction in which the firm should proceed in an overseas market there is a need to understand the extent to which the new capabilities acquired as a result of exposure to one overseas market can be leveraged so as to provide the firm with competitive advantage in another. Initially, when entering an overseas market the firm's core competencies centre on production capabilities but, as the market develops, attention shifts to taking the competencies and leveraging them internationally both across products and across product lines within a single country. Leveraging takes three forms: shared physical assets, shared external relationships and shared information and expertise.

## SHARED PHYSICAL ASSETS

Apart from the case of branching into new product lines in a country because of excess capacity, the firm may share its physical assets by undertaking work for another firm in the form of contract manufacture, contract packaging or partial (or component) manufacture. It may also perform functions for an affiliate in another country so that the sharing of physical assets takes place across national borders. In most cases this sharing of physical assets is based on the firm using those physical resources in which it has a competitive advantage.

## SHARED EXTERNAL RELATIONSHIPS

The very fact of commencing operations or even exporting to another country leads to the firm becoming involved with established networks in that country. These networks are an important asset of the firm and form part of its competitive advantage in that market. In such circumstances the phrase 'one thing leads to another' applies and these relationships in the overseas market can be used to the advantage of the firm. The network applies to all elements of the value chain in the overseas market. There are differences between countries as to the extent to which business is conducted on a competitive as opposed to a cooperative basis. Although in reality, even in marketing-oriented countries, there is a great deal of collaboration between enterprises, there are strong indications that collaboration is increasing globally. This is illustrated by the fact that the share of the international market held by countries where cooperation is a strong feature of business life, for example Japan, South Korea, Taiwan, India, China and the countries of ASEAN, is expanding.

## SHARED INFORMATION AND EXPERTISE

There is a powerful incentive for the sharing of information and leveraging expertise—the costs of developing and bringing a product to market are escalating. An example of this is in the pharmaceutical industry where the costs of developing, trialling and obtaining approval for a new drug can run into several million dollars. The need to achieve large market size becomes more and more important in order to amortise these costs, so relationships of this kind are becoming increasingly necessary in order to be able to compete. By leveraging information and expertise overseas through these relationships, reciprocal benefits are likely to flow. This in turn may improve the firm's competitive position in the Australian or New Zealand markets as the overseas involvement may yield economies of scale because costs of development can be defrayed over a larger base. The sharing of information and expertise applies not only to R&D and production activities, but also to sources of supply and marketing functions. There are many cases where involvement overseas as an exporter has led to the Australian firm becoming the importer of products that fit well into their existing distribution network in Australia.

# Understanding product market structure

The structure of the market for a product varies from one overseas country to another and often from market to market within an overseas country. This is particularly so where there are different ethnic groups in the one country, as is the case with Malaysia, which has significant populations of Malay, Chinese and Indian ethnic origin. This structure is defined by market boundaries, differentiation, branding and the size of the market.

## IDENTIFYING THE PRODUCT MARKET BOUNDARIES

The boundaries of a market are likely to differ from country to country in terms of the product's use, the functions it performs, what the product category includes and the activities of competitors. As Craig et al. (2000) point out, this is the case with soft drinks. In Australia beer is viewed as an alcoholic beverage whereas in some other markets it is treated as a soft drink. In the USA the soft drink market includes sodas (fizzy drinks) only whereas in South-East Asia it includes fresh fruit juices and in other countries, such as Europe, cordials and fruit concentrates.

The form in which the product is currently available in the overseas market is important, for example whether soft drink is sold in bottles or cans. Also to be considered is whether the product to be offered should be differentiated from competitor's offerings by changing the form in which it is presented or the benefits claimed for it, such as varying the size of the pack or the claimed end-use application. In addition, the nature of the other products with which the use of the product is associated can vary and influence the need to differentiate the offering. In countries such as India, where washing of clothes is done by hand, bar soap is used, whereas in countries such as Australia, where washing is usually done by machine, synthetic detergents are most commonly employed.

The significance attributed to branding in a market can also influence its structure. In markets emerging from a subsistence level or markets which are changing from a command to a market economy, branding is less important than it would be in a highly market oriented environments such as Australia or New Zealand. The significance of brands differs between segments within an overseas market. This is evidenced by Japanese yuppies' preference for imported designer-label clothing. The significance of branding in market-oriented economies will also vary according to positioning of the product in that market. This aspect will not be as important if the product is retailed through discount chains, which also sell buyer's label products such as Big W in Australia, as it would be if retailed through boutique outlets or 'category killers' such as Toys R Us.

The above issues point to a need to place some dimension on the market for the product or service in the overseas country. In some countries, where the product is at a mature stage of the product life cycle, the potential is likely to be low and the market mainly a replacement one. In markets where the stage of the life cycle is one of growth, the potential is much larger, especially if these countries have large populations and high rates of economic growth (e.g. ASEAN countries). Other factors include the age distribution of the population and the degree to which the market is concentrated in major cities or dispersed throughout the country. Also relevant is the extent to which the market is fragmented and in the hands of many small firms or concentrated in the hands of several major conglomerates.

# Modifying products for overseas markets

## TAILORING PRODUCTS TO SUIT OVERSEAS MARKETS

In some cases it may be possible to take a product made in Australia or New Zealand and modify it to enhance its appeal in selected markets overseas. In other cases it will be necessary to create a product from scratch for the target overseas market. In other situations it may be necessary to design a product to appeal to global markets from the outset. International Highlight 13.1 illustrates how aggressive strategies with a unique product can pay off.

The extent to which modification of products is required will vary according to whether it is a consumer good or an industrial product. Even within these groupings the need for modification will vary according to the environmental sensitivity of the item being offered overseas. In some instances product modifications are voluntary in order to enhance its appeal to customers; in other instances they are compulsory in order to conform to product standards or government legislation.

### 13.1 INTERNATIONAL HIGHLIGHT

## China turns onto Tim Tams

The iconic Australian biscuit, the chocolate-covered Tim Tam manufactured by Arnott's (which is now owned by Campbell Soups of the USA), is being targeted at the Chinese biscuit market worth A$2.8 billion and growing at 10% a year. Traditionally a market for savoury biscuits, penetrating the Chinese market with Tim Tams will involve changing Chinese taste preferences. As part of the launch of the product in 700 stores in the coastal cities of Guangzhou and Shenzen, awareness of the brand is being created by an extensive sampling campaign in the stores, Tim Tam-painted buses plying the crowded streets and a saturation prime time TV campaign. Also of assistance is the fact that the Chinese translation of the brand name Tim Tam is 'have a little more', which Arnott's hope the Chinese customers will do.

## PRODUCT STANDARDS AND REGULATIONS

Product standards in different countries determine whether or not the Australian or New Zealand product needs to be adapted to conform to the local standard in that country. Standards can be either technical or mandated by government. Technical standards are enforced by the market in that consumers will not or cannot buy the product unless it conforms to the accepted standards. Often standards issued by government are a device for keeping out foreign products. Some countries such as Japan may demand that, despite tests having been completed in the country of origin, tests must also be carried out in their country, often at considerable expense. This exclusion can also be achieved by requiring the overseas firm to comply with cumbersome certification requirements. Onerous and costly testing and certification requirements are illustrated in the case of electrical goods entering the USA which are required to undergo Underwriters Laboratory testing. This time-consuming and costly process has served to exclude many imported electrical products and whitegoods (including items from Australia) from the US market.

Most countries have a national standards body such as Standards Australia that sets standards, often in the interests of protecting the consumer. Sometimes these bodies are in the public sector and sometimes in the private sector, for example the Underwriters Laboratories in the USA. There is also a trend to set international standards such as the international quality management standard ISO 9000. Standards are most common in pharmaceuticals, automobiles, electrical appliances and foods. In some instances regulations may prevent a product from entering an overseas market and in others the regulations may operate as a disguised non-tariff barrier.

## MEASUREMENT AND CALIBRATION

Another reason to modify products for sale overseas is to ensure that they conform to weights and measures legislation in the overseas country. Not only do some countries use imperial rather than metric measures, but the norm or legal requirement is that the weight or measure must be stated on the pack in a specific manner, such as in *mL* rather than *cL* or by volume rather than by weight. With products there can be requirements relating to statement of capacity, voltage or speed. Increasingly, with products intended for sale in several markets, it is necessary to show measurement or calibration in multiple ways in conformity with varying requirements in each market. This may involve a significant modification to the product or its packaging, as happens with multi-voltage electrical appliances.

## TRADEMARKS

Trademarks and other forms of protection for intellectual property, such as patents and copyright, may necessitate modification of the product together with its branding and packaging. The Australian or New Zealand brand might already be registered in an overseas country. It may be that this brand, due to intellectual piracy, has acquired a poor reputation in the target overseas market, which means that a different brand name should be used when introducing the product. It sometimes happens that another party in the overseas country has a patent on the process used that prevents the Australian or New Zealand firm selling or at least manufacturing the product in the target country without further modification. Abuses of trademarks and patents are particularly prevalent in developing countries.

## CLIMATE AND USAGE

If products need to be modified in order to be able to operate effectively under different environmental or climatic conditions, then changes will be necessary in the interests of both utility and marketability. Climatic conditions need to be borne in mind, particularly when packaging a product for shipment overseas to ensure that the goods arrive in good condition. For example, strong waterproof packaging would be more necessary if the customer was in Laos, and could only be reached via a bumpy road from Thailand in the rainy season, than it would be for a customer in a port city in New Zealand.

Another factor is that of usage patterns. These often reflect affordability, as with the sale of cigarettes in single sticks in parts of Asia. Usage patterns also reflect the environment as exemplified in the demand for small, quiet air-conditioning units in Tokyo. Here, people live in very small flats in close proximity to each other in a very humid climate. Usage patterns also reflect social customs; for example, in parts of Europe people shop daily because shopping is a social event.

## LANGUAGE AND SYMBOLISM

This issue has an impact particularly on the packaging and labelling of products because different symbols are interpreted differently from country to country and they can affect the way the product is perceived. The same applies to the use of brand names because the use of an Australian or a global brand name can give a negative connotation to a product if the brand has a different meaning in another language. This is discussed in more detail later in this chapter.

Other issues relating to the need to modify the product are the acceptability of colours used on the product and its packaging, the need for visual as opposed to written instructions and, in the case of products destined for a number of markets, the use of several languages on the packaging, labelling and instructions for use.

## STYLE, DESIGN AND TASTE

The above factors may necessitate modification to the product in order to improve its marketability overseas. This will affect the size of packaging in relation to the size of the product and the quality and nature of the packaging. For example, the Japanese tend to judge the quality of the product by the elaborate nature of its packaging, whereas the environmentally conscious Germans are critical of unnecessary packaging and highly conscious of environmental issues associated with disposing of packaging materials. Colour preferences and religious/social acceptability of specific colours vary from country to country and need to be taken into account in the formulation of the product as well as its packaging. Taste is another variable that is particularly important with foods and beverages. In 1990 the Commonwealth Scientific and Industrial Research Organisation (CSIRO) of Australia set up a sensory perception laboratory in Japan. This was to test Australian products being offered for sale in that country in terms of their acceptability as far as Japanese taste and sensory preferences were concerned. The CSIRO subsequently expanded this operation to other countries, including Indonesia.

Although modifying products involves extra costs the costs can be more than offset by enhancing the appeal of the product to a wider market in the target overseas country. It is often necessary to change the formulation of the product and its design features. Sometimes design changes may be a matter of local taste but, in other situations, the changes are virtually mandated because government-imposed tariff or non-tariff barriers require the use of local inputs if the barriers are not to be prohibitive. A further aspect is that features associated with a product in one country may be different or not be required for the product in another. An example is motor vehicles that must be sold with air-conditioners in countries such as Saudi Arabia and with heaters in other countries such as Sweden. Even within the one geographic area the features required of a product may vary due to affordability. For this reason a fully optioned vehicle is likely to be more marketable in the United Arab Emirates than on the other side of the Gulf in Iran.

## TECHNOLOGY ISSUES AND PERFORMANCE STANDARDS

With high-tech products, performance standards are likely to differ from one country to another. This is often because the degree of technical infrastructure varies between countries. In a country plagued with power blackouts or brownouts a high-tech product that is sensitive to inconsistent voltage in the power supply may be of dubious value unless it can be supplied with its own generator, which significantly increases its cost. In addition, products developed in technologically advanced countries often exceed the performance standards needed in less-developed countries where labour is a more significant factor of production than is capital. In these countries customers prefer products that are simpler but which will last longer under local conditions, especially as the purchase is likely to account for a greater percentage of average annual income.

## WARRANTY AND SERVICING ISSUES

Customers buying products are buying utility, function and performance as well as image and status. This utility, function and performance involves warranty provision. In many cases products are sold with a package of service attributes. These can take the form of linked servicing programs such as free service for one year, or warranty programs like 30 000 km or three years with a motor vehicle. Expectations regarding these, as well as the cost of providing them, will also vary from country to country on the basis of use conditions, government regulation, cost of providing the warranty service and the availability of competent persons to provide that service in the overseas country. During the oil price hikes of the late 1970s and early 1980s, there was a healthy appetite for luxury motor vehicles in oil-rich countries such as Libya. However, because local repair and servicing facilities were primitive, it was not uncommon to see relatively new vehicles abandoned by the side of the road because they had been driven without major servicing until they stopped. In circumstances of this kind, having a standardised servicing and warranty policy worldwide does not work. Another related challenge and dilemma is whether to conform to the local expectation, knowing that this may affect the firm's international reputation, or whether to provide the same service package/warranty provision as in Australia or New Zealand when this may make the firm less competitive in the overseas market.

The next aspect of tailoring a product for overseas markets involves the decision as to how to develop a product specifically for the new market.

## Developing a product for an overseas market

In cases where it is not possible either to export a product in an unaltered form to an overseas market or to modify it to ensure its appeal in an overseas market, it may be necessary to develop a product specifically for that market. Robinson (1961), when considering the implications for developing products specifically for less-developed countries, listed a number of factors and their implications for product design as follows:

- level of technical skills may necessitate product simplification;
- level of labour costs will impact on automation or manualisation of the product;
- level of literacy will impact on visualisation of instructions and simplification of the product;
- level of income will impact on the degree to which quality is built in and price charged;
- level of interest rates will impact on inventory holding decisions;
- level of maintenance will impact on changes in tolerances and nature of guarantee offered;
- climate will impact on operating conditions and packaging to protect product;
- isolation will create the need for a simplified and reliable product due to difficulties and expense of repairs; and
- different standards will require recalibration and resizing of the product.

As an alternative to designing a new product for an overseas market from scratch it may be possible to take existing technology and apply it to the needs of the overseas market. Applied research, as opposed to fundamental research, has been a strong point with the Japanese and has made a significant contribution to their success in international business. Czinkota and Kotabe (1990) describe this process as incrementalism, as opposed to the giant leap. The incremental approach of the Japanese emphasises continued technological improvement aimed at making an already successful product even better for the customer. It also enables the pace of new product introductions to be accelerated.

The stages to be followed in developing a new product for an overseas market are listed below:

- *Generating ideas*: The ideas to be generated should tap new or existing markets, complement existing product lines or improve existing products in the overseas market. Such ideas should not only come from local sources such as consumers, employees and competitors, but also from sources in both the target overseas market as well as from other countries.

- *Screening ideas*: As not all ideas generated from the search process may be suitable for the selected overseas market, some sorting out will be necessary. A list of acceptable ideas should be developed based on compatibility with the firm's distinctive competence, ability of the firm to convert the idea into a product offering, the export potential of the idea and the fit of the idea with the firm's competitive position in the industry of which it is a part.

- *Business evaluation*: Although new product ideas might be acceptable to the firm, they may not represent the best use of funds and should be subject to a cost–benefit analysis. This analysis with respect to the selected country would consider current and potential demand, likely competitor response and potential for expansion into other markets.

- *Product development*: This is the next stage for those ideas which still indicate promise following the cost–benefit analysis. Details of the product are worked out and tangible and intangible benefits are specified. Considerations influencing the development of the product include its core benefits, where it is to be positioned in the overseas market and the role of the other marketing mix variables in enhancing the product's appeal.

- *Test marketing*: This involves selecting a small section of the overseas market to test consumer reaction to the product. The town or area selected should be a microcosm of the wider market so that the results of the test can be assumed to predict the average reaction of those to be targeted in the wider market. On the basis of results from the test market decisions can be made as to whether to launch the product in the wider market and if so whether any modifications are necessary to the product before the launch.

- *Product introduction*: This is the final stage of product development. Further modification might still be required. This may depend on whether reaction in the wider overseas market proves to be the same as in the test market, or whether the conditions under which the product is used or consumed in the target overseas market affect the acceptability of the product or the nature of the reaction of competitors.

An alternative to exporting a tailored product is to offer the same product overseas as manufactured in Australia or New Zealand. This involves the issue of the relative merits of standardisation as opposed to adaptation.

## Standardisation versus adaptation

One of the frequently debated issues in international marketing is whether the firm should modify and adapt products when offering them overseas or only offer a standardised product to all markets. Standardisation is offering a common product on a national, regional or, more usually, a worldwide basis. Levitt (1983) argues that firms should treat the world as one large market and ignore regional and national differences that he claims are superficial. To support his argument he claims that with improvements in communication knowledge is being rapidly disseminated across national borders. This means that with the advent of the multinational company and the internet as a promotion vehicle, the ability of national governments to protect both their firms and citizens from foreign activities and influences is diminishing. With growing middle classes (Jacob 1994), global segments and the rise of global as opposed to national competitors, proponents of standardisation argue that the only way to be internationally competitive is to offer a standardised product worldwide. This will enable the firm to be more competitive globally because of the resulting economies of scale.

Adaptation, on the other hand, involves making appropriate changes in a product to match the requirements of customers in specific markets. The arguments for adaptation reflect the essential elements of the marketing concept—tailoring a product specifically for the needs of the customer. Japan is an example of where firms find it necessary to adapt the product to local conditions if they wish to achieve a worthwhile market share. It is also a market where the customers are very discriminating and have considerable choice. To offer an unchanged product in such a market is unlikely to win many customers.

The *factors that encourage standardisation* of a product are:

- *high costs of adaptation*: Where these are high and the volume of anticipated sales modest, adaptation can be uneconomic because by including costs of adaptation in the price the product would become uncompetitive.

- *nature of the product*: Where the nature of the product is such that technical specifications are critical, such specifications tend to be internationally uniform resulting in a standardised product as with many industrial goods. Consumer goods, on the other hand, tend to be more adapted because they are more likely to reflect personal preferences.

- *convergence of tastes between countries*: Such convergence is most likely to occur with countries that have similar income levels and consumption patterns. The greater this convergence, the greater the potential for standardisation.

- *economies of scale in manufacture*: Standardising a product at the point of manufacture results in scale economies in production. This benefit decreases as firms increase the number of their manufacturing sites around the world.

- *economies in research and development*: If the firm offers a standardised product to all countries it gets more mileage from its R&D activities because it is not using its R&D resources to modify its products for each overseas market. Furthermore, less R&D effort is consumed in product modification.

- *economies in marketing*: When the product is standardised, marketing costs will fall as product literature, salesforce training, advertising and promotional activity will require less modification.

- *economic integration between countries*: This is enhancing similarities between markets especially in terms of standards of living and information flows. To this can be added the effect of industrial rationalisation between markets within the trade bloc.

- *competition*: The absence of competition improves the likelihood that a standard product will be accepted in another country. However, if established or new competitors offer a product tailored to needs in that country, the acceptability of the standard product is likely to be less.

## 13.2 INTERNATIONAL HIGHLIGHT

# Australian business must research the way to success

Today Australia invests about 1.65% of its gross domestic product on research. Among advanced countries it is the fourth highest for government investment and the 17th highest for business investment. This shows up the tendency of Australian business to leave innovation up to others and highlights its failure to commercialise 'Aussie' ingenuity.

Although there is some validity in the excuse that our firms are relatively small in scale and size, the real challenge for business, government and researchers is to develop technology-based companies that can participate in global growth without being taken over. The CSIRO (Commonwealth Scientific and Industrial Research Organisation) can act as a catalyst in this connection.

In a 'coals to Newcastle' story, a small Australian company, Cotton Seed Distributors, is selling Australian-bred cotton seed to the USA, one of the world's largest producers of cotton. Its activities showcase local science producing world-best cotton varieties, and an entrepreneurial group of farmers adopting a global approach to marketing for their product. Some Australian firms involved in similar activities will develop into global companies in their own right while

*Image courtesy of Cotton Seed Distributors*

others such as Memtec will become part of much larger global enterprises, but will continue to generate significant Australian employment and income. An example of a promising world enterprise at the formative stage is the CSIRO's partnership with the Queensland Metals Corporation and Ford Motor Company to develop a magnesium metals industry that could earn A$4 billion in its first decade of operation.

**SOURCE:** *Adapted from* Business Review Weekly, *10 March 2000, p. 60.*

The *factors that encourage adaptation* are:

- *variation in consumer needs and tastes*: Variations in consumption patterns may require different products. As an example, the number of cycles required for a washing machine may be a function of clothes-wearing habits in a country. Fast-food franchisers have often been faced with this need to adapt—the food portions offered by McDonald's in Japan are smaller than those offered in Australia or the USA.

- *differing conditions under which the product is used*: Where the conditions under which the product is used vary as between countries, the greater the need is for adaptation. This is particularly the case with products whose demand is climate related or whose utilisation depends on certain levels of skill.

- *variations in ability to afford the item offered*: Given that average per capita annual incomes in countries range from around US$350 to US$60 000, price-sensitive items will require adaptation to expand market reach in many parts of the world. In countries where the product has a utility role (as do bicycles and outboard motors in the developing world), the demand is likely to be for a basic 'no frills' item. In developed countries where the same product is used in leisure activities, the product sought will be required to have a range of features that enhance both its appearance and performance.

- *the influence of government*: This will be reflected in the presence or absence of regulations on products driven by a desire to protect local industry, safeguard the environment, guard local intellectual property, enforce cultural and religious mores and save citizens from harm. The greater the volume of government regulation the greater the need to adapt. Whereas with market-driven differences adaptation is voluntary, with government-driven regulations adaptation is mandatory if the firm wishes to do business with that country.

- *legal requirements*: A country's laws may require adaptation of the product. Different countries have different laws relating to standards, patents, tariffs, non-tariff barriers and taxes.

- *different tastes and behaviours on the part of consumers*: Cultural differences affect tastes, consumption habits and product acceptance. With culturally sensitive products the greater the cultural similarity between Australia and the overseas market, the less the need for adaptation.

- *physical environment*: The climate, topography and resources of a country may necessitate adaptation of the product. Appliances need to be designed differently if they are to operate in humid as opposed to dry climates, if maintenance facilities are primitive and if power fluctuations are common. Differences in average size of accommodation affect the design of appliances and home furnishings.

- *lack of adequate support systems*: The nature of the systems that support the sale of the product varies between countries and may affect the acceptability of offering a standard product. Examples include mode of transport, warehousing, distribution channels and credit facilitators. Selling butter in packets into a market in Asia such as Myanmar is a problem if retailers and households in that country are not generally equipped with refrigeration. In these circumstances it may be necessary to offer butter in another form, such as canned.

Debate on the issue has become polarised on standardisation versus adaptation rather than reflecting the reality that there is a continuum between the two extremes. The international marketer must take into account the circumstances of the firm, the nature of the product on offer and the requirements of the market. Then a decision can be made as to where along the continuum from full standardisation to full adaptation the product should be pitched. The factors discussed above need to be taken into account when making this decision for the target overseas market.

The question of standardisation leads to consideration of whether a global product should be created by the firm from the outset.

## Creating a global product

An alternative to the usual approach of taking an Australian or New Zealand product and offering it overseas in a standard or an adapted form is to design a product which can be offered overseas as well as in domestic markets virtually simultaneously. Several examples are portrayed in International Highlight 13.3.

The phrase 'born global' is increasingly being used to describe firms that commence operations with a focus on the global market rather than simply on the Australian or New

## 13.3 INTERNATIONAL HIGHLIGHT

# Born global

Whittle, a programming company of Melbourne, can claim to be a 'born global' company. Because of the specialised nature of its product (a computer software program for the design of open-pit mines to maximise extraction) and the necessary size of the customer's operation to support the purchase, the Australian market was too small to support Whittle's activities. From the outset, the product was designed to be sold globally and the company's first sale was to a mining firm in Spain. Currently, Whittle has licensed the software to more than 200 companies, half of which are outside Australia.

Another 'born global' company is Novasoft Technology, a small Australian start-up company, which has released a new operating system designed for the internet. Its first users include the ANZ, Bankers Trust, CBA and Macquarie Bank—operating on a free trial basis to trade foreign exchange options over the internet. This is offered as an alternative to the existing broker market in which open voice phone lines are used. Because of its speed the new system offered by Novasoft has wide application for professionals who want to create real-time interactive applications. Its success among the giants in the industry such as Microsoft and Sun Microsystems remains to be seen, but Novasoft illustrates the myriad specialised internet applications and possibilities that can launch a 'born global' firm.

Born global firms are often global technology firms like WebSpy and Proteome Systems, both of which are included in the *BRW* Fast 100 list. WebSpy Ltd, which is a Perth-based internet and email monitoring specialist, came 18th in the 2004 Deloitte Technology Fast 50 awards with 189% growth (<http://www.webspy.com.au>) and Proteome Systems focuses on advancing the understanding of biology in humans and other living systems by using proteomics to develop breakthrough technologies, diagnostic products and drugs.

SOURCES: *Butler, G. (1998)* Australian Financial Review, *14 May, p. 34; and more recent newspaper reports.*

---

Zealand markets. Often these firms offer products or services that are suitable for small niche markets and the size of that niche in the above markets is insufficient to ensure the viability of the concept underlying the product. In other cases the product requires such large upfront costs to get it to a stage where it can be offered to the market that a much wider demand than exists in Australia or New Zealand is essential to ensure its survival. In these circumstances the design of the product and its proposed marketing must ensure its appeal to potential buyers in a wide variety of countries. Products that are not culturally sensitive are likely to be able to be offered with little modification on a global basis. However, products that are culturally sensitive may need to be designed so that a base product which is capable of modification in the overseas market to enhance its acceptability is offered. In some cases 'born global' firms need a reference client in an overseas market before they have the credibility to sell in their domestic market.

Designing global products is very much a concern of transnational companies. No longer is the focus on the Italian subsidiary designing products for the Italian market, the German subsidiary designing for the German market and the Malaysian subsidiary designing products for the Malaysian market, but rather on a global product to which each subsidiary contributes according to the relative advantage each has to offer. The Italian subsidiary in this example might contribute the design, the German subsidiary the R&D and the Malaysian subsidiary the labour-intensive elements of the manufacture. Another advantage of this new approach is that experience and technology are able to be more rapidly transferred between subsidiaries as the desire of each subsidiary to 'protect its own turf' is lessened.

To date, the discussion in this chapter, when referring to product, has generally treated it as synonymous with consumer goods. Industrial products are widely marketed between countries and have features additional to those mentioned above. These must be taken into account if international marketing efforts for industrial goods are to be successful.

# MARKETING INDUSTRIAL PRODUCTS OVERSEAS

## Industrial products

Firms marketing industrial products internationally face similar problems to those encountered when marketing consumer goods overseas. However, these firms also face a number of problems unique to industrial products; these problems in part derive from the different nature of industrial marketing.

Demand for industrial products is characterised by four features. The first of these is that industrial products are usually purchased for reuse in creating other products. It may well be that the product is also a consumer good in some applications, for example a computer. However, the intent behind the purchase is important. When the product is purchased to create another product it is an industrial product. When selling products to industrial buyers as opposed to consumers different marketing campaigns are needed.

The second feature is that demand for industrial products is usually derived from consumer demand for a particular product. As a result, demand tends to fluctuate more widely than demand for consumer goods. This is because firms such as Holden use forecasts of consumer demand for vehicles to make decisions about their purchase of industrial components. Often the industrial buyer seeks to purchase a system, rather than a single product, to solve a problem/address an issue. This requires suppliers to collaborate.

The third feature of demand for industrial products is that it is often reciprocal—two companies may buy and sell to each other at the same time. As an example, a producer of ceramic components for brick-making machinery may be expected to purchase raw materials such as kiln bricks from a firm owned by the brick manufacturer. Associated with this is the concept of networking that was discussed in detail in Chapter 12. Frequently transactions take place between firms within a network of established relationships.

A final demand feature is that, with industrial goods, demand often rests in the hands of a few buyers only. This is particularly the case where investment in a process is high or technology very advanced, as in the aircraft industry. In these circumstances industrial marketers experience a high volume of demand per customer, with the value of individual transactions being higher than with consumer goods.

As a consequence of the above demand features industrial buyers value service, performance and reliability as well as cost. In overseas markets environmental aspects such as the level of economic development are also major determinants of both the nature and level of demand for industrial products.

These features are also likely to influence the way industrial products are marketed overseas, especially the way industrial buying decisions are made, the industrial buying situation and the unique features of marketing industrial products overseas. As a consequence, internationalisation in industrial marketing involves integrating networks and supply relationships across national borders.

# INDUSTRIAL BUYING DECISIONS

Whereas in consumer marketing the decision to purchase is usually made by the individual or the immediate family, in industrial marketing the decision is either made by a much wider group or is influenced by a wide range of people in the organisation. In some cases companies have purchasing committees which make the decision to purchase. Bonoma (1982) categorised those who make or influence decisions relating to the purchase of industrial products as follows:

- *initiator*: the person who makes the initial request for the product such as the foreperson on the factory floor;

- *decider*: the individual (or group) who formally decides what product to buy;

- *influencer*: those within the organisation who influence buying decisions. They can be located in a variety of different sections, from sales to accounts, to R&D to production;

- *gatekeeper*: the person who controls access to those who make or influence purchasing decisions. For an executive this may be a secretary, and for a person on the factory floor or in the laboratory it may be a supervisor;

- *user*: the person who uses the product; and

- *purchaser*: the person who agrees to the purchase and negotiates the terms of sale. Often this is the purchasing department.

In international marketing, the problem is how to reach those parties when they are located offshore. Because of this difficulty it is important that the network of agents and distributors established in the target overseas market have contacts at all levels and lobby for the Australian or New Zealand firm's interests.

# INDUSTRIAL BUYING SITUATION

Buying decision making is likely to be influenced by the nature of the purchase. In general, the less routine and the larger the purchase, the more people are likely to be involved in making and influencing it. There are three categories of buying situations, all of which influence decision making for industrial products in the international market:

1. *extensive problem solving*: This usually applies when the buying situation is unique or unusual such as with a one-time purchase of an expensive piece of capital equipment. In this situation there is unlikely to be any initial preference for a supplier.

2. *limited problem solving*: This usually involves industrial products of considerable importance to the buyer on technical or financial grounds. The buyer usually has had some experience with purchasing these products previously and there tends to be supplier preferences. With these products partially structured purchasing procedures are likely to be in place.

3. *routinised purchasing behaviour*: This applies when products are purchased on an ongoing basis. Supplier preferences are well established and purchasing procedures are likely to be well structured. Raw materials inputs and standardised products such as stationery purchases typify products in this category.

# Features of the international market for industrial products

There are a number of unique features of international markets for industrial products. The most important are summarised below:

- *Different characteristics of buyers*: While it can be argued in general that cultural and other local differences are likely to be more important with consumer than with industrial products, in Asian countries cultural norms can also be very important in industrial procurement. This is especially the case with those countries where relationships are considered to be equally if not more important than price, functionality or quality.

- *Overseas market potential*: The levels of economic development and industrialisation in other countries can be critical factors in the demand for industrial products. The existence of an abundance of cheap labour will influence demand for products such as capital plant.

- *Targeting decision makers*: This is complicated in other countries because it is often difficult to pinpoint who is involved in the decision-making process. In Asian countries many buyers are family-owned companies which compounds the problem.

- *Government control*: Foreign governments exercise control over supply from offshore for security, protectionist, political or revenue reasons. The nature of the regime in the overseas country also determines the extent to which the government is a major purchaser of industrial products. In some countries there are very close relationships between business and government as in Japan and this can affect the ability of the Australian or New Zealand firm to supply products in competition with local sources.

- *Service support*: The need for service support varies greatly for different types of industrial goods. For this reason selling industrial products requiring high levels of support will create problems in countries such as Libya, where the available level of such support is basic.

- *Direct contact between buyer and seller*: In cases where the supplier does not operate in the overseas country there will be a need for an intermediary between buyer and seller in than market. This will reduce the likelihood of direct contact between buyer and seller with the result that there will be a reduction in the degree of control that the Australian or New Zealand firm is able to exercise over the marketing of its industrial products overseas.

- *Terms of sale*: Because costs of industrial products tend to be higher than with consumer goods and the contracts may cover a longer period of time, the critical factors in the terms of sale in overseas markets may extend beyond price and include credit terms and countertrade proposals.

When marketing industrial products overseas it is necessary to segment the market so as to ensure reaching those customers to whom the technology is the most relevant and to identify those customers a firm merely wishes to sell to as opposed to those with whom it wishes to form a long-term relationship. Criteria for segmentation of international markets for industrial products include industry, firm size, operating characteristics, purchasing modes and personal characteristics of buying decision makers and influencers.

Morgan and Katsikeas (1998, p. 173) found that manufacturers of industrial products need to regularly visit export markets so as to develop 'in-depth' relationships with those that both make and influence purchasing decisions; ensure that their relationships with intermediaries result in a 'win–win' outcome for all parties; use specialised salespeople with successful track records in doing business overseas, and avoid markets subject to rapid changes in exchange rates due to the longer-term nature of contracts for supply of industrial products.

Apart from direct involvement, manufacturers of industrial products can internationalise by following their customers abroad and, for example, supplying them in Indonesia with the same inputs as they do in Australia or New Zealand and by integrating their activities into the supply chains of trans-national firms so that their goods are supplied not only to the plants in Australia and New Zealand, but also to the plants the transnational operates in other parts of the world, as is often the case in the automotive industry.

## 13.4 INTERNATIONAL HIGHLIGHT

## A James Hardie assault

Since 1990 James Hardie Industries (JHI) has transformed its diversified business of energy, electronics, services and building products around its core competencies in the fibre cement business. While the Australian market has become subject to pricing pressures from competitors and a decline in overall residential construction, JHI has made successful inroads into the large US building materials market as well as entry into Asia, primarily through its fibre cement business in the Philippines. It has captured 90% of the fibre cement market in the USA, with sales of US$1.2 billion.

JHI is the lowest cost and most profitable producer of fibre cement in the USA. Its growth in recent years has seen JHI become the leading producer of siding in the USA. Its products are primarily used in residential construction for the exterior and interior of homes. The James Hardie US fibre cement business is continuing to expand. JHI implemented the largest ever expansion of capacity to meet the growing demand and more new products have been launched. This followed a strategy of more than 10 years in the USA offering the unique Australian fibre cement product range with localised pricing, advertising and distribution.

The longer-term outlook for JHI in the Philippines remains positive with sales running at US$242 million, although sales volumes in the near term are below targets. Plans for a fibre cement plant in Indonesia have been deferred. Recently, however, the image of the company has been tarnished in Australia by its action in incorporating itself in the Netherlands in a way that minimises its liability for compensating those suffering from ill-health as a result of using or being exposed to its asbestos products. It remains to be seen whether this negative image will affect its operations and markets outside Australia.

**SOURCE:** *Based on James Hardie Australia website (2007), <http://www.jameshardie.com.au/AboutUs>.*

# BRANDING AND PACKAGING FOR OVERSEAS MARKETS

Branding and packaging are two important additional issues related to the international marketing of products that need to be taken into account when modifying products for overseas markets. A brand is a name, term, symbol, sign, design or combination of these, created with the objective of differentiating the offering from those of competitors. A brand can reduce the search costs for the buyer also.

## Branding

Brand names are a critical element in making an impact on the customer. Should there be one international brand or different brands for each market? If the company uses its own brands, it may want to use multiple brands in the same overseas market to target different customer segments as it does in Australia or New Zealand. However, if the brand name does not travel well and create positive images in the mind of the overseas customer, modification of the brand name will be necessary. A major issue is whether to promote local country-specific brands or establish global and regional brands with appeal across countries.

In countries where the language is ideographic (word pictures) English brand names will require change; for example, in China the translation gives an international brand not just a Chinese name, but also a distinctive local image. In part, this is because in China brands have historically been used as vehicles for conveying social distinctions in an environment where social class divisions have been ambiguous due to the rapid rise and fall of family wealth. In these circumstances, there was a need for material symbols to both indicate status and cement social relationships.

A good brand name in Chinese should have desirable connotations, desirable sound and tonal associations and attractive calligraphy. Chinese native speakers tend to encode verbal information in a 'visual mental code' according to Fan (2001), whereas English native speakers rely more on a 'phonological code' and judge a brand name based on whether the name sounds appealing. Often there can be a paradox between the global brand and the image that the translated version creates.

When the former Ansett Airlines of Australia commenced its service to Hong Kong a decade ago, it was surprised to discover that the Chinese strongly disliked the name Ansett. Inquiry revealed that the word Ansett, when translated, meant 'to die peacefully', which was not regarded as a confidence-building name for an airline! A new translation which meant 'safe and fast' was created.

Obviously there is a need to use ideographs which create a favourable image for the product. As Fan (2001) points out, this situation also provides an opportunity to treat the renaming as a value-adding process and create a unique global–local image that enhances the original brand equity.

## BUILDING GLOBAL BRANDS

Building a global brand also usually involves creating or having a partially or totally standardised product. Its success depends on a growing convergence of consumer tastes and the coordination of global promotion. One of the advantages of global branding is economies of scale in advertising—a uniform image appeals to globe-trotting consumers. Global brands are also important in accessing the best distribution channels and intermediaries in other countries. In developing global brands it is necessary to decide what brand image to project. This is often referred to as the brand's personality. Research by Roth (1995) found that in countries where the degree of separation between high- and low-power-distance individuals in great (as in China), brand images should stress social and sensory needs. In individualistic cultures, brands should have unique, distinct and consistent characteristics whereas in collectivist cultures, the brand personality should be projected as part of the wider social environment. This is reflected in the fact that, whereas Western-based companies have concentrated on promoting product brands, Asian companies have tended to promote corporate brands (de Mooij 2004, p. 97).

Quelch (1999, pp. 2–3) proposes six measures by which a brand might be judged as global. These are:

1 it dominates the domestic market, which generates cash flow to enter new markets;

2 it meets a universal consumer need;

3 it demonstrates balanced country-market coverage;

4 it reflects a consistent positioning worldwide;

5 it benefits from positive country of origin image; and

6 the focus is on the product category.

Even with multinational firms with a reputation for global brands, few have the same brands in all markets in which they operate and many of their brands are available in one country only, as shown in Table 13.1.

## MODIFICATION OF BRAND NAMES

Czinkota and Ronkainen (2004, p. 261) refer to the work of NameLab of California which offers the following suggestions in connection with checking the appropriateness of a brand name in an overseas market:

- *translation*: Translate the local brand name directly into the foreign language. Although this is achievable with languages using the same script as English, problems arise with languages that use ideographic script such as Japanese or Mandarin.

- *transliteration*: Test the local brand name to see if it denotes the same meaning in another country as it does in Australia or New Zealand. Whereas in Australia Coca-Cola has no meaning in itself, in China it means 'tasty and happy'.

- *transparency*: This avoids the brand-name problems of transliteration, translation and prior registration of trademarks by developing an essentially meaningless brand name. Victa is an example.

---

**TABLE 13.1   Brands of six multinational companies in 67 countries**

| Company | Total no. of brands | Brands found in 50% or more countries | | Brands in only one country | |
|---|---|---|---|---|---|
| | | Number | % of total | Number | % of total |
| Colgate | 163 | 6 | 4 | 59 | 36 |
| Kraft GF | 238 | 6 | 3 | 104 | 44 |
| Nestlé | 560 | 19 | 4 | 250 | 45 |
| P&G | 217 | 18 | 8 | 80 | 37 |
| Quaker | 143 | 2 | 1 | 55 | 38 |
| Unilever | 471 | 17 | 4 | 236 | 50 |
| Total | 1792 | 68 | 4 | 784 | 44 |

**SOURCE:** *Boze, B.V. and Patton, C.R. (1995) 'The future of consumer branding as seen from the picture today',* Journal of Consumer Marketing, *Vol. 12, No. 4, p. 22. Reproduced with permission from Emerald Group Publishing.*

## 13.5 INTERNATIONAL HIGHLIGHT

# Global branding and emerging markets

China is dominating world manufacturing because of its low-cost labour. To date most of its companies have been content to be original equipment manufacturers (OEMs) supplying the world's biggest brands and retailers' private labels. The government is now urging firms to sell branded goods abroad instead because branded products can be more profitable than generics. A focus on branded goods will also help China move away from its current image as a producer of cheap goods. Some companies have already established a reputation in emerging markets for their own brands in product categories such as domestic appliances, consumer electronics and motorcycles. Companies involved include Haier (appliances), Legend (computers), Kenjian (mobile phones) and SVA (plasma televisions). In so doing these companies face a substantial challenge. The issue is not whether they can make the grade in terms of product features and quality, but rather whether they can develop marketing strategies for branded products. Some firms have already begun to export to developed markets in an attempt to get their leading edge products in front of consumers so as to create an image for their brands. In 2002, Chinese firms such as SVA exported 33% of their product (turnover US$3.2 billion), Midea 27% (turnover US$1.3 billion), and Haier 11% (turnover US$8.6 billion).

In the case of Haier, initially the company attempted to enter the US market by offering to purchase an American firm, Maytag, that had well-established brands such as Hoover. When this failed, Haier was faced with the challenge of marketing its own brand internationally. As part of its new thrust towards a globalised brand strategy, the firm is now constructing an R&D centre in Sydney to create and test whitegoods models for Western markets to be marketed under its own brand. The firm is also building up awareness of its brand in the US by tapping market niches based on technology innovation where local firms do not have a strong presence. Examples of such niches are small refrigerators for dorm rooms and free-standing wine cellars holding around 30 bottles.

SOURCES: *Adapted from Gao, P., Woetzel, R. and Wu, Y. (2003) 'Can Chinese brands make it abroad?',* The McKinsey Quarterly Special Edition: Global Directions; *'Haier goals',* New York Times, *20 November 2005, p. 38; and Chong, F. (2006) 'Why China must have world class brands',* Asia Today International, *April, pp. 14–16.*

* *transculture*: because the product category has a foreign image that is associated with desirable attributes, the brand name used is a foreign word associated with the country having a positive image for the product category. The use of a French word such as 'Poisson' as a brand name for perfumes is an example.

## BRAND NAME STRATEGIES

For a firm operating in a number of markets or on a global basis, a range of options is available:

* *Use the same brand name worldwide.* This is appropriate when the company markets one product and has wide international distribution for it. This approach works when there is no conflict between the brand name and the culture of different countries. 'Pepsi' is an example of this. The use of a single brand name worldwide both creates customer identification and results in savings in promotion costs.

* *Modify the brand name in each market.* This is appropriate when the marketing strategy is to identify with the local market. While the same brand name is used, add-on words create local identification, for example coffee called 'Nescafé' and shampoo called 'Sunsilk'.

- *Use different names in different markets.* This is necessary when the brand name cannot be translated into the local language or when the firm wishes to create a local identity. Often local brands are adopted as a result of acquisition. These may have a strong local loyalty due to promotion by the previous owners; for example, Unilever markets the Streets brand of ice-cream in Australia and the Wall's brand in most other countries. It acquired Streets in the early 1960s.

- *Use the company name as a brand name.* Many firms use standard trademarks for all their products and allow the use of local brand names in different countries. These trademarks, which can take the form of letters, symbols and logos, act as a form of corporate identification. Because the trademark is identified with both the product and the company it often conveys a stronger corporate message to the consumer than the brand by itself. When successfully undertaken, this approach can create an umbrella that lends strength to the individual brands and creates the impression of strong corporate identity, for example the 3M company.

One of the benefits of global branding is brand equity—the value attributed to the firm because of the brands it owns. With well-known brands such as Coca-Cola the value placed on the brand may well exceed the value of the firm's assets many times. However, Rust et al. (2004) argue that brands exist to serve customers and what is really of value is customer equity rather than brand equity. As customers vary widely from international market to international market, the value of the brand is unlikely to be the same in all markets as customers may have widely differing perceptions of the value of the brand. For this reason, in international marketing brands should be built around customer segments, not the other way around.

Over recent years global brands have become the target of anti-globalisation protests: demonstrators smashed the windows of McDonald's in Davos (World Economic Summit) and stomped on Coke cans in Seattle (World Trade Organization meeting). According to Holt et al. (2004) this has had a negative impact on the onward march of global brands. As a consequence many marketers of global brands have shifted their focus to striving for global scale in backroom activities such as technology, production and organisation, but are tailoring 'front of house' activities such as product features, communication, distribution and selling approaches to local consumer tastes. These authors recently conducted a study of global brands and concluded that with these brands, quality signal (the more who buy a brand, the better the quality is likely to be), global myth (global brands as symbols of cultural ideals) and social responsibility (firms willing to address social problems linked to what they sell and how they conduct their business) were most important and American values were not important.

# Packaging and labelling

The main function of packaging is to ensure that the product gets to its intended recipient in a serviceable shape and pleasing form. It provides:

- *protection*: Protecting the product is particularly important in international marketing as the product usually travels longer distances, is handled and transferred more frequently and its transit involves changes in both climate and temperature to a greater extent than in the Australian or New Zealand markets. The degree to which packaging will need to be different for exported products will depend on transit time, mode of transport and transportation conditions. Another problem affecting packaging requirements is the higher incidence of pilfering in a number of overseas markets.

Although containerisation has reduced this, pilfering can still occur at the stage when the container is opened for inspection on arrival at the overseas port. Clear handling instructions in both English and the languages used at the transit points as well at the final destination will facilitate safe handling. The use of universal symbols, such as a glass to denote 'fragile', is becoming increasingly common.

- *promotion*: Packaging can also act as a vehicle for promoting the product or the company's image in overseas markets. The same cultural sensitivities that are taken into account with labelling should also be observed when designing the outer package. The size and the shape of the package can be important for those markets where the goods are displayed in or sold from the outer container and where the package in an empty or after-use form still has value. There should be consistency between the colours, messages and logos used on both the product and the outer packaging so as to maximise the packaging's promotional value.

- *convenience*: This applies to both intermediaries in the overseas distribution channel and the final consumer. For the intermediary convenience is a matter of ease of handling, ease in opening to facilitate bulk-breaking, conformity to shelf layouts, efficient pricing and retail labelling and protection of the product. From the consumer's point of view, the package should be one that is easy to carry or shift, is aesthetically pleasing and, where appropriate, has use or assembly instructions that are clearly illustrated or written in the consumer's language. The packaging should be in a form that is compatible with storage facilities in the user's household. For example, in countries where refrigerators are not the norm or are very small a six-pack is not a convenient way of packaging beverages.

Another aspect of packaging in international marketing concerns environmentalism. There is increasing concern as to the environmental implications of disposing of packaging materials. This is particularly the case in the more-developed countries where the volume of packaging generated has increased in line with the greater focus on elaborate packaging as a form of marketing. The European Union, led by Germany, wants to reduce the amount of packaging material that is generated and increase the recycling of the essential packaging that remains. Its requirements initially were that 60% of all packaging material must be recyclable and now the figure that applies is 90%. These regulations affect Australian and New Zealand firms marketing their products to countries in the European Union.

There are a number of areas where governments impose regulations on packaging. Regulations mostly relate to labelling and marking and are designed both to inform and protect consumers. These vary from country to country as indicated by 'warnings' on cigarette packets. The languages used on packages are often prescribed by governments, as is the form in which volume or weight of contents should be indicated. Government regulations may specify that a list of ingredients is shown on the pack and the manner in which this must be shown also varies between countries.

The use of multiple languages in the labelling of products in international marketing is a primary consideration in providing information to consumers. Regulations in many countries require that detailed product composition and nutritional data be provided, as well as a warning of any hazards that might ensue from the use of the product. Firms may wish to provide instructions for correct assembly or use which have implications for how the message is communicated on the label. In these cases, simply translating the text from English into the other language is unlikely to be sufficient. In some countries, such as Canada, information on the label is required to be in all official languages used in a country or a region. Often this can result in crowded or impractical labels, with the result that manufacturers are increasingly using icons, diagrams and cartoons to instruct consumers in the use of their products. These regulations impose significant costs on exporters and indirectly act as a form of protection. In line with the reduction of tariffs to free up the flow of trade, discussions are now taking place to arrive at more standardised labelling requirements internationally as is evidenced by recent moves in the wine industry.

# The internet and marketing products overseas

The internet leads to faster discovery of customer needs, greater customisation of products to customer needs and shorter product life cycles. According to Craig et al. (2000), there will be three categories of products in the internet environment:

- *physical products*: With physical products (e.g. cosmetics), information search can be conducted online and in many countries, but completion of the transaction either requires the consumer to go to a physical location to purchase the product or for the product to be delivered to the consumer in a given location. In this case, the final stage of the transaction relies on traditional market infrastructure and the merchant relies on physical infrastructure to deliver the goods (e.g. Amazon.com's warehouses in each major geographic region);

- *transaction-related products*: With transaction-related products (services such as rental cars, air tickets), information search is conducted online, but actual consumption is tied to a given time and location. Although delivery of a physical product is not involved, an organisational infrastructure is needed to ensure delivery at the time and location requested (e.g. at the airport check-in desk).

- *virtual products*: With virtual products (such as music, software, news broadcasts) there is no physical location and consumption is anywhere in the world. There are no physical or geographic constraints to search, transaction or consumption. Table 13.2 provides a typology for each of these categories of product.

Figure 13.2 shows the physical value chain. By contrast, Figure 13.3 shows the value chain for e-business and indicates that with e-business, between the inventory and fulfilment logistics phases, there are two intermediate steps on the platform for conducting e-business and ensuring that the transaction is processed in a secure manner.

Figure 13.4 illustrates that when e-business crosses national borders, the intermediate steps in the e-business value chain become more complicated as do the subsequent stages of fulfilment logistics and support. These complications reflect the environmental variables discussed in Part A of the textbook.

### TABLE 13.2 Internet product typology

| | PRODUCT TYPE | | |
|---|---|---|---|
| Key Dimensions | Physical products | Transaction-related products | Virtual products |
| Ease of reaching a global segment | Difficult | Moderate | Easy |
| Degree of product standardisation | Varies | Moderate | Customised |
| Role of information | Complement | Enhancement | Equivalent |
| Role of infrastructure | Infrastructure constrained | Conforms to infrastructure | Unconstrained by infrastructure |

SOURCE: *Craig, C.S., Douglas, S.P. and Flaherty, T.B. (2000) 'Information access and internationalisation–the internet and consumer behaviour in international markets',* Proceedings of the eCommerce and Global Business Forum, *Santa Cruz, CA, 17–19 May, Andersen Consulting Institute for Strategic Change.*

### FIGURE 13.2 The physical value chain

SOURCE: *Plumley, B.J. (2000)* Global e-Commerce: The Market, Challenges and Opportunities, *Browne Global Solutions, Irvine, CA.*

### FIGURE 13.3 The e-business value chain

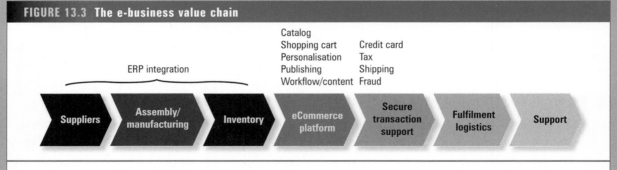

SOURCE: *Plumley, B.J. (2000)* Global e-Commerce: The Market, Challenges and Opportunities, *Browne Global Solutions, Irvine, CA.*

In the case of business to business transactions on line, as shown in Figure 13.5, the customer (top left) accesses the website and orders equipment. As part of this process, the customer accesses applications on the site as well as internal data from the company. These processes ensure that the customer is ordering a viable configuration of equipment and that the necessary parts are available.

The transaction flows directly into the company's own system. Payment information is sent to the appropriate bank and the transaction processing system (middle of the figure) exchanges the necessary information with the company's customer database, product database and financial/billing databases.

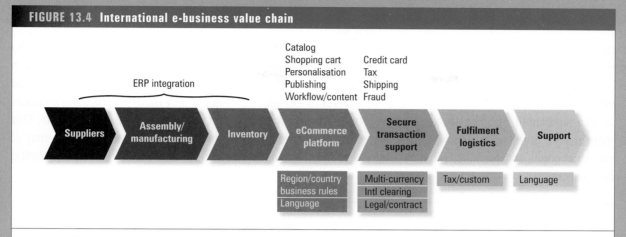

**FIGURE 13.4  International e-business value chain**

**SOURCE:** *Plumley, B.J. (2000)* Global e-Commerce: The Market, Challenges and Opportunities, *Browne Global Solutions, Irvine, CA.*

If the customer has questions, they too can be directed to the website. This then transmits them to the customer service centre, which also has access to customer, product and billing data and can respond appropriately.

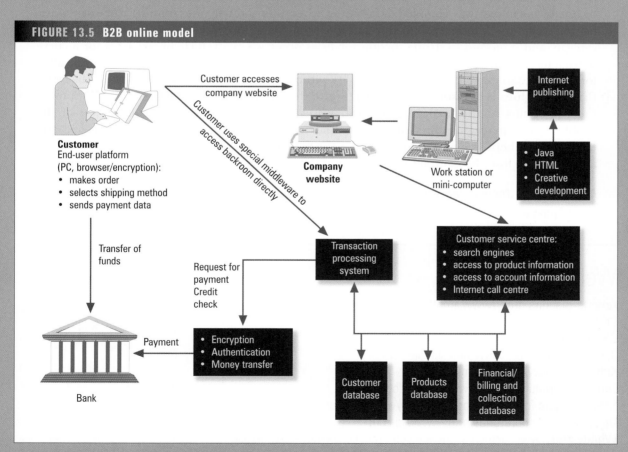

**FIGURE 13.5  B2B online model**

# Summary

Developing a strategy to embrace international as well as domestic markets is one of the challenges faced by the firm when management decides to engage in international business. The strategic marketing approach of the firm no longer is focused just on the Australian or New Zealand market, but is also focused on the international markets. Tailoring products to suit overseas markets requires not only modifying existing products to improve their fit, but also developing new products from scratch to meet specific offshore requirements. This may involve creating a global product. There are a number of unique issues relating to the marketing of industrial goods and services, and these need to be taken into account as do specific issues relating to branding and packaging.

## ETHICS ISSUE

James Johnson is the director of product development for Australia's only manufacturer of automobile axles. Johnson's company received a large contract from Malaysia six months ago to manufacture axles to be used in a new line of four-wheel-drive vehicles, which are to be introduced to the market by the Proton company. The contract is vital to Johnson's firm, which has recently fallen on hard times due to import competition. Just before receiving this contract half the employees, including Johnson, were scheduled for indefinite layoff. Final testing of the transaxle assemblies was completed. However, when Johnson began examining the test reports he noted that the transaxles tended to fail when both were loaded at more than 20% over rated capacity and subjected to strong torsion forces as occur when a vehicle breaks hard for a curve down a mountain road. Although the specifications accompanying the order from Proton called for transaxles to carry 130% of rated capacity without failing, Johnson knows that the Malaysian firm has no means of testing the transaxles once they have arrived in Malaysia. Johnson showed the test results to the managing director, who indicated that he was already aware of the problem. The managing director advised that, given the low likelihood of occurrence and the fact that there was no time to redesign the assembly, he had decided to ignore the report as they would lose the contract if they did not deliver on time.

*If you were James Johnson, would you show the results to the Malaysian automobile manufacturer?*

## Websites

Arnotts Biscuits http://www.arnotts.com.au
Cotton Seed Distributors http://www.csd.net.au/
CSIRO http://www.csiro.au
James Hardie http://www.jameshardie.com.au
Kirby http://www.kirbyjn.com.au
Lennox International http://www.lennox.com
Search engine for Asian products http://www.asianproducts.com
Underwriters Laboratories http://www.ul.com
Whittle http://www.gemcomsoftware.com./products/Whittle.default/asp

# Discussion questions

1 Prepare a matrix showing the following countries along the horizontal axis: Canada, Vietnam, Thailand and Japan. On the vertical axis list each of the six factors to be taken into account when redefining the business and considering overseas markets. In the cells indicate how these factors would differ for each of the four countries.

2 How would leveraging capabilities with respect to the Indonesian market differ between an Australian/New Zealand producer of computer software and an Australian/New Zealand manufacturer of automotive parts?

3 Modifying a product to facilitate its sale overseas will involve extra costs. To what extent are these costs discretionary and how would you assess whether the costs are worthwhile?

4 For what kinds of products do you expect customer needs to be worldwide? Why?

5 In what ways does the product's packaging need changing when the product is being marketed in another country?

6 You have been asked to develop a product for sale throughout the ASEAN region. What are the criteria you would apply in the development process and what are the stages from conceptualisation to market introduction?

7 What factors decide whether the same product can be marketed in each ASEAN country and whether modifications are necessary?

# References

Ambler, T. and Styles, C. (2000) *The Silk Road to International Marketing–Profit and Passion in Global Business*, Prentice Hall, London.

Bonoma, T.V. (1982) 'Major sales: who really does the buying?', *Harvard Business Review*, May–June.

Boze, B.V. and Patton, C.R. (1995) 'The future of consumer branding as seen from the picture today', *Journal of Consumer Marketing*, Vol. 12, No. 4, pp. 20–41.

Bradley, F. (2004), *International Marketing Strategy*, 4th edn, Financial Times Prentice Hall, Harlow, UK.

Butler, G. (1998) *Australian Financial Review*, 14 May, p. 34.

Chong, F. (2006) 'Why China must have world class brands', *Asia Today International*, April, pp. 14–16.

Craig, C.S., Douglas, S.P. and Flaherty, T.B. (2000) 'Information access and internationalisation—the internet and consumer behaviour in international markets', *Proceedings of the eCommerce and Global Business Forum*, Santa Cruz, CA, 17–19 May, Andersen Consulting Institute for Strategic Change.

Czinkota, M.R. and Kotabe, M. (1990) 'Product development the Japanese way', *The Journal of Business Strategy*, November–December.

Czinkota, M.R. and Ronkainen, I.A. (2004) *International Marketing*, 7th edn, Thomson South Western, Ohio.

De Mooij, M. (2004) *Consumer Behaviour and Culture–Consequences for Global Marketing and Advertising*, Sage Publications, Thousand Oaks, California.

Fan, Y. (2001) 'The national image of global brands', *Proceedings of the Academy of Marketing Conference*, Cardiff, 2–4 July, University of Cardiff.

Gao, P., Woetzel, R. and Wu, Y. (2003) 'Can Chinese brands make it abroad?', *The McKinsey Quarterly Special Edition: Global Directions*.

'Haier goals', *New York Times*, 20 November 2005, p. 38.

Holt, D.B., Quelch, J.A. and Taylor, E.L. (2004) 'How global brands compete', *Harvard Business Review*, September, pp. 68–75.

Jacob, R. (1994) 'The big rise: middle classes explode around the globe', *Fortune*, 30 May.

Keegan, W.J. and Green, M.C. (2005) *Global Marketing*, 4th edn, Pearson Prentice Hall, NJ.

Kotler, P., Keller, K.L., Ang, S.H., Leong, S.M. and Tan, C.T. (2006) *Marketing Management—an Asian Perspective*, Pearson Prentice Hall, Singapore.

Levitt, T. (1983) 'The globalisation of markets', *Harvard Business Review*, May–June.

Morgan, R.E. and Katsikeas, C. (1998) 'Exporting problems of industrial manufacturers', *Industrial Marketing Management*, Vol 27, pp. 161–76.

Onkvisit, S. and Shaw, J.J. (1983) 'An examination of the international product life cycle and its applications within marketing', *Columbia Journal of World Business*, Fall.

Plumley, B.J. (2000) *Global e-Commerce: The Market, Challenges and Opportunities*, Browne Global Solutions, Irvine, CA.

Porter, M. (1990) *The Competing Advantage of Nations*, Macmillan, London, p. 41.

Quelch, J. (1999) 'Global brands: taking stock', *Business Strategy Review*, Vol. 10, No. 1, pp. 1–14.

Robinson, D. (1961) 'The challenge of underdeveloped national markets', *Journal of Marketing*, October.

Roth, M.S. (1995) 'The effects of culture and socio-economics on the performance of global brand image strategies', *Journal of Marketing Research*, May, pp. 163–75.

Rust, R.T., Zeithaml, V.A. and Lemon, K.N. (2004) 'Customer-centred brand management', *Harvard Business Review*, September, pp. 110–14.

## go online

Go online to <www.pearsoned.com.au/fletcher> to find more case studies.

CASE STUDY 13

# 'Green' international wine marketing

**Mary Pugh and Richard Fletcher**

*The Banrock Station brand, owned by wine producer BRL Hardy, has been highly successful in the UK and USA, and in the Australian premium wine market. In part, success has arisen from the positive attributes of being a New World wine, but this case study shows that it is its branding as a 'green' wine that supports the conservation activities that have given Banrock Station a distinctive edge. The experience of BRL Hardy points to a number of key lessons in international marketing that may help other companies break free from the competitive pack.*

## INTRODUCTION

One of the major challenges facing Australian firms in the international marketplace is how to differentiate their products from those of competitors. This case explores the challenges facing BRL Hardy Ltd of Australia and how it met the challenge in a global wine market that is highly competitive and characterised by multiple players, labels and products.

Although Australia has captured only a small percentage of the world's wine market, Australian wines are the fastest growing import category in key markets such as the UK and USA, stealing market share from traditional Old World wine producers such as France, Italy, Germany and Spain. Australia's success to date stems not only from its comparative advantage of producing quality wines at reasonable prices, but from the ability of Australian wine companies to build brands to compete internationally.

This case study demonstrates that BRL Hardy has identified a unique global market segment of a wine targeted at the environmentally conscious. The case covers the initial stages of the implementation of the strategy to position its BRL Hardy's Banrock Station brand of wines in the environmentally conscious segment, through to a promotional program of 'green' international wine marketing.

## BACKGROUND

BRL Hardy Ltd was formed after the 1992 merger of South Australian-based wineries Berri Renmano Ltd and Thomas Hardy and Sons Pty Ltd. It is one of the top wine producers in Australia and one of the largest wine groups in the world. Its Banrock Station brand, produced from grapes grown mostly in the Riverland region of South Australia, is the star of the company's wine portfolio. The first wine stock was produced as recently as 1995, and now production is 2.4 million cases a year.

In 1994 BRL Hardy acquired Banrock Station with 250 hectares of good soil for producing premium grape varieties. The rest of the property is made up of 900 hectares of wetland and 600 hectares of protected Mallee Woodland ecosystem. The property was suffering from the impact of prolonged farming and grazing. BRL Hardy, together with Wetland Care Australia, undertook

Banrock Station wines postcard

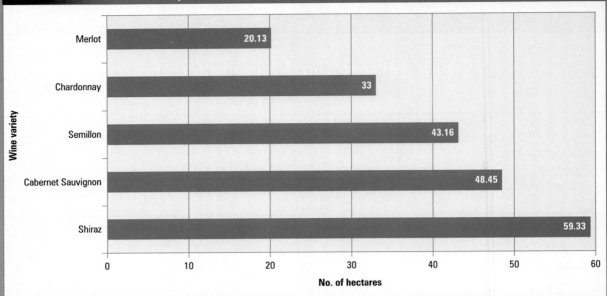

FIGURE 1 Banrock Station major wine varieties

a huge revegetation program to remove stock, install fish barriers and reintroduce natural wetting and drying cycles in the wetland. This has resulted in the native birds and fish, water plants, frogs and insects returning to restore the health of the River Murray.

The 250 hectares of new vineyard is used to produce five major wine varieties. As Figure 1 shows, red wines are more favoured than white wine varieties.

The vineyard's total yield per year was then 5000 tonnes, which converts to 3 500 000 litres of wine, or 380 000 cases. The additional tonnage required to meet domestic and export demand of more than two million cases came from purchasing grapes from other local producers in the Riverland.

## AUSTRALIA AND THE GLOBAL WINE MARKET

In the late 1990s, market conditions were ripe for Australian wine producers to increase exports. The Old World wine producers such as France and Italy, which had historically held a large market share of the global export market, were in decline. In 1997 France accounted for 41.7%, Italy 17.2% and Spain 9.2% of world wine exports by

value as shown in Table 1. In total these Old World producers represented 68% of the export wine market by value. Although this differs on a volume basis, the picture is much the same with France accounting for 26%, Italy 23% and Spain 14% of the volume of wine exported. However, it is the New World wine producers such as Australia, New Zealand, Chile and South Africa which were experiencing growth. While holding only a relatively small market share of export volume, they were stealing share from the Old World producers.

Following centuries of quality wine being associated with Old World wine producers, Australian wines were at the forefront of a new consumer trend led by New World producers—the supply of good quality, good value, ready to drink, good tasting fruity wines. As Table 1 shows, in 1997 Australia was ranked number four on export value and was the market leader in New World wines.

Australia's remarkable success in the UK market was being demonstrated by delivering wine products that were relevant to everyday living and enjoyed by all. The wine brand 'Australia' was leveraging the effect of country of origin image (Ahmed and D'Astous 1996) in

## TABLE 1 — 1997 world wine export value

| Country | Export value as a % of world wine exports | Old or New World wines |
|---|---|---|
| 1. France | 41.7 | Old |
| 2. Italy | 17.2 | Old |
| 3. Spain | 19.2 | Old |
| 4. Australia | 14.8 | New |
| 5. Portugal | 14.3 | Old |
| 6. Germany | 13.8 | Old |
| 7. Chile | 13.6 | New |
| 8. USA | 13.3 | New |
| 9. Former Soviet Union | 13.2 | Old |
| 10. South Africa | 11.5 | New |

**SOURCE:** *Berger, N., Spahni, P. and Anderson, K. (1999)* Bilateral Trade Patterns in the World Wine Market 1988 to 1997: A Statistical Compendium, *Centre for International Economic Studies, University of Adelaide.*

transferring favourable perceptions of quality fruit and a relaxed lifestyle to its food and wine. This positioning in the UK and US markets stimulated demand for premium category wines (i.e. those that are categorised above basic 'good-quality/good-value' wines).

Australian wine exports have grown substantially since the mid-1980s. At the end of the 2000/01 financial year Australia exported 339 million litres, which was a 17% increase on the previous year. The export market volume for Australian wine is projected to double in size over the first decade of the millennium to 676 million litres, accounting for 61% of production compared to 47% at present. This is illustrated in Figure 2.

There are five key quality/price segments in the wine industry. The principal driving force behind increased export sales is considered to be in the branded premium wine segment, estimated to account for 34% of world wine sales.

## FIGURE 2 Australian domestic market versus international market growth

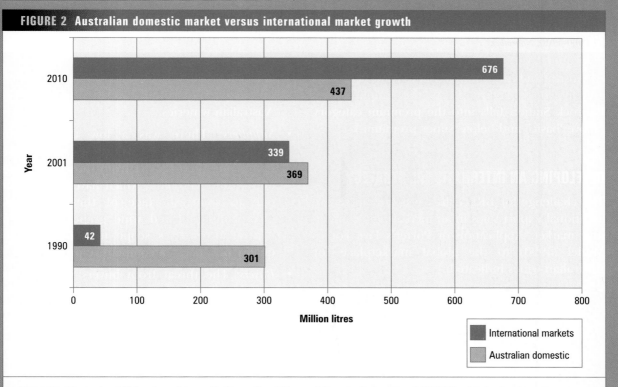

**SOURCE:** *Winemakers' Federation of Australia/Australian Wine and Brandy Corporation (2000)* The Marketing Decade 2000–2010, *November.*

brands exported to the USA. In the 13-week period ending 17 May 2001, Banrock Station's overall ranked position in the US market was 189th and it is the fastest growing brand in the BRL portfolio. Banrock Station is the number one fastest growing brand in the UK as shown in Table 3.

There is no doubt that much of this success has been due to the 'green' international wine marketing of Banrock Station wines. Future growth is dependent upon maintaining and building the brand through continued investment in conservation projects and the development of new markets with significant segments of environmentally friendly wine buyers.

## KEY LESSONS

The success of BRL's Banrock Station brand in the UK and US markets to date can be explained in part by its being a New World wine, priced in the attractive premium wine category with a country of origin image associated with sunshine, health and wide open spaces—an attractive image consistent with wine production. However, of themselves these New World wine characteristics do not explain Banrock Station wines' rapid rise in overseas sales, or their major market share among the Australian premium wine segment. Success is also due to the niche marketing strategy pursued by the firm of positioning the brand as a

'green' wine that supports conservation activities. This strategy has positioned the brand in a new marketspace that includes environmentally conscious consumers. This strategy appeals to a different set of values, and values not targeted by other wine producers. Although the magnitude of this segment may differ between countries, environmentally conscious consumers are a global segment that offers considerable potential for the future marketing of the Banrock Station brand.

The experience of BRL Hardy points to a number of other key lessons in international marketing that may help other companies also break free from the competitive pack. The first of these is that innovative marketing approaches are a useful vehicle for companies to create new overseas markets and/or reposition themselves in existing markets. BRL's approach was to look at its market from a new perspective and create new value for stakeholders in those markets. This was achieved by tapping into the values and beliefs of its customers and creating new product attributes to influence the purchasing decisions of customers. In this case it was by creating a brand associated with caring for the environment as illustrated by investing sales receipts back into conservation projects.

The second lesson relates to the need to pursue a strategy in depth rather than superficially if it is to be effective in overseas markets. In this case a

| TABLE 3 | UK brands top wines, 2000 listing | |
|---|---|---|
| **Brand** | **Company** | **Off trade % growth** |
| Ernest & Julio Gallo | E&J Gallo Winery | 22% |
| Jacob's Creek | Orlando Wyndham | 24.3% |
| Hardy | BRL Hardy Wine | 33.3% |
| Stowells of Chelsea | Matthew Clark | 28.1% |
| Rosemount | Rosemount Wine Estates | 69.1% |
| Lindemans | Southcorp Wines | 52.9% |
| Penfolds | Southcorp Wines | 2.8% |
| Blossom Hill | UDV | 143.3% |
| Le Piat D'or | Piat Pere Et Fils | (−14.6%) |
| Banrock Station | BRL Hardy Wines | 164.8% |

**SOURCE:** *Macquarie Bank Research (2001)* Essentials, *March.*

- *Substitutes*: Although there are other alcoholic products that compete with wine, wine was the fastest growing alcoholic beverage on a global basis. Australia has a comparative advantage in producing innovative, high-quality wines which, because they can be consumed without ageing, attract new wine consumers and young drinkers in Old World countries.

As illustrated in Figure 4, BRL countered the reaction of industry competitors to overseas market entry. BRL differentiated itself by pursuing a niche market strategy in its target overseas markets. This was achieved by positioning the Banrock Station brand initially in the two major markets of the UK and USA as a 'green' wine that supports conservation activities. This involved looking at the market from a different perspective and looking at areas to create value to differentiate the selected brand from the competitive pack. The key to discovering new value was asking four basic questions, as outlined in the Kim and Mauborgne model (1999) shown in Table 2.

Addressing these key questions allowed BRL to create 'Banrock Station'—a wine that was positioned as 'good wine, good earth, good living'.

Kim and Mauborgne (1999) suggest that 'the value curve'—a graphic depiction of the way a company or industry configures its offering to customers—is a powerful tool for creating new marketspace. It is drawn by plotting the performance of the offering relative to other alternatives along the key success factors that define competition in the industry. Identified in Figure 4, the creation of a new value curve appeared to be possible for Banrock Station wine, by adopting a marketing positioning strategy based on a 'green' wine that supported conservation activities.

## CREATING A 'GREEN' BRAND

Creating a 'green' brand meant tapping into the values and beliefs of wine buyers. As a starting point, BRL Hardy recognised that its investment in and achievement of restoring the magnificent Banrock Station wetlands might be shared with its customers. This strategy has proven to be successful in Australia. With every bottle of Banrock Station wine sold, a portion of the sale proceeds is donated to conservation projects to ensure environmental havens are restored and preserved for future generations. All proceeds in Australia go to

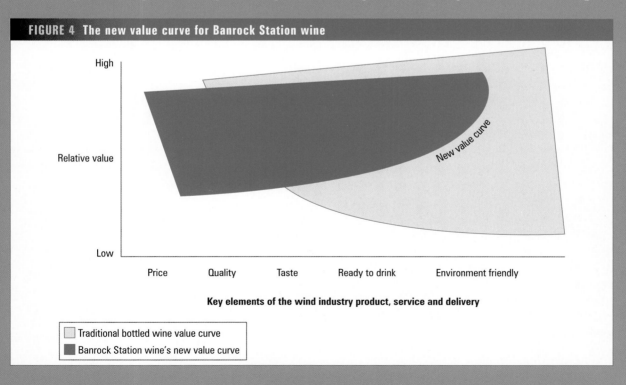

**FIGURE 4  The new value curve for Banrock Station wine**

Traditional bottled wine value curve

Banrock Station wine's new value curve

| TABLE 2 | Creating new value |
|---------|-------------------|

| Key questions | Areas for innovation |
|---------------|---------------------|
| 1. **Reduce**—What factors should be reduced well below the industry standard? | • Price<br>• Length of time to markets from the vine to the table<br>• Alcohol content |
| 2. **Create**—What factors should be created that the industry has never offered? | • A representation of healthy living<br>• An environmentally friendly wine |
| 3. **Eliminate**—What factors should be eliminated that the industry takes for granted? | • Standard labels<br>• Intimidation factor<br>• Wine speak |

Wetland Care Australia and Landcare Australia.

An analysis of the demographics of wine consumption in developed country markets such as Australia indicates that the bulk of wine consumers typically fall into the 40–60-year-old age group with a skew towards women. This generation is often referred to as 'baby boomers' and represents about 24% of the Australian population and around 33% of the US population. It is a group that is sensitive to environmental concerns. They were the original activists and are pro-environment. They created the first Earth Day back in 1970. However, the values of this group have not previously been tapped as far as wine marketing is concerned.

For this strategy to be implemented it must be conveyed to the customer via the brand. The brand is a bond with the customer. Keegan et al. (1992, p. 448) define it as a 'perception in the mind of consumers who ascribe beliefs, values and personalities to products' and Kotler (2000, p. 404) describes it as a 'seller's promise to deliver a specific set of features, benefits and services consistently to buyers'. Strategically, it has been the brands that have made Australian wine producers successful over other market competitors—not the name of the wine producer. Successful wine, the brand and the attitude it engenders must relate to the wine consumer's own sense of individuality and unique style. For a 'green' wine, the brand image should appeal to consumers who are seeking a product that fits with their values of good living, being healthy and their desire to act in an environmentally friendly way. Wine buyers

are thinking about the quality connection with where the product comes from and what they are purchasing.

Ottman (1992) claimed that while quality, price and convenience are still uppermost in consumers' purchasing decisions, a fourth attribute, environmental compatibility, that is, a product's 'greenness', is fast becoming a tie-breaker at the shelf.

By linking Banrock Station's brand attributes of good-value, quality wines that are ready to drink with a conservationist personality it was intended to create a new source of competitive advantage for BRL Hardy's 'Banrock Station' brand. The brand slogan 'good earth, fine wine' easily identifies Banrock Station with supporting the environment. Additional in-store promotional material highlights Banrock Station wines' conservation initiatives—for example, a bottle flyer with a pelican. This saves the consumer time in evaluating other brands and helps to easily distinguish the point of difference in retail outlets. In addition, Banrock Station's 'green' brand image is reflected in the advertising, good news stories about conservation projects, packaging, point-of-purchase promotions, wine shows and on the website where consumers can take a virtual tour of Banrock Station (see <www.banrockstation.com.au>).

## APPLICATION OF 'GREEN' BRAND EQUITY TO INTERNATIONAL MARKETS

As the 'green' marketing approach was successful in Australia, BRL Hardy decided to apply it to selected overseas markets that were considered to offer long-term growth potential. The eight selected international wine markets were the USA, Netherlands, Canada, Sweden, New Zealand, UK, Finland and Denmark. All are developed markets with environmentally sensitive baby boomers. In these markets BRL aimed to build strategic alliances with local conservation groups, as it did in Australia. A key to the market entry strategy was establishing strategic alliances with 'green' groups so as to increase consumers' confidence in and credibility of the brand's environmental claims. In each case a certain percentage of profit from the sale of each bottle of wine would go to the alliance partner to fund environmental projects. Implementation of this international approach was facilitated by hiring an environmental scientist, Tony Sharley, who manages the Banrock Station Wine and Wetland Centre in Australia. In this role, he manages conservation projects with organisations in key international markets and can verify Banrock Station's 'green' credentials.

High on the agenda was Australia's number one wine market, the UK, where BRL sells a number of successful brands. In the UK, Banrock Station wines and the Wildfowl and Wetlands Trust (WWT) are working together to save wetlands and wildlife. Funds from Banrock Station wines are being used to support the continual monitoring and maintenance of 4000 acres of WWT's wetland reserves and their wildlife.

In Canada, BRL established its own organisation to coordinate environmental projects to help conserve and protect endangered birds and wetlands (the Banrock Station Wine Wetland Foundation, Canada). In the USA, Banrock Station has partnered with the Arthur R Marshall Foundation to champion restoration and preservation of America's Greater Everglades ecosystem and sponsored Cypress Tree Planting Day in an effort to restore the Everglades ancient forest.

In Europe, Banrock Station wines are working with the Swedish Wetland Fund, with proceeds supporting OsterMalma, Lida and other wetlands in the area; in Finland, with Liminganlahti Bay, a high-profile and highly regarded wetland region in the north of Finland; and in the Netherlands Banrock Station wines, Staatsbosbeheer and Wetlands International are working together to save wetlands. Recently, Banrock Station commenced a partnership with Danish Nature which will use the funds to restore wetlands in the Langelands region.

Closer to home, Banrock Station wines have combined with the environment group Wetland Care New Zealand to sponsor wetland restoration projects throughout New Zealand. The first year's proceeds under the sponsorship helped to develop a wetland within the widely acclaimed Karori Sanctuary in Wellington and this year a wetland has been created at Masterton in the Wairarapa region.

## INTERNATIONAL SALES GROWTH

Figure 3 shows that Banrock Station is in the premium wine category offering good value for money. A similar price positioning was adopted in selected overseas markets. As such, it is priced below some of its major Australian competitors. In the UK, BRL Hardy had to contend with a distribution system where the retailers are gatekeepers and 10 accounts can represent 70% of the market. Here, buyer label wines account for a considerable share of the market. To counter this it was necessary for Banrock Station to create an awareness of its own brand. This is being achieved via the use of cinema and outdoor advertising, including the London Underground. By contrast, in the USA the distribution of wines approximates that of fast moving consumer goods (FMCG) and there is little wine sold under the labels of buyers. The value for money claim is being augmented in all markets with the 'support conservation' theme and point-of-sale support that reinforces the conservation image. It is this support that provides the brand with its unique selling proposition.

This approach has proved to be a deciding factor at the point of purchase among the growing number of environmentally conscious consumers in the USA and the UK.

Banrock Station wines are proving to be a standout performer for BRL Hardy in international markets. They are ranked number seven in the top 10 selling Australian wine brands in the US market and third in volume of the premium Australian brands exported to the USA. In the 13-week period ending 17 May 2001, Banrock Station's overall ranked position in the US market was 189th and it is the fastest growing brand in the BRL portfolio. Banrock Station is the number one fastest growing brand in the UK as shown in Table 3.

There is no doubt that much of this success has been due to the 'green' international wine marketing of Banrock Station wines. Future growth is dependent upon maintaining and building the brand through continued investment in conservation projects and the development of new markets with significant segments of environmentally friendly wine buyers.

## KEY LESSONS

The success of BRL's Banrock Station brand in the UK and US markets to date can be explained in part by its being a New World wine, priced in the attractive premium wine category with a country of origin image associated with sunshine, health and wide open spaces—an attractive image consistent with wine production. However, of themselves these New World wine characteristics do not explain Banrock Station wines' rapid rise in overseas sales, or their major market share among the Australian premium wine segment. Success is also due to the niche marketing strategy pursued by the firm of positioning the brand as a

'green' wine that supports conservation activities. This strategy has positioned the brand in a new marketspace that includes environmentally conscious consumers. This strategy appeals to a different set of values, and values not targeted by other wine producers. Although the magnitude of this segment may differ between countries, environmentally conscious consumers are a global segment that offers considerable potential for the future marketing of the Banrock Station brand.

The experience of BRL Hardy points to a number of other key lessons in international marketing that may help other companies also break free from the competitive pack. The first of these is that innovative marketing approaches are a useful vehicle for companies to create new overseas markets and/or reposition themselves in existing markets. BRL's approach was to look at its market from a new perspective and create new value for stakeholders in those markets. This was achieved by tapping into the values and beliefs of its customers and creating new product attributes to influence the purchasing decisions of customers. In this case it was by creating a brand associated with caring for the environment as illustrated by investing sales receipts back into conservation projects.

The second lesson relates to the need to pursue a strategy in depth rather than superficially if it is to be effective in overseas markets. In this case a

| TABLE 3 | UK brands top wines, 2000 listing | |
|---|---|---|
| **Brand** | **Company** | **Off trade % growth** |
| Ernest & Julio Gallo | E&J Gallo Winery | 22% |
| Jacob's Creek | Orlando Wyndham | 24.3% |
| Hardy | BRL Hardy Wine | 33.3% |
| Stowells of Chelsea | Matthew Clark | 28.1% |
| Rosemount | Rosemount Wine Estates | 69.1% |
| Lindemans | Southcorp Wines | 52.9% |
| Penfolds | Southcorp Wines | 2.8% |
| Blossom Hill | UDV | 143.3% |
| Le Piat D'or | Piat Pere Et Fils | (−14.6%) |
| Banrock Station | BRL Hardy Wines | 164.8% |

**SOURCE:** *Macquarie Bank Research (2001)* Essentials, *March.*

company embarking on a 'green' brand strategy needs to realise it has to be more than just a gimmick. The company has to excel in delivering not just the product benefits but also the 'green' benefits that customers truly desire. BRL's experience shows its 'green' brand has to stay relevant and credible. This was achieved by ongoing restoration of its own wetland, employing an environmental scientist and consistently communicating the brand's environmental initiatives and project involvement via publication of 'good news' stories and distinctive product packaging and labelling and through the focus of its sales team. Only in this way can a company continue to grow the market in its chosen segment.

Finally, the application of brand management to overseas markets often requires the building of strategic alliances with local groups if brand equity is to be sustained or further developed in these overseas markets. In the case of BRL Hardy, the strategic alliances were with local conserva-tion groups similar to those with whom alliances had been forged in Australia. The lesson from Australia was in this case applied in overseas markets—that the brand must associate itself with the projects of its alliance partner and should do this by the firm's management maintaining an active interest in the quality of those environmental projects. Banrock Station's environmental scientist developed quality controls to ensure that funds directed to those conservation groups from Banrock Station sales were invested in technically sound and rewarding conservation projects. If 'green' projects are important, well supported and understood by the consumer, the brand will build and increase its 'green' brand equity.

In summary, BRL Hardy has shown how important a 'green' brand is to increasing market share and how innovation in marketing can help a company create a point of difference that redefines the attributes on which buyers base their purchasing decision.

## Bibliography

Ahmed, S.A. and D'Astous, A. (1996) 'Country of origin and brand effects: a multidimensional and multi-attribute study', *Journal of International Consumer Marketing*, Vol. 9, No. 2, pp. 93–115.

Berger, N., Spahni, P. and Anderson, K. (1999) *Bilateral Trade Patterns in the World Wine Market 1988 to 1997: A Statistical Compendium*, Centre for International Economic Studies, University of Adelaide.

Keegan, W., Moriarty, S. and Duncan, T. (1992) *Marketing*, Prentice Hall, NJ.

Kim, C. and Mauborgne, R. (1999) 'Creating new market space', *Harvard Business Review*, January–February, pp. 83–93.

Kotler, P. (2000) *Marketing Management: The Millennium Edition*, Prentice Hall, NJ.

Macquarie Bank Research (2001) *Essentials*, March.

Ottman, J. A. (1992) *Green Marketing: Challenges and Opportunities for the New Marketing Age*, NTC Business Books, Chicago.

Porter, M. (1990) *The Competitive Advantage of Nations*, Macmillan, London.

Winemakers' Federation of Australia/Australian Wine and Brandy Corporation (2000) *The Marketing Decade 2000–2010*, November, <http://www.awbc.com.au>.

## Acknowledgements

The authors of this case are grateful to Mr Stephen Millar (Managing Director, BRL Hardy Ltd); Mr David Woods (International Trading Director, BRL Hardy Ltd) and Mr Tony Sharley (Manager, Banrock Station Wine and Wetland Centre) for agreeing to be interviewed and for their valuable insights.

## Questions

1 How can innovation help a wine company break free from the competitive pack and tap existing and new markets for growth?

2 BRL Hardy has tapped baby boomers' concerns for the environment to attract Banrock Station customers. What strategy would you employ to attract 'generation X' to drink Banrock Station wines?

3 Do you think a 'green' brand is just a gimmick or a unique and valuable offering in the wine industry?

# 14

# MARKETING SERVICES OVERSEAS

## LearningObjectives

**After reading this chapter you should be able to:**

- appreciate the increasing role of services in international marketing;

- recognise ways in which marketing services overseas differs from marketing goods overseas;

- determine how the unique characteristics of services marketing require a different strategic approach when introducing services into an overseas market;

- appreciate issues involved in major services export sectors such as tourism, education, retailing and professional services;

- develop market entry strategies for services; and

- assess ways in which the internet can overcome some of the problems traditionally encountered in international services marketing.

# Marketing education overseas—from rags to riches

Until 20 years ago tertiary education in Australia was intended for Australians and most overseas students were on scholarships. In 1986 the Australian government began offering full fee paying places to overseas students and promoting 'study in Australia' in overseas countries. Today, rather than the few thousand overseas students of two decades ago, there are 200 000 foreign students in Australia, raising A$7 billion a year for the economy. This has enabled the government to reduce funding for universities, in turn forcing academic institutions to become more aggressive in marketing their courses overseas. In the process, Australia has taken share of the market from traditional providers of tertiary education such as the UK and the USA and is now the fourth-largest global destination for overseas students.

*Taylor's University College Main Campus in Subang Jaya, Malaysia*

As with most exports, when foreign governments see a drain of foreign exchange, they introduce barriers to both reduce the drain and transfer the expertise to their own country. The 'stages' approach to internationalisation discussed in Chapter 7 applies to education and Australian academic institutions have variously entered into twinning arrangements as did the University of Technology, Sydney (UTS) with Taylor's University College in Malaysia (Australian academics delivered lectures in Kuala Lumpur, locals gave the tutorials for the first half of the degree and students came to UTS in Sydney for the second half of the degree); set up joint degree programs where students undertook one degree in their own country, often under supervision of the Australian university, and undertook the second degree in Australia (48 of China's 164 joint degree programs are with Australian universities); and taught the total degree in the overseas location (using either local academics or flying in Australian academics or a combination of both, or set up a campus in the overseas country as RMIT has done in Vietnam or the University of Wollongong has done in Dubai). The overseas partners in the above arrangements can be local universities, industry groups such as the Singapore Employers' Federation or entrepreneurs such as Ceylinco in Sri Lanka.

One cloud on the horizon is the cloning of competitors, as happens when countries that used to send large numbers of students to Australia, such as Philippines and Singapore, establish their own facilities and compete with Australia for students from other countries in the region.

# INTRODUCTION

The international services trade is increasingly important to the economies of most countries, especially industrialised countries. The marketing of services in an international context needs to be considered separately from goods. This is because opportunities for growth are better and the barriers to trade in services are different from those for goods. The services trade is now around 30% of total world trade. The international services trade is growing at 16% per year compared to only 7% per year for goods. In the case of Australia, services exports in 2005 were worth A$37 billion and now exceed the value of rural exports. Services account for in excess of 70% of gross domestic product and employ 80% of the Australian workforce. Considering the fact that services are also embedded in goods that are exported and account for approximately a fifth of their value, services are estimated to account for around 40% of Australian exports overall. The main markets for Australian services exports are the USA, Japan, UK, New Zealand and China. The main services export sectors for Australia are tourism valued at A$11 billion (5.5 million visitors); passenger transport valued at A$7.5 billion; education valued at A$7 billion (200 000 students a year) and financial and insurance services valued at A$1.5 billion.

The growth of services in international trade is due to a combination of changing lifestyles, a changing world and changing technology. This is modelled in Figure 14.1.

In order to appreciate the intricacies of marketing services overseas, it is necessary to recognise the difference between the marketing of goods and the marketing of services.

This issue is addressed in the first part of the chapter. This leads to a discussion of the marketing of services overseas. In this connection, the impact of the overseas environment is considered, the factors that drive internationalisation of services are discussed and the issues, such as culture and standardisation, involved in international services marketing are considered. The next section of the chapter considers the various ways of categorising services for marketing internationally as these often require different strategies. The chapter concludes with a review of Australia's situation regarding the international marketing of services and in particular reviews areas of major interest such as the international marketing of tourism, education, retailing and professional services.

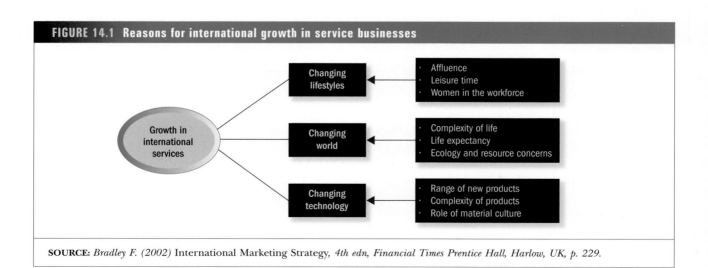

**FIGURE 14.1  Reasons for international growth in service businesses**

**SOURCE:** *Bradley F. (2002)* International Marketing Strategy, *4th edn, Financial Times Prentice Hall, Harlow, UK, p. 229.*

# THE NATURE OF SERVICES

Services are different from products and have a number of distinguishing characteristics that are critical in their marketing overseas. Services are anything that can be bought or sold but cannot be dropped on your foot! Services can be distinguished from products in that they can bring about a change in those who use them, as happens with education; can bring about changes to the goods to which they are applied, as with engine design; can be embedded in products, as with after-sales service on a car; or can exist on a stand-alone basis, as with a haircut.

Other features of services are that they can combine both tangible (e.g. aircraft and food and drink served on board) and intangible elements (e.g. in-flight service and transportation); they can be experiential (i.e. you don't know what you will get until it is delivered, for example an operation); they can be delivered in real time (e.g. filling a tooth); they can be delivered face to face (as with a university lecture); and often they need to be taken on trust (e.g. when you have your car serviced).

## The marketing paradigm for services

The marketing characteristics of services are:

- *intangibility*: The fact that services often cannot be touched or felt can be compensated for by stressing the tangible cues associated with the service, by using word-of-mouth to promote them, by creating a strong image for the company supplying the service, and finally by having a program of post-purchase communication to lessen any feeling of cognitive dissonance.

- *simultaneity*: Because production and consumption of many services occur at the same time and the consumer becomes part of the service, selection and training of personnel become very important. The degree of simultaneity can influence the firm's decision to adopt a particular mode of overseas market entry and the lesser the degree of simultaneity between production and consumption, the more likely it is that the mode of entry will involve some degree of direct investment (Jack 2006, p. 62).

- *heterogeneity*: Because of the high labour content in the provision of most services, output can vary in quality. This can be reduced by customising the service (as with ladies' hairdressing) or by industrialising it (as with carpet cleaning).

- *perishability*: Because services cannot be saved or stored, it is necessary to devise strategies to cope with fluctuating demand. These might take the form of having a flexible pool of part-time employees to call on at periods of peak demand, as in the hotel industry, or by implementing yield management strategies, as with airlines.

Figure 14.2 shows the additional marketing mix variables that apply with services.

Most marketing textbooks point out that marketing is driven by the *four Ps* of product, price, promotion and place (distribution). When they do so, they are generally referring to the marketing of goods. As with goods, the four Ps can apply to services. The *product* could be the content of a degree; the *price* could be A$2000 per subject; the *promotion* would be to advertise the MBA in the *Australian Financial Review*; and the *place* would be delivery on campus or delivery in a downtown location or delivery via a residential program. In addition, with services marketing, three additional Ps apply. These are *personnel* as with the lecturer; *process* as with enrolment in the degree program; and *physical* facilities as with the quality of lecture halls and the content of the library.

**FIGURE 14.2  7Ps—service paradigm**

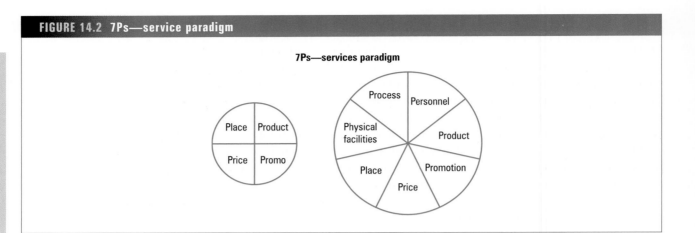

Lovelock et al. (2004) argue that, rather than focusing on generic differences between services and goods, you should focus on the process by which services are delivered. They categorise services as explained below:

- *People-processing services*: Customers become part of the production process, which usually is simultaneous with consumption (e.g. passenger transportation, lodging and health care). Customers must either travel to the place in which the service is provided or the service provider must travel to the customer. In both cases the service provider needs to maintain a local geographic presence.

- *Possession-processing services*: These involve doing something to physical products to improve their value to customers (e.g. transporting freight; repairing motor vehicles; servicing capital/plant). The service provision facility may be either in a fixed location or mobile. A local geographic facility is necessary when the service supplier needs to provide service to physical products in a location on a repeated basis. In some cases electronic technology obviates this by enabling diagnosis of a problem from a distance, as with telemedicine and computer support.

- *Information-based services*: These involve collection, interpretation and transmission of data to create value (e.g. banking, consulting, accounting, education). Customer involvement in the production of these services is minimal and modern global telecommunication enables them to be delivered from a central hub to almost any location. Local presence requirements are limited to an automatic teller machine or a fax or a computer.

## The content of services marketing and delivery

The services encounter involves not only traditional elements of marketing but also marketing within the organisation. Because of the high involvement of people in the supply of the service, there will need to be considerable emphasis within the company on training people to provide the service and the development of a service culture within the firm. It will also involve a greater emphasis on relationship marketing than is necessary when simply dealing with goods, because services marketing emphasises retaining and managing relationships with customers on an ongoing basis especially when there is a face-to-face element in the service provision. This is reflected in Figure 14.3.

The delivery of services typically involves backstage or invisible elements such as the kitchen in a restaurant, and front-stage or visible elements such as the actual meal, the table setting and the waiter service. In general, the backstage elements are low in contact with the customer whereas the front-stage elements are high in contact with the customer. Services will vary according to the extent to which they are low contact or high contact and this will affect the relative weight given in the firm to the operations system to provide the service, the system to deliver the service and the system to market the service. Figures 14.4 and 14.5 illustrate the differences between low- and high-contact services.

In recent years, there has been an increase in the extent of low-contact services due to both self-service and electronic delivery of an increasing range of services.

## FIGURE 14.3  Framework for analysing services marketing

SOURCE: *Lovelock, C.H., Patterson, P.G. and Walker, R.H. (2004)* Services Marketing: An Asia–Pacific and Australian Perspective, *3rd edn, Prentice Hall, Sydney, p. 23.*

## FIGURE 14.4  The service marketing system for a low contact service

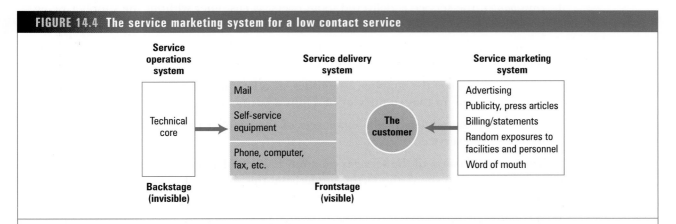

SOURCE: *Lovelock, C.H., Patterson, P.G. and Walker, R.H. (2004)* Services Marketing: An Asia–Pacific and Australian Perspective, *3rd edn, Prentice Hall, Sydney, p. 48.*

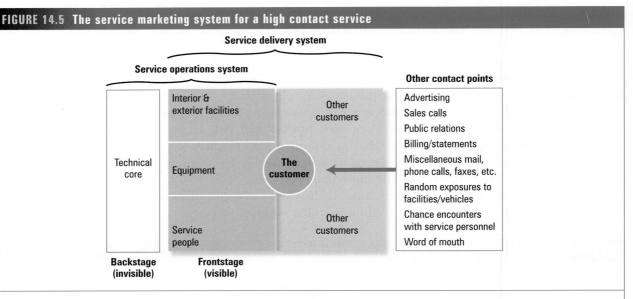

**FIGURE 14.5  The service marketing system for a high contact service**

SOURCE: *Lovelock, C.H., Patterson, P.G. and Walker, R.H. (2004)* Services Marketing: An Asia–Pacific and Australian Perspective, *3rd edn, Prentice Hall, Sydney, p. 46.*

With the increasing mechanisation of service delivery as exemplified by ordering taxis via speech recognition facilities, purchasing shares over the internet and buying insurance over the phone, more emphasis is being placed on scripts to be used in the selling episode so as to reduce the variability that comes with a high dependence on people. In the international domain such scripts are culturally sensitive and cannot be transported from one country to another.

# MARKETING SERVICES IN THE INTERNATIONAL MARKETPLACE

There are four ways of exporting services overseas. They are:

1  *cross border*: the service is delivered to an overseas customer without the supplier being present;

2  *consumption abroad*: the overseas customer comes to the country of the supplier of the service to receive that service as with tourism and education;

3  *commercial presence*: the supplier establishes an office in the overseas country or appoints a representative in that country or develops a partnership overseas;

4  *movement of natural persons*: the employees of the supplier travel to the overseas country to deliver the service.

The transformation of the services economy has stimulated the international marketing of services. Figure 14.6 shows the factors underlying this. Issues to be considered in relation to each of the above factors are described below:

• *Internationalisation in general*: There has been a hollowing-out effect caused by low-tech, labour-intensive operations being transferred to the less-developed countries. This has resulted in a demand for the value-added intelligent services necessary to support a

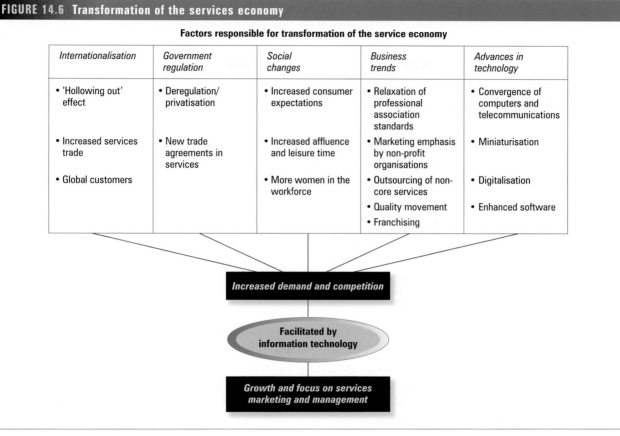

**FIGURE 14.6** Transformation of the services economy

**Factors responsible for transformation of the service economy**

| Internationalisation | Government regulation | Social changes | Business trends | Advances in technology |
|---|---|---|---|---|
| • 'Hollowing out' effect<br><br>• Increased services trade<br><br>• Global customers | • Deregulation/ privatisation<br><br>• New trade agreements in services | • Increased consumer expectations<br><br>• Increased affluence and leisure time<br><br>• More women in the workforce | • Relaxation of professional association standards<br>• Marketing emphasis by non-profit organisations<br>• Outsourcing of non-core services<br>• Quality movement<br>• Franchising | • Convergence of computers and telecommunications<br><br>• Miniaturisation<br><br>• Digitalisation<br><br>• Enhanced software |

*Increased demand and competition*

**Facilitated by information technology**

*Growth and focus on services marketing and management*

SOURCE: *Lovelock, C.H., Patterson, P.G. and Walker, R.H. (2004)* Services Marketing: An Asia–Pacific and Australian Perspective, *3rd edn, Prentice Hall, Sydney, p. 9.*

more high-tech manufacturing sector. Firms in this sector find there is a need to go international in order to survive and when they do so their service suppliers are forced to follow them overseas. This factor has partly been responsible for the growth of service trade internationally.

• *Decreased government regulation*: This is especially the case internationally in the service industry with banks, airlines and telecommunications. The World Trade Organization has been working on freeing up trade in services and has introduced the agreement on Trade-Related Aspects of Intellectual Property Rights (TRIPS). Increasingly, government is privatising its business undertakings as it has with utilities and outsourcing the services it needs, as opposed to undertaking them 'in-house'. Deregulation has often occurred in response to public pressure, as with shopping hours. This has strengthened private sector provision of services and its ability to compete in service provision internationally.

• *Social changes*: Rising expectations, greater affluence and more focus on leisure and quality of life have caused increased expenditure on services such as tourism. Furthermore, the increase in the percentage of women in the workforce has brought about a larger demand for labour replacement services such as purchasing food supplies via the internet (for example, <http://www.GreenGrocer.com.au>).

- *Business trends*: A number of business trends have facilitated internationalisation of services. The spread of franchising is one such trend, as is the creation of international standards relevant for services (e.g. ISO 9000 quality management standard and ISO 14000 environmental management systems and standards) and moves towards international recognition of standards of professional practice (e.g. accountancy standards).

- *Advances in technology*: These have lessened the constraints on provision of services traditionally imposed by national boundaries and caused international service providers to rationalise activities on a global basis. This is evident in the media, transportation and telecommunications sectors. Advances in technology have also created new international markets for services, as exemplified by the internet, and facilitated existing services activities such as the tracking of international airfreight.

# Drivers of internationalisation of service firms

These can be divided into drivers at the firm-level and drivers at the industry-level. Within each category are a number of specific drivers. These apply to the marketing of both goods and services. Their application to services is outlined below.

## FIRM-LEVEL DRIVERS

- *Market seeking*: This usually involves small and medium-sized service exporters seeking new markets because of their apparent higher growth potential.

- *Client following*: This involves service firms following their Australian clients into overseas markets to provide the same services as they do in Australia. This often happens in the mining industry, for example when a firm supplying Rio Tinto in Australia supplies their operation in Indonesia.

- *Domestic market pressure*: This occurs when the domestic market becomes saturated and there is pressure from forces within the market for the service provider to go international. This has happened in the Australian education system.

- *Unsolicited orders*: These usually result from the service firm having an international reputation or a technology that is innovative and which has application to an overseas project. For example, Australian land titling firms receive unsolicited inquiries from managers of urban development schemes in Asia because of Australia's reputation in this field.

## INDUSTRY-LEVEL DRIVERS

- *Common customer needs*: In general, standardisation is less likely with services than with goods. Within services, the potential for standardisation is greater the less the provider is involved in the delivery because this increases the extent to which customer needs are likely to have more features in common.

- *Scale economies*: These are driven by the opportunity to spread fixed costs. With services, such economies are more likely to come from standardised processes than from a physical concentration of activities.

- *Government drivers*: These can take the form of incentives from your own government for exporting services, as with the Australian Export Market Development Grants Scheme, or barriers placed in the way of services exports by the government in the overseas market to protect local service industries.

- *Competition drivers*: These often occur because the service provider finds it necessary to go overseas in order to protect its position in the domestic market, especially if costs can be lowered. If the service provider does not take this step, then there is an increased risk that firms in the overseas market may use that market as a base from which to enter the Australian market. This has been a motive behind several Australian insurance firms going into Asia.

- *Information technology drivers*: The ability to centralise information hubs on a global basis is a motive because it strengthens the firm's competitive position. Rupert Murdoch's involvement in satellite TV in order to monopolise sports coverage is an example of this factor.

## Issues in services exports

When firms engage in international trade in services they face most of the same problems as they would with international trade in goods. There are, however, a number of additional problems that influence firms' international marketing strategies:

- *Delivery issues*: Unlike goods, the export of services can also be inbound. This happens when the recipient of the service enters the provider's country to receive the service (e.g. tourism and education). In some cases the international services export can be inbound (e.g. telemedicine) or outbound (e.g. surgeon flies to the overseas country to perform the operation).

- *Infrastructure requirements*: Services exports are often dependent on the presence of an existing infrastructure in the overseas market. Taking tourism as an example, there is a need for the existence of airports and resorts in the country before tourists can be attracted to the market. With financial services and call centres, there is a requirement for telecommunications and informational facilities. Exports of technology require an education infrastructure that fosters creativity and innovation as well as the provision of an R&D infrastructure to create an entrepreneurial environment. In essence, few services can be exported without the accompanying service delivery system.

- *Direct contact needs*: When the export of services involves simultaneous production, exchange and consumption there is a need for much more face-to-face contact and for buyer and seller to be in the same location. The Australian firm has to supply the service in person direct to the foreign market because it cannot be shipped there and, when direct contact is involved, each service transaction is unique. In these circumstances controlling quality is likely to be a greater problem than with goods. Finally, because services cannot be inventoried the opportunity to reduce variance in overall demand by diversification of production/supply from overseas is lessened.

- *Greater protectionism*: Government often regards the service sector of its economy as having special cultural or strategic significance. It strives to protect this sector via the use of non-tariff barriers or by prohibiting investment in service sectors of the economy. Reducing the barriers to the entry of services is more difficult than for goods due to foreign limitations on equity, lack of recognition of qualifications, restrictions on the issue of licences and impediments to the establishment of a commercial presence in the market (Department of Treasury 2006, p. 96). Table 14.1 provides examples of barriers to the international marketing of services.

- *Economies of location*: Because services tend to be more jointly demanded, supplied and consumed than goods, there is advantage to be gained from concentrating some service activities in certain cities or in certain countries. The creation of 'technology parks' is an example of this. The concentration of global banking, insurance and financial services in specific centres such as Singapore, Tokyo and London reflects the above, as do current moves by Sydney and Melbourne to become regional headquarters for global service providers.

- *Quantifying international services trade*: One of the problems with services exports is that they have not received the same focus of attention as goods exports do. Possibly this is because media and government tend to underplay export achievement in the services sector due to their embedded nature. Certainly this factor, together with their intangibility as well as their variability in location of delivery, have made it difficult to measure accurately the volume of services exports.

There are two particular issues in the international marketing of services that need to also be taken into account. These are cultural sensitivity and the potential for standardisation.

## SERVICES EXPORTS AND CULTURAL SENSITIVITY

As a general rule services are more culturally sensitive than goods. This is because services are delivered in real time, the process of service delivery involves interaction, services are

**TABLE 14.1    Selected barriers to the international marketing of services**

| Type | Example | Impact |
|------|---------|--------|
| *Tariff* | Tax on imported advertising | Discriminates against foreign agencies |
| | Tax on computer services contracts | Prices international service providers higher than domestic providers which stand alone |
| | Higher fees for university students from outside the country | Decreases foreign student enrolment |
| *Non-tariff* | | |
| National buying policies | US government buying training services only from US companies | Discriminates against foreign suppliers |
| Prohibited employment of foreigners | Priority to Canadian citizens | May prevent supplier from going to buyers |
| Distance | International business education | May raise cost of bringing supplier to buyer, buyer to supplier |
| Direct government competition | Indonesian monopoly on telecommunications | Must market services to government |
| Scarce factors of production | Lack of trained medical workers in Biafra | Limits production of services |
| Restriction on service buyers and sellers | North Korea limiting the number of tourists allowed to enter and exit the country | Limits the restricted industry |

**SOURCE:** *Adapted from Dahringer, L. D. (1991) 'Marketing services internationally: barriers and management strategies',* Journal of Service Marketing, *Vol. 5, No. 3, pp. 5–17. Reproduced with permission from Emerald Group Publishing.*

**TABLE 14.2**   Cultural influences on the service encounter

| Cultural dimension | High context | Low context | Service encounter implication |
|---|---|---|---|
| Relationship with nature | Control over nature | Controlled by nature | Customer expectation of degree of control in service encounter |
| Relationship with time | Past (tradition) oriented | Future (goal) oriented | Customer expectation of provider flexibility in time spent at service encounter |
| Relationship with activity | Task (doing) oriented | Experience (being) oriented | Customer emphasis on process versus outcome of service |
| Relationship with others | Group oriented | Individual oriented | Customer expectation of significance of personal relationship in service encounter |

people specific, services are delivered in a cultural setting and customers judge the process as well as the outcome. Table 14.2 illustrates cultural influences on the service encounter. It shows that this influence will vary according to whether the culture is low in context or high in context (see Chapter 3). In the former, most meaning is conveyed by what is said, as is the case in the USA, whereas in the latter much of the meaning is in who says it, when it is said and where it is said, as in Japan.

Specific implications of culture on the international service encounter are:

- *relationship with nature*: in cultures where the tendency is to avoid uncertainty the customer seeks more control over the service encounter;

- *relationship with time*: the service encounter is likely to be influenced by whether the orientation of the culture is towards the past, the present or the future;

- *relationship with activity*: context influences whether the customer for the service places emphasis on the process (as in high-context cultures) or on the outcome of the service delivery (as in low-context cultures); and

- *relationship with others*: in high-context cultures, frontline employees are more likely to respond to the wishes of the customer, whereas in low-context cultures they are more likely to implement management directives regardless of customer wishes (e.g. whereas airline check-in staff and gate agents in Asia tend to be polite and, where possible flexible, in the USA such staff are often inflexible and abrupt in manner, citing company regulations).

## SERVICES MARKETING AND STANDARDISATION

The possibilities of standardisation of the offering across countries are less with services than with products. This is due to personal elements involved in their provision. However, some services are more amenable to standardisation than others. This has implications for marketing overseas because of the search for economies of scale when transferring the offering from one country to another. Table 14.3 illustrates this by comparing the source of the service with the type of service provider. The more local the service provider and the more local the delivery of the service, the less likely the service is to be amenable to standardisation. Examples of services falling in cell 1 would be the local restaurant; in cell 2 selling insurance via a local agent; in cell 3 offering a Mastercard credit card via a local bank; and in cell 4 TNT parcel express.

| TABLE 14.3 | Potential for standardisation of different services | | |
|---|---|---|
| | Local service provider | Multinational service provider |
| Local service product | Local service provided locally for domestic market (1) | Local service provided by multinationals in various countries (2) |
| Transnational service product | Transnational service provided locally only (3) | Transnational service provided internationally (4) |

## Services and international market entry

Figure 14.7 shows that the range of overseas market entry options for services differs from that for goods. While each stage involves the same trade-off between commitment of resources and desire for control, the role of the agent may not be as important and licensing is replaced by franchising.

As with the export of goods, protectionist pressures from overseas governments can force Australian providers of services to change their entry strategy from one of export to one of greater involvement in the overseas market.

Even within forms of involvement, pressures to increase local content occur. The experience of the University of Technology, Sydney (UTS), illustrates such pressures in the education sector. With the UTS twinning program in Malaysia, the Malaysian government several years ago insisted that the percentage of the degree offered in Kuala Lumpur be increased and the percentage offered in Sydney reduced.

## Categorisation of services exports

According to the L/E/K Partnership (1994), services exports can be categorised according to the function they perform—as either 'facilitational' or traded. Within the category of 'facilitational', services exports can be logistical or support. With the traded services category, exports can be either business services or consumer services. This is reflected in Figure 14.8, which shows Australian exports of services in financial year 2000–01, organised according to each category and subcategory of services exports and is based on a model developed in 1994.

Services exports can also be categorised according to different stages of development of

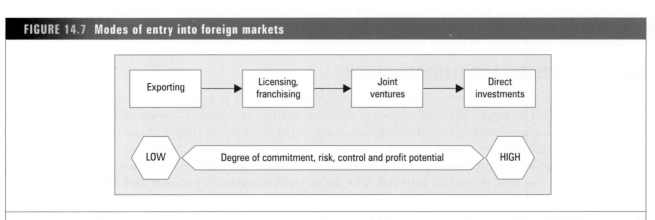

FIGURE 14.7  Modes of entry into foreign markets

**SOURCE:** *Lovelock, C.H., Patterson, P.G. and Walker, R.H. (2004)* Services Marketing: An Asia–Pacific and Australian Perspective, *3rd edn, Prentice Hall, Sydney, p. 371.*

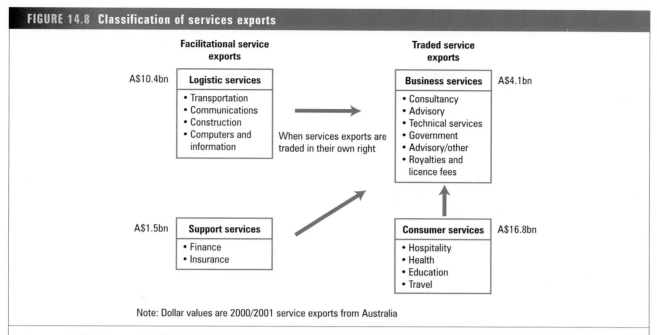

**FIGURE 14.8  Classification of services exports**

**Facilitational service exports**

A$10.4bn **Logistic services**
- Transportation
- Communications
- Construction
- Computers and information

*When services exports are traded in their own right*

A$1.5bn **Support services**
- Finance
- Insurance

**Traded service exports**

**Business services** A$4.1bn
- Consultancy
- Advisory
- Technical services
- Government
- Advisory/other
- Royalties and licence fees

**Consumer services** A$16.8bn
- Hospitality
- Health
- Education
- Travel

Note: Dollar values are 2000/2001 service exports from Australia

**SOURCE:** *L/E/K Partnership (1994)* Intelligent Exports and the Silent Revolution in Services, *Commonwealth of Australia, Canberra, Fig. 9. Copyright Commonwealth of Australia. Reproduced with permission.*

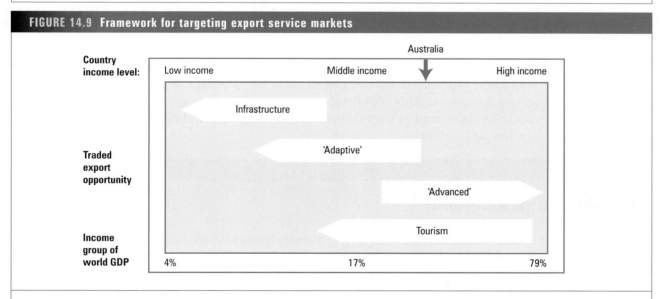

**FIGURE 14.9  Framework for targeting export service markets**

Country income level:
Australia
Low income      Middle income      High income

Infrastructure

'Adaptive'

Traded export opportunity

'Advanced'

Tourism

Income group of world GDP
4%      17%      79%

**SOURCE:** *L/E/K Partnership (1994)* Intelligent Exports and the Silent Revolution in Services, *Commonwealth of Australia, Canberra, Fig. 45. Copyright Commonwealth of Australia. Reproduced with permission.*

overseas markets. Figure 14.9 contrasts the nature of the services export with the stage of development attained by a market:

- *Infrastructure-related services exports*: These are essential for a nation's industrialisation and the flow is usually from a provider in a middle-income country to a buyer in a low-income country.

- *Adaptive services exports*: These are services exports that facilitate trade (often computer-aided) and because of the technology involved the flow tends to be from high-income or middle-income countries to countries with growing middle classes such as Thailand.

- *Advanced services exports*: These are generally high-tech or information-based exports and the flow is from middle-income to high-income countries or from one high-income country to another.

- *Tourism exports*: Because of the importance of levels of disposable income for tourism, the flow tends to be from high-income to middle- and low-income countries.

Patterson and Cicic (1995) have developed an alternative framework for classifying firms involved in the export of services. Based on research in Australia among service firms, their typology focuses on the dimensions of face-to-face contact on the one hand and 'intangibility of the service' on the other. This is shown in Figure 14.10 and the categories are explained below:

- *Location-free professional services*: A permanent presence in the overseas market is not necessary to deliver these services. Firms exporting these services internationalise using direct representation such as sending their personnel to the foreign market.

- *Location-bound customised projects*: These are longer term and require considerable personal interaction between client and service provider as well as the need to establish a permanent presence in the overseas country. Firms in this category mostly internationalise by following major clients into the foreign market.

- *Standardised service packages*: Generally, these services are linked to the supply of goods, such as software and technological training, and as such tend to be standardised. Services in this category are mostly exported by small firms whose internationalisation involves direct representation, agency arrangements or franchising.

- *Value-added customised projects*: Because of their nature these services require considerable interaction with the customer if delivery is to be successful. With these services, the service component adds considerable value to the physical goods element. Firms exporting these tend to internationalise both by following their customers into overseas markets and by filling unsolicited orders.

## 14.1 INTERNATIONAL HIGHLIGHT

# Healthcare goes global

In increasing numbers, Australians are turning to countries like India and Thailand for elective medical and dental treatment provided by the private sector. Thirty-five thousand Australians visited Thailand for this purpose in 2004. The treatment is supplied by mostly foreign-trained professionals in an oasis of privilege away from the teaming masses. The service is targeted at a specific global segment and supplied at rates less than 30% of those that apply in developed countries. Apollo Hospitals in India package medical treatment with tourism and currently handle 115 000 'medical tourists' a year. This is in a country where government spending on health care is less than 1% of gross domestic product (GDP) and which is home to 40% of the world's poor. A similar trend is apparent in Thailand where, in 2004, 1.1 million foreign patients received medical or dental treatment. The above trend is a result of new global realities such as the Asian economic downturn, the fallout from terrorism, internet access to price information and the globalisation of health services.

**SOURCE:** *Levett, C. (2005) 'A slice of the action',* Sydney Morning Herald, *29–30 October, p. 27.*

**FIGURE 14.10 A typology of service firms in international markets**

**Degree of face-to-face contact**

| | Low | High |
|---|---|---|
| **Degree of tangibility** **Pure services** (Low) | **Cell 1** **Location-free professional services** Typical firms: executive recruitment, market research, environmental science consulting, transportation, finance and insurance, information technology, product design services. • Degree of customisation: low • Firm size: small (median size = 25 employees) • Foreign ownership = 14% of sample | **Cell 2** **Location-bound customised projects** Typical firms: project management, engineering consulting, management consulting, human resource development consulting, larger market research firms, legal services. • Degree of customisation: high • Firm size: largest in sample (median size = 160 employees) • Foreign ownership = 9% of sample |
| **Services bundled with goods** (High) | **Cell 3** **Standardised service packages** Typical firms: software development, installation/testing of new hardware/ equipment, development of distance education courses, compact discs. • Degree of customisation: low • Firm size: small (median size = 40 employees) • Foreign ownership = 13% of sample | **Cell 4** **Value-added customised services** Typical firms: on-site training, computer hardware consulting, facilities management, accommodation services, catering, software training and support. • Degree of customisation: high • Firm size: medium (median size = 55 employees) • Highest incidence of foreign ownership = 21% of sample |

**SOURCE:** *Patterson, P. G. and Cicic, M. (1995), 'A typology of service firms in international markets: an empirical investigation',* Journal of International Marketing, *Vol. 3, No. 4, pp. 57–83. Reprinted with permission from* Journal of International Marketing. *Published by American Marketing Association.*

## AUSTRALIAN TRADE IN SERVICES

For almost the last two decades services have been Australia's fastest-growing export sector. In 2005–06 there was a deficit in Australia's trade in manufactures of A$15.3 billion, but a surplus in Australia's trade in services of A$1.2 billion. In the case of Australia, services exports in 2005 were worth A$37 billion and now exceed the value of rural exports. Services account for in excess of 70% of gross domestic product and employ 80% of the Australian workforce. Considering the fact that services are also embedded in goods that are exported and account for approximately a fifth of their value, services are estimated to account for around 40% of Australian exports overall. The main markets for Australian services exports are the USA, Japan, UK, New Zealand and China. The main services export sectors for Australia are tourism valued at A$11 billion (5.5 million visitors); passenger transport valued at A$7.5 billion; education valued at A$7 billion (200 000 students a year) and financial and insurance services valued at A$1.5 billion.

Collectively the countries of ASEAN represent a substantial market for Australian services exports and, as shown in Figure 14.11, exports to the region now exceed A$6 billion a year.

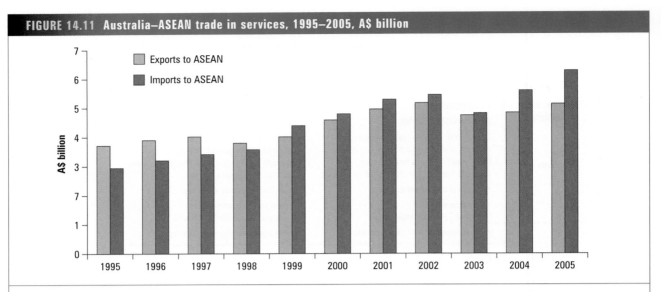

**FIGURE 14.11   Australia–ASEAN trade in services, 1995–2005, A$ billion**

SOURCES: *Department of Foreign Affairs and Trade Economic Analytical Unit (2006)* ASEAN: Building an economic community, *Commonwealth of Australia, Canberra; and Australian Bureau of Statistics, Catalogue No. .5368.0.*

## International marketing of tourism

In the last two decades tourists to Australia have increased from one million to 5.5 million and tourism in now Australia's largest services export. It is now a A$49 billion industry accounting for 8.6% of GDP in 2005 (according to <http://www.tourismvictoria_ significance_tourism>). The international tourism market is becoming increasingly competitive and requires much larger national expenditure on promotion since the Paul Hogan-led campaign to 'put a shrimp on the barbie' and 'come and say g'day' of two decades ago. In order to distinguish itself in a crowded market the Commonwealth government and the Australian Tourism Commission plans to spend A$210 million on international marketing from 2004 to 2008 (Dennis and Lee 2004, p. 32) and this was evident in the G'day LA campaign of 2006 in the USA. Australian tourism is benefiting from the current global terrorism threat and its focus on a clean, green image and environmental tourism. Tourism is closely linked to education as each student that comes to Australia attracts an average of 1.3 friends or family members to visit the country during their stay here.

## International marketing of education

The future of Australia's third largest services export, education, is inextricably linked to the future of globalisation, as students from overseas travel here to acquire not only skills but also to experience the ways people behave and do business in another environment. It is linked to the expansion of the middle class in developing countries (especially in Asia) and their increasing levels of affluence. Furthermore, it is argued that education is a two-way street, the continued sustainability of which will depend not only on academic providers (mostly from developed countries) being able to offer courses at a profit, but also on the ability of education to increase prosperity in less-developed countries. This latter aspect is due to mobility among students stimulating development in the student's country of origin. Australia is the fourth-largest provider of education (after the USA and UK and Germany), but there

**TABLE 14.4** | Overseas student enrolments in Australia from our top 10 source countries

| Country | 2002 | 2003 | Change |
|---|---|---|---|
| China | 47 931 | 57 579 | 20.1% |
| Hong Kong | 22 091 | 23 803 | 7.7% |
| South Korea | 18 658 | 22 159 | 18.8% |
| Indonesia | 20 985 | 20 336 | −3.1% |
| Malaysia | 17 530 | 19 779 | 12.8% |
| Japan | 17 329 | 18 987 | 9.6% |
| Thailand | 15 643 | 17 025 | 8.8% |
| India | 11 364 | 14 386 | 26.6% |
| USA | 11 064 | 12 189 | 10.2% |
| Singapore | 12 062 | 11 843 | −1.8% |
| Other countries | 79 198 | 85 238 | 7.6% |
| **Total** | **273 855** | **303 324** | **10.8%** |

SOURCE: *Department of Education, Science and Training as reproduced in* Australian Financial Review, *5 March 2004. Copyright Commonwealth of Australia. Reproduced with permission.*

are signs of increasing competition at the lower end of the price range from Asian countries such as the Philippines and Singapore, with Malaysia and Thailand likely to follow.

# International retailing and wholesaling

An important facet of international services marketing is that of wholesalers and retailers going offshore. They are usually motivated by the desire to spread risk by being involved in more than one country, a need to form international alliances (often to improve the efficiency of their procurement activities) and obtaining a presence in a leading-edge market so as to spot new trends that can be introduced into the home market.

Modes of internationalisation in wholesaling and retailing can include acquiring an established retail operation as did David Jones Ltd with their ill-fated purchase of Buffums of Southern California; setting up your own stores as did Barbeques Galore in California; franchising a retail format overseas as did Sweathog in the UK; licensing the concept as did Done Art and Design in Japan; entering into a joint venture as did Mitre 10 in New Zealand; or selling management know-how as did David's Wholesale in Cambodia. Successful wholesaling and retailing requires a unique and differentiated format as was the case with the Dutch wholesaler Macro going into Thailand; a format that is capable of being replicated offshore; the existence of a similar type of target market offshore to that in Australia or New Zealand; and finally the presence of a niche market of sufficient size that can be profitably serviced in the overseas market while growing your business among locals in that market (e.g. the expatriate market or a market of international sophisticates). The growth of the middle class in Asia has attracted Western retailers as with Marks and Spencer's franchising involvement with the Central Department Store Group in Thailand.

## 14.2 INTERNATIONAL HIGHLIGHT

# In services marketing, service counts

Asian firms are 'taking on' the West by offering relationship-based approaches their local competitors have long since abandoned in the search for profit based on price advantage. Family Mart of Japan, which took over 7-eleven in that country in 1991, has become a household word in Asia by anticipating customer needs and catering for them. In the process it has earned almost unheard of profit margins of 31%. Not only does this chain of convenience stores sell groceries and beverages, but it also offers customers high margin products such as meals, tickets to movies and sporting events, dry cleaning and DVD rentals.

As the convenience store market became saturated in Japan, Family Mart expanded overseas and now 50% of its 12 000 stores are located elsewhere In Asia. The company then targeted the USA with four stores opening In Los Angeles by the end of 2006 and a total of 200 scheduled to open nationwide by 2009. In the USA the aim of Family Mart is to be a premium grocery, quick service restaurant and convenience store combined, targeting customers aged between 21 and 44 whose household incomes exceed US$80 000. Although the local competition in the USA is the existing 140 000 convenience stores, Family Mart are banking on their mastery of information technology to cater for the requirements of current convenience store customers in a manner that offers superior service and focus on detail, so as to appeal to the needs of this affluent customer segment.

**SOURCE:** *Adapted from Caryl, C. and Kashiwagi, A. (2006) 'High convenience', Newsweek, 3–10 July, pp. 49–50.*

## 14.3 INTERNATIONAL HIGHLIGHT

# Westfield hops around

Shortly before the horrific events of 11 September 2001, the Westfield Group in April of that year made a US$420 million (A$797 million) investment in New York's World Trade Center, and at the time this was likely to be just the first of similar acquisitions in the USA. It followed a series of investments in British shopping centres. Although Westfield has invested in the USA since the 1970s, its move into Britain has been more recent with its first involvement in February 2000.

Not widely recognised is that Australia has a comparatively high proportion of retail space to population and, as a consequence, both local retailers and retail owners have become efficient at managing their assets and developing a very sophisticated approach to retailing.

Westfield is the largest retail property group in the world by market capitalisation and has 4400 employees worldwide. It now manages or has interests in 128 shopping centres in four countries with a total value of A$57.5 billion and it has 21 retail developments under way, worth another A$5.6 billion. The major location of these centres is now the USA (67) followed by Australia (50), the UK (7) and New Zealand (4).

Westfield's strategy in the USA is similar to that in Australia—to have shopping centres clustered in big cities. It is now the owner of the largest number of regional malls in California. Other areas for expansion include Europe, following further activities in Britain, Canada and eventually Japan, where it is anticipated the market will eventually open up through the establishment of Japanese real estate investment trusts.

**SOURCES:** *Adapted from Lindsay, B. (2006) 'Westfield plans $1.5 billion fund', Wall Street Journal, 30 August, p. 29; and <http://www.Westfield.com/corporate>, accessed 28 January 2007.*

# International marketing of professional services

A report by the Allen Consulting Group (2001), prepared for the Department of Industry, Science and Resources and Austrade, found that since 1997 business and professional services exhibited a strong growth in exports. Involved in the transformation of data into knowledge and knowledge into valuable advice, the business and professional services sector has four subsectors, which range from relatively traditional legal and accounting services to technical services through to computer services and finally to marketing and business management services.

Globalisation, facilitated by e-commerce, has been a major factor in the development of this sector, but it is the big firms in each of the four subsectors above that have been the major players in developing export markets. In many cases firms have ventured offshore because their clients have gone global and because they attempt to even out risk by diversifying activity and operating in a number of countries. In the process, however, firms have come up against a number of international trade barriers to both the services themselves as well as to the providers of the services. Trade in legal and accounting services faces barriers from regulations in some countries that restrict provision of the services to specific practitioners (e.g. nationals of the country); and computer, marketing and business management services face regulations governing the services provided. For example, in many countries, trade in computer services is constrained by regulations similar to those traditionally applied to telecommunications and broadcasting; and trade in marketing and business management services is often limited by regulations governing advertising content (Allen Consulting Group 2001, p. 3).

Each of the subsectors of professional services export is considered below.

## ACCOUNTING AND LEGAL SERVICES

This subsector has made a positive contribution to Australia's balance of trade since the beginning of 1992. Exports are hampered by a variety of overseas impediments, according to the Department of Foreign Affairs and Trade (Allen Consulting Group 2001, p. 31), such as:

- *accountancy*:
  - licensing and qualification requirements: these could include residency or citizenship requirements and the requirement to complete qualifying examinations in the other country;
  - requirements for foreign accountancy firms to enter into joint ventures and other foreign equity limitations;
  - differences in accounting standards, especially the non-use of international accountancy standards; and
- *legal*:
  - restrictions on foreign lawyers providing some legal services: different restrictions may exist for practising host country law, home country law, international law or third party law;
  - geographical restrictions on licences;
  - difficulty in gaining recognition of qualifications, citizenship and residency requirements; and
  - restrictions on foreign firms associating with local legal firms and hiring local lawyers.

# Building blocks

Although Australians are used to their sportsmen and sportswomen winning awards, they are less aware of their fellow citizens winning awards in the international services sector, as occurred when Glen Murcutt won the Pritzker Prize—architecture's most prestigious award. Australian architects have recently won prestigious projects overseas, including buildings for the Beijing Olympics, restoration of historic sites and the building of hotels and stadiums in Asia, the Middle East and in parts of Europe. Australian architecture is noteworthy because of its freshness of design and concern for the environment.

Now firms such as Denton Corker Marshall (DCM) of Melbourne and the Cox Group and Peddle, Thorpe and Walker (PTW) of Sydney obtain most of their commissions from overseas. Notable successes in this field include Professor Mark Burry, New Zealand-born head of RMIT's Spatial Information Architecture Laboratory, who cracked the geometry code used by Gaudi in his uncompleted art noveau cathedral, La Sagradia Familia, in Barcelona. Gaudi's great church was never finished, partly because no one knew how to complete the project. Burry cracked the code and has been leading the completion project for the last 24 years. More recently, PTW was awarded the design for both the National Swimming Centre and the athlete's village at the Beijing Olympics.

At the 2004 Olympics a network of experienced Australian firms in the services sector helped to ensure that the Athens Olympic Games ran smoothly. Firms involved range from Great Big Events (which won the contract to provide announcers, video systems, scoreboard operation and cueing athlete introduction systems) to Cleanevent, which not only had the A$85 million cleaning contract but also a major advisory role because, according to part-owner Craig Lovett, 'everything was running so late we walked into a construction zone'. Another Australian services operation at the Athens Olympics was TAFE Global, which prepared

training programs for the ATHOC workforce and for the staff of two major sponsors of the games. The ATHOC contract, worth A$7 million, involved provision of a curriculum on how to train Athens volunteers and paid staff. Bidding for Olympic business can have pitfalls, however, as a major firm of Australian architects discovered when they were paid A$150 000 to prepare a plan of a sailing centre for the 2008 Beijing Olympics. The firm spent three times that amount, confident they would win the tender. But the Beijing organisers rejected the tender and retained the plans so as to build the sailing centre themselves.

**SOURCE:** *Masters, R. (2004) 'Gameplan has silver lining for Aussies', Sydney Morning Herald, 23 August, <http://www.smh.com.au/ articles/2004/08/22/1093113054656.html>.*

The export of legal services from Australia was valued at A$121 million in 2004–05 with the major markets being UK, USA, North Asia and South-East Asia (Parkes 2006).

## TECHNICAL SERVICES

These consist of architectural, surveying, consulting engineering and other technical services. The work is non-standardised and project-specific with a major emphasis on design skills and creativity. For most years during the last decade, exports in this subsector have been greater than imports, but the picture fluctuates depending on the economic situation in major overseas markets due to the linking with project work. The 1997 Asian currency crisis had a major effect on exports but these have now recovered.

Architect Philip Cox currently has 20 projects under way in China, including the Quing Dao sailing club, and now cannot cope with the requests his firm receives. With offices in Dubai, Kuala Lumpur, Shanghai and Beijing, as well as having a Chinese language website, 60% of Cox's work now comes from outside Australia. Architect John Bilmon of PTW Architects won the contract to design the Water Cube Aquatic Centre for the Beijing Olympics which combines the symbolism of the Chinese square and the natural structure of soap bubbles. This was assisted by having established an office in Beijing to service other projects either on the go or already completed.

SOURCE: *Adapted from* Export, *August–September 2004; and Carswell, A. (2007) 'Designs on Chinese deals'*, Daily Telegraph, *5 June.*

## COMPUTER SERVICES

International trade in computer services has generally been positive. This has especially been the case since the beginning of 1997. Isolating exports in this subsector is difficult because IT and information management are central to the value propositions that most business and professional firms offer (Allen Consulting Group 2001, p. 56). International opportunities in this sector are linked to the overall growth in overseas markets and the degree to which the firms are embracing e-business, as evidenced by numbers of secure servers and hosts.

## MARKETING AND BUSINESS MANAGEMENT SERVICES

This subsector includes firms in advertising, commercial art and display, market research, business administration and business management services. In this subsector Australia's imports almost always exceed exports although over the last decade the gap between the two appears to be steadily narrowing. To a significant extent this is due to firms in this sector in Australia being overseas owned. Globalisation was found (Allen Consulting Group 2001, p. 89) to have a major affect on both advertising and business management. Research by Styles et al. (2005), based on 17 case studies of Australian exporters of knowledge-based services, found that the tangible and intangible assets of the firm determined success and that, in cases where face-to-face contact was essential to the delivery of the service, personnel-related factors leading to the creation of relationships and networks were essential to export success.

# The internet and the international marketing of services

As the internet matures into a global medium for the trading of services, cross-border online trade will increase dramatically in both scale and diversity. This is most likely to occur in business-to-business trade in services because firms use the internet to link international supply chains. Digitally delivered services have the potential to intensify international trade, particularly in financial and professional services. This is because the internet gives firms more flexibility in locating their operations and it facilitates the internationalisation of small and medium-sized enterprises (SMEs). The web is a developing marketing channel for services and not only transcends national boundaries but also informs, investigates, interacts, distributes, elicits feedback and supports the services transaction.

As pointed out earlier, difficulties in the international marketing of services are sometimes created by the fact that they are characterised by intangibility, simultaneity, heterogeneity and perishability. These difficulties can often be reduced by using the web as a vehicle for international services marketing:

- *Intangibility*: The web can be used to provide tangible cues when marketing the intangible, that is, something to compensate for the fact that customers cannot see the service they are receiving. This happens when airlines sell you an electronic ticket and you receive confirmation via electronic means. The web can also address the issue of intangibility by providing the customer with a sample in cyberspace as happens with the MP3 music site. Having a 'visitor's book' on your site also addresses this issue as it provides a record of who visited the site and when.

- *Simultaneity*: Because of the simultaneous nature of production and consumption of the service, demands for a customised offering are frequent. The web is ideally suited for customisation because its capacity is based on information technology, data storage and data processing instead of reliance on employees at a physical location. The web facilitates the customer by innovating and offering suggestions to improve the service outcome. It also facilitates interactivity between customer and provider as exemplified by a customer being able to customise the content of a web page so that it allows people to interact with each other.

- *Heterogeneity*: The web facilitates standardisation of customer treatment as when you receive the same form of greeting when logging onto a website. It removes some of the variable treatment in the service encounter due to different personalities encountered in the marketplace. This is evident, for example, when booking travel via the web as opposed to booking travel through a travel agent. Data gathering is facilitated by web usage. The conduct of focus groups via the internet enables focus groups to be conducted with more customers, more attentively and in real time. It also means that everyone in the firm can listen to what the customer has to say about the service, not just the interviewer.

- *Perishability*: To overcome this problem, international service marketers are using websites to manage both supply and demand. On the supply side, the web gives the international marketer the ability to provide a 24-hour service to customers anywhere in the world. On the demand side, firms can use the web for promotion, pricing and service bundling to stimulate demand (e.g. to dispose of last-minute remaining seats on a flight or at a concert).

There are strategic implications for using the internet in marketing services internationally. Lovelock et al. (2004, p. 387) point out the strategic implications:

- *Customer service*: The web enables SMEs to provide almost the same level of service when marketing services internationally as would be the case if they had used a salesperson. Given the cost differences, the web enables SME service providers to internationalise more easily.

- *Pirating the value chain*: Participants in the value chain have the opportunity with the web to take over the role of other members in the chain and provide customers with better value as a consequence. This happens when the producer of the service uses the web to replace physical delivery and the use of intermediaries overseas. An example would be when a publisher delivers the content of publications via these means to libraries in other countries.

- *Digital value chain creation*: Innovation can be achieved and new services provided from afar. SMEs located anywhere can engage in online collaboration in R&D, service design and promotion with overseas alliance partners.

- *Creating a customer magnet*: Firms that create a strong brand equity on the internet will create confidence among their customers about returning to the site again.

# Summary

The international marketing of services is different from that of products because of both the different nature of services and the way they are delivered to the customer. Although the categorisation of goods and services is arbitrary because many services are dependent on goods and vice versa, the general differentiating characteristics of services which decide their being offered internationally are their perishability, their intangibility, their simultaneity and their heterogeneity. Because services are more dependent on people, on availability of information and material infrastructure for delivery, their provision to overseas customers is often complicated, especially as they may be delivered in the supplying country, as with tourism, or in the overseas country, as with consultancy. Because of their characteristics the provision of services overseas is more culturally sensitive than with products and more subject to government regulation and non-tariff barriers. It is more difficult to standardise the service offering in overseas markets and most attempts to do so focus on the mode of service delivery rather than on the service itself.

## ETHICS ISSUE

Your company has been asked by Thai Farmer's Bank to carry out a preliminary audit of a publicly listed, large sugar mill operation in which the bank is a minor shareholder. This audit is necessary following a notification by the Thai Stock Exchange of reports of some minor irregularities in the operations of the firm. Your investigations reveal that the major shareholders are a Thai business conglomerate, a division of the Thai army and powerful interests in an adjacent country whose shares are held by Thai nominees. Furthermore, the financial affairs of the sugar mill operation are not what they seem; their actual debt to equity ratio substantially exceeds prudent limits and there is strong evidence that the operation is being used by parties in an adjacent country to launder money. When you raise your concerns with the management of the sugar mill operation, you are strongly advised to stick to your brief of preparing a preliminary report that is confined to the issue raised by the Thai Stock Exchange. You are further advised that exceeding this brief could result in no further business for your firm in Thailand, may cause trade relations problems between the adjacent country and Thailand, and may place you personally at risk.

*Caught between expediency on the one hand and protecting the international reputation of your accounting firm on the other, what would you do?*

## Websites

Additional thoughts on international services marketing http://www.globaledge.msu.edu/
Cleanevent http://www.cleanevent.com
David Maister http://www.davidmaister.com
Great Big Events http://www.greatbigevents.com.au
IDP Education Pty Ltd http//www.idp.com
IP Australia http//www.ipaustralia.gov.au
PTW Architects http://www.ptw.com.au
QBE Insurance Group http//www.qbe.com
Tourism Australia http://www.australia.com
Tourism Victoria http://www.tourismvictoria_significance_tourism
Treasury http://www.treasury.gov.au
TRIPS (Trade Related Intellectual Property) http//www.wto.org/english/tratip_e/trips_e
Westfield http://www.westfield.com/corporate

## Discussion questions

1  Discuss how marketing services overseas involves different marketing approaches to those required when marketing products in overseas markets.

2  Which of the ways of categorising services exports are the most appropriate in the internet age?

3  Why are services exports more subject to cultural sensitivity issues than the exports of products?

4 What are the factors responsible for the increased attention now being focused on the international marketing of services?

5 Take a service provider with which you are familiar and outline various strategic options for entering the Thai market.

# References

Allen Consulting Group (2001) 'Creating value by transforming knowledge: Australia's business and professional services sector', report prepared for the Services Industry Section of the Department of Industry, Science and Resources and Austrade, Commonwealth of Australia, Canberra.

*Australian Financial Review*, 5 March 2004.

Bradley, F. (2002) *International Marketing Strategy*, 4th edn, Financial Times Prentice Hall, Harlow, UK.

Carswell, A. (2007) 'Designs on Chinese deals', *Daily Telegraph*, 5 June, p. 53.

Caryl, C. and Kashiwagi, A. (2006) 'High convenience', *Newsweek*, 3–10 July, pp. 49–50.

Dahringer, L.D. (1991) 'Marketing services internationally: barriers and management strategies', *Journal of Service Marketing*, Vol. 5, pp. 5–17.

Dennis, A. and Lee, J. (2004) 'Sun, sand and salesmenship', *Sydney Morning Herald*, 17–18 April, p. 32.

Department of Foreign Affairs and Trade (DFAT) Economic Analytical Unit (2006) *ASEAN: Building an Economic Community*, Commonwealth of Australia, Canberra.

Department of the Treasury (2006) *Australia's Services Exports*, Treasury Submission to House of Representatives Economics, Finance and Public Administration Committee Public Inquiry, August 2006.

*Export*, August–September 2004.

<http://www.tourismvictoria_significance_tourism>.

Jack, R. (2006) 'The impact of services embeddedness and inseparability on firms' entry mode: an appraisal', unpublished PhD thesis, *Monash University*.

L/E/K Partnership (1994) *Intelligent Exports and the Silent Revolution in Services*, Commonwealth of Australia, Canberra.

Levett, C. (2005) 'A slice of the action', *Sydney Morning Herald*, 29–30 October, p. 27.

Lindsay, B. (2006) 'Westfield plans $1.5 billion fund', *Wall Street Journal*, 30 August, p. 29.

Lovelock, C.H., Patterson, P.G. and Walker, R.H. (2004) *Services Marketing: An Asia-Pacific and Australian Perspective*, 3rd edn, Prentice Hall, Sydney.

Masters, R. (2004) 'Gameplan has silver lining for Aussies', *Sydney Morning Herald*, 23 August, <http://www.smh.com.au/articles/2004/08/22/1093113054656.html>.

Parkes, J. (2006) 'Export and the Law', *Export*, July 1, pp. 22–26.

Patterson, P.G. and Cicic, M. (1995) 'A typology of service firms in international markets: an empirical investigation', *Journal of International Marketing*, Vol. 3, No. 4, pp. 57–83.

Styles, C., Patterson, P. and La, V.Q. (2005) 'Exporting services to Southeast Asia: lessons from Australian knowledge-based service exporters', *Journal of International Marketing*, Vol. 13, No. 4, pp. 104–28.

**go online**

Go online to <www.pearsoned.com.au/fletcher> to find more case studies.

# Cognition Consulting—marketing a 'knowledge rich' firm overseas!

**Greg Walton, School of Marketing and International Business, Victoria University of Wellington, New Zealand**

The New Zealand education export industry is a shining example of a services industry. Along with professional services and tourism, the education industry is a relatively new foreign exchange earner. The tertiary sector (New Zealand universities and vocational trainers/polytechnics) and the English language sector were the first sectors to leap into exporting, effectively beginning the industry's export development. More recently, the secondary school sector recognised revenue earning and other benefits from internationalising its core function/business as well. Export earnings began with elementary student recruitment— revenue earnt from fees paid by foreign fee paying students. Student recruitment now supplements more sophisticated forms and components of internationalisation that include collaborative research (typically between academics), curriculum development, institutional strengthening, staff swaps and in-market curriculum delivery.

Many of these latter and more sophisticated forms represent in-market investment activities.

Built on the success of New Zealand's educa-

tion reforms, Cognition Consulting is a fast-growing export business, winning an international reputation for performance and delivery from Asia to the Middle East.

Cognition Consulting is the export arm of Multi Serve Education Trust, a charitable trust and New Zealand's largest independent supplier of consulting services to the education community. Most of Cognition Consulting's work is within individual schools, coaching and mentoring them through the reform process. It also works at a strategic level with government agencies, as in the case of Qatar, where it is currently assisting with development of a new early childhood education strategy. The range of Cognition Consulting's expertise spans 'institutional strengthening' and 'structural reformation' work within education systems. Specific services include:

- new school establishment projects;
- community consultation;
- policy development and reviews;
- assessment, recording and reporting;
- governance training;
- evaluation and auditing;
- financial management;
- project management;
- information and communications technology (ICT) management, including cyber safety;
- personnel management;
- school leadership and leadership training;
- management, including performance management;
- curriculum solutions;

*Chris Sullivan, Cognition Consulting Consultant, in Doha, Qatar.*

- strategic planning and school self-review;

- recruitment;

- teacher professional development;

- coaching and mentoring; and

- financial consulting.

Multi Serve Education Trust was launched in 1989 at the time of the Tomorrow's Schools reform program to take over some of the business divested by the Department of Education. Being a charitable trust, the net surplus arising from its activities directly benefits New Zealand schools.

Des Hammond, Chief Executive of Multi Serve Education Trust and Chairman of Cognition Consulting, says the trust started exporting in 1996 after it was approached by several offshore education contacts and it became apparent that New Zealand's education reform program was held in very high regard internationally.

Multi Serve Education Trust's annual turnover is about NZ$20 million with about 50% being generated offshore through Cognition Consulting. Mr Hammond anticipates revenue to reach NZ$40 million by 2010, with 80% generated from its international consultancy work.

Exports have grown hugely in the past three years, says Mr Hammond, driven by the opening up of the Middle East market, 'a new and exciting market for New Zealand educators'. Other export markets where Cognition Consulting has experience include Thailand, Malaysia, Brunei, China and Hong Kong (see Figure 1). Des Hammond says:

*We target markets where governments are committed to significant education reforms. The reform changes in these markets often mirror New Zealand's own education journey since 1989 and which Multi Serve Education Trust was an integral part of, including self-management of schools, governance reforms, modernisation of the curriculum, new learning techniques and changes in the art of teaching itself. Sometimes the reforms in international markets are even more dramatic, and go beyond self-management to privatisation of the school sector.*

The quote above discusses two key themes. The first statement indicates a little about Cognition Consulting's customer characteristics. It describes who they are and what they look like. The statement specifically details important selection criteria. This criterion is directly related to the second key point—the nature of the business Cognition Consulting is in. These clear statements are about 'positioning.' They detail how Cognition Consulting positions itself in the marketplace based on defined competences, clear customer definition and where it develops areas of competitive advantage. Des Hammond says, 'We are very proud of what we've contributed to reforms in Qatar. In just over two years we have moved from being a minor player in the education reform movement to being acknowledged openly and in publicity material as the leading

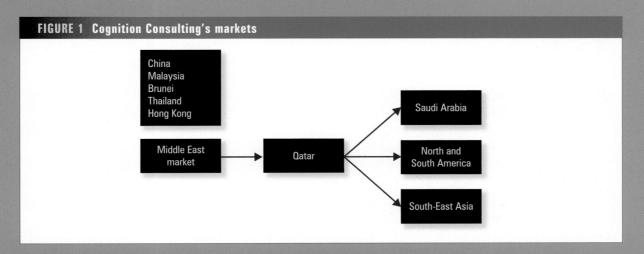

**FIGURE 1  Cognition Consulting's markets**

service provider.' Success in Qatar has also led to approaches from other Middle East markets, such as Saudi Arabia and interest from new regions, notably North and South America and parts of South East Asia.

Cognition Consulting has continued to expand its operations in the Middle East with a new school support project in Dammam, a city in the Eastern Province of the Kingdom of Saudi Arabia. Des Hammond says the Saudi contract involves the provision of support to teachers and school leadership for the Al Bassam Group, a significant private education provider in the region. This venture into Saudi Arabia represents a new and challenging direction for Cognition Consulting. The company has swiftly capitalised on its very successful operations in Qatar in order to create additional opportunities and anticipates that this will be the beginning of even wider operations in Saudi Arabia. Des Hammond says:

> Cognition Consulting is competing with multi nationals who operate as global education consultancy companies. Given their scale of economy it's crucial we retain key points of difference in our delivery and operations. We continue to win business from these competitors through the strength of our local and international brand, based on our reputation, our people and the quality of our work as well as our experience in the New Zealand educational reforms. A key success factor in education consultancy is building really strong relationships in the market with key people in agencies that are responsible for the contracting. And you must build the depth of capability within your own organisation in order to deliver on the promise; that's absolutely critical; otherwise service quality falls down quickly.

Supply chain management and value chain management are contemporary management disciplines. More pronounced in services marketing than in consumer product supply is the need for strong personal relationships. This is an important component of networking and networks. The importance of interpersonal relationships is a direct response to understanding the 'intangibility' and 'perishability' of services and services marketing. It concerns recognising the importance of trust, credibility of the people designing and delivering the service and the capability of the supplier. Just as important, however, is how an understanding of personal relationships informs and shapes market entry mode choice.

Cognition Consulting's employees have increased in number from 15 in 2004 to more than 70. Its consultants are a combination of highly qualified and experienced educators, current and/or former principals, senior teachers and managers from the Ministry of Education and other government agencies. It also contracts suitably qualified expatriate New Zealanders.

Des Hammond says: 'It's a fascinating and exciting role for New Zealand educators. It uses all of their professional learning over their education careers in terms of student and business management techniques, curriculum development and pedagogy'.

Contracts typically range from three months to two years, though Cognition Consulting currently has a bid on the table for a five-year project in the Middle East. It has a formal quality assurance and evaluation process in place to measure performance. Mr Hammond says the high number of approaches it receives from new clients and the high level of repeat business it wins from existing clients are also measures of how well the consultancy is performing.

Cognition Consulting's vision is to expand its capacity as a global consultancy firm while retaining its unique New Zealand character, which it sees as a valuable marketing tool internationally. Des Hammond says, 'We have tapped into a new exciting export market and the rewards of that are the growth of the business and the professional satisfaction that our educators get from contributing to education reform in other markets. There's a lot of potential for this to become a really important export industry. Out of our growth, our beneficiaries, the New Zealand school sector, will be rewarded.'

## Bibliography

New Zealand Trade and Enterprise, <http://www.nzte. govt.nz/section/14606/16260.aspx>.

## Questions

1   What determines an internationally competitive services firm? What elements of firm international competitiveness are more important for a services firm like Cognition Consulting than a products manufacturer? What models of competitiveness would be useful to understand this?

2   Some services exporters (especially professional services like Cognition Consulting) have a more complex definition of their customer groups than manufactured goods exporters. This case study suggests two customer groups. Draw a diagram to illustrate how different these two groups are and explain the importance of this in understanding international services marketing.

3   How should a services firm develop market entry strategy and determine market entry mode? How does this compare to a non-services firm?

4   Describe the importance and value of an operational/tactical marketing plan for a services provider like Cognition Consulting.

5   What tactical marketing considerations should Cognition Consulting consider? What is the relevance of the 4Ps in international marketing?

# PROMOTION IN INTERNATIONAL MARKETING

## Learning Objectives

**After reading this chapter you should be able to:**

- identify the stages which apply to the international communications process;

- evaluate the factors which cause international communication to differ from domestic communication;

- assess the extent to which modifications are necessary when using print media overseas;

- recognise the advantages and disadvantages of visual and aural media for promotion in the international marketplace;

- prepare a plan for effective participation in trade displays overseas;

- maximise the benefits of joining a trade mission; and

- appreciate the advantages of taking into account country of origin and of standardisation versus differentiation when promoting overseas.

# Putting a 'brand' on your country

# G'DAY LA and NY

The inaugural Anholt-GMI Nation Brand Index looked at consumer's attitudes towards a number of countries and Australia rated as the most attractive of all. This indicates that products marketed as 'made in Australia' are likely to be viewed by overseas buyers in a positive way.

The Australian government has moved swiftly to capitalise on this with moves to promote a range of Australian goods and services in overseas countries under the Australian 'brand', beginning with the USA.

The G'day LA campaign of 2006 took a wide variety of activities in which there was already an awareness of Australia and used them to extend the positive image to goods and services by involving 200 companies from all over Australia in the campaign. Commencing with the Penfold's Icon Black Tie Dinner, the promotion featured an AFL match, a private INXS concert and a golf day with Ian Baker Finch.

Australian entities already established in Los Angeles were recruited to the cause, including Westfield Shopping Malls, which featured an Australian theme, and well-known Australian entertainment celebrities such as Steve Irwin, Olivia Newton-John and Delta Goodrem.

In 2007, the event broadened its scope with a G'day USA program based in New York. This enabled Austrade to involve some major new media partners and tackle the fashion and business centres that are focused on New York. Australian celebrities based in the US included in the New York promotion were Russell Crowe, Naomi Watts, Cate Blanchett, Rachel Griffiths and Olivia Newton-John. Australian firms reported more than A\$14 million in sales from their connection with Australia Week involvement.

**SOURCES:** *'Aussie brand is number one'*, Export, *October 2005; 'They love us in the US'*, Export, *March 2006; and 'US says hello to Aussie exports'*, Export, *March 2007. Image courtesy of Australia Week Committee.*

# INTRODUCTION

This chapter focuses on promotion in international marketing rather than on international promotion. It is primarily concerned with the management of promotion both in and across a number of nations. Promotion in international marketing plays the same role as it does in domestic marketing—that is, communication with audiences to achieve desired outcomes. Any consideration of communications strategy in the international marketplace must take into account that there are four elements in the promotional mix. The first is advertising—a non-personal presentation through any medium that is paid for by a sponsor. The second is public relations—a non-personal form of communication based on conveying messages to many 'publics' (stakeholders) or exchange partners designed to create a favourable image for the organisation. The third is personal selling, which involves direct communication between buyer and seller. The final element is sales promotion, which involves techniques to stimulate a short-term response. The relative importance of these techniques will vary from overseas market to overseas market, depending on government regulation, media availability, marketing acceptability and promotions infrastructure. As a consequence, the relative importance of elements within the promotion mix will vary when the Australian firm promotes offshore, as will the need to modify each element of the promotion mix prior to its implementation.

## COMMUNICATION THEORY

Promotion is a major form of communication in international business. Its essence is the transmission of a message from the seller or exporter to the buyer or importer. However, the Australian firm will have many 'publics' (otherwise referred to as stakeholders) with which to communicate besides the overseas customer. These 'publics', located both in Australia and overseas, include the general public, the government, its suppliers, its employees, the media, its stockholders, other firms in the industry and its intermediaries. The communication objective will vary from 'public' to 'public'. Whereas, for example, the objective with the media might be to obtain favourable coverage, the objective with the government may be to obtain fair or favourable treatment. Also, the most appropriate promotional tool will vary according to the 'public', with public relations being used to influence government in contrast to using advertising to influence customers or intermediaries.

### The communication process

Figure 15.1 shows the communication process. There are three major elements. These are the sender, the medium through which the message is conveyed and the receiver of the message. This process of communication is influenced by both environmental factors and noise or interference in the transmission of and/or receiving of the message.

#### SENDER

The sender of the message, although usually a person, can also be a brand or a company or a combination of all three. The message must be appropriate to the medium being used and in a form that the intended recipients can understand. As an example, an Australian TV commercial intended for use in the USA should not involve broad Australian accents because these will not be comprehensible to Americans.

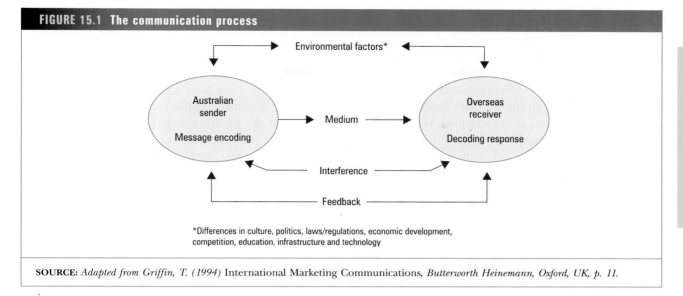

**FIGURE 15.1 The communication process**

*Differences in culture, politics, laws/regulations, economic development, competition, education, infrastructure and technology

**SOURCE:** *Adapted from Griffin, T. (1994)* International Marketing Communications, *Butterworth Heinemann, Oxford, UK, p. 11.*

Before being sent, the message is encoded so that it is suitable for the medium to be used and will appeal to its intended audience. Encoding ensures that the message will be interpreted correctly and, for this reason, literal translations on the one hand and plays on words on the other should be eliminated.

## MEDIUM

The medium can take a wide variety of forms, ranging from a letter to a phone directory to a billboard to a television commercial. Not only must the medium be appropriate for the environment in which it is to be used, but it must also be appropriate for the product or service being promoted. Some media are more appropriate for some products than for others. As an example, expensive perfume is more likely to be promoted in glossy magazines than on billboards because of the image that accompanies the product and the expectations that have been created by the product. It is necessary first to check that the medium used in Australia or New Zealand is available in the overseas country. Then it should be determined whether it has a similar impact in terms of cost per potential customer reached, is technically able to convey the message without distortion and is similarly regarded in relation to the image of the product category. The medium selected must be suitable for conveying the attributes of the product. For example, television is most appropriate for demonstrating a product whereas direct mail is most appropriate for sampling a product.

## RECEIVER

Those receiving the message can be from a wide spectrum and can include employees, intermediaries, media editors and those who can influence decision makers as well as past, present and future customers. How the message is received will depend on many factors. These include whether the content is interesting, the message clear and the language translation appropriate, and whether the pictures, sounds, words and actions used are suitable in relation to the message, its purpose and its subject. How the receiver responds to the message is likely to be a function of whether something was learned, or attitudes changed or further action stimulated.

## INTERFERENCE

Interference creates noise, which has the effect of disrupting communication. A major source of noise is competitive activity that often takes the form of confusion created by competitors' messages being transmitted at the same time. If faced with this problem one solution is to seek a different medium for the message. Interference can also occur because of distortion due to poor-quality reproduction or transmission of print, audio or visual material. Another source of interference is that of appropriateness of the medium. Apart from its suitability for the target audience, there is also the issue of editorial compatibility between product and medium, as with contraceptives and a Roman Catholic-owned radio station. Also, this includes location of the advertisement and editorial content. For example, in a magazine an advertisement on a feminine hygiene product should be adjacent to an article on beauty rather than to an article on cooking. A final source of interference relates to the degree to which receivers were receptive to the message. For example, were they distracted at the time the message was received? Were they preoccupied with other things? Would receiving the message at that time cause irritation? An example would be the screening of soap commercials during coverage of the opening ceremony of the Olympic Games.

## ENVIRONMENTAL FACTORS

The effectiveness of promotion as a form of communication will be influenced by a number of factors. These include sensitivity to social norms, the degree to which local tastes and preferences are catered for, the extent to which religious mores and standards of behaviour are conformed to, the awareness of media alternatives and the constraints attaching to each in the overseas market.

## FEEDBACK

The feedback loop in Figure 15.1 enables an assessment as to whether the communications objectives are being achieved. Depending on the form of promotion employed, this feedback can be immediate, as with personal selling, or drawn out, as with assessing the effectiveness of advertising. Also, the feedback may be voluntary, as indicated by orders placed, or involuntary, as with research to assess the effect of print and visual advertising.

# Constraints in international marketing communication

The more important of these constraints are outlined below:

- *Language differences*: The diversity of languages in world markets, even within the one country, provides a challenge because, when venturing overseas, the firm will need to communicate in a variety of languages other than English. Technological accuracy or perfect translation is not sufficient as use of the other language must be motivating— what Terpstra and Sarathy (2000, p. 449) term 'language of the heart'.

- *Marketing acceptability*: This varies from country to country depending on politics, history (e.g. former Centrally Planned Economies) and level of economic development (generally speaking, marketing is less acceptable in the poorest countries).

- *Media availability*: The media available in Australia or New Zealand may not be available in many countries or, if they exist, they may not be allowed to be used for promotion other than by government. In addition, the volume of each medium available in each country varies. Even in developed countries this is the case, with a lesser volume available in rural as opposed to urban areas. Associated with this is the variation between countries in terms of the number of viewers, listeners or readers per TV set, radio set or newspaper copy.

- *Intermediary availability*: The availability and effectiveness of advertising agencies, media buying groups and market research institutions also vary from country to country and this variation can be a constraint on international promotion, especially where it is intended to replicate an Australian or New Zealand approach in an overseas market.

- *Activities of competitors*: In some markets the competitors are other international firms, local firms and, in many, a combination of both. This creates a different situation from market to market. Competitor activities may require either an increase or a reduction in promotion in a given market at any time.

- *Government controls*: The final constraint is that national governments regulate promotional activities within their borders in the interests of protecting their citizens, their firms and their culture. Such regulations can have an impact on the media, the message, the budget, media ownership and operations of promotional intermediaries.

# FACTORS IN INTERNATIONAL COMMUNICATION

International communication, whether it be verbal, visual, written or oral, will be influenced by a variety of contextual factors. These may be a mix of culture, language, education, economic development, media infrastructure or government regulation.

## Culture

The factor in the application of the communications model with the most impact on international promotion is culture. This is because the message encoded in one culture may not work in another. In international promotion it is necessary to establish a common frame of reference for both sender and receiver. Included in this is overstatement versus understatement as the norm, as well as harmony in expectations as to size, distance, punctuality and location. The message to be conveyed should also take account not only culturally influenced differences in spoken or written language, but also differences in the silent language of the body and accompanying gestures.

Culture affects what people like and dislike, how they interpret signals and symbols, as well as their attitudes towards and biases against particular products and services. These issues need to be taken into account when developing the message to be communicated and deciding on the medium to be used. As a consequence, symbols, brand names, celebrity endorsements and copy platforms used in Australia may be inappropriate in another country. Albaum et al. (2006) argue that the successful communicator relies upon symbols when establishing empathy with a person in another country. Colour is one type of visual symbol. In the case of colours, the associations and meanings attributed to certain colours in different countries explain why some colours are preferred in advertisements to others. Figure 15.2 provides detail as to colours and numbers that would be appropriate to use when promoting products in Chinese communities.

Aircraft manufacturers bidding to secure new aircraft orders from the fastest growing market in the world for new aircraft—China—are very conscious of Chinese preferences in

**FIGURE 15.2  Perceptions of colours and numbers**

| Colour | Perception |
|---|---|
| Grey | Inexpensive |
| Blue | High-quality |
| Green | Pure<br>Trustworthy<br>Dependable<br>Sincere |
| Red | Happy<br>Love<br>Adventurous |
| Yellow | Happy<br>Pure<br>Progressive |
| Purple | Expensive<br>Love |
| Brown | Good tasting |
| Black | Powerful<br>Expensive<br>High quality<br>Dependable<br>Trustworthy |

The Chinese consider the following numbers lucky and would prove advantageous if used with a product: 8, 11, 13, 15, 16, 17, 18, 25, 29, 31, 32 and 39.

**SOURCE:** *Jacobs, L., Keown, C., Worthley, R. and Ghymn, J. (1991) 'Cross-cultural colour comparisons',* International Marketing Review, *Vol. 8, No. 3, pp. 21–30. Reproduced with permission of Emerald Group Publishing.*

numerology. According to Wallace (2005), Boeing's decision to name its new 300-seat 7E7 aircraft the 787 was an influential factor in Chinese Airlines placing an order for approximately 100 of this new model. Eight is considered a lucky number in Chinese numerology.

Hall (1976) divided cultures into those that were high-context cultures and those that were low-context cultures and argued that cultures fell somewhere along a continuum between these two extremes. High-context cultures are those where the social context that surrounds the act is much more important than written or legal documentation. China is an example of a high-context culture. Low-context cultures are those where the social context is unimportant and it is the written word or legal agreement that counts, as in Australia or the USA. Knowing where a culture falls along this continuum provides a useful guide as to how to communicate effectively with people in different cultures. In high-context cultures communications approaches should imply rather than directly state the obvious. whereas in low-context cultures the reverse applies. Dulek et al. (1991) categorise the application of context to international communication as described below.

## CONVERSATIONAL PRINCIPLES

The first of the four conversational principles involves recognising that in high-context cultures people want to know considerable detail about the executive and the company represented. This means that advertising and promotion should feature the company, its credibility and its background to a greater extent than in Australia or New Zealand. The second relates to clarity in communication and the need to avoid assuming that elements of the message which are taken for granted in Australia or New Zealand will also be taken for granted in the other country. In promoting overseas, it is necessary to speak clearly, use a presenter without a strong accent, speak slowly and avoid jargon, clichés or slang. The third principle focuses on identification with the overseas recipient. This can be achieved by including phrases or words from the language spoken by the recipient and by allusion to history or contemporary events in the receiver's country. The fourth requires attention to body language. When recipients of the message cannot understand the spoken word they are likely to rely for meaning on the body language of the presenter or the tone of voice used when the communication is made. The body language in commercials needs to be consistent with the message being communicated.

## PRESENTATION PRINCIPLES

The first of these presentation principles involves respect for cultures that are more formal than those in Australia or New Zealand. The desire for structured as opposed to more natural presentations will influence the format and content of the promotional communication. The second presentation principle involves respecting and appealing to the different way foreign audiences react to promotional messages. The third requires patience with cultures where messages are drawn out or subject to interruption—rather than fast-paced or brief. In some cultures the length of the message is often viewed as an indication of the importance the promoter attaches to its subject.

## WRITTEN-WORD PRINCIPLES

It is important to vary the structure of the message according to the context of the culture. Only in low-context cultures should communication be organised so that the central point is directly and immediately stated.

A second principle requires that the style of writing be adapted to the culture to which the readers belong. In high-context cultures this means that there should be more emphasis on politeness and decorum in the message. In cases where there is doubt about the ability of the recipient of the communication to understand the language in which it is conveyed, it is necessary either to provide a translation or communicate the message visually as well as verbally.

Trade names, brands and slogans may have to be changed as well as translated when used in other markets. A brand name or slogan that is effective in Australia or New Zealand may mean something offensive or ludicrous in another language.

Commercial and General Acceptance Company of Australia use the brand name CAGA. They acquired a large office block in the commercial heart of Sydney and had CAGA emblazoned on the building. The building housing the Consulate-General for Spain faced the CAGA building and the Consul-General's office faced directly onto the sign. A formal protest was lodged to the Australian government about the sign which both the Consul-General and his Spanish visitors found offensive—in Spanish, caga means 'to shit'.

Other cultural issues that can affect communication overseas are whether social hierarchies are respected or egalitarianism prevails. This will affect the content of the message, the presenter used and possibly on the background employed in the promotion or advertisement. The role of women in a culture also has an impact on the target of the communication and the content of the message.

De Mooij (2005) studied the applications of Hofstede's (2001) dimensions of culture (see Chapter 3) to advertising messages and found that in high power distance cultures egalitarian appeals should be avoided and that advertisements showing respect for age and status are more acceptable; in collectivist cultures appeals should not relate to individual achievements, but rather to group benefits and should avoid use of the personal pronoun 'I'; in feminine cultures masculine traits such as a focus on winning and aggressive typology and layout should be avoided and a focus on relationships and affiliation is preferred; and in high uncertainty avoidance cultures the content of messages needs to be more highly structured and detailed information provided. As well, the presenters of the message should be well groomed and exude an air of competence, and in cultures where a short-term orientation prevails, messages should demand immediate action rather than calm consideration.

## Language

The ability to translate words from one language to another is no guarantee that the same message is being communicated. Often meaning is culturally influenced and a portion of meaning is often lost in translation. For this reason it is preferable to translate the idea or concept into the other language rather than the words used in English. Furthermore, because English tends to be the language of international business, it is mostly American, English or Australian cultural norms that are communicated when English is translated into other languages. These cultural norms are often not those of the target market overseas. In promotion, the culturally sensitive elements of the other culture need to be taken into account to enhance the impact.

Languages also vary in the degree to which they convey meaning precisely. In markets where language tends to be imprecise the communication needs to be more extended than in markets where a more precise language is used. Finally, languages vary as to the extent to which words commit the speaker. As an example, does 'yes' mean 'yes' as in Australia, or 'maybe' as in Thailand, or 'I hear what you are saying' as in Japan?

Chinese written language is composed of pictures rather than a sequence of words. As a consequence, Chinese thinking tends towards a more holistic processing of information and Chinese are better at seeing 'the big picture' whereas Westerners are more at ease with describing details and thinking sequentially in parts. Messages directed at Chinese should as a rule skip the details and focus on the benefit of the whole proposition.

Context is important as this will influence the interpretation put on the message. For this reason it is necessary to check the context in the overseas market where the target of the promotion is located. The context consists of the people involved in the communication, when the communication is made and where it is made. The way the message is projected will influence the way it is interpreted. This can be a matter of the tone of voice, the overlap of conversations in the communication, the speed of speaking, the degree of personal involvement in what is said and the emphasis on talking rather than listening. All the above vary from country to country and can influence how the message is received. This is illustrated by the following story.

The slogan 'Put a Tiger in Your Tank', although often regarded as a perfect example of a standardised advertising campaign, is not as standardised as it might seem. It is not fully equivalent from one country to another. A study of the back translations of the advertisements shows that in Northern European countries, such as Holland and Germany, the power of the tiger is located in the tank; and in France the power of the tiger is located in the engine. In Asian countries, such as Thailand, the tiger may be regarded as a danger for the local population and its image is that of the jungle rather than of power.

SOURCE: *Adapted from Usunier, J.C. and Lee, J.A. (2005)* Marketing Across Cultures, *4th edn, Financial Times Prentice Hall, Harlow, UK, p. 387.*

There are three aspects of language and mass media that require comment. These are the use of foreign words, the impact on advertisement layout and translation problems. Foreign words are often used in advertisements to enhance the image of the product. The foreign word can create an association with a country or a region and this can enhance awareness as well as identification. For example, French words are commonly used when perfume is promoted internationally. Foreign words are often embodied in logos that result in their reinforcing the image of the product being promoted. Sometimes foreign words are used in advertising because the local language is incapable of conveying the precise meaning or because a technical term exists in one language only and most in the field are familiar with that term. Usually, it is European words that are used as foreign words in advertisements.

Language affects the layout of advertisements because different languages, regardless of whether written in characters or script, require different amounts of space to convey the same message. Thai, for example, requires 35% to 50% more space than English. This means that in an advertisement the balance between visual and written elements may need to be reviewed when advertising overseas or more space paid for per advertisement. Similarly, with spoken advertising the number of words required to convey the idea or concept may result in a longer radio or TV commercial.

It is important to translate the concept rather than the words when translating an advertisement from one language to another. Failure to do so results in mistakes; for example, 'full aeroplane' in English becomes 'pregnant aeroplane' in French; and 'body by Fisher' becomes 'corpse by Fisher' in German. Any translation must be made culturally relevant in the target language and this may cause not only the original English text to change, but also the tone of the advertisement to alter. It is desirable once the advertisement has been translated into the other language to arrange for a back translation from the other language into English, to ensure that the correct concept and message is being conveyed.

## Education

Different media have different educational requirements. In markets where literacy is low it may be necessary to communicate messages in visual or aural modes rather than in writing Figure 15.3 shows how most instincts can be tapped by using primitive visual symbols. In addition, the level of education in an overseas country will influence the content of the promotional or advertising message. In countries such as India where literacy rates are low it may be necessary to use media that are visual or aural and, if print media is used, then ensure that it is the visual elements which convey the message. Other media may need to be considered, such as billboards, mime performances, puppet shows, movies and posters. Those

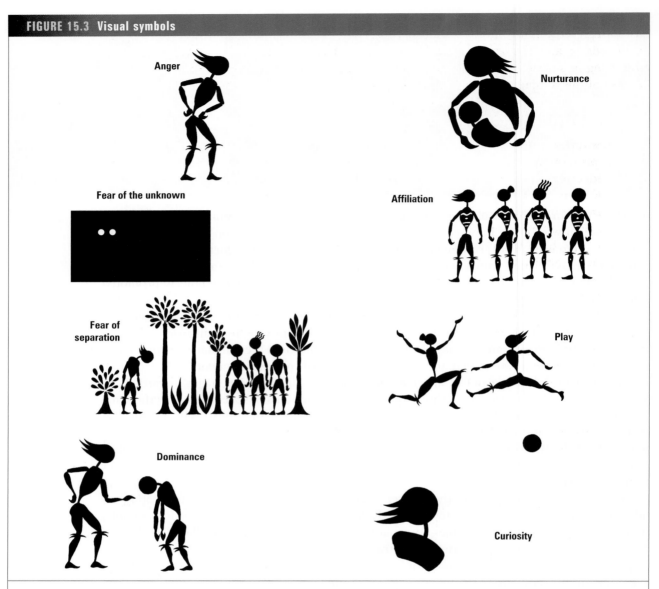

**FIGURE 15.3  Visual symbols**

Anger

Nurturance

Fear of the unknown

Affiliation

Fear of separation

Play

Dominance

Curiosity

**SOURCE:** *Rossiter, J.R. and Bellman, S. (2005)* Marketing Communications: Theory and Applications, *Pearson Prentice Hall, Sydney, NSW, p. 54. Reproduced with permission.*

promoting social services, such as health and contraception in less-developed countries, frequently have to devise innovative promotional vehicles for communicating with people with limited education and literacy.

## Economic development

The level of economic development has an impact on how many people in the overseas market can afford the product. It also influences who has a need for the product and the acceptable level of sophistication of the product to be offered to that market. This factor can also affect which media the people can afford to patronise as well as which media are available. In some countries the higher the per capita GNP, the higher the percentage of GNP accounted for by advertising expenditure. However, as a country's income rises, so does the incentive to engage in advertising and promotion. This has the side effect that, despite the greater need for advertising in such countries, the effectiveness of particular advertising messages is reduced because of the volume of persuasive messages.

# Media infrastructure

Countries differ as to availability, reach, cost and effectiveness of media and this alters the optimal promotional mix from one country to another. Whereas in some countries the same media might not be available, even in countries where it is, it may not be available in the same form. To achieve national coverage in India would require 100 newspapers and involve overlap in coverage and scheduling problems. By contrast, national coverage in Japan could be achieved by advertising in three newspapers.

Another problem has to do with differing levels of demand from one country to another. Where media availability is limited in relation to demand, either because of controls on advertising volume or lack of media, the time lag for advanced bookings may restrict its use for promotional purposes. In South Africa, for example, TV advertising must be booked one year in advance. A further constraint may relate to the production of commercials. Some countries, such as Australia, have local content requirements for commercials that specify that they must either be produced in Australia or employ a number of Australian actors.

The issue of reach is also important in comparing effectiveness between countries. In many countries it is not only circulation or home viewing figures which count, but also the number of readers per copy or the number of viewers per TV set which is important. In the villages in India it is not uncommon for up to 20 people to watch the communal village TV set. The degree to which various media are used and what are acceptable forms of promotion and advertising varies from country to country.

# Government regulation

Governments in most countries regulate the use of media for promotion in the interests of protecting their citizens from undesirable influences. Such regulations relate to the product that can be promoted, the content of what is said, by whom it is said, how it is said, the time at which it is said and the medium used. The above influences advertising and promotion to differing degrees in one country or another. Restrictions on media access may take the form of bans on advertising on certain media. For example, until the last decade advertising was not allowed on TV in Indonesia.

Regulations can also govern the ratio of advertising to editorial and can set a limit on the maximum number of minutes of advertising allowed per hour on TV. In some countries, advertising is banned altogether (e.g. in Libya) because it is contrary to the prevailing political philosophy. Government regulation can also apply to the content of advertising or promotion. In some countries, content regulations are motivated by a concern to protect moral and religious values (e.g. in Thailand the showing of underwear on billboards is prohibited). In other instances the ban is driven by a desire not to expose children to undesirable influences. In this case the ban may apply to promoting certain products in publications read by children or on TV or radio in the hours before children go to bed. Regulations on promotion to children vary markedly from country to country and change frequently. Finally, government can ban its citizens from accessing media lest the message conveyed has a destabilising influence or cause dissatisfaction. An example is the control on access to the internet in some countries.

## There's no accounting for taste

Australians and Americans consider that they have an affinity with each other. Among other things this affinity is based on a common language. However, although the language is the same, often the meaning conveyed is not. This confusion may be a function of accent, such as when the Australian asking for a 'scotch and soda' in Los Angeles is given a 'scotch and cider'. It may also be a result of the fact that parts of meaning that are assumed and taken for granted in one culture are not taken for granted in the other. An example of this is when the Australian asking for a 'brandy and dry' in San Francisco receives 'dry vermouth' rather than 'dry ginger ale' with the brandy.

Australian beer has been exported to the USA for several decades. For most of that time the second most popular beer has been the Queensland brew XXXX. This is despite the hilarity that results from the verbalisation of the brand name being Fourex, which is the name of a major selling brand of condoms. Even the adventurous Madison Avenue types baulked in the mid-1980s when it was proposed to replicate the highly successful Australian promotional program for XXXX in the USA. This was because the campaign was built around the slogan 'I feel a XXXX coming on'.

Government regulations can also apply to sales promotion and can influence which sales promotion tools are allowed in the interests of ensuring that consumers are protected and that competition is conducted fairly. Not only do these regulations vary from country to country, but also within a country as is the case in Australia where mail competitions are not allowed in some states.

The above factors often mean that an innovative approach to international promotion and advertising will be necessary.

## CONTENT OF INTERNATIONAL COMMUNICATION

Although words are a means of communication and not the communication itself, many of the blunders in international advertising and promotion are due to words being translated literally rather than the meaning being translated. This is often the case when the language of the other country is written in a script based on symbols rather than letters, for example Japanese or Chinese. Even when the language of the other country is in letters, as with Bahasa Indonesia, misunderstandings can easily occur.

An Australian Trade Commissioner newly arrived in Indonesia was advised that the translation of his title was 'Commisaris Perdaganan', which is literally correct. When cards with this title were presented to Indonesian executives they invariably inquired of the Trade Commissioner what hidden commission they should reserve for him if the transaction with the Australian firm proved successful. They were puzzled by his disclaimer of the need for any commission. After this happened several times, the Trade Commissioner found that his title should have been translated as 'Perwakilan Perdaganan', which means trade representative, rather than 'Commisaris Perdaganan', which meant commission agent—there being no direct translation in Bahasa Indonesia for Trade Commissioner.

This example highlights that richness of language and ability to convey shades of meaning vary from country to country. Where the language is less able to convey shades of meaning it may be necessary to alter the balance in the advertisement between copy and visuals in print media or between voice and visuals in TV, so that the visual elements convey the shades of meaning. This requires an understanding as to how consumers in the overseas market arrive at a decision to purchase and how the message to capitalise on this process must be modified in order to maximise the advertisement's appeal overseas. Promotion must be undertaken to fit in with the decision process involved in purchasing.

## The management of promotional communication

The content of the international communication will be influenced by the process to be followed in designing and managing the communications activity. The management of international communication involves six steps. These are illustrated in Figure 15.4 and discussed below:

1 *Isolate the communication problem to be solved*. This may be a matter of increasing awareness, improving brand image, increasing sales, differentiating the product or service from that of the competition or increasing market share.

2 *Identify the target population*. Are there specific segments and what are their characteristics in terms of demographics, lifestyle and consumption habits?

3 *Define the communications objective*. Is the objective to convince buyers to like the product, or to stimulate repeat purchase or to motivate people to act? Alternatively, the objective might be one of general education.

4 *Establish the creative strategy*. This may involve selecting particular themes for the promotion or stressing a unique selling proposition.

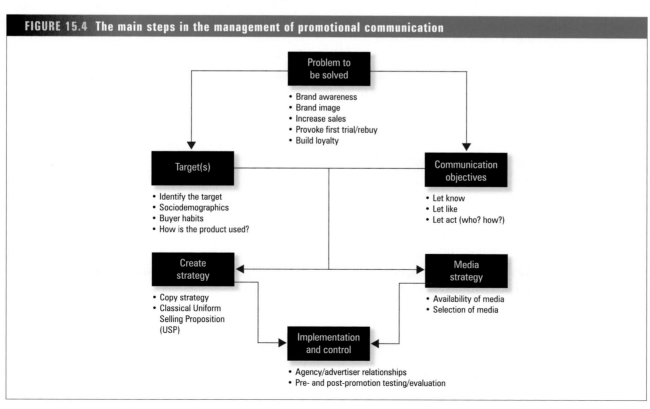

**FIGURE 15.4 The main steps in the management of promotional communication**

Problem to be solved
- Brand awareness
- Brand image
- Increase sales
- Provoke first trial/rebuy
- Build loyalty

Target(s)
- Identify the target
- Sociodemographics
- Buyer habits
- How is the product used?

Communication objectives
- Let know
- Let like
- Let act (who? how?)

Create strategy
- Copy strategy
- Classical Uniform Selling Proposition (USP)

Media strategy
- Availability of media
- Selection of media

Implementation and control
- Agency/advertiser relationships
- Pre- and post-promotion testing/evaluation

5 *Design a media plan.* This will specify which media to use, when to use it and how to optimise the media mix so as to reach the target audience best. Critical to this will be whether the media is available in the overseas market and its degree of effectiveness.

6 *Implement and monitor the promotional campaign.* This can involve pre- and post-promotion tests to determine the promotion's effectiveness as well as research into different aspects of the campaign.

## Buyer's decision process

The decision process of buyers will also influence the content of the communication in overseas markets. There are five stages in the decision process:

1 *Need recognition*: This involves the recipient being made aware that they have a need for the product or service. The communication should reinforce or draw attention to the basic need that the product/service fulfils.

2 *Information search*: This will vary with the nature of the product. With impulse purchases the search is instantaneous; with frequent purchases the search is casual; and with high-involvement purchases the information search is extensive. The message should provide information commensurate with the expected search needs for each of the above categories in the overseas market.

3 *Evaluation and comparison*: As part of this process, potential purchasers may seek information from independent assessors of quality and value, such as *Choice* magazine in Australia. They may also try a number of products before making a final decision or they may base their decision on that of a referent, for example a well-known local figure who endorses the product. At this stage the communications objective is to assess the importance in the overseas market of the comparison process and facilitate it in such a way that the Australian product is not disadvantaged.

4 *Vendor and product purchase decision*: This aspect of the decision process involves deciding the type of outlet to buy from such as supermarket versus pharmacy; incentives to purchase such as couponing, bundling, free gifts or discounts; unique packaging or point-of-sale material; product support such as warranties or extended periods of free maintenance; and the extent of information provided with the purchase as to its ingredients or contents.

5 *Post-purchase evaluation*: This element of the decision-making process involves convincing the customer after the purchase has been made that they have made the right decision. This will ensure that the customer becomes an unpaid advocate for the product with friends and acquaintances and may encourage repeat purchasing by the customer. Attention at this stage will reduce cognitive dissonance.

As the above five stages of the decision-making process vary between overseas markets, it is necessary to ascertain how each operates in the chosen market and formulate a message strategy.

## Message strategy formulation

The content of the communication in overseas markets is likely to differ depending on whether national or international appeals are to be used. If national appeals are employed, then the message will need to differ from that used in Australia or New Zealand for a number of reasons:

- *Linguistic and cultural nuances*: These give rise to various subtleties which affect how the message will be received and need to be taken into account to improve the effectiveness of the communication. An associated issue is that of language overlap. The message, while directed to one country market, may also be received in an adjacent market, as happens with radio and TV in Europe. To maximise this benefit the message should also be crafted to appeal to customers in this adjacent market.

- *Different products*: Some product groups are more sensitive to cultural differences between markets than others and the extent of such sensitivity for the same product will vary between overseas markets. This degree of cultural sensitivity will need to be taken into account in deciding on the extent to which the advertising message should be localised.

- *Different users*: Some products will have different uses in different markets from those in Australia or New Zealand. For example, outboard marine engines, which are mostly used for pleasure craft in Australia, in Indonesia are mainly used for commercial craft (including smuggling boats). Differences in the buyer's consumption pattern need to be taken into account because similar appeals are less feasible where the product does not meet the same needs or is not used in the same way.

- *Different media alternatives*: Not only does availability vary from market to market, but also the relative importance of different media varies within each market. The suitability of different media for communicating different messages varies and if the same media as could be used in Australia or New Zealand are not available in the overseas location, then a different message strategy may need to be devised.

- *Communication sophistication*: The expectations both of media and the messages they convey vary from country to country and especially between developed and developing countries. This must be taken into account when formulating messages. As local needs vary, the above should be evaluated in the light of these needs, otherwise the message may be irrelevant.

- *Business priorities*: Whereas in some countries, such as Australia or New Zealand, business priorities are driven by the short-term goal of maximising returns to shareholders, in other countries, such as Japan, business priorities focus on achieving long-term growth in market share. Where the former priorities dominate, the communication strategy is likely to concentrate on stimulating instant purchase, whereas in countries where the latter predominate the communication strategy is more likely to concentrate on image creation.

- *Status of marketing*: This varies throughout the world. In countries such as the USA, where marketing is highly acceptable, the volume of promotional expenditure is likely to be high and sizeable promotion is expected to accompany market entry. In countries, such as the former Centrally Planned Economies, promotional expectations remain low despite moves towards a market economy.

The above points are exemplified in the situation several years ago when Proctor and Gamble ran television advertisements in Japan. The advertisements compared its Pamper brand of babies' nappies to Brand X in a way which aimed to show that Brand X was inferior to the Proctor and Gamble product. The advertisements were unsuccessful because hard-edged comparative advertising that is acceptable in Australia, New Zealand and the USA is considered insulting in Japan.

# PULL STRATEGIES IN INTERNATIONAL PROMOTION

Strategies that are targeted directly towards overseas customers or end-users will need to be crafted correctly so as to appeal to those customers or end-users, who are likely to differ from their Australian or New Zealand counterparts. Pull strategies involve advertising, publicity and public relations.

## Advertising

This can include newspapers, magazines, trade publications, telephone directories, television, radio, cinema and outdoor and transit advertising. In general, advertising is the most high profile of the various communications activities. Although it is the most powerful aid to positioning a product or service in a market, it is also the most expensive. It differs from other forms of promotion in that it is paid for; it involves non-personal presentation; and it uses media.

### BETWEEN-COUNTRY DIFFERENCES

Advertising differs from one country to another in various ways:

- *Usage*: Variations relate to the extent of advertising, the expectations of local buyers as to what advertising will achieve and the degree to which advertising is politically acceptable.
- *Form*: The relative weight given to press, radio, TV and other media will vary from country to country as will the availability of different media for promotional purposes.
- *Content*: What can be said or included, and what cannot be included, is a matter of both taste and government ruling (see earlier). As already mentioned, it is often not appropriate to replicate Australian or New Zealand advertising approaches in other countries because of cultural differences and sensitivities.
- *Presentation*: This should conform to local expectations and, if there is doubt, 'play it straight'. Humour in advertising or advertisements that are situation-specific rarely cross national boundaries. In the presentation of the message, either go for a neutral background or one that most readers/listeners/viewers can identify with regardless of their background.

Until 1990 advertising was not common in Vietnam. Now, although advertising is in its formative stages, it is growing strongly. Radio, print media and television remain under tight state control and any advertising still requires the completion of much paperwork before it is approved. The government screens the content of most advertisements. Misleading or untrue advertisements and advertisements damaging the interests of the state or that are contrary to the country's history or culture are not allowed. Advertising rates in Vietnam are relatively inexpensive and, because it is a relatively new industry, it has a substantial influence. However, the downside is that the boom in advertising has led to inflation in media costs of about 40% per year.

International Highlight 15.2 indicates the way in which promotional strategies and techniques are received and how they can differ markedly between countries.

Media usage by form varies widely between countries. The usage in Asia is shown in Table 15.1

---

**15.2 INTERNATIONAL HIGHLIGHT**

# A tale of two cities

n Tokyo companies are not concerned about differentiating themselves from competitors, as is the case in Australia. This is because they feel that if the approach worked for others, then it should also work for them. The Japanese approach towards using celebrities also differs. Whereas in Australia celebrities are used because their association lends strength to the claim for the product, in Japan they are used to lend dignity and elegance to the image of the product rather than aggressively marketing it. In South-East Asia advertisements that virtually ask for the order, as many do in Australia or New Zealand, are considered impolite because asking for the order is bad manners. And while, in Australia, an advertisement that boasts about one's wealth would not be well received because of Australian people's aggressive egalitarianism, such advertisements would be perfectly acceptable in South-East Asia. The above examples illustrate

the need to tailor the advertisement to the preconceived notions existing in the overseas market.

A study of advertisements on buses in Bangkok is illuminating. The first thing noticed is that on most buses the advertisements on the side of the bus adjacent to the footpath are different from the advertisements on the rear of the bus or on the side of the bus adjacent to the traffic. Further examination reveals that the advertisements on the side of the bus adjacent to the footpath are usually for low-unit price, high-volume consumer goods, whereas the advertisements on the other parts of the bus body are for higher-value luxurious items. Investigation reveals that this is deliberate because it is assumed that those who walk can only afford low-cost basic items whereas those who drive cars are the only ones in a position to purchase high-priced luxury products, many of which are imported.

---

**TABLE 15.1    Media allocation in Asia**

| Medium | 2004 (%) | 2003 (%) |
|---|---|---|
| Radio | 3 | 4 |
| CRM/digital/interactive | 8 | 6 |
| Out-of-home | 9 | 6 |
| Magazine | 15 | 14 |
| Total print | 28 | 30 |
| Total TV | 36 | 40 |

**SOURCE:** *Keegan, W.J. and Green, M.C. (2005)* Global Marketing, *4th edn, Pearson Prentice Hall, NJ, p. 458.*

---

## MEDIA SELECTION

Of the media available in the overseas market, a selection will need to be made based on a number of criteria, each of which will vary in terms of its relevance to the overseas market. In the first place, it is important to be specific as to which is the target of the campaign. It may be that the target audience should be the total population or it may be special interest groups only. A second factor affecting media selection is the nature of the product or service to be promoted. Different media will be more suitable for promoting some products rather than others: if the product needs to be demonstrated, TV would be a preferable medium to press or radio; if the product is at an early stage in its life cycle, then a medium which appeals to innovators and early adopters may be most appropriate. A third factor is the type of message to be conveyed: if it is a complex message, then print may be preferred to radio (because of the limitation of the voice medium) or TV (because of cost due to the need for lengthy explanation and demonstration). A fourth factor affecting overseas media selection is the objective of the campaign: if the campaign is to inform rather than to persuade, then technical journals or specialist publications may be preferable to newspapers or mass-circulation magazines.

## PRINT MEDIA

Print media consists of headlines, illustrations, body copy and signature/theme/incentive to action. To ensure the advertisement's appeal each of these components of the print advertisement may need to be modified when the advertisement is used offshore. In general, the major disadvantage of print media is that it is restricted to the visual senses, whereas some products may also need an audio effect (e.g. the throaty roar of a powerful car engine).

**Newspapers** Although being the print medium with the greatest global spread, newspaper circulation characteristics vary considerably; this influences the cost-effectiveness of this medium. Newspapers can have morning or afternoon editions or be circulated less frequently than daily. In addition, newspapers can be tabloid or broadsheet and this has implications for advertising layout and positioning. Newspapers vary widely in terms of both number of copies sold per thousand of population and the number of readers per copy. The scope of distribution varies and the fact that the newspaper is distributed nationally does not always indicate a larger circulation. For example, in the USA the local *Los Angeles Times* newspaper has a much larger circulation than the national *US News and World Report* newspaper.

The language used in the newspaper will influence its suitability as a promotional vehicle. It is necessary to inquire whether all newspapers are printed in the same language or if there is a bilingual press. In India, for example, the daily metropolitan newspapers containing economic and financial news are in English, while regional daily newspapers are printed in the language of the region. The physical characteristics of newspapers will influence advertising. This is not only a matter of tabloid versus broadsheet, but also of column width and column direction. Figure 15.5 shows the differences in typical page layout between US and Japanese newspapers. Finally, newspapers can carry a number of different forms of print advertisement—classified, display and supplement.

The advantage of newspapers from a promotional perspective is that newspapers can cope with detailed information and are flexible in terms of coverage. The immediacy of the news that they feature improves the currency of the advertising messages, there is scope for cooperative advertising with retailers if consumer goods are being promoted and there is flexibility as regards shape and size of advertisements. The disadvantages of newspapers are that more than one newspaper may be required to cover the target market, that much of the circulation is likely to be wasted and that the paper and printing ink used can reduce the quality of the reproduction. There are also limitations on the use of colour, the life of the message is very short, usually only one day, and the medium is not suitable for the conveying of emotion or for demonstration.

**Magazines** Magazines are a selective way of reaching a more targeted audience as, in general, magazines are audience-specific rather than general in appeal. Their availability varies

## FIGURE 15.5 Differences in page layout for newspapers

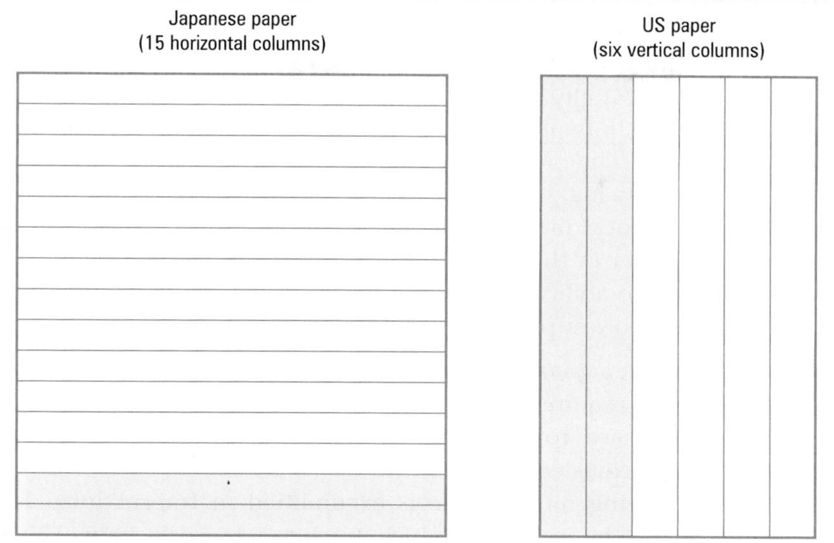

Japanese paper
(15 horizontal columns)

US paper
(six vertical columns)

SOURCE: *Griffin, T. (1994)* International Marketing Communications, *Butterworth Heinemann, Oxford, UK, p. 219.*

considerably from overseas market to overseas market and, in general, the less-developed the country, the fewer the number of magazines likely to be available. Due to the nature of the editorial content magazines are likely to have a higher reader involvement than newspapers. Also, magazines are likely to have a longer life and a greater number of readers per copy. The placement of magazines in waiting rooms and office foyers extends both their life and readership. This medium uses better quality paper and colour reproduction than newspapers, enhancing the suitability of it for promotion of products requiring quality in graphic representation. The image of the magazine lends prestige to the goods and services promoted therein. To a greater extent than newspapers, magazines can provide reader attention devices, such as samples and perfume strips.

The disadvantages include the fact that magazines appear usually monthly and sometimes weekly. There are long lead times for placement of advertising, deadlines are less flexible and greater forward planning is necessary. Readership is not as immediate and separate language issues can be a problem. In developing countries, infrastructure shortcomings can make magazine circulation a problem and the auditing of circulation numbers in such countries is problematic. The production costs for full-colour advertisements are high relative to circulation, and the purchase price can be a disincentive as far as the target audience is concerned. In Australia newspapers sell for around $1.50 each and magazines sell for around $6.50 each.

There is a range of regional magazines such as the *Far East Economic Review* or global magazines with regional editions such as *Vogue* or *Time*. In-flight magazines of airlines are another category of publications which cross national borders. In evaluating such magazines, it is desirable to undertake research to make sure that they cater for the segment claimed and that this segment is relevant to the international aspirations for the Australian or New Zealand product.

**Other print media** There is a plethora of *trade publications* available in the more-developed countries and some of these find their way to the less-developed countries. These are particularly useful if marketing industrial products internationally because they cater for a select audience, most of whom are either in a position to buy the product/service or influence the purchasing decision. One advantage of such media is their interest in new product development and a willingness to feature, along with the advertisement, an editorial piece on the product and its underlying technology.

Commercial sections of telephone directories are another print medium that is available in most countries. The *Yellow Pages* are available, for example, in Vietnam in Ho Chi Minh City, Hanoi and Danang. Often *Yellow Pages* are the first reference point in the search process. A predominantly local medium, the challenge when using this form is how to get noticed. This can be a matter of the size of the advertisement, the illusion created of the firm's status in the industry, the ability to convey a message of reliability and a 'bait for action', such as 'phone us for the lowest prices'. A key feature of this medium is its wide usage.

**Posters, billboards, signage and transit media** Although not print media, these are forms of advertising which require careful research as to consumer response patterns in overseas countries if they are to be effective. Table 15.2 shows the percentage of advertising expenditures in various countries.

Transit advertising on a vehicle is exemplified in International Highlight 15.2. Transit advertising can also be inside the vehicle, such as a bus or a train. This form of advertising is important in countries where private transportation is expensive (Japan) or restricted (Singapore, where mass transit is the norm).

Posters, billboards and signage can also lead to additional publicity in other media. When TV covers an event in Piccadilly Circus in London, Foster's beer, which has an enormous sign there, gets a free plug for its product. It is necessary to ascertain in advance whether there are any regulations in the overseas country governing what products can be promoted in this manner and what can be said about or claimed for the product, using this medium. Cigarette advertising in Australia is subject to restrictions where outdoor advertising is concerned, as is lingerie in Thailand. Other advantages of this form of advertising are that it can achieve a striking effect due to size, it can build audience coverage quickly and it can reach a broad or selective audience depending on placement. It has geographic and seasonal flexibility and it is not dependent on outlay by the recipient, as with papers, TV or radio. On a cost per

**TABLE 15.2  Outdoor advertising expenditures as a percentage of total advertising spending**

| Country | Percentage |
|---|---|
| France | 11.7 |
| United Kingdom | 5.8 |
| Spain | 5.4 |
| Italy | 4.3 |
| Canada | 4.2 |
| United States | 4.0 |
| Germany | 4.0 |
| Worldwide | 5.9 |

**SOURCE:** *Published in Keegan, W.J. and Green, M.C. (2005) Global Marketing, 4th edn, Pearson Prentice Hall, NJ, p. 458. Reproduced with permission from Advertising Expenditure Forecasts, Zenith Optimedia.*

viewing basis, it is relatively inexpensive. Its disadvantages are that the viewing span is brief when viewed from a moving vehicle and that, because it is usually non-intrusive, it may blend into the background and not be noticed. There is the possibility of a high percentage of wasted viewers, and there is limited opportunity to deliver a written message. Because of its outdoor location there is likelihood of weather and climate damage, and if small quantities are required the cost of design and artwork may be prohibitive.

## VISUAL MEDIA

The main forms of visual media are television and cinema, although some might consider the internet a visual medium.

**Television** The key promotional factors with television are its ability to incorporate attention-getting devices, conveying the message with drama, suspense or humour, and the ability to make a claim and prove it. These advantages are facilitated by its having a continuous story line from introduction to close; using a mix of voices, sounds and music; and being able to capture the way the product appears and performs by showing 'in use' situations. Although regulations on television commercials vary from country to country, new forms such as satellite TV and some forms of cable TV may reduce the ability of nations to control what their citizens view when the signal is beamed in from outside its borders. Because different countries gained TV at different times, the quality of transmission can vary, as does the audience reach. These factors need to be taken into account when evaluating the cost per reach of this medium in overseas markets.

Advantages include the ability to involve the additional sensory effects of sound and motion and an ability to show change and demonstrate outcomes. In addition, it delivers a captive audience because viewers must make a deliberate effort to avoid seeing the commercial. Furthermore, TV can deliver a national or a major regional audience and it can impart credibility to the advertiser's message because it tends to be regarded as a source of informed opinion.

The main disadvantage is one of cost and this excludes many advertisers. Cost is not just in the rate per minute, but also in the expense of producing TV commercials. The audience receiving the message tends to be non-selective. Also the availability of advertising time in association with programs that deliver large audiences is limited, costly and often subject to government regulation. The life of the message is short; this means that this medium cannot be used by the customer as a vehicle for search and product selection. Finally, advertising intensity on this medium often causes noise due to conflicting claims by other advertisers of similar products. Table 15.3 shows the number of estimated television households in Asian countries.

**Cinema** Overall its importance is diminishing, but it is still important in some countries, especially those with lower per capita incomes. It is a medium targeted at a local audience and therefore suitable for overseas test market activities.

The audience characteristics need prior research as audiences differ from country to country. In India, for example, cinema audiences are predominantly male.

## AUDIO MEDIA

**Radio** This is the main form of audio media and it relies on the sense of sound. The mental picture created can be added to by use of sound forms other than voice. Commercials are usually measured by the number of seconds, and the number of words that can be conveyed in a 30-second slot can vary according to the language used. In English, for example, it would

| TABLE 15.3 | Estimated television households in the Asia–Pacific region | |
|---|---|---|
| **Country** | **Households (millions)** | **Television households (%)** |
| Australia | 7.35 | 99 |
| China | 351.20 | 94 |
| Hong Kong | 2.10 | 99 |
| India | 192.00 | 43 |
| Indonesia | 56.00 | 59 |
| Japan | 48.00 | 99 |
| Malaysia | 3.60 | 96 |
| New Zealand | 1.30 | 98 |
| Philippines | 13.80 | 71 |
| Singapore | 1.00 | 99 |
| South Korea | 13.80 | 100 |
| Taiwan | 7.23 | 90 |
| Thailand | 17.12 | 94 |

SOURCE: *<http://www.worldscreen.com/asiapacific.php>, accessed 29 January 2007.*

be 65 words. When creating a radio message it is necessary to address a number of issues in relation to the overseas audience and market. These include adherence to strategy and ensuring that the script contains the essential elements of the message to be communicated. Also required is that the commercial be sufficiently simple for the listener to grasp the principal idea; that the commercial stimulates interest (rather than a yawn!) by having some attention-getting device at the start; and that the language used is simple and the sentences short. Finally, the commercial should be memorable and suitable for frequent repetition—the use of a jingle or a catchy tune can help achieve this outcome.

The advantages of radio are its relatively low cost and its ability to deliver messages at or away from home as with drive-time radio. Some stations have a highly selective audience and radio also has the advantage of short lead times for placing advertisements, low production costs and a large number of local radio stations whose existence facilitates geographic segmentation. Disadvantages involve the limited effectiveness of this medium in delivering a nationwide audience, a fatigue factor from listeners hearing the same message over and over again and noise from competing stations all airing a large number of commercials each hour. Figure 15.6 shows that even in developed countries the split between different advertising media varies markedly from country to country.

## GLOBAL MEDIA

There are an increasing number of media that transcend national boundaries. There are media that operate in a region rather than in a country, such as the footprint map of satellite TV (e.g. Rupert Murdoch's Sky Channel based in Hong Kong). In addition, there are media that are targeted at a global segment (e.g. prestige magazines like *National Geographic*), and there are new forms of media that are global in design (e.g. the internet).

**Global print media** Global print media consists of general newspapers, such as *US News and World Report* and the *International Herald Tribune*. It can also involve a newspaper that has a

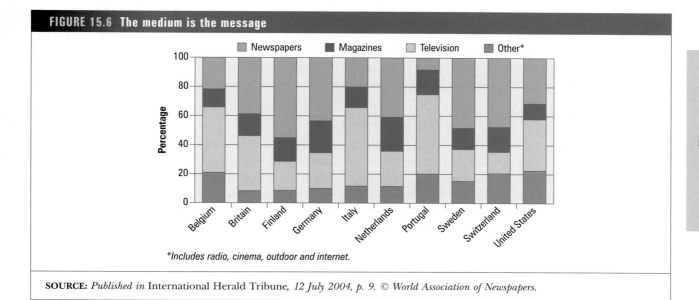

**FIGURE 15.6  The medium is the message**

Legend: Newspapers, Magazines, Television, Other*

*Includes radio, cinema, outdoor and internet.

Countries: Belgium, Britain, Finland, Germany, Italy, Netherlands, Portugal, Sweden, Switzerland, United States

**SOURCE:** *Published in* International Herald Tribune, *12 July 2004, p. 9.* © *World Association of Newspapers.*

number of different country editions such as the *Wall Street Journal* (European and Asian editions plus special editions in 25 countries). The *China Daily* of the People's Republic of China is published by satellite simultaneously in China, the USA and Europe. Magazines are more likely to be global because the news they contain is not so perishable. Some magazines emanate from one location and are distributed in many countries, such as the *Economist*, and others are produced in a number of languages in a number of different locations, such as *Time*, which publishes 133 different editions, or *Reader's Digest*, which publishes 41 editions. The internationalisation of magazines has increased with international consolidation among magazine publishers.

**Global visual media** CNN is the leader and reaches consumers in more than 100 countries and has a number of competitors. The biggest growth is in satellite television, which is the most prominent form of global visual media and has already influenced other media with local or regional coverage. Satellite messages can be received via rebroadcasting in traditional form on the cable network or per medium of a satellite dish. Beaming messages into other countries, as happens with Star TV in Hong Kong, which is able to access 4.8 million homes in mainland China, opens up new opportunities for promotion overseas. The Australian Broadcasting Corporation launched its Australian Television International Service in 1993 using Indonesia's Palapa satellite whose footprint covers eastern India, southern China and South-East Asia. Although intended as an image-creation vehicle rather than a direct commercial medium, this activity indicates that governments are recognising the value of global media.

**Global audio media** International commercial radio is important, especially in Western Europe where a number of commercial stations reach several nations (e.g. Radio Luxembourg). Such global media are useful for reaching non-literate populations. In addition, there are a number of national radio networks (many with global reach), such as the BBC (UK) and the ABC (Australia) that currently do not accept advertising. Should this change with privatisation, then this will create another powerful medium for global or regional promotion.

**Internet** The internet removes many barriers to communication with customers by eliminating the obstacles created by geography, time zones and location and in the process creates a 'frictionless' business environment. The long-term growth of the internet raises the opportunity for cross-border information flows and transactions. At present the internet is mostly an English-language medium. This is in the process of change and soon the majority of internet traffic will be in languages other than English. This trend is likely to be the result of increased adoption of the internet in less-developed countries.

# Publicity and public relations

These activities can be regarded as communication between an organisation and its 'publics' to achieve specific objectives based on mutual understanding. The publics of the firm are broader than the market it serves and include all those affected by the firm's operations—customers, general public, stockholders, government, media, suppliers, employees, activist groups, financial community and distributors (Terpstra and Sarathy 2000, p. 505). In normal situations publicity and public relations can be used to create or enhance a favourable image. In the international arena it is a useful way of combating nationalistic criticism. In crisis situations publicity and public relations not only facilitate a response to criticism, but also provide the opportunity to explain proposed remedial action and to head off criticism harmful to the corporate image. In the international scene, however, publicity and public relations must be culturally sensitive and attuned to local customs and commercial practices. In developing countries, public relations communication can be via the 'gong man', the town crier, announcements in the market square or the chief's courts (Keegan and Green 2005, p. 463).

Apart from public relations activities, sponsorships and loyalty programs are becoming increasingly important publicity activities in international marketing. Underlying the increasing importance of public relations is the view that marketing today must do more than manage the 4Ps—it must also try to influence factors in the environment, especially political power and public opinion. This concept of megamarketing is particularly important when doing business in countries where the Australian firm is likely to lack a deep understanding of the culture and the politics.

## NEWS RELEASES

In many countries, being 'foreign' may be newsworthy itself. One way of securing news coverage is to hold press conferences overseas to announce a new product, a different strategy or a significant linkage with a local interest. No matter how good the public relations consultant might be, it is always necessary to have a newsworthy message to convey, otherwise the 'take up' of the press release will be less than enthusiastic. Associated with this is support for good causes in the overseas country. This lessens the image of the Australian or New Zealand firm being yet another foreign company 'trying to rip us off'. This support might take the form of a donation, an endowment, making a gift of physical property with the name of the firm carved/labelled on the gift, or a promotional campaign with a percentage of sales/earnings going to a nominated local charity.

## SPONSORSHIPS

These relate a company or a brand to an event in order to benefit from the exploitable commercial potential associated with that activity. The most talked about event in this connection is the 2008 Beijing Olympic Games. Globally, sponsorships are big business with the value exceeding A$6 billion annually. Sporting activities attract most sponsorships, with the arts coming second. Usually the sponsor contributes funds to defray a portion of the production costs of the event.

Sponsorships have grown as a promotional vehicle. This is because funding by public bodies has been cut back and funds have to be obtained from other sources. The globalisation of mass media increases the reach of the sponsor's message in relation to a specific event such as the global coverage Coca-Cola obtained as a result of its sponsorship of the 1996 Olympic Games in Atlanta. Changing lifestyles and technology have delivered larger audiences for sports and arts events. As traditional forms of promotion become more expensive and message clutter via these media increases, there is a desire for new, 'less spoilt' forms of promotion and extensive possibilities exist for a sporting or arts figure to endorse the sponsor's product.

> Robert Timms used sponsorship of the 2000 Sydney Olympic Games as a vehicle to create both domestic and international awareness for its brand of coffee. The event was viewed as an opportunity for the company to become a major player in the Australian coffee market and to generate awareness in overseas markets of the firm's strong position in the Australian market. This wider awareness would have been enhanced by the fact that more than three billion people watched the games on TV. During the games events Robert Timms served more than two million cups of coffee to spectators, and provided coffee to people in ticket queues every morning of the games. It provided coffee to the Business Club organised by Austrade which hosted networking sessions for more than 10 000 business leaders during the games period and Robert Timms undertook a number of good corporate citizen activities such as sponsoring thousands of young Olympic hopefuls.

The above activities of Robert Timms support the research by Thompson and Quester (2000), which found that sponsorship effectiveness is directly related to the degree to which sponsors are willing to leverage their investment with additional forms of promotional expenditure.

## PUBLIC RELATIONS ACTIVITIES

The attraction of public relations is that the resulting messages come across as news and therefore have more credibility than advertising. Public relations consultants value the space occupied by the PR release in the print media or the number of minutes coverage on TV or radio as being worth around three times the value of advertising rates. Public relations does not lead to immediate sales, but improves cumulative favourable awareness. In international marketing, public relations is particularly useful if the product is not widely known or if there is a country of origin image problem. When used overseas, PR releases should not simply be newsworthy, but should have an intriguing application, identify with the needs of the overseas market and be supported with good-quality photographs, preferably showing 'in use' situations with which overseas readers/viewers can identify.

The use of public relations in Asian markets varies considerably, depending on how the market and the government view it as a promotional vehicle. In China, it has long been used to promote official policies to the population and was used extensively in the international domain by the government to support its successful bid to host the 2008 Olympic Games. By contrast, in Vietnam many local businesses still view it as advertising, although this is slowly changing due to the public relations activities of foreign firms operating in that country.

In the mid-1980s an Australian manufacturer of leather riding saddles visited Los Angeles to market his products in Southern California. He was horrified at the cost of media advertising. With the help of the Australian Trade Office, a program was devised whereby several film personalities were persuaded to be photographed riding horses bearing his saddles and these photographs were distributed to the media aimed at the horse riding fraternity. Almost every one of these specialised magazines featured the photographs and accompanying story and almost 1000 of these highly priced saddles were sold.

Public relations can also be used to correct misleading impressions or unfavourable images in an overseas country.

### LOYALTY PROGRAMS

These are sales promotions in which loyalty is acknowledged in the form of meaningful rewards to the customer—usually in the form of the marketer's own product. This reduces the cost of the program as happens with frequent flyer schemes. When using such schemes in international marketing, it is necessary to ascertain whether the scheme is regarded favourably or suspiciously in the overseas country and whether the reward is perceived as offering the same value as it would in Australia or New Zealand. For example, a free domestic flight or hotel night might be a most attractive reward in a poor nation, but a lesser incentive in a rich nation. Other issues concern differing tax treatment of rewards in various countries as this can lessen the value of the rewards, and whether in the overseas country the reward is viewed as an added cost element in the price which, if so, creates a negative perception of the value of the Australian or New Zealand offering.

## PUSH STRATEGIES IN INTERNATIONAL PROMOTION

Push strategies in the overseas marketplace primarily involve sales promotion and personal selling.

## Sales promotion

Sales promotion plays a much more important role in international marketing than it does in domestic marketing. In part this is due to the focus in international marketing on introducing new products to the marketplace and getting them into local distribution channels. Whereas in the Australian and New Zealand markets sales promotion is often in the form of contests, coupons, sampling, premiums, cents-off deals etc., in international marketing the most important form is the trade show.

### TRADE SHOWS

One of the oldest forms of trade promotion, trade shows date back to the medieval fairs. They are an affordable form of promotion for smaller firms venturing offshore for the first time and are a convenient way of testing market reaction to the product. They are particularly important for business-to-business marketing overseas because trade promotion is more important than advertising where industrial products are concerned. Trade shows provide the opportunity for meeting potential purchasers without making an appointment and, because there are exhibitors of both local and imported competitive products, they provide an opportunity for gathering intelligence on the market. As complementary products are being promoted at trade shows, they are also a means of finding potential agents and distributors from among other exhibitors at the show, as well as from visitors to the show. Trade shows provide the opportunity for potential buyers to see and demonstrate the product. They are important in creating credibility for an imported product from an unknown source of supply. They are also an economic medium for sales promotion. It is generally accepted that a visitor to a trade show costs the exhibitor around A$150 compared to around A$350 for making a sales call.

Figure 15.7 shows that trade shows can perform a selling function, a promotion function and a network-creating function. The selling function involves primarily customers and other buyers, while the promotion function includes suppliers, influencers of the purchasing decision and industry analysts. The network-creating function includes other stakeholders, such as competitors, regulators, show organisers, partners and industry associations.

Trade shows take a number of forms. They can be open to the public or to the trade only, or be a combination of trade-only days followed by one or two public days. Shows open to the public are useful for consumer goods or products already available in the overseas country or in cases where the specific objective is to reinforce awareness. Trade-only shows in foreign markets are more suitable for industrial products, for firms seeking representation or for promoting items of large unit value.

Trade shows can also be classified according to whether they are general or specialised. General trade shows cover a wide variety of unrelated products and are usually mounted to create an awareness of the range of products a country wishes to promote in an overseas market. They are often mounted in countries where the trade show infrastructure, such as

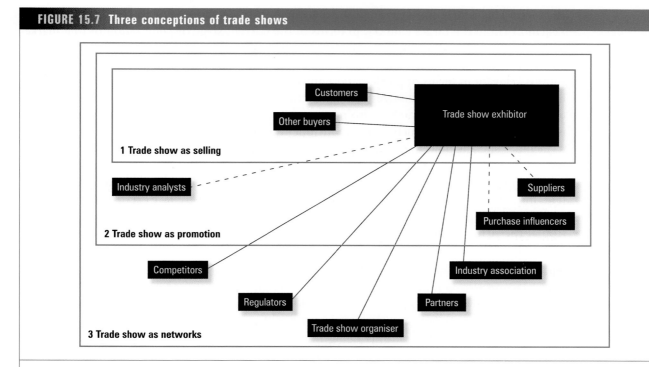

**FIGURE 15.7  Three conceptions of trade shows**

Customers

Other buyers

Trade show exhibitor

**1 Trade show as selling**

Industry analysts

Suppliers

Purchase influencers

**2 Trade show as promotion**

Competitors

Industry association

Regulators

Partners

Trade show organiser

**3 Trade show as networks**

**SOURCE:** *Adapted from Rossen, J.R. and Seringhaus, F.H.R. (1996) 'Trade fairs as international marketing venues: a case study', paper presented at the 12th IMP Conference, University of Karlsruhe, p. 1181.*

convention centres and exhibition halls, is sparse and specialised trade shows are non-existent. The emphasis is on a public rather than a trade audience, especially if the show is to mark a specific event of an 'Expo' type.

Specialised trade shows concentrate on narrow product categories, such as mining equipment, and are usually open only to the trade. Although they are smaller than general trade displays, some can be quite large, such as the COMDEX computer show in the USA where the number of exhibitors runs into thousands. Often the specialised show is the major event in the calendar of a specific industry and may attract a regional or global audience rather than just a national one. In many cases new product launches are timed to coincide with the industry's annual trade show.

The range of opportunities to display goods in an overseas country is extensive. For an Australian firm these include:

- the firm hiring space in a hotel and setting up its own display and inviting potential buyers to view it;

- mounting a display in Austrade or embassy premises and arranging for the Trade Commissioner to issue invitations;

- the firm participating in an organised trade show on its own account; and

- participating in an exhibition organised by Austrade in an overseas market where they are responsible for attracting the audience.

Effective participation in trade shows overseas usually requires research in advance, active involvement in attracting an appropriate audience, contingency plans to overcome infrastructure problems, an understanding of visitors' motivations and a realistic appraisal of results.

**Research** This is necessary to establish what the best trade show is for the Australian or New Zealand firm in the target country, in terms of the current stage of penetration of that market and objectives for that market. Research is also necessary to ensure that the audience profile matches objectives and to see whether a significant percentage of the audience attracted to the show is relevant in terms of participation objectives. In this connection it is useful to obtain an indication as to what percentage of the audience likely to attend the show is local as opposed to regional or global. Research is also necessary to establish the full cost of participation as this is easy to underestimate. Such costs can include renting space, dressing the exhibit, connection to facilities such as power and water, shipment and clearance of exhibits, establishing customs bonds, provision for emergency airfreight if shipment is delayed, hire of furniture and equipment for the exhibit and hire of local people to assist and interpret. Costs should also take into account the expense of sending executives from Australia to staff the exhibit and supplementary promotional activities in conjunction with participation to attract visitors to stop at the firm's exhibit. These include direct mail, advertising and public relations activities. There should also be a contingency amount of at least 10% of the total costs.

**Attracting an audience** Although in many cases the trade show organisers promise an audience and have a publicity campaign to attract an audience, it is desirable for the firm to supplement this with its own campaign. Such a campaign should be aimed at both ensuring that the visitors it wants stop by its stand, and that they make a point (in advance of their visit) of noting the Australian stand as being one they must visit. Advertising in the trade show catalogue is useful, particularly if the catalogue is distributed in advance of the trade show. Publicising a competition in advance, entry to which requires a visit to the stand, is also useful.

Another way of attracting an audience is to operate additional events timed to coincide

A technique employed in a number of Austrade-sponsored specialised trade displays in the USA was to have a competition which would be drawn from business cards left in a large goldfish bowl at the Australian stand. In advance of the show, the competition would be publicised in industry publications or via notices slipped under the door of delegates' hotel rooms. The prize was usually two return business class tickets to Australia, donated by Qantas.

with exhibiting at the trade show. These could take the form of a technical seminar or a cocktail party held at the hotel recommended for the accommodation of exhibitors by the trade show organisers.

**Infrastructure issues** Unless the firm already has an agent in the country and the exhibits are supplied from the agent's stock, then the exhibit material has to be shipped from Australia. Also, unless the exhibits are part of a consolidated shipment for the trade display, goods should be shipped 50% in advance of the normal shipping time to allow for contingencies. The manager of the exhibit should arrive in the country at least three days before the show opens. This enables full recovery from jet lag and allows time to take action to correct mistakes at the exhibit site and to oversight the dressing of the stand. It also provides the manager with the opportunity to telephone key contacts and invite them to visit the stand. A local person should be hired as a translator and a 'Mr (or Ms) Fixit'. It is important to become familiar with customs procedures for entry and disposal/reshipment of exhibit material. It is also necessary to develop a fallback plan to cater for contingencies. This could include knowing what type of generator to hire if power is not connected to the exhibit and having plenty of spares in the exhibit shipment in case of local problems, such as damage in transit or pilferage. It is also desirable to remain in the city several days after the display closes to oversee disposal/reshipment of display goods and to follow up promising contacts made as a result of participating in the trade display. A final infrastructure problem relates to staffing the exhibit. It is essential that the exhibit be staffed at all times. Because staffing trade displays is exhausting and local conditions can create health problems for those from overseas staffing the stands, it is important to have sufficient people to staff the stand to give reasonable breaks and to allow for any of the above contingencies.

**Visitor motivations** Visitors attend trade shows for different reasons. Adopting a customer orientation to attracting the right prospects to the Australian exhibit requires an understanding of their reasons. Research has shown that these reasons can be categorised as viewing new products or developments; strong interest in the field of activity covered by the display; seeing a particular product or meeting a specific company; attending a training session held in conjunction with the trade display; or obtaining technical information. Exhibition organisers are often able to provide this information based on questionnaires completed by visitors to the display in previous years. Table 15.4 shows the results of research in this connection.

**Measuring outcomes** Outcomes should be measured against specific rather than 'rubbery' objectives. Specific measures could include: (1) the number of leads generated and the quality of sales from those leads; (2) the number of potential agents/distributors located and the likelihood of establishing a good distribution network as a result; (3) the number of visitors to the exhibit and the percentage who displayed active interest and accepted literature on the product; (4) the sales which were actually made at the display; and (5) a realistic appraisal of sales likely to directly result over the next 12 months.

| TABLE 15.4 | What the visitor is looking for at a trade show |
|---|---|

| | Totally unimportant (1) | Unimportant (2) | Medium (3) | Important (4) | Essential (5) | Average (6) |
|---|---|---|---|---|---|---|
| Buying exhibited products | 43.3 | 24.2 | 17.2 | 9.6 | 5.7 | 2.10 |
| Contacting potential suppliers | 5 | 3.1 | 9.4 | 34.6 | 47.8 | 4.17 |
| Seeking new ideas/carrying out market research | 2.5 | 6.3 | 12.6 | 41.5 | 37.1 | 4.04 |
| Finding out about competitors | 8.8 | 11.3 | 21.4 | 33.3 | 25.2 | 3.55 |
| Discovering new lines or new products | 1.9 | 1.3 | 6.9 | 47.8 | 42.1 | 4.27 |
| Discovering new applications of the product | 24.1 | 15.2 | 17.1 | 25.9 | 17.7 | 2.98 |
| Obtaining information about the operation of industrial machinery not easily transportable and investigating technical features by specialised staff | 24.3 | 13.5 | 20.9 | 24.3 | 16.9 | 2.96 |
| Meeting specialists | | 23.6 | 24.8 | 36.9 | 14.6 | 3.29 |
| Comparing market prices | 14.5 | 10.7 | 17.6 | 32.7 | 24.5 | 3.42 |

**SOURCE:** *Munvera, J. and Ruiz, S. (1993) 'Trade fairs: visitors' viewpoint',* Proceedings of the 23rd Conference of the European Marketing Academy, *Barcelona, 25–28 May, p. 1032.*

## TECHNICAL SEMINARS

This form of international promotion is particularly useful when marketing a product or service overseas that embodies a technology new to that market. It involves hiring a venue with audiovisual or screening capability and mounting a seminar designed to attract people interested in the technology being promoted. The invitees can be those who make the purchasing decision, those who influence the decision and those in regulatory authorities whose approval might be needed to market the new technology. Seminars are particularly appropriate for reaching 'influencers', as opposed to purchasers, and can facilitate their early involvement in development projects where new technology is relevant. A prestigious venue is necessary and the seminar must have educational or information value. It is also very suitable for products which require demonstration or complex explanation. Technical seminars are valuable in cases where there is a degree of uncertainty about the technology if it has not been seen in the country before, or where it has not yet been accepted as a natural solution to a specific type of problem situation.

Using the theatre at the Australian Embassy in Bangkok, the Australian promoters of the EFTPOS technology in the late 1980s mounted a technical seminar targeted at the Thai banking community to disseminate their expertise in this new technology. Included in the audience were officials from the Thai Central Bank, major commercial banks, the Thai Ministry of Finance as well as representatives of several firms which might be potential agents.

Details of overseas trade shows where the Australian government is facilitating participation can be found on the Austrade website, <http://www.austrade.gov.au>.

# Personal selling

Although personal selling overseas involves both salesforce activities and trade missions, it is the latter which is a promotional activity mostly found in international marketing.

## TRADE MISSIONS

Trade missions are like a series of blind dates as they are designed to introduce parties who for the most part are unknown to each other. The facilitation is via the mediation of a government or chamber of commerce which acts as a sponsor for the members of the trade mission. Trade missions can be inward or outward. Inward trade missions involve bringing the buyers to Australia, paid for by the Australian parties such as the government or a chamber of commerce. The members of the inward mission are then introduced to firms that wish to develop relations with them. Inward missions can also be organised by the government of the overseas country, but paid for by the Australian government as part of the country's aid activities or under the framework of a bilateral agreement between Australia and the other country. Thai Investment Missions to Australia are an example of this form of trade mission. Research by Wilkinson and Brouthers (2000) shows that trade missions are a highly effective vehicle for attracting foreign direct investment.

Outward trade missions, however, are the most common and involve Australian or New Zealand exporters visiting the overseas market. These missions can be:

- *general* and designed to create an awareness of Australia as a source of supply as with the Australian Trade Mission to Vietnam in 1988. Usually these missions do not include competing firms;

- *policy related* such as creating an awareness of Australian capability in an area of activity involving government as with Australian Offsets Missions to the USA. Usually this type of mission does not involve competitors;

- *product category* and confined to an industry or industry segment, such as automotive manufacturing equipment trade missions to the US mid-west. This type of mission can often involve competing firms; and

- *project related* and consisting of a range of non-competing firms with the collective capability to undertake the project for which tenders are likely to be called.

Most trade missions from Australia are sponsored by the Australian government or the government of an Australian state. This gives them credibility and improves the access in the overseas country for members of the mission. This sponsorship results in appointments being made by Austrade or the embassy.

Trade missions are led by a senior political figure as is often the case with general trade missions, or by a senior government official as with policy-related or project-related missions, or missions to promote defence related products and services, or by a leading industry figure as with product-category missions. The leadership is important because it influences the level and extent of access, the degree of publicity obtained and the attendance at mission hospitality functions.

Trade missions can also be sponsored by industry associations or chambers of commerce, and participation confined to members of that association or chamber. The credibility tends to be less although this can be compensated for in part by having the commercial section of the Australian Embassy make VIP appointments for the mission leader and host mission

When Malaysian Prime Minister Dr Mahatir made his last overseas visit before retiring, it was to Papua New Guinea, which is Malaysia's second largest trading partner. On this visit he was accompanied by four jet loads of Malaysian business leaders who used the umbrella of the visit to consummate deals in a much more conducive environment than if they had visited the country separately and on their own account. In association with the visit the Malaysians organised an investment seminar to boost the commercial relationship between the two nations. Implicit in this activity was capitalising on the downturn in relationships between Australia and Papua New Guinea on the one hand and the increase in positive relations between Malaysia and Australia on the other.

**SOURCE:** *Report on* Dateline, *television program, SBS Television, Sydney, 29 October 2003.*

social functions. Often trade missions coincide with an exhibition of products at one or more locations ('showcases') as happened with the Australian Defence Industry Mission to South East Asia in 1998 led by the then Minister for Defence Industry, Science and Technology, Bronwyn Bishop.

The advantages of a trade mission as a form of international trade promotion are that it facilitates the acquisition of information on the overseas market, enables access to decision makers at a senior level and puts mission members in contact with planners and regulators.

A trade mission also generates publicity for the members' products/services as the mission has news value and assists in relationship building because the initial introduction was as a member of the trade mission. In addition, there is the benefit of sharing experiences with other mission members which leads to synergy (resulting in a deeper investigation of the market) and the production of a trade mission report which assists future credibility in the market. Because the trade mission is mobile it can cover more ground by visiting regional areas. It is better than many other forms of international trade promotion which are anchored in one place. There are also efficiencies in the amount of time spent in the overseas market due to the organisation of appointments, transport and hospitality in advance of the mission's arrival. Disadvantages relate to the possible existence of competitors on the mission, the long planning time required, the fact that participation is generally by invitation only and that fewer contacts can be made than at trade displays.

## SALESFORCE ACTIVITIES

Personal selling overseas is different from personal selling in Australia or New Zealand because it involves crossing national borders and managing relationships with people from a different cultural background. Often the Australian or New Zealand firm is unknown in the other country and there may be a country of origin problem with Australia or New Zealand offering the product or service. These problems, which do not exist back home can be overcome by a sensitive approach and a selling strategy that concentrates on relationship building. Selling overseas requires an understanding in advance of the norms regarding introductions to new contacts, the getting-to-know-you phase of the relationship and expectations as to the conduct of the initial interview. Some strategies in selling in a new overseas market are noted below.

• Be prepared. Study the culture, the politics, the geography, the history, the industry structure, the role of the client in that industry and the background to the client's operation. This will create the impression that the salesperson has taken the trouble to learn about the client and the environment within which the client operates.

## 15.3 INTERNATIONAL HIGHLIGHT

# Mission incredible

Australia every year runs hundreds of trade missions promoting services and products of local businesses to overseas customers. In almost any month of the year Australian trade missions can be found in places as distant as Mumbai in India and Manhattan in the USA. It is not only Austrade that leads such missions, but also chambers of commerce and state governments. These trade missions for the most part produce positive results. Some mission operators concentrate on specific regions, for example the Northern Territory focuses on Asia's BIMP markets (Brunei, Indonesia, Malaysia and the Philippines). Victoria casts its net more widely and in 2002 dispatched 35 missions involving 318 companies, all of which

according to Dom Tassone of the Victorian Department of Innovation, Industry and Regional Development, were 'export ready'. New South Wales has a more sector-targeted approach and coordinates three kinds of mission—for groups of business-people from mixed industries, market visits for specific industry sectors and individual market visits for single firms. All mission organisers claim that making contacts is the most valuable part of mission participation and that spot sales are an accidental bonus. They also caution that success is dependent on carrying out detailed market research before departing Australia and that membership of a trade mission can help in the selection of the right agent in the overseas market.

**SOURCE:** *Parkes, J. (2003) 'Mission incredible',* Export, *November, pp. 32–4.*

- Slow down the pace of negotiation if you're in Asia, or speed up the pace if you're in the USA, depending on the norm in that country. Exercise patience because delays in reaching a decision may be due to time being spent on researching the accuracy of your firm's claim.

- It is important not to try to hurry a decision in countries where the time taken to arrive at a decision is proportional to the importance of the decision. In the eyes of the other party, to hurry a decision diminishes the importance the Australian or New Zealand firm attaches to the negotiation.

- Be careful of body language and the way it is interpreted in the other country. It is important to be sure that body language is consistent with the meaning of the spoken words, and that any gestures/actions are not offensive in the local culture.

- Spend time on relationship building in cultures where this is valued before getting down to business. It is important to understand the role of entertainment in the target market, especially when to offer, how lavish is the expectation, the form it should take and the preferred location.

The criteria for recruiting, selecting and managing the salesforce in another country will differ markedly from that in Australia or New Zealand for a variety of social and cultural reasons as exemplified in the following:

- *Japan*: individual recognition of sales representatives is still at odds with the nation's team approach to business;

- *Saudi Arabia*: finding qualified sales representatives is difficult because of a labour shortage and the low prestige of selling; and

- *India*: salesforce management is difficult in a market fragmented by language divisions and the caste system.

One of the issues that will need to be addressed is whether the selling should be undertaken in the overseas market by a member of your own sales team or by a national of the overseas country. Often this depends on the technical sophistication of the product or service involved as illustrated in Table 15.5.

The advantages and disadvantages of using professional expatriates as opposed to third-country nationals as opposed to locals are set out in Table 15.6.

## BROCHURES

It is not sufficient for the salesperson to be knowledgeable about and culturally sensitive regarding the overseas market. Such sensitivity must also be reflected in the material they distribute. Apart from local regulations with hand-out material relating to content, local expectations/norms as to size and quality, cultural requirements, appropriate colours etc, care is also needed with translation, graphics and what is depicted in the brochure lest its impact is misleading, irrelevant, irreverent or inappropriate.

---

**TABLE 15.5    Contingency factors in selecting salesforce nationality**

| Technology level | Management orientation | | | | | |
| | Ethnocentric | | Polycentric | | Regiocentric | |
| | Developed | Less developed | Developed | Less developed | Developed | Less developed |
| --- | --- | --- | --- | --- | --- | --- |
| High | Expatriates | Expatriates | Expatriates | Host-country nationals | Expatriates | Third-country nationals |
| Low | Expatriates | Expatriates | Host-country nationals | Host-country nationals (agents) | Third-country nationals | Third-country nationals (agents) |

**SOURCE:** *Reprinted from Honeycutt, E.D. and Ford, J.B. (1995) 'Guidelines for managing an international sales force'*, Industrial Marketing Management, *Vol. 24, p. 139, with permission of Elsevier Science.*

**TABLE 15.6**    Advantages and disadvantages of different sales types

| Category | Advantages | Disadvantages |
|---|---|---|
| Expatriates | Superior product knowledge<br>Demonstrated commitment to high customer service standards<br>Train for promotion<br>Greater HQ control | Highest cost<br>High turnover<br>Cost of language and cross-cultural training |
| Host country | Economical<br>Superior market knowledge<br>Language skills<br>Superior cultural knowledge<br>Implement actions sooner | Need product training<br>May be held in low esteem<br>Language skills may not be important<br>Difficult to ensure loyalty |
| Third country | Cultural sensitivity<br>Language skills<br>Economical<br>Allows regional sales coverage | Face identity problems<br>Blocked promotions<br>Income gaps<br>Need product or company training<br>Loyalty not assured |

SOURCE: *Reprinted from Honeycutt, E.D. and Ford, J.B. (1995) 'Guidelines for managing an international sales force',* Industrial Marketing Management, *Vol. 24, p. 138, with permission of Elsevier Science.*

## DIRECT MARKETING

Previously, direct marketing has mostly taken the form of mail or telephone selling. However, the internet is becoming an alternative method of direct marketing. Essential elements in direct marketing are an accurate database, an ability to filter the purchased database to remove incorrect listings and a capacity to merge the database with your promotional message.

At the consumer level in international marketing, direct mail is used to reach high-income groups and international travellers. At the commercial level it is often used as a substitute for a repeat sales call and as a supplement to other forms of promotion such as inviting attendance at an exhibit at a trade display. It can also be used as a means of obtaining qualified sales leads for local agents to follow up in the overseas market.

Difficulties with operating international direct mail campaigns from Australia or New Zealand relate to differing postal regulations between countries, different envelope and paper sizes, and variable quality of direct mail lists especially in terms of recency and targeting. Other problems can be due to the decision-making units in companies being different from country to country or there being different reactions in the country to direct mail solicitations. Whereas in some countries there is a tendency to treat commercial direct mail as junk (as in the USA) or environmentally wasteful (as in Germany), in other countries it tends to be regarded more as a source of information (as in Indonesia).

## CATALOGUE MARKETING

This medium is useful when the overseas customer is located some distance from the nearest sales office handling the product. To be effective, the catalogue, according to Albaum et al. (2006, p. 521) must be able to close the gap between buyer and seller. To do this, the catalogue must create interest and attract readers, arouse a positive response from the readers, impel action and supply all the information needed to make a decision (e.g. colour, size, prices and shipment cost).

## INTERACTIVE MARKETING COMMUNICATIONS

Increasingly marketers around the globe are experimenting with multimedia tools that facilitate interactive advertising and promotion. Although the internet is the prime vehicle for this, there are others such as text messaging and the mailing of DVDs containing interactive advertising. SMS messaging is becoming very popular as a promotion medium in Asia where the number of mobile phones now exceeds the number of fixed line phones. Another element of interactive marketing communications is direct and online database marketing. This entails the development and updating of electronic databases so as to interact with past, present and potential customers on a one-to-one basis. The databases have value apart from their content as they are a relationship maintenance tool and can generate a measurable response.

---

**15.4 INTERNATIONAL HIGHLIGHT**

# Swimming in international waters

I n a business which is famously unforgiving, Seafolly, Australia's best-selling swimwear label, has grown and prospered at home and is now growing in Europe where its garments can be found in Harrods, Selfridges and the House of Fraser chain of stores. Furthermore, Seafolly is about to be featured in that highly respected catalogue of the US lingerie giant, Victoria's Secret. It's all part of a plan for the label to become the number one swimwear seller in the world within 10 years.

Catalogue marketing is a commonly used promotional vehicle for the firm in all its markets. Five years ago the catalogue was a straightforward practical aid for retailers. More recently, the catalogue was shot on Fraser Island with *Sports Illustrated* model Kristy Hinze on the cover and is a glossy 36-page publication aimed directly at the Seafolly consumer—women aged 18 to 35.

Recently the firm has concentrated on building its international business, which now accounts for a significant percentage of its turnover. Managing director Peter Hallas believes that Australia has always done well in businesses that grew out of the surf culture and points to labels such as Billabong, Mambo and Quicksilver as examples. All have capitalised on Australia's attractive country of origin image in this category. For Seafolly, which now sells into 28 overseas markets as varied as Switzerland, Holland, France, Austria, Iceland, Dubai, Thailand and Lebanon, globalisation is not a dirty word. When it's winter in Australia, it's summer in Europe and people are buying swimwear.

**SOURCES:** Sun Herald, *11 July 2001; and <http//:www.seafolly.com.au>, accessed 29 January 2007.*

---

## AGENCIES

There are intermediaries available in overseas markets to assist with many forms of promotion, including advertising, media buying, exhibition organisation and public relations. The intermediary not only knows the local scene and what is culturally acceptable, but also knows how to work with what is available in the overseas market. When engaging a promotional intermediary overseas the Australian firm is buying access to a network of contacts as well as the service the intermediary provides. Table 15.7 shows the world's leading advertising agencies in terms of both gross income and billings.

Advertising agencies can be local or international and many international agencies were

| TABLE 15.7 | Top 10 global advertising agencies, ranked by worldwide revenue, 2006 | |
|---|---|---|
| **Agency** | **Headquarters** | **US$million** |
| Dentsu | Tokyo | 2490 |
| McCann Erickson Worldwide | New York | 2130 |
| BBDO Worldwide | New York | 2100 |
| DDB Worldwide | New York | 2080 |
| Ogilvy Mather | New York | 1710 |
| Young and Rubicam | New York | 1590 |
| TBWA Worldwide | New York | 1520 |
| JWT | New York | 1500 |
| Publicis Worldwide | Paris | 1230 |
| Leo Burnett Worldwide | Chicago | 1190 |

**SOURCE:** *Adapted from <adage.com/datacenter>, accessed 25 April 2007.*

domestic agencies that followed their clients overseas, such as Lintas of the UK and Dentsu of Japan. In some cases these agencies operate autonomously in overseas markets and in others, such as Dentsu, they form joint ventures with local agencies. Australian companies will need to decide whether all communications services in the overseas market should be provided by one full service agency or whether different services, such as creative or media buying, should be supplied by local specialist firms. Because the exporter is highly dependent on the agency in the overseas market, selection should be undertaken carefully. Whether to choose a local or the subsidiary of an international agency may be determined by what is available in the overseas market and the international strategy of the firm. Of particular relevance will be the extent and the quality of the coverage the agency provides, the other marketing services it can provide (e.g. market research, public relations) and its size relative to the exporter.

If the agency is large and the exporter's billings are modest, the service provided by the agency may be indifferent. If the reverse is the case, or the size of client and agency are in balance, then the agency is likely to try harder and devote more attention to the account.

Exhibition organisers offer similar advantages to locally based advertising agencies overseas and can facilitate not only participation in a trade show, but also involvement in associated promotional activities. Media buying is a specialist activity and media buyers can plan advertising strategies in the overseas market. Using the strength of their local media contact networks and bulk buying shared among their clients, they can obtain media exposure at favourable rates. They are also useful in countries where media availability is restricted and in evaluating alternatives when the media used in Australia is not available. Public relations firms are important in promoting in markets where cultural sensitivity is an issue because they can assist in positioning the product or service in an acceptable way.

# ISSUES

There are a number of issues unique to promotion and advertising in the international marketplace. Three of the most important are country of origin, standardisation versus differentiation and consumer versus B2B promotion overseas.

## How sweet it is!

The Sydney-based Whybin Lawrence TBWA has scored a rare coup for an Australian advertising agency with its appointment to develop worldwide 'masterbrand' campaigns for Cadbury Schweppes. The agency won the business after a global pitch and will work on the business alongside its affiliate agency TBWA in London.

To launch the new campaign the Sydney agency has developed a television commercial to 'spearhead the global marketing effort'. The commercial, which features the actress Pia Miranda, was launched in Britain in mid-March 2001, with other countries to follow. According to the chief executive of the agency, Neil Lawrence, the campaign represents a significant evolution in Cadbury's advertising. It is their first ever truly global campaign and the first time the Cadbury brand and its values, as distinct from individual products, have been communicated. 'That the work was conceived and produced by an agency here in Australia for a global market is great testament to the creative talent that this country has to offer. It is nice to be exporting.'

**SOURCE:** B & T, *7 April 2005.*

## Country of origin

Country of origin provides the customer with a tangible cue for evaluation when other less obvious features are difficult to assess. Its importance is directly linked to product and brand knowledge and the greater the knowledge of the product or brand, the less the need to use country of origin for evaluation (Lampert and Jaffe 1998). The country of origin can either add to the image or detract from the image of the product, depending on whether the image of the country in the specific product category is positive, negative or non-existent. With globalisation, country of origin is becoming a more complex issue.

Research by Mort and Duncan (2000) in Australia found that, increasingly, 'owned by' was just as important a country of origin cue as 'made in'. As the following indicates, 'made in' often does not mean what is implied. Volkswagens are now German-engineered rather than German-made; Ikea furniture is now Swedish-designed rather than Swedish-made; although 'Yoplait is French for yogurt', the product is made in Australia, not France; and the nuts in 'Queensland Fruit and Nuts' are from China rather than Queensland. Known as 'captious cues', the use of misleading, deceptive or ambiguous country of origin cues is a widespread practice in international marketing (Mueller et al. 2001).

The above examples indicate that, with the increase in the number of global firms, although products are produced in a variety of locations they are being promoted as associated with whichever country has the strongest country of origin image. Country of origin image can be embedded in the brand name as with Alitalia Airlines or *France-Soir* newspaper; it can be indicated through a brand name that sounds like a word in a particular language, such as Lamborghini or Toyota; or it can be in the manufacturer's name, such as Nippon Steel. Country of origin can also be included as part of the logo or package design, such the stylised kangaroo on the Qantas logo, or implied by the uniforms worn by salesforce or delivery people; for example, the red, white and blue uniforms of Domino's pizza delivery people could indicate association with the USA. Country image can also be conveyed by images, such as a bowler hat to indicate British, by use of personalities identified with a country, such as Paul Hogan for Australia, or by geographic association, for example the Rocky Mountains for Coors beer.

One subject of current research is whether the country image comes first, followed by

The Country of Origin image for Australia represents a lifestyle and a perception of the quality of life enjoyed by its people. A relaxed way of life, a beach culture and a 'green' healthy environment are all ingredients of this image. This has proved attractive to overseas buyers of men's clothing (Driza-Bone, R.M. Williams), women's fashion (Sass and Bide), men's casual and beachwear (Billabong, Quicksilver), underwear (AussieBum), ladies swimwear (Seafolly, Lustythreads) and food and wines (Maggie Beer paté, Beerenberg jams, Casella wines). Success in organising major international sporting events like the 2000 Olympic Games and the Rugby World Cup have created the image that Australians, while friendly and 'laid back' are also fair minded, efficient and hard working. To capitalise on this Country of Origin image, around 8000 products now carry the green-and-gold kangaroo logo and the Australia-made logo is used on a range of goods marketed in more than 30 countries.

**SOURCE:** *Adapted from* Export, *June 2007.*

beliefs and then attitudes, or whether beliefs or attitudes come first and lead to an evaluation about products from that country. The first is termed the 'halo construct' and operates where consumers are unfamiliar with the product. The second is termed the 'summary construct' and operates where consumers know the product and form conclusions about the country of its origin based on their experience of products from that source.

Country of origin has value in cases where the association permits the charging of a premium for products or services associated with that country. Mueller et al. (2001) coined the term 'captious cues' to describe marketing cues that mislead, confuse or create ambiguity for customers as far as country of origin is concerned. Fletcher and Bell (2002) showed that this practice leads to hijacking the country of origin's image, as evidenced by the Outback Steakhouse chain of restaurants in the USA implying Australian identity and the Irish pub phenomenon in many countries outside Ireland.

In the future, country of origin may become less important because as multinationals expand globally and become less identified with the country of their original establishment, it may well be their brand rather than country of origin which is 'top of mind' for the international buyer.

## Standardisation versus differentiation

Earlier discussion points to the need for promotion and advertising overseas to be tailored to the needs of each country. Yet there is a move towards globalisation; this implies that promotion and advertising approaches should be standardised in the interests of economies of scale and because customers worldwide are being driven by the same needs. Also, communications improvements are making customers in one country aware of what customers are demanding in another. Despite this, only about 10% of the *Fortune* 500 firms were committed to standardised global advertising. Although the trend is increasing, even transnational firms are not adopting this practice on a wide scale.

In deciding whether to try for a global approach in promotion and advertising overseas it is necessary to establish the extent to which the product or service on offer appeals to global customers. These are customers that read, watch or listen to global media, who travel widely, are reasonably homogenous in their tastes and have universal needs. A standardised approach can reduce communication costs. Although creating a global advertisement is very expensive, as British Airways discovered with its 'Manhattan Landing' campaign, it can be amortised over a large number of markets. It also needs to be kept in mind that, of total advertising costs, media costs are far greater than production expenses.

Market segmentation on the basis of lifestyle can facilitate a global approach to international promotion and advertising. Firms such as Rolex, Mercedes-Benz, Levi's and Gucci have successfully pursued this strategy with a standard form of promotion to secure global reach using international media.

Global campaigns also enable greater control over the promotion activities of a subsidiary and improve the firm's ability to maintain a consistent brand image. In general, standardisation of campaigns is more likely to succeed with luxury goods because of the nature of the customers and their ability to afford the luxury item. Such campaigns will need to be print or poster campaigns, which are more dependent on graphics than text. Technical products are also more likely to be amenable to standardised campaigns because of the limited and more specialised nature of the target audience. Products targeted at the youth market may also be amenable to standardised campaigns. This is because there is an increasing youth culture stimulated by music, film and communication and youth tend to be more homogenised because they have not yet internalised traditional cultural values to the same extent as their parents.

Coca-Cola's latest global advertising campaign, involving over US$300 million, is the largest in the company's history and illustrative of things to come. Its creation involved marketing directors from 13 regions around the world creating ads for their own markets based on 11 story ideas, all with the tag line 'Life tastes good'. It reflects the 'act local' approach. It includes 31 television implementations tailored to consumer tastes and trends in different countries and a radio song that will run in 20 versions recorded by local artists worldwide. This approach will mean that ads will differ from country to country, but will have a consistent message.

**SOURCE:** *Adapted from* USA Today, *20 April 2001, p. 5b.*

However, for most products and services, having one standardised campaign for a global audience is akin to prescribing Panadol for every ailment or illness. While it may work for some in all markets, it may not work for most and, although cost effective, it may not be commercially successful. This leads to the argument that a different promotion and advertising strategy should be adopted for each overseas market. Between these two extremes lies the doughnut approach. As a general rule, the most successful global firms in their promotion use local advertising and marketing strategies to express the global objectives of the brand.

Many transnational firms adopt a variation of the doughnut approach to standardisation. This involves having a standard frame of reference for all advertisements (the ring of the doughnut containing brand name and uniform global message) and a core which relates content or application to the individual country market. The standardisation can be further extended by all advertisements using similar colours and similar layout.

As the following commentary indicates, when a company with a principal domestic orientation becomes involved in international activities a standardised promotional approach will be riddled with pitfalls unless it is careful to take national preferences and behaviours into account.

Because of the large numbers of fiascos in international advertising due to cultural insensitivity and failure to undertake sensitivity research in advance, awards are given each year for the most notable fiasco. These are known as the Chevy Nova awards, in honour of GM's fiasco in trying to market this car in South and Central America where in Spanish 'No va' means 'it doesn't go'. Some recent nominees for the award are:

The Tourism Australia global campaign 'Where the bloody hell are you?' appears to have fallen on deaf ears in Japan. At a time when there has been an upsurge in Japanese travelling overseas, the number of Japanese visitors to Australia barely changed. 'Where the bloody hell are you' did not translate well into Japanese and came out as a rather flat message of 'So? Why don't you come?' which, according to Masato Takamatsu, vice president of marketing for the Japan Tourism Marketing Company, is an expression that does not fit with the Japanese mindset.

**SOURCE:** *Adapted from Cameron, D. (2006) 'Bloody well not there, that's for sure', Sydney Morning Herald, 25 August 2006, p. 3.*

- *Coors*—which put its slogan 'Turn it loose' into Spanish where it was read as 'Suffer from diarrhoea';

- *Clairol*—which introduced its curling iron under the brand name 'Mist Stick' into Germany, only to find out that 'mist' is slang for manure;

- *Gerber*—which, when it started selling baby food in Africa, used its US packaging with a smiling baby on the label. This led customers to believe that they were buying canned babies because in Africa, owing to illiteracy, it is common to illustrate the contents of the product on the packaging;

- *Frank Perdue's*—whose chicken slogan 'It takes a strong man to make a chicken tender' was translated in Spanish as 'It takes an aroused man to make a chicken affectionate'; and

- *American Airlines*—which, when it wanted to advertise its new first-class leather seats in Mexico, translated its 'Fly in leather' campaign literally, which came out as 'Fly naked' (*vuela en cuero*) in Spanish.

## Consumer versus B2B promotion overseas

With consumer promotion, often the push strategy is adopted. It implies that communication is something that is done to people. This is certainly not the case with business-to-business (B2B) promotion, which is more of an interactive process. The differences between the two are summarised in Table 15.8, which takes into account the relative lack of mass media available for B2B marketing. These differences should be taken into account when promoting overseas.

**TABLE 15.8    Differences between B2B and consumer communications**

| Consumer markets | B2B markets |
| --- | --- |
| Availability of mass media | Mass media of little use |
| Greater use of emotional appeals | More rational approach used |
| Tendency by consumers to avoid the message | Greater willingness to seek out information |
| Communications quickly forgotten | Communications often stored for future reference |
| Copy mostly short and punchy | Copy tends to be much longer and information laden |
| Communication aimed at individuals | Communication aimed at multiple decision makers |
| Involves mass media reaching broad segments | Involves industry-specific media widely read by those in the industry |

**SOURCE:** *Adapted from Blythe, J. and Zimmerman, A. (2005)* Business to Business Marketing Management; a Global Perspective, *Thomson Learning, London, p. 223.*

# The internet and international promotion and advertising

A survey by the *Economist* in 1997 revealed that 75% of customers who shopped on the internet went on to purchase goods through traditional channels. This suggests that the internet plays a more important role as a worldwide advertising and promotional vehicle than it does as a selling tool. However, compared with other media the spread of the internet has been much faster. The internet has the characteristics of both broadcast mass media and direct response advertising. It is more like newspapers than TV, but the medium and response convenience are closer to TV than newspapers from the perspective of impact on consumers.

Whereas in the traditional model of communications in the international marketplace there are clear-cut distinctions between the sender, the message and the recipient with control of the message being with the sender, in marketspace control of the message is shared between the sender and the receiver. This is because of the interactivity of the medium, the ability of the medium to carry back a message in reply and the impact of information technology on time, space and communication.

The web represents a move away from a push strategy in international promotion, where a producer focuses on convincing an agent or a distributor to stock products, towards a pull strategy in which the producer communicates direct with the customer. The web, in comparison with other forms of advertising, tends to be high on information, low on generating an emotional response and poor on reinforcing existing behaviour.

Web advertisements are often targeted at a user profile, which in turn influences the way the message is received. Increasingly, the ads displayed on this international medium are specific to user interests and pop up as these interests are revealed when the user navigates the web. In order to provide value to the potential international customer and maintain interest, the website must be attractive and user-friendly. This involves an appealing design, being available in the buyer's language (or one with which the buyer is likely to be familiar) and being aesthetic in terms of colour and background (taking into account the buyer's cultural norms). It should be easy to navigate, contain the information the buyer is likely to want and be easy to access.

Having a website is not enough in itself to attract 'hits' from international buyers. It is necessary to promote the site by both traditional and electronic means. Some recommended techniques are to put the firm's URL address on all correspondence, in traditional advertisements and highlight it as part of other marketplace promotion activities.

Apart from the website itself being an international promotional medium for the company owning the site, the websites can be used to promote specific products for the firm or for products of other firms, especially other products that are linked to the firm's offering. This promotion is achieved by linking websites of other firms to the site or by banner advertisements on the site. Not only does this banner advertising drive traffic to a particular website, but it also can provide more detailed information on the offer, enhance the credibility of the firm and create additional awareness of the brand. In cases where the firm is unrelated to the company owning the site, the banner advertisements can be placed through advertising networks of brokers who specialise in placing banner advertisements. Banner advertisements are usually paid for on the basis of the number of 'hits' on the banner (i.e. costs per thousand ad impressions).

In traditional brand relationships, according to Albaum et al. (2006), communication flows between the marketer and the consumer. With the internet, brand-based online communities have sprung up, with dialogue flowing between consumers via real-time chat taking place in chat rooms and interaction over time via discussion forums or bulletin boards. Although these online communities may be geographically dispersed in time and space, they share a common interest that can best be served via the internet rather than via other media. Such interactive communication gives a brand website considerable free input from the consumer community about the brand over time.

# Summary

Promotion and advertising overseas requires a different blend of activities to promotion and advertising in Australia. Some promotional techniques, such as trade displays and trade missions, are much more important when promoting overseas than in Australia. All forms of advertising and promotion will require substantial modification to take into account the specific circumstances of specific overseas markets. Although there are unique issues when promoting overseas, such as country of origin and the potential for standardisation, research in advance is essential if promotional activities in other countries are to be effective. In a nutshell, both the elements of the promotion mix will need modifying, as will the balance between various forms of promotional activity.

## ETHICS ISSUE

You are in Ho Chi Minh City for the first Australian Trade Display where your exhibit is a feature attraction. The display is due to open in three days' time. An hour ago you received a fax from Australia advising that, due to a mistake at your firm's warehouse, there were a large number of items in the consignment not mentioned in the list of goods on the manifest previously submitted to the Vietnamese customs authorities. The customs clearance agent for the Australian display responsible for handling all exhibit goods has advised that if the discrepancy is drawn to the attention of the Vietnamese authorities they will impound your consignment for at least a week. This will mean it will not be available for the trade show. However, the customs agent has mentioned that through a contact he could arrange that the consignment not be inspected, but this would require a 'donation' of A$5000 to the Customs Officers Welfare Fund.

***How would you respond if faced with this predicament?***

## Websites

**ACNielsen** http://www.acnielsen.com
**Advertising Age** http://adage.com
**Anholt-GMI Nation Brand Index** http://www.nationbrandindex.com
**Austrade** http://www.austrade.gov.au
**COMDEX** http://www.comdex.com
**Dentsu** http://www.dentsu.com
**Lintas** http://www.lintas.com
**McNair Ingenuity Research** http://www.mcnairingenuity.com
**Seafolly** http://www.seafolly.com
**Tourism Australia** http://www.tourismaustralia.com

# Discussion questions

1 How does each stage of the communications process require modification when promoting overseas?

2 Rate in terms of importance factors in international communications when promoting machine tools in India.

3 What are the factors affecting the effectiveness of communicating messages to overseas markets?

4 How do newspapers differ from magazines as promotional print media for accessing overseas customers?

5 Will global media eventually replace national media? What are the factors that underlie the rise of global media?

6 Why are trade shows an ideal medium for the new exporter to introduce products into an overseas market?

7 How do technical seminars differ from trade shows? When would you use a technical seminar in preference to a trade show?

8 What are the key features of a trade mission which facilitate its use as a vehicle for researching opportunities in an overseas market?

9 What are the characteristics of an effective international as opposed to a domestic salesperson?

10 Under what circumstances is the doughnut principle preferable to complete differentiation when promoting in overseas markets?

# References

Albaum, G., Duerr, E. and Strandskov, J. (2006) *International Marketing and Export Management*, 5th edn, Financial Times Prentice Hall, London.

'Aussie brand is number one', *Export*, October 2005.

*B & T*, 7 April 2005.

Blythe, J. and Zimmerman, A. (2005) *Business to Business Marketing Management; a Global Perspective*, Thomson Learning, London.

Cameron, D. (2006) 'Bloody well not there, that's for sure', *Sydney Morning Herald*, 25 August, p. 3.

*Dateline*, television program, SBS Television, Sydney, 29 October 2003.

De Mooij, M. (2005) *Global Marketing and Advertising: Understanding Cultural Paradoxes*, Sage Publications, Thousand Oaks, California.

Dulek, R.E., Fielden, J.S. and Hill, J .S. (1991) 'International communication: an executive primer', *Business Horizons*, January/February, pp. 20–5.

*Export*, June 2007.

Fletcher, R. and Bell, J. (2002) 'Hijacking country of origin image', *Proceedings of the United Kingdom Academy of Marketing Conference*, University of Nottingham, Nottingham, UK, 2–5 July.

Griffin, T. (1994) *International Marketing Communications*, Butterworth Heinemann, Oxford, UK.

Hall, E.T. (1976) *Beyond Culture*, Anchor Press/Doubleday, New York.

Hofstede, G. (2001) *Culture's Consequences*, 2nd edn, Sage Publications, Thousand Oaks, California.

Honeycutt, E.D. and Ford, J.B. (1995) 'Guidelines for managing an international sales force', *Industrial Marketing Management*, Vol. 24, March, pp. 138–9.

<http://www.worldscreen.com/asiapacific.php>, accessed 29 January 2007.

*International Herald Tribune*, 12 July 2004, p. 9.

Jacobs, L., Keown, C., Worthley, R. and Ghymn, J. (1991) 'Cross-cultural colour comparisons', *International Marketing Review*, Vol. 8, No. 3, pp. 21–30.

Keegan, W.J. and Green, M.C. (2005) *Global Marketing*, 4th edn, Pearson Prentice Hall, New Jersey, USA.

Lampert, S.I. and Jaffe, E.D. (1998) 'A dynamic approach to country of origin effect', *European Journal of Marketing*, Vol. 32, pp. 61–78.

Mort, G.S. and Duncan, M. (2000) 'The country of origin effect: a study of the "owned by" cue', *Proceedings of the Conference of the Australia–New Zealand Marketing Academy*, Griffith University, Gold Coast, 28 November–1 December.

Mueller, R.D., Broderick, A.J. and Mack, R. (2001) 'Captious cues: the use of misleading, deceptive or ambiguous country of origin cues', *Proceedings of the Conference of the European Marketing Academy*, Bergen, 8–11 May, Norges Handelshoyskole.

Munvera, J. and Ruiz, S. (1993) 'Trade fairs: visitors' viewpoint', *Proceedings of the 23rd Conference of the European Marketing Academy*, Barcelona, 25–28 May, p. 1032.

Parkes, J. (2003) 'Mission incredible', *Export*, November, pp. 32–4.

Rossen, J.R. and Seringhaus, F.H.R. (1996) 'Trade fairs as international marketing venues: a case study', paper presented at the 12th IMP Conference, University of Karlsruhe.

Rossiter, J.R. and Bellman, S. (2005) *Marketing Communications: Theory and Applications*, Pearson Prentice Hall, Frenchs Forest, NSW.

*Sun Herald*, 11 July 2001.

Terpstra, V. and Sarathy, R. (2000) *International Marketing*, 8th edn, Dryden Press, Fort Worth, Texas.

'They love us in the US', *Export*, March 2006.

Thompson, B. and Quester, P. (2000) 'Evaluating sponsorship effectiveness: the Adelaide Festival of Arts', *Proceedings of the Conference of the Australia–New Zealand Marketing Academy*, Griffith University, Gold Coast, 28 November–1 December.

*USA Today*, 20 April 2001, p. 5b.

Usunier, J.C. and Lee, J.A. (2005) *Marketing Across Cultures*, 4th edn, Financial Times Prentice Hall, Harlow, UK.

Wallace, J. (2005) 'Boeing lands huge Chinese order of 7E7s', *The Sydney Morning Herald*, 29–30 January, p. 44.

Wilkinson, T.J. and Brouthers, L.E. (2000) 'Trade shows, trade missions and state governments: increasing FDI and high-tech exports', *Journal of International Business Studie*s, Vol. 31, No. 4, pp. 725–34.

## go online

Go online to <www.pearsoned.com.au/fletcher> to find more case studies.

# Taking Tasmanian Pure and Natural to Asia: lost in translation

### Al Marshall, ACU National

## THE BRAND

Tasmanian Pure and Natural is a brand of still bottled water that is harnessed at its source in a valley near Hobart. The brand has been in the domestic market for around 10 years, and after meeting some success in its home state, the owners and marketers of the brand expanded into the Melbourne market. The brand name had been carefully chosen by business partners Todd and Luis to appeal to Tasmanian's sense of pride in their own state. They felt that Tasmanians, living on an island state, consider themselves to be a little different from those in mainland Australia. Having 'Tasmanian' in the brand name would appeal to state pride. 'Pure and Natural' would refer to the source that the water is bottled from and to the process of bottling it, would also differentiate it from other brands (while subtly suggesting that these other brands are less 'pure and natural'), and most importantly convey the central consumer benefit.

Todd and Luis also believed that the brand name would give them traction in mainland markets like Melbourne, where the same brand images would help conjure up ideas of clean, plentiful and unpolluted water from fresh Tasmanian mountain streams. The packaging and labelling were designed to reinforce this positioning. The glass bottle is an icy blue, and the paper label (which wraps around the centre of the bottle) features an image of a stream cascading over rocks with verdant ferns on either side of the stream and a snow-capped mountain backdrop meant to represent Mt Wellington (which is near the bottling source). The non-transparent nature of the icy-blue bottle took its cue from the dark-green Perrier bottle. The main inspiration for the in-house label design was the Cascade beer label. Both the business partners had observed how this

state-based beer brand had been able to carve out a niche for itself in mainland markets, and indeed in some overseas markets. As researchers such as Belch and Belch have discovered, brand image can be a powerful source of differentiation and competitive advantage in crowded and competitive markets (Belch and Belch 2004).

## DOMESTIC MARKETING COMMUNICATIONS

After five years in its home state market, Tasmanian Pure and Natural was launched in the Melbourne market. The marketing communications for this had their genesis in the marketing communications that Todd and Luis had used in Hobart and Launceston for their initial launch of the brand. This involved point of sales sampling of the product in supermarket and delicatessens. A sales promotion company was able to supply a team of attractive demonstrators. The product was offered to customers in these stores in small ice-blue, non-translucent disposable sampling glasses from a tray set up on a metal stand. The demonstrators were provided with matching ice-blue T-shirts. The signage on the stand read 'Pure and Natural Virgin Tasmanian', and the words were also printed in small writing with the company's logo on the T-shirts worn by the female demonstrators. Shelf talkers in the same colour and with the same body copy were used in the adjacent aisle shelving where the product was stocked. The partners were particularly happy that the whole look was integrated. Indeed it appeared to conform to the principles of integrated marketing communications.

After being in this metropolitan market for two years the business partners felt that it was time for Tasmanian Pure and Natural to expand its share of the premium bottled water market. They were also aware that the packaging, labelling and repeat point of sale sampling were not enough to reinforce the brand image, or to reach new consumers not previously exposed to the campaign.

Accordingly, a small Hobart advertising agency was appointed to create a 30-second television commercial. This subsequently went to air in less-expensive time slots in Hobart, Launceston and in Melbourne. The advertisement features an attractive young female model reaching for a bottle of Tasmanian Pure and Natural, unscrewing the bottle top, drinking straight from the bottle, and then (looking highly refreshed) mouthing the words 'Pure and Natural Virgin Tasmanian'. The advertising agency reassured Todd and Luis that consumers who could lip-read would immediately be able to understand what the model was saying. For other consumers who would not immediately understand, but who would be intrigued (and therefore be drawn into the advertisement) the model was wearing a T-shirt with 'Pure and Natural Virgin Tasmanian' on it in big lettering. On this basis they would quickly work out what the model was saying. The fact that the television commercial had no audio sound track (the model does not speak and there is no music) was intended to differentiate it from the relatively noisy advertisement aired before and after it, and to get consumers to pay attention. It also saved considerably on costs! The advertisement also appeared to be effective, with sales increasing each time after it went to air.

## THE INTERNATIONAL OPPORTUNITY

Todd and Luis were subsequently approached by a Hong Kong-based beverage importing company who to their surprise expressed interest in obtaining rights to the product for the Hong Kong, Macau and the mainland China market. Involvement in international markets is not always the result of the domestic marketer having international marketing objectives. The company proposed that it would ship the brand to its distribution warehouse in Hong Kong. It would use its already established marketing channels to distribute Tasmanian Pure and Natural to retailers in its home market of Hong Kong, and the geographically close southern Chinese mainland provinces, as well as Macau. It would be responsible for selling to the retailers, and for keeping them stocked. The Hong Kong company, however, would not take legal title to the products at the docks in Melbourne or when they arrived by container ship in the port of Hong Kong. Rather, what they proposed was a joint venture whereby production, branding and marketing would remain the responsibility of Todd and Luis in Australia, and the Hong Kong company would take responsibility for shipping from Melbourne, warehousing, transportation to the retailers and invoicing. They proposed a 50/50 joint venture. As was discovered by Belch and Belch, as a form of market entry strategy joint ventures require both parties to bring complementary core competences to the proposed relationship (Kotler 2004).

The Tasmanian partners realised that their brand might well have appeal beyond their own previously limited ideas for expanding the brand. In fact it appeared to be a very exciting idea. While Perrier and Evian had been in their sights in Hobart, Launceston and Melbourne, these brands are also present in the Chinese markets. Marketing Tasmanian Pure and Natural in these markets would allow them to position the brand in a similar way to the home market, and take on Perrier, Evian and possibly other premium brands in these markets. The potential Hong Kong joint venture partner had also painted a very positive picture of the market potential, particularly for the southern Chinese provinces, with fast economic growth, rising disposable incomes and increasingly Westernised consumer tastes. The joint venture partner had also pointed out that the high levels of water pollution (along with air and land pollution as a result of fast industrial growth with few environmental controls) in southern China mean that consumers are increasingly turning to bottled waters, to fulfil their daily water consumption needs. Macro environmental factors can have a direct impact on overseas consumers' consumption patterns, just as they can with local consumers.

On this basis the joint venture partnership was signed and the two Tasmanian business partners, from their small beginnings with the spring in the valley near Hobart, found themselves suddenly responsible for marketing Tasmanian Pure and Natural in the three Chinese markets. The Hong Kong joint venture partner had explained right from the outset that as a company it knew very little about marketing, and that its strengths lay in identifying gaps in the Chinese beverage market, importing beverages and building and maintaining channel relationship, as well as in logistics and supply chain management. Not all organisations are imbued with the marketing or the relationship marketing orientations. Hence what Todd and Luis had learnt from their experiences in the Tasmanian market and in the Melbourne market would need to form the basis for their foray into the brave new world of international marketing.

## INTERNATIONAL MARKETING COMMUNICATIONS

The first initiative they took was to ship 15 of the point-of-sale steel stands, with the associated signage, and a large supply of the ice-blue plastic disposable sampling glasses, along with a supply of the ice-blue T-shirts for the in-store demonstrators. Their Hobart printer also produced 1000 shelf talkers. Todd and Luis were really pleased that the television commercial did not have an audio soundtrack, since this meant that dubbing into Cantonese would not be required. They were not concerned that the advertisement featured an attractive Australian model (rather than a Chinese model), since this would emphasise that the brand really is from Tasmania, and would help sustain its aspirational positioning.

In consultation with the Hong Kong partner the decision was made to launch the brand initially

in the Hong Kong market, with subsequent launches in Macau, followed by southern China, specifically Guangdong province. The Hong Kong company already supplies the Hong Kong supermarket chain Pack n Pay with imported beverages, and the chain agreed to also stock Tasmanian Pure and Natural, provided it was offered trade support, and there was a commitment to television advertising to build brand awareness and imagery. On their first business trip to Hong Kong Todd and Luis signed a contract with a sales promotion company to run the point-of-sale sampling program. They also negotiated a deal to run an initial one-month campaign using a major Cantonese language TV network.

The advertisements were scheduled to run later in the evening to avoid the expensive peak time rates. It was felt that the chosen time spots could reach a target market not dissimilar to the Australian target market. The point of sales sampling of the product in Pack n Pay was timed to commence two days after the first television commercial went to air, and would run for 10 days. The TV spots would run for another 20 days after this to continue to build brand awareness and imagery. The Tasmanian partners flew home confident that the campaign conformed to integrated marketing communications principles and that the communications elements being used had been tried, and proven as sales builders. Strong arguments exist for standardising communications as much as possible across national markets to avoid issues like inconsistent messaging, and ending up with different positionings in different markets.

## STAKEHOLDER AND CONSUMER REACTIONS

The shock came one week after the campaign commenced. The Hong Kong joint venture partner called to complain about the television commercial, and to report that Pack n Pay was also not happy. Individual stores were receiving a number of complaints about the point-of-sale sampling program. The Hong Kong partner reported that the TV network had also received some complaints from its viewers.

The partner pointed out that they personally really had little idea about what the Australian-made advertisement was about. It did not seem to be saying anything (literally), and while their own English was good, it had taken them some time to work out the words that the model was mouthing in the ad. They had only managed to work it out after seeing the advertisement a few times, and noticing the words on the T-shirt worn by the model. They argued that there was little hope that Cantonese speakers with limited or no knowledge of English would understand. They therefore felt that the advertisement would fail to build much brand awareness, and rather than building brand image it might simply confuse and frustrate those in the identified target market.

The complaints received by the supermarkets principally related to two customer concerns. The first concern by some customers was that they were not sure what they were being offered. Some thought what was in the non-translucent ice-blue bottles was probably a vodka, or even liquor. When it was poured into the ice-blue disposable glasses more of them thought it was vodka. They were surprised and some were plainly annoyed to be offered a vodka or clear liquor when they went grocery shopping. Many had refused to sample the product, either because they did not drink alcohol, or else because they thought that a supermarket during the day is not an appropriate place to sample an alcoholic beverage.

The other concern by customers related to their understanding (or rather lack of understanding) of the brand name and the associated slogan. In particular they objected to the slogan 'Pure and Natural Virgin Tasmanian' on the metal stands and on the T-shirts worn by the sales promotion company demonstrators. Tasmanian Pure and Natural did not exactly indicate to them what they were being offered, since the script used by the demonstrators simply required them to say 'Would you like to try Tasmanian Pure and Natural?'. 'Tasmanian' itself did not have an immediate association for them. Those who read and translated 'Pure and Natural Virgin Tasmanian' on the T-shirts of the attractive local demonstrators into Cantonese were less than impressed. They wondered exactly what was being promoted, and some had moral objections.

The Hong Kong joint venture partner, while maintaining its claim that it lacked expertise in marketing, pointed out that it did not feel this was a good start to the relationship, and the marketing communications campaign instituted by the Tasmanian bottler and marketer did not give it confidence about the marketing abilities of its new Australian partner. Todd and Luis were perplexed that their sophisticated and well-thought-through Tasmanian Pure and Natural campaign appeared to have been lost in translation! Customisation of marketing communications campaigns in international marketing is often necessary.

## Bibliography

Belch, G. and Belch, M. (2004) *Advertising and Promotion: An Integrated Marketing Communications Perspective*, 6th international edn, Irwin/McGraw-Hill, New York.

Kotler, P., Brown, L., Adam, S. and Armstrong, G. (2004) *Marketing*, 6th edn, Pearson Prentice Hall, Sydney.

## Questions

1 Identify the strengths and the weaknesses of Tasmanian Pure and Natural in its domestic market, and its potential strengths and potential weaknesses in the Chinese markets. What led Todd and Luis to believe the brand could succeed internationally?

2 If Todd and Luis decided to persist with their month-long marketing communications campaign for Tasmanian Pure and Natural in the Hong Kong market, what modifications to the campaign could they make to reassure Pack n Pay, their joint venture partner and potential consumers?

3 Design a new campaign for Tasmanian Pure and Natural for the Hong Kong market that could also be used in Macau and Guangdong province. You do not have to restrict yourself to point-of-sale sampling and a television commercial, but the campaign should not be elaborate or expensive.

4 What general lessons can Todd and Luis learn from their first experiences of international marketing? In particular, what do these indicate about the application of sound international marketing communications principles and strategies?

# INTERNATIONAL PRICING FOR PROFIT

## LearningObjectives

**After reading this chapter you should be able to:**

- assess the importance of the pricing decision in the international context;

- learn how to apply a range of alternative international pricing strategies;

- discuss factors that must be considered in setting prices;

- compare different approaches to setting international prices so as to ensure an optimal outcome;

- appreciate the variety of payment terms and techniques that operate in international marketing;

- determine the constraints that apply to setting international prices; and

- appreciate the role of international pricing for the global firm and the rationale for transfer pricing.

# The Japanese approach to price setting—competing on value

The Japanese do not treat costs as given. Rather they decide in advance what costs they must achieve in order to ensure a price that will deliver them dominance of the international market. The target cost is then used as a target for the designers, the engineers and for those who wish to be suppliers or subcontractors for the Japanese firm. Once initial profitable entry into an overseas market has been achieved, the pressure to lower the target costs continues so as to ensure that the market position is protected and expanded.

International marketing by Japanese companies, such as Honda and Toyota, is based on 'value'—quality products at prices lower than their direct competitors. Although most Japanese international marketers think of product quality and function first, 'value' is also seen to be created by low price. Starting with 'value packaging', which combines high quality and low price, the Japanese marketer then adds value through advertising and after-sales service backed by strong distribution channels. Over time additional service, image and status is provided through advertising and styling to sell 'value' at a higher price.

Often the international marketer in an Australian firm does not control price. Accountants and top management monitor prices and margins, as do corporate legal counsel, to avoid allegations of dumping or price discrimination. To compensate for this lack of control Australian overseas marketers will set list prices at an acceptable price positioning, then make frequent short-term price changes. This is particularly the case for packaged consumer goods.

Japanese marketers prefer to hold prices so that intermediaries maintain margins and they are against

sudden price wars. Sony, Panasonic and Sharp prefer to compete on product features and brand image, not price. The Japanese strategy is to set a low price, then position the product in terms of features and image (see Figure 16.1).

Thus, when a Japanese company enters a foreign market for the first time, the product usually enters with a very low price. In the past this was at the lower end of the market. Today it is more likely to be at a higher price point— but, relative to competition, lower prices are still common. This strategy differs from Australian firms and perhaps from some US and European firms, who expect to exchange their success at home for a killing abroad. Firms from a variety of industries, such as McDonald's, Kodak and Ericsson, tend to flaunt their domestic market leadership as a reason for premium prices abroad. European auto companies, such as Saab and BMW, also use their foreign connection to extract consumer goodwill in the form of higher prices. So far, with less confidence in the status of their own country, the Japanese have largely avoided this strategy.

**SOURCE:** *Adapted from Johansson, J.K. and Nonaka, I. (1996)* Relentless—the Japanese Way of Marketing, *Harper Business, USA, pp. 126–9.*

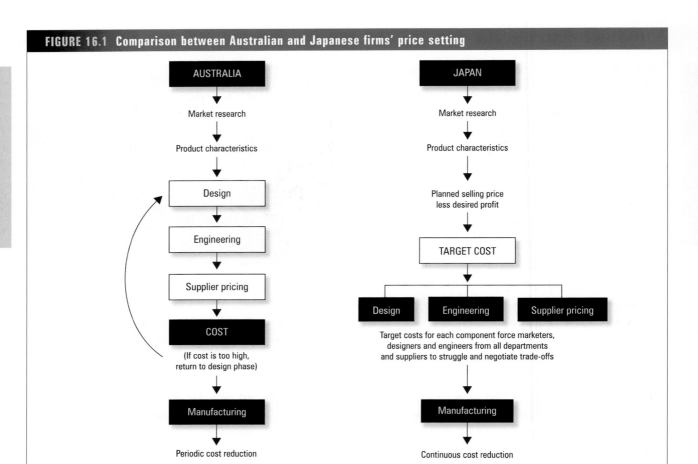

**FIGURE 16.1  Comparison between Australian and Japanese firms' price setting**

**SOURCE:** *Robert, M. (1993)* Strategy Pure and Simple, *McGraw-Hill, London, UK. Reproduced with permission of The McGraw-Hill Companies.*

# INTRODUCTION

The role of pricing in international marketing is analogous to the selection and purchasing of a fine expensive wine. In the same way as wine to be tasted is sipped rather than gulped, international price setting requires research to establish the most appropriate price to charge. Just as the making of fine wine is a compromise between the objectives of the winemaker and the wishes of the consumers, so the setting of prices in overseas markets is a compromise between the strategic objectives of the firm and the estimated demand at various price levels. The winemaker does not totally control the price to be charged because of the requirement to add excise or sales taxes and prices charged for products sold in other countries are often regulated by governments. There are elements such as import duties which add to the price and the consumer's perception of value over which the Australian or New Zealand supplier has no control.

# INTERNATIONAL PRICING ISSUES

International pricing is a more complex activity than domestic pricing because of the larger number of variables involved and the greater degree of uncertainty. For this reason international pricing requires more care and effort, and approaches that merely extend domestic pricing rarely succeed. A number of issues influencing the setting of prices in the international environment need to be considered in advance of a decision as to the most advantageous price. These include a variety of interrelated internal and external factors. First, the role of price and the nature of the pricing decision are considered.

## The role of price

Price is the only marketing variable that produces revenue. It is an integral part of the product when marketed overseas as it is difficult to think of a product without considering its price. Price is important because it affects demand. Demand and price are usually inversely related. Price, however, is also related to other elements of the international marketing mix and does not exist in isolation from them. Price can be the subject of controversy, not because consumers object to paying for products or services, but because they wish to see a relationship between price and perceived value. Price must be set at equivalent or lower than perceived value for this reason.

## Reference prices

The price that an international buyer pays for a product or sees being demanded for a product becomes the reference price against which other products are likely to be evaluated. Reference prices are not constant and are modified by market experience. In international marketing, buyers establish a range of prices for a product around the reference price and anything outside this range is unlikely to be acceptable unless it has unique or different features, in which case it becomes a different product. Within this range of prices, however, price in international marketing is often used as an indicator of quality until experience indicates otherwise. When price is perceived as being similar for alternative products, then product quality or value as communicated through the brand becomes the deciding factor in the decision to purchase. For example, regardless of relative merits, the locally manufactured Proton Saga, which sells for less than the Volkswagen in Malaysia, tends to be regarded as being of lesser quality because of both its lower price and the international reputation of the Volkswagen brand.

## Nature of the pricing decision

Pricing is the only variable in the international marketing mix which can be changed at short notice without cost implications. The form of market entry will depend on whether the price is decided by the firm or by an intermediary, such as an agent overseas. In cases where the firm sets the price the pricing decision when the product is being introduced to an overseas market for the first time will be different from the decision to change the price in an existing market. With a new product, flexibility to set prices will be increased the more innovative the product and/or the greater the capacity of consumers to afford the product and/or the less the degree of competition in the market. With existing products, the ability to change prices will be increased as the firm acquires more knowledge about the overseas market and increases the share it already holds in that market. This ability will also be influenced by the extent to which the market is free or regulated.

## THE FIRM'S FACTORS

These include corporate goals, the degree to which the firm wishes to control prices charged to the overseas consumer, the firm's usual approach to costing and the extent to which the company is internationalised. For example, does it insist on the same free on board (FOB) price for all overseas markets or does it charge different FOB prices to different markets to take account of varying circumstances? This may be a matter of whether the firm views export as an extension of its domestic sales effort or as a separate strategic activity.

**Nature of the product or industry** The nature of the product or industry influences the degree of price discretion available to the firm. A firm with a specialised or technically advanced product or with a knowledge-based competitive advantage is likely to have fewer competitors than a 'me too' product. When the product has unique advantages price will have a more static role in the international marketing mix. With consumer goods local income levels will be critical in the pricing decision. However, some industries face dramatic fluctuations in the price of raw materials or are more susceptible to predatory pricing practices by foreign competitors. This can have an impact on prices of the finished product offered overseas. For example, a rise in the price of Australian coal might cause a rise in the price of Japanese steel that in turn might result in a price rise in the cost of Japanese automobiles. Technically complex products in general have greater servicing requirements, longer production times and greater sales lead times than simple, non-technical products. A final product-related issue affecting price is the level of service expected to be provided to support the product in the overseas market. Expectations as to service provision differ from country to country and constitute a cost that must either be factored into the price or charged for separately.

**Location of production facilities** Companies with production or assembly facilities in other countries find it easier to respond to fluctuations in exchange rates and cost of inputs. This is because they are able to supply from a variety of sources rather than simply one source and can source from the plant in whichever country offers the greatest competitive advantage at a particular time.

Several years ago one of the authors was visiting the Philippines together with a group of students undertaking projects in international marketing research. He noticed in a major supermarket chain that the Kellogg's products came from five different countries. Inquiries from the chain's buying office revealed that the office varied its sourcing of Kellogg's lines according to whichever source had the most advantageous exchange rate to the peso at the time of the purchasing decision.

## CUSTOMER FACTORS

**The price element of the purchase** The price that is charged for a product is not only for the physical product, but also for an associated bundle of other attributes that come with the purchase, any one of which can positively or negatively impact on the perceived value. This can be illustrated in the case of a motor vehicle. Here the price may include extra features such as air conditioning or power steering and a warranty that has a greater perceived value if it is for three years/30 000 kilometres instead of one year/10 000 kilometres. It may also include servicing in the original price or extended servicing available at a concessional price;

discount for repeat purchase; affiliation with credit card frequent flyer programs as with Holden; or discount for bulk purchase as with fleet owner discounts. When pricing for overseas markets it is useful to ascertain what bundling of benefits is included with the price of competing products so these can be matched if necessary or introduced if not usual in the market, so as to gain a competitive edge.

## ENVIRONMENT FACTORS

**Culture** Because price is a decisive element in the interaction between buyer and seller, culture plays a role in price setting and negotiation. In the first place, culture influences the bargaining over price. In some cultures, everything is negotiable and no one believes that the first price offered by the seller is anything but a negotiating ploy and a ceiling that can be negotiated downward. In these cultures the alternative price offered by the buyer is treated as a floor price that can be negotiated upwards. In other cultures prices are not negotiable and the price sought is the result of careful consideration as to what is a fair price and, once put on the table, is inflexible. In markets where negotiation is the norm the Australian or New Zealand firm should consider having a higher list price so as to leave room for negotiation.

In some cultures (e.g. in many Islamic countries), interest is regarded as usury, yet buyers still want extended payment terms. In such cases the firm may need to load the opportunity cost of funds 'tied up' into the price, rather than charge interest for delayed payment.

Another culturally influenced aspect of pricing is that price is viewed as a surrogate indicator of quality. The degree to which this occurs will vary between cultures as illustrated by Usunier and Lee (2005, p. 322) who contrast northern and southern Europeans. The former consider that goods should be expensive in order to limit their consumption based on the Lutheran value system, and prefer durable, lasting goods in line with a thrifty, austere view of life. The southern Europeans are less concerned with a price–quality relationship and support instant spending in order to satisfy immediate needs—allegedly more in line with the Roman Catholic philosophy.

A final cultural variable is the acceptability of loading the price to cater for various pay-offs in order to get the business. This is a form of disguised bribery that influences price setting. The degree to which this practice is the norm varies from country to country. Inquiries in this connection will enable the Australian or New Zealand firm to decide whether it wishes to do business on this basis.

From the above, it is apparent that there are many factors that cause prices to escalate between production in Australia or New Zealand and sale to overseas customers. These factors will also cause the gap between local and overseas price to vary from country to country. Figure 16.2 illustrates the impact of factors on price escalation.

**Location and environment of the foreign market** The location of the overseas market also affects the operational costs of exporting to that market. Such costs include undertaking market research, visits to that market by company executives, communicating with the market and promoting in that market.

One environmental factor is climate. Climatic conditions can add to price. Examples include climatic conditions in overseas markets requiring termite-proofing or stronger packaging because the product is being transported over unpaved roads, or weatherproofing because of monsoon rains.

Economic factors can also influence the price that can be charged in international markets. These include the rate of inflation and fluctuations in the exchange rates. Also

**FIGURE 16.2 Factors influencing price escalation in international markets**

Inflation

Taxes, tariffs and administrative costs

Exchange rate fluctuations

Price escalation

Varying company values

Transportation costs

Intermediary margins

**SOURCE:** *Cateora, P.R. and Ghauri, P.N. (1999) International Marketing, McGraw-Hill, Maidenhead, UK. Reproduced with permission.*

having an impact on price are political factors such as the perceived risk of dealing with a particular country. The firm may wish to charge a higher price to compensate for such factors. Certainly its credit insurer, such as the Australian Export Finance Insurance Corporation, will charge a higher premium to compensate for the greater risk of doing business in the overseas market. Such premiums become a cost that will need to be reflected in the price charged.

**Government regulations** Government regulations can affect prices charged overseas and in Australia these regulations can involve export inspection costs (particularly with agricultural products) and the costs of conforming to standards imposed by the domestic government on export products. Other costs include the effect of local taxes when applied to products to be exported. These include payroll tax and excise rates and have the effect of reducing a nation's competitive advantage when doing business overseas. Import duties can also add to costs of exported products. Although there is provision for the refund of duties paid on components used in finished products that are subsequently exported, the bureaucratic procedures involved may make the claiming of duties not worthwhile.

**International trade relations** Membership of regional trade groupings can influence price setting. Companies that are selling to one member of the European Union, especially those that are members of the euro zone, have to deal with the fact that prices in one country will be readily known by consumers in another because of cross-border transparency in prices in regional trade groupings.

## DISTRIBUTION CHANNEL FACTORS

The channels of distribution often dictate export pricing. The nature of distribution influences the degree of control the Australian firm is able to exercise over the price charged to the final customer in the overseas market. The length of distribution channels varies from country to country. When the firm has a subsidiary in that market it is able to exercise more control over the final price than when the firm operates in the market through an independent agent or distributor. By reducing the number of intermediaries between the Australian manufacturer and the final customer in the foreign market the firm is able to

## 16.1 INTERNATIONAL HIGHLIGHT

# Passing the buck

In February 1998 the Australian Taxation Office (ATO) announced that it would carefully peruse the financial affairs of companies controlled by media magnate Rupert Murdoch. Although Murdoch operated on a global basis, his companies were for the most part headquartered in Australia and in the previous financial year Murdoch had paid only A\$130 million tax on profits of A\$1.65 billion. This represented an effective tax rate of 7.8% compared with the company tax rate in Australia of 36%. It is alleged that Murdoch minimised tax liability by a variety of international pricing strategies that, although not necessarily illegal in themselves, had the effect of siphoning off into profits taxes that the company should return to the country as a good corporate citizen. Included in these practices were transfer pricing, use of tax havens and taking advantage of differing interpretations of tax liability. The actions were also characterised by differing degrees of enthusiasm for enforcement of pricing legislation between countries and inflating the costs of intercompany transfer of goods and services in order to reduce profits earned in high-taxing countries. The ATO considers transfer pricing to be a very significant source of revenue leakage and recently extended its review of international transfer pricing to small business. Transactions that will attract increasing scrutiny from the ATO include:

- sale of stock to an overseas parent company or vice versa;
- cross-border sales of plant and equipment;
- cross-border loans that are interest free or have non-commercial interest rates;
- charges between head office and foreign subsidiaries;
- use of trade names, patents, trade marks, etc. without appropriate consideration;
- cost allocations to Australian or foreign branches.

Transnational companies are becoming increasingly concerned at the attention transfer pricing is receiving from the ATO. Multinational subsidiaries in Australia represent about 1.5% of companies in Australia, but account for 47% of company tax paid. If they do not pay their fair share of tax, the economy suffers. In the three-year period since July 1999, the ATO collected A\$492 million in transfer pricing penalties and insisted firms adjust their taxable income upwards by \$2 billion to account for transfer pricing arrangements. In order to ensure the practice is not used for tax avoidance, the ATO is now persuading companies to sign advance pricing agreements for a five-year term whereby a company agrees on a method to calculate appropriate allocation of income and expenses it transfers overseas.

SOURCES: *Adapted from* Tax News, *Winter; 2002; and 'ATO gets tough on transfers',* Business Review Weekly, *24 April–1 May 2002, p. 84.*

reduce the international escalation in the price of its product. In international business, intermediaries are usually employed because the manufacturer does not have a physical presence in the overseas market. For this reason the distribution channel in international marketing usually adds more to costs than in the domestic market. This disadvantage can be overcome if the firm is able to localise manufacture in the overseas market by techniques such as partial assembly or shipment in bulk and contract packing. The costs and margins of a given channel vary from country to country. Research by Terpstra and Sarathy (2000, p. 561) shows that, even within the one geographical area (Europe), there are extreme differences in the mark-ups of various goods. With medicines wholesale mark-ups varied from 25% in the case of Germany to 10% in the case of Italy, and retail mark-ups varied from 99% in the case of Switzerland to 38% in the case of Italy (see Table 16.1).

One of the problems encountered by Australian firms in competing in the Japanese market has been the extended and complex nature of the Japanese distribution system, which

| TABLE 16.1 | Cost variability of the same channel in different countries: medicines (US$) | | | | |
|---|---|---|---|---|---|
| Country | Manufacturer's price $ | Wholesaler's markup $ | Retailer's markup $ | VAT $ | Total $ |
| Germany | 100 | 25 | 92 | 24 | 214 |
| Switzerland | 100 | 21 | 99 | none | 220 |
| France | 100 | 12 | 56 | 34 | 202 |
| United Kingdom | 100 | 18 | 59 | 14 | 191 |
| Italy | 100 | 10 | 38 | 9 | 157 |

**SOURCE:** *Terpstra, V. and Sarathy, R. (2000) International Marketing, 8th edn, Dryden Press, Fort Worth, Texas, p. 561. © 2000. Reprinted with permission.*

involves several layers of distributors and subdistributors. Each of these adds to the price of the final product often making Australian products uncompetitive. Firms such as CIG Gas Cylinders (now Luxfer Gas Cylinders) and the Great Australian Pie Company have been able to compete in that market by dealing direct with wholesalers or major end-users, thus bypassing several layers of intermediaries.

## COMPETITION FACTORS

When setting prices for the overseas market it is necessary to take competitors' prices into account. It is also necessary to take into account the price of substitute products which perform the same or a similar function. The OPEC price hike of the 1970s illustrates this. In this case it was substitute energy products such as coal tar sands and wind power, as well as the advent of competition from non-OPEC producers such as Britain and Norway, that created a ceiling on the price which OPEC countries were able to impose on the global market for oil. In setting overseas prices it should be remembered that the entry by an Australian or New Zealand firm into a new foreign market is likely to provoke a competitive reaction that may manifest itself in price cutting. The likelihood of competitor reaction will be influenced by the firm's relationship to the overseas market. If the Australian or New Zealand firm is a leader in the market the reaction will be different from that if the Australian or New Zealand firm is a challenger or a follower. The anticipated competitor reaction should be taken into account in setting prices.

## INTERNATIONAL PRICING STRATEGY

In the preceding section of this chapter, a number of issues that have an influence on the setting of prices in the international marketplace were discussed. These influence pricing strategy and can be summarised as follows:

- Firm factors—including corporate objectives, cost policies, marketing activities and range of products offered;

- Customer factors—perceptions of the product, affordability and what value the offering represents;

- Environmental factors—the situation in the overseas economy, inflation, currency stability and government regulations;

- Distribution channel factors—the costs and margins in the channel, the need to control what happens to the offering in the overseas market and the potential for grey market activities;

- Competitor factors—how the firm's offering compares to that of competitors, their pricing strategies, competitors' likely reactions to a new firm's entry/activities and their cost base.

The impact of these on pricing strategy is illustrated in Figure 16.3.

Having considered the issues influencing the setting of international prices, it is necessary to set prices within the context of the overall strategic approach of the firm.

Price is an essential element of the overall marketing mix, but only one factor in the buying decision. Because of this there needs to be a high degree of consistency between the approach to product market pricing and other aspects of the marketing program. Not only must the marketing strategies of the supplying firm be taken into account, but also the distributor's needs, the requirements of trade buyers, competitor activities and the market environment. This is shown in Figure 16.4.

In addition, it is necessary to factor into the price the terms of sale and the terms of payment that fit with the firm's overall approach to international business. The strategic approach to pricing differs between companies and between the differing cultures of countries. A comparison of the difference in strategic orientation taken to pricing by Japanese companies and their Western counterparts is depicted in the vignette at the introduction to this chapter.

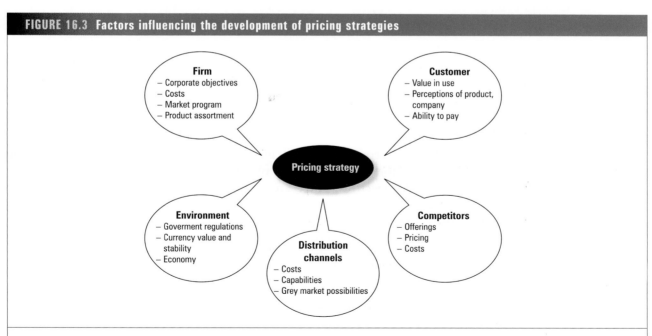

**FIGURE 16.3  Factors influencing the development of pricing strategies**

**Firm**
– Corporate objectives
– Costs
– Market program
– Product assortment

**Customer**
– Value in use
– Perceptions of product, company
– Ability to pay

**Pricing strategy**

**Environment**
– Goverment regulations
– Currency value and stability
– Economy

**Distribution channels**
– Costs
– Capabilities
– Grey market possibilities

**Competitors**
– Offerings
– Pricing
– Costs

**SOURCE:** *Blythe, J. and Zimmerman, A. (2005)* Business to Business Marketing Management: A Global Perspective, *Thomson Learning, London, p. 177.*

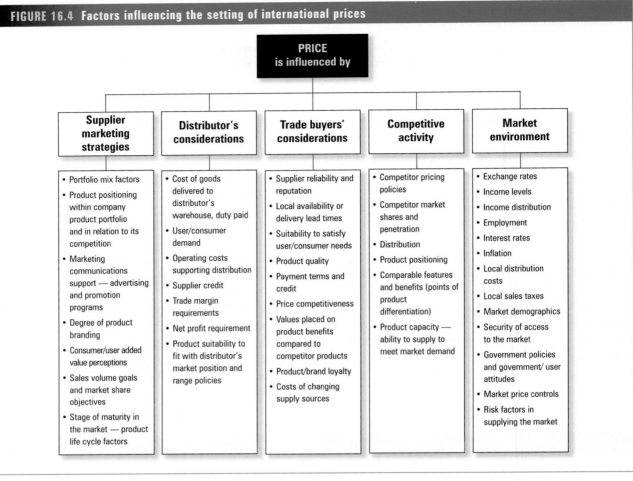

**FIGURE 16.4 Factors influencing the setting of international prices**

**PRICE** is influenced by

| Supplier marketing strategies | Distributor's considerations | Trade buyers' considerations | Competitive activity | Market environment |
|---|---|---|---|---|
| • Portfolio mix factors<br>• Product positioning within company product portfolio and in relation to its competition<br>• Marketing communications support — advertising and promotion programs<br>• Degree of product branding<br>• Consumer/user added value perceptions<br>• Sales volume goals and market share objectives<br>• Stage of maturity in the market — product life cycle factors | • Cost of goods delivered to distributor's warehouse, duty paid<br>• User/consumer demand<br>• Operating costs supporting distribution<br>• Supplier credit<br>• Trade margin requirements<br>• Net profit requirement<br>• Product suitability to fit with distributor's market position and range policies | • Supplier reliability and reputation<br>• Local availability or delivery lead times<br>• Suitability to satisfy user/consumer needs<br>• Product quality<br>• Payment terms and credit<br>• Price competitiveness<br>• Values placed on product benefits compared to competitor products<br>• Product/brand loyalty<br>• Costs of changing supply sources | • Competitor pricing policies<br>• Competitor market shares and penetration<br>• Distribution<br>• Product positioning<br>• Comparable features and benefits (points of product differentiation)<br>• Product capacity — ability to supply to meet market demand | • Exchange rates<br>• Income levels<br>• Income distribution<br>• Employment<br>• Interest rates<br>• Inflation<br>• Local distribution costs<br>• Local sales taxes<br>• Market demographics<br>• Security of access to the market<br>• Government policies and government/ user attitudes<br>• Market price controls<br>• Risk factors in supplying the market |

**SOURCE:** *Noonan, C. (1999)* Export Marketing, *2nd edn, Butterworth Heinemann, Oxford, p. 343. Reprinted with permission of Butterworth Heinemann.*

## Preliminary planning

When dealing with multiple country markets, international marketers must develop pricing objectives and strategies for achieving those objectives. The preliminary planning stage involves establishing such objectives. There are a number of approaches to establishing the price to be charged in overseas markets. These relate to both the firm's corporate and marketing objectives and conditions in overseas markets. The corporate and marketing objectives could include earning an acceptable return on investment. They may also involve maintaining prestige and image, as is the case with consumer goods sold in many countries, for example brands of perfume. It may also include a desire not to trigger a competitive reaction that could destabilise the overseas market or to defend an existing position in a country where the firm already operates.

To achieve these objectives it is necessary to decide upon the pricing strategy to be adopted. One strategy is *price skimming*. This is akin to skimming the cream off the top of the milk. This strategy is appropriate when the intent is to achieve the highest possible return in the quickest period of time. It assumes that the product is unique and that there exist groups of customers prepared to pay a high price. It also assumes that competitive reaction will be sufficiently slow so that a return can be obtained before competitors force down the price. Another strategy is *market pricing*. This applies when there are similar products to those of the firm already available in the overseas market. Competitive prices determine the price to be charged and both production costs and marketing of the Australian product must be adjusted to this price. This approach assumes a good knowledge of the competitive situation in the overseas market. It also assumes that the life cycle for the product in that market will be of sufficient duration to warrant entry by the Australian firm into the new overseas market.

A third strategy alternative is *penetration pricing*. Here, the product is offered at a low price so as to rapidly build sales volume and market share. The downside is low returns per unit sold. For success, this strategy requires mass markets, price-sensitive customers and a situation whereby production and marketing costs fall as sales volumes rise. Another pricing strategy is *product line pricing* where one element in the line is sold cheaply so as to stimulate sales of a related item that is more profitable.

> The Omark Company of Portland, Oregon, in the USA had its rivet guns made in Australia by its subsidiary Omark (Australia). These guns were sold at very low prices in the USA to encourage the purchase of high-margin rivets made by the Oregon-based principal that could only be used on the Omark rivet guns. A more contemporary example is the sale of mobile phones at 'give away' prices in anticipation that the customer will become a heavy user of the mobile network linked to the phones.

A final strategy is that of *relationship pricing*. This is driven by the notion that the relationship with the customer should be long term and beneficial to both parties. It should also involve a willingness to modify prices in the interests of the relationship and build mutual dependency between exporter and importer. It often results in both parties working together to deliver benefits in time, costs and quality. In relationship pricing a special relationship is created with no immediate effect on price. This then moves to the enrichment phase where price is set on the basis of perceived benefit by the customer. This then moves to a shared risk and reward phase where price is replaced by a sharing arrangement based on value delivered to both parties.

As far as market conditions and pricing strategy are concerned, answers should be obtained to the following questions:

- What international market segments should the firm concentrate on?
- Who are its major international competitors?
- What are the competitive strengths of the international competitors?
- Why and how do the international consumers buy?
- What are the major segments in the international market for the product/service?

However, it may not always be possible to apply the same pricing strategy in all overseas markets, as a product may be positioned as a low-priced item with appeal to the mass market in one country and as a premium-priced item appealing to a niche market in another. In addition the overall strategy of the firm towards the product will change at various stages of the product life cycle. So do the pricing strategies in an overseas market. This is because pricing is a critical element of overall strategy and the constraints on a firm's freedom to price the product also vary at each stage of the product life cycle.

# Terms of sale

One of the aspects in which international pricing differs from domestic pricing is in the terms of sale. Terms of sale have evolved with experience of the requirements of international trade over time.

Recently these have been codified to yield uniformity by the International Chamber of Commerce and a series of international commercial terms (incoterms) have been arrived at. The most common are:

- *ex-works* (EXW)—the price at the point of origin (the factory). All other charges are to the account of the buyer.
- *free alongside ship* (FAS) at a specified Australian or New Zealand port of export. This is the price of the goods delivered to and unloaded at the wharf of the port from which they will be exported. The buyer is responsible for the cost of loading, freight and insurance.
- *free on board* (FOB)—the price of goods delivered and loaded onto an overseas vessel. The buyer is responsible for freight and insurance.
- *cost and freight* (C&F)—the price of the goods delivered to a nominated overseas port where the goods will be disembarked. The buyer is responsible for insurance, customs clearance, etc.
- *cost, insurance and freight* (CIF)—the landed price at the port of destination including insurance. It is a more comprehensive basis for sale and can also include port charges, unloading, wharfage, storage, heavy lift, demurrage, documentation charges and certification charges.
- *delivered duty paid* (DDP) or *delivered duty unpaid* (DDU)—the price delivered to the premises of the overseas customers and includes inland transportation. The difference between DDU and DDP is whether the seller also pays the duty.

Increasingly, exporters are quoting more inclusive terms such as CIF or DDP, as this makes it easier for the overseas buyer to compare the price of the goods on offer with the price already being paid or quoted by other potential sources of supply in the buyer's home market, be they domestic or international. The overseas offer is more attractive if the seller assumes responsibility for the goods until they are delivered to the buyer and the buyer is not burdened with extra administration because the goods are being supplied from overseas rather than from local sources.

The point of delivery determines the point at which the risk shifts from seller to buyer as shown in Table 16.2—the closer the point of delivery to the buyer's operation, the lower the risk for the buyer; the further the point of delivery from the buyer, the lower the risk for the seller.

# Terms of payment

Terms of payment are extremely important because they affect how payment is received. If payment is not received, or not received in a timely fashion, the entire international marketing effort is likely to be defeated. An integral part of any international marketing strategy is the method of payment that is acceptable and the terms and costs of alternative payment methods. Decisions on this subject need to be related to the firm's reasons for going international, international market entry, growth strategies and resources available for international marketing activities.

## TABLE 16.2 Shift of risk from seller to buyer

| Terms of Sale | EXW | FAS | FOB | C&F | CIF | DDP |
|---|---|---|---|---|---|---|
| *Point of delivery* | | | | | | |
| Suppliers warehouse | X | | | | | |
| Export dock | | X | | | | |
| On board vessel | | | X | X | X | |
| Buyer's warehouse | | | | | | X |
| Transit insurance met by | Buyer | Buyer | Buyer | Buyer | Seller | Seller |

**SOURCE:** *Adapted from Onkvisit, S. and Shaw, J.J. (1997)* International Marketing: Analysis and Strategy, *Prentice Hall, Upper Saddle River, NJ, p. 696. Reproduced with permission from the authors.*

In a more specific context, the terms of payment relate to the degree of risk the Australian or New Zealand exporter is willing to assume and the terms of sale that are most preferred. Often it is not the price alone that motivates purchase, but also the payment terms that go with it. The extent of credit allowed on the export transaction will not only affect the profitability of the transaction, but also involve credit insurance premiums. If the exporter funds the credit this may require inclusion of either interest on borrowings in the price at the Australian or New Zealand end or the opportunity cost of interest forgone. In deciding whether it is necessary to offer credit, the exporter will need to take into account the amount involved together with the likelihood of default; the terms offered by competitors; and the ability to finance the transaction or secure funds to be able to offer the finance. The basic methods of payment vary in attractiveness to both buyer and seller, as illustrated in Figure 16.5.

## FIGURE 16.5 Attractiveness of different methods of payment

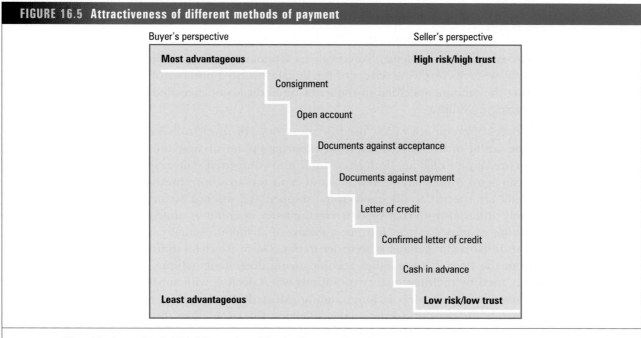

**SOURCE:** *Chase Manhattan Bank (1984)* Dynamics of Trade Finance, *Chase Manhattan Bank, New York, p. 5.*

Most attractive to the Australian or New Zealand exporter is cash in advance because there is no risk and funds are immediately available. Most attractive to the overseas importer is shipment on consignment, which means that, although the seller retains ownership, any outlay of funds is deferred until the buyer receives the goods. However, rarely in international business are overseas buyers willing to deal on a cash in advance basis or sellers willing to deal on a consignment basis. The next most attractive option for the overseas importer is selling to them on open account. This involves delivering the goods or services without a guarantee of payment and is generally only used in cases where the exporter has already had successful dealings with the importer from whom continuing constant business is expected in the future. Supporting the open account transaction is usually an underlying sales contract or agreement. Documentary collection provides the exporter with additional security in that transfer of goods from seller to buyer occurs only if accompanied by documents transferring ownership (title) from seller to buyer. Included in such documents is usually a bill of exchange or draft. This is a written order addressed from the seller to the buyer requiring the buyer to pay immediately (sight draft), or at some time in the future (time draft), a specific sum of money in favour of the seller. The main disadvantage of this payment method is that it does not obligate the buyer to accept the goods unless this is specified in an underlying sales contract.

The most common term of payment instrument is the *letter of credit*. It is issued by a bank (usually in the overseas country) at the request of the buyer, following the buyer depositing funds with the bank. The letter of credit contains a promise by the bank to pay the specified amount of money on presentation of a draft or written demand to receive payment by the seller or the seller's representative. There are various types of letters of credit:

- *Irrevocable or revocable*: An irrevocable letter of credit cannot be changed or cancelled without the agreement of the beneficiary (the exporter). This guarantees payment. All letters of credit are irrevocable unless stated otherwise.

- *Confirmed or unconfirmed*: When the letter of credit is confirmed, another party (usually a bank) assumes any risk that the exporter will not receive the sum in the currency specified, including risk due to foreign exchange movements.

- *Revolving or non-revolving*: Non-revolving letters of credit are valid for one transaction only, whereas revolving letters of credit can involve a number of transactions, provided that the amount specified in the letter of credit is not exceeded at any point in time during its validity.

Letters of credit are widely used because they effectively substitute the credit of the bank for the credit of the buyer. From the exporter's point of view the most attractive letters of credit are those which are both irrevocable and confirmed. The availability of letters of credit also can assist Australian or New Zealand exporters to secure preshipment financing. Letters of credit are specific to the goods to be shipped and will not be met if the consignment is in any way different from that specified in the letter of credit or attached documents. Letters of credit are promises to pay, but not a means of payment. Actual payment is made by a *draft*. A draft is like a cheque and is an order to pay. There are clean drafts, which are orders to pay without the need for any other accompanying documents (shipping documents); these are mainly used by multinational corporations when dealing with subsidiaries or in cases where the business relationship is longstanding. Most drafts, however, must be accompanied by documents. In cases of documentary collection the seller ships the goods and then shipping documents and the draft demanding payment are presented to the importer through the banks acting as the agent for the seller. These drafts may be either payable on sight or at some time in the future (in which case they are known as time drafts). Time drafts may be 30, 60, 90, 120 or 180 days. These time drafts, once accepted by the bank, may be sold at a discount in order to obtain funds immediately. Table 16.3 illustrates different payment methods, and the way risk is shifted from importer to exporter, as payment is deferred and goods are shipped in advance of payment being received.

In deciding which method of payment to accept the Australian or New Zealand exporter should consider the creditworthiness of the importer, the previous track record of the importer in meeting payment obligations and the credit terms offered by competitors. Also to be considered are whether political and economic conditions in the importer's country create risk of not being paid, the value of the consignment (whether this is a one-off order or the start of a long commercial relationship) and finally the nature of the product. If it is a standardised product it could be sold to another buyer at a discount, but if it is a customised product it has a much lower resale value.

---

**TABLE 16.3    Attractiveness of payment methods to buyer versus seller**

| Method | Payment | Goods available to buyer | Risk to exporter | Risk to importer |
|---|---|---|---|---|
| Cash in advance | Before shipment | After payment | None | Relies on exporter to ship goods as ordered |
| Letter of credit | When goods shipped and documents comply with L/c* | After payment | Little or none depending on L/c* | Relies on exporter to ship goods described in documents |
| Sight draft, documents against payment | On presentation of draft to buyer | After payment | Buyer can refuse goods | Same as L/c* unless he or she can inspect goods before payment |
| Time draft, documents against acceptance | On maturity of draft | Before payment | Relies on buyer to pay draft | Same as above |
| Open account | As agreed | Before payment | Relies completely on buyer to pay his or her account | None |

*L/c: denotes letter of credit.

**SOURCE:** *Unibac Trust (1985)* International Workbook, *Unibac Trust, Chicago, p. 1.*

---

# INTERNATIONAL PRICE SETTING

In establishing the price to be charged it is first necessary to decide which principles of costing are to be applied. Following this, the exporter should estimate the minimum price that is acceptable to the firm and assess the maximum price that the market is prepared to pay. Finally, it is necessary to determine which price point between the minimum and maximum price is likely to yield the greatest profit.

## Full versus marginal cost pricing

An issue to determine in advance of calculating the price to be charged in the overseas market is the cost recovery strategy to be adopted. It needs to be decided whether full costs, which include both fixed costs and variable costs, should be recovered. The alternative is to recover in the price charged overseas only the variable costs associated with the specific international business transaction. These are known as marginal costs and are basically the costs of producing the extra units for the overseas order. It is assumed with marginal costing that the fixed costs have been amortised in the price charged in the Australian or other markets. There is, however, a range of price-setting strategies between these two extremes.

It may be argued that fixed costs have already been covered during activities in Australia and therefore the costs of production for the overseas market should be based on variable costs only. This argument has merit as long as the firm has excess capacity in its Australian operation. When this capacity is exhausted additional capacity must be installed and to amortise this it is necessary to recover full costs (both fixed and variable) from the overseas market. On the assumption that excess capacity does exist, Table 16.4 details the circumstances when marginal costing is most appropriate and when full costing is likely to be achievable.

| **TABLE 16.4** | **Assessment of the need for marginal costing** | | | | | | |
|---|---|---|---|---|---|---|---|
| **Factor** | **Strongly agree 2** | **Agree 1** | **Neutral 0** | **Disagree −1** | **Strongly disagree −2** | **Weight** | **Score** |
| Low product differentiation | | | | | | | |
| Committed to exporting | | | | | | | |
| Strong financial resources | | | | | | | |
| High excess capacity | | | | | | | |
| Possible economies of scale | | | | | | | |
| Strong growth potential in the export market | | | | | | | |
| Follow-up sales potential good | | | | | | | |
| Price sensitivitiy high | | | | | | | |
| Competitive intensity high | | | | | | | |
| Can offer favourable terms of sale and financing | | | | | | | |
| | | | | | Total | 1.0 | |

If the total score for the weighted rating of the 10 factors is positive, then serious consideration should be given to some degree of marginal costing.

Traditionally, there are two approaches to setting overseas prices—cost-plus and marketplace pricing. Used separately they won't lead to the optimal price to be charged. The optimal price may result by combining the two approaches.

## Cost-plus pricing

| | A$ |
|---|---|
| Cost of production in Australia (depending on strategy and corporate policy, this can be either full or marginal cost) | 100.00 |
| Costs of getting goods to the overseas customer (freight A$10; insurance A$5; delivery to wharf A$2; agent's margin A$15; additional costs of marketing in overseas market A$5) | 37.00 |
| Less export incentives and subsidies (e.g. Export Market Development Grants Scheme—EMDG) | −10.00 |
| Minimum acceptable profit | 13.00 |

| TOTAL | 140.00 |
|---|---|

**This is the floor price below which the business is not worth having.**

The cost-plus approach is simple to calculate from Australia, requires little if any market research and may be suitable if the product to be exported is of leading-edge technology and has no competitors in the overseas market. However, this approach ignores most of the factors that should be considered when setting prices discussed earlier in this chapter.

## Marketplace pricing

| | A$ |
|---|---|
| The price of a competitive product in the overseas market (excluding duty) | 240.00 |
| Adjust for quality difference between competitive product and Australian product (assuming it is slightly better than the Australian item) | −5.00 |
| As the Australian product is unknown in the overseas market it will need to be priced at a lower figure to encourage switching | −25.00 |
| Costs of getting product to the overseas customer (freight A$10; insurance A$5; delivery to wharf A$2; agent's margin A$15; additional costs of marketing overseas A$5) | −37.00 |
| Add subsidies and export incentives (EMDG) | 10.00 |
| Pro-rata costs of management time to develop overseas market | −3.00 |
| TOTAL | 180.00 |

**This is the ceiling price, which is the most that can be expected.**

The marketplace price requires research to establish the competitive prices in the overseas market, and includes more of the factors influencing price discussed earlier in this chapter. This approach is suitable for products already available in the selected overseas market and takes account of the competitive environment.

## Optimal price setting

If there is no positive gap between the ceiling and the floor price, then the market cannot be pursued at a profit and should be abandoned unless favourable price and cost dynamics are expected in the future. If there is a positive gap, then the challenge is to decide which price should be charged in the range between the floor and the ceiling price. Basic laws of demand and supply indicate that the lower the price, the greater the quantity demanded and the greater the probability of a sale. However, the profit levels per item will vary at different price levels. The challenge is to set a price between the floor price and the ceiling price which yields the largest overall profit. One technique for establishing this price is decision analysis. In the case above, this price will be somewhere between the floor of A$140 and the ceiling of A$180. To work out the optimal combination of profit per unit and volume it is necessary to estimate the probability of sales at each price point.

| Unit price A$ | Unit profit A$ | Probability A$ | Expected profit (per unit) A$ |
|---|---|---|---|
| 140 | 13 | 0.80 | 10.4 |
| 145 | 18 | 0.70 | 12.6 |
| 150 | 23 | 0.60 | 13.8 |

*continued*

| Unit price A$ | Unit profit A$ | Probability A$ | Expected profit (per unit) A$ |
|---|---|---|---|
| 155 | 28 | 0.50 | 14.0 |
| 160 | 33 | 0.40 | 13.2 |
| 165 | 38 | 0.30 | 11.4 |
| 170 | 43 | 0.20 | −8.6 |
| 175 | 48 | 0.10 | −4.8 |
| 180 | 53 | 0.05 | −2.6 |

Based on the hypothetical example above, the price most likely to yield the optimum profit is A$155 per unit.

## Mismanagement of price setting

It was argued earlier in this chapter that price often sends a signal to buyers as to the quality that they might expect, especially if buyers are unfamiliar with the product. Mismanagement of price setting can send the wrong signal to the buyer. In addition, mismanagement of price setting can result in different prices being charged in different countries and, unless there are substantive reasons for this difference, 'grey markets' can result. This is an issue touched upon later in the chapter and explored in depth in Chapter 17. Once customers in the target market learn of discrepancies between the price charged in their market and the price charged in other markets, they are likely to pressure the Australian or New Zealand firm for price reductions or larger discounts. Finally, mismanagement of price setting creates an adverse impression of the Australian or New Zealand firm as either a 'gouger' or an 'incompetent'.

## An alternative approach to price setting

Traditional approaches to price setting in international marketing tend to view the product as being a tangible item rather than a bundle of services or satisfactions. Given the increasingly augmented nature of products traded internationally and the fact that in many cases what is traded and has value is the service rather than the tangible product, an alternative approach to international pricing is to charge for the service rendered rather than the product. In the process, a fixed cost can be converted into a variable cost, adding to the appeal of the offer. An often cited example of this is the aircraft tyre manufacturer who, instead of putting a price on each tyre, offered a contractual arrangement where the airline was supplied with tyres as needed and charged on the basis of the number of aircraft take-offs and landings.

Another approach is to make changes to the production process so that the product is price competitive in the overseas market. This may involve switching manufacturing locations to take advantage of lower labour costs, the redesign of the product so that its manufacturing costs are reduced, or the sourcing of cheaper materials and inputs.

## Responding to price changes in international markets

Accelerating technological advances, shorter product life cycles and more rapidly changing input costs increase the likelihood that either prices of competitive products will change or the ability to afford the Australian product will vary after the product has been introduced into an overseas market. This will necessitate a review of the firm's pricing policy with respect to that market. Alternatives include:

- maintaining current price as a holding action until it can be established how deep the price change will be and how long it is likely to last. This is especially useful when price escalation is due to a movement in the exchange rate which could well drop back to its earlier level;

- reducing the price if there is an immediate likelihood of losing customers because most competitors have already reduced their prices;

- raising the price and justify the increase by offering a demonstrable product improvement; and

- reducing the price and enhance the perceived value as a way of creating barriers to other firms contemplating entering the market.

Other ways of responding to price changes in overseas markets focus on reducing the cost of goods as supplied to that market. These include:

- reducing the number of intermediaries in the distribution channel or have the firm undertake some intermediary functions itself. If the market is large enough a sales office might be established in the market to replace the local agent;

- eliminating costly features, reduce product quality or offer an 'economy' version of the product. The extent to which this is possible will depend on what features competitors offer with their product in the overseas market;

- shipping and assembling from components in the overseas market for this purpose—a contract assembler might be employed (e.g. motor vehicle assembly in Thailand) or you might establish your own assembly operation. Establishing such an operation in a free-trade zone can be very attractive because duty is not paid on the components until the assembled product leaves the free-trade zone. As well, governments often provide incentives to set up in such zones, such as tax holidays and concessional rents;

- modifying the product so that it is classified for tariff purposes in the other country as eligible for a lower rate of duty. This requires an expert to study various eligible tariff classifications and convince local authorities that the product is eligible for the lowest one;

- reducing the basis of valuation for duty by switching from full cost to marginal cost, or by reimbursing distributors for service functions performed instead of including this cost in the price;

- manufacturing the product in the overseas country or in another country where costs are less. As duties are less if products are supplied from a fellow member of a regional trade grouping to the target country, it may be possible to source some components or accessories from such countries as a way of lowering costs; and

- for markets where sales are declining, allowing 'grey markets' to develop (see Chapter 17 for a full discussion of this topic).

# Pricing and foreign currency fluctuations

Devaluation and revaluation are other aspects of international marketing affecting price over which the Australian or New Zealand exporter has little control. Until the 1980s one currency was usually pegged to another and currency movements were reasonably stable. Since that time most countries have moved to a floating exchange rate system whereby the currency is pegged to a basket of currencies reflecting the country's most important trading partners. This has resulted in much greater volatility in exchange rates. With this floating exchange rate system, devaluation and revaluation automatically take place when currencies fluctuate in relation to each other. Devaluation of the importing country's currency causes the costs of goods imported from Australia or New Zealand to be more expensive in the importing country. However, if the goods being imported contain components from another country the relationship to final price of those imported components will have an impact. This depends on moves in the exchange rate between Australia or New Zealand and the country from which the components are imported.

Revaluation of the importing country's currency, on the other hand, causes Australian or New Zealand goods to be cheaper in the importing country. Because price affects demand in the overseas market the firm will have to decide whether to vary its prices in response to a movement in the currency relativity between the Australian or New Zealand dollar and the currency of the importing nation. In some circumstances the firm may wish to absorb some loss by not passing on the full cost of the devaluation in the importing country. In other cases it may take a windfall profit by not passing on all the gain resulting from a revaluation of the currency of the importing country. As discussed earlier, the impact of this factor on price and profit can be reduced by taking out forward foreign exchange cover through the company's bank.

Since the early 1970s an increasing number of currencies have been allowed to float or have been linked to a basket of other currencies rather than to a single currency such as the US dollar (see Chapter 2). This volatility in foreign exchange rates has important implications for pricing.

The Indonesian rupiah was trading at around 2200 to the Australian dollar in August 1997, whereas six months later the rate was about 8000 to the Australian dollar. If the price had been quoted in August in rupiah the Australian exporter would have received around 27.5% of the anticipated amount in Australian dollars in February 1998. On the other hand, if the price had been set in Australian dollars, then the product would have cost 3.6 times as much in Indonesia and the demand would be likely to fall.

The Australian exporter can either maintain a stable Australian dollar price, which will cause the foreign currency price to rise or fall; maintain a stable price in the foreign currency, which will cause the Australian dollar price to fluctuate; or arrive at a combination of the two policies so as to protect returns to the Australian exporter without pricing the product beyond the capacity of the overseas market to afford it. Table 16.5 explores options for the Australian exporter to cope with currency fluctuations.

A change in the exchange rate between the $A or the $NZ and an overseas currency will directly affect the price charged in the overseas market and will often force a reappraisal of prices charged in local currency in order to remain competitive. Table 16.6 illustrates this in the hypothetical case of the exchange rate for the Thai baht and the Australian dollar changing following the Asian currency crisis of 1997. On this occasion the exchange rate went from A$1 = 20 baht to A$1 = 30 baht.

As a result of the devaluation of the Thai baht by 50%, the retail price of the Australian product went from 2670 baht to 3948 baht—an increase of 48%.

It is not always the case that variations in exchange rates will be passed on to the importer by the exporter in the form of higher or lower prices. This is known as 'exchange rate

## TABLE 16.5 — Strategies for Australian exporters to cope with currency fluctuations

| When the A$ is weak | When the A$ is strong |
| --- | --- |
| • Stress price benefits | • Undertake non-price competition by improving quality, delivery and after-sales service |
| • Expand product line and add features | |
| • Shift manufacturing and sourcing to Australia | • Improve productivity and engage in cost reduction |
| • Exploit export opportunities in all markets | • Shift sourcing and manufacturing offshore |

## TABLE 16.6 — Impact of a 50% devaluation of the Thai baht on the price of an Australian product in Thailand

| Item | A$1 = 20 baht | A$1 = 30 baht |
| --- | --- | --- |
| Total manufacturing cost A$ | 20.00 | 20.00 |
| Mark-up A$ | 8.00 | 8.00 |
| Ex-factory cost A$ | 28.00 | 28.00 |
| Ex-factory cost baht | 560 | 740 |
| Export credit insurance (EFIC)  A$ | 0.20 | 0.20 |
| Freight and handling Australia A$ | 3.00 | 3.00 |
| Finance costs A$ | 0.25 | 0.25 |
| Bank charges A$ | 0.40 | 0.40 |
| Documentation A$ | 1.00 | 1.00 |
| Export packaging A$ | 3.00 | 3.00 |
| Export marketing A$ | 2.15 | 2.15 |
| FOB Australia | 38.00 | 38.00 |
| Freight  A$ | 10.00 | 10.00 |
| Insurance  A$ | 5.00 | 5.00 |
| CIF Price A$ | 53.00 | 53.00 |
| CIF Price in baht | 1060 | 1590 |
| Handling/delivery Bangkok (est.) baht | 10 | 10 |
| Customs clearance Bangkok baht | 20 | 20 |
| Tariffs/Duty (20% ex-factory cost) | 112 | 148 |
| Landing charges (3% CIF value) | 32 | 48 |
| Landed cost in baht | 1234 | 1816 |
| Agency distributor mark-up 20% baht | 249 | 377 |
| Agency/distributor price baht | 1483 | 2193 |
| Wholesale mark up 20%  baht | 297 | 439 |
| Wholesale price baht | 1780 | 2632 |
| Retail mark-up 50% baht | 890 | 1316 |
| Retail price in baht | 2670 | 3948 |

pass-through' (Clarke et al., 1999), and research has shown that the extent of such pass-through will be influenced by:

- the size of the economy of the export market (pass-through greater for small countries);
- the level of industry concentration in the target overseas market (the greater the concentration, the greater the pass-through);
- whether the exchange rate variation in the export market is an appreciation or a depreciation (greater likelihood of pass-through for appreciations than for depreciations);
- the proportion of foreign exporters to domestic firms in the overseas market (pass-through greater as the number of export competitors in a market increases);
- the type and height of non-tariff barriers in the export market (import quotas discourage pass-through);
- country of origin of exporter—some countries use export pricing in a more strategic manner (e.g. Japan) than others do (e.g. European countries)—the more strategic the approach to pricing, the less the likelihood of pass-through.

## CURRENCY INCONVERTIBILITY

It may be that the country has restrictions on the convertibility of its currency or that due to balance of payments reasons or political change, currencies that were previously freely convertible are no longer so. This has cost and pricing implications as the artificial exchange rate may diverge significantly from the freely floating or the black market rate. This may result in having to deal on a countertrade basis and the additional cost of doing so will need to be factored into prices asked.

## CONSTRAINTS ON SETTING PRICES

The foregoing assumes that the firm is free to set any price it wishes to charge in the overseas market. Even in Australia this is not always possible because there may be regulations controlling prices or regulatory bodies, such as the ACCC, which influence prices charged. This occurred when the Prices Justification Tribunal was in operation in Australia. There may be moral pressure as to what is an appropriate price, which can happen when a firm's pricing activities receive unwelcome publicity on widely watched TV consumer programs. Additional constraints operating in the overseas market are mostly due to governments wishing to protect domestic firms from foreign competition and from restrictive pricing practices by foreigners which may drive domestic firms from the market.

## Restrictive trade practices

Knowing what constitutes a restrictive trade practice in a country is important for making pricing decisions. What is acceptable as a pricing strategy in one country may be viewed as a restrictive trade practice in another. For example, an Australian industrialist who is accustomed to an uncompromising attitude by the Australian government towards price fixing must be careful not to adopt an antagonistic attitude towards this practice in a country where price fixing is an acceptable practice. Restrictive trade practices take many forms, the most common of which are:

- horizontal price fixing, such as price fixing between competing firms;

- vertical price fixing, such as price fixing in the distribution chain as between suppliers, distributors and retailers to maintain retail prices;

- allocating or dividing up markets;

- export or import cartels;

- boycotts;

- monopolies or monopolising practices;

- mergers or consolidations;

- price discrimination.

Most of these restrictive trade practices are price-related. The application of legislation against restrictive trade practices can result in:

- complete prohibition (where the act is illegal and courts are not interested in motives or results such as with 'antitrust' legislation);

- practices having to be notified and subsequently investigated (to establish whether the public interest has been adversely affected, or whether injury has occurred, as with mergers);

- practices being permitted to continue without interference (unless it can be demonstrated that an abuse has occurred, as with price discrimination).

Restrictive trade practices are not only regulated by national laws, but may also be covered by multinational arrangements such as the World Trade Organization, regional agreements like the European Union and bilateral undertakings such as the Closer Economic Relations Agreement between Australia and New Zealand.

## Administered pricing

The government of the overseas country can dictate to the foreign supplier what prices can be charged in the market. It does this because it considers its main responsibility is to its citizens, not to the foreign supplier. It can dictate prices by establishing margins, establishing price floors and ceilings and making its approval necessary before price changes can be made. US pharmaceutical manufacturers argue that the Australian government does this in relation to the Pharmaceutical Benefits Scheme (PBS). It can also dictate prices by competing in the market on its own account, by granting subsidies and by taking over control of all purchasing or selling of the product. This happens in many socialist countries. Sometimes the government will import the product at world market prices and subsidise the price to the local consumer, in pursuit of political objectives (as happened with colour TV sets in Libya in the 1980s).

Government may either directly or indirectly control the price at which products can be sold in other ways. If it wants to discourage consumption as with luxury items, for example, it can mandate a very high price or load the products with duty and tax to ensure a high price. If the products are politically sensitive or necessities, it can dictate a low retail price. When selective price controls are implemented, usually foreign companies are more susceptible than local companies because they lack political influence with government that local firms are able to bring to bear. Subsidies provided by overseas governments to producers of products often make it difficult for Australian or New Zealand firms to compete in an overseas market.

Australian agricultural producers have found this to be the case over several decades in both Europe (with the Common Agricultural Policy) and the USA (with the Grain Enhancement Program).

Not only do governments in foreign markets interfere with the ability of the firm to charge a price of their own choosing, but competitors in the market also interfere. They can band together and collude to fix prices, reduce price competition and reduce foreign competition. Because no country favours or permits totally free competition, it is relatively easy for local industry to have their government turn a blind eye to restrictive practices when directed against foreign firms, especially if the domestic industry is likely to be injured by the import competition. Industry groups also engage in price setting and disguise these activities under a variety of names (e.g. trade associations, communities of profit, informal inter-firm arrangements, licensing agreements and cartels).

One example of government setting and controlling prices is in the pharmaceutical industry. In many countries government meets part of the cost of prescription drugs which enables them to influence prices charged. In December 1997 in Australia the government considered that pharmaceutical firms were charging too much for a range of drugs used for treating major health problems such as heart disease. One of these was Monopril. A publicity campaign was mounted by the government advising that the Pharmaceutical Benefits Scheme (PBS) prescription costs for these drugs would exceed the normal $20 figure. Patients were urged to request their doctor to prescribe an equally effective alternative for which the PBS prescription cost would remain at $20.

## Dumping

Dumping refers to the practice of selling products at a price lower than the current domestic value in the country of origin. It would be logical to expect that because of freight, insurance and the involvement of an extra party in the distribution channel prices would be more expensive for the firm's product in an overseas country than in Australia where it is made. Exceptions to this occur when taxes are imposed on domestic products by the Australian government that do not apply when the goods are sold overseas. Examples of such taxes are import duty on components, sales taxes and payroll taxes. However, when the Australian firm uses profits obtained in the Australian market to subsidise entry into an overseas market, or engages in predatory pricing to obtain market share quickly in another country, it may be accused of dumping its products.

Governments, via export incentive schemes, facilitate dumping by Australian firms. On several occasions other countries (especially the USA) have invoked the GATT Anti-Dumping Code against Australia. It can be argued that the Export Markets Development Grants Scheme, which refunds part of the expenses incurred in promoting an Australian product in overseas markets, constitutes dumping. The rationale for this is that marketing costs are incurred with products sold in Australia and, in this case, the government is enabling firms to sell overseas at prices which do not include the same proportion of marketing costs as would be incurred in Australia.

Past export incentive schemes, such as the Payroll Tax Rebate Scheme and the Export Expansion Grants Scheme, were also susceptible to accusations of dumping. On the other hand, obtaining products from overseas firms cheaply is to the advantage of firms and governments in the foreign country. For this reason it is unlikely that a country will accuse

BHP Billiton has for a number of years sold its steel products on the west coast of the USA. In earlier years, its exporting to that market was opportunistic and designed to dispose of periodic surpluses. On most occasions its efforts attracted the attention of US steel producers who complained to the US government that BHP was dumping the steel. The alleged justification for the dumping accusations varied, but frequently was based on the export incentive programs of the Australian government. Dumping claims on these grounds were usually upheld by the US government agency investigating the dumping claim.

Australia of dumping unless the same product or a close alternative product is being produced domestically. Many countries such as Australia apply an 'injury' test to evaluating dumping charges—the Australian firm must prove that it has been actually injured by the dumped goods from the other country.

Dumping can take several forms:

- *predatory dumping*, which occurs when a foreign firm intentionally sells at a loss in another country in order to increase its share of market, usually at the expense of domestic producers;

- *sporadic dumping*, which occurs when a firm solves excess inventory problems in the home market by selling at any price it can get in an overseas market. This avoids a competitive war in the domestic market;

- *unintentional dumping*, which occurs when there are time lags between the dates of the transaction and the arrival of the goods in the overseas market. The firm's involvement in dumping in this case is usually because there has been a movement in the exchange rates in the intervening period, making the landed price to the overseas customer less that the cost of production in Australia.

When a firm feels that it is being injured by dumping from overseas it can complain to its government, which may take action to impose a penalty to nullify the price advantage from the dumping action. The government can either impose an anti-dumping duty equivalent to the dumping margin, or in cases where the foreign government is subsidising exports, as with an export incentive program, impose a countervailing duty to offset the price advantage the imported product has received as a result of the subsidy. Sometimes the threat of potential anti-dumping action against a product from an overseas country is used as a device to 'persuade' that country to restrain voluntarily the volume of its exports of the product to that market. The USA has used this approach to restrict imports of motor vehicles and semiconductors from Japan.

## Inflation

Once price is set it may need to be adjusted periodically because of inflation. Although the Australian or New Zealand exporter has no control over such inflation or its rate, sensitivity to inflation is necessary in order to protect the long-term profitability of involvement in the overseas country. In countries which experience very high inflation rates (e.g. some South American countries), consumers cannot commit themselves to purchases over a period and the pricing proposal will need to take this into account. At the wholesale level, this affects inventory holding and, at the promotion level, it stimulates use of instant media, such as the daily press and TV, rather than long-term promotional vehicles, such as catalogues and magazines. One answer for the exporter when dealing with a country with high inflation levels is to post prices in the currency of a less inflationary country such as Australia, New Zealand or the USA.

# GLOBAL PRICING STRATEGIES

Just as with the other marketing mix variables the transnational firm needs to consider the degree to which it will benefit from a global pricing strategy as opposed to operating a different pricing strategy for each individual market.

## Global versus local pricing strategies

While some products and services are more amenable to a global pricing approach than others, such as those targeted at affluent segments and those with a technical edge, for most products and services affordability will vary from country to country and from segment to segment within each country. This will influence the extent to which a global as opposed to a differential pricing policy is realistic. Three alternative pricing strategies are explained below.

### STANDARD WORLD PRICES

This approach calls for the unit price charged for an item to be the same no matter in which country it is sold. This ethnocentric strategy involves setting a standard price at corporate headquarters and applying it in all markets, after taking into account exchange rates and sales taxes imposed at the other end. The importer is responsible for paying freight and insurance. Such an approach ignores both the competitive environment and conditions in that market.

### MARKET-DIFFERENTIATED PRICES

This polycentric approach involves a different price for each market to reflect market conditions such as affordability and source and nature of competition, as well as the strategic objectives of the Australian or New Zealand firm. There is no requirement that prices be coordinated from one country to another. Usually, subsidiaries or intermediaries in the overseas country are allowed to charge whatever they feel 'the traffic will bear'. Although sensitive to local market conditions, such an approach isolates the subsidiary from the global pricing strategies of the parent firm. Another of the dangers of this approach is grey markets, where others buy the product from markets where it is cheaper and make a windfall profit by reselling in a market where prices are higher.

### MODIFIED PRICING POLICY

This geocentric approach balances the global strategic objectives of the firm with the recognition that market conditions in each overseas market will vary. With this approach, the company does not set a single price worldwide, nor does it allow subsidiaries/local distributors to make independent pricing decisions. Local costs plus a return on invested capital create the long-term price. This will be modified by short-term strategic considerations of the company, such as rapid market penetration or disposing of a domestic surplus or testing the market. This is a more dynamic and proactive approach to international price setting.

In developing pricing strategies for global markets, firms will need to consider how their actions will be interpreted by buyers in various countries. Research has shown that, in countries with individualistic cultures, negative outcomes of a price increase are more likely to be blamed on others such as the retailer, whereas in collectivist cultures negative outcomes of a price increase are more accepted by the individual and are not as likely to be blamed on the retailer or other party (Maxwell 2001).

# Transfer pricing

Transfer pricing does not happen with simple exporting, but rather with overseas investment when a firm has divisions operating in different countries. Multinationals are able to exert a huge influence on the global economy. Multinationals derive their competitive advantage from utilising operations in a variety of countries to their advantage. Their normal operations involve the transfer of raw materials, goods and services between divisions both within and between countries. Since the entities are related but operate separately, some method must be arrived at to value these intercompany transfers. The usual mechanism is transfer pricing, which applies to goods sold within the corporate family from an operation in one country to an operation in another. It is a means of maximising the profit of the corporation as a whole rather than that of a branch or a division. It is achieved by arranging corporate affairs so that profits are brought to account as far as possible in the country with the lowest taxation regime. This is effected by reducing the prices of goods shipped from a subsidiary in a high-tax country to a subsidiary in a low tax country so little profit is earned in the high-tax country. While this practice might be rationalised as tax avoidance and not tax evasion, it effectively denies the high-tax country a legitimate tax return on activities undertaken within its borders. This leads to the government of the high-tax country accusing the transnational of not being a good corporate citizen. It also leads to bad public relations resulting from critical press articles attacking, for example, the small tax contribution to the Australian or New Zealand economies by transnational companies as a whole. The Internal Revenue Service in the USA alleges that foreign companies overcharge their American subsidiaries and in the process have avoided paying up to US$8 billion in taxes annually (Fraedrich and Bateman 1996, pp. 17–22).

## 16.2 INTERNATIONAL HIGHLIGHT

## Transfer pricing in the spotlight

Transnational companies are becoming increasingly concerned at this attention transfer pricing is receiving from the Australian Tax Office (ATO). Multinational subsidiaries in Australia represent about 1.5% of companies in Australia but account for 47% of company tax paid. If they do not pay their fair share of tax, then the economy suffers. In the three-year period since July 1999, the ATO collected A$492 million in transfer pricing penalties and insisted firms adjust their taxable income upwards by $2 billion to account for transfer pricing arrangements. In order to ensure the practice is not used for tax avoidance, the ATO is now persuading companies to sign advance pricing agreements for a five-year term whereby a company agrees on a method to calculate appropriate allocation of income and expenses it transfers overseas.

**SOURCES:** *Adapted from* Tax News, *Winter, 2002; and 'ATO gets tough on transfers',* Business Review Weekly, *24 April–1 May 2002, p. 84.*

There may be motives other than tax avoidance for transfer pricing. These include liquefying frozen assets. When restrictions on foreign currency transfers prevent a firm extracting its profits from a country with foreign exchange problems, transfer pricing enables such profits to be repatriated by under-invoicing goods to a subsidiary in another country. Yet again, such action is designed to circumvent the regulations of the host country. Transfer pricing may also be used to maintain or create a competitive position in another country. The transfer price can enable profits earned in one country to subsidise entry into another. In this case it has a result akin to dumping and, as such, may be contrary to regulations in the host country. Transfer pricing may also allow the firm to institute price reductions in response to slack demand or a decline in the wellbeing of the economy of the overseas country. A final transfer pricing objective includes the acquisition of goods or raw materials—in this case the price set is such that the manager, forced by company policy to purchase from an overseas affiliate, pays no more than world market price despite the affiliate's product being more expensive. Table 16.7 (see Cravens 1997) summarises the motivations for transfer pricing. It indicates that, although tax avoidance is not the only motivation, it continues to be the most important.

There are five possible methods of transfer pricing between national divisions of a company and these vary in terms of their intent to evade host country regulations and taxes:

1  sale at the local manufacturing cost;

2  sale at local manufacturing cost plus a standard mark-up;

3  sale at the cost of the most efficient producer in the company plus a standard mark-up;

4  sale at negotiated prices based on those prevailing in the overseas market;

5  arm's length sale using the same prices as quoted to independent customers.

Of these, arm's length pricing is most acceptable to tax authorities in the host country. With this 'Basic Arm's Length Standard' the tax authority compares the sale price with the selling price set by independent buyers and sellers in similar business environments. Although

| TABLE 16.7 Motives for transfer pricing | |
|---|---|
| **Objectives** | **%** |
| **Taxation related** | |
| Manage tariffs | 4 |
| Comply with tax regulations | 7 |
| Manage the tax burden | 40 |
| | 51 |
| **Internal management-oriented** | |
| Equitable performance evaluation | 7 |
| Motivation | 9 |
| Promote goal congruence | 5 |
| | 21 |
| **International or operational** | |
| Cash transfer restrictions | 2 |
| Competitive positions | 21 |
| Reflect actual costs and income | 5 |
| | 28 |

SOURCE: *Cravens, K.S. (1997) 'Examining the role of transfer pricing as a strategy for multinational firms',* International Business Review, *Vol. 6, No. 2, pp. 127–45.*

| TABLE 16.8 | Basic principles of transfer pricing |
| --- | --- |

| Country X (high tax) | | Transfer price manipulation | |
| --- | --- | --- | --- |
| 'Ex-factory' costs | 100 | | 100 |
| Transfer price ('arm's length') to subsidiary in market Z | 120 | Artificially low transfer price | 105 |
| Profit | 20 | | 5 |
| Local tax (50%) | 10 | | 2.5 |
| Net profit | 10 | | 2.5 |
| Country Z (low tax) | | | |
| Buys from X | 120 | | 105 |
| Duty (20%) | 24 | | 21 |
| Cost warehouse | 144 | | 126 |
| Sells at (marketable price) | 160 | | 160 |
| Profit | 16 | | 34 |
| Tax (5%) | 0.8 | | 1.7 |
| Net profit | 15.2 | | 32.3 |
| Corporate net profit | | | |
| (Two markets) | 25.2 | | 34.8 |
| Government tax/duty | 34.8 | | 25.2 |

SOURCE: *Keegan, W.J. and Schlegelmilch, B.B. (2001)* Global Marketing Management: A European Perspective, *Prentice Hall, Harlow, UK, p. 414.*

governments in many countries including Australia are targeting firms using transfer prices to evade taxes and regulations, eliminating the practice is proving difficult. Table 16.8 illustrates the principles of transfer pricing and shows how profits can be manipulated through transfer pricing.

# The internet and international pricing

The most prevalent form of information on the internet relates to prices. And because prices on the internet are known worldwide, the internet encourages standardisation of prices across borders. There are a number of features of the internet that can directly or indirectly influence international pricing. The first of these is that the internet lowers the cost of acquiring information by making the buyer's search more efficient, and this can translate into lower prices in terms of the quality of competitive data obtained and the costs of obtaining general market information on the potential in selected overseas markets. In the second place, the internet reduces transaction costs because of its interactivity and timeliness. This reduction in transaction costs improves efficiency which can also translate into lower prices. The third area where the internet can influence international pricing is its potential to link the Australian or New Zealand exporter directly to the overseas buyer. This eliminates the agent, or at least the distributor, in business-to-business marketing and also the wholesaler and possibly the retailer in business-to-consumer marketing. Known as 'disintermediation', this has a major impact on pricing in international marketing where there is likely to be at least one more step in the distribution channel than is the case with domestic marketing. Each extra stage in the channel results in one more profit margin being added to the final price. A fourth area where the internet influences pricing is its ability to provide the consumer with a customised offering. Generally, customers are prepared to pay more for a product or service that is specifically tailored to their needs, especially if they have had an input into the design of the offering, which is possible due to the interconnectivity of the internet.

With the internet, geography becomes less relevant and competition increasingly comes from elsewhere in the world. In international marketing, the internet exposes the Australian or New Zealand firm to a greater degree of international competition, especially when buying is conducted via internet auctions. As pointed out earlier in this chapter, governments in many countries influence prices charged within their domain so as to support domestic policies and protect national enterprises. With the internet, government power over pricing is reduced, consumers become aware of different prices prevailing in other countries and will either pressure government to reduce the differential or use the internet to evade existing government regulations. As an example, some governments ban the use of 'price off' coupons. When such coupons are offered over the internet, government can do little to stop their nationals making purchases using such coupons. The purchase may be at a dumped price and government can do little to stop this and applying countervailing duties is unlikely to be practical, especially on small-value consumer items. Finally, the goods entering the country as a result of an internet purchase may be liable for duty so as to protect local producers or raise revenue. But will it make economic sense to collect the duty on a small-value item, such as a book from Amazon.com?

The paperless world of the internet has the ability to reduce shipping costs by as much as 30%. Furthermore, costs will fall further as online networks come on stream with the facility to handle both fulfilment and settlement of international trade transactions. Already TradeCard has formed an alliance with the Thomas Cook Group whereby, once exporter and importer have decided to transact, TradeCard provides an electronic payment guarantee charging customers one-tenth of the average cost of a letter of credit. In the area of shipping the internet facilitates small shippers banding together under the aegis of a trade portal and achieving the same rates that apply to large shippers thus enabling small exporters to lower their delivered price and compete more effectively.

# Summary

In this chapter most of the factors influencing pricing for overseas markets have been discussed. Cavusgil (1988, 1996) summarises these in his decision framework for export pricing. He argues for a formal decision-making procedure that incorporates and weights the relevant variables. This framework, he suggests, will result in a more profitable pricing policy. The steps in this decision framework are listed below:

• *Verify the potential of the market*—use formal sources such as Austrade, market research firms and industry bodies such as the Australian Business Chamber, as well as informal sources such as trade shows, trade journals and local intermediaries.

- *Estimate the target price range*—calculate both the floor and the ceiling price discussed earlier in the chapter.

- *Estimate sales potential*—estimate the size and concentration of customer segments, likely consumption patterns, competitive reaction and distributor expectations.

- *Analyse the barriers to import, distribution and transactions in the overseas market*—these barriers may include quotas, tariffs, taxes, anti-dumping measures, price maintenance, exchange rates, remittance of funds and relevant government regulations.

- *Review in relation to corporate goals and preference for pricing policy*—make a decision as to whether to insist on full-cost pricing or accept marginal cost pricing (if full cost is not attainable), and the ability to obtain normal profit margins.

- *Check consistency of proposed pricing approach with the current pricing approach*—if the firm already operates in the target market the recommended pricing strategy should be compared to the strategy currently in place. It is also important to ensure that export-pricing policies are consistent between overseas markets to reduce potential problems such as those with grey markets.

- *Implementation*—decide on specific prices for both distributors and end-users, arriving at a recommended pricing strategy and deciding on specific pricing tactics.

- *Monitoring*—this should be a continuous activity, because the overseas market is likely to be more volatile than the Australian market due to daily movements in the exchange rates, an increased level of competition and government restrictions of pricing activities, especially by foreign firms.

---

## ETHICS ISSUE

Your company has enjoyed a successful business exporting concrete pumping equipment from Australia to Thailand over the last decade. Due to the Asian currency crisis, the rate of the Thai baht to the Australian dollar has moved from 20 baht to 30 baht to A$1. This has forced the major customer, the Ministry of Public Works, to seek cheaper sources of supply. You have heard that a Malaysian firm is likely to be awarded the next tender as the movement of the Malaysian ringgit to the Thai baht has only been from 15 to 18 = M$1. Currently your product incurs an import duty of 50% due to its being classified as construction equipment. Your Thai agent advises that because of his political connections he could 'arrange' for your concrete pumping equipment to be classified on entry as pumps that incur a duty of 5%. This difference in duty would comfortably enable you to compete and retain the business, but would require you to falsely describe your equipment on shipping invoices and bank documents.

*If you were the Australian firm's export manager, would you recommend the above course of action to the managing director? List both the positive and negative side effects of reclassifying the Australian product for duty purposes in this way.*

# Websites

**Australian Tax Office (ATO)** http://www.ato.gov.au
**Closer Economic Relations Agreement** http://www.dfat.gov.au/cer_afta
**Common Agricultural Policy** http://ec.europa.eu/agriculture/capreform
**Export Finance and Insurance Corporation (EFIC)** http://www.efic.gov.au
**Export Markets Development Grants Scheme (EMDG)** http://www.austrade.gov.au/exportgrants
**International Chamber of Commerce** http://www.iccwbo.com
**Omark Corporation** http://www.omarksafety.com
**OPEC** http://www.opec.org
**US Grain Enhancement Program** http://www.ers.usda.gov/features/FarmBill

# Discussion questions

1 In what ways is the role of pricing in the international market (a) similar to and (b) different from the role of pricing in the domestic market?

2 What influence do distribution strategies have on international price setting?

3 Outline an international pricing strategy that is a win–win outcome for both importer and exporter.

4 Under what circumstances does marginal costing for export constitute dumping?

5 How would you ensure stable returns from international marketing activities in the face of volatile foreign exchange rate movements between the Australian dollar and the Indonesian rupiah?

6 Develop a strategy for reducing potential constraints by an overseas government on the price you can charge in the overseas market.

7 Under what circumstances is transfer pricing likely to be acceptable to an overseas government and when is it regarded as impugning their national sovereignty?

8 Discuss the circumstances when a global price is (a) the most appropriate course of action, and (b) an inappropriate course of action for an Australian or New Zealand firm.

# References

'ATO gets tough on transfers', *Business Review Weekly*, 24 April–1 May 2002.

Blythe, J. and Zimmerman, A. (2005) *Business to Business Marketing Management: A Global Perspective*, Thomson Learning, London.

Cateora, P.R. and Ghauri, P.N. (1999) *International Marketing*, McGraw-Hill, Maidenhead, UK.

Cavusgil, S.T. (1988) 'Unravelling the mystique of export pricing', *Business Horizons*, May–June, pp. 54–63.

Cavusgil, S.T. (1996) 'Pricing for global markets', *The Columbia Journal of World Business*, Winter, pp. 67–78.

Chase Manhattan Bank (1984) *Dynamics of Trade Finance*, Chase Manhattan Bank, New York, p. 5.

Clarke, T., Kotabe, M. and Rajaratnam, D. (1999) 'Exchange rate pass-through and international pricing strategy: a conceptual framework and research propositions', *Journal of International Business Studies*, Vol. 30, No. 2, pp. 249–68.

Cravens, K.S. (1997) 'Examining the role of transfer pricing as a strategy for multinational firms', *International Business Review*, Vol. 6, No. 2, pp. 127–45.

Fraedrich, J.P. and Bateman, C.R. (1996) 'Transfer pricing by multinational marketers: risky business', *Business Horizons*, January–February, pp. 17–22.

Johansson, J.K. and Nonaka, I. (1996) *Relentless–the Japanese Way of Marketing*, Harper Business, USA, pp. 126–9.

Keegan, W.J. and Schlegelmilch, B. (2001) *Global Marketing Management: A European Perspective*, Prentice Hall, Harlow, UK.

Maxwell, S. (2001) 'Biased attributions of a higher than expected price: a cross-cultural analysis', *Proceedings of the European Marketing Academy*, 8–11 May, Bergen, Norges Handelshoyskole.

Noonan, (1999) *Export Marketing: A Practical Guide to Opening and Expanding Markets Overseas*, 2nd edn, Butterworth Heinemann, Oxford.

Onkvisit, S. and Shaw, J.J. (1997) *International Marketing: Analysis and Strategy*, Prentice Hall, Upper Saddle River, NJ, Chapter 16.

Robert, M. (1993) *Strategy Pure and Simple: How Winning CEOs Outthink their Competition*, McGraw-Hill, London, UK.

Rugman, A.M. and Hodgetts, R.M. (2003) *International Business*, 3rd edn, Financial Times Prentice Hall, Harlow, UK.

*Tax News*, Winter, 2002.

Terpstra, V. and Sarathy, R. (2000) *International Marketing*, 8th edn, Dryden Press, Fort Worth, Texas.

Unibac Trust (1985) *International Workbook*, Unibac Trust, Chicago.

Usunier, J.C. and Lee, J.A. (2005) *Marketing Across Cultures*, 4th edn, Financial Times Prentice Hall, Harlow, U.K.

### go online

Go online to <www.pearsoned.com.au/fletcher> to find more case studies.

# CASE STUDY 16

# Proactive pricing on the internet

**Al Marshall, ACU National**

Ozi Native Clothing is a small clothing manufacturer based in Melbourne and manufactures clothing and accessory items made from the hides of Australian native animals, including emus, kangaroos and wallabies.

The company was established in the late 1980s at the time Australia had started to become a highly popular tourist destination and there was a growing general interest in Australia in many overseas markets.

The company manufactures a range of products including women's and men's winter coats, women's skirts, waistcoats, handbags and purses. These products have proved to be very popular with overseas visitors.

To date, Andy Scelly, the managing director of Ozi Native Clothing, has distributed these products through a limited range of tourist and souvenir shops in the Melbourne CBD, in close proximity to a number of four- and five-star hotels in the area.

Feedback from these distribution outlets indicates that the great majority of the buyers are upper-income tourists from Japan, the USA and South Korea, with a more limited number from other Asian markets. The clothing and accessories do not appear to appeal to British and other European tourists or to New Zealand tourists. Nor does it appear that Australians themselves want to wear Australian native animals.

The raw materials are sourced from a variety of suppliers in Victoria, with emu farms supplying the emu skins, and with commercial shooters supplying the kangaroo and wallaby skins via an intermediary. Emu skins are relatively expensive to source, whereas a plentiful supply of kangaroo and wallaby skins means that supplier prices have historically been fairly low. Accordingly, Andy Scelly has priced the emu products above the other products.

The overall mark-up is around 50% over and above the company's variable and fixed costs (including all overheads), and Ozi Native Clothing supplies the retailers with a recommended retail price, allowing them a substantial margin as well. The great bulk of the company's fixed costs, including the overheads, is covered by the sales to the tourist and souvenir shops in the Melbourne CBD. Volume over a certain amount covers the variable costs.

The company expanded until the downturn in many Asian markets in 1997 resulted in the number of tourists from countries like South Korea, Thailand and Taiwan decreasing sharply. The decreases in the number of tourists from these markets has since been in part made up for by increases in the number of American visitors. In both volume and value terms, however, the market for Australian native animal clothing and accessories is now stable, rather than growing.

Furthermore, the recent downturn in the American economy also appears to be having an effect on sales of Ozi Native Clothing products. The tourist and souvenir shops have noted a decrease in the number of buyers from this market. (Note that a certain volume is required to meet the variable costs.)

As a result these retail outlets have had a build-up in their inventory and in the last few months have been placing fewer orders for items right across the Ozi Native Clothing product range, from the big ticket emu winter coats to small ticket items like kangaroo purses.

Andy has considered lowering the percentage mark-up the company has historically used in supplying the retail outlets, and at the same time has considered encouraging the latter to lower their retail prices, even for the more expensive emu skin products.

His intuitive belief, however, is that lowering both the price to the suppliers and the retail prices will not necessarily attract more buyers, since pricing may not ultimately be a very significant factor for the typical well-heeled overseas buyers.

In addition, lowering the percentage mark-up would have a major impact on Ozi Native Clothing's ability to cover its fixed costs, while not necessarily attracting a greater volume of business to meet most of the variable costs.

Rather, Andy feels that the key problem facing the business is that it is vulnerable to the cyclical nature of economic growth and development in the source countries his customers come from.

He had seen in the media that negative or slow economic growth leads to a downturn in inbound tourism, even among upper-income consumers who may instead visit less long-haul destinations, or (in the case of his business) at least be less attracted to buying relatively highly priced Australian native animal clothing and accessories.

Andy is also wondering what occupancy rates have been like in recent months in the four- or five-star hotels in the Melbourne CBD, where the bulk of the visitors appear to stay. It may be that his market is drying up, albeit only in the short or medium term.

A friend of his, Danny Winter, who works for the internet division of a large management consultancy, has suggested that Ozi Native Clothing is too dependent on its current distribution system, and that marketing to overseas tourists visiting Australia may simply be too limiting.

Danny has pointed out to Andy on several occasions that since Ozi Native Clothing's final customers are overseas consumers he should consider more direct ways of accessing them without having to use local retailers, who impose their own margins and make decisions about the retail prices charged.

Since the retailer's margins are themselves around 50%, Danny has been trying to convince Andy that marketing directly could potentially allow Ozi Native Clothing to make a full 100% margin over and above the fixed and variable costs.

This assumes that the current retail prices to customers (which they appear willing to accept) could be maintained, and that the current variable costs could be controlled, without additional distributional expenses being incurred.

Andy was not entirely convinced by this argument, and had real reservations about his ability as the owner of a relatively small business to market directly to overseas customers, and at the same time make healthy margins, even after meeting the fixed and variable costs.

The advice given to him by Danny was to establish an internet site for the retailing of the products, linked to a number of search engines using key words, so that potential customers could find the site with relative ease and purchase online.

The site would need to be supported by promotional materials in traditional media, such as brochures, magazines and books about Australia, distributed in key markets like Japan, the USA and South Korea as well as other Asian markets.

In addition, Danny suggested that Andy should attempt to get the potential site listed as a link on the more significant sites about Australia. He even offered to assemble a list of these sites, including the main government tourism marketing sites.

This suggested strategy seemed to Andy to be a radical departure from the company's current marketing strategy, though the ability to have control of the prices charged for items in the clothing and accessory range had considerable appeal.

In selling the idea to Andy, Danny also pointed out that an Ozi Native Clothing site would have the potential to reach potential customers all over the world, not just in the key markets, and that clothes and accessories purchasing via the internet is becoming an accepted consumer behaviour.

He further suggested that the pricing of the various items on the proposed site be in US dollars with the site also featuring a currency converter calculator, and that the site should offer full ordering and credit card payment online. This would have a number of advantages, including insulation against further possible falls in the value of the Australian dollar against the US dollar, and the ability to receive payment more rapidly than is often the case with the traditional outlets. Those visiting the site from markets other than the USA would have an immediate idea of the cost of the various items, since many consumers have a reasonable idea at any one point in time of the value of their national currency against the US dollar. Those who were less sure, or who wanted to know precisely the cost of the items, could always use the currency converter on the site.

Andy also liked the fact that the site would accept major credit and charge cards only, since such payments were backed by the substantial resources of global credit and charge card companies, guaranteeing certainty in payment, with fewer potential debtors to chase.

He noted that some of the tourist and souvenir shops were rather slow in their payment cycles and that, as small businesses, on occasion had cash flow problems, meaning that he had to supply items in the product line on credit. For some of the bigger ticket items, like three-quarter-length winter emu coats, this presented somewhat of a financial management problem. It was less of a problem though for the smaller ticket items like the kangaroo and wallaby purses.

What concerned Andy more was the fact that if he took Danny's advice in establishing such a site he would in effect be abandoning the strategy which Ozi Native Clothing had been pursuing since its establishment in the late 1980s. He wondered whether the site should simply replace his current distribution arrangements with the tourist and souvenir shops in the Melbourne CBD, or whether he should run it in parallel with these existing distribution arrangements.

Beyond this, there was also the concern that he would have to develop some understanding of the international marketplace over and above his current understanding of the overseas visitors to Australia who have been buying the clothing and accessories. As he saw it, this would involve becoming familiar with logistical issues such as transportation, insurance and customs regulations, because Ozi Native Clothing would have responsibility for the delivery of the items ordered online by the customers overseas.

While Danny had suggested that the margins could be a lot better than the current 50% made on sales to the retailers, and that they could even be double this, Andy was worried that the logistical costs would negate such potential gains.

Becoming an international marketer by using the internet certainly offered the potential to have greater control of the pricing strategy (in addition to the other advantages noted earlier), but what if the variable costs blew out and had a negative effect on margins?

Andy wondered if he would need to price the items on the site higher than the recommended retail prices in the current outlets to cover such eventualities. Alternatively, Ozi Native Clothing could simply absorb the costs (particularly for the bigger ticket items such as the emu winter coats which had better margins on them anyway).

More broadly, Andy wondered if upper-income customers in Japan, the USA, South Korea and some of the other Asian markets were really price-sensitive anyway, particularly when it came to unique items like emu coats or kangaroo skirts, which they would otherwise have to travel all the way to Australia to purchase.

After all, emus are unique to Australia and surely a premium could be charged for owning clothing and accessories not available anywhere else in the world!

## Questions

1   Is the downturn in Ozi Native Clothing's overseas-oriented business a temporary phenomenon, and should Andy Scelly remain committed to the current distribution and pricing strategy?

2   Is Danny Winter's advice about establishing an internet site with links to search engines and other sites about Australia and supported by traditional promotions a sound idea?

3   What advice, if any, can you give Andy about the additional logistical costs that he would incur if Ozi Native Clothing became an international marketer using the internet?

4   Is one option to continue selling to the tourist and souvenir shops to cover the great bulk of the company's fixed costs, while planning to cover the variable costs via the new distribution and pricing strategy?

5   Is the idea of following the current domestic pricing strategy (traditional mark-up pricing) in the international market sound, or does Andy Scelly in fact have more choices?

# EFFECTIVE DISTRIBUTION OVERSEAS

## LearningObjectives

**After reading this chapter you should be able to:**

- appreciate the role of distribution in the international marketing mix;

- compare alternative international channels of distribution;

- integrate the alternative distribution strategies available to the international marketer;

- discuss techniques for managing distribution channels overseas;

- perceive how differences in wholesaling and retailing overseas impact on other elements of the distribution channel;

- relate global issues of standardisation and grey markets to international distribution; and

- examine the impact of physical distribution in international marketing on international competitiveness.

# Getting your goods to market

You have found an overseas buyer, but how you service that buyer will determine whether your sale is a 'flash in the pan' or the start of a long-term relationship. The supply chain and logistics of getting your product to the overseas market is often treated as an afterthought by international marketers when in reality it requires long-term planning and integration into the offering to the customer.

One aspect is getting permission for your goods to leave the country on the one hand and permission for your goods to enter the overseas market on the other. In Australia for example, most agricultural and fresh food products require the approval of the Australian Quarantine and Inspection Service (AQIS) who issue certificates following testing that the products meet Australia's international obligations and conform to certain requirements (e.g. absence of disease in growing area, use of certain pesticides etc). Such certificates testify that the goods are as described. The AQIS inspection usually is carried out at the port of shipment; however, if this inspection involves destroying the packaging, then the inspection may have to be undertaken at the firm's premises before being packed, as Mountain Top Coffee discovered when it changed its export packaging from Hessian bags to vacuum-packed, gas-flushed plastic foil bags.

Quarantine inspection also takes place at the point of entry into the overseas country and it is essential that the exporter knows well ahead what quarantine regulations apply to both the product and the packaging materials used lest the shipment be rejected on arrival. Not only should the International Phytosanitary Portal (<https://www.ipc.int>) be consulted, but also the website of the quarantine body in the overseas country.

Getting goods to an overseas market is not only a matter of sea or air shipment, but rather of the total logistics package from factory door to point of consumption. Often the speed and efficiency of the total supply chain can command a substantial premium in price, as with perishable foodstuffs or the supply of a critical replacement component for a production line so as to reduce the downtime and get the production line up and running again. Ian Murray, national executive director of the Australian Institute of Export, cites Casepan of South Africa as a model. It is an organisation that has become a word leader in the marketing of fresh fruit internationally by giving detailed attention to the logistics task from farm gate to end-user—in, between and within the markets it supplies.

Sending goods to overseas markets by sea or air is not as straightforward as it seems on the surface, and considerable savings are possible by studying the demand patterns on different sectors or routes. As an example, because Australia is a net importer of containerised goods, there are often large numbers of empty containers to be returned to the port of origin. Rather than pay to ship back an empty container, there is an incentive to offer a cheap rate to fill it—often this can be achieved by sending it to another country from whence there is a demand for full containers returning to the point of origin. The hire of a container to move goods from China to Australia is about US$2000, but if it is reassigned to move goods from Sydney to Thailand, the cost is only US$350. Savings on freight can also be made by shipping via an indirect route, often with little sacrifice of delivery time. Fidax Foundry, which exports 35% of its production of iron components, has found that for goods destined for the East Coast of the USA, it is cheaper to ship to the West Coast and truck overland than ship direct via the Panama Canal, and that for goods destined for Dortmund in Germany it is less expensive to route them to Rotterdam and barge them to Dortmund than to ship them to the nearest German port of Hamburg.

**SOURCES:** *Adapted from Murray, I. (2007) 'Use logistics wisely',* Australian Freight Logistics, *December/January, p. 16; 'Indirect solutions',* Dynamic Export, *October 2006, p. 26; and Spicer, S. (2006) 'Coping with quarantine',* Dynamic Export, *August, pp. 8–12.*

# INTRODUCTION

Channel distribution is different from physical distribution described above. A channel of distribution is an organised network of agencies that combine to link producers with users. Distribution is the physical flow of goods through channels. A channel is useful in that it makes a product or service available in a convenient location to the customer (place), makes the product or service available when the customer wants it (time), packages or reprocesses the product or service into a form that the customer can use (form) and advises the public about the product and its attributes (information).

Distribution channels in international marketing can be a basic source of competitive advantage on the one hand and a cause of problems on the other. This is because small exporters have difficulty in establishing effective channels to distribute their products in the overseas market and because the headquarters of transnational firms often fail to understand that channels differ from country to country. In addition, channels involve relationships, and skill at managing these relationships will determine the success of firms' international marketing efforts. They also often involve long-term legal commitments and obligations to another party in another country that can be difficult to terminate or change. It is important that the right distribution channels be established in an overseas market because when goods cross borders title is transferred to persons in another country, control is more difficult to exercise and the competitive environment is fiercer. Distribution channels in international marketing can be of varying length as indicated in Figure 17.1.

# ROLE OF CHANNEL INTERMEDIARIES

International channels of distribution are characterised by intermediaries who perform a number of functions including:

- coordinating buyer demand with product availability and facilitating negotiation between exporter and importer;
- protecting both buyer and seller from opportunistic behaviour in a cross-cultural context by establishing trust with each party;
- reducing transaction costs due to smoothing out the bargaining process and matching demand with supply;
- matching buyers and sellers in different countries and facilitating the transaction by supplying information one party may not be aware of about the other or the requirements for doing business in the market; and
- providing physical distribution/logistical support necessary to facilitate the business.

**FIGURE 17.1  Long versus short channels of distribution**

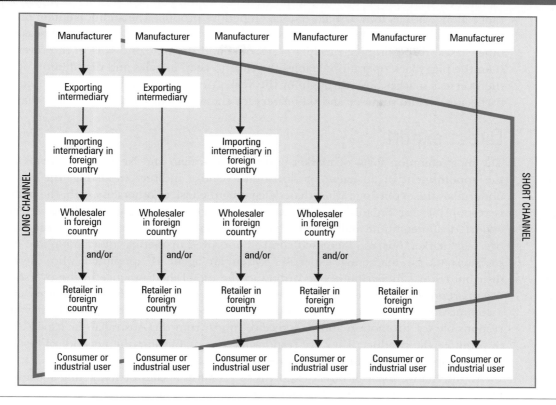

**SOURCE:** *Adapted from Keegan, W. (1995)* Global Marketing Management, *5th edn, © 1995. Adapted with permission from Pearson Education, Inc., Upper Saddle River, NJ.*

# CHANNELS OF DISTRIBUTION

There are a number of different forms by which products can be entered into overseas markets. These have already been discussed in Chapter 7 as far as their implications for market entry are concerned. These forms can be categorised as follows.

## Use of an export intermediary

Export intermediaries can be export merchants. These merchants, based in Australia or New Zealand, buy the goods from the local firm and ship them to customers offshore. The merchant takes title to the goods and the sale in this instance is like a domestic sale.

With the export agent, the agent sells goods in the overseas market on behalf of the Australian or New Zealand producer and receives a commission on the sale, although it does not take title to the goods. Overseas firms also establish buying offices in Australia or New Zealand and these offices take title to the goods at the time of purchase and usually are responsible for shipment of the goods to their overseas headquarters or affiliates. In all cases where an export intermediary is involved, the producer has little influence over the final price or control over the marketing of the products overseas. The benefit is that the producer does not have to spend time developing an overseas market.

Another form of indirect export is 'piggybacking'. Here a manufacturer uses its established distribution network in an overseas country to sell another company's product range along with its own. Usually a non-competitive product, the additional item often fleshes out the product range that the established exporter is able to offer in the overseas market. In other cases, if the original product is seasonal and the new one sells in the reverse season, then the piggyback operation enables the firm to keep its sales and distribution operation in the overseas market busy throughout the year. An example would be a firm that sells both barbecues for the summer and oil heaters for the winter in the same overseas market.

## Direct export

The most common form of market entry for Australian and New Zealand firms is through the appointment of an agent or distributor. Unlike indirect exporting, the manufacturer undertakes the exporting rather than delegating the task to others. As such, the manufacturer is responsible for organising initial market contact, market research, physical distribution, export documentation and pricing. The advantages are not only direct contact with the overseas market, but also increased control, improved marketing information and acquisition of international marketing expertise. Often an agent is appointed who then appoints distributors or subdistributors according to the established practice in the overseas market. Agents represent the Australian or New Zealand company in a defined territory and receive a commission on sales made. They do not take title to the goods, although they are usually responsible for promotion and may receive funds from the Australian or New Zealand firm to promote the product. They are responsible for establishing the network of distributors in the territory for which they are appointed.

An alternative form of direct export is to establish a sales or marketing subsidiary in the overseas country. This office then performs agency functions and may sell direct or through a network of distributors depending on the nature of the market. The sales/marketing subsidiary enables the firm to get closer to the customer and have more control over what happens in the market than direct export to an agent overseas. However, maintaining overseas offices is very expensive and involves more management time.

### 17.1 INTERNATIONAL HIGHLIGHT

## Exports of Japanese trading companies

The top nine Japanese trading companies, which are referred to as the *sogo shosha* (Mitsui, Mitsubishi, Itochu, Sumitomo, Marubeni, Nichimen, Nissho, Iwai and Kanematsu), represent a significant force in the world economy. The top five are in the top 20 companies in the *Fortune* 'Global 500' list and had combined annual revenue of US$530 billion in 2000. They still operate as procurer for Japan's industry and door-to-world markets, although this role has diminished a little as their Japanese client base has become more directly involved in world trade. In Australia, the *sogo shosha* are prominent on the *BRW* 1000 list and Mitsui, Marubeni and Itochu are on the top 100. In 2000, the *sogo shosha* in Australia had combined exports of almost A$10 billion and they remain the principal mode of entry for Australian sales to the Japanese market. The *sogo shosha* also have significant investments in Australia, most notably in the mining, metals and energy industries. As an example, Mitsui and Mitsubishi are partners in a one-sixth share of the North West Shelf development.

**SOURCE:** *Adapted from Walters, R. (2002)* The Big End of Town and Australia's Trading Interests, *Department of Foreign Affairs and Trade, Canberra. p. 37.*

# Exporting intellectual content

This takes two common forms—licensing and franchising. Licensing involves allowing someone in another country to manufacture the product on their own behalf. This may involve assigning the patent rights, copyright, trade marks or know-how on products or processes. The licensee undertakes to produce the nominated products and market them in the territory covered by the agreement. In return for providing this know-how and technology (and possibility supervision and quality control) the overseas firm (licensee) may make a lump sum payment for the technology transferred and a royalty in relation to volume of output. Licensing usually applies with products rather than services. Advantages to the licensor include the fact that it does not require an outlay of capital and therefore is a means for small firms to enter overseas markets. It is also a quick way to gain entry because it does not involve the firm erecting a factory or establishing its own distribution channels. Furthermore, the firm immediately gains local knowledge and many foreign governments favour licensing over direct investment because no surrendering of local ownership or control is involved. Other advantages are that the licensor is able to retain technological superiority in product development in its field, overcoming barriers to import into the overseas country and gain additional revenue from a product at the tail end of its life cycle. Licensing agreements usually cover one or more of the following: a patent covering the product or process involved in its manufacture; manufacturing know-how not subject to patent protection; technical assistance; marketing assistance; and the use of trade marks.

Franchising is somewhat similar and usually applies at the wholesale/retail level, and particularly with services. Hollensen (2004) describes it as a marketing-oriented method of selling a business service to usually small independent investors with working capital, but little business experience. In international marketing, franchising involves allowing the party in the other country access to brand names, design, packaging, marketing systems, training, bulk buying advantages and production systems. In return, the Australian or New Zealand firm receives payment for items provided and a royalty or share of profits for the marketing and systems support supplied. The rapid recent growth in international franchising has been largely due to the general decline in international trade in manufactures and its replacement by services. The 'business package' supplied by the franchisor is likely to include, where relevant, trade marks, copyright, patents, trade secrets, business know-how and geographical exclusivity. It may also include the right for the franchisee to appoint subfranchisees. Other elements of the package might include managerial assistance in setting up the operation, centrally coordinated advertising and store fit-out.

With both forms of distribution based on intellectual property, the firm runs the risk of being 'ripped off' unless it sets a minimum amount for royalty payments and establishes a system for monitoring turnover. Another risk is that the transfer of intellectual property can result in the Australian or New Zealand firm 'cloning a future competitor'.

# Manufacture overseas

This can take the form of assembly, contract manufacture, joint venture or acquisition. The extent of the firm's involvement in production and marketing varies with the approach it chooses. Assembly involves shipping the product to the overseas market either in 'knocked down' form, as with motor vehicles, or as component parts. Frequent motives for this include duty rates on parts being much lower than on the finished product, transport costs on components or kits being lower than on built-up units, and assembly being a relatively unskilled task which can often be done more cheaply in the overseas market, especially if that market is in a developing country. Figure 17.2 shows various motives for forms of foreign direct investment.

## ASSEMBLY

Often such assembly takes place in a Foreign Trade Zone (FTZ), sometimes referred to as an Export Processing Zone (EPZ). These have been established in more than 50 countries by or with the blessing of government, with the aim of attracting industry to their shores and creating employment that would normally be driven away because of trade barriers. Usually, the government and/or zone administrators provide a range of incentives to encourage foreign firms to locate there. These incentives can include tax holidays, duty-free admission of goods and plant, subsidised rents, infrastructure and facilities (e.g. power and water). Specifically, such facilities enable the foreign firm to bring goods into the country without paying duties as long as it remains within the zone or bonded warehouse. Many allow processing, assembly, sorting and repacking within the zone. Other advantages include the economies of being able to ship in bulk to a country without paying customs duties until the goods are released into the distribution channel, and taking advantage of the lower labour costs available in that market for relatively unskilled assembly. To a large extent, the advantages of operating in an FTZ will depend on the duty rates because the zones are designed to compensate for high tariff barriers. Where barriers are low these zones are not as attractive, as many of the other advantages such as bulk shipping and low-cost labour can be obtained outside them. Savings that can accrue from using a FTZ include:

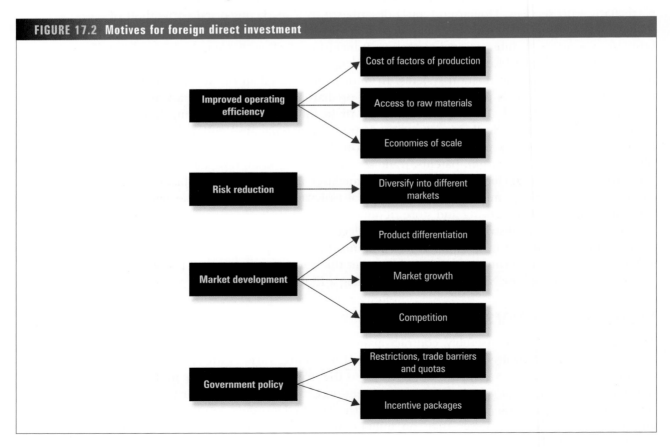

**FIGURE 17.2  Motives for foreign direct investment**

- inventory—if inventory is held outside the zone the funds tied up include the duty levied, but if the inventory is held in a FTZ, the funds tied up only relate to the value of the product:

- goods for re-export—if goods are imported outside the zone, duty has been paid on them before processing/repackaging occurs and this duty must be recovered in the export price. However this is not the case if the activity takes place within the FTZ as no duty has been imposed:

- components for processing into finished goods and sale in the domestic market—if goods are processed outside the Zone, duty is levied on the value of the components when they enter the country. However, if the components enter a FTZ duty on them is only levied when the finished product exits the zone for the domestic market. In some cases these duties may be waived by government as a way of encouraging processing within the FTZ.

Examples of such zones are the Northern Territory Trade Development Zone (renamed Darwin Business Park) in Australia and the Bataan Export Processing Zone in the Philippines.

## CONTRACT MANUFACTURE

Contract manufacture occurs when an overseas firm produces goods for an Australian or New Zealand company, has no title or rights to the output and is paid for the manufacturing process. Marketing remains the responsibility of the Australian or New Zealand firm. The goods could be destined for the country in which they are manufactured, for third countries or, as is increasingly the case, for the Australian or New Zealand markets. Contract manufacture is usually driven by the attraction of cheap labour costs and access to raw materials. It involves relatively little risk to the firm (apart a potential for pirating of the technology) and no outlay of investment capital. Contract manufacturing is an attractive option if the firm's expertise is in marketing or branding rather than in manufacturing. This is often seen with packaged foods, textiles, clothing and footwear. It avoids problems due to unfamiliarity with the country, such as labour issues, while at the same time allows the firm to claim that the product is made locally.

## JOINT VENTURES

Joint ventures are the most common form of manufacture overseas undertaken by Australian or New Zealand firms. Joint ventures are foreign operations in which the international company has sufficient equity to have a say in management, but not enough to dominate the venture. The firm, in conjunction with a partner in the overseas market, builds and operates a manufacturing facility. The contribution by the local firm can vary and may include equity, buildings, local contacts, market knowledge and access to raw materials. Often the percentage of equity that the local firm must have is dictated by the local government as a condition of the awarding of investment approval. In a number of developing countries this must be at least 51%, which can cause problems when the contribution of the local firm is far less than that of the Australian or New Zealand company. In order to encourage development of new industries, export-generating industries or location of new industries in poorer parts of the country, overseas governments often grant new joint ventures investment incentives ranging from tax holidays to duty-free import of raw materials and components. Compared with other forms of manufacture discussed above, joint ventures potentially deliver greater returns from equity participation compared with royalties, greater control over production and marketing, better feedback from the market and greater hands-on experience in international marketing.

## ACQUISITION

A final form of manufacture overseas involves acquiring an existing operation or building a plant from scratch (greenfield operation). This option requires considerable investment, involves building up a base of contacts and requires considerable research as to conditions in the market. Another disadvantage is that it is more susceptible to expropriation than the joint venture because of its lack of local equity. It does have the advantage that the firm retains total control of the operation from production to marketing, to delivery to the final customer. The laws of many countries put conditions on greenfield investments and prohibit or restrict acquisition of existing businesses.

## Strategic alliances

Strategic alliances are another way of being able to distribute products in overseas markets. They cover a variety of non-equity contractual relationships, frequently between competitors in different countries. Cross-border strategic alliances have become a popular vehicle for international expansion in cases where firms face internationalisation pressures. Internationalisation is an increasing phenomenon in international marketing and these pressures are discussed in depth in Chapter 12 as are the advantages and disadvantages of strategic alliances.

## DISTRIBUTION STRATEGIES

Developing distribution strategies for getting goods to the international marketplace often involves dependence on intermediaries. Kim and Frazier (1997) have developed a typology for the necessary degree of commitment between supplier and intermediary under different situations. They contrast the circumstance of high versus low environmental uncertainty with both the extent to which intermediaries add value to the finished product in the hands of overseas customers (low value added versus high value added) and the degree to which the intermediary can replace the Australian or New Zealand firm as a supplier. An adaptation of their typology is shown in Figure 17.3.

*Cell 1 depicts 'market exchanges'.* In this form of interaction between supplier and intermediary both parties have a very low commitment to the relationship and can easily change partners.

*Cell 2 depicts 'short-term relationships'.* In this form of interaction both parties have a 'low' rather than a 'very low' commitment to the relationship influenced by the higher perceived degree of environmental uncertainty and volatility in the distribution channel.

*Cell 3 depicts 'supplier domination'.* In this form of interaction intermediaries have greater difficulty in replacing suppliers than suppliers have in replacing intermediaries. Because the environment is stable this domination of the channel by the supplier is likely to continue beyond the short term.

*Cell 4 depicts 'supplier leadership'.* In this form of interaction suppliers are dominant because of the low value added by intermediaries, but the uncertainty of the environment makes it difficult for suppliers to manage without the intermediary, with the result that both parties have a medium degree of commitment to the overall relationship.

*Cell 5 depicts 'intermediary domination'.* In this form of interaction the intermediary adds considerable value to the product and suppliers are not difficult to replace. In this situation suppliers have a greater stake in investing resources in the relationship than do intermediaries.

## FIGURE 17.3 A typology of channel systems

|  |  | Low value added in downstream channel | | High value added in downstream channel | |
|---|---|---|---|---|---|
|  |  | Replaceability of suppliers | | Replaceability of suppliers | |
|  |  | High | Low | High | Low |
| Environmental uncertainty | Low | **Cell 1** Market exchanges | **Cell 3** Supplier domination | **Cell 5** Intermediary domination | **Cell 7** Long-term relationships |
|  | High | **Cell 2** Short-term relationships | **Cell 4** Supplier leadership | **Cell 6** Intermediary leadership | **Cell 8** Partnering |

**SOURCE:** *Adapted from Kim, K. and Frazier, G.L. (1997), in Doole, I. and Lowe, R. (eds)* International Marketing Strategy, Contemporary Readings, *International Thomson Business Press, London, p. 302.*

*Cell 6 depicts 'intermediary leadership'.* In this form of interaction intermediaries are in the dominant position because the value they add is high. However, because environmental uncertainty is high, intermediaries have a greater need to coordinate with suppliers.

*Cell 7 depicts 'long-term relationships'.* In this form of interaction both parties are highly committed to each other because suppliers are difficult to replace and intermediaries add significant value. The combination of the right channel member and strong channel ties can yield a distinct competitive advantage.

*Cell 8 depicts 'partnering'.* In this form of interaction the uncertain environment reaffirms the need for both parties to work closely with each other and creates a strong motivation to coordinate closely the channel relationship. It leads to a high level of joint activities between the parties.

The above typology can assist the firm in developing a strategy for deciding on the relationship that it needs to establish with a potential intermediary. It involves balancing a realistic perception of the relative strengths of both itself and the overseas intermediary with the degree of uncertainty in the overseas environment.

The specific factors to be considered when planning the distribution system should take into account the following:

- a distribution system is the major link between a company and its customers;

- a distribution system takes considerable time and capital to build and is not changed easily;

- the way the distribution system is structured will have a strong influence on both the market segments that can be reached and the ability to execute certain marketing strategies; and

- the distribution system influences companies' ability to penetrate new overseas markets or expand existing ones.

# Cost

In deciding on the distribution strategy to be adopted, cost plays a part. These costs can be managerial time as well as financial outlay. Basically, it is usually cheaper to use an intermediary in an overseas market than it is for the exporter itself to perform the function. Establishing a sales office in another country can be an expensive undertaking. Whereas the intermediary can amortise costs over a range of products including those of the Australian or New Zealand firm, with a sales office the costs can usually only be amortised over the Australian firm's products. The greater the involvement of the firm in the overseas market (see forms of involvement outlined in the introduction), the greater the initial outlay is likely to be.

There are costs involved in setting up the distribution channel, such as visiting the overseas market, interviewing and negotiating with and appointing members. Maintaining the channel also involves expenses such as those that would be incurred by regular visits to the overseas market and providing promotional support for channel members. Finally, there are associated logistics costs, such as providing, funding and replenishing inventory. Costs vary according to the relative power of the supplier as opposed to the intermediary. The greater the power of the intermediary, the greater the likelihood that costs such as promotion and inventory carrying will be met by the Australian or New Zealand firm.

Another issue is that of cash flow to parties in the distribution channel. A decision needs to be made as to who extends credit to customers—is it the supplier of the goods or is it the intermediary in the overseas market?

# Control

The use of intermediaries will lead to a degree of loss of control over how the firm's products are marketed in the overseas market. The looser the relationship between the firm and the intermediary (see the Kim and Frazier typology discussed earlier), the less control the supplier can exert. In addition, the longer the distribution channel, the less the likelihood that the supplier can have any say over the marketing mix variables of price and promotion in the overseas market. Therefore, the greater the importance of exercising control over the distribution channel, the greater the likelihood that the Australian or New Zealand firm will become directly involved in distribution activities in overseas markets.

From a strategic point of view there is a trade-off between desire for control and the wish to minimise commitment of resources to the overseas market. Where control is important the firm is more likely to establish its own salesforce in the overseas market as opposed to working through agents and distributors. Often firms new to a market commence operations using an intermediary because of the intermediary's specialised knowledge of the market. With experience of dealing in the market, the firm may replace the agent with its own local sales office so that it can directly monitor the network of distributors.

# Commitment

Commitment affects distribution strategy. One indicator of commitment is the manner in which it is intended to cover the selected overseas market. Alternatives are to distribute the product through the largest number of intermediaries catering for the largest number of market segments; to select one market segment only and choose a limited number of intermediaries for that segment; to select multiple segments, but only one or several intermediaries for each chosen segment; or, finally, select one intermediary only who will cater for all segments in the overseas market. One constraint on the above is that of the potential profit for the intermediary. It may be necessary for the intermediary to seek exclusive distribution for the whole market on the basis that without it the line would not be worth handling. On the other hand, a single agent may be a better strategy when entering a new overseas market because:

* single representation eliminates confusion among local buyers;
* the larger volume represented by the sole agent may attract larger distributors;
* promotion of the product to the trade will be without contradictory claims because it is coordinated by one agent only;
* sales and promotional activities can be more effectively coordinated;
* logistics will be more economical;
* a sole agent is more likely to cover minor (and possibly currently unprofitable) segments of the overseas market because of its exclusivity for the whole market;
* the relationship between the principal and the overseas intermediary is likely to be better because of the larger stake each has in the success of the other.

## Nature of the market

Distribution strategy will be affected by the economic health of the country. This is because the investment of resources will vary according to the distribution mode employed. Whereas, before the currency crisis of 1997 in Indonesia, Australian firms may have contemplated opening their own sales office in Jakarta, such firms in 1998 were more likely to rely on an Indonesian agent until they could see how the crisis and subsequent political upheavals would be resolved.

Another issue is whether the selected distribution channel is vulnerable to political change, such as being outlawed or nationalised. In some countries (e.g. Libya), intermediaries are not allowed, in others they must be government undertakings (as in many former socialist countries). In a number of countries, retailing is also controlled by the government. In some cases (e.g. Japan) this control is exercised to protect the small retailer who is considered part of the social fabric. Regulations on retailing can take the form of zoning the location of stores (especially supermarkets and large retail complexes), control over hours of opening and requirements governing health and safety. In non-socialist countries governments often engage directly in retailing (e.g. various State Government Liquor Control Board retail outlets in Canada) and in wholesaling (e.g. Thailand Tobacco Monopoly).

Customer characteristics in the overseas market influence distribution channels because they dictate how buyers prefer to acquire their products. In this connection, it is necessary to research not only what customers need, but also why they buy, when they buy and how they buy. Different distribution channels are likely to be needed for food products in Japan. This is because people are more likely to buy small quantities on a daily basis due to space being at a premium in their small apartments and refrigerators being small as a result. This contrasts with the scene in the USA where accommodation is larger, shopping more infrequent and refrigerators larger.

Other factors deriving from the nature of the market that impact on distribution strategies include the potential for the Australian or New Zealand product in the overseas market. The larger the potential, the greater the likelihood that it will be worth investing resources to ensure control over the distribution channel. Another factor is the way the market operates—cartels or trade associations will influence whether direct involvement is a possibility and, if not, the nature of the intermediary arrangement.

## Nature of product/service

Product attributes, such as degree of standardisation, extent of perishability, bulk, servicing requirements and unit price, influence both channel design and the distribution strategy. Products with a high price per unit are more likely to be sold direct to the end-user/customer, whereas bulky products often only justify direct marketing. Products that are complex, such as computers, require intermediaries to provide installation and after-sales service. Sophisticated products may justify a more direct form of distribution than fast moving consumer goods, while other products such as cosmetics need large margins to 'incentivise' the salesforce and, as a result, may be sold door to door. Perishable products need direct channels of distribution because of their limited lifespan and bulk commodities usually require channels which minimise the number of intermediaries because of buyer resistance to high prices.

Viewed from another perspective, transportation and warehousing are critical factors for basic industrial goods; direct selling and servicing are critical factors for more sophisticated industrial products such as computers, machinery and transportation equipment; and durability, ease of servicing and type of servicing required are factors influencing the distribution of durable consumer goods. There are different channel configurations for consumer goods, industrial products and services:

- With consumer goods, the channels tend to be longer and include more intermediaries, as wholesalers and retailers are involved due to the lower unit value of the final sale.

- With industrial products, the sale is often direct to the customer, with either an agent or an agent and distributor involved because of higher price and/or larger volume orders placed by the final customer.

- With services, there is usually only an agent as an intermediary, due to the provider of the service being involved in the delivery of the service.

## Objectives of the firm

The design of the international distribution channel will be influenced by and will also be a vehicle for implementing the objectives of the firm. Any channel of distribution must meet company objectives for overall profitability and market share. However, international channels may change as the firm's operations in an overseas market expand. For example, initially a firm may distribute in an overseas market through an agent, then it might establish its own salesforce and, finally, once significant market share is in prospect, it might establish its own retail network as happened with the Australian firm Country Road in the USA.

Figure 17.4 compares alternative international distribution strategies in terms of profit potential, credit exposure, control, information and risk/commitment.

# DISTRIBUTION CRITERIA

It is important that the structure of distribution channels is considered in advance of entering an overseas market because, once put in place, distribution structures are difficult to change and a wrong decision may have long-lasting negative consequences. In designing a distribution channel decisions about the following features should be made in advance.

**FIGURE 17.4  Comparing strategies**

| Strategy | Contractual relationship | Profit potential | Credit risk exposure | Control | Market information | Risk/ commitment |
|---|---|---|---|---|---|---|
| **Direct sales** | No | Excellent | High | Yes | Low | Low |
| **Agent/representative** | Yes | 5%–15% of price to agent/rep. | Med. high | No | Moderate | Low |
| **Distributor** | Yes | Good after discount | Low | No | Fair | Low/moderate |
| **Licensing** | Yes | You get 3%–15% | Very low | No | Fair | Low |
| **Joint venture/subsidiary** | Yes | Very good | N/A | Maybe/yes | Very good | High |

SOURCE: *Adapted from* World Trade *(1999), May, p. 46.*

# Structure

## LENGTH

How many levels is it necessary to have in a distribution channel overseas? In general, the more economically developed the country, the shorter the distribution channel. However, this may not always be the case and other factors may intervene, as in Japan where shortage of storage space necessitates an extended channel of distribution so that stock can be held at various points along the channel.

## WIDTH

This is determined by the number of each type of intermediary in the channel. The larger the number of similar intermediaries, the greater the width of the channel and the higher the level of competition. However, the wider the channel, the easier it is to locate effective distributors.

## DENSITY

This is the exposure or coverage desired for the product to achieve a profitable penetration of the overseas market (e.g. the number of sales outlets necessary to cover the whole market).

## ALIGNMENT

This refers to the extent of coordination between members of the channel so as to achieve a uniform and integrated approach in getting the product to the final consumer.

## LOGISTICS

This is the physical transfer of the product from the plant in Australia to the customer in the overseas market.

# Availability of channels

One aspect to appreciate in overseas marketing is that the channels of distribution that exist in Australia or New Zealand cannot be taken for granted in an overseas country. Distribution structures differ from country to country and the availability of channel members affects both strategy and pricing of the product. It also impacts on whether a 'pull' strategy (promote to the customer who then demands the product from the retailer who then demands the product from the wholesaler) or a 'push' strategy (promote the product to the wholesaler who in turn promotes the product to the retailer) is most appropriate.

It is important to establish in advance whether the channel that is desired actually exists in the selected market. A second issue to research is that if the channel exists in the overseas market, is it still available to the Australian or New Zealand firm or does it belong to an established competitor? If the latter is the case, then it needs to be determined whether it is worth the investment seducing the channel member away from the competitor or whether an alternative distribution channel should be pursued. It may be that the channel exists, but is devoted to a non-competing organisation. If this is the case, then one possibility is to negotiate an arrangement whereby the channel is shared with this non-competing firm. Finally, the channel may exist in the overseas market, but is not interested in handling the Australian or New Zealand product. If this situation applies, then a review of the attractiveness of the 'package' may need to be undertaken so as to improve the possibility of effective distribution in the target market.

One feature of channels of distribution in less-developed countries is the large number of people engaged in selling very small quantities of merchandise. Although such a situation often attracts criticism from those in developed countries, given the low cost of labour and limited availability of capital, the distribution system is a rational one given the constraints under which less-developed countries operate.

## Cultural issues

Distribution channels are designed to bridge the gap between Australian/New Zealand sellers and overseas buyers. There are two dimensions to this gap (see Chapter 3)—one is the physical distance between buyer and seller, and the other is the attitudinal and perceptual distance between buyer and seller. This latter dimension, often referred to as the psychic distance, is largely culturally influenced due to the role played in distribution channels by the formation of interpersonal relationships. Researchers such as Gatignon and Anderson (1986) have found that the greater the degree of psychic distance of the domestic from the foreign market, the less will be the firm's commitment of resources to the overseas market and the greater the likelihood that involvement will be via an agent rather than on a direct basis. As psychic distance is usually based on a perception of risk and lack of knowledge, where this is the case great use of intermediaries is a preferred option.

Japan provides a good illustration of the impact of culture on the distribution system. Because the Japanese are extremely fastidious about detail and quality of service, retailers provide home delivery, stay open 12 or 13 hours a day, are open most days, readily accept return of goods and are liberal in offering credit to regular customers. This cultural expectation of service and loyalty is passed back through the distribution channel to wholesalers and producers.

# Government and legal constraints

Government regulation of distribution can impact on the design of the channel, especially when it is necessary to structure the channel to circumvent the government-regulated elements of the distribution system. In some countries government regulation has been designed to protect small businesses (e.g. the 'large-scale retail law' in Japan). Protective regulation can relate to store location, store opening hours and the establishment of government-controlled monopolies.

Channel activities in overseas markets are also subject to varying legal regulations, such as retail price maintenance, turnover taxes, liability legislation, legislation covering intermediaries and dealer rights, laws governing termination of agents, restrictions on territory to be covered and reciprocal selling arrangements. Legal factors such as the above will make some distribution arrangements in an overseas market more attractive to some Australian firms than others.

# Commercial and environmental constraints

Differences in the nature of the distribution channels between countries are due to a number of commercially related factors: in some countries the intermediary function may rest with a particular group; in many South-East Asian countries this function is controlled by the Chinese minority; in other countries, such as in Africa, the intermediary function is undertaken by more recently arrived immigrants (often Indians). This can engender specific attitudes in that country towards intermediaries. Customer orientation also plays a role because in some countries intermediaries perform a distribution function only (e.g. United Arab Republic) whereas in other countries (e.g. India) intermediaries provide full customer service.

Another variable is the breadth of the line carried by the intermediary. This can involve a wide variety of products as is the case with the indigenised successors of the trading companies from the pre-World War II era (e.g. Dieltem or the East Asiatic Company in Thailand); whereas other intermediaries may specialise in a narrow product line. Costs and margins levied by intermediaries will also vary substantially between countries because of the degree of local competition, the differing expectation as to service to be provided and local salespeople's wages.

A competitive issue alluded to earlier is whether the best agents and distributors in the overseas market are already committed to competitors. If this is the case, then different channels of distribution may need to be used to access target customers. Veering away from the established pattern of distribution in a country may be a way of gaining a competitive advantage. Several Australian firms (e.g. CIG Gas Cylinders—now Luxfer) have tried this approach successfully in the Japanese market and not only secured a worthwhile market position, but also improved their competitiveness by bypassing several layers in the traditional Japanese distribution system.

Finally, the general characteristics of the overall environment in a country are a major consideration in designing the distribution channel. The purchasing power of the customers, the demographic characteristics of the population, the lifestyle preferences of the target group, percentage of females in the workforce, the nature and size of homes and the nature/adequacy of infrastructure (power, water, transport by road, rail or sea) are just some of the factors in the wider environment which can impact on distribution. They impact on the number of stages in the channel, the size of the wholesalers and retailers and the breadth of the line carried.

market. Not only is the trade commissioner in a position to provide a list, but they can also provide background information and often a credit check on potential intermediaries. Once a shortlist has been developed based on the factors previously discussed, then those firms remaining on the list should be compared on the basis of a grid similar to that in Table 17.1.

This grid will enable a firm to rate those intermediaries that appear most promising. The next step should be to visit the overseas country to interview those remaining firms. Unfortunately, many Australian and New Zealand firms only view the agent's office, not the agent's activity. An important part of the appraisal is to go with the agent's salespeople on calls to see how they conduct their representation of other imported products and how they are received by the trade. To illustrate the above, Table 17.2 hypothetically compares two distributors in Sri Lanka.

### TABLE 17.1 International agent selection criteria

| | | Distributor 1 | | Distributor 2 | | Distributor 3 | |
|---|---|---|---|---|---|---|---|
| Criteria | Weight | Rating | Score | Rating | Score | Rating | Score |
| 1. Financial soundness | | | | | | | |
| 2. Marketing management expertise | | | | | | | |
| 3. Satisfactory trade, customer relations and contacts | | | | | | | |
| 4. Capability to provide adequate sales coverage | | | | | | | |
| 5. Overall positive reputation and image | | | | | | | |
| 6. Product compatibility (synergy or conflict?) | | | | | | | |
| 7. Pertinent technical know-how at staff level | | | | | | | |
| 8. Adequate technical facilities and service support | | | | | | | |
| 9. Adequate sales infrastructure | | | | | | | |
| 10. Proven performance record with client companies | | | | | | | |
| 11. Positive attitude toward the company's products | | | | | | | |
| 12. Trading area or region covered | | | | | | | |
| 13. Excellent government relations | | | | | | | |
| 14. Warehousing and storage facilities | | | | | | | |
| 15. Experience in representing foreign firms | | | | | | | |
| 16. Willingness to promote product/service | | | | | | | |

**SCALES**

| Rating | Weighting |
|---|---|
| 5 Outstanding | 5 Critical success factor |
| 4 Above average | 4 Prerequisite success factor |
| 3 Average | 3 Important success factor |
| 2 Below average | 2 Of some importance |
| 1 Unsatisfactory | 1 Standard value |

**SOURCE:** *Adapted from Business International Asia/Pacific Limited (1983)* Finding and Managing Distributors in Asia, *Business International Asia/Pacific Limited, Hong Kong, p. 92.*

| TABLE 17.2 | Comparison of distributors in Sri Lanka | | | | | |
|---|---|---|---|---|---|---|

| | | Distributor 1: Duncan Macneil & Co. Ltd | | Distributor 2: Global Tea & Commodities Ltd | |
|---|---|---|---|---|---|
| Criteria | Weight | Rating | Score | Rating | Score |
| 1. Financial soundness | .08 | 5 | .4 | 5 | .4 |
| 2. Marketing management expertise | .07 | 4 | .28 | 4 | .28 |
| 3. Satisfactory trade, customer relation and coverage | .09 | 4 | .36 | 3 | .27 |
| 4. Capability to provide adequate sales coverage | .08 | 4 | .32 | 3.5 | .28 |
| 5. Overall positive reputation and image | .07 | 4 | .28 | 4 | .28 |
| 6. Product compability (synergy or conflict) | .07 | 3 | .21 | 3.5 | .25 |
| 7. Adequate technical facilities and service support | .05 | 4 | .20 | 4 | .20 |
| 8. Adequate sales infrastructure | .06 | 5 | .30 | 5 | .30 |
| 9. Proven performance record with client companies | .05 | 4 | .20 | 3.75 | .19 |
| 10. Positive attitudes towards companies products | .04 | 5 | .20 | 4.5 | .18 |
| 11. Trading area or region covered | .06 | 4 | .24 | 4 | .24 |
| 12. Excellent government relations | .04 | 3 | .12 | 2.5 | .1 |
| 13. Warehousing and storage facilities | .08 | 4 | .32 | 4.25 | .34 |
| 14. Experience in representing foreign firms | .09 | 4.25 | .38 | 4 | .36 |
| 15. Willingness to promote product | .07 | 4.75 | .33 | 4 | .28 |
| Total score | | | 4.14 | | 3.95 |

SOURCE: *Hettigoda, R., Yahzampath, U., Gunasena, P., Puwakgolla, S. and Krishnanand, T. (2004) 'Bogawantalawa Tea Gardens', unpublished report, Sydney Graduate School of Management, p. 24.*

# Appointment

Once it has been decided which agent is to be appointed, then an agreement should be drawn up which clearly spells out the details of the arrangement. The agreement should specify which products will be represented and the boundaries of the area within which the agent will represent the firm. While the agent may wish to represent the total range, care needs to be taken to ensure that the agent has the capability and distribution network in all the product areas for effective representation. If not, then it is best to restrict the range to areas where the agent is competent and appoint other agents for other areas.

Often agents will seek representation rights for a whole country or even a geographical region such as ASEAN. It is important to check in which areas within the country or region the agent has an effective distribution network. To give an agent rights to a whole country (e.g. USA) when the agent only operates in part of it (e.g. California) is to exclude the Australian range from a major market area. If there is uncertainty as to the area of effective representation it may be best initially to confine representation to the agent's current area of effectiveness and review the issue in two years subject to the agent's results.

Usually, agents seek an exclusive arrangement that prevents the Australian or New Zealand firm appointing another agent in the country. If this is the case it is important that the agreement be for a specified time period so that another agent can be appointed if the appointed agent does not perform or if the Australian or New Zealand firm wishes to establish its own sales office or manufacturing arrangement in the market. It is also useful to check that the agent does not handle any competing lines and a clause preventing the agent from doing so should be included in the agreement. There have been cases where firms with a number of similar products have taken on the Australian line and done nothing to promote it—their motive being to keep it out of the market. Generally speaking, both parties should have an exclusive arrangement with each other, or neither party should have an exclusive arrangement with the other.

## Communication and control

This phase of activity should be driven by the notion of creating a positive operating climate so as to improve chances of a long-term satisfactory relationship. To achieve this, it is desirable to answer correspondence promptly in a sympathetic and friendly manner, and to provide the agent with copies of all company material—even if this material is not directly related to the agent's duties for the overseas principal. Such material should include company bulletins, company newsletters, staff bulletins, new product information, public relations releases and fact sheets on new products. This assists in making the agent feel part of the firm's corporate family. In addition, mention of the agent's activities should be included in the above information where possible.

Once appointed, the agent should be visited regularly. The visit should be by the executive responsible for the agency (e.g. not by the managing director or other employee on a junket!), be planned well in advance and have specific objectives that have been agreed upon with the agent in advance.

It is also important to bring the agent to Australia or New Zealand shortly after appointment—the visit could be timed to coincide with a national sales conference. This visit is desirable, not only to enable the agent to meet managers and view the production process, but also to enhance the agent's credibility in the overseas country as the Australian or New Zealand firm's representative. When the agent's customers ask details about where the product is made and the agent admits that he has never seen the manufacturing process, his credibility as the firm's representative suffers.

## Motivation and termination

Any relationship should be operated on the basis that it is a win–win exercise for both parties rather than an arrangement where each party tries to be opportunistic and take advantage of the other. This is especially the case with agency arrangements. It is essential to create strong loyalty throughout the overseas distribution network. This leads to a good image in the overseas market and is good public relations. The philosophy underlying the relationship is that both parties have a long-term horizon for their relationship and each is willing to invest in it.

Remuneration of agents is another issue on which many overseas agency arrangements founder. It should conform to or preferably exceed general rates of commission in the overseas market. If it exceeds the prevailing rate, then the agent might be more likely to put extra effort into promoting the product. If training and development is provided at the expense of the Australian or New Zealand principal, this also provides an incentive, not only for the agent, but also for salespeople and distributors. In most cases the agent handles a number of lines of which the new Australian or New Zealand product is only one. However, because this product is unknown it requires extra effort during the first year of its introduction to the market. The remuneration package should reflect this.

In order to ensure that the agent devotes extra effort to a new overseas product during the initial year when it is being introduced into the new overseas market, some firms pay the salary of one of the sales personnel of the agent or distributor. In return, that person sells only the Australian product. The agent wins because he still receives commission on all products sold and the Australian firm wins because of the effort being devoted to the Australian product. Also, at varying times, some of this outlay may be claimable by the Australian firm against the government's export incentive programs.

Transfer of knowledge and identification with the Australian or New Zealand principal is important. This may be facilitated by the firm training the agent's staff—either in the country or in Australia or New Zealand. Training should be frequent and involve knowledge of the company and its products in general, in-depth knowledge of the products included in the agency arrangement, servicing of the products if applicable, how the product should be sold (taking into account cultural and commercial differences in the foreign market) and communications activities (e.g. the form and style of reporting and effective presentation of the product).

It is necessary from the outset to reach a clear understanding with the agent as to how performance of the product in the overseas market will be measured. This could be on the basis of market share, sales volume, number of times inventory turns over per annum, annual growth rates or extent of floor/shelf space secured for the product. Such standards should be included in the agreement if at all possible. Some of the above measures require access to industry-based market research that may not be available or reliable in many developing countries. If this is the case, objectives should be set in terms of sales volumes. Not only should performance be evaluated in relation to agreed objectives, but also in terms of performance by the industry in that country and in relation to customary business practices. Furthermore, in evaluating performance it is necessary not to accept excuses for non-performance for which the agent is responsible while also being understanding about non-performance due to situations over which the agent has no control (e.g. the financial crisis in Asia in late 1997). Figure 17.5 encapsulates many of the above factors.

If it is decided to terminate the arrangement this must be handled with tact and in accordance with both the contract and accepted practice in the overseas country. Perceived unfair termination can provoke hostility in the trade which could impact on efforts to attract an alternative agent or on the reception of the Australian or New Zealand product if the firm decides to establish its own sales office or manufacturing facility in that country. Such termination can cause insecurity among others in the established distribution channel and can provoke government hostility, especially if the agent is well connected politically. Sometimes termination of agency arrangements can give rise to claims for substantial legal compensation especially if grounds for termination are not clearly spelt out in the agency agreement. This is because local courts overseas tend to be favourably disposed towards local firms. In some countries termination might not be possible (e.g. Saudi Arabia). In others (e.g. Latin America) it is time consuming, expensive and requires considerable advance notice resulting in a period in which little promotion or selling of the Australian or New Zealand product is likely to occur.

## Wholesaling and retailing

The next stages in the distribution channel for most consumer goods have traditionally been wholesaling and retailing. However, patterns of distribution in many countries are changing

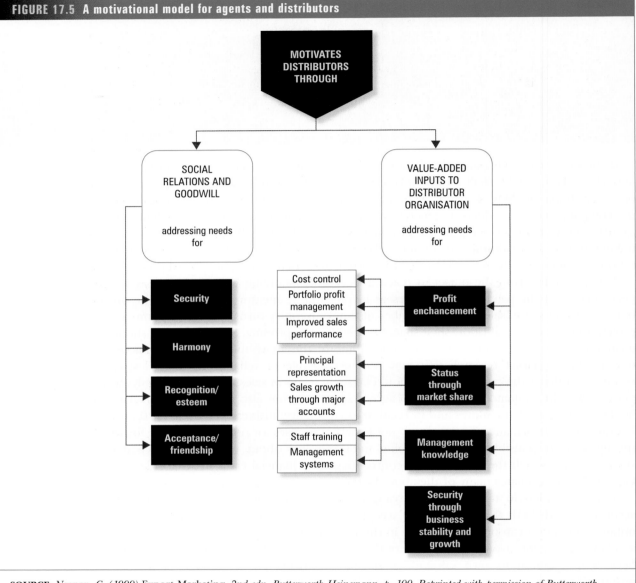

**FIGURE 17.5  A motivational model for agents and distributors**

**SOURCE:** *Noonan, C. (1999)* Export Marketing, *2nd edn, Butterworth Heinemann, p. 100. Reprinted with permission of Butterworth Heinemann.*

and various intermediaries in the distribution channel between manufacturer and retailer or between manufacturer and customer are disappearing.

## WHOLESALING

Wholesalers undertake purchasing, selling, transportation, storage, financing and to an extent information gathering. In some countries, however, one or more of these functions may be undertaken by the manufacturer or the retailer. The status and role of wholesalers vary from country to country. In developing countries they play an important role in financing the flow of goods between manufacturer and retailer. Because wholesalers trade rather than manufacture and because the wholesale trade in developing countries is often dominated by minority groups of distinct ethnic origin, wholesalers often tend to be held in low esteem.

The size of wholesaling operations varies substantially, with some countries such as Finland having very few but very large wholesalers and others such as Japan having a multitude of small wholesalers. The quality of service often relates to the size of the wholesaler, especially in developing countries with smaller wholesalers having limited capital and less know-how. In markets with fragmented wholesaling incomplete market coverage is likely to result, with the consequence that the Australian or New Zealand firm may need to undertake promotion direct to the consumer.

The services provided by wholesalers also depend on the nature of the competition because this influences the margins that prevail and the variety of services provided. In countries where wholesalers are numerous, margins low and competition fierce, wholesalers are likely to provide a variety of services from financing to maintenance of inventory. This is especially the case where the retail sector is small and under-financed as in Pakistan. In industrialised countries wholesalers are facing pressure from both manufacturers who are increasingly dealing direct with retailers and from retailers who are increasingly dealing direct with manufacturers. In this situation, to justify their continued existence wholesalers are having to provide services tailored to the needs of both manufacturer and retailer. Whereas smaller wholesalers in many countries handle only a particular category of goods, they can coexist with larger wholesalers who deal in a wide variety of unrelated products. As mentioned earlier, in developing countries some of these larger wholesalers are the successors of the pre-World War II trading companies that used to dominate international business throughout Asia. Many of these firms have integrated backward into manufacturing and forward into retailing. A recent development has been wholesalers integrating further forward and selling direct to the more affluent consumer.

In many Asian countries most retailing continues to involve small shops and roadside stalls selling products in small units (e.g. one cigarette stick), despite the advent of supermarkets, department stores and shopping malls. The Dutch wholesaler Macro decided in Thailand in the late 1980s to bypass the established distribution channel for these small retailers and erect large warehouses with cash and carry facilities for wholesalers, enabling them to buy several units at a time as opposed to cases. At the same time, they emulated the US concept of forming a buyer's club allowing more affluent consumers to buy, thus bypassing the supermarket. The Macro approach has caught on and there are now similar approaches in operation in most Asian countries.

## RETAILING

International retailing has its origins in the colonial era when British, Dutch, French and German trading companies established retail operations in their various colonies. Retailing operations vary considerably between countries—not only in terms of size of outlet, but also in terms of population served and the role of retailing in the social life of the country. Table 17.3 illustrates the relative average size of retail operations between countries.

However, with developing countries these figures do not reflect the total picture because unlicensed shops, street stalls and street vendors, which play an important role in retailing in such countries, are not included in the statistics.

Although the number of retailers is not strongly influenced by stage of economic development attained, retailing practices are. Even within developing countries retail patterns in major cities with large numbers of affluent people differ from patterns in smaller towns

| | **TABLE 17.3** | **Size of retailers in selected countries** | |
|---|---|---|---|

| Country | Average employment per retailer | Country | Average employment per retailer |
|---|---|---|---|
| Pakistan | 1.2 | Japan | 4.4 |
| Belgium | 1.2 | Brazil | 4.5 |
| Spain | 2.1 | France | 4.5 |
| Mexico | 2.2 | Sweden | 5.3 |
| Israel | 2.3 | Venezuela | 7.2 |
| China | 2.4 | Canada | 8.6 |
| Argentina | 3.8 | Ghana | 10.7 |
| United Kingdom | 3.9 | United States | 13.3 |
| New Zealand | 4.3 | Germany | 13.4 |

**SOURCE:** © *Euromonitor PLC.*

and rural communities. Size can have an impact on the level of service that retailers provide. Large retailers usually carry inventory, whereas smaller retailers hold little inventory creating a need for wholesalers in the channel. Often larger retailers undertake promotion of products either on their own account or in conjunction with manufacturers (cooperative advertising). Smaller retailers expect all promotion to be provided by the manufacturer or wholesaler. It is worth keeping in mind that the Australian concept as to what is meant by a supermarket, a pharmacy and a department store differs from other developed countries (e.g. the USA) and other developing countries (e.g. Indonesia).

Differing environments within countries cause the nature of retailing to vary. The level of a country's development and its infrastructure is likely to impact on the pattern of retailing. As an example, supermarkets and larger retail outlets tend to be more prevalent in countries where GNP per capita is high. Also the concentration of population within the country and concentrations of pockets of affluence are other environmental determinants of retail patterns. As a consequence, Western patterns of retailing are not often appropriate for serving the needs of consumers in Third World countries where traditional labour-intensive retailing is more suitable for the marketing of staples, which account for the bulk of retail spending.

In these poorer countries, retailing is much more labour-intensive and time-consuming than in the West. There is a lack of specialisation in the assortment offered and often the venue of the retail operation is a 'hole in the wall', a single small room or the footpath. Where department stores exist they are often government owned, subject to frequent stock outages and involve a series of stages from viewing the merchandise to selecting the merchandise to wrapping the merchandise to finally paying for the merchandise. These stages often take place in different parts of the store and are accompanied by much paperwork and recording of the transaction—all of which do much to create employment, but do nothing for providing the customer with service.

In such countries, to replace labour-intensive retailing on a widespread basis with supermarkets and department stores would add to the growing unemployment and possibly destroy the social fabric of shopping as a daily event involving social intercourse.

Retailing itself has gone international. For the most part this has been motivated by saturation of the domestic market and the desire to export a particular retail offering which might occupy an unfilled niche in the foreign market. Stores have opened branches in other countries and international alliances between stores have evolved to enhance their buying power. Manufacturers, having established a retail chain to sell their products in the home country, then establish retail outlets in other countries when they decide to export to that market (e.g. Country Road of Australia). The internationalisation of retailing is often stimulated by regional trade groupings, which account for the expansion of UK department stores such as Marks and Spencer into continental Europe and Japanese department stores such as Isetan, Daimaru and Sogo into South-East Asia. The internationalisation of retailing has been littered with failures, illustrating that retailing is basically an operation that has evolved within national boundaries. It is inherently traditional and any innovation is culturally sensitive. This explains why most attempts by Australian retailers to expand offshore have not been successful.

Legislation also has had an impact on the degree to which retailing has gone international. In France, Belgium, Japan and Italy legislation regulates the establishment of retail operations and controls over foreign ownership to preserve the role of local firms in this sector. The way these laws operate in Japan is illustrated in International Highlight 18.5 in Chapter 18.

# GLOBAL DISTRIBUTION ISSUES

There are two issues that often arise when distribution is considered on a global as opposed to a national basis. These are the practicality of achieving standardisation and the frequently occurring problem of grey markets.

## Standardisation

Of the marketing mix variables that are usually discussed in connection with the debate on standardisation versus differentiation, distribution receives the least attention. Most academics and practitioners believe that distribution cannot be standardised. This is true if a dichotomised approach is adopted that the firm either standardises or adapts. The reality of international marketing is that there is a continuum between standardisation and adaptation and that feasible standardisation exists somewhere along this continuum. Moreover, there are two aspects to standardisation. One aspect is *process standardisation*—this refers to the development of uniform management practices. Experience indicates that it is easier to standardise global planning and decision making than it is to standardise the global marketing mix. The other aspect is *program standardisation*—this refers to the development of a uniform marketing mix for all international markets. As far as distribution is concerned, while it may be possible to standardise aspects of process such as types and numbers of intermediaries, difficulties are more likely to arise with program standardisation due to the influence of both culture and tradition on distribution channels overseas. To achieve the greatest practical degree of standardisation for distribution channels, the factors relating to the firm, its objectives and the distinctive features of the overseas market should be consciously taken into account.

## Grey markets and unofficial distribution channels

A grey market is the unauthorised distribution into an external market and can take three forms:

- parallel importation—export of the product to one of the product's existing export markets by a party other than the manufacturer;

# Not your cup of coffee

This is what Nestlé Australia thought when supermarket chain Aldi began importing Nestlé Coffee from Indonesia and Brazil rather than buying from Nestlé Australia. Before the Australian Competition and Consumer Commission (ACCC), Nestlé Australia argued that Aldi should present and display imported blends of coffee differently from Australian blends. In fact Nestlé Australia, in order to 'persuade' Aldi to conform to this company requirement, refused to sell its other branded products (e.g. Milo and Nescafé Blend 43) to Aldi stores, arguing that consumers need to be made aware of the difference between Australian-made Nestlé products and those from Nestlé's operations overseas. The ACCC rejected the submission of Nestlé Australia on the grounds that it had the purpose of substantially lessening competition in the instant coffee market in Australia.

**SOURCE:** *Adapted from* Sun Herald, *13 August 2006, p. 29.*

- re-importation—importing the product back into the home market;
- lateral importation—moving a product from one overseas market to another (Assmus and Wise 1995).

Most commonly it involves unauthorised distributors circumventing authorised channel arrangements by buying a firm's products in low-price countries (usually from authorised distributors in that country) and selling them in high-price countries at prices lower than those offered by authorised members of the distribution channel. The goods involved are genuine branded merchandise and not counterfeit goods. They are different only in that they are sold in the market by unauthorised distributors. This reduces sales for legitimate distributors and disrupts both pricing and distribution strategies. On the other hand grey markets (parallel imports) may help the producer extend the number of countries in which the product can be sold and hence boost global profit according to Ahmadi and Yang (2000).

Grey markets have become more of a problem during recent years due to the growth in the number of global products, the easier availability of price information and increased international product standardisation. Being opportunistic, grey market operators are able to respond more quickly to rapidly changing differences between markets than can global firms. As well, fluctuations in exchange rates have been more pronounced since the major currencies in which international trade is denominated have been allowed to float. Prices are usually set by the supplier with a foreign exchange rate in mind and the price is unlikely to vary unless there is a major movement in the exchange rate. This provides the opportunity for grey market operators to take advantage of day-to-day exchange rate fluctuations. Another reason relates to price discrimination. This occurs when the manufacturer sets different prices for different markets as part of the marketing strategy, competitive reaction or discount for bulk purchase. Finally, due to fluctuations in demand a distributor in one country may be left with large inventory that needs to be liquidated for cash flow reasons by severe discounting. The grey market operator buys the stock and resells it in a higher-price market.

When faced with a grey market situation, many manufacturers do nothing because the cost of litigation is likely to be very expensive and judgments difficult to obtain, especially if the suit is bought in another country where the action is not viewed as intrinsically illegal. In addition, legal challenges involving grey marketing have mostly failed in the courts. An alternative to seeking legal redress is to change marketing mix strategies. Changing the product strategy can involve localising the product for the specific overseas market. This works only if the volume in that market is sufficiently large to amortise the costs of the modification without a major increase in local prices. The manufacturer can change pricing to authorised distributors in different countries to minimise price differences between markets and/or change discount strategies to reduce overstocking. Changing the distribution strategy may involve refusal to supply dealers that stock the grey market product, or refusal to honour warranties on products distributed via grey market channels.

Prices of prescription drugs made in the USA are considerably cheaper (30% to 50%) in Canada than in the USA because the Canadian government controls prices. Those living close to the Canadian border frequently drive to Canada to purchase their pharmaceuticals. Recently, a Canadian firm, Canada RX.net, set out to cater for others in the USA and set up a warehouse in Freeport in the Bahamas. This firm buys drugs from wholesalers in Europe and elsewhere and then ships these drugs at lower prices directly to US customers, bypassing intermediaries in the USA.

**SOURCE:** *Adapted from Dorschner, J. (2004) 'Pharmacy pipeline',* Miami Herald, *10 October, pp. E1–2.*

Discussion so far has implied that all drivers in the economic environment of a nation are official and legal. In many economies, particularly in the developing world, this is not the case and a significant proportion of economic activity does not appear in official records or statistics.

In Burma (now Myanmar), prior to the advent of the State Law and Order Reform Commission (SLORC) government, anecdotal comment suggested that 85% of the country's international trade did not appear in official statistics. One reason for this was that the central government only controlled 40% of the land area because the remainder was controlled by various revolutionary groups, such as the Karen. In addition, the central government had no power in that part of Burma which was part of the 'golden triangle' where opium was the major source of income. The extensive common border between Burma and Thailand meant that much of the country's imports entered free of duty by being physically carried across the border. In the supply of products to Burma, a significant distribution channel was via agents in Thailand.

How to tap such a market is a challenge for the international marketer. Both markets and activities are not all the same shade of black and different shades apply to varying forms of illegal activity. They can range from criminal behaviour to unofficial business practices that are widely condoned. Some of the advantages of the black economy can be higher levels of employment due to the economic activity undertaken, increased availability of products in the marketplace due to greater currency liquidity and increased availability of goods and services. Apart from its illegality, disadvantages of a black economy include negative impact on the growth of the official economy, diversion of resources from public infrastructure projects into private consumption and lack of control over a significant sector of the economy. These can operate to the country's overall detriment.

Black markets are especially prevalent where the rule of law is deficient or applied in an erratic or subjective fashion. For those desiring to tap this segment it may be necessary to trace the foreign source of the black market goods and promote to that party, for example a Singapore agent for goods smuggled into eastern Indonesia. There are of course risks involved because the practice is illegal in that it avoids payment of duty and often contravenes intellectual property or safety laws. Black marketing is particularly prevalent in markets such as Russia, India, China and Brazil—countries characterised by government-owned enterprises, volumes of government regulation, corruption and a history of the involvement of organised crime in business activities.

The growth of the internet will further add to the use of unofficial channels because manufacturers and users can contact and transact directly on the internet.

In summary, it is important for the international marketer to take into account the nature of the trading environment in the overseas country when preparing a strategic plan for activity in that country. The trading environment will also impact on the price that can be charged as well as on the most appropriate form of entry.

## The internet and international distribution

The internet, by connecting producers and end-users directly, has the potential to replace traditional intermediaries in international marketing. The most promising products for trading internationally via the internet are those where existing intermediaries do not perform the traditional wholesaler functions due to the high cost of servicing small, diverse and geographically dispersed players. In international marketing this results in an opportunity for SMEs to engage in international trade from which they were formerly excluded. If the internet can perform a useful set of functions undertaken in marketplace distribution, then potentially it can absorb or render unnecessary the jobs of existing providers of those services. When this happens the internet reduces transaction costs because it cuts out the need for intermediaries. This withering away of intermediaries because firms contact their customers direct is termed 'disintermediation'. While you can eliminate the intermediary, you cannot always eliminate the function performed. Either you do it or your customers do it—if they don't want to, then despite the internet channel functions are unlikely to disappear entirely. There is evidence that marketplace channels may be replaced with marketspace channels, which are sometimes called cybermediaries. The functions that a channel performs are largely fixed (providing information and distributing goods and services), but the institutions that perform these functions are not. For this reason the internet should be regarded as a component of a firm's international marketing plans rather than a new phenomenon that replaces conventional methods of doing business.

Disintermediation is less likely to be the case in international marketing than in domestic marketing as one of the reasons for intermediaries in international marketing is to replace the absent principal in the overseas country. This function will still need to be performed in many cases and as a result the eradication of channel intermediaries and the forging of closer producer-to-consumer relationships has not occurred in the international market to the extent anticipated. Re-intermediation has, however, taken place in a number of instances—this happens when traditional intermediaries find new niches for themselves in the electronic marketplace by gathering customers and information, extending online credit and providing services to complete transactions.

The disintermediation caused by the internet is more likely to occur in B2B marketing than in B2C (business-to-consumer) marketing as in consumer markets, with large numbers of products and infrequent purchases, the matching role of intermediaries is generally more important. Despite exponential growth in access to the internet, consumers still confine their purchases to relatively few product lines: 40% of all internet purchases are for travel, 26% for purchases of tickets to concerts and similar events, and 25% for books and CDs.

In summary, the reality is that although the internet may eliminate some of the 'physical' intermediaries in the distribution channel, these may well be replaced by new types of intermediaries in the international value chain.

# PHYSICAL DISTRIBUTION

Physical distribution is the means by which products are made available to customers where and when they want them. It includes customer service, packaging and protection, transportation, warehousing and storage and documentation.

## Customer service

The level of customer service provided to customers in overseas markets tends to be lower than the level in the domestic market. This is because of geographic distance, the greater possibility of mistakes, inadequate packaging, transportation delays and customs clearance problems. If the firm establishes its own distribution facilities in the overseas market some of these problems can be overcome. It is not usually desirable for the Australian or New Zealand firm to try to maintain the same level of customer service in all markets. This is because customer service is subjective and expectations as to level vary substantially from country to country and from market to market within countries, especially between urban and rural areas. If the level of service being provided is lower than that available from domestic suppliers in the overseas market, then this needs compensation if the resulting competitive disadvantage is to be removed.

## Packaging and protection

Because of the extended transit times and the distances travelled by imported products in getting to market, the usual problems in physical distribution of goods are compounded. Scope for pilfering is greater and the possibility of damage in transit increases the greater the distance involved and the more stages there are involved in transit. Because imported goods often have to travel through different climatic zones there is an increased possibility of damage due to heat, rain or cold. Furthermore, as transport infrastructure in many countries in the developing world is poor, damage to consignments due to poor handling becomes more likely. Although containerisation reduces the above problems to an extent, when goods arrive in a country and containers are unloaded, pilferage and damage in transit become real problems. Thus goods destined for other countries will usually need better packaging and protection which adds to cost. The size of outer containers used in Australia or New Zealand may not be suitable either for the transportation infrastructure of the overseas market or for the local requirements of wholesalers or retailers. It is worth investigating in advance of shipment what handling and transport conditions the product is likely to be subjected to, so that goods can be packaged in ways appropriate to the overseas market.

*In the late 1980s Haiphong, the main port in northern Vietnam, was chaotic due to the flood of goods entering the country following the 'doi moi' liberalisation of the economy. As a result, goods were mostly stored in the open, were handled manually or moved by untrained forklift drivers and remained for long periods at the dock before being cleared. Many arriving consignments had been packed assuming containerised transport 'door to door', but there was no containerisation at Haiphong. Damage and pilfering were rife.*

## Transportation

Choice of mode of transportation is an issue that often does not receive sufficient attention. This can be broken up into its different stages:

1   *Transport of goods from factory to port of shipment*: Other shipment stages and modes might dictate the type of outer packaging and whether containers are used, even if not required for transport to the docks.

2   *Transport from Australian or New Zealand port to overseas port*: Careful analysis needs to be undertaken as to the relative cost of air versus sea. Although airfreight rates are usually more expensive, they may have a lower overall impact on costs. This is because the period for insurance coverage is less and the opportunity cost of funds tied up in goods in transit is lower. In addition, there is greater value due to increased customer satisfaction because transit time is shorter and goods can be delivered nearer to inland customers by air than by sea, thus reducing inland transport costs.

3   *Transportation of goods from point of arrival in the overseas country to the customer*: Transportation infrastructure within a country varies considerably from truck and rail (e.g. in the USA) to barge (in parts of Thailand) to handcart and bullock dray (in the Indian subcontinent).

Another factor influencing the selection of transport mode is the nature of the product. If the product is a spare part, then the cost of machine or plant lying idle is far greater than the difference between air and sea freight rates. If the article is perishable, as with vegetables, then air may be the only feasible transport mode. In some cases, if the shipment is small air will be cheaper because of the larger minimum quantities required for sea shipment. Freight rates are influenced by the nature of the demand for cargo. If the demand is seasonal or irregular, then rates will be higher and if the flow of goods between Australia or New Zealand

and other countries is mostly one way, then rates are likely to be higher because there is no 'backloading' cargo available (as is the case with most countries in the Middle East).

As far as specific modes of transportation are concerned, the main ones are as follows:

- *Road*: This is very efficient for short hauls of goods with high value, and this mode has the virtue that the goods can be delivered direct to the customer's premises. Problems arise when the goods have to cross national boundaries as border controls are time consuming and, on occasion, sea crossings are involved as the truck moves from one road system to another. In developing countries road surfaces are often poor with resulting damage to the goods.

- *Water*: The key mode for transport of goods from country to country, sea transport provides a low-cost means to transport bulky products such as iron ore and petroleum. It also is a convenient means of carrying general cargoes in containers, which reduce the risk of pilfering. Water transport is slow and subject to delays caused by weather. And it needs to be combined with other transport modes to achieve door-to-door delivery. It requires the construction of expensive port facilities and if these are not adequate cargo can be delayed in the port as happened in Iran in the 1970s when port delays as long as nine months were experienced.

- *Air*: Airfreight can be used to get goods to most countries and there has been a huge growth in the volume of international cargo during recent decades. Air cargo is the fastest form of transport and is particularly useful for high-value goods and spare parts. Offsetting the higher freight rates is the opportunity cost savings due to the goods being in transit for a much shorter period of time. In addition, goods sent by air do not require the same strength of packaging as do many sea consignments. It accounts for less than 1% of the volume of goods transported internationally, but is responsible for about 20% by value.

- *Rail*: Rail is a good method for transporting bulky goods over long distances and the increasing use of containers has led to a multi-modal concept whereby rail is combined with road or sea to achieve more efficient transportation. In countries where high-speed trains operate, such as in Europe, rail is accounting for a greater percentage of transport. In developing countries and countries where rail infrastructure has not been modernised, this is not the case. In the case of Australia, there is the recently opened Adelaide to Darwin rail link which is aiming to deliver goods to Asian markets more cheaply.

Hollensen (2004) argues that the decision as to which transportation mode to use is contingent on the following factors:

- cost of different transport alternatives;

- distance to the location;

- nature of the product;

- frequency of the shipment;

- value of the shipment;

- availability of transport.

Table 17.4 provides a comparison of the various transportation modes available for supplying overseas customers.

| TABLE 17.4 | Comparison of major international transportation modes | | | | | |
|---|---|---|---|---|---|---|
| **Mode** | **Reliability** | **Cost** | **Speed** | **Accessibility** | **Capability** | **Ease of tracing** |
| Rail | Average | Average | Average | Average | High | Low |
| Water | Low | Low | Slow | Low | High | Low |
| Truck | High | Varies | Fast | High | High | High |
| Air | High | High | Fast | Low | Moderate | High |
| Pipeline | High | Low | Slow | Low | Low | Moderate |
| Internet | High | Low | Moderate to fast | Moderate; increasing | Low | High |

**SOURCE:** *Keegan, W.J. and Green, M.C. (2005)* Global Marketing, *4th edn, Pearson Prentice Hall, NJ, p. 425. Reproduced with permission of Pearson Education, Inc., Upper Saddle River, NJ.*

## 17.4 INTERNATIONAL HIGHLIGHT

# *Cormo Express*—lessons learned

On 6 August 2003 a consignment of 57 000 live sheep left Fremantle on the *Cormo Express* for Jeddah to feed the pilgrims on their journey to Mecca for the Haj. The live sheep trade has evolved over the last 30 years into a highly profitable Australian export, particularly to Muslim countries, and is worth over A$1 billion a year.

The sheep arrived in Jeddah, but were not disembarked. The Saudi authorities rejected the sheep due to claims that an unacceptably high proportion of the sheep were suffering from scabby mouth. A remarkable series of events followed. The Saudi authorities were resolved not to accept the sheep so a new destination had to be found. The *Cormo Express* and its cargo endured fires, food shortages and spurious offers of acceptance by other countries before the cargo was off-loaded in Eritrea some two months after being rejected by Saudi Arabia.

Although the sheep were born in Australia, it is likely that they ceased to be Australian when they wandered up the gangway of the *Cormo Express* as by that time the sheep had been sold to Saudi Importer Hamood Alali Alkhalaf Trading and Transportation Co. on a free on board (FOB) basis. Under such a contract the title to the sheep would have passed from the Australian exporter to the Saudi importer as the sheep were loaded. If this were the case the Saudi importer would have contracted with the carrier to transport the cargo of sheep from Fremantle to Saudi Arabia under a voyage charter or time charter arrangement. On this basis the Australian sellers would be in the clear unless there were stipulations in the contract that they were liable for the condition of the sheep until they arrived in Saudi Arabia.

It is common for sellers to pass this risk onto buyers by stipulating that the condition of the goods is final at the port of shipment and this is demonstrated by provision of a veterinary certificate. A disgruntled buyer may or may not have recourse against the carrier, depending on the contract for the carriage of the goods. By taking these precautions the seller will be paid regardless of the condition of the sheep when they arrived in Jeddah. In rejecting the sheep, was the Saudi government endeavouring to exert pressure over the long haul to reduce the live sheep process from imported sources? In the event, the issue became one involving trade relations between Australia and Saudi Arabia and the problem was eventually solved by the Australian government buying the sheep for A$4.5 million and giving them as aid. A small price to pay given the value of the trade being over A$1 billion a year.

**SOURCE:** *Adapted from* Export, *February 2004, pp. 12–13. Thanks to* Export Magazine, *The Australian Institute of Export and Geoff Farnsworth of Norton White.*

# Warehousing and storage

Warehousing and storage facilities can be set up by the Australian or New Zealand firm in the overseas market or provided by others in the distribution channel. If the latter is the case, the nature of warehousing in the other country needs to be investigated in advance because it can impact on the strength and design of packaging. Size requirements and storage practices for products in warehouses vary as do location and transportation distances from port or airport. One aspect of relevance is the availability of foreign trade zones (FTZs) where prior to duty being paid goods can be stored, repackaged into smaller containers for in-country shipment, assembled from shipped components and relabelled. It is only when goods leave the FTZ to be sold elsewhere in the country that they become liable to local tariffs and taxes.

# Documentation

Physical distribution of products in global markets is complicated by the need for considerable documentation. The most important documents that should accompany a shipment are:

- *export declaration*—used for statistical purposes by the Australian government to keep track of the value and volume of goods being exported from Australia;
- *bill of lading*—acknowledges receipt of goods by the carrier and serves as proof of ownership;
- *commercial invoice*—describes in detail the goods sold and the conditions accompanying the sale; and
- *certificate of origin*—specifies the exact origin of the goods and is used by the customs authority at the point of importation for specifying the applicable tariff.

# Freight forwarders

Use of facilitating firms such as freight forwarders is essential for small firms and novice exporters and desirable for most other firms, as the forwarding of freight can be a very complex activity and one that easily lends itself to outsourcing. Freight forwarders (sometimes referred to as consolidators) can either arrange to forward a shipment from the point of origin of the goods to the customer in the other country, or just to book space on the transportation carrier.

From the point of view of the novice exporter, there are considerable advantages in the freight forwarder attending to matters such as documentation, export inspection, arranging insurance and booking space on all transport modes involved in the shipment. Furthermore, the freight forwarder is able to consolidate shipments from a number of exporters and obtain a much better rate than if each firm's product were shipped individually. These firms, because of their continuous involvement in the international domain, can also provide advice on markets, government regulations and potential problems. In addition, they are able to track the movement of goods at each stage en route to the final destination.

# The internet and international physical distribution

A substantial level of traditional trade will be influenced by the internet and made more efficient through speedier delivery using internet-based transport, logistics and border-crossing procedures. The Department of Foreign Affairs and Trade (1999) estimates that internet trade across borders could amount to 20% to 30% for many products because the internet reduces the traditional barriers to international trade of distance, time and language. Whereas for bricks-and-mortar businesses the value chain involves inbound logistics (shipping product from manufacturer/wholesaler to distribution centres) and outbound logistics (shipping product from distribution centres to retail stores), with e-business the distribution value chain can differ widely depending on the configuration of the value chain and the level of sourcing. Specific areas of difference are that e-business companies may ship small shipments to individual customers, so that warehousing and consolidation operations may not be required.

Although paperless trade is a reality in international business it is still not all encompassing and does not address the problems of customs clearance, especially in the developing world. Costs most likely to be affected by differences in the configuration of the value chain for bricks-and-mortar businesses and e-business companies are:

- *inventory costs*: while with bricks-and-mortar firms some inventory needs to be located at a physical store location, e-business companies can hold inventory at a more centralised location or even not take possession of the inventory until the order arrives.

- *order-handling costs*: although bricks-and-mortar firms offer a greater variety to choose from, order costs will be greater for e-business firms because the handling of individual customer orders is labour intensive. As a result, e-business firms may shift their distribution centres to low-labour-cost countries.

- *transportation costs*: e-business firms are involved in delivering product from the manufacturing facility to the customer. As the distance from distribution centre to customer is greater and the volume of product smaller with e-business companies, transportation costs are likely to be higher.

The internet involves a de-linking of value creation from location and this affects the motivation to locate value-adding activities in different parts of the world. There are two elements of the impact of the internet on choice of international location:

1 digitisation of value-adding content and delivery;

2 the ability of the internet to form at low cost an electronic network that connects various corners of the world.

# Summary

International distribution is a critical aspect of successful international marketing. If the product cannot be delivered to the customer in the overseas market sales will not occur regardless of how good the product or service is, the attractiveness of the price at which it is offered or the volume and impact of the promotion. Whether the channel is direct or indirect, the international marketer faces a major challenge in matching the international distribution system to both the objectives of the firm and the competition it faces in the international marketplace.

It is important that the channel selected by the international marketing manager will both reach the overseas customer and take their characteristics into account. It is also important that in the process care is exercised not only in establishing the channel and selecting its members, but also in managing and motivating members of the channel. Differences need to be appreciated between countries as far as wholesaling and retailing are concerned as these differences can have a backward effect on other stages in the channel.

The international manager needs to be conscious of how the channels set up in one country compare with channels set up in others. Such consciousness enables the manager to be on the lookout for economies resulting from standardising aspects of distribution on the one hand and problems which can result from differences on the other, such as grey markets.

Finally, the characteristics of the physical distribution channel need to be explored as these affect the product, its pricing and its promotion. Measures must be taken to ensure that the problems of physical distribution, especially those manifested in an inability to maintain competitive levels of customer service with domestic or closer suppliers, are either overcome or compensated for in other ways.

## ETHICS ISSUE

In Singapore, Australian Pumps Pty Ltd has had a long-established agent whose performance has been disappointing. This is because the local price at which its electric motors sell makes them only just competitive due to the high margin added by the agent, which is normal for this category of product in Singapore. Recently, the volume of the firm's pump products entering Singapore has trebled. Investigation reveals that this increase is due to product being imported directly by Singaporean end-users from the Australian firm's Indonesian agent who operates on a commission rate half that which prevails in Singapore. As a result the landed product from this source is 20% cheaper. The Singapore agent is demanding Australian Pumps stop the Indonesian agent selling into its territory and insists that it cease supplying the Indonesian agent if he does not desist. Although there is nothing in the agency agreement with the Singapore firm to prevent supplying this grey market operator, to do so is contrary to the spirit of the agency arrangement.

*If you were the export manager for Australian Pumps Pty Ltd would you comply with the Singapore agent's request or allow the situation to continue?*

## Websites

Australian Quarantine and Inspection Service (AQIS) http://www.aqis.gov.au
Country Road http://www.countryroad.com.au
Daimaru http://www.daimaru.co.jp
Department of Foreign Affairs and Trade (DFAT) http://www.dfat.gov.au
International Phytosanitary Portal http://www.ipc.int
Isetan http://www.isetan.co.jp
Luxfer http://www.luxfercylinders.com

**Marks and Spencer** http://www.marksandspencer.com
**Northern Territory Trade Development Zone (now Darwin Business Park)**
  http://www.ldc.nt.gov.au/pages/darwin_business_park.cfm
**Sogo** http://www2.sogo-gogo.com

## Discussion questions

1  Why is global distribution more difficult than domestic distribution?

2  What are the advantages and disadvantages of the Australian or New Zealand firm establishing its own distribution in an overseas market and what forms might this take?

3  How do the characteristics of the final consumer affect a decision as to the most appropriate distribution option in international marketing?

4  What steps should be taken when selecting an overseas agent?

5  What criteria should be applied when managing an overseas agent or distributor so that the relationship might be long lived?

6  What differences are likely to be encountered when setting up a distribution channel overseas for industrial products as opposed to consumer goods?

7  What are the possible risks in engaging in a partnership with an overseas intermediary who already handles a competitor's product?

8  How does international physical distribution differ from international channel distribution?

9  Discuss the advantages and disadvantages of the Australian or New Zealand firm undertaking warehousing and storage in the overseas market.

## References

Ahmadi, R. and Yang, B.R. (2000) 'Parallel imports: challenges from unauthorised distribution channels', *Marketing Science*, Vol. 19, No. 3, Summer, pp. 279–94.

Assmus, G. and Wise, C. (1995) 'How to address the grey market threat using price coordination', *Sloan Management Review*, Spring, Vol. 36, No. 3, p. 31.

Business International Asia/Pacific Limited (1983) *Finding and Managing Distributors in Asia*, Business International Asia/Pacific Limited, Hong Kong, p. 92.

Classen, T.F. (1991) 'An exporter's guide to selecting foreign sales agents and distribution', *Journal of European Business*, Vol. 3, No. 2, pp. 28–32.

Department of Foreign Affairs and Trade (1999) *Creating a Clearway on the New Silk Road–International Business and Policy Trends in Internet Commerce*, Commonwealth of Australia, Canberra.

Dorschner, J. (2004) 'Pharmacy pipeline', *Miami Herald*, 10 October, pp. E1–2.

*Export*, February 2004.

Gatignon, H. and Anderson, E. (1986) 'The multinational corporation's degree of control over foreign subsidiaries: an empirical test of a transaction cost expansion', Working Paper No. 86-041R, The Wharton School, University of Pennsylvania.

Hettigoda, R., Yahzampath, U., Gunasena, P., Puwakgolla, S. and Krishnanand, T. (2004) 'Bogawantalawa Tea Gardens', unpublished report, Sydney Graduate School of Management.

Hollensen, S. (2004) *Global Marketing–A Decision-Oriented Approach*, Financial Times Prentice Hall, Harlow, UK.

'Indirect solutions', *Dynamic Export*, October 2006, p. 26.

Karunaratna, A.R. and Johnson, L.W. (1997) 'Initiating and maintaining export channel intermediary relationships', *Journal of International Marketing*, Vol. 5, No. 2, pp. 11–32.

Keegan, W. (1995) *Global Marketing Management*, 5th edn, Prentice Hall International, Sydney, pp. 542, 545.

Keegan, W.J. and Green, M.C. (2005) *Global Marketing*, 4th edn, Pearson Prentice Hall, New Jersey.

Kim, K. and Frazier, G.L. (1997) in Doole, I. and Lowe, R. (eds) *International Marketing Strategy, Contemporary Readings*, International Thomson Business Press, London, pp. 297–315.

Murray, I. (2007) 'Use logistics wisely', *Australian Freight Logistics*, December/January, p. 16.

Noonan, C. (1999) *Export Marketing: A Practical Guide to Opening and Expanding Markets Overseas*, 2nd edn, Butterworth Heinemann, Oxford.

Spicer, S. (2006) 'Coping with quarantine', *Dynamic Export*, August, pp. 8–12.

*Sun Herald*, 13 August 2006.

Walters, R. (2002) *The Big End of Town and Australia's Trading Interests*, Department of Foreign Affairs and Trade, Canberra.

*World Trade*, May 1999.

## go online

Go online to <www.pearsoned.com.au/fletcher> to find more case studies.

# CASE STUDY 17

# Grey markets

### Chloe Savage and Richard Fletcher

During the normal course of business, manufacturers of goods are able to deliver them to consumers through predefined and negotiated distribution channels. These usually involve contracts and agreements which set out the rules of distribution, such as point of sale, recommended retail price and warranty issues. Outside these distribution channels there operate grey markets. A 'grey market' refers to the flow of goods through distribution channels other than those authorised by the manufacturer and often involves the goods being bought and sold at prices lower than those that prevail in the local market. Grey markets affect a broad range of products including, but not limited to, recording companies, publishing houses, makers of computer software and computer games, food and beverage companies, automobiles, pharmaceuticals and fashion accessories.

To the manufacturers of products so affected, grey markets pose a significant concern. The main advantage of grey markets to consumers is the significant savings they receive from the products they purchase.

KPMG LLP in the USA conducted research into the effects of grey markets on the IT industry. It showed that average savings when buying products from grey markets instead of from authorised distribution channels can be significant. Fifty-seven percent of respondents cited savings of between 10% and 30%, as illustrated in Figure 1.

However, this price advantage often comes with many drawbacks that various manufacturers try to highlight when defending orthodox distribution channels. Products available through grey market sources are often sourced from oversupply in another distribution channel. They are sold off at significantly lower prices to get rid of excess

stock and are then sold to the consumers at lower prices, often in different countries, without the knowledge of the producer.

In the past, parallel imports for certain goods were considered unlawful as they infringed on copyright and trade marks, and were in common law viewed as passing off and misleading or deceptive conduct. Intellectual property rights' owners and their licensees often blocked such imports. In the past 15 years however, the government of Australia has passed legislation which restricted the rights of the intellectual property (IP) owners and made parallel importation a lawful conduct (Barraclough 2006).

Provisions in both the *Copyright Act 1968* and the *Trade Marks Act 1995* relating to parallel imports adopt the principle of international exhaustion. This theory provides that once a trade mark or copyright owner places goods onto the market, the owner's ability to control subsequent dealings with the goods or services is exhausted (Barraclough 2006).

Under section 123 of the *Trade Marks Act*, a person may import goods which bear the trade mark of another party as long as the trade mark was applied to those goods with the Australian registered trade mark owner's consent, even if this has occurred outside Australia. This provision

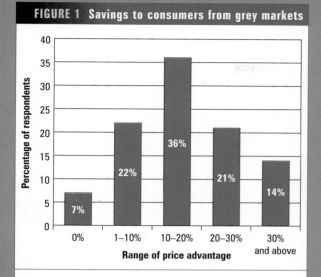

**FIGURE 1 Savings to consumers from grey markets**

SOURCE: *KPMG LLP (2000)* The Grey Market, <*www.kpmg.ca*>.

has been part of the *Trade Marks Act* since it came into force in 1995 (Barraclough 2006).

Some retailers that resell products on the grey market are not able to provide the same quality of customer support as would be the case if they had dealt with authorised distributors. The grey market products usually have limited or no warranty as in most cases the warranty is only valid in countries in which the product was purchased through the authorised distributor and the manufacturer will not honour warrantees on grey market purchased goods. In these situations the customer often has to pay the manufacturer to perform repairs that would have been provided free of charge had the purchase been through authorised distribution channels.

Generally grey markets are not illegal, but some illegal products can be masked as parallel imports, causing consumers to purchase counterfeit goods. Another risk of grey markets is that consumers may be buying obsolete products. Warehouses clear stock at below market prices in anticipation of a new product which is more technologically advanced and often cheaper. The consumers then fall into the trap of buying what they believe is a new product at a very discounted price only to realise a short time later that they could have purchased a far better product at a lower price. When designing and distributing products to different markets, producers of consumables especially make the product based on the tastes and requirements of the market of the intended point of sale. Consumers are usually not aware that they purchased the product on the grey market and subsequently after experiencing the problems outlined become disgruntled with the producer of the product.

On occasion grey markets can be encouraged by a retailer looking for a larger margin on a product and the retailer seeks out a different distributor, often in another country. This is sometimes referred to as parallel importing. Parallel importing can be defined as goods that are imported through 'non-official' channels from low-price to high-price countries (Find Law Australia for Students 2006).

This case study will examine the grey market dispute between Nestlé and the new supermarket chain in Australia—Aldi. In late 2005 Aldi became involved in a dispute with its supplier Nestlé over what Nestlé claimed was the deliberate attempt by Aldi to circumvent Nestlé's established distribution channels in Australia.

Aldi sourced its Nescafé Blend 43 coffee from its Indonesian distributor. Aldi claimed that Nestlé prevented Aldi from access to the same buying conditions it extended to the Woolworths and Coles chains in Australia and to compete with them it would have to sell the product at a loss. Frustrated, Aldi initially turned to a Singaporean distributor and later to a Brazilian distributor in its efforts to bypass Nestlé Australia (Baker McKenzie 2006).

One of the risks entailed in such action is that since the product has been acquired from a different country, it may not be compatible with the standards that apply in the country of final sale— as with electrical products that are not compatible with Australian power outlets. In Australia, this can be a breach of sections 52 and 53 of the *Trade Practices Act 1974*).

Nestlé claimed that it received large amounts of negative formal and informal feedback and complaints due to customers purchasing Nescafé

Blend 43 that was manufactured to a weaker strength to conform to Indonesian tastes. Aldi responded by putting stickers on both the product and the surrounding shelf areas to inform its consumers of the origin of the product. Nestlé argued that this action was inadequate and refused to supply Aldi with any more products, including other coffee products and the energy drink Milo, until 'Aldi improved in-store information about the parallel imported coffee'. Nestlé also proceeded to file a claim with the Australian Competition and Consumer Commission (ACCC) in December 2005, outlining the reasons for its actions.

On 9 August 2006 the ACCC revoked Nestlé's notice and therefore its immunity from prosecution for exclusive dealings (i.e. barred further supply of Nestlé products to Aldi) under the *Trade Practices Act*. The ACCC chairman, Graeme Samuel, stated that:

*Aldi had taken adequate steps to ensure consumers were making informed choice.*

The ACCC response further elaborated that Nestlé's reasoning behind the notice and its discontinuance of the supply of its products to Aldi:

- substantially lessened competition in the instant coffee market;
- discouraged and eliminated a new source of competition for the local (Australian) Nescafé instant coffee brands; and
- removed the stimulus to other Australian grocery retailers, who might have responded to Aldi's sale of the imported Nescafé instant coffee by discounting Nescafé Blend 43 or importing similar products.

The ACCC's judgement showed that it viewed the refusal to supply Aldi as going much further than was needed to inform consumers.

## Questions

1   What are the effects of grey markets on producers and manufacturers? Explain in relation to:
    a   profits; and
    b   brand/company image.
2   Name some specific products and companies which relate to the grey market and parallel imports issues.
3   Outline ways in which companies may protect their products against appearing in grey markets.
4   Draw a product distribution network map representing this case study. It must show the distribution channels from Nestlé to the final consumer, depicting the normal distribution channels alongside Aldi's grey market distribution channel.

## Bibliography

Baker McKenzie (2006) *Nestlé Australia Ltd—Exclusive Dealing Notification N31488*, <www.accc.gov.au>, accessed 23 October 2006.

Barraclough, E. (2006) 'Companies rapped over grey market policies', *Managing Intellectual Property*, <www.proquest.umi.com>, accessed 22 October 2006.

Coffee Scout (2006) *The Australian Coffee War*, <www.coffeescout.net>, accessed 20 October 2006.

Dibb, S., Simkin, L., Pride, W. and Ferrell, O.C. (2006) 'Modifying the marketing mix for various markets', in *Marketing*, 4th edn, Houghton-Mifflin, Warwick, UK.

Find Law Australia for Students (2006) *Nestlé vs Aldi*, <www.findlaw.com.au>, accessed 22 October 2006.

Gittins, R. (2006) 'Why what we don't know can hurt us', *Sydney Morning Herald*, <www.smh.com.au>, accessed 23 October 2006.

Kayasit, P. (2006) 'Asia's rules on grey market goods', *Managing Intellectual Property*, <www.proquest.umi.com>, accessed 22 October 2006.

KPMG (2006) *The Grey Market*, <www.kpmg.ca>, accessed 28 September 2006.

Venu, S. (2004) 'Should parallel imports be regulated at all?', *The Hindu Business Line*, <www.thehindubusinessline.com>, accessed 23 October 2006.

## go online

Go online to <www.pearsoned.com.au/fletcher> to find more case studies.

# The Wiggles

**Dr Susan Dann, consultant**

## INTRODUCTION

For a country whose economy is traditionally associated with sport, agriculture and mining it has come as a surprise over the past decade that Australia also excels in the arts and entertainment. Although Australian performers have individually succeeded in the overseas market for many years, it has only been relatively recently that entertainment has been taken seriously as an Australian export.

According to Austrade, Australian entertainment as an export category has grown massively in recent years. Between 2003 and 2005 export growth in the music industry alone increased by 50%. This translates to annual sales of around $100 million. In 2005–06 entertainment and arts companies working with Austrade completed 459 export deals for a total value of $301 000 000.

The impact and influence of the Australian entertainment industry, and the importance that the government places on it, is evident from the regular inclusion of entertainers in trade missions to key markets such as the USA. The G'Day LA annual promotion of Australian exports to the USA regularly features influential figures from the Australian entertainment industry such as Nicole Kidman, Olivia Newton-John and Bindi Irwin.

A second indicator of the fact that entertainment is now considered a serious export is the peer recognition of entertainers in the annual Australian export awards. Not only does entertainment and the arts have its own industry category award equal in consideration to more traditional industries such as mining, agribusiness and technology, in 2005 the entertainment category winners—The Wiggles—took out the overall Australian Exporter of the Year Award.

## OVERVIEW—THE WIGGLES

The Wiggles is a band that targets the children's music market and consists of four members who dress in distinctive, colourful outfits. The original members of the group, identified by the colour of their costumes, were Jeff Fatt (purple), Anthony Field (blue), Murray Cook (red) and Greg Page (yellow). The group is well known for its large number of short and catchy original children's songs. The band performs a large number of live shows every year and also has five television series, which are shown internationally. Their show also includes a number of other characters— Dorothy the Dinosaur, Wags the Dog, Henry the Octopus and Captain Feathersword.

The Wiggles' success as children's entertainers is now an international phenomenon. With an estimated gross annual revenue in excess of A$50 million The Wiggles are listed as Australia's highest earning entertainers. Over the past 16 years The Wiggles have grown from a group

© 2007 The Wiggles Pty Ltd

of local entertainers playing to audiences in shopping centres to a major international act with approximately two-thirds of their revenue coming from the US market.

The history of The Wiggles is relatively well known. Three of the original Wiggles, Anthony Field, Greg Page and Murray Cook met at Macquarie University while studying early childhood education. Anthony Field knew musician Jeff Fatt from earlier days in the band, 'The Cockroaches'. Together they wrote and recorded children's songs as part of a music project. The completed tape was then sent to the ABC, which released it as a self-titled album in 1991. In 1992 The Wiggles adopted their distinctively coloured skivvies as costumes.

Based on these songs the band developed a show that they performed initially at shopping centres and for preschools. In 1993 their spent 10 months touring around Australia and by 1996 were performing 500 shows across Australia.

From these relatively simple beginnings, the band's popularity amongst its target audience of preschoolers has grown to the extent that in 2005 they performed for more than a million fans at live concerts, sold $17 million in DVDs and $5 million in CDs. In addition there is now a wide range of Wiggles merchandise as well as other licensing deals.

During 2006, the 15th anniversary of the creation of The Wiggles, the group faced a significant threat to their ongoing existence. Due to illness, the 'Yellow Wiggle' Greg Page had to leave the group. Potentially this could have meant the end of The Wiggles. However, as the following demonstrates, the way in which The Wiggles have developed as an act and as an export product allowed the band to continue its success despite the loss of an original member.

## ENTERTAINMENT AS A SERVICE

Marketing arts and entertainment products of any kind is a difficult process. Like all services, entertainment has to deal with marketing issues surrounding the four key characteristics of services:

1  intangibility—the fact that a 'service' cannot be seen, held or evaluated independently prior to use;

2  heterogeneity—labour-intensive services differ in delivery due to the varying competence of service providers; however, even technically identical services will be subjectively experienced differently by different people and at different times;

3  inseparability—the production and consumption of a service occurs simultaneously; and

4  perishability—the fact that services are time-based and cannot be stored for later use.

Arguably, for entertainers the easiest of these characteristics to address is perishability. Like many other services, technology provides entertainers with the ability to capture their service, in this case a performance, and allow it to be consumed at the leisure of the individual. Recordings of music and film can be played and replayed multiple times without any degradation or alteration in product quality, allowing fans to consume and reconsume elements of the entertainment experience on demand.

However, it is clear that for any entertainment, multiple experiences of the same product result in different levels of enjoyment. Hearing a song for the first time is very different to hearing it for the fifth, tenth or hundredth time. For some people, increasing repetition brings increased enjoyment; for others, the opposite is true. This phenomenon brings into play the dual issues of inseparability and inconsistency.

Inseparability and inconsistency also vary across the different types of entertainment product being created. For example, the same performer will be perceived very differently in a live performance when compared to a recorded performance.

Inseparability also leads to issues surrounding co-production. The enjoyment of an entertainment experience is as much a consequence of the individual audience member's frame of mind and willingness to participate as it is due to the entertainer's skill.

The key defining feature of the entertainment product, like all services, is its intangibility. It is

difficult to define exactly what it is about one entertainer or type of entertainment that makes it a success. The inherent intangibility of entertainment is simultaneously the biggest asset and biggest liability in determining the entertainment product.

The indefinable and intangible quality of specific entertainers contributes to varying levels of success at different times and is an asset in that it cannot be copied by rivals. However, because this intangible quality cannot be replicated, the entertainment product remains one of the most volatile of all services.

Services in the international marketplace face additional problems. These have been discussed in detail in the text, but there are two specific problems for the entertainment export industry. These are distribution and ensuring that the target audience has a shared frame of reference.

Distribution is the key to success for all export industries. In entertainment, distribution is often handled at an international level from the outset, for example in the film industry. However at an individual level, entertainers still need to break into these multinational distribution networks.

What is considered appropriate entertainment varies significantly according to local cultural norms. Consequently, although significant progress is being made exporting Australian arts and entertainment into new markets, much of the focus of successful export entertainers has been on the traditionally similar markets of the USA, UK and Europe.

## INTERNATIONAL EXPANSION

The Wiggles members maintain that they did not have a clear strategic plan for international expansion and export from the outset. Based on their Australian success, The Wiggles made their first trip to the US in 1998 where they signed a music and DVD deal with Lyric Studios. The following year they released *The Wiggles Movie* in the USA and toured the country as a support act for Barney the Dinosaur. However, their big breakthrough in the USA came in 2001 when they appeared in the Macy's Thanksgiving Parade, signed a licensing deal with Walt Disney International and toured the

UK for the first time. Since then the popularity of The Wiggles on the international stage has continued to grow, creating some unique problems for a people-focused service product.

## CONSUMER UNDERSTANDING

One of the keys to success for The Wiggles is their understanding of their core target market—preschool-age children. Coming from a background in early childhood education has given The Wiggles an important insight into the way in which young children think and what appeals to them.

Shows and songs are written from a child's perspective about topics of interest to them—usually involving food or animals. Mindful of the fact very young children can become confused or distressed by the unexpected, any surprises in live shows are explained before they happen and children are communicated with in a way that is relevant but never patronising.

The visual and sound appeal of The Wiggles across nationalities and cultures is based on this strong understanding of the developmental needs of preschool children. The fact that Wiggles songs, and accompanying dance moves, are equally popular with very young children in Australia, Europe, Asia and the USA demonstrates how deep the group's understanding of their market's needs and preferences are.

The secondary target market which The Wiggles must address is that of the parents. Considering the age of their audience, parents are the key gatekeepers to access to the market. It is the parents who control television viewing, as well as purchasing decisions, amongst this age group.

Parents are attracted to The Wiggles and their products for a number of reasons, key amongst these being the educational component of the group's materials. The rise of The Wiggles' popularity has coincided with an increased market demand for early childhood educational products. However, this level of trust is difficult to maintain in the long term, especially when the group is involved in commercial franchising decisions. If, for example, The Wiggles endorse a product that parents believe is inappropriate, this could have a strong negative effect on their ability to reach their core consumers.

## THE WIGGLES' PRODUCT

In services, the expanded marketing mix always includes the additional element of 'people'. In the case of The Wiggles, the people element has been core to the development of the product portfolio. Despite their huge financial successes, The Wiggles still see themselves primarily as educators, rather than businesspeople. However, increasing demand for The Wiggles and their products has meant that a more strategic approach to the product is needed; hence the decision in 2001 to recruit a general manager to focus on the commercial elements of the brand.

The Wiggles' product portfolio is extensive. In particular, the commercial opportunities that are presented through licensing and merchandising mean that Wiggles-branded products are available across a range of categories and through a variety of partners (see Table 1).

In 2005 Wiggles World opened at the Dream World amusement park on the Gold Coast and has been a huge success. Three Wiggles World's have also just been introduced into theme parks with US theme park giants, Six Flags. Wiggly Play Centres, purpose-built indoor play centres, are also being introduced in the USA and Australia.

Despite the vast range of licensed and accessory products, the core products of The Wiggles remains education and entertainment. Unlike many other entertainers, The Wiggles do not rely on CD and DVD sales to interact with their audience base. Instead they spend up to six months a year touring. This emphasis on live performances differentiates The Wiggles' approach to children's entertainment and provides the opportunity for ongoing direct interactions with their fan base.

To maximise the benefits and reach of live performances, The Wiggles have perfected stadium shows with high quality performances aimed at very large audiences. The extent of these live performances also provides a direct comparison of success with other entertainers. For example, when touring the USA, The Wiggles

| TABLE 2 | Wiggles' partnerships |
| --- | --- |
| **Product category** | **Partners** |
| Toys | Funtastic |
| | Timat |
| | TGA |
| | Tree Toys |
| | Leisure Dynamics |
| | MTA |
| | CA Aust |
| | Croftminster |
| | Learning Curve |
| Apparel and accessories | Turning Point: outerwear and swimwear |
| | Casco Blu: outerwear and sleepwear |
| | Brand Direct: footwear |
| | Funtastic: Rainwear, underwear |
| | Engelite: headwear, scarf and gloves |
| | Samsonite: luggage bags and backpacks |
| | Vimwood: fashion jewellery, wallets, key chains |
| Food and beverages | Heinz |
| | Pauls |
| | Ital Biscuits |
| Health and beauty | Johnson & Johnson: sticking plasters |
| | Vimwood: hair accessories |
| Other consumer products | Hallmark: all party goods |
| | Anagram: balloons |
| | Hunter Leisure: carnival showbags |
| | Ride on entertainment: Dorothy and Big Red Car coin-operated ride |
| Media | Australia: ABC Network, Disney Channel |
| | UK: Nick Jr |
| | USA: Playhouse Disney |
| | Italy: Jim Jam TV |
| | New Zealand: TV3 |
| | South America: Disney |

played 12 shows in Madison Square Garden at a time when renowned rock band 'Coldplay' were considered the biggest band in the world after playing only eight shows at the same venue.

The inseparability of the performance allows The Wiggles to provide an experience that creates an enduring relationship with the audience. For most children, a Wiggles concert is their first experience of live performance. Despite the size of the venues, and the number of people in the audience, The Wiggles' performances are characterised by a perception of individual attention. This is achieved through highly interactive performances that encourage children to participate in the show.

Wiggles songs are always short, catchy and easy to remember. Not only have they been a commercial success, but the quality of The Wiggles' musical contributions has been recognised by their peers, as is evidenced by their winning of multiple music awards including four ARIAs (Australian Recording Industry Awards) in addition to winning the Outstanding Achievement Award in 2003.

The Wiggles have succeeded in standardising a highly personal and differentiated entertainment product, as well as making it tangible through the use of characters and other cues. It is the consistency of message and quality which helps to position the group as an enduring entertainment product and helps to explain their international appeal.

This consistency is drawn from the basic philosophy underpinning the group's existence. The Wiggles have set in place a set of values and behavioural standards that are consistent and central to the brand. The 'Wiggles Way' is based around ensuring all products reflect positive and ethical ideas and that all members of The Wiggles and support staff adhere to a strict code of conduct regarding what constitutes acceptable behaviour. For example, The Wiggles are never seen riding in their Big Red Car unless they are wearing seatbelts. Similarly, they are never seen eating junk food. By creating an intangible set of consistent standards, it is possible for The Wiggles philosophy and concept to expand beyond the four original band members.

## MULTIPLE WIGGLES

Increasing success, especially in the international market, created extreme time pressures on The Wiggles. Demands for personal appearances and live performances throughout the world could not all be met. Further, the inherent attractiveness of the sight and sounds of The Wiggles meant that this demand extended beyond the traditional English-speaking markets for Australian entertainers to multi-lingual markets.

The most obvious way to enter the non-English-speaking market was to simply dub existing DVDs and re-record CDs in the appropriate language. However, with a strong live component to The Wiggles' appeal, the solution to this problem of meeting public demand for a live product with finite limits to the amount of time available was highly innovative. In effect, The Wiggles have developed a franchise approach to meet increasing international demand.

This solution was initially trialled in the Latin American market where an alternative group of Wiggles, including two female Wiggles, was created. These Spanish-speaking Wiggles dress in a similar way, perform the same songs and embody the same approach to children's entertainment as the originals. Similarly there are alternative Wiggles in Taiwan with further bands planned for other countries.

The franchise option is not without its risks. Most notably, it is difficult in any franchise operation to maintain full control of the product in multiple venues and even more difficult for such a person-centred service. However, this solution does allow the original Wiggles more time to spend with family as well as on creating new shows, programs and songs.

Ultimately the franchise solution, originally created to serve the needs of a non-English-speaking market as part of their international expansion, provided the original Wiggles with the means to overcome the potential crisis of the loss of Greg Page in 2006.

The 'Yellow Wiggle' was able to be divided off from the person playing the role with the result that the transition to Sam Moran was effected relatively smoothly. Again highlighting the group's understanding of very young children and their need for consistency, the change of Wiggle was open and transparent. A short film was made to explain, in child-friendly terms, the change, why it was happening and to introduce the new Yellow Wiggle.

By adopting an innovative approach to

defining and controlling a variable entertainment product, The Wiggles have succeeded as a major Australian export product. The lessons learnt from the international experience have in turn provided a model to ensure the longevity of the group over time and in changing circumstances.

## Bibliography

Harcourt, T. (2006) 'Exporters get a Wiggle on', Australian Trade Commission, <http:www.austrade.gov.au>.

<http://www.thewiggles.com.au>.

Ross, E. (2006) 'It's a Wiggly world', *Intheblack*, November, pp. 24–28.

'The Wiggles: The fab four', *Brand Strategy*, 9 May 2007, p. 20.

Wright, G. (2005) 'The Wiggly way', *The Age*, 5 May, <http://www.theage.com.au/news/TV—Radio/The-Wiggly-way/2005/05/19/1116361668574.html>.

## Questions

1   What characteristics of entertainment as a service product make it difficult to export?
2   How have The Wiggles addressed these in their strategy?
3   What are the benefits and potential problems associated with the franchise model that The Wiggles are adopting for international markets?
4   What lessons can be taken from The Wiggles' international experience to help their domestic marketing activities?
5   How has the development and expansion of The Wiggles business differ from most other competitors in the entertainment market?

PART E

# CONTEMPORARY CHALLENGES IN INTERNATIONAL MARKETING

In this final part of the book a number of contemporary issues in international marketing are explored in depth. The first of these is the impact of international trade relations (Chapter 18) on international marketing and its role in gaining access to overseas markets. International trade relations are examined from a multilateral, regional and bilateral perspective, as are ways firms can lobby their governments to have their concerns raised in trade relations negotiations between countries. The second contemporary issue is that of winning projects offshore (the first part of Chapter 19). The balance of decision making in awarding contracts at each stage of the project cycle, between the government agency in the receiving country and the provider of finance/aid, is explored in depth. An understanding of the drivers underlying both bilateral and multilateral aid is needed, as is an appreciation of financing techniques including mixed credits. A third issue is that of countertrade (the second part of Chapter 19), which operates as a vehicle for international trade facilitation in situations where the availability of foreign exchange is restricted. Various countertrade techniques are analysed in terms of how their relative merits may fit with the strategic objectives of the firm. The section on countertrade concludes with a discussion of strategies to cope with requests for countertrade as a condition of doing business offshore. The final issue explored in this chatper is that of doing business at the bottom of the pyramid (BOP) in developing countries—with the 4 billion who live on less than US$1500 a year. Ways in which the behaviour of these buyers differs from that of their more affluent colleagues are explored, as are the techniques for modifying each of the marketing mix variables if firms in Australia and New Zealand are to be able to profitably supply customers in this group.

# 18 INCORPORATING INTERNATIONAL TRADE RELATIONS INTO OVERSEAS MARKETING

CHAPTER

## LearningObjectives

**After reading this chapter you should be able to:**

■ appreciate the role of international trade relations in marketing products and services overseas;

■ recognise how the role of government impacts on international marketing;

■ learn how multilateral trade relations have evolved and their likely directions in the years ahead;

■ assess the impact of the various Regional Trade Groupings which have emerged and the rationale for their existence;

■ appreciate the reasons for the increase in the number of free trade agreements;

■ recognise how bilateral trade relations operate and how they can be used by businesspeople to address problems of access or impediment in an overseas market; and

■ discuss the advantages and disadvantages of managed trade.

# Food to go

Nowhere are the barriers to international trade between countries more in evidence than in the agricultural sector. Why would the European Union spend more of its budget on supporting its Common Agricultural Policy (and creating subsidised agricultural surpluses) than on any other item? Why have the Japanese for years banned the import of rice? When they finally succumbed to intense trade relations lobbying to open their market, the imported rice went into storage and was earmarked for industrial purposes or cattle feed so that the Japanese consumer would not be exposed to imported rice. Possibly this is because food products engender an emotional response involving an affinity with the land and a hearkening back to a bye-gone era when most of us lived off the land. It is this deep-rooted sentiment that may account for the barriers to the trade in agricultural products and the ingrained reluctance of countries to eliminate or reduce them. Often these barriers are not even necessary to protect the livelihoods of local farmers and are kept on the books for political reasons, for supposed quarantine reasons or as bargaining chips for future trade negotiations.

For Australia and New Zealand with their 'clean green image' such barriers are a source of frustration and prevent the natural endowments of these countries being capitalised upon despite arguments of comparative advantage and the virtues of free trade. Traditionally, with many potential overseas markets, if one part of Australia had a quarantine problem, products from anywhere in Australia were declared a prohibited import. Japan banned Tasmanian apples because of fruit fly in mainland Australia, despite the fact that the distance between Tasmania and mainland Australia was not that much shorter than the distance between Japan and the rest of Asia.

Due to trade relations lobbying this ban has now been lifted—first for Tasmanian Fuji apples in 1997 and recently for all Tasmanian apples. A similar situation existed with Australian citrus exports to the USA. Again because of fruit fly, there was a ban on the import of citrus. Extensive lobbying managed to convince the US Department of Agriculture that there were no fruit fly in the Riverina area and exports of Riverina oranges into the US are now allowed. These are likely to be worth A$4 million a year because they are produced in the reverse season to the California and Florida oranges. In the USA, part of the explanation for this more liberal attitude may be because of the signing of the Australia-US Free Trade Agreement, which came into effect on 1 January 2005. Tariffs on items like beef (Australia's largest export) and citrus fell, making agricultural products more competitive in the US market.

**SOURCES:** *Parkes, J. (2006) 'Food to go', Dynamic Export, August, pp. 16–20; and 'A boost to fruit', Dynamic Export, October 2006, p. 3.*

# INTRODUCTION

International trade relations are part of a country's total relationship with other countries. They are interrelated with political relationships, which are increasingly influenced by trade considerations; cultural relationships, which frequently operate as a vehicle to expand services exports such as stage productions, films, music and art works; defence relationships, which are influenced by the potential to sell military hardware; civil aviation relationships, which involve landing rights and bilateral agreements to access other markets; immigration relationships including issues such as business migration; and finally development assistance relationships where the tying of aid to trade is a common practice. Figure 18.1 illustrates how political relationships are perceived to facilitate commercial relationships in various countries in the region.

A series of recent global changes have served to shift the focus of international relations further towards trade. The redrawing of the global atlas following the collapse of communism has caused a shift in Eastern Europe and the former USSR from politics to trade, especially obtaining benefits from the World Trade Organization and membership of regional trade groupings such as the European Union. In addition, with the absence of a Cold War threat, global defence expenditures have fallen and political competition between countries is more by trade than by war. The increase of tribalism, rather than the nation state, is now the major source of conflict. In places such as Africa and the former Yugoslavia, a dilemma for overseas governments is whether they should also target their trade relations activity towards the tribal group or the alternative government as opposed to just the government in power.

Globally there has been an overall reduction in aid from the richer to the poorer nations. This reduction has been in grants as well as in low-interest, long-term loans. The political motivation for aid has diminished as the Cold War recedes and debt levels in the wealthy nations increase. Reduction in aid increases the pressure to trade and developing countries are increasingly exploring trade expansion as an alternative to aid.

## THE GENERAL CONTEXT

International trade relations (ITR) activity has significantly contributed to globalisation—a fact appreciated by those protesting against globalisation who use the occasion of trade relations discussions to voice their protests. This contribution of ITR is manifested in its:

- reducing trade barriers during the period when the General Agreement on Tariffs and Trade (GATT) operated from 1947 to 1994 and in the activities of the World Trade Organization (WTO) over the last 12 years;

- facilitating growth in the flow of capital and foreign direct investment (FDI) via multinational corporations until the 1980s and by transnational corporations since;

- fostering the growth of newly industrialising countries such as China and India and their ability to provide goods and services on a global scale;

- recognising the expanding role of services in the global economy;

- shifting the emphasis on protection from tariff to non-tariff barriers where measures of protection were unavoidable; and

- supporting developments in the areas of transport and communication in the interests of expanding global trade.

**FIGURE 18.1  Love thy neighbour**

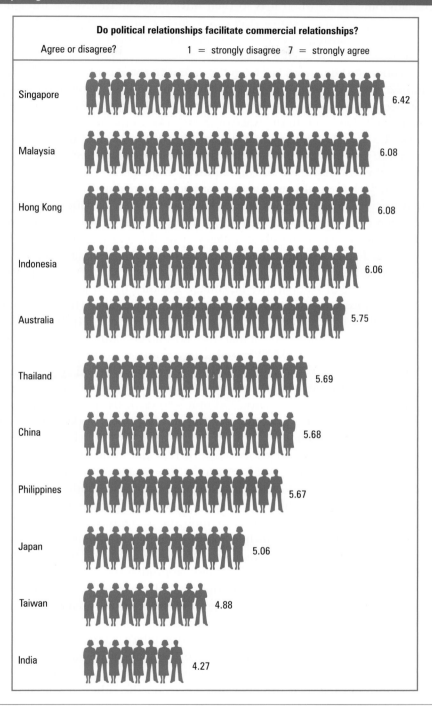

Do political relationships facilitate commercial relationships?

Agree or disagree?        1 = strongly disagree   7 = strongly agree

| | |
|---|---|
| Singapore | 6.42 |
| Malaysia | 6.08 |
| Hong Kong | 6.08 |
| Indonesia | 6.06 |
| Australia | 5.75 |
| Thailand | 5.69 |
| China | 5.68 |
| Philippines | 5.67 |
| Japan | 5.06 |
| Taiwan | 4.88 |
| India | 4.27 |

**SOURCE:** International Business Asia, *17 November 1997. Reproduced with permission of the Charlton Group.*

However, although most countries pay 'lip service' to the concept of free trade, they usually only do so when it is to their advantage, and most see foreign trade as a zero sum game in which one country attempts to give up as little as possible in exchange for another country liberalising access to its market. As national sovereignty and the ability of governments to guarantee prosperity erode, the reaction to problems is often an upsurge in protectionist rhetoric, as has been the case with the recent increase in the offshoring of goods and services. Although the rhetoric about the necessity of freeing up trade between nations has been around since the end of World War II, from time to time events cause a move in the reverse direction. In the wake of the attacks on the World Trade Center and the Pentagon in the USA on 11 September 2001, cross-border movement of goods and people has become more difficult and the costs of the security measures in themselves can reduce the expansion of global trade in pursuit of comparative advantage.

With global trends, such as the formation of regional trade groupings and the spread of globalisation, small countries such as Australia and New Zealand face the prospect that both they and their companies may be 'left out in the cold'. This prospect has encouraged the use of trade relations to minimise the disadvantages of its size and its dependency on agriculture and raw materials. The government needs to create trade alliances that protect the national interest and ensure that they are not the target of unfair or discriminatory trade practices by others.

The theory of comparative advantage assumes free trade. However, the barriers to trade prevent nations maximising their comparative advantage. This is the situation with a number of Australia's basic exports, such as sugar. For the most part, it is government assistance and intervention that distorts comparative advantage. Much of the focus in Australia's trade relations activity over recent decades has been towards reducing or eliminating distorting practices, such as those in agriculture as practised by the European Union (EU) with its Common Agricultural Policy and the USA with its Grain Enhancement Program.

Recently Australia has supported moves towards freer trade and embraced the concept of a 'level playing field'. Unfortunately this concept only works if other countries play by the same rules. This has not been the case and, in view of the rise in protectionism via non-tariff barriers and the increasing formation of regional trade groupings, Australia's stance seems somewhat naive. As an example, Australia sees protectionism in terms of tariffs or quotas and other static instruments, whereas most Asians see it as subtle and flexible rather than static. They have more of a 'tilted' rather than a 'level' playing field approach. Their approach involves provision of assistance to industry as required, in return for which industry is expected to deliver a worthwhile share of the world market. In addition, their approach to protectionism is driven by the concept of long-term benefit to the nation as opposed to short-term benefit to the firm. Because there is a much stronger sense of unity between firms in the one industry in most Asian countries, they are able to impose unwritten barriers to protect their interests and adopt a unified front in negotiations, as Australians have found when negotiating coal contracts with Japan.

In the first decade of the new century Australia's trade relations will need to focus on steps to reduce the trade deficit and on ways of expanding the nation's narrow export base. It will need to avoid continuing to be caught in the crossfire between the USA and the EU on the one hand and between the USA and Japan on the other. It will also need to reduce trade dependency on the Asian region as the currency crisis of 1997 highlighted the extent of Australia's exposure in this connection.

There may be merit in Australia adopting a more proactive trade relations approach whereby trade policy becomes an instrument of its global competitive strategy. Trade relations

## 18.1 INTERNATIONAL HIGHLIGHT

# Australia looks to its Pacific neighbours

Following the creation of the World Trade Organization (WTO) in 1995, it appeared that the trend towards regionalism and bilateralism in international trade relations was over. In the years since, the rhetoric has not matched the reality and the new environmental variables discussed in Chapter 5 and the macro aspects of globalisation discussed in Chapter 11 have yielded a progressive disenchantment with the WTO, especially on the part of developing nations. This has led the Australian government to move towards bilateral trade agreements with real teeth in the form of bilateral free trade agreements (FTAs). Apart from the currently negotiated Australia–United States Free Trade Agreement (see Department of Foreign Affairs and Trade 2005a) discussed later in this chapter, free trade agreements have been signed with Singapore and Thailand, and another is being negotiated with China.

The Singapore–Australia Free Trade Agreement (SAFTA—see Department of Foreign Affairs and Trade (2004b)), which began in July 2003, was the first bilateral free trade agreement entered into by Australia since the Closer Economic Relations Agreement with New Zealand in 1983. It is consistent with WTO rules and secures for Australia outcomes that are better than could have been achieved through the WTO in the areas of trade in services,

intellectual property, investment and competition policy. This is in addition to eliminating all tariffs. It provides a more open and predictable business environment in a number of areas including telecommunications regulation, government procurement, technical standards, e-commerce, customs procedures and business travel. It is to be reviewed every two years and can be added to and updated as bilateral trade and investment evolves over time.

The Australia–Thailand Free Trade Agreement signed in 2004 (see Department of Foreign Affairs and Trade (2004a)) is Australia's third free trade agreement and Thailand's first. It is intended to enhance Australia's A$2.5 billion exports to its 11th largest export market. It will lead to the elimination of all Thai tariff and quota barriers on imports from Australia. This will significantly improve prospects in the Thai market for Australian grains, dairy products, meat, horticulture, sugar, foodstuffs and wine. In the industrial sector, among the many items to benefit will be motor vehicles and parts and the current 80% tariff on passenger cars will be phased out and disappear entirely by 2010. More than three-quarters of current Australian exports will gain immediate tariff-free access to Thailand. In the area of investment, Thailand will permit majority Australian ownership in many fields of activity including mining, and further negotiations are planned to allow further liberalisation of two-way services trade.

**SOURCES:** *Adapted from Department of Foreign Affairs and Trade (2004a)* Australia–Thailand Free Trade Agreement, *Commonwealth of Australia, Canberra; and Department of Foreign Affairs and Trade (2004b)* The Singapore–Australia Free Trade Agreement—A Business Guide, *Commonwealth of Australia, Canberra.*

can be used to generate protectionist measures as a means of discouraging overseas entrants from entering the Australian market on the one hand and eliminating trade barriers in the interests of microeconomic efficiency on the other.

# MARKETING CONTEXT

Both international trade relations and marketing are about access—to world markets, to regional markets or to single country markets. The bottom line is that a firm cannot market its goods overseas if the goods are not allowed entry. Issues of access can be short term, as with temporary quarantine bans such as that engendered in the UK by 'mad cow disease', or long term, as with the ban until recently on rice imports into Japan. Impediments to access are driven by:

- firms in the other country that want to keep out imports;

- governments which want to raise revenue by using tariffs as with Thailand; and

- firms or governments that wish to favour specific countries as with fellow members of ASEAN, or national groups as with the ethnic Chinese.

The principal vehicles for impediments are tariff and non-tariff barriers.

Marketing is also about maximising international competitiveness. Trade relations and trade policy activities by governments can have an adverse impact on the ability to compete. It can do this by reducing the value offered to the overseas customer, by creating different relationships in the market and by placing different emphasis on the importance of government in the value chain for the product or service being offered. The role of government in the value chain is often overlooked in Australia where there is more of a confrontational attitude between business and government than is the case in many of the overseas markets with which Australian firms trade.

# ROLE OF GOVERNMENT

Both the Australian and overseas governments can influence the ability of the Australian firm to compete internationally.

## Domestic governments

The government operates as a partner in the Australian firm's network as a regulator, as a facilitator and as a customer. Each of these roles by the government can become the subject of trade relations representations should another government feel it has an adverse impact on its firms entering the Australian market.

### REGULATOR

The government can impose bans on its firms exporting to specific overseas countries as happens when it supports UN embargoes on trade with countries such as formerly occurred with Iraq. Its actions in the domestic market can raise the costs of exporting. Examples of such actions are export inspection fees, stamp duties and transaction charges and either not allowing or making difficult the claiming back of import duties paid on the imported content of products subsequently exported.

Another area where the government operates as a regulator is in the imposition of standards. Standards may be deliberately set as different from other countries so as to make it difficult for foreign products to enter the Australian market, or may be imposed for (allegedly) quarantine or health reasons.

Government acts as a regulator when it controls exports by imposing bans on the export of certain products for security reasons. Examples include actions by the USA under its foreign military sales program, and Australia protecting its distinctive competitive advantage— as illustrated by the former ban on the export of Merino sheep.

### FACILITATOR

There are many ways in which the government can act as a facilitator of exports if it chooses to do so. When a product is exported, it can refund any taxes or import duties paid. Many governments have a program of export incentives. Often other countries argue that these incentives amount to dumping or in other ways result in injury to their domestic suppliers. When this occurs the matter becomes one that is settled via trade relations representations and discussion. In some cases domestic governments deliberately create a favourable financial environment for exported products. This can take a number of forms including establishing specific exchange rates to apply to exported products.

Domestic government representatives overseas such as Australian Trade Commissioners and embassy officials can provide assistance to firms. Not only do these representatives provide direct assistance and market information to firms, but they also lobby overseas government departments and ministers on behalf of the interests of firms.

Other ways in which the government facilitates firms is via the provision of investment incentives. These encourage firms from overseas to invest in Australia, especially in joint ventures.

## CUSTOMER

The government is also a customer for many Australian firms. In the process they add credibility to firms' claims of expertise, especially in countries where government endorsement is respected. Governments also give preference to local products and legislation such as 'Buy Australian' Acts allow governments to buy from local sources even if they are more expensive than overseas sources. Often the domestic government gives aid to overseas countries and this aid is often given to advance the donor's commercial interests. There may be a requirement for the aid to be tied to procurement of Australian products, or the aid is given to an overseas country as part of a joint government–private sector assistance package, which resulted from bilateral trade discussions between Australia and the other country.

# Foreign governments

A foreign government can also operate as a regulator, facilitator and customer.

## REGULATOR

Foreign governments can impose duties on products entering their domain. They can also impose a variety of non-tariff barriers, such as quotas, licences, quarantine regulations and health requirements. They may impose standards not only on the product, but also on the way it is promoted, the way it is distributed and the way it is priced.

## FACILITATOR

A foreign government can act as a facilitator, not so much with exports unless a countertrade arrangement is involved, but more when investment in their country is involved. Governments often offer incentives to foreign firms to invest in either priority regions in the country, in priority industries or for the transfer of unique technology or in all three areas. The incentives can relate to free or concessional duties on the importation of capital equipment, components or raw materials; tax holidays; absence of restrictions on the repatriation of profits, capital or dividends; or concessions on local taxes and imposts.

## CUSTOMER

Because of the large volume of purchasing in the government sector, overseas governments can be major customers for imported products, services and projects. Often their trade relations activities reflect their using the leverage of their purchasing to facilitate other commercial objectives. This often happens with offsets programs (see Chapter 19).

## Influence and government

If the Australian firm is able to involve its government as a partner in its international network, this is likely to improve its international competitiveness. The government using its 'trade relations clout' can assist firms' entry into overseas markets. Government involvement improves the attractiveness of the offer because in many overseas countries buyers want the security of dealing with overseas firms that have the active support of their government.

Another issue is how the firm can enlist the support of its government to help it win business overseas. The firm can directly approach the relevant government department for assistance. It can also initiate an approach through indirect means, such as via the industry association to which it belongs; by lobbying ministers and officials through third parties such as professional lobbyists; by approaching local political representatives such as a member of parliament or responsible minister; or it can work through local or regional government bodies. Some of these may have a pre-existing relationship with the overseas market such as a 'sister city' relationship.

There are five major ways for government to influence the trade activities of other countries. These are participation in multilateral forums, membership of regional trade groupings, bilateral trade relations with countries on an individual basis, entering into commodity agreements, and insisting on managing the trade in certain product categories. The Australian businessperson can influence each of the above in order to improve business prospects overseas. A trade relations approach by the firm need not be confined to one of the above, but may include several as they interact and overlap.

International trade issues can be addressed on a multilateral basis, on a regional basis or on a bilateral basis.

# MULTILATERAL TRADE RELATIONS

## Purpose

The purpose of multilateral trading systems such as the General Agreement on Tariffs and Trade (GATT) is to remove restrictions on trade worldwide. In pursuit of this objective, they support structural change and economic growth in the overall world economy. They do this in two ways. The first is by promoting trade liberalisation. Bodies such as the GATT (now the World Trade Organization) believe that overall economic growth will be enhanced if all countries remove their barriers to trade and liberalise their existing measures for protecting local producers and using imports to raise revenue. The second is by establishing a framework of rules for the conduct of trade policy by nations.

## History

Following the depression of the 1930s, in the years leading up to World War II there was chaos in international trade. Following World War II it was felt by the victorious nations that, in order to facilitate world recovery, there should be introduced a new trading order which allowed each member nation to pursue its comparative advantage and stimulate the flow of trade which World War II had interfered with. It was presumed that the main barriers to trade were tariff barriers and the reduction of these should be targeted. It was also considered that the main reason for the introduction of tariffs by a nation was to protect its infant industries. Therefore the focus of this new world trade order was on manufactures.

The above resulted in the formation of the GATT in 1947. This body aimed to provide a secure and predictable international trading environment in which the progressive liberalisation of trade could continue. Since its formation and its renaming, there were a number of major forums where GATT members came together to debate major issues of concern. Known as GATT rounds, these went on for several years at a time. The last GATT round was the Uruguay Round. This was arguably the most significant of all and resulted in the GATT renaming itself the World Trade Organization (WTO). As of 1 March 2007, there were 150 signatories to the WTO, accounting for more than 90% of world trade. Like its predecessor the GATT, the WTO has rounds of negotiations. The first of these, the Seattle Round, collapsed in chaos largely due to anti-globalisation protests. The current round is the Doha Round.

## Operation

The GATT operated on the basis of a set of rules agreed on a multilateral basis governing the behaviour of governments. It provided a forum for trade negotiations designed to liberalise the international trading environment. It also provided an international court in which governments could resolve disputes on trade issues with other governments.

The objectives of the GATT were to reduce tariffs on goods, prohibit restrictions on the quantities of goods that could be traded and eliminate other non-tariff barriers to trade in goods. It also aimed to eliminate all forms of trade discrimination through the operation of the Most Favoured Nation Principle (MFN). All GATT members agreed to the MFN principle by which they undertook to accord to any GATT member the same treatment as they accorded to their most favoured trading partner.

The GATT objectives were to be achieved by a range of measures:

1 *Non-discrimination*: This involved ensuring that nations did not discriminate in their trade and treated all other nations equally. Both the MFN and an agreement by GATT members not to introduce any new preferences were to be the means for eliminating discrimination.

2 *Open markets*: Signatories agreed that any forms of protection they implemented would be transparent to all and not hidden; that they would work towards reducing tariffs and that, once reduced, these tariffs would not be subsequently increased; and that restrictions on the quantities of a product allowed to be imported would only be imposed if a country was experiencing serious balance of payments problems.

3 *Fair trade*: All the world's exporters were to have the chance to compete with each other on fair and equal terms. To this end, export subsidies on manufactures were prohibited and limits were imposed on subsidisation of primary products.

4 *Settlement of trading disputes*: If both parties to the dispute were GATT members, then they were required to consult with each other. If they could not settle the dispute by consultation, then the GATT would arbitrate the issue.

5 *Stability and predictability*: All members were to facilitate stable trading conditions and governments should not subject importers to constant changes in regulations or other aspects of gaining access to their markets.

# Current focus

Although earlier GATT rounds had endeavoured to update GATT rules and provisions to take into account the changing international trading scene, in reality little had changed in the two decades prior to the conclusion of the Uruguay Round in 1994. There was considerable dissatisfaction with the operation of the GATT. The less-developed nations, although members, claimed that they were disadvantaged compared to the developed nations. The GATT appeared to be unable to address issues of agricultural protectionism that resulted in inefficient agricultural producers in developed countries receiving subsidies to produce agricultural products surplus to domestic requirements. These surpluses were then dumped on world markets to the detriment of efficient producers who were mostly from the developing countries. Protection of intellectual property was another area which GATT did not cover and this was of concern to developed countries the products of which were being copied by operators in the developing countries. The growth in international trade in services was expanding faster than that of goods and was not adequately catered for by existing GATT rules. Increasingly, investment in manufacturing in the overseas country was the alternative to supply of goods and this facet of international activity also was not covered in the GATT. Finally, there was increasing dissatisfaction with the effectiveness of the GATT in resolving disputes.

During the period of the Uruguay Round considerable lobbying took place among like-minded countries, and groupings were formed as a means of applying pressure. One such group was the Cairns Group of non-subsidising agricultural nations. An Australian initiative, this group of 14 agricultural producers, which met regularly and lobbied aggressively, were successful in focusing attention on the rise of agricultural protectionism.

These shortcomings led to the Uruguay Round. This was the toughest of the eight GATT rounds and lasted seven and a half years. The results represented a major achievement in addressing the shortcomings mentioned above. However, there is always a gap between the rhetoric and the implementation. The most important outcomes are listed below:

- *Agriculture*: Because an average cut of 36% in tariffs was agreed to, access for agricultural products to other markets was likely to improve significantly. In addition, the extent of subsidisation of agricultural products for export was curtailed both by agreement to reduce measures to support agricultural production by 20% and by the cutting of export subsidies by 36%.

- *Industry*: Tariffs on most industrial products were reduced by one-third, which was considerably in excess of tariff cuts negotiated at previous GATT rounds.

- *Services*: For the first time international trade in services was to be governed by the rules of fair trade. This is the fastest growing segment of world trade. Seventy nations entered into binding commitments as far as their trade in services was concerned. This resulted in the General Agreement on Trade in Services (GATS).

- *Intellectual property*: A new agreement covering intellectual property, Trade Related Aspects of Intellectual Property Rights (TRIPS), was drawn up, providing both specific rules and rules for dispute resolution. Because individual countries had different laws and varying degrees of enforcement where a breach of intellectual property was concerned, transition periods were provided to enable countries to bring their practices into line with the provisions of the TRIPS agreement. The transition periods were one year for developed countries, five years for developing countries and 11 years for the least developed of the developing countries.

- *Investment*. A new agreement covering investment (TRIMS) was arrived at. This limited the scope for foreign governments to attach onerous conditions to investment approvals or link such approvals to receipt of other advantages, which might be viewed as being discriminatory. The importance of addressing investment on a multilateral basis is highlighted by the creation of some 2500 bilateral investment treaties in the decade to 2006 and the fact that, in the two decades prior to 2006, global investment expanded faster than global trade.

The Uruguay Round resulted in the formation of the WTO, which commenced with 120 members. This number has now risen to 150 and there are other countries seeking membership. The WTO has inherited a substantial agenda for implementation from the Uruguay Round. Some of the major issues confronting the WTO are its focus on single-sector negotiations such as telecommunications and providing less opportunity for trade-offs and mutual concessions. It will also have to grapple with the growing friction between the USA and the EU over issues of extraterritoriality, such as trade with Cuba and Libya, and the feeling of many developing countries that they got relatively little out of the Uruguay Round.

## Australian involvement

Australia was pleased with the final outcome of the Uruguay Round. The general outcomes mentioned earlier in the chapter would result in specific benefits to Australia as outlined below:

- *Agriculture*: No subsidised beef would be shipped to Australia's growing markets in Asia; no duties would be imposed on sheep meat exports to the EU; the markets for rice in both Japan and South Korea were to be opened; the USA would no longer sell subsidised rice to these markets and there would be greater access for Australian dairy products to the US, EU, Japanese, Thai and Malaysian markets.

- *Industry*: Access for Australian coal and metals to the EU, Japanese and Thai markets would be improved and the value of trade-weighted tariff cuts Australia received from its major trading partners were to be 55%. This meant that, on average, duties on manufactures entering the markets of Australia's major trading partners would be 55% less than was formerly the case.

- *Intellectual property*: Bringing this issue within multilateral rules of trade is likely to boost Australia's role as an innovator in intellectual property, especially in the sectors of film, music, design and patentable inventions.

In bilateral negotiations, usually anything agreed upon is matched by a concession from the other party, whereas in multilateral negotiations no reciprocal concession is required. As a small to middle-sized nation, Australia is more likely to benefit from multilateral negotiations than bilateral negotiations where it is likely to be disadvantaged by its size and lack of economic muscle. It is for this reason that the Australian government strongly supported the GATT Uruguay Round and spent so much effort lobbying to have the issue of agricultural protectionism fully addressed. The benefit of so doing is illustrated in the following example.

As an extension of this support for multilateralism, Australia wishes to see a reversal in the trend towards a weakening of the GATT rules and also wants the implementation of a dispute resolution mechanism, which will produce rapid settlements and minimise protracted trade conflicts. GATT procedures were very cumbersome and often markets were lost while protracted deliberations took place.

Research by the Australian Bureau of Agricultural and Resource Economics (ABARE) shows that cutting trade barriers and subsidies by 50% would yield a US$94 billion increase in global income. Australia's terms of trade if this were to happen would improve by about 1.4% (i.e. the prices we get for the goods sold overseas would increase by 1.4% compared with the prices we pay for our imports).

**SOURCE:** Business Review Weekly, *8 June 2001, p. 24.*

## MILLENNIUM ROUND

In order to implement the above agreed outcomes, a new round of multilateral trade talks known as the 'Millennium Round', was held in Seattle in 1999. This was a disaster and this can be attributed to a number of factors, including disenchantment with globalisation and suspicion by the developing countries that the WTO would continue the GATT tradition of being a 'rich man's club'. Despite the rhetoric, little had been done by the developed countries to address agricultural subsidies that prevented efficient agricultural producing nations (many in the developing world) from selling into developed country markets. Subsidies paid to farmers in the EU, the USA and Japan are now valued at US$29.4 billion, a figure not seen since the mid-1980s. The USA continues to hide behind the requirement that agreements made by the President had to be referred to Congress so as to delay implementation—the Clinton administration allowed the 'Fast Track Legislation' (FTL) that would overcome this anomaly to lapse in 1994. Although the FTL was restored by the current Bush administration, in reality there has been little change. The consequence is a lack of enthusiasm by a number of Asian countries for the WTO, as illustrated by their entering into free trade agreements with their trading partners. This renewed FTL again expired in June 2007 which is likely to delay decisions of the Doha Round, if any, being implemented until 2009.

The WTO, like its predecessor, is frequently called upon to resolve disputes between its members. Although the emphasis is on conciliation, it also arbitrates disputes and this activity is undertaken by the Disputes Settlement Body (DSB). This body appoints panels of experts who consider cases and make recommendations to the DSB. In the eight years to 2003, the WTO considered some 300 disputes compared with the GATT hearing only 300 disputes throughout its 47-year existence.

One issue that will pose a challenge for the WTO is the enforcement of penalties for breaches of its rules. According to the *Financial Times* of 1 September 2004 (p. 3), the WTO has allowed the EU and seven other members to impose sanctions of up to US$150 million a year on the USA for its failure to repeal a trade law declared illegal by the WTO. This was the Byrd amendment, which requires US Customs to distribute the proceeds of anti-dumping and anti-subsidies duties to the companies that initiated the cases.

## DOHA ROUND

The Doha Round began in 2001 with the objective of focusing on the needs of developing countries and addressing their areas of complaint regarding the implementation of the Uruguay Round and the issue of the use of Trade Related Aspects of Intellectual Property Rights (TRIPS) to impede their access to affordable life-saving drugs.

Items discussed at the Cancun meeting of the Doha Round were how to keep the trade talks alive, how real progress can be made to help the world's poor, how farm trade can be

One area where developing countries have been disappointed at the lack of progress has been in implementing the Trade Related Aspects of Intellectual Property Rights (TRIPS) Agreement. In theory, TRIPS should benefit both rich and poor nations alike. However, it was pushed onto the trade agenda by the USA, Europe and Japan, which hold the lion's share of world patents and whose companies wanted more protection abroad. It required the developing countries to bring their legal protection and enforcement systems up to Western levels, but to date has given them nothing in return. In fact, the recent disputes over 'copycat' life-saving drugs to treat AIDS have highlighted the gulf between developed and developing countries over patent protection and related TRIPS issues.

liberalised and how intellectual property issues can be managed so that life-saving drugs are made available to the poor at affordable prices. Also yet to be resolved is how far countries are willing to reduce trade barriers and the role and responsibility of the poor countries themselves.

However, this round of trade negotiations was suspended in 2006 due to failure to make progress on freeing up trade in farm products. China, a new member of the WTO, played a low-key role in the Doha Round, preferring to let countries such as Brazil and India represent the interests of developing nations.

## Lobbying

It is business, not government, that actually undertakes most of Australia's international trade. Therefore, the formulation and conduct of Australia's multilateral trade policies should involve the private sector. This can take the form of advisory panels involving businesspeople. In the final stages of the Uruguay Round negotiations a trade negotiations advisory group was established in Australia. Another way that private sector involvement can be achieved is for the Australian delegation to include representatives of affected businesses as advisers. Finally, industry associations such as the Australian Business Chamber have a role to play in bringing to the attention of government unfair practices, restricted access and lost opportunities that have impeded the internationalisation of their members in areas where the WTO rules and guidelines appear to have been breached.

As an alternative to settling international trade issues on a global basis, like-minded countries, usually located in the same region, can band together and improve their international trade position and negotiating strength via the resulting synergy.

## REGIONAL TRADE GROUPINGS

Regional trade groupings (RTGs) are being pursued to a greater extent than at any time during the last 50 years and today about 40% of world trade takes place under the umbrella of these RTGs. This increased focus on RTGs is a sign of loss of faith in the multilateral trade system. The move towards RTGs gained additional stimulus during the early years of the Uruguay Round when few thought that it would be successful. One of the ironies is that the USA, which has been a major champion of non-discrimination, has itself entered into a major RTG—the North American Free Trade Agreement. Given this scenario, should countries like Australia and New Zealand continue to put faith in the WTO or should it seek to become a member of a wider RTG than their Closer Economic Relations Agreement with each other?

# China embraces the world market

A topical issue for a number of years was the admission of China to the WTO. When the GATT was established, nations did not have to demonstrate their credentials on non-economic issues in order to be included as members. However, since that time some Western developed countries (especially the USA) have endeavoured to use the membership issue as a device to impose on other countries their approach to non-economic issues such as human rights and democracy. This was behind the delay in China being admitted to the WTO. It was realised, however, that China's membership would facilitate resolving trade disputes (e.g. that between Japan and China on the entry of Chinese foodstuffs).

China's accession to the WTO in December 2001 was a major step in its reintegration into the world economy. It will have a profound impact not only on East Asia, but also on the rest of the world. As a WTO member, its products will receive Most Favoured Nation (MFN) treatment. In the USA this will mean that its products will enter at an average tariff of 8% compared with 40% formerly. As Table 18.1 shows, its share of world exports and world imports is likely to rise substantially.

Table 18.1 explains why China is willing to submit itself to WTO constraints and rules. Its eagerness to be accepted into the WTO has caused it to make the most far-reaching commitments in the history of the WTO. It will move swiftly to lower tariffs on imports (on cars these will fall from 80% in 2001 to 25% in 2006). On the export side, direct export subsidies will be eliminated and China has agreed that its trading partners can use 'safeguard' procedures against a surge in imports for 12 years. It has undertaken to increase the transparency of its work practices and extend the protection of intellectual property rights. In addition, China's restrictions on foreign investment in the services sector will be eased and majority or total foreign ownership of businesses will be allowed in many cases.

| **TABLE 18.1** | **Impact of China's accession to the WTO** | | | | | |
|---|---|---|---|---|---|---|
| | China's exports as a share of world exports (%) | | | China's imports as a share of world exports (%) | | |
| | 1995 | 2005 | | 1995 | 2005 | |
| | | Without WTO | With WTO | | Without WTO | With WTO |
| Apparel | 19.6 | 18.5 | 47.1 | 1.0 | 1.1 | 3.7 |
| Textiles | 8.4 | 8.8 | 10.6 | 13.4 | 18.0 | 25.5 |
| Beverages & tobacco | 2.4 | 1.0 | 1.0 | 0.9 | 1.3 | 16.2 |
| Automobiles | 0.1 | 0.7 | 2.2 | 2.0 | 1.8 | 4.8 |
| All products | 3.7 | 4.8 | 6.8 | 3.4 | 5.3 | 6.6 |

**SOURCE:** *Ianchovichina, E., Martin, W. and Fukase, E. (2000)* Assessing the Implications of Merchandise Trade Liberalisation in China's Accession to WTO, *World Bank. Cited in* Insights, *2003, Vol. 3, No. 1, p. 6.*

As mentioned in Chapter 1 RTGs can take different forms (from simplest to complex):

- They can be preferential tariff arrangements whereby the members extend lower tariff rates to other members, but apply normal tariffs to non-members.

- They can be a grouping committed to the free trade area, where tariffs between member countries are dropped completely.

# Cambodia's accession to the WTO

Some 13 years after emerging from two decades of war and isolation, Cambodia is set to join the WTO. The likely long-term gains of doing so, however, are likely to be partially offset by short-term pain. Will Cambodia have to pay too high a price to join the global club? Anticipated gains are increased market access, non-discrimination rights and access to a dispute-settling mechanism. Membership will also boost Cambodia's poor international image and attract back foreign investors. In the longer term, membership could help the country lessen its dependence on its major foreign exchange earners of garments and tourism. The downside is that Cambodia will have to adhere to WTO requirements that it should have transparent laws and regulations. This means a crackdown on corruption and government red tape, as, if these continue unabated, the country's ability to profit from increased market access under the WTO will be severely restricted. It is joining the WTO even though it lacks many laws considered as essential, such as bankruptcy and incorporation statutes. New negotiating procedures have been introduced by the WTO to help developing countries join it more quickly. Cambodia's entry is an indication that the new negotiating procedures for least developed countries are proving effective. Cambodia's ratification, largely driven by new WTO rules for textiles and apparel that could have stifled Cambodian industry in these sectors, imposes pressure on Vietnam, which could now lose international business for its textile and apparel industries.

SOURCES: *Adapted from the Bradsher, K. (2004) 'Cambodia legislature approves WTO entry'*, International Herald Tribune, *1 September, p. 14; and Sloan, B. (2004) 'A whole new world'*, Far Eastern Economic Review, *2 September, pp. 18–19.*

In November 2004, Australia and New Zealand commenced negotiations with the Association of South East Asian Nations (ASEAN), leading to a free trade agreement (FTA). The FTA will cover goods, services and investment and build on the existing WTO commitments of each of the parties. This proposal is still under negotiation, but it is planned to fully implement the arrangement by 2014. It would complement Australia's existing bilateral FTAs with Singapore, Thailand and Malaysia.

SOURCE: *Adapted from Department of Foreign Affairs and Trade (2006) ASEAN: Building an Economic Community, Department of Foreign Affairs and Trade, Canberra, p. 71.*

- They can be a customs union in which members have standard external barriers to imports.
- They can form a common market where labour and capital flow freely across members' borders.
- They can be an economic union where there is coordination of fiscal and monetary policies.

## Purpose

An RTG is a preferential economic arrangement between a group of countries. This arrangement is intended to reduce intra-regional barriers to trade in goods, services or investment, or all three. It stimulates trade between members of the group. Successful RTGs usually contain members with similar per capita GNP, geographic proximity, compatible trading regimes or a political commitment to membership of a regional organisation.

There are a number of factors that have stimulated the formation of RTGs. These are listed below:

- *Political*: A joining of forces in trade activities may be viewed as a prelude to some form of political unity. This was an important reason underlying the moves towards European economic unity. It is likely that the former Centrally Planned Economies in Europe were admitted to the European Union for this reason. It is also an underlying reason for the recent signing of a free trade agreement between Australia and the USA.

- *Trade, economics and investment*: This results from a desire to eliminate unnecessary customs and transport procedures, to reduce technological and regulatory barriers to production and to rationalise and concentrate production to achieve economies of scale. Economic factors also come into play, particularly when an RTG moves from a free trade area to an economic union. For example, underlying the transition from the European Economic Community to an economic union were issues such as control over interest rates, inflation and employment. RTGs are also motivated by a desire to achieve gains from intensified competition within the wider economic grouping and attract foreign investment to the wider region because of its enhanced attractiveness as a market.

- *Globalisation*: The increasing movement towards globalisation is resulting in greater mobility in factors of production. Firms wish to operate in wider markets than in single countries and RTGs provide insider status in a much larger market.

- *Marketing*: Reasons in this category include the need for multinationals to access consumers in new countries. As domestic markets become saturated, smaller nations and their companies are defending themselves against global competition by securing the protection of being a member of an RTG and firms are rationalising their production within a region by having separate plants in each country produce separate components of the final product. In addition, other factors include the willingness of nations to cede partial sovereignty to supra-national organisations so as to obtain benefits in international trade, increased consumer mobility and convergence of their needs.

## History

Since World War II the formation of a regional grouping in Europe has been the most prominent example of the move towards RTGs and has created a situation which others sought to emulate. There are now around 35 such groupings in operation. They can take a number of different forms. These forms involve varying degrees of commitment and the surrendering of differing degrees of national sovereignty. In terms of commitment and lessening of national sovereignty, forms include preferential trade agreements, such as the Caribbean Basin Initiative; free trade areas, such as the North American Free Trade Agreement; customs unions, such as the South African Customs Union; common markets, such as the Central American Common Market; and economic unions, such as the European Union.

RTGs are here to stay. They discriminate explicitly and implicitly against outsiders by granting preferences to member countries only. They are not a violation of the WTO as long as barriers are not raised against third countries—however, most RTGs do involve such barriers. Despite this apparent breach the formation of RTGs has not been strongly contested. This is because very few members of the WTO are not members of an RTG and some RTGs also have a political agenda, such as the promotion of democracy in their region.

# Operation

RTGs can vary between two extremes. At one extreme, they aim to free up trade, they are open to new members and they have common agreements covering all members. As such they complement rather than inhibit free trade. This type of grouping usually takes place between countries that are natural partners in that they are contiguous and undertake a substantial percentage of their overall international trade with each other. The Closer Economic Relations (CER) Agreement between Australia and New Zealand is an example. These types of RTGs are known as GATT+ types on the presumption that the reduction of barriers is negotiated by like-minded participants and extended on an MFN basis to all other WTO members.

At the other extreme are RTGs that are limited in product coverage, have different rules for different countries, are antagonistic to outsiders and only admit new members on discriminatory conditions. The European Union is an example of this type. Those RTGs that limit free trade are often referred to as 'hub and spoke' agreements as they are usually between a large country and several smaller countries, as is the case with the North American Free Trade Agreement. These RTGs are more likely to resist rather than pursue multilateral trade liberalisation. Figure 18.2 shows the main regional trading groupings.

RTGs can be viewed from both an insider and an outsider perspective. The perspective of a firm already operating within an RTG or wishing to operate in a region will be different from that of a firm outside a region wishing to trade with countries in the region.

## INSIDER PERSPECTIVE

The insider perspective involves considerations as to how to expand business, where to produce, the potential for rationalising operations and opportunities for standardisation:

- *Expansion*: One attraction of RTGs to firms is the resulting access to a larger market. There is also the potential for the firm to establish itself in one country in the grouping and, once successful there, expand to other countries in the group.

- *Production*: The next decision involves deciding which of the member countries the Australian firm should begin operation in. This situation is illustrated in International Highlight 18.4.

- *Rationalisation*: If the Australian company is already operating in several countries within the newly formed RTG, then the formation of the RTG provides the firm with the opportunity to rationalise its existing operations.

- *Standardisation*: Associated with the potential for rationalisation is the opportunity for standardisation offered by the RTG. Instead of producing different products for each market in the group it may be possible to produce the same product or at least to reduce the differences because of the likelihood of increasing homogenisation of demand within the group. The potential for standardisation will vary according to the nature of the product, the racial composition of the region and differences in per capita GDP, religion, climate, stage of industrial development, languages spoken and levels of education.

Considering the marketing mix variables, with product there will be a need to adjust positioning strategy of brands because of differences in strategy between countries in the

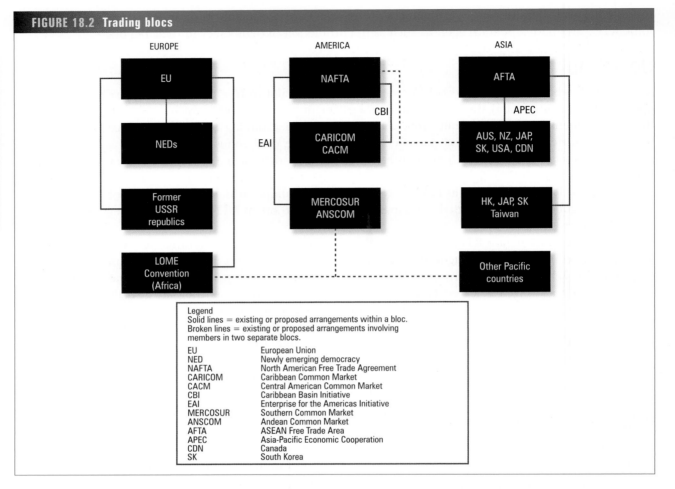

**FIGURE 18.2 Trading blocs**

Legend
Solid lines = existing or proposed arrangements within a bloc.
Broken lines = existing or proposed arrangements involving members in two separate blocs.

| | |
|---|---|
| EU | European Union |
| NED | Newly emerging democracy |
| NAFTA | North American Free Trade Agreement |
| CARICOM | Caribbean Common Market |
| CACM | Central American Common Market |
| CBI | Caribbean Basin Initiative |
| EAI | Enterprise for the Americas Initiative |
| MERCOSUR | Southern Common Market |
| ANSCOM | Andean Common Market |
| AFTA | ASEAN Free Trade Area |
| APEC | Asia-Pacific Economic Cooperation |
| CDN | Canada |
| SK | South Korea |

group—for example, Palmolive is positioned as a beauty soap in Italy and as a family soap in the UK. With price, reductions will be possible because of the absence of tariff and non-tariff barriers. Tax harmonisation within the group and the need for price coordination in the light of differences in affordability across member countries will also be a consideration. As far as promotion is concerned, the need for multilingual sales personnel and executives who can operate in all member countries will increase. Also, media focus may need to switch from national media to regional media and from national facilitators such as advertising agencies and market research agencies to firms competent to operate across the region. Finally, with distribution, the RTG will eliminate border controls on transportation and reduce grey markets within the region.

## OUTSIDER PERSPECTIVE

If it is possible, the ideal situation from the perspective of a firm in a country outside the RTG is to lobby its own government to bring pressure to bear on the overseas governments to exclude from the arrangement products currently exported to countries in the new RTG. For example, most products Australia supplies to ASEAN countries are excluded from the ASEAN Free Trade Area arrangement. Where this is not possible the greatest worry to the outsider is loss of a traditional market because competitors within the new group no longer face the same barriers

## 18.4 INTERNATIONAL HIGHLIGHT

# What should Ansell do?

The Ansell Company, manufacturers of medical and industrial gloves and condoms, hypothetically wishes to establish a presence in ASEAN. Should Ansell:

- be close to the source of its major raw material, which is rubber? If so, then it should commence operations in Malaysia or Thailand;

- locate where labour is cheapest? If so, then it should set up in the Philippines or Indonesia;

- commence business where the commercial infrastructure is best? If so, then Singapore would be best;

- select the country with the greatest political stability? If so, then Singapore would be the most attractive location;

- begin production where the domestic demand is largest? If so, then Indonesia would be preferable;

- set up in the country which has the most preferential arrangements with export markets outside the RTG? If so, then Singapore would be desirable;

- locate in the country with the best capital market so that additional funds can be mobilised if necessary? If so, then Singapore would be the favoured location; or finally,

- establish operations in the country that would be the best distribution hub for the RTG as a whole? If so, then again Singapore would be the most attractive location.

as the outsider. This problem caused considerable concern when the UK entered the European Common Market and Australian products were no longer accorded preferential entry to the UK market under the British Commonwealth Preference Scheme. In this circumstance the challenge is to acquire insider status. Possible ways of achieving this are as follows:

- the Australian government becomes a member of the RTG;

- the Australian government applies for associate membership. A number of former colonies and small countries in the region obtained associate membership of the European Community (e.g. Malta prior to its becoming a full member in 2002);

- Australia secures a continuation of privileged access or negotiates phased-down arrangements, as New Zealand was able to do when the European Common Market was formed;

- Australian components are assembled in one of the member countries. The Japanese automobile manufacturers achieved this with their automotive transplant factories in the European Community;

- the Australian firm forms a strategic alliance with a firm already operating inside the RTG. This could take the form of a manufacturing under licence arrangement (MUL); or

- manufacture in a country that is a member of the RTG. This could involve acquiring a firm already there or entering into a joint venture.

## Current focus

Because of the momentum with the formation of RTGs and fear of the isolation of not being a member of one of them, countries in increasing numbers are seeking membership of existing RTGs. Figure 18.3 shows how the original 'triad' of the EU, North America and Japan has expanded to the North American Free Trade Agreement (NAFTA), Western Europe and Japan, Australia and the Asian 'tiger' economies. The figure also shows South and Central America seeking to join NAFTA, Central and Eastern Europe seeking to join Western Europe (which they have now done) and developing countries in Asia seeking to join Japan, Australia and the 'tigers'. The potential for expansion of RTGs is illustrated by the Third Summit of the Americas in Quebec City, held 20–22 April 2001. The agenda included discussions on expanding NAFTA to include all countries (34) from the Bering Strait to Cape Horn—800 million people and a combined GDP of US$11 trillion, making it the largest free trade zone on the planet.

Expansion of RTGs can bring with it a host of problems, as illustrated by the proposed enlargement of the EU as shown in Figure 18.4. The EU admitted 10 new members on 1 May 2004 and its membership increased from 15 to 25 nations. The newly admitted were Cyprus, the Czech Republic, Estonia, Hungary, Poland, Slovenia, Latvia, Lithuania, Malta and Slovakia. Bulgaria and Romania joined in 2007, bringing membership to 27 countries. Many people within the current EU view the enlargement as a vehicle for the creation of a homogenous superstate that will be marked by loss of national identities, national cultures and national languages. However, in the same way that China's membership of the WTO was delayed until it modified its political and legal systems, countries wishing to join established RTGs are also having to establish their credentials in non-economic areas, as was the case with Bulgaria trying to become a member of the European Union (EU).

## Australian involvement

From Australia's perspective, recent trends in the formation of RTGs that are of most interest are outlined below.

The EU originated with the formation of the European Economic Community (EEC) in 1957 as an outcome of the Treaty of Rome. When the UK joined the EEC in 1973 Australia lost its major market for agricultural exports and faced new competition in other traditional markets because the Common Agricultural Policy (CAP) resulted in dumping surpluses of

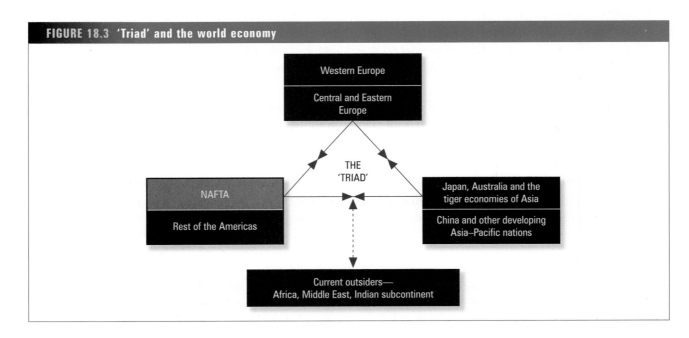

**FIGURE 18.3 'Triad' and the world economy**

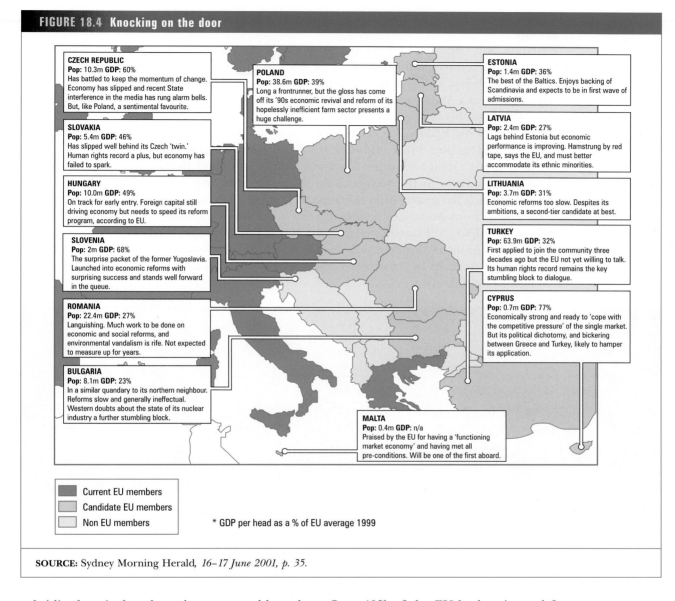

**FIGURE 18.4 Knocking on the door**

**CZECH REPUBLIC**
**Pop:** 10.3m **GDP:** 60%
Has battled to keep the momentum of change. Economy has slipped and recent State interference in the media has rung alarm bells. But, like Poland, a sentimental favourite.

**SLOVAKIA**
**Pop:** 5.4m **GDP:** 46%
Has slipped well behind its Czech 'twin.' Human rights record a plus, but economy has failed to spark.

**HUNGARY**
**Pop:** 10.0m **GDP:** 49%
On track for early entry. Foreign capital still driving economy but needs to speed its reform program, according to EU.

**SLOVENIA**
**Pop:** 2m **GDP:** 68%
The surprise packet of the former Yugoslavia. Launched into economic reforms with surprising success and stands well forward in the queue.

**ROMANIA**
**Pop:** 22.4m **GDP:** 27%
Languishing. Much work to be done on economic and social reforms, and environmental vandalism is rife. Not expected to measure up for years.

**BULGARIA**
**Pop:** 8.1m **GDP:** 23%
In a similar quandary to its northern neighbour. Reforms slow and generally ineffectual. Western doubts about the state of its nuclear industry a further stumbling block.

**POLAND**
**Pop:** 38.6m **GDP:** 39%
Long a frontrunner, but the gloss has come off its '90s economic revival and reform of its hopelessly inefficient farm sector presents a huge challenge.

**MALTA**
**Pop:** 0.4m **GDP:** n/a
Praised by the EU for having a 'functioning market economy' and having met all pre-conditions. Will be one of the first aboard.

**ESTONIA**
**Pop:** 1.4m **GDP:** 36%
The best of the Baltics. Enjoys backing of Scandinavia and expects to be in first wave of admissions.

**LATVIA**
**Pop:** 2.4m **GDP:** 27%
Lags behind Estonia but economic performance is improving. Hamstrung by red tape, says the EU, and must better accommodate its ethnic minorities.

**LITHUANIA**
**Pop:** 3.7m **GDP:** 31%
Economic reforms too slow. Despite its ambitions, a second-tier candidate at best.

**TURKEY**
**Pop:** 63.9m **GDP:** 32%
First applied to join the community three decades ago but the EU not yet willing to talk. Its human rights record remains the key stumbling block to dialogue.

**CYPRUS**
**Pop:** 0.7m **GDP:** 77%
Economically strong and ready to 'cope with the competitive pressure' of the single market. But its political dichotomy, and bickering between Greece and Turkey, likely to hamper its application.

Current EU members
Candidate EU members
Non EU members

\* GDP per head as a % of EU average 1999

**SOURCE:** Sydney Morning Herald, *16–17 June 2001, p. 35.*

subsidised agricultural products on world markets. Over 40% of the EU budget is used for the CAP which supports agriculture that yields less than 4% of GDP for the European Union ('The battle of the budget', *Economist*, 25 March 2005, p. 47).

The North American Free Trade Agreement was an outcome of the US–Canada Free Trade Area of 1989. When Mexico joined in 1993 and the NAFTA came into being, the nature of the RTG changed from one involving two countries of similar economic backgrounds and considerable economic dependency to one that now included a totally different partner with a much weaker economy.

ASEAN established the ASEAN Free Trade Area (AFTA) in 1992. Its aim was that by 2003 all tariff barriers for non-agricultural products would be removed, as would most non-tariff barriers on these items. It also aimed to increase the volume of intra-ASEAN trade. It employs the Common External Preferential Tariff System that operates in two phases, depending on the prior tariff level. Its formation was a reaction by ASEAN members to changes in the world economy.

Vietnam was admitted in 1995 and Myanmar, Laos and Cambodia in 1997. ASEAN and China have agreed to establish a free trade area by 2010 and AFTA indicated that it would begin talks with Japan, South Korea, Australia and New Zealand by 2006 on the creation of a free trade area ('Asean sets trade-talk dates', *Asian Wall Street Journal*, 6 September 2004, p. A3), although this has yet to be realised.

The Asia-Pacific Economic Cooperation Group (APEC) was the result of an initiative in 1989 attributed to then Prime Minister Hawke. It was originally envisaged as a consultative body akin to the Organisation for Economic Cooperation and Development (OECD) where like-minded countries in the region could discuss current and anticipated trade problems. Since its genesis it has grown from the original 12 member countries to currently 21 members. Its conception from Australia's perspective was a reaction to 'outsider' status with respect to the EU and NAFTA. APEC is located in Australia's perceived area of trade expansion and trade surplus as the countries involved account for two-thirds of Australia's trade. Since the Bogor declaration in 1994, APEC has moved towards becoming a Pacific Area Community rather than a consultative body.

A recent APEC initiative is the proposal to create a 'single window' to reduce the paperwork now needed to move containers around member countries—paperwork that is required in order to address health, quarantine, customs and security issues. Under the proposed change there will be one clearance—a Secure Trade APEC Region (STAR) certificate that will save billions of dollars for the shipment of the 3.5 million containers around the region each year. Also proposed is an APEC nations business travel card to function as a visa for preferential travel for 17 of the APEC countries.

SOURCE: *Adapted from Akerman, P. (2007) 'Parochial view gets APEC in the eye'*, Daily Telegraph, *29 May, p. 16.*

APEC is still evolving and, unlike other RTGs, has little other than shared economic interests to bind its members together. Its members face no joint security threat: they have no common borders and no cultural or ethnic similarity. APEC represents 2.5 billion people and accounts for about 60% of the world's economic activity. Its focus has been expanded to include non-trade issues that have an impact on trade, such as international terrorism and its effect on transport security. Figure 18.5 shows the members of APEC and illustrates the diversity in its membership. At each of its annual talks a specific issue is addressed. At the talks in 2004 in Chile the focus was on flexible foreign exchange systems—timely in view of the dispute between the USA and China on this issue. APEC points the way to a future development in RTGs—that of RTGs between developing and developed countries rather than just between developed or just between developing countries. This is also evident in the case of the expansion of the EU from 15 to 25 members in 2004 where the majority of the new members were developing countries, in the inclusion of Mexico into NAFTA and in the current talks about a FTA between ASEAN, Australia and New Zealand.

The concern from Australia's point of view regarding RTGs is that, if everyone else is becoming a member of an RTG, can Australia afford to be left out? Although Australia has for many years been a member of a grouping with New Zealand, this is a very small grouping

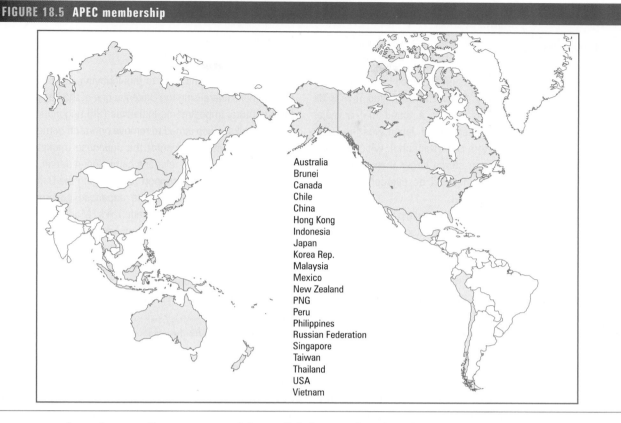

**FIGURE 18.5  APEC membership**

Australia
Brunei
Canada
Chile
China
Hong Kong
Indonesia
Japan
Korea Rep.
Malaysia
Mexico
New Zealand
PNG
Peru
Philippines
Russian Federation
Singapore
Taiwan
Thailand
USA
Vietnam

that accounts for only a small percentage of Australia's international trade. One possibility is for Australia to seek membership of the ASEAN Free Trade Area (AFTA) as already mentioned. Initial overtures in this connection did not met with an encouraging response because some ASEAN nations do not regard Australia as part of their region. This explains why Australia has been an enthusiastic supporter of APEC in its transition from a consultative group to becoming a free trade area.

## Lobbying

RTGs such as APEC provide Australian firms with an opportunity to have the Australian government raise problems of access or operation in member countries. APEC meets once a year at heads of government level, and businesspeople are often included in the delegation as advisers or form a separate group and hold parallel talks with business interests at the same time. Firms should lobby the Australian government to join an RTG (on either a full or associate membership basis) if:

* creation of an RTG is likely to result in loss of an established overseas market;

* creation of an RTG is likely to result in loss of markets in third countries because these countries have been accorded associate membership of the RTG;

* the firm's market in Australia is under threat because the new RTG results in more competitive imports; or

* the combined market of the RTG is now much more attractive.

## Toys R Us

The Japanese market is renowned for its numerous barriers to entry. When the US-based Toys R Us investigated this market it found that a major impediment to operating in Japan was the Large Scale Retail Store Law (Daitenho), which made it virtually impossible to open stores larger than 450 square metres. Unless this problem could be overcome the firm could not enter this new market.

Its first move was to form a partnership with McDonald's of Japan, which had excellent contacts with Japanese politicians and officials, especially those in the Ministry of International Trade and Industry (MITI). The key factor, however, was the joint approach (adopted with the US government) to persuade the Japanese government to liberalise the Daitenho. Due to this lobbying, Toys R Us was able to make liberalising the Daitenho one of the key issues in the Structural Impediments Initiatives (SII) negotiations with Japan—talks which aimed to remove non-tariff barriers faced by US firms wishing to enter the Japanese market. At the same time, via a public relations campaign in Japan, the firm actively sought popular support for changing the Daitenho so that it would be easier for the Japanese government to concede on this issue in the trade talks. Modification of the law enabled the US firm to commence operations in Japan. The second store was opened by then US President George Bush Senior during his state visit to Japan, as a symbol of how the SII negotiations had begun to tear down structural barriers to trade and investment in Japan.

**SOURCE:** Cohen, L. (1997) *Si-Well International, presentation to the Association of Japanese Business Studies Conference, Washington DC,* 13–15 June.

Traditionally, countries have negotiated trade issues directly with each other and if issues cannot be settled in multilateral forums or within RTGs to which both parties belong, then negotiations on a bilateral basis are the most likely vehicle to achieve resolution.

## BILATERAL TRADE RELATIONS

This is the oldest and most common form of international trade relations. Issues of 'fair' trade and market access are often dealt with bilaterally, outside the scrutiny of the WTO and in ways that may be at variance with WTO rules. One of these rules is that of non-discrimination, and, by their very nature, bilateral agreements tend to discriminate in favour of both parties. Because some of the bilateral undertakings entered into are not always a matter of public record the WTO principle of transparency is sometimes breached in bilateral trade relations.

## Purpose

Bilateral trade relations are used as a vehicle for addressing trade problems between two countries. When issues are not being addressed fully by the WTO or its predecessor the GATT, then nations may address these issues on a bilateral basis in order to achieve a more immediate result. As mentioned, during the Uruguay Round a number of countries became frustrated with the slow pace of discussions and attempted to address areas of friction, such as services, foreign investment and intellectual property rights, on a bilateral basis. This frustration is again on the rise following the failure of the WTO meeting in Seattle, the current pause in the Doha Round and overall the lack of progress in implementing the Uruguay Round outcomes. The way bilateral arrangements operate to solve problems between trading partners is illustrated in the following:

Subsidies and collusion are in theory anathema to the WTO, but are regularly practised by its members. Two of its members, Canada and Brazil, have for years not only dominated the world market for a category of small jet aircraft (Bombadier and Embraer respectively), but have also been arguing over subsidies that their governments pay to these manufacturers of regional jet aircraft. On many occasions each side has complained about the other to the WTO. Agreement between the two is now in prospect and is likely to result in a bilateral deal. This will enshrine the continuance of subsidies that are against WTO principles and also allow both parties to collude to obtain a larger share of the global market for regional jets.

**SOURCE:** *Adapted from Tuck, S. and Marotte, B. (2004) 'Canada, Brazil to resume subsidy talks',* Globe and Mail, *Toronto, 30 September 2004, p. B3.*

## Operation

A bilateral trade agreement is an agreement between two countries to regulate the conduct of their trade to the mutual benefit of both parties. It seeks to provide stable conditions for market access on equal terms. These agreements are usually entered into between countries that share a large volume of mutual trade or are viewed as having the potential to develop significant mutual trade. The basic bilateral agreement is based on MFN principles and most agreements follow a standard pattern. Within this context, bilateral trade agreements cover customs duties and internal taxes, issues relating to import and export licences, and other issues of mutual interest. However, they go beyond these principles by the use of words such as 'take measures to facilitate, strengthen and diversify so as to expand trade further'. This type of statement implies that the parties to the agreement may discriminate against outsiders to their mutual benefit. Figure 18.6, a trade agreement between the government of Australia and the government of the Hashemite Kingdom of Jordan, is a typical bilateral trade agreement of the MFN type. After a number of general articles, it lists products that each country would like to be a focus of its trade with the other.

Bilateral trade agreements may be called by other names, such as the Basic Treaty of Friendship and Cooperation (as between Australia and Japan in 1977) or Agreement on Trade, Economic and Technical Cooperation (as between the government of Australia and the government of the Republic of Turkey in 1988). Bilateral agreements may be entered into for specific commercial purposes, such as the agreement between the government of the Kingdom of Thailand and the government of the Federal Republic of Germany concerning financial cooperation (1983). The agreement between Australia and the Republic of Hungary titled the Reciprocal Promotion and Protection of Investments (1992) is another example. Bilateral agreements, because of their 'umbrella' nature, tend to remain in force a considerable period of time. They may be updated by the addition of a supplementary document. An example is the Exchange of Notes (1973) between Australia and Canada, constituting an agreement concerning the future operation of the Trade Agreement of 12 February 1960.

The implementation of bilateral trade agreements is usually via regular rounds of trade discussions held alternately in each country. Basically, the trade agreement serves as an umbrella under which discussions between the two countries on trade matters can take place. It is at these discussions that specific problems can be raised. The Australian firm needs to ensure that it has input into the matters on the agenda for the discussion. Often this can be

## FIGURE 18.6 Trade agreement

Department of Foreign Affairs and Trade
Canberra

# Trade Agreement

between the

# Government of Australia

and the

# Government of the Hashemite Kingdom of Jordan

(Amman, 14 February 1988)

*Entry into force: 14 February 1988*

TREATY SERIES 1988
No. 4

Australian Government Publishing Service
Canberra

2

### Article 2

1.     For the purpose of promoting trade between the two countries, each Party shall, within its competence and subject to the laws and regulations of each country, encourage and facilitate:

(a)   the interchange of commercial and technical representatives, groups and delegations;

(b)   the holding of, and participation in, trade fairs, trade exhibitions and other promotion activities in the fields of trade and technology in its country by enterprises and organisations from the other country,

2.     Each Party shall, in accordance with the laws and regulations of its country, exempt from the payment of import duties and taxes, articles for display at fairs and exhibitions, as well as samples of goods for advertising purposes, imported from the country of the other. Such articles and samples shall not be disposed of otherwise than by re-exportation except with prior approval of the competent authorities in the importing country and the payment of appropriate import duties and taxes, if any.

### Article 3

1.     The Parties shall, as appropriate, and subject to the laws, regulations and policies of their respective countries in force from time to time, encourage and facilitate the development of industrial and technical co-operation, including investments on a joint venture or other basis, between relevant enterprises and organisations in their respective countries.

1

TRADE AGREEMENT BETWEEN THE GOVERNMENT OF AUSTRALIA AND THE GOVERNMENT OF THE HASHEMITE KINGDOM OF JORDAN

The Government of Australia and the Government of the Hashemite Kingdom of Jordan, hereinafter referred to as the Parties, desiring to promote and expand mutually beneficial trade and trade relations between Australia and Jordan,

Have agreed as follows:

### Article 1

1.     Each Party shall, subject to the laws and regulations in force in its country, facilitate as far as possible imports from, and exports to, the territory of the other, particularly of the goods and services enumerated in Schedules A and B annexed to this Agreement.

2.     This Article shall not be construed in such a manner as to limit the exchanges of goods and services between the two countries to the goods and services enumerated in Schedules A and B annexed to this Agreement. The Schedules to this Agreement may be amended by mutual consent at any time by an exchange of letters between the Parties.

3

### Article

2.     The decision to enter into individual co-operation projects and the contractual arrangement for their implementation shall be the responsibility of the relevant enterprises and organisations, subject to the laws, regulations and policies of their respective countries in force from time to time.

### Article 4

All payments arising from trade between the two countries shall be effected in mutually acceptable convertible currency subject to the foreign exchange laws in force from time to time in the two countries.

### Article 5

1.     For the purpose of promoting the aims of this Agreement, a Joint Trade Committee, which shall consist of representatives designated by the respective Parties, is hereby established.

2.     The Committee shall meet as often as may be mutually agreed, alternately in Australia and Jordan.

3.     The Committee shall examine the state of trade between the two countries, shall explore measures for the expansion of mutual trade and of industrial and technical co-operation between relevant commercial enterprises and organisations, and shall seek solutions to problems which may arise in the course of the development of trading relations between the two countries.

achieved through membership of groups involved in advising the official delegation. In the case of Australia, members may be drawn from the relevant panel of the Trade Development Council or the appropriate business cooperation committee or chamber of commerce between Australia and the other country. There are about 30 Business Councils, Business Cooperation Committees or Chambers of Commerce with either a country or a regional focus.

A bilateral trade agreement can also operate as an umbrella for the discussion of a single major issue. This was the case with the negotiations between Australia and South Korea in 1993 on beef access.

Bilateral trade relations can be advanced by regular meetings of officials from both countries. Often these are called joint trade committees. Increasingly, the 'official' talks take place at the same time as talks between business groups from both countries. At the conclusion of both sets of talks, officials and businesspeople come together for a joint meeting. The Thai–Australia talks in Chiang Mai in late 1988 operated along the above lines and paved the way for the visit of the Australian Prime Minister to Thailand early the following year.

Bilateral trade relations can also be advanced by regular meetings of ministers from both countries. Known as joint ministerial meetings, these meetings provide opportunity for private sector involvement. There may be opportunity for businesspeople to accompany the ministerial party as advisers, as happened with the 1994 visit to Vietnam by Australia's Foreign Minister.

Finally, bilateral trade relations can be advanced by visits of appropriate ministers to the other country. When the then Australian Deputy Prime Minister and Minister for Trade, Tim Fischer, visited Latin America in June 1996 he raised the issue of the impact on Australian coal supply of Chile's agreement with Canada, added credibility to Australian promotion of mining equipment, negotiated improved air links between Australia and the region and raised Australia's concern over Brazil's 25% tax on shipping freight.

## 18.6 INTERNATIONAL HIGHLIGHT

# Free trade with strings attached

When the Australian Prime Minister went to Washington in September 2001 he was expecting the Americans to provide him with a free trade agreement (FTA) that would boost his chances at the polls. Interrupted by the events of 11 September, PM Howard again visited the USA in February 2002. Given that the Americans have a history of tough trade negotiating dating back to when they purchased Manhattan from the Indians for a handful of beads and trinkets, Howard faced the possibility that he might come away with a document of good intentions that would amount to nothing in the end or that he would be confronted with a protracted negotiation haggle in a situation where the dice were loaded in America's favour.

For the negotiations that followed, the USA wanted Australia to dispense with its price caps on drugs supplied under its Pharmaceutical Benefits Scheme (PBS), a removal of stringent quarantine rules, abolition of local content rules for Australian TV shows, modification of labelling laws for genetically modified foods and an investment agreement that neutered or removed the Foreign Investment Review Board (FIRB). Selling such demands to the electorate in Australia posed real problems. With foot-and-mouth disease, SARS and CJD causing global concern, it would be a brave politician who would argue against Australia's tough quarantine laws. With PBS subsidies imposing a burgeoning burden on the Australian health budget, siphoning off taxpayers' funds to the coffers of transnational pharmaceutical companies was unlikely to be an electoral winner. The Americans could argue that local content rules discriminate against Hollywood studios, but those rules are permitted under international trade agreements so as to stop other countries being swamped by cut-price Hollywood TV programs that are sold cheaply abroad once their costs have been recovered in the huge US market. Howard could not support a situation whereby popular Australia TV dramas would be axed so as to allow the spread of US cultural imperialism in the name of free trade. Likewise, he could not side with US chemical companies that don't like Australia's labelling laws on genetically modified foods. To get rid of the FIRB would most likely result in reduced employment and investments the value of which to the Australian economy is marginal.

Even if the Prime Minister had been willing to 'sell the family silver' in pursuit of a trade agreement with the US, what could he realistically expect to receive in return? Given the Coalition's falling support in the bush, something for the farmers, such as a reduction on barriers to our agricultural exports entering the market, would have top priority. Logic would appear to be on Australia's side as, according to a report to the US Congress in February 2001, government subsidies account for 47% of farm incomes in the United States. Australian sugar exporters face stiff barriers erected to protect local producers, many of whom come from Florida, the state that was the key to President George W. Bush's electoral victory. Also critical in supporting Bush are the mid-west farm-belt states which benefit from the massive subsidies on beef and grain. On the manufacturing front, opening the American market for Western Australian and Tasmanian fast catamaran ferries could be electorally popular. This too may prove to be illusory, as the chances of

Congress changing the *Jones Act* that prohibits the importation of foreign-built ships is remote.

The question may be asked: should we have a free trade agreement with the US? After all it continues to be our second largest trading partner and our largest source of imports. Given that Australia's deficit in merchandise trade with the USA in 2003 was more than A$11 billion, some may be tempted to suggest that instead of a free trade agreement we should stop trading with them—but that is not the way of the world!

In November 2004, after much negotiation, it was 'full steam ahead' for ratification of the agreement. Both Howard and Bush were re-elected with increased majorities and this has resulted in diminished opposition to the FTA in both countries. Coming into force on 1 January 2005, this agreement:

* eliminated duties on over 97% of US tariff items for Australian non-agricultural exports;

* reduced tariffs on 66% of Australian agricultural items to zero and on a further 9% within four years;

* provided full access for Australian goods and services to the US government procurement market; which is worth A$200 billion a year; and

* enhanced legal protections that guarantee market access and non-discriminatory treatment for Australian providers of services.

It is estimated that the signing of this agreement could boost Australian GDP by A$6 billion within a decade.

**SOURCE:** *Adapted from Department of Foreign Affairs and Trade (2005a)* Australia and the United States: Trade and the Multinationals in a New Era, *Economic Analytical Unit, Department of Foreign Affairs and Trade, Canberra, p. 10.*

## Current focus

As reflected in the above International Highlight, the trend to bilateralism has moved away from bilateral trade agreements to a free trade agreement between the two countries. Australia signed free trade agreements (FTAs) with Singapore (2003), Thailand (2004) and the USA (2004). Currently under active negotiation are FTAs with China, Malaysia, the UAE and Japan.

The current focus of bilateral agreements and associated rounds of trade talks and the issues raised for Australian firms are outlined below:

* *Exchange of information* as far as areas of joint interest are concerned: From the Australian firms' perspective would this exchange of information benefit its international activities?

Australia could become the first developed country to conclude a FTA with China. Negotiations began in May 2005 and one area of focus is liberalising services trade between the two countries—especially in education and tourism. Also under discussion are measures to improve regulatory transparency as far as investment is concerned, and reduce barriers that cause Australian investors additional costs and reduce their access in China. Allied to this is the mutual recognition of professional qualifications. It is estimated that the FTA, once signed, could boost Australia's economy by US$18 billion and China's by US$64 billion in its first decade of operation.

**SOURCE:** *Adapted from Department of Foreign Affairs and Trade (2005b)* Unlocking China's Services Sector, *Economic Analytical Unit, Department of Foreign Affairs and Trade, Canberra, p. 99.*

- *Exchange of representatives*: These could be commercial, industrial or technical representatives. The Australian firm might consider providing a person who would be placed in a key decision-making or advisory area in the overseas country. Alternatively, there is the opportunity to favourably predispose officials from the overseas country towards the Australian firm's technology by providing a short-term placement within their company in Australia.

- *Holding of trade fairs/exchange of trade missions* in each country: The issue for Australian firms is whether they should participate in the activity directed towards the other country because of the blessing of both governments.

- *Lists of products* which each side wishes to trade with the other: Are the products or services of Australian firms included in the list? If not, can the firms lobby the Department of Foreign Affairs and Trade to have them included at the next round of bilateral trade talks?

- *Investment clauses*: These detail areas in which new investment is sought. Is the Australian firm's industry covered?

- *General problems in the bilateral trade*: These could include a wide variety of issues, such as shipping services, cost of insurance or need for concessional credit. If a firm faces a general problem that impedes its trade with the country, can it arrange for it to be discussed under the umbrella of the trade agreement?

- *Specific problems in the bilateral trade*: These may also take the form of barriers to future trade development. If a firm has a specific problem, can it arrange for it to be included in trade talks between the two countries?

- *Establishment of new groups to facilitate trade objectives*: An example would be the establishment of the Australia–Indonesia Institute to promote people-to-people contacts. Groups of this nature provide opportunities for Australian firms to network and they may consider membership because of this.

Bilateral trade agreements do not usually cover:

- goods supplied under aid, whether grant or loan;

- advantages of access with bordering countries to facilitate frontier traffic;

- tariff preferences currently in force and which result from multilateral activities;

- existing obligations or measures resulting from international commodity agreements; or

- measures necessary for balance of payments or health, safety or quarantine reasons.

Basically, enforcing the provisions of bilateral trade agreements depends on the goodwill of both parties. Often, the rhetoric of cooperation is pushed far ahead of reality due to a lack of genuine interest. It often boils down to how important the parties are to each other. Goodwill in the associated trade discussions largely depends on reciprocal advantage. If Australia wants a concession from the other country it has to offer something in return. As an example, a bilateral trade initiative may ease import barriers in the other country against exports from Australia. However, success in this connection is likely to depend on whether Australia is willing to reduce existing barriers against the other country for products which they produce more efficiently.

Sometimes in bilateral trade relations problems are created so as to provide negotiating coin for future discussions. For example, a perceived health or quarantine problem may result in a blanket prohibition of a product. Individual nations then lobby to prove that the prohibition should not apply to them as the problem does not exist in their country. In return for accepting this representation, the first country requests as a trade-off a solution to a pre-existing problem in their trade with the second country. In negotiating reciprocal reductions to barriers to trade, it is preferable to focus on areas of growth in the other economy. This is because growth areas are better placed to weather any additional competition as a result of the reduction in protection, whereas barriers are more entrenched in declining industries or sectors and more difficult to dislodge because of greater employment effects.

According to Stiglitz (2004), bilateral treaties between developing and developed countries can often operate to the disadvantage of the former. In the case of a treaty between the USA and Morocco, the USA used the same approach that has earned it enmity in many other parts of the world in lobbying the interest of domestic special interests groups such as drug companies.

It is also easier to negotiate away revenue-motivated as opposed to protectionist-motivated barriers because the latter have social implications and are more sensitive in terms of domestic politics. Barriers to trade are driven by different reasons in each country. It is useful to research these differing motivations as this will assist in formulating the optimal negotiation strategy. Often these motivations are reflected in vested interest groups in the other country, such as the agricultural lobby in a Coalition government in Australia or the rice lobby in Japan.

## Lobbying

An Australian firm may lobby its government to raise an issue under a bilateral trade agreement. This is particularly the case where the problem relates to gaining access to the market in that country, to restrictions on operating in that country, to being able to market its products and services in that country, or to a regulatory practice in that country discriminating against the Australian product. In order to improve its lobbying effectiveness an Australian firm with a strong interest in a particular overseas country should consider joining the bilateral business group, participating in government-sponsored trade missions to that country, asking to brief ministers and officials prior to trade talks and supporting government advertising or public relations activities in the overseas market.

## MANAGED TRADE

Managed trade is not free trade as envisioned by the WTO because it restricts the operation of the market by government decision or decree.

The EU and the USA have reached agreement to resolve outstanding disputes over the operation of the 1996 D'Amato Act penalising firms investing more than US$40 million in Iranian or Libyan energy sectors and the Helms Burton Law banning trade with Cuba. Triggered by US sanctions against a consortium, led by Total, being involved in Iranian gas development, the agreement will apply to Gazprom of Russia and Petronas of Malaysia as well. It heralds a weakening in the US propensity to impose sanctions on firms outside its jurisdiction who trade with its perceived enemies.

In addition, it is not appropriate to call it protectionist as government involvement may be motivated by other reasons, such as to assist reduction of national debt, achieve investment goals or acquire new technology. Managed trade can be defined as direct intervention by government in trade and investment so as to manage better its own economy and its interaction with the international economy. There are two main forms of managed trade. These are government intervention and voluntary restraints.

## Government intervention

With managed trade, governments are exercising their sovereign rights. Intervention can include the following forms:

* *Embargoes*: Often embargoes are imposed for political reasons. As long as the resulting restraint of trade is predictable and non-discriminatory, then embargoes are defensible.

* *Import quotas*: These are generally protectionist in motivation and are subject to more criticism than tariffs. The excuse that they are imposed for balance of payments reasons has been used so frequently that this form of managed trade is viewed with suspicion.

* *Other non-tariff barriers*: These include health and safety regulations, standards for products, certification and recognition requirements for professional services, giving preference to domestic providers when government purchases are involved, and import inspection procedures and costs.

* *Countertrade*: An increasing number of governments mandate countertrade as a condition of contract when government purchases are involved, or when the availability of foreign exchange is scarce. While all forms of countertrade can be mandated, offsets is the most usual form of mandated countertrade (see Chapter 19).

* *Export assistance*: This takes a variety of forms, including tax incentives, low-interest loans, assistance with promotion overseas, provision of information on the potential of and restraints in overseas markets, trade representation and formation of export groups or consortia to bid on projects. A number of these are alleged to interfere with free-market activities and, when they do so, they can be regarded as managed trade. The current trend with export assistance is to help firms further back along the supply chain. One example is the provision of investment incentives for export-generating industries.

If an Australian firm feels that it is disadvantaged by any of the above forms of intervention by an overseas government, it can lobby the Australian government to provide advice and possibly compensatory assistance or to apply pressure to the other government to reduce the disadvantages faced by the firm.

# Voluntary restraints

Despite the high-sounding diplomatic phrases which surround them, voluntary restraints are akin to blackmail because there is nothing genuinely voluntary about them. Governments are often subject to intense lobbying by sectoral interests to restrict imports because of their impact on higher-priced domestic products. Approaches to the WTO can be time-consuming and may not succeed. As the competitive threat may come from a variety of countries, neither an appeal to relevant RTGs nor bilateral negotiation is likely to yield a speedy resolution.

As an alternative, the country threatens to impose highly restrictive import quotas on the product, but offers to negotiate much more liberal quotas if interests in the major supplying countries agree to accept the restriction on imports. All parties often agree to this negotiated arrangement. This is because the importing country can avoid seeking approval from the WTO for the quota system it proposes, and because the exporting country receives guaranteed access for a fixed quantity for an agreed period. The operation of voluntary restraints is illustrated in the case of the operation of the US Meat Importation Law (MIL) on exports of Australian manufacturing-grade beef.

Originally introduced in 1979, the US MIL limits the amount of beef, veal and mutton that can be imported into the USA in times of domestic surplus so as to protect domestic industry. A minimum base level was set of 56 000 tonnes and a quota arrived at for each year by varying the base level in the light of domestic production. Supplying countries agree not to exceed the annual quota by more than 10% in total. Should the likely imports for a year look like exceeding this figure, then voluntary restraint arrangements (VRAs) are negotiated with each supplying country to ensure that the quota, plus the 10% trigger, is not exceeded. In 1992 the figure was set at 594 750 tonnes (540 000 quota + 10% trigger) of which Australia's share was expected to be 335 000 tonnes. If Australia refused to restrain its exports so that they did not exceed the VRA, then the quota figure of 540 000 tonnes would be imposed, of which Australia's share would be 302 000 tonnes. By agreeing to the VRA, Australia sold the USA an additional 33 000 tonnes in that year, valued at A\$97 million.

Voluntary restraint arrangements particularly tend to apply to 'smokestack industries', such as steel and automobiles, and examples exist in both these areas where the USA has used VRAs as a form of protectionism. Prior to the conclusion of the Uruguay Round, VRAs increased in incidence and it was estimated in 1993 that one-third of imports of manufactures into the USA were covered by VRAs. The conclusion of the Uruguay Round raised hopes that VRAs would disappear as it was recognised that it was a trade-distorting practice. In Australia's case, the MIL was scrapped and replaced by a tonnage quota of 380 000 tonnes, which would make the trade more predictable. However, as many of the WTO's measures have not yet been implemented and global economic circumstances are likely to stimulate protectionism, it would be premature to say that VRAs will shortly disappear.

# ISSUES IN INTERNATIONAL TRADE RELATIONS

## Subsidies

An issue increasingly raised in bilateral trade relations discussions is that of governments subsidising exports. Frequently, the subsidy issue is raised when there is a downturn in the

The prospect of America's farmers being weaned from government subsidies appears as remote as ever with Congress about to pass a new farm bill that will be similar to the 2002 bill and will simply extend the subsidies enshrined in the current bill. With a presidential election scheduled for 2008, no politician is likely to oppose a continuation of the current situation. However, there are signs that the public at large is becoming tired of funding these subsidies to the tune of US$20 billion a year, which, along with the escalating cost of the war in Iraq, is touching the 'hip pocket nerve'. Given that subsidies to farmers cost more than twice what the US spends on foreign aid, criticism is mounting. This criticism has been fuelled recently by a number of anti-subsidy rulings by the WTO and has led to a desire to make the new farm bill 'WTO proof'. The impact of these subsidies on other countries is illustrated in the case of the cotton industry in the USA. America's lavish handouts to its farmers cause poverty throughout the developing world. The *International Herald Tribune* of 29 April 2004, p. 6, reported this conclusion when commenting on the hearing by the WTO of Brazil's challenge to the US cotton subsidies on the grounds that they belie the commitment by the US to free and fair trade. Cotton is West Africa's cash crop and the only field in which the region has a competitive advantage. By underwriting much of the costs of America's 25 000 cotton farmers with cheques totalling US$3 billion a year, the USA wipes out that advantage. Recently the WTO ruled against US subsidies to cotton farmers. The implementation of this resolution will be difficult, however, as the subsidies were approved by the US Congress and it will also have to approve the removal of the subsidies.

SOURCES: *Adapted from* International Herald Tribune, *29 April 2004, p. 6; 'Facing the scythe',* Economist, *28 May 2005, p. 64; and 'Uncle Sam's teat',* Economist, *9 September 2006, p. 39.*

domestic industry, as periodically happens with Australian steel when there is a recession in the USA. Many subsidies are disguised, and often they are embedded in the structure of the economy or industry in such a way that they are inseparable from its operation.

# Negotiation

Although many of the issues discussed in Chapter 3 under the heading of negotiation apply to negotiations in the trade relations domain, there are differences when multilateral negotiation as opposed to bilateral negotiations take place. Multilateral negotiations differ in three ways:

1  Coalitions inevitably form between parties involved in the negotiations. Such coalitions have the effect of facilitating problem solving in negotiation (Money and Allred 2006).

2  Negotiators tend to oversimplify the problem in the interests of maintaining harmony.

3  Various parties take on wider roles such as mediator, leader, scapegoat and blocker.

In addition, bilateral negotiations tend to favour the stronger power player; this may not be the case with multilateral negotiations (Turner 1988). In all ITR negotiation there is pressure from outside bodies and interests on those who conduct the actual negotiation; together these and the negotiating team constitute a network.

Those undertaking the ITR negotiation are likely to be heavily influenced by whether they come from a cultural background that is high context or low context (see Chapter 3); those from the former will engage in more innuendo, face saving and implied communication whereas those from the latter will be much more explicit in their communication. Failure to appreciate this issue often causes misinterpretation of the meaning the other party is trying to convey in the ITR negotiation.

# Commodity agreements

Hitherto discussion has centred on trade relations applying to products and services in general. There are trade relations activities that are confined to specific product groups. These are known as commodity agreements. Commodity agreements were introduced to create predictability and security in the international trade for specific commodities. They evolved when the percentage of world trade that was resources- or agriculture-based was much greater than it is today. They usually involve both the buyer and the seller, and sometimes include a price support or buffer stock mechanism, as was the case with the previous wool stockpile in Australia. The intention is to increase stability for both buyer and seller by ironing out sharp price fluctuations. In this way it was hoped to increase overall consumption of the product. Furthermore, the security of agreed remunerative prices permits the gradual expansion of production of the commodity. Membership of these arrangements could involve both public and private sectors.

The position today is that commodity agreements have diminished in significance. Their role has changed from a market-stabilising role to more of an information-exchange function. This is because some of the previous economic-type commodity agreements that regulated production, for example the International Tin Agreement, collapsed,. The focus of current commodity agreements is on the threat of substitute products and the gathering and supply of worldwide data and statistics on production and trade in the commodity covered.

Commodity agreements can benefit a firm involved with a commodity covered in this way as synergies arise from exporting as a group, and the exchange of information enables early warning of threats which might arise from producers outside the arrangement or from substitute products. Cooperating with customers to the mutual advantage of both parties has a stabilising effect on the trade in what might otherwise be a volatile commodity.

# The internet and international trade relations

E-business is an issue that affects the ability of countries to compete with each other and one that has the potential to confer monopoly power on some countries at the expense of others due to its interactive, borderless and timely nature. As such, it is a subject that is increasingly likely to appear on the agendas of countries' multilateral, regional and bilateral trade relationships. However, historically nation states have had only limited success at creating global treaties that succeed in practice. Furthermore, such treaties take a very long time to negotiate (e.g. the GATT Uruguay Round) and, given the pace of internet technology, they run the risk of limping behind economic reality. In the multilateral arena, the WTO is focusing on e-commerce issues, such as privacy, customs duties, modes of delivery, international procurement, intellectual property, standards and the use of telecommunications networks. WTO agreements applicable in this context are the General Agreement on Trade in Services (GATS), the Agreement on Basic Telecommunications of 1997 and the Information Technology Agreement of 1996. In 1998 the WTO set up a Work Program on Electronic Commerce to examine trade-related aspects of e-commerce that would be likely to involve it in the future. Given the borderless nature of e-commerce, these issues in the future could be many.

The World Intellectual Property Organisation (WIPO) has established benchmarks for treating various forms of intellectual property in cyberspace and has set up an Arbitration and Mediation Centre. The Organisation for Economic Cooperation and Development (OECD) hosted an international conference on e-commerce in 1998 and operates a number of working parties on e-commerce issues.

At the regional level, various bodies are addressing e-commerce issues. For example, the Asia-Pacific Economic Cooperation (APEC) Group has created an interconnection framework that aims to foster competitive network development and an authentication task group with the objective of fostering user confidence in e-commerce.

As the importance of e-commerce grows in international trade, it is likely to be included in bilateral negotiations between countries. It may be included in general trade agreements between countries or be the subject of specific agreements as with the Australia–United States Joint Statement. This latter agreement provides that both countries will work together to provide certainty and build confidence for government, business and consumers in key areas of e-commerce.

# Summary

Although there is much in the media about international trade relations in their various forms—multilateral, regional and bilateral—there is a tendency on the part of Australian business executives to regard them as a political exercise undertaken by bureaucrats and ministers. There is considerable advantage to a firm to become actively involved in international trade relations activities concerning overseas markets in which the firm is involved or interested, or in issues which affect the future profitability of the firm in Australia or overseas.

In the first place it is necessary for the firm to strengthen its relations with the Australian government. If this happens, its interests are more likely to be taken into account when issues of interest to the firm are being negotiated in a multilateral context. It will also improve chances that impediments faced by the firm in specific overseas markets are raised by government in either regional trade forums or in bilateral discussions. To facilitate this improvement in relations with the home government, the firm should become actively involved in business groups focusing on trade development with an area or with a region. Such involvement is likely to result in collective strength when lobbying government, being called upon to offer advice to government on trade with the country/region involved, and possible invitation to become a member of an official trade delegation to the country.

The second step is for the firm to strengthen its relationship with the overseas government. Although this may be achieved via the firm's agent or joint venture partner in the other country, it should also be undertaken directly by the firm. Membership of bodies involved in advancing trade between Australia and the other country adds credibility to the Australian firm's approach to officials, as does involvement in official talks as an adviser or by accompanying Australian ministers on their visits to the overseas country.

Such relationships with government will improve the competitiveness of the networks involved in international operations and serve both to minimise impediments overseas and maximise facilitation by government.

## ETHICS ISSUE

**Y**ou are a major exporter of fresh fruit and an industry spokesperson from the state of Tasmania. The Minister for Trade has asked that you attend the next meeting of the Australia–Indonesia Ministerial Commission where Indonesian restrictions on the import of Australian fresh fruit on quarantine grounds will be debated. Given the general level of health problems in Indonesia, it is felt that the restriction is motivated more by protectionist than quarantine reasons. The minister will be arguing that the ban on Australian apples should not apply to produce from Tasmania as, being an island state, it does not have the disease problems that plague the mainland. The day before you were scheduled to leave for Jakarta, you are advised of an isolated instance of mainland fruit fly in the north-east part of the state. This was immediately treated.

***If you were the industry spokesperson, would you inform the minister and would you advise the minister to inform the Indonesians of the recent occurrence of fruit fly?***

# Websites

**Ansell** http://www.ansell.com.au
**APEC** http://www.apecsec.org.sg
**ASEAN** http://www.aseansec.org
**Australia–Thai Free Trade Agreement** http://www.dfat.gov.au/trade/negotiations/aust-thai_agreement
**Australia–US Free Trade Agreement** http://www.dfat.gov.au/trade/negotiations/us
**Australian Federal Government** http://www.australia.gov.au/
**Australian Wheat Board** http://www.awb.com.au
**Cairns Group** http://www.cairnsgroup.org
**Closer Economic Relations Agreement (ANZCER)** http://www.dfat.gov.cer
**European Union** http://europa.eu
**General Agreement on Trade in Services (GATs)** http://www.wto.org/english/tratop_e/serv
**NAFTA** http://www.nafta-sec-alena.org
**OECD** http://www.oecd.org
**Singapore–Australia Free Trade Agreement**
  http://www.dfat.gov.au/trade/negotiations/australia_singapore_agreement
**Toys R Us** http://www.toysrus.com
**Trade Related Intellectual Property Agreement (TRIPs)** http://www.wto.org/english/tratop_e/trips
**World Intellectual Property Organization (WIPO)** http://www.wipo.int
**World Trade Organization** http://www.wto.org

# Discussion questions

1  Why has the prime emphasis in international relations shifted from the political to the commercial?

2  How do international trade relations affect marketing?

3  Discuss the role of government as both a regulator and as a facilitator in international trade.

4 Comment on ways in which the Australian or New Zealand government can be an ally in overcoming impediments and facilitating access to overseas markets.

5 In what ways has the World Trade Organization gone beyond the GATT in its approach to international marketing issues?

6 Why is the World Trade Organization sometimes referred to as 'the rich man's club'?

7 What caused Australia to play a pivotal role in proposing APEC?

8 How do bilateral trade relations differ from multilateral trade relations? Under what circumstances can the latter be more effective than the former?

9 Does managed trade still have a future, given recent developments in implementing the outcomes of the Uruguay Round?

# References

'A boost to fruit', *Dynamic Export*, October 2006, p. 3.

Akerman, P. (2007) 'Parochial view gets APEC in the eye', *Daily Telegraph*, 29 May, p. 16.

'Asean sets trade-talk dates', *Asian Wall Street Journal*, 6 September 2004.

Bradsher, K. (2004) 'Cambodia legislature approves WTO entry', *International Herald Tribune*, 1 September, p. 14.

*Business Review Weekly*, 8 June 2001, p. 24.

Cohen, L. (1997) Presentation to the Association of Japanese Business Studies Conference, Washington DC, 13–15 June.

Department of Foreign Affairs and Trade (2004a) *Australia–Thailand Free Trade Agreement*, Commonwealth of Australia, Canberra.

Department of Foreign Affairs and Trade (2004b) *The Singapore–Australia Free Trade Agreement–A Business Guide*, Commonwealth of Australia, Canberra.

Department of Foreign Affairs and Trade (2005a) *Australia and the United States: Trade and the Multinationals in a New Era*, Economic Analytical Unit, Department of Foreign Affairs and Trade, Canberra.

Department of Foreign Affairs and Trade (2005b) *Unlocking China's Services Sector*, Economic Analytical Unit, Department of Foreign Affairs and Trade, Canberra.

Department of Foreign Affairs and Trade (2006) *ASEAN: Building an Economic Community*, Department of Foreign Affairs and Trade, Canberra.

'Facing the scythe' *Economist*, 28 May 2005, p. 64.

*Financial Times*, 1 September 2004, p. 3.

Ianchovichina, E., Martin, W. and Fukase, E. (2000) *Assessing the Implications of Merchandise Trade Liberalisation in China's Accession to WTO*, World Bank. Cited in *Insights*, 2003, Vol. 3, No. 1, p. 6.

Money, R.A. and Allred, C.R. (2006) 'An exploratory test of a model of social networks, national culture and international multilateral negotiations', *Proceedings of the Conference of the Academy of International Business*, July, Beijing.

Parkes, J. (2006) 'Food to go', *Dynamic Export*, August, pp. 16–20.

Sloan, B. (2004) 'A whole new world', *Far East Economic Review*, 2 September, pp. 18–19.

Stiglitz, J.E. (2004) 'US treaties hurt the poorest partners', *International Herald Tribune*, 12 July, p. 8.

*Sydney Morning Herald*, 16–17 June 2001.

'The battle of the budget', *Economist*, 25 March 2005, p. 47.

Tuck, S. and Marotte, B. (2004) 'Canada, Brazil to resume subsidy talks', *Globe and Mail*, Toronto, 30 September 2004, p. B3.

Turner, J.N. (1988) 'There is more to trade than trade: an analysis of the US/Canada Trade Agreement 1988', *California Management Review*, Vol. 33, No. 2, pp. 109–16.

'Uncle Sam's teat', *Economist*, 9 September 2006, p. 39.

## go online

Go online to <www.pearsoned.com.au/fletcher> to find more case studies.

# CASE STUDY 18

# Organic products in Japan: an issue of quality analysis

## Tina Slattery and Richard Fletcher

## BACKGROUND

The organic boom in Japan started around 12 years ago at the time Japanese consumers were becoming increasingly aware of the excessive use of fertilisers and pesticides in conventional food. Around 25% of Japan's 120 million people suffer from allergies and in particular are sensitive to environmental poisons. Japan is now the third largest organic market in the world after the USA and Germany; however, only 0.09% of Japan's agricultural land area (approximately 5000 hectares) is farmed using organic methods. It is estimated that the market volume for organic products in Japan grew from approximately US$1.5 billion to US$3 billion between 1997 and 2000. It must be noted, however, that up until 2001 products produced using fewer pesticides and chemical fertilisers were also sold as organic.

In 1993 the Japanese Ministry of Agriculture passed the first Japanese organic directive, but it remained non-binding and was not controlled. The six different descriptions for organic products, which included products with fewer chemicals, confused Japanese consumers and made them suspicious of their domestic organic standards. Imported organic products from coun-

tries such as the USA, Europe and Australia, which were considered to have stricter standards, profited greatly from this situation.

In April 2001 a new Japanese organic standard (JAS–Japan Agricultural Standard) issued by the Ministry of Agriculture, Forestry and Fisheries (MAFF) was implemented based on the international standards (Codex Alimentarius, IFOAM). The JAS label is now essential for the sale of organic agricultural products and the criteria for use of this label for the first time clearly defines the conditions under which products can be classified as organic in Japan. Foreign certifiers and products must now be recognised by MAFF and the certifier may also be forced to have a registered office in Japan in order to bear the JAS label. However, it took nearly six months after the implementation of the JAS standards before a foreign certifier was recognised by MAFF, during which time imported organic products without the JAS label were not allowed to be labelled as organic. The first country to be recognised under country equivalence status of organic standards was Australia, followed a couple months later by the European Union (EU).

Sokensha, a major Japanese natural products company, had been importing packaged organic safflower oil since 1999; this product is certified by the National Association for Sustainable Agriculture Australia (NASAA), one of Australia's largest certification bodies administered under the Australian Quarantine and Inspection Service (AQIS). Sokensha would always conduct quality testing of the finished product at a laboratory in Japan (the Japan Food Analysis Centre (JFAC)) before payment for the shipment from Australia. This was to ensure that the product complied with the Japanese organic standards and Japanese labelling laws. The JFAC is owned and operated by MAFF, which regulates the food quality standards in Japan; however, the JFAC is not an internationally accredited testing laboratory. Up until 2001 Sokensha had not experienced any major problems with the quality of the product from Australia nor did it experience any discrepancies in analysis results between Japan and Australia. It was in fact feeling very confident and comfortable with its supplier, Devexco International, and was looking to increase the import volume by developing brands for other types of organic oils from Australia.

## THE CONTAMINATION INCIDENT

In December 2001 Devexco International shipped 2241 cartons of packaged organic safflower oil worth A\$120 000 to Sokensha. This shipment was the first to Sokensha since the formal acceptance of Australian certification bodies to administer the JAS label on their licensee's products. As usual, one bottle off the production line was couriered to Sokensha for analysis at the JFAC. The agreement was that Sokensha would notify Devexco within 10 days from receipt of the sample of the analysis results. Prior to shipment, Devexco would also conduct its own analysis with Amdel Ltd, an internationally accredited testing laboratory, to ensure that the product met the Japanese specifications. The analysis results received from Amdel for this shipment indicated that all of Sokensha's specifications were met and therefore Devexco was confident that the product would be accepted and payment remitted.

On 28 December 2001, two days after the agreed notification period, Devexco received a phone call from Sokensha informing it that the JFAC had found BHA (a synthetic antioxidant used in some conventional vegetable oil) in the sample at a level above the specification (1 part per million). Although BHA is approved for human consumption up to a level of 200 parts per million in Japan, Sokensha informed Devexco that the Japanese organic standards and labelling laws require it to identify BHA's presence on the label if it is above 1 part per million. To include a synthetic ingredient on the label of an organic product, it

said, would not be acceptable to its customers and therefore it could not accept the shipment.

Devexco was puzzled by the JFAC result. Its staff have extensive knowledge and experience of the Japanese market and therefore was well aware of the strict standards in Japan. It also knew the importance of maintaining the integrity of organic products throughout the production process. It had taken every precaution to prevent contamination through sampling and testing at each critical stage of production. All tests conducted showed no presence of BHA, so the firm could not identify at what stage the contamination could have happened. Devexco could only assume that the tests conducted by Amdel were wrong.

## JAPANESE VERSUS AUSTRALIAN LABORATORIES

Soon after receiving the news of contamination from Sokensha, Devexco rang Amdel's technical manager to inform him that it had received conflicting results from the JFAC. The technical manager was adamant that Amdel's results were correct but he agreed to retest the samples, this time under his close personal supervision. A few days later Devexco received a call from Amdel informing it that all test results were correct and BHA was definitely not present above 1 part per mullion. Devexco asked if it was possible that there could be BHA at a level less than 1 part per million. Amdel agreed that it was possible, but explained that the internationally recognised testing methodology is not quantifiable for less than 1 part per million (that is, you could not be definitive about the presence of BHA in quantities of less than 1 part per million as equipment interference could occur). Devexco presented this information to Sokensha and asked for the JFAC to retest the sample.

Sokensha believed that the first analysis from the JFAC was correct. It was of the opinion that the JFAC is a government laboratory with the most sophisticated testing methodology and equipment and is also the arbitration laboratory for any food analysis disputes in Japan. Sokensha strongly felt that the Australian laboratory had made the mistake, so there was no need to retest the sample. Devexco wondered how a laboratory that is not internationally accredited could be considered more sophisticated than an accredited one. Was this just a case of national pride taking over rational thinking?

In order to determine the differences in methods used by the two laboratories, Devexco requested a copy of JFAC's methodology and equipment for Amdel to retest the samples on an equivalent testing level. This request was denied by the JFAC, which stated that its methodology was developed internally and superior to any international method, and therefore 'commercial in confidence'. This reasoning was unacceptable to Devexco and it demanded that Sokensha have unmarked random samples from the shipment tested again. Sokensha was initially reluctant, but agreed to take six random samples from the container, transfer them into another container and send them to the JFAC for testing.

A week later the JFAC submitted the results of the six unmarked random samples: all six samples had different results. This clearly proved the inconsistency in the JFAC's testing. Due to the production process that occurs for vegetable oils, both Sokensha and Devexco knew that if a contamination were detected in the final product the level would be consistent throughout the whole shipment. Despite having been presented with the new evidence that the JFAC may possibly have made a mistake in its initial testing, Sokensha still refused to accept the shipment. It believed that once the JFAC determined there was contamination then it would be a waste of time arguing with it about whether it was right or wrong because it is the government laboratory that makes the final ruling on all disputes—in other words, it has the final say, no matter what the circumstance. At this point Devexco noticed that the reluctance by Sokensha to challenge the JFAC seemed to come from the fear of possible retribution in some way by the Japanese government body (MAFF).

## THE SETTLEMENT

Sokensha had been a very good customer to Devexco in the previous three years with an annual purchase level of approximately A$1 million.

Although the loss of income worth A$120 000 would affect Devexco's cash flow in the short term, it was a loss it knew it could withstand over time. Devexco's major concern was over whether this testing discrepancy would occur again in further shipments and, if it did, whether it would make business between them unsustainable.

Despite the clear inconsistency of the JFAC's results, Sokensha requested that Devexco reimburse it for the following costs:

- importation and transportation costs within Japan;

- warehousing costs in Japan;

- export documentation fees;

- shipping cost back to Australia;

- extra testing costs for the six bottles.

The total of these costs came to approximately A$10 000. Sokensha also hinted at compensation for loss of shelf space in retail outlets and loss of income from lack of supply, but this was not pursued any further than a passing comment.

Devexco pondered over a number of options it could pursue in its negotiation for settlement of this shipment. The options it had were these:

- Because Sokensha was a valuable customer Devexco could accept all the costs and hope that the situation would not happen again and that business would continue in the same way as during the previous three years.

- Since Sokensha had breached the purchase agreement by not informing Devexco of the result within the specified time period, Devexco could demand that Sokensha accept and pay for the shipment. This option would most certainly damage the good relationship Devexco had enjoyed with Sokensha and put at risk the continuation of the business.

- Get an internationally recognised third-party laboratory to arbitrate and force Sokensha to accept this result, and lobby appropriate Australian government body officials to negotiate with MAFF officials on the discrepancy between test results. From discussions held with Sokensha, it was evident that it was unwilling to accept any other result but the JFAC's and it was unlikely that MAFF would acknowledge a mistake. This option would also involve a lengthy process during which time the product would be accumulating warehousing charges.

- Ask Sokensha to help with disposal of the product within Japan. This option would require relabelling and packing and would cost much more than A$10 000. The sale price of the product would also be only about one-third of its original price.

- Negotiate with Sokensha to share the costs incurred. That is, Sokensha would pay for the importation and transportation within Japan, warehousing and extra testing. Devexco would pay for export documentation and costs of shipping back to Australia. Since Sokensha was in breach of agreement and did not clearly define in its agreement which laboratory result would determine the final acceptance of the product, Devexco felt it was only fair that they share the risk.

Devexco had to think carefully. Sokensha was an important customer to them and it wanted the business to continue yet it did not want to give the impression that it had accepted the JFAC's results. If it did, then it would have no grounds for negotiation on all future shipments. Devexco also knew that the Japanese would always consider their equipment and methodology to be more accurate than that of others. This was a deep-rooted cultural aspect and way of thinking that cannot be changed and one that could destroy a business relationship if disputed too vigorously. Devexco decided that the only option to take in order to minimise loss, ensure the business continued and not to concede total responsibility was to share the risk.

On 22 January 2002 Devexco contacted Sokensha with the counter settlement. To Devexco's surprise, Sokensha accepted the counter settlement without further negotiation. It even apologised for the problems caused to Devexco and asked for its understanding, stating that in the overall Japanese food industry it was only a small company and did not have the resources or power to tackle a government body over issues. It requested that the next production start as soon as possible as it was rapidly running out of stock.

## FUTURE PRODUCTION

Over the previous three years Devexco and Sokensha had enjoyed a good and strong business relationship. Devexco staff visit Japan at least twice a year and Sokensha staff also visit Australia for facility inspections once a year. Once a close and reliable relationship with a Japanese company has been built, it is not likely to switch suppliers easily. Over the years Sokensha has had offers from Devexco's competitors, but these offers were all declined. It can take several years and involve many information exchanges and visits before a firm can finally make a sale to a Japanese company. Many foreign companies find it too difficult and give up halfway through this process. Having been through the struggle to enter the Japanese market, Devexco was not about to give up so easily. It had to find a solution to the BHA testing problem to ensure that it did not occur again.

Without a definitive outcome on the discrepancy in test results, Devexco was in a dilemma as to whether or not BHA was present in the oil. Without this knowledge Devexco could not identify the problem source if it existed. Devexco decided that the best way to restore Sokensha's confidence and find a solution was to invite Sokensha staff to Australia to help pinpoint possible contamination danger points in the production process.

In February 2002 Sokensha staff arrived in Australia and together with Devexco's staff inspected all the production facilities to identify possible problem sources. After several days of inspections and discussions it was decided that one section in the refining process posed the greatest danger for contamination. Devexco quickly moved to rectify this problem by investing in new stainless steel piping and pumps at the refinery, costing A$30 000. Sokensha staff left Australia feeling confident and pleased with Devexco's effort and willingness to cooperate.

Although the new piping and pumps would almost eliminate the possibility of contamination in the future, Devexco wondered whether the

Japanese laboratory would still find contamination in future shipments. Was the JFAC's initial test right or wrong? If it was wrong, why was it wrong? Was it an honest error by the analyst or a deliberate act to create a trade barrier or to discourage importation of organic products? Is this the risk that foreign food and agricultural companies must take to export to Japan? The answer to these questions will probably never be known. Meanwhile, business has continued as usual between Devexco and Sokensha, but there will always be the feeling of uncertainty that the situation might happen again and the outcome will be undisputable.

## Questions

1 Do you think that the option Devexco took to resolve the dispute was the best choice? Explain why.

2 This case study clearly demonstrates that foreign food and agricultural companies exporting to Japan must accept the ruling by a Japanese laboratory with regard to the quality of a product. Why do you think the Japanese insist on this criterion to determine acceptability of a product when there are international standards and testing methodologies that are used for international trade in most other countries?

3 How could Devexco minimise its risk in the future?

4 Despite the capital investment and extra precautionary measures Devexco has made to ensure the product is BHA free, if the Japanese laboratory finds its presence again in the future, what action should Devexco take?

5 In cases of this nature, would any purpose be served by involving the local Australian Trade Commissioner in Japan? What would be the upside and what would be the downside in Japan of this course of action?

# CONTEMPORARY INTERNATIONAL MARKETING ISSUES

## LearningObjectives

**After reading this chapter you should be able to:**

- develop strategies for securing consultancy and construction work associated with projects overseas;

- recognise the different stages involved in the project cycle and the criteria applied to the evaluation of bids;

- assess the relative importance of bilateral and multilateral aid in decision making in overseas projects;

- appreciate the role of countertrade in international marketing;

- recognise the different forms countertrade can take and when each applies;

- develop an appreciation of the advantages and disadvantages of countertrade from both a macro perspective and a firm's perspective;

- develop a strategic approach for including countertrade in the firm's international marketing activities;

- recognise the unique problems of marketing to consumers at the bottom of the pyramid; and

- appreciate how each element of the marketing mix needs modification if the offering is to be relevant to this group.

# CHAPTER OVERVIEW

In this chapter three contemporary issues will be discussed in depth. These are winning projects overseas, international countertrade and marketing to customers at the 'bottom of the pyramid' (BOP). Although most international marketing textbooks give scant attention to these issues, they are particularly important when doing business with developing countries—the countries that have the greatest market potential in the future.

# WINNING OVERSEAS PROJECTS

## Winning international projects: Leighton Holdings—projects by the dozen

Leighton Holdings is the parent company of Australia's largest project development and contracting group. The Leighton Group's overseas operations are all in Asia and are the responsibility of Leighton Asia, Leighton International and Thiess. This geographic spread outside Australia is part of the Group's strategy to diversify its earnings base and insulate itself from a downturn in any one location. It has three overseas divisions—Leighton International, which is responsible for activities in Malaysia, Brunei, Indonesia, Sri Lanka, India and the Arabian Gulf with over 1900 employees; Leighton Asia, which is responsible for activities in Hong Kong, China, Macao, the Philippines, Thailand, Vietnam, Laos and Cambodia with over 1100 people; and Thiess Indonesia with over 7000 employees in that country and India. The Leighton Group operates through a number of companies including Thiess, Leighton Contractors, Leighton Asia, Leighton International and John Holland. The acquisition of Thiess in 1983 introduced a major German contractor, Hochtief, as the group's largest shareholder. This relationship has provided the Group with access to construction technology and additional business connections to develop new business in Asia. Currently, around 17% of the Group's revenues and 23% of assets derive from Asia. Revenue from offshore operations was

A$1.7 billion for the 2005/06 year and work in hand was valued at A$3.2 billion as at 30 December 2006. In February 2007, the company announced it had been awarded a A$330 million contract by Reliance Industries, India's largest private company.

The Group has regional headquarters in Hong Kong, Kuala Lumpur and Jakarta, and ongoing business in Indonesia (mostly related to coal mining), Malaysia, Thailand, Vietnam, the Philippines, India and the Gulf region. It takes a long-term view of business in Asia and is judicious in taking on projects, not getting involved where there are any doubts about being paid. Its Asian activities have led to many business opportunities for Australian consultants and suppliers.

**SOURCES:** *Adapted from Walters, R. (2002)* The Big End of Town and Australia's Trading Interests, *Department of Foreign Affairs and Trade, Canberra, p. 79; and <http://www.leighton.com.au>, accessed 8 February 2007. Image compliments of Leighton Holdings Limited.*

# INTRODUCTION

The marketing of projects overseas is an important form of services marketing. This is because those who bid on a project are providing the service of offering a turnkey solution to a problem. This usually involves packaging various services and goods to achieve the desired outcome. Overseas projects provide opportunities for two broad groups of firms—those involved in consultancy and those involved in construction. These projects mostly involve infrastructure development and are part of a long-term development program in a country.

The value of these projects is large and the costs of bidding on such projects are high. Without such large values, firms would find it uneconomic to lodge bids because of the complex nature of the bidding process. Often there is a requirement for interested bidders to prequalify. This involves preparing copious information to demonstrate to the agency calling for bids that the firm is competent to carry out the work. The costs of preparing and lodging bids include the need to purchase the tender documents. These are often priced at a high figure in order to discourage frivolous bids. Then there is the cost of preparing the tender documents and submitting them in multiple copies. Usually, a bid bond must accompany the bid. If the firm is awarded the contract, then a performance bond is also often required as surety that it will perform as specified in the tender. This bond should be refunded if performance is satisfactory. There have, however, been cases where these bonds are retained on specious grounds, as occurred with some projects in Libya in the 1980s. Overall, in addition to any bonds that are required, the costs of bidding on projects are likely to exceed 5% of the tender value.

A characteristic of project marketing is that the project does not exist in a concrete form before it is delivered and installed. It involves selling an idea and the capability to transform the idea into something concrete that will deliver an expected outcome. Usually the provider of the idea (the prime contractor) will not be providing all the inputs, as many will be provided by others (subcontractors) for whose performance the prime contractor will be held responsible.

In project marketing the transfer of information is also critical. This, together with social influence, can be more crucial in being awarded the contract than the tangible elements. Because a buyer does not know what will be delivered at the time of entering into the contract, to allay uncertainty the buyer is likely to put more store on reputation, connections and obligations than would be the case with the purchase of a product.

Often project marketing involves providing a solution to a problem and the more innovative and cost-effective the solution, the more attractive the proposal. This 'solution selling' is labour-intensive and is likely to involve multiple parties in both the buying organisation and the funding body.

## Marketing issues

There are three major forms that projects can take in the international domain. These are:

1   partial projects—these involve delivery of an element or component of a total project such as a pumping station for a water reticulation project;

2   turnkey projects—these involve delivery of the complete project and its commissioning;

3   turnkey plus projects—these involve supply of extra services in addition to the project such as training of staff and/or maintenance activities.

International project activities are characterised by:

- discontinuity—they are not continuous in demand and the relationship between buyer and seller may end when the project is finished. This creates the challenge of keeping the relationship alive between projects;

- uniqueness—the resources applied and relationships developed must be customised to each project as each is a 'one off' and not amenable to a standardised approach;

- complexity—there are myriad actors and activities involved in a project and, apart from the prime contractor, there are likely to be a number of subcontractors; this plethora of involved parties adds to the complexity of delivering the project in an operational form on time.

Marketing projects overseas will require modifying the four usual marketing mix variables and catering for two additional variables. With *product*, it is technical competence rather than a physical product that is being offered. Because of this, the firm will need to demonstrate its capability in relation to the proposed project. In addition, this capability will need to be congruent with the overall planning goals of the country in which the project is being undertaken. Former socialist and developing countries, where most overseas project opportunities exist, operate on a long-term planning basis—usually five years. Agencies in these countries submit a list of their long-term infrastructure development requirements to the national planning agency, such as the National Economic and Social Development Board in Thailand. These requirements are then put in priority order and those for which funding is likely to be available from domestic, aid or loan sources are included in the five-year plan. This plan may have overriding criteria, such as attraction of a particular technology or acquisition of specific skills. It is expected that any bids would take these objectives into account.

In terms of *price*, often the financial terms of the bid are more important than its dollar value because government is involved and many of the economies offering project opportunities are strapped for cash. Also, as will be explained later in the chapter, the country from which the funds are available will often exercise an influence on who will be awarded the project.

*Promotion* will need to focus more on image than on product and will need to create positive feelings towards the firm, its 'country of origin' and its capabilities. As a consequence, promotion in the project sector often involves potential overseas clients making trips to Australia, New Zealand or elsewhere to witness firms' projects in operation and to receive extravagant entertainment, and also regular visits by Australian or New Zealand executives to the overseas market to keep up the lobbying pressure. The target of these promotion activities will be the risk-averse bureaucrats in the managing agency in the overseas country, and local and headquarter representatives of the body providing the funds.

With *place* it is important to appreciate that the role of the principal is more important due to the value of the project and its conceptual nature. It is expected that the CEO will regularly visit the market and participate directly in negotiations. The role of the agent differs in this environment. The intermediary must be technically competent and have excellent social connections with those in the managing agency who influence the award and those who actually award the contract. The agent in project marketing is a facilitator and representative rather than an intermediary.

The first of the additional variables in project marketing is *politics*. The party in power in the overseas country is likely to use the project, once completed, as a showcase for its political achievements and may use the awarding of the project as a vehicle for augmenting party funds. It is essential for the bidder to cultivate a good relationship with the party in power and to ascertain well in advance who in government will have prime responsibility for awarding or approving the bid. Where the government is a coalition it is useful to know which of the parties in the coalition will be involved in and influence the awarding of that particular project.

In the late 1980s Thailand had a coalition government and most government departments had a minister and two deputy ministers, each drawn from a different coalition partner. Each of these ministers was responsible for a different section of the department and controlled the awarding of infrastructure projects within the section of the department for which they were responsible.

Another political factor that can influence the awarding of projects is the relationship between the party in power and the governments of both the home and host countries. Considerable lobbying and use of influence at a government-to-government level takes place with the awarding of projects. If the relationship between governments is not good this can eliminate the likelihood of the project not being awarded to a firm from the offending country, despite it offering 'the best solution to the problem'.

This may have been the case in 1993 when an Australian consortium led by Transfield Corporation looked set to be awarded a contract to supply patrol boats to the Malaysian Navy—a situation which resulted from considerable financial assistance and lobbying by the Australian government. Australia's Prime Minister, Paul Keating, then accused Malaysia's Prime Minister, Dr Mahatir, of being 'recalcitrant' for not having attended the APEC leaders' summit in Seattle. The patrol boat contract was 'put on hold' and ultimately the contract went to Germany and not to Australia.

The second additional variable affecting project marketing is that of *people*. This is because successful negotiation and implementation of projects require coordination of Australians or New Zealanders, locals and other nationals. It requires sensitivity to the objectives of the client and an appreciation as to what motivates the senior public servants in the host country. It also involves an ability to attract to the project team people with innovative problem-solving skills, willingness and skill in training local people and finally an ability to negotiate effectively at all levels in a totally different culture. These modified and additional variables have influenced past successes by firms in winning project work overseas.

## Australia and overseas projects

Australia has a number of advantages when bidding for project work in other countries. These derive from the background to its construction industry and its position in the world marketplace.

### BACKGROUND

After World War II Australia needed to create infrastructure projects in the areas of dams, power generation, housing development and railways/transportation. This led to the establishment of a highly trained and experienced design, construction and engineering sector typified by firms such as the Snowy Mountains Corporation. This phase of development was followed by the mineral boom, which created a demand for infrastructure projects to facilitate the exploitation of mineral resources. This involved the building of ports, towns, harbours, rail and road links, airports and schools. However, the development needs of the past decades were reduced due to constraints on government spending, a change in the pattern of migration, infrastructure development not being as essential to maintain quality of life, environmental constraints on mining and Australia entering a high-tech era. With the consequent slackening in demand, Australian consultants and construction firms were in a position to offer a series of proven skills to developing countries in Asia where there was a lack of infrastructure. As an example, the Snowy Mountains Corporation became the Snowy Mountains Engineering Corporation (SMEC) and began focusing on Asia. As with many other Australian firms, initially SMEC's exposure was through undertaking Australian government aid projects in the region. It then graduated to bidding successfully on projects funded by multilateral development agencies such as the World Bank and the Asian Development Bank. Now the emphasis is on exporting skills to countries where there is a lack of infrastructure, or where natural disasters occur and Australian experience is of relevance, as with the Kobe earthquake of 1995. Basically, the strategy of the Australian industry is to avoid being held hostage to the business cycle in Australia and to achieve a spread of risk.

The focus of Australian construction and consultancy firms during the last two decades reflects a market life cycle approach. Initially, the focus was on Singapore and Hong Kong, then it was on Malaysia, Indonesia and Thailand, more recently on the Philippines, Vietnam, China, India and the Middle East, and possibly in the future it will be on Cambodia, Myanmar and Laos.

## POSITIONING

In marketing their abilities in overseas markets firms in the project sector need to analyse their situation carefully so as to arrive at the most appropriate positioning strategy. Their strengths are that, unlike many countries, Australia is not viewed as a threat to anyone, has world-class skills and has a wide variety of terrain and climatic conditions, with the result that its firms are likely to have undertaken projects in similar environments to those found most places in the world. In addition, Australia has rural/urban divisions, is located close to Asia and, since the inauguration of the Colombo Plan after World War II, has been a training ground for Asian professionals.

Australia's weaknesses include the small size of its market, its country of origin image being one of hedonism rather than engineering and construction skills, and a naivety in international negotiation. Other weaknesses include a laid-back approach as typified in the frequently heard phrase 'she'll be right, mate', high foreign ownership levels and poor relations between government and business.

Some areas of opportunity are those where Australian domestic experience some years ago is directly relevant to the needs of developing countries today. These include telecommunications over long distances and through variable climates and areas where Australian expertise has a worldwide reputation, such as dry land farming, land titling and water management.

Threats mostly derive from politics in the overseas country. There can be instances (as in Myanmar) where the central government does not control all the regions within the national borders, or where governments outside the country exert a dominant influence (as in Lebanon), or where there are politically related trade pressures favouring specific interest groups as was formerly the case with the operation of the extended Suharto family in Indonesia. Other threats can arise from competitors who might badmouth the firm, or from a change in the financial situation of the other country (as happened with the devaluation of the Mexican peso shortly after Mexico joined NAFTA).

## ALTERNATIVE STRATEGIES

There are several strategies firms can adopt when seeking project work overseas. These are illustrated in Figure 19.1.

The first strategy is *going it alone*. Firms pursuing this strategy often establish their own facility or representation overseas. This improves chances of obtaining work, both in the country in which the operation is established and in adjacent countries.

Another strategy is *piggybacking*. This involves teaming up with other firms to undertake a project offshore. Experience has indicated that often such consortia experience difficulties, as Australian firms are not good at cooperating with each other, especially in cases where they compete with each other in the Australian market.

A third strategy is that of *government showcasing*. This involves the Australian government funding a prestige project so as to showcase the abilities of Australian consultants and contractors in the hope that it will improve their chances of obtaining other work in the country. It is expected that the obligation created by the gift will result in future work for Australian companies. This approach enables the firm to gain experience in a particular market and provides the firm with the opportunity to use its presence in that market during the project as a base from which to seek other work. An example of showcasing is the 'Friendship Bridge' constructed by Australia in the early 1990s between Thailand and Laos.

A final strategy is that of entering into a *strategic alliance* with a view to establishing an effective presence offshore. This involves the sharing of skills, benefits and market

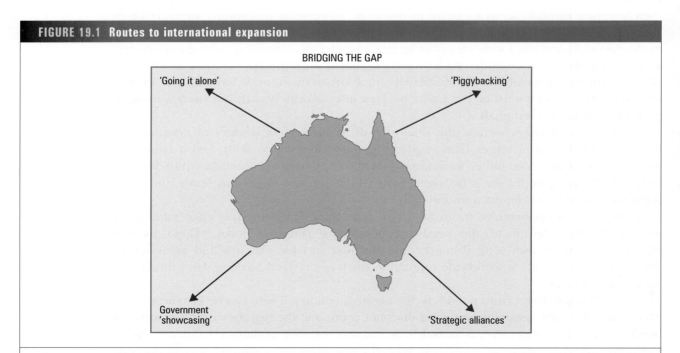

**FIGURE 19.1  Routes to international expansion**

BRIDGING THE GAP

'Going it alone'

'Piggybacking'

Government 'showcasing'

'Strategic alliances'

**SOURCE:** *L/E/K Partnership (1994)* Intelligent Exports and the Silent Revolution in Services, *Austrade, p. 101. Copyright Commonwealth of Australia. Reproduced with permission.*

information with the other firms in the alliance that might be from other countries or (more likely) from the host country.

Often such alliances take the form of a joint venture. The L/E/K Partnership (1994) found that the most effective joint ventures in the project field were in situations where the venture was between an Australian firm and a firm in the host country and each complemented the other in terms of the skills brought to the venture.

## PROBLEM AREAS

There are several areas where problems arise for Australian firms when bidding for project work offshore. The first results from competitive reaction when more than one Australian firm is bidding on the same project. Often the firms badmouth each other and in the process destroy the credibility of any proposal from Australian firms and the likelihood of any Australian firm being awarded the project. This is because the end-user becomes confused by the criticism, especially where it is not the norm in that country for competitors to criticise each other.

A second area of difficulty arises when the Australian firm doing the bidding is an offshoot of a multinational company, for example when Siemens Australia or Ericsson Australia bid on overseas telecommunications projects. The Australian subsidiary may find itself bidding in competition with its parent or face accusations that it is not a genuine Australian bid because of its foreign affiliation. The problem becomes more difficult when Australian aid funds are involved, such as in the feasibility study that led to the project.

A final problem area relates to Australia's image. What is good for tourism may be counterproductive for bidding on overseas projects. A hedonistic lifestyle and laid-back approach do not create the image of technical excellence or a capacity to deliver according to deadlines. This shortcoming needs to be compensated for in bid proposals by stressing positives and experience relevant to project work. These might include the ability to cope with the 'tyranny of distance', experience in operating in all types of climate and weather and the ability to undertake activities associated with mineral extraction and agricultural development.

There are a number of stages in the bidding and awarding of international project and consultancy work, and a detailed understanding of each stage is essential if the bid is to lead to a successful outcome.

# The project cycle

The project cycle describes the stages through which an international project proceeds from inception to completion and its final evaluation. The cycle outlines the relationship between the borrowing country and the funding agency. It applies to projects funded by multilateral aid agencies and by development agencies in specific countries or regions. Table 19.1 summarises the stages of the project cycle, shows how long on average each stage takes and indicates who has prime responsibility at each stage.

## PARTIES INVOLVED

The first of the parties involved is the borrower. Often known as the executing agency, this is usually a government agency or ministry in the developing country, such as the department of communications. Most developing and former socialist countries have a national planning agency responsible for preparing five-year plans. Examples are Bappenas in Indonesia and the National Economic and Social Development Board (NESDB) in Thailand. The departments

| TABLE 19.1 | Summary of project cycle | |
|---|---|---|
| **Stage** | **Approximate time** | **Responsibility** |
| 1. Identification | 1–2 years | Borrower |
| 2. Preparation | 3 years | Borrower |
| 3. Appraisal | 3–6 months | Bank |
| 4. Negotiation | 1–2 months | Borrower and bank |
| 5. Implementation | 6+ years | Borrower |
| 6. Evaluation | 6 months | Bank |

SOURCES: *Austrade (1994) 30 Billion Reasons to Enter the Market—Doing Business with Multilateral Development Banks and United Nations Agencies, Aidab and Austrade, Canberra, p. 14, <http://www.aidab.org/Projects/cycle>; and <http://www.web. worldbank.org/WEBSITE/EXTERNAL/PROJECTS>, accessed 8 February 2007.*

or ministries make submissions to the planning agency as to which projects should be undertaken in the forthcoming five-year plan period and the national planning agency accords priority to these requests. This planning body also decides which of these requests are suitable for funding by a multilateral or national development agency that is henceforth referred to as the lender. Once approved, the department or ministry assumes responsibility for the project.

The second party involved is the lender, which is usually a multilateral development agency such as the World Bank, a regional development agency such as the Asian Development Bank or a national development agency such as Australia's AusAID. The lenders, especially in the case of multilateral or regional development bodies, provide funds on a long-term, low-interest basis. The countries contributing funds to these bodies hope that their firms will be awarded contracts. A principal function of the lender is to ensure that the tendering procedures are fair to its members. They also examine the feasibility of the project and the capacity of the country to pay off the loan, and they are interested in the quality of work undertaken. Finally, the funding body wishes to be satisfied that the project will provide added benefits to the recipient country, such as training the workforce or being a catalyst for new business ventures.

The third party involved is the potential supplier. Suppliers may be numerous and include consultancies, construction services and suppliers of equipment for the project. Selection of projects involves ascertaining in advance whether suitable suppliers exist. It is possible for potential suppliers to suggest a project for consideration by the managing agency and the lender.

## PROJECT IDENTIFICATION

The decision as to which projects should be undertaken is a result of ongoing dialogue between the borrowers and the lenders. These lending agencies may select projects on the basis of previous studies of developmental needs of the country.

On the other hand, borrowers select projects on the basis of the developmental priorities of their country, the aims of their five-year plans and internal or external pressures. It is the borrowing country that selects the agency to approach to give or lend money for the project.

Once both parties have approved a project it forms part of the lending agencies' multi-year aid program for that country. Consultants are then hired to undertake a pre-feasibility study

For many years after the Vietnam War the USA used its veto to prevent multilateral development agencies funding development projects in that country. However, during that period the United Nations Development Programme (UNDP) maintained an office in Hanoi and conducted feasibility studies of areas where development assistance was likely to be needed. As a consequence, when the US embargo was lifted there were a number of projects presented to the World Bank and the Asian Development Bank which were feasible for funding.

if this has not already been undertaken. The hiring of the consultant is usually by the borrowing country although funds are often provided for the pre-feasibility study via aid from another country or the lending body.

## PROJECT PREPARATION

Formal responsibility for the project preparation stage rests with the borrower, although it involves close cooperation with the lender. Technical alternatives are considered so that the project solution selected is the one that is most appropriate to the country's stage of development and resource endowment. This does not mean that the most technically advanced alternative is selected, as social issues may make the most technically advanced solution inappropriate.

The borrower prepares a project brief, in which the objectives are detailed, the principal issues identified and a timetable established. Technical, institutional, economic and financial conditions necessary to achieve the project objectives are spelt out. In cases where a country is unable to carry out the above tasks, the lending agency may hire a consultant to do so.

Consultants are then hired to undertake the feasibility study, design the project and draw up procurement specifications. It is at this stage that the host government nominates the ministry or department that will be the executing agency. This is followed by the appraisal of the project that is the culmination of the preparatory work.

## PROJECT APPRAISAL

This stage is the prime responsibility of the lending agency. It involves the multilateral or regional development body reviewing the feasibility study and visiting the country in which the project is to be undertaken so as to hold discussions with the executing agency. There are four areas of appraisal:

1 *Technical appraisal*: Issues investigated include whether the project is soundly designed and engineered, the physical aspects of the project, its appropriateness to local conditions, the accuracy of cost estimates and likely adequacy of contingency provisions.

2 *Institutional appraisal*: Issues investigated include the extent to which the project will contribute to the country's overall development, its contribution to the objectives of the managing agency in the country, its impact on the local environment and the extent to which it is congruent with local cultural norms.

3 *Economic appraisal*: The project is studied in its sectoral setting. For example, a dam would be assessed in terms of the needs of the local community for water. The strengths and weaknesses of local public and private institutions are examined, as is the likely impact of key government policies on the project. A cost–benefit analysis of different ways of undertaking the project is carried out, as is a qualitative and quantitative

assessment of the project in relation to the development objectives of the country. The final aspect relates to ensuring that the project is likely to have a satisfactory economic return.

4 *Financial appraisal*: Issues here include whether there are likely to be sufficient funds available to finance that portion of the project not being funded by the multilateral development body. Appraisal will also consider whether there is a finance plan that will make funds available to implement the project on schedule and consider the financial viability of the project in terms of cash flow and return on assets.

Following the above appraisals, a report that recommends the terms and conditions of the loan as well as any modifications or redesign of the project is prepared.

## PROJECT NEGOTIATIONS

During this stage the lender and the borrower negotiate on conditions necessary for the success of the project, such as the charge for power once the dam is completed. Loan documents are prepared covering issues that have emerged at earlier stages, interest rates are agreed upon and repayment conditions are established.

An agreement is then signed between the lending body and the borrowing country and funds begin to be disbursed as conditions of both borrower and lender are met.

## PROJECT IMPLEMENTATION

Responsibility for implementation rests with the borrower, whereas responsibility for supervision lies with the lending agency, which also prepares regular progress reports. At this stage regular feedback is gathered so as to improve the design of future projects of a similar nature. In projects of this kind there are a large number of individual contracts. The average split would be civil works, such as earthworks for a dam, 30%; procurement of equipment, such as power generators for the dam, 60%; and consultancies, 10%.

## PROJECT EVALUATION

Once completed, the project will be evaluated by the lending agency with a view to identifying future projects that might flow from that just completed.

## SUCCESS IN OBTAINING WORK

Success for Australian firms will depend on understanding the international competitive bidding system favoured by multilateral and regional development agencies, appreciating the various stages at which consultants are used and knowing at what stage information about projects is available and from whom.

# International competitive bidding

This is preferred because the multilateral and regional development agencies have a responsibility to both the borrowers and those that contribute their funds. International competitive bidding is fair to contributing countries. It is used when the contract is of a reasonable size; otherwise, the bidding is usually limited to local suppliers. These bids have a closing date that must be rigorously adhered to and it is the responsibility of the Australian or New Zealand bidder to ensure that the bid arrives on time. In addition, the bids have specific tender conditions that must be observed. Bidders are invited to attend bid openings as these can be a source of additional information. It should be kept in mind that the evaluation criteria in the bid document might mean that the award does not always go to the lowest bidder.

## Consultancy opportunities

Consultants are used at all stages of the project cycle. They are used in pre-feasibility studies to identify projects, in feasibility studies to prepare projects for funding and in environmental impact studies for project appraisal. Consultants are also used during the project implementation stage to undertake engineering and detailed design, furnish project supervision and provide advisory services and technical assistance. Finally, consultants are used during the evaluation stage to carry out additional studies and recommend remedial action if necessary.

## Information sources

A register of consultants is maintained by both the World Bank and the Asian Development Bank—it is known as DACON (Data on Consulting Firms). Australian consultants should register on DACON and update their registration on an annual basis. Whereas formerly registration was in writing, now this can be by logging onto the website of these bodies. Consultants can also register their interest in specific projects. For contractors and suppliers, the multilateral development agencies also publish handbooks on the procurement of goods and civil works.

Different types of data are available on the requirements for a project at various stages. At the project identification stage data is available on the types of goods and construction services likely to be needed, on the market itself (such as standards and past supply patterns) and on local capabilities—knowledge of which is essential if a possible requirement is to use local contractors or supply sources.

At the project appraisal stage, equipment and civil works requirements are likely to be more clearly defined as tender lists are drawn up at this time. As this stage precedes the actual calling of tenders, leads in the borrowing country can be followed up.

Once the loan has been approved technical data sheets are likely to be available from the public relations offices of the lending agencies. In addition, at this stage the borrower must publicise the procurement opportunity in the magazine *Development Business*, within the borrowing country and at the same time they must alert the commercial representatives in the host country of all countries that are members of the funding agency.

## Projects and multilateral aid agencies

Wealthy nations are very influential in determining the nature of the aid and the underlying philosophy of the aid offered by the multilateral aid agencies. This is because wealthy nations are the main contributors of funds to such bodies as the World Bank and the Asian Development Bank. The original approach of these nations was that what had worked in the developed world would work in the developing countries. This resulted in a focus on the transfer of high technology or encouraging the growth of a middle class and promoting a population shift from country to city. The case of Iran and the removal of the Shah showed that this does not work. This is because such an approach tends to enrich the elite without improving the lot of the masses in the country and this can lead to social unrest.

The subsequent approach was to focus on the transfer of appropriate technology. This resulted in the transfer of technology being slower because the technology to be transferred was more labour-intensive. In addition, this more recent approach has delayed the creation of a large middle class in many developing countries.

## AID ISSUES

The volume of aid on a global basis approximates US$90 billion of which the World Bank provides US$33 billion, Japan US$15 billion, the Asian Development Bank US$6.2 billion and Australia US$2.3 billion. In deciding the most appropriate form of assistance to developing countries the following issues need to be considered:

* *Relative advantage*: It is important to ensure that the recipient country perceives the technology offered to be an improvement over the existing technology in terms of the prevailing culture.

* *Compatibility*: The technology offered should be consistent with the present needs, values, practices and rituals in the receiving culture and, where possible, should be delivered through existing channels in that country.

* *Complexity*: The technology needs to be easy to use and easy to understand. In some cases it may be necessary to introduce an intermediate technology and then switch to a more complex technology at a latter date.

* '*Trialability*': To improve ultimate acceptability of the new technology it is useful if the new technology can be made available to local people on a trial basis for a limited period prior to its full-scale introduction.

* *Observability*: The results or benefits of the innovation to be introduced should be observable. If this is not possible, then the benefits should be communicated in the receiving country in a form that is easy to understand.

By paying attention to the above factors the acceptability of the foreign assistance is likely to be improved. This is because such an approach does not assume members of developing countries do things for the same reasons as people in developed countries or seek the same benefits from the products they use.

## MULTILATERAL DEVELOPMENT AGENCIES (MDA)

These are international financial institutions established to help developing countries promote their economic growth and alleviate poverty. They provide finance on concessional terms and consulting services to member developing countries to undertake development projects and structural reforms.

The projects funded cover activities in infrastructure, income generation and social welfare fields. The MDAs fund only that part of the project involving foreign exchange and the balance is funded by the developing countries themselves or from other sources. As a consequence the value of projects supported by the MDAs is much greater than the financial assistance they extend.

**The World Bank** The World Bank group comprises:

* *International Bank for Reconstruction and Development*—the lending operations of this body are financed by borrowing on the world capital markets. Loans are directed towards the more developed of the developing countries, have a modest grace period and are repayable at between 15 and 20 years;

- *International Development Association*—this is the main facility for the poorer developing countries. The loans have a 10-year grace period and are repayable over 35 to 40 years without interest;

- *International Finance Corporation*—this body assists the development of the less developed countries by mobilising domestic and foreign capital to help the growth of their private sectors; and

- *Multilateral Investment Guarantee Agency*—this arm of the World Bank encourages equity investment flows to developing countries by offering investment guarantees so as to reduce both perceived risk and barriers to investment.

The World Bank has approximately 10 000 staff and 100 offices around the world. There are 185 member countries that contribute capital and it is headquartered in Washington. Its assistance for new projects in 2005 was US$22.3 billion and covered 278 projects. As mentioned earlier, countries contributing to the World Bank look for their contributions to result in contracts being awarded to their firms. It is estimated that Australian firms receive about 1% of the value of contracts awarded by the World Bank. This is equivalent to A$240 million. Looked at in another way, it is estimated that for every $1.00 Australia puts into the World Bank, its firms receive $1.40 in contracts awarded.

**Asian Development Bank** The Asian Development Bank is the largest regional development bank in the Asia–Pacific region and administers four sources of finance:

- *Ordinary Capital Resources*—this is the bank's non-concessional lending arm, which makes funds available on a commercial basis;

- *Asian Development Fund*—this is the arm which makes funds available to the less developed countries on a concessional basis;

- *Technical Assistance Special Fund*—this fund finances technical assistance to developing countries that are members of the bank; and

- *Japan Special Fund*—these funds provided by Japan are also used to finance technical assistance packages.

The Asian Development Bank has staff of about 2000 and, apart from its headquarters in Manila, has 26 other offices. Its largest shareholders are Japan, the USA, China, India and Australia. It has 66 member countries of which 47 are from the region and 19 are from outside the region. It uses the capital subscribed by its members as collateral to borrow funds on world markets. It lends around US$6 billion a year for projects and a further US$186 million for technical assistance projects.

It is estimated that Australia receives 1.5% of the value of contracts awarded by the Asian Development Bank. This is equivalent to A$80 million. From another perspective, for every $1.00 Australia puts into the Asian Development Bank, its firms receive $1.30 in contracts awarded.

**United Nations bodies** The United Nations consists of more than 50 agencies, many of which are major sources of funding for developmental projects and technical assistance. The UN has established an Inter-Agency Procurement Service Office to assist its agencies with procuring supplies and equipment for their projects. This body also publishes a general business guide outlining the UN procurement system.

Australian firms have been successful in obtaining consultancy work and supplying equipment to the United Nations Development Programme, the United Nations Children's

Fund, the World Meteorological Organisation and the United Nations Transitional Authority in Cambodia.

In general, however, it has been found that UN agencies are difficult to deal with, their funding is subject to sudden cutbacks, and obtaining the business is very much dependent on personal contacts and the employment of a well-connected agent. Of total UN procurement that approximates to A$5 billion annually, Australian firms obtain only about 0.45% of the business. From another perspective, for every $1.00 Australia puts into United Nations agencies, its firms receive $0.21 in contracts awarded. This is very low by comparison with the World Bank and Asian Development Bank.

## MARKETING TACTICS

With projects funded by multilateral development agencies it is necessary to lobby both the funding body and the executing agency in the developing country. The Australian firm should use such projects to demonstrate its competencies and become familiar with an overseas market in which it wishes to secure further business. Such exposure will enhance the chances of the firm obtaining non-aid-funded contracts in the future.

When quotes exceed the budget for the project, then it is likely that the project will be rebid and this could involve the Australian firm in lodging another bid with a reduced scope of works. With both the World Bank and the Asian Development Bank, even if the firm does not win the bid, it should attend the debriefing sessions that both institutions conduct in conjunction with the executing agency. Attendance at these sessions facilitates learning what the firm needs to do to improve its chances of success in bidding on similar projects in the future.

In general, business with multilateral development agency-funded projects is very competitive. Firms cannot expect that just because Australia contributes to the agency they will get a piece of the action. The margins in this business are meagre. Firms new to this area should try to gain initial exposure by subcontracting to another firm with experience in bidding for this kind of work.

### 19.1 INTERNATIONAL HIGHLIGHT

## Australian firms blossom in the Middle East market

It is now 10 years since the Australian firm, Multiplex, turned its attention to the Middle East. It has formed a subsidiary in the United Arab Emirates, Nasa Multiplex, to pursue contract work in the region. It successfully built the Emirates Towers Office complex in Dubai and was recently awarded a contract to build 12 residential towers in an expensive area of Dubai valued at A$392 million, bringing to A$4 billion the value of work Multiplex has won in the Middle East.

Australia's well-regarded technology and expertise played a key role in the Australian professional services company GHD winning the contract for the strategic plan for the 2006 Doha Games, following its acquisition of the local firm MME. This acquisition gave GHD local offices in both Qatar and the United Arab Emirates, to be used as a basis for enhancing local credibility and pursuing further work in the region. Previously GHD had been contracted in 2004 by the Sharjah government to produce an expansion and redevelopment program for the Sharjah International Airport. The firm has also been involved in the expansion of the Doha and Al Ain airports and in planning the US$180 million Dubai Maritime City.

**SOURCE:** *Adapted from Department of Foreign Affairs and Trade (2005)* More than Oil: Economic Developments in Bahrain, Kuwait, Oman, Qatar and the United Arab Emirates, *Economic Analysis Unit, Canberra, pp. 53, 58.*

# Projects and bilateral aid

The other major form of aid, much of which is spent on projects and consultancy, is bilateral aid—that is, aid given by an individual country.

## AID ISSUES

Altruism, charity and humanitarian concerns on the part of their citizens motivate countries that give aid. In democratic countries people must be convinced that their government should give the aid. Aid is also given for political reasons, such as the promotion of stability, the encouragement of democracy and the facilitation of strategic alliances. A final motivation is enlightened self-interest, as aid can promote potential benefits for business interests in the donor country.

In positively responding to the request of Thai Prime Minister Chatchai that Australia should fund the erection of the first bridge across the Mekong River between Thailand and Laos (the Friendship Bridge), the Australian Cabinet saw as one of the benefits the possibility of the Australian firms involved winning other infrastructure projects in Thailand, both because of the obligation incurred and the demonstration of Australian engineering capabilities.

Aid given on a bilateral basis can be either tied or untied. Tied aid must be spent on the products or services of the country giving the aid. This makes the giving of the aid more acceptable to the electors of the donor country. It also increases the possibility that the aid will become the foundation of an ongoing economic relationship between the donor and the recipient country. Untied aid, on the other hand, can be spent on the products or services of any country and conforms to the concept that aid should be altruistic. It also enables the aid dollar to go further, as it allows the recipient country to buy from the cheapest source of supply and results in more flexibility in the way the aid money is spent.

Bilateral aid can take a number of forms. It can be by grant. This means that projects are funded by gifts of money and intended to promote goodwill towards the country giving the aid. As with the Friendship Bridge above, grant aid can operate as an advertisement for the donor country and may lead to follow-on commercial work funded on a commercial basis or via multilateral aid.

Bilateral aid can also take the form of loans that are usually extended at concessional rates of interest for longer terms than offered by commercial banks. If the loans are mobilised in the domestic capital market of the donor country, there is an expectation that they will be used to fund purchases from the donor country. Loans from the Japanese post office savings accounts are an example of this loan source. As with all loan forms of aid, bilateral loans can mortgage the future of the developing country, as the increasing debt service commitments may dampen growth momentum and divert scarce capital away from its development priorities.

Bilateral aid can also take the form of technical assistance that aims to strengthen human resources and technical skills in the recipient country. Often it involves education or 'in-house' training programs. One result of this form of aid is that people likely to influence the awarding of contracts become used to the way things are done in the donor country, its technical specifications and its standards. Technical assistance also facilitates the creation of networks of relationships, which can be to the long-term advantage of the overall relationship between the giving and the receiving countries.

## MIXED CREDIT FACILITIES

An increasingly common form of bilateral aid is the mixed credit facility whereby countries use their aid to enhance prospects for their firms to secure project business in developing countries. This is achieved by deploying aid monies to subsidise the interest rates offered by the firm as part of its bid on a project. Until the advent of the Liberal–National Party government in 1996, Australia offered a mixed credit facility known as the Development Import Finance Facility (DIFF). Although no longer in operation, this facility is typical of what Australian firms have to compete against when seeking project work overseas. The DIFF involved a commercial rate loan offered by the Export Finance Insurance Corporation (EFIC) being blended with aid monies from Australia's aid agency. It could take the form of either the EFIC loan and the grant aid being offered separately, or a combination of the two, resulting in a low-interest-rate loan.

Such an arrangement was available only where it could be demonstrated that the market was 'spoilt' by the activities of other countries and that business was not available without offering such a loan. DIFF packages also had to conform to the OECD guideline for export credits that the grant element should not exceed 35%. During its life, the DIFF accounted for an increasing percentage of Australian aid expenditure. It was estimated that for every $1 spent on DIFF, $5 was returned to the Australian economy.

## AUSTRALIAN AID

Australian aid is primarily delivered by AusAID (formerly Australian International Development Assistance Bureau) and approximates to 0.30% of gross national income. It was originally motivated totally by altruism and was all grant aid; that is, commercial linkages were avoided. As other countries increasingly used their aid for commercial advantage, Australia changed its posture and moved towards a more commercial approach to its aid, adopting the 'enlightened self-interest' approach. There has now been a reversal back towards the 'untied' approach.

Currently, of Australia's approximate A\$2.95 billion aid per annum (2006–07), 71% is bilateral, 22% is spent on contributions to multilateral aid agencies and 7% on other forms such as emergency relief. The bilateral aid is divided between human resource development and project assistance to specific countries (AusAID Annual Budget 2006–07; see <http://www.ausaid.gov.au>, accessed 26 April 2007).

The human resource development aspect involves providing government officials from developing countries with postgraduate training in Australia and a scholarship scheme for bright overseas students to undertake tertiary studies in Australia. The project assistance aspect, on the other hand, usually focuses on areas that are developmental in nature and where Australian organisations have competence. In addition to AusAID, other government departments at both state and federal levels provide some overseas aid.

# Financing issues and overseas projects

Discussion so far of bilateral and multilateral aid has treated each of these as being separate from the other. In actual fact many individual projects are funded from a variety of different sources and co-financing is an effective way for collaboration between different sources of funds.

## CO-FINANCING

A significant percentage of projects assisted by the multilateral development banks (MDBs) receive financial support from a co-financier. With the World Bank the figure is 33% of projects with the value of the co-financing being US$9 billion. With the Asian Development Bank the value of co-financing is US$3.15 billion.

**General** The underlying rationale for co-financing is that the MDBs cannot provide all the external funds needed to stimulate growth in member countries. Therefore they seek additional funds from the bilateral aid programs of other countries, or other multilateral agencies, such as regional development banks. They also seek assistance from export credit agencies via loans, guarantees or provision of insurance to commercial banks extending export credit. They may even be provided with funds by commercial banks. Because the MDB is involved, the risk to the lender is reduced as the MDB undertakes activities such as project appraisal and supervision. In addition, this involvement is likely to result in more favourable terms for the commercial portion of the funded project.

The co-finance arrangement will need to be tailored to the objectives and terms of each source of co-financing and will require a sharing of information between the co-financiers. Such an arrangement will also need to be responsive to the restrictions on the use of funds by each party involved. This may require the project being split into different packages, each financed from a different source. The borrowing country may use different procurement procedures for those parts of the project not financed by the MDB. These can be divided into joint and parallel financing:

- *Joint financing* arrangements occur where there is a common list of goods and services and the cost of procuring the goods and services is shared between the MDB and the co-financier in agreed proportions. In this case the bidding procedures and the conditions regarding the opening of the bid must conform to the guidelines of the MDB. Because of these requirements joint financial arrangements are not as acceptable to co-financiers as parallel financial arrangements.

- In *parallel financing* the MDB and the co-financier fund different goods/services or different parts of the project under separate loan agreements. Parallel financing is used where co-lenders put different conditions on the use of their funds with the result that different procurement procedures are applied to different funded segments. As an example, a hydro-electric project could have the following segments each separately funded:
  - roads to the dam site;
  - the dam structure;
  - water control gates;
  - powerhouse and turbines; and
  - transmission lines.

## RISK IDENTIFICATION

There are five major categories of risk in international projects. These need to be identified so that action to minimise risk can be undertaken at each stage.

1 *Start-up cost risk*: At this stage, it is tempting to underestimate initial costs so as to be awarded the business.

2 *Operating cost risk*: At this stage it is important to check that the actual output of the project will be sufficient to service the loan and that the currency is hedged against devaluation, making the imported elements of the project more expensive.

3   *Technology risks*: It is important to guard against the technology employed becoming obsolete. There is also a concept applied at this stage known as the MPT (market × product × technology) index. A high index may increase the rate of return obtained by the lenders and hence the financial attractiveness of the project.

4   *Market risk*: This can be due to loss of competitive position in the market where the project is being implemented, or a delay in introducing the product into the local market.

5   *Political risk*: This can result in currency restrictions, repatriation problems and demands for increased equity. All of these have an adverse impact on the lender.

## BUILD AND OPERATE SCHEMES

There are a number of problems with forms of development assistance discussed to date in this chapter. Given the restraints in developing countries of poor indigenous technology, lack of finance and limited managerial expertise, difficulties often arise once the project is completed and handed over. These difficulties can be due to insufficient training of locals to operate the project, poor maintenance, resort to short-term, cost-driven solutions when something goes wrong, lack of necessary associated infrastructure and inadequate management skills. An alternative, which is becoming increasingly popular, involves the firm or consortium undertaking the project and operating it until its outlay plus profit are recovered from the earnings of the project. At that stage ownership usually reverts to the agency that commissioned the scheme.

These 'build and operate' schemes (Figure 19.2) have a number of variants. These are build, operate and own, in which case the facility is owned by the consortium; build, operate, own and maintain, whereby a maintenance function is added to the responsibility of the consortium; and build, operate and transfer, in which case the facility is transferred to the host government after a specified period.

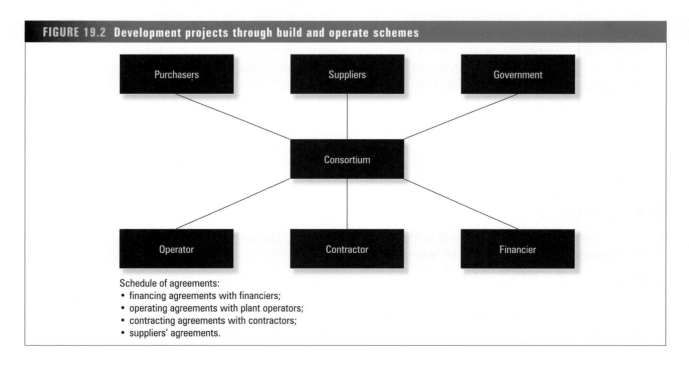

**FIGURE 19.2  Development projects through build and operate schemes**

Schedule of agreements:
- financing agreements with financiers;
- operating agreements with plant operators;
- contracting agreements with contractors;
- suppliers' agreements.

These schemes usually involve the formation of a consortium that includes private sector interests. The consortium funds the cost of the project and builds it. Then it is the consortium that operates and maintains the project. To attract private sector involvement, guarantees are usually required from the host government, so that revenue generation is ensured, and concessions are given to enhance profitability, such as duty-free entry of imports and equipment.

> In India today there is a focus on replacing ageing infrastructure, especially in the power, roads, telecommunications, railway, ports and airport sectors. Public-private sector partnerships are springing up to address this need on a build, operate and transfer basis as illustrated by the US$38 billion program for the rehabilitation of India's roads.

The advantages of build and operate schemes are that they promote investment in developing countries, reduce pressure on local governments to finance their own infrastructure developments and reduce overall potential debt burden and repayment obligations. A single group assumes responsibility for the project and both contractors and financiers have a vested stake in its being successfully completed. The likelihood of overpricing and the risk of inappropriate technology being employed are reduced because this will affect the return on the project. A final advantage is that both appraisal and project evaluation will be more rigorous. This is because those who build it are going to have to operate it for a number of years.

The disadvantages of build and operate schemes are that they cannot be applied to all infrastructure projects. To make the returns commercially attractive, high charges for the resulting product or service must be levied. In addition, to avoid currency risks the resulting revenues have to be either generated in hard currency or pegged to a hard currency. The anticipated revenues are spread over a long period, and both guarantees and extensive legal arrangements are usually required as a prerequisite for the investment. Finally, there is increased risk and uncertainty as opposed to simply constructing a project. This will need to be incorporated into the pricing structure for the project.

## Issues in winning overseas projects

There are a number of additional issues that can have an impact on winning projects overseas. One of the most important of these is to form a consortium of firms that can work together and deliver the completed project on time.

### CONSORTIA FORMATION

Consortia, which are groups of organisations that join together for a specific purpose, are becoming an increasingly common feature of international projects. The first attempt to form consortia for international projects by Australian firms was the Australian Airports Consortium's bid on an airport project in Iran in 1976. Several years later an Australian Overseas Projects Corporation was formed to put together consortia to bid on international projects. It was found that a major problem was the reluctance of Australian firms to work together because they were used to operating on a competitive rather than a cooperative basis. Recent research indicated that of Australian companies operating in Asia, only 9% had joint ventures or strategic alliances with other Australian companies and only 7% had joint ventures or strategic alliances with foreign firms.

The advantages for the Australian firm of entering into consortia with other Australian firms are that:

- it can bid on a project which is too large for it to handle alone;
- it can bid on a project that requires a range of skills that a single firm might not have;
- it can offer greater depth of backup and after-sales service;
- it can reduce the bidding costs for the single firm;
- it can reduce the costs of operating an office in the overseas country where the project is being undertaken; and
- it is a way of spreading risk.

In addition to the above, entering into a consortium with foreign firms enables an Australian firm to bid on a project where it has a unique skill, but lacks the necessary commercial, political or trade relations leverage. It also means that the governments and local commercial representatives of several countries, rather than one country, can lobby the host government as far as the project is concerned. In addition, the aid funds of several countries can be tapped to facilitate the financing of the project.

Some of the disadvantages of consortia include problems in finding the right partners, the decision as to which firm takes the spokesperson role and the nature of the formal partnership, such as joint venture or strategic alliance, between consortia members. Other disadvantages are determining which firm has prime responsibility for relationships with government ministers, officials and business leaders in the host country, and the risk that one of the members of the consortium will adapt your technology and become an eventual competitor.

The Australian Hospital Design Group (AHDG) is a consortium of architectural, engineering and health-care consultants which have been active in the Gulf for the past five years. In conjunction with its local partner, Ishmail Khonji Associates, this consortium in 2003 won a major project to design and construct the A$180 million King Hamad General Hospital in Bahrain. This consortium has also undertaken projects In the Emirates working with its local partner in Dubai, Al Hashemi.

**SOURCE:** *Adapted from Department of Foreign Affairs and Trade (2005)* More than Oil: Economic Developments In Bahrain, Kuwait, Oman, Qatar and the United Arab Emirates, *p. 56.*

# The internet and marketing projects overseas

Project marketing overseas is an offering that combines services and products, with the competitive ingredient usually being the ability to coordinate a series of different inputs to deliver a solution to a problem. Costs are driving construction firms to consider the use of online exchanges to facilitate delivering a solution to the problem. Two large exchanges have been developed to service the Australian market. One, AECventure in the USA, consists of Bovis Lend Lease, AMEC, Hochtief, Turner Corporation and Skanska and is aimed at the global market, including Australia. The other, a local grouping, the Construction Industry Trading Exchange, involves Leighton Holdings and its subsidiaries, Barclay Mowlem, Baulderstone Hornibrook, Clough, Henry Walker Eltin, Transfield and Multiplex. The construction industry has been attracted to online exchanges because of the potential for accessing a wide range of products and facilitating collaboration among the many parties involved. In a single project the exchanges will aim to offer one-stop shops for cataloguing and purchasing goods and services, managing jobs, bidding for tenders and other industry services. In addition, they will facilitate electronic tendering, obtaining updates on new products, support for transactions, streamlined document flows and speedy access to industry news and information—all most important when involved in a project in a developing country.

## Summary

The following technique, based on the work of Luqmani (1988), summarises the main thrust of the discussion in this chapter concerning winning overseas projects.

## The screening process in bid selection

Elements at each stage of the screening process can be classified according to whether they are intrinsic, or unique to the region, or extrinsic, or international practices. Examples of intrinsic factors are local conditions and requirements, whereas examples of extrinsic factors are related to international practices and procedures. With this screening process a large number of firms initially interested in bidding on a project are narrowed down to a few from which one is finally awarded the contract. This is illustrated in Figure 19.3; it is assumed that 100 firms are interested in bidding on the project.

### ELIGIBILITY SCREEN

At this stage intrinsic factors include the cost of the tender documents. These are often very expensive so as to deliberately discourage small or faint-hearted firms.

The requirement to prequalify involves the firm providing details as to legal status, financial status, technical ability and the background and capability of managers. There will also be selection criteria developed by the local managing agency.

Extrinsic factors at this stage consist of external criteria developed by the outside consultant appointed to advise on the project. It may be useful to find out which country the consultant comes from, how the consultant was funded or appointed and what are the consultant's predilections. After this stage only about 50 firms remain.

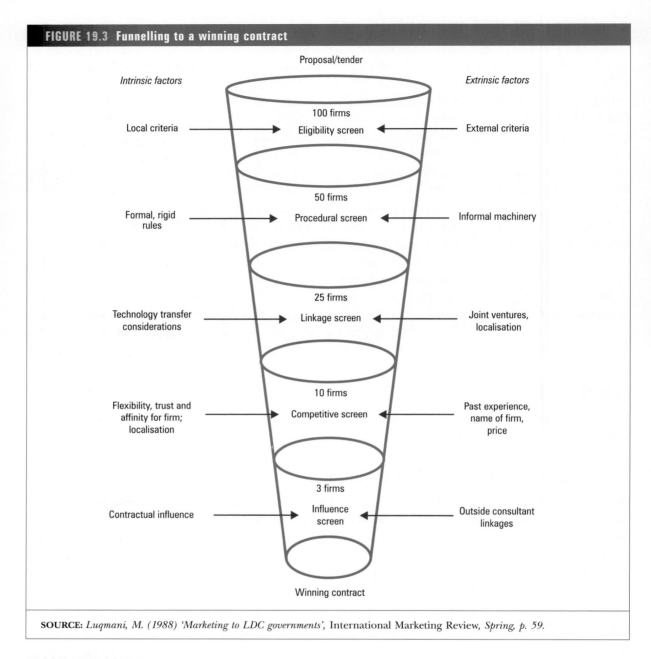

**FIGURE 19.3 Funnelling to a winning contract**

Proposal/tender

*Intrinsic factors*                                          *Extrinsic factors*

100 firms

Local criteria ———————▶ Eligibility screen ◀——————— External criteria

50 firms

Formal, rigid rules ———————▶ Procedural screen ◀——————— Informal machinery

25 firms

Technology transfer considerations ———————▶ Linkage screen ◀——————— Joint ventures, localisation

10 firms

Flexibility, trust and affinity for firm; localisation ———————▶ Competitive screen ◀——————— Past experience, name of firm, price

3 firms

Contractual influence ———————▶ Influence screen ◀——————— Outside consultant linkages

Winning contract

**SOURCE:** *Luqmani, M. (1988) 'Marketing to LDC governments',* International Marketing Review, *Spring, p. 59.*

## PROCEDURAL SCREEN

At this stage the intrinsic factors relate to safeguard procedures designed to get better value for the project's budget and reduce the likelihood of fraud and cheating. The layers of bureaucracy to achieve this can result in 'scrutiny without substance', job creation and cronyism. In addition, bids must conform to specifications. This mindless insistence on conformity to specifications acts as a protection for risk-averse public servants in the managing agency and provides a convenient excuse for disqualifying firms.

From an extrinsic perspective the Australian firm may feel that its experience results in it being able to undertake the project in a more cost-effective way than that prescribed in the tender specifications. Lodging a non-conforming bid instead is not recommended because immediate disqualification is likely to result. A preferable alternative is for the firm to lodge both a conforming and non-conforming bid. The latter can be the subject of negotiation at a more advanced stage of the evaluation. At the conclusion of this stage, about 25 firms remain.

## LINKAGE SCREEN

Intrinsic factors relate to technology transfer. Bidders are required to demonstrate that they will use local technology where available, will diffuse their technology among local firms and will introduce to the country innovative and high technology. The bidder is also required to detail how its proposed activity will train locals and improve their skill levels.

From an extrinsic perspective, the bidder at this stage will also be evaluated on the extent to which it is proposed to enter into partnerships with local firms. At the completion of this stage 10 firms are still under active consideration.

## COMPETITIVE SCREEN

In the intrinsic area, issues will be the sensitivity the bidder displays towards local customs and traditions, the extent of trust built up in dealings to date with the managing agency and evidence that, if awarded the contract, the firm would have a long-term commitment to the host country. From the extrinsic side, factors are the extent of previous experience the firm has had in the host country or, if not in the host country, then in similar environments. Also important is the ability to offer a creative financial package that takes into account the buyer's circumstances. At the end of this stage, possibly three firms remain.

## INFLUENCE SCREEN

This screen comes into play in determining which of the remaining three bidders are successful. Extrinsic factors relate to the foreign consultant and ways of influencing that person. Often it is this consultant who had prepared the tender specifications, who may have oversight in the execution of the project and who has a responsibility to the lending agency for smooth operation of the bidding process.

Intrinsic factors at this final stage relate to those associated with the managing agency that influences the decision. It may be made up of technical officers in the relevant ministry, regional interest groups or provincial administrations operating in the area where the project is to be located, local firms or politically powerful figures or a political party. Then there are those who actually make the award. These include government departments, a minister or a ruler of a state.

# ETHICS ISSUE

Y ou are one of three firms short-listed as managing consultant of a project in Myanmar being funded by OECF of Japan. The value of the consultancy is US$10 million. When you initially submitted prequalification data you appointed as your local representative a retired army officer well connected to the SLORC government. The initial lobbying by this agent has resulted in you now being one of the remaining three bidders. Your agent has now advised that all firms on the shortlist are required to make a 'donation' of US$25 000 to the welfare fund for widows of former army officers. You understand that failure to make this payment will result in your bid not being further considered. This 'unforseen expense' was not factored into your bid price.

***Given the above circumstances, would you make the requested 'donation'?***

## Websites

**AECventure** http://www.aecventure
**Asia Pacific Economic Cooperation (APEC)** http://www.apecsec.org.sg
**Asian Development Bank** http://www.adb.org
**AusAID** http://www.ausaid.gov.au
**Bappenas** http://www.bappenas.go.id
**DACON** http://www.dgmarket.com/dacon
**Export Finance and Insurance Corporation (EFIC)** http://www.efic.gov.au
**GHD** http://www.ghd.com.au
**Leighton Holdings** http://www.leighton.com.au
**Lend Lease** http://www.lendlease.com.au
**Multiplex** http://www.multiplex.com.au
**NESDB** http://www.nesdb.go.th
**Snowy Mountains Engineering Corporation (SMEC)** http://www.smec.com.au
**Transfield Corporation** http://www.transfield.com.au
**United Nations** http://www.un.org
**United Nations Development Programme** http://www.undp.org
**World Bank** http://www.worldbank.org

## Discussion questions

1   Do you consider that the positioning of Australian/New Zealand consultants and contractors when seeking project work overseas could be improved upon? If so, in what ways?

2   What are the relative advantages of multilateral as opposed to bilateral aid from the perspective of an Australian/New Zealand firm bidding on a project overseas?

3   What marketing approaches would you suggest to improve the success rate of Australian/New Zealand consultants and contractors securing projects funded by United Nations agencies?

4   Why do build and operate schemes provide an attractive alternative to concessional loans for implementing projects overseas?

# COPING WITH COUNTERTRADE

## When the going gets tough, the tough turn to countertrade!

When economic circumstances are difficult for a country and foreign exchange is scarce governments move to control foreign exchange. When this happens firms are forced to swap their goods for the goods they want from other countries. An examination of countertrade in Asia reflects this. When times were tough in the early 1980s Indonesia, Malaysia, the Philippines and Thailand arranged for government procurement to be offset by exports of locally produced products instead of payment in hard currency. At that time firms facing restricted access to fully convertible currency (free foreign exchange) also sought to trade internationally using countertrade. However, although these countertrade requirements remained on the books they were not enforced from the mid-1980s to 1997 because circumstances in these countries improved. By early 1998 the Asian currency crisis had resulted in Indonesia's currency having depreciated by 72%, Thailand's by 54%, Malaysia's by 39% and the Philippines' by 31% against the US dollar. This situation has again caused these countries to focus on countertrade as a medium for doing business. Australian firms who refuse to contemplate countertrade during these difficult times when doing business with cash-strapped Asian economies are likely to lose their hard-won position in these markets. As an example, Australian firms that have contracted with Indonesian manufacturers to produce shirts for the Australian market may supply them with cotton and take delivery of the shirts in exchange. This would be at a lower price than before because, although the imported cotton

costs more in Indonesia, the labour element is much cheaper. This would require an arrangement with an Australian cotton exporter to take part in the countertrade deal.

Since the late 1990s times have improved for many countries, especially in Asia, and there is less attention given to countertrade. It still occurs, but the extent to which it is mandated by government has declined due to diminishing government involvement in business worldwide since the fall of the Berlin Wall. Now it is more often at the intra-firm level as evidenced by the implementation of off-shoring, international outsourcing, BOT (build, operate and transfer) arrangements or operation of international strategic alliances. Where countertrade operates at arm's length it is often managed by trading companies with offices worldwide, such as the Japanese trading companies and the South Korean *chaebols*.

# INTRODUCTION

One of the major problems in international marketing, particularly in emerging markets such as the developing economies and the former Centrally Planned Economies, is concluding the transaction and getting paid. While the marketing function may create interest in a product or service and result in an order being placed, often political, legal and economic constraints may result in the international transaction not proceeding because of payments difficulties or impediments from other sources. As far as politics is concerned, governments may influence import sourcing in line with their bilateral or regional trade relations commitments, their industrialisation objectives and their political relationships. These may result in selective or blanket prohibitions on importing from a specific source (e.g. boycotts or embargoes). Regarding legal constraints, transactions might not proceed because they involve breaches of international law or of the national law of the countries whose firms are party to the transaction. One mechanism for addressing these problems is a range of trade practices collectively known as countertrade that can be defined as the linking of an import and an export transaction in a conditional fashion (Fletcher 1996). The various forms of countertrade will be discussed in detail later in this chapter, but can be summarised as follows:

- barter (direct exchange of goods/services without involvement of money);

- counterpurchase (separate contracts covering goods offered and goods received linked by another contract making the performance of one conditional on the performance of the other with some settlement in cash is required);

- offsets (involving a mandated government requirement and driven by a desire to acquire technology as well as to reduce foreign exchange outlay);

- buyback (building or rehabilitating a production facility and being paid in resulting output); and

- debt (discharging debt for goods/services so as to improve future borrowing collateral).

Countertrade can address problems of concluding transactions and getting paid because it operates as an alternative means of undertaking international trade without the use of money (e.g. barter) for all or part of the payment. It can also be a means of attracting foreign involvement and securing innovative technology (e.g. offsets and buyback); of either improving or bypassing traditional trade relations obligations (long-term counterpurchase arrangements or individual barter transactions); and evasion of international prohibitions (e.g. triangular countertrade with a third country that is not party to the embargo–see Fletcher 2003). From a legal perspective countertrade operates as an avoidance mechanism because when full settlement is not required it is difficult to prove that the law has been broken, especially when the law relates to breaches measured in monetary terms as with dumping. When money is not involved the point at which title to the goods is transferred is also more difficult to prove. It is factors like the above that have enabled countries such as Libya, Iran and Iraq regularly to breach OPEC guidelines. Countertrade operates as an alternative to aid when foreign exchange is in short supply and debt countertrade can improve a nation's credit rating and future borrowing potential.

## Forces fuelling countertrade

The last 20 years have seen greater changes in the global geo-political system than at any other time since the aftermath of World War II and have involved major change in the region that was most commonly associated with countertrade in popular consciousness. Developing countries tend to be pushed towards countertrade because of declining foreign exchange reserves. The decline has been largely due to adverse long-term movement in the terms of trade for developing countries. Being largely dependent on agricultural products and resources, these countries were finding that prices for these products were not rising as fast as the prices they were having to pay for the manufactures and high-tech products they imported. As a result, they were having to export larger volumes of agricultural products and raw materials to fund the same volume of imports as the terms of trade continued to move against them.

Coinciding with this development were moves by developed countries to restrict their imports of agricultural products in response to pressure from their own farmers. Not only did this reduce demand from developed countries for the agricultural exports of developing countries, but it resulted in the developed countries subsidising farmers to grow surpluses, which were then dumped on the other markets traditionally supplied by more efficient producers from developing countries. The initiators were the European countries with the Common Agricultural Policy of the EC, and they were matched by the USA which introduced a similar measure under the US Farm Bill—the Grain Enhancement Program.

The resulting trade deficits coincided with a reduction in aid from developed to developing countries. Developed countries claimed that the global recession did not enable them either to give aid or extend long-term, low-interest loans to developing countries to the same extent as previously. The hike in oil prices of the 1970s also severely affected many developing countries, especially those dependent on imported energy—increasing the pressure on them to engage in countertrade. Ironically, it also resulted in increased countertrade by OPEC members such as Libya, Iran and Iraq as a way of circumventing the minimum prices and maximum quantities previously agreed to.

The desire for technology has been a similar stimulus to countertrade. Historically, technology has been acquired by surrendering equity, as with a joint venture, or by payment of fees, as with licensing arrangements. Countries facing foreign exchange shortages may be unable to afford the fees, and socialist countries may be unwilling to surrender equity on philosophical grounds. Certain forms of countertrade such as buyback can enable the acquisition of technology without payment of fees in foreign exchange or giving up ownership.

Hennart (1989) argues that saving on foreign exchange is not the only reason for countries to engage in countertrade. Another is to reduce transaction costs by building up reciprocity. This is because countertrade includes a variety of contracts with very different characteristics. In addition, with intermediate products, technology and distribution services, countertrade is more about reducing transaction costs than saving foreign exchange. Countertrade here involves transforming a unilateral supply relationship into a bilateral one, in which A's sale to B will be contingent on B selling to A, and reciprocity is used to equalise the exposure of the parties.

Due to recent major changes in the international marketing environment, such as the rise of transnational companies, the information revolution and the increasing problems national governments face in protecting themselves from international trends and developments, there have been changes in countertrade. The classical forms such as barter and counter-purchase are on the decline, and there is greater emphasis placed on long-term and development-oriented forms of countertrade such as offsets and buyback.

Involving industrial cooperation and compensation arrangements, these countertrade forms also extend to financial arrangements, such as swapping debt for equity and equity arrangements like build, operate and transfer projects. In addition, in recent years there has been a change in government policy towards countertrade away from direct reciprocity to broader-based economic objectives, such as solving economic problems, creating regional employment, establishing export industries, acquiring new technology and meeting other national agendas.

## Incidence of countertrade

A precise calculation of the extent of countertrade is impossible as statistics related to countertrade are not collected by any one country, let alone by any international body. Estimates of countertrade range from 5% to 40%, but this is a matter of what is included in countertrade; countries such as the USA do not include offsets whereas others such as Australia do. A consensus view would be that countertrade accounts for approximately 15–20% of world trade. Whatever the proportion, there is no doubt that countertrade is a significant and permanent feature of the international trade scene.

## Forms of countertrade

The term 'countertrade' covers transactions of a variety of types. These are explained in more detail below. Often barter is used synonymously with countertrade, but countertrade involves activities other than barter. The main forms of countertrade are barter, counterpurchase, offsets and buyback. There are a number of variants, such as switch trading or swaps, clearing arrangements or countertrade involving debt. There are differing opinions as to what each form of countertrade includes, and there is some overlapping between forms.

### BARTER

Barter is the direct exchange of goods or services between two principals, technically without any flow of money taking place. In reality, with a number of barter transactions banks finance the operations and money changes hands between a number of parties. It is, however, the original form of countertrade and the simplest form. It involves a double coincidence of wants: the buyer must want what the seller is offering and the seller must want what the buyer is offering.

In cases where one party does not really want what the other is offering, the transaction is unlikely to proceed unless there is a third party, such as a trading company that is willing to take the goods and dispose of them on the open market. Barter is a one-time transaction and involves only one contract, covering the offsetting deliveries between the two parties. The goods to be exchanged are specified at the time the contract is signed. Barter takes place over a relatively short time to minimise the effect of price fluctuation in the market value of the goods being exchanged. Because of the difficulty of matching needs and wants the significance of barter is diminishing and it now accounts for around 8% of global countertrade. As an example of a barter arrangement, in 2001 Malaysia purchased diesel locomotives from General Electric in the USA in exchange for 200 000 tons of palm oil.

### COUNTERPURCHASE

Counterpurchase is the most common form of countertrade, although recently its importance has been diminishing. At present about 45% of global countertrade takes this form. With counterpurchase, the exporter agrees to buy goods and/or services equivalent to an agreed proportion of the firm's deliveries. The proportion can vary from as little as 10%

to as much as 150%. Counterpurchase agreements are often part of a package put together in the absence of traditional financing, and can be combined with aid, loans or part payment in cash (Holmes 1995). Often the goods received relate to the activities of the exporting firm. Where the goods are unrelated, as with barter, complicated commercial arrangements may be required to dispose of the goods (these are discussed under the variant of switch deals).

Counterpurchase arrangements, sometimes referred to as parallel barter, usually involve two separate contracts for the deal, each of which is linked by a third contract. The first of the contracts (the primary contract) covers the sale of the seller's goods; the second (secondary contract) covers the undertaking by the seller to buy the countertrade goods; the third (contract protocol) links the primary and secondary contracts.

From the above it will be appreciated that the exchange is not necessarily equal and that the transactions are of longer duration than is the case with barter. This is especially the case when evidence accounts (discussed later) are included. An example of this is Lockheed Martin Corporation of the USA, which sold 48 F-16 Falcons to Poland, paid for by a variety of Polish manufactured goods.

## OFFSETS

Offsets are described by the World Trade Organization as measures used in government procurement to encourage local development or improve the balance of payments account by means of domestic content, licensing of technology, investment requirements, countertrade or similar arrangements. Waller (2003) argues that in the current competitive environment in the global defence industry, a selling firm must offer offsets to the buyer if they are to have a chance of winning the business.

Often referred to as mandated countertrade because it is a requirement for doing business with many overseas governments, offsets are routinely required by at least 50 countries and a further 50 countries have the legislative provisions to require offsets if this is expedient. Offsets are associated with foreign purchases made by governments, government instrumentalities or private sector corporations subject to government regulation, such as parties to the previous two-airline agreement in Australia. Originally motivated by government desire to use the leverage of its large-volume procurement to offset the foreign exchange cost, the focus is now on using the leverage to achieve the transfer of technology. As a consequence, the quality of what is offered as an offset is more important than the percentage of the offset offered, and multipliers are applied to offset credits when the offset proposal is particularly attractive in technology or investment terms. Offset arrangements are usually of long duration because of the need to prequalify and often upgrade the technology of overseas suppliers and train their personnel (see International Highlight 19.2).

Current government thinking in Australia regarding offsets is that criteria in evaluating proposals should change from an examination of offsets for individual projects to consideration of the long-term benefit offered to Australia's industrial capability by partnership involvement at a conceptual stage, as with the Joint Strike Fighter (JSF) program, which will involve Australia being responsible for a piece of the action in all units produced.

Government purchases may be in the defence sector, as with the procurement by the Royal Australian Air Force of F/A-18 fighter-bombers from McDonnell-Douglas of St Louis, USA, or in the civil sector, as with the purchase by Qantas of aircraft from Boeing Corporation of Seattle, USA. *Military offsets* may be motivated by security considerations as well as technology and financial reasons. This happens when a country sees advantage in an ally's having compatible equipment in a location considered vital to its strategic interests, or when it is

## 19.2 INTERNATIONAL HIGHLIGHT

# The Australian government and Boeing

I n the late 1960s the Australian government wanted to offset the foreign exchange outlay involved in the procurement of new-generation aircraft from Boeing. Approaches to the US company resulted in three trial work packages for the new 747—angle gearbox assemblies, acrylic passenger windows and escape chute packing boards. Accompanying these work packages were stringent requirements and tolerances, as Boeing could take no risk of aircraft falling out the sky due to faulty overseas components. Once these trial packages demonstrated a capacity to meet Boeing's standards, work commenced to isolate packages of work in which Australian industry had the capability to become a long-term supplier to Boeing or its major subcontractors. Two areas were selected: spars and ribs for the tail assemblies of aircraft supplied directly to Boeing, and turbo fan blades supplied to engine manufacturers such as General Electric. In both cases the Australian firms involved became either sole or one of the two or three supply sources. This generated sufficient work volume to comply largely with the offset requirements imposed by the Australian government. Today, Australian firms continue to supply these and other components to Boeing and reciprocal purchasing is a factor taken into account when orders are placed for new aircraft. Today a typical 747 aircraft is likely to have landing gear doors from Northern Ireland, wing tip assemblies from Korea, rudders and spars for tail assemblies from Australia, outboard wing flaps from Italy and fuselages from Japan.

necessary to have maintenance and servicing facilities in another country. Liesch (1991) explores government-mandated countertrade in the case of Australia and the technical transfer imperative underlying it. *Civil offsets*, on the other hand, may be motivated by the desire to have the foreign supplier establish manufacturing facilities in the country imposing the offsets, possibly in undeveloped regions of the country. Due to the cessation of the Cold War the emphasis in offsets has shifted during the last decade from defence to civil. Many countries have either introduced or refined offsets programs so that they now extend beyond the traditional defence, aerospace and telecommunications sectors.

Offsets may be direct or indirect. *Direct offsets* relate to the product being sold, and their cost is included in the total bid. They include licensed production, co-production and transfer of technology. The nature of the direct offset package offered was a significant factor in the award by the Royal Australian Air Force to British Aerospace of a contract to supply Hawk jet aircraft worth US$800 million. Eighty per cent of this contract took the form of co-production and industrial cooperation between British Aerospace and its Australian subcontractors. *Indirect offsets* are not related to the product being delivered. They may be products that can be disposed of via the established distribution channels of the seller; they may involve using the seller's expertise and contacts to establish an agency/distribution network; or may be an unrelated product which the seller has to dispose of through a third party. Careful research is necessary before accepting products as indirect offsets, as the following story illustrates.

*In the 1970s Douglas Aircraft Company of Long Beach, California (now a division of the Boeing Corporation), sold a DC9 aircraft to an East European airline. Payment was in canned ham. However, after the contract was consummated, it was found that the ham did not conform to the requirements that would allow it to be sold commercially in the USA. As a result, the ham was on the menu of staff canteens at various facilities of the McDonnell-Douglas Corporation for many years.*

Anecdotal evidence also suggests that, overall, direct forms of offsets are declining and indirect forms are rising. Over 20% of global countertrade takes the form of offsets.

## BUYBACK

Buyback, otherwise known as compensation payment, occurs when the seller of capital equipment or a project development, as with a turnkey operation or upgrading of an obsolete plant, accepts part or all of the payment in annual deliveries of goods produced by the factory. Buyback operates as a vehicle for industrialisation and facilitates technology transfer. It is linked to the expansion of exports because a significant percentage of the goods produced may be shipped offshore to defray the cost of the equipment and services supplied.

As previously mentioned, it is an important form of countertrade in cases where investment and technology transfer is desired, but foreign exchange is in short supply and there are philosophical impediments to surrendering equity to foreign interests. Buyback has increased substantially in the former Centrally Planned Economies over recent years as they strive to upgrade obsolete plants to produce the goods consumers are clamouring for. One of the advantages of buyback is that the supplier of the plant and equipment is forced to be concerned with quality, as shortcomings in this connection are likely to be reflected in the product received. Buyback is the fastest-growing form of countertrade and, although it fluctuates, it now approximates 20% of global countertrade. Increasingly, overseas joint ventures in the developing and former communist world are being financed by buyback. From this countertrade arrangement, non-countertrade business followed.

In the mid-1980s Bulk Materials Coal Handling of Sydney (BMCH) learnt of an opportunity in Vietnam to rehabilitate two coal washeries operating at about one-third capacity. The Vietnamese were seeking a buyback arrangement, with payment being in the form of coal resulting from expansion of washery capacity. Being an engineering firm, BMCH had no use for the coal, so contracted with White Industries to accept the coal at the Port of Haiphong. White Industries found a customer for the coal in Hong Kong and, once they received payment, they credited the funds to the BMCH bank account in Sydney. In subsequent years in Vietnam, BMCH won a privately funded coal washery rehabilitation project and then two aid-funded projects of a similar nature.

The interrelationship between these four major forms of countertrade is shown in Figure 19.4.

## DEBT

Reports of countertrade transactions increasingly mention the countertrading of debt. This may take the form of a seller accepting goods to discharge an obligation involving a party in another country. Once the goods are received they can then be sold and the debt discharged in whole or in part. Such an arrangement assists the firm in the other country because it reduces its indebtedness and improves its future borrowing collateral. As far as debt is concerned, it is often undesirable to have 'too many eggs in one basket', and to achieve a more balanced debt portfolio it may be in the interests of the firm to countertrade debt for debt. In cases where the firm wants to discharge some of its debt and cannot repay in either cash or goods, it may elect to countertrade debt for equity, and the party to which it owes money becomes a shareholder in the firm. The number of transactions involving the countertrade of debt, especially among the former Centrally Planned Economies, has risen during recent years and now transactions involving debt probably account for about 10% of global countertrade.

A rise in the number of these transactions was triggered after the collapse of the USSR, and the Russian payments system degenerated into countertrade operations. Typical of such transactions was the swapping of truckloads of aspirin for poultry, which in turn was bartered

## FIGURE 19. 4  The complex web of countertrade transactions

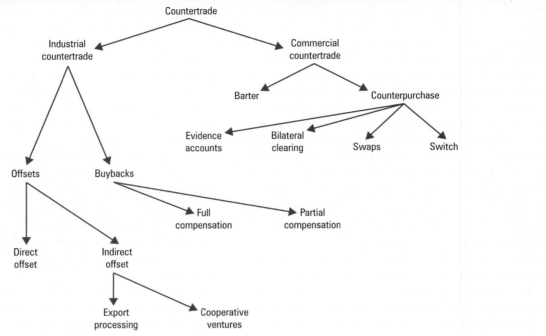

**SOURCE:** *Brennan, M. (1998) 'Government pro-active countertrade: a decade of deals', Working Paper, Economics Department, Murdoch University. Reproduced with permission.*

for lumber, which was then exchanged for X-ray equipment from Kazakhstan so as to settle debts.

## VARIANT: CLEARING ARRANGEMENTS

Particularly with barter and counterpurchase, when the projected annual trade turnovers are likely to be substantial, countertrade can be conducted under an umbrella arrangement that allows for the inclusion of multiple trading parties. When the agreement is between a private sector exporter and a government entity in the other country, it is known as an evidence account. When the agreement is between the governments of two countries, it is known as a bilateral clearing arrangement. In both cases, the parties agree to countertrade nominated items of interest to each other over a specified period, usually one to three years, up to a specified level. The flows both ways are recorded in the same currency and regularly monitored. At the end of the period or after an agreed time, any outstanding balance is settled in free foreign exchange or liquefied by switching the rights to the trade imbalance to third parties at discounted prices. Clearing arrangements were widespread in the trade of the communist countries, both between themselves and between them and developing countries. The oil crisis led to a number of clearing arrangements with some oil-producing nations. With the fall of communism and the world decline in oil prices, clearing arrangements are a less common feature of countertrade. In the early 1990s Indonesia signed clearing arrangements with both Iran and Iraq.

## VARIANT: SWITCH TRADING

In the operation of clearing accounts, credit balances can accumulate in favour of one of the signatories. These credits can be sold at a discount to a third party. This party, often referred to as a switch trader, can on-sell them to someone else or use the credit to buy goods to export to the debtor country. In the process the title to the goods can be switched from one party to others. Switch traders can also be used when the goods offered in countertrade are of little interest to the seller, who wants to receive cash without delay. The goods are sold at a discount to a switch trader who finds another party interested in them.

# Content of countertrade transactions

Australian firms, when contemplating entering new overseas markets, especially those in developing countries or former socialist countries, are likely to be asked to consider accepting countertrade. Even firms that have been exporting to markets for some time may be asked to consider countertrade when those markets encounter economic turmoil, and to accept countertrade if they want to retain their position in such markets. Firms will need to decide whether countertrade is unavoidable because being paid in cash is preferable and less complicated. If the countertrade is unavoidable the firms should then decide whether they would be better off considering other markets instead. Such decisions require some understanding of the global pattern of countertrade.

Fletcher (2001) addressed this problem by analysing reported countertrade transactions (which numbered 3544) over a 12-year period from 1987 to 1999 in terms of products, region, size, form and interactive aspects. His findings are discussed below.

## PRODUCTS

The most frequently countertraded product group on a global basis is industrial equipment. Over the period this replaced basic manufactures as the most frequently countertraded category, reflecting the rise in more sophisticated forms of countertrade such as offsets and buybacks and the decline in less sophisticated forms such as barter and counterpurchase, which were more suitable for mature products that were difficult to dispose of and lacked technological uniqueness. The pattern varies markedly from region to region and from country to country within each region, reflecting differing resource endowment and distinctive competence in international trade. This information provides managers with a guide as to what product categories are countertraded on a global basis, and managers will need to ascertain whether the potential countertrade partner can supply goods that can easily be disposed of if received as a result of a countertrade transaction.

## REGIONS

The current and former Centrally Planned Economies, followed by developed countries, were the groups most often involved in countertrade. The involvement of the developed countries suggests that countertrade tends to take place between countries at different stages of economic development, reflecting the need for less fortunate countries to obtain technically advanced products and services. It also reflects the importance of offsets in countertrade, as offsets usually involve the more developed countries. Over the 12 years of the study, there appears to have been a decline in the involvement of low-income developing countries, reflecting their deteriorating economic situation and increasing inability to offer for countertrade anything their more developed potential countertrade partners might want. Knowledge about whether specific regions are increasing or reducing their involvement in countertrade compared with the global trend can be useful to managers, as this may indicate how countertrade approaches are likely to be received, especially by governments. A knowledge of the motivation for regions and countries to engage in countertrade is also useful.

## SIZE

The complexities of international countertrade suggest that more managerial time is required when countertrade is involved, and disposing of goods received will involve either additional management effort or expense due to offloading the transaction onto a specialist intermediary. Either way, it is unlikely that firms will bother with countertrade unless the value of the transaction is sufficiently large to justify the additional time and expense involved. A majority of countertrade transactions are in excess of US$100 million on a global basis. Before accepting a countertrade proposition Australian managers will need to decide whether their firm is large enough to undertake the countertrade successfully and, if not, to assess whether the transaction contains sufficient profit to enable the products received to be on-sold at a discount to another party.

## FORM

In the earlier discussion of various forms of countertrade, the consensus view was given as to the share of global countertrade accounted for by each major form of countertrade. This pattern is not the same for all countries, as is illustrated in the case of Australia, where offsets are more important than buyback, and Malaysia, where offsets were the most frequently used form of countertrade. The tendency of one region to engage more in one type of countertrade than another region may affect the attractiveness of a countertrade proposition. In addition, as discussed earlier, different factors drive different forms of countertrade. Therefore, when considering a countertrade approach it is desirable to evaluate the potential countertrade partner in terms of factors that drive the form of countertrade that is being proposed.

## INTERACTIVE ASPECTS

Countertrade involves a conditional relationship—therefore it is necessary to consider not only the frequency of participation by each group of countries, and frequency of product categories countertraded, but also the extent to which countries in one group countertrade with countries in another group as opposed to countries in the same group, and products in one category are countertraded with products in another category as opposed to products in the same category.

A knowledge of interactive patterns in the countertrade of products can be useful, as a guide as to what categories of products are likely to be offered when countertrade is proposed for a specific product group. A knowledge of whether or not there is the tendency to countertrade within the same product category may enable managers to locate better products which they can use within their own operation, handle through their established distribution channels or more easily dispose of to other organisations. If a switch deal is necessary a knowledge of product interactions in countertrade may assist in locating a switch partner.

# Macro perspective

Countertrade is often a response to conditions in the international environment—whether political, commercial, legal or financial. In evaluating a countertrade proposition the firm needs to consider how these macro issues affect involvement with the country concerned.

## POLITICAL AND COMMERCIAL PERSPECTIVES

Countertrade offers political advantages. The willingness of another country to accept countertrade can strengthen bilateral ties between nations, and often countertrade will be the subject of bilateral trade talks between countries. In 2004, offsets were an issue considered in the context of the proposed free trade area between Australia and the United States (Williams 2004). In some cases it may be included in bilateral trade agreements as an incentive to organisations in both countries to countertrade with each other a list of designated items. This is particularly relevant when the arrangement is on a clearing account basis. Developing countries are susceptible to falling commodity prices and this is of concern to their governments. Countertrade can alleviate the problem by linking the sale of one commodity to the procurement of another product, thus eliminating price fluctuation in the short term.

Governments wanting to boost the technology base in their country can use countertrade as a vehicle to attract the technology they seek. The Australian government has used offsets for this purpose, and the former Centrally Planned Economies have used buybacks in the same way. Also, when a country has a pool of unemployed labour, countertrade, by providing additional employment, can be attractive to government.

One of the major disadvantages of countertrade is that it is opposed by the World Trade Organization on the grounds that it contravenes the spirit and intent of GATT principles. These include non-discrimination, as countertrade is a relationship whereby each party discriminates in favour of the other; multilateralism, as countertrade is a bilateral arrangement; non-distortion of the natural flow of trade, as countertrade distorts the flow of trade towards the countertrade partner; and transparency, as countertrade is not transparent and is surrounded with secrecy. The developed countries have done well from the GATT system of open trade, and over the past half century have become richer while the developing countries as a group have become poorer. Many of the developed countries view countertrade as eroding their natural competitive advantage.

## LEGAL PERSPECTIVE

Disadvantages relate to there being no specific body of law covering countertrade—nor is countertrade provided for in the body of international law. Those international trade laws that might apply to countertrade are not generally enforced. Because countertrade transactions can often involve a number of actors in a number of countries, the issue of whose law applies in the event of a dispute is even more complex than with normal international transactions. In addition, as countertrade often involves the government as one party, the potential for resolving a dispute is lessened due to the difficulty of a foreign company successfully pursuing legal action against a sovereign government.

Advantages of countertrade from a legal perspective relate to its use as a legal avoidance mechanism. With countertrade, price is not transparent. This enables the use of countertrade as a device to mask a price cut. Libya and Iran use countertrade for this purpose in the case of oil. In the same way, countertrade can be used to disguise dumping. As it is difficult to assess the true value placed on goods exchanged in a countertrade transaction, proving dumping in a court of law is problematic. Countertrade is used on occasion, in a similar way to transfer pricing by multinational firms, to minimise tax liability. As it is possible to switch title to the goods so that a number of different parties are involved in a transaction before the goods are finally disposed of, the transaction can be structured so that the resulting profit is brought to account in a low-tax regime. Countertrade has even been used to evade embargoes: anecdotal comment suggests that US oil firms with investments in Iran evade the US embargo on the export of oil from Iran through countertrade with countries in Central Asia. Finally, countertrade can be used to delay the repayment of debt. If certain South American organisations with large debts to US banks export products for cash, they face pressure to use the resulting receipts to reduce their indebtedness. If, on the other hand, payment for the boatload of bananas is in steel billets, pressure is less likely due to the non-liquid nature of the payment received for the bananas.

## FINANCIAL PERSPECTIVE

The financial advantages from a macro perspective include the use of countertrade as an antidote to dependence on aid. With the drying up of long-term, low-interest loans and a reduction in grant aid, developing countries increasingly turned to countertrade. Whereas aid promotes continued dependence, it can be argued that countertrade promotes independence, as the countries concerned have to produce items to pay for the infrastructural developments they need or for the technology transferred to them.

Another advantage of countertrade is that it can be used to liquefy frozen assets. From a country perspective, if foreign exchange shortages force it to freeze or limit the repatriation of funds from that country, the country becomes unattractive as a location for foreign investment. Funds can be unfrozen by being used to buy goods on the local market. These goods are then shipped and, when sold overseas, converted into cash.

There are several financial disadvantages associated with countertrade. Because of the possibility of multiple parties in the transaction and because recourse to a boatload of bananas is not as attractive as recourse to cash, there are often problems with insuring countertrade transactions. Even where insurance is available it is more expensive and the additional premiums must be included in the arrangement. On average, the extra premiums in Australia for insuring countertrade transactions approximate to 5%. Countertrade also adds to the cost of conducting the transaction. This can be measured by the discount applied when the countertrade obligation is offloaded onto a third party. This discount, which is termed 'disaggio', can vary from 2% to 20%, depending on the products and countries involved. Countries such as Malaysia will not approve countertrade transactions involving the use of intermediaries as they claim they inflate the cost of the transaction and reduce the returns to the Malaysian parties involved. In 2007, the Philippines government called for tenders for the supply of 500 000 tonnes of rice and asked tenderers to supply a price if countertrade were to be involved and a price if it were not, so they could calculate the cost of countertrade (Reuters 2007).

A final problem relates to establishing a basis for value for duty and other imposts where countertrade is concerned.

## Micro perspective

Apart from weighing up advantages and disadvantages of entering into countertrade with organisations in the overseas market, it is necessary to assess the advantages and disadvantages to the Australian firm itself.

## ADVANTAGES TO THE FIRM

If the firm is prepared to accept countertrade its immediate offer becomes more attractive to the other party and it is more attractive as a source of imports in the longer term. Willingness to accept countertrade is likely to facilitate entry into overseas markets, especially into those that actively seek to do business on a countertrade basis. The firm is also likely to find attractive the using of countertrade as a vehicle for recovering outstanding debt and for unfreezing frozen assets. Apart from overcoming currency and foreign exchange problems, countertrade is a useful way of building close relationships with overseas customers. It is possible that these customers will appreciate the Australian firm's willingness to countertrade during a period of difficulty and will show this appreciation by trading with the Australian firm on a normal basis when times improve. For example, Bulk Materials Coal Handling of Sydney won its first coal washery rehabilitation contract in Vietnam using buyback. Subsequently it has been awarded other projects that did not involve the use of countertrade.

Although not common, it is possible for a firm engaging in countertrade to experience a double opportunity to make profit—profit on the goods exported to the overseas customer, and profit on the goods received in countertrade when on-sold. A final advantage of countertrade to the firm is its use for lining up a long-term source of supply, especially of items whose availability is subject to fluctuation. Independent Seafoods of Western Australia faced a shortage of shrimp for the Asian restaurant trade in Australia. Traditional sources of supply in Thailand, Malaysia and Indonesia were already committed, but they discovered abundant supply of this shrimp in the waters off the southern part of Vietnam. However, the catching, processing and packing of these shrimp did not meet either Australian quarantine or market requirements. The company set up a program with two major seafood processors in Ho Chi Minh City whereby Independent Seafood's personnel supervised the trawling operation, provided equipment for the hygienic processing and freezing of the catch, supplied packaging materials and oversaw the packaging operation. In return, they were paid for their involvement and equipment/materials supply in shrimp and had first call on buying additional product for the Australian market.

## DISADVANTAGES TO THE FIRM

For every countertrade proposal the firm receives the number that come to fruition can be as low as one in 15 (Holmes 1995). Countertrade is costly. It inevitably raises the price of goods being sold. It involves a reduction in liquidity and can affect cash flow from international activities. Often there is insufficient time available before the deal must be signed, to undertake a market analysis—both of what will happen to the goods supplied and prospects of disposing of the goods received in exchange. Of constant concern is how to cater for the day-to-day fluctuations in the price of the goods involved during the period of the negotiations. Governments of some countries insist that, in countertrade deals, the valuation on the commodities from their country must be at world market prices, which leaves no room for the cost of countertrade and shifts the cost back onto the Australian party involved. Discounts are often required to dispose of the goods received in countertrade, and both inflation and fluctuating exchange rates complicate pricing issues in countertrade, making it more onerous than with normal international transactions.

Countertrade involves greater risk. This relates to the buyer's ability to supply the goods, the reliability and punctuality of deliveries, the possibility of anti-dumping action when disposing of the goods and bureaucratic delays and obstacles. Another source of risk is arriving at a realistic value for the goods involved in the transaction. Countertrade is expensive in terms of management time because negotiations for finalising a countertrade deal are lengthy and may continue for years. Further disadvantages relate to the products received in countertrade: often these will need modification before they can be sold in Australia or elsewhere. It was found with pepper received as a result of countertrade with Vietnam that it was necessary to reclean and repack it before it could be sold. Another product-related problem relates to the fact that the source of supply of the countertrade product is often not well known, and extra expense is incurred in marketing the product. This may involve publicity to convince buyers that the Vietnamese pepper is as good as the Indian pepper with which they are familiar, or selling the Vietnamese pepper at a discount.

A final product problem relates to shipment of commercial quantities. This is particularly a problem when the countertrade is with a socialist country, where there are national import–export companies for each product category. Although a contract signed with the Vietnamese National Import/Export Company for spices will specify quantities and delivery dates, the company relies on a number of widely spread cooperatives to deliver the pepper to the dock. If one or more do not meet the deadline imposed by the company, shipment may be delayed or be less than anticipated.

## USE OF INTERMEDIARIES

Intermediaries can be professional countertrade firms, such as those operating from Vienna to assist firms counter-trading with Eastern Europe, or those established in Singapore under that nation's pioneer industries program to countertrade with socialist states in Asia. Intermediary functions are also performed by international trading firms, such as the Japanese *sogo sosha* or the South Korean *chaebol*. These trading companies are well placed to act as intermediaries because their network of international offices enables them to stitch countertrade deals together. An issue for the firm to consider when confronted with a countertrade proposal is whether to undertake the countertrade itself or use the services of an intermediary. Using an intermediary will add to costs and may eliminate the financial viability of the transaction. On the other hand, the intermediary may, through its experience and contacts, be the only means of consummating the countertrade. The issue for decision is: when should an intermediary be used by the Australian firm?

Firms with countertrade experience such as Elders would argue that intermediaries should be used when firms are inexperienced with the concept of countertrade, when the product received cannot be used within the firm, when the product being offered is one outside the firm's normal sphere of activity, or when it cannot be disposed of through the distribution channels which the firm controls. It is necessary to enquire in advance whether there is any impediment to the use of an intermediary because, as mentioned, some countries prohibit countertrade involving intermediaries.

# Strategic considerations in international countertrade

Apart from the decision as to whether to include countertrade in the firm's overall international marketing strategy, there are several strategic considerations relating directly to countertrade that need to be considered.

## WHOSE ADVANTAGE?

Often the firm responding to a countertrade request views the matter from the perspective of the firm's advantage alone and how both to minimise the countertrade and get rid of the obligation as quickly as possible. As pointed out earlier, countertrade is a lengthy process, often extending over a number of years. Some countertrade forms also involve high degrees of mutual obligation. Therefore, instead of viewing countertrade in terms of company advantage, it may be preferable to view it in terms of mutual advantage and use the initial transaction as a vehicle to create a long-term commercial relationship from which both parties benefit.

## PRICING STRATEGIES

Because of the importance of price in international countertrade it is desirable to determine in advance a pricing strategy. As Paun and Albaum (1995) point out, this involves establishing the marketing objectives of both buyer and seller. From these marketing objectives the pricing strategies of both buyer and seller are derived. These strategies can be categorised as to premium pricing strategy, going-rate pricing strategy and discount pricing strategy. In the case of both buyer and seller in countertrade the premium pricing strategy involves a price above market value, the going-rate pricing strategy involves a price equal to market value and the discount strategy involves a price below market value. Figure 19.5 matches the seller's and buyer's strategies.

Where the seller's pricing strategies result in a pricing policy the same as or less than that of the buyers, there is potential for countertrade to take place. Such a situation applies in cells 1, 4, 5, 7, 8 and 9.

## PROACTIVE VERSUS REACTIVE

Often Australian firms wait until countertrade is requested of them and then react. By this time they have usually already indicated the terms of sale such as price, quantities and

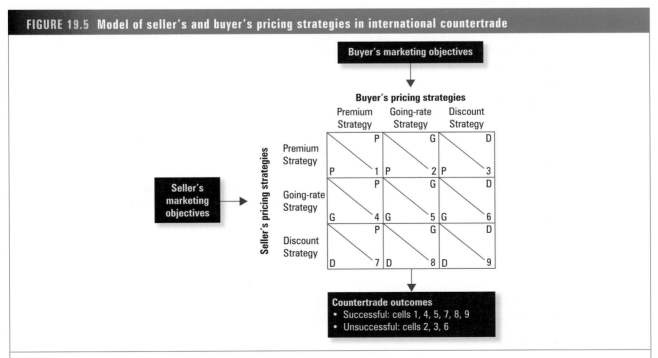

**FIGURE 19.5  Model of seller's and buyer's pricing strategies in international countertrade**

**SOURCE:** *Paun, D. and Albaum, G. (1995) 'A conceptual model of seller and buyer's pricing strategies in international counter-trade'*, Journal of Global Marketing, *Vol. 7, No. 2, pp. 75–95.*

deliveries. When subsequently confronted with the countertrade request, they are faced with a dilemma. Do they adhere to the price already quoted and bear the additional cost of the countertrade from their margin of profit? Or do they demand a higher price if countertrade is involved? In either case, the Australian firm is likely to lose out—on the one hand in terms of profit, and on the other by upsetting the potential buyer. Had they known that countertrade would be required they would have been better off pricing on this basis in the first place. Research can often reveal whether countertrade is a likely requirement or an attractive feature. Public sector purchases in Malaysia, Indonesia, the Philippines and Thailand are likely to require countertrade, and trade with Vietnam is generally on a countertrade basis. Both China and the Commonwealth of Independent States (CIS) republics seek to use countertrade, especially buyback when industrial or infrastructural projects are involved.

If countertrade is likely to be requested or if it is likely to improve the attractiveness of the offer, a proactive approach of pricing for that market on a countertrade basis should be adopted. Australian trade with the CIS has developed since the break up of the USSR, much of it on a countertrade basis. Australian firms have taken a proactive stance. As an example, fresh and canned meat have been supplied to the Russian far east in exchange for canned salmon and other seafoods.

## IS THERE ANOTHER WAY OF SOLVING THE PROBLEM?

Countertrade, which attracted academic interest during the 20-year period 1980–99, has had less exposure since 2000 in both the academic and the general literature. However, many of the reasons for the use of countertrade as a payment mechanism and a technique for international trade are still in evidence, despite changes in the world geo-political scene. Although the underlying reasons are still present in the least-developing countries, the need for countertrade has partly diminished in the former centrally planned economies. In many instances, countertrade in its more sophisticated forms of offsets and buyback has been replaced by other practices that perform the same function, but in a different manner. This is possible because of a reduction in barriers to world trade, easier access to information and advances in technology such as fibre-optic cable and satellite communication facilitate new forms of linked internationalisation.

One such technique is international outsourcing, often referred to as offshoring. Two major developing nations have largely turned around their balance of payments using this technique—India by being the recipient of outsourcing of services and China by being the recipient of outsourcing of products. International outsourcing is driven by many of the same underlying factors as countertrade, especially those of overcoming imperfections in the market, the desire to acquire innovative technology and the need to boost foreign exchange earnings. Williams and Maull (2006) show that offsets and offshoring are similar in that they are both driven by the need to access inputs and access markets. In both cases the outcome is a global value chain facilitated by advances in communication, data management and other technologies. As with countertrade, international outsourcing can vary from simple procurement to establishing complete production operations in another country.

Also, as with countertrade, figures on the extent of international outsourcing are incomplete or unavailable. However, given that international outsourcing is driven by many of the same factors underlying countertrade, in the current millennium it is likely that it, along with build, operate and transfer schemes and strategic alliances, has replaced activities previously considered as countertrade.

# The internet and countertrade

The internet is likely to facilitate the conduct of international countertrade as it addresses some of the difficulties firms encounter when using this international business mechanism. To conduct countertrade there is a need for up-to-date information as to trading conditions, level of interest in countertrade by government and private sectors in overseas countries and what products are available for countertrade. The web is a source of such information on a timely basis.

Another problem in countertrade is that of disposing of goods that a firm has been forced to accept, but which can neither be used in its own operation nor disposed of through its established distribution channels. The internet facilitates the search process to ascertain who might have a requirement for these goods and enables the firm to canvass their availability on a much wider basis, with less risk of having to bear a large loss when selling them.

Countertrade transactions, because of their complexity, often involve the use of intermediaries whose commission charges can add substantially to the cost of the transaction. One of the features of the internet is the potential to eliminate intermediaries—disintermediation. Although in some cases the marketplace intermediaries may be replaced by cybermediaries, the intermediary costs are likely to be much less, improving the possibility of undertaking the countertrade transaction at a profit.

The internet facilitates the bargaining process when endeavouring to arrive at an equitable exchange in the countertrade arrangement. A firm can be in instant touch with other potential parties to the transaction and better placed to respond to offers instantly. Online auctions take this process further and enable the firm to place a quantity of product on offer and solicit bids.

A final feature of e-business is that of interactivity. Such interactivity is important when negotiating complex transactions, often with multiple parties, across national boundaries. This enables multiple party negotiation in circumstances where face-to-face interaction is not possible and where the sale is conditional on the purchase as with countertrade. The interaction in marketspace takes much less time than in marketplace transactions and as a result countertrade decisions can be arrived at much more quickly.

# Summary

Countertrade is an established practice in international trade. It is not diminishing in significance and will possibly grow due to recent economic changes in Asia. Countertrade is becoming more sophisticated and increasingly involves services and projects. With the collapse of communism it is being appreciated that the motivation for countertrade is economic rather than political, and as a result there is growing global recognition of countertrade as a legitimate form of international business. By its very nature, it will be difficult to measure and will continue to be surrounded by secrecy, and in part this will be due to countertrade being used as a vehicle for intercompany transfers between divisions of transnational corporations. It is likely that intermediaries, particularly the Japanese and other Asian general trading companies, will play an increasingly important role in countertrade. The specific markets insisting on countertrade will wax and wane according to economic circumstances, as the recent Asian currency crisis has shown. However, the conclusion is inescapable: countertrade is significant, it is here to stay and will not go away!

## ETHICS ISSUE

You are the international manager of an Australian manufacturer of aluminium extrusions contemplating vertical integration into the door and window security latch business. A range of latches, identical to those you propose to produce, is available from an associated firm in Malaysia. You want to use their products to test the market in Australia before commencing manufacture. You know that if the full cost of production in Malaysia were taken into account, the landed cost of these latches in Australia would result in a price to the consumer 25% above those of the competition. Although the Malaysian firm is willing to supply you at 75% of its cost of production, it is nervous of Australian manufacturers taking anti-dumping action against it. It has proposed a countertrade arrangement, whereby you supply your aluminium extrusions at 25% above world market prices and you receive the latches as countertrade, valued at a price that reflects their full cost of production.

*If you were the international manager, would you agree to this countertrade proposal to circumvent Australian anti-dumping regulations?*

## Websites

**Asea Brown Boveri** http://www.abb.com
**Bartercard** http://www.bartercard.com.au
**Boeing Corporation** http://www.boeing.com
**Elders** http://www.elders.com.au
**World Trade Organization (WTO)** http://www.wto.org

## Discussion questions

1   Why did the Asian currency crisis of 1997 stimulate an upsurge of interest in countertrade?

2   Why are some forms of countertrade increasing in popularity while others are diminishing?

3   As the former Centrally Planned Economies adopt more of a marketing orientation, are they more or less likely to become involved in countertrade?

4   Discuss recent trends in the content of countertrade transactions.

5   When would you adopt a proactive and when would you adopt a reactive approach to countertrade?

6   How effective is countertrade as a legal avoidance mechanism?

7   On balance, do you consider that the advantages to the firm of countertrade outweigh the disadvantages?

8   Should the Australian/New Zealand government assist Australian/New Zealand firms with international countertrade? If so, what specific forms should this assistance take?

# MARKETING TO CUSTOMERS IN DEVELOPING COUNTRIES AT THE BOTTOM OF THE PYRAMID (BOP)

## Credit the poor and end poverty

Muhammad Yunus and the Grameen Bank he founded 30 years ago received the Nobel Peace Prize for 2006, indicating global recognition that the poor could be helped by tailored commercial programs and offerings and in the process break out of the cycle of perpetual dependency. Yunus began his 'bank for the poor' with a loan to 42 people that totalled US$27—less than a US$1 per loan. His loans were provided to women for small rather than large amounts and without collateral or paperwork. His security was the cultural norms that characterised women at the BOP and the subsequent almost non-existent defaulting on loans proved his intuitive judgment correct. The mission of the Grameen Foundation is 'to empower the world's poorest people to lift themselves out of poverty with dignity through access to financial services and to information'.

His revolution in banking practice has spread to 22 countries and the foundation he established works with 52 microfinance institutions reaching 2.7 million clients. The plan is that, by 2115, 175 million of the world's poorest families will have microcredit, and 100 million families will

be enabled to rise above the US$1 per day threshold and lifted out of poverty—this would mean cutting the US$1 per day poverty level in half. Grameen commercial activities have spread beyond microfinance, but the principle of empowerment remains in these other commercial endeavours, such as the Grameen phone company where female entrepreneurs are provided with a mobile phone on credit and they then sell usage of the phone to friends and acquaintances on a per minute basis.

SOURCE: *Adapted from <http:en.wikipedia.org/wiki/Grameen_Foundation>, accessed 8 February 2007. Image AP Photo/Bjoern Sigurdsoen/SCANPIX/POOL.*

# INTRODUCTION

As developed markets become saturated, international marketers have been turning increasingly to markets in developing countries. In most cases they have been targeting the wealthy elite at the top of the income scale in such countries and when considering the future potential of such markets, their focus has usually been on the expanding middle class in these countries. Rarely do international marketers focus on the masses, be they the urban poor or occupants of rural towns and villages. When they do attempt to research these markets, their market research is often flawed because, as Liu and Leach (2005, p. 1) state:

*parsimonious models developed for Western individualistic markets, may not be the most appropriate models for use in collective and high context markets.*

Prahalad and Lieberthal (1998) attribute these shortcomings to firms having an 'imperialist mindset', which drives them to sell the same products as in the West in an unchanged form to established upscale markets in developing countries. London and Hart (2004) claim that this approach only captures the tip of the iceberg of commercial potential in such markets and this is shown in Figure 1.1 in Chapter 1.

This figure shows that the number of potential customers whose annual purchasing power parity is less than US$1500 per year amount to 4 billion people (estimated to be 6 billion by 2045). This group at the bottom of the pyramid (BOP) accounts for 65% of the world's population and it is amongst this group that future growth prospects are likely to be greatest. However, a different mindset will be necessary to tap this potential particularly in the short term. A standardised developed country marketing mix offering will not make sense to this group, whose circumstances will require a highly customised approach.

Furthermore, such a standardised offering is unable to cope with the informal economy that accounts for between 30 and 60% of total economic activity in a number of developing countries (de Soto 2000), due to the fact that such markets often have underdeveloped legal systems with inconsistent enforcement (Rubesch 2005). In this situation, those at the bottom of the pyramid are likely to be involved in the informal economy which can extend from simple barter to piracy of intellectual property, smuggling and corruption. Prahalad (2005, p. 125) cites a retailer in Brazil as advising that there the informal market is twice as big as the formal market, especially with the lower income population and that the retailer has to believe what his customers are telling him as they do not declare their income.

## Unique features of the market at the BOP

There are a number of unique features operating at the BOP which need to be taken into account when doing business with consumers in this market. These are age, gender, rural or urban location, size of dwelling, degree of uncertainty and turbulence in the environment, nature and adequacy of infrastructure and the extent of the informal economy.

The age demographic is different at the BOP as, whereas in the West the populations are ageing, the median age is much younger in the developing countries where the BOP consumers are mostly to be found. Traditionally, the young have different values, are more individualist, and tend to have a more short-term orientation. This may result in a group at the BOP that differs from older respondents, one which focuses on different products and is most likely to act as a catalyst for change.

Gender is also an issue as in many BOP countries—women have less opportunity to speak out, and to directly determine purchasing decisions. It is likely they will respond differently to males and that their influence on purchasing decisions may be more indirect than in the West. Because of these factors, sensitivity will be needed and, in any research undertaken, care will be needed so that their espoused views rather than 'acceptable' views are obtained. Mahajan and Banga (2005) argue that younger females may react differently to older females at the BOP as, with increasing access to global values, younger women may want to engage in purchasing behaviour that 'leaves behind' restrictions on education and careers in cultures that traditionally have offered them restricted opportunities.

Whether at the BOP urban consumers differ from rural consumers is also an issue. There is a trend of migration from country to town and 2007 marks the first time on a global basis that the urban population exceeds the rural population. Age is also a factor here, as often the move to the cities is led by the members of the younger demographic. At the BOP however, there is the complicating factor of large numbers of breadwinners working in the city to support a family in the village. Urban and rural consumers at the BOP may need to be treated separately, as their responses to offerings may differ.

Purchasing behaviour is often influenced by the size of the dwelling and the number of occupants per dwelling. In developed countries sizes are usually larger and number of occupants fewer, as reflected in the fact the average dwelling in the US is 2200 square feet—26 times larger than the average in Africa (Mahajan and Banga 2005). This suggests that, at the BOP, small dwellings will create a requirement for small, space-saving appliances and furniture, and for small sizes in consumer goods. For this reason, as far as many products and services are concerned, information will need to be sought as to the size of the dwelling and the number of occupants per dwelling.

Countries where those at the BOP tend to reside are more likely to be subject to turbulent change and those at the BOP are least likely to be able to do anything to influence the consequences, protect their interests or seek legal remedy. This creates on their part a mindset of having 'portable assets' (e.g. money or jewellery rather than property) and a 'just in time' philosophy regarding purchases, resulting in their buying goods for immediate consumption rather than storage. The varying impact of political and economic instability will need to be taken into account.

In developing countries, infrastructure is inadequate and unreliable. BOP consumers are most likely to be inconvenienced as the upper/middle classes in these countries can often fund their way around the problem by sinking their own bore wells or installing their own power generators. This infrastructure inadequacy poses challenges to those wishing to supply the BOP and will require product design innovation (e.g. solar-powered units) to avoid using the existing infrastructure. This is evidenced by the number of mobile phones in India now exceeding the number of land-line-connected phones. This also will be a relevant factor for those seeking to tap the BOP market.

Customers at the BOP also are deprived due to lack of information. Khanna and Palepu (1997) attribute this to three causes—the communications infrastructure is not sufficiently developed, they have no redress if a product/service does not deliver on its promise and there are no mechanisms to corroborate claims made by sellers.

A final factor is degree to which those at the BOP see themselves as being in the formal or informal economy, as this may well influence their purchasing behaviour and consumption patterns. Given that 80% of employment in India, Pakistan, Indonesia and Philippines is in the informal economy and that in India only 3% of the population pays income tax (Mahajan and Banga 2005), it is likely that most at the BOP are outside the formal economy.

## Buyer behaviour

Culture influences the behaviour of buyers. It is for this reason that models of buyer behaviour derived from developed countries need to be modified when doing business in developing countries. Different tastes, customs and habits are likely to result in different preferences. Also, the popularity of developed country luxury goods among developing country consumers may be due to different factors, such as saving or giving 'face', or peer pressure, rather than because of perceptions of value. These factors explain why people at the BOP are often brand-conscious, especially for aspirational or confidence reasons. Arnold and Quelch (1998) cite Coca-Cola as an example of this and point out that the sales rates for Coca-Cola doubled every three years in markets such as China, India and Indonesia, whereas in developed country markets the growth rates averaged less than 5%.

The model of innovation adoption, for example, does not apply uniformly to all international markets. In many respects this is due to differences in culture. Different cultures have a different attitude towards the past, present and the future, which in turn influences the degree of enthusiasm for adopting new technologies. Also, different cultures exhibit different degrees of individualism and collectivism, and this influences the readiness to adopt something new or a preference to wait until many others have adopted the technology. Some research has been undertaken on differences in buyer behaviour between the West (reflecting developed countries) and the East (reflecting developing countries). Figure 13.2 from Bradley (2002) in Chapter 13 shows that in Eastern countries the response pattern is different to that in the West and the life cycle much shorter.

Another model affecting the way buyers behave is Maslow's hierarchy of needs—this shows the order in which needs are satisfied by buyers. Research by Schutte and Ciarlante (1998) shows that in Asia (reflecting developing countries) not only is the order in which these needs are satisfied different, but the needs themselves vary compared with the West (reflective of developed countries). This is illustrated in Figure 3.4 in Chapter 3. These models of buyer behaviour illustrate that in emerging or less-developed markets consumers are driven by different motivations to those that operate in Western, developed markets.

The problem with these models is that they view developing country markets as a whole and do not differentiate between groups within such markets on socio-economic lines. In these countries, buyer behaviour is likely to be markedly different between the wealthy elite and growing urban middle class on the one hand and the urban poor/rural masses (BOP) on the other. Although advocates of globalisation argue that over time such consumers will become more Westernised (reflective of behaviour of developed country consumers), to the extent that this is true it is only likely to apply to the upper and middle class elements of such markets. Those in these markets at the bottom of the pyramid are much less likely to be exposed to Western influences as disseminated by e-commerce and the media. Only 50% of those at the BOP in many developing markets actually have access to the media (Prahalad 2005, p. 193). Therefore, the observed buyer behaviour differences commented upon above are more likely to be evident at the BOP. This is because embedded cultural differences are likely to be greater or subject to less modification by exposure to Western influences.

# Marketing mix issues

Tapping the market at the BOP will involve revamping one or more elements of the marketing mix. Prahalad (2005) cites cases of multinational firms such as Hindustan Lever Limited, which has been successful in tapping this group by totally revamping one or more elements of the marketing mix. The literature is reviewed briefly with respect to each element of the mix as follows.

## PRODUCT

Coca-Cola has 400 brands in 200 countries so as to tap markets that cannot be penetrated by its flagship brand. Prahalad argues that developed country entrepreneurs are caught up in form instead of functionality. Washing clothes in an outdoor stream is generally a communal activity and will require a different soap product formulation to washing clothes in a washing machine that adjusts itself to levels of soiling and for coloured or white garments. There may also be deeper cultural significance to acts that to Westerners may seem unnecessarily labour-intensive. Mahajan and Banga (2005) point out that in rural India, the act of rubbing a bar of soap on clothes is viewed as a labour of love and that a time-saving washing product could have a negative connotation. As a result, Hindustan Lever developed a detergent bar that offered all the benefits of traditional bar soap as well as superior performance in water. Overcoming the above challenges and tapping BOP markets may require making units of sale smaller and therefore affordable—cigarettes sold by the stick instead of by the packet of 25 or 50; shampoo sold by the single-use sachet instead of by the bottle. Approaching the market in this way brings the product into the consideration set of the poor for the first time—even if they only buy the sachet once a month as a luxury when they have extra money. This is particularly the case with non-durable consumer goods where, according to D'Andrea, Ring and Lopez-Aleman (2005), expenditure accounts for a very high percentage of total income amongst respondents at the BOP. In this category, they argue, consumers are willing to pay a premium for leading brands as a means of reducing the risk of purchase. Collectively these purchases can result in a substantial volume of product. London and Hart (2004) argue that products offered to BOP markets will need local content added to the product design so as to improve both their credibility and acceptability. Also there is the problem in some product categories of quality. Scaling down some products at the expense of quality can make minimal the difference in perceived quality between a pirated and an authentic version of a product—therefore, as computer firms have found, the need is to offer cheap products, but not poor ones.

Contrary to popular perception, the BOP market is not averse to technology, as evidenced by the rapid expansion of PC kiosks. Technology often enables firms in developing countries to leapfrog several stages in the product development life cycle that previously occurred in developed countries, and in the process facilitate providing products that customers at the BOP can afford. The example of the US$12.5 billion Tata Group of India is informative. Its CEO, Rattan Tata, plans to reach into the BOP market, not by stripping down an existing vehicle, but by designing a quality vehicle from scratch, aligned to the cost structure necessary to tap this market. This compact car will sell for US$2200 compared with the current lowest priced offering—Suzuki's US$5000 Maurati.

In addition, the infrastructure at the bottom of the pyramid is often hostile and products may need to be adapted to withstand shortcomings such as fluctuating voltage, impure and intermittent water and movement over unsealed roads or tracks.

Because of this, the product designed needs to reflect the circumstances of the local environment—in other words 'don't build a car when you need a bullock cart'!

Hindustan Motors, the manufacturers of the Ambassador car in India, teamed up with an Australian partner to design a vehicle for rural India so as to compete against the bullock cart. The result was a box-like Rural Transport Vehicle (RTV) designed to move both people and goods and narrow enough to move down narrow village streets. It had a tight turning radius and a high ground clearance to cope with potholes. Fitted with eight gears it was able to creep along rough rural roads and race along paved highways. It was equipped with folding seats so it could move 20 people or shift two tonnes of cargo. It was also designed as a low maintenance vehicle as competent serving facilities are rare in rural India.

**SOURCE:** *Mahajan, V. and Banga, K. (2005) The 86% Solution: How to Succeed in the Biggest Market Opportunity of the 21st Century', Wharton School Publishing, NJ, p. 33).*

## PRICING

Research by London and Hart (2004) found that multinational companies usually tried to impose their pricing formulae on developing country markets with little success at the bottom of the pyramid. This is because they overlook the need to both make products affordable and price the offering in a way that takes into account the unique circumstances faced by BOP consumers commented upon earlier. Dramatic cost reductions are often necessary to achieve this. The technique required is low margins and high volumes. By virtue of their numbers, those earning less than US$2 per day represent a significant potential purchasing power. Firms who have been successful in this sector have recognised that millions of small sales can yield big profits, and that this is achieved by providing goods and services at a lower price point while still maintaining margins. This may involve taking the goods or services, reducing them to their bare essentials and offering them on a massive scale. It also involves ways of making the offering cheap enough to appeal to this larger, poorer market. This requires low price points, minimum marginal costs, de-skilling services so non-experts can deliver them and the use of local entrepreneurs. Creating affordability may require repackaging and recovery of cost so that the upfront cost of access is reduced for potential consumers with little or no disposable income. Often this requires innovative financial mechanisms involving small repayments so as to put the offering within the reach of a broader segment of the population. This might be achieved through charging a small upfront payment and a monthly usage fee, instead of selling the product outright. This will inject a performance promise into the transaction, as the monthly fees will continue only as long as the product performs. In such circumstances, low price cannot equate to low quality. To achieve affordability in the face of smaller units of sale is likely to require innovative financial techniques such as that adopted by the Grameen Phone Operation in Bangladesh, where the firm lends a female entrepreneur the price of a phone so she can resell it in minute increments to individuals in the village. The BOP causes considerable emphasis on the price-performance relationship and, to be successful, firms must focus on all aspects of cost. In essence, it is availability, affordability and access that creates a new market at the BOP by taking advantage of the consumer's capacity to consume at a particular point of time.

In BOP markets, the Western logic of pricing is often turned on its head with consumers paying less per unit for items offered in small packs than for items offered in large packs. In India, Proctor and Gamble charges 80% more for its family size package of Tide than for the same volume offered in small sachets. In developed country markets, consumers buy small packages for convenience and are willing to pay a premium to do so, whereas in BOP markets consumers buy smaller packages for price because of their limited resources. Companies still make money as they are focusing on economies of volume rather than on economies of scale and sachet sales do not cannibalise sales of larger packets, but rather add to overall volume of product sold.

SOURCE: *Mahajan, V. and Banga, K. (2005)* The 86% Solution: How to Succeed in the Biggest Market Opportunity of the 21st Century', *Wharton School Publishing, NJ, pp. 116–17.*

## DISTRIBUTION

Developing countries are often composed of a series of highly fragmented local markets in which local brands flourish to the chagrin of many multinationals. Many areas of BOP markets are not accessible by traditional distribution modes and can only be reached in innovative ways such as by combining the selling and delivery function using bicycles, 'hole on the wall' stores and locals who are insiders to local BOP networks. The small stores account for one-third of the retail outlets in India and 90% of retail outlets in the Philippines. An additional layer in the distribution channel is needed to reach them. There are areas of the BOP where even these small stores do not exist and a further layer of salespeople on bicycles is required to cater for this market. In some areas at the BOP, the market can only be breached intermittently, such as carnivals and market days or by vans that infrequently visit the village and create the market. Creating distribution systems to cater for unique local circumstances is marketing in action—imposing Western distribution systems on the BOP is the antithesis of marketing. Nowhere is this better illustrated that in the dabbawala lunch delivery system.

The dabbawala lunch delivery system in Mumbai (Bombay) has been in operation for 120 years and caters for the tradition of having home-cooked meals delivered to your place of work. A cooperative run by illiterate and semi-illiterate entrepreneurs, it uses various modes of transport, but mostly bicycles, to deliver 175 000 lunches a day. These are collected from home by 9 am and delivered to work by 12.30 pm. Each tiffin box containing the lunch has a code that directs it through the delivery network and results in the equivalent of a modern 'packet switching' system.

Reaching the bottom of the pyramid, therefore, is likely to involve breaking the economic and physical bottlenecks created by traditional systems of distribution and extending the 'break-bulk' functions of the distribution channel even further. Contrast the milk collection arrangements of the Kaira District Coop in Anand in Gujerat, India where for years at dawn ladies deliver the milk of a single cow carried in a bowl on their head to the collection site, with methods used in intensive dairy farming in countries like Australia and New Zealand. Research by London and Hart showed that existing local partners in an overseas market often do not have the knowledge and capabilities to reach customers in the BOP section of the market. Such partners were unable to create sufficient incentives for current distributors to promote the product, because promoting to the BOP sector was viewed by them as cannibalising existing, more lucrative product lines. This suggests that a new distribution channel may be needed for the BOP sector. Innovations in the distribution system are critical for tapping the BOP market. Distribution at the BOP may need to involve networks at the BOP built on existing relationships. This is illustrated in the case of firms in one country accessing a BOP market in another via the ethnic group in the first country. Gateway Pharmaceuticals collected remittances from Vietnamese in Australia, converted them into its medicines on a favourable basis and shipped the medicines to the relatives in Vietnam. It is also illustrated in the preference for shopping at small stores, as relationships are a significant determinant of purchase and ad-hoc credit is provided. Finally, at the BOP informal channels are likely to exist because of the circumstances outlined above, and these informal channels can co-exist with authorised channels, providing in the case of the former a lower priced entry strategy. Such informal channels can also provide value-creating services that are not catered for by authorised channels. Unilever's Indian affiliate, Hindustan Lever, recognises that at the BOP it needs to not merely sell its products, but also educate potential customers in how to use its products. It is for this reason that its vans visit villages to distribute boxes of low unit price packs accompanied by personnel to explain how the products should be used. In the evenings, the vans show videos and include in the shows product communications to generate product awareness.

Opportunities at the BOP can be indirect. In their book, *The 86% Solution*, Mahajan and Banga (2005), refer to the ricochet economy, which is the market of recent immigrants (both legal and illegal) in developed countries who use their increased income to fund purchases in their country of origin for family and relatives there. Stores and intermediaries in developed countries such as the USA have sprung up to exclusively service this market segment. To cater for this market, Australian and New Zealand firms will need to establish contact with those in developed countries that specialise in this networked economy that stretches between developed and developing markets.

## PROMOTION

Research to date has little to say about promotion at the bottom of the pyramid. The issue of communication is equally as important as other marketing mix variables when doing business at the BOP. Like the variable of product, significant modification is likely to be needed with promotion. Many at the BOP live in 'media dark' zones where they do not have access to the print media due to illiteracy, variable access to the radio, little access to TV and no access to the internet. Some research such as that by Thomas (1996) stresses that unique innovative promotion methods will be necessary to communicate with potential BOP customers. He illustrates this by citing 'wokabaut' marketing in the highlands of Papua New Guinea, where promotion is achieved by a troupe of actors going from village to village undertaking plays from the back of a truck that promote products, supplies of which have been previously augmented at the little shops or stalls along the route. Fletcher (2006) conducted studies on differences in promoting to upper/middle classes on the one hand and those at the BOP on the other in Vietnam, Thailand and Sri Lanka. He took a standard communications model (see Figure 15.1 in Chapter 15), and asked respondents a number of questions regarding 'sender' issues, 'medium' issues 'receiver' issues, 'interference' issues and 'feedback' issues. He found the following:

- Indications were that, as far as 'sender-oriented' aspects were concerned, lower income customers (BOP) were perceived as preferring local presenters of messages and liked messages containing testimonials (especially from authority figures/glamorous people) reflecting acceptance of power distance. They also preferred message appeals directed to group rather than to individual benefit.

- Concerning 'medium' issues, differences in media usage was apparent between high/middle and lower income groups (BOP). The latter were heavier users of radio, purchased fewer magazines, were less likely to watch TV, had little if any exposure to the internet and considered direct marketing of little appeal compared to the upper/middle income group. Their choices of media were heavily influenced by their lower literacy and education levels.

- With 'receiver-oriented' elements of the model, affordability of the equipment to receive the message was a greater problem for the lower income group (BOP) as was the reliability of overall communications infrastructure, especially in rural areas. Also, for this group it was more common for them to receive the message in a communal situation (e.g. around the village TV set) and messages couched in terms of group norms rather than individual preferences had greatest appeal. This group was more likely to respond to emotional appeals.

- Sources of 'interference' in the interpretation of the message, such as group influence, local and regional loyalties, had more impact on the lower income group (BOP) compared with the upper/middle group.

- Finally, with 'feedback', the lower income group were perceived as being more reluctant to provide information or express an opinion; this has implications for conducting market research.

From this exploratory research into communication, it appears necessary for managers wishing to do business in BOP markets to develop separate marketing strategies for these markets.

# The internet and the bottom of the pyramid

This adoption of the internet is likely to be very slow at the BOP because in many cases the infrastructure is not in place to support it. If power is not available, is unreliable or is intermittent, then the ability to operate a personal computer is limited even assuming the BOP customer can afford one. In addition, the internet presupposes literacy and the majority of the world's illiterate are likely to be found at the BOP. Also, most websites are in English or other major languages—they are unlikely to be in the regional dialects spoken by those at the BOP.

For most at the BOP, their access to the internet is most likely to be via internet cafés. These are more likely to be found in towns than in the countryside; this indicates that the urban BOP customers are more likely to access the internet ahead of the rural BOP customers. From the perspective of communication with those at the BOP via the internet, research by Fletcher (2006) found that in Thailand, Vietnam and Sri Lanka, the internet was viewed as being the least-effective medium to use to market to the BOP.

# Summary

To successfully access markets at the BOP requires approaches tailored to such markets rather than a global approach. This is because those in the BOP markets have not had the exposure to developed country influences, as they do not have the same media access as do the upper and middle income groups in developing countries. Appeals to those at the BOP will need to be tailored more to their cultural differences and take into account local conditions. Approaches to BOP consumers will need to capitalise on existing relationships and employ those who are insiders as far as local networks are concerned. Offerings to the BOP segment will require a deep understanding of the local environment and involve a 'bottom-up' approach resulting from identifying, leveraging and shoring up the existing social infrastructure. Strategies need to be culturally sensitive and relationship based. They might include:

- creation of a unique business model tailored to the local market that is both culturally sensitive and economically feasible;
- identification of the real needs of the consumer and product adaptation to meet these needs in a way that creates opportunity for local participation;
- development of tactics to overcome the infrastructure problems faced by BOP consumers;
- detailed research into the BOP market, its needs and characteristics;
- collaboration with non-traditional partners in the market so as to gain expert knowledge of the existing social infrastructure; and
- a conscious and publicised plan to develop local talent.

---

## ETHICS ISSUE

Your company has a joint venture in Pakistan producing long-life soy milk in 500 mL cartons selling to the more affluent in urban areas. A strong brand image has been created for the product amongst all sections of society, particularly as an alternative to milk for the lactose intolerant. Your joint venture partner has suggested that a valuable market could exist for 100 mL cartons of the product marketed under the same brand amongst the urban poor. He advises, however, that in order to make the product affordable to this group, it would be necessary to dilute the contents by 50%, thus reducing the nutritional properties. Under Pakistan law, this is permissible as long as the list of ingredients shown in small print on the side of the pack is accurate.

**Given that most of the urban poor in Pakistan are illiterate, should you agree to this proposal?**

# Websites

**Grameen Bank** http://www.grameenfoundation.org
**Hindustan Lever** http://www.hll.com
**Tata Group** http://www.tata.com

# Discussion questions

1   What factors differentiate those at the BOP from the middle class in developing countries?

2   Why have Yunus and the Grameen Bank been so successful and what accounts for the success of the Grameen Foundation in other developing countries, despite the cultural differences between them?

3   When targeting the BOP, should you modify your existing product offering or devise a totally new offering for the BOP?

4   What routine purchases for the affluent in developing countries are occasional luxury purchases for those at the BOP? What impact does this have on the way you tailor your marketing mix?

# References

Arnold, D.J. and Quelch, J.A. (1998) 'New strategies in emerging markets', *Sloan Management Review*, Fall, pp. 7–18.

AusAID Annual Budget 2006–07; see <http://www.ausaid.gov.au>, accessed 26 April 2007.

Austrade (1994) *30 Billion Reasons to Enter the Market–Doing Business with Multilateral Development Banks and United Nations Agencies*, Aidab and Austrade, Canberra.

Bradley, F. (2002) *International Marketing Strategy*, 4th edn, Financial Times Prentice Hall, Harlow, UK.

Brennan, M. (1998) 'Government pro-active countertrade: a decade of deals', Working Paper, Economics Department, Murdoch University.

D'Andrea, G., Ring, L.J. and Lopez-Aleman, B. (2005) 'Retail value creation for emerging customers', Paper delivered at the CIMAR Conference, 29–31 May, Barcelona, Spain.

de Soto, H. (2000) *The Mystery of Capital: Why Capitalism Triumphs in the West and Fails Everywhere Else*, Basic Books, New York.

Department of Foreign Affairs and Trade (2005) *More than Oil: Economic Developments in Bahrain, Kuwait, Oman, Qatar and the United Arab Emirates*, Economic Analytic Unit, Canberra.

Fletcher, R. (1996) 'Network theory and countertrade transactions', *International Business Review*, Vol. 5, No. 2, pp. 167–89.

Fletcher, R. (2001) *Lifting the lid on countertrade*, Working Paper 1.01, School of Marketing, University of Technology, Sydney.

Fletcher, R. (2003) 'Countertrade in the electronic age', World Marketing Congress, Perth, Academy of Marketing Science, 11–14 June.

Fletcher, R. (2006) 'International marketing at the bottom of the pyramid–a three country study', Paper delivered at the CIMAR Conference, 26–30 May, Barcelona, Spain.

Hennart, J.F. (1989) 'The transaction-cost rationale for countertrade', *Journal of Law, Economics and Organisation*, Vol. 5, No. 1, pp. 127–53.

Holmes, J. (1995) *Countertrade for Australian Exporters*, Australia New Zealand Bank, Sydney.

Khanna, T. and Palepu, K. (1997) 'Why focused strategies may be wrong for emerging markets', *Harvard Business Review*, Vol. 75, July/August, pp. 41–51.

L/E/K Partnership (1994) *Intelligent Exports and the Silent Revolution in Services*, Austrade, Commonwealth of Australia, Canberra.

Liesch, P. (1991) *Government Mandated Countertrade–Deals of Arm Twisting*, Avebury, Sydney.

Liu, A.H. and Leach, M.P. (2005) 'The importance of product attributes in high context cultures: implications for managing business relations in Asia', *Proceedings of the IMP Asia Conference*, 11–15 December, Phuket.

London, S.L. and Hart, T. (2004) 'Reinventing strategies for emerging markets: beyond the transitional model', *Journal of International Business Studies*, Vol. 35, pp. 350–70.

Luqmani, M. (1988) 'Marketing to LDC governments', *International Marketing Review*, Spring, p. 59.

Mahajan, V. and Banga, K. (2005) *The 86% Solution: How to Succeed in the Biggest Market Opportunity of the 21st Century*, Wharton School Publishing, New Jersey.

Paun, D. and Albaum, G. (1995) 'A conceptual model of seller and buyer's pricing strategies in international counter-trade', *Journal of Global Marketing*, Vol. 7, No. 2, pp. 75–95.

Prahalad, C.K. (2005) *The Fortune at the Bottom of the Pyramid*, Wharton School Publishing, New Jersey.

Prahalad, C.K. and Liebethal, K. (1998) 'The end of corporate imperialism', *Harvard Business Review*, Vol. 76, No. 4, pp. 67–89.

Reuters (2007) 'Philippines: Manila seen buying rice from Vietnam', <http://www.flexnews.com/pages/6683/Philippines/rice>, accessed 8 February 2007.

Rubesch, E. (2005) 'Incorporating informal channels into market entry strategies for emerging markets', *Proceedings of the ANZMAC 2005 Conference*, 5–7 December, Perth.

Schutte, H. and Ciarlante, D. (1998) *Consumer Behaviour in Asia*, Macmillan Business Press, London.

Thomas, A.O. (1996) 'Advertising to the masses without mass media: the case of wokabaut marketing', in Johnson, D.W. and Kaynak, E. (eds) *Marketing to the Third World*, Haworth Press, London, pp. 75–88.

Waller, R.L. (2003) 'The use of offsets in foreign military sales', *Acquisition Review Quarterly*, Summer, pp. 225–32.

Walters, R. (2002) *The Big End of Town and Australia's Trading Interests*, Department of Foreign Affairs and Trade, Canberra.

Williams, B.G. (2004) 'Submission to the Senate Standing Committee on the free trade agreement between Australia and the United States of America', Sydney Centre for International and Global Law, University of Sydney.

Williams, T. and Maull, R. (2006) *Global Operations Strategy and the Impact of Offsets*, Exeter Centre for Strategic Processes and Operations, University of Exeter, UK.

## go online

Go online to <www.pearsoned.com.au/fletcher> to find more case studies.

# Negotiation to win international projects—Cardno MBK in Indonesia

**Trevor Morgan and Richard Fletcher**

## BACKGROUND

Cardno MBK is an Australian-based firm that has 550 employees, 200 of whom live and work outside Australia. There are 13 directors who are responsible for all of the firm's contract negotiations and the firm's wellbeing. Cardno MBK has more than 35 years of experience exporting to foreign countries, and today has constructed projects in more than 20 different countries. Cardno MBK specialises in the design and construction of long-spanning bridges, urban design, roads and many environmental engineering projects such as sewage treatment plants. In Indonesia, Cardno MBK has been operating for more than 20 years and now boasts that if all of the bridges it has built were lined up end to end they would stretch for more than 144 kilometres.

Negotiation is the process of bargaining with one or more parties to arrive at a solution that is acceptable to all (Hodgetts and Luthans 1997, p. 196). The negotiation process involves a number of different steps including planning; interpersonal relationship building; task-related exchange of information; persuasion; and agreement. Planning starts with the negotiators identifying those objectives they would like to attain. This includes setting limits on single point objectives, dividing issues into short- and long-term considerations and determining the sequence in which to discuss the various issues (Tse et al. 1994, p. 537). Interpersonal relationship building involves getting to know the people on the other side. This period is characterised by the desire to identify those who are responsible and those who are not. In the exchange of task-related information, each group sets forth its position on the critical issues. This allows the participants to find

out what the other party wants to attain and what it is willing to give up. Persuasion is another vital aspect of the negotiation process. The success of persuasion depends on how well the parties understand each other's position, the ability to identify each other's similarities and differences, the ability to create new options and the willingness to work towards a solution that allows all parties to walk away feeling they have achieved their objectives. The last phase of negotiation is the hammering out of a final agreement. This may require resolving each issue one at a time, or negotiating a final agreement on everything.

Negotiation in the engineering and construction industry is different from that in many other industries because it provides a service that is intangible. The intangible aspect makes negotiation and bargaining difficult as the clients cannot see the final product before deciding if it is exactly what they expected. However, a successfully negotiated contract usually dictates the profitability of an engineering firm. The techniques to successful contract negotiation could result in millions of dollars of extra profit for a firm such as Cardno MBK.

Cardno MBK is required to negotiate at least one major tender per week. A major tender is one with more than $100 000 in fees. However, up to five or six smaller tenders are placed each week and at least one director will be involved in a smaller project's negotiation. In an international environment, this places a great deal of strain upon directors who travel to as many as 20 different countries in a year. Cardno MBK have a number of standard procedures which its directors try to follow and which enable them to have a greater chance of success in being awarded contracts. As soon as Cardno MBK is shortlisted for a tender, it attempts relationship building with the client as soon as possible. This requires understanding exactly what the client needs and expects, as well as whom Cardno MBK may have to compete against to win the bid. If the client is an international client then Cardno MBK tends to employ local personnel from the client's country to enhance the relationship building with the client. Once Cardno MBK starts building a relationship with the client, one of the first priorities is to find out who has the strongest influence, and to try to work with that person. When Cardno MBK has to negotiate with an aid agency as a client, it is often very difficult to develop a relationship with a particular person, as frequently there are many people to deal with compared to a firm or company. Thus, there are many different strategies that Cardno MBK employs when facing a client across a negotiating table.

Cardno MBK ensures that for every major contract negotiation there are at least two directors who are involved in the negotiation process. Often when negotiating a contract in a foreign country a local consultant may be employed to assist the directors with any problems they may encounter. Cardno MBK has 13 directors within the company and between them they must decide which of the directors will be required to negotiate the contracts for a particular project or country. Some directors, such as Syd Gamble, are responsible for a particular country, in Syd's case the Philippines, but for any major projects he will be accompanied by another director for contract negotiation on a projects tender. Other directors, such as Trevor Johnson and Doug McMillan, have functional roles and are responsible for environmental and structural engineering respectively. While the Philippines has a director in charge of all its operations, Indonesia has a variety of directors dealing with various projects, and all company directors are familiar with Indonesia due to the company's 20-year involvement with the country. The chairperson of Cardno MBK, Richard Kell, tends to be involved in the contract negotiation for most of the major projects. However, due to his time constraints he may be able to spend only one or two days in a country discussing a contract before having to leave. This tends to leave little time for relationship building with the client.

In the engineering/construction industry it is not just one contract that is awarded covering all aspects of a project. Numerous contracts tend to be set out in stages and any engineering company could bid for the contracts no matter what level of completion a project is at. Generally, a project will have a contract for a feasibility study, an early works contract and a project-completion contract as well as many other smaller well-defined contracts related to the main project. While any company may bid for these contracts, the company that completes the feasibility study and satisfies the client in the process will gain a greater chance of winning future contracts.

The official international engineering contracts are produced by the FIDIC international body. FIDIC was established in France and is an abbreviation for International Federation of Consulting Engineers. These official documents are widely used throughout the world by all engineering firms. These documents simplify most of the fine print that is included in a contract. FIDIC contracts have standards such as a set period for liability on the construction of projects, methods of payments and types of construction procedures. However, a contract that is not recognised by FIDIC might include a reduced fee if the project is not completed on time, or a range of other clauses that often penalise and restrict the engineering firm attempting to complete the task. Generally, a FIDIC contract provides confidence for both the client and the engineering firm, as each understands exactly what the other party expects. If, however, a client insists on using a non-FIDIC contract this will usually cause the negotiation process to be extended, as both parties will be required to discuss each minor point of the contract in great detail.

## CARDNO MBK AND INDONESIA

Cardno MBK became involved in a contract negotiation for a second container terminal to be constructed in Jakarta. The client comprised three different partners who formed a joint venture. The first firm was BJLT (Koperasi Pegawai Maritim), a local Indonesian company, which was awarded the 'right' to build the port by the Indonesian government. This company was owned by one of Suharto's sons, and contributed no financial input to the joint venture. The second joint venture partner was Persero (Pelabuhan 2), which is the Indonesian Port Authority (a government authority). This partner was to contribute 30% of the project's funding. The third joint venture partner was Hutchison Ports (<http://www.hph.com>). Hutchison is a multi-billion dollar Hong Kong-based company, which was to provide 70% of the project's funding.

In 1994, Cardno MBK won the contract for the new container terminal in Jakarta. All the client partners were satisfied with Cardno MBK's feasibility study. The contract for the feasibility study was US$1.5 million and this was paid in three parts during the feasibility study. The final payment was made after the feasibility study was completed, as per standard procedure. In January 1997 the feasibility study had been approved and Cardno MBK was appointed project manager and engineering consultant for the new container terminal in Jakarta. The total project value was US$300 million. While Cardno MBK had won the tender on the project, a final contract was yet to be agreed upon. The contract specified for an early work stage to commence the project, with the finer details to be agreed upon with the directors of Cardno MBK and the three partners who comprised the client.

The chairperson of Cardno MBK, Richard Kell, has had a long association with two of the Indonesian partners, Persero and BJLT. Because of this, he felt comfortable discussing the project's details directly with his Indonesian associates, and possibly less comfortable discussing the same details with Hutchison, the Chinese-based partner. A rift occurred with the latter partner due to personality clashes between the Hutchison management and Richard Kell. During the contract negotiation Richard Kell was available to spend only two days in Indonesia every two weeks before having to move onto the next project. While this would be a sufficient time period when dealing with an ordinary client, this was not an ordinary client. Dealing with a client composed of three different partners amplifies the complexity of contract negotiation, and these potential complexities should have been recognised at an early stage of the contract negotiation. Despite some tension with Hutchison, Cardno MBK had friendly associations with the two Indonesian partners. Because of this, it could have been assumed that the contract negotiation would still remain in the simple standard FIDIC format, as the two Indonesian partners should be able to influence the third partner in the contract formation process.

Due to cultural reasons, Australian managers are very keen to 'do business' straight away, which is in direct contrast to the approach of many Asian managers. Chinese or Asian managers tend to have luncheons, dinners, receptions, ceremonies and tour invitations before any business is even mentioned. Effective negotiators should regard this process as an opportunity for interpersonal relationship building. Even if business has yet to be mentioned, Western managers need to realise that a successful negotiation has already begun. For Cardno MBK, the directors who were in charge of the negotiation process would fly into Indonesia, spend two days 'doing business' and then fly back home to their families, leaving little time for the relationship-building process. In their reasoning, they had already completed a contract with the same client just a few years before, and so the directors felt that there was little point in going through the dinner, reception and ceremony process all over again. As the project was being conducted in Indonesia, and there were two Indonesian partners out of the three partners comprising the client, it could have been assumed by Cardno MBK that one of the Indonesian partners would lead the client group, especially because of its government connections. However, Hutchison, the Hong Kong-based partner, was certainly the most ambitious partner within the client group. While it was not local to Indonesia it was providing 70% of the project's funding, and this was a very important tool for controlling the other two partners and persuading them to do what it wanted. Even if the two Indonesian partners disagreed with Hutchison on a particular issue they were frequently silenced by Hutchison's persistence at completing a task in a certain way.

In February 1997 the client agreed that Cardno MBK begin construction on the new container terminal for the early works stage of the project. During the contract negotiation, Hutchison refused to use a standard internationally recognised FIDIC contract and insisted on having its own solicitors write up the contact's terms and conditions. This was quite unacceptable to Cardno MBK, which pressured the other partners within the client group to have a contract written up in the standard FIDIC format. After two days of intense negotiations, Cardno MBK realised that Hutchison would not budge on the issue and that if it wanted to start work on the project it would have to agree to a non-FIDIC contract. With enhanced relationship building with Hutchison before negotiations, a non-FIDIC contract may have been avoided.

Eventually, Cardno MBK agreed to a non-FIDIC contract with the client. The major contractual issues, such as remuneration, were resolved and this allowed the early works stage to commence within a few days. Having work begin before a contract has been finalised is not uncommon practice in the engineering industry. The client agreed that the fees at the completion

of the project would be US$2.5 million, paid to Cardno MBK in three different stages. The details of the contract would be finalised within the coming weeks once work had commenced.

The unresolved issues, however, became a problem. One such issue related to insurance—specifically the request for insurance to cover the liability of all workers in the port for the next 20 years when the standard length of time was only five years under an FIDIC contract. The contract details remained unresolved throughout the first half of 1997 for a variety of reasons. One factor was that the negotiation of the contract details had reached a stalemate, and the directors of Cardno MBK had not decided what to do next. In the meantime, Cardno MBK went about completing the early works stage of the project, assuming that these minor contract details would be ironed out in due course. Just as the early works stage had began, three other tenders were put out on the new container terminal. Cardno MBK focused its energies on the new contracts, which were more lucrative than the early works contract it had already been awarded. To ensure that Cardno MBK had greater success with these three new contracts put out to tender, the directors 'backed off' in their pursuit of the early works project contract details. When pursuing a new contract it is logical not to offend the client, and Cardno MBK's engineering prowess would be exhibited by completing the early works stage on time and under budget.

By August 1997 the early works stage of the project had been completed. Cardno MBK had been paid US$1.6 million for its work, but it still required the final payment of US$0.9 million. The timing of this, however, proved to be unfortunate, as the Asian financial crisis hit Indonesia very hard during the coming weeks. The money that had been held in Indonesia ready for Cardno MBK's final payment vanished almost overnight. The result was dramatic. The client, which had the three contracts still out to tender, put them on hold. Suddenly, a project that was valued at US$300 million was halted completely as Indonesia was thrown into economic and political turmoil. It was soon apparent to Cardno MBK that it should try to resolve the payment for the outstanding amount of US$0.9 million. Hutchison, the Chinese partner within the client group, flatly refused to pay the outstanding amounts owed. Even though the finer details of the contract had not been resolved, Cardno MBK was still legally entitled to the final payment of US$0.9 million as every aspect of the draft contract had been complied with and completed.

Persero and BJLT agreed that Cardno MBK was still owed the US$0.9 million, but Hutchison refused any final payments and indicated to Cardno MBK that it could try to sue if it wished. As Cardno MBK's contract was with the client comprising the three partners, it would have to sue all three. After careful consideration, Cardno MBK decided not to proceed with any further legal action as it was highly unlikely that Cardno MBK would be successful suing an Indonesian company and Indonesian government body in an Indonesian court. The non-payment caused Cardno MBK serious cash flow problems, but the company still managed to maintain a reduced profit. After two years of continued discussions and negotiations Cardno MBK wrote off the amount owed from its books as bad debt. There is still a slim chance that the amount owed will be paid as Persero and BJLT have promised Cardno MBK that it will be paid if work on the container terminal continues. Today the new Jakarta container terminal project is still on hold. The non-payment of the US$0.9 million has turned out to be a very expensive lesson for Cardno MBK, but fortunately not a fatal one. Although bad luck did play a part in the turn of events, it is interesting to ponder how different the events may have been if more time had been spent on relationship building with all three firms comprising the 'client'.

## Bibliography

Hodgetts, R.M. and Luthans, F. (1997) *International Management*, McGraw-Hill, New York.

Tse, D.K., Francis, J. and Walls, J. (1994) 'Cultural differences in conducting intra- and inter-cultural negotiations', *Journal of International Business Studies*, Vol. 25, pp. 537–56.

## Questions

1 What did Cardno MBK do wrong in its negotiation process, if anything? In which area of the process did it fail?

2 Do you think that the Chinese-based partner was more aggressive in its negotiation process due to cultural reasons?

3 Do you think that Cardno MBK should have waited for the contract to be finalised before it committed any resources, even though it may have missed out on more lucrative contracts?

4 Has Cardno MBK's company structure affected its ability to identify problems and does the company have too many or too few directors?

5 To what extent is cultural insensitivity to blame for the problems encountered by Cardno MBK and should there have been more inclusion of locals, as opposed to Australians, in the negotiation process?

6 Refer to Bazerman, M. and Gillespie, J. (1999) 'Betting on the future: the virtues of contingency contracts' *Harvard Business Review*, September/October, pp. 155–60, and discuss the merits of FIDIC-based contracts versus contingency contracts with reference to the Cardno MBK case.

**go online**

Go online to <www.pearsoned.com.au/fletcher> to find more case studies.

# Nestlé Waters and the global issue of water supply: integrating social responsibility in the management process

**Sebastien Vaccari and Richard Fletcher**

## INTRODUCTION

Nestlé Waters—part of Nestlé SA—is considering water supply as one of the most important issues in relation to its position in the global bottled-water market. It is aware that numerous international organisations—both governmental and non-governmental—strongly defend human rights and will do almost anything to protect such rights and to ensure social responsibility issues are given primary consideration. As part of their global campaigns, some organisations give the message that access to water is not a matter of choice, but a human right regarding which water should not be bought and sold. As a consequence, Nestlé is aware that the issue of putting a price on bottled water is increasingly important and its performance in the global marketplace depends on its ability to demonstrate that it is taking corporate social responsibility into account. There is also a need for manufacturers of bottled water to provide a clear message for consumers as to its safety and healthy properties to blend competitiveness on the one hand with responsibility on the other. Conforming to these requirements has created a water supply problem for all bottled water manufacturers around the world.

The corporate social responsibility of multinational firms has become a crucial issue for both international relations and the international political economy. The ethics involved are viewed differently from one country to another and now the issue has expanded to cover other ethical matters such as human rights. Nestlé SA has now given its international business operation—Nestlé Waters—the challenge of finding solutions to the issues outlined above.

## NESTLÉ SA BACKGROUND

Nestlé SA is a Swiss-based company launched in 1866. Nestlé produces a variety of goods and has a large portfolio including popular brands such as Vittel, Perrier, Nescafé, Sveltesse and Nestlé Ice Cream. It is the world's largest food and beverage company, employing 265 000 people. The company operates 481 factories worldwide, achieving success with its aggressive strategy of acquisition and business agreements. However, the company faces tough competition, especially from Danone.

In 2002, Perrier Vittel, with a portfolio of 72 brands including Acquarel and Pure Life—two strategic brands covering the globe, changed its name to Nestlé Waters. Sales were US$7.8 billion, with an 19% market share. Although the company is currently strongest in developed markets, it is pushing aggressively into emerging markets with its bottled water products.

*Image copyright Bob Randall/iStockphoto.com*

| TABLE 1 | Global bottled water market: leading countries' consumption and compound annual growth rates (1999–2004) | | | |

| Rank 2004 | Countries | Millions of gallons | | Compound annual growth rates |
| | | 1999 | 2004 | 1999–04 |
|---|---|---|---|---|
| 1 | United States | 4579.9 | 6806.7 | 8.2% |
| 2 | Mexico | 3056.9 | 4668.3 | 8.8% |
| 3 | China | 1217.0 | 3140.1 | 20.9% |
| 4 | Brazil | 1493.8 | 3062.0 | 15.4% |
| 5 | Italy | 2356.1 | 2814.4 | 3.6% |
| 6 | Germany | 2194.6 | 2722.6 | 4.4% |
| 7 | France | 1834.1 | 2257.3 | 4.2% |
| 8 | Indonesia | 907.1 | 1943.5 | 16.5% |
| 9 | Spain | 1076.4 | 1453.5 | 6.2% |
| 10 | India | 444.0 | 1353.3 | 25.0% |
| | Top 10 subtotal | 19 159.8 | 30 221.6 | 9.5% |
| | All others | 6833.5 | 10 535.0 | 9.0% |
| | World total | 25 993.3 | 40 756.6 | 9.4% |

**SOURCE:** Rodwan, J.G. Jr (2005) 'Bottled water 2004: US and international statistics and developments', <www.beveragemarketing.com/news>.

## THE BOTTLED WATER MARKET

The global bottled water market involved 177 billion litres in 2006, becoming the most dynamic sector of the refreshment beverage market. In developed countries, key factors in this increase in importance of the bottled water market included rising consumer concerns about health, wellbeing and natural products, along with a need for practicality as lifestyles become increasingly mobile. In developing countries, the factors are different: the demand for safe water is increasing due to weaker sanitary infrastructures and accessibility and availability of water. Disparity between countries (see Table 1) and regions (see Figure 1) remains important, creating inequality between developed and developing countries. Three common types of bottled waters are provided: natural mineral water, spring water and purified water. These sell using different materials for the packaging: glass, plastic (PVC or PET) and aluminium. In addition, although bottled waters tend to look alike on store shelves, there are significant differences regarding their chemical composition and these vary from one country to another. Although bottled water is a world market product involving global companies, 75% of the actual water is still controlled by local actors and thus multinational corporations such as Nestlé use joint ventures and acquisitions in order to facilitate their entry into foreign markets.

## CHALLENGES FACING NESTLÉ WATERS

A company like Nestlé faces numerous human rights and ethical issues when selling its bottled waters overseas, especially to developing countries. Attracted by economic conditions in some countries, companies can incur criticism, both in their country of origin and in other countries, for their activities in developing country markets. By putting pressure on governments to stop privatisa-

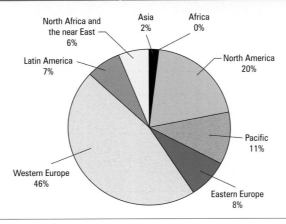

**FIGURE 1  World bottled water consumption in 1999**

- North Africa and the near East 6%
- Asia 2%
- Africa 0%
- Latin America 7%
- North America 20%
- Pacific 11%
- Western Europe 46%
- Eastern Europe 8%

**SOURCE:** *Adapted from Belot, L. (2000) 'L'eau en bouteille, bataille des géants de l'agroalimentaire', Le Monde, 23 May.*

tion of water, the public, institutions and associations, as well as legal bodies and the media, force companies to take into account the ethical and environmental consequences of their actions.

## Price and consumption

Sales of bottled water have been steadily growing in the world for the past 30 years as it is increasingly viewed as an alternative to tap water (Ferrier 2001). The current increase in bottled water consumption poses a threat to local water resources and this is one of the main factors in the overconsumption of bottled water in developed countries. This problem implies much more than environmental issues—it also involves the issue of the right of human beings to access water free of charge. People have effectively no alternative to using water, even when price increases threaten their accessibility to it. The price of bottled water tends to be excessive, considering that the cost of the water itself in bottle production does not exceeded A$0.02 per bottle (Ferrier 2001). The rest of the price is attributed to bottling, packaging, labelling, marketing, retailing and other expenses. The fact that three-fifths of the population in the developing world lack access to basic sanitation and almost a third has no access to clean water means Nestlé needs to consider the issue of charging for a perceived

natural resource when communicating its message in such markets, and take into account the costs and benefits of acting in a socially responsible manner. Furthermore, the political and social contexts significantly differ from one nation to another, and often companies are ignorant of cultural sensitiveness. Building a social network can positively influence the marketing leading to cooperation with nongovernmental organisations, activists and business interests. On the other hand, these issues raise the moral concern regarding multinational companies and their perceived wish to increase profits regardless of the impact on equality and damage to the environment.

## Packaging and transport

The function of the packaging used for bottled water is important in response to criticism. First, it protects the product when transported over long distances (Ferrier 2001). The choice of materials is also increasingly important due to specific requirements, which vary from one country to another. For instance, PET is chosen instead of PVC for its environmental benefits. It can be re-manufactured into many different products and it does not release chlorine into the atmosphere when burnt, unlike PVC. However, emerging and developing countries may not have the necessary infrastructure to incinerate or recycle the bottles. Trading and transporting bottled water all over the world also has an important environmental impact, in particular on atmospheric pollution and climate change because of fuel combustion. This impact varies a lot depending on many factors—the type of transport used, the type of fuel used and the distance travelled. It also varies according to the degree of sanitary concerns of the host country. Consequently, information on packaging and labelling remains an important issue in communication, especially regarding the firm's position on human rights and environmental issues. Regulations requiring bottled water producers to list the chemical contents and origin of the water on the label also vary from one to country to another.

Companies like Nestlé are often confronted by humanitarian movements criticising their activities in the developing world. Companies receptive to human rights face a lesser problem, create a better image for their product and thus create a more sustainable competitive advantage. Integrating social responsibility into the management process can bring numerous benefits, but can also lead to a conflict of interest between key decision makers including stakeholders, governments and non-government organisations. Furthermore, taking human rights into consideration tends to be more difficult when doing business overseas due to different legal bodies, different interests and differing levels of sensitivity regarding human rights. In effect, companies have to place themselves on a continuum from capitalism to socialism as far as this issue is concerned. Moreover, key decision makers need to be aware of differences in doing business in foreign countries, especially when the level of corruption is high, as ethical behaviours generally differ from one country to another.

In 2006, Nestlé continued to focus on positioning itself as a company committed to health and nutrition. However, the question facing many organisations like Nestlé selling a natural resource such as water is whether such organisations can at the same time sell their bottled water and promote themselves as social and ethical groups serving the community. By integrating social corporate responsibility and environmental considerations, Nestlé Waters is certainly hoping to overcome these barriers.

## Bibliography

Belot, L. (2000) 'L'eau en bouteille, bateille des geants de l'agroalimentaire', *Le Monde*, 23 May.

Euromonitor International (2005) *Nestlé SA in Soft Drink*, October.

Ferrier, C. (2001) 'Bottled water: understanding a social phenomenon', *AMBIO: A Journal of the Human Environment*, Vol. 30, No. 2, p. 118.

Hamprecht, J., Corsten, D., Noll, M. and Meier, E. (2005) 'Controlling the sustainability of food supply chain', *Supply Chain Management: An International Journal*, Vol. 10, No. 1, pp. 7–10.

Nestlé official website, <http://www.nestle.com>.

Rodwan, J.G. Jr (2005) 'Bottled water 2004: US and international statistics and developments', <www.beveragemarketing.com/news>.

## Questions

1 What are the potential advantages of using social responsibility in the marketing strategy of a company?

2 Ethical views differ between people. To what extent do these views on ethics differ?

3 What are the main factors that account for ethical differences between countries?

# INDEX

Page numbers in *italics* indicate figures.